Siberia
SIA
Lake Baikal
Ulaanbaatar
MONGOLIA
Mountains
Gobi Desert
Shenyang
Beijing
NORTH KOREA
P'yongyang
Sea of Japan
Seoul
SOUTH KOREA
CHINA
Huang River
Yellow Sea
Pusan
Fukuoka
Kyushu
JAPAN
Sapporo
Tokyo
Kobe
Osaka
Chengdu
Chang River
Shanghai
30°N
East China Sea
Okinawa
Naha
Taipei
TAIWAN
PACIFIC OCEAN
BHUTAN
Brahmaputra R.
Irrawaddy R.
Red River
Dhaka
Calcutta
MYANMAR (BURMA)
Guangzhou
Hong Kong
Macao
Hanoi
LAOS
Chiang Mai
Vientiane
Mekong River
Udon Thani
Yangon
Bay of Bengal
THAILAND
VIETNAM
South China Sea
Luzon
Philippine Sea
Manila
PHILIPPINES
Bangkok
Tonle Sap
CAMBODIA
Phnom Penh
Andaman Islands
Gulf of Thailand
Ho Chi Minh City
Spratly Islands
Cebu
Mindanao
PALAU
Koror
Nicobar Islands
Strait of Malacca
Songkhla
Bandar Seri Begawan
BRUNEI
Medan
MALAYSIA
Kuala Lumpur
Sarawak
Singapore
SINGAPORE
Sumatra
Kalimantan
Borneo
0°
Irian Jaya
PAPUA NEW GUINEA
INDONESIA
Jakarta
Surabaya
Java
Bali
Dili
EAST TIMOR
Port Moresby
OCEAN
120°E
150°E
90°E
AUSTRALIA

Encyclopedia of Modern Asia

Editorial Board

Encyclopedia of Modern Asia

Volume 4

Malaysia to Portuguese in Southeast Asia

A Berkshire Reference Work

David Levinson · Karen Christensen, Editors

CHARLES SCRIBNER'S SONS®

New York • Detroit • San Diego • San Francisco • Cleveland • New Haven, Conn. • Waterville, Maine • London • Munich

Encyclopedia of Modern Asia

David Levinson and Karen Christensen, Editors

Charles Scribner's Sons
An imprint of The Gale Group
300 Park Avenue South
New York, NY 10010

Gale and Design™ and Thomson Learning™ are trademark s used herein under license.

For more information, contact
The Gale Group, Inc.
27500 Drake Rd.
Farmington Hills, MI 48331–3535
Or you can visit our Internet site at
http://www.gale.com

The paper used in this publication meets the requirements of ANSI/NISO Z39.48-1992 (Permanence of Paper).

LIBRARY OF CONGRESS CATALOGING-IN-PUBLICATION DATA

Levinson, David, 1947-
Encyclopedia of modern Asia : / David Levinson, Karen Christensen,
p. cm.
Includes bibliographical references and index.
ISBN 0-684-80617-7 (set hardcover : alk. paper)
1. Asia—Encyclopedias. I. Christensen, Karen, 1957- II. Title.
DS4 .L48 2002
950'.03—dc21

2002008712

Printed in United States of America
1 3 5 7 9 11 13 15 17 19 20 18 16 14 12 10 8 6 4 2

Contents

Volume 1

List of Maps ix
Preface xi
Acknowledgments xxi
Survey of Asia's Regions and Nations xxv
Regional Maps xxxiii
Reader's Guide xxxix
Abacus to *China*

Volume 2

List of Maps vii
Survey of Asia's Regions and Nations ix
Regional Maps xvii
Reader's Guide xxiii
China-India Relations to *Hyogo*

Volume 3

List of Maps vii
Survey of Asia's Regions and Nations ix
Regional Maps xvii
Reader's Guide xxiii
Iaido to *Malay-Indonesian Language*

Volume 4

List of Maps vii
Survey of Asia's Regions and Nations ix
Regional Maps xvii
Reader's Guide xxiii
Malaysia to *Portuguese in Southeast Asia*

Volume 5

List of Maps vii
Survey of Asia's Regions and Nations ix
Regional Maps xvii
Reader's Guide xxiii
Possession to *Turkey*

Volume 6

List of Maps vii
Survey of Asia's Regions and Nations ix
Regional Maps xvii
Reader's Guide xxiii
Turkic Languages to *Zuo Zongtang*
Directory of Contributors 225
Index 271

List of Maps

Front Matter of All Volumes
Central Asia
China and East Asia
South Asia
Southeast Asia—Insular
Southeast Asia—Mainland
West and Southwest Asia

Volume 1
Afghanistan .21
Altay Mountains .89
Amu Dar'ya .94
Andaman and Nicobar Islands .101
Aral Sea .122
Armenia .159
Azerbaijan .205
Bangladesh .237
Bay of Bengal .269
Bhutan .287
Borneo .308
Brahmaputra River .317
Brunei .329
Cambodia .408
Caucasus .449
Chang River .488
China .504

Volume 2
East Timor .314
Euphrates and Tigris .352
Fergana Valley .375
Ganges River .423
Gobi Desert .438
Great Wall .449
Gulf of Thailand .461
Himalayas .513
Hong Kong .548
Huang River .558

Volume 3
India .9
Indonesia .53
Indus River .77
Iran .96
Iraq .123
Irian Jaya .144
Irrawaddy River .147
Jammu and Kashmir .203
Japan .207
Java and Bali .267
Kalimantan .302
Karakoram Highway .317
Kara-Kum Canal .319
Kara-Kum Desert .320
Kazakhstan .337
Killing Fields—Cambodia (1999) .369
Kyrgyzstan .424
Laos .443
Luzon .530
Macao .532

Volume 4
Malaysia .3
Maldives .22
Mauritius .86
Mekong River and Delta .136
Mindanao .148
Mongolia .165
Myanmar (Burma) .245
Nepal .307
North Korea .348
Pakistan .424

Pamir Range .457
Persian Gulf .480
Philippines .492

Volume 5

Red River and Delta .60
Réunion .82
Sarawak .130
Siberia .195
Silk Road .208
Singapore .212
South Korea .270
Spratly Islands .314
Sri Lanka .317
Strait of Malacca .339
Sumatra .354
Syr Dar'ya .362
Taiwan .380
Tajikistan .394
Taklimakan Desert .406
Thailand .452
Tian Shan .481
Tibet (Xizang) .484
Tonle Sap .513
Turkey .540

Volume 6

Turkmenistan .7
Uzbekistan .43
Vietnam .60

Survey of Asia's Regions and Nations

The *Encyclopedia of Modern Asia* covers thirty-three nations in depth and also the Caucasus and Siberia. We have divided Asia into five major subregions and assigned the thirty-three nations to each.

West and Southwest Asia

The West Asian nations covered in detail here are Turkey, Iran, and Iraq. Afghanistan and Pakistan form Southwest Asia, although in some classifications they are placed in Central and South Asia, respectively. Afghanistan, on the crossroads of civilizations for thousands of years, is especially difficult to classify and displays features typical of Central, West, and South Asia.

Despite diversity in language (Persian in Iran, Arabic in Iraq, Turkish in Turkey) form of government (theocracy in Iran, dictatorship in Iraq, and unstable democracy in Turkey) and international ties (Iran to the Islamic world, Iraq to the Arab Middle East, Turkey to the West), there are several sources of unity across West Asia. Perhaps the oldest is geographical location as the site of transportation routes between Europe and Central, East, and South Asia. Since ancient times, people, goods, wealth, and ideas have flowed across the region. In 2002 the flow of oil was most important, from the wells of Iran and Iraq through the pipelines of Turkey. Another source of unity is Sunni Islam, a major feature of life since the seventh century, although Iran is mainly the minority Shi'a tradition and there have long been Zoroastrian, Jewish, Christian, and Baha'i minorities in the region. Diversity is also evident in the fact that Turkey is a "secular" state while Iran is a theocracy, and in the conflict between fundamentalist and mainstream Islam in all the nations.

Another important common thread is the shared historical experience of being part of the Ottoman Empire and having to cope with British and Russian designs on their territory and, more recently, American influence. And, in the twentieth century, all three nations have sought to deal with the Kurdish minority and its demands for a Kurdish state to be established on land taken from all three nations.

Unity across Afghanistan and Pakistan is created by adherence to Sunni Islam (although there is a Shi'ite minority in Afghanistan) and the prominence of the Pashtun ethnic group in each nation. Both nations also experienced British colonialism, although the long-term British influence is more notable in Pakistan, which had been tied to India under British rule. West Asia is the only region in the world never colonized by Britain, although some experts argue that it did experience significant British cultural influence. In all nations resistance to external control—British, Russian, or United States—is another common historical experience.

Across the region (although less so in Afghanistan) is the stark contrast between the traditional culture and the modernity of liberation from imperial rule, still not complete across the region. This contrast is apparent in clothing styles, manners, architecture, recreation, marriage practices, and many elements of daily life.

In 2002 all the nations faced a water crisis of both too little water and water pollution. They all also faced issues of economic and social development, including reducing external debt, controlling inflation, reducing unemployment, improving education and health care, and continually reacting to the ongoing Arab-Israeli conflict, which exacerbates many of these problems. The governments also faced the difficult task of solving these problems while resisting Americanization and also while controlling internal political unrest. Political unrest is often tied to efforts at creating democratic governments and the persistence of elite collaboration with tyrannical governments.

Central Asia

Central Asia is known by many names, including Eurasia, Middle Asia, and Inner Asia. At its core, the region is composed of five states that became independent nations following the collapse of the Soviet Union in 1991: Kazakhstan, Kyrgyzstan, Tajikistan, Turkmenistan, and Uzbekistan. Scholars sometimes include Afghanistan, Mongolia and the Xinjiang province of China within the label Central Asia. For this project, Central Asia is restricted to the five former Soviet countries, while Afghanistan is classified in Southwest Asia, and Mongolia and Xinjiang as part of East Asia. These states have a shared landmass of 1.5 million square miles, about one-half the size of the United States.

The region's unity comes from a shared history and religion. Central Asia saw two cultural and economic traditions blossom and intermix along the famed Silk Road: nomadic and sedentary. Nomadic herdsmen, organized into kinship groupings of clans, lived beside sedentary farmers and oasis city dwellers. Four of the countries share Turkic roots, while the Tajiks are of Indo-European descent, linguistically related to the Iranians. While still recognizable today, this shared heritage has developed into distinct ethnic communities.

The peoples of Central Asia have seen centuries of invasion, notably the legendary Mongol leader Genghis Khan in the thirteenth century, the Russians in the nineteenth and the Soviets in the twentieth century. For better or worse, each invader left behind markers of their presence: the Arabs introduced Islam in the seventh century. Today Islam is the predominant religion in the region, and most Central Asians are Sunni Muslims. The Russians brought the mixed legacy of modernism, including an educated populace, alarming infant mortality rates, strong economic and political participation by women, high agricultural development, and environmental disasters such as the shrinking of the Aral Sea. It was under Russian colonialism that distinct ethno-national boundaries were created to divide the people of the region. These divisions largely shape the contemporary Central Asian landscape.

Today the five Central Asian nations face similar challenges: building robust economies, developing stable, democratic governments, and integrating themselves into the regional and international communities as independent states. They come to these challenges with varied resources: Kazakhstan and Turkmenistan have rich oil reserves; several countries have extensive mineral deposits; and the Fergana Valley is but one example of the region's rich agricultural regions.

Finally, the tragic events of September 11, 2001, cast world attention on Afghanistan's neighbors in Central Asia. The "war on terrorism" forged new alliances and offered a mix of political pressure and economic support for the nations' leaders to suppress their countries' internal fundamentalist Muslim movements.

Southeast Asia

Southeast Asia is conventionally defined as that subregion of Asia consisting of the eleven nation-states of Brunei, Cambodia, East Timor, Indonesia, Laos, Malaysia, Myanmar, Philippines, Singapore, Thailand, and Vietnam. Myanmar is sometimes alternatively classified as part of South Asia and Vietnam as in East Asia. The region may be subdivided into Mainland Southeast Asia (Cambodia, Laos, Myanmar, Thailand, and Vietnam) and Insular Southeast Asia (Brunei, East Timor, Indonesia, Philippines, and Singapore). Malaysia is the one nation in the region that is located both on the mainland and islands, though ethnically it is more linked to the island nations of Indonesia, Brunei, and the Philippines.

Perhaps the key defining features for the region and those that are most widespread are the tropical monsoon climate, rich natural resources, and a way of life in rural areas based on cooperative wet-rice agriculture that goes back several thousand years. In the past unity was also created in various places by major civilizations, including those of Funan, Angkor, Pagan, Sukhothai, Majapahit, Srivijaya, Champa, Ayutthaya, and Melaka. Monarchies continue to be significant in several nation—Brunei, Cambodia, Malaysia, and Thailand—today. Subregional unity has also been created since ancient times by the continued use of written languages, including Vietnamese, Thai, Lao, Khmer and the rich literary traditions associated with those languages.

The region can also be defined as being located between China and India and has been influenced by both, with Indian influence generally broader, deeper, and longer lasting, especially on the mainland, except for Vietnam and Singapore, where influences from China have been more important. Islamic influence is also present in all eleven of the Southeast Asian nations. Culturally, Southeast Asia is notable for the central importance of the family, religion (mainly Buddhism and Islam), and aesthetics in daily life and national consciousness.

In the post–World War II Cold War era, there was a lack of regional unity. Some nations, such as Indonesia under Sukarno, were leaders of the nonaligned nations. Countries such as Thailand and the Philippines joined the U.S. side in the Cold War by being part of the Southeast Asia Treaty Organization (SEATO). A move toward greater unity was achieved with the establishment of the Association of Southeast Asian Nations (ASEAN) in 1967, with the founding members being Indonesia, Malaysia, the Philippines, Singapore, and Thailand. Subsequently other Southeast Asian nations joined ASEAN (Brunei, 1984; Laos, Myanmar, and Vietnam 1997; Cambodia 1999). As of 2002, communism was still the system in Laos and Vietnam and capitalism in Brunei, Cambodia, East Timor, the Philippines Thailand, Indonesia, Malaysia and Singapore. Political, economic, and cultural cooperation is fostered by the Association of Southeast Asian Nations (ASEAN), with headquarters in Jakarta, Indonesia. Economically, all the nations have attempted to move, although at different speeds and with different results, from a reliance on agriculture to an industrial or service-based economy. All nations also suffered in the Asian economic crisis beginning in July 1997.

Alongside these sources of similarity or unity that allow us to speak of Southeast Asia as a region is also considerable diversity. In the past religion, ethnicity, and diverse colonial experience (British, Dutch, French, American) were major sources of diversity. Today, the three major sources of diversity are religion, form of government, and level of economic development. Three nations (Indonesia, Malaysia,

Brunei) are predominately Islamic, five are mainly Buddhist (Vietnam, Laos, Cambodia, Thailand, Myanmar), two are mainly Christian (Philippines and East Timor), and Singapore is religiously heterogeneous. In addition, there is religious diversity within nations, as all these nations have sizeable and visible religious minorities and indigenous religions, in both traditional and syncretic forms, also remain important.

In terms of government, there is considerable variation: communism in Vietnam and Laos; state socialism in Myanmar; absolute monarchy in Brunei; evolving democracy in the Philippines, Thailand, Cambodia, and Indonesia; and authoritarian democracy in Malaysia and Singapore. The economic variation that exists among the nations and also across regions within nations is reflected in different levels of urbanization and economic development, with Singapore and Malaysia at one end of the spectrum and Laos and Cambodia at the other. Myanmar is economically underdeveloped, although it is urbanized, while Brunei is one of the wealthiest nations in the world but not very urbanized.

In 2002, Southeast Asia faced major environmental, political, economic, and health issues. All Southeast Asian nations suffer from serious environmental degradation, including water pollution, soil erosion, air pollution in and around cities, traffic congestion, and species extinctions. To a significant extent all these problems are the result of rapid industrial expansion and overexploitation of natural resources for international trade. The economic crisis has hampered efforts to address these issues and has threatened the economies of some nations, making them more dependent on international loans and assistance from nations such as Japan, Australia, and China. The persisting economic disparities between the rich and the poor are actually exacerbated by rapid economic growth. Related to poverty is the AIDS epidemic, which is especially serious in Cambodia, Myanmar, and Thailand and becoming more serious in Vietnam; in all these nations it associated with the commercial sex industry.

Politically, many Southeast Asian nations faced one or more threats to their stability. Political corruption, lack of transparency, and weak civic institutions are a problem to varying degrees in all the nations but are most severe in Indonesia, which faces threats to its sovereignty. Cambodia and Thailand face problems involving monarch succession, and several nations have had difficulty finding effective leaders. Myanmar's authoritarian rulers face a continual threat from the political opposition and from ethnic and religious separatists.

In addition, several nations faced continuing religious or ethnic-based conflicts that disrupt political stability and economic growth in some provinces. The major conflicts involve Muslim separatists in the southern Philippines, Muslims and Christians in some Indonesian islands and Aceh separatists in northern Sumatra, and Muslims and the Karen and other ethnic groups against the Burman government in Myanmar. Since the economic crisis of 1997, ethnic and religion-based conflict has intensified, as wealthier ethnic or religious minorities have increasingly been attacked by members of the dominant ethnic group. A related issue is the cultural and political future of indigenous peoples, including the so-called hill tribes of the mainland and horticulturalists and former hunter-gatherers of the islands.

In looking to the future, among the region's positive features are the following. First, there is Southeast Asia's strategic location between India and China, between Japan and Europe, and between Europe and Oceania. It stands in close proximity to the world's two most populous countries, China and India. Singapore, the centrally located port in Southeast Asia, is one of two major gateways to the dynamic Pacific Basin (the other is the Panama Canal). Second, there is the region's huge population and related economic market, with a total population approaching that of one half of China's. Indonesia is the world's fourth most populous nation. Third, there is enormous tourist potential in sites and recreational locales such as Angkor Wat, Bali, Borobudur, Phuket, and Ha Long Bay. Fourth, there is the region's notable eclecticism in borrowing from the outside and resiliency in transcending tragedies such as experienced by Cambodia and Vietnam. Fifth, there is the region's significant economic potential: Southeast Asia may well have the world's highest-quality labor force relative to cost. And, sixth, there is the region's openness to new technologies and ideas, an important feature in the modern global community.

South Asia

South Asia is the easiest region to demarcate, as it is bounded by the Hindu Kush and Himalayan ranges to the north and the Bay of Bengal and Arabian Sea to the south. It contains the nation-states of Bangladesh, Bhutan, India, Nepal, and Sri Lanka and the more distant island nations of the Maldives and Mauritius. Myanmar and Pakistan, which are considered part of South Asia in some schemes, are here classified in Southeast Asia and Southwest Asia, respectively.

While the region is diverse economically, culturally, linguistically, and religiously, there is unity that, in some form, has existed for several thousand years. One source of unity is the historical influence of two major civilizations (Indus and Dravidian) and three major religions (Hinduism, Buddhism, and Islam). Regionally, Sikhism and Jainism have been of great importance. There is also considerable economic unity, as the majority of people continue to live by farming, with rice and especially wet-rice the primary crop. In addition, three-quarters of the people continue to live in rural, agricultural villages, although this has now become an important source of diversity, with clear distinctions between urban and rural life. A third source of unity is the caste system, which continues to define life for most people in the three mainland nations. Another source of unity is the nature and structure of society, which was heavily influenced by the several centuries of British rule. A final source of political unity in the twentieth century—although sometimes weakened by ethnic and religious differences—has been nationalism in each nation.

South Asia is diverse linguistically, ethnically, religiously, and economically. This diversity is most obvious in India, but exists in various forms in other nations, except for the isolated Maldives, which is the home of one ethnic group, the Divehi, who are Muslims and who have an economy based largely on tourism and fishing.

The dozens of languages of South Asia fall into four major families: Indo-European, Austroasiatic, Dravidian, and Tibeto-Burman and several cannot be classified at all. Because of its linguistic diversity, India is divided into "linguistic" states with Hindi and English serving as the national languages.

Hinduism is the dominant religion in South Asia, but India is the home also to Buddhism, Jainism, and Sikhism. India also has over 120 million Muslims and the world's largest Zoroastrian population (known in India as Parsis) and Bangladesh is a predominately Muslim nation. India also has about twenty-five million Christians and until recently India had several small but thriving Jewish communities. Nepal is mainly Hindu with a Buddhist minority, and Bhutan the reverse. Sri Lanka is mainly Theravada Buddhist with Hindu, Muslim, and Christian minorities. Mauritius, which has no indigenous population, is about 50 percent Hindu, with a large Christian and smaller Muslim and Buddhist minorities.

Linguistic and religious diversity is more than matched by social diversity. One classification suggests that the sociocultural groups of South Asia can be divided into four general and several subcategories: (1) castes (Hindu and Muslim); (2) modern urban classes (including laborers, non-Hindus, and the Westernized elite); (3) hill tribes of at least six types; and (4) peripatetics.

Economically, there are major distinctions between the rural poor and the urban middle class and elite, and also between the urban poor and urban middle class and elite. There are also significant wealth distinctions based on caste and gender, and a sizeable and wealthy Indian diaspora. There is political diversity as well, with India and Sri Lanka being democracies, Bangladesh shifting back and forth between Islamic democracy and military rule, the Maldives being an Islamic state, and Nepal and Bhutan being constitutional monarchies.

In 2002, South Asia faced several categories of issues. Among the most serious are the ongoing ethnic and religious conflicts between Muslims and Hindus in India, the conflict between the nations of Pakistan and India; the ethnic conflict between the Sinhalese and Sri Lankan Tamils in Sri Lanka; and the conflict between the Nepalese and Bhutanese in both nations. There are also various ethnic separatists movements in the region, as involving some Sikhs in India. The most threatening to order in the region and beyond is the conflict between India and Pakistan over the Kashmir region, as both have nuclear weapons and armies gathered at their respective borders.

A second serious issue is the host of related environmental problems, including pollution; limited water resources; overexploitation of natural resources; destruction and death caused by typhoons, flooding, and earthquakes; famine (less of a problem today), and epidemics of tropical and other diseases. The Maldives faces the unique problem of disappearing into the sea as global warming melts glaciers and raises the sea level. Coastal regions of Bangladesh could also suffer from this.

There are pressing social, economic, and political issues as well. Socially, there are wide and growing gaps between the rich and middle classes and the poor, who are disproportionately women and children and rural. Tribal peoples and untouchables still do not enjoy full civil rights, and women are often discriminated against, although India, Sri Lanka, and Bangladesh have all had women prime ministers. Economically, all the nations continue to wrestle with the issues involved in transforming themselves from mainly rural, agricultural nations to ones with strong industrial and service sectors. Politically, all still also struggle with the task of establishing strong, central governments that can control ethnic, religious, and region variation and provide services to the entire population. Despite these difficulties, there are also positive developments. India continues to benefit from the inflow of wealth earned by Indians outside India and is emerging as a major technological center. And, in Sri Lanka, an early 2002 cease-fire has led to the prospect of a series of peace negotiations in the near future..

East Asia

East Asia is defined here as the nations of Japan, South Korea, North Korea, China, Taiwan, and Mongolia. It should be noted that Taiwan is part of China although the People's Republic of China and the Republic of China (Taiwan) differ over whether it is a province or not. The inclusion of China in East Asia is not entirely geographically and culturally valid, as parts of southern China could be classified as Southeast Asian from a geographical and cultural standpoint, while western China could be classified as Central Asian. However, there is a long tradition of classifying China as part of East Asia, and that is the approach taken here. Likewise, Mongolia is sometimes classified in Central Asia. As noted above, Siberia can be considered as forming North and Northeast Asia.

Economic, political, ideological, and social similarity across China, Korea (North and South), and Japan is the result of several thousand years of Chinese influence (at times strong, at other times weak), which has created considerable similarity on a base of pre-existing Japanese and Korean cultures and civilizations. China's influence was greatest before the modern period and Chinese culture thus in some ways forms the core of East Asian culture and society. At the same time, it must be stressed that Chinese cultural elements merged with existing and new Korean and Japanese ones in ways that produced the unique Japanese and Korean cultures and civilizations, which deserve consideration in their own right.

Among the major cultural elements brought from China were Buddhism and Confucianism, the written language, government bureaucracy, various techniques of rice agriculture, and a patrilineal kinship system based on male dominance and male control of family resources. All of these were shaped over the centuries to fit with existing or developing forms in Korea and Japan. For example, Buddhism coexists with Shinto in Japan. In Korea, it coexists with the indigenous shamanistic religion. In China and Korea traditional folk religion remains strong, while Japan has been the home to dozens of new indigenous religions over the past 150 years.

Diversity in the region has been largely a product of continuing efforts by the Japanese and Koreans to resist Chinese influence and develop and stress Japanese and Korean culture and civilization. In the twentieth century diversity was mainly political and economic. Japanese invasions and conquests of parts of China and all of Korea beginning in the late nineteenth century led to hostile relations that had not been completely overcome in 2002.

In the post–World War II era and after, Taiwan, Japan, and South Korea have been closely allied with the United States and the West; they have all developed powerful industrial and postindustrial economies. During the same period, China became a Communist state; significant ties to the West and economic development did not begin until the late 1980s. North Korea is also a Communist state; it lags behind the other nations in economic development and in recent years has not been able to produce enough food to feed its population. In 2002 China was the emerging economic power in the region, while Taiwan and South Korea hold on and Japan shows signs of serious and long-term economic decline, although it remains the second-largest (after the United States) economy in the world. Mongolia, freed from Soviet rule, is attempting to build its economy following a capitalist model.

Politically, China remains a Communist state despite significant moves toward market capitalism, North Korea is a Communist dictatorship, Japan a democracy, and South Korea and Taiwan in 1990s seem to have become relatively stable democracies following periods of authoritarian rule. Significant contact among the nations is mainly economic, as efforts at forging closer political ties remain stalled over past grievances. For example, in 2001, people in China and South Korea protested publicly about a new Japanese high school history textbook that they believed did not fully describe Japanese atrocities committed toward Chinese and Koreans before and during World War II. Japan has refused to revise the textbook. Similarly, tension remains between Mongolia and China over Mongolian fears about Chinese designs on Mongolian territory. Inner Mongolia is a province of China.

Major issues with regional and broader implications are the reunification of Taiwan and China and North and South Korea, and threat of war should reunification efforts go awry. Other major regional issues include environmental pollution, including air pollution from China that spreads east, and pollution of the Yellow Sea, Taiwan Strait, and South China Sea. A third issue is economic development and stability, and the role of each nation, and the region as a unit, in the growing global economy. A final major issue is the emergence of China as a major world political, economic, and military power at the expense of Taiwan, South Korea, and Japan, and the consequences for regional political relations and stability.

Overview

As the above survey indicates, Asia is a varied and dynamic construct. To some extent the notion of Asia, as well as regions within Asia, are artificial constructs imposed by outside observers to provide some structure to a place and subject matter that might otherwise be incomprehensible. The nations of Asia have rich and deep pasts that continue to inform and shape the present—and that play a significant role in relations with other nations and regions. The nations of Asia also face considerable issues—some unique to the region, others shared by nations around the world—as well as enormous potential for future growth and development. We expect that the next edition of this encyclopedia will portray a very different Asia than does this one, but still an Asia that is in many ways in harmony with its pasts.

David Levinson (with contributions from Virginia Aksan, Edward Beauchamp, Anthony and Rebecca Bichel, Linsun Cheng, Gerald Fry, Bruce Fulton, and Paul Hockings)

Regional Maps

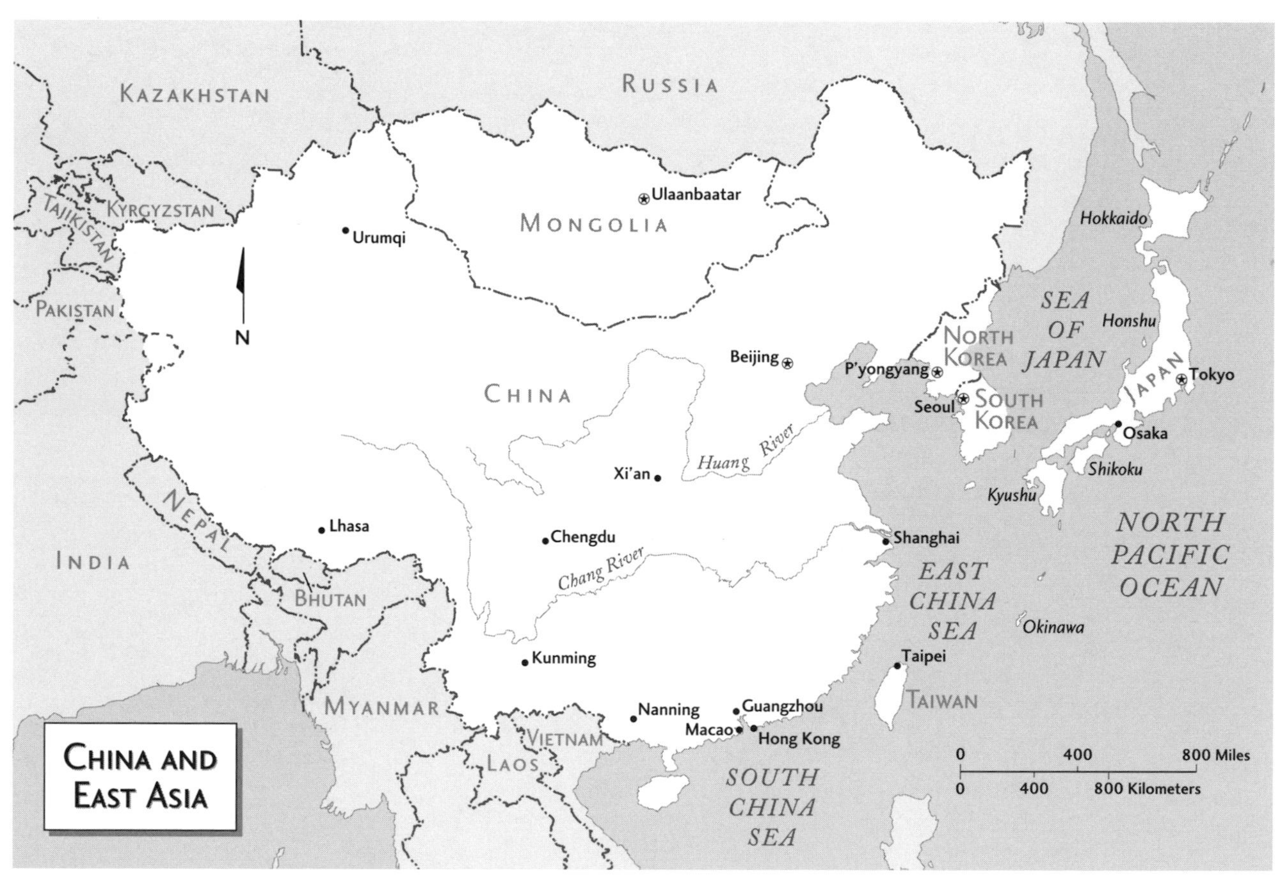
Kazakhstan
Russia
Kyrgyzstan
Tajikistan
Pakistan
Urumqi
Ulaanbaatar
Mongolia
N
Hokkaido
Sea of Japan
Honshu
North Korea
Beijing
P'yongyang
China
Seoul
South Korea
Japan
Tokyo
Osaka
Huang River
Xi'an
Shikoku
Kyushu
Nepal
Lhasa
Chengdu
Shanghai
North Pacific Ocean
India
Chang River
East China Sea
Bhutan
Okinawa
Kunming
Taipei
Myanmar
Nanning
Guangzhou
Taiwan
Macao
Hong Kong
Vietnam
Laos
China and East Asia
South China Sea
0
400
800 Miles
0
400
800 Kilometers

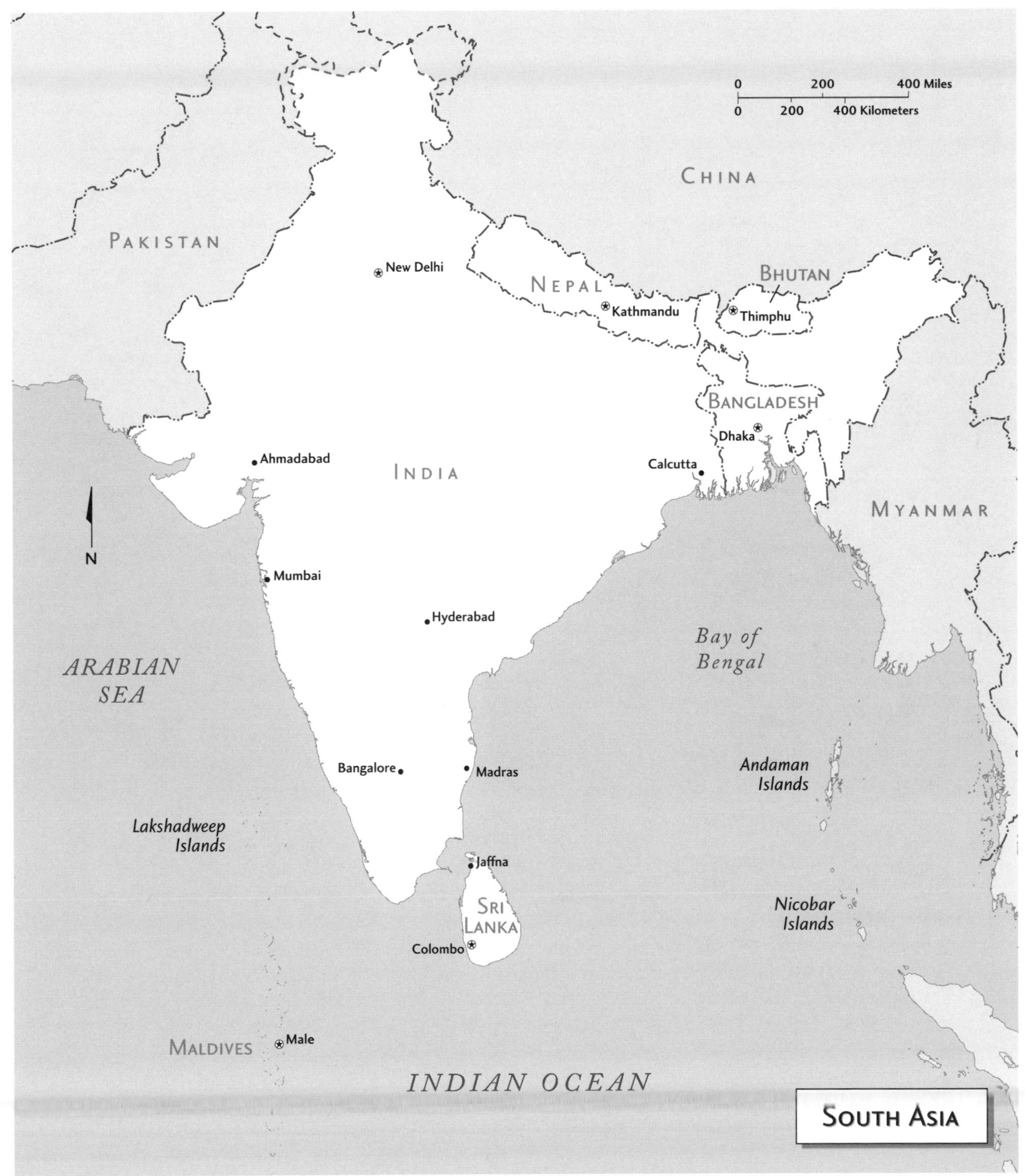
0 200 400 Miles
0 200 400 Kilometers
CHINA
PAKISTAN
New Delhi
NEPAL
Kathmandu
BHUTAN
Thimphu
BANGLADESH
Dhaka
Calcutta
Ahmadabad
INDIA
MYANMAR
N
Mumbai
Hyderabad
Bay of Bengal
ARABIAN SEA
Bangalore
Madras
Andaman Islands
Lakshadweep Islands
Jaffna
SRI LANKA
Colombo
Nicobar Islands
MALDIVES
Male
INDIAN OCEAN
SOUTH ASIA

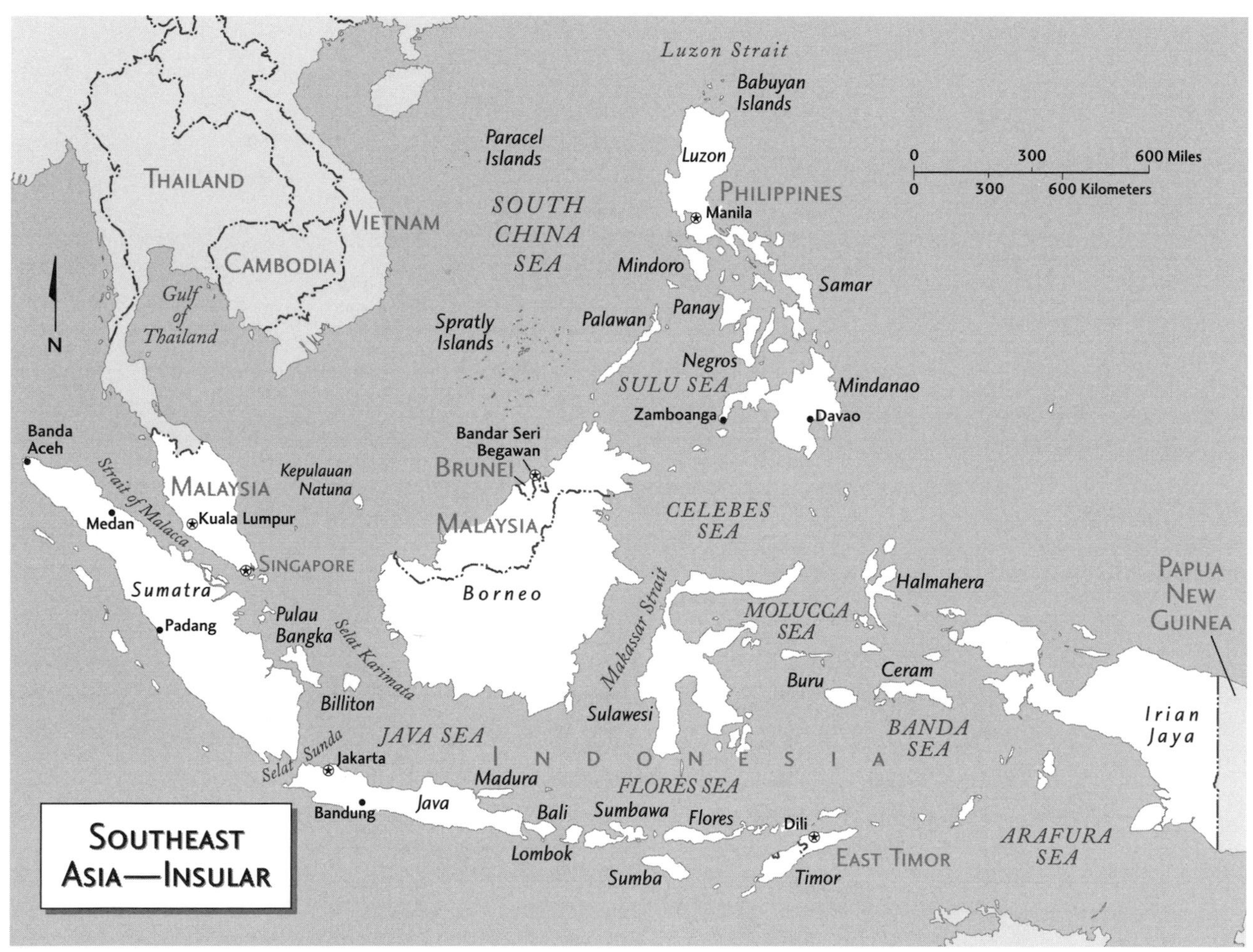
Southeast Asia—Insular
Luzon Strait
Babuyan Islands
Paracel Islands
Luzon
0 300 600 Miles
0 300 600 Kilometers
Thailand
Philippines
Manila
Vietnam
South China Sea
Cambodia
Mindoro
Samar
Gulf of Thailand
Panay
Palawan
Spratly Islands
Negros
Sulu Sea
Mindanao
Zamboanga
Davao
Banda Aceh
Bandar Seri Begawan
Brunei
Strait of Malacca
Malaysia
Kepulauan Natuna
Medan
Kuala Lumpur
Malaysia
Celebes Sea
Singapore
Halmahera
Papua New Guinea
Sumatra
Borneo
Molucca Sea
Pulau Bangka
Padang
Selat Karimata
Makassar Strait
Buru
Ceram
Billiton
Sulawesi
Irian Jaya
Banda Sea
Java Sea
Selat Sunda
Jakarta
Indonesia
Madura
Flores Sea
Bandung
Java
Bali
Sumbawa
Flores
Dili
Arafura Sea
Lombok
East Timor
Sumba
Timor

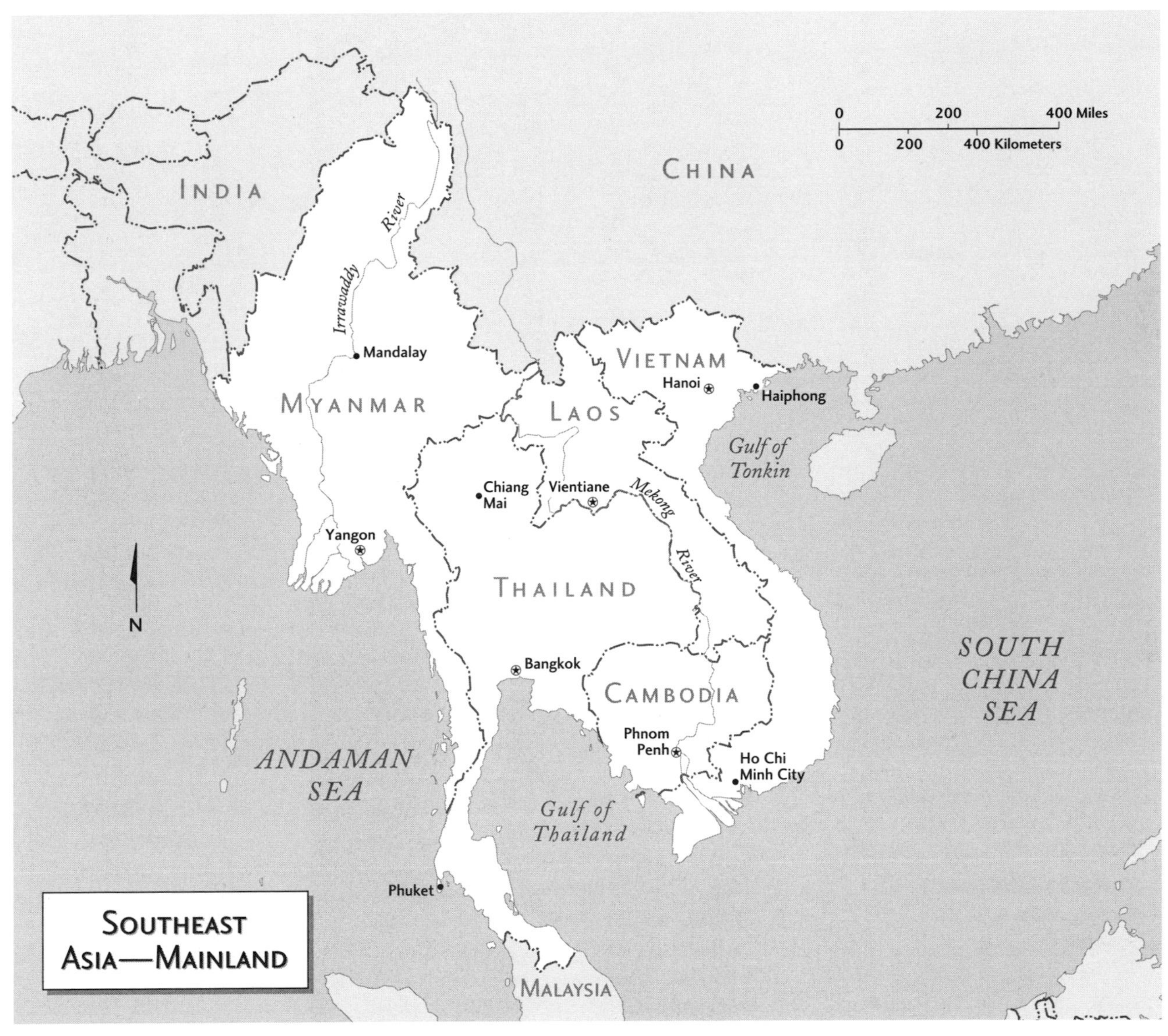
0 200 400 Miles
0 200 400 Kilometers
CHINA
INDIA
Irrawaddy River
Mandalay
MYANMAR
VIETNAM
Hanoi
Haiphong
LAOS
Gulf of Tonkin
Chiang Mai
Vientiane
Mekong River
Yangon
N
THAILAND
SOUTH CHINA SEA
Bangkok
CAMBODIA
Phnom Penh
Ho Chi Minh City
ANDAMAN SEA
Gulf of Thailand
Phuket
SOUTHEAST ASIA—MAINLAND
MALAYSIA

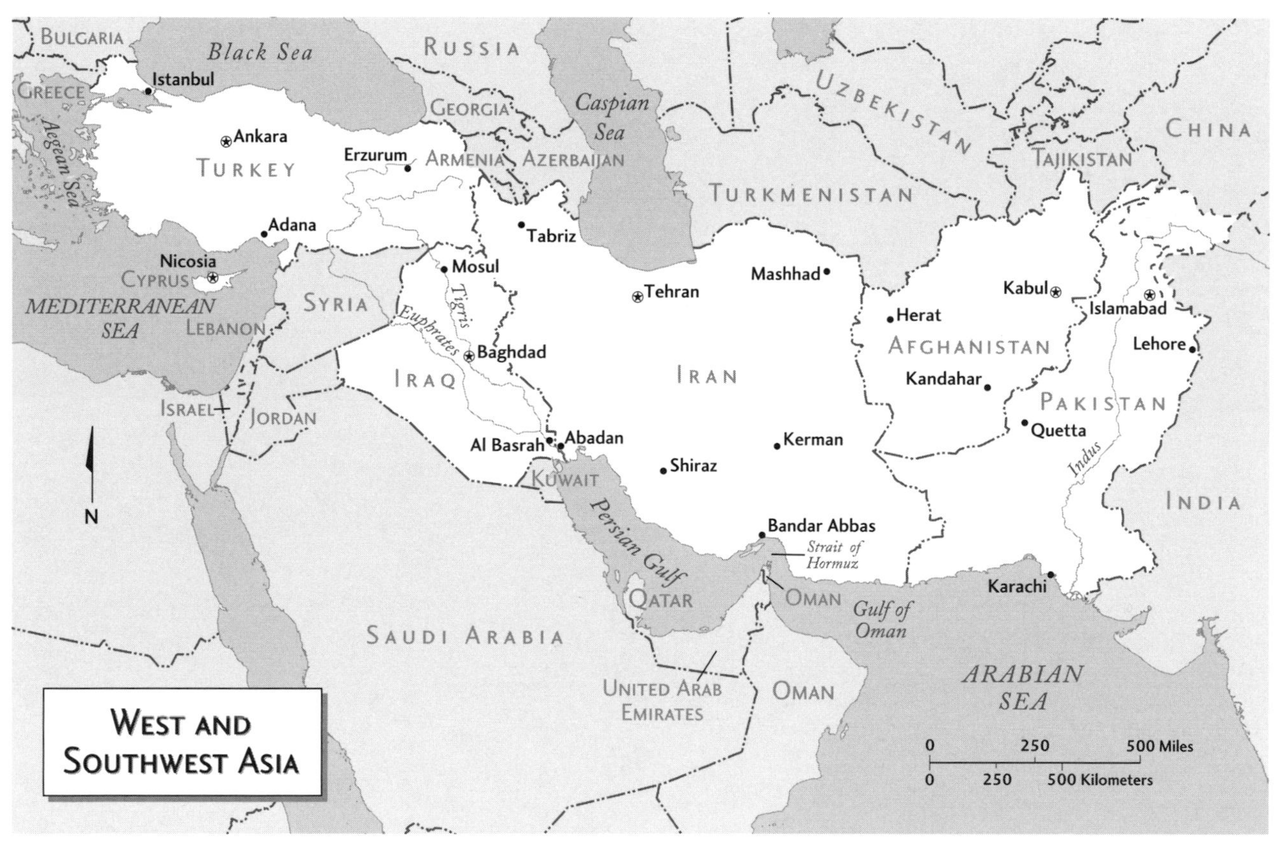
WEST AND SOUTHWEST ASIA
BULGARIA
Black Sea
RUSSIA
GREECE
Istanbul
Aegean Sea
Ankara
TURKEY
GEORGIA
Caspian Sea
UZBEKISTAN
CHINA
Erzurum
ARMENIA
AZERBAIJAN
TAJIKISTAN
TURKMENISTAN
Adana
Tabriz
Nicosia
CYPRUS
Mosul
Mashhad
Kabul
Islamabad
MEDITERRANEAN SEA
SYRIA
Tigris
Tehran
Herat
LEBANON
Euphrates
Baghdad
AFGHANISTAN
Lehore
IRAQ
IRAN
Kandahar
ISRAEL
JORDAN
PAKISTAN
Quetta
Al Basrah
Abadan
Kerman
N
Shiraz
KUWAIT
Indus
INDIA
Persian Gulf
Bandar Abbas
Strait of Hormuz
Karachi
QATAR
OMAN
Gulf of Oman
SAUDI ARABIA
ARABIAN SEA
UNITED ARAB EMIRATES
OMAN
0
250
500 Miles
0
250
500 Kilometers

Reader's Guide

ASIA

Arts, Literature, and Recreation

Asian Games
Board Games
Chinese New Year
Jade
Kabaddi
Kites and Kite Flying
Mountaineering
Olympics
Storytelling

Economics, Commerce, and Transportation

Asian Development Bank
Asian Economic Crisis of 1997
Asia-Pacific Economic Cooperation Forum
Automobile Industry
Bogor Declaration
Drug Trade
Export-Led Development
Golden Crescent
High-Technology Industry
Information Technology Industry
Intellectual Property
Islamic Banking
Manila Action Plan
Measurement Systems
Osaka Action Plan
Shanghai Cooperation Organization
Silk Road
Spice Trade
Sustainability
Tin Industry
Tourism
World Bank in Asia

Geography and the Natural World

Air Pollution
Bamboo
Buffalo, Water
Camel, Bactrian
Caspian Sea
Chicken
Cormorant
Deforestation
Duck and Goose, Domesticated
Earthquakes
Endangered Species
Goat
Mangroves
Monsoons
Opium
Pacific Ocean
Pacific Rim
Pig
Rhinocerous, Asiatic
Rice and Rice Agriculture
Soil Loss
South China Sea
Surkhob River
Tiger
Toxic-Waste Disposal
Typhoons
Volcanoes
Water Issues

Government, Politics, and Law

Corruption

International Relations

Africa-Asia Relations
Australia-Asia Relations

ASIA *(continued)*
International Relations *(continued)*
Europe-Asia Relations
International Monetary Fund
Land Mines
New Zealand-Asia Relations
Nuclear Arms
United Nations
World War I
World War II
Language and Communication
Altaic Languages
Austroasiatic Languages
English in Asia
Hmong-Mien Languages
Indo-European Languages
Language Purification
Media
Self-Censorship
Sinitic Languages
Tibeto-Burman Languages
Turkic Languages
Uralic Languages
Peoples, Cultures, and Society
Fertility
Homosexuality
New Rich
Orientalism
Religion and Philosophy
Asian-Christian Religious Dialogue
Baraka
Muslim Saints
Religious Self-Mortification
Shamanism
Shariʿa
Zoroastrianism
Science,Technology, and Health
AIDS
Disease, Tropical
Terrace Irrigation

CENTRAL ASIA
Arts, Literature, and Recreation
Alpamish
Architectural Decoration—Central Asia
Architecture—Central Asia
Buzkashi
Carpets—Central Asia
Chagatay
Cuisine—Central Asia
Dance—Central Asia
Dastan, Turkic
Dombra
Edige
Felting—Central Asia
Fine Arts—Central Asia
Folklore—Central Asia
Gorkut Ata
Koroghli
Literature—Central Asia
Minaret
Music—Central Asia
Nava'i, Mir' Ali Shir
Tile Work—Central Asia
Woodworking—Central Asia
Kazakhstan
Auezov, Mukhtar
Dauylpaz
Dulatov, Mirzhaqyp
Kalmakanov, Bukharzhrau
Kobyz
Kunanbaev, Abai
Mailin, Beiimbet
Makhambet Utemisov
Seifullin, Saduakas
Taimanov, Isatai
Valikhanov, Chokan
Aitmatov, Chingis
Manas Epic
Tajikistan
Bun Bang Fai
Turkmenistan
Kuli, Maktum
Uzbekistan
Abdalrauf Fitrat
Abdullah Quaisi
Mamadali Mahmudov
Economics, Commerce, and Transportation
Agriculture—Central Asia
Caravans
Energy—Central Asia
Oil and Mineral Industries—Central Asia
Kazakhstan
Kazakhstan—Economic System
Kyrgyzstan
Kyrgyzstan—Economic System
Tajikistan
Tajikistan—Economic System
Turkmenistan
Turkmenistan—Economic System
Uzbekistan
Uzbekistan—Economic System
Education
Madrasahs
Kazakhstan
Altynsarin, Ibrahim
Kazakhstan—Education System

Kyrgyzstan
Kyrgyzstan—Education System
Tajikistan
Tajikistan—Education System
Turkmenistan
Turkmenistan—Education System
Uzbekistan
Alisher Navoiy Samarkand State University
Uzbekistan—Education System

Geography and the Natural World
Altay Mountains
Aral Sea
Bactria
Balkhash, Lake
Camel, Arvana Dromedary
Fergana Valley
Horse, Akhal-teke
Horse, Karabair
Horse, Lokai
Kara-Kum Desert
Khwarizm
Leopard, Snow
Murgab River
Pamir Range
Paracel Islands
Radioactive Waste and Contamination—Central Asia
Sheep, Karakul
Sheep, Marco Polo
Syr Dar'ya
Tedzhen River
Tobol River
Trans Alai
Tura Lowland
Turugart Pass
Ustyurt Plateau
Zerafshan River
Kazakhstan
Irtysh River
Ishim River
Kazakh Uplands
Mangyshlak Peninsula
Turgay Plateau
Tajikistan
Kafirnigan River
Sarez Lake
Turkmenistan
Garabil Plateau

Government, Politics, and Law
Basmachi Movement
Communism—Central Asia
Great Game
Russification and Sovietization—Central Asia
Timur
Tribes and Tribal Federations—Central Asia
Urgench
Kazakhstan
Almaty
Astana
Bokeikhanov, Alikhan
Kazakhstan—Political System
Kunaev, Dinmukhamed
Nazarbaev, Nursultan
Oral
Petropavlovsk
Saryshaghan
Semipalatinsk Movement
Seralin, Mukhammedzhan
Suleimenov, Olzhas
Kyrgyzstan
Akaev, Askar
Aksakal
Bishkek
Kurmanjan Datka
Kyrgyzstan—Political System
Osh
Usubaliev, Turdakun Usubalievich
Tajikistan
Dushanbe
Gafurov, Bobojan Gafurovich
Islamic Renaissance Party—Tajikistan
Khorog
Khujand
Kulob
Nabiev, Rakhmon
Qurghonteppa
Rakhmonov, Imomali
Tajikistan—Political System
Tajikistan Civil War
Turkmenistan
Ashgabat
Mary
Niyazov, Saparmurat
Turkmenabat
Turkmenistan—Political System
Uzbekistan
Bukhara
Guliston
Karakalpakstan
Karimov, Islam
Karshi
Mahalla
Nukus
Rashidov, Sharof Rashidovich
Samarqand
Tashkent
Termez
Uzbekistan—Political System

CENTRAL ASIA *(continued)*

History and Profile

Bukhara, Khanate of
Central Asia—Early Medieval Period
Central Asia—Late Medieval and Early Modern
Central Asia—Modern
Khiva, Khanate of
Paleoanthropology—Central Asia
Quqon, Khanate of

Kazakhstan

Kazakhstan—History
Kazakhstan—Profile

Kyrgyzstan

Kyrgyzstan—History
Kyrgyzstan—Profile

Tajikistan

Tajikistan—History
Tajikistan—Profile

Turkmenistan

Turkmenistan—History
Turkmenistan—Profile

Uzbekistan

Uzbekistan—History
Uzbekistan—Profile

International Relations

Central Asia—Human Rights
Central Asia-China Relations
Central Asian Regionalism
Central Asia-Russia Relations

Language and Communication

Central Asian Languages
Farsi-Tajiki
Media—Central Asia

Kazakhstan

Ai Qap
Baitursynov, Akhmet
Kazak
Leninshil Zhas

Peoples, Cultures, and Society

Dungans
Germans in Central Asia
Kalym
Kishlak
Koreans in Central Asia
Marriage and Family—Central Asia
Nomadic Pastoralism—Central Asia
Pamir Peoples
Russians in Central Asia
Westernization—Central Asia
Women in Central Asia
Yurt

Kazakhstan

Kazakhs

Kyrgyzstan

Clothing, Traditional—Kyrgyzstan
Kyrgyz

Tajikistan

Clothing, Traditional—Tajikistan
Tajiks

Turkmenistan

Clothing, Traditional—Turkmenistan
Turkmen

Uzbekistan

Clothing, Traditional—Uzbekistan
Karakalpaks
Uzbeks

Religion and Philosophy

Buddhism—Central Asia
Bukharian Jews
Christianity—Central Asia
Islam—Central Asia
Ismaili Sects—Central Asia
Jadidism
Minaret
Muslim Religious Board of Central Asia
Naqshbandiya

Science,Technology, and Health

Ariq Water System
Ibn Sina
Kara-Kum Canal
Kariz Irrigation System
Medicine, Traditional—Central Asia

EAST ASIA

Arts, Literature, and Recreation

China

Ang Lee
Architecture—China
Architecture, Vernacular—China
Ba Jin
Beijing Opera
Birds and Bird Cages
Calligraphy—China
Cao Xueqin
Chen Kaige
Chuci
Ci
Cinema—China
Cloisonne
Cui Jian
Cuisine—China
Dazu Rock Carvings
Ding Ling
Dragon Boat Festival
Drama—China
Du Fu
Five Classics

Fu Baoshi
Gao Xingjian
Gardening—China
Ginseng
Gong Li
Guo Moruo
Hong lou meng
Hong Shen
Humor in Chinese History
Hungry Ghost Festival
Imperial Palace
International Labor Day—China
Jin ping mei
Lao She
Li Bai
Literature—China
Longmen Grottoes
Lu Xun
Mei Lanfang
Mid-Autumn Festival
Mogao Caves
Music—China
National Day—China
Nu Shooting
Painting—China
Poetry—China
Qi Baishi
Qigong
Qin Tomb
Qingming
Qiu Jin
Quan Tangshi
Shadow Plays and Puppetry
Shen Congwen
Shi
Shijing
Social Realism—China
Sports—China
Spring Festival—China
Summer Palace
Tai Chi
Tea—China
Temple of Heaven
Thirteen Ming Tombs
Tian Han
Tofu
Twelve Muqam
Wang Yiting
Wu Changshi
Wushu
Xiqu
Xu Beihong
Xu Zhimo
Zhang Yimou
Dance, Modern— East Asia
Lacquerware
Masks—East Asia
Porcelain—East Asia

Japan

Aikido
Ando Tadao
Anime
Aoi Matsuri
Arata Isozaki
Architecture—Japan
Architecture—Modern Japan
Baseball—Japan
Basho
Bento
Biwa
Bon Matsuri
Bonsai
Bunjinga
Bunraku
Calligraphy—Japan
Ceramics—Japan
Children's Day—Japan
Chugen
Cinema—Japan
Cinema, Contemporary—Japan
Cuisine—Japan
Dazai Osamu
Drama—Japan
Edogawa Rampo
Emakimono
Enchi Fumiko
Endo Shusaku
Eto Jun
Fugu
Fujieda Shizuo
Fujisawa Takeo
Fujita Tsuguhara
Fukuchi Gen'ichiro
Fukuzawa Yukichi
Funakoshi Gichin
Futabatei, Shimei
Geisha
Gion Matsuri
Haiku
Hakata Matsuri
Hayashi
Hina Matsuri
Hiratsuka Raicho
Iaido
Ito Noe
Judo
Jujutsu
Kabuki

EAST ASIA *(continued)*

Arts, Literature, and Recreation *(continued)*

Japan (continued)

Karaoke
Karate
Kawabata Yasunari
Kendo
Koto
Kouta
Kurokawa Kisho
Literature—Japan
Manga
Mori Ogai
Murasaki Shikibu
Music—Japan
Music, Ryukyuan
Naguata
Natsume Soseki
Nihonga
Noh-Kyogen
Oe Kenzaburo
Oh Sadaharu
Origami
Pachinko
Painting—Japan
Poetry—Japan
Shakuhachi
Shamisen
Shimazaki Toson
Sports—Japan
Tange Kenzo
Tanizaki Jun'ichiro
Tatsuno Kingo
Tea Ceremony
Teahouses
Three Imperial Regalia—Japan
Utai
Yoga

Koreas

Architecture—Korea
Calligraphy—Korea
Ceramics—Korea
Chajon Nori
Ch'oe Nam-son
Ch'usok
Cuisine—Korea
Dance—Korea
Dance Drama, Mask—Korea
Drama—Korea
Hanshik
Hwang Sun-won
Kim Myong-sun
Kim Sowol
Literature—Korea
Music—Korea
Paik, Nam June
Painting—Korea
Pak Kyung-ri
P'ansori
Paper Crafts and Arts—Korea
Poetry—Korea
Pojagi
Shin Saimdang
So Chongju
Sol
Sottal
Sports—Korea
Ssirum
Tae Kwon Do
Tanch'ong
Tano
Yi Kyu-bo
Yi Mun-yol
Yun Sun-do

Mongolia

Buh
Cuisine—Mongolia
Damdinsuren, Tsendiyn
Geser Khan
Khararkhi
Natsagdori, Dashdorjiyn

Economics, Commerce, and Transportation

China

Agriculture—China
Agricultural Collectivization—China
China—Economic System
Defense Industry—China
Development Zones—China
Energy Industry—China
Fishing Industry—China
Household Responsibility System—China
Machinery and Equipment Industry—China
Privatization—China
Rural Workers, Surplus—China
Salt Tax
Shanghai Pudong New Area
Shenzhen Special Economic Zone
South Manchuria Railway
Special Economic Zones—China
Taiwan Economic Miracle
Taiwan Investment in Asia
Toy Industry—China
Transportation System—China
Department Stores—East Asia
Textile and Clothing Industry—East Asia

Japan

Danchi
Denki Roren

Economic Planning Agency
Economic Stabilization Program
Electronics Industry—Japan
Farmer's Movement
Financial Crisis of 1927
Fishing Industry—Japan
Furukawa Ichibei
Japan—Economic System
Japan—Money
Japanese Firms Abroad
Japanese Foreign Investments
Japanese International Cooperation Agency
Kawasaki
Nikkyoso
Overseas Economic Cooperation Fund
Quality Circles
Ringi System
Settai
Shibusawa Eiichi
Shunto
Whaling—Japan

Koreas

Chaebol
Fishing Industry—Korea
Food Crisis—North Korea
North and South Korean Economic Ventures
North Korea—Economic System
South Korea—Economic System
Steel Industry—Korea

Mongolia

Cashmere Industry
Forest Industry—Mongolia
Mongolia—Economic System
Trans-Mongolian Railway

Education

China

Academia Sinica
China—Education System
Hu Shi
National Taiwan University
Peking University
Taiwan—Education System

Japan

Asiatic Society of Japan
Cram Schools
Daigaku
Ebina Danjo
Gakureki Shakai
Ienaga Saburo
Imperial Rescript on Education
Japan—Education System
Kyoiku Mama
Nitobe Inazo
Shiga Shigetaka

Koreas

Korea Institute of Science and Technology
North Korea—Education System
Seoul National University
South Korea—Education System

Mongolia

Mongolia—Education System

Geography and the Natural World

Siberia
Yellow Sea

China

Bramaputra River
Cathaya Tree
Chang River
East China Sea
Emei, Mount
Famine—China
Greater Xing'an Range
Hengduan Ranges
Huang River
Huang Shan
Huanglongsi
Jiuzhaigou
Kunlun Mountains
Lu, Mount
Panda
Qinling Range
Tai Shan
Taiwan Strait
Taklimakan Desert
Tarim Basin
Tian Shan
Wudang Shan
Wulingyuan
Wuyi, Mount
Yak

Japan

Amami Islands
Chrysanthemum
Chubu
Chugoku
Etorofu Island
Fuji, Mount
Hokkaido
Honshu
Iriomotejima Island
Kansai Region
Kanto Region
Kinki Region
Kunashiro Island
Kyushu
Sado Island
Setouchi Region
Shikoku

EAST ASIA *(continued)*
Geography and the Natural World *(continued)*
Japan (continued)
Tohoku Region
Tokaimura Nuclear Disaster
Tsushima Island
Yakushima Island
Koreas
Amnok River
Han River
Kaema Plateau
Keumkang, Mount
Korea Bay
Korea Strait
Kum River
Naktong River and Delta
Nangnim Range
T'aebaek Mountains
Taedong River
Tumen River
Mongolia
Gobi Desert
Hangai Mountains
Hentii Mountains
Horse, Przewalski's
Government, Politics, and Law
China
Anhui
Beijing
Cadre System—China
Chen Duxiu
Chen Shui-bian
Chen Yun
Chengde
Chengdu
Chiang Kai-shek
Chilung
China—Political System
Chinese Civil War of 1945–1949
Chinese Communist Party
Chongqing
Ci Xi, Empress Dowager
Civil-Service Examination System—China
Communism—China
Corruption—China
Cultural Revolution—China
Deng Xiaoping
Fujian
Gang of Four
Gansu
Great Leap Forward
Guangdong
Guangxi
Guangzhou
Guizhou
Guomindang
Hainan
Hangzhou
Harbin
Hebei
Heilongjiang
Henan
Hong Kong
Hu Jintao
Hu Yaobang
Hubei
Hunan
Hundred Days Reform
Hundred Flowers Campaign
Jiang Zemin
Jiangsu
Jiangxi
Jilin
Kang Youwei
Kao-hsiung
Kong Xiangxi
Lee Teng-hui
Lhasa
Li Hongzhang
Li Peng
Liang Qichao
Liaoning
Lin Biao
Liu Shaoqi
Long March
Macao
Manchuria
Manchurian Incident
Mao Zedong
May Fourth Movement
Nanjing
Nei Monggol
Ningxia
Northern Expedition
People's Liberation Army
Political Participation, Unofficial—China
Qinghai
Quemoy and Matsu
Red Guard Organizations
Republican Revolution of 1911
Self-Strengthening Movement
Shaanxi
Shandong
Shanghai
Shanxi
Sichuan
Socialist Spiritual Civilization—China
Song Ziwen

Sun Yat-sen
Suzhou
Tainan
Taipei
Taiping Rebellion
Taiwan—Political System
Thought Work—China
Three and Five Antis Campaigns
Tiananmen Square
Tianjin
Tibet
Tibetan Uprising
Wang Jingwei
White Terror
Wu Zetian
Xi'an
Xi'an Incident
Xinjiang
Yen, Y.C. James
Yuan Shikai
Yunnan
Zeng Guofan
Zhang Zhidong
Zhao Ziyang
Zhejiang
Zhou Enlai
Zhu De
Zhu Rongji
Zuo Zongtang

Government, Politics, and Law

Japan

Abe Iso
Aichi
Akita
Aomori
Araki Sadao
Aum Shinrikyo Scandal
Baba Tatsui
Buraku Liberation League
Chiba
Citizen's Movement
Constitution, Postwar—Japan
Constitutional Crisis of 1881
Democratic Socialist Party—Japan
Eda Saburo
Ehime
Enomoto Takeaki
Fukuda Hideko
Fukuda Takeo
Fukui
Fukumoto Kazuo
Fukuoka
Fukushima
Gifu
Goto Shinpei
Gumma
Hara Takashi
Hatoyama Ichiro
Higashikuni Naruhiko
Hirohito
Hiroshima
Hyogo
Ibaraki
Ichikawa Fusae
Ikeda Hayato
Ishihara Shintaro
Ishikawa
Iwate
Japan—Political System
Japan Communist Party
Japan Socialist Party
Kagawa
Kagoshima
Kanagawa
Kanno Suga
Kato Takaaki
Kishi Nobusuke
Kochi
Kodama Yoshio
Komeito
Konoe Fumimaro
Kumamoto
Kyoto
Liberal Democratic Party—Japan
Lockheed Scandal
Maruyama Masao
Mie
Minobe Tatsukichi
Miyagi
Miyazaki
Mori Arinori
Nagano
Nagasaki
Nakasone Yasuhiro
Nara
Niigata
Ogasawara
Oita
Okayama
Okinawa
Osaka
Recruit Scandal
Saga
Saionji Kinmochi
Saitama
Sapporo
Sasagawa Ryoichi
Sato Eisaku

EAST ASIA *(continued)*
Government, Politics, and Law *(continued)*
Japan (continued)
Sendai
Shiga
Shimane
Shipbuilding Scandal
Shizuoka
Showa Denko Scandal
Siemens Incident
Tanaka Giichi
Textbook Scandal
Tochigi
Tojo Hideki
Tokushima
Tokyo
Tottori
Toyama
Wakayama
Yamagata
Yamagata Aritomo
Yamaguchi
Yamamoto Isoroku
Yamanashi
Yoshida Shigeru
Yoshida Shoin
Koreas
April 19 Revolution—Korea
Chagang Province
Cheju Province
Ch'ongjin
Chun Doo Hwan
Communism—North Korea
Corruption—Korea
Democratization—South Korea
Haeju
Hamhung
Han Yong-un
Inchon
Juche
Kaesong
Kangwon Province
Kim Dae Jung
Kim Il Sung
Kim Jong Il
Kim Pu-shik
Kim Young-sam
Kim Yu-sin
Kwangju
Kwangju Uprising
Kyonggi Province
March First Independence Movement
Namp'o
North Cholla Province
North Ch'ungch'ong Province
North Hamgyong Province
North Hwanghae Province
North Korea—Political System
North Kyongsang Province
North P'yongan Province
Park Chung Hee
Pusan
Pyongyang
Rhee, Syngman
Roh Tae Woo
Sadaejuui
Sejong, King
Seoul
Sinuiju
South Cholla Province
South Ch'ungch'ong Province
South Hamgyong Province
South Hwanghae Province
South Korea—Political System
South Kyongsang Province
South P'yongan Province
Taegu
Taejon
Three Revolutions Movement
Ulchi Mundok
Wang Kon
Yanggang Province
Yi Ha-ung
Yi Song-gye
Yi T'ae-yong
Yu Kwan Sun
Yushin
Mongolia
Aimag
Batmonkh, Jambyn
Choybalsan, Horloogiyn
Chormaqan, Noyan
Darhan
Erdenet
Genghis Khan
Golden Horde
Gurragchaa, Jugderdemidiyn
Karakorum
Khubilai Khan
Mongolia—Political System
Mongolian Social Democratic Party
Narantsatsralt, Janlavyn
Ochirbat, Punsalmaagiyn
Sukhbaatar, Damdiny
Tsedenbel, Yumjaagiyn
Ulaanbaatar
United Party of Mongolia

History and Profile

East Asia

Paleoanthropology—East Asia

China

China—Profile
Han Dynasty
Hongcun and Xidi
Jurchen Jin Dynasty
Lijiang, Old Town of
Ming Dynasty
Pingyao, Ancient City of
Qin Dynasty
Qing Dynasty
Republican China
Shang Dynasty
Sixteen Kingdoms
Song Dynasty
Sui Dynasty
Taiwan—Profile
Taiwan, Modern
Tang Dynasty
Warring States Period—China
Yuan Dynasty
Zhou Dynasty

Japan

Choshu Expeditions
Heian Period
Heisei Period
Japan—Profile
Jomon Period
Kamakura Period
Meiji Period
Muromachi Period
Nara Period
Showa Period
Taisho Period
Tokugawa Period
Yayoi Period

Koreas

Choson Kingdom
Korea—History
Koryo Kingdom
North Korea—Profile
Parhae Kingdom
South Korea—Profile
Three Kingdoms Period
Unified Shilla Kingdom

Mongolia

Mongol Empire
Mongolia—History
Mongolia—Profile

International Relations

Chinese Influence in East Asia
United Front Strategy

China

Boxer Rebellion
Central Asia-China Relations
China—Human Rights
China-India Relations
China-Japan Peace and Friendship Treaty
China-Japan Relations
China-Korea Relations
China-Russia Relations
China-Taiwan Relations
China-United States Relations
China-Vietnam Relations
Chinese Influence in East Asia
Chinese Influence in Southeast Asia
Hart, Robert
Japan-Taiwan Relations
Mongolia-China-Russia Relations
Nanjing Massacre
Open Door Policy
Opium War
Sino-French War
Spratly Islands Dispute
Taiwan—Human Rights
Taiwan-United States Relations
Tibet—Image in the Modern West

Japan

China-Japan Peace and Friendship Treaty
China-Japan Relations
Comfort Women
Japan—Human Rights
Japan-Africa Relations
Japan-France Relations
Japan-Germany Relations
Japan-Korea Relations
Japan-Latin America Relations
Japan-Pacific Islands Relations
Japan-Philippines Relations
Japan-Russia Relations
Japan-Taiwan Relations
Japan–United Kingdom Relations
Japan–United States Relations
Japanese Expansion
Nixon Shock
Northern Territories
Nuclear Allergy
Plaza Accord
Russo-Japanese War
San Francisco Peace Treaty
Sino-Japanese Conflict, Second
Sino-Japanese War
Status of Forces Agreement
United States Military Bases—Japan
United States-Japan Security Treaty
Yasukuni Shrine Controversy

EAST ASIA *(continued)*
History and Profile *(continued)*
Koreas
China-Korea Relations
Japan-Korea Relations
Korea-Japan Treaty of 1965
Korean War
North Korea—Human Rights
North Korea-South Korea Relations
North Korea-United States Relations
South Korea—Human Rights
South Korea-European Union Relations
South Korea-United States Relations
Mongolia
Mongolia—Human Rights
Mongolia-China-Russia Relations
Mongolia-Soviet Union Relations
Polo, Marco
Language and Communication
China
Chinese, Classical
Dai Qing
Hakka Languages
Mandarin
Media—China
Min
Romanization Systems, Chinese
Sino-Tibetan Languages
Wu
Xiang
Yue
Japan
Feminine Language
Japanese Language
Matsumoto Shigeharu
Media—Japan
Koreas
Hangul Script
Korean Language
Media—South Korea
Romanization Systems, Korean
Mongolia
Khalkha
Mongolian Languages
Tungus Languages
Peoples, Cultures, and Society
Marriage and Family—East Asia
Westernization—East Asia
China
Aboriginal Peoples—Taiwan
China—Internal Migration
China—Population Resettlement
Chinese, Overseas
Clothing, Traditional—China
Clothing, Traditional—Hong Kong
Clothing, Traditional—Taiwan
Clothing, Traditional—Tibet
Courtyards
Foot Binding
Guanxi
Hakka
Han
Hmong
Hui
Manchu
Marriage and Family—China
Miao—China
Moso
Muslim Peoples in China
National Minorities—China
Qingke
Single-Child Phenomenon—China
Social Associations—China
Social Stratification—China
Tibetans
Tujia
Uighurs
Women in China
Yao
Yi
Zhuang
Japan
Aging Population—Japan
Ainu
Burakumin
Chinese in Japan
Clothing, Traditional—Japan
Ijime
Koreans in Japan
Social Relations—Japan
Women in Japan
Koreas
Ch'onmin
Clothing, Traditional—Korea
Koreans
Koreans, Overseas
Kye
Nobi
Women in Korea
Yangban
Mongolia
Clothing, Traditional—Mongolia
Mongols
Russians in Mongolia
Religion and Philosophy
Ancestor Worship—East Asia
Zodiac System—East Asia

China
Analects
Atheism, Official—China
Buddhism—China
Buddhism, Chan
Buddhism—Tibet
Buddhism, Pure Land
Bureau of Religious Affairs
Christianity—China
Confucian Ethics
Confucianism—China
Confucius
Cult of Maitreya
Dalai Lama
Falun Gong
Feng Shui
Five Phases
Four Books
Judaism—China
Laozi
Marxism-Leninism-Mao Zedong Thought
Mencius
Mozi
Neo-Confucianism
Potala Palace
Religion, Folk—China
Ricci, Matteo
Taoism
Xunzi
Zhu Xi
Japan
Atsuta Shrine
Buddhism—Japan
Christianity—Japan
Confucianism—Japan
Hayashi Razan
Honen
Ikkyu
Ise Shrine
Iwashimizu Hachiman Shrine
Izumo Shrine
Kukai
Motoori Norinaga
Nichiren
Nishida Kitaro
Religion, Folk—Japan
Religions, New—Japan
Saicho
Shinran
Shinto
Suzuki Daisetsu Teitaro
Twenty-Six Martyrs
Uchimura Kanzo
Yamato Damashii
Yasukuni Shrine
Koreas
Buddhism—Korea
Ch'ondogyo
Christianity—Korea
Confucianism—Korea
Religions, New—Korea
Seshi Customs
Taejonggyo
Tan'gun Myth
Taoism—Korea
Tonghak
Unification Church
Yi I
Mongolia
Bogdo Khan
Buddhism—Mongolia
Gandan Lamasery
Islam—Mongolia
Shamanism—Mongolia

Science, Technology, and Health

Calendars—East Asia
China
Abacus
Acupuncture
Dujiangyan
Grand Canal
Great Wall
Gunpowder and Rocketry
Junk
Li Shizhen
Magnetism
Massage—China
Medicine, Traditional—China
Moxibustion
Needham, Joseph
Printing and Papermaking
Science, Traditional—China
Sericulture—China
Three Gorges Dam Project
Xu Guangqi
Koreas
Science Towns—Korea

SOUTH ASIA

Arts, Literature, and Recreation

Chitra/Ardhachitra/Chitrabhasha
Conveyance Arts
Cricket
Cuisine—South Asia
Drama—South Asia
Farid, Khwaja Ghulam
Indigo
Islam, Kazi Nazrul

SOUTH ASIA *(continued)*

Arts, Literature, and Recreation *(continued)*

Jatra
Kama Sutra
Kipling, Joseph Rudyard
Literature, Bengali
Literature, Sanskrit
Literature, Tamil
Mahabharata
Manto, Sadaat Hasan
Nur Jehan
Painting—South Asia
Persian Miniature Painting
Raga
Ramayana
Rubab
Sarangi
Sarod
Sculpture—South Asia
Shah, Lalon
Shehnai
Veena

Bangladesh

Dance—Bangladesh
Music—Bangladesh

Bhutan

Textiles—Bhutan

India

Anand, Mulk Raj
Architecture—India
Bachchan, Amitabh
Chatterjee, Bankim Chandra
Chaudhuri, Nirad Chandra
Chughtai, Ismat
Cinema—India
Dance—India
Diwali
Drama—India
Forster, E. M.
Ghalib, Mirza Asadullah Khan
Holi
Kalidasa
Khan, Vilayat
Khusrau, Amir
Kumar, Dilip
Literature—India
Mangeshkar, Lata
Music—India
Music, Devotional—India
Narayan, R.K.
Nataka
Poetry—India
Prakarana
Premchand
Rahman, A.R.
Rao, Raja
Rasa
Ray, Satyajit
Sports—India
Taj Mahal

Sri Lanka

Coomaraswamy, Ananda Kentish
Dance, Kandyan
Literature, Sinhalese

Economics, Commerce, and Transportation

Agriculture—South Asia
British East India Company
French East India Company
Hawkins, William
Nomadic Pastoralism—South Asia
Tea—South Asia

Bangladesh

Bangladesh—Economic System
Grameen Bank

India

Agriculture—South Asia
British East India Company
French East India Company
Hawkins, William
India—Economic System
Nomadic Pastoralism—South Asia
Remittances
Salt Tax
Tea—South Asia

Nepal

Nepal—Economic System

Sri Lanka

Sri Lanka—Economic System

Education

Panini
Sayyid, Ahmad Khan

Bangladesh

Bangladesh—Education System

India

India—Education System

Nepal

Nepal—Education System

Sri Lanka

Sri Lanka—Education System

Geography and the Natural World

Andaman Sea
Bay of Bengal
Bramaputra River
Bustard, Hubara
Chagos Archipelago
Elephant, Asian
Green Revolution—South Asia
Himalaya Range

Indian Ocean
Indian Subcontinent
Indo-Gangetic Plain
Jhelum River
Jute
K2, Mount
Kangchenjunga, Mount
Kaveri River
Kistna River
Mongoose
Punjab
Reunion Island
Sundarbhans
Tarai
India
Abu, Mount
Andaman and Nicobar Islands
Bhopal
Chenab River
Dekkan
Eastern Ghats
Ganges River
Godavari River
Hindu Kush
Jumna River
Lion, Asiatic
Mahanadi River
Narmada Dam Controversy
Narmada River
Rann of Kachchh
Satpura Range
Sutlej River
Thar Desert
Tungabhadra River
Vindhya Mountains
Western Ghats
Zebu
Nepal
Everest, Mount
Kathmandu Valley
Government, Politics, and Law
Bahadur Shah
Birla Family
Colombo Plan
Hastings, Warren
Humayun
Ibn al-Qasim, Muhammad
Jahangir
Marxism—South Asia
Poros
Raziya
Roy, Rammohan
Shah Jahan
Singh, Jai
Tata Family
Tipu Sultan
Bangladesh
Awami League
Bangladesh—Political System
Bangladesh Nationalist Party
Chittagong
Dhaka
Ershad, H.M.
Hasina Wajid, Sheikh
Jatiya Party
Rahman, Mujibur
Rahman, Ziaur
Zia, Khaleda
Bhutan
Thimphu
Wangchuck, King Jigme Singye
India
Afzal Khan
Agartala
Agra
Ahmadabad
Ajanta
Ajodhya
Akbar
Ali Janhar, Mohamed
Allahabad
Ambedkar, B.R.
Amritsar
Andhra Pradesh
Arunachal Pradesh
Asoka
Assam
Aurangabad
Aurangzeb
Awadh
Azad, Abu'l-Kalam
Babur
Bangalore
Bengal, West
Bentinck, William Cavendish
Bhosle, Shivaji
Bhubaneshwar
Bihar
Bodh Gaya
Bose, Subhas Chandra
Calcutta
Calicut
Canning, Charles John
Chandigarh
Chhattisgarh
Coimbatore
Constitution—India

SOUTH ASIA *(continued)*

Government, Politics, and Law *(continued)*

India (continued)

Cranganur
Curzon, George Nathaniel
Dadra and Nagar Haveli Union Territory
Daman and Diu Union Territory
Darjeeling
Dehra Dun
Delhi Union Territory
Devi, Phoolan
Fazl, Abu'l
Gandhi, Indira
Gandhi, Mohandas K.
Gangtok
Goa
Godse, Nathuram Vinayak
Gujarat
Guwahati
Haidar, Ali Khan
Harsa
Haryana
Himachal Pradesh
Hindu Law
Hindu Nationalism
Hyderabad
Imphal
India—Political System
Indore
Jaipur
Jammu and Kashmir
Jharkhand
Jodhpur
Kanpur
Karnataka
Kautilya
Kerala
Khilafat Movement
Kohima
Ladakh
Lakshadweep
Laxmibai
Leh
Lucknow
Macaulay, Thomas B.
Madhya Pradesh
Madras
Madurai
Maharashtra
Mangalore
Manipur
Mathura
Meghalaya
Mizoram
Montagu-Chelmsford Reforms
Morley-Minto Reforms
Mumbai
Muslim League
Mysore
Nagaland
Nehru, Jawaharlal
Nehru, Motilal
Nilgiri District
Ootacamund
Orissa
Patna
Pondicherry
Pune
Puri
Raipur
Rajagopalachari, Chakravarti
Rajasthan
Rajkot
Ramachandran, Marudur Gopalamenon
Sarnath
Satyagraha
Shillong
Sikkim
Simla
Sindhia Family
Srinagar
Tamil Nadu
Thanjavur
Tripura
Trivandrum
Uttar Pradesh
Uttaranchal
Varanasi
Vishakapatnam

Nepal

Kathmandu
Nepal—Political System
Rana

Sri Lanka

Bandaranaike, Sirimavo Ratwatte Dias
Bandaranaike, Solomon West Ridgeway Diaz
Colombo
Jaffna
Kandy
Polonnaruva
Sri Lanka—Political System
Trincomalee

History and Profile

British Indian Empire
Chera
Chola
Dogra Dynasty
Gupta Empire

Harappa
Holkars
Mauryan Empire
Mughal Empire
Paleoanthropology—South Asia
Pandya
South Asia—History
Vijayanagara Empire
Bangladesh
Bangladesh—History
Bangladesh—Profile
Bhutan
Bhutan—History
Bhutan—Profile
India
Anglo-Mysore Wars
India—Medieval Period
India—Profile
Mutiny, Indian
Quit India Movement
Maldives
Maldives—History
Maldives—Profile
Mauritius
Mauritius—Profile
Nepal
Nepal—History
Nepal—Profile
Sri Lanka
Sri Lanka—History
Sri Lanka—Profile
International Relations
Bangladesh
Bangladesh-India Relations
Bangladesh-Pakistan Relations
India
Bangladesh-India Relations
China-India Relations
India—Human Rights
India-Myanmar Relations
India-Pakistan Relations
India-Southeast Asia Relations
India-Sri Lanka Relations
India-United Kingdom Relations
India-United States Relations
Sri Lanka
India-Sri Lanka Relations
Sri Lanka—Human Rights
Language and Communication
Bengali Language
Dravidian Languages
Indo-Aryan Languages
Media—South Asia
Munda Languages
India
Hindi-Urdu
Sanskrit
Tamil Language
Sri Lanka
Sinhala
Peoples, Cultures, and Society
Bengalis
Ethnic Conflict—South Asia
Gama, Vasco da
Ismaili Sects—South Asia
Marriage and Family—South Asia
Nagas
Panjabi
Refugees—South Asia
South Asians, Overseas
Westernization—South Asia
Women in South Asia
Bhutan
Bhutanese
Clothing, Traditional—Bhutan
India
Anglo-Indians
Aryan
Assamese
Bhil
Brahman
Caste
Clothing, Traditional—India
Garo
Gond
Gujarati
Hill Tribes of India
Khasi
Oriyas
Pahari
Pandit
Parsi
Peripatetics
Rajput
Sanskritization
Santal
Sati
Tamils
Telugu
Untouchability
Sri Lanka
Sinhalese
Vedda
Religion and Philosophy
Buddhism—South Asia
Chishtiya
Christianity—South Asia

SOUTH ASIA *(continued)*

Religion and Philosophy *(continued)*

Islam—South Asia
Jones, William
Judaism—South Asia
Khwaja Mu'in al-Din Chishti
Nurbakhshiya
Pilgrimage—South Asia
Sankara
Siddhartha Gautama
Sufism—South Asia
Vivekananda, Swami
Wali Allah, Shah

Bhutan

Bhutan—Religion

India

Blavatsky, Helena Petrovna
Bhakti
Dev, Nanak Guru
Hindu Philosophy
Hindu Values
Hinduism—India
Jainism
Jesuits— India
Lingayat
Nagarjuna
Nizam ad-din Awliya
Possession
Ramakrishna
Ramanuja
Sai Baba, Satya
Sikhism
Tagore, Rabindranath
Teresa, Mother
Upanishads

Science,Technology, and Health

Calendars—South Asia
Climatology—South Asia

India

Medicine, Ayurvedic
Medicine, Unani

SOUTHEAST ASIA

Arts, Literature, and Recreation

Architecture—Southeast Asia
Batik
Cockfighting
Drama—Southeast Asia
Hari Raya Puasa
Kain Batik
Kain Songket
Mendu
Sepak Takraw
Thaipusam

Cambodia

Angkor Wat
Literature, Khmer

Indonesia

Arja
Bali Barong-Rangda
Balinese Sanghyang
Bedaya
Borobudur
Cuisine—Indonesia
Dance—Bali
Gambang Kromong
Gambuh
Gamelan
Hikayat Amir Hamza
Ludruk
Masks, Javanese
Music—Indonesia
Noer, Arifin C.
Pramoedya Ananta Toer
Puisi
Randai
Rendra, W.S.
Riantiarno, Nano
Sandiwara
Wayang Beber
Wayang Golek
Wayang Kulit
Wayang Topeng
Wayang Wong
Wijaya, Putu

Laos

Ikat Dyeing
Luang Prabang
Music, Folk—Laos
Palm-Leaf Manuscripts
Textiles—Laos
That Luang Festival
Wat Xieng Khouan

Malaysia

Bangsawan
Chang Fee Ming
Chuah Thean Teng
Cuisine—Malaysia
Dance—Malaysia
Dikir Barat
Gawai Dayak
Jikey
Jit, Krishen
Labu Sayong
Lim, Shirley
Mak Yong
Maniam, K.S.
Manora

Pesta Menuai
Petronas Towers
Songket
Tarian Asyik
Tarian Portugis
Tay Hooi Keat
Myanmar
Burmese Arts
Literature—Myanmar
Mandalay Palace
Pagodas, Burmese
Philippines
Arnis
Bagonbanta, Fernando
Balisong
Baltazar, Francisco
Bulosan, Carlos
Cuisine—Philippines
Guerrero, Fernando M.
Literature—Philippines
Luna Y Novicio, Juan
Poetry—Philippines
Thailand
Bidyalankarana
Cuisine—Thailand
Damkoeng, Akat
Dokmai Sot
Drama—Thailand
Emerald Buddha
Fish Fighting
Khun Chang, Khun Phaen
Literature—Thailand
Longboat Racing
Muay Thai
Nirat
Phumisak, Chit
Ramakien
Siburapha
Sot Kuramarohit
Vietnam
Ao Dai
Cuisine—Vietnam
Dai Viet Su Ky
Doan Thi Diem
Ho Xuan Huong
Hoang Ngoc Phach
Hoat, Doan Viet
Khai Hung
Linh Nhat
Literature—Vietnam
Nguyen Du
Nguyen Thieu Gia
Opera—Vietnam
Plowing Ritual—Vietnam
Poetry—Vietnam
Puppetry, Water
Tet
Tran Do
Truong Vinh Ky
Tu Luc Van Doan
Wandering Souls
Economics, Commerce, and Transportation
Agriculture—Southeast Asia
Burma-Thailand Railway
Fishing Industry—Southeast Asia
Forest Industry—Southeast Asia
Golden Triangle
Ho Chi Minh Trail
Rubber Industry
Cambodia
Cambodia—Economic System
Indonesia
Indonesia—Economic System
Manufacturing Industry—Indonesia
Repelita
Laos
Chintanakan mai
Laos—Economic System
Mittaphap Bridge
Malaysia
Malaysia—Economic System
Manufacturing Industry—Malaysia
Mineral Industry—Malaysia
New Economic Policy—Malaysia
Rubber Industry—Malaysia
Timber Industry—Malaysia
Myanmar
Burma Road
Myanmar—Economic System
Philippines
Manufacturing Industry—Philippines
Pan-Philippine Highway
Philippines—Economic System
Suki
Singapore
Banking and Finance Industry—Singapore
Singapore—Economic System
Thailand
Thailand—Economic System
Thompson, Jim
Vietnam
Doi Moi
Ho Chi Minh Trail
Mekong Project
New Economic Zones
Vietnam—Economic System

SOUTHEAST ASIA *(continued)*

Education

Brunei

Universiti Brunei Darussalam

Cambodia

Cambodia—Education System
Royal University of Phnom Penh

Indonesia

Bandung Institute of Technology
Gadjah Mada University
Indonesia—Education System
University of Indonesia

Laos

Laos—Education System
Sisavangvong University

Malaysia

Malaysia—Education System
Universiti Sains Malaysia
University of Malaya

Myanmar

Myanmar—Education System

Philippines

Philippines—Education System

Singapore

Nanyang Technological University
National University of Singapore
Singapore—Education System

Thailand

Chulalongkorn University
Thailand—Education System

Vietnam

Vietnam—Education System

Geography and the Natural World

Andaman Sea
Banteng
Borneo
Dangrek Range
Green Revolution—Southeast Asia
Leopard, Clouded
Mongoose
Orangutan
Sun Bear

Cambodia

Cardamon Mountains
Elephant Range
Kompong Som Bay
Tonle Sap

Indonesia

Babirusa
Bali
Banda Sea
Flores Sea
Java Sea
Komodo Dragon
Maluku
Nusa Tenggara
Timor Sea

Laos

Bolovens Plateau
Plain of Jars

Malaysia

Cameron Highlands
Kinabalu, Mount
Strait of Malacca

Myanmar

Arakan Yoma Mountains
Inle Lake Region
Irrawaddy River and Delta
Salween River
Sittang River

Philippines

Agno River
Cagayan River
Caraballo Mountains
Celebes Sea
Cordillera Central
Luzon Group
Maguey
Mindanao
Philippine Sea
Sierra Madre
Sulu Archipelago
Visayan Islands
Zambales Mountains

Thailand

Chao Phraya River and Delta
Doi Inthanon
Gulf of Thailand
Khon Kaen
Nakhon Ratchasima
Peninsular Thailand
Three Pagodas Pass

Vietnam

Cam Ranh Bay
Central Highlands of Vietnam
Con Dao Islands
Ha Long Bay
Ho Dynasty Citadel
Hoan Kiem Lake
Karun River and Shatt al Arab River
Mekong River and Delta
Red River and Delta
Tonkin Gulf

Government, Politics, and Law

Albuquerque, Afonso de
British Military Administration
Doumer, Paul
Dutch East India Company

Romusha
Weld, Frederick
Brunei
Azahari, A.M.
Bandar Seri Begawan
Brooke, James
Hassanal Bolkaih
Parti Rakyat Brunei
Cambodia
Buddhist Liberal Democratic Party—Cambodia
Cambodia—Civil War of 1970-1975
Cambodia—Political System
Cambodian People's Party
Fa Ngoum
FUNCINPEC
Heng Samrin
Hun Sen
Jayavarman II
Jayavarman VII
Khieu Samphan
Khmer Rouge
Killing Fields
Lon Nol
Phnom Penh
Phnom Penh Evacuation
Pol Pot
Ranariddh, Norodom
Sam Rainsy
Sihanouk, Norodom
East Timor
Belo, Bishop Carlos
Dili
Dili Massacre
Fretilin
Gusmao, Xanana
Ramos-Horta, José
Indonesia
Airlangga
Amboina Massacre
Bandung
Batavia
Bosch, Johannes van den
Budi Utomo
Coen, Jan Pieterszoon
Cukong
Daendels, Herman
Darul Islam
Ethnic Colonial Policy—Indonesia
Gajah Mada
Gerindo
Gestapu Affair
Golkar
Habibie, B.J.
Hamengku Buwono IX, Sri Sultan
Hatta, Mohammad
Hizbullah
Indonesia—Political Parties
Indonesia—Political System
Indonesian Democratic Party
Indonesian Revolution
Irian Jaya
Jakarta
Jakarta Riots of May 1998
Java
Kalimantan
Malik, Adam
Medan
Megawati Sukarnoputri
Military, Indonesia
Moerdani, Leonardus Benjamin
New Order
Old Order
Pancasila
Partai Kebangkitan Bangsa
Partai Persatuan Pembangunan
Rais, Muhammad Amien
Sarekat Islam
Solo
Speelman, Cornelius
Suharto
Sukarno
Sulawesi
Sumatra
Surabaya
Taman Siswa
Treaty of Giyanti
Umar, Teuku
Wahid, Abdurrahman
Yogyakarta
Laos
Bokeo
Chao Anou
Civil War of 1956–1975—Laos
Kaysone Phomvihan
Lao People's Revolutionary Party
Laos—Political System
Louangnamtha
Pathet Lao
Setthathirat
Souphanuvong, Prince
Souvanna Phouma, Prince
Vientiane
Xayabury
Malaysia
Abdul Razak
Abu Bakar
Anwar, Ibrahim
Badawi, Abdullah Ahmed

SOUTHEAST ASIA *(continued)*

Government, Politics, and Law *(continued)*

Malaysia (continued)

Bendahara
Birch, James W. W.
Bumiputra
Clifford, Hugh
Federal Territories—Malaysia
Federation of Malaysia
Haji, Raja
Hussein Onn
Iskandar Muda
Johor
Kapitan Cina
Kedah
Kelantan
Kota Kinabalu
Kuala Lumpur
Kuching
Laksamana
Light, Francis
Lim Chong Eu
Mahathir Mohamad
Mahmud Shah
Malay States, Unfederated
Malayan People's Anti-Japanese Army
Malayan Union
Malaysia—Political System
Malaysian Chinese Association
Mansur Shah
Mat Salleh Rebellion
May 13 Ethnic Riots— Malaysia
Melaka
Negeri Sembilan
Ningkan, Stephen Kalong
Onn Bin Jaafar
Pahang
Pangkor Treaty
Penang
Perak
Perlis
Raffles, Thomas Stamford
Resident System
Rukunegara
Sabah
Sarawak
Straits Settlements
Swettenham, Frank
Tan Siew Sin
Temenggong
Templer, Gerald
Trengganu
Wan Ahmad
Yap Ah Loy

Myanmar

All Burma Students Democratic Front
Anawratha
Anti-Fascist People's Freedom League—Myanmar
Aung San
Aung San Suu Kyi
Bassein
Burma Independence Army
Chin State
Communist Party of Burma
Irrawaddy Division
Kachin Independence Organization
Kachin State
Karen National Union
Karen State
Kayah State
Magwe Division
Mandalay
Mandalay Division
Mon State
Mong Tai Army
Moulmein
Myanmar—Political System
National League for Democracy—Myanmar
National Unity Party—Myanmar
Ne Win, U
Nu, U
Palaung State Liberation Party
Pao National Organization
Pegu
Rakhine State
Sagaing Division
Shan State
Shan State Army
State Law and Order Restoration Council—Myanmar
Tenasserim Division
Thakins
Than Shwe
Thant, U
Union Solidarity and Development Association—Mya
United Wa State Party
Yangon
Yangon Division

Philippines

Aquino, Benigno
Aquino, Corazon
Autonomous Region of Muslim Mindanao
Baguio
Cebu
Davao
Estrada, Joseph
Garcia, Carlos P.

Huk Rebellion
Macapagal, Diosdado
MacArthur, Douglas
Magsaysay, Ramon
Manila
Marcos, Ferdinand
Marcos, Imelda
Moro Islamic Liberation Front
Moro National Liberation Front
Nur Misuari
People Power Movement
Philippines—Political System
Ramos, Fidel
Rizal, José
Romulo, Carlos Peña
Urdaneta, Andres de
Zamboanga

Singapore

Barisan Sosialis
Goh Chok Tong
Goh Keng Swee
Jeyaretnam, Joshua Benjamin
Lee Kuan Yew
Lim Chin Siong
Marshall, David
Singapore—Political System
Singapore Democratic Party
Workers' Party—Singapore

Thailand

Anand Panyarachun
Bangkok
Bhumipol Adulyadej
Chart Thai
Chavalit, Yongchaiyudh
Chiang Mai
Chuan Leekpai
Chulalongkorn, King
Ekaphap
Manhattan Incident
Mongkut
National Peacekeeping Council—Thailand
Nation-Religion-Monarch
October 6 Crisis—Thailand
Phalang Dharma Party
Phuket
Phya Taksin
Pibul Songgram
Pridi Banomyong
Rama Khamheng
Rama Tibodi I
Sarit Thanarat
Student Uprising of 1973—Thailand
Sulak Sivaraksa
Thai Revolution of 1932
Thailand—Political Parties
Thailand—Political System
Thaksin Shinawatra
Thanom Kittikachorn
Trailok
Ungphakorn Puey

Vietnam

An Duong Vuong
Anh Dao Duy
Army of the Republic of Vietnam
August Revolution
Ba Trieu
Bac Son Uprising
Bao Dai
Co Loa Thanh
Communism—Vietnam
Da Nang
Dalat
Duong Van Minh
Haiphong
Hanoi
Ho Chi Minh
Ho Chi Minh City
Ho Tung Mau
Hoi An
Hue
Huynh Tan Phat
Iron Triangle
Lac Long Quan
Le Duan
Le Duc Anh
Le Duc Tho
National Front for the Liberation of South Vietnam
Ngo Dinh Diem
Ngo Dinh Nhu
Nguyen Cao Ky
Nguyen Thi Minh Khai
Nguyen Van Thieu
Nhu, Madame Ngo Dinh
People's Army of Vietnam
Phan Boi Chau
Phieu Le Kha
Revolt of the Short Hair
Revolutionary Youth League of Vietnam
Tay Son Rebellion
Tran Van Giau
Trung Sisters
Vietnam—Political System
Vietnam Communist Party
Vo Nguyen Giap
Vo Van Kiet

History and Profile

British in Southeast Asia
Dutch in Southeast Asia

SOUTHEAST ASIA *(continued)*

History and Profile *(continued)*

Paleoanthropology—Southeast Asia
Portuguese in Southeast Asia
Srivijaya

Brunei

Brunei—Political System
Brunei—Profile

Cambodia

Cambodia—History
Cambodia—Profile
Khmer Empire

East Timor

East Timor—Profile

Indonesia

Aceh Rebellion
Amangkurat
British-Dutch Wars
Candi of Java
Indonesia—History
Indonesia—Profile
Java War
Konfrontasi
Majapahit
Mataram
Netherlands East Indies
Padri War
Pakualaman
Sailendra

Laos

Laos—History
Laos—Profile

Malaysia

Anglo-Dutch Treaty
Federated Malay States
Malaysia—History
Malaysia—Profile
Melaka Sultanate
White Rajas

Myanmar

Myanmar—History
Myanmar—Profile
Pagan

Philippines

Philippines—History
Philippines—Profile

Singapore

Singapore—History
Singapore—Profile

Thailand

Ayutthaya, Kingdom of
Ban Chiang
Sukhothai
Thailand—History
Thailand—Profile

Vietnam

Vietnam—History
Vietnam—Profile

International Relations

Association of South-East Asian Nations
Bali Summit
Bandung Conference
Bangkok Declaration
Chinese Influence in Southeast Asia
Five Power Defence Arrangements
India-Southeast Asia Relations
Indochina War of 1940–1941
Piracy—Southeast Asia
Southeast Asia—Human Rights
Southeast Asia Treaty Organization
Treaty of Amity and Co-operation of 1976
ZOPFAN

Cambodia

Cambodia-Laos Relations
Cambodia-Vietnam Relations
United Nations Transitional Authority in Cambodia

East Timor

United Nations in East Timor

Indonesia

Indonesia-Malaysia Relations
Indonesia–United States Relations
Irian Jaya Conquest
Volksraad

Laos

Cambodia-Laos Relations
Laos-Thailand Relations
Laos-Vietnam Relations

Malaysia

Indonesia-Malaysia Relations
Malayan Emergency
Malaysia-Europe Relations
Sabah Dispute

Myanmar

India-Myanmar Relations
Myanmar—Foreign Relations
Myanmar—Human Rights

Philippines

Japan-Philippines Relations
Philippines—Human Rights
Philippines–United States Relations

Thailand

Laos-Thailand Relations

Vietnam

Cambodia-Vietnam Relations
China-Vietnam Relations
Franco-Viet Minh War
Laos-Vietnam Relations
Soviet-Vietnamese TFOC

Vietnam War
Vietnam–United States Relations

Language and Communication

Austronesian Languages
Malay-Indonesian Languages
Media—Insular Southeast Asia
Media—Mainland Southeast Asia
Mon-Khmer Languages
Tai-Kadai Languages

Indonesia

Bahasa Indonesia
Javanese
Mohamad, Goenawan
Tempo

Laos

Lao-Tai Languages

Myanmar

Burmese

Philippines

Philippine Languages

Singapore

Chinese-Language Newspapers—Singapore
Straits Times, The

Thailand

Saek

Vietnam

Chu Nom
Vietnamese Language

Peoples, Cultures, and Society

Adat
Akha
Borneo Peoples
Chinese in Southeast Asia
Clothing, Traditional—Tribal Southeast Asia
Ethnic Relations—Southeast Asia
Hmong
Khmu
Marriage and Family—Insular Southeast Asia
Marriage and Family—Mainland Southeast Asia
Refugees—Southeast Asia
Westernization—Southeast Asia
Women in Southeast Asia

Cambodia

Clothing, Traditional—Cambodia

Indonesia

Acehnese
Balinese
Clothing, Traditional—Indonesia
Coastal Malays
Madurese
Peranakan
Pribumi
Priyayi
South Asians in Southeast Asia
Sundanese

Laos

Clothing, Traditional—Laos
Khmer

Malaysia

Clothing, Traditional—Malaysia
Orang Asli

Myanmar

Burmans
Chin
Chinese in Myanmar
Ethnic Conflict—Myanmar
Kachin
Karen
Mon
Rohingya
Shan

Philippines

Godparenthood—Philippines

Thailand

Clothing, Traditional—Thailand
Mechai Viravaidya
Thai

Vietnam

Boat People
Chinese in Vietnam
Clothing, Traditional—Vietnam
Sino-Vietnamese Culture
Vietnam—Internal Migration
Vietnamese
Vietnamese, Overseas

Religion and Philosophy

Basi
Buddhism, Theravada—Southeast Asia
Christianity—Southeast Asia
Islam—Mainland Southeast Asia
Muang
Pali Canon
Protestant Fundamentalism—Southeast Asia
Zikir

Brunei

Islam—Brunei

Indonesia

Abangan
Hosen, Ibrahim
Islam—Indonesia
Muhammadiyah
Nahdlatul Ulama
Prambanan Hindu
Santri

Laos

Prabang
That Luang

SOUTHEAST ASIA *(continued)*

Religion and Philosophy *(continued)*

Malaysia

Angkatan Belia Islam Malaysia
Islam—Malaysia

Myanmar

Christianity—Myanmar
Islam—Myanmar
Spirit Cults

Philippines

Catholicism, Roman—Philippines
Iglesia ni Christo
Islam—Philippines
Philippine Independent Church
Ruiz, Saint Lorenzo
Sin, Jaime

Thailand

Buddhadasa, Bhikku
Dhammayut Sect
Hinduism—Thailand
Phra Pathom Chedi

Vietnam

Buddhism—Vietnam
Cao Dai
Catholicism, Roman—Vietnam
Hoa Hao
Thich Nhat Hanh

Science,Technology, and Health

Bedil
Calendars—Southeast Asia
Gunpowder and Rocketry

SOUTHWEST ASIA

Arts, Literature, and Recreation

Alghoza
Bhitai, Shah Abdul Latif
Jami, 'Abdurrahman
Khushal Khan Khatak
Shah, Waris

Afghanistan

Cuisine—Afghanistan

Pakistan

Ali Khan, Bade Ghulam
Bhit Shah
Faiz Ahmed Faiz
Gulgee
Hir Ranjha Story
Iqbal, Muhammad
Makli Hill
Naqsh, Jamil
Nusrat Fateh Ali Khan
Sabri Brothers
Sadequain

Economics, Commerce, and Transportation

Afghanistan

Afghanistan—Economic System

Pakistan

Karakoram Highway
Pakistan—Economic System

Education

Pakistan

Pakistan—Education System

Geography and the Natural World

Badakhshan
Kabul River
Karakoram Mountains
Khyber Pass
Ravi River

Afghanistan

Afghan Hound
Dasht-e Margo
Hunza
Wakhan

Pakistan

Azad Kashmir
Baltistan
Bolan Pass
Indus River
Indus River Dolphin
Khunjerab Pass
Sutlej River

Government, Politics, and Law

Afghani, Jamal ad-din
Baluchistan
Dost Muhammad
Taxila

Afghanistan

Afghanistan—Political System
Amanollah
Bagram
Bamian
Bin Laden, Osama
Daud, Muhammad
Dawai, Abdul Hadi
Din Mohammad, Mushk-e Alam
Ghazna
Herat
Kabul
Mahmud of Ghazna
Mazar-e Sharif
Mujahideen
Omar, Mullah Muhammad
Taliban
Zahir Shah

Pakistan

Abdullah, Muhammad
Anarkali

Ayub Khan
Bhutto, Benazir
Bhutto, Zulfiqar Ali
David, Collin
Hadood
Islamabad
Jama'at-e-Islami
Jinnah, Mohammed Ali
Karachi
Khan, Abdul Ghaffar
Lahore
Mohenjo Daro
Muhajir Qawmi Movement
Multan
Musharraf, Pervez
North-West Frontier Province Sarhad
Pakistan—Political System
Pakistan People's Party
Peshawar
Rahmat Ali, Chauduri
Rohtas Fort
Sehwan
Sind
Zia-ul-Haq, Mohammad

History and Profile

Afghanistan

Afghanistan—History
Afghanistan—Profile
Durrani

Pakistan

Federally Administered Tribal Areas—Pakistan
Pakistan—History
Pakistan—Profile

International Relations

Afghanistan

Afghanistan—Human Rights
Treaty of Gandomak

Pakistan

Bangladesh-Pakistan Relations
India-Pakistan Relations
Pakistan—Human Rights

Language and Communication

Pashto

Afghanistan

Dari

Peoples, Cultures, and Society

Afridi
Baluchi
Brahui
Pashtun
Pashtunwali
Waziri
Clothing, Traditional—Afghanistan
Ethnic Conflict—Afghanistan
Hazara

Pakistan

Sindhi
Siraiki
Women in Pakistan

Religion and Philosophy

Bakhsh, Data Ganj
Islam—Southwest Asia
Shah, Mihr Ali
Shahbaz Qalandar Lal
Sufism—Southwest Asia

Afghanistan

Ansari, Abdullah
Bitab, Sufi

Pakistan

Mawdudi, Abu'l-A'la
Muhajir

WEST ASIA

Arts, Literature, and Recreation

Architecture—West Asia
Architecture, Islamic—West Asia
Cinema—West Asia
Music—West Asia
Rudaki
Shahnameh Epic
Sports—Islamic Asia
Twelver Shi'ism

Iran

Cuisine—Iran
No-ruz
Literature, Persian

Iraq

Cuisine—Iraq
Poetry—Iraq

Turkey

Children's Day—Turkey
Cuisine—Turkey
Guney, Yilmaz
Literature—Turkey
Music—Turkey
Nesin, Aziz
Pamuk, Orhan

Economics, Commerce, and Transportation

Agriculture—West Asia
Industry—West Asia
Oil Industry—West Asia
Organization of Petroleum Exporting Countries

Iran

Iran—Economic System

Iraq

Iraq—Economic System

Turkey

Etatism—Turkey

WEST ASIA *(continued)*
Economics, Commerce, and Transportation *(continued)*
Turkey—Economic System
Education
Iran
Iran—Education System
Iraq
Iraq—Education System
Turkey
Turkey—Education System
Geography and the Natural World
Caucasia
Euphrates River
Sistan
Tigris River
Iran
Abkhazia
Amu Dar'ya
Dagestan
Elburz
Gulf of Oman
Persian Gulf
Zagros Mountains
Turkey
Aegean Sea
Anti-Taurus
Ararat, Mount
Black Sea
Bosporus
Cappadocia
Cilician Gates
Dardanelles
Gaziantep
Izmir
Kizel Irmak River
Marmara, Sea of
Tarsus
Taurus Mountains
Yesilirmak River
Government, Politics, and Law
Aleppo
Karabag
Yerevan
Iran
Abadan
Ardabil
Azerbaijan
Bakhtaran
Bandar Abbas
Bazargan, Mehdi
Constitution, Islamic—Iran
Esfahan
Fars
Hamadan
Iran—Political System
Islamic Revolution—Iran
Kandahar
Kerman
Khomeini, Ayatollah
Khurasan
Khuzestan
Mashhad
Qom
Sana'i
Shariati, Ali
Shiraz
Tabriz
Tehran
Veleyet-e Faqih
Iraq
Al-Najaf
Baghdad
Basra
Hussein, Saddam
Iraq—Political System
Karbala
Kirkuk
Mosul
Sulaymaniya
Turkey
Adalet Partisi
Adana
Afyon
Amasya
Anatolia
Ankara
Antakya
Antalya
Ataturk
Bayar, Mahmut Celal
Bodrum
Bursa
Constitution—Turkey
Demirel, Suleyman
Democrat Party—Turkey
Diyarbakir
Edirne
Erzurum
Halide Edib Adivar
Hikmet, Nazim
Inonu, Mustafa Ismet
Istanbul
Iznik
Kars
Kas
Kemal, Yasar
Konya

Kutahya
Menderes, Adnan
Mersin
North Cyprus, Turkish Republic of
Ozal, Turgut
Pergamon
Refah and Fazilet Parties
Republican People's Party—Turkey
Rize
Samsun
Sardis
Sinop
Sivas
Tanzimat
Trabzon
Turkey—Political System
Urfa
Van
Zonguldak

History and Profile

Iran

Iran—History
Iran—Profile
Pahlavi Dynasty
Qajar Dynasty

Iraq

Iraq—History
Iraq—Profile

Turkey

Archaeology—Turkey
Byzantines
Hittites
Ottoman Empire
Turkey—Profile
Turkey, Republic of

International Relations

Ibn Battutah

Iran

Iran—Human Rights
Iran-Iraq Relations
Iran-Russia Relations
Iran–United States Hostage Crisis
Iran–United States Relations

Iraq

Iran-Iraq Relations
Iraq—Human Rights
Iraq-Turkey Relations
Persian Gulf War

Turkey

European Union and Turkey
Iraq-Turkey Relations
North Atlantic Treaty Organization and Turkey
Turkey—Human Rights
Turkey-Russia Relations
Turkey–United States Relations

Language and Communication

Arabic
Media—West Asia
Persian

Peoples, Cultures, and Society

Arabs
Armenians
Kurds
Marriage and Family—West Asia
Turks—West Asia
Westernization—West Asia
Women in West Asia

Iran

Azerbaijanis
Bakhtiari
Persepolis
Persians

Iraq

Clothing, Traditional—Iraq
Marsh Arabs

Turkey

Albanians
Bulgarians
Circassians
Clothing, Traditional—Turkey
Greeks in Turkey
Miletus
Tatars

Religion and Philosophy

Alevi Muslims
Baha'i
Islam—West Asia
Judaism—West Asia
Muslims, Shi'ite
Muslims, Sunni
Oriental Orthodox Church
Qadiriya
Saint Paul

Iran

Babism

Turkey

Eastern Orthodox Church

Science, Technology, and Health

Calendars—West Asia
Kariz Irrigation System
Medicine, Traditional—West Asia

Encyclopedia of Modern Asia

MALAYSIA—PROFILE (2001 est. pop. 22.2 million). An independent federation in Southeast Asia, Malaysia is a constitutional monarchy whose capital is Kuala Lumpur, and whose major ports are Penang city and Klang. Its total area is 329,750 square kilometers.

Malaysian Territories, Geography, and Climate

Malaysia consists of two parts: West Malaysia, also called Peninsular Malaysia or Malaya, on the Malay Peninsula, including the states of Perlis, Kedah, Pinang, Perak, Kelantan, Terengganu, Pahang, Selangor, Negeri Sembilan, Melaka (Malacca), and Johor, and coextensive with the former Federation of Malaya and one federal territory, Wilayah Persekutuan, which is coextensive with the city of Kuala Lumpur; and East Malaysia, including the island states of Sabah and Sarawak (the former British colonies of North Borneo and Northwest Borneo) on the island of Borneo and two federal territories, Putrajaya and the island of Labuan. The two parts are separated by about 640 kilometers of the South China Sea.

West Malaysia borders Thailand on the north and Singapore on the south (separated by the narrow Johore Strait), with the South China Sea on the east and the Strait of Malacca and the Andaman Sea on the west. East Malaysia is bordered on the north by the South China Sea and the Sulu Sea, on the east by the Celebes Sea, and on the south and west by Kalimantan (Indonesian Borneo). Along the coast in Sarawak is the independent nation of Brunei.

Both East and West Malaysia have coastal plains and narrow, steep mountains in the interiors. In Peninsular Malaysia the Main Range, or Banjaran Titiwangsa, runs from the Thai border southward to Negeri Sembilan. The highest point is in Sabah—Mount Kinabalu (4,101 meters). The longest rivers in the country are the Rajang (approximately 760 kilometers) in Sarawak, the Kinabatangan (560 kilometers) in Sabah, and the Pahang (322 kilometers) in West Malaysia.

Lying close to the equator, Malaysia has a tropical, rainy climate with high temperatures and high humidity. Nearly three-fourths of the land area is covered with tropical rainforest. Rice cultivation is practiced throughout the country.

Ethnic Mix

West Malaysia, with more than 80 percent of the total population of Malaysia, is more densely populated than East Malaysia. Most of the population of East Malaysia is concentrated on the west coast, which is economically more developed. Of the total population, about 60 percent are of Malay or indigenous descent, over 30 percent are Chinese, and some 10 percent are Indian or Pakistani. In West Malaysia, Malays make up about one-half of the population, Chinese one-third, and Indians and Pakistanis one-tenth. In East Malaysia, the two largest groups are the Chinese and the Iban (Sea Dayaks), an indigenous people, who together make up about three-fifths of the total population. Conflict between the ethnic groups, particularly between Malays and Chinese, has played a defining role in Malaysian political history.

Religion and Language

Islam is the religion of about half the people of Malaysia and is the official religion; nearly all Malays are Muslims. The Chinese are largely Buddhist,

MALAYSIA

Area: 329,750 sq km
Population: 22,229,040 (July 2001 est.)
Population growth rate: 1.96 % (2001 est.)
Birth rate: 24.75 births/1,000 population (2001 est.)
Death rate: 5.2 deaths /1,000 population (2001 est.)
Net migration rate: 0 migrant(s)/1,000 population (2001 est.)
Sex ratio—total population: 1.01 male(s)/female (2001 est.)
Infant mortality rate: 20.31 deaths/1,000 live births (2001 est.)
Life expectancy at birth—total population: 71.11 years, male: 68.48 years, female: 73.92 years (2001 est.)
Major religions: Islam, Buddhism, Taoism, Hinduism, Christianity, Sikhism; Shamanism is practiced in East Malaysia
Major languages: Bahasa Melayu (official), English, Chinese dialects (Cantonese, Mandarin, Hokkien, Hakka, Hainan, Foochow), Tamil, Telugu, Malayalam, Panjabi, Thai
Literacy—total population: 83.5 %, male: 89.1 %, female: 78.1 % (1999 est.)
Government type: constitutional monarchy
Capital: Kuala Lumpur
Administrative divisions: 13 states and 2 federal territories
Independence: 31 August 1957 (from U.K.)
National holiday: Independence Day/Malaysia Day, 31 August (1957)
Suffrage: 21 years of age; universal
GDP—real growth rate: 8.6% (2000 est.)
GDP—per capita (purchasing power parity): $10,300 (2000 est.)
Population below poverty line: 6.8% (1997 est.)
Exports: $97.9 billion (2000 est.)
Imports: $82.6 billion (2000 est.)
Currency: ringgit (MYR)

Source: Central Intelligence Agency. (2001) *The World Factbook* 2001. Retrieved 22 April 2002, from: http://www.cia.gov/cia/publications/factbook.

Confucian, or Taoist, and the Indians are mostly Hindu. Christianity is also embraced by a small minority, and in Sabah and Sarawak the indigenous peoples generally follow traditional beliefs.

Bahasa Malaysia (Melayu), based on the Malay language, is the country's official language. Other principal languages are English, Chinese, and Tamil, an Indian language. Education is free between the ages of six and nineteen years. Primary education is provided in the four major languages, with English as the compulsory second language. Malaysia's institutions of higher education have increased to twelve in recent years. They include Universiti Kebangsaan Malaysia (National University of Malaysia) and the University of Malaya in Kuala Lumpur, Universiti Sains Malaysia in Pulau Pinang, International Islamic University, University of Technology, and Universiti Utara.

Economy

The Malaysian economy is based principally on the production of raw materials for export, including petroleum, rubber, tin, and timber. The country also has significant textile and electronic-equipment industries. It has been onc of thc fastest-growing economies in Southeast Asia, largely because of its steadily expanding manufacturing, industrial, and electronic sectors, which propelled the country to an 8 to 9 percent yearly growth rate from 1987 to 1992.

During the early 1990s the Barisan government, dominated by the United Malay National Organiza-

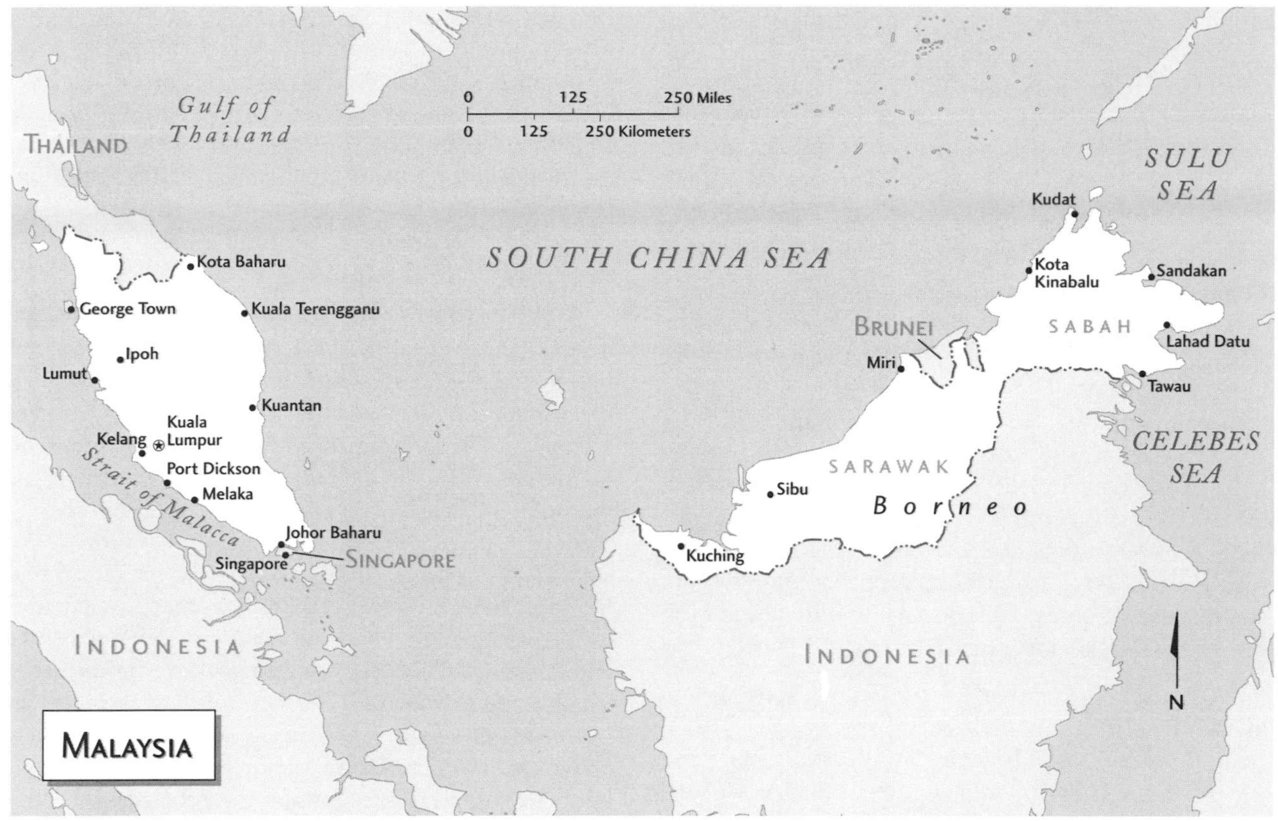

tion and including the Malaysian Chinese Association, the Malaysian Indian Congress, and other parties representing ethnic groups, privatized large industries that had been under state control, but there were allegations of political corruption and nepotism in awarding privatization contracts. The Asian financial crisis of 1997 slowed the economic development of the country, but it quickly recovered toward the end of the 1990s as a result of the introduction of capital-control measures aimed at creating stable domestic conditions along with price stability.

The major cities on the Malay Peninsula are connected by railroads with Singapore, and an extensive road net covers the west coast, with the North-South Highway forming a main artery. The country has six international airports—Kuala Lumpur, Pulau Pinang, Kota Kinabalu, Johor Bahru (Senai), Kuching, and Tawau.

Government

Malaysia is a federal constitutional monarchy with a parliamentary democracy. The Malaysian constitution is derived from the constitution of the Federation of Malaya, which was promulgated on Merdeka (Independence) Day, 31 August 1957. The constitution of the Federation was the product of a constitutional commission consisting of constitutional experts from Australia, India, and Pakistan. The Malaysian head of state is the king (the Yang di-Pertuan Agong), who is elected every five years by the nine hereditary rulers of Perlis, Kedah, Perak, Kelantan, Terengganu, Pahang, Selangor, Negeri Sembilan, and Johor. The king appoints the cabinet, headed by the prime minister, who must be a member of the cabinet and have the confidence of the house of representatives (Dewan Ra'ayat). The prime minister is the chief executive officer of the government and has tremendous power of patronage.

The parliament has two chambers. In 2000, the house consisted of 180 members, all elected by popular vote in single-member districts. Representatives of the lower house are popularly elected for five-year terms. Legislative power is divided between the federal and state legislatures. Senators serve for six years. Two senators are elected by each state legislature, and the rest are appointed by the head of state. Malaysia has universal adult suffrage.

Political Parties

The leading national political organization of Malaysia is the National Front, a multiracial coalition of thirteen parties. Its predecessor was the Alliance Party; in one incarnation or the other it has controlled the government since 1957. It is dominated by the United Malay National Organization, with the Malaysian Chinese Association, GERAKAN (the Malaysian People's Movement Party), and the Malaysian Indian Congress as other major parties. Other major opposition parties include the Democratic Action Party, the Pan-Malayan Islamic Party, and the Justice Party.

Legal System and International Associations

The Malaysian legal system reflects British influence as it adheres closely to the Westminster model of the U.K. parliament. It has two houses of parliament, namely the elected House of Representatives and the appointed House of Lords. The king is the supreme head of the government, assisted by the prime minister and the cabinet ministers. The judicial system consists of lower courts at urban and rural centers, two high courts having original and appellate jurisdiction, and a supreme court. Certain civil and domestic matters are under the jurisdiction of Islamic courts.

Malaysia is a member of the United Nations and many of its specialized agencies, such as the World Bank, International Monetary Fund, and the General Agreement on Tariffs and Trade. It also has membership in the Asian Development Bank, the Commonwealth of Nations, the Five-Power Defense Arrangement, the Movement of Nonaligned Nations, and the Association of Southeast Asian Nations.

Ho Khai Leong

Further Reading

Means, Gordon P. (1991) *Malaysian Politics: The Second Generation.* Singapore: Oxford University Press.

Ryan, N. J. (1969) *The Making of Modern Malaysia and Singapore.* Kuala Lumpur, Malaysia: Oxford University Press.

Winstedt, R. O. (1969) *Malaya and Its History.* London: Hutchinson University Library.

MALAYSIA—ECONOMIC SYSTEM

MALAYSIA—ECONOMIC SYSTEM Malaysia, consisting of peninsular Malaysia (Malay Peninsula) and East Malaysia (Sabah and Sarawak), came into being as a political entity in 1963. The nation has experienced various economic systems from the maritime-based trading empire of the Malay sultanate of Melaka of the fifteenth century to the mixed-market economy of the late twentieth century.

Melaka, established in the early 1400s by a Majapahit refugee prince, was a maritime-based trading power with hegemony over the Malay Peninsula and central Sumatra. The Malay-Hindu rulers of Melaka embraced Islam, which was consistent with Melaka's role as a port serving the East-West trade then under Muslim domination that stretched from the Red Sea to the Indian Ocean. Melaka's control of the Malacca Strait was the key to its economy in the long-distance East-West commerce in spices from the Moluccas (Spice Islands) to Venice. Described as the emporium par excellence, Melaka functioned as an entrepôt for the products of Southeast Asia and China in exchange for manufactures from India and Europe.

Trade was the lifeblood of fifteenth-century Melaka. The sultan, at the apex of the ruling hierarchy, derived his income from trade. Commercial tribute was exacted in a number of forms, namely as import and export tax on trade goods passing through the seaport, fees paid by merchants for the license to trade in selected commodities, and harbor dues imposed on vessels passing through the Malacca Strait. Melaka's navy enforced the sultan's pretensions. Although the palace engaged to a limited extent in direct trading, commercial activities were largely in the hands of foreign merchants (Arabs and Chinese), who were accorded trading rights by the sultan in return for tribute. The sultanate ensured an environment conducive to trade by maintaining law and order, security from piracy, provision of infrastructure facilities (for example, warehouses for storage of goods), and standardization of weights and measures. Barter trading coexisted with a fairly developed monetized economy.

Paralleling Melaka, the Malay sultanate of Brunei emerged as the dominant power over the northwestern part of Borneo (present-day Sabah and Sarawak) from the fifteenth to the seventeenth century. Brunei derived its power and wealth from trade with the Malay Archipelago and southern China. The Brunei ruler, at best, had only nominal overlordship over the coastal regions, where Brunei *pangeran* (chieftains) located at river mouths controlled and exacted commercial tribute. The *pangeran* possessed little authority over the various ethnic communities, who owed allegiance to none but themselves. The indigenous peoples of the interior engaged in subsistence cultivation of hill rice and root crops complemented by hunting and gathering of jungle produce; others, like the Penan, led a nomadic existence relying exclusively on hunting and gathering. In the coastal areas, the native peoples collected sea produce and swamp sago and fished. Although certain jungle and sea produce supplied the China trade, the majority of the inhabitants lived in subsistence-farming communities.

The Coming of the Portuguese

Melaka's preeminence in trade made it a coveted possession of European imperialists. Melaka featured

FIVE LARGEST COMPANIES IN MALAYSIA

According to *Asia Week*, the five largest companies in Malaysia are the following:

Company	Sector	Sales ($ millions)	Rank in Asia
Petroliam Nasional	Oil, Gas, Refining	19,302.9	51
Tenaga Nasional	Energy	3,610.3	368
Sime Darby	Trading, Commodities	3,147.3	426
Malaysian Airline	Air Transport	2,356.9	567
Telekom Malaysia	Telecommunications	2,319.9	579

Source: "The Asia Week 1000." (2001) *Asia Week* (9 November): 114.

prominently in Portuguese expansionist goals and subsequently fell in 1511. The Malay ruling house fled to Johor in the southern part of the peninsula and attempted in vain to recapture Melaka. The Portuguese at Melaka continued the entrepôt trade in spices and other Southeast Asian products for the European market based at Lisbon. Like their predecessor, the Portuguese acquired commercial tribute in the form of import and export tax and harbor dues from trading vessels passing the Malacca Strait.

The transformation of Melaka from a Muslim to a Catholic entrepôt center under Portuguese control witnessed a resuscitated prosperity for Brunei as some of the Muslim mercantile elite relocated their commercial operations there. Other Muslim traders moved to the northern Sumatran Muslim port of Acheh.

Meanwhile, on the Malay Peninsula there emerged Malay sovereign principalities, such as Pahang and Perak, possessing ties with the former Melakan sultanate. These were followed later by Selangor and other states. The ruling elite of the peninsular Malay states imitated Melaka's economic system, albeit on a much lesser scale, by establishing hegemony over river systems. Unlike the sultan of Melaka, who had supreme control over his chiefs, rulers of Malay states possessed little authority over territorial chiefs, who might be more powerful than the rulers themselves. The sultan and the chiefs occupied strategic positions at river mouths and confluences to tax river-based commerce. As in Melaka, commercial tribute was the main source of income for the ruling class of the Malay states.

The livelihood of the Malay peasantry revolved around the production of rice. Where flat alluvial plains were abundant in the coastal areas, permanent sedentary wet-rice cultivation was the chief means of subsistence; in the hilly interior, cultivation of hill rice predominated. It is uncertain if land rent was imposed by Malay rulers on their *rakyat* (peasant producers); it was, however, commonplace for the ruling class to act in an arbitrary manner toward the peasantry, such as by confiscating their produce without compensation. Furthermore, the peasantry was subjected to corvée *(kerah)*, the forced labor demanded by the palace. Owing to the rapacious character of the ruling class and *kerah*, peasant cultivation was limited to subsistence and a little surplus for exchange (rice for cloth or salt). There was no capital investment in peasant production nor innovation or technical progress.

The economic situation in the Malay States, including Melaka, did not exhibit capitalist relations of production, namely involving the exploitation of free wage labor. The existence of slavery and debt-bondsmen and *kerah* afforded the needed labor required by the ruling class and worked against the emergence of a class providing free wage labor. Although capital existed, often in its usurious form, there was little capital investment in agrarian productive activities; likewise, commercial capital was negligible until the nineteenth century.

The Coming of the Dutch and the British

Denied access to Lisbon for spices, Dutch traders ventured to the Malay Archipelago themselves. By 1641, the Dutch seized Melaka from the Portuguese and sought to impose their monopolistic trade practices in the region. Attempts to exact a monopoly over the tin trade in the western Malay states proved problematic. The main focus of Dutch mercantilist ambition, however, was to make Batavia (Jakarta) in Java, and not Melaka, the center of the spice trade. The

Vereenigde Oostindische Compagnie (VOC, Dutch United East Indies Company), through force and treaty arrangements, asserted its political and economic hegemony over the entire Malay Archipelago. Meanwhile, the advent of the Spaniards in the Philippines from the mid-sixteenth century and the ascendance of the VOC in Java served to weaken Brunei's commercial and political power, which began to wane in the seventeenth century.

During the eighteenth century, individual English country traders and others associated with the English East India Company (EIC) vied against the VOC for control of the trade throughout the Malay Archipelago. EIC priorities were in the China trade. Circumstances in the last quarter of the eighteenth century—the Anglo-French struggle in India and the Anglo-Dutch rivalry in the Malay Archipelago—pressured the EIC to secure a land base on the western shores of the Malay Peninsula for naval and commercial purposes. In 1786, the EIC acquired Penang to protect British interests in the Strait of Malacca, the prime sea route to China.

Championing the principles of free trade, the British declared Penang a free port. Penang attracted Chinese merchants and European planters. Penang enjoyed moderate success as an entrepôt and port of call for the China trade. The opening of Singapore in 1819 by the EIC was an unqualified success; within a brief period, Singapore became the ultimate entrepôt port for the British in the Malay Archipelago. Both Penang and Singapore were collecting centers for Southeast Asian products for exchange in the lucrative China trade in tea and silks. Both these British free ports had a sizeable Chinese mercantile population.

Anglo-Dutch rivalry in the Malay Archipelago culminated in an agreement signed at London in 1824 that delineated spheres of influence between the British and the Dutch, with present-day Malaysia falling in the British sphere and Indonesia in the Dutch. In exchange for Bengkulu, the British acquired Melaka. In 1826, the British coordinated the administration of Penang, Melaka, and Singapore, which became the Straits Settlements that primarily served the British China trade.

Meanwhile, in the 1820s, Chinese from southwestern Borneo crossed into the mineral-rich upper Sarawak area to work the alluvial gold at and around Bau. The discovery of antimony ore in the vicinity brought Brunei's attention to the area. Forced labor was exacted from the local population to work the antimony. Disaffection with Brunei resulted in a revolt in the late 1830s. James Brooke, an English gentleman-adventurer, intervened to end the trouble. In return the Brunei ruler proclaimed Brooke raja of Sarawak in 1841.

Tin had long been produced in small quantities in the Malay Peninsula. However, the discovery of large alluvial tin in Larut, Perak, in the late 1840s ushered in large-scale capitalist production of tin. Whereas in the past Malay chiefs relied on slaves and debt-bondsmen to undertake the mining, the chiefs now farmed out mines in return for a lump sum to Chinese entrepreneurs from the Straits Settlements, who in turn recruited labor from southern China. Chinese by the thousands entered the western Malay states of Perak, Selangor, and Sungei Ujong (later Negeri Sembilan). British capitalist investors represented through the agency houses (trading firms) in Penang and Singapore invested in tin mining owing to tin's high demand in the expanding Western tin-plating industry.

Unsettling conditions in the tin-producing Malay states throughout the 1850s and 1860s—marked by political and economic disputes among Malay chieftains, clashes between rival Chinese groups over tin concessions, and the pirate menace off the coast—combined to disrupt tin production and its trade. By the early 1870s, it became imperative on the part of the British to stabilize the troubled situation, thereby ensuring an uninterrupted supply of tin for the Western market, in which British capitalists had a substantial stake. The 1874 Pangkor Engagement opened the door for the imposition of British colonial rule over the Malay Peninsula. Pax Britannica over the Malay Peninsula was complete following the conclusion of the Anglo-Siamese treaty of 1909, which brought the northern peninsular Malay states of Kedah, Perlis, Kelantan, and Terengganu into the British colonial system.

Attempts to colonize North Borneo (Sabah) beginning in the 1850s culminated in the establishment of the British North Borneo Chartered Company (BNBCC) in 1881. Both the sultanates of Brunei and Sulu that possessed nominal sovereignty over Sabah's western and eastern parts, respectively, relinquished their rights to BNBCC.

British Malaya

Capitalist exploitation of the natural resources of British Malaya (the peninsular Malay states and the Straits Settlements) began in earnest from the last quarter of the nineteenth century and throughout the first half of the twentieth century. Tin and rubber were the main focus of the colonial economy of British Malaya, primarily fueled by British capital and immigrant (Chinese and Indian) labor. The colonial state sought to provide the necessary infrastructure, particularly in transportation (rail and road) and legislation to regulate smooth exploitation of resources aimed at facilitating maximum returns for entrepreneurs for their investments.

In the tin industry, Chinese capital and labor predominated from the mid-nineteenth century to the first decade of the twentieth century. In order to ensure success in mining ventures, Chinese capital (mainly from the Straits Settlements) utilized a variety of means for exercising control over Chinese labor through recruitment systems, kinship links, provincial connections, and operation of the powerful politico-socioeconomic organization of the *hui* (brotherhood). From the 1890s, the colonial state passed legislation (for example, in labor recruitment) to weaken the control of Chinese capital over Chinese labor and, at the same time, promoted British mining capital. By the first decade of the twentieth century, most of the surface alluvial tin deposits had been exhausted, resulting in greater financial investment for access to the deeper deposits via mechanization, namely utilizing the tin dredge. Under the circumstances and with greater resources, British capital that enjoyed support from the colonial state dominated the tin industry (mining, smelting, and trade).

Chinese miners exploited the gold fields of upper Sarawak. The Brooke government operated the Sadong collieries from the 1860s for local consumption. Owing to Brooke's pronative policies and an aversion to Western capital, only the Borneo Company Limited (BCL), a British company, was given the privilege to tap the mineral resources of the nation (antimony, mercury, and later gold). The BCL utilized new technology such as the cyanidization process for gold extraction. By the turn of the twentieth century, the BCL dominated the mining industry in upper Sarawak, whereas Anglo-Dutch Shell monopolized the petroleum industry from the time it sank Sarawak's first oil well in 1910 at Miri. Despite the Brooke government's cautionary stance toward Western capitalist ventures, the mining sector was solely controlled by British capital. The majority of the labor force in Sarawak's extractive industry was drawn from immigrant Chinese recruited from southern China.

The Rubber Industry

As in the extractive industries, British capital was favored by the colonial state in commercial agriculture in British Malaya. Several cash crops—spices, sugarcane, tapioca, and coffee—were tried during the nineteenth century, but it was rubber *(Hevea brasiliensis)* that paid handsome dividends to shareholders during its boom years early in the twentieth century. The

A fisherman and a crowded fishing boat in Kota Kinabalu, Sabah, Malaysia. (NIK WHEELER/CORBIS)

agency houses played a pivotal role in convincing British capital to invest in rubber during the late 1890s and early 1900s. Falling coffee prices, coupled with blight in the industry, paved the way for the emergence of rubber as the premier plantation crop. The expansion of the American auto industry during the first decade of the twentieth century dramatically pushed up the demand for plantation rubber. The colonial state again rendered almost exclusive support for British capital, which invested in thousands of acres of rubber estates. The colonial state not only improved upon the transport system already in place for the tin industry but also conveyed the best available land for rubber to British capital and invested in research to improve the rubber industry. The colonial state coordinated the recruitment of immigrant labor from southern India to offer a cheap and plentiful supply of workers for the hundreds of British-owned estates.

On a lesser scale, the rubber industry in Sabah developed along lines similar to those in British Malaya, with the company lending full support and granting privileges to British capital not unlike the preferential treatment it had accorded to European tobacco planters in the nineteenth century. In contrast, the Brooke government blocked the entry of Western capital into the state. Instead, family-owned native and Chinese rubber smallholdings were the rule, with a handful of European-owned large estates being the exception.

In addition to rubber, Sarawak exported pepper and gambier, which were grown by Chinese smallholders. Sabah was one of the major producers and exporters of tropical hardwoods, largely worked by British capital and Chinese labor.

In British Malaya, the agricultural policy of the colonial state worked against the Malay peasantry. It

WAWASAN 2020

Wawasan 2020 or Vision 2020 is the ambitious vision of Malaysia's longest-serving prime minister, Mahathir Mohamad. It was launched in 1991. Through this vision Mahathir aspires to see Malaysia an industrialized nation by the year 2020. Ideally, he wants to see Malaysia become a great country equipped to compete effectively in the information age.

One of the goals is to have Malaysia double its gross national product every ten years so that by the year 2020 Malaysia's economic output will be eight times what it was in 1990. However, the 1997 financial crisis that struck the entire Asian region, including Malaysia, could be a setback in meeting these goals.

With this vision in mind, the prime minister has launched a series of ambitious infrastructure projects to help Malaysia realize its goals. Among these are the Express Rail Link, Kuala Lumpur City Center, Kuala Lumpur International Airport (replacing the former Subang International Airport), Kuala Lumpur Sentral, Multimedia Super Corridor, Putrajaya, and many other large projects.

The vision is based on the nine challenges that are facing the nation as defined by Mahathir. They are:

> [E]stablishing a united Malaysian nation with a sense of common and shared destiny. . . .
>
> [C]reating a psychologically liberated, secure, and developed Malaysian Society with faith and confidence in itself. . . . This Malaysian Society must be distinguished by the pursuit of excellence. . . .
>
> [F]ostering and developing a mature democratic society, practising a form of mature consensual, community-oriented Malaysian democracy that can be a model for many developing countries.
>
> [E]stablishing a fully moral and ethical society, whose citizens are strong in religious and spiritual values and imbued with the highest of ethical standards.
>
> [E]stablishing a mature, liberal and tolerant society in which Malaysians of all colours and creeds are free to practise and profess their customs, culture and religious beliefs and yet feeling that they belong to one nation.
>
> [E]stablishing a scientific and progressive society, a society that is innovative and forward-looking. . . .
>
> [E]stablishing a fully caring society and a caring culture, a social system in which society will come before self. . . .
>
> [E]nsuring an economically just society. . . .
>
> [E]stablishing a prosperous society, with an economy that is fully competitive, dynamic, robust and resilient. (Mahathir 2002)

Mala Selvaraju

Sources: Denison Javasooria. (1994) *Vision 2020 and Challenges Facing the Marginalized Communities in Malaya.* Kuala Lumpur, Malaysia: Centre for Community Studies.

Mahathir Mohamad. (2002) "Malaysia As A Fully Developed Country." Retrieved 9 April 2002, from: http://www.wawasan2020.com/vision/p2.html.

was the expressed aim of the colonial state to maintain a Malay yeoman peasantry engaged in food crop (mainly rice) production to meet the consumption needs of the large and increasing immigrant labor force in the capitalist sector (mining and commercial agriculture). The goal of this policy was to minimize the outflow of foreign exchange in payment of rice and other food imports. In line with this policy, the colonial state discouraged rubber cultivation by the peasantry, for example, by restricting rubber cultivation on certain lands, such as Malay Reservation Land. Notwithstanding the official preference for large rubber estates managed by British capital, there emerged a considerable number of Malay smallholdings. These smallholdings suffered continuous discrimination by the pro-estate stance of the colonial state, particularly during the implementation of restriction schemes during the 1920s and 1930s.

The Effects of the Great Depression and World War II

The production and export of commodities—tin, gold, petroleum, rubber, timber—made British Malaya, Sabah, and Sarawak players in the world economy with its vicissitudes of price booms and slumps. Whereas British Malaya and Sabah, on a lesser scale, suffered severe dislocations during the Great Depression (1929–1931), Sarawak braved the depression years with minimal repercussions. British Malaya was dealt a crushing blow with the forced closing of mines and estates, widespread and massive layoffs of workers, repatriation of Indian and Chinese laborers, and bankruptcies. The extent of suffering mirrored the extent of involvement of British Malaya in the world economy. Owing to the restrictions placed by the Brooke government on large capitalist ventures and the continuous discouragement of rubber monoculture by native and Chinese smallholders, Sarawak experienced little economic dislocation. Sarawak's indigenous peoples, who had never discarded their subsistence mode of livelihood, were deprived of only the extra income derived from the sale of rubber.

The wartime economy during the three years and eight months of Japanese military occupation (1941–1945) of British Malaya, Sabah, and Sarawak was focused on food-crop production aimed at food self-sufficiency. Notwithstanding the relentless efforts largely achieved through coercion, there were widespread shortages of food, especially rice. Worst hit was the urban population, which had always relied on imported foodstuffs. Subsistence-based rural communities fared better during the occupation. The tin and rubber industries came to a halt during the war years. The Japanese managed to reactivate petroleum production at Miri despite scorched-earth tactics implemented prior to the Japanese landings. By 1944, the Japanese attained almost half the prewar output.

Malaysia after Independence

Sabah and Sarawak became British Crown colonies in 1946. In 1957, Malaya attained independence, excluding Singapore, which remained a British Crown colony. In 1963, Singapore, Sabah, and Sarawak joined the Federation of Malaya to form Malaysia. Two years later, Singapore seceded from Malaysia.

Malaysia's economic landscape experienced dramatic changes in the postcolonial period. The market economy of the nation at the time of independence was largely dependent on the production and export of primary commodities—tin, rubber, petroleum, and timber. At the same time, a conspicuous feature of the economy was a large concentration of indigenous peoples (Malays in Peninsular Malaysia and the various native communities in Sabah and Sarawak) in the subsistence agricultural sector, with nonindigenous groups (mainly Chinese) playing pivotal roles in the modern rural and urban sectors.

Several major policy shifts were made in agricultural and industrial development during the four decades after independence. The immediate postindependence period was devoted to diversifying the agricultural and industrial bases, which during the colonial period had focused on the monoculture of rubber and the processing of raw materials for the world market. Oil palm cultivation was introduced in the early 1960s as an alternative to rubber. Growth in palm oil production was spectacular; by the mid-1990s, Malaysia accounted for half of world production. Cacao production expanded promisingly throughout the 1980s; by the early 1990s, cacao became the fourth most important agricultural commodity after palm oil, timber, and rubber. Sabah accounted for more than 86 percent of the nation's total cacao output. Whereas Sabah led in timber production and export during the colonial period, Sarawak took the lead in the 1960s. In the last quarter of the 1990s, Sarawak accounted for 36 percent of total timber production, Peninsular Malaysia 24 percent, and Sabah 20 percent.

Initially the strategy for industrial development was to promote import-substituting industrialization, which was pursued after independence until the late 1960s. Then, in the early 1970s, industrial policy was shifted to emphasize export-oriented industrialization whereby manufactures were added to the list of exports that hitherto comprised raw materials, hence broadening the ties to the world economy. During the 1980s, policy was shifted to emphasize the manufacturing sector. Consequently, by 1987, manufacturing overtook agriculture as the lead growth sector. The major manufactured exports then were electronic and electrical products, chemical products, wood-based and fabricated metal products, textiles and clothing, and transport equipment. The 1990s witnessed another reorientation in Malaysia's economy. In an effort to transform Malaysia into an industrialized nation by the year 2020, a strategic shift was undertaken to replace low-skill, low-value-added output with high-skill, high-value-added output. After the early 1970s, foreign direct investments were greatly encouraged through various incentives (free-trade zones, tax exemptions, and so on).

The extractive industries that had long relied on the tin industry shifted to petroleum and natural gas in the 1970s. Offshore oil and gas fields in Terengganu, Sabah, and Sarawak boosted the mineral sector, which by the late 1990s accounted for 40 percent of industrial production. Tin output has steadily declined since the 1980s.

The New Economic Policy (NEP), launched in 1970, focused on two objectives. First, the NEP sought to reduce and eventually eradicate poverty, regardless of ethnicity, by increasing income levels and generating employment opportunities. Second, the NEP sought to restructure Malaysian society to correct economic imbalances between racial groups and uneven geographical development, thereby gradually eliminating the identification of race with economic function. At the end of the scheduled twenty-year period of the NEP, its achievements were encouraging. In 1991, the New Development Policy (NDP), which laid the basis of Malaysia's Vision 2020 program, was inaugurated to attain industrialized status for the nation by the year 2020. Emphasis was placed on the manufacturing sector to propel the economy forward; its share of exports was expected to increase to more than 90 percent by 2020. But the regional economic crisis of 1997–1998 has set back Vision 2020 by at least a decade.

Ooi Keat Gin

Further Reading

Allen, G. C., and A. G. Donnithorne. (1954) *Western Enterprise in Indonesia and Malaya.* London: Allen & Unwin.

Faaland, J., J. R. Parkinson, and Rais Saniman. (1990) *Growth and Ethnic Inequality: Malaysia's New Economic Policy.* London: Hurst.

Gullick, J. M. (1987) *Malay Society in the Late Nineteenth Century: The Beginnings of Change.* Singapore: Oxford University Press.

Jomo, Kwame Sundaram. (1986) *A Question of Class: Capital, the State, and Uneven Development in Malaya.* Singapore: Oxford University Press.

———, and Greg Felker, eds. (1999) *Technology, Competitiveness, and the State: Malaysia's Industrial Technology Policies.* London: Routledge.

Kaur, Amarjit. (1998) *Economic Change in East Malaysia: Sabah and Sarawak since 1850.* New York: St. Martin's Press.

Kratoska, Paul H. (1998) *The Japanese Occupation of Malaya: A Social and Economic History.* London: Hurst.

Lim, Teck Ghee. (1977) *Peasants and Their Agricultural Economy in Colonial Malaya, 1874–1941.* Kuala Lumpur, Malaysia: Oxford University Press.

Mahathir, Mohamad. (1998) *The Way Forward.* London: Weidenfeld & Nicolson.

Ooi Keat Gin. (1997) *Of Free Trade and Native Interests: The Brookes and the Economic Development of Sarawak, 1841–1941.* Kuala Lumpur, Malaysia: Oxford University Press.

———. (1999) *Rising Sun over Borneo: The Japanese Occupation of Sarawak, 1941–1945.* New York: St. Martin's Press.

Rajah, Rasiah. (1995) *Foreign Capital and Industrialization in Malaysia.* New York: St. Martin's Press.

Rokiah, Alavi. (1996) *Industrialization in Malaysia: Import Substitution and Infant Industry Performance.* London: Routledge.

Wolters, O. W. (1970) *The Fall of Srivijaya in Malay History.* Kuala Lumpur, Malaysia: Oxford University Press.

MALAYSIA—EDUCATION SYSTEM

MALAYSIA—EDUCATION SYSTEM Education and society in Malaysia, as in other nations, are inherently linked. The form of Malaysia's educational system can be traced to the era of British colonialism starting at the beginning of the nineteenth century. The impact of colonialism was twofold. First, under British rule, Malaya (Malaya was the preindependence [1957] term and Malaysia the postindependence one) developed into a multiethnic society, incorporating Chinese and Indians (brought to the colony primarily as laborers) within the indigenous Malayan society. Educational policies have since been highly influenced by this social structure. Second, Malaysia's educational system bears a heavy imprint of Britain's.

Today the Malaysian education system is a reasonably successful one, responding to the demands for equity among the different ethnic groups as well as the needs of a rapidly developing economy. The literacy rate is 84 percent, the figures for males and females being 89 percent and 79 percent, respectively. Primary school enrollment is above 90 percent for both males and females, while enrollment at the secondary level is 66 percent for females and 58 percent for males, presumably reflecting the higher labor force demands on males. At the tertiary level enrollment is 11 percent overall.

Religious education is found under the rubric "moral education," which allows for religious instruction without offending any specific ethnic group. The Malay language (Bahasa Malaysia) and English are compulsory subjects, with the latter recently receiving increasing attention. The other subjects taken at the secondary level depend on what options are chosen in addition to the usual required academic subjects—commercial studies, home science, agricultural science, and industrial arts.

Education in the Colonial Era

By the end of the colonial era in the 1950s, Malaya had four distinct educational systems. One was the English system, a result of the increasing need, from the late nineteenth century, for more English-speaking people to work in commerce and government. The other three, following the ethnic divisions in Malaya, were vernacular schools for the Malays, Chinese, and Indians. Whereas the vernacular schools provided ba-

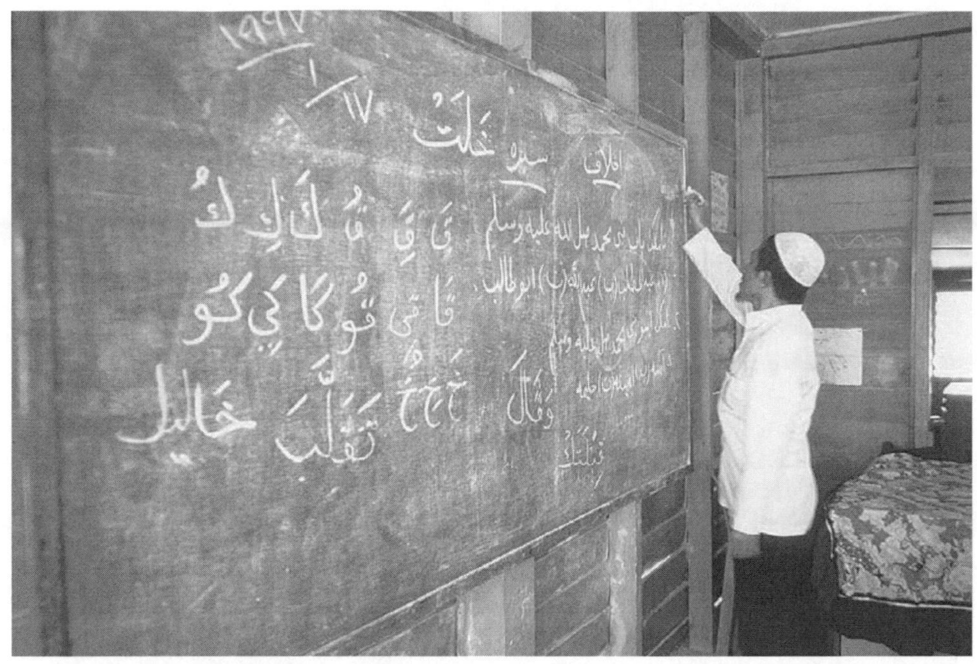

A Muslim teacher writing in Arabic on the blackboard in a school on Pangkor Island in 1997. (EARL & NAZIMA KOWALL/CORBIS)

sic education in the Malay language or a Chinese or Indian dialect, the English system aimed at higher educational levels and was the path for upward mobility in the colony. It was not possible to attain higher education in the vernacular schools.

Education in Malaya after World War II

After World War II, British policy was oriented toward self-determination for Malaya. The primary purpose of the new educational system was to develop a common sense of identity among the peoples of Malaya with a view to furthering social stability following the granting of independence.

The Education Act of 1961 was one of compromise. Although the vernacular school system was retained, the Malay language was made compulsory as a subject and it became apparent that a long-term goal of the government was to make Malay the language of instruction for all children in Malaya—it would be the new national language (Bahasa Malaysia). In this regard, English was relegated to a secondary position for political reasons, although basic British educational structures, including the examination system, were retained.

Communal riots following the 1969 federal election led to significant social and economic changes in Malaysia, and issues related to language and education were of particular importance. Malay claims for parity became the basis for policy formulation. With regard to the medium of instruction in schools, the minister of education announced a timetable for the progressive implementation of Bahasa Malaysia in all schools beginning in 1970 (it had become the nation's official language in 1967). This was a critical issue because, as in the past, ability in English had dominated access to higher education and therefore employment prospects and socioeconomic mobility.

The revised educational policies were set out in the New Economic Policy (NEP), the aims of which were included in the Second Malaysia Plan (SMP) of 1970–1975. The goal was to raise the socioeconomic circumstances of the Malay population and thereby dampen ethnic and racial frictions within Malaysia. An integral part of the NEP was a program designed to raise the number of *bumiputra*s (meaning "sons of the soil," referring for the most part to ethnic Malays but including a small number of other indigenous groups) in the universities in Malaysia. A quota system in favor of the Malays was therefore established.

Ethnic Groups and Tertiary Places in Contemporary Context

The NEP has been quite effective at redressing the imbalances. This trend differs considerably from the trend early in the twentieth century, when non-*bumiputra*s were overrepresented in the system in general, education in the English medium in particular, and later at the tertiary level (college or university level). However, the ethnic quotas—which were adopted initially to redress Malay underrepresentation in universities and which were administered by implementing a requirement of higher entry marks for Chinese and Indians—resulted in the Malays being overrepresented in tertiary institutions.

Malaysia's educational system reflects a history of British colonialism, not only in the basic form of its structures, but also in the fact that educational policies are a response to the multiethnic society created under British colonialism. Although vernacular schools continue to function, funded primarily by private means, the educational system is dominated by publicly funded institutions in which Bahasa Malaysia is the medium of instruction. Recently there has been increased concern over the decline in the quality of students' English, and it appears that this language is enjoying a resurgence in the educational system.

The Malaysian government faces a dilemma in its policies. On the one hand, it must satisfy demands from the Malays for a greater role in the economy of the nation. To this end, the government has given this group preferential treatment in terms of access to higher education. On the other hand, if too many restrictions are placed on the other ethnic groups in terms of access to a reasonable share of the wealth of the nation, including entrance to tertiary institutions, communal tension could again build up. Moreover, non-*bumiputras* still play a dominant role in the economy of the nation. If people from this group feel that the restrictions placed on them are too great, they may emigrate, taking their skills and assets with them. Those who cannot emigrate are likely to become frustrated in the extreme. One safety valve for middle-class ethnic Chinese and Indians has been access to tertiary education in foreign branch campuses in Malaysia or educational institutions in other nations.

Curtis A. Andressen

Further Reading

Andaya, B. W., and L. Y. Andaya. (1982) *A History of Malaysia*. London: Macmillan.

Andressen, C. (1993) *Educational Refugees: Malaysian Students in Australia*. Monash Papers on Southeast Asia no. 29. Melbourne, Australia: Monash University Press.

Chee, T. S. (1979) "Issues in Malaysian Education: Past, Present, and Future." *Journal of Southeast Asian Studies* 10, 2 (September): 321–350.

Chien, D. J. (1986) *University Places: Options for a Creative Response*. Kuala Lumpur, Malaysia: Institute of Strategic and International Studies.

Jayasuriya, J. E. (1983) *Dynamics of Nation-Building in Malaysia*. Colombo, Sri Lanka: Associated Educational Publishers.

Karthigesu, R. (1986) "Distribution of Opportunities in Tertiary Education in Malaysia: A Review of the Fifth Malaysia Plan." *Educators and Education: Journal of the School of Educational Studies, Universiti Sains Malaysia* 8, 34–47.

Loh, P. F. S. (1974) "A Review of the Educational Developments in the Federated Malay States to 1939." *Journal of Southeast Asian Studies* 5, 2 (September): 225–238.

Sharma, C. L. (1979) "Ethnicity, Communal Relations and Education in Malaysia." *Southeast Asian Journal of Educational Studies* 16, 1–2 (December): 9–22.

Thomas, R. M. (1983) "Malaysia: Cooperation versus Competition—or National Unity versus Favored Access to Education." In *Politics and Education*, edited by R. M. Thomas. Oxford: Pergamon Press, 149–169.

MALAYSIA—HISTORY

MALAYSIA—HISTORY Malaysia is one of the most developed countries in Southeast Asia, surpassed in per capita income only by Singapore and the small but oil-rich sultanate of Brunei Darussalam. In developing its economy, Malaysia traditionally relied on commodity exports of rubber, tin, palm oil, and petroleum. More recently, however, it gained competitiveness in export manufactures, especially in the electronics sector. Malaysia's mines and plantations have thus been transformed into urban high-rises, industrial estates, and middle-class housing tracts.

Over the past few decades, this rapid economic development has distinguished Malaysia in the region, capturing the attention of economists seeking strategies for eradicating poverty, as well as foreign investors searching for markets. But Malaysia has also confronted—and in some measure overcome—other challenges. For example, political struggles and great social pressures have periodically tested the country's democratic procedures, first introduced during the final phase of British colonialism. Yet unlike many other former British possessions, Malaysia has managed to perpetuate at least some of its formal democratic structures, including regular elections and a reasonably competitive party system. On the social level, Malaysia has often been characterized as a "plural" or "divided" society, with ethnic rivalries forming principally between Malays and Chinese. Ethnic imbalances and resentments have been alleviated over time, however, through a program of affirmative action known as the New Economic Policy, while some sense of cross-ethnic unity has been forged through a new notion of *bangsar Malaysia* (Malaysian race).

In 1997–1998, Malaysia's record of economic development was challenged by the financial crisis that struck Asia. The government responded imaginatively, if somewhat heretically, with capital controls that enabled Malaysia to recover more rapidly than neighboring countries that conformed to the dictates of the International Monetary Fund (IMF). Nonetheless, as

KEY EVENTS IN MALAYSIA'S HISTORY

15th century The Melaka sultanate flourishes.
1511 Melaka is captured by the Portuguese, then the Dutch.
1824 The Dutch trade Melaka to the British, who combine it with Singapore and Penang to form the Straits Settlements.
1941–1945 Malaya is controlled by the Japanese.
1946 The United Malays National Organization is founded.
1957 British colonial rule ends.
1963 Malaya federates with Singapore, Sarawak, and Sabah to form Malaysia.
1965 Singapore becomes an independent nation.
1960s Ethnic politics emerges as a major issue.
1969 The riots known as the May Thirteenth incident take place.
1970s The New Economic Policy is enacted.
1981 The government under Mahathir becomes more repressive.
1980s–1990s The economy grows rapidly.
1997–1998 The economy falters during the Asian economic crisis.

the twenty-first century dawned, Malaysia's industrial development was once again under strain as the contraction of the global economy reduced the demand for electronics goods. At the same time, the military action against the Taliban in Afghanistan quickened the pace of Islamic resurgence; although Islamic leaders cast their renewed fervor in nonracial terms, they still threatened to rekindle social unrest.

It is these features, then, that give Malaysia greater significance on the world scene than its population suggests. It has developed rapidly over the past few decades, earning a World Bank ranking as a middle-income country. It has preserved enough democratic procedures that its politics can be understood as a stable semidemocracy. And its pluralistic society, while not having converged in tight nationalist unity, displays much tolerance and accommodation.

Colonial Legacies and Independence

In precolonial times, the societies found on what is today the west coast of peninsular Malaysia reached their apogee in the fifteenth century, forming a maritime empire known as the Melaka sultanate. In 1511, however, Melaka was captured by the Portuguese, then seized by the Dutch. In 1824, it was traded to the British, who were already established in the port cities of Singapore and Penang. During the final quarter of the nineteenth century, the British used these three coastal outposts, known collectively as the Straits Settlements, to move deeper into the peninsula, gaining control over the tin trade (which flourished thanks in part to new food-canning technologies that had developed during the U.S. Civil War) and rubber plantations (markets for rubber latex having emerged with the introduction of the pneumatic tire). British colonialists also ranged farther afield into north Borneo, which included the territories of Sarawak, the sultanate of Brunei, and what would later be christened Sabah.

Beyond the Straits Settlements, the British practiced "indirect rule" on the peninsula, relying upon local Malay sultans and aristocrats to exercise traditional forms of authority over the indigenous population. In order to perpetuate these social patterns and the political deference they encouraged, the British insulated the indigenous community from new economic undertakings. Hence, to operate the rapidly expanding tin mines and rubber plantations, the British recruited large numbers of immigrant workers, mainly from south China and India. Although the Chinese thus entered the economy's modern sectors and occasionally amassed great personal fortunes, they were viewed as sojourners without political rights. In this way, the politically sovereign but collectively poor Malays were counterbalanced by the economically empowered but politically disenfranchised Chinese. Most Indians remained both poor and disenfranchised, subsisting as tappers on often-remote rubber plantations. Meanwhile, behind the facade of traditional Malay sovereignty and indirect rule, British civil servants administered the territory through a deeply penetrative bureaucratic apparatus. And atop the labor of Chinese tin miners and artisans, British investors and managers reaped the benefits of increasingly large-scale commercial activities.

At the start of World War II, the Japanese occupied Malaya, disrupting the complex ethnic balance that had been perpetuated by the British. In particular, the Japanese encouraged the political aspirations of Malay aristocrats, who could set their sights on the bureaucratic positions opened up by the flight or internment of British officials. At the same time, the Japanese neglected the wider Malay community and harshly discriminated against the Chinese. This triggered some Chinese guerrilla resistance, fortified by ethnic resentments and Marxist ideology.

After the war the British returned, and having conceptualized Malay wartime behaviors as collaborative, proposed a new governing arrangement, known as the Malayan Union. In this scheme, the standing of Malay sultans would be sharply diminished, while the Chinese would be rewarded with full citizenship and political rights. The Malay community was soon roused from its torpor, first protesting the Malayan Union, then forming a variety of organizations that cohered in 1946 under the leadership of Dato Onn bin Jaafar (1895–1962) as the United Malays National Organization (UMNO). The British then dropped the union proposals, thereby precipitating a new militancy among the Chinese, which gained force through the Malayan Communist Party (MCP), which launched an insurgency known popularly as the Emergency.

The British responded to the Emergency with a two-track approach, first mounting a counterinsurgency that was distinguished by innovative techniques. But they sought also to forge a moderate Chinese political party, one whose leaders could compete with the MCP for Chinese loyalties and effectively interact with leaders of the UMNO. To this end the British recruited a prominent Chinese businessman, Tan Cheng Lock (1883–1960), and assisted him in forming the Malayan (later Malaysian) Chinese Association (MCA). They also convened a series of Community Liaison Committee meetings through which elite-level cooperation could be forged across ethnic lines. In this way, the British encouraged both the competitive party organizations and interpersonal restraint that would make peaceful yet meaningful elections possible.

During the 1950s, the British introduced a staggered series of electoral contests, proceeding from local to national levels. In the course of waging these contests, the UMNO and the MCA formed a winning coalition called the Alliance. These parties also recruited a third partner, the Malayan (later Malaysian) Indian Congress. Within this coalition, UMNO remained pivotal. However, the MCA and the MIC attracted significant support from the Chinese and Indian communities, respectively, thus bolstering the Malay support won by the UMNO. The Communist insurgency subsided, democratic procedures took root, and the party system grew more firmly institutionalized, encouraging the British to decolonize Malaya in 1957. The country grew in size in 1963, when the peninsula merged with Singapore, Sarawak, and Sabah, thereby transforming Malaya into Malaysia. Singapore departed from the new federation two years later, however, in somewhat acrimonious circumstances.

During the 1960s, the Alliance continued to flourish, winning parliamentary elections in 1964 and most state-level contests. However, as urbanization took place, many Malay rice farmers and fishermen gathered on the fringes of the cities, there to observe the market activities and relative prosperity of the Chinese. In these circumstances, many Malays turned gradually from UMNO to an opposition party, the more stridently ethnic Pan-Islamic Party of Malaysia (PAS). Many Chinese voters, equally alienated by what they viewed as the compromising outlook of the MCA, turned to new Chinese parties in opposition, the Democratic Action Party and the Gerakan Rakyat Malaysia (Malaysian People's Movement). Thus, when general elections were held on 10 May 1969, the Alliance won at the federal level, but with a much reduced majority in parliament. It was also defeated outright in several state assemblies.

In these circumstances, the Malay community contemplated the erosion of UMNO preeminence. Many Chinese, for their part, responded by celebrating the rise of the opposition. Three days after the election, street confrontations broke out between Chinese and Malays in the capital of Kuala Lumpur; these caused significant loss of life and extensive property damage, an event that is locally recorded as the May Thirteenth incident. After diagnosing the loss of Malay support for the government and the causes of the rioting, UMNO leaders began to restructure Malaysia's democratic political system and the largely free-market economy.

The Present

In order to renew its grip on state power, the UMNO coopted PAS and Gerakan into its ruling coalition, rechristening the Alliance as the Barisan Nasional ("National Front"). In expanding its coalition, the UMNO further heightened its own standing while effectively di-

FORMING A UNIFIED MALAYA

After World War II the British resumed control in Malaya and proposed a new governing arrangement, known as the Malayan Union. The scheme included granting citizenship to residents as set forth in the 1948 Federation of Malaya Agreement below and weakening the authority of the sultans.

> Agreement dated the twenty-first day of January, 1948, and made between Sir Gerard Edward James Gent . . . on behalf of His Majesty and the [nine rulers of Johore, Pahang, Negri Sembilan, Selangor, Perak, Kedah, Perlis, Kelantan, and Trengganu]:
>
> Whereas it has been represented to His Majesty that fresh arrangements should be made for the peace, order and good government of the Malay States of Johore, Pahang, Negri Sembilan, Selangor, Perak, Kedah, Perlis, Kelantan and Trengganu, the Settlement of Penang and the Settlement of Malacca:
>
> And whereas His Majesty in token of the friendship he bears towards their Highnesses, the subjects of Their Highnesses, and the inhabitants of the Malay States, is pleased to make fresh arrangements as aforesaid to take effect on such day as His Majesty may, by Order in Council; appoint . . . :
>
> And Whereas His Majesty has accordingly entered into a fresh agreement with each of Their Highnesses . . . for the purpose of ensuring that power and jurisdiction shall be exercised by Their several Highnesses in their several States and it is in each of such Agreements provided that it shall come into operation on the appointed day:
>
> And Whereas it seems expedient to His Majesty and to Their Highnesses that the Malay States, the Settlement of Penang and the Settlement of Malacca should be forced into a Federation with a strong central government and that there should be a common form of citizenship in the said Federation to be extended to all those who regard the said Federation or any part of it as their real home and the object of their loyalty:
>
> And Whereas it is the desire of His Majesty and Their Highnesses that progress should be made towards eventual self-government, and, as a first step to that end, His Majesty and Their Highnesses have agreed that, as soon as circumstances and local conditions will permit, legislation should be introduced for the election of members to the several legislatures to be established pursuant to this Agreement:
>
> Now, Therefore, it is agreed and declared as follows:
>
> 1. There shall be established a Federation comprising the Malay States, the Settlement of Penang and the Settlement of Malacca, to be known as the Federation of Malaya . . . .
>
> Provided that His Majesty and Their Highnesses the Rulers reserve to themselves the power by mutual agreement from time to time to admit within the Federation any other territory or territories as they shall see fit.
>
> 2. His Majesty shall have complete control of the defence and of all the external affairs of the Federation and undertakes to protect the Malay States from external hostile attacks, and for this and other similar purposes, His Majesty's Forces and persons authorised by or on behalf of His Majesty's Government shall at all times be allowed free access to the Malay States and to employ all necessary means of opposing such attacks.

Source: Federation of Malaya Government Gazette. (1948) Kuala Lumpur: Federal Government (5 February), vol. 1, no. 1.

minishing opposition forces. Furthermore, a series of constitutional amendments and sedition laws were passed, effectively prohibiting criticisms of the ruling coalition's policies by the opposition in parliament, while truncating civil liberties more broadly.

After Mahathir Mohamad (b. 1925) became prime minister in 1981, additional controls were incrementally imposed on free communication and assembly and were enforced through regular applications of preventive detention under the Internal Security Act, first

People march in the 31 August 1999 parade in Merdeka Square, Kuala Lumpur, marking the 42nd National Day after independence from British rule in 1957. (AFP/CORBIS)

introduced in 1960 as a way to control Communists. Indeed, amid a leadership challenge mounted from within the UMNO in 1987, Mahathir ordered the detention of over a hundred opposition leaders and members of nongovernmental organizations, an exercise known as Operation Lallang. He also brought an independent judiciary to heel, replacing many of its judges with more compliant functionaries.

The extent to which the judiciary had become subservient to the executive was made plain a decade later, during a challenge to Mahathir mounted by his deputy, Anwar Ibrahim (b. 1947). Amid the regional economic crisis of 1997–1998, forces aligned with Anwar tried to discredit Mahathir at a UMNO party assembly. In a highly publicized case that attracted the attention of legal observers from around the world, Mahathir expelled Anwar from the party and the cabinet, while his attorney-general brought charges against Anwar of corruption and sexual misconduct. Although the evidence appeared scant, Anwar was convicted and sentenced to fifteen years in prison. Meanwhile, security forces suppressed a broad-based movement for political reform that had been triggered by Anwar's downfall.

The New Economic Policy

After the May Thirteenth incident, the UMNO not only consolidated its political grip, but also entered deeply into the economy in order to reenergize its support among its ethnic Malay constituencies. The UMNO introduced a series of quotas on public and private employment, the distribution of equity ownership, and the issuance of state contracts, credit, and business licenses that heavily favored the Malays. This affirmative-action program, known as the New Economic Policy (NEP), is one of the most systematic programs of cross-ethnic redistribution ever attempted.

During the 1970s, when NEP quotas were most rigorously enforced, the Chinese community grew proportionately alienated, and many people emigrated. But over time, many members of the Malay community grew sophisticated in business dealings, while a new urban Malay middle class emerged. Hence, while the NEP doubtless fueled corruption in the UMNO, spawning a series of financial abuses and scandals, it appeared to mitigate ethnic Malay resentment. In this context, many Chinese came grudgingly to recognize NEP's social benefits. Put simply, with greater equality between ethnic communities established, violence on the scale of May thirteenth has never recurred in Malaysia. Furthermore, as part of Malaysia's Vision 2020 program for full economic and social development, Mahathir heralded the formation of a new national identity, with Malays and Chinese converging as *bangsawan Malaysia*.

Greater ethnic forbearance in Malaysia was encouraged not only by redistribution, but also by Malaysia's rapid industrialization. During the 1970s, the inefficiencies associated with NEP quotas were offset by the discovery and export of natural gas. And from the late 1980s to the late 1990s, the economy grew through foreign investment in Malaysia's electronics-manufacturing sector. Indeed, Malaysia attained some of the highest growth rates in the world during this decade, helping sustain new business conglomerates, a burgeoning middle class, relative ethnic harmony, and even a new nationalist identity and pride. It was during this time that Malaysia celebrated its achievements with a number of grand projects, including the world's tallest building, the Petronas Twin Towers.

During 1997–1998, however, the economic crisis that swept Asia halted Malaysia's record of development. Unlike other national leaders, however, who turned to the IMF for support, Mahathir invoked a series of capital controls that pegged the national currency to the U.S. dollar, banned the currency's offshore trading, and blocked the repatriation of capital gains by foreign investors. Despite attracting much international criticism, these measures were cheered by local businesspeople and consumers. Moreover, they appeared to promote faster economic recovery in Malaysia than IMF strictures facilitated in neighboring countries.

Nonetheless, Malaysia, like most of Asia, was beset by new economic difficulties in 2001, with global markets for electronics exports and tourism shrinking dramatically. Unemployment increased commensurately, rekindling social pressures. However, Malaysia's new nationalist identity appeared in some degree to take hold; social tensions were manifest less in terms of renewed conflict between the Malay and Chinese communities than between UMNO members and the more stridently Islamist PAS.

William Case

See also: **Malayan Emergency; Malayan Union; Malay States, Unfederated; Melaka Sultanate; Straits Settlements**

Further Reading

Case, William. (1996) *Elites and Regimes in Malaysia: Revisiting a Consociational Democracy*. Clayton, Australia: Monash University.

Crouch, Harold. (1996) *Government and Society in Malaysia*. Ithaca, NY: Cornell University Press.

Kahn, Joel S., and Francis Loh Kok Wah, eds. (1992) *Fragmented Vision: Culture and Politics in Contemporary Malaysia*. Sydney, Australia: Allen and Unwin.

Means, Gordon P. (1991) *Malaysian Politics: The Second Generation*. Singapore: Oxford University Press.

Milne, R. S., and Diane K. Mauzy. (1999) *Malaysian Politics under Mahathir*. London and New York: Routledge.

MALAYSIA—POLITICAL SYSTEM A former British colony, Malaysia attained independence on 31 August 1957. The nation is a federation of thirteen states, governed by a Westminster-style parliamentary system. It includes the nine states of peninsular Malaya and the two Borneo territories of Sabah and Sarawak. The population is approximately twenty-five million, 52 percent of whom are ethnic Malays, 35 percent ethnic Chinese, and 10 percent Indians.

Paramount Ruler

The head of state, the paramount ruler, is one of nine hereditary sultans who serve rotating five-year terms; he is constitutionally required to act with the advice of the prime minister. The paramount ruler is elected by the conference of rulers, which includes the nine hereditary sultans and four appointed governors and meets three to four times a year.

Parliament

There is a bicameral parliament consisting of a nonelected upper house and a popularly elected lower house. The senate, or Dewan Negara, has sixty-nine seats, forty-three of which are appointed by the paramount ruler and twenty-six by the state legislatures. The house of representatives, or Dewan Rakyat, has 193 seats; members are elected by popular vote to serve five-year terms. Malaysia has universal suffrage for all adults over twenty-one years of age. The electoral system is weighted toward the rural Malay population.

Head of Government

The head of the government is the prime minister, who is chosen from among the members of the house of representatives. Following legislative elections, the leader of the party that wins a plurality of seats in the house of representatives becomes prime minister and appoints a cabinet. The prime minister is in charge of day-to-day governance. Beneath the prime minister is a cabinet made up of the heads of all government ministries and ministerial-level commissions and bodies. The cabinet meets once a week. If the prime minister loses the confidence of parliament, he or she must resign, along with the cabinet, and ask the paramount ruler to dissolve parliament; popular elections must be held within sixty days (ninety days in Sabah and Sarawak), and a new government is formed after legislative elections are held.

National Parties and Government Stability

Malaysia has experienced relative political stability. There have been only four prime ministers since the

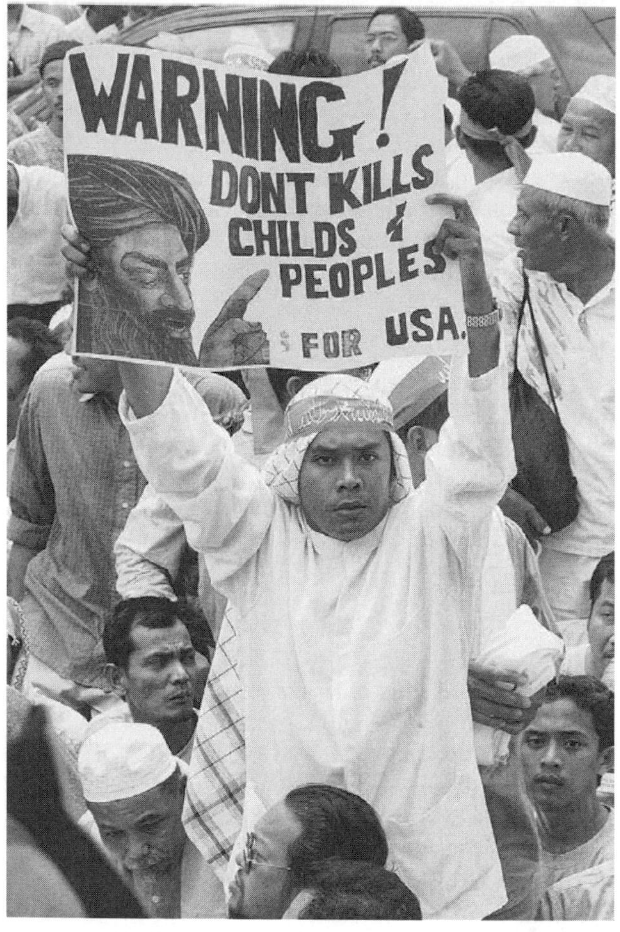

Demonstrators from Malaysia's opposition Parti Islam Se-Malaysia protest the United States military action in Afghanistan in Kuala Lumpur in October 2001. (AFP/CORBIS)

country's founding, the first three all scions of the sultanates. Mahathir Mohamad (b. 1925), the current prime minister, chosen in 1981, is the longest-serving premier.

The National Alliance, the grouping of the three major ethnic-based parties—the United Malay National Organization (UMNO), the Malaysian Chinese Association, and the Malaysian Indian Congress—has dominated the government since the first federal elections in 1955. As ethnic minorities, many Chinese and Indians believe that their interests are best served by working with the dominant Malay party, UMNO. Since the founding of the country, all four prime ministers have belonged to the UMNO, including the incumbent, Mahathir Mohamad.

There are several opposition political parties, including Parti Islam SeMalaysia (PAS), an Islamic party that is the main opposition party for ethnic Malays. Although an opposition party at the federal level, PAS controls two states in northeastern Malaysia, Kelantan and Teregganu, and has succeeded in winning ethnic Malay support away from the UMNO. The Democratic Action Party (DAP) is modeled on Singapore's dominant party, the People's Action Party. The DAP remains dominated by ethnic Chinese and has been unable to broaden its base of support; hence it wins only a portion of the Chinese vote. The National Justice Party (NJP), founded in 1998 by the wife of the former deputy prime minister Anwar Ibrahim, has helped to win ethnic Malay support away from the UMNO, especially from those Malays who want a more secular opposition party than PAS. In the house of representatives, the National Front coalition holds 148 of the seats; PAS has 27; DAP has 10; NJP has 5; and the Parti Bersatu Sabah has 3. Although the power of opposition parties has grown, they have been unable to forge a durable coalition to challenge the UMNO-dominated National Alliance.

Although the government has an electoral system that virtually guarantees that it gets returned to power each election because of the National Front's alliance with the three largest ethnic-based parties, it also uses a variety of authoritarian measures to keep the opposition weak. Several draconian laws were inherited from the colonial era, including the Internal Security Act (ISA), the Sedition Act, and the Official Secrets Act. Press freedoms are severely restricted as the government has the right to revoke or deny licenses to newspapers that aggravate national sensitivities or fail to serve national development goals. Journalists, editors, publishers, and printers are all punishable, and there is a lot of self-censorship. The government keeps tabs on all newspapers and maintains control over some media through direct ownership.

The ISA allows the minister of home affairs to detain anyone without trial if he or she is satisfied that such detention is necessary to prevent the person from acting in a way prejudicial to the security of Malaysia or to the maintenance of essential services. The supreme court has upheld the ISA, which however was slightly amended in 1988, so that the court can now review cases on procedural, though not factual, grounds.

The Sedition Act deters political discussion and debate on the country's most controversial issues. The Official Secrets Act is another broad British-based law that covers the publication of any information in the hands of the government, no matter how significant or widely known. This law has prevented journalists or opposition politicians from attacking the government on corruption charges.

Parliamentary rule was suspended once, following race riots in 1969 in which 169 people were killed after opposition gains at the polls. Martial law was imposed, and the country was ruled by decree by the National Operations Council for twenty-one months, until 1971. The government then implemented a radical affirmative-action program, the New Economic Program, designed to redistribute wealth and educational and career opportunities to the majority, but poorer, Malay community. The government believes that the dissolution of parliamentary rule and draconian laws and controls are necessary to maintain order in an ethnically divided society. But it also uses these controls to stifle opposition.

Federal System

Malaysia has a federal system of government, with thirteen states and two federal territories. On 16 September 1963, Sabah, Sarawak, and Singapore were constitutionally added to Peninsular Malaya to create the Federation of Malaysia; Singapore was subsequently expelled from the Federation on 9 August 1965. On Peninsular Malaysia, all states are governed by hereditary rulers; the governors of Melaka and Penang, as well as of the two Borneo territories of Sabah and Sarawak, are appointed by the federal government. Two federal territories are directly administered by the federal government: Wilayah Persekutuan, the national capital region that includes Kuala Lumpur and the new administrative capital of Putrajaya, and the island of Labuan. The federal system is quite weak, and most decision-making power and fiscal authority reside with the central government. Although all thirteen states have their own legislatures, there is a strong bias toward the federal parliament, and the federal government is able to control most states through the allocation of resources and transfer payments. The concept of federal supremacy pervades the legislative process, and federal law always takes precedence in cases of inconsistency or conflict with state law. It is illegal for states to pass laws that undermine the authority of the federal government.

Constitutions and Judiciary

Malaysia has had two constitutions, the Independence Constitution of 1957 and a 1963 constitution that saw the incorporation of Sarawak, Sabah, and Singapore. The legal system is based on English common law. The supreme court has the right of judicial review over legislative acts at the request of the paramount ruler.

Although Malaysia inherited a British system of common law, the judicial branch has lost much of its independence from the government. Supreme Court justices are appointed by the paramount ruler on the advice of the prime minister. But in 1988, Prime Minister Mahathir Mohamad took the unprecedented step of sacking the chief justice and two of his associates. Since then the court has become highly politicized and infrequently adjudicates against the interests of the government. In addition to the secular court system, Malaysia has a parallel Islamic—or *shari'a*—court system that adjudicates matters of family law and religion.

Zachary Abuza

Further Reading

Crouch, Harold. (1996) *Government and Society in Malaysia.* Ithaca, NY: Cornell University Press.

Gomez, Edmund Terrence, and K. S. Jomo. (1997) *Malaysia's Political Economy.* New York: Cambridge University Press.

Tarling, Nicholas, ed. (1999) *The Cambridge History of Southeast Asia.* New York: Cambridge University Press.

Watson Andaya, Barbara, and Leonard Y. Andaya. (2001) *A History of Malaysia.* 2d ed. Honolulu: University of Hawaii Press.

MALAYSIA-EUROPE RELATIONS

In world affairs, Malaysia maintains close relations with the United States, the European Union (EU), and Japan. Malaysian relations with the European nonmembers of the EU are still insufficiently developed, and there is a growing need for reinforcement of these relations, especially more effective economic cooperation. Trade between non-EU European countries and Malaysia is the most dynamic feature of this relationship, which also includes cultural and scientific exchange. The EU's dialogue with Malaysia has always been an inseparable part of the EU's (and before it the European Community, or EC's) relations with the Association of Southeast Asian Nations (ASEAN). The EU has no bilateral cooperation agreement with Malaysia. Economic cooperation between the EU and Malaysia is carried out mainly through regional programs, both within the framework of the 1980 EC-ASEAN Cooperation Agreement and through other programs.

Between 1967, when ASEAN was established, and the beginning of the 1990s, there were no particular political disagreements between the EC and ASEAN. In the 1990s, however, different approaches to political and social questions—particularly human rights, trade policy, and the impact of globalization—emerged. After the collapse of the Soviet bloc, the conflicting interests of these two regions became clearer. These conflicts have been mostly ideological, rather than economic, since both regions are trying to develop their own political and ideological cultures.

The Cenotaph, a British World War I memorial in Kuala Lumpur, Malaysia, is a reminder of the British colonial presence in Southeast Asia. (PAUL ALMASY/CORBIS)

In 1995 the European Parliament accepted the EU's new Asian strategy, wherein the ASEAN situation was considered. With the issuance of "Creating a New Dynamic in EU-ASEAN Relations" in 1996, a renewed focus was placed on the dialogue between Europe and Malaysia. During their official visit to Malaysia in 1996, EU leaders declared that they wished to develop a more meaningful political dialogue with Malaysia through a more frequent and direct exchange of views.

Asia-Europe Institute

There were series of Asia-Europe ministerial meetings in the 1990s, in which Malaysia took part. One important result was the establishment of the Asia-Europe Institute at the University of Malaya, the main mission of which is to further the integration of the Malaysian and European economies. Other principal tasks of the institute are promotion of the exchange of information on strategic business issues, analysis of the role of European banks in Asia before and after the 1997 Asian financial crisis, and comparison of the investment strategies of Asian and European banks. These tasks are undertaken in an effort to support the integration of the two financial systems.

EU-Malaysia Trade

In 1998, the EU was the third most significant export destination of Malaysian goods (behind ASEAN members and the United States), with a share of 16 percent ($12 billion). Among EU members the main Malaysian export partners were the United Kingdom and Germany, with 4 percent and 3 percent of total exports respectively. The EU was the fourth largest source of Malaysian imports (behind ASEAN members, Japan, and the United States) with a share of 12 percent ($7.1 billion). Among EU members the main Malaysian import partners were Germany and the United Kingdom, with 4 percent and 3 percent respectively. In 1998, Malaysia had a trade surplus of $5.1 billion with the EU, compared to a surplus of $250 million in 1997.

Malaysia's main exports to the EU are electronic equipment, textiles, and palm oil and palm oil products. The main imports from the EU are machinery, chemicals, and transportation equipment. Malaysia has adopted a broad range of import restrictions, especially on automobiles and heavy machinery.

EU Aid

The EU has never provided general development aid to Malaysia, but some specific activities have been funded, including forestry and pharmaceutical projects and support for refugees. European development assistance began in 1987 and for the most part has been limited to the environmental sector. The EC-Malaysia Forest Programme was agreed upon in 1992, after which several projects were implemented. The main purpose is to improve the efficiency of forest harvesting and reduce logging damage. Another aim of forestry projects is to contribute to the conservation and sustainable management of natural forests and their biological diversity. Forestry projects for Sabah, totaling $419,000, were implemented in 1998. Total funding since 1980 for other activities amounted to nearly $6.5 million.

Along with Singapore, Japan, the United States, and Taiwan, the EU is among the largest sources of foreign investment in Malaysia. In Sarawak, the EU is the main source of foreign investment, accounting for 30 percent of the total between 1995 and 2000. EU industrial investments in Sarawak come mainly from six countries: Netherlands (natural gas), United Kingdom (forestry and nonmetallic minerals), Germany (metals), Portugal (electronics), Finland (chemicals), and France (food manufacturing).

Anglo-Malaysian Relations

Great Britain has a special relationship with Malaysia, as it was the colonial power that controlled the Malaysian peninsula from the late eighteenth into the twentieth century. In 1786, the British acquired Penang Island, establishing a settlement called Georgetown. In 1826, the British formed the Straits Settlements, a colony that included Melaka (Malacca) and the islands of Penang and Singapore. The British later colonized the interior of the Malayan peninsula when tin was discovered. By the beginning of the twentieth century, Britain had established many protectorates on the Malayan peninsula, as well as in East Malaysia (the states of Sabah and Sarawak in North Borneo). By 1914, Britain had either direct or indirect colonial control over all the lands that now comprise Malaysia. After World War II, Britain united its territories on the peninsula as the Union of Malaya (1946); Sabah and Sarawak became crown colonies. In 1948, Britain created the Federation of Malaya, which became an independent state within the Commonwealth in 1957.

Several critical issues affected Anglo-Malaysian economic and business relations in the last decades of the twentieth century. In the early 1980s, diplomatic relations deteriorated when Mahathir Mohamad, Malaysia's prime minister, launched a "Buy British Last" campaign to protest skyrocketing fees for overseas students and restricted landing rights at London Heathrow airport. In 1981, "Buy British Last" became state policy, the goal of which was to decrease Malaysia's economic dependence on England. The policy was reversed later in the decade. In February 1994, Anglo-Malaysian relations were disturbed for a second time, when Malaysia's cabinet decided that British companies would be excluded from competing for any new government construction contracts. As a whole, the Malaysian relationship with Britain was cool in the 1990s, but commercial relations began to pick up in the latter half of the decade.

The Future

In the latter half of the 1990s, EU-ASEAN relations were complicated by Myanmar's joining ASEAN, as the EU looked unfavorably on Myanmar's record in supporting democracy and human rights. The future of Malaysia-Europe relations to a large extent depends on the political situation in Malaysia—in particular political stability and human rights. Street protests in the fall of 1998, calling for the resignation of Mahathir Mohamad, unsettled Malaysia's reputation as one of the most politically stable countries in Southeast Asia. By 2000, the human-rights situation in Malaysia had deteriorated, largely because of Mahathir's determination to crush his political rivals.

Dimitar L. Dimitrov

Further Reading

Milne, Robert, and Diane Mauzy. (1999) *Malaysian Politics under Mahathir.* London and New York: Routledge.

Palmujoki, Eero. (1997) "EU-ASEAN Relations: Reconciling Two Different Agendas." *Contemporary Southeast Asia: A Journal of International and Strategic Affairs* 19, 3: 269–285.

Saravanamuttu, Johan. (1996) "Malaysia's Foreign Policy in the Mahathir Period, 1981–1995: An Iconoclast Comes to Rule." *Asian Journal of Political Science* 4, 1: 1–16.

MALAYSIAN CHINESE ASSOCIATION

The Malaysian Chinese Association (MCA) was established on 27 February 1949 by Tan Cheng Lock (1883–1960) a legislator in the British Straits Settlement and a leader of the Chinese community. The association was founded to protect the interests of the Chinese community of the British-controlled Federation of Malaya. The British colonial authorities had imposed a state of emergency in 1948 because of an insurgency led by the Malayan Communist Party, which was dominated by ethnic Chinese, and began to deport large number of Chinese. The British established some six hundred "strategic hamlets" where other Chinese and Malays could live away from Communist-controlled zones. The MCA began by working with colonial authorities to resettle and provide humanitarian aid to refugees from the insurgency. The MCA believed that only by allying with the majority Malay population could the rights and interests of the Chinese, who comprised 27 percent of the population, be defended.

In 1952, the MCA formed an alliance with the dominant Malay political party, the United Malay National Organization (UMNO). They later allied with a third communal or ethnically based party, the Malaysian Indian Congress, to form the National Front, which since its founding in 1957 has ruled first the Federation of Malaya and then Malaysia. The MCA favored the establishment of the Federation of Malaysia in 1963, but it had to compete for Chinese votes with the Singapore-based People's Action Party (PAP), led by Lee Kwan Yew (b. 1923). (Singapore was at that time part of the Federation of Malaya.) Owing to the PAP's electoral success, in 1964 Lee asked the Malaysian prime minister to drop UMNO's alliance with the MCA in favor of the PAP, but he was rebuffed. The MCA supported UMNO's decision to eject Singapore from the Federation of Malaysia in August 1965.

The MCA tacitly supported the notion of Malay dominance in government. After the race riots of 13 May 1969, the MCA supported the New Economic Program, which called for a radical redistribution of corporate wealth from Chinese ownership to Malays, as well as for an affirmative-action program in education and government that favored the Malays. The MCA is the dominant political party representing the interests of Malaysian Chinese, and though it continues to advocate "Malaysianization" for the Chinese community, it is also the main advocate for Chinese language, education, and culture.

Zachary Abuza

Further Reading

Andaya, Barbara Watson, and Leonard Y. Andaya. (2001) *A History of Malaysia*. Honolulu: University of Hawaii Press.

Lee Kwan Yew. (1999) *Singapore Story: Memoirs of Lee Kwan Yew*. Englewood Cliffs, NJ: Prentice Hall.

MALDIVES—PROFILE (2001 est. pop. 311,000). Nature has blessed the Maldives with a living environment of tropical atolls and coral reefs that form a highly vulnerable marine ecosystem. Located in the Indian Ocean, approximately 700 kilometers off the southern tip of India and the west coast of Sri Lanka, the whole Maldivian archipelago spreads over 1 million square kilometers, and comprises a total of 1,190 islands belonging to twenty-four distinct atolls. Arranged in a long, narrow double chain of coral atolls stretching 820 kilometers from north to south and 130 kilometers from west to east, the total island area above the sea surface covers a mere 300 square kilometers, rarely more than two meters above sea level. As a result, the Maldives face serious infrastructural, communication, and developmental problems. Extreme isolation, remoteness, and global warming threaten the existence of the Maldives.

Geologically, the double chain of atolls are the tips of two parallel submarine ridges that rise 300 to 400 meters from a flat submarine plateau. Atolls vary in shape from circular and elliptical to pear-shaped. The lagoon, 40 to 60 meters deep, located around each atoll, is encircled by a fringing reef that serves as a natural barrier, sheltering the islands against the tides and floods. Eighty percent of all the islands are lower than one meter above mean high tide level. The islands vary in shape from small sandbanks to elongated strip islands and in size from 0.5 to 2 square kilometers.

Year-round temperatures are tropical, with a daily mean at around 28°C. Precipitation is high, at around 2,000 millimeters annually, mostly occurring as heavy showers. Comparably dry months coincide with the peak season of tourist traffic from January to April. Strong monsoon winds (and storms) do not hit the Maldives, and tropical cyclones are unknown.

The Maldives were first settled in the fifth century CE by settlers from Sri Lanka and southern India. The Dutch controlled the region in the seventeenth century, and it was a British protectorate from 1887 to 1965, when the Maldives achieved independence. In the year 2001, only 202 islands were populated, with a further 87 uninhabited islands that were converted into tourist resort islands. With a total population of approximately 311,000 people on all 202 inhabited islands, the Maldives are overpopulated. The capital, Malé, located on an island in the center of the Maldivian archipelago, holds 75,000 people on only 1.5 square kilometers—therefore, a population density of 50,000 persons per square kilometer. Nearly half the population is under fifteen years of age, causing serious challenges of education and employment. Education levels in the Maldives are for the most part high, with a literacy rate of more than 90 percent, both for males and females. Secondary and higher secondary schools are located mainly in Malé, while primary schools are found on all islands, and a free education is offered to all. The Maldives, however, lack a uni-

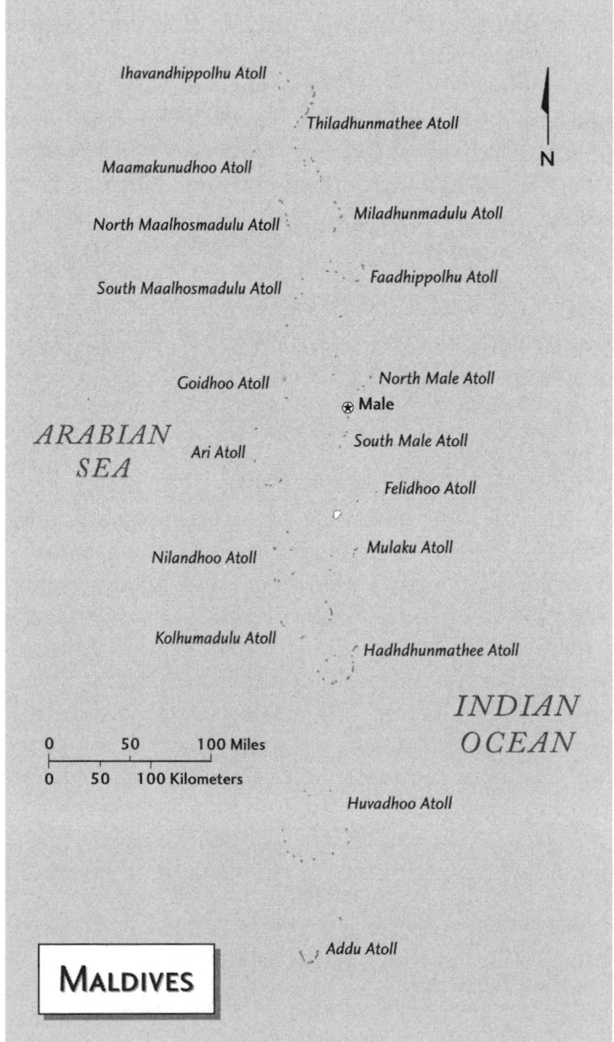

MALDIVES

Country name: Republic of Maldives (Dhivehi Raajjeyge Jumhooriyyaa)
Area: 300 sq km
Population: 310,764 (July 2001 est.)
Population growth rate: 3.01% (2001 est.)
Birth rate: 38.15 births/1,000 population (2001 est.)
Death rate: 8.09 deaths/1,000 population (2001 est.)
Net migration rate: 0 migrant(s)/1,000 population (2001 est.)
Sex ratio—total population: 1.05 male(s)/female (2001 est.)
Infant mortality rate: 63.72 deaths/1,000 live births (2001 est.)
Life expectancy at birth—total population: 62.56 years, male: 61.39 years, female: 63.8 years (2001 est.)
Major religions: Sunni Islam
Major languages: Maldivian Dhivehi, English
Literacy—total population: 93.2%, male: 93.3%, female: 93% (1995 est.)
Government type: republic
Capital: Malé
Administrative divisions: 19 atolls and 1 other first-order administrative division
Independence: 26 July 1965 (from U.K.)
National holiday: Independence Day, 26 July (1965)
Suffrage: 21 years of age; universal
GDP—real growth rate: 7.6% (2000 est.)
GDP—per capita (purchasing power parity): $2,000 (1999 est.)
Population below poverty line: not available
Exports: $88 million (f.o.b., 2000)
Imports: $372 million (f.o.b., 2000)
Currency: rufiyaa (MVR)

Source: Central Intelligencc Agency. (2001) *The World Factbook* 2001. Retrieved 18 October 2001 from: http://www.cia.gov/cia/publications/factbook.

versity. Major economic and employment sectors are tourism, fishery, manufacturing, and public and private services. As the coral soils are not very fertile, agriculture only plays a meager role.

Housing and urban problems seriously affect Malé. As the only urban center, Malé suffers from land shortage, traffic overcrowding, and declining freshwater quality and quantity. A large portion of Malé is reclaimed land on the reef flat; the island shores of Malé are in close proximity to the edges of the underlying reef platform. Malé is greatly burdened by a heavy migration of workers from other atolls and islands attracted by more favorable economic opportunities and better health and education services. Under the pressure of population, Malé capital was extended to the nearby former tourist island of Villingili; additionally, a new suburban town quarter is under construction through land reclamation on the reef platform between Hulule airport island and Farukolhufushi island, formerly known as Club Med Tourist Resort island.

Interatoll and interisland traffic and transportation is handicapped by the large distances over sea and the slowness of the still prevailing traditional, albeit mechanized, Maldivian *dhoni* boats. Transportation problems represent a major constraint to equitable distribution of goods and services throughout the country. *Dhoni* craft satisfy the basic interisland trade and commerce of goods as well as of passengers. Speedboats and air taxis are in service only for quick transportation of tourists, mostly between the international airport and the tourist resort islands. Internal air transport is limited; the national carrier, Air Maldives, serves four domestic airports in addition to Hulule. Domestic air transportation is too expensive for

Maldivians, hence the continued popularity of *dhoni* sea-transport. There is a modern telecommunication network across all of the atolls and inhabited islands. Health services options are best in Malé, with outpost hospitals on several islands.

As the Maldive islands abound in rich marine biodiversity, international tourism has become the leading component of the economy. After a mild start in 1972, tourism developed aggressively from the 1980s, under the First Tourism Master Plan. Resort islands were developed mainly in North and South Malé atolls, in close proximity to Hulule. When the Second Tourism Master Plan, valid for 1996 to 2005, came into effect, resort islands were regionally diversified to other atolls adjacent to Malé and Ari atolls, in order to spread the benefits of tourism.

Resort islands are restricted to foreign tourists only; the number of resort islands is projected to increase to more than one hundred in the early part of the twenty-first century. Tourist arrivals increased to an annual total of 465,000 in 2000. Two-thirds of all tourists come from central and western Europe; the remaining one-third comes from Asia.

Tourism development is under the strict control of the government of the Maldives, mainly to ensure a minimum impact of tourism on the marine environment and on cultural integrity. Tourism in the Maldives has an exclusive nature; this is manifested in the clublike style of most of the resort islands. Environmental problems are, in fact, the biggest threat to sustainable future development of the Maldives. Sea-level rise, due to global warming, is the one thing most seriously threatening the future of the Maldives.

Manfred Domroes

Further Reading

Domroes, Manfred. (2001) "Conceptualising State-Controlled Resort Islands for an Environment-Friendly Development of Tourism: The Maldivian Experience." *Singapore Journal of Tropical Geography* 22:122–137.

———. (1999) "Tourism in the Maldives: The Resort Concept and Tourist-Related Services." *Insular International Journal of Island Affairs* 8: 7–14.

Government of Maldives, Ministry of Planning, Human Resources and Environment. (1994) *The Maldives, State of the Environment.* Global Conference on the Sustainable Development of Small Island Developing States, Barbados. Malé, Republic of Maldives: Ministry of Planning, Human Resources and Environment.

———. (1981) *Statistical Yearbook of Maldives*. Malé, Republic of Maldives: Ministry of Planning and Development.

Government of Maldives, Department of Tourism. (1983) *Maldives: A Nation of Islands*. Bangkok, Thailand: Maldives Department of Tourism.

MALDIVES—HISTORY

The history of the Maldives is buried in obscurity owing to the islands' geographical isolation and their comparative insignificance throughout the centuries, even though they are strategically located along the sea routes between Europe and the Far East and were well known to ancient Arabian sailors. Significantly, the Arabs converted the people of the Maldives to Islam in 1153. Since then Islam has been the state religion. As stipulated in its constitution, each Maldivian citizen is a Muslim. The history of the Maldives under the ruling sultans is recorded continuously from 1153 to 1821 in the Maldivian *Tarikh* (a chronicle); it covers the reign of eighty-three sultans. Sultans continued to rule the Maldives until 1968, though their political power steadily diminished. The last sultan, Muhammad Fareed Didi, was a titular ruler only.

Early Visitors to the Maldives

At certain times casual visitors to the Maldives and sailors recorded valuable eyewitness accounts of the islands and their inhabitants. It is not known when the Maldives were discovered or who the first settlers were, and whether they migrated from India or Sri Lanka is disputed. Probably the oldest historical source, the work of the fourth-century classical writer Ammianus Marcellinus (320–390), carefully differentiated the islanders of the Maldives, whom he called "Divi," from the islanders of Ceylon (now Sri Lanka), whom he called "Serendivi." However, the famed Maldivian "Koimala Kalo" legend of the twelfth century describes the peaceful arrival on the Maldives of Ceylonese royalty, who were invited to settle there with the consent of the friendly aboriginal community of Giravaru Island.

Brief and vague notices of the Maldives appear in writings by Ptolemy (second century) around 150 CE, Moses Chorenensis in the late fourth century, and Cosmas Indicopleustes between 530 and 550. Arab travelers recorded valuable historical accounts, among them those of Lamma Mas-Oodhi in 947, Al-Becrooni in 1030, and Al-Idrisi (1099–1186). The greatest early Arab traveler, Ibn Battutah (1304–1368/69) visited the Maldives twice: first for a year and a half, from the beginning of 1343 until middle of 1344, and again two years later for a short visit at the end of 1346. Married to several Maldivian women, he was assimilated into the indigenous society.

The Coming of the Europeans

Until the European colonial era beginning in the sixteenth century, practically all of the Indian sea trade remained in the hands of Arab traders. The early Portuguese commander Afonso de Albuquerque (1453–1515) in 1510 forced the sultan of the Maldives to pay a tribute to the Indian Cannanore Raja. After two unsuccessful expeditions to the Maldives, the Portuguese in 1558 captured the capital, Malé, which they ruled for fifteen years, until expelled by a Maldivian guerrilla force. The Portuguese introduced Christianity for the only time in Maldivian history. In the seventeenth century, when Dutch, British, and French vessels also competed for the Maldivian trade, the Portuguese launched two fresh, unsuccessful attacks. Several times in the middle of the century Indian rulers attacked the Maldives, particularly Malé, from the Malabar Coast. In 1752 an expedition of the raja of Cannanore conquered Malé, destroying the palace and most of the town. The Malabar rulers, supported by the Portuguese colonial power in India, constantly harassed the Maldives. Subsequently the Maldivian sultan formed an alliance with the French rulers in Pondicherry, India, to protect the Maldives.

In 1887 the Maldivian sultan formalized an alliance with the British, who ruled the neighboring country of Ceylon. While the British government promised to protect the Maldives from foreign enemies and to abstain from interfering in local administration, the sultan agreed to pay tribute to the British government. The tribute obligation was lifted in 1948, but the Maldives retained the status of British protectorate. During World War II the British built a staging post on Gan Island in the South Maldivian Addu Atoll. In 1957 the post was converted into a British Royal Air Force base, which was abandoned in 1976. In 1953 the Maldives experienced a brief seven months as a republic with Amin Didi (d. 1954) as president. Though very modern (Westernized), the people of the Maldives disagreed with his politics and banished him on 31 December 1953 to Kurumba island, where he died. In spite of his ouster, Didi is considered the father of Maldivian nationalism. In 1965 the Maldives gained independence and membership in the United Nations.

Recent History

On 11 November 1968, President Ibrahim Nasir, who had taken over government from the last sultan, Muhammad Farid Didi, that same year, declared the (second) Republic of the Maldives and promulgated a new constitution that declared the Maldives an Islamic republic and vested great power in the president. He aimed at improving the economy and promoted the Maldives as a tourist destination. The political climate became unfavorable in 1974, escalating to actual revolt. Nasir resigned and fled to Singapore amid charges of political mismanagement. In 1978 Maumoon Abdul Gayoom (b. 1937) was elected president of the Maldives. Credited with bringing economic and social progress to the country, he has subsequently been reelected four times. The Maldives is a strong member of the Nonaligned Countries and the Small Island States.

Manfred Domroes

Further Reading

Bell, H. C. P. (1881, 1921) "The Maldive Islands: Monograph on the History, Archaeology, and Epigraphy." Ceylon Government Sessional Papers nos. 53 (1881) and 15 (1921).

MALIK, ADAM (1917–1984), vice president of Indonesia. Adam Malik was Indonesia's vice president from 1978 until 1983. He also was one of Indonesia's most successful foreign ministers, a position he held during the early New Order from 1966 to 1976. He was distinguished as a shrewd diplomat, known by the nickname "mouse-deer," derived from a popular Malay fable, as well as for his diplomatic words, "everything can be managed." Born in Pematang Siantar, North Sumatra on 22 July 1917, Malik dropped out of secondary school because of his interest in political activism. At the age of twenty, he left his hometown for Batavia (Jakarta). With only one typewriter, he built the Antara News Agency, which became Indonesia's national news agency. During the struggle for independence, he was jailed several times by the Dutch. As one of the young emerging leaders in 1945, he and his friends kidnapped Sukarno (1901–1970) and forced him to declare the independence of Indonesia.

Malik served many government positions under both the Sukarno (1945–1966) and Suharto (1966–1998) regimes. Having no diplomatic background, he initially questioned Sukarno's decision to appoint him as ambassador to the Soviet Union in 1959. He nevertheless proved to be a capable diplomat, and Suharto entrusted to him the project of building a new image of Indonesia as a capitalist and pro-Western country. As foreign minister, Malik was active in reducing tensions between Indonesia and neighboring nations. He also was one of the founders of the Association of Southeast Asian Nations (ASEAN) in 1967. Malik was appointed the twenty-sixth president of the U.N. General Assembly in 1971 and was a member of the Willy Brandt Commission in 1977. Prior to becoming vice president of Indonesia, Malik briefly was the Speaker of People Consultative Assembly (Majelis Permusyawaratan Rakyat, MPR) in 1977. He died on 5 September 1984.

Abubakar Eby Hara

Further Reading

Malik, Adam. (1980) *In the Service of the Republic*. Singapore: Gunung Agung.

Salam, Solichin. (1990) *Adam Malik dalam Kenangan (In Memoriam Adam Malik)*. Jakarta, Indonesia: Yayasan Adam Malik.

MALUKU (2002 est pop. 2.3 million). Maluku (Moluccas), a region of Indonesia formerly known as the Spice Islands, was once the source of cloves and nutmeg, spices highly valued for their aroma, preservative ability, and use in medicine before people learned how to cultivate the plants in other parts of the world. Maluku is a cluster of about one thousand islands totaling 74,504 square kilometers, forming part of the Malay Archipelago in eastern Indonesia near New Guinea. The region is divided into two provinces, Maluku (2002 estimated population 1.4 million), with its capital in Ambon, and North Maluku (2002 estimated population 913,000), with its capital in Ternate; other important islands in the group include Halmahera, Seram, and Buru.

Maluku lies in the transition zone between Asiatic and Australian flora and fauna and has a tropical climate. Maluku's flora include *meranti* trees and many kinds of orchids; distinctive fauna include *cuscuses*, birds of paradise, wild goats, and parrots. The economy is based on subsistence agriculture, especially sago (the sago palm, producing a starch used in food), and on the export of such products as spices, cacao, coffee, coconuts, fish, and minerals. Important indigenous groups include the Ambonese.

The Portuguese reached Maluku in 1511, but the region was later colonized by the Dutch, who arrived in 1599. In recent times, there has been conflict between the large Ambonese Christian minority and the Muslim majority.

Michael Pretes

Further Reading

Andaya, Leonard Y. (1993) *The World of Maluku: Eastern Indonesia in the Early Modern Period*. Honolulu: University of Hawaii Press.

Ricklefs, Merle Calvin. (2001) *A History of Modern Indonesia since c. 1200*. Basingstoke, U.K.: Palgrave.

MAMADALI MAHMUDOV (b. 1940), Uzbek writer. A prominent Uzbek writer, Mamadali Mahmudov gained literary fame in the former Soviet Union in the 1980s. In 2001, he was given the PEN/Barbara Goldsmith Award. His most famous work is the historical novella *Immortal Cliffs*, which was published in 1981. It won the Cholpan Prize in 1992.

Mahmudov believes in the unity of the Central Asian Turkic people and suggests that foreign concepts, such as Islam and Russian domination, have sapped their strength. His notion of unity implies understanding the shared heritage of these people and overcoming the alien elements that have crept into Central Asian culture, especially Islam and its ensuing Arabic influences.

In his work, Mahmudov draws heavily upon the oral *dastan* (accounts) tradition of Central Asia. A repository of a tribe's historical memory, a *dastan* is composed to commemorate an event, a person, or a battle and is often used to memorialize the struggles of the Turkic people against foreign invaders. *Dastans* are recited throughout Central Asia.

With independence, Mahmudov's aggressive nationalistic stance found little favor with the newly created nation of Uzbekistan. On 19 February 1999, he was arrested by order of the Committee for National Security and disappeared into the Uzbek prison system. He was officially charged with threatening the president, Islam Abduganievich Karimov, and seeking to destroy the nation's constitutional order. His arrest followed a series of explosions in Tashkent. He was allegedly tortured and forced to sign a confession, and in August 1999, he was sentenced to fourteen years in prison. He is presently in Chirchik Prison. Organizations such as PEN have taken up his cause and are seeking his freedom.

Nirmal Dass

Further Reading

Bohr, Annette. (1998) *Uzbekistan: Politics and Foreign Policy*. London: Royal Institute of Internal Affairs, Russia and Eurasia Programme.

Melvin, Neil. (2000) *Uzbekistan: Transition to Authoritarianism on the Silk Road*. Amsterdam: Harwood Academic.

MANAS EPIC Among Turkic oral traditions, that of the Kyrgyz is justly celebrated as one of the richest and finest. The main Kyrgyz epic is *Manas*, an epic cycle of monumental proportions. In this century the cycle has been recorded by a number of singers; the most famous versions are those by Saghymbay Orozbakov, Sayakbay Karalaev, and Dzhusup Mamay (from the Chinese Xinjiang Uighur Autonomous Region). Saghymbay's version comprises over 180,000 lines, Mamay's around 210,000 verse lines, containing eight instead of the canonical three branches of the *Manas* cycle, and Sayakbay's version no less than 500,000 verse lines. Generally, the epic cycle has three main parts. In *Manas* proper the subject is the miraculous birth of the hero, his fight against the enemies of his tribe, in particular the Kalmucks, his marriage to Kanykey, and his eventual death through treason. In the center of the second part is Manas's son Semetey, and his grandson Seytek is the subject of the third part. The epic cycle is full of detailed descriptions and lively dialogue and is packed with heroic and sometimes also romantic action. Not without reason, it has been ranked with the Homeric epics. The epics are in verse; the meter is a verse line of seven or eight syllables; the verses are linked together by rhyme and verse-initial alliteration to form stanzas of irregular length. Kyrgyz singers, called *manaschy*, perform the epic by singing and chanting the words to a number of melodic formulas without the use of instruments. The art of singing the epic is still alive among the Kyrgyz.

Karl Reichl

Further Reading

Bogdanova, M. I., V. M. Zhirmunskiy, and A. A. Petrosyan, eds. (1961) *Kirgizskiy geroicheskiy èpos Manas* (The Kyrgyz Heroic Epic Manas). Moscow: Izd. Akademii Nauk SSSR.

Chadwick, N. K., and V. Zhirmunsky. (1969) *Oral Epics of Central Asia*. Cambridge, U.K.: Cambridge University Press.

Hatto, Arthur T., ed. and trans. (1990) *The Manas of Wilhelm Radloff*. Asiatische Forschungen 110. Wiesbaden, Germany: Harrassowitz.

Karypkulov, A., et al., eds. (1995) *Manas Entsiklopediya* (Manas Encyclopedia). 2 vols. Bishkek, Kyrgyzstan: Muras.

MANCHU The Manchus (or Man) are a minority people concentrated in the northeastern provinces of Liaoning, Heilongjian, Jilin, and Inner Mongolia in China. In the 1990 national census, the number of Manchus in China was 9.84 million. The Manchus are descended from a group of peoples of northeast Asia collectively termed the Tungus. The Manchus also claim descent from rulers of the Jurchen Jin dynasty (1126–1234). In the late sixteenth century, the Manchu tribes were organized into a collective nation under the rule of the greatest of their chiefs, Nurhaci (1559–1626). Nurhaci's successor, Abahai (1592–1643), changed the name of his people to Manchu in order to remove the historical memory that as Jurchens they had been under Chinese rule. The Manchus continued to grow in military power in the border region northeast of the Great Wall and eventually overthrew the Ming dynasty (1368–1644) and established China's last imperial era, the Qing, or Manchu, dynasty (1644–1912). The Manchus remained an important symbolic people in China during the twentieth century, as was demonstrated by their being named in 1912 as one of the five races that constituted the new Chinese Republic.

The Manchu language is a member of the Tungusic branch of the Altaic language family and has some structural similarities to Japanese, Korean, and Mongolian. During the Jin dynasty, Jurchen official documents were transcribed using a modified form of the Khitan script. In 1599, as part of his nation-building, Nurhaci commissioned two scholars to modify the Mongolian script in order to create a written form of the Manchu language. This form of written Manchu is called the Old Manchu script because it was further modified in the 1620s by the addition of dots and circles, which eliminated some of the linguistic ambiguities that had resulted from the first attempt to modify the Mongolian script. This new script remained the standard form of the written language throughout the Qing dynasty. Few native speakers of Manchu remain in China, although volumes of the written script are preserved as official documents of the Qing dynasty and are housed in the national archive in Beijing and provincial archives in the northeast.

Robert John Perrins

Further Reading

Crossley, Pamela Kyle. (1990) *Orphan Warriors: Three Manchu Generations and the End of the Qing World*. Princeton, NJ: Princeton University Press.

Li, Gertraude Roth. (2000) *Manchu: A Textbook for Reading Documents*. Honolulu: University of Hawaii Press.

Michael, Franz. (1972) *The Origin of Manchu Rule in China: Frontier and Bureaucracy as Interacting Forces in the Chinese Empire*. New York: Octagon Books.

State Statistical Bureau. (1998) *China Statistical Yearbook*. Beijing: China Statistical Publishing House.

MANCHURIA (1997 est. pop. 105 million). Manchuria, the region of northeastern China comprising the provinces of Heilongjiang, Jilin, and Liaoning (Fengtian), is referred to as Dongbei ("Northeast") in China. This Chinese terminology is part of a larger effort to distance the region's history from the colonial overtures associated with the term "Manchuria," the nomenclature of which was partly the creation of Russian and Japanese imperialists who hoped that the name would imply the region's separateness from the rest of China. Originally peopled by a number of tribal groups, the largest of whom were Mongols, Tungus, and Manchus, Manchuria is rich in natural resources, including coal, iron, timber and forest products, furs, and ginseng. During the twentieth century, Manchuria's transportation infrastructure and industrial base were developed by foreign occupiers and later by Chinese administrators. Today the region, bordered to the southeast by Korea and to the north and northeast by Russia, is one of the most important industrial heartlands in the People's Republic of China.

The presence of Han Chinese in Manchuria can be traced back to the Qin dynasty (221–206 BCE) when a prefecture was established on the Liaodong Peninsula at the southernmost point of Liaoning Province. It was during the reign of the fifth Han emperor, Wu Di (reigned 140–87 BCE), that a more significant Chinese presence was established when Wu Di encouraged the settlement of Chinese both on the Liaodong Peninsula and in an area of what is today western Liaoning in order to strengthen the northern borders against the Xiongnu peoples. For much of China's imperial past, however, there was only a minimal presence of Chinese in this region that lay beyond the northeast border of the Great Wall. After their conquest of China in the mid-seventeenth century, the Manchu rulers of the Qing dynasty (1644–1912) sought to preserve Manchuria as an undeveloped ancestral homeland, and the early emperors, including Shunzhi (1638–1661), Kangxi (1654–1722), Yongzheng (1678–1735), and Qianlong (1711–1799), all issued edicts, of dubious effectiveness, forbidding the settlement of Chinese in the region.

Russian Annexation Feared

With the growing Russian presence in the Far East in the late eighteenth and early nineteenth centuries, the Qing emperors grew to fear Russian annexation of Manchuria more than the presence of Chinese settlers. The last of the old edicts were repealed, and northern Chinese were encouraged to settle in Manchuria. The arrival of British and French warships off the coast of southern Manchuria during the Opium Wars of the mid-nineteenth century had also alerted the Manchus that the region had strategic importance and that the development of its population and fortifications was required. These belated efforts by the Qing rulers were ineffective, and by the 1890s Manchuria was largely lost to foreign imperialists, first Russian and then Japanese.

In 1896, following the Sino-Japanese War (1894–1895), the Qing rulers, now more fearful of Tokyo's colonial ambitions than Russia's, granted permission to czarist Russia to build the Chinese Eastern Railway across Manchuria as a shortcut and alternative route to the Trans-Siberian Railway. In 1898, Russia secured further concessions from a weakening Manchu court, including a twenty-five-year lease of the southern portion of the Liaodong Peninsula and the right to construct an additional southern route to the region's railway that would have the added benefit of having a year-round ice-free port as its terminus in the new leasehold. Following the Russo-Japanese War (1904–1905), the new Russian rights in southern Manchuria, along with the region's railway and harbors at Lushun (Port Arthur) and Dalian (Dairen in Japanese and Dalny in Russian), were transferred to Japanese control.

Manchuria as a Japanese Colony

The new Japanese governors in southern Manchuria continued to build on the original Russian plans, and their new colony blossomed during the soybean boom of the late 1910s. By the late 1920s, tension was building as Japanese colonial ambitions in Manchuria could no longer be satisfied by a small leasehold on the Liaodong Peninsula and the attempts by commanders in the local Japanese garrison force, the Guandong (Kwantung) Army, to manipulate the region's de facto ruler, the warlord Zhang Zuolin (Chang Tso-lin). On 18 September 1931, the Guandong Army launched an invasion of Manchuria. The following year, the birth of a new "independent" nation of Manchukuo ("Country of the Manchus") was proclaimed. The reality was that Manchukuo was a creation of the Japanese military and a puppet state with no real independence. Until the end of the Pacific War, Manchuria remained under Japanese occupation, supplying raw materials to the home islands and playing an important role in the creation of Japan's colonial ideology. Manchuria was viewed by many Japanese not only as a strategic buffer zone between their empire and the Soviet Union but also as a colonial frontier, even a potential utopia, awaiting the arrival of brave Japanese settlers who would develop the region's untapped potential.

Following Japan's surrender in 1945, the Russians returned to Manchuria. Having secured the restoration of Russia's former rights in the region at the Yalta Conference in February 1945 in return for a promise to enter the war against Japan, Soviet troops invaded the region in the final days of the Pacific War. Over the next couple of years, the Russians plundered the region, dismantling factories and sending them in pieces back to the Soviet Union on railcars. Because of its industrial capacity and abundant natural resources, Manchuria was a hotly contested territory during the Chinese Civil War (1947–1949) between the Communists and Nationalists.

Since the 1950s, Manchuria has been developed as China's industrial heartland. The steel mills at Anshan, the Fushun colliery, the giant factory complexes in the industrial cities of Shenyang (Mukden) and Changchun, and the commercial port of Dalian played important roles in the industrialization strategies of the Communist regime. With the move to create a market economy in China in the late 1980s and early 1990s, industrial Manchuria began to experience new challenges. Many of the inefficient state-owned enterprises either closed or severely downsized their workforces. One of the results was a high level of unemployment in a region that had traditionally been prosperous under the old state-planned economy. Decades of industrialization have also created serious environmental problems in China's Northeast, including high rates of respiratory diseases among its populace and high levels of toxins in its rivers and waterways. The former pristine reserve of the Manchus is now polluted and home to tens of millions of Han Chinese factory workers.

Robert John Perrins

Further Reading

Chao, Kang. (1982) *The Economic Development of Manchuria: The Rise of a Frontier Economy*. Ann Arbor: University of Michigan Press, Center for Chinese Studies.

Elliott, Mark C. (2000) "The Limits of Tartary: Manchuria in Imperial and National Geographies." *The Journal of Asian Studies* 59, 3 (August): 603–646.

Hosie, Alexander. ([1904] 1980) *Manchuria, Its People, Resources, and Recent History*. Reprint ed. New York: Garland Publishing.

Janhunen, Juha. (1996) *Manchuria: An Ethnic History*. Helsinki, Finland: Finno-Ugrian Society.

Lattimore, Owen. (1935) *Manchuria: Cradle of Conflict*. New York: Macmillan.

Young, Louise. (1999) *Japan's Total Empire: Manchuria and the Culture of Wartime Imperialism*. Berkeley and Los Angeles: University of California Press.

MANCHURIAN INCIDENT On 18 September 1931, the Japanese Kwantung Army (Japanese forces in Kwantung, China) claimed that Chinese bandits had blown up the main tracks of the Japanese-controlled South Manchuria Railway outside Mukden (Shenyang) in southern Manchuria. Japan had pinned much of its hopes for gaining economic self-sufficiency and being a world power on the slender thread of its control of the South Manchuria Railway.

Although Japanese trains traveled the railway soon after the "incident," Japanese forces, apparently acting without formal approval from the government in Tokyo, used this incident as an excuse for a year-long campaign to gain control over all of Manchuria, a resource-rich Chinese province that had been the scene of increasing tension between rising Chinese and Japanese nationalisms and also between Japanese civilian and military officials in southern Manchuria and the government at home.

The Chinese government complained to the League of Nations, which appointed Lord Victor Bulwer-Lytton of England to lead a commission of inquiry. The resulting report harshly criticized the Japanese, and the Japanese government responded by withdrawing from the league.

Japan eventually sought to demonstrate the "independence" of Manchuria and established a government for what they termed Manchukuo ("Manchu country") under the last Qing (or Manchu) emperor, Henry Pu-yi, in early 1932. (The emperor had abdicated in 1912, ending the reign of the Qing dynasty over China, which it had ruled since 1644.) But despite the appointment of some Chinese officials, power clearly rested with Japanese "advisers."

Thereafter, Japan sought to force Chinese recognition of Manchukuo's independence and began a war of aggression. Throughout the 1930s, Japanese military forces took one Chinese province after another without being able to compel China to concede the independence of Manchuria. Eventually, to support this increased military commitment in China, Japan looked to widen the war into Southeast Asia and against the United States, leading to the disastrous Pacific theater of World War II.

Charles Dobbs

Further Reading

Iriye, Akira. (1965) *After Imperialism: The Search for a New Order in the Far East, 1921–1931*. Cambridge, MA: Harvard University Press.

Yoshihashi, Takehiko. (1963) *Conspiracy at Mukden: The Rise of the Japanese Military*. New Haven, CT: Yale University Press.

MANDALAY (2002 est. pop. 1.1 million). Mandalay, located in the central dry zone of Myanmar (Burma) 620 kilometers (400 miles) north of Yangon (Rangoon), is Myanmar's second-largest city, with a population of between 653,000 and 1 million (including unregistered aliens). The sprawling city, built on a grid pattern of roads, covers an area of 25 square miles bounded on the west by the Irrawaddy River. Mandalay has lost much of its traditional char-

An elaborate Buddha statue in Kuthodaw Pagoda in Mandalay in 1992. (GEORGE W. WRIGHT/ CORBIS)

acter due to devastating fires in the 1980s and massive development by Chinese entrepreneurs, the Myanmar military, and other investors following legalization of the lucrative Myanmar-China border trade in 1989. Many local residents have been forced to relocate to peripheral satellite towns. Mandalay is at the hub of a trading and communications network and, besides its river, rail, and road links, has a new international airport (inaugurated in 2000).

The last in a succession of royal capitals, Mandalay was founded in 1857 by King Mindon (1853–1878) in fulfillment of a prophecy that a great Buddhist center would be built at the foot of Mandalay Hill on the 2,400th anniversary of the Buddhist faith. Mandalay was also known by its classical name of Yatanapon (City of Gems) and Shwe-myo-daw (Golden Royal City). Mindon was renowned for his piety, and during his reign many new monasteries and temples were endowed, ancient sites restored, the Buddhist scriptures carved on 729 marble slabs, and the Fifth Buddhist Council convened. In 1885 Mandalay was occupied by the British, who deposed and exiled King Thibaw (reigned 1878–1885) to India and incorporated Upper Burma into British Burma with Rangoon as its capital.

Although Mandalay was Myanmar's capital for less than three decades, its royal past and religious patronage have ensured that it remains Myanmar's cultural heartland and a flourishing center of traditional crafts as well as an important religious center, with approximately 60 percent of the nation's Buddhist monks resident there. Mandalay Hill is a place of pilgrimage and affords a spectacular view. The royal palace and fort dominate the north of the city and occupy a perfect square, bounded by crenellated brick walls, each over a mile long and aligned with the cardinal points of the compass and encircled by wide moats. Mandalay Palace, which incorporated many carved teak structures from the old Amarapura Palace, was destroyed in the closing stages of World War II and reconstructed only in the 1990s. Part of the palace compound is occupied by army command headquarters. Besides the royal palace, Mandalay's most famous monuments include the Mahamuni (or Arakan) Temple, the Shwe-nan-daw Monastery, the Atumashi Monastery (destroyed by fire in 1890 and reconstructed in 1996), the Kutho-daw, the Kyauk-taw-gyi Temple, the Ein-daw-ya Temple, and the Shwe-in-bin Monastery.

Patricia M. Herbert

Further Reading

Dhida Saraya. (1995) *Mandalay: The Capital City, Center of the Universe*. Bangkok, Thailand: Muang Boran Publishing House.

Mya Maung. (1994) "On the Road to Mandalay: A Case Study of the Sinonization of Upper Burma." *Asian Survey* 34, 5: 447–459.

Strachan, Paul. (1994) *Mandalay: Travels from the Golden City*. Gartmore, U.K.: Kiscadale Publications.

MANDALAY DIVISION

MANDALAY DIVISION (2002 est. pop. 6.6 million). The Mandalay Division plays a pivotal role in the life of Myanmar (Burma) and accounts for approximately 15 percent of the national economy. With an area of 37,024 square kilometers (14,295 square miles), it is located on the major transport and communication crossroads between the north and south of the country. Consisting of 29 townships and 1,796 wards or village tracts, its 1992 population was calculated at 5.54 million, the majority of whom were ethnic Burmans. The political and economic hub is Mandalay, Myanmar's second largest city.

The main economy is agriculture. Lying in the dry zone, various dams and reservoirs have been constructed to promote irrigation, including thirty new such projects since 1988. The main crops are paddy rice, wheat, maize, peanut, sesame, cotton, legumes, tobacco, chili, and vegetables. A number of industries are also located within the division, including the Mandalay Brewery, textile mills at Meiktila and Paleik, and the sugar mill at Pyinmana. In addition, the division contains the important gem mines at Mogok.

Mandalay is the main tourist center. There are also the remains of other royal capitals at Amarapura, Ava (Innwa), and Pagan. Other destinations include the 4,981-foot (1,518-meter) Mount Popa, which has been a center of *nat* (spirit) worship and pilgrimage for centuries, and the former British hill station at Maymyo (Pyin Oo Lwin), which is situated on the main trade road to Shan State and China.

Martin Smith

Further Reading

Bunge, Frederica M., ed. (1983) *Burma: A Country Study.* Washington, DC: American University Foreign Area Studies, U.S. Government Printing Office.

O'Connor, Vincent C. Scott. (1907) *Mandalay and Other Cities of the Past in Burma.* London: Hutchinson.

Tinker, Hugh. (1967) *The Union of Burma: A Study of the First Years of Independence.* Oxford: Oxford University Press.

MANDALAY PALACE

MANDALAY PALACE Mandalay Palace was the last Burman palace resided in by independent royalty during the latter part of the Konbaung Dynasty. Soon after Mindon (reigned 1853–1878) seized power from his brother King Pagan, in January 1857 he gave the order to move the palace from Amarapura to the new palace grounds in the new royal capital, Mandalay. The palace itself was completed and occupied in July 1858, but the outer walls were completed later.

After British conquest in 1885, the British neglected Mandalay Palace. Under Lord Curzon (viceroy 1899–1905) the largely wooden palace was declared a museum in 1901. In 1945 the palace compound was destroyed during the Allied bombardments, leaving only the outer walls in place with a few broken buildings. During the Burma Socialist Programme Party (BSPP) period it functioned as a military station. Mandalay Palace is a symbol of Burmese sovereignty in particular to the BSPP–State Law and Order Restoration Council government, which by 1989 made a decision to renovate and rebuild from scratch 89 of the originally recorded 114 buildings, with the aim of bolstering legitimacy and attracting tourists. This was completed in 1996. It is surrounded by a 7-meter wall backed by an earth rampart, and by a moat 68 meters wide and 3 meters deep.

Gustaaf Houtman

Further Reading

Duroiselle, Charles M. (1925) *A Guide to the Mandalay Palace.* Yangon, Myanmar: Superintendent of Government Printing.

Ministry of Union Culture. (1963) *Mandalay Palace.* Yangon, Myanmar: Directorate of Archaeological Survey.

MANDARIN

MANDARIN The term Mandarin is generally believed to be a translation of Chinese *guanhua*—literally "official talk," which originated as a form of common language among speakers of different Chinese dialects. In linguistic terms, there are four different views of Mandarin: as a Chinese lingua franca, as Modern Standard Chinese, as a branch of the northern Chinese dialect family, and as Premodern Chinese. Each of these senses of the term Mandarin will be examined in detail.

Mandarin as a Chinese *Lingua Franca*

Mandarin is believed to have originated as a form of common language among speakers of different Chinese dialects, loosely based on some form of northern Chinese. The precise locale of this prestige northern dialect is not clear, but Beijing, Nanjing, and Luoyang are likely candidates. The Jesuit missionary Matteo Ricci (1552–1610), for instance, wrote in his travel journals (1583–1610) of a spoken language called "Quonhoa," which was used throughout the empire for civil and forensic purposes. In a way, the status of *guanhua* is similar to that of the "cultivated pronunciation" of the American Atlantic states existing alongside the local vernacular, with each state having its own version—its best approximation of the prestige dialect.

Mandarin as Modern Standard Chinese

The second meaning of Mandarin focuses on the area around Beijing—the Chinese capital for the past 500 years—whose local speech presumably had a prestige that conflicted with the prestige status of the *guanhua*. By the end of the nineteenth century, the two were extremely similar, with remnants of the old *guanhua* known as the "literary stratum" of Beijing Mandarin, and the local vernacular as the "colloquial stratum." An example of differences would be the word "to learn," which is pronounced *xue* in the literary stratum, but *xiao* in colloquial Beijing. Differences exist also in vocabulary, with *guanhua* leaning towards classical Chinese and colloquial Beijing being more abundant in localisms.

From the demise of the Qing dynasty (1644–1912) through to the early days of the Republican era (1912–1927), the recognition of Beijing Mandarin as a national standard took a more convoluted route. At a meeting of linguists in 1913 to decide upon the new official language, the standard of choice was not the speech of the capital, but an artificial language incorporating the maximum number of distinctions found in the major dialects, envisaged as a compromise between north and south. But it soon became clear that no one, not even the linguists themselves, could speak this linguistic Frankenstein, and the movement failed miserably. In 1920 Shiyi Zhang, a professor from Nanjing, called for replacement of the man-made standard with "the speech of Beijing locals educated to the level of secondary school." Though Zhang's proposal initially met with resistance, Beijing Mandarin gradually took over as the de facto national standard. In 1926, when the national language was revised, pronunciations were largely based on the literary readings of Beijing.

The new national language, up to this point, had been known as *guoyu*—"national language," a term borrowed from Japanese usage—and still goes by this name in Taiwan. On the mainland, however, the national language underwent a second revision in 1955, and switched to the name *Putonghua* ("commoners' language"), which is normally translated as Modern Standard Chinese. Differences between *putonghua* and *guoyu* are few, mainly in the adoption of colloquial pronunciations in the case of *putonghua* where *guoyu* retains the 1926 literary norms. A 1955 revision managed to define the nature of the national language, basing "its pronunciation on the speech of Beijing, its lexicon on the core vocabulary of Northern Chinese, and its syntax on the norms of exemplary vernacular literature" (Li 1999: 32).

Tone aside, Modern Standard Chinese contains between 398 and 419 syllables, depending on whether we are to include certain Beijing colloquialisms not part of the educated vocabulary. The syllable is traditionally analyzed into an initial consonant and a final. The possible initials and finals of Modern Standard Chinese are listed in Tables 1 and 2, given in both pinyin romanization (in italics) and the international phonetic alphabet (square brackets).

TABLE 1

Modern Standard Chinese initials

Labial	*b* [p]	*p* [pʰ]	*m* [m]	*f* [f]
Alveolar (nonsibilant)	*d* [t]	*t* [tʰ]	*n* [n]	*l* [l]
Alveolar (sibilant)	*z* [ts]	*c* [tsʰ]	*s* [s]	
Retroflex	*zh* [tʂ]	*ch* [tʂʰ]	*sh* [ʂ]	*r* [ɹ]
Alveopalatal	*j* [tɕ]	*q* [tɕʰ]	*x* [ɕ]	
Velar	*g* [k]	*k* [kʰ]	*h* [x]	

Full syllables in Modern Standard Chinese carry one of four tones, which play a role in distinguishing word meaning. (See Table 3.)

Tone 3 often rises when it occurs at the end of a sentence or utterance, and as such is sometimes referred to as the dipping tone. Grammatical particles, suffixes, and unstressed syllables in Mandarin Chinese are often stripped of their tonal value, a condition referred to as being in the neutral tone.

Regarding syntactic properties, it is worth noting that Mandarin, like most other varieties of Chinese, is relatively free of inflection—nouns generally are not marked for case, number, or gender, and verbs need not agree with the person, number, or gender of the subject or object. Therefore, much essential information is encoded in the word order of a sentence.

There is however much controversy regarding the characterization of Mandarin word order. While the simple declarative sentence in Mandarin retains the

TABLE 2

Modern Standard Chinese finals

	i [i]	*u* [u]	*ü* [y]
a [a]	*ia* [ia]	*ua* [ua]	
o [o]		*uo* [uo]	
e [ɤ]			
ê [ɛ]	*ie* [iɛ]		*üe* [yɛ]
ai [ai]		*uai* [uai]	
ei [ei]		*ui* [uei]	
ao [ɑu]	*iao* [iɑu]		
ou [ou]		*iu* [iou]	
an [iou]	*ian* [iɛn]	*uan* [uan]	*üan* [yɛn]
en [ən]	*in* [in]	*un* [uən]	*ün* [yin]
ang [ɑŋ]	*iang* [iɑŋ]	*uang* [uɑŋ]	
eng [əŋ]	*ing* [iŋ]		
ong [ʊŋ]	*iong* [iʊŋ]		
er [əɹ]			

TABLE 3

Tones in Modern Standard Chinese

	Description	Contour	Example
Tone 1	high	HH	*mâ* "mother"
Tone 2	rising	LH	*má* "linen"
Tone 3	low	LL	*ma* "horse"
Tone 4	falling	HL	*mà* "to scold"

(Note: H = high pitch; L = low pitch.)

Subject-Verb-Object (SVO) order of Old Chinese (600 BCE–265CE), Modern Standard Chinese contains characteristics of languages with the basic word order Subject-Object-Verb (SOV), such as the ordering of relative clauses and genitives before head nouns, the placement of aspect markers after verbs, and the presence of operations that change word order from SVO to SOV. In the early 1980s, some linguists saw this as evidence that Mandarin Chinese is in the process of switching over from SVO to SOV, most likely due to influence from the Altaic languages of northern China. But recent scholarship in language acquisition and Chinese corpus analysis point to the contrary, namely, that SOV structures in Mandarin are infrequent, marked forms that are not easily acquired by young children, and that such properties are not unusual in rigid SVO languages such as English and Biblical Hebrew. The prevailing view, for now at least, seems to be that Mandarin Chinese, like most other languages of southern and southeastern China, is a typical SVO language.

Mandarin as a Branch of Northern Chinese

In Chinese dialectology, Mandarin or *guanhua* refers to a branch of Northern Chinese, which includes dialects used throughout most of northern and southwestern China, the majority of which are descended from or have had extensive contact with the *guanhua* lingua franca. Mandarin, in this context, refers to an entire dialect family, the largest family in the Chinese branch of Sino-Tibetan in fact, in terms of both geographical distribution and number of speakers.

Within the Mandarin family, there are three main divisions comprising eight subdialects: (1) Southern Mandarin includes the Yangtze (*Jianghuai guanhua*) and Southwestern (*Xinan guanhua*) subdialects, (2) Central Mandarin includes the Central Plains (*Zhongyuan guanhua*) and Northwestern (*Lanyin guanhua*) varieties, and finally (3) Northern Mandarin includes Northeastern (*Dongbei guanhua*), North Central (*Jilu guanhua*), Peninsular (*Jiaoliao guanhua*), and Beijing Mandarin (*Beijing guanhua*).

Mandarin as Premodern Chinese

From the demise of the Tang dynasty (907) onward, the homeland of Mandarin's northern Chinese roots was successively occupied by peoples of Turkic, Mongol, and Tungus-Manchu stock. This resulted in the drastic simplification of Middle Chinese (265–1269) and produced *guanhua*, or Mandarin. Thus Mandarin, as a historical phonological entity, is synonymous with what historical lexicographers call Premodern Chinese, and refers to the language of northern China from the Yuan dynasty (1279–1368) to the present day.

Historical phonologists further divide the Mandarin period into three parts: Early Mandarin (1269–1455) is typified by the opera manual *Zhongyuan yinyun* (Rhymes of the Central Plains, 1324) of Zhou Deqing (1277–1365); Middle Mandarin (1455–1795) is preserved in Chinese-Korean pedagogical texts such as *Hongmu chŏngyun yŏkhun* (Standard Rhymes of the Reign of Hongwu, Annotated and Transcribed, 1455) and *Sasŏng t'onghae* (Thorough Investigation of the Four Tones, 1517), as well as the *Yunlue huitong* (1642) and other Chinese rhyme manuals. Mandarin from the mid-nineteenth century to the present is considered to have changed very little, and is referred to as Modern Mandarin or Modern Chinese.

Chris Wen-Chao Li

Further Reading

Chen, Ping. (1999) *Modern Chinese: History and Sociolinguistics.* Cambridge, U.K.: Cambridge University Press.

Cheng, Robert Liang-Wei. (1985) "A Comparison of Taiwanese, Taiwan Mandarin, and Peking Mandarin." *Language* 61, 2: 352–377.

Coblin, Weldon South. (1997) "Notes on the Sound System of Late Ming *Guanhua.*" *Monumenta Serica* 45: 261–307.

———. (2000) "A Brief History of Mandarin." *Journal of the American Oriental Society* 120, 4: 537–552.

Gallagher, Louis Joseph. (1953) *China in the Sixteenth Century: The Journals of Matthew Ricci, 1583–1610.* New York: Random House.

Kim, Kwangjo. (1991) "A Phonological Study of Middle Mandarin Reflected in Korean Sources of the Mid Fifteenth and Early Sixteenth Centuries." Ph.D. diss., University of Washington.

Li, Rong. (1989) "Hanyu Fangyan de Qufen" (Classification of the Chinese Dialects). *Fangyan* 4: 241–259.

Li, Wen Chao. (1999) *A Diachronically-Motivated Segmental Phonology of Mandarin Chinese.* Berkeley Insights in Linguistics & Semiotics, no. 37. New York: Peter Lang.

Liu, Xunning. (1995) "Zailun hanyu beifanghua de fenqu" (Dialect Regions of Northern Chinese Revisited). *Zhongguo yuwen* 249: 447–454.

Norman, Jerry. (1988) *Chinese.* Cambridge, U.K.: Cambridge University Press.

MANGA *Manga* are Japanese comic magazines. These large, softcover magazines printed in monochrome are by far the most broadly read literary genre in Japan. Around 2 billion copies are produced annually. Some magazines are printed in 1 million copies or more each week. Many *manga* are reprinted later in pocketbook format.

Each *manga* magazine features stories and serials of broadly the same theme: education and training, romance, action, humor, history, or even violent pornography. Characters and stories from *manga*, *anime* (animated films), and computer games are often reproduced in each other. Drawing and dialogue conventions are more complex than are generally seen in, for example, American comics: odd-shaped panels, reduction or addition of detail for emphasis, use of varied camera point of view, and mixed (Japanese/Latin) script for effect are common.

Manga artists are generally organized into schools or studios, in traditional Japanese *iemoto* pattern, where a senior or master instructs junior artists, who eventually instruct juniors of their own. Members of a studio tend to have broadly similar drawing and expressive styles.

Otaku, young Japanese males who are obsessed with *manga* and *anime*, are considered something of a social problem in Japan because they are said to develop limited and difficult social relationships.

Michael Ashkenazi

Further Reading

Kinsella, Sharon. (2000) *Adult Manga: Culture and Power in Contemporary Japanese Society.* Honolulu: University of Hawaii Press.

Schodt, Frederik L. (1996) *Dreamland Japan: Writings on Modern Manga.* Berkeley, CA: Stone Bridge Press.

MANGALORE (2001 pop. 399,000). Mangalore, which was earlier known as Kodial Bunder, is the headquarters of the modern district of Dakshin (south) Kannada in the Indian state of Karnataka. Located on the Arabian Sea coast at the mouths of the Netravati and Gurpur rivers, it is marked by undulating landscape with areca nut (betel palm) groves, coconut palms, and other trees. The town has a tropical climate. Tulu is the most popular language. Mangalore is believed to have derived its name from the Managaldevi Temple located there. In addition, the town has several famous pilgrim centers.

This strategic port town had strong commercial links with the Persian Gulf for many centuries, and various powers have fought for control over it. In 1526, Mangalore was taken over by the Portuguese from its Bidanur Nayaka rulers. In 1695, the town was burned by the Arabs in retaliation for Portuguese restrictions on Arab trade. In 1763, when the Mysorean ruler Hyder Ali (1722–1782) conquered the town, he built a dockyard and an arsenal here. The town was annexed by the British in 1799. The modern port is ten kilometers north of the town, and is now India's ninth largest cargo handling port. Mangalore's economy is dominated by agricultural processing and port-related activities, and it is also the major banking center for the region. The population is about 60 percent Hindu with significant Muslim, Christian, and Jain minorities.

R. Gopinath

Further Reading

Mangalore University, Editorial Committee. (1991) *Perspectives on Dakshina Kannada and Kodagu.* Mangalagangottri, India: Mangalore University.

MANGESHKAR, LATA (b. 1929), Indian singer. Lata Mangeshkar's mellifluous voice has enthralled millions of people for the last five decades. Born in Indore, Madhya Pradesh, India, Lata showed her talent early, acting and singing in scores of Hindi movies since childhood. *Pahili Mangalagaur*, released in 1942, was her first acting assignment. At the age of thirteen she recorded her first film song in Vasant Joglekar's *Kirti Hasaal.* Singing with equal ease in Marathi, Hindi, and Urdu, Lata performed thirty thousand solos and duets that entranced millions of people throughout the world. Purity, sharpness, clarity, and lyrical notes are hallmarks of her songs. Lata's song "Aye Mere Watan Ke Logon" (People of My Country) sung during the Sino-Indian war of 1962 aroused a patriotic fervor and brought tears to many, including the premier, Jawaharlal Nehru.

She has won many laurels during her career: a place in the *Guinness Book of Records* (for singing the most songs in twenty different languages); a platinum record for EMI London, *Padma Bhushan*, *Padma Vibhushan*; and the Dadasaheb Phalke award. In 2001, Lata won India's highest civilian award: the Bharat Ratna.

Patit Paban Mishra

Further Reading

Bhimani, Harish. (1995) *In Search of Lata.* New Delhi: Indus Publishing.

MANGROVES Mangroves are communities of plants and animals existing within swampy intertidal mudflats in the Tropics, mainly at estuaries, riverbanks, and coastal regions subject to brackish water. Asia has 46 percent of the world's mangroves.

Diverse communities are found in mangroves. Frequent inundation and continual silting make the soil soft and clayey in texture, lacking aeration. Mangrove flora are uniquely adapted to such conditions. The red mangrove *(Rhizophora mangle)* has prop roots growing from the trunk for stability and bears germinated seedlings with long radicles. The white mangrove *(Laguncularia racemosa)* develops a dense network of cable roots within the soft mud for stability. A feature of this and several other species is spongy vertical structures growing from the cable roots, protruding several centimeters above the soil surface. These breathing roots (pneumatophores) help the plants obtain air. The black mangrove *(Avicennia germinans)* achieves stability by a massive growth of knee-shaped pneumatophores around the collar of the tree.

An abundance of animal species inhabits mangroves, including mollusks, crustaceans, insects, and fish. The fauna feed on organic matter mainly derived from leaf litter. The group of crabs called sesarmids may rely on fresh mangrove leaves as a food source.

Humans also benefit from mangroves. In countries such as Bangladesh, mangroves are the main source of livelihood for coastal populations. They derive fuel, medicines, and building materials from mangrove trees. Mangroves are also reliable sources of food: fruit such as Nipah palm nuts, and crabs, prawns, snails, and bivalves are constantly harvested. The complex structure of pneumatophores and fallen branches, and the abundant detritus, make mangroves nursery grounds for commercial varieties of fish, prawns, and crabs. Mangroves also help prevent erosion of the shore or riverbanks as their dense root networks help stabilize the soil.

More than 75 percent of the coastlines of tropical and subtropical countries were once covered with mangrove forests, which help to protect the shorelines. However, it is estimated that fewer than 50 percent of these remain today. The loss of mangroves in several countries is caused largely by urbanization, land reclamation, deforestation for charcoal and timber, mounting pollution problems, as well as the recent pressure from commercial shrimp farming. Industrial shrimp aquaculture has led to the clearing of large tracts of mangrove forest in Southeast Asia, Latin America, Africa, and the Pacific Islands. Furthermore, the pollution caused by organic waste from shrimp is an additional problem. In view of the importance of mangroves, several initiatives are being implemented in several of the countries mentioned to restore degraded mangrove forests and regenerate these on new mudflats. Active research is also being conducted internationally to develop sustainable models on how to derive benefits from the mangrove forests without destroying the ecosystem.

Leo Tan and Sing Kong Lee

Further Reading

Lee, S. K., W. H. Tan, and S. Havanond. (1996) "Regeneration and Colonisation of Mangrove on Clay-Filled Reclaimed Land in Singapore." *Hydrobiologia* 319: 23–35.

Mangrove Action Project. (1990) "Mangrove Ecosystems." Retrieved 30 November 2001, from: http://www.earthisland.org/map/mngec.htm.

Ng, P. K. L., and N. Sivasothi, eds. (1999) *A Guide to the Mangroves of Singapore.* 2 vols. Singapore: Singapore Science Centre.

Tomlinson, P. B. (1986) *The Botany of Mangroves.* Cambridge, U.K.: Cambridge University Press.

Watson, J. G. (1928). "Mangrove Forest of the Malay Peninsula." *Malayan Forest Records* 6: 1–275.

MANGYSHLAK PENINSULA The Mangyshlak Peninsula (in Kazakh: Mangghystau Tubegi), is located along the western boundary of the Republic of Kazakhstan, an internal political division of the USSR until its independence in 1991. It is part of a greater political-administrative region of Kazakhstan known as the Manggystau Province (Oblysy). The peninsula extends westward into the Caspian Sea.

The Mangyshlak Peninsula is at the heart of a larger oil and gas region that Kazakhstan inherited with independence from the Soviet Union in 1991. Rich in fossil fuels and other natural resources, the peninsula yielded over half the republic's oil output in the early 1990s. The peninsula sits at the southern margins of the giant Tenghiz oil field, which extends to the north. Tenghiz oil reserves have been estimated to be around 25 billion barrels, or about twice the amount of Alaska's north slope. Chevron Oil entered into a joint venture with the Kazakh government in 1992, called Tengizchevroil, to extract oil in the region. Several problems have limited the development of the field in recent years, including decreased demand by Russian Siberian refineries that imported most of the oil, and pipeline access across the borders of the Russian Federation. In addition, the high sulfur, paraffin, asphalt, and tar content of much of the oil makes it difficult (that is, more expensive) to process.

Kazakhstan also inherited the Soviet Union's only fast breeder nuclear reactor, built in 1972 and located on the Mangyshlak Peninsula near the port city of Aqtau (Shevchenko). The reactor was built mainly to desalinate brackish Caspian Sea water for both personal and industrial uses. For economic as well as security concerns, the Kazakh government shut down the reactor in 1992.

The Caspian Sea is in reality the world's largest lake, with the Volga River supplying more than 80 percent of its inflow. It has no outlet and loses water through evaporation. Regional climate changes and changes in river flow into the Caspian have caused it to rise in the latter part of the twentieth century, leading to the evacuation of small towns and villages along the coast due to flooding.

Because of its high latitude (50°N), far from the moderating influences of oceans, the peninsula experiences a very continental climate. It sits on the western margins of the dry Kazakh steppe region. Horse, sheep, and camel herding, as well as some irrigated farming, are the main occupations of the inhabitants of the peninsula.

David R. Smith

Further Reading

Lydolph, Paul. (1977) *Geography of the USSR*. New York: Wiley.

National Imagery and Mapping Agency (NIMA). (2000) "GEOnet Names Server." Retrieved 3March 2002, from: http://gnpswww.nima.mil/geonames/GNS/.

MANHATTAN INCIDENT Thailand's *Manhattan* Incident of 1951 was the result of a bitter interservice rivalry between the more politically moderate navy and the conservative, royalist army, which was in turn tied up in the ongoing conflict between Pridi Banomyong (1900–1983) and Field Marshall Pibul Songgram (1897–1964), the leaders of Thailand's 1932 Revolution, which ended the absolute monarchy. Following World War II, Premier Pibul was forced to resign because of his alliance with the Japanese. He was replaced by the leading democrat, Pridi, who implemented sweeping constitutional changes designed to keep the military out of politics. Pridi's leftist economic reforms worried many in the army and royal family, who implicated him in the 1946 death of King Ananda. Therefore, despite his 1946 electoral victory, Pridi resigned, installing his close friend Admiral Dhamrong as premier.

In March 1947 Pibul reentered politics, resigning from the army and founding an ultranationalist party. Dhamrong was ousted in a 7 November 1947 army coup; he and Pridi were given refuge by the navy before fleeing abroad. Pibul denied planning the coup and was immediately named chief of Thailand's armed forces; he consolidated his power by September 1948, scrapping Pridi's liberal constitution and giving the army full control over the legislature. Corrupt and authoritarian, Pibul saw his legitimacy wane.

Pridi had a lot of popular support but had already disbanded his wartime Free Thai Movement, which had been allied with the West against Pibul's pro-Japanese government. Pridi also feared the prospect of a full-scale civil war, and both the United States and Great Britain urged the navy not to participate in a civil war against the army-led government. Pridi lived in exile but remained a threat to the regime as the navy laid the groundwork for his return, and on 26 February 1949 he secretly returned to lead an abortive coup by the navy and marines that was quickly crushed, forcing Pridi back into exile.

Pibul sought to improve the economy and began to shore up his anti-Communist credentials, winning American aid. As part of the aid program, the United States provided Thailand with a dredger, the USS *Manhattan*. At the 29 June 1951 ceremony transferring the dredger to the Thai government, a naval officer forced Pibul into a naval launch at gunpoint. He was taken to the battleship *Sri Ayudhya*, where he was held.

The navy, which had been biding its time since the February 1949 coup attempt, was hoping to oust Pibul, but army, air force, and police units responded quickly and on 30 August, the air force bombed the battleship. Pibul survived, and swam ashore, and within thirty-six hours was back in full control. In total, there were some 603 civilian casualties and an untold number of military casualties. Pridi died in exile, and Pibul was ousted in a September 1957 coup by Field Marshall Sarit Dhanaret. The lasting result of the 1951 *Manhattan* Incident was that the army consolidated its political power and would continue to dominate Thai politics for decades.

Zachary Abuza

Further Reading

Fineman, Daniel M. (1997) *A Special Relationship: The United States and Military Governments in Thailand, 1947–1958*. Honolulu: University of Hawaii Press.

MANIAM, K. S. (b. 1942), Malaysian writer. K. S. Maniam was born in Bedon, Kedah, Malaya. Trained as a teacher in Britain, he taught for several years in

Kedah before graduating from the University of Malaya in 1973. He is the author of some of the most significant Malaysian fiction in English. In 2000, he won the international Raja Rao Award for literature, which was conferred by the Samvad India Foundation. His novel *The Return* is considered a landmark for creating a distinctive Malaysian voice in the English language. His national award–winning short story "Haunting the Tiger" is similarly regarded as a groundbreaking piece of stylistic innovation for the genre of the Malaysian short story.

The Return has been included in the newly formed national canon of English-language writing for the national secondary schools curriculum. This inclusion is also the first official acknowledgment of contributions by Malaysian writers in languages other than the national Malay language.

Two of Maniam's plays, *The Cord* and *Sandpit*, marked the beginning of a resurgence in original Malaysian theater in English, which took off in the early 1980s. His work draws on the historical experiences of Indian-Malaysians and is concerned with the creation of new mythological and symbolic languages that integrate immigrant experiences into the multiracial national psyche of Malaysia. K. S. Maniam was associate professor of English at the University of Malaya and is now an independent writer.

Mohan Ambikaibaker

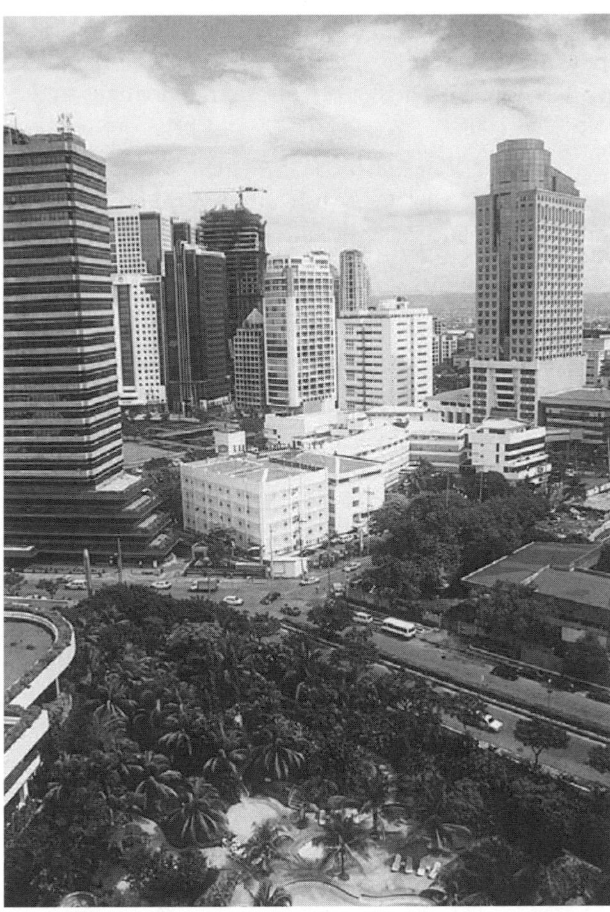

The skyline of Quezon City, Manila, in 1998. (STEPHEN G. DONALDSON PHOTOGRAPHY)

MANILA (2002 Metropolitan Manila est. pop. 10 million). Manila is the capital and the primary city of the Philippines. Manila proper (1995 population 1.6 million) is the Philippines' second-largest city after Quezon City (1995 population 2 million) in terms of population. Manila is located in southern Luzon Island on the Pasig River and Manila Bay. The Pasig River divides the city into north and south sections, with the old city, government buildings, and tourist facilities in the south and commerce, large slums, and Chinatown in the north. Present-day Manila is a major manufacturing, commercial, educational, cultural, and political center. It is a major port, the endpoint for the island's highways and railroads, and it has the nation's major airport. Major industries include processing plants for hemp and tobacco, pharmaceuticals, chemicals, steel, automobile assembly, and textiles. It also has over twenty colleges and universities and a reputation as the entertainment center of East and Southeast Asia with many restaurants, nightclubs, and theaters.

From the twelfth century, the territory that was to become Manila was a Muslim trading port with ties to Brunei and Melaka to the south and west. It was conquered by the Spanish colonizer Miguel Lopez de Legazpi (c. 1510–1572) in 1571; Legazpi made it the center of Spanish colonization of the Philippines. The name Manila is a Spanish corruption of Maynilad, meaning "where the *nilad* grows." (The *nilad* is a small white flower that used to flourish on Pasig riverbanks.)

Under the Spanish, Manila became the center of education, commerce, and religion; it was administered from distant Mexico City. The Spanish actually created two cities: the Intramuros, a walled city south of the river, where the Spanish lived, and an Extramuros, outside the walls, where the Malays and Chinese lived. For two centuries it was mainly a regional trade center for the flow of goods and wealth between China and Mexico. After the Spanish developed the Philippines as an agricultural colony early in the nineteenth century, Manila became the primary trade city both for intra-island and external trade. As the major trading center, it attracted the Spanish elite and became a cosmopolitan city and the home to Spain's major educational and religious organizations in Asia. It was this elite that played a major role in the Philippine revolution (1896–1898) and who worked with U.S. colonial officials to create an independent Philippines in 1946.

Manila was occupied by the Japanese from January 1942 until February 1945. It suffered much damage in both the Japanese assault and the American recapture, with the old city almost entirely destroyed. In 1948 Quezon City was made the national capital; Manila became the capital again in 1976. Since the end of World War II the city has been rebuilt and has experienced enormous growth.

Metropolitan Manila, or Metro Manila, is an administrative region composed of twelve cities (Quezon City, Manila, Caloocan, Makati, Pasig, Marikina, Mandaluyong, Pasay City, Muntinlupa, Paranaque, Las Pinas, and Valenzuela) and five municipalities (Taguig, Malabon, Navotas, San Juan, and Pateros). Metro Manila was created in 1975 by Ferdinand Marcos (1917–1989), the Philippines' leader from 1966 to 1986, to make coordination of regional services such as sewage disposal, garbage collection, housing, and water supply more efficient. Marcos appointed his wife, Imelda, the first governor of the district. Each of the cities and municipalities maintains its autonomy and elects its own mayor and council.

Further Reading

Reed, Robert R. (1978) *Colonial Manila: The Context of Hispanic Urbanism and Process of Morphogenesis.* Berkeley and Los Angeles: University of California Press.

Solon, Orville. (1996) "Global Influences on Recent Urbanization Trends in the Philippines." In *Emerging World Cities in Pacific Asia*, edited by Chen-lo Fu and Yue-Man Yeung. Tokyo: United Nations University, 268–285.

Von Naerssen, Ton, Michel Ligthart, and Flotilda N. Zapanta. (1996) "Managing Metropolitan Manila." In *The Dynamics of Metropolitan Management in Southeast Asia*, edited by Jürgen Rüland. Singapore: Institute of Southeast Asian Studies, 168–206.

MANILA ACTION PLAN

On 24 and 25 November 1996, the Asia-Pacific Economic Cooperation (APEC) nations held their annual meeting in Manila, the Philippines. Security at the meeting was especially tight, as the host nation was undergoing considerable political unrest and it feared possible violence from Islamic fundamentalists.

The Manila meeting followed a lackluster conference in Osaka the previous year where little of substance was accomplished. Some anticipated a similar result for Manila because of differences among the member countries over tariff reductions.

The signature issue of the conference was loosening restraints on the trade in advanced technology, especially computers and communication equipment. As the world's leader in these areas, the United States pressed for liberalized trade rules. But other nations had developing industries in these market segments and were reluctant to let them fend for themselves in a brutally competitive world market. China, especially, was reluctant to go along with U.S. proposals.

Rather than let a second consecutive conference end in relative failure, President Bill Clinton proposed a compromise that set the year 2000 for the elimination of national tariffs on technology. The resulting "action agreement" was, however, nonbinding and no enforcement provision was adopted. This somewhat lame agreement was the only real item of business for the conference, which also split over the issue of human rights, with China and the United States once again in opposition.

Robert K. Whalen

MANIPUR

(2001 est. pop. 2.4 million). Bordering Myanmar (Burma), Manipur is a small state in northeastern India. The state is a rough rectangle with an area of 22,327 square kilometers. One-third of the people, living in the rugged hills, belong to twenty-nine tribes, which are part of either the Kukis or the Nagas ethnic groups. The other two-thirds of the population, in the valley, are primarily Meitei. In the 1700s Bengali influence led to the adoption of Vaishnavism by the elite. British conquest in 1891 increased the social distance between the elite and the masses. Efforts to revive Meitei culture and religious rituals and to replace Bengali with Manipuri script strongly challenged the national government and the Vaishnavite Brahmans. Resistance in the hills was violent, with a 1917 rebellion against the British and a union of Naga groups into the anti-Christian Zeliangrong movement in Nagaland (1927–1932).

During World War II Manipur was occupied by the Japanese, with 250,000 British and Indian troops trapped under siege. Since 1972 violent self-rule campaigns and a war between the Kukis and Nagas have disturbed the state. Agriculture and forestry predominate; small-scale industries produce cotton and silk textiles, milled rice, crude sugar, and wooden wares. More than 200,000 hand looms yield designed cloth in demand throughout India.

C. Roger Davis

Further Reading

Gangle, Thangkhomany S. (1993) *The Kukis of Manipur.* New Delhi: Gyan Publishing House.

MANORA *Manora*, also known as *menora*, *nora chatri*, or simply *nora*, is a traditional Malaysian folkdance drama. Some scholars believe that *manora* originated in India and later spread to Java and Malaya before reaching southern Thailand. Other scholars believe that *manora* is a primitive performing art, originating in southern Thailand, and could have evolved from the ritual of propitiation of hunters. Today, *manora* is largely performed as an art form for the common people.

The word *manora* derives from the name of the heroine in the Manohra tale in Buddhist literature. There are two types of *manora*. One is performed for a specific ritual purpose (e.g., the release of a vow, or to celebrate coming of age). The other is performed purely for entertainment at weddings, fairs, or festivals. *Manora* is popular in the northern and eastern states of Malaysia (Kedah, Perlis, and Kelantan), as well as in various provinces in southern Thailand.

Manora is similar to Mak Yong, another traditional Malay dance drama. However, they are different in terms of their presentation of music and dance. The musical instruments that accompany the dancing and singing in a *manora* are much more numerous than those in Mak Yong. *Manora* is performed on a low platform with the audience sitting or standing on three sides. Mak Yong, on the other hand, is performed on the level ground and is open on all sides so that performers can sit and move freely and are visible to the audience at all times. *Manora* emphasizes the dance rather than the stories, which derive from *Ramayana* and *Mahabharata* epics. Unlike Mak Yong, all performers of *manora* are men, who cross-dress to play female roles. The language used depends upon the local dialect. In Kelantan, for example, actors use the Kelantanese dialect, while in Perlis, a mix of Thai and Perlis dialects is used. *Manora* music is adapted from Thai folk music, and instruments usually include a double-reed oboe, a pair of single-headed stick drums, cymbals, and bamboo or wooden clappers.

Nor Faridah Abdul Manaf

See also: **Mak Yong**

Further Reading

Yahaya, Ismail. (1989) *The Cultural Heritage of Malaysia.* Kuala Lumpur, Malaysia: Dinamika Kreatif.

Yousof, Ghulam Sarwar. (1994) *Dictionary of Traditional South-East Asia Theatre.* Kuala Lumpur, Malaysia: Oxford University Press.

MANSUR SHAH (d. 1477), Malay Melakan sultan. During Mansur Shah's reign (1459–1477), the sultanate of Melaka reached the zenith of its political, territorial, and religious influence in the Malay Archipelago. Mansur succeeded his father, Muzaffar Shah (reigned 1445–1459), owing to the support of his powerful and influential uncle Tun Perak, the *bendahara* (prime minister). Throughout his reign, Mansur was assisted by Tun Perak, Tun Ali, the treasurer, and Hang Tuah, the *laksamana* (admiral).

The power and status of the sultan was consolidated due to the efforts of Tun Perak. Melaka expanded its hegemony through diplomacy, political maneuvering, religious influence, and military conquest, and Tun Perak planned and executed this expansionist policy. Eastern Sumatra, the Malay Peninsula, and the Riau-Lingga archipelago submitted to Melaka. Through trade and Islamic propagation, Banda, Brunei, and the northern Javanese ports also came within Melaka's sphere of influence. Mansur's marriage to both a Chinese and a Javanese princess further strengthened relations with China and Majapahit, respectively.

The pleasure-loving Mansur was neither an efficient administrator nor an exemplary ruler. He presided over a royal court rich with ceremonies. He preferred literature and religious discourse and left state affairs to his ministers. The well-known Tuah-Jebat duel exemplified Mansur's misuse of his power as an absolute monarch. Out of blind loyalty to his ruler, the *laksamana* Tuah killed his friend, Jebat, who had revealed the monarch's injustices. The Tuah-Jebat conflict struck at the heart of the traditional Malay concepts of unquestioned loyalty and justice.

Ooi Keat Gin

Further Reading

Muhammad Yusuf Hashim. (1992) *The Malay Sultanate of Malacca: A Study of Various Aspects of Malacca in the 15th and 16th Centuries in Malaysian History.* Trans. by D. J. Muzaffar Tate. Kuala Lumpur, Malaysia: Dewan Bahasa dan Pustaka.

Sejarah Melayu or Malay Annals. (1983) Trans. by C. C. Brown. Kuala Lumpur, Malaysia: Oxford University Press.

Sheppard, Mubin C. (1966) *The Adventures of Hang Tuah.* Singapore: Donald Moore for Eastern University Press.

Wheatley, Paul. (1966) *The Golden Khersonese: Studies in the Historical Geography of the Malay Peninsula before A.D. 1500.* Kuala Lumpur, Malaysia: University of Malaya Press.

MANTO, SAADAT HASAN (1912–1955), Indian writer. Saadat Hasan Manto, the much acclaimed and controversial South Asian Muslim literary figure, was born in Sambrala, in the Ludhiana district of the Punjab. As a young man, Manto began his literary career with an Urdu translation of Victor Hugo's *The Last Days of a Condemned Man.* Early in his career, Manto was deeply influenced by French and Russian realist writers such as Hugo, Guy de Maupassant, Anton Chekhov, and Maksim Gorki. During the 1930s, Manto was also peripherally involved with the Indian Progressive Writers Association, a literary movement committed to articulating the ideals of social uplift and justice through literature.

During his career, Manto wrote more than two hundred stories and a number of essays, film scripts, and radio plays. However, his greatest contributions to Indian literature were his mastery of the short story genre and his use of the Urdu language. Some of his well-known Urdu short stories include "Bu" ("Odor"), "Khol Do" ("Open It"), "Thanda Gosht" ("Cold Meat"), and "Toba Tek Singh," translated into English after Manto's death.

After the partition of India in 1947, Manto left his home in Mumbai (Bombay), where he had lived since 1936, and returned to Lahore, Pakistan, in January 1948. Although Manto's last years in Pakistan were filled with financial hardship, failing health, and relative obscurity, they were also witness to some of his greatest literary achievements. Manto was survived by his wife Safiyah and three daughters.

Ami P. Shah

Further Reading

Manto, Saadat Hasan. (1985) *The Life and Works of Saadat Hasan Manto.* Introduction by Leslie Flemming; trans. by Tahira Naqvi. Lahore, Pakistan: Vanguard Books Ltd.

MANUFACTURING INDUSTRY—INDONESIA

Indonesia's economic performance from 1969 to 1996 has been remarkable. From the mid-1960s to the early 1980s, gross domestic product (GDP) grew by more than 7.5 percent per annum (p.a.). After a mild economic recession due to the collapse of the price of oil in 1980–1985, the economy rebounded again and grew by 6.7 percent p.a. from the mid-1980s to 1996.

Continued economic growth transformed the structure of Indonesia's economy. In 1970, agriculture accounted for 45 percent of GDP, and manufacturing 12 percent. By 1996, agriculture had declined to 17 percent of GDP, whilst manufacturing rose to 24 percent.

Structural Transformation—Key Features of the Manufacturing Sector

Between 1970 and 1980, the manufacturing sector grew by more than 14 percent per year. However, Indonesia was confronted with a series of problems in the 1980s, and a large decline in oil prices hurt Indonesia's balance of payments. The government then launched economic liberalization programs to increase economic efficiency, and made development of non-oil and gas exports a top priority. The impact of these measures on non-oil manufacturing exports was quite remarkable; they experienced a 57 percent growth in 1987. After experiencing slower growth in 1980–1985 (8.5 percent), the sector grew by 10.7 percent in 1985–1990 and 10.4 percent in 1990–1995.

In 1997, however, Indonesia faced a serious economic crisis. The rupiah fell to a record low of 17,000 to the dollar in January 1998, and the economy shrank by 13.2 percent. In 1998 the manufacturing sector experienced negative growth of –11.4 percent while the overall economy declined by –13.2 percent. The overall economy slightly improved in 1999, experiencing 0.2 percent growth while the manufacturing sector grew by 2.2 percent. The share of the manufacturing sector to the total GDP was relatively stable during that period, implying a stagnation in structural change in this sector.

To understand about the structure of the manufacturing sector, it is important to observe how the structural change took place within it. Food products (International Standard Industrial Classification number 31, or ISIC 31), which accounted for 47 percent of total non-oil manufacturing in 1975, had declined to 23 percent of total manufacturing by 1995. On the other hand, the share of labor-intensive industry (ISIC 32 and 39) in total manufacturing continued to rise, from 11 percent in 1975 to 19 percent of total manufacturing by 1995.

Internationally, Indonesian exports were dominated by non-oil manufacturing products, particularly after the mid-1980s. In the 1970s, manufacturing exports contributed less than 3 percent to total exports, and primary goods dominated, but by 1987 the share of manufacturing exports had surpassed that of primary exports.

Before the mid-1980s, manufacturing exports were dominated by the Agriculture Resource Intensive (ARI) group. In the 1970s, ARI exports represented 90 percent of all non-oil manufacturing exports, and Unskilled Labor-Intensive (ULI) only 5 percent. But ULI exports grew rapidly, surpassing the ARI share in 1985. That year, ULI was 44 percent of total manufacturing exports, while ARI was 42 percent. The share of ULI continued to increase, reaching 54 percent in 1992, while that of ARI continued to decline, to 25 percent. This notable performance of labor-intensive

The Arco oil company's offshore facility in the Java Sea. (HANAN ISACHAR/CORBIS)

exports can be attributed to the trade liberalization that began after 1985, which allowed Indonesia to exploit its potential comparative advantage in labor-intensive products.

Another important feature of the Indonesian manufacturing sector was the high dispersion of trade protection among the industries, particularly during the period 1975 to 1998. But trade protection in the manufacturing sector was not random. In the 1970s it was mainly influenced by national policy, such as protection for infant industries. Particularly after the mid-1980s, it was strongly influenced by crony capitalists and various interest groups.

The period since 1985 has seen outstanding performance in the Indonesian manufacturing sector. This rapid expansion can be credited to factors such as the devaluations of the rupiah in 1983 and 1986, high savings and investment rates, and economic liberalization since 1985. Indonesia's remarkable growth in the manufacturing and export sectors during the pre-crisis era and this achievement can be attributed to credible macroeconomic management, a political predisposition towards moderate inflation, and trade liberalization during the 1980s.

During the 1997 economic crisis, the share of manufacturing in the total GDP remained relatively stable. After 1998 the manufacturing sector rebounded in line with the improvement of Indonesia's economic growth.

Muhammad Chatib Basri

Further Reading

Basri, Muhammad C. (2001) "The Political Economy of Manufacturing Protection in Indonesia, 1975–1995." Ph.D diss. Australian National University, Canberra.

Chenery, Hollis, and Moshe Syrquin. (1975) *Patterns of Development, 1950–1970.* New York: Oxford University Press.

MANUFACTURING INDUSTRY—MALAYSIA

MANUFACTURING INDUSTRY—MALAYSIA The manufacturing industry in Malaysia became a significant contributor to the country's economy in the postindependence period beginning in the 1960s. During the colonial period, the country had been a major producer of raw materials, namely, tin and rubber. Secondary industries then were related to tin, rubber, timber, foodstuffs, and petroleum.

Historical Overview

Tin smelting started in Kuala Lumpur in the early 1880s. In 1885, a reverbatory furnace was in operation in Telok Anson (now Telok Intan), Perak (now a state in Malaysia), for smelting low-grade ores. The Straits Trading Company erected smelting plants on Pulau Brani (c. 1887) and at Butterworth (1902) in Penang state. A Chinese-owned smelter at Datuk Keramat that started operation in 1897 was bought by the Eastern Smelting Company.

Oil was struck at Miri, Sarawak, in 1910. A Shell-owned distillation plant for crude oil at Lutong came into operation in mid-1919 to serve the needs of the oilfields of Miri and Seria, Brunei. The Borneo Company processed gold by utilizing the cyanidation process at its plants in Bau (1899) and Bidi (1900) in Sarawak.

Some light-engineering works involved motor repairs of machinery in tin mining, irrigation, and transportation (road and rail) equipment. Service maintenance of locomotives and coaches was an industry supporting the transportation sector. The manufacture of consumer goods (soap, matches, etc.) for domestic consumption was on a very small scale. There were also indigenous handicraft and cottage industries (textiles, foodstuffs, etc.). Beginning in the 1960s concerted efforts and programs were implemented to promote and develop the manufacturing industry in the country.

Contemporary Status

The manufacturing sector is now a dynamic and flourishing component of the national economy, accounting for about one-third of the gross domestic product (GDP) as shown in Table 1.

The electrical, electronics, and machinery-products industries experienced rapid growth and expansion during the 1970s. Malaysia progressed from assembling electrical goods and machinery to manufacturing a wide range of these products by the 1980s. The electronics industry is the largest in the region, and Malaysia is the leading exporter of semiconductor components to the United States. Multinationals like Intel, AMD, Sony, Sharp, Motorola, and others are well entrenched with huge amounts of capital investments.

The Rubber Industry

Complementing its market position as the world's major producer and exporter of natural rubber, Malaysia also leads in the manufacture of latex goods. The manufacture of rubber-based products has attracted a constantly growing number of foreign manufacturers and investors, including Goodyear of the United States, Viking Askim of Norway, Ansell of Australia, BDF Beiersdorf AG of Germany, Pirelli of Italy, Sagami of Japan, Dongkuk Techco of South Korea, and others.

TABLE 1

Gross Domestic Product (GDP): Sectoral Performance, 1999

	Growth	Share of GDP	Contribution to growth
Agriculture, Forestry, and Fishing	4.6	9.4	10.1
Mining	–1.2	7.6	–2.3
Manufacturing	8.9	29.2	68.0
Construction	–3.6	3.7	–3.4
Services	2.4	54.6	31.3
Less imputed bank service charges	3.7	7.4	6.4
Plus import duties	21.6	2.9	12.7
GDP	4.3	100.0	100.0

SOURCE: Ministry of Finance, Malaysia (1999/2000).

The Food Industry

The food, beverages, and tobacco industries are the province of small- and medium-scale (SMIs) establishments. Food manufacturing continues to be heavily dependent on imported inputs. Efforts are being undertaken to encourage import substitution in this sector.

The Petroleum Sector

Optimism is high for the petroleum industry and the manufacture of related products. From its beginning in Lutong in 1919, Malaysia had five oil refineries by 1998: two are owned by PETRONAS (Petroliam Nasional Berhad), the national petroleum company, two by Shell, and one by Exxon Mobil. The PETRONAS-owned Liquefied Natural Gas (LNG) plant at Bintulu, Sarawak, which started operation in 1983, is the world's third-largest LNG exporter. The Association of Southeast Asian Nations (ASEAN) Bintulu Fertiliser plant, an ASEAN joint-venture project that commenced operation in 1985, is reputedly the world's largest in terms of production-train capacity. Another joint venture, the Middle Distillate Synthesis plant that converts natural gas into diesel, kerosene, solvent, and so on, is a project by PETRONAS, Shell Gas BV, Mitsubishi Corporation, and the Sarawak state government. It started production in 1993. There are also several petrochemical industries operating under PETRONAS.

Heavy Industry

The heavy-industry sector can trace its beginnings to the period of large-scale tin mining in peninsular Malaysia from the mid-nineteenth century. The manufacture of cast-iron parts for tin mines was important then. When railways were introduced, steel casting of replacement parts for locomotives and coaches was undertaken by this sector. In 1967, the country's first integrated commercial steel mill (Malayawata Steel Bhd.) was established. Foreign vehicle giants like Toyota, Honda, and Volvo have had assembly plants in Malaysia since the 1960s. Two national car projects and one national motorcycle project boosted the heavy-industry sector. Malaysia has emerged as a producer and exporter of motor vehicles since the ap-

A customer examines a pirated VCD copy of a Star Wars movie at a stall in Jakarta in May 1999. At the time, the government had initiated a campaign to shut down the video piracy industry. (AFP/CORBIS)

pearance of the Proton Saga (1985), Perodua Kancil (1992), and Modenas Kriss (1995). In Malaysia, Proton held more than 60 percent of the market share for automobiles throughout the 1990s.

The Chemical Industry

The chemical industry in Malaysia continues to rely on imported intermediate chemical and petrochemical products in production ranging from household items to material inputs for the rubber, palm-oil, and timber industries. The chemical-industry sector has a conspicuous foreign participation, including ICI, Unilever, Colgate Palmolive, Borden, Exxon Mobil, Shell, and Mitsubishi Chemical Industries.

The Timber, Textile, and Plastics Industries

The timber-based industries manufacture a wide range of wood products including sawn timber, plywood, prefabricated houses, doors, window frames, wall panels, fiberboard, particleboard, wood briquette, wood wool, timber moldings, veneer, and block board. Furniture and wood fixtures are produced for the domestic and foreign markets.

The textile industry focuses on textiles and yarn production and garments and knitwear that cater for local and international markets. The industry is dominated by local enterprise.

The manufacturing sector also produces plastics (containers, pipes and hoses, electrical components), precision products (surgical, dental, photographic, optical), palm oil–based products (margarines, shortenings), clay-based products (bricks, ceramic articles), and leather goods.

Industrial Organizations and Government Organs

The Federation of Malaysian Manufacturers (FMM, 1968) focuses on creating and sustaining a dynamic business environment. Its membership of more than two thousand is representative of the various subsectors of the Malaysian manufacturing industry. The FMM Institute of Manufacturing offers skills training. FMM operates and manages the Malaysian Product Numbering System as well as being the authorized body for issuing and endorsing certificates of origin.

The manufacturing industry in Malaysia comes under the purview of the Ministry of International Trade and Industry (MITI). Specifically the Industrial Policy Division and the Industries Division in MITI oversee the promotion and development of the manufacturing sector. Other related government organizations and agencies include the Malaysian Industrial Development Authority (1965), Malaysian Industrial Development Finance Berhad (1960), and Malaysian Industrial Estates Sdn Bhd (1964).

In concert with the National Development Policy, the Second Outline Perspective Plan (1991–2000) and the Seventh Malaysia Plan (1996–2000), the Second Industrial Master Plan (IMP2) targets the manufacturing sector as a major contributor to the national economy. The industrial sector is entrusted with the pivotal task of propelling the country toward industrialization and sustainable economic growth and development. IMP2 emphasized the strengthening of Malaysia's industrial base as well as diversifying the export of manufactured products. The promotion of foreign investment in the manufacturing sector will continue to be adopted as one of the pivotal strategies in developing and expanding the sector.

Ooi Keat Gin

Further Reading

Allen, George Cyril, and Audrey G. Donnithorne. (1954) *Western Enterprise in Indonesia and Malaya: A Study in Economic Development*. London: Allen & Unwin.

Brookfield, Harold, ed. (1994) *Transformation with Industrialization in Peninsular Malaysia*. Kuala Lumpur, Malaysia: Oxford University Press.

Esderts, Hans J., and Ismail Muhammad Salleh, eds. (1990). *Promotion of Small-Scale Industries and Strategies for Rural Industrialization: The Malaysian Experience*. Kuala Lumpur, Malaysia: Friedrich-Ebert-Stiftung.

Fong, Chan Onn. (1986) *Technological Leap: Malaysian Industry in Transition*. Singapore: Oxford University Press.

Jomo, Kwame Sundaram, ed. (1994) *Malaysia's Economy in the Nineties*. Petaling Jaya, Selangor: Pelanduk Publications.

Kok, Swee Kheng. (1994) *Malaysia to 2003: From Redistribution to Growth*. London: Economic Intelligence Unit.

Ministry of Finance, Malaysia. (1999) *Economic Report, 1997/1998*. Kuala Lumpur, Malaysia: Kementerian Kewangan Malaysia.

Ministry of Finance, Malaysia. (2001) *Economic Report, 1999/2000*. Kuala Lumpur, Malaysia: Kementerian Kewangan Malaysia.

Rasiah, Rajah. (1995) *Foreign Capital and Industrialization in Malaysia*. New York: St Martin's Press.

MANUFACTURING INDUSTRY—PHILIPPINES A critical goal of the Philippine economy has been an expansion of its product manufacturing base to take advantage of its labor surplus and position itself favorably in the regional economy. The Philippines is a labor-surplus country, and the government has traditionally encouraged the development of labor-intensive industries, such as textile production and the assembly of electrical and electronic equipment. However, manufacturing has made only a relatively small contribution to employment. So far, the Philippine manufacturing industry has not exhibited the same structural changes as have neighboring countries.

Historical View

The roots of modern manufacturing in the Philippines can be found in the closing years of Spanish rule in the last decades of the nineteenth century. Few industrial establishments began operations in the 1880s, and most of those that did produced food, tobacco, and beverages. Over the first four decades of the twentieth century, manufacturing developed slowly and irregularly. Industrial expansion was primarily directed to the processing of agricultural products (sugarcane and coconuts), the manufacture of apparel, and the production of ceramics, cement, glassware, and wooden and rattan furniture. During the period immediately following World War II, industrial production was geared to the domestic market, and manufacturing was assisted by high levels of protection. Protection depended initially on import quotas and foreign exchange control. Later, in the 1970s, the main forms of protection became tariffs and foreign-exchange controls administered by the Central Bank.

Much industrial growth took place in the 1950s. By 1960 manufacturing accounted for 20 percent of the gross domestic product (GDP), whereas the range in the other member countries that would later join the Association of Southeast Asian Nations (ASEAN) was 9 to 13 percent. However, growth rates dropped appreciably after the late 1950s, as the main opportunities for import substitution became exhausted. The government made a mistake in not moving away from the policy of import substitution in the 1960s. The 1970s experienced some reorientation toward exports, stimulated by the floating of the Philippines peso, the Export Incentive Act (1970), and the Export Processing Zone project (1972). However, in the beginning of the 1980s, the main thrust of industrial policy continued to be the protection of domestic manufacturing aimed at import substitution.

Since the mid-1980s, the performance of nontraditional manufactured exports has shown its growing importance to the Philippine economy. Within this category are electronics, furniture, wood products, and fashion garments, shoes, and leather goods. Most of these industries depend on imported raw materials that are assembled or fashioned in some of the Philippine special economic zones: the Bataan Free Trade Zone, Baguio, and Cebu.

Contemporary Status

Manufacturing is the second most important economic sector after services, employing 9.8 percent of the labor force and contributing 22 percent of the GDP in 1998. In the 1990s, manufacturing was the most dynamic sector in the Philippine economy. According to the Asian Development Bank, the GDP of the manufacturing sector increased by an annual average of 2.8 percent in the 1990–1997 period; manufacturing GDP declined by 1.1 percent in 1998 (as a result of the 1997 Asian financial crisis) and increased by 1.4 percent in 1999.

Manufacturing is dominated by the private sector. Firms employing over 100 workers together contribute 75 percent of the added value. Concentration is most pronounced in beverages, tobacco, cosmetics, paper and paper products, and household appliances. Many factories are licensees of foreign companies or act as subcontractors for foreign firms, turning out finished products for export from imported intermediate goods. In 1997 the most important branches of manufacturing, measured by gross value of output, were food products, machinery and transport equipment, and chemicals. (See Table 1.)

Modern manufacturing production is concentrated on processing and assembly operations of the following: food, beverages, tobacco, rubber products, textiles, clothing and footwear, pharmaceuticals, paints, plywood and veneer, paper and paper products, small appliances, and electronics. Heavy manufacturing contributes less than 40 percent of the total added value in the 1990s. It is dominated by the production of cement, glass, industrial chemicals, fertilizers, iron, steel, and copper and refined petroleum products. (See

TABLE 1

Structure of Manufacturing

(percentage of total)

Year	Value added in manufacturing, (in billions of dollars)	Food, beverages, and tobacco	Textiles and clothing	Machinery and transport equipment	Chemicals	Other manufacturing
1980	8.354	30	13	12	14	31
1997	18.333	33	9	15	13	29

SOURCE: National Statistical Information Center (1999).

Table 2.) In the 1990s the electronics industry was the fastest growing sector not only in manufacturing but also in the Philippine economy as a whole. Exports of electronic production increased from $3 billion in 1992 to $20 billion in 1998; they contributed two-thirds of Philippine exports in 1998. The electronics industry is also the branch where the most employment has been gained.

Manufacturing is highly dualistic, consisting of a modern sector, which has considerable export potential, and a cottage sector, which contributes only a small amount to total added value but employs over half the manufacturing labor force.

Urban Base

The government's industrial strategy places high priority on the dispersal of manufacturing capacity outside the capital. However, the industrial sector remains concentrated in the urban areas, especially in the metropolitan Manila region, and has only weak links to the rural economy. Over 60 percent of the manufacturing establishments are still concentrated in the Manila area and the southern Luzon region. The ability of the Philippines to reach a new level of industrial growth may depend on its achieving diversification outside urban areas.

Dimitar L. Dimitrov

TABLE 2

Manufacturing—Selected Products

(in thousands of metric tons, unless otherwise indicated)

Product	1987	1990	1993	1996
Raw sugar	1,304	1,629	2,020	1,775
Footwear, total production, excluding rubber (in thousands of pairs)	10,600	10,000	15,000	N/A
Veneer sheets (in thousands of cubic meters)	75	49	65	82
Wrapping and packaging paper and paperboard	144	78	270	269
Nitrogenous fertilizers, total production	120	121	165	N/A
Phosphate fertilizers, total production	193	199	186	N/A
Cement	3,984	6,360	7,932	N/A
Crude steel, ingots	250	600	623	500
Copper, refined, unwrought	132.1	125.9	166.0	155.8

SOURCE: National Statistical Information Center (1999).

Further Reading

Boyce, James K. (1993) *The Philippines: The Political Economy of Growth and Impoverishment in the Marcos Era.* Honolulu: University of Hawaii Press.

Corpuz, Onofre D. (1997) *An Economic History of the Philippines.* Quezon City, Philippines: University of the Philippines Press.

Kunio, Yoshihara. (1985) *Philippine Industrialization: Foreign and Domestic Capital.* Oxford: Oxford University Press.

National Statistical Information Center. (1999) *Center Philippine Statistical Yearbook.* Makati City, Philippines: National Statistical Information Center.

Vos, Bob, and Josef T. Yap. (1996) *Philippine Economy: East Asia's Stray Cat? Structure, Finance and Adjustment.* New York: St. Martin's Press.

MAO ZEDONG (1893–1976), leader of the Chinese Communist Party and chairman of the People's Republic of China. Mao was one of the leading figures of the twentieth century. Beyond serving as the head of the Chinese Communist Party (CCP), his ideas and policies served as a model for many other political leaders in the Communist world.

Mao was born in the village of Shaoshan, Xiang Tan County, Hunan Province in 1893. As a boy he resisted working on the family farm and instead sought every opportunity to obtain an education. In 1911 he joined the army and after six months service returned

Mao Zedong in a classic portrait. (ROMAN SOUMAR/CORBIS)

to his education. Six months spent reading on his own in the library proved of immense value and in 1913 he returned to formal schooling. Patriotism was perhaps the major motivating force in his life, and he saw education as a means to improve the lot of the Chinese people and the nation.

In 1919 he became involved in the May Fourth Movement (a reform movement aimed at strengthening China); through the movement he met Chen Duxiu and Li Dazhao, the founders (1921) of the Chinese Communist Party, of which Mao was an original member. In July 1921 he led the Hunanese delegation to the First Congress of the Chinese Communist Party in Shanghai. Thereafter, he devoted himself to revolutionary activities mainly in Hunan and Guangzhou. At first shut out of CCP leadership by a pro-Soviet faction that favored a traditional urban proletariat revolution, Mao came to power after the Long March (1934–1935) from southeastern to northwestern China. From that time forward, Mao's vision of a peasant revolution took hold. Mao's agrarian Marxism won the CCP the support of the people to the detriment of the Nationalists. His supremacy in the party was confirmed at the Seventh CCP Congress in April 1945, where "Mao Zedong Thought" was adopted as the official ideology. Following Japan's surrender in 1945 at the end of World War II, the CCP defeated the Nationalists in China's civil war (1945–1949).

In the first ten years after the establishment of the People's Republic (1 October 1949), Mao, as the chairman both of the government and the party, worked to unify the nation and rebuild it after decades of war. He instituted land reform and oversaw the transition to a socialist economy. However, de-Stalinization in the USSR from 1956 brought about a radical shift in Mao's thinking.

Determined to avoid what he saw as the rise of bourgeois elements in the Soviet Union, he instituted his Great Leap Forward (1958–1960), an attempt to industrialize China at the rural level. Not only was the attempt a failure, the diversion of resources from agriculture caused widespread famine. Undeterred from his vision, Mao launched the Cultural Revolution in 1966; it was an attempt to keep the CCP and society at large from restratifying, but its result was societal chaos. Nevertheless, the CCP concluded officially in 1981 that Mao's contributions to the Chinese revolution far outweighed the "gross mistakes" he committed during his final years. Mao died on 9 September 1976 and his body remains on display in Tiananmen Square in Beijing.

Noriyuki Tokuda

Further Reading

Chen, Jerome. (1965) *Mao and the Chinese Revolution*. Oxford: Oxford University Press.

Meisner, Maurice. (1986) *Mao's China And After: A History of the People's Republic*. New York: The Free Press.

Spence, Jonathan. (1999) *Mao Zedong*. New York: Penguin.

MARCH FIRST INDEPENDENCE MOVEMENT The March First Independence Movement *(Samil undong)* was a Korean popular movement against Japanese colonization that resulted in a Korean declaration of independence from Japan and the fostering of Korean national liberation movements worldwide.

In 1919, Korean nationalists both in Korea and living abroad were inspired by President Woodrow Wilson's concept of national self-determination for all peoples, hoping that Korea could regain its independence from Japan, which had annexed it in 1910. As a result, nationalist Korean intellectuals planned an appeal for independence from Japan to coincide with the World War I peace negotiations at Versailles. The death of Korea's former Emperor Kojong (reigned 1864–1907) in early 1919, and his planned public funeral for March of that year, gave the opportunity for Korean nationalist leaders to express their call for independence. In March, thousands of Koreans gathered, no doubt angered by rumors of the emperor's poisoning at the hands of the Japanese. Demonstrations were also planned in regional cities.

On 1 March 1919, Korean intellectuals presented to the Japanese governor-general in Seoul a "Declaration for Korean Independence" signed by Korean religious, political, and intellectual leaders. The declaration was proclaimed publicly the same day. The independence movement that erupted in Seoul on March 1 soon spread throughout the country in the form of spontaneous demonstrations for national independence. Among the demonstrators were farmers and craftsmen, Christians and Buddhists, housewives and school children, as well as intellectual and political leaders. The Japanese authorities were caught completely off guard by the movement's scale and spontaneity and their first reaction was one of brutal repression. Throughout the year conflicts between Koreans and Japanese resulted in thousands of deaths before the Japanese authorities were able to regain control.

The movement ultimately failed to free Korea of Japanese rule. The symbolic Declaration of Independence and national show of solidarity, however, provided the needed impetus for the Korean nationalist movement, which had languished since the time of annexation. Nationalist organizations began to appear both in Korea and among Koreans overseas. The Provisional Government of the Republic of Korea was established in Shanghai in April 1919, and became a focal point for subsequent independence efforts. Japanese policy in Korea also changed, as the authorities relinquished their initial heavy-handedness. Greater freedom of the press and organization was allowed, which aided the development of nationalist writings in Korea. After the suppression of the movement, however, the incentive towards Korean national independence moved overseas.

Daniel C. Kane

Further Reading

Ch'on, Kwan-u. (1971) "The Samil Revolt Considered as a Mass Movement." *Korea Journal* 11, 3: 9–14.

Eckert, Carter J., et al. (1990) *Korea Old and New: A History.* Cambridge, MA: Harvard University Press.

Ko, Seung Kyun. (1972) "The March First Movement: A Study of the Rise of Korean Nationalism under Japanese Colonialism." *Koreana Quarterly* 14, 1–2 (Spring–Summer): 14–33.

Lee, Chong-sik. (1963) *The Politics of Korean Nationalism.* Berkeley and Los Angeles: University of California Press.

Pak, Ch'an-Sung. (1990) "Current Issues in the Study of the March First Movement." *Seoul Journal of Korean Studies* 2: 133–146.

Shin, Yong-ha. (1987) *Formation and Development of Modern Korean Nationalism.* Seoul, South Korea: Dae Kwang Munhwasa.

MARCOS, FERDINAND (1917–1989), Philippines president. Ferdinand Marcos was president of the Philippines; he was deposed and his initial successes overshadowed by his imposition of martial law, systematic human rights abuses, and massive corruption. Born on 11 September 1917 in the northern province of Ilocos Norte to a family of teachers, Marcos attended the University of the Philippines, obtaining a law degree in 1939. A year earlier, he had

Ferdinand Marcos at his inauguration in January 1966. (TED SPIEGEL/CORBIS)

been implicated in the murder of Julio Nalundasan, a congressman and political rival of his father. Marcos was imprisoned and subsequently posted bail to enable himself to take the bar examinations. He topped the exams amid allegations of cheating. He successfully defended his high scores with the university dean but months later was found guilty of murder and sentenced to imprisonment. He appealed his own case before the Supreme Court and was acquitted. During World War II, Marcos asserted that he was an anti-Japanese guerrilla, but documents appeared to show substantial collaboration with the Japanese. In 1949, Marcos successfully ran for Congress on the Liberal Party ticket, becoming the youngest member of Congress.

In 1954, Marcos married Imelda Romualdez, a beauty queen who belonged to a prominent political family in the south. They had three children. Marcos was reelected to Congress twice (1953 and 1957) and successfully ran for the Senate in 1959. In the 1961 presidential race, he supported Diosdado Macapagal, with the understanding that Macapagal would serve for only one term and would support Marcos's presidential run in 1965. When it was clear that President Macapagal was going to run for reelection, Marcos joined the rival Nacionalista Party and easily won the presidential nomination. He defeated Macapagal and became the nation's sixth postwar president. He was reelected in 1969, but, facing a constitutionally imposed term limit, he declared martial law in 1972, dismantled Congress, suspended civil and political rights, outlawed political parties, and shut down the independently owned press. In 1973, he promulgated a new constitution and rigged a nationwide referendum that allowed him to remain in office. In 1981, Marcos decided to lift martial law and call for elections. In what critics called a "cosmetic" lifting, he was reelected president for another six-year term. Two years later, he declared that congressional elections would be held in 1984. In preparation for these elections, Benigno Aquino, Marcos's long-time rival and head of the opposition party, returned from exile in 1983. He was assassinated as he was led from the plane to the airport tarmac, sparking mass unrest. In 1985, Marcos called a presidential "snap" election and was quickly challenged by Aquino's widow, Corazon Aquino. In 1986, Marcos declared himself the winner in an election fraught with voter intimidation, fraud, and violence. A popular uprising ensued, and in a clear demonstration of people power, Marcos was removed from office. He and his wife Imelda fled to Hawaii, where he died on 28 September 1989. Marcos was accused of plundering the nation's treasury of up to $5 billion. In 1988, he, Imelda, and eight others were indicted in a U.S. court for racketeering. To date, much of the Marcos family assets remains in family hands despite attempts by the Philippine government at recovery.

Zachary Abuza

Further Reading

Hamilton-Paterson, James (1999) *America's Boy: A Century of Colonialism in the Philippines*. New York: Henry Holt.

MARCOS, IMELDA (b. 1929), Philippine former first lady. Born on 2 July 1929 in Manila, onetime beauty queen Imelda Romualdez Marcos is best known as the spouse of Ferdinand Marcos (1917–1989), whom she married in 1954 when he was a young member of the Philippine congress. After her husband was elected president in 1965, as first lady she embarked on a beautification program for run-down Manila, commissioned orphanages, homes for the aged, and daycare centers, distributed seeds for backyard gardens, and arranged free medical care for the poor—while allegedly confiscating wealth from the rich for her personal bank accounts. In 1974, Marcos appointed her governor of Metro Manila. In 1978, after she was elected to the interim parliament, the Batasan Pambansa, she became minister of human settlements. As her husband's health deteriorated, Imelda began to run the civilian government, even campaigning for him. In 1986, when he was ousted by the People Power movement, she fled with him to Honolulu. In 1991 she returned to the Philippines and ran unsuccessfully for the presidency. In 1993, Imelda Marcos was convicted of corruption but appealed the case, which in 2002 was still pending. In 1995, she was elected to the Philippine House of Representatives. Although for a time the

Imelda Marcos, rumored to be seeking public office, at a mosque in Manila in July 2000. (AFP/CORBIS)

world's richest woman, she has been accused of helping her husband steal nearly $5 billion, for which she faces lawsuits in the Philippines for alleged illegal money transfers and tax evasion.

Michael Haas

Further Reading

Ellison, Katherine. (1988) *Imelda: Steel Butterfly of the Philippines*. New York: McGraw-Hill.

Mijares, Primitivo. (1976) *The Conjugal Dictatorship*. San Francisco, CA: Union Square Publications.

Psinakis, Steve. (1981) *Two Terrorists Meet*. Dobbs Ferry, NY: Morgan & Morgan.

MARMARA, SEA OF The Sea of Marmara, in northwest Turkey, is a small intercontinental basin that covers about 11,474 square kilometers between the Aegean Sea and the Black Sea and partly separates the Asiatic and European parts of Turkey. It is 280 kilometers long and 80 kilometers wide. On the east it is connected to the Black Sea through the Bosporus and on the west to the Aegean through the Dardanelles.

The Sea of Marmara derives its name from the Greek word for marble *(marmaros)*, which has been quarried since ancient times on the island of Marmara to the west of the Marmara Sea. Istanbul, Turkey's largest city, is situated at the entrance of the Bosporus into the Sea of Marmara.

The Sea of Marmara has become severely contaminated due to the flow of heavily polluted Black Sea waters and the waste discharges from Istanbul. Turkish authorities and environmentalists fear further environmental degradation in the Sea of Marmara because of the increasing passage of oil tankers carrying Caspian and Central Asian oil through the Turkish straits from the Black Sea.

Earthquakes are common in the Marmara Sea area. The epicenter of the devastating earthquake of 17 August 1999, which claimed over 17,000 lives and caused widespread destruction of property, was located near Golcuk, a town near the city of Izmit at the eastern end of the Sea of Marmara.

Tozun Bahcheli

Further Reading

Ozturk, Bayram, and Nesrin Algan, eds. (2001) *Problems of Regional Seas 2001: Proceedings of the International Symposium on the Problems of Regional Seas*. Istanbul, Turkey: Turkish Marine Research Foundation.

MARRIAGE AND FAMILY—CENTRAL ASIA "A person separated from the family will be eaten by wolves." This Central Asian proverb reveals much about the pervasive belief system in this region regarding the importance of families and the need for members to remain interconnected. The central imperative to preserve the family unit is also seen in various marriage practices, such as giving *kalym* (bride wealth) and dowry, bride stealing, and the appointment of guardian parents for newlyweds.

Prior to Soviet collectivization in the 1920s, the economic demands of pastoral nomadism as practiced in parts of Kazakhstan, Kyrgyzstan, Tajikistan, Turkmenistan, and Uzbekistan required alliances among the patrilineal kinship groups to maintain grazing pastures and water rights for their horses, sheep, or cattle. Solidifying economic relationships with neighboring tribes was accomplished through arranged exogamous marriages. These agreements formed the foundation of economic relations that often lasted for several generations, since new wives had to originate from their mother's tribal group. Members of these two groups were expected to share grazing lands and to protect one another's animals from raids by neighboring tribes. Often matchmakers arranged marriages between tribal groups prior to the births of children. Families honored the agreements even in the event of the death of a husband, when the customary law of levirate required that a brother or another relative marry the widow. When a wife died, the children of that marriage remained with their father. The husband was free to remarry.

Marriage

In Central Asia the good of the family is considered a higher priority than the good of an individual, therefore traditional marriages are based more on productive relations between the families than on the bride and groom themselves. In the early twentieth century, in accordance with Islamic and customary laws, marriages typically were arranged by close relatives or a matchmaker. A girl might marry at the age of nine, and a man might have up to four wives if he could support each wife equally. The Soviet laws introduced in the 1920s prohibited girls from marrying before they were sixteen years of age and permitted men to have only one wife.

Following the dissolution of the Soviet Union, the five individual governments of Central Asia took over legal regulation of matrimonial relations. Nevertheless, the customary practices of marriage arrangements and the dowry and *kalym* traditions bestow upon the bride greater status and increased security over official marriage registration. As a practical result the Muslim traditional marriage remains of far greater importance than the state-granted contractual marriage.

Kalym and Dowry

Giving *kalym* and dowry is among the more enduring marriage practices in spite of Soviet laws that once opposed it. In pre-Soviet times *kalym* was not only a reflection of highly developed property relations among Central Asians but also a sign of wealth, influence, and prestige. Cattle originally were central in the *kalym*, which was given to the bride's tribe instead of directly to the father of the bride. The size of the *kalym* depends to a large extent on the social and material position of the groom's family. For many families in rural regions, *kalym* consists of cash and animals (sheep or horses) as well as gifts of fabric, warm coats, hats, boots, and blankets to every member of the woman's extended family. The worth of the dowry is often based on the size of *kalym*. Since *kalym* is given at the time of engagement, it often assists the bride's family in preparing the dowry, even though the collection of a dowry begins when a female child is born.

Kalym and dowry gifts have significantly increased in value since 1991, when Soviet constraints were removed. By 1994 the wedding itself was estimated to cost between $1,000 and $5,000, depending on the economic status of the family. Given the low salary of the average Central Asian ($35 per month according to 1999 figures), the costs associated with this ritual often leave a family in debt.

Bride Stealing

With the changing economic conditions, paying *kalym* to the bride's family has become excessively burdensome. Many men have chosen to "steal a bride" instead, which does not involve *kalym* and consequently costs a family much less money. Bride stealing is also an alternative when a bride's relatives are uncooperative or when the parents of both the bride and groom oppose the marriage.

In the rural regions bride stealing has long been a common feature of marriage agreements. Even though it is illegal, perpetrators are rarely brought to court since it brings only additional disgrace to the bride's family. Stolen brides are expected to capitulate so as not to shame their relatives.

Bride stealing typically occurs when a family is not able to pay the high price of *kalym*, so an agreement is made to "steal" the girl. Afterward the groom's father asks the bride's father to pardon his son. Settlements usually include a smaller fee than would be expected with the payment of *kalym*.

Although bride stealing was illegal during the Soviet period, it nevertheless occurred, especially in the rural villages. Since 1991 the practice has experienced a resurgence. The Kyrgyz historian Anara Tabyshalieva has estimated that one in five marriages involves bride stealing and attributes the increase, especially in the cities, to people considering it a fashionable fad signifying that the bride is a good Muslim.

Guardian Parents

The practice of arranging guardian parents (*okul apa* and *okul ata* in Kyrgyz) for the newly married is highly important to Central Asian marriages. In this custom the parents of the groom arrange for an established married couple to act as sponsors, confidants, and mentors to the newlyweds. The practice reflects the societal belief that it is better for the couple to take their marital problems to someone other than their own parents. It also expresses the importance of maintaining positive relations between the families of the bride and groom.

According to the tradition, after the guardian parents have been identified it is left up to the young couple to contact them. If the new couple makes no contact, it is just a formal process, and no gifts are exchanged. But if the young couple seeks out the guardian parents, the relationship serves two aims. First, the guardian parents provide a good role model for the couple, and second, the guardian parents strengthen ties between unrelated families.

The guardian parent relationship is seldom discussed among Central Asians, as it is understood to be a private and confidential relationship. In part it is kept confidential also because it was once considered anticommunist to have guardian parents.

In summary, marriage practices in Central Asia must be considered more as building alliances between families than as creating unions of two individuals. Although formal laws regarding marriages exist, many customary regulations take precedence over the state institution of marriage. The giving of *kalym* and dowry is still paramount for forging family alliances through marriage, even though they are not legal. Similarly, the old custom of bride stealing has been rejuvenated in post-Soviet times due to the excessive costs of traditional weddings. Nevertheless, the aim remains the same, that is, to preserve the institution of marriage not only for the individuals but also for the respective families. Therefore, the guardian parent custom plays a unique role in protecting family alliances through the preservation of the marriage.

Kathleen Kuehnast

Further Reading

Abramzon, Saul M. (1978) "Family-Group, Family, and Individual Property Categories among Nomads." In *The Nomadic Alternative: Modes and Models of Interaction in the African-Asian Deserts and Steppes*, edited by Wolfgang Weissleder. The Hague, Netherlands: Mouton, 179–188.

Argynbaev, Kh. (1978) "Marriage and Marriage Rites among the Kazakhs in the Nineteenth and Early Twentieth Centuries." In *The Nomadic Alternative: Modes and Models of Interaction in the African-Asian Deserts and Steppes*, edited by Wolfgang Weissleder. The Hague, Netherlands: Mouton, 331–342.

Brown, Bess. (1988) "The High Cost of Getting Married in Central Asia." In *Radio Liberty Research*. Munich, Germany: Radio Free Europe/Radio Liberty.

Tabyshalieva, Anara. (1995) "Kultyrno-religioznie traditcsii i polozhenie zhenschin" (Cultural-Religious Traditions and Roles of Women). In *Zhenshchiny Kyrgyzstana: Traditsii I novaia real'nost'* (Women of Kyrgyzstan: Tradition and Reality), edited by E. Shukurov. Bishkek, Kyrgyzstan: Uchkun, 12–29, 87–89.

MARRIAGE AND FAMILY—CHINA

For 2,500 years of Chinese history, through stable and relatively secure times, and through stormy catastrophic times, China's family system has provided powerful continuity in the social structure. In keeping with the precepts of Confucius (551–479 BCE), clans based on male kinship coordinated village life under the autocratic rule of China's dynasties and subordinate elites. Even today, after a century of wrenching changes and social development, China retains a family system remarkably similar to its historical pattern.

The patriarchal system was perpetuated through marriages arranged between the family of the prospective groom and a family, usually from a different village, whose daughter was a suitable bride. Marriage was so nearly universal that the vast majority of people found their social place in this family structure. At the beginning of the twenty-first century, the previous century of modernization and liberation of women have still not deeply shaken China's patrilocal (brides living with the groom's family) marriage and family system in the rural areas.

The Traditional Ideal and Reality

The ideal Confucian family was an extended family consisting of three or four generations living under the same or nearby roofs. Family decisions were supposed to be made by the highest-ranking male, perhaps in consultation with other male kin, and obediently followed by all others in the rigid family hierarchy under him. The result, theoretically, was family harmony and smooth functioning. Land, houses, animals, tools, furniture, and other possessions were to be held by the extended family unit. When the patriarch died or became unable to function, his sons were supposed to become the heads of their extended families, with family land and other possessions distributed among them. The practice of ancestor worship provided cultural support for this system, as reverence for dead ancestors was extended into reverence for the living older generation, especially the family patriarch. Sons were needed to lead some of the ceremonies—daughters did not qualify.

Nearly every male outranked almost every female, except that young boys had to obey adult women in the family. Females were considered perpetual outsiders, because the marriage system brought a bride from an outside family and village into her husband's village and family. Even daughters born into the extended family were seen as low-status temporary sojourners there, as they were destined to marry out.

The reality bore some resemblance to this ideal, because females and subordinate males were economically dependent on the patriarchal family. They risked social isolation and even destitution or starvation if they rebelled against the system of patriarchal controls. But China's people were not necessarily as pliant and submissive as portrayed in this harmonious ideal. Their different personalities, perspectives, and preferences naturally clashed with some of the system's expectations. Dire poverty also necessitated adjustments at odds with the prescribed scenario. Besides, demographic reality prevented the achievement of the extended family ideal most of the time. Illness was frequent and the death rate was extremely high. Data from 1929–1931 show that females and males in Chinese rural farm families had average life expectancies of only twenty-four and twenty-five years, respectively. The low average life expectancy was due in part to extremely high infant and young child mortality rates (three-fifths of children died before age five). However, even those children who were lucky enough to survive to age five could expect to live only to age thirty-eight on average. It was difficult to have both parents in a nuclear family live long enough to raise their children to adulthood. Three-generation families tended to last a short time, as death claimed the older generation and many in the younger generations. Four-generation families were very rare.

WIVES AND THEIR MOTHERS-IN-LAW

In China, and in some other East Asian societies, the most difficult relationship for a young, married woman is with her mother-in-law. This is especially the case in rural areas where a woman goes to live in the house or village of her husband. The text below outlines the difficulties faced by the young wife and also some factors that might make the situation easier.

> In the household situation as Fei described it, the most difficult relationship for the young wife was that with her mother-in-law. It was taken more or less for granted that the mother-in-law was a potential enemy of the daughter-in-law, who had come as an unloved stranger into the house where the mother-in-law had been the female authority. The mother-in-law would wish to retain her authority and would seek to make the daughter-in-law subservient by constant criticizing and scolding. She also resented her daughter-in-law for breaking the singleness of her son's affectionate relationship with her. The son himself was in a difficult situation. To side with his wife in quarrel with her mother-in-law meant a quarrel against his mother, which besides being unpleasant and contrary to both his ideals and natural affection added fuel to her resentment of the daughter-in-law. Generally in the early years of the marriage he sided with his mother, which meant that his wife suffered doubly.
>
> In cases of extreme conflict, the daughter-in-law might be repudiated, usually on the initiative of the mother-in-law, who might repudiate her against the will of her son. If she could find any recognized ground for such action, such as adultery or sterility, no compensation would be asked. Otherwise compensation, amounting to sixty or seventy yuan, had to be given to the daughter-in-law.
>
> There were positive checks on the mother-in-law. There was, first, the positive value which the community placed on harmony between mother-in-law and daughter-in-law, making it the subject of special praise. Secondly, there was the negative sanction of harmful action by the daughter-in-law. She might threaten to commit suicide. Since she would then become a spirit, able to revenge herself, the threat was usually enough to effect a reconciliation. Furthermore her brothers might seek a physical revenge, even destroying part of her husband's house. Finally a husband might decide to support his wife against his mother and the household would be divided in two.
>
> Fei says that the extent of the disharmony which could result from conflict between mother-in-law and daughter-in-law should not be exaggerated. The danger of it, however, was great enough to influence the form of marriage.

Source: W. R. Geddes. (1963) *Peasant Life in Communist China: Monograph #6*. Ithaca, NY: Society for Applied Anthropology, 27–28.

Changes in the Twentieth Century

China entered the twentieth century with the Qing dynasty (1644–1911/12) in near collapse and colonial and imperialist powers intruding on China from all sides. In desperation, Qing government leaders and revolutionary leaders alike searched for a new path to save China from disintegration and foreign incursions. They considered importing and implementing foreign ideas and systems, such as foreign-style industrial and military production, a new form of government, such as a republic or a democracy, and modern educational systems. China's leading thinkers also noted that China's autocratic and patriarchal family and marriage system was a powerful conservative force preventing or slowing necessary change. Therefore, they adopted ideologies that would overturn China's traditional family system. In particular, Nationalist leaders and Communist leaders opposed arranged marriage and supported the concept of equality between men and women. Notably, both the Communists and the Nationalists opposed the oppressive practice of female foot binding.

Marriage From the beginning, China's Communist government was determined to overturn China's patriarchal family and marriage customs. The very first major law passed by the People's Republic of China (PRC) was the Marriage Law of 1950, which outlawed arranged marriage, child marriage, prostitution, polygamy, and concubinage; it also allowed divorce and free choice of marriage partner and set a minimum marriage age of eighteen for women and twenty for men. The government promoted the idea of male-female equality. The government also weakened the economic power of the family, especially by collectivizing agriculture under the commune system.

During the second half of the twentieth century, China's system of marriage underwent a slow transformation under the government's leadership. Ages at marriage rose slowly in the early PRC decades and rapidly in the 1970s. In 1929–1931, the average age at first marriage was 17.5 years for women and 21.3 years for men. By the late 1990s, the mean age at first marriage had risen to twenty-two for women and twenty-four for men. Some marriages in China are still arranged by the families, but the law requires that marriages be registered, and that the marrying man and woman tell the registration official that the marriage is voluntary. Some marriages today are love marriages freely chosen by the two young people. But most marriages in China are contracted through a system of introductions, in which family, friends, or colleagues introduce the potential partners and their families to one another. After a number of meetings, if the man and woman and their parents all agree, the marriage is contracted.

Marriage in China is still essentially universal: in 1995, 99.7 percent of women aged thirty-five through thirty-nine had married, as had 95.4 percent of men in the same age bracket. The remaining single men cannot marry because of China's constant shortage of women caused by earlier female infanticide and maltreatment of girls.

The Position of Males and Females Males were traditionally so important in Chinese society and females so unimportant that many historical family genealogies recorded males only, generation after generation, entirely overlooking the female half of the family. The birth of a son was cause for rejoicing. From birth, sons were groomed for eventual dominance. If food or money for medical treatment were in short supply, these scarce commodities were directed toward the boys and men. As China's economy has industrialized, most of the nonagricultural jobs have gone to men, and the men in the family are still seen as its economic core.

China's Communist Party has worked with determination against this formidable belief system since coming to power, with significant positive results. Yet even today, most families in China, particularly rural families, believe that they must have a son. There are objective reasons, such as the lack of an old age security system in rural China. Parents feel that they require a son to take care of them when they grow old (a daughter will marry out of the family, but a son will bring in a daughter-in-law to help care for all their needs). Yet even if such practical needs can be met in other ways, the emotional preference for sons remains.

Female Infanticide Female infanticide was common in imperial times at all economic levels in society. Selective neglect of daughters also meant that they died in excess throughout childhood. In the Communist period, killing infants was outlawed. Female infanticide and maltreatment of girls gradually declined. The lowest point of female losses was reached in the 1960s and 1970s, when excess female child mortality (mortality beyond the expected rates) killed about 2 percent of girls in each birth cohort. But after the introduction of China's one-child family-planning policy in 1978–1979, excess deaths of young girls rose suddenly to 3 percent of each birth cohort. In the 1980s and 1990s, the introduction of technology that can be used for sex-selective abortion of female fetuses has led to major losses of females in utero. In 1999, there were 120 boys per hundred girls at ages 0–4, one of the worst sex imbalances in the world. Analysis of data from successive censuses of China suggests that life-threatening discrimination against females is now mostly confined to the prenatal period and the first couple of years of life. After that, girls still experience discrimination, but the most recent data suggest that it seldom leads to death after the first two years of life.

Family Planning In the 1950s and 1960s, women in China averaged six births each. After the famine of the Great Leap Forward, China's government began to take seriously the need to slow down population growth. Cities conducted a vigorous campaign to persuade or require couples to have fewer children. Urban fertility declined to three births per woman by 1966. Then, in the early 1970s, the government waged an increasingly compulsory campaign in China's rural areas, demanding that couples cease childbearing at three births, then two births. In the late 1970s, based on population projections, the PRC government decided that the only way to stop population growth soon was to require couples all over China to stop childbearing at one child. Financial rewards were given for couples who pledged to have only one child, with special education and health benefits given to the single child. But urban and rural couples who resisted the one-child limit were penalized with fines, forced abortion, required use of an intrauterine device (IUD) after one birth, and required sterilization (usually of the wife) after two or more births. Rural fertility dropped from 6.4 births per woman in 1970 to 3.1 in 1977; meanwhile, urban fertility declined further to 1.6 births per woman. China's population growth rate was reduced from almost 3 percent per year in the late 1960s (for a population doubling time of about twenty-five years) to 1.5 percent in the 1980s (doubling time just under fifty years).

The most concentrated campaign of coercive family planning was waged in 1983, when medical teams went to the villages to carry out forced sterilizations, abortions, and IUD insertions. This led to a popular backlash, and the government lessened the coercion temporarily. Meanwhile, an associated rise in female infanticide alarmed the government. The demand for a son in rural families was so great that most provinces changed their rural family-planning policies to allow couples with a firstborn daughter to have a second child, while sticking with the one-child limit if the first child was a son.

From the 1970s on, China's family-planning policy has required couples that want a child to apply for permission to have a pregnancy and birth. If the authorities give them a "birth quota," they may proceed to have a child; otherwise they are in potentially serious political and economic trouble. For most women, insertion of an IUD is required after one birth, and a sterilization operation is required after a second birth whether the birth was allowed or not. These are "passive" forms of birth control that will stop pregnancy even if the couple actually wants a child; this is why China's government usually insists on these tech-

A family planning billboard in Chengdu in 1985. The signs reads, "Family Planning—a Basic National Policy of China." (OWEN FRANKEN/CORBIS)

GIRLS AND THE "ONE-CHILD" RULE

Between 1985 and 2000, there were approximately 24,000 adoptions of children from China—primarily girls—by families in the United States. The excerpt below attempts to explain to these young girls how their birth parents could love them yet abandon them.

> Remember that China is a very old country, so some ideas have been around for thousands of years. One of those ideas is that a son should take care of his parents when they get older. You see, parents usually live with their son until they die. Of course parents love their daughters very much. But if they only have daughters, the daughters will get married and move away to live with their husbands, where they will help take care of their husband's parents.
>
> Most people in the countryside do not have enough money to take care of themselves when they get old. So if a mother and father are allowed to have only one or two children, they feel they desperately need at least one son—someone to take care of them when they become too old to work.
>
> But what does this have to do with you? Well, when you were born in China, you may have been born to parents who did not have a son. Your birthparents so much wanted to take care of you *and* try to give birth to a son. But having another child would break the government's rule about the number of children they could have in their family, and they would be punished. They would have to pay a very big sum of money, more money than they had. Your birthparents couldn't find a way to keep a daughter in their family and still have a son to take care of them later in life.
>
> *Source:* Sara Dorow. (1997) *When You Were Born in China: A Memory Book for Those Children Adopted from China*. St. Paul, MN: Yeong & Yeong Book Company, 15–16.

niques. Of couples using contraception, 48 percent have one partner sterilized and 45 percent are using an IUD. In the 1990s, China's fertility level was below replacement-level fertility, at about 1.8 births per woman. Since 1998, China's population growth rate has been below 1 percent per year, which is extremely low for a developing country.

China's compulsory and often coercive family-planning program has been condemned by some international funding organizations and some governments. In response, China is conducting a high-profile pilot program in selected localities to implement a more client-friendly family-planning program. The new program gives couples more choices of birth-control techniques, but they are still not allowed to have more children than permitted before. China remains the only country with a compulsory family-planning program.

China's low death and birth rates have had mainly good effects. Today in China, most people live to advanced years. Therefore, health and educational and other financial investments in children and adults pay off because the recipients live relatively long lives and can contribute to society. Small numbers of births combined with rising incomes means that each child can get more food, health care, education, clothing, and attention than was the case with larger families in the past. Low fertility reduces female deaths from pregnancy and childbirth; it also frees women to pursue careers and opportunities beyond childrearing. Nevertheless, compulsory family planning is harmful to families, couples, and women in many ways. Those who love children and want another are usually prevented from having more than their assigned limit. Ubiquitous family planning clinics use either x-ray or ultrasound to inspect the abdomens of women every few months to confirm that the IUD is still in place; use of frequent x-rays may harm the women's health. Forced abortions are often in the second and third trimester, which is dangerous for the health of the mother. Even putting aside health issues, compulsory abdominal x-ray or ultrasound inspections, IUD insertions, abortions, and sterilizations are violations of women's bodies and their rights.

Almost everyone in China now marries, as in the past, and almost every couple has at least one child. This means that the family structure is very much intact, in spite of low fertility. Currently, people mostly live as part of an extended family, or a "stem" family (three generations living together, but with just one son and his wife and child or children in the household), or a nuclear family (parents and children only). Often, the families of the older parents, the sons and their spouses and children, and sometimes the married daughters in urban areas, continue to have very frequent contact even if they live in separate dwellings.

But low fertility and mortality mean that China's population is aging. In future decades, the proportion of elderly will rapidly increase; there is great concern that the smaller numbers of children and grandchildren will be unable to cope with or financially support their family elderly, and there are grave doubts about the government's ability to step into the breach.

Divorce Divorce remains rare in China. Of the population aged fifteen and older, only 1.1 percent of men and 0.7 percent of women are divorced (more divorced women than divorced men have remarried). In the leading cities, however, divorce rates are rising.

Economic Reform and the Family

Since the death of Mao Zedong (1976) and the implementation of economic reforms (started 1978), the proportion of the total population living in cities has increased from 18 percent to 36 percent. Chinese urban life has weakened the patriarchal nature of the family (partly because access to agricultural land is not a factor), raised the position of women, reduced illiteracy, and improved educational levels.

In rural China, economic reforms have renewed the power of the family, because the rights to use agricultural land, to make decisions about its use, and to sell the products for profit have reverted to the family unit from the communal "production team." Income and wealth once again belong to the patriarchal family unit, though the gradual shift out of agriculture gives some decision-making power to the men and women who earn outside income. Rural marriage is still usually patrilineal and patrilocal. Continuing limits on permanent migration out of the village reinforce the rural family's control over its members. While temporary migration from the village is allowed, most migrants have to assume that they cannot permanently get out of the rural areas.

Today China's strengthened rural family is, from an economic perspective, a flexible and positive force in the midst of rapid economic change. The rural family keeps its tiny pieces of arable land and farms them, but at the same time, frees up its surplus laborers to work in rural industry or services, or to migrate for work. The family diversifies its sources of income and spreads its risk across different economic sectors and into different places. It pools its resources for family goals. Meanwhile, the rural family supports its dependents—children, elderly, the unemployed and underemployed, the sick and disabled. This is important, given that there is barely any social safety net in China's vast rural areas.

The Family as a Source of Stability

China's rural families today are robust in the face of considerable uncertainty. The historic transition from agriculture into nonagricultural sectors of the economy in rural China today is happening inside the family, as it has for the last century in the rural families of the United States. The strong family is also helping urban China weather the destabilizing storms of massive layoffs of workers in state-owned industries and widespread loss of medical insurance benefits.

China's traditional marriage and family systems have been buffeted by political attacks, legal changes, communal farming, economic development, the sharply rising status of women, and foreign ideas and influences. Certain changes have been real and deep, such as the decline of arranged marriage. Within today's families, decision making is less hierarchical, and more shared and consultative, than in the past. Ancestor worship is no longer a strong belief system.

But in spite of the genuine changes that have taken place, China's patrilineal and patrilocal family remains very strong. It has survived and has experienced renewal because it works. As China tries to move toward a market economy, hundreds of millions of people have to change what they are doing to earn a living. Many tens of millions are displaced or sidelined during the transition, and the confusion and dislocation are profound. China's people need their families to fall back on, and that is what they are doing. Family life and the institution of marriage are surprisingly strong in China today, and they show few signs of weakening.

Judith Banister

See also: **Single-Child Phenomenon; Women in China**

Further Reading

Aird, John S. (1990) *Slaughter of the Innocents: Coercive Birth Control in China.* Washington, DC: AEI Press.

Banister, Judith. (1987) *China's Changing Population.* Stanford, CA: Stanford University Press.

Barclay, George W., Ansley J. Coale, Michael A. Stoto, and T. James Trussell. (1976) "A Reassessment of the Demography of Traditional Rural China." *Population Index* 42, 4 (October 1976), 606–635.

China National Bureau of Statistics. (2000) *China Population Statistics Yearbook 2000.* Beijing: China Statistics Press.

———. (2000) *China Statistical Yearbook 2000.* Beijing: China Statistics Press.

Coale, Ansley J., and Judith Banister. (1994) "Five Decades of Missing Females in China." *Demography* 31, 3 (August 1994), 459–479.

Lee, James Z., and Wang Feng. (1999) *One Quarter of Humanity: Malthusian Mythology and Chinese Realities, 1700–2000.* Cambridge, MA: Harvard University Press.

THE GENERATION GAP IN EAST ASIA

According to surveys in Japan and South Korea reported in *Asia Week*, there is a growing generation gap between adults who value tradition and serving society and their children who are most interested in their own happiness and success. In Japan, for example, 27.3 percent of teenagers wanted "to live each day happily" and only 50 percent felt responsible for looking after their elderly parents. Similarly, in South Korea, some 20 percent of youths say that they don't respect their parents. Other research suggests that the trend is not confined to East Asia as young people feel the same way in Thailand and Hong Kong. Experts say this is part of a global trend of youths wanting happiness, freedom, and wealth.

Source: Davena Mok. (2001) "What's in It for Me?" *Asia Week* (7 December): 16.

MARRIAGE AND FAMILY—EAST ASIA

Until the early part of the twentieth century, marriage and the family system in East Asia (China, Japan, and Korea) followed patrilineal and patriarchal principles with some variations. In traditional East Asian families, the family head, whose position was taken by the most senior male member of the most senior generation, possessed great authority and responsibilities. He managed family property and made important decisions for family members regarding their marriages and living arrangements. He was also responsible for offering appropriate respect to the ancestors by officiating at memorial rites and making sure that descendants were produced and family traditions were preserved. The concept of family *(jia)* included the lineage that would be preserved from generation to generation. Under the traditional patrilineal family system, the daughters were normally excluded from their family of birth upon marriage.

In China, the extended family system was viewed as the ideal, whereas in Japan the stem family system prevailed. Under China's extended family system, all sons brought their brides to their parental home and lived there until the death of the parents. The brothers formed separate households after the death of their parents and, in general, inherited an equal share of their father's property. The extended family system necessarily required large and growing landholdings or ownership of a business by the family. It is not surprising, then, that the practice of the extended family system was largely limited to upper-class Chinese.

Under the stem family system practiced in Japan, the eldest son brought the bride to his parental home and lived there while other sons established their own households upon marriage. In Japan the eldest son inherited nearly all of the father's property. Kin networks played lesser roles in the socioeconomic lives of individuals.

In Korea the residential patterns followed the stem family system. The social and economic aspects of family life, however, resembled the extended family system. The eldest son lived with the parents and enjoyed the privilege of being the designated heir of the family, but the concept of family extended beyond the "main" household where the eldest married son lived with his parents. Other married sons, who usually resided in separate houses, were under the control of their father and eldest brother and were obligated to participate in important family affairs such as memorial rites for the ancestors. Unequal division of family property was the common practice of inheritance in Korea, with the eldest son taking a larger share than other sons.

MARRIAGE, FAMILY, AND THE COMMUNITY

This extract of text from an anthropological study of a Taiwanese village makes it clear that marriage in East Asia is not just about the woman and man who are getting married. Because of the importance of kinship, family and community attitudes matter a great deal.

> The preference for marriage beyond the village limits also rests on the feeling that it is not a good thing to have one's in-laws too close or to have the bride in too close proximity to her parents' home. When the two families live nearby, there is too much opportunity for bad feeling to develop between them. When the two families are in the same village, every detail of how the daughter-in-law is treated by her husband's family immediately reaches her own family, and it is far too easy for the girl to run home with complaints about every hardship, real or imaginary, in her new family. This sort of thing can easily cause interfamily conflict. In intravillage marriages in Hsin Hsing there have also been instances where a daughter-in-law has spent too much time in her old home, helping her mother instead of always being available in her husband's house to do whatever work is asked of her. Of the twelve marriages between Hsin Hsing families, relations between the two families in five cases were not considered good for a variety of reasons.
>
> Another factor favoring marriage outside the village is the village parents' fear of gossip about the circumstances of the marriage. If both families live in Hsin Hsing village there is a good chance that the boy and girl knew each other before marriage; this in itself is considered improper, and people are very likely to say that this was a "love marriage" forced upon the two families because the young couple had been secretly seeing each other and having sexual intercourse. When one hears village discussions of marriages having taken place between Hsin Hsing villagers, one gets the idea that almost all of them have been the result of a secret love affair. Such secret affairs do usually force the two families to agree eventually to a union between the two young people. Thus, in most instances, neither the couple nor their parents will willingly discuss the reasons for an intravillage marriage. When they do, they usually say that the marriage was arranged because both families felt the boy and the girl were well suited. They feel it is necessary to defend such a marriage from the inevitable talk. Family members usually remark that they had firsthand knowledge without needing the word of a matchmaker, that the girl would be a good worker and an asset to the family. However, no matter what reasons are given, other villagers openly discuss the matter, often good-naturedly teasing those involved and making jokes about the "real" basis for the marriage.
>
> *Source:* Bernard Gallin. (1966) *Hsin Hsing, Taiwan: A Chinese Village in Change*. Berkeley and Los Angeles: University of California Press, 150.

In China and Korea, families that shared a common ancestor, that is, members of the same clan, usually lived in clusters and owned some property jointly. Villages where families from one or two clans constituted the majority of the population were common. The kin network played important roles in educating children and providing economic assistance and social welfare to its members.

Under the patrilineal family system, marriage and child rearing were regarded not only as important steps in life but as essential duties for loyal family members. At the same time, filial piety was viewed as the most important and basic human behavior. Thus, fathers were obligated to produce sons, and sons were obligated to obey fathers. When a couple failed to bear a son, one was adopted. In Korea, the adopted son had to come from the paternal kinship group of the appropriate generation. In China and Japan, adoption of the son-in-law was frequently practiced. Adoption of nonrelatives was also practiced in Japan. Moreover, even when a biological son was available, adoption of an "heir" was still possible in Japan if the head of the family so desired. Thus, in China and Korea, preservation of family lineage had to be accomplished through biological descendants, whereas in Japan it was the preservation of the social institution of the *ie* that was viewed as important.

In China and Korea, the most commonly practiced marriage pattern was for the bride and groom not to come from closely related families, and not from the same clan. In contrast, marriage between close relatives was common in Japan. The marriage process often began with the groom's parents seeking a future daughter-in-law. An intermediary, or a go-between, played a major role, especially in China and Korea, in searching for appropriate candidates and in negotiating the terms of marriage. The prospective bride and groom had no say in deciding whom they would marry. The decision was made by the head of household. A woman, in effect, "moved to her permanent family" after marriage. She would spend the rest of her life with this family, and after death she would be remembered by the descendants in this family. It was considered a great dishonor for her natal family if a married daughter was sent back to her parents' home. From an early age, women were taught to obey and serve their future husbands and parents-in-law.

Marriage was universal and early in China and Korea. Married couples, in turn, were expected to have as many children as possible and as early as possible in China and Korea. In Japan, marriage was universal but relatively late, and having many children was not emphasized. Although having many children was

A dairy farming family eating breakfast on Hokkaido in 1989. (MICHAEL S. YAMASHITA/CORBIS)

viewed as one of life's blessings, evidence indicates that married couples in historic Asian populations often practiced fertility control as a strategy for sustaining a desired living standard. Fertility control was more widespread in Japan than in China and Korea.

Sons were viewed as much more precious than daughters in China and Korea, where the continuation of the family line depended more heavily on male descendants. This attitude resulted in female infanticide and high female infant and child mortality in China and Korea, creating a shortage of adult women and leading to a large proportion of men living their entire lives as bachelors as well as to a large number of prostitutes. In Japan, due to the custom of adoption of a son-in-law or a nonrelative as heir, daughters did not suffer higher levels of infanticide or child mortality.

The rules of divorce and remarriage were different for men and women. Women were not allowed to divorce their husbands, but men could divorce (or send wives back) for reasons such as committing a crime, not bearing a son, being unfaithful, being jealous, or being too talkative. Men were allowed or even encouraged to remarry after a divorce or after the death of a spouse, but women were not allowed to remarry after divorce or widowhood. A widow would spend the rest of her life with the family of a deceased husband unless she was sent back to her parents for committing a crime such as adultery. Norms about extramarital sexual behavior also differed for men and women. It was considered natural for adult men to engage in sexual activity outside marriage, but women's sexual activity was strictly limited to within marriage.

The lives of men and women were separate both conceptually and physically. Economic and other "external" roles were reserved for men. Although wives helped their husbands in farms and family businesses, their economic role was considered secondary; their main role was the management of housework and providing care for the elderly, men, and children. In upper-class families in East Asia, women rarely went outside their residences. Within the family, interaction among men and women was minimal. Even interaction between husbands and wives was restricted and reserved and often was subject to supervision by the members of an older generation. Men often sought sexual pleasure from concubines and female entertainers rather than from their wives.

Beginning of Changes

The family system in East Asia began to change with the modernization process in the region. Political and social reform began to take place with the Meiji Restoration (1868) in Japan, with the fall of the Qing dynasty (1911) in China, and with the Japanese occupation of Taiwan (1885) and Korea (1910). Modern education became accessible to the majority of the population, and the concept of equal individual rights became popular. Critical evaluation of the patriarchal family system began, and efforts were made to abolish parental dictation of the marriage decision, child marriage, concubinage, widespread prostitution, exclusion of women from inheritance, and unfair divorce and remarriage customs.

By the mid-twentieth century, family laws in East Asian countries took a modern form, establishing a minimum age for marriage and women's legal and economic rights. Women and men have equal legal bases for employment and inheritance of their parents' assets. The family registration system, which forms the legal basis for such rights as citizenship, however, continues to favor men over women in the inheritance of family lineage even after the latest amendment of the civil code.

Post–World War II

Further changes in marriage behavior and the family system took place after World War II. It is generally believed that the change was brought about by rapid economic development, migration, urbanization, a higher level of education, especially among women, and increased contact with the outside world. In mainland China, economic development and contact with the outside world started late, but government policies and programs played a large role in changing family lives after 1948.

Extended families disappeared, nuclear families became more common, and the kinship network weakened. The fertility level declined, marriage became late and nonuniversal, and intergenerational relationships weakened. More women took employment outside the home, and increasing proportions of women refused to give up employment for family responsibilities. To a lesser extent, the divorce rate increased, and premarital sexual relationships became more common.

As of the late 1990s, marriage was very late in Japan, Taiwan, South Korea, and some urban areas in China. Furthermore, some women, especially well-educated women, were not marrying at all. For example, among thirty-five- to thirty-nine-year-old women with a college education, in Japan 11 percent were not married in 1994, and in Taiwan 14 percent were not married in 1990. Nonmarital cohabitation and childbearing, however, were rare in East Asian populations even in the late 1990s. Increasing proportions of adolescents and young adults, however, were sexually active before marriage. As of the mid-1990s, most men and a substantial proportion of women in East Asia had sexual experience before marriage. The level of premarital sexual activity was higher among men than among women. Gender differences in premarital sexual behavior and remarriage patterns reflected the influence of the patriarchal family system. Women's premarital sexual activities were closely related to marriage: most women engaged in sexual activity only with men they intended to marry. Conversely, large proportions of men engaged in sexual activity with women they did not intend to marry. The gap was often filled by commercial sex workers. Divorce increased in all East Asian populations. The pattern of remarriage after divorce or widowhood was less common among women than among men up to the mid-1990s.

In general, intergenerational ties weakened. Parents' involvement in selecting children's spouses declined dramatically. In Taiwan and Japan, only about 10 percent of marriages that took place in the 1995–1998 period were acknowledged to have been arranged. Economic dependence of elderly parents on adult children weakened, and the proportion of married adults living with their parents declined. The intergenerational residential pattern observed in the mid-1990s, however, continued to reflect patriarchal tradition: eldest sons were much more likely to live with their parents after marriage than were other sons and daughters. At the same time, changes were taking place. The proportion of elderly parents who lived with married sons who were not the eldest or with married daughters became more common, especially in Japan. Married daughters, although not living with their parents, were maintaining close relationships with natal parents.

Two aspects of intergenerational relationships, parents' devotion to and involvement in their children's ed-

THE JAPANESE HOME

Japanese homes reflect the Japanese cultural traditions of precision, detail, and craftsmanship. The following is a description of some of the design details found in Japanese homes in the late nineteenth century.

> Simple and unpretending as the interior of a Japanese house appears to be, it is wonderful upon how many places in the apparently naked rooms that the ingenuity and art-taste of the cabinet-maker can be expended. Naturally, the variety of design and finish of the *tokonoma* and *chigai-dana* is unlimited save by the size of their areas; for with the sills and upright posts, the shelves and little closets, sliding-doors with their surfaces for the artists' brush, and the variety of woods employed, the artisan has a wide field in which to display his peculiar skill. The ceiling, though showing less variety in its structure, nevertheless presents a good field for decorative work, though any exploits in this direction outside the conventional form become very costly, on account of the large surface to deal with and the expensive cabinet-work required. Next to the *chigai-dana* in decorative importance (excepting of course the ceiling, which, as we have already seen, rarely departs from the almost universal character of thin boards and transverse strips), I am inclined to believe that the *ramma* receives the most attention from the designer, and requires more delicate work from the cabinet-maker. It is true that the areas to cover are small, yet the designs may be carved or latticed—geometric designs in fretwork, or perforated designs in panel—must have a strength and prominence not shown in the other interior finishings of the room.

Source: Edward S. Morse. ([1896] 1961) *Japanese Homes and Their Surroundings*. New York: Dover Publications, 168.

ucation and their support of adult children before marriage, did not change much or can even be characterized as having intensified. Parents in East Asian countries are known to have invested excessively in their children's education to the extent of affecting mothers' employment patterns in the mid-1990s. A large proportion of adult children lived with their parents and often were supported economically by their parents.

The nature of women's economic activity changed drastically with economic development in East Asia. In all of the East Asian populations, employment among single women increased substantially and by the end of 1990s had come close to being universal. Patterns of employment among married women showed substantial variations. The most traditional pattern was observed in South Korea, where the employment rate among married women was low and most women stopped their employment at the time of marriage. Some women returned to work after they had passed the prime childbearing age, but they did so at low rates. In addition, the proportion of women working in semiprofessional, technical, or clerical occupations drastically decreased after marriage, whereas the proportion of those working in sales and service areas increased. In Japan, women's employment was disrupted by marriage and childbearing to a lesser extent than in South Korea. Married women's employment in Japan, however, continued to be affected by their husbands' income and their family situation (for instance, the presence of a preschool-aged child in the family), and not by their personal characteristics, such as their level of education. In fact, among married women, the most educated were the least likely to be employed in Japan. In Taiwan, women's employment was minimally interrupted by marriage and childbearing. Furthermore, the employment pattern of married women was affected mostly by their own characteristics, such as their level of education. There, the most educated women were most likely to be employed even after marriage.

Current Trends

While the role of women has expanded to include employment outside the home, their role within the family sphere has not been reduced, mainly because the role of men has not changed much. In East Asia, women continue to carry most of the responsibilities of managing household affairs and providing care for the elderly, men, and children regardless of their hours of employment. Thus, married employed women often face the extreme difficulty of balancing their responsibilities at work and in the family. Many women in East Asia seem to respond to potential conflict between work and family life by postponing marriage until a very late age or by not marrying at all. Some marry but do not have any children. Surveys conducted in the mid-1990s in Japan and Korea document that single women tend to anticipate their lives changing for the worse after marriage, whereas single men tend to view their lives as not changing much after marriage.

The continuing trend toward later marriage and the increasing numbers of those who decide not to marry at all are threatening an even further decline of fertility in East Asia, as well as an ever heavier social and economic burden of caring for the elderly.

Minja Kim Choe

See also: **Marriage and Family—China; Women in Korea**

Further Reading

Choi, Jai-Seuk. (1970) "Comparative Study on the Traditional Families in Korea, Japan, and China." In *Families in East and West: Socialization Process and Kinship Ties*, edited by R. Hill and R. Konig. Paris: Mouton, 202–210.

Freedman, Maurice, ed. (1970) *Family and Kinship in Chinese Society*. Stanford, CA: Stanford University Press.

Fukutake, Tadashi. (1989) *The Japanese Social Structure: Its Evolution in the Modern Century*. 2d ed. Translated by Ronald P. Dore. Tokyo: University of Tokyo Press.

Hanley, Susan B., and Arthur P. Wolf, eds. (1985) *Family and Population in East Asian History*. Stanford, CA: Stanford University Press.

Kendall, Laurel. (1996) *Getting Married: Of Gender, Morality, and Modernity*. Berkeley and Los Angeles: University of California Press.

Lebra, Takie Sugiyama, ed. (1992) *Japanese Social Organization*. Honolulu: University of Hawaii Press.

Lee, James, and Cameron Campbell. (1997) *Fate and Fortune in Rural China: Social Organization and Population Behavior in Liaoning, 1774–1873*. Cambridge, U.K.: Cambridge University Press.

Lee, James, and Wang Feng. (1999) "Malthusian Models and Chinese Realities: China's Demographic System, 1700–2000." *Population and Development Review* 25, 1: 33–65.

Lee, Kwang-Kyu. (1972) "The Korean Family in Changing Society." *East-West Cultural Studies* 11, 1–4: 28–43.

Mason, Karen O., Noriko. O. Tsuya, and Minja K. Choe, eds. (1998) *The Changing Family in Comparative Perspective: Asia and the United States*. Honolulu, HI: East-West Center.

Mattielli, Sandra, ed. (1977) *Virtues in Conflict: Tradition and the Korean Woman Today*. Seoul, Korea: Samhwa.

Thornton, Arland, and Hui-Sheng Lin, eds. (1994) *Social Change & the Family in Taiwan*. Chicago: University of Chicago Press.

Wang Feng and Yang Quanhe. (1996) "Age at Marriage and the First Birth Interval: The Emerging Change in Sexual Behavior among Young Couples in China." *Population and Development Review* 22: 299–320.

Whyte, Martin King, and William L Parish. (1984) *Urban Life in Contemporary China*. Chicago: University of Chicago Press.

Wolf, Margery. (1972) *Women and the Family in Rural Taiwan*. Stanford, CA: Stanford University Press.

MARRIAGE AND FAMILY—INSULAR SOUTHEAST ASIA

The large number of ethnic groups in insular Southeast Asia accounts for the variety of patterns and practices relating to marriage and the family. However, intermarriage between ethnic groups means that the situation is never totally straightforward, and conceptions of kinship and behavior relating to them have always been fluid. There are also differences between urban and rural groups; economic and social development has led to more rapidly changing patterns in recent times.

Kinship Patterns

In the eastern islands of the Indonesian archipelago as well as in North Sumatra, patrilineal groups trace descent through the male line. In West Sumatra the matrilineal Minangkabau trace descent through the female line. In such unilineal descent systems, individuals belong to one kin group according to their parentage. In one or two parts of the archipelago, as in the Toraja highlands, kinship may be traced down both male and female lines, with individuals choosing the group to which they wish to belong. In a few other cases, such as the island of Savu, an individual may belong to two groups: one patrilineal and one matrilineal. However, the majority of the population of island Southeast Asia belong to ethnic groups whose kinship patterns are normally termed "cognatic," as is the case with the Javanese, Malays, and the Filipinos. Among such groups, equal recognition is given to the relatives of both parents in deciding who are kin.

In Javanese, Malay, and Filipino societies, the core of the family unit is the conjugal couple and their children. However, the boundaries of the household are very flexible, and many others may join, either through adoption or fostering. Children may move from one household to another, often being raised by persons other than their biological parents. Members of the extended family are expected to help each other on a reciprocal basis both in everyday life and in crisis. In the Philippines, as in Malay and Javanese systems, when a man and wife marry, each becomes a part of the spouse's family, and the two families are united as kin.

A characteristic feature of many families in Southeast Asia is the importance of seniority and of siblingship. In many societies, the link between brothers and sisters is considered as important as the link between parent and child. In terms of deference and respect, age differences between family members are more important than differences in gender, with older siblings especially having responsibilities toward their younger siblings.

To win favor with the ancestors, a woman makes an offering at the family shrine in Bali, Indonesia. (JACK FIELDS/CORBIS)

Courtship and Choice of Marriage Partner

Although in the past Malay, Javanese, and Minangkabau men were free to take more than one wife, this practice has become increasingly rare in Southeast Asia. Among Filipinos, marriage is strictly monogamous. Among all groups, there is usually strong pressure to marry, and widowed or divorced individuals are expected to find a new partner and marry again. Although families take a considerable interest in their children's marriage partners, children are not normally forced to marry against their will, and many find their own partners. In Malay, Javanese, and Filipino groups, courtship is generally carefully supervised, and dalliance by either sex is frowned upon. Parents in these groups are more concerned about their daughters than their sons in terms of courtship and sexual activity, and during adolescence, young people tend to go out in groups rather than as separate couples. Among the Batak of Indonesia, however, premarital chastity is not highly valued, and meetings between adolescent boys and girls are less strictly supervised.

In Java, marriages between distantly related couples are preferred. Ideally, a husband should be older than his wife, and after marriage she will address him respectfully as "older brother." In the Philippines, there is a tendency to take a partner from a similar background in terms of class, religion, and ethnic grouping.

Unilinear groups such as the Minangkabau and the Batak have rules and prohibitions concerning the choice of marriage partner. The Minangkabau are forbidden to marry someone of their own matriline, and there is a preference for marriage within the village. In Batak society, a boy will ideally marry his mother's brother's daughter, thus reinforcing relations between the two families, and he should not marry a bride from his own lineage.

Marital Residence

Among the Javanese, Malay, and Filipinos, newly married couples may live with either set of parents but will most often live with the wife's parents initially, setting up an independent home when they have the resources, often after the birth of the first child. Family ties are important in ensuring basic security. Among Malays, there is a tendency for new homes to be established near the wife's parents, and in traditional rural contexts, clusters of related females are often found, providing a supportive network of local ties.

In accord with tradition, the families of the bride and groom negotiate the wedding arrangements on Sumba Island, Indonesia. (WOLFGANG KAEHLER/CORBIS)

In both Malay and Javanese societies, one married daughter usually remains behind to care for the parents in their old age and to take over the house after their death.

Child Rearing

Relationships between husband and wife are relatively egalitarian in most cases, with each responsible for his or her own domain. In all parts of insular Southeast Asia, generally the mother has overall responsibility for child rearing. However, because she is likely to be engaged in some sort of economic activity as well, this responsibility is likely to be shared by older siblings, aunts, uncles, and grandparents as well as between the biological parents themselves. Age commands respect, and there is an emphasis on strong sibling relationships.

Divorce

In Java, divorce is relatively rare in urban areas but common among the rural population, particularly in the early years of the marriage. In the event of divorce, traditional Javanese law provides for each spouse to retain personal property, usually property brought into the marriage. Anything acquired by the husband and wife during their marriage is divided between them, generally in a 2:1 ratio favoring the husband. These rules are flexible and depend on circumstances. If a couple divorces, the question of the custody of children arises. Young children tend to stay with the mother, whereas older children may be allowed to choose.

The divorce rate has been high among Malays, although it has decreased in recent years. Experts have suggested that this decrease is a result of the influence of Islam, which strongly discourages divorce. As in Java, in Malaysia customary law is more likely to be invoked than Muslim law in determining how property should be divided and what arrangements will be made for the custody of children after a divorce.

In the Philippines, arrangements are relatively equitable in the division of property between the divorcing husband and wife. The mother's position is quite strong in respect of the custody of children, but she may be expected to become wholly responsible for them.

Patterns of marriage and family life in insular Southeast Asia are undergoing change. In general, there has been in recent decades a tendency toward living in smaller household units. Especially in urban areas, family planning programs have had some impact, and couples are choosing to reduce the number of births. Geographic mobility and social mobility have also contributed toward making the extended family a less central institution than before. Nevertheless, traditional patterns of family relationships continue to have a fundamental importance that permeates social intercourse.

Fiona Kerlogue

See also: **Marriage and Family—Mainland Southeast Asia**

Further Reading

Atkinson, Jane M., and Shelly Errington. (1990) *Power and Difference: Gender in Island Southeast Asia.* Stanford, CA: Stanford University Press.

Banks, David J. (1983) *Malay Kinship.* Philadelphia: Institute for the Study of Human Issues.

Djamour, Judith. (1959) *Malay Kinship and Marriage in Singapore.* London: Athlone Press.

Dube, Leela. (1997) *Women and Kinship: Comparative Perspectives on Gender in South and Southeast Asia.* New York: United Nations University Press.

Jones, Gavin W. (1994) *Marriage and Divorce in Islamic South-East Asia.* Kuala Lumpur: Oxford University Press.

Karim, Wazir J., ed. (1995) *"Male" and "Female" in Developing Southeast Asia.* Washington, DC: Berg.

MARRIAGE AND FAMILY—MAINLAND SOUTHEAST ASIA

Practices and patterns relating to the family vary widely in mainland Southeast Asia for a number of reasons. The present population is made up of a variety of ethnic groups speaking many languages and being influenced by cultural traits introduced partly through migrations from the north in historic and prehistoric times. The cultural practices of these groups differ in many ways, and although there has been much assimilation, with war, globalization, and their effects having blurred the boundaries to some extent, there is still considerable variation in the forms and behavior relating to marriage and the family.

In terms of family structure, there is a key distinction between those groups who consider family membership in terms of descent from a common ancestor and those with a broader notion of family membership that includes relatives on both the mother's and the father's side. In general, it is chiefly the many and varied upland groups who follow the former pattern, where there are rights and obligations between lineage members that extend to fairly distant relatives. The mainly lowland Buddhist peoples who form the majority of the population of mainland Southeast Asia, such as the Tai (the ethnic group, not to be confused with Thai, the nationality), ethnic Burmese, and Khmer, fall into the latter category, and here the family is a smaller entity.

Marriage and Family Life among Burmese and Tai Peoples

Among the Burmese and the ethnic Tai (the latter group including the majority population of Laos), conception of who belongs to the family group is loose. Both the male and female lines are relevant in determining descent, so that each individual regards relatives on both his or her mother's and father's side as belonging to the same family grouping. The nuclear family is emphasized more than the extended family.

Tai marriage partners are generally chosen by the individuals themselves, subject to parental approval. Elopement to avoid parental objections is relatively common. Young Burmese are also generally allowed to find marriage partners for themselves, though this may still be supervised to some extent. Parents make arrangements for the actual marriage, so that their approval is important. As with the Tai, marriages by elopement are not uncommon because the recognition by the community that a couple are cohabiting is the chief essential in marriage, and parents tend to agree to a wedding if cohabitation is already established.

In Burmese societies, polygyny (having more than one wife) was in the past officially condoned, but in practice few men had more than one wife. Some Tai men take a "minor" wife, a practice that usually causes some distress to the first wife. For a first marriage, choice of partner is essentially voluntary for both daughters and sons among the Burmese and the Tai, though parents have always been concerned that their children should make "good" marriages, and many attempt to influence their children. However, elopement is a source of shame for parents, and they will generally fall in with the choice of their child, even if they disapprove of it, to avoid an elopement. Parents prefer their children to choose a partner who is of the same ethnic group and religion (Buddhist) and of similar or superior socioeconomic status. Ideally the husband should be a few years older than the wife, and there is a preference for a local choice. Astrological considerations are another factor, though a relatively minor one, in determining whether the choice of partner is a good one. Courtship among the Burmese is initiated by the boy, usually through a go-between. In traditional Burmese communities, courtship is strictly supervised, and sexual contact of any kind is strictly prohibited.

Tai marriages are accompanied by the payment of bride-price, that is, the parents of the groom offer property to the family of the bride. This differs from the Burmese custom, in which the groom brings with him to the marriage a "dower," that is, property from his family that is offered specifically to the couple and

CARING FOR INFANTS IN SOUTHEAST ASIA

"*Capturing a Cold.* Young babies are liable to become ill easily, because their bodies are still delicate. For example, they might take cold and have blocked noses so that they cannot breathe easily. If a child has these symptoms they must make a medicinal poultice to apply to the top of the head. They use onion or bulbs of sweet *pron* pounded and mixed with turmeric, red lime and liquor. They dip cotton into this medicine and form it into a flat, thin plaster, and apply this to the child's head. The juice of the pounded onions remaining from making the poultice for the head is used to apply to the bridge of the nose and to the body. This method of applying a poultice to the head and smearing the body of the child until it appears red and blotched all over is called 'capturing a cold.' "

Source: Donn V. Hart, Phya Anuman Rajadhon, and Richard J. Coughlin. (1965) *Southeast Asian Birth Customs: Three Studies in Human Reproduction*. New Haven, CT: Human Relations Area Files, Inc., 167.

over which they have control. It has been suggested that the importance of the wedding ceremony is that it is the occasion when the amount and nature of the dower are announced. The dower is a symbol of the girl's and her family's status, and thus the wedding is an important occasion even though a marriage can in fact be established without such a ceremony.

Young Tai couples may live with the wife's parents for a time, but they will normally hope to set up an independent household after a while, and this may be some distance away. Relationships with friends and neighbors are likely to be as important as relationships with relatives beyond the immediate family. Burmese couples are also likely to set up a new home after marriage. Again, if they do stay for a short while in the home of a parent, it is likely to be the house of the bride.

Divorce is in principle relatively easy for both husband and wife in Tai groups, as it is with the Burmese. Desertion, cruelty, a wife's adultery, and a husband's remarriage are considered proper grounds for divorce. The rate of divorce is relatively low, however. Traditionally, a spouse seeking divorce should ask the village headman, and the headman's intervention may be one reason why, despite frequent quarreling and dissatisfaction within marriages, the actual divorce rate is low in rural areas. Divorce is in any case a difficult choice for a woman because it is often hard to obtain support for any children of the marriage. A divorce is not usually granted without the consent of both parties unless the matter is taken to court, and few women have the resources to do this. Male children of a divorced Tai couple normally stay with the mother, whereas girls stay with the father.

A Burmese man whose wife dies may be expected to marry the sister of his deceased wife; a similar situation occurs if the husband dies, though in this case the new husband may already have a wife.

Marriage and Family Life among the Khmer

It has been argued that there is a matrilineal bias in the Khmer kinship system that has been obscured by other sociopolitical factors, but the ideology of descent is clearly cognatic (bilateral, that is, descent is traced on both mother's and father's sides). For example, the spirits of the mother and father are worshiped and commemorated and are consulted at life crises. Relationships beyond the nuclear family group are not formally structured.

Most Khmer marriages are arranged by the families of the bride and groom, and it is considered the duty of parents to arrange their children's marriage. The marriage may be organized by a go-between, and in rural areas the arrangements are made while the children are quite young. The groom's family offers compensation in the form of bride-price to the bride's family for the loss of their daughter; the amount varies according to the girl's position in the family and the reputation and wealth of the family. The oldest and youngest daughters are most highly valued. In the past, it was common for the son-in-law to move in with his wife's family and to work for the father-in-law until the young couple were ready to set up a household of their own, usually near the wife's parents' home.

In rural Cambodia, widows and women without husbands for whatever reason lose status to a considerable degree and rarely participate in temple festivals and other village ceremonies. Unless they have children to support them, they are likely to live without proper means of subsistence, and because of the shame of poverty many do not participate in village decision making or public life.

Vietnamese Marriage and Family Life

The Vietnamese as a nation regard themselves as having common descent, and this means that there is an underlying sense of brotherhood generally. However, ancestry is the key element in Vietnamese concepts of the family, with descent counted through the male line. Allegiance to one's clan is very important, and the most honored place in every home is reserved for the ancestors' altar. Traditionally it is the oldest son who presides at ceremonial rites of death and burial. In a burial procession, the eldest son walks in front of the coffin, whereas the rest follow behind it.

Vietnamese households may include three or four generations, and in rural contexts neighboring households in a village will almost certainly be made up of closely related kin. It was traditionally the pattern for the eldest son to live with his wife in his father's house, other sons settling in the vicinity with their wives. Although the pattern is changing in urban areas, these traditions are still strong. The concept of the family is thus reinforced by the presence of large numbers of kin from the same lineage living close by. Although in the modern Vietnamese family some members may move into the city a long distance away, they are likely to return at New Year's, and their shared feasting and offerings to ancestors reinforce the sense of kinship.

In Confucian models, on which the Vietnamese notions of family life were broadly based in the past, women had little status and few rights outside their relationship with their fathers, their husbands, or their sons. They had no legal right either to own personal property or to inherit anything from their parents. Marriage was arranged by the parents, often through an intermediary, who made certain that there was no existing family relationship between the man and woman. For the woman, marriage was an official transference of loyalty from her father's family to that of her husband. A wife would be expected to serve her husband and comply with his wishes absolutely. After his death her service was transferred to her eldest son.

In practice, however, the Vietnamese never followed the Confucian code strictly. For example, women in north and central Vietnam often inherited land alongside their brothers. They also took part in the administration of land held by the lineage. Only in aristocratic groups was the Confucian code adhered to rigidly. Another aspect of Vietnamese society, derived from a Chinese model, is that of polygyny and the taking of concubines. This was once common practice in Vietnam, especially among the more affluent, but it was made illegal by legislation passed in South Vietnam in 1958. Attitudes toward women and their role have changed under Communism, although within the home there are still strong echoes of such traditional values.

In South Vietnam, divorce and separation were declared illegal without government approval in 1958, whereas in the north, the right to divorce for both men and women was established under the Communist regime. However, formal channels for reconciliation were established, and couples were encouraged to settle their differences and stay together. Since unification, this has become the norm across Vietnam.

Marriage and Family Life among the Hmong

The Hmong, who live in the border areas in the north of Vietnam, Thailand, and Laos as well as in southwestern China, trace their descent from a common ancestor, and women marry into their husband's lineage. Among the Hmong there are about twenty surname groups or clans. The household may consist of just one nuclear family, but it is more likely to include three generations. The eldest male is the household head. In addition to parents and children, there may be grandparents, unmarried uncles or aunts, and widowed relatives. Adoption is also quite common. Those adopted are usually girls and almost invariably of non-Hmong origin, but they are treated as close kin.

The man and woman in Hmong couples must come from different clans. A woman may have only one husband, whereas a man may have as many wives as he can afford. However, most marriages are monogamous because only the wealthy can afford more than one wife. A first wife is the most privileged in any case and has authority over subsequent wives.

Parents may have preferences, but the Hmong are relatively free to choose their marriage partners, and premarital sex is tolerated. The Hmong New Year in December is the best opportunity for a young man to find a bride or for a couple to demonstrate their intentions toward one another. Boys must find a girl from outside their clan to marry; the ideal is for a boy to marry his father's sister's daughter or his mother's brother's daughter. This strengthens the alliance between two families who are already related. It also allows the girl to remain in contact with family and friends.

When a boy has found a girl to marry, his father has to provide bride-price to be handed to the father of the girl. The amount of this, usually a considerable sum, must be agreed to on both sides. It is traditionally paid in silver, acquired from the proceeds of as much as an entire year's opium harvest. The size of the bride-price required means that a son is dependent on his father until he is married and that his father has considerable control over his behavior. Similarly, the groom is under pressure to treat his wife well. If he does not, the girl may return to her family, and the bride-price will be lost.

If a Hmong couple elope, the boy's father is still obliged to pay the bride-price. Sometimes the couple have children before the transfer of the bride-price, and in this event the children are deemed to belong to the bride's father's clan. The groom may be allowed to work for his father-in-law for a year or two instead of paying the bride-price, but this is regarded as demeaning for the boy, and the situation is generally avoided.

Divorce is rare among the Hmong. A man has the right to divorce if his wife misbehaves badly by becoming addicted to opium or committing adultery, and in such cases he can demand the return of the bride-price. A woman is also free to leave her husband, but unless her husband is proved guilty of cruelty her family must return the bride-price, and this would be humiliating both for her and her family. If she does decide to leave her husband, she returns to her original clan. Custody of the children normally goes to the man, but rarely, if the woman is the innocent party, she may retain custody.

If a Hmong woman is widowed, she should normally marry her husband's younger brother if he is willing (in which case no bride-price need be paid), but this rarely happens in practice, and she may marry elsewhere.

Family Life Today

Family life is still an important feature of life in mainland Southeast Asia, despite greater geographic and social mobility connected with new employment opportunities, urbanization, and global influences. For the majority, particularly those who belong to the lowland cognatic societies, the definition of the boundaries of the family is fairly loose. Even so, there is generally a strong sense of duty and obligation between members of the nuclear family. For unilineal societies, such as the Hmong and the Vietnamese, common ancestry and residence near the husband's family mean that the sense of what constitutes the family is both larger and more clearly defined. Although globalization, industrialization, and the migration associated with them have affected traditional values, fundamental structures in society have been fairly resilient, and especially in rural areas the pace of change in attitudes toward marriage and the family is still relatively slow.

Fiona Kerlogue

Further Reading

Cooper, Robert G., ed. (1998) *The Hmong: A Guide to Traditional Lifestyles.* Singapore: Times Editions Pte. Limited.

Dube, Leela. (1997) *Women and Kinship: Comparative Perspectives on Gender in South and Southeast Asia.* New York: United Nations University Press.

Eisen, Arlene. (1984) *Women and Revolution in Vietnam.* London: Zed Books.

Keyes, Charles. (1995) *The Golden Peninsula: Culture and Adaptation in Mainland Southeast Asia.* Honolulu: University of Hawaii Press.

Ovesen, Jan, Ing-Britt Trankell, and Joakim Ojendal. (1996) *When Every Household Is an Island: Social Organisation and Power Structures in Rural Cambodia.* Uppsala Research Reports in Cultural Anthropology, no 15. Uppsala, Sweden: Department of Cultural Anthropology, Uppsala University.

Potter, Sulamith Heins. (1979) *Family Life in a Northern Thai Village: A Study in the Structural Significance of Women.* Berkeley and Los Angeles: University of California Press.

Somswasdi, Virada, and Sally Theobald. (1997) *Women, Gender Relations and Development in Thai Society.* Chiang Mai, Thailand: Women's Studies Center, Faculty of Social Sciences, Chiang Mai University.

Spiro, Melford E. (1977) *Kinship and Marriage in Burma: A Cultural and Psychodynamic Analysis.* Berkeley and Los Angeles: University of California Press.

UNDP (United Nations Development Programme). (1998) *Human Development Report 1998.* New York: Oxford University Press.

MARRIAGE AND FAMILY—SOUTH ASIA

Almost every form of marriage is practiced by cultural groups in South Asia. In some districts in mountainous Himachal Pradesh, bride-capture initiates a marriage, while among the Garo in mountainous Assam, bridegroom-capture initiates a marriage. Fraternal polyandry, marriage of one wife to two or more brothers—a rare form of marriage from a worldwide perspective—occurs among some of the hill people in northwest India and among Tibetan residents in Nepal, as well as among the Todas in the Nilgiri Hills in the southern Indian state of Tamil Nadu. Nonfraternal polyandry, also rare, was found in the matrilineal caste of Nayars of Kerala and among groups in Sri Lanka. In the Jaunsar-Bawar hilly area of Uttar Pradesh is practiced what the anthropologist D. N. Majumdar called polygynandry, a simultaneous combination of polygyny (the custom of one husband married to two or more wives) and polyandry—within the same family.

About a quarter of the population of South Asia is Muslim. The Qur'an permits polygyny; a man may have as many as four wives. In practice, almost all South Asian Muslims are however monogamous, as are the vast majority of Hindus, Christians, Sikhs, Jains, and Parsis.

More than half of the people of the Indian subcontinent are peasants living on the northern riverine plains and on the Deccan plateau to the south. This account focuses on them.

Marriage and Family in the Context of the Caste System

Marriage and family in peasant South Asia should be seen in the context of the Indian caste system. "Indian" is used here rather than "Hindu" because non-Hindus—Muslims, Sikhs, Christians, even those residing in Bangladesh and Pakistan—are organized into castes (a system of ranked segments of society). An individual is born into a caste, that of his or her parents, and he or she must marry within caste—that is, castes are endogamous. Due to rigidly enforced rules of inheritance and endogamy, a caste as a lived-in institution is a set of families whose children marry only among themselves.

For example, the potters residing in perhaps fifty villages in an area, all within walking distance of one another, may form a *jati*, the term anthropologists use for the endogamous caste group. The potters of this set of fifty villages do not marry among other potters of other villages, even though outsiders may see all potters in a region as belonging to a single caste of potters—caste as an occupational specialty group.

Within a South Asian village, from one to three dozen castes may be represented. Castes are ranked, with (among Hindus) Brahmans often at the top and untouchables almost always at the bottom, and castes such as cultivators of land, merchants, various artisans, and servants between the two extremes. In some villages, there may be no untouchable castes; in some, there may be so-called tribals, who hunt, fish, or both, whom villagers may consider lower than untouchables. Families of a particular caste, almost always related through ties of blood and marriage, usually reside near one another, often in their own section of a village.

Patrilineal and Fraternal Joint Families

A widespread South Asian ideal is a patrilineal joint family—one composed of an older couple, their unmarried children, and one or more of their married sons with their wives and children. Less common is a fraternal joint family—one composed of two or more married brothers and their wives and children. While a joint family is generally the ideal, such families are usually in the minority in any count of family households in a village because of the low life expectancy for South Asians. Furthermore, due to crowding or problems in maintaining fraternal harmony, adult married brothers in most parts of South Asia usually do not continue to live together in the same house, and parents may live with only one married son at a time.

Most of South Asia emphasizes patrilineal descent, although something will be said about matrilineal people below. The north requires patrilocal residence; that is, after marriage a couple lives with the husband's relatives, usually with his parents and unmarried siblings, until crowding in the living quarters or disharmony among members of the different nuclear families prompts the decision to have a junior couple and their children move out.

A multigenerational Indian family in a small village in Rajasthan, India, c. 1996. (VINCE STREANO/CORBIS).

The 1961 census of India showed that the highest proportions of joint families in India were found in the states of Rajasthan and in eastern Uttar Pradesh. What facilitated the high frequency of joint families in these places was the comparatively early age of marriage; several districts had unusually high proportions of married females in the five-to-nine-years age group and unusually high proportions of married males in the ten-to-fourteen-years age group. In a marriage system with very young brides and bridegrooms, a joint family is required, since a young-teenaged couple is too inexperienced to run their own economic enterprise or to rear children without help. The older couple, either the groom's parents or his older brother and his brother's wife, are both protectors and teachers of the young married couple (who in general would not cohabit before puberty).

Whether an Indian lives in a joint family or not, he or she is likely to live among many relatives. Among patrilinealists, brothers' or father's brothers' houses are likely to be next door to one another. Among the much less common matrilinealists, sisters' or mother's sisters' houses are likely to neighbor one another. It is not uncommon for an individual to be related to all the other members of his caste-chapter within a village.

Rules of family hierarchy are almost universal. Juniors should defer and show respect to seniors. Females should defer and show respect to both adult male and female members of the family, especially in their husbands' families. A daughter-in-law must obey her mother-in-law. A son must obey his father and his elder brother. Given the emphasis on the importance of patrilineal descent, the most important duty for a newly married bride is to produce a son or sons to carry on her husband's patrilineage into the future.

Matrilineal Families

There continue to be some castes and ethnic groups that trace descent and structure of families on matrilineal lines—in Kerala and Karnataka in the southwest and in Assam and other parts of the northeast. Most famous are the Nayars of Kerala and the Naga groups of Assam.

Until about 1900, among the Nayars, adult brothers and sisters ideally resided together. The fathers of the women's children did not reside with the women, but rather with their sisters and their mother and her sisters and brothers. Many of the Nayars, until about one hundred years ago, had extensive agricultural estates with large households of matrilineally related kin. Children born to female members were raised in their mother's home with her siblings and her mother and her mother's siblings. The head of the matrilineal household was usually the eldest mother's brother or mother's mother's brother. As in patrilineal households, children had to obey their elders, but especially they had to obey the *karnavan*, the mother's brother who was head of the household.

Among matrilineal groups and even among a few patrilineal groups in south India and Sri Lanka, women inherit landed property. This is rarely the case in patrilineally oriented north India, Pakistan, or Bangladesh.

Characteristics of Marriage in Northern South Asia

Almost universally in South Asia, marriages are not romantic attachments but are arranged by the bride's and bridegroom's older male relatives—father, grandfather, uncle—although possible mates for children are often suggested by the women of a family. In much of the north, there is a rule of three- or four-*gotra* (a named patriline of fathers and children over generations, which has no function other than proscribing marriage between its members) exogamy. One inherits the name of a *gotra* from one's father. If there is a three-*gotra* rule, then a child should not marry someone with the same *gotra*, or with the *gotra* of his or her mother or of the mother's father. If there is a four-*gotra* rule, then the child is also prohibited from marrying someone in the mother's mother's *gotra*. The French social anthropologist Louis Dumont figured out that the three- or four-*gotra* rule had the effect of prohibiting marriage between a bride and groom related to each other more closely than third cousins. The rule facilitates marriage between strangers, although strangers of the same *jati*.

In the north, there is also a rule of village exogamy. That is, marriages must take place between a couple from different villages. A bride must marry a bridegroom from her own caste, but from a *gotra* other than the three or four prohibited and from another village. The patrilocal residence rule requires that after the wedding ceremonies have taken place in her village home, she must leave to join her husband's home in another village.

North Indians tend not to have two daughters married into the same family or into the same village. In parts of Rajasthan among Hindus, and in parts of Pakistan among Muslims, however, marriages between sets of brothers and sets of sisters are preferred. Two or three brothers of one family and village marry two or three sisters of another family and village, which can be achieved while still obeying a three- or four-*gotra* rule of exogamy. Since double or triple weddings may also accompany such an arrangement, wedding expenses are less than they would be for two or three separately timed weddings. At the same time, one wedding party represents both or all three bridegrooms, thus reducing the number of guests the bride's relatives must feast and entertain at the wedding and in the future. Many Rajasthani cultivators also like the strengthening of the fraternal joint families. Not only do brothers live together in the same household and work together in the fields, but their wives are sisters, more likely to get along well than if they were strangers, and so willing to take care of each other's children, freeing one sister to gather wood or to work in the fields.

A girl should be married between the ages of twelve and twenty to a boy of fifteen to thirty years. William Crooke in the late nineteenth century and others more recently have reported that infant marriage occurred and was even preferred and esteemed in some communities in both north and south India. Nowadays most of the youngest brides—those between the ages of eight and fourteen years—are found in Rajasthan, Uttar Pradesh, and Bihar, three north Indian states. In all these child-marriages, sexual relations between a couple do not occur until both have reached puberty. Widely in the north, there are two wedding ceremonies. In western Uttar Pradesh, for example, the first wedding ceremony is called *shadi*, the second *chala*. With rare exceptions, sexual relations between husband and wife do not take place until the bride is mature (after first menstruation), so that she may have gone through both wedding ceremonies some time before she begins conjugal relations with her husband. In earlier decades, there may have been as many as five years between *shadi* and *chala*. A bride may be taken by the groom and his all-male party back to his village after the first wedding ceremony. During this visit, she stays with the women of her husband's family—her mother-in-law, her husband's brothers' wives, her husband's sisters—and might not see her husband at all. Then after a few days, she is taken back to her parents in her home village; she stays with her parents until the groom and his party come for the second wedding ceremony. She again goes to her husband's home and village after the second ceremony; if she is mature by now, sexual relations between husband and wife commence. If not, she again returns to her parental home until she is mature.

This scenario is still more or less accurate for the north, except for girls who have gone ahead in school. Only a minority of girls in Pakistan, Bangladesh, Nepal, and the north Indian states of Uttar Pradesh, Bihar, Rajasthan, and Madhya Pradesh go to school, even today. Probably a majority of girls in states such as Haryana and the Punjab go at least through elementary school, as do most girls living in cities. Relatively few girls go beyond fifth grade, but those who do generally have their marriages postponed until they have finished their education—whether at eighth, tenth, twelfth grade or higher. For such brides, the two wedding ceremonies may take place on the same day, since the bride is already mature and can begin married life right away. Boys' marriages similarly are usually postponed until boys have completed their education.

Much of Pakistan, Bangladesh, and northern India continues to practice purdah, the seclusion of married women. Housing arrangements separate women's quarters from men's quarters. The women of the joint family may each have a room in the ribbon of rooms around a courtyard. Men may have their own sleeping quarters in their cattle yard, clubhouse, or entryway to the women's quarters. A husband slips into his wife's room at night for sexual relations and then returns to his own quarters. The woman in a nuclear family often has a small one- or two-room house, while her husband sleeps with men in a neighborhood clubhouse.

A girl between the ages of four and thirteen years may move about freely in her parental village, but a married girl in her husband's village seldom goes out of the women's quarters, and when she does, she is carefully chaperoned. All married women cover their heads, and in the presence of men of the family older than their husband, or when they sally outside the house, they cover their faces with the outer edges of their head scarves or the borders of their saris covering their heads; some Muslim women wear *burqa*s in public, long, dark coats with hoods that cover the head with attached veiling in front of the face.

An Indian bride and groom at a traditional wedding ceremony in 1961. Both are adorned with garlands of flowers. (BETTMANN/CORBIS)

Characteristics of Marriage in Southern South Asia

As one moves south to Maharashtra and beyond, one finds that with rare exceptions women no longer cover their heads, and, except for unmarried pubescent girls and young married women, females generally move about their locales outside their houses more freely than in the north.

The northern three- or four-*gotra* prohibitions in mate selection contrast with preferences for cousin marriage among most south Indian Hindus and Christians and among some Muslims of both north and south. Until about twenty years ago, south Indians, including Christians, preferred marriages between cross-cousins (a father's sister's child marrying a mother's brother's child; in other words, a marriage between children of brother and sister) or between children of a mother's younger brother and an older sister's daughter (maternal uncle-niece marriage). Among some Muslims, there is or was a preference for marriage between parallel cousins, either between the children of brothers or between the children of sisters. Imtiaz Ahmad, however, has written that most Muslims in India do not follow this rule, although it is often followed among Muslims of the Middle East. Indian Muslims, he suggests, have been influenced by the north Indian Hindu idea that cousins are equivalent to siblings, so that cousin marriage is considered a form of incest and is avoided. Both forms of cousin-marriage, the cross-cousin marriage of the south and the parallel-cousin marriage of some Muslims, are justified by assertions that such marriages keep property within the family. South Indians tend not to have two children married to the children of the same mother's brother or father's sister.

Marriages between cross-cousins and maternal uncle and niece have become less frequent in recent decades due to at least two factors: education (parents prefer that their son marry into a wealthy stranger family rather than marrying one of his poor cross-cousins or elder sisters' daughters) and increasing awareness that marriage between close relatives is considered by Western science to be deleterious to offspring.

In south India generally, there is no rule of village exogamy, and a sizable proportion of marriages may be between bride and groom of the same village. South India differs from north India also in the equality between the two sides in a marriage. In north India, the bride's side is usually considered to be inferior to the groom's, while in south India, the two sides are more likely to be considered equal.

Weddings, Dowries, and Bride-Price

South Asians are often criticized for their elaborate and costly weddings. The bridegroom's party, until recently in the north composed entirely of male relatives and friends of the groom, comes to the bride's village and stays for three or four days, during which time the bride's family must house and feed them lavishly. In south India, the groom's party may include women, even the groom's mother, and since many couples in the south come from the same village, the burdens of entertainment may not be so heavy on the bride's people. In both north and south, relatives of the bride, such as her married sisters and mother's brothers and their families who reside in other villages, are also invited, as are members of her local caste-chapter.

In north India, the bride is also expected to bring a *dahej*, or dowry, composed in part of household goods and gifts—cooking vessels, beds and bedding, embroidered linens, toys for the children in the groom's family, saris for the women in the groom's family, her own saris, cosmetics, and silver and gold jewelry, and the gift of a finger ring for the groom. Accumulation of these dowry goods may begin as soon as a daughter is born.

Dahej may also include cash to be given by the bride's father to the groom's father. Until recent decades, only wealthy families gave cash or impressively sumptuous gifts in dowry. Most brides' families in the north bore the greater part of the expenses of the feasting and the household goods and gifts, the most onerous expense being that for the bride's jewelry. According to the Indian social anthropologist M. N. Srinivas, the giving of dowry in south India began only in the twentieth century. In south India generally, and in the mountainous parts of north India, bride-price given by the groom's people in the form of all or some of the following—food, clothing, cash, jewelry—made up most of the wedding expenses among almost all communities until recently.

Since Indian independence in 1947, there has been a considerable increase in modern education, especially for males. Many parents and elders with girls to marry off seek educated bridegrooms because they are believed to have excellent potential earning capacity. While literacy among males in India is now over 50 percent, there are still relatively few males who are well enough educated to achieve good occupations with good salaries, such as teaching, government work, or professional work. The elders in charge of arranging the marriage of a young engineer or medical doctor can demand a very large amount of cash and modern consumer goods in dowry from the bride's people—hundreds of thousands of rupees in cash, a television set, a scooter or automobile, and so on. Such elders usually also enjoy a wide choice in selecting a bride for their educated son. The parents of the bride selected may be hard pressed to provide all the items in dowry that they agree to and may postpone some payments until after the wedding. "Dowry-deaths" sometimes occur when the bridegroom's parents press the bride to persuade her parents to come up with the agreed-upon dowry payments, but they are unable to do so. The usual story is that the bride's sari caught fire in a fireplace used for cooking and she was burned to death—but in fact she has been murdered. In cities, and it is in cities that such cases may be reported to police and newspapers, some women's advocacy groups have managed to have the bride's parents-in-law prosecuted for such deaths in a few instances. With few exceptions, the elders of the educated groom can select another bride for him.

Dowry-deaths are a new phenomenon in India, just as the great increase in dowry giving is new. Both have come about with the increase in higher education for males and the consumerism that has arisen with new manufacturing and imports. It is relatively well-off middle-class people who perpetrate dowry-murders, not poor, uneducated villagers.

MATCHMAKING IN TWENTY-FIRST-CENTURY INDIA

In India, it is common for young men and women or their families to place advertisements for brides and grooms in the newspaper. The ads below are excerpted from actual classifieds in the *The Tribune* of Chandigarh.

Brides Wanted

Match for Ramagarhia Sikh handsome boy Electronics and Microcomputers Engineer, senior British government executive, annual income pound 55,000. Divorced after short marriage, no children, girl should be up to 32 years from status family.

Status alliance for very handsome Brahmin boy Engineer in reputed American Delhi based company drawing 6 lakhs pa, 5'-10"/26yrs; status family—father Chief Engineer in Coal India; attractive girl preferably Computer/IIT Engineer/having professional qualification.

Wanted—dependable slim simple companion For civil engineer Doaba (Punjab) based Hindu SC boy 29, 5'8", religion/caste/horoscope/dowry no bar.

Alliance for 21, 5/11" Jak Sikh Bhuliar boy, diploma Mechanical Engineer. Rural urban property. Mediocre family.

Alliance for very handsome, fair, Canadian citizen, 29 year old, 5'6" Hindu Punjabi, BE-Mechanical Computer networking Engineer, presently engaged in computer IT consulting, boy own property in India as well as Canada. Short marriage annulled. Wanted beautiful, educated girl willing to migrate, from a well educated decent family, caste no bar, the boy will visit India in late February, 2002 for 15 days.

Grooms Wanted

Extremely beautiful, educated Canadian citizen 29 yrs, 5'8", Ramagarhia girl working at Royal Bank of Canada, looking for compatible Canadian or US born professional or well established Indian resident. Caste no bar.

Khatri Sikh parents seek USA settled well educated Medico/Computer professional match for their smart intelligent professional daughter BE, MS, Database developer, working in USA green card shortly. 31/162, highly educated liberal professional family.

Dowry-deaths are more likely to be northern events than southern, because in north India the bride and groom in an arranged marriage are commonly almost total strangers to each other, as are the two families allied by marriage. In south India, even when the bride and groom are not cross-cousins or uncle and niece, they are likely to be more distant relatives and to be acquainted with each other, at least from their childhood days, since *jati*s in south India are smaller on average than in the north, and marriages can take place between a bride and groom from the same village. Gift giving at south Indian weddings is also more likely to be balanced between the two sides. Dowry giving is a much more recently adopted custom, among even high-ranking south Indian castes, than in the north.

As in north India, dowry is becoming more important in southern India, as educated bridegrooms are allied with brides from unrelated wealthy families. Such marriages sometimes cross *jati* lines but are in the same occupational caste, since it may be difficult to find educated bridegrooms for educated brides.

The Logic of Arranged Marriages

Why arranged marriages? There are at least four reasons. First, ancient Hindu religious law states that a father would be punished in afterlife if he has not got his daughter married off before her first menstruation. Second, arrangement of marriages by elders ensures that marriages take place within the *jati*. The stability of the caste system depends on arranged marriage. A third practical reason in areas where village exogamy is the rule is the impossibility of children's knowing potential mates in other villages. A fourth reason is the general disapproval of self-selection of a mate, called all over South Asia a "love marriage." There is the assumption that a love marriage must have involved some kind of premarital sexual contact between the couple, which violates the requirement that a bride be a virgin at the time of her wedding, held by all religious and caste communities in South Asia. This requirement that a bride be virginal encourages Muslims and Christians to arrange marriages for their daughters at young ages and to chaperone marriageable girls carefully.

Remarriage

High-caste Hindu women generally are not allowed to marry a second time. A high-caste widow may remain in her dead husband's joint household; if she is young, she may return to her parents' or married brother's home; if she is old and has no relative whom she can reliably turn to, she may have to try to find some means to support herself. Some Hindu widows become holy women visiting pilgrimage places such as Varanasi (Benares) and Haridwar on the Ganges. Many Hindu middle and lower castes allow widows to remarry, many following the rule of junior levirate, encouraging a widow to take her husband's younger brother as a second mate. Muslim and Christian widows are allowed to remarry.

Divorce was made legal in India after independence, but it is usually said that Hindus do not allow divorce. What this means in practice is that a barren first wife (for it is almost always due to infertility that a Hindu woman is abandoned by her husband) is taken home to her parents or to her married brother and left there. Her husband never comes again to get her; he then takes another wife. The abandoned wife usually cannot remarry. Muslim family law explicitly allows men to divorce their wives. Such divorces are probably more common among urban Muslim merchants than among rural Muslims, however, and are very easily achieved.

Kinship and caste ties are strong in Indian life. One's relatives and members of one's *jati* are ready to help, and in turn, one should help them. Loyalty and duty, toward one's family especially, but also toward one's *jati*, are emphasized in child rearing. Many Western observers of Indian family life have commented on the collectivistic ethic at its core and the absence of an individualistic ethic. Indeed, what might be interpreted as healthy individualism by a person from the West maybe seen by South Asians as selfishness.

Recent Developments

There has been much movement of Indians from their villages into towns and cities, especially since the mid-nineteenth century and increasingly in the twentieth century. Studies suggest that in towns with long-settled stable populations, there were neighborhoods associated with particular castes, but in rapidly growing metropolises such as Mumbai (Bombay), Delhi, Calcutta, and Madras, people are segregated more by economic class than by caste. Wealthy people live in certain estates or "colonies," poorer people in others. Even though the caste-cum-kinship neighborhood milieu may be gone in the city, and households may be nuclear in structure—a working man plus his wife and children—urban families are often joined by other relatives, by a nephew attending school or by an elderly parent of the husband or wife. Marriages continue to be arranged by elders and arranged almost always within the *jati*. The *jati* for the city dweller may be located around his home village, or it may be merely a network of scattered families, few in his own neighborhood. If enough families of his *jati* migrated to a town or city and have been there for a few generations, a new urban *jati* may have developed.

There has been much discussion of the so-called decline in the joint family in South Asia. With the increase in average life expectancy in South Asian countries during the twentieth century, there should be more lineal joint families since there should be more grandparents available to fill joint-families' upper generations. However, there are countervailing forces, such as outmigration from rural areas to cities, plantations, and abroad. There also has been an increase in the average age of marriage for both females and males, so that there are fewer junior members to fill the middle generation in the joint family. To the extent that more children survive infancy and early childhood than in past centuries, the problem of crowding is greater. Crowding tends to force some of the component couples in a joint-family household to take their children and move elsewhere. Population pressure and the patrilineal South Asian pattern of dividing land among all male descendants has resulted in land fragmentation and a decline in resources for people in rural areas, making it difficult to accommodate a joint family.

Pauline Kolenda

See also: **Westernization—South Asia**

Further Reading

Ahmad, Imtiaz. (1976) *Family, Kinship, and Marriage among Muslims in India.* Columbia, MO: South Asia Books.

Burling, Robbins. (1963) *Ransanggari: Family and Kinship in a Garo Village.* Philadelphia: University of Pennsylvania Press.

Census of India. (1961) *Village Studies in Himachal Pradesh: Village Kanum, Village Nachar.* Delhi: Government of India.

Crooke, William. (1896) *The Tribes and Castes of the North-Western Provinces and Oudh.* Calcutta, India: Government Printing.

Gough, E. Kathleen. (1961) "Nayar: Central Kerala; Nayar: North Kerala; Tiyyar: North Kerala; Mappilla: North Kerala." In *Matrilineal Kinship*, edited by David M. Schneider and E. Kathleen Gough. Berkeley and Los Angeles: University of California Press, 298–442.

Kolenda, Pauline. (1985) *Caste in Contemporary India: Beyond Organic Solidarity.* Prospect Heights, IL: Waveland Press.

———. (1989) "The Joint Family Household in Rural Rajasthan: Ecological, Cultural, and Demographic Conditions for Its Occurrence." In *Society from the Inside Out: Anthropological Perspectives on the South Asian Household*, edited by John N. Gray and David J. Mearns. New Delhi: Sage Publications, 55–106.

———. (1987) *Regional Differences in Family Structure in India.* Jaipur, India: Rawat.

Majumdar, D. N. (1962) *Himalayan Polyandry.* Mumbai, India: Asia Publishing House.

Van der Veer, K. W. (1971) *I Give Thee My Daughter: A Study of Marriage and Hierarchy among the Anavil Brahmans of South Gujarat.* Assen, Netherlands: van Gorcum.

MARRIAGE AND FAMILY—WEST ASIA

Family and marriage are important in the social economy of West Asia. The dominant religion of the area is Islam, and therefore the mores that govern marriage and family life in the region are derived from, and firmly rooted in, Islamic traditions. As such, society is strictly male-dominated, with women often serving the dual roles of mother and housewife. It is not unusual to see men in public while women are seen but rarely; when women are seen, they are draped in an all-encompassing veil, for a veil is said to protect and guard the virtue of a woman.

Family Structure

A typical family in West Asia is an extended one, in that several generations of the same family live in one abode. Generally the eldest male is the head of the household. Family life is best described as clannish, wherein each member works for the benefit of the whole. It is highly unusual for sons to leave their parents home and set up a household of their own. Traditionally, a son gets married and his wife comes and lives in the family home. Conversely, the girl children of the household are married off and go to live with their in-laws. This sort of familial arrangement has age-old roots in West Asia. Certainly, the extended family predates the arrival of Islam, since earlier civilizations in the area show the same pattern of family life. In modern urban West Asia (that is, in the larger cities of Turkey and Iran), however, the nuclear family is becoming more common. Most modern Turkish and many Iranian young people, while recognizing the prevalence of the traditional pattern, would resist including themselves in it.

Choice of Marriage Partners

Traditionally, marriage is arranged by the parents, with the son or the daughter having little say in the matter. The concept of young people choosing their own life partners is alien to the culture of the region. Arranged marriages tend to be based on the concept of gain, in that a marital union will further the economic or social standing of the family. Also, it is often customary that marriages are arranged within the larger family group. Thus, there are frequent consanguineous arrangements with either first or second cousins. Such practices derive from ancient concepts of blood ties and the idea that marriages must be kept within the family. No doubt such customs stem also from the need to safeguard the family's property, and are fueled by ancient notions of procreation, in which the father is deemed the full progenitor of children, with the mother contributing little other than her womb as a place for the child to grow. In this context, the question of incest cannot occur.

Women are expected to be virgins at the time of their marriages. Indeed, there are many dire consequences if an unmarried woman is not a virgin. Traditionally, the sexual life of young women is strictly controlled and the mingling of boys and girls is not encouraged.

Dowry Gifts

The bride's family provides a substantial dowry to the groom, although the groom's family also gives the bride marriage gifts. Traditionally, the dowry ensured the marriage would remain stable, since dissolution of the bond would mean the groom would have to return much of the dowry the bride brought with her.

A dowry is often a heavy responsibility for the girl's family and contributes to the common view that girls are a burden. Traditionally, girls are married off as soon as they reach puberty. Although this practice of early marriage is now abating, it persists in many areas of the region.

Widowhood and Divorce

If the husband dies at a young stage, it is not atypical for the wife, who is already living with her in-laws, to be married to one of her brothers-in-law. This levirate arrangement serves to ensure the economic well-being of the woman, since she cannot fend for herself in a traditional society and needs the umbrella of a family. Traditionally, a widow would not be accepted back into her parents' home.

Given that the larger culture of the region is Islamic, it is perfectly permissible for a man to take four wives. Indeed, it is the duty of a Muslim man to marry. Each wife has equal rights in the eyes of the law, and her children are deemed full heirs to the father's property. However, having more than one wife implies that a man is rich enough to take care of them all; polygamy is thus also a status symbol within the larger society. A man is free to divorce as many times as he chooses. A man may divorce a woman by simply stating so, four times, without witnesses, and the pronouncement becomes binding. Divorce often results when children are not produced. It is perceived that the woman is literally barren, in that the man's seed cannot grow in her womb. Such ancient notions still predominate in the region.

Pleasure Marriages

Where Shi'a Islam prevails, another marriage pattern exists. This is the "temporary" or "pleasure marriage." In such arrangements, any woman (whether a divorcee, a widow, or a virgin) may unite with a man for a clearly defined period of time (anywhere from a few hours to many years) by simply uttering a phrase of consent. This verbal contract has loose rules, takes place without witnesses, and is not officially registered, although it is fully backed by Islamic religious tradition. Once the marriage expires, according to the dictates of the preset period of time, the woman must abstain from sexual intercourse for a period of three months, in order to determine the father in case of pregnancy. If during the pleasure marriage the woman falls pregnant, the father must take charge of the child. Such marriages are becoming popular in certain parts of West Asia, because they involve less financial commitment on the part of the husband. Critics of this practice view it as little more than prostitution. However, many men and women in parts of West Asia are now involved in such marriages.

Nirmal Dass

Further Reading

Farsoun, Samih K. (1985). *Arab Society: Continuity and Change*. London and Dover, NH: Croom Helm.

Landau, Jacob M. (1972). *Man, State, and Society in the Contemporary Middle East*. New York: Praeger.

MARSH ARABS Until the middle 1990s, when the Iraqi government began extensive drainage works that destroyed much of their traditional homeland, the Marsh Arabs inhabited much of the area extending southward from Kut on the Tigris River and Hilla on the Euphrates River, to Basra on the Shatt al- 'Arab. The area is alternately desert and marsh and originally covered 52,000 square kilometers (20,000 square miles). In the rainy season (March–July), 10,400 square kilometers (4,000 square miles) would be completely inundated; during the rest of the year the area was part marsh, part lake, and part dry land, covered with reeds and bulrushes. The inhabitants of the area, all nominally Shi'ite Muslims, were members of a number of different tribes, notably the Albu Muhammad, the Bani Lam, the Albu Salih, the Bani 'Isad, and the Bani Hashsham. Traditionally, villages were formed on small islands, with huts made of reeds; transport was by canoe or raft.

The only academic anthropological study of part of the region (published in 1962, based on research carried out in 1953) divides the inhabitants occupationally into cultivators (of rice, millet, wheat, barley, and vegetables), reed gatherers, and buffalo breeders; some of the larger tribes, especially the Albu Muhammad, had members in all three categories, buffalo breeding being the most socially prestigious. In 1947, when the population of Iraq was about 5 million, there were about 300,000 Marsh Arabs. Although the nation's population in 2001 was over 20 million, rural to urban migration has been a major feature of the last five decades, so there were probably no more than 600,000 Marsh Arabs as of 1990.

Traditionally, the marshes provided a place of refuge for those fleeing from conscription or from the tax collector. However, the system of air control introduced by the British mandatory authorities in the 1920s meant that recalcitrant tribes could be and were bombed for various acts of disobedience or for non-payment of taxes. Increasingly, the inhabitants of the rural south settled in larger villages or left the area al-

A Marsh Arab man prepares dough for baking near Nasiriya, Iraq, in 1974. (NIK WHEELER/CORBIS)

together. In the autumn of 1967, a splinter group of the Iraq Communist Party (the ICP–General Command, led by ʿAziz al-Hajj) conducted a brief guerrilla campaign based in the marshes. After the uprisings in southern Iraq following Desert Storm in 1991, groups of rebels took refuge in the marshes, which caused the Iraqi regime to lay siege to the area. Movement in and out of the marshlands was forbidden, and two huge canals were constructed and a number of rivers diverted, deliberately draining the marshes to make them uninhabitable by their traditional population (because the water was a vital part of their way of life). Most of the population has fled to refugee camps across the Iranian border. It may be that the damage done so far is irreversible; in any case, if the new hydraulic works were to be abandoned immediately, it would take many years for the ecology of the area to recover.

Peter Sluglett

Further Reading

Al-Bayati, Hamid. (1994) "Destruction of the Southern Marshes." In *Iraq since the Gulf War: Prospects for Democracy*, edited by Fran Hazelton. London: Zed Press, 141–146.

Maxwell, Gavin. (1957) *People of the Reeds*. New York: Harper.

Salim, S. M. (1962) *Marsh Dwellers of the Euphrates Delta*. London: Athlone Press.

Thesiger, Wilfred. ([1964] 1983) *The Marsh Arabs*. Reprint ed. Harmondsworth, U.K.: Penguin.

Young, Gavin. (1977) *Return to the Marshes: Life with the Marsh Arabs of Iraq*. London: Collins.

MARSHALL, DAVID (1908–1995), Singapore politician. David Marshall was born in Singapore on 12 March 1908. Educated in Singapore and London, he was called to the Singapore bar in 1938. A volunteer in World War II, he was taken prisoner in 1942 and sent to Japan; he returned to Singapore in 1946 and established his reputation as a leading criminal lawyer. His involvement in politics began in 1949, when he joined the Progressive Party. In 1954, he founded the Labour Front and became its chairman. In 1955 Singapore became a self-governing colony of the United Kingdom and an election was held; Marshall was elected chief minister when his party won ten out of twenty-five contested seats. He resigned in May 1956, after failing to secure full independence from the British government. In 1957 Marshall formed the Workers' Party, which, with Communist support, emerged as a political force in the December 1957 city council election, but then faded, except as a vehicle for winning Marshall a parliamentary seat in the 1962 Anson by-election. He resigned from the party in 1963 because of ideological differences, and returned to the practice of law. Marshall was admired for his courage and integrity, and for his willingness to stand up to authority on issues of conscience. In 1978 he was made Singapore's ambassador to France; later his portfolio expanded to include Spain, Portugal, and Switzerland. He retired from the diplomatic corps and returned to Singapore in 1993, where he practiced law until his death in 1995.

Kog Yue Choong

Further Reading

Chan Heng Chee. (1984) *A Sensation of Independence: A Political Biography of David Marshall.* Singapore: Oxford University Press.

Marshall, David Saul. (1995) *Memorial Service, 1908–1995.* Singapore: Maghain Aboth Synagogue.

Mulliner, Kent, and Lian The-Mulliner. (1991) *Historical Dictionary of Singapore.* Metuchen, NJ: Scarecrow Press.

MARUYAMA MASAO (1914–1996), Japanese political scientist. Maruyama Masao is one of the most influential intellectuals in postwar Japan and is a representative political thinker. The son of a political journalist, he was born in Osaka Prefecture in 1914. In 1937, he graduated from the Law Faculty of Tokyo Imperial University (as the University of Tokyo was called until after World War II) and became a faculty member there. In 1950, he was appointed full professor and gave lectures on the history of political ideas in the East until his retirement in 1971.

Throughout his career, Maruyama analyzed Japan's social aspects and ideology from the perspective of democratic humanism (a philosophy promoting the worth of all people). His 1946 book *Chokokka shugi no ronri to shinri* (The Logic and Psychology of Ultranationalism) cataloged Maruyama's thoughts on the Japanese government. His analysis of the country's postwar democracy and the psychology of the Japanese imperial system revealed his criticism of Japan's system of government with an emperor as head of state. He wrote a series of other works that include the *Nihon seiji shisosho kenkyu* (Studies on the Intellectual History of Tokugawa Japan, 1952), *Gendai seiji no shiso to kodo* (Thought and Behavior in Modern Japanese Politics, 1965–1967), and *Senchu to sengo no aida* (Between the War and Postwar Eras, 1976).

Nathalie Cavasin

Further Reading

Kersten, Rikki. (1996) *Democracy in Postwar Japan: Maruyama Masao and the Search for Autonomy*. New York: Routledge.

Maruyama Masao (1963) *Thought and Behavior in Modern Japanese Politics*. London: Oxford University Press.

MARXISM—SOUTH ASIA Marxist ideas have had a deep and enduring influence on political, economic, and literary thinking in South Asia, even though Communist parties have been in power in only a few regional pockets. This influence has advanced along two routes: anticolonial political movements and thoughts on economic development.

The Communist Party of India was established in 1925. From 1920, the idea of class struggle was closely linked with the nationalist movement, partly because such a connection was favored by Moscow and inspired by Lenin's thesis that imperialism was a mature stage of capitalism. Partly, it appealed to a section of nationalists disillusioned by the Indian National Congress's elite leadership. That feeling was strengthened after the sudden withdrawal of the noncooperation movement (1920–1922). This connection between class struggle and nationalism was for the Communists a source of both strength and weakness. Strength because it was expected to bring the working classes into the nationalist movement while staying at a distance from the Congress, which was seen as representing the national bourgeoisie, and weakness because it led to intellectual division. In the most famous dissent, M. N. Roy argued and almost persuaded the Comintern (the international association of Communist parties) that the two agendas, class struggle and nationalist movement, needed to be separate. Soon after, in 1926, Roy was expelled from the Comintern. The Communist Party of India, which followed Moscow closely thereafter, suffered credibility when it abruptly changed its line on anticolonial struggles after Russia entered World War II as an ally of the British.

Following India's independence from Britain (1947) and the creation of Bangladesh (1971), new national Communist parties were formed. These parties splintered for a variety of reasons: intellectual tensions arising from the appeal of Maoism and the emphasis on peasant struggles, regional tensions arising from local concerns, and political tensions concerning participation in parliamentary politics. A major development came in 1957 in Kerala when, for the first time in world history, a Communist state government was voted into power as a result of a democratic election. In the last six elections West Bengal, too, has produced Communist governments.

Before India's independence, a main current within the Indian National Congress was convinced of the need for state control of productive resources to ensure a more equal distribution of income and wealth. This socialist strand was inspired directly by the Soviet developmental model, with the emphasis on state ownership, redistribution, and central planning, and indirectly by classical Marxism with its accent on equity and fair distribution. Between the 1950s and the 1980s, these ideas were incorporated into India's developmental policy and philosophy and became part of an informal consensus among Indian intellectuals. Such Soviet-influenced developmental ideas were popular in greater South Asia as well. In this way, gaps were bridged between the political parties of the left and the mainstream intellectual tradition in political economy. The collapse of the Soviet Union, China's economic reforms and rapid economic growth in Southeast Asia and East Asia were some of the major forces that weakened the socialist development strategy and the link between leftist politics and policy discourse.

At the beginning of the twenty-first century, Marxism was on the wane both politically and intellectually. Struggles for representation and empowerment of the underprivileged carry on, but are not focused on the concerns of workers. Still, Marxism has left a deep and enduring impact on ideas about rural political change, on the trade-union movement, on historiography, and, in the cultural sphere, on theater and film.

Tirthankar Roy

Further Reading

Seth, Sanjay. (1995) *Marxist Theory and Nationalist Politics: The Case of Colonial India*. New Delhi: Sage.

Sherlock, Stephen. (1988) "Bȩrlin, Moscow and Bombay. The Marxism that India Inherited." *South Asia* 21, 1 (June): 63–76.

MARXISM-LENINISM-MAO ZEDONG THOUGHT

Marxism-Leninism-Mao Zedong Thought is a complex set of philosophical ideas and views, economic and historical theories and conceptions, and political doctrines, each integral part of which has its own history of emergence and development in China.

Marxism

The first Chinese to fasten their eyes on Marxism at the beginning of the twentieth century were reformers and revolutionaries. Due to their efforts, some writings of the classics of Marxism began to be translated and published in 1906. The founding of the Chinese Communist Party (CCP) in July 1921 was a landmark in the development of Marxism in China. Since then, Marxism has been tightly connected to the CCP, and Marxism has been proclaimed the ideological basis of the party, which is engaged in the struggle for revolutionary transformation of society.

As a matter of fact, Marxism was ill-suited to this mission. The reason is that even Marxist theories about the general laws of historical development (let them be called "scientific Marxism" here) aimed in the long run to prove the inevitability of capitalist society's revolutionary transformation into a socialist society, characterized by a higher level of development, and therefore qualified as postcapitalistic in nature. As for Marxist revolutionary doctrines (let them be called "political Marxism" here), they dealt altogether with revolutionary transformation and the construction of the postcapitalist society only. But the CCP conducted its struggle in a precapitalist society and for this purpose had nothing to do with the transformation of capitalism into a "higher" stage of development. Moreover, contrary to the Chinese Communists' claims, this struggle was in essence intended not to build any "postcapitalist" society at all, but to prevent the emergence of a capitalist society. However, it is at this very point that the Chinese Communists' efforts coincided with the utopian views of political Marxism about both capitalism and socialism, which in fact neglected capitalism from the standpoint of precapitalist rather than postcapitalist society. That is why the Chinese Communists armed themselves with Marxism, using it as an ideological cover rather than an ideological basis. The CCP inherited Marxism from the Russian Bolsheviks in the form that later was proclaimed to be Leninism (the formula "Marxism-Leninism" came to usage in China only after its invention in the Soviet Union, after Lenin's death). The main feature of this form of Marxism was Lenin's representation of a struggle against capitalism from the standpoint of precapitalist society as a striving for a new, postcapitalist society. At the same time, once the Chinese Communists adopted Marxism, scientific Marxism provided a solid theoretical and methodological base for Chinese scholars who were conducting research in social sciences and humanities.

Mao Zedong Thought

Mao Zedong Thought developed in China during the second half of the 1930s and the first half of the 1940s, as Mao Zedong (1893–1976) consolidated his leadership position in the CCP. The term "Mao Zedong Thought" appeared for the first time in 1943, when it was declared to be an amalgam of Chinese Marxism-Leninism, Chinese Bolshevism, and Chinese Communism, as well as the correct road for Chinese

Communists. Mao Zedong Thought evidently referred to new policies adopted by the CCP. Their main features were revealed by Mao Zedong in his work *On New Democracy* (1940).

The new policies' cornerstone became the statement that China had not been ready for socialism. Therefore, the revolution conducted by the Chinese Communists had not been a proletarian and socialist revolution, but a bourgeois-democratic one. And it had to be guided, as before, by the CCP, not by the proletariat. The CCP was declared to be the leader of the peasantry and all the other democratic forces. The revolution was designed to establish a bourgeois-democratic regime of what was termed the "New Democracy" and to clear the way for the development of national capitalism. Therefore the Chinese Communists sought support for such a revolution not from the Soviet Union, but from the United States.

However, for quite a number of reasons, the New Democracy and the attempts to enlist the support of the United States failed. The Soviet Union remained the only potential source of external aid for the Chinese Communists. As a result, in the second half of 1948, on the eve of their victory over the Nationalist Chinese forces of the Guomindang Party, the Chinese Communists began to revise the New Democracy course and to return to orthodox Marxist lines, based on the leadership of the working class and on the principles of Marxism-Leninism and of Proletarian Internationalism. This process was finally completed after the establishment in October 1949 of the People's Republic of China (PRC).

Coalescence into Marxism-Leninism-Mao Zedong Thought

After independence, Marxism-Leninism regained its former dominant status. Mao Zedong Thought was subsumed into Marxism-Leninism, and Marxism-Leninism-Mao Zedong Thought as a whole was elevated to the status of something like a state ideology. In full accordance with this ideology's demands, China was declared to be "a socialist country," and the policies of the CCP fluctuated toward what was termed "Socialist construction."

The elevation of Marxism-Leninism-Mao Zedong Thought to the status of an official state ideology meant that the obligation to demonstrate loyalty to this ideology, to study its doctrines, and to use its theories as a methodological basis for scholarly research of all kinds, which had earlier been imposed on party members only, was extended to the entire citizenry. In the late 1950s and the early 1960s, a new elevation of Mao Zedong Thought set in. Once again, it became tightly connected to a fundamentally new political course. Mao Zedong's leftist conceptions of the Great Leap Forward economic movement and class struggle under socialism, of continued revolution under proletarian dictatorship, and of the Cultural Revolution formed its theoretical and ideological basis and determined its domestic policies. Its foreign policy aspects included confrontation with the Soviet Union during the late 1950s and early 1960s and improvement of China's relations with the United States and the West as a whole in the early 1970s. In 1967, Mao Zedong Thought was proclaimed to be "the perfection of Marxism-Leninism" and Mao himself to be the "Lenin of the present age."

The failure of the Cultural Revolution's domestic policies and the adoption of the Four Modernizations course in 1978 led to the restoration of the status quo in the hierarchical relations between Marxism-Leninism and Mao Zedong Thought. Moreover, those aspects of Mao Zedong Thought that were considered the theoretical underpinnings of the rejected policies were strongly criticized. Simultaneously, the criticism was extended to many basic nonscientific and utopian doctrines of Marxism-Leninism itself, regarding the fundamental features of capitalist and socialist societies. Also, a considerable number of scholarly inquiries were published that were designed to eliminate from Marxist scientific theories of precapitalist societies' development all of the perversions generated by Soviet interpretations of Marxism. Nevertheless, the official status of Marxism-Leninism-Mao Zedong Thought as the leading ideology of the state was not called into question in China.

Alexandre Tiourine

See also: **Chinese Communist Party; Cultural Revolution—China; Mao Zedong**

Further Reading

Brugger, Bill, and David Kelly. (1990) *Chinese Marxism in the Post-Mao Era.* Stanford, CA: Stanford University Press.

Fogel, Joshua A. (1987) *Ai Ssu-chi's Contribution to the Development of Chinese Marxism.* Cambridge, MA: Council on East Asian Studies/Harvard University.

Ladany, Laszlo. (1988) *The Communist Party of China and Marxism, 1921–1985: A Self-Portrait.* Foreword by Robert Elegant. Stanford, CA: Hoover Institution Press, Stanford University.

Meisner, Maurice. (1967) *Li Ta-chao and the Origins of Chinese Marxism.* Cambridge, MA: Harvard University Press.

———. (1982) *Marxism, Maoism, and Utopianism.* Madison: University of Wisconsin Press.

ANCIENT MERV—WORLD HERITAGE SITE

The ruins of Merv in Mary, Turkmenistan, an important city on the Silk Route, were designated a UNESCO World Heritage Site in 1999. The exceptionally well-preserved oasis city's architecture bears witness to four millennia of trade and cultural cross-pollination through its walls.

MARY (1998 est. pop. 123,000). Mary (formerly Merv), the third-largest city in Turkmenistan, lies near the very ancient settlement of Merv; in Hindu, Parsi, and Arab tradition Merv was thought to be the site of paradise and the home of the Aryans. Mary is situated in the southeastern part of the country, in a large oasis in the Kara-Kum desert, at the intersection of the Murghab River and the Kara-Kum Canal, a 1,400-kilometer-long waterway linking the Caspian Sea and the Amu Dar'ya River.

Mary was founded in 1884 under the name of Merv during the Russian conquest of Central Asia, 30 kilometers west of the ruined ancient city of Merv, known from early times under the names of Mouru, Margush, Margiana, and Maru. After establishment of the Turkmen Soviet Socialist Republic (1924), Merv, renamed Mary in 1937, was the administrative center of the Mary province until the dissolution of the Soviet Union in 1991.

Since 1991 Mary is the administrative center of the Mary province of the republic of Turkmenistan. At present it is a major railway junction and an important center for cotton growing and gas extracting. The major Shotlyk ("joy") gas field with recoverable resources of 460 billion cubic meters is located 20 kilometers west of Mary.

Natalya Y. Khan

Further Reading

Allworth, Edward, ed. (1994) *Central Asia, 130 Years of Russian Dominance: A Historical Overview.* 3rd ed. Durham, NC: Duke University Press.

Herrmann, Georgina. (1999) *Monuments of Merv: Traditional Buildings of the Karakum.* London: Society of Antiquaries of London.

MASHHAD (2000 pop. 2 million). Mashhad (Mashad, Meshed), a city in northeastern Iran in the province of Khorasan, is located in the Kashaf River valley near the borders of Turkmenistan and Afghanistan. The city was always an important center for travelers from India and for those moving north-south. Today, Mashhad is the provincial capital and Iran's second largest city.

Mashhad was once a small village called Sanabad, twenty-five kilometers southeast of Tus, Khorasan's urban center throughout antiquity. Following the Shi^cite Imam Reza's death in 817 CE and his burial in Sanabad, however, the village became a key pilgrimage destination for Shi^cites and was eventually known as Mashhad-e Moghaddas ("place of martyrdom"), or just Mashhad. Since that time locals and notables built mosques, *madrasahs*, (religious schools), libraries, and numerous other structures adjacent to Reza's tomb. The resulting religious complex is an impressive urban center and one of the holiest pilgrimage sites for Shi^cites. Today millions visit Mashhad each year as pilgrims.

After Mongol armies razed Tus in 1220, Mashhad emerged as a true city and eventual provincial capital. Though raided or seized by invading armies of Oghuz Turks, Mongols, Uzbeks, and Afghans through the centuries, Mashhad endured and grew. In 1736, Mashhad was made capital of Persia under Nadir Shah, and his tomb and museum are important monuments in the city. In the nineteenth and early twentieth centuries, Mashhad was a significant center in the Anglo-Russian struggles over Eurasia, and the shrine of Imam Reza was even bombarded by Russians in 1912. During the past two decades Mashhad has also been a major destination for thousands of Afghan refugees.

Kyle Evered

Further Reading

Cronin, Stephanie. (1997) "An Experiment in Revolutionary Nationalism: The Rebellion of Colonel Muhammad Taqi Khan Pasyan in Mashhad, April–October 1921." *Middle Eastern Studies* 33, 4: 693–750.

Melville, Charles Peter. (1996) "Shah ʿAbbas and the Pilgrimage to Mashhad." In *Safavid Persia: The History and Politics of an Islamic Society*, edited by Charles Peter Melville. London: I. B. Tauris, 191–230.

Patai, Raphael. (1997) *Jadid al-Islam: The Jewish "New Muslims" of Meshhed.* Detroit: Wayne State University Press.

MASKS—EAST ASIA From prehistoric to present times, masks in China, Korea, and Japan have been used in religious rites and theatrical performances. Made of varying materials and configurations, masks were often believed to have magical powers. The use of masks enabled the wearer to assume another identity, either divine, human, or animal.

Masks in China have been traced to Neolithic times (c. 5000 BCE). Copper masks were in use in the Zhou dynasty (1045–256 BCE) and huge gilt bronze masks with protruding eyes and fantastic brow crests were found at Sanxingdui (thirteenth to tenth centuries BCE). Nuo Xi, ritual exorcisms enacted as masked dance, were performed to frighten away evil and to avoid disasters. Masked stilt dancers in Anhui province brought good fortune. The masks of Di Xi, worn atop the forehead, have stern visages, sharp features, and beards. Beijing opera, traditionally performed without masks, gave rise to renditions of *jing* (painted face) character masks. Enacting rituals and theater in the outdoors required masks to be brightly colored and exaggerated.

Korean masks owe their origins to shamanism and Buddhism, as well as to Chinese influences. The oldest known mask, from the fifth to sixth century during the Shilla kingdom (57 BCE–935 CE), is of black lacquered wood from Ho'u-chong in Kyongju Province. The Korean masked dance drama *(t'al ch'un)* was performed at the New Year and Tano Festival, which was on the fifth day of the fifth moon and which was when women washed their hair in iris and swung on swings while men participated in traditional Korean wrestling *(ssirum)* matches. Dramas were also performed on Chosuk, the seventh day of the seventh moon, a festival when ancestors were honored in order to ensure prosperity for families; women and children performed ceremonies at wells to ensure abundant water for the coming year, and books and clothing were aired in the sun. The often bawdy drama ridicules the *yangban* (landed aristocrats) and Buddhist monks. The masks, either wood, papier-mâché, or gourd, were often burned after performances, except the wooden masks of Hahoe village, which were kept in a sacred place. Guardian masks also adorned the wooden poles at the village entrances. Funeral masks *(pangsangsi)* were made of carved wood, paper, or straw, according to the status of the deceased, and were either carried in front or worn by a performer who danced in front of the procession and frightened evil from the burial site.

In Japan, early masks were used for *gagaku*, elegant ritual music brought to Japan from China or Korea in the early Nara period (710–794 CE), and *bugaku*, court dance and music also dating from the Nara period. The most renowned Japanese masks, however, are Noh masks representing gods, warriors, beautiful or aged women, and demons. Created by actor, playwright, and critic Zeami (c. 1363–c. 1443), Noh drama incorporated parts of ritual dances to form a slow-moving tragic genre. Noh mask carvers such as the Deme family of Echizen Province carefully guarded their skills, which were passed down for over eight generations.

Noelle O'Connor

See also: **Drama–China; Drama–Japan; Drama–Korea; Noh, Kyogen**

Further Reading

Portal, Jane. (2000) *Korea: Art and Archaeology*. New York: Thames and Hudson.

Tokugawa Yoshinobu and Sadao Okochi. (1977) *The Tokugawa Collection: No Robes and Masks*. Trans. by Louise Allison Cort and Monica Bethe. New York: Japan Society.

Xue Roulin, ed. (1999) *The Art of Chinese Ritual Masks*. Taipei, Taiwan: Oriental Book Store.

MASKS—INDONESIA, JAVANESE Java has a strong tradition of the cultural use of face masks. Probably ritual in origin, today they are important in many traditional styles of drama, while their carving is a major Javanese folk art

The Javanese term *topeng* (from a root meaning "to cover up") refers to all face masks, whether for performance, ceremonies, or decoration. While masks for ritual exist in other parts of Indonesia, in Java and Bali masks are principally associated with theatrical performance and are also collected as objets d'art. Javanese masks are carved from a single block of wood and then painted. Performance masks are either gripped between the performer's teeth by means of a strap attached to the inner surface, or held on with a string passing over a headdress.

Javanese masks are differentiated according to well-established types closely related to the characterization of *wayang kulit* (shadow puppets), and dance types from *wayang wong* (court ballet). Characters are either *halus* (refined), *gagah* (strong), clowns, or ogres. *Halus* character masks have pointed noses and narrow eyes, while *gagah* masks have round eyes and prominent noses. Some clown characters are represented by half masks, allowing actors wearing them to speak more freely. Female characters normally fall within the *halus* type. As with Javanese shadow puppets, there are regional variations, and details of eye shape, face color, and nose and mouth representation represent distinctions between characters.

While some craftsmen still specialize in carving and painting performance masks, many cruder masks are produced as tourist souvenirs and for interior decoration.

Masks are used in folk-theater, but their use in classical theater is now more common in Bali than in Java.

In some modern forms of dance-drama such as *sendratari* (the "Ramayana ballet" developed in the 1960s), masks are used only for nonhuman characters. Classical masked dances also exist in Java, dances such as the *klana topeng gagah*, in which a male dancer represents an ogre king. There are traditional theatrical forms (*topeng pajengan*) in which a single performer represents a number of characters by using different masks, a feat requiring dexterity and skill.

Many dancers specializing in masked performance spend considerable time with new masks, even wearing them around their houses to get the feel of the new character inhabiting the mask.

The concept of masked theater is still strong today in the work of avant-garde theater groups and choreographers, while a growing number of dealers in Indonesia and overseas provide support for the craft of mask-making.

Tim Byard-Jones

Further Reading

Yousouf, Ghulam-Sarwar. (1994) *Dictionary of Traditional South-East Asian Theatre*. Kuala Lumpur, Malaysia: Oxford University Press.

MASSAGE—CHINA

Massage is an ancient healing art in China. Archaeological studies show that as early as 2700 BCE the Chinese in the Huang (Yellow) River Valley were using massage for healing purposes. During the period of Warring States (475–221 BCE), a folk doctor, Bianqie, used massage and acupuncture successfully for a patient suffering from shock.

Methods of massage include rubbing, stroking, kneading, or tapping with the hands as well as with the healer's arm and elbow on the patient's body and extremities. The principles of massage developed alongside the essential principles of traditional Chinese medicine, that is, the theory of yin and yang, and the belief in flows of energy through the channels and the collaterals. In accord with these beliefs, massage is thought to not only heal an injury at one particular location but also to influence the entire body or other parts of the body through energy flowing through the channels and the collaterals that regulate the balance of yin and yang, correct the pathology and physiology of body fluid, *qi* (vital energy), and stimulate circulation. The effect of the manipulation is directly related to the methods used—mild or powerful manipulations, vigorous or soft performance, quick or slow frequency, direction of the force, and so forth.Currently, therapeutic massage is used in China as a conservative treatment for orthopedic disorders such as frozen shoulder, lumbago, protrusion of spinal disc, and joint sprains. Chinese orthopedic surgeons do not consider therapeutic massage and surgical treatment as opposites, but as complementary treatments. Therapeutic massage, using only the doctor's hands, relieves the patient's pain and avoids the side effects of chemical agents such as repeated local injections of steroids. It can also frequently eliminate the side effects of unnecessary surgical procedures. In most Chinese hospitals today, a section of massage treatment is often affiliated with the department of physical therapy.

Chen Bao-xing and Garé LeCompte

Further Reading

Gulling, A. (1988) *Essentials of Tuinaology: Chinese Medical Massage and Manipulation.* Hilo, HI: Cao's Fire Dragon.

Feng, Tianyu. (1983) *Treatment of Soft Tissue Injury with Traditional Chinese and Western Medicine.* Beijing: People's Medical Publishing House.

Zhang, Enqin. (1990) *Chinese Acupuncture and Moxibustion.* Shanghai, China: Publishing House of the Shanghai College of Traditional Chinese Medicine.

MAT SALLEH REBELLION

The Mat Salleh Rebellion of 1894–1905 reflected the failure of the British North Borneo Chartered Company to administer British North Borneo (Sabah) after two decades and was a culmination of opposition since the 1880s.

Mat (Mohamed) Salleh (d. 1899), of mixed Bajau-Sulu heritage, was a trader and minor chief in the upper reaches of the Sugut River. A military tactician believed by the indigenous peoples to be endowed with supernatural powers and invulnerability, he utilized both Muslim and native symbols of authority (Islamic standards, flags, silk umbrellas) and commanded prestige and mystique amongst Muslims and non-Muslims alike.

The right and wrong of the conflict between Mat Salleh and the company remain obscure. Apparently an initial misunderstanding escalated into a series of attacks, followed by retribution by either side that created a hostile situation on the western coast and interior. The conflict erupted in late 1894 with the killing of two Iban traders on the Sugut River. A show of force by Mat Salleh at Buli Sim Sim, outside Sandakan, in August 1895 was followed by an attack on his village on the island of Pulo Jambongan. Salleh escaped to the village of Lingkabau and was declared an outlaw in July 1896. He sacked and burned Gaya Island, then Ambong in 1897; the company destroyed his fort at Ranau in 1898.

W. C. Cowie, managing director of the company's Court of Directors in London, felt that Governor Leicester P. Beaufort had mishandled the situation. Cowie met Mat Salleh at the town of Menggatal in April 1898 and verbally promised amnesty to him and his followers. They could reside in the Tambunan region without interference. Mat Salleh agreed but felt deceived when the written agreement refused to pardon his followers who were escaped felons. He began raiding and pillaging in the Tambunan Valley. Furthermore, a company outpost was established in the valley in June 1898, clearly breaking Cowie's pledge.

By the time a company force was sent to attack Mat Salleh's fort at Tambunan in December 1899, Cowie had given up on the whole affair. On 31 December 1899, during the siege of the fort, a chance shot hit and killed Mat Salleh. But it was another five years before the last of his henchmen were killed, surrendered, or captured.

The resistance of the people to the company was generally attributed to discontent over the introduction of taxes, including a levy on rice (a staple food) to fund railway and telegraph construction. But the lack of manpower forced the company to rely on local chieftains to collect revenue; subsequently they abused their mandate, creating dissatisfaction among the people, who readily supported Mat Salleh. The rebellion was not a unified territory-wide uprising, nor was it a nationalist-type struggle; it was a typical type of resistance to intrusion and curtailment of freedom from without.

Ooi Keat Gin

Further Reading

Black, Ian. (1983) *A Gambling Style of Government: The Establishment of the Chartered Company's Rule in Sabah, 1878–1915.* Kuala Lumpur, Malaysia: Oxford University Press.

Leong, Cecilia. (1982) *Sabah: The First 100 Years.* Kuala Lumpur, Malaysia: Percetakan Nan Yang Muda.

Ranjit Singh, D. S. (2000). *The Making of Sabah, 1865–1941: The Dynamics of Indigenous Society.* Kuala Lumpur, Malaysia: Penerbit Universiti Malaya.

Tarling, Nicholas. (1985) "Mat Salleh and Krani Usman." *Journal of Southeast Asian Studies* 16, 1 (March): 46–68.

Tregonning, Kennedy Gordon. (1956) "The Mat Salleh Revolt, 1894–1905." *Journal of the Malayan Branch of the Royal Asiatic Society* 29, 1 (May): 20–36.

MATARAM This great Javanese kingdom was centered in present-day Central Java in Indonesia. Its history divides into Hindu and Islamic Mataram periods, with a long interregnum between. The history of Hindu Mataram is obscure, and this kingdom is mainly known for building numerous *candi* (temples) in Java. The earliest records of this kingdom date from 732 CE, but by the tenth century Mataram's glory faded for unknown reasons. The center of power in Java moved to the east to what eventually became several great kingdoms, most notably Majapahit.

Islamic Mataram was the last great Javanese kingdom in modern Java, lasting from 1587 until its breakup in 1745. This reborn Mataram resulted from integrating various small principalities that remained following Majapahit's fall. Its court, initially located in Kota Gede, on the outskirts of present-day Yogyakarta, moved several times in the agricultural area between Yogyakarta and Surakarta—the heartland of Javanese civilization.

Islamic Mataram actually started as a Hindu kingdom led by Panembahan (Prince) Senopati. Contacts with Islam came immediately after the court's establishment, especially with the small Islamic sultanates on Java's northern coast, which led Islamic propagation in the island. In 1641, the greatest Mataram lord, Sultan Agung, embraced Islam, making Mataram an Islamic sultanate. While pious in carrying out Muslim practices, Sultan Agung did not order the abandonment of existing Hindu practices. Islamic rituals did not replace previous traditions, but were regarded as complementary. Many attributes and rituals of the Mataram court remained, but glossed over by Islamic words and titles. Because of Mataram practice, Islam in Java was embraced in a manner syncretic with previous traditions. This still remains true.

Mataram peaked during the reigns of Sultan Agung and his successor, Amangkurat I (1645–1677). Its influence extended to all of Java, parts of Sumatra, and even present-day Malaysia. A legal code, taxation, and bureaucracy were all established at this time. While basically agricultural, Mataram traded with other kingdoms in the archipelago and with European traders—especially the Dutch East India Company—who ventured into the region.

In the late seventeenth and early eighteenth centuries, relations between Mataram and the expansionist Dutch administration grew tense. The Dutch took advantage of court sibling rivalries over the issue of succession, as conflicting noblemen each sought backing from the now-dominant Dutch. Fearing rivalry might get out of hand, the Dutch brokered a deal among the lords, which led to the disintegration of the Mataram court. Through the Treaty of Giyanti (1755), Mataram was divided into the Sunanate of Surakarta under Pakubuwono I, and the Sultanate of Yogyakarta under Hamengkubuwono I. Later, these two kingdoms would be split again: the court of Mangkunegaran was established in Surakarta in 1757, and Pakualaman was established in Yogyakarta in 1813.

Though Mataram no longer exists, its successor courts in Yogyakarta and Surakarta remain active cultural centers, though without political or legal functions after the Republic of Indonesia was established. Mataram's legacy remains salient to this day, especially for Indonesia's political culture and bureaucracy.

Irman G. Lanti

Further Reading

Hall, Kenneth R. (1999) "Economic History of Early Southeast Asia." In *The Cambridge History of Southeast Asia*, vol. 1, pt. 1, edited by Nicholas Tarling. Cambridge, U.K.: Cambridge University Press.

Koentjaraningrat. (1985) *Javanese Culture*. Singapore: Oxford University Press.

Lombard, Denys. (1990) *Le Carrefour Javanais*. Paris: Éditions de l'École des hautes études en sciences sociales.

Taylor, Keith W. (1999) "The Early Kingdoms." In *The Cambridge History of Southeast Asia*, vol. 1, pt. 1, edited by Nicholas Tarling. Cambridge, U.K.: Cambridge University Press.

MATHURA (2001 est. pop. 299,000). Mathura (formerly Muttra), on the Yamuna River 155 kilometers south of Delhi, India has been a mercantile city since the fourth century BCE. It hosted Jain and Buddhist establishments and produced much Brahmanic sculpture. In Hindu mythology Mathura was founded by Satrugna, youngest brother of Rama, hero of the *Ramayana*. After 78 CE the city peaked under the Indo-Bactrian Kushan people. A Chinese pilgrim, Fa Hian, reported that in 400 CE Mathura held twenty Buddhist monasteries with a total of 3,000 monks. Its situation on a busy trade route ensured its prosperity until plunderings by the Afghan sultan Mahmud of Ghazni in 1017 and its later destruction in 1500 by Sikander Lodi, the second Lodi sultan of Delhi.

Hindu tradition stipulates that Mathura is one of seven major places of pilgrimage on the subcontinent. Believers hold that it was to rescue the throne of Mathura from usurpation by the wicked king Kamsa that Krishna, an incarnation of Vishnu, descended to earth. The focus of Krishna's story later shifted from this confrontation to his idyllic childhood in the surrounding countryside. Another major pilgrimage destination *(tirtha)* is Vrindavan, twenty kilometers upriver, where Krishna first danced his amorous musical drama *(rasa lila)* with local cowherding maidens. In Mathura the Curzon Museum of Archaeology contains Buddhist, Jain, and Hindu artifacts, stone inscriptions, and art treasures of many dynasties.

C. Roger Davis

Further Reading

Yadav, Jagdish S. (1991) *Cultural Heritage of Mathura: A Bibliography*. New Delhi: Manohar Publications for American Institute of Indian Studies.

MATSUMOTO SHIGEHARU (1899–1989), Japanese journalist and internationalist. Born in Osaka Prefecture, Matsumoto Shigeharu graduated from the Tokyo Imperial University (now University of Tokyo) and then went abroad to study in the mid-1920s at Yale University in the United States and at Oxford University in England, before choosing his career as a journalist. In 1933, he was appointed bureau chief in Shanghai for the *Nihon Shimbun Rengosha* (Associated Press of Japan). During his stay in China, he built a reputation as an internationalist by making contacts with Chinese people and speaking out against Japan's military activities in China. In 1936, he garnered international attention by reporting on the kidnapping of China's president Chiang Kai-Shek. After World War II, he created an opinion journal (*Minpo*) to promote a new kind of journalism, but the journal was unsuccessful. In 1952, he established the International House of Japan, an institution that promotes international cultural exchange by hosting scholars, journalists, and opinion leaders from different countries. He published his memoirs from his time as a journalist in China in a three-volume book entitled *Shanhai jidai* (Shanghai Days). In 1979, he received the Japan Foundation Award for his outstanding contributions to cultural exchange and mutual understanding between Japan and other countries.

Nathalie Cavasin

Further Reading

Jansen, Marius B. (1995) *Japan and Its World: Two Centuries of Change*. Princeton, NJ: Princeton University Press.

Matsumoto Shigeharu. (1975) *Shanghai jidai* (Shanghai Days). 3 vols. Tokyo: Chuo Koron Shinsha.

MAURITIUS —PROFILE (1999 est. pop. 1.15 million). Mauritius, a tiny, pear-shaped volcanic island of barely 1,865 square kilometers, lies 900 kilometers northeast of Madagascar in the Indian Ocean. Mauritius is 61 kilometers long and 47 kilometers wide, or

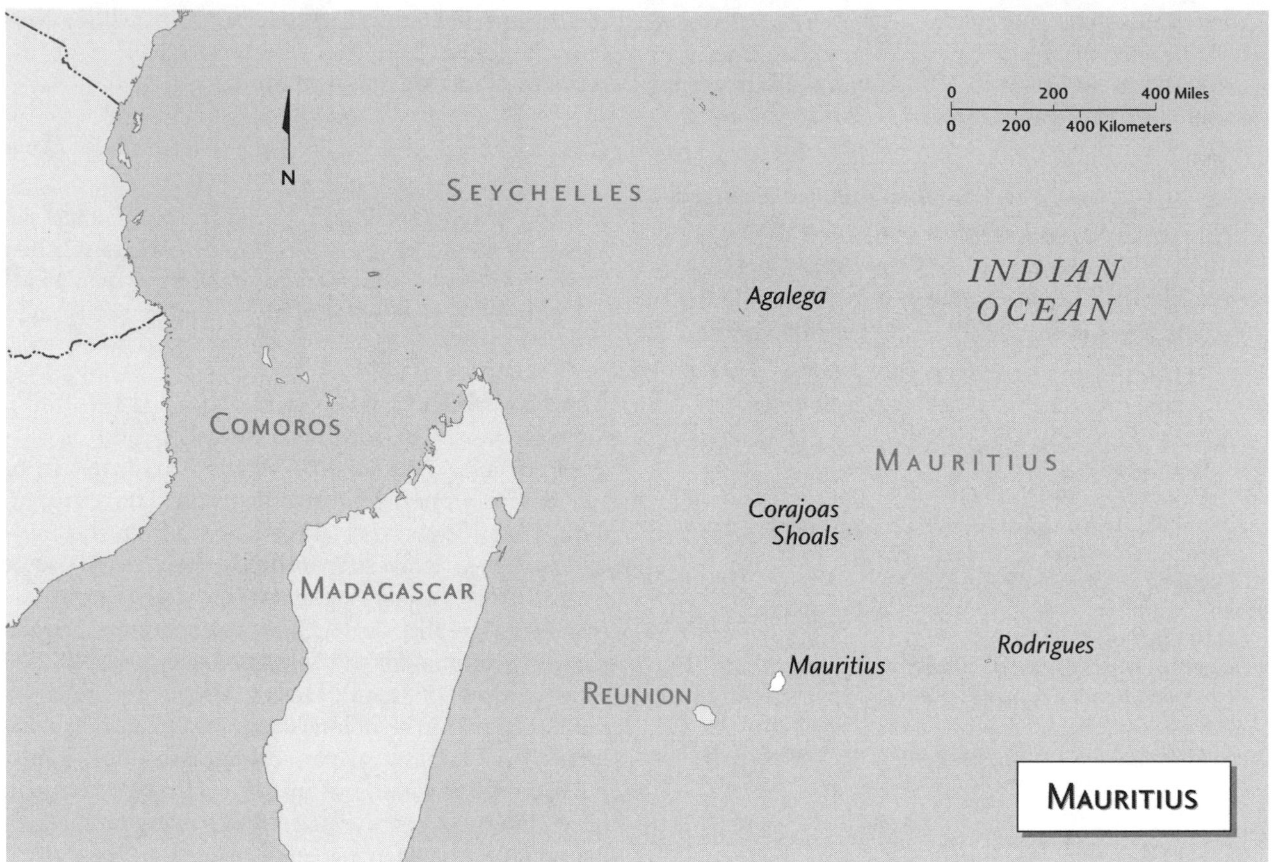

about the size of Connecticut plus Delaware or one-tenth the size of Wales. Mauritius is known for its vast white beaches, rugged volcanic mountains, and its large plateau at 550 to 730 meters above sea level.

The island lies 20 degrees south of the equator, just within the Tropic of Capricorn. Mauritius enjoys an equable maritime climate, tropical in summer and subtropical in winter, with an average summer temperature of 27°C and a winter temperature averaging 17°C.

The island's coastline runs over 200 kilometers and is surrounded by beautiful coral reefs, clean white sands, and clear lagoons full of tropical fish. The nearest Asian neighbor of Mauritius in the Indian Ocean is Sri Lanka: Colombo is 3,200 kilometers from Port Louis, the capital of Mauritius. Both Aden in Yemen and Cape Town in South Africa are 3,680 kilometers from Mauritius.

In addition to the island of Mauritius and the small island of Rodrigues, the state of Mauritius includes two tiny dependencies laying to the north—Agalega Islands (70 square kilometers) and the Carajoas Shoals (1.3 square kilometers), which are virtually unpopulated. There are also five small islands off the northwest coast of Mauritius, and the Chagos Archipelago lies midway between Mauritius and Sri Lanka. This archipelago was long a dependency of Mauritius.

People

In the sixteenth century, the island was uninhabited; at the beginning of the twenty-first century, it is one of the world's most densely populated countries. The capital city, Port Louis, is not particularly impressive, and, apart from some old buildings displaying features of European art and architecture, most of the buildings and roads are in a poor state. Port Louis is linked by narrow winding roads with the other towns of the island: Curepipe, Rose Hill, Mahebourg, and smaller villages such as Poste de Flacq, Poudre d'Or, and Souillac. Most of the villages on the plateau are inhabited by Indo-Mauritians, and there are a few Chinese shopkeepers as well. The Franco-Mauritians live in the towns or on large sugarcane plantations. The Chinese live mostly in the towns, and the Creoles live in Port Louis and in towns such as Beau Bassin, Quatre, Bornes, and Vacoas.

Present-day Mauritians have their origins on three continents: Europe, Asia, and Africa. The Mauritian population is composed of four ethnic groups and four major religious groups: the Franco-Mauritians and Creoles who are Catholic; the Indian community, comprising both Muslims and Hindus; and the small Chinese community, who are either Buddhist or Catholic. All Mauritians are, in a manner of speaking, immigrants, and the Franco-Mauritians, Indo-Mauritians, and Chinese still maintain some cultural ties with their original homelands. The Creoles, however, who are descended from East African slaves brought to Mauritius, have no such ties.

The Indo-Mauritians constitute the largest ethnic group in the island. Most of them are descendants of the indentured laborers who came from various parts of India to the island between 1832 and 1855. Three-quarters of them are Hindus, while the rest are Muslims, with a very small number of Christians. The Muslims maintain their separate cultural and religious identity and have their own political organizations.

The Chinese constitute approximately 3 percent of the total population. Half of them are Catholic, while the rest are Buddhists. The majority of them live in Port Louis; a few are engaged in small-time business in the villages. Most of the older generation of Chinese were born in China. The younger generation are gradually realizing that as they cannot be a strong political force, they must depend on the good will of the government.

The island also is inhabited by people of European and African descent. Most of those of European descent, who comprise only 2 percent of the total population, have French ancestors. Very few of them are British, although Mauritius is now a member of the Commonwealth. The Creoles, the largest group within the general population, are mostly descendants of slaves who were brought to the island by the French. Until very recently, the small but powerful Franco-Mauritian elite occupied the top of the Mauritian hierarchy, followed by the light-skinned Creole professional and middle class. The Creoles, however, did not enjoy all the privileges enjoyed by the white minority. At the bottom of the society, there were the Indian laborers and dark-skinned Creoles. To a large extent, this social stratification was a result of the hierarchical organization of the sugar industry.

History

Mauritius appeared in seventh-century Arab navigational charts, so it may be presumed that Arab traders did land on the island to collect food, water, and fuel. The Portuguese also stopped in Mauritius en route from Cape Town to Goa from 1505 onward. But it was the Dutch who in 1598 claimed the island and named it after their ruler, Prince Maurice Van Nassau. Twice the Dutch tried to establish their settlements, but they failed because of lack of food and efficient administration. Finally, in 1710, they abandoned Mauritius.

Subsequently, the French were drawn to the island. In 1715, the French East India Company claimed the island for France, and in 1721, the French established their first permanent settlement in Mauritius. In 1734, the French East India Company appointed Mahe de Labourdonnis, who had some earlier private trading experience in Pondicherry (a French colony in South India) as governor of both Bourbon and Isle de France (the French name for Mauritius). The French undertook a large-scale importation of African slaves from Madagascar and Africa to boost the sugarcane economy of the island. The governor also imported some Tamils from Pondicherry to work as artisans and domestics.

The French governor also distributed large tracts of government land freely among his relatives and close friends, who not only received the most fertile lands but also obtained free African slave labor to work on the sugar plantations established there.

The French domination in Mauritius did not last long, however. The British, realizing the strategic importance of Mauritius, decided to capture it. In 1810, while the Napoleonic wars raged in Europe, the English took over the island. The British possession was confirmed by the Treaty of Paris, which gave Britain not only Mauritius but also its dependencies, including Rodrigues and Seychelles. The British continued to import slaves. By 1833, the population of the island had reached 100,000, of which more than 70 percent were African slaves. Then, during 1834–1839, the slaves were freed by abolitionists, and were paid over 2 million pounds in compensation.

In the early decades of the nineteenth century, Indians migrated to Mauritius as indentured laborers or as free immigrants. The Indian laborers came mainly from Bihar, from Madras Presidency, and from certain parts of western India. The majority of the indentured Indian laborers, however, came from Bihar. Among them, a sizable section belonged to lower castes or were classed as untouchables by Hindu society. Since the indentured laborers mostly hailed from Bihar, Bhojpuri—a dialect of Hindi—became widely spoken in Mauritius.

Apart from the Biharis, there also was a large-scale migration of tribal peoples from the Bengal Presidency, who were popularly called the "Hillcoolies." Most of them were unskilled laborers and domestic servants, and some had no agrarian background or knowledge of agriculture. Significantly, after the Indian Mutiny of 1857 in British India, a large number of Indian troops went to Mauritius to escape punishment and harassment at the hands of their British superiors.

Between 1837 and 1910, more than 450,000 Indians emigrated to Mauritius, and of them, 160,000 returned home to India. Interestingly, the 1974 census pointed out that 96 percent of the Indians were native-born, and they numbered 600,000 out of a total population of 850,000 (roughly 70 percent of the total population).

Agitation for Equality and Economic Improvement

The French system of indenture as it operated in Mauritius led to a bitter legacy of distrust and dislike between Franco-Mauritians, who were the plantation owners, and the Indian laborers.

The Franco-Mauritians were apprehensive about the loss of their social and economic prestige and differed with the British rulers over the issues of slavery and indenture. The colonial government also differed with the Franco-Mauritian community over Indian immigration and the treatment of Indian labor in Mauritius. In addition, the Franco-Mauritians faced a threat from the Creole elites. Ultimately, in 1886, the British Governor Sir John Pope-Hennessey, in order to restore the sociopolitical equilibrium in the island, introduced a new constitution that strengthened the power of the Franco-Mauritian and Creole elites at the expense of the Indian population.

Meanwhile, the issue of indentured labor was gaining prominence in the British official circles. Since the 1870s, individuals such as Alophe de Plevitz had been carrying out extensive campaigns pleading for certain basic rights for Indians. Those campaigns gathered momentum with the visit of Mohandas (Mahatma) Gandhi (1869–1948) to Mauritius in October 1901. Under Gandhi's influence, a young Indian lawyer, Manilal Maganlal Doctor, published a newspaper—*The Hindustani*—to publicize the wretched conditions of Indian laborers. In 1910, the indenture system finally came to an end.

Throughout the first half of the twentieth century, Indians tried to gain political representation in the legislature. Their efforts in most cases were thwarted by the Franco-Mauritian and Creole elites. It was not until 1926 that two Indians were elected from rural districts to the Council of Government. In the 1930s and 1940s, however, Indian candidates suffered defeats as the system of restricted franchise operated to effectively prevent election of members of the majority community in the island.

The adoption of a new constitution in 1947, which stressed the creation of a legislative body and an advisory council to the governor, slowly moved Mauritius toward self-government. Indian independence in the same year acted as a catalyst for those demanding self-rule in Mauritius. Seewoosagur Ramgoolam of the Labour Party emerged as the most popular political figure in Mauritius. In 1964, he became the premier of Mauritius. On 12 March 1968, after 158 years of British rule, Mauritius became independent, and Ramgoolam became its first postindependence prime minister.

At the turn of the twenty-first century, Mauritius continues to be an independent sovereign member of the British Commonwealth. The governor-general of Mauritius, who represents the British monarch, is an Indo-Mauritian. Sugarcane cultivation still forms the backbone of the economy, but tourism is fast catching up. The economy is thriving, and there is very little political turmoil.

Rajshekhar Basu

Further Reading

Allen, Richard B. (1985) *Creoles, Indians, Immigrants and the Restructuring of Economy in Mauritius, 1767–1885.* Ann Arbor: Michigan University, Microfilm International.

——— (1999) *Slaves, Freedom and Indentured Labourers in Colonial Mauritius.* Cambridge, U.K.: Cambridge University Press.

Burton, Benedict. (1961) *Indians in a Plural Society: A Report on Mauritius.* London: Her Majesty's Stationery Office.

Chandrasekhar, Sripati. (1990) *The Population of Mauritius: Fact, Problem and Policy.* New Delhi: Indus Publishers.

Hazareesingh, K. (1975) *History of Indians in Mauritius.* London: Macmillan.

Simmons, Adele Smith. (1982) *Modern Mauritius: The Politics of Decolonization.* Bloomington: Indiana University Press.

MAURYAN EMPIRE (322–184 BCE). The age of the Mauryas heralded a new chapter in the history of the Indian subcontinent; the people witnessed for the first time a unified empire covering most of present-day India and Pakistan. The founder of the dynasty, Chandragupta Maurya (reigned 322–298 BCE), deposed the unpopular ruler, Dhana Nanda (reigned 334–322 BCE) of Pataliputra (now Patna), with the help of Chanakya (fourth century BCE). In 305 BCE Chandragupta Maurya defeated the Greek General Seleucus Nikator (358?–281 BCE) and became master of the trans-Indus region. Bindusara (reigned 298–273 BCE) inherited from him not only a vast empire covering the Indo-Gangetic plains of the Ganga and Indus rivers, as well as the Deccan, but also a well-organized administrative system.

The Buddhist tradition speaks about Bindusar's successor Asoka's (reigned 273–236 BCE) cruel nature in the early part of his life and holds that this cruel nature changed under the influence of Buddhism, but most scholars regard this as mere fiction. The actual coronation of Asoka took place in the year 269 BCE, and he turned his attention toward the prosperous province of Kalinga in the eastern part of India. Asoka attacked Kalinga in 261 BCE, which resulted in the large-scale killing of about one hundred thousand people including both sides. Although Kalinga became a part of the Mauryan Empire, Asoka had a change of heart and relinquished war in favor of victory by *dhamma* (righteous path/piety). Converted to Buddhism, he convened the Third Buddhist Council in 251 BCE; sent missionaries to far-off places such as Sri Lanka, Myanmar (Burma), Thailand, central Asia, and so on; granted large endowments; built monasteries; and erected commemorative pillars and eighty-four thousand stupas. Under Asoka's patronage, Buddhism spread to Southeast Asia and the Far East.

In tune with the policy of *dhamma*, Asoka insisted on high ethical standards for his subjects and set a high ideal for himself. Asokan edicts engraved on rocks and pillars throughout his empire are living testimony to the greatness of the emperor. Here was a king who was concerned for the material and moral welfare of his subjects and said, "All men are my children." Spending substantial amounts from the royal treasury, Asoka left no stone unturned for the welfare of his subjects by his benevolent measures. As a testimony to his rule, the Indian government on 26 January 1950 adopted the four-lion capital of the Asokan pillar as its national emblem, and the wheel of *dhamma* is embedded in the center of Indian national flag.

The successors of the emperor were not worthy of Asoka and the Mauryan Empire began to disintegrate. The empire officially ended in 184 BCE, after Pushyamitra Sunga (reigned 187–151 BCE) assassinated the last Mauryan ruler, Brihadratha (d. 187 BCE).

Patit Paban Mishra

See also: **Asoka**

Further Reading

Majumdar, R. C., ed. (1989) *The Age of Imperial Unity (600 BC–320 AD)*. Vol. 2. Bombay, India: Bharatiya Vidya Bhavan.

Sharma, Ram Sharan. (1977) *Ancient India*. New Delhi: NCERT.

Thapar, Romila. (1977) *A History of India*. Aylesbury, U.K.: Penguin.

MAWDUDI, ABU'L-A'LA (1903–1979), South Asian Muslim leader. Abu'l-A'la Mawdudi was the founder of the most important South Asian fundamentalist Islamic movement and a leading ideologue. Born in Hyderabad (south-central India) in 1903, he worked as a journalist before being recognized as an influential intellectual and a political leader. Before Indian independence he was opposed to the Congress Party as well as to the secularist Muslim League. Instead, he advocated the necessity of an Islamic state where *shari'a* (Islamic law), interpreted in a conservative way, would be the only source for civil, criminal, and constitutional laws. An autodidact, he contested the authority of the ulama (traditional religious scholars) by interpreting religious sources on his own, and he developed an original understanding of Islam as a complete system and the only ideological alternative to both Western liberalism and Marxism. He engaged in political activism in 1941 by creating the Jamaʿat-e-Islami and was its leader until 1972. In 1953 he was sentenced to death for sedition; the sentence was commuted to life imprisonment and later canceled. From 1956 to 1974 he traveled widely in the Middle East; he also visited Canada and the United States. In April 1979 he traveled to the United States, where he received medical treatment from one of his sons (a doctor) for kidney and heart problems. Although he died in the United States, he is buried in Pakistan.

Amélie Blom

Further Reading

Nasr, Seyyed Vali Reza. (1996) *Mawdudi and the Making of Islamic Revivalism*. New York: Oxford University Press.

Mawdudi, Sayyid Abu'l-A'la. (1st ed. 1932; English ed. 1940) *Towards Understanding Islam (Risalah-i diniyat)*. Delhi: Markazi Maktaba Islami.

———. (1965)*The Political Theory of Islam*. Lahore, Pakistan: Islamic Publications.

MAY 13 ETHNIC RIOTS—MALAYSIA The 13 May 1969 ethnic riots that broke out in Malaysia represented a milestone in the history of the young nation-state's ethnic relations since its independence from the British colonial government in 1957. Malaysia's population is multiethnic and includes a large Malay majority, which is mostly indigenous, and two relatively large minority ethnic groups—Chinese and Indians—who are descended mainly from migrants from China and India. The Chinese form a larger ethnic minority than the Indians. Ethnicity has also been politicized in independent Malaysia because each ethnic group has its own political party.

During the British colonial administration, the migrant Chinese, who had been more economically successful than either the Malays or the Indians, were largely concentrated in the urbanized and developed parts of present-day Malaysia. Most Malays and Indians lived and worked in the rural agricultural sectors. After independence, the Malay political party, the United Malay National Organization (UMNO), was more powerful than other parties, in terms of its political support by the larger Malay population and its representation in the political leadership. Tensions therefore gradually developed between the politically powerful Malays and the economically successful Chinese.

In the 1969 Malaysian national elections, the national Chinese political party, the Malayan Chinese Association (MCA), which had won the elections in 1959 and 1964, won only thirteen of the thirty-three seats it contested. The opposition Chinese parties, the Democratic Action Party (DAP) and the Gerakan Rakyat, gained 26.2 percent of the total vote and twenty-five parliamentary seats, compared with 13.5 percent garnered by the MCA. The Malay national party also suffered losses because of the popularity of its major rival, the Pan-Malaysian Islamic Party.

With the rejection of the MCA by Chinese voters, the party decided to pull out of the government, although it remained within the Alliance Party, the coalition of the national Malay, Chinese, and Indian political parties. The withdrawal of the MCA from government led to a worsening of the tensions already created by the DAP's victory parade in the capital city of Kuala Lumpur. During a counterdemonstration organized by UMNO activists on 13 May, racial violence broke out and escalated. An estimated six thousand residents in Kuala Lumpur, which was 90 percent Chinese at the time, lost their homes and properties during the riots. Hundreds of buildings in Kuala Lumpur were razed to the ground. Although the unofficial figures and nongovernmental sources put the number of people who died in the riots in the hundreds, official figures set down the death toll at 196. Three-quarters of the casualties were reportedly Chinese.

The riots and government response showed the Chinese in Malaysia the difficulty of challenging Malay dominance, given the Malay-controlled military and police forces, which in any confrontation could impose their will on any issue of concern to the Malays.

Since 1969, there has been a gradual increase in Malay dominance and the growth of a Malay-dominated state. In 1971, the New Economic Policy was launched, which aimed at eradicating poverty and putting Malays, who make up more than half the population in Malaysia, into the mainstream of Malaysia's economic life. Preferential policies have been introduced, which have set quotas for the number of Malays to be admitted to universities as well as government and private-sector employment. At first set for twenty years, the policy was extended in 1991 for another decade.

Ooi Giok-Ling

Further Reading

Ho, K. L. (1997) "Political Indigenisation and the State in Peninsular Malaysia." In *ASEAN in the Global System*, edited by H. M. Dahlan, H. Jusoh, A. Y. Hing, and J. H. Ong. Bangi, Selangor, Malaysia: Penerbit Universiti Kebangsaan Malaysia, 210–224.

Lee, K. H. (1997) "Malaysian Chinese: Seeking Identity in Wawasan 2020." In *Ethnic Chinese as Southeast Asians*, edited by L. Suryadinata. Singapore: Institute of Southeast Asian Studies, 90

Mee, W. (1998) "National Difference and Global Citizenship." In *Southeast Asian Identities—Culture and the Politics of Representation in Indonesia, Malaysia, Singapore, and Thailand*, edited by J. S. Kahn. Singapore: Institute of Southeast Asian Studies, 227–259.

Pan, L., ed. (1998) *The Encyclopedia of the Chinese Overseas.* Singapore: Chinese Heritage Centre.

MAY FOURTH MOVEMENT

During the 1910s and early 1920s, China was plagued by the twin forces of warlordism and imperialism. Military commanders had seized control over various sections of China, resulting in incessant fighting. Taking advantage of this situation, numerous foreign powers carved out spheres of influence up and down China's coast. Despite this chaotic environment, this period—known either as the May Fourth era or the New Culture era—was an exciting and vibrant time for Chinese intellectuals. Individuals of this time called for cultural rejuvenation and the development of a more modern worldview. Without these changes, they warned, China would not free itself from the oppressive forces of warlordism or imperialism or both. Between 1915 and 1923, "new culture" advocates from various groups scrutinized and derided many of China's literary, philosophical, and social traditions.

The Beginning of the May Fourth Era

Many scholars suggest that the May Fourth era started with the 1915 publication of the journal *Xin qingnian* (New Youth). Edited by Chen Duxiu (1879–1942), the first issue of *Xin qingnian* called on its readers to be progressive, cosmopolitan, utilitarian, and scientific. In short, Chen asked the youth of China to overthrow the old elements of society and to bring about a national awakening. Confucianism, the preferred symbol of Chinese traditionalism, was a frequent target of the journal. With its emphasis on filial piety, ritualism, hierarchy, and orthodoxy, Confucianism was seen as antimodern and regressive. Within a few months, *Xin qingnian* became a widely read and influential publication among China's student population.

Peking University as a Center of Liberalism

In 1917, Chen was made dean of the School of Letters at Peking (Beijing) University, and the academy quickly became the focal point of what was to be the May Fourth Movement. Cai Yuanpei (1867–1940), the university president, was committed to making the school a center of academic freedom and intellectual liberalism. By the late 1910s, Peking University was a hotbed of intellectual debate involving students, faculty, and independent writers.

In addition to Chen, Cai also brought Hu Shi (1891–1962), a young literature professor, to the campus. Educated in the United States, Hu believed that literature was at the heart of China's cultural problems. With its emphasis on specialized norms, obscure vocabulary, and terse diction, the classical written language was inaccessible to all but the most educated. Hu suggested that the solution was to write in the vernacular, enabling those with a more rudimentary education to participate in China's world of letters. In the pages of *Xin qingnian*, Hu argued that writers should avoid the use of classical allusions, discard stale literary phrases, and quit imitating the ancients. Instead, he suggested that writers be true to their own feelings. Only then would they produce something with meaning and substance. This emphasis on vernacular literature, or *baihua*, led to a greater democratization of China's literary world.

Though Hu advocated *baihua* literature, its greatest practitioner was Lu Xun (1881–1936). Lu Xun was a frequent contributor to *Xin qingnian*, writing short stories designed to jolt the reading public out of its cultural complacency. One of his better-known stories of this period is "*Kuangren riji*" ("Diary of a Madman"). In the story, the protagonist repeatedly sees the words "eat people" inscribed in the margins of classical Confucian texts. Convinced that he is living in a cannibalistic society, he becomes mad with suspicion. By the end of the story, Lu Xun has satirically demonstrated that the Confucian social order is based, figuratively if not literally, on cannibalism. By shocking his readers with such imagery, Lu Xun hoped to awaken them to the need for cultural renewal.

As with literature, intellectuals of the time called for democratization in the political arena. Democracy and science, Chen argued in the pages of *Xin qingnian*, formed the foundation of modern society. Many of China's backward practices, he claimed, could be eliminated or reformed with the assistance of De Xiansheng ("Mr. Democracy") and Sai Xiansheng ("Mr. Science"). By 1919, these and a handful of other eclectic catchphrases circulated around Peking University and, by way of *Xin qingnian*, throughout China's intellectual communities.

The May Fourth Movement and the 1919 Demonstrations

While it is difficult to mark definitively the beginning of the May Fourth era, its chronological focal point is much more precise. The May Fourth Movement refers, in its most limited sense, to the demonstrations of 4 May 1919. On that day, throngs of irate students, educators, and urban workers converged on Beijing's Tiananmen Square to protest the Paris Peace Conference ending World War I. Years earlier, in August 1914, Japan had declared war on Germany and had occupied all German-held territories in China. Since China also participated in the war against Germany, many believed China would regain control over the properties following the war. Bolstered by their faith in self-determination as championed by Woodrow Wilson, the Chinese delegates attending the conference were confident the European powers would recognize the validity of their claims. Instead, Japan's delegates unveiled a handful of treaties signed by Britain, France, and Italy recognizing Japan's demands in China.

The public reaction to the news was swift and powerful. Led by students of Peking University, concerned individuals from throughout the Beijing area congregated to denounce Japan's underhanded and aggressive maneuvers. They also demanded that China's representatives reject the resulting treaty. The crowd, which eventually numbered in the thousands, marched through the streets of Beijing until government troops restored order. Although the whole affair lasted only a few hours, historians consider this May Fourth event vitally important in the development of modern Chinese nationalism.

Despite the protesters' actions in Beijing, the peace conference concluded, and Japan retained control over the Chinese territory (though the Chinese delegation refused to sign the treaty). The incident, however, was far from insignificant. In the days after 4 May, similar protests erupted throughout China. Furthermore, many intellectuals intensified their demands for "national salvation" through cultural reform. In many ways, the May Fourth protest symbolized the concerns of the new culture advocates, and consequently the intellectual movement that swept through China between 1915 and 1923 is often referred to as the May Fourth movement.

The Aftermath of May Fourth and the Rise of Communism

In the years after 1919, the May Fourth movement became increasingly ideological. Advocates of anarchism, socialism, syndicalism, and even pragmatism competed in the marketplace of ideas. It was also during this time that the Chinese Communist Party was formed. Organized in Shanghai during summer 1921, the Communist Party embraced the antiestablishment ideals of the May Fourth movement. Since that time, official Communist histories have portrayed the May Fourth era as a period of great patriotic fervor, the turning point between an old, bourgeois democracy and a new, proletarian democracy. Not surprisingly, 4 May is still a national holiday, and May Fourth intellectuals such as Lu Xun are considered patriotic heroes.

By the mid-1920s, China's intellectual debates had become more political and less cultural. The iconoclasm of the earlier years was replaced by new orthodoxies, as political organizations expected their members to conform to the official party line. For this reason, most historians suggest that 1923 marks the approximate end of the May Fourth era. Others, however, contend that the advocates of the movement remained active well beyond 1923. Regardless of the outcome of such debates, the May Fourth movement, with its emphasis on democracy, science, and antitraditionalism, has cast a long shadow over twentieth-century Chinese history.

David L. Kenley

Further Reading

Chow Tse-tsung. (1960) *The May Fourth Movement: Intellectual Revolution in Modern China*. Cambridge, MA: Harvard University Press.

Dirlik, Arif. (1986) "Ideology and Organization in the May Fourth Movement: Some Problems in the Intellectual Historiography of the May Fourth Period." *Republican China* 12, 1 (November): 3–19.

Schwarcz, Vera. (1986) *The Chinese Enlightenment: Intellectuals and the Legacy of the May Fourth Movement of 1919*. Berkeley and Los Angeles: University of California Press.

Schwartz, Benjamin, ed. (1972) *Reflections on the May Fourth Movement: A Symposium*. Cambridge, MA: Harvard University Press.

MAZAR-E SHARIF

(2002 est. pop. 240,000). Mazar-e Sharif is a major city in northern Afghanistan, located about 320 kilometers northwest of the capital city of Kabul. The city was founded by pilgrims when the tomb of Ali, the brother-in-law of the Prophet Muhammad and an important figure for Shi'ite Muslims, was discovered in 1480. The tomb, which today dominates the skyline, had been buried by the residents of the Greco-Bactrian town of Balkh in 1220 to hide it from Genghis Khan's rampaging armies, and then forgotten. After the establishment of the community, pilgrimages by Shi'ite Muslims to the tomb for the New Year's celebration of Nao Roc and a brisk trade in the melons, high quality cotton, and grains grown in the fertile river plains enabled Mazar-e Sharif to become the region's largest city. In 1852 it was consolidated as part of the Afghan state, controlled at that time by the British.

Mazar-e Sharif's proximity to the border of Uzbekistan and large Uzbek minority made it irresistible to Soviet forces during the Soviet-Afghan conflict of 1979–1989. The Soviets established a military command there during their ill-fated invasion in 1979. Thousands were killed when the Taliban took control of the rebel city in 1998. In November 2001 Mazar-e Sharif was retaken by Northern Alliance troops, providing a beachhead for U.S. troops battling the Taliban.

James B. McGirk

Further Reading

Afghan-Info. (2002) "City of Mazar-i-Sharif Home." Retrieved 9 March 2002, from: http://www.afghan-info.com/mazar.htm.

Ewans, Martin (2002) *Afghanistan: A Short History of its People and Politics*. New York: HarperCollins.

Sabawoon.com. (2002) "Afganapedia." Retrieved 9 March 2002, from: http://www.sabawoon.com/afghanpedia/City.Mazar-e-Sharif.htm.

Shah, Sirdah Ikbal Ali. (2002) *Afghanistan of the Afghans*. New Delhi: Bahvana Books.

Goodman, Larry P. (2002) *Afghanistan's Endless Rule*. Seattle: University of Washington Press.

MEASUREMENT SYSTEMS

Metrology, the science of measurement, evaluates how people assess quantities. People throughout Asia devised indigenous measurement systems or adopted foreign measurement units to describe quantities representing the

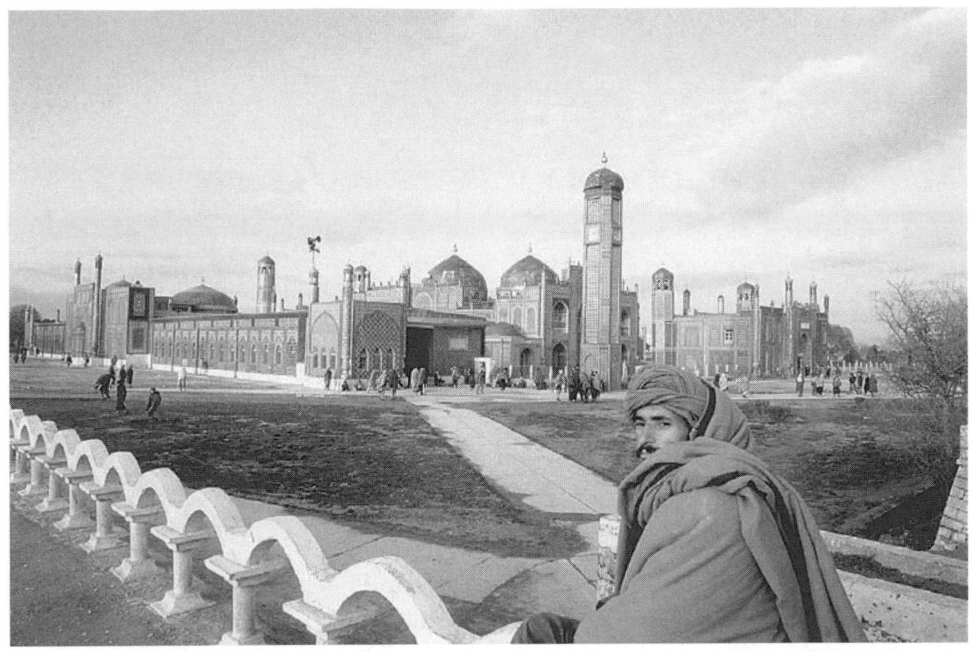

The Mazar-e Sharif mosque, purported to be the burial place of Ali, son-in-law of the Prophet Muhammad. (BACI/CORBIS)

physical size, capacities, or proportion of materials or areas. Precise, reliable measurements are crucial for governmental, legal, professional, domestic, and public needs; they ensure accurate communications and quality control.

In Asian countries, various units were developed to describe length, width, distance, circumference, and thickness. Units signify the mass, weight, volume, and density of solids and liquids. Movement is measured by velocity, force, and pressure. Energy is depicted by power units. Time, temperature, and humidity measurements provide information about duration and climate. The World Meteorological Organization oversees pollution-measurement systems to evaluate Asian environmental conditions.

Traditional Units

Early Asians measured portions, magnitudes, and distances based on the adult male body, such as limb and digit lengths or the area one person could travel or work in one day. The cubit represented the measurement from the middle fingertip to the elbow, and the palm signified the width of an outstretched hand. These measurements were imprecise because of the variation of individuals' size, speed, and endurance. Traders often encountered difficulties because of cultural measurement differences, varying terms, and changing definitions for units. The catty, a unit that measured tea and rice, had numerous sizes throughout Asia.

The ancient Chinese emperors Qin Shi Huangdi (c. 259–210 BCE) and Wang Mang (45 BCE–23 CE) initiated measurement-standardization reform. Some units became obsolete as new measurements were created. Over time, most Asian countries converted local units in favor of modern measurement systems. Many Asians, however, continue to refer to traditional measurement units unique to their geographical regions.

In Singapore, Hong Kong, India, and the Philippines, both traditional *(man* and *tola)* and British (feet-pound system) units are routinely used in many herbal and pawn markets and in property management. Rural Indonesians often use traditional measurements during grain harvests. Such Korean units as *ri* (length), *kun* (weight), *mal* (volume), and *pyong* (area) are retained. Malaysian jewelry shops rely on traditional units, and buildings are measured by feet. In modern Thailand, weight is sometimes referred to by *picul* and land area as amount of *rai.*

Asian time measurements differ from other countries. In Afghanistan, India, Myanmar (Burma), Iran, French Polynesia, and Sri Lanka, time is offset by half-hour increments from other areas; thus when it is 10:30 a.m. in Thailand, it is 8 a.m. in Afghanistan. Sources do not list any time measurement units unique to Asia except that the *kalpa*, in the Hindu calendar, equals about 4.32 billion years. Also, Asian calendars are often measured by periods of time based on the reigns of emperors or leaders. Chinese years have

THE COMPLEXITY OF MEASURES

The following description of weights used in Afghanistan in the early twentieth century indicates just how complicated the issue was across much of Asia. As is the case here, there often was no central standard (or the standard was one imposed by a colonial government), and each region or city had its own system.

> At Kabul: 16 *khurds* = 1 *charak*; 4 *charaks* = 1 seer (7 seers 13 ½ chittacks of British Indian weight); 6 seers = 1 *man*; 10 *mans* = 1 *kharwar* (15 maunds 27 ½ seers, British).
>
> At Kandahar: 20 *miskals* = 1 seer (8 5/8 *tolas* of British Indian weight); 40 seers = 1 *man* (4 seers 25 *tolas*, British); 100 *mans* = 1 *kharwar* (10 maunds 31 seers 10 *tolas*, British).
>
> The weights used in Herat province are practically the same as at Kandahar. In Afghan-Turkistan, Kabul weights are in common use as far as Haibak: beyond that place local weights are used, which vary greatly in different districts. Those of Mazar-I-Sharif are in most general use. They are: 1 Mazar Seer = 1¾ Kabuli seers (14 British seers); 16 seers = 1 Mazar *man* (5 maunds 24 seers, British); 3 *mans* = *1* Mazar *kharwar* (16 maunds 32 seers, British).
>
> *Source: Imperial Gazetteer of India: Afghanistan and Nepal. (1908)* Calcutta: Superintendent of Government Printing, 41–42.

names that are used in sixty-year cycles. These names have a celestial stem such as *bing* and a terrestrial branch, represented by types of animals such as the tiger, rat, dragon, and so forth.

Asian calendars reflect different measuring systems to designate year numbers, based on religious beliefs and varying annual cycles. Asian years are sometimes measured as tropical or sidereal, based on seasonal or celestial cycles. Seasons divide the year into three or fewer phases according to weather patterns of rain and heat. The dates of holidays such as Ramadan (the Islamic month of fasting), and Loy Krathong (the Thai flower boat festival) are variable because they depend on time measurement based on moon phases and periods of darkness and daylight.

The Metric System

During the twentieth century, Asian countries adopted the metric system, which aided the achievement of global measurement standardization, especially in scientific endeavors, regardless of language and cultural differences. The Philippines, Afghanistan, and Cambodia began converting in the early twentieth century. By mid-century, Iran, Iraq, Turkey, Thailand, Indonesia, and Korea became metric. From the 1950s to the 1970s, Taiwan, India, Japan, Laos, Vietnam, Pakistan, and Singapore accepted the metric system. Myanmar is the only Asian country that has not officially adopted the metric system. The International Bureau of Weights and Measures coordinates traditional measurement systems unique to countries and cultures and national metrology institutes with international metrology standards.

Most Asian countries accept fundamental metric units including kilograms (mass), seconds (time), liters (volume), Celsius (temperature), and amperes (electromagnetic), from which other metric units were derived. Greek and Latin prefixes indicate larger and smaller quantities, which have been incorporated in the international system of units (SI) adopted in 1960 by the General Conference of Weights and Measures. All measurements are interrelated with seven base SI units: meter, kilogram, second, ampere, kelvin, candela, and mol. Because 99 percent of the world is metric, the metric system facilitates competitive trade between countries that might refuse to import goods that are not issued in metric dimensions and that are incompatible with other devices, machinery, and tools.

The CGS system used in parts of Asia refers to the measurement of small quantities by centimeters, grams, and seconds.

In 1875, a Meter Convention was held, and the Ottoman empire was one of the participants, but Turkey did not pursue metrification until a 1931 law of weights and measures initiated gradual implementation. By 1992, TUBITAK, the Scientific and Technical Research Council of Turkey, established the National Metrology Institute.

A 1908 Chinese imperial law recommended that traditional measures be redefined according to the metric system. Because metric terms consisted of unfamiliar words and sounds, the Chinese were reluctant to accept that system. In 1959, the metric reform of the People's Republic of China retained traditional unit names and adjusted them to metric dimensions.

An 1891 Japanese law recognized the *shaku* and *kan* as traditional length and mass measurement units, respectively, and by 1909 three measurement systems—traditional, British, and metric—were used. During the 1920s, legislation implemented plans for a single metric system. Public resistance, World War II, and the Allied occupation delayed efforts until a 1958 law. By 1981, Japan was completely metric with the exception of sake bottles, which were assessed by a traditional unit, and Japanese-style houses, which are still described by traditional dimensions.

Elizabeth D. Schafer

Further Reading

Campbell, Paul D. Q. (1995) *An Introduction to Measuration and Calibration.* New York: Industrial Press.

Drazil, J. V. (1983) *Quantities and Units of Measurement: A Dictionary and Handbook.* London: Mansell; Wiesbaden, Germany: Oscar Brandstetter Verlag.

Ellis, Keith. (1973) *Man and Measurement.* London: Priory Press.

ISO Information Centre, comp. (1979) *Units of Measurement: Handbook of International Standards for Units of Measurement.* ISO Standards Handbook 2. Geneva: International Organization for Standardization.

Johnston, William D. (1975) *For Good Measure: A Complete Compendium of International Weights and Measures.* New York: Holt, Rinehart and Winston.

Klein, H. Arthur. (1974) *The World of Measurements: Masterpieces, Mysteries, and Muddles of Metrology.* New York: Simon and Schuster.

Kula, Witold. (1986) *Measures and Men.* Trans. by R. Szreter. Princeton, NJ: Princeton University Press.

Rossini, Frederick D. (1974) *Fundamental Measures and Constants for Science and Technology.* Cleveland, OH: CRC Press.

United Nations Economic Commission for Asia and the Far East. (1955) *Glossary of Commodity Terms Including Currencies, Weights, and Measures Used in Certain Countries of Asia and the Far East, Prepared by the Secretariat.* Bangkok, Thailand: United Nations Department of Economic Affairs.

Young, Richard A., and Thomas J. Glover. (1996) *Measure for Measure.* Littleton, CO: Blue Willow.

MECHAI VIRAVAIDYA (b. 1941), Thai contraceptive advocate. Known as the Condom King, Mechai (meaning "victory" and later "condom" in Thai) Viravaidya is the son of physicians, his father a Thai and his mother a Scot. Born in 1941, he spent much of his early life studying in Australia. Upon his return to Thailand, Mechai worked for the National Economic Development Board, which gave him a firsthand view of serious rural poverty.

Mechai viewed Thailand's rapid population growth and pronatalist policies as a major obstacle to the nation's development. During the period 1974–1980, he launched one of the world's most dynamic and creative campaigns to promote contraceptive usage, utilizing a rice-roots approach and transforming the condom into an acceptable, clean, healthful product. Key to his campaign was the establishment of the Population and Development Association (PDA), which grew dramatically and became Thailand's largest and most influential nongovernmental organization.

In 1989, Mechai took on a new challenge: to convince the Thai government to break its silence on an emerging AIDS problem of potentially epidemic dimensions. Subsequently Mechai and PDA became a leader in promoting extensive AIDS education in Thailand.

Mechai has served in many other important capacities, including deputy minister of industry, government spokesman, governor of the Provincial Water Works, chair of the Telephone Organization of Thailand, and most recently as chairman of the troubled Krung Thai Bank. In 2000, Mechai was elected to the Senate. In recognition of his public service, Mechai in 1994 received the Magsaysay Award, considered to be the Nobel Prize of Asia, and *Asiaweek* named Mechai as one of the twenty great Asians for the period 1975–1995.

Gerald W. Fry

Further Reading

D'Agnes, Thomas. (2001) *From Condoms to Cabbages: An Authorized Biography of Mechai Viravaidya.* Bangkok, Thailand: Post Books.

MEDAN (2000 est. pop. 2 million) Medan is the largest city in Sumatra, which is part of the Republic of Indonesia, and is among the larger cities in Indonesia. The city is the capital of the province of North Sumatra, as well as a leading port. Its location makes it the gateway and entry point to this part of northern Sumatra from neighboring countries such as Malaysia and Singapore. Described as congested and crowded, Medan has proved to be less popular as a tourist destination than Lake Toba, which is located near the city.

The word *medan* means "battleground," and the city was the site of wars waged between the sultans of Deli and Aceh. Medan is located on the Deli Plain, and oral traditions and local writings claim that it was first ruled by generals who came from Delhi in India. The city was founded by Sultan Mahmud Perdasa Ahmad in the seventeenth century.

Beginning with a number of small villages *(kampung)* located in marshy lowlands, the city has thrived mainly because of its location on the northeast Deli coastal area, which fronted a major shipping route in the region. The coastal swamp area developed into a major plantation district, given the hot, humid climate and the fertility of the area.

The Dutch subdued the Deli Sultanate in 1872. In 1886, the Dutch colonial administration made Medan the capital of the northern Sumatra region. The success of enterprises like Deli Tobacco contributed to the city's continuing growth, and it became incorporated as a municipality in 1909.

Medan is a business and industrial city rather than a cultural capital. With its long-standing history as a port and trading center, it has developed into a major banking and commercial capital. Many of the region's exports of petroleum and other agricultural produce, including rubber, coffee, and tobacco, pass through the port of Belawan, which lies north of Medan. The location of the city and business opportunities in Medan have attracted Indonesians of all ethnic backgrounds. The Chinese control much of the city's commerce, but there are also Javanese, Sikhs, Acehnese, Minangkabaus, and Malays, as well as Christian and Islamic Batak groups. The city is actually the hub of the Batak people (an Indonesian people not under Dutch control until the mid-nineteenth century). Essentially, some 40 percent of the city's population is not Muslim.

Due to its historical background as a Dutch colonial center, the city has old colonial buildings and living quarters in what is known as the European Town. There is also a Chinatown, but the majority of people live in crowded residential areas.

Ooi Giok Ling

Further Reading

Dalton, Bill. (1988) *Indonesia Handbook*. Chico, CA: Moon Publications.

The Grand Mosque in Medan in 1996. (STEPHEN G. DONALDSON PHOTOGRAPHY)

de Jongh, R. C. (1973) *Indonesia—Yesterday and Today.* Sydney: Ian Novak.

Oey, Eric. (1987) *Insight Guides—Indonesia.* Hong Kong: Apa Productions.

Taylor, Maurice, with the Trailfinders. (1976) *Island Hopping through the Indonesian Archipelago.* London: Wilton House Gentry.

MEDIA

MEDIA The media of mass communication, usually called "mass media" or "media," include newspapers, magazines, books, film, radio, television, recorded music, and the Internet. Mass communication usually involves the production of content (such as information, entertainment, or art) by an institution (such as a radio station or a publishing enterprise); this content is transmitted to large, scattered, and heterogeneous "mass" audiences who potentially may be interested in receiving it. Unlike much interpersonal communication, which is face-to-face and unfiltered, this type of communication is mediated by complex technologies of recording (for example, film or television cameras), transmitting (radio transmitters, satellites, computers), and receiving (radio sets, satellite dishes). In this way, the contemporary media are complex, technology-based economic, political, cultural, social, and ideological institutions.

Historical Context

Asia is the birthplace of the world's most important communication revolutions, including writing as well as the mechanization of writing, i.e., printing. Writing emerged some six thousand years ago in the civilization of Sumer in western Asia, while printing, paper, and ink were invented in China and Korea in the first half of the second millennium CE. Although printed books first appeared as early as the ninth century in China, the invention of printing did not immediately create mass media such as newspapers and magazines. This was due less to the nonalphabetic nature of Chinese writing than to the social and economic system of feudalism, which thrived in the absence of mass literacy.

With the rise of capitalism in Europe, the West replaced Asia as the leader in the development of communication technologies. The modern media appeared after Johannes Gutenberg printed the first book around 1455 in Germany. In contrast to East Asia, printing in Western Europe facilitated the advent of capitalist economic relations, and, within the next two centuries, contributed to the intellectual and social movement known as the Enlightenment, often seen as the turning point in the rise of modern Western society and democracy.

Colonialism and Modernization

Asia began its modern media under conditions of European colonization, when missionaries, administrators, and business interests launched commercial printing presses. The first newspapers, in European and Asian languages, appeared in the latter part of the eighteenth century and visibly expanded throughout the nineteenth. The print media, especially periodicals, soon turned into sites of rhetorical struggle between, among others, colonial powers and local independence movements, modernity and tradition, socialism and nationalism, and patriarchal power and women's movements.

Twentieth-century products of the West's Industrial Revolution, the post-print media, i.e., recorded music (gramophones), motion pictures, and radio, all arrived in Asia during colonial times. The state and private institutions adopted these media quickly, though unevenly. India emerged as one of the world's most productive centers of filmmaking, while many Asian nations did not produce any movies until the 1960s. Unlike recorded music and film, radio was monopolized by the state (under colonial rule and in the nascent independent states) for nation building and external broadcasting purposes.

Asia's media environment is, more than on any other continent, distinguished by uneven and conflicting trends of development and extreme diversity. Asia has two-thirds of the planet's population—at about 3 billion, the world's largest potential audience. It has the largest number of daily newspapers (3,536 out of the world figure of 8,896 in 1994), radio receivers (696 out of 2,183 million in 1996), and television receivers (652 out of 1,361 million in 1996). In terms of the diffusion of media, however, Asia is below the world average and lags markedly behind other continents, excepting Africa. For instance, the circulation of daily papers per thousand inhabitants in 1994 was 63—lower than 96 for the world, and much lower than 135 for America, 278 for Europe, and 214 for Oceania; however, it is higher than Africa's 17. In broadcast media, the number of television receivers per thousand inhabitants in 1996 was 187, which is considerably lower than 236 for the world, 431 for America, 442 for Europe, 421 for Oceania, but, again, higher than 50 for Africa.

The discrepancy between Asia's potential audience, the largest in the world, and its actual audience, proportionately the smallest after Africa, can be explained by the persistence of poverty, illiteracy, and state control of the media. The percentage of illiterate adults (fifteen years and over) was 74.3 in Pakistan (1981), 70.8 in Bangladesh (1981), 59.2 in India (1981), 22.2 in China (1990), and 18.5 in Indonesia (1990). In India, advanced computer and space industries coexist with high illiteracy rates and the continuing phenomena of serfdom and even slavery. By contrast, Japan has one of the world's most developed media and communication technologies markets, full literacy, and extensive press freedoms, and Hong Kong is known as the "advertising capital" of Asia.

New Media

At the beginning of the twenty-first century, the unceasing revolution in communication technologies and the globalization of media markets is reshaping Asian societies. The Internet is blurring the borders that divided the rather distinct media of the past, creating media convergence—a "hypermedia," "multimedia," or "post–mass media" era. This involves the production, transmission, and reception of diverse media content—film, radio, television, newspapers, magazines, and books—through the single medium of the Internet and the rise of multichannel satellite and cable television. Equally important is the increasing privatization of the media or "cultural industries" market and open-door policies encouraged by the West, the World Trade Organization, the World Bank, and the International Monetary Fund. Many Asian states have resisted the introduction of the Internet and continue to restrict citizens' access to the medium. By 1999, however, Saudi Arabia, staunchly opposed to freedom of the press, had allowed controlled access to the Internet.

Language is an indispensable component of the life of media. Linguistically and culturally, Asia is the most diverse continent. It is the site of the world's oldest and most important classical languages and literatures (Chinese, Sanskrit, Arabic, and Persian) and the homeland of half of the twelve largest languages (Mandarin, Hindi, Arabic, Bengali, Japanese, and Malay-Indonesian). Still, it offers the most colorful linguistic map, with 2,165 (32 percent) of the world's 6,703 languages in 1996. The densely media-penetrated urban cultures of Japan, Hong Kong, and Taiwan coexist with the mosaic of surviving oral cultures of tribal and rural communities in other parts of the continent. The new electronic media intervene in this environment more intensively and differently than print media and allow extensive cultural and linguistic interaction. Satellite television, for instance, delivers round-the-clock programming in English and the major languages of the continent, while smaller languages, once excluded, increasingly find access to radio and television broadcasting through cable and the Internet. English-language (especially American) content was more widely disseminated at the turn of the century, but Asia's media culture has experienced both globalization and localization, homogenization and heterogenization.

Contemporary Asian economies, like their Western counterparts, are increasingly characterized as "information" or "knowledge" economies. Privately owned media are major players in the shift in economic emphasis from agriculture and industry to information. These media produce and deliver entertainment and information and by doing so create audiences, which are sold profitably to advertisers. Not surprisingly, there has been a global scramble for Asia's potentially lucrative media market. However, precapitalist relations still persist in parts of the continent, where the communications infrastructure remains underdeveloped. For instance, the number of telephone lines per hundred people in the mid-1990s was 1.1 in India and 2.9 in China, compared with the high "teledensity" of the "tiger economies" of Hong Kong (54.0), Korea (39.7), Singapore (47.3), and Taiwan (40.0). At the same time, the proliferation of pirate media and software throughout Asia has undermined the idea of copyright and intellectual property, which are central to the functioning of information economies. Some Asian states, including socialist China, Vietnam, and Laos, have promoted what are billed as free-market economic reforms, and the telecommunications and media markets were growing fast by the turn of the century. However, the gulf between "information-rich" and "information-poor" regions and countries seems to persist, if not grow, in spite of promises of prosperity generated by the information superhighway. In fact, earlier, in the 1950s, Western economists had optimistically assigned the media a prominent role in the modernization of the continent's underdeveloped economies.

The media are active participants in the political life of Asia; they have played important roles in democratic and socialist revolutions (e.g., Iran in 1906–1911 and 1977–1979; Turkey in 1908; China in 1911, 1919, and 1949; and the Philippines in 1986). By the late 1990s, many dictatorial states had initiated economic liberalization but were reluctant to tolerate media freedoms. From Korea and Singapore to Turkey and Iran, states engage in widespread censorship and commit violence against the media. However, a marginalized majority, including women, labor, rural communities, nonstate nations, ethnic, linguistic, and religious minorities, disabled people, and social movements continue to engage in democratization struggles by creating alternative, usually small-scale, media. As in the past, though much more intensively, Asia's media remain a site of struggle among the globalizing market, states, and citizens.

Amir Hassanpour

Further Reading

Ayalon, Ami. (1995) *The Press in the Arab Middle East: A History*. New York: Oxford University Press.

Boyd, Douglas. (1999) *Broadcasting in the Arab World: A Survey of the Electronic Media in the Middle East*. 3d ed. Ames: Iowa State University Press.

Emirates Center for Strategic Studies and Outreach. (1998) *The Information Revolution and the Arab World: Its Impact on State and Society*. Abu Dhabi, United Arab Emirates: Emirates Center for Strategic Studies and Outreach.

International Telecommunication Union (ITU). (1995) *World Telecommunication Development Report*. Geneva: ITU.

Sreberny-Mohammadi, Annabelle, and Ali Mohammadi. (1994) *Small Media, Big Revolution: Communication, Culture, and the Iranian Revolution*. Minneapolis: University of Minnesota Press.

United Nations Educational, Scientific and Cultural Organization (UNESCO). (1998) *Statistical Yearbook 1998*. Lanham, MD: UNESCO Publishing and Bernan Press.

MEDIA—CENTRAL ASIA The first independent television and radio stations in the five former Soviet republics in Central Asia—Kazakhstan, Kyrgyzstan, Tajikistan, Turkmenistan, and Uzbekistan—appeared as early as 1991. Since their independence in the early 1990s, these nations have developed a market for independent media in contrast to the state-owned media outlets of Soviet times, which remain a major part of the media even today. Improvements in civil society and a higher demand for information after the decline of the Soviet Union led to the founding of the first independent television and radio stations, but economic hardships and governmental pressure have so far prevented the independent media from flourishing. During the late 1990s, most leaders of the Central Asian nations frequently cracked down on the media and had a tendency toward authoritarian rule to preserve their power and undermine democratic changes.

The Media in Central Asia

Television is the most important source of information for the population of Central Asia. The majority of the inhabitants receive Moscow-based stations as well as the government stations of the respective nations. Television-set ownership was high during Soviet times and has remained so ever since. Radio programming focuses more on entertainment through music than on information and therefore does not play a predominant role in the opinion-building process. Newspapers are important in the capitals and in regional centers, but their influence sharply decreases in rural areas due to the lack of a functioning infrastructure.

Countries with Partly Free Media

Although all five Central Asian nations were exposed to the same Soviet media before the collapse of the USSR, they developed in different directions in the 1990s. The most democratic nation was Kyrgyzstan under President Askar Akaev (b. 1944). As the first former Soviet republic in Central Asia to declare independence in 1991, the mountainous nation soon became a member of both the United Nations and the International Monetary Fund, thus officially joining the global community as an independent nation. Freedom of the press is guaranteed in the constitution of Kyrgyzstan, which was adopted in May 1993. The early 1990s saw an increasing number of independent media outlets, and today all seven regions of Kyrgyzstan receive information from independent television, radio stations, or both. In 1999 and especially in 2000, however, the Kyrgyz authorities started to crack down on the independent media; this campaign reached a climax during the parliamentary and presidential elections in 2000. The Vienna-based Organization for Security and Cooperation in Europe, the largest regional security organization in the world with fifty-five participating states from Europe, Central Asia, and North America, stated in its election report that the Kyrgyz government had tried to limit coverage of opposition candidates during the election campaign by pressuring independent media and that the state media presented biased coverage of incumbents.

The Kazakh media were similarly open-minded during the early 1990s, and they remain the most professional in the whole of Central Asia. While there were only a limited number of private media outlets in Kazakhstan right after the country's independence, there are now more than seventy nongovernmental television and radio stations and more than one hundred newspapers, most of which are based in regional capitals. However, beginning in 1996, the government of Kazakhstan began placing increasingly strict regulations on media access and use. In 1999, Kazakhstan passed a law that restricts the formation and activities of television and radio stations and newspapers. A media holding led by the eldest daughter of President Nursultan Nazarbaev (b. 1940), Dariga Nazarbaeva (b. 1963), was founded in the mid-1990s and now controls a number of television and radio stations, newspapers, and production studios.

The situation of the media in Tajikistan is marked by a severe economic crisis and the repercussions of the civil war that took place in the nation in the mid-1990s. Between 1994 and 1996, more than forty journalists were killed in connection with their professional duties. What makes the situation even more complicated is that although the Tajik government had made a commitment to freedom of speech and of the media, it was nevertheless responsible for murdering journalists between 1994 and 1996. More than twenty media outlets were closed during this time, and journalists were forced into exile. Some have still not returned, fearing persecution by the authorities in Dushanbe, Tajikistan's capital. The consequence of these incidents is a high degree of self-censorship among journalists in Tajikistan. The absence of daily newspapers in the whole nation is just one indicator of the economic and political problems that have led to a stagnation of media development in Tajikistan.

Nations with Media under Direct Censorship

The Uzbek media suffer under direct censorship that has not changed very much since Soviet times. Censors read every item, even obituaries, in all the Uzbek newspapers and may delete whatever they choose. Journalists are frequently brought to court and heavily fined; others leave the country to avoid being jailed. The Uzbek government has almost full control over the media, especially in the capital of Tashkent. There are a number of independent broadcast outlets and print media, but their influence on public opinion is very small.

The situation of the media in neighboring Turkmenistan is even worse. There are no independent media outlets, and virtually all information is filtered through the authorities in Ashgabat, Turkmenistan's capital. President Saparmurat Turkmenbashi (b. 1940) controls the nation with an iron fist and has put harsh restrictions even on access to the Internet. The three state-owned television channels are little more than state propaganda tools and rarely show anything but pictures of the president and the Turkmen countryside. Satellite dishes are still available in the capital, but experts expect the government to restrict their sale soon as well. The population of Turkmenistan is suffering under a serious information blackout, and there are no signs of a positive change in sight.

Chris Schuepp

Further Reading

Eurasianet. "Turkmenistan Media Links." Retrieved 8 April 2002, from: http://www.eurasianet.org/resource/turkmenistan/links/media.shtml.

Loersch, Andre. (2000) "Cimera." Retrieved 7 April 2002, from: www.cimera.org/files/reports/Media_Report_Tajik2000.pdf.

Lotus, Adele. (2001) "The 'Sound of Silence.' " In *Dangerous Assignments: Covering the Global Press Freedom Struggle*, edited by Richard McGill Murphy. Retrieved 7 April 2002, from: http://www.cpj.org/dangerous/2001/uzbek/uzbek.html.

Organization for Security and Cooperation in Europe. (2000) "Kyrgyz Republic: Presidential Elections: OSCE/ODIHR Final Report." Retrieved 7 April 2002, from: http://www.osce.org/odihr/documents/reports/election_reports/kg/kgz2000fin.pdf.

Sigal, Ivan. (1998) "Survey of Non-Governmental Kazakhstani Electronic Media." *Internews Network*. Retrieved 7 April 2002, from http://www.internews.ru/report/kaztv/.

MEDIA—CHINA

MEDIA—CHINA The media play a pivotal role in Chinese society. Since reform and opening began in 1978, the media have evolved from a tool of Communist Party propaganda to a market-oriented vehicle for advertising. The effect on society has been to stimulate the desire for conspicuous consumption necessary to goad people into working hard to make the money necessary to enjoy the fruits of material plenty. At the same time, many Chinese critics charge that for these same reasons the media have contributed to spiritual pollution and the debasing of people's value systems. The critics hope that the media will continue to secure greater freedom from state control but that they will also act more responsibly in selecting content.

The change in Chinese media from the Maoist period (1949–1976) is striking. Only a few thousand people owned television sets in 1976, but today almost every household has at least one set. Under Mao Zedong (1893–1976), all public communication was—in principle, at least—centralized under the control of the Communist Party's Central Propaganda Department (CPD) in Beijing. The media's responsibility was to relay the CPD's heavily politicized news and cultural programs throughout the system, down to the village level, where public loudspeakers conveyed the state's message to almost every Chinese citizen. The content of the media under Mao was extremely staid. Most of it consisted of extraordinarily distorted Communist "news" and sanitized revolutionary films and music.

Chinese Media in the Period of Reform

The reformers who assumed power in 1978 believed that heavily propagandistic media content acted as a drag on China's development. They decided to pour huge funds into television while at the same time making almost all media outlets—television and radio stations, newspaper and book publishers, and film studios—responsible for their own profits and losses. This meant that the outlets would no longer receive the state subsidies that had kept them afloat in the past. On the other hand, they would be allowed for the first time to sell advertising and to use large proportions of the proceeds to improve their own personnel's living standards. The way to sell advertising was to provide viewers, listeners, and readers with the content they demanded. Only in this way could ratings and circulation be increased. As a result, beginning in the 1980s, the content of the Chinese media changed dramatically—from Communist propaganda to market-oriented glitz. It did not take long for things to get out of hand. Illegal cable television stations transmitted pirated pornography tapes from Hong Kong, Taiwan, Japan, and the West. Factories installed illegal satellite receiving dishes so that workers could watch Hong Kong television. Journalists began selling news to advertisers so that they could make extra money. Many people in the Communist Party—as well as outside intellectuals—complained that society was awash in cultural garbage. They feared that children coming of age in such a setting would become excessively materialistic and culturally tasteless. It was good that people could now watch and read more of the things they liked, but what should be done about the fact that they liked such vulgar content? The media outlets resisted attempts to tighten central control. They were making far too much money off advertising to accept that. They also argued that China could develop economically only if its people were materialistic.

Even as media content became increasingly vulgar, except on a few occasions, the media never openly challenged the Communist Party politically. There was a tacit deal between the party and media outlets (in which the party was represented): the media would be allowed to serve up spiritual pollution to the population and make money—but only in exchange for steering firmly clear of politics. News programs were to faithfully retransmit the state's propaganda, and they were to avoid politically sensitive topics in television programs and films. For the Chinese people, only depoliticized programs would be acceptable. This prompted many Chinese critics to angrily denounce the Communist Party for pursuing a policy of stupidifying the people so that it could maintain control.

The Internet

New challenges appeared with the advent of the Internet in the late 1990s. Within just a few years tens of millions of Chinese people had Internet access—from homes, schools, offices, and Internet cafes. The Chinese state struggled to control the kinds of sites Chinese people could visit and encouraged China's own media companies to establish sites of a flashy but nonpolitical nature so that Chinese people would be less tempted to visit banned sites abroad. The state also approved message boards so that web surfers could post their own views on controversial topics—although the posts were heavily censored.

It seems unlikely that the Chinese state will succeed in its efforts to establish a great firewall around China. The technological challenges are far too daunting. It quickly became easy for Chinese web surfers to access proxy servers abroad for the purpose of visiting banned foreign sites. In fact, new sites were being added so rapidly that it was practically impossible for the government to keep its list of banned sites up to date. E-mail presented further problems because its volume increased so rapidly that the government found it impossible to monitor effectively. Naturally, the possibility—however small—of being monitored did deter many people from using the Internet or e-mail to discuss forbidden subjects. A few high-profile imprisonments of Internet activists acted as a further deterrent. Nevertheless, in absolute terms many people did use the Internet for political purposes. For example, the Falun Gong religious movement used the Internet to mobilize thousands of people to demonstrate in the face of brutal hostility by the state.

The merging of the mass media with telecommunications that the Internet exemplifies had become the single biggest challenge facing the Communist Party as it continued to try to shape the way Chinese people think. Within the next decade, up to 100 million Chinese people will enjoy access to an Internet far more developed than today's—an Internet that facilitates easy downloading of multimedia programs of all stripes, including political programs. Moreover, the continued diffusion of telephones and computers means that the Chinese people will increasingly be able to talk with each other about the things they see online. Because the state will not be able to control either the content or the conversations, its grip on the way Chinese people view the world will loosen further. This may pave the way for eventual political change of a democratic nature.

Daniel C. Lynch

Further Reading

Lee, Chin-Chuan, ed. (2000) *Power, Money, and Media: Communication Patterns and Bureaucratic Control in Cultural China*. Evanston, IL: Northwestern University Press.

Lynch, Daniel C. (1999) *After the Propaganda State: Media, Politics, and "Thought Work" in Reformed China*. Stanford, CA: Stanford University Press.

Zhao, Yuezhi. (1998) *Media, Market, and Democracy in China: Between the Party Line and the Bottom Line*. Champaign: University of Illinois Press.

MEDIA—INSULAR SOUTHEAST ASIA

The media in insular Southeast Asia—a regional label that generally refers to Indonesia, the Philippines,

Malaysia, Singapore, Brunei, and East Timor—has seen dramatic changes in recent years. Indonesia's media has been greatly liberalized following the 1998 fall of Suharto (b. 1921), that country's dictator of thirty-two years, while media control by the socioeconomic elite in the Philippines has been credited with a large role in the 2001 ouster of former president Joseph Estrada (b. 1937), over the objections of the more populous working classes. Strong governments in Malaysia and Singapore have, in contrast, maintained tighter control over the media, and have held onto power through the Asian economic crisis of the late 1990s.

Both Indonesia and the Philippines—the region's most populous nations—are archipelagic, meaning that they are composed of numerous islands rather than a contiguous landmass. This makes the media's role particularly important in creating a sense of national identity among their culturally and linguistically diverse populations. Indonesia, for example, comprises more than seventeen thousand separate islands, which are home to over three hundred distinct languages and cultural groups. Whereas Singapore, a highly developed multiethnic city-state, has allowed the media marketplace to deliver ethnically and linguistically targeted products, Indonesia's attempt to culturally bind its far-flung islands together has proved a trying task in which the government has relied heavily on media control, propagation, and use of the national language, Bahasa Indonesia. Media of all varieties continue to play an increasingly critical role in the political, economic and cultural development of Southeast Asia.

One significant contrast between Indonesia and its neighbors in the region lies in the difference between print and broadcast; higher literacy levels, particularly in Malaysia and Singapore, but also in the Philippines, are dramatically reflected in their newspaper circulations, whereas poorer Indonesians show surprisingly high levels of television ownership despite having had only one government station broadcasting before the 1990s. Singapore's high media consumption and infrastructure levels put it in a class with developed nations such as the United States and Japan. (See Table 1.)

Television

Indonesia did not begin television broadcasting until 1962, when then-president Sukarno (1901–1970) commissioned a station to broadcast the first Asian Games in Jakarta. In contrast to the Philippines' rapid commercial development, Indonesia did not license commercial stations until 1989. Instead, it kept strict control of content through a single government station. In 1976 Indonesia became only the third nation to launch its own communications satellite, named Palapa, which carried the government network TVRI. Suharto's government continued its nation-building

TABLE 1

Intraregional Comparison

	Indonesia	Malaysia	Philippines	Singapore
Population† (in millions, 2001)	228	22	81	4
Daily newspapers (per thousand people, 1996)	24	158	79	360
Radios (per thousand people, 1997)	156	420	159	822
Radio broadcast stations† (in 1998–1999)	AM: 678, FM: 43, shortwave: 82	AM: 56, FM: 31, shortwave: 5	AM: 366, FM:290, shortwave: 3	AM: 0, FM: 16, shortwave: 2
Television sets (per thousand people, 1998)	136	166	108	348
Television broadcast stations† (in 1998–1999)	41	27	31	6
Telephone mainlines (per thousand people, 1998)	27	198	37	562
Mobile telephones (per thousand people, 1998)	5	99	22	346
Personal computers (per thousand people, 1998)	8.2	58.6	15.1	458.4
Internet hosts (per ten thousand people, 2000)	1.00	25.43	1.58	452.3

Note: The less populated nations (Brunei and East Timor) are discussed in the final section.

SOURCES: Data drawn from the World Bank (2001) *World Development Report 2000/2001: Attacking Poverty;* †Central Intelligence Agency (2000) *The World Factbook 2001.*

Indonesian Vice President Megawati Sukarnoputri speaks on national television on 20 June 2001. It was the first nationwide broadcast and the speech commemorated the 100th anniversary of the birth of Sukarno, the founder of Indonesia, and Megawati's father.

project via television with a 1980s program that placed televisions and satellite dishes in remote villages throughout the nation. This was intended to promote nationalism not only through program content, but also through propagation of Bahasa Indonesia. Private television flourished in the 1990s, and in the early 2000s there were eight networks broadcasting in major cities, two of which had near-nationwide coverage.

Malaysian and Singaporean television began broadcasting in 1963, but their governments restricted private broadcasting until 1984 and 1994, respectively. Although these countries' broadcasters have yet to experience the freedom visible in post-Suharto Indonesia, they have long been allowed to exploit ethnic divisions with television stations that cater to their nations' particular linguistic and cultural groups. In Malaysia, this amounts to stations targeting Malay (TV1) and Chinese-Malaysian (TV2) audiences; in Singapore, English- and Tamil-language stations are added to the mix. Singapore is also the regional hub for U.S. cable broadcasters, including MTV, HBO, and the Discovery Channel, who must edit their content to conform to conservative Singaporean standards. Singapore launched an international Asian news service in 1999. Malaysia's prime minister, Mahathir Mohamad (b. 1925), has been accused of controlling television broadcasts and orienting them toward the promotion of his government's point of view.

The Philippines was relatively early in starting its television industry, with the first station broadcasting by late 1953. To overcome high import taxes, the country also developed a significant domestic television manufacturing company, becoming in 1971 the third nation in the world to produce color sets. In the early 1960s, competition between Philippine stations was already strong, and the major players moved to secure their piece of the U.S. programming pie by developing exclusive relationships with the "big three" American networks. The haphazard but politically open nature of Philippine television news was brought to a sudden halt when Ferdinand Marcos (1917–1989) rose to power in 1972; within hours the military had shut down all stations that were critical of him. Although stations were later allowed to regulate their own content, their freedoms were greatly restricted and many became the mouthpieces of government propaganda. Marcos's 1986 fall from power, which was sealed by the military takeover of Manila's MBS Channel 4, returned many stations to their original owners and restored commercial competition to the industry.

Print Media

Indonesia's print media have experienced a surge since the fall of Suharto's New Order government in 1998, which brought a sudden lifting of media restrictions that had previously placed severe limits on press freedom. In the opinions of many cultural leaders, however, the surge has not been an unmitigated positive step, and has sparked an ongoing debate over how to cultivate more responsible and high-quality journalism in Indonesia. This is partly a reaction to the rise in radical and religious-oriented newspapers that have been faulted for provoking a deterioration of interethnic and interfaith relations in the predominantly Muslim nation. Nevertheless, these new freedoms have quickly led to a bold press corps that routinely questions the government and offers the sort of critical analyses that were all but unknown for more than thirty years. The most respected daily is *Kompas*, while the weekly *Tempo*—which was banned by Suharto in 1994—is highly regarded for its impartial analysis. Other major papers include *Republika*, a Muslim-themed daily, and the *Jakarta Post*, an English language daily.

BORNEO BULLETIN

The *Borneo Bulletin* newspaper first made its appearance as an English-language newspaper on 7 November 1953. Published in Kuala Belait, Brunei, it was initially a daily, then became a weekly tabloid until August 1990. It reverted to a daily on 3 September 1990. Its coverage generally focuses on Brunei affairs as well as developments in the neighboring East Malaysian states of Sabah and Sarawak and Kalimantan, Indonesia. There is a section in Brunei Malay. There is also a *Borneo Bulletin (Sarawak Edition)*, a weekly tabloid published since 1975 that offers greater emphasis on Sarawak and Malaysian news.

Ooi Keat Gin

David Leake. (1989) *Brunei: The Modern Southeast Asian Islamic Sultanate*. Jefferson, NC: McFarland.

As in television broadcasting, print media in Malaysia and Singapore are largely geared toward particular ethnic readerships. Among others Malaysia's *Utusan Malaysia* caters to Malay readers, *Sin Chew Jit Pau* is the major Chinese language daily, and the *New Straits Times* caters to English speakers. In Singapore, popular newspapers include *Lianhe Wanbao* and *Shin Min Daily News*, both in Chinese; *Berita Harian*, in Malay; *Tamil Murasu* in Tamil (with a largely ethnic Indian and Sri Lankan readership); and the *Straits Times* in English, which is the language of government administration. The presses of Malaysia and Singapore are more tightly controlled by their governments than are many of their Southeast Asian neighbors. Although major media companies across the region have traditionally had strong political ties, these connections are still a powerful source of influence and censorship in both Malaysia and Singapore, both of which also maintain strict laws curtailing press freedoms. The 1999 jailing of a journalist for the *Far Eastern Economic Review*, who published an article on the growing number of lawsuits in Malaysia, shocked much of the international community.

The pre-Marcos print media in the Philippines was known for sensational and unsubstantiated reporting, but was also willing to expose corruption at the highest levels of government. As with television, Marcos reined in the press by shutting down critical news outlets and by supporting newspapers owned by his family or cronies. Reporting began to become more open after the 1983 assassination of his main opponent, Benigno Aquino (1932–1983), and following Marcos's 1986 ouster, government papers were confiscated and many returned to their former owners. Most influential newspapers continue to be owned by powerful elite families, and have been criticized by the international press for undue bias toward the interests of their owners. Many of the more responsible papers are in English, while sensational tabloids often use Tagalog or Cebuano languages. Major dailies include the *Manila Bulletin* and the *Inquirer*. The close historic association between the Philippines' press and elite political interests has led to widespread distrust of media among the working classes.

Internet

Although the Internet continues to make inroads in the region, infrastructure development was seriously set back by the Asian economic crisis of the late 1990s, particularly in Indonesia. Singapore remains the exception to the rule in this region, with some of the highest levels of computer ownership and Internet access in the world, and has made major inroads into building a fiber-optic infrastructure that will allow widespread broadband access throughout the city-state. Nevertheless, the government has gone to great lengths to regulate access to Internet content, seeking to avert its use as a forum for political dissent.

In the region's developing nations, Internet access has become most popular among university students and young urban professionals, and has been cited (along with cell-phone messaging) as having facilitated the nationwide coordination of student protests that brought down Indonesia's Suharto. It has also given a voice to radical Islamic groups of that country, some of which have developed sophisticated, English-language websites to publicize their cause among international readers. In Malaysia, the Internet has become home to various banned print publications and government opposition groups.

The prohibitive cost of home computers compels most in the region to log on at the office, the university, or at Internet cafes. Cable Internet access has recently become available in major cities, but often suffers from low bandwidth and unstable infrastructure. It should be remembered that access to information technologies in this region remains largely a privilege of the wealthy, who comprise only a small percentage of the general population and do not necessarily share the interests of the larger populace.

Brunei and East Timor

The World Wide Web's advent in the mid-1990s gave a boost to the East Timor independence movement, thanks to numerous activist websites that helped to consolidate international opinion against Indonesia's 1975 annexation of the former Portuguese colony. Since gaining independence from Indonesia in 1999, East Timor has sought to institute a free press with the help of the United Nations, but remains in a rebuilding phase at the time of this writing.

Brunei has one Internet service provider, two television and thirteen radio stations, as well several newspapers, all of which operate under the close scrutiny of the royal family. The country also receives television transmissions from neighboring Malaysia, which are reportedly more popular than the domestic alternatives.

In this politically volatile region, the media plays a tremendously important role in the stewardship of democracy and political reform, but its history of government control remains visible and problematic. Small elites maintain disproportionate influence over major media outlets, setting the tone of public discourse and propagating wealthy, international lifestyle models among some of Asia's poorest peoples.

Gareth Barkin

Further Reading

ABS-CBN Broadcasting Corporation. (1999) *Pinoy Television: The Story of ABS-CBN.* Pasig City, Philippines: Benpres Publishing Inc.

Anderson, Benedict. (1983) *Imagined Communities: Reflections on the Origin and Spread of Nationalism.* London and New York: Verso.

Central Intelligence Agency. (2001). *The World Factbook 2001.* Washington, DC: Central Intelligence Agency.

Kitley, Philip. (2000) *Television, Nation, and Culture in Indonesia.* Columbus: Ohio State University Press.

Nain, Zaiharom. (2000) "The State, the Market and the Malaysian Media." In *De-Westernizing Media Studies,* edited by J. Curran and M-J. Park. London: Routledge, 139–155.

Williams, Louise, and Roland Rich, eds. (2000) *Losing Control, Freedom of the Press in Asia.* Canberra, Australia: Australian National University.

Wong, Kokkeong. (2001) *Media and Culture in Singapore: a Theory of Controlled Commodification.* Cresskill, NJ: Hampton Press.

World Bank. (2001) *World Development Report 2000/2001: Attacking Poverty.* Washington, DC: World Bank.

MEDIA—JAPAN

Japan has a highly developed media system with newspapers, magazines, books, and public and commercial television networks, as well as mobile phone and Internet services. Japanese readers can choose from more than 120 daily newspapers. Japan's five major daily national newspapers—the *Asahi Shinbun*, the *Yomiuri Shinbun*, the *Mainichi Shinbun*, the *Nikkei Shinbun*, and the *Sankei Shinbun*—have a daily combined subscription-based circulation rate of more than 53 million copies and reach almost all of Japan's approximately 48 million households (2001 data).

Despite the extensive readership of newspapers, television is the most significant medium in Japan at the beginning of the twenty-first century. According to a 2001 survey, Japanese viewers over the age of seven years watch on average approximately three hours and forty-five minutes of television every day. Japan's public television, NHK (Nippon Hoso Kyokai. or Japan Broadcasting Corporation), has fifty-four broadcasting stations and employs more than 12,600 staff across Japan, in addition to more than twenty-five offices overseas. Japan's 127 commercial television broadcasters are organized in five major commercial networks with so-called key stations in Tokyo.

NHK provided Japan's first analog satellite television service in 1989, followed by commercial satellite television in 1997 and digital satellite broadcasting in 2000. Subscription rates to cable-television services, many of which also provide Internet access, reached a total of 18.7 million households in March 2001, with other telecommunication services such as digital terrestrial broadcasting and broadband services expected to reach a mass clientele before 2005.

The Beginnings of Modern Mass Media in Japan

The path to the development of modern mass media in Japan was paved in the early Tokugawa period (1600/1603–1869), when illustrated pamphlets, so-called *kawara-ban* ("tile block prints"), reported on the struggle between the Tokugawa clan and their opponents and the fall of Osaka Castle. For most of the following two centuries, however, *kawara-ban* were almost exclusively devoted to personal tragedies, love suicides, natural disasters, and other human-interest stories, with hardly any interest in politics.

The first modern newspaper published in Japan was the English-language paper *Nagasaki Shipping List and Advertiser* of 1861, followed a few years later by the first Japanese-language newspaper, the fortnightly *Kaigai Shinbun.* The early Meiji government (1868–1912) considered newspapers an important part of modernization and encouraged their publication and distribution. The next four decades saw the development of a varied and at times highly politicized press. Many of Japan's leading newspapers of today were founded in the late nineteenth century, including the *Yomiuri Shinbun* (1874), the *Nihon Keizai Shinbun* (1876), and the *Osaka Asahi Shinbun* (1879).

Another Japanese media institution, the press club *(kisha kurabu)*, also has its roots in the Meiji period. The first press club was founded in 1890 to cover the opening of the Diet (parliament). Today, all significant public and commercial organizations in Japan, ranging from the prime minister's office and the Bank of Japan to the municipal fire services, have an associated press club. While allowing journalists easy access to official information, the press clubs are also a major reason for the relative uniformity of the modern Japanese press, as journalists from all media outlets obtain their information from the same limited pool of informants.

Media Freedom and Censorship: From Prewar Democracy to Allied Occupation

While the late Meiji period initially saw an increase in relative journalistic autonomy, the Newspaper Law of 1909 set the trend for a more restricted press environment, which continued throughout the years of prewar democracy. The law, administered through the Home Ministry, allowed various levels of censorship. Ministry officials instructed publishers about public events, and publishers had to submit inspection copies to the ministry at the time of their circulation. The ministry could then prohibit the publication or suspend the offending newspaper. Press control was substantially tightened under military rule (1937–1945). Prepublication censorship replaced the previous system of suspending offending material, and many intellectuals and writers from the center-left were either arrested or blacklisted and banned from publishing. Another form of control was the rationing of paper, which led to a rapid drop in the number of newspapers. By 1941, only 54 of the over 1,200 newspapers that had been in circulation in 1936 had survived.

Radio broadcasting in Japan began on 22 May 1925 with a program by the Tokyo Broadcasting Station, the first commercial radio broadcaster in Japan, followed by the opening of two further commercial radio stations in Osaka and Nagoya. Independent commercial radio broadcasting did not continue for long, as the government forced the merger of the three stations in 1926 into a new broadcaster, NHK. The expansion of NHK's broadcasting network throughout Japan and the mass production of cheaper radio sets led to a rapid increase in audience numbers. NHK held a broadcasting monopoly in Japan until 1951.

From the beginning, the communications ministry imposed strict control over radio content. After the Mukden Incident of 1931, when Japan occupied Chinese-held Manchuria, NHK radio became a significant tool for mobilization. NHK's unwavering support for the war effort ended only with Japan's surrender on 15 August 1945.

In the following years, American-led occupation forces prosecuted those media owners and newspaper journalists responsible for Japan's war propaganda and restructured NHK to foster demilitarization and democratization. However, many of those earlier removed from their positions returned to the media as America's concern moved from promoting democracy to combating Communism, a shift that occurred with the advent of the Korean War.

The Media and Politics in Contemporary Japan: The Case of Television

Japanese broadcasting laws make Japan's public broadcaster, NHK, one of the most autonomous public broadcasters in the world. The Japanese public holds NHK in high regard for its reliability and trustworthiness. However, the long incumbency of the ruling Liberal Democratic Party (LDP), which has governed Japan almost without interruption since 1955, has led to many unofficial methods by which the LDP can exert control over the public broadcaster. NHK's annual budget must be approved by the LDP-dominated parliament. The LDP also has strong links to NHK's board of governors, which elects NHK's president, and to the Ministry of Public Management, Home Affairs, Posts, and Telecommunications, which oversees compliance with media laws and controls media licenses. To avoid friction with the authorities, NHK tends to shun coverage of controversial issues and presents mostly neutral and authoritative news.

Until the mid-1980s, commercial-television networks focused almost exclusively on entertainment, with little interest in news or current affairs. While entertainment in the form of popular television-drama series, variety programs, and game shows continues to dominate commercial television, all commercial stations now also broadcast regular news shows, which provide opinionated coverage of current affairs, in contrast to NHK. The surge in commercial news reporting was sparked by the success of TV Asahi's *Newsstation*, which first aired in 1985. The show's main presenter, Hiroshi Kume, combines entertainment, analysis, and in-depth news reporting in a highly popular program. In 1993, the program's critical stance on many political issues almost cost TV Asahi its broadcasting license when the LDP attributed its first defeat in a general election since 1955 to *Newsstation*'s political reports. Subsequently, the amount of politi-

IRON CHEF

One of the most popular Japanese television programs of the 1990s was *Ryori no Tetsujin* (Cooking Iron Man). The show first aired on 10 October 1993 in the Kitchen Stadium of the Gourmet Academy. The shows were hosted by Takeshi Kaga, chairman of the Gourmet Academy, who introduced each week's "Iron Chef"—one of the show's "home team" of master chefs. A visiting chef competed against the show's Iron Chef to produce four or five dishes, all of which had to be based on a core ingredient unveiled at the start of the show. The dishes were then rated by a panel of experts and celebrities, and the winner declared. Camera crews and commentators followed the chefs and their assistants as they prepared the dishes in elaborate on-set kitchens. As a cultural drama, the show combined elements of samurai warrior ethos, the excesses of global materialism, and modern sports culture and drew a large audience of mainly young, affluent men. The appeal spread beyond Japan, and French and American chefs participated. The show began airing on the U.S. Food Network in July 1999 under the title *Iron Chef*, with an American version introduced later.

Source: Fuji Television, Inc. (2000) *Iron Chef: The Official Book.* New York: Berkley Books.

cal reporting decreased until 2001, when the unprecedented popularity of the LDP prime minister Junichiro Koizumi during his first year in office created a renewed interest in political reporting with high viewer ratings for political news and talk shows.

The long incumbency of the LDP has not diminished the demand for reliable and trustworthy news media in Japan. Despite the legally established freedom of the public broadcaster and the best efforts by some journalists in commercial television, Japan's defacto one-party government system has impeded the development of independent and serious journalism since the mid-1950s and has restrained the media's ability to provide a forum for public debate.

Barbara Gatzen

Further Reading

Altman, Albert A. (1976) "*Shinbunshi*: The Early Meiji Adaptation of the Western-Style Newspaper." In *Modern Japan: Aspects of History, Literature, and Society*, edited by W. G. Beasley. Tokyo: Charles E. Tuttle, 52–66.

Feldman, Ofer. (1993) *Politics and the News Media in Japan.* Ann Arbor: University of Michigan Press.

Gatzen, Barbara. (2001) *Fernsehnachrichten in Japan: Inszenierungsstrategien im interkulturellen Vergleich mit Deutschland* (Reports on Television in Japan: Production Strategies in Intercultural Comparison with Germany). Tübingen, Germany: Gunter Narr Verlag.

Kasza, Gregory J. (1993) *The State and the Mass Media in Japan, 1918–1945.* Berkeley and Los Angeles: University of California Press.

Kim, Young C. (1981) *Japanese Journalists and Their World.* Charlottesville, VA: University Press of Virginia.

Krauss, Ellis S. (2000) *Broadcasting Politics in Japan: NHK and Television News.* Ithaca, NY: Cornell University Press.

———, and Susan J. Pharr, eds. (1996) *Media and Politics in Japan.* Honolulu: University of Hawaii Press.

MEDIA—MAINLAND SOUTHEAST ASIA

The peoples of Southeast Asia, including Vietnam, Cambodia, Laos, and Myanmar (Burma until 1989), live in much poorer and less free conditions than their neighbors in Thailand. Myanmar remains under military rule, Vietnam and Laos are Communist, while Cambodia's fledgling democracy has emerged only since the 1998 United Nations–supervised elections. In each, except Cambodia, communications are under direct or indirect government control.

Neither the press nor television has significant penetration in Vietnam, Laos, or Myanmar, where both media are intended above all for regime maintenance, nor are they a significant presence in Cambodia. By contrast,

TABLE 1

Media Density in Southeast Asia

	Vietnam	Cambodia	Laos	Myanmar	Thailand
Population (in millions)	77.5	11.8	5.1	45	61.7
Mainline telephones (1998 per thousand)	26	2	6	5	84
Cellular phones (1998 per thousand)	2	6	1	0	32
Press circulation (1996 per thousand)	4	2	4	10	63
Radios (1997 per thousand)	107	127	143	95	232
TVs (1998 per thousand)	47	123	4	7	236
Personal computers (1998 per thousand)	6	1	1	0	22
Internet hosts (1998 per 10,000)	.02	.13	0	0	6

SOURCE: World Development Report 2000/2001.

the media have been used for national development and for promoting consumerism in Thailand. (See Table 1.)

Media Density

The reasons for this underdevelopment are historical. Southeast Asia is still rebuilding after the ravages of the Vietnam War. Despite conditional moves to open their economies by Vietnam *(doi moi)* and Laos (New Economic Measures) since the late 1980s, these countries remain stagnant. Cambodia is still recovering from the Khmer Rouge, while Myanmar's generals have kept a stranglehold on the polity and its declining economy since 1988. Thailand's media are more fully developed and are comparable with the media in insular Southeast Asia.

The Press

Vietnam's largest daily is the tabloid *Cong An Thanh Pho HCM* (Ho Chi Minh City Police). Other dailies include *Tuoi Tre* (Young Age) and *Lao Dong* (Labor)—youth and trade-union papers that reach wider readerships. There are also women's papers, such as *Phu Nu Thu Do* (Hanoi) and *Phu Nu Thanh Pho HCM* (Ho Chi Minh City). There are also the Party paper *Nhan Dan* (The People), the elite intellectual paper *Dai Doan Ket* (Great Unity), and two army papers. English-language papers include the *Saigon Times Daily* since 1996 and the *Vietnam Economic Times*. There are also a French monthly and a Chinese weekly.

The press is supervised first at the national level by the Ideology Department and the Ministry of Culture and Information, then by the paper's own internal committee. There are also provincial supervisory committees. The net effect is that the Vietnamese press—and indeed all media—are brought under the control of the Communist Party.

In contrast, Myanmar, which had a large number of papers before the 1962 coup, publishes only two main national titles—*Myanmar Alin* and *Kyemon* (The Mirror)—two regional dailies, and the English-language daily *New Light of Myanmar*. In the year 2000, a new English-language weekly *The Myanmar Times*, started up; it focused on business news, and a Burmese-language version was added in 2001.

Cambodia has twice the population of Laos but almost ten times as many papers. Since a degree of press freedom has emerged in Cambodia, there has been a boom in the Khmer-language press. The largest is the pro-government paper *Rasmei Kampuchea*, which has some 35 percent of all advertising, followed by others such as *Koh Santepheap* and *Monearsekar Kampuchea*. A weekly *Cambodia Times* has been published in English and Khmer since 1995, rivaling the smaller *Cambodia Daily* begun three years earlier in English, Khmer, and Japanese. The Cambodian press is wildly partisan, reflecting the chaotic freedom of recent politics. The Lao press is smaller and not at all democratic. There is one main Lao-language daily, *Siang Prachachon*, and the English-language weekly *Vientiane Times*.

Thailand's press was often censored by the army and the government until 1992, but it has since been increasingly free. Thai-language papers are dominant, with tabloids including *Thai Rath* and *Daily News*, and elite papers such as *Matichon* and *Siam Rath*. The English-language papers, the *Bangkok Post* and *The Nation*, are read by elite Thais and expatriates, but have much smaller circulations. The Thai Chinese-language papers have small readerships and are declining.

Radio and Television

With the exception of Thailand, the nations of mainland Southeast Asia have low levels of literacy. Adult illiteracy levels in Cambodia and Laos in 1998 were 61 and 54 percent, respectively. Radio is therefore still an important communication channel. In Vietnam, for example, twice-daily half-hour broadcasts are made to villages through public loudspeaker systems. Some state channels aimed mainly at metropolitan listeners carry advertising.

The Voice of Vietnam (VOV) Radio began in 1945 and currently has five domestic and eleven overseas channels. One of the domestic services broadcasts in five minority languages, as do twenty of the sixty provincial stations. Cambodian stations are mainly in the capital of Phnom Penh, though national FM broadcasting began in 1999. Lao National Radio covers most of the country, supplemented by two Vientiane Radio stations. Broadcasting in Myanmar, where radio and television penetration is low, is controlled by the Myanmar Television and Radio Department.

Television began in Vietnam in the south in the 1960s with channels run by Royal Vietnam TV and the U.S. military. The day after the war ended in 1975, it was renamed Liberation Television, later becoming VTV (Vietnam Television). Hanoi's VTV runs VTV 1 and 2, while Ho Chi Minh City (HCMC) has VTV 7, 28, and Song Be TV. There are three regional relay stations in Da Nang, Hue, and Can Tho, servicing sixty local stations. A commercial channel, VTV 3, was introduced in 1996, three years after VTV, VOV, and the Vietnam News Agency had been split from the Ministry of Culture and Information as part of *doi moi*. VTV began some satellite relay services in 1996 with twelve channels in HCMC and nine in Hanoi. While Vietnam television is tightly controlled, there are some local differences. In 1994, for example, HCMC TV refused to carry the Japanese serial *Oshin* as requested by VTV.

There are six broadcast television channels in Cambodia and three cable services, most of which are very recent. The proceedings of the National Assembly are taped for rebroadcast. Cambodia and Laos experimented with importing commercial services from Thailand from the Shinawatra group in the mid-1990s, but canceled them after disputes over their management. Laos has only one national service, Laos National TV on Channel 9, but many Laos watch the Thai programs that spill over their borders. Myanmar has two channels (Myanmar Television and Army Television) as well as satellite channels, but these are restricted to tourists and elite officials.

Television began in Thailand in 1955. Thailand now has six free-to-air channels; satellite-delivered cable-TV services were established in 1991. Thai broadcast television is almost exclusively in Thai. Foreign-program content on Thai television was an issue in the early 1990s; because of language barriers and government policy, there is little foreign programming. When U.S. or Chinese movies or Japanese cartoons are screened, they are dubbed with Thai voice-overs.

High school students in Bangkok watch a video on television in 1989. (ED ECKSTEIN/CORBIS)

Thai broadcasting has traditionally been controlled by the army, but the degree of control has been significantly reduced since 1992. The army still runs Channel 5, which is also broadcast internationally by satellite. Thailand first allowed private broadcasting in 1996, when iTV became the first channel not owned by the state; it pioneered freer news programs, but in 2000 control of the channel went to the telecom magnate Thaksin Shinawatra, who became prime minister in January 2001.

New Media and Information Technology

Recent attempts being made to introduce the information technologies and new media that are important in Singapore and Malaysia have yet to have any significant impact in Southeast Asia. The Internet was introduced to Vietnam in December 1997, and some newspapers, such as *Nan Danh*, have developed web presences. Myanmar has no laws regarding Internet use. The Internet is mainly used by offshore critics of the regime to run critical news reports about the government (for example, *The Irrawaddy* website).

On the other hand, Malaysia and Singapore are providing significant business investment for Cambodia, Vietnam, and Myanmar in transport, leisure, and telecoms. Sweden conducted a major regional radio-improvement program for Laos between 1993 and 1995. Thai communications companies such as Shinawatra and Jasmine also have telephone investments in Laos and Cambodia, while Australia's Telstra, France's Telecom, and Japan's NTT have helped to build Vietnamese telecom services.

Some initiatives also aim at boosting regional communications. China and Thailand have joined the four states to form a Greater Mekong Subregion Telecommunications Group, while in late 2000 an e-Association of Southeast Asian Nations (ASEAN) was formed to promote e-commerce in ASEAN, in which Vietnam, Laos, Cambodia, and Myanmar are now members. However there remain major obstacles to the success of these schemes, not least of which are the widespread bureaucratic corruption and political repression that continue.

Glen Lewis (Cambodia, Laos, Thailand, Vietnam) and editorial staff of Berkshire Publishing (Myanmar)

Further Reading

Barisoth, Sek. (2000) "Media and Democracy in Cambodia." *Media Asia* 27, 4: 206.

Irrawaddy Publishing Group. (2002) *The Irrawaddy*. Retrieved 1 May 2002, from: http://www.irrawaddy.org

Irvine, D. (1997) *The Guide to Asian Media*. Beaumaris, Australia: Asian Media Access.

Marr, D. G., ed. (1998) *The Mass Media in Vietnam*. Canberra, Australia: Australian National University, RSPAS.

MEDIA—SOUTH ASIA

There have been protean transformations in the media landscape in recent years in the countries of South Asia. This change presents both opportunities and challenges to the countries in the region: India, Pakistan, Bangladesh, Nepal, and Sri Lanka. These nations' reform programs and active engagement in the world economy are now paying off in terms of higher foreign investment, a fallout that is also noticeable in the media industries. However the rate of progress is far from equal in all the countries.

Radio

Until recently radio has been under state control in most South Asian countries, but it is opening up now in India. Bangladesh Betar (Radio Bangladesh) is government controlled, as is Radio Nepal, which broadcasts programs in Nepali and English to over 90 percent of the country's population.

Newspapers

Bangladesh has about forty daily newspapers, published mainly in Dhaka. Of these, *Dainik Ittefaq*, *Dainik Inquilab*, and *Dainik Janakantha* have the highest circulation. The major newspapers in Nepal include the *Gorkhapatra*, *Nepali Hindi Daily*, *Samaya*, and the *Daily News*. Sri Lanka has nine daily newspapers, the one with the largest circulation perhaps being the *Dinamina*. Over 275 daily newspapers, mainly printed in Urdu and English, are published in Pakistan, the best selling among these being perhaps the *Daily Jang* and the *Dawn*. The major dailies are concentrated in Lahore and Karachi. Around 35,000 newspapers, 10 percent of which are dailies, are published in India. These include such English-language publications as the *Times of India*, the *Indian Express*, the *Hindu*, the *Deccan Herald*, and the *Statesman*.

Television

Since the early 1990s, there has been an exponential growth in television viewing, spurred on in part by the spread of private cable systems and television broadcasts via satellite that provides access to news, sports, and entertainment from around the globe. As satellite channels have proliferated across the South Asian subcontinent, distinct forms of localized entertainment and news channels have emerged. The entertainment channels, including the STAR TV network, have largely been dominated by the Indian film industry and its offshoots, and these continue to be popular across the subcontinent.

The South Asian countries are now at a crossroads regarding development, particularly in the field of satellite television and the information superhighway. Some of them have large numbers of technically trained, English-speaking workers, particularly India. Earlier, the major stumbling block was the lack of financial flows to sustain this market. Today, the problem is more keeping pace with developments that are taking place so rapidly worldwide and with the issues of regulatory control.

Telecommunications Infrastructure and the Internet

The South Asian region has had a telecommunications infrastructure since the mid-nineteenth century, when the British held power in the region. The Telegraph Act of 1885 still operates in many parts of the region, though it recently has been amended in India, for instance. The management of telecommunications in all the countries of South Asia began with state control. There were various reasons for this choice, chief among which were the high investment required to support the infrastructure and the desire of the government to exercise control. Rapid expansion of technology in the past two decades, however, made it possible to deliver service to more areas than ever before.

The growth of the information superhighway via the Internet has outstripped any previous information technology innovation in recent times. While its greatest advantage is that it needs no new infrastructure to get started, it does demand a complete revamping of

WHO WANTS TO BE A MILLIONAIRE—IN INDIA

Kuan Banega Crorepati, India's version of *Who Wants to Be a Millionaire*, is one of the most watched television shows in the entire world, edging close to *Baywatch*'s record of 1.1 billion viewers in 142 countries. In 2000 the show had an approximate viewership of more than 100 million worldwide. *Kuan Banega Crorepati* (which translates as "who wants to be a deca-millionaire") awards its prizes in Indian rupees, worth approximately US$219,000.

Kuan Banega Crorepati is a little different from the U.S. original—in India delighted spouses prostrate themselves in front of the host, and host Regis Philbin has been replaced by the Indian film star Amitabh Bachchan—but the agony and ecstasy of the game show remain the same.

James B. McGirk

Source: Barry Bearak. (2000) "Many, Many in India Want to Be a Millionaire. *The New York Times* (30 August). Retrieved 5 April 2002, from: http://www.nytimes.com.

the way the existing infrastructure of telecommunications is used. The growth of the telecommunications infrastructure in South Asia has not been demand-driven; it has been almost entirely investment-driven and dependent on the priority level possible for the allocation of funds from limited public resources. This means that the current situation in South Asia faces some major problems that limit the utility of the information superhighway. One, of course, is the cost of computer ownership; another is the cost of telecommunication access. But above all, there is limited access to the telecommunications medium itself.

India is the only country in the region with a reasonably high level of engineering hardware and software technology and state- as well as privately owned provision for international connectivity. Nepal gained access to the Internet via India's education and research network, ERNET. This limited arrangement was later routed through Singapore and Australia. Bangladesh, Sri Lanka, and Pakistan also have very limited international connectivity. One of the reasons for this is that those countries use a single government agency for both domestic and international services.

All the countries in the area have liberalized access to the Internet in one way or another. India for the first time set up a ministry of information and technology in the autumn of 1999. In Pakistan, the government has an open policy for data communications and the Internet to encourage their spread and use. Telecommunications in Bangladesh remain the responsibility of the government, whereas the Nepal Telecommunications Authority has loosened the controls placed on the private sector, with an eye toward attracting private investment. All these steps, however, have not been easy processes, facing as they do considerable resistance from the government-owned telecommunications monopolies. So, while all the countries in the South Asian region have tried to

A newsstand in Nuwara Eliya, Sri Lanka, that sells English- and Sinhalese-language newspapers. (ARVIND GARG/CORBIS)

deregulate and liberalize their data and voice services and have been encouraging private investment, this process has been unevenly implemented.

With the coming of age of new technologies in digital and electronic communications, a major upgrading of systems in the countries of South Asia is called for. The costs of online access remain extremely high, and availability of telephone lines remains very restricted. Even where telephone lines exist, poor quality and service remain stumbling blocks. The entire purpose of telecommunications needs reexamination so that maximum efficiency can be obtained for mediums of transmission, including copper cable, fiber-optic cable, terrestrial radio waves, and satellite communications.

The information superhighway has a lot to offer to the regions of South Asia, but successful utilization requires a paradigm shift in traditional funding and management models. Otherwise, new technologies in the media sphere will just continue to exacerbate the digital divide between rural and urban, non-English- and English-speaking South Asia. Private (profit-driven) agencies and nongovernmental organizations (NGOs) must be brought in as participants if benefits are to be productive for the South Asian region in any meaningful time frame.

Shoma Munshi

See also: **Cinema—South Asia**

Further Reading

Azad, Abul Kalam, and Nazrul Islam. (1997) *Overview of Internet Access in Bangladesh: Impact, Barriers, and Solutions.* Retrieved 22 April 2002, from: http://www.isoc.org/inet97/proceedings/E3/E3 1_HTM.

Chowdhury, Jamilur Reza. (1999) *Information Technology in Bangladesh.* Retrieved 22 April 2002, from: http://som.scudh.edu/fac/lpress/devnat/nations/Bangladesh/jrc.html.

French, David, and Michael Richards, eds. (2000) *Television in Contemporary Asia.* New Delhi: Sage Publications,

Gunaratne, Sheldon. (2000) *Handbook of the Media in Asia 2000* New Delhi: Sage.

Herman, Edward S., and Robert W. McChesney (1997) *The Global Media.* London: Cassell Academic Publication.

Jeffrey, Robin. (2000) *India's Newspaper Revolution: Capitalism, Politics and the English Language Press.* New Delhi: Oxford University Press.

Joshi, Ila. (1999) "Communication Revolution in South Asia" Orbicom column (January 1999). Retrieved 22 April 2002, from http://www.orbicom.uqam.ca/en/column/january99.html.

Mody, Bella, Johannes M. Bauer, and Joseph D. Straubhaar, eds. (1995) *Telecommunications Politics: Ownership and Control of the Information Highway in Developing Countries,* Mahwah, NJ: Erlbaum.

Page, David, and William Crawley. (2000) *Satellites Over South Asia: Broadcasting Culture and the Public Interest.* New Delhi: Sage

Pohjola, Matt, ed. (2001) *Information Technology, Productivity & Economic Growth: International Evidence and Implications for Economic Development.* Oxford: Oxford University Press.

Press Council Nepal, Worldview Nepal, and Nepal Press Institute (1998) *Nepal National Mass Media Directory, 1998.* Kathmandu, Nepal: Press Council Nepal, Worldview Nepal, Nepal Press Institute.

Press, Larry. (1999) *Against All Odds, The Internet in Bangladesh.* Retrieved 22 April 2002, from: http://som.csudh.edu/fac/lpress/devnat/nations/Bangladesh/bdmosaic.htm.

Singhal, Arvind, and Everett Rogers. (2001) *India's Communication Revolution: From Bullock Carts to Cyber Marts.* New Delhi: Sage

MEDIA—SOUTH KOREA

MEDIA—SOUTH KOREA The development of mass media in South Korea has been one of the most dramatic in Asia. Development was significantly delayed during the Japanese occupation (1910–1945) of Korea, when the media were used as the Japanese colonial government's propaganda tools, and further delayed by the Korean War (1950–1953). Since the 1950s, virtually all major changes in the structure of the media have followed a change in government. Many media scholars have attributed South Korea's media democratization to President Rho's June Declaration in 1987, which guaranteed freedom of the press in South Korea. Prior to this, the media in South Korea were under the strict control of the governments of Park Chung Hee (1961–1979) and Chun Doo Hwan (1980–1987), with each new government deciding the role and function of the media. The changes in domestic politics since 1987, however, have brought more media freedom.

Broadcast Media

Radio in Korea was introduced in 1927 by the Japanese colonial government in order to promote and disseminate its policies. Despite a poor economy and political instability, which continued until the 1950s, radio gradually attracted an audience with its news and entertainment programs. Its growing popularity also attracted commercial interest, and, as a result, both commercial and national radio coexisted until 1979. Although television was introduced in 1956, the first regular television broadcasting started in 1961 by a national broadcaster owned and operated by the state. Following this, television came to consist of both commercial and state operations (1965–1979). Then both television and radio became a monopoly of public broadcasting (1980–1990), and they are currently a duopoly of commercial and public broadcasting.

There are three major land-based broadcasters: two public broadcasters, Korean Broadcasting System (KBS) and Munhwa Broadcasting Company (MBC), and one commercial broadcaster, Seoul Broadcasting System (SBS). KBS and MBC provide television and radio (AM and FM) services through their own nationwide networks; SBS broadcasts in Seoul and surrounding areas. These major broadcasters are complemented by nine local commercial broadcasters that provide television and FM radio service in the nine largest cities in South Korea, and each of them covers its respective geographical area. Apart from national and local broadcasters that provide both television and radio services, seven broadcasters provide radio-only service. Some of them, such as BBS (Buddhist Broadcasting System), CBS (Christian Broadcasting System), and TBN (Traffic Broadcasting Network), have their own local stations in large cities. Yonhap News Agency is the only news agency in South Korea. It was established in 1981, after the merger of two major news agencies, Tongyang News Agency and Haptong News Agency.

Cable television in South Korea started in 1995 with twenty-nine channels. It is operated by three sectors: station operators, program providers, and network operators. Despite optimistic predictions, cable television in South Korea, except for a handful of channels, has undergone difficult times. This has been largely due to the government's poor management of the industry. South Korea's own broadcasting satellite was launched in 1997; however, by December 1999, satellite broadcasting in the country was yet to commence, mainly due to the absence of legal structure. With the new Broadcast Law in effect, Korea Digital Satellite Broadcasting (KDB), the sole satellite operator, started satellite broadcasting in March 2002.

Print Media

The first Korean newspaper *(Hansong Sunbo)* and magazine *(Sonyon)* appeared in 1883 and 1908, respectively. Korea had a flood of newspapers in the second half of the 1940s when the Korean government allowed all newspaper publishers to operate provided they register with the government. Under South Korea's license system, which was introduced in 1952–1953, the number of newspapers significantly dropped. Under the military regimes in the 1960s, 1970s, and 1980s, newspaper companies were required to have a license to publish, and journalists were required to have a press card issued by the government to access government information. On the other hand, the military governments provided newspaper companies with financial benefits, such as tax exemption and pay raises, in return for positive coverage of their policies.

Newspaper companies in South Korea have been centered around Seoul. In addition to general-interest dailies, companies publish specialized newspapers, such as sports and economic/business newspapers. They also publish magazines, such as weekly and monthly news magazines and women's magazines, which target specific readers. Most of the regional newspapers, however, have been struggling to attract readers in their region, mainly due to the dominance of the large Seoul-based newspapers, such as *Choson Ilbo, Chungang Ilbo,* and *Tonga Ilbo,* in the regional markets.

The expansion of print media in South Korea can be attributed partly to the country's booming economy in the 1980s, which created a strong advertising market and strong revenue for the print media, and partly to the media liberalization of June 1987. Although the print media are largely free to criticize the government, some critics point out that many of the newspaper companies, to varying degrees, still operate as family businesses. This family nature, together with their strong competition to dominate the market, has been the main concern voiced by civil organizations since the end of the 1990s. South Korea's president Kim Dae Jung (b. 1925) in early 2001 ordered a tax examination, which was a serious challenge for newspapers, which had enjoyed tax exemption. The newspapers claimed that the government was trying to control the media, whereas the government maintained that all companies must abide by the Tax Law and Fair Trade Law.

Ownership

In South Korea, newspaper companies and business conglomerates were allowed to own and operate broadcasting stations in the 1960s and 1970s. The 1980 media reform, which was enforced by the Chun Doo Hwan government, prohibited private companies from providing broadcasting service. The reform also banned cross-media ownership by placing all broadcasters under the umbrella of public broadcasting and allowing only a handful of national newspapers in Seoul and just one newspaper in each of the eight provinces. This restriction, however, provided Seoul-based newspaper companies with an opportunity to expand by publishing newspapers and magazines.

Foreign ownership and foreign investment in the South Korean media were strictly prohibited until 1995, when the government partially lifted restrictions on foreign ownership of cable television. Faced with financial problems caused by the devaluation of Asian currencies against the U.S. dollar at the end of 1997, the South Korean government was forced to further deregulate industry sectors, including broadcasting. As a result, the government opened the media industry to foreign investors, with the exception of land-based broadcasting.

State Control

The regulatory structure of media in South Korea has been characterized by a strong centralized bureaucratic-authoritarian state. Mass media have been controlled by successive military governments until the end of the 1980s. They have used explicit measures to control the media, such as direct intervention in management and personnel affairs, overt censorship, and the arrest of antigovernment journalists without warrants. Although the degree of state control over the media since then has weakened, some scholars argue that the state still controls media, broadcasting in particular, indirectly, such as by administrative guidance, which requests broadcasters' cooperation. To Western scholars, South Korea remains a conservative nation with conservative media.

State control of broadcasting in South Korea has been exercised mainly by two government ministries (the Ministry of Information and the Ministry of Communication, which were merged and renamed the Ministry of Information and Communication in 1998) and by two seemingly independent regulators: KBC (Korean Broadcasting Commission) and KCCC (Korean Cable Communications Commission). Unlike the broadcast media, the print media have been loosely regulated and encouraged to practice self-regulation.

The New Broadcast Law

South Korea is undergoing a major change in its regulatory structure of broadcasting after passage of the new Broadcast Law by the National Assembly in December 1999. The new Broadcast Law consolidates all laws relating to broadcasting, namely broadcast law and cable law. The new Broadcast Law empowers the KBC with broader structural and administrative authority. All types of broadcasting—land-based, cable, and satellite—will be placed under the control of a single regulator, the KBC. The law also empowers the KBC with ultimate licensing power, that is, to issue, cancel, and renew licenses. The law relaxes the restriction on cross-media ownership and foreign ownership by allowing newspaper companies, conglomerates, and foreign investors to own up to 33 percent of one satellite broadcasting operator.

Ki-Sung Kwak

Further Reading

Kim, Chie-woon, and Tae-sup Shin. (1994) "The Korean Press: A Half Century of Controls, Suppression and Intermittent Resistance." In *Elite Media amidst Mass Culture: A Critical Look at Mass Communication in Korea*, edited by Chie-woon Kim and Jae-won Lee. Seoul: Nanam Publishing House, 43–64.

Kim, Kyu, Won-Yong Kim, and Jong-Geun Kang. (1994) *Broadcasting in Korea.* Seoul: Nanam Publishing House.

Korean Press Foundation. (1999) *The Korea Press 2000.* Seoul: Korean Press Foundation.

Kwak, Ki-Sung. (1999) "The Role of the State in the Regulation of Television Broadcasting in South Korea." *Media International Australia Incorporating Culture & Policy* 92: 65–79.

Vanden Heuvel, Jon, and Everette Dennis. (1993) *The Unfolding Lotus: East Asia's Changing Media.* New York: Freedom Forum Media Studies Center.

MEDIA—WEST ASIA

MEDIA—WEST ASIA West Asia—made up of the two non-Arab nations of Iran and Turkey as well as Iraq, which has a sizable non-Arab population—is home to the world's richest written traditions in extinct languages as well as living languages such as Arabic and Persian. Writing, the world's first major communication revolution, began six thousand years ago in the civilization of Sumer, which flourished in southern Iraq. Writing used diverse media, including stone, clay, metals, wood, parchment, and finally paper, which was adopted from China and later transferred to Europe.

Unlike paper, printing came to West Asia from Europe rather than China or Korea and was not welcomed by Ottoman sultans, who issued decrees in 1485 and 1515 in order to deny the Muslim population access to the technology. However, book publishing began in the eighteenth century, and by the mid-nineteenth century, the first periodicals emerged in Arabic, Persian, and Turkish. Publishing in languages used by Christian and Jewish populations had an earlier start.

Media and Modernity

The transition from a rich scribal culture to a print culture occurred under conditions of mass illiteracy, which continued until the 1970s. Unlike the West, where the rise of print media was associated with the formation of civil societies and "public spheres," in West Asia illiteracy and the persistence of tribal, nomadic, and feudal relations were not hospitable to the development of print media. Still, these media had, by the late nineteenth century, turned into sites of struggle between the Ottoman and Iranian despotic states and new social forces such as the emerging mercantile class, women, labor, the modern intelligentsia, students, peasants, nationalities, and ethnic and religious groups. The press constituted a major force of modernity and played a crucial role in the democratic and anticolonial movements of the region, including Iran's Constitutional Revolution (1906–1911) and the Young Turk Revolution of Ottoman Turkey (1908). Newspapers and magazines were also a major factor in the rise of nationalism, feminism, socialism, and the modernization of linguistic and literary traditions among Arabs, Armenians, Kurds, Persians, Turks, and others.

Recorded music was introduced to the region through Western phonograph and gramophone companies in the 1910s. Cinema was also introduced through private initiatives, with early commercial screenings in 1904 (Tehran), 1905 (Istanbul), and 1909 (Baghdad); film production began in 1916 (Turkey), 1930 (Iran), and 1946 (Iraq). The medium was secular and urban, and promoted the official language and culture.

The advent of radio coincided with the rise of nationalist, secular, and modernizing regimes in Turkey (1923) and Iran (1925), which monopolized broadcasting and used it along with other media as vehicles for state- and nation-building and assimilating ethnic and national minorities. Broadcasting began in Turkey in 1927, Iraq in 1939, and Iran in 1941. In the 1950s, there were major propaganda "radio wars" between Egypt on one side and Iran, Iraq, and Turkey on the other. Clandestine and state radio stations also engaged in numerous broadcasting wars involving the Soviet Union and the nations of the region. Television broadcasting began in Iraq in 1956, Iran in 1958, and Turkey in 1968. By the latter part of the 1990s, satellite broadcasting to and from the region had visibly transformed the audiovisual culture of the region.

State Control of the Media

In Iraq, the consolidation of power by the Baʿath Party after its 1968 coup d'etat led to the strict control of the media and eventually to the elimination of private journalism. The destabilization of the Iraqi state after the Persian Gulf War (1990–1991) allowed the Kurds in the north to establish an autonomous government, where Kurdish language media flourished. In Iran, print journalism, "small media" such as cassette tapes, and "xerox literature" (oppositional leaflets and other literature printed as photocopies) played an important role in the 1978–1979 revolution against the Pahlavi monarchy (1925–1979), which was replaced by an Islamic theocracy. The Islamic republic used the media intensively to Islamize state and society.

The nations of West Asia have exercised strict control over the media. In the late 1990s, Turkey, Iran, and Iraq ranked highest among the world's violators of press freedom. State violence against the media included assassinating, jailing, and abducting reporters and media personnel, smashing satellite dishes, arresting viewers, and attacking media outlets and institutions. Ayatollah Khomeini's 1989 *fatwa* (religious decree) authorizing the assassination of British writer Salman Rushdie for blasphemy was typical of a policy that eliminated hundreds of Iranian intellectuals, especially journalists and their publications, after 1979.

However, technophiles and technological optimists see in new technologies such as the Internet the demise of state control and the rise of a civil society that never took off in the old technopolitical order. The Turkish republic allowed private broadcasting in the early 1990s, and by the mid-1990s, the monolithic state broadcasting system found itself in an ocean of radio (over 1,200) and television (over 250) stations. Moreover, satellite television from other nations brought to audiences programs that challenge the state (for example, the Europe-based Kurdish-language channel Med-TV, later called Medya TV, and Iranian television channels from California).

Although the unprecedented growth of channels introduced diverse programming, Turkey remained the top violator of freedom of the press by the early 2000s. The media were tolerated only if they subscribed to the official ideology and politics, and the Kurdish citizens, numbering about 10 million, were denied the right to broadcast in their language. Unlike Turkey, Iraq and Iran have banned satellite dishes, although dishes continue to be used in the course of a "guerrilla war" between audiences and the police.

By 2001, access to the Internet was most extensive in Turkey, growing in Iran, and most limited in Iraq. Surveillance of the Internet was commonplace in West Asia. At the same time, satellite broadcasting and the Internet allowed round-the-clock contact between Iraq, Iran, and Turkey and the numerous diasporas formed by the refugees and emigrants from these nations.

Amir Hassanpour

Further Reading

Kamalipour, Yahya R., and Hamid Mowlana, eds. (1994) *Mass Media in the Middle East: A Comprehensive Handbook.* Westport, CT: Greenwood Press.

Leaman, Oliver, ed. (2001) *Companion Encyclopedia of Middle Eastern and North African Film*. London: Routledge.

Sreberny-Mohammadi, Annabelle, and Ali Mohammadi. (1994) *Small Media, Big Revolution: Communication, Culture and the Iranian Revolution*. Minneapolis: University of Minnesota Press.

MEDICINE, AYURVEDIC Ayurveda is the oldest traditional system of healing in India, still widely in use today. Developed by the people of the Indo-Gangetic plain, Ayurveda was at first transmitted by verbal instruction; texts and commentaries were later written in Sanskrit. Ancient Indian medicine, like all of life in India, was interwoven with philosophy and religion. Ayurveda was and remains holistic; that is, it emphasizes keeping the entire person healthy rather than addressing specific ailments in isolation. The basic Hindu texts for Ayurveda are the four Vedas, ancient Hindu sacred texts. All four Vedas have sections dealing with healing and prevention and cure of sickness; the approach to treatment is generally one of magic or prayer to the deities of the Vedic pantheon. Later, specific tracts dealing with health and disease were compiled.

Some Problems of Chronology

The exact dates of the Ayurvedic texts are impossible to determine, except that they are known to be later in date than the four Vedas. Because early Indian texts were written on palm leaves or tree bark, they were perishable in the humid climate. Texts were often ascribed to sages or gods to establish their validity, and the authors of the Ayurvedic texts seldom clearly defined who they were and where they lived. Thus it is difficult to establish the dates of the authors' lives. Scholars estimate that the codification of Ayurveda probably occurred around the sixth century BCE. The Ayurvedas are believed to have taken their current form by the sixth or seventh century CE.

Medical Texts

Collections of texts with medical significance were known as tantras. Tantras were codified and made compact so that they were easily transmitted by verbal instruction, and instructors could easily explain the verses that students had memorized. The mainly medical *Agnivesa-tantra* and the surgical *Sushruta-tantra* were either never written down or did not survive, and are known only because they are mentioned in other texts.

In their later systematized forms the texts are known as *samhita*s (Sanskrit term for any systematically arranged collection of texts or verses that convey information). Five *samhita*s are known. The three major *samhitas*—*Charaka* (mainly internal medicine), *Sushruta* (mainly surgery), and *Astangasamgraha/Astangahrdaya* (a combination of both)—are together termed the *Brddhatrayee* (ancient triad). Their complete texts are available in a number of copies and commentaries. Two other incomplete texts, the *Bhela* and the *Kashyapa*, are available in one or two copies. The *Kashyapa samhita* deals almost exclusively with pediatrics (which are dealt with less extensively in the other texts). Some doubt exists about the authenticity of a sixth and also fragmentary text—the *Harita samhita*. The *Madhavanidanam* is a text that deals specifically with the causation and diagnostic features of diseases.

Theory of Ayurvedic Medicine

Ayurveda deals with life (human and animal) in all its aspects, including areas that do not fall in the domain of Western medicine today. The Ayurvedic texts discuss dietetics, geographic pathology (disease as affected by the environment), medical ethics, the selection and teaching of medical students, and even the philosophical basis of existence.

Ayurvedic medicine was based on a theory of the balance of three essential vital forces in the individual. Somewhat similar to the Western concept of humors (a notion propounded by Hippocrates in the fifth century BCE that the human body contained four humors, or fluids, on whose equilibrium health depended), these vital forces called *Tridosha*s or "three *dosha*s" are *vayu* or *vata* (loosely translated as wind), *pitta* (bile), and *kapha* or *sleshman* (mucus). The terms are conceptual and do not equate with the physical bile or mucus in a Western sense.

The balance of those vital forces gives each person his or her specific mental and physical characteristics. Imbalance—resulting in disease—arises from either congenital or inborn causes and acquired or external factors. Such external agents could be diet, addictions and habits, inappropriate foods and drinks, sexual habits, place of residence, climate, or injuries. Some diseases are also called *raktaja*—arising from impure blood—though blood is not considered a *dosha*. In the diagnosis and cure of any disease, the nature of the cause is important, as is the individual constitutional (humoral) characteristics of the patient.

***The* Charaka *and the* Sushruta** The *Charaka* and the *Sushruta* are divided into a number of sections, each dealing with some special aspect of diseases and their treatment. The *Charaka samhita* supposedly contained the version of the medical teaching of Atreya Punarvasu (a mythical sage) put forward by Agnivesa (another mythical sage). The currently available text is a redaction by Dridhabala (probably ninth century CE).

In both the *Sushruta* and the *Charaka*, medicine is broadly divided into eight areas—surgery; diseases of the ears, nose, throat, and eyes; internal medicine; mental diseases; pediatrics, including pregnancy and its complications; chemicals used in treatment (which

HYMNS FOR THE DISEASE DEMON *BALASA*

The two hymns below are used by Ayurvedic healers to treat an internal disorder that results in swelling in the limbs. The healer attempts to remove the disease agent (*balasa*) by cutting it out, applying a herbal remedy, and reciting hymns.

Destroy every *balasa*, who is seated in the limbs and in the joints, the indwelling one who loosens the bones and the joints and afflicts the heart.
I eradicate the *balasa* of the *balasa* victim, like the muskara (or *pushkara*, 'lotus') [and] I cut through his link [to the body] as the root of the *urvaru*-plant (gourd).
O *balasa*, fly forth and out of here, as the very young asumga (-bird?), and like the annual grass, pass away without destroying [our] men.

O tree, O herb, do not let even a small bit of the red *balasa*, the *vidradha* (abscess), the *visalpaka* (swelling) remain.
O *balasa*, your two withdrawn testicles which are hidden in the armpit, I know a splendid medicine for that—*cipudru*.
We tear away the *visalpaka* (swelling) who is in the limbs, in the two ears and in the two eyes, the *vidradha* (abscess) [and] the heart-affliction; [likewise] we dispel down [and] away that unknown *yaksma*.

Source: Kenneth G. Zysk. (1993) *Religious Medicine: The Historical Evolution of Indian Medicine.* New Brunswick, NJ: Transaction Publishers, 33.

at a later time developed into an extensive treatment of chemistry, especially of metals); rejuvenation; and aphrodisiacs.

The *Charaka* and particularly the *Sushruta* also describe the selection of medical students. Students were chosen from the three highest castes, and their physical and mental attributes were carefully considered. During a ceremony with a sacrificial fire as witness, teacher and student agreed on their respective roles. The student stayed with the teacher as a member of the teacher's family through the long years of apprenticeship.

The *Charaka* and especially the *Sushruta* discuss medical ethics in addition to other topics. The dress and conduct of physicians and especially their behavior toward the women in a patient's family are clearly enunciated. Both texts insist that patients should be treated with the same care and respect that one would give one's own child, without consideration of the patient's caste or position in society. The physician is asked to cure when possible, palliate when cure cannot be achieved, but under no circumstances to attempt the impossible (thus hurting the patient.) In return, a physician becomes financially successful and is praised by the king and the community.

Sexual activity was an overt and recognized part of Ayurveda. The major texts have a section—*Vajikarana*—that deals with rejuvenation and aphrodisiacs. Books such as the *Kama sutra* (Essentials of Physical Love) and *Anangaranga* (Games of Cupid) examine the physical aspects of male and female genitals and homo- and heterosexual lovemaking in great detail, but in a clinical, not lascivious fashion.

In discussing human beings in health and illness, the *Charaka* mentions the necessity of examining the following aspects: structure, function, causation, symptoms, methods of treatment, objectives of treatment, influence of the seasons and age, capabilities of the physician, nature of the medications and appliances used in treatment, and procedures used and their sequence. Structurally, the eight sections of the *Charaka* include an introduction and general principles, causes of disease, general pathology and dietetics, development of the fetus and anatomy, diagnosis and prognosis, methods of treatment, pharmacy, and cure of diseases. All together the *Charaka* has 150 chapters of varying lengths.

The *Sushruta* has been edited, with commentary, a number of times. The earliest known text is by Dallanacharya (twelfth century CE), who states that he

An Ayurvedic physician in Bhubaneswar, India, uses a hot iron rod and fabric soaked in herbs to heal an arthritic hip. (LINDSAY HEBBERD/CORBIS)

worked on an earlier commentary by Nagarjuna. The original text is the teachings of the sage Dhanvantari collected by Sushruta. It must be mentioned, however, that Dhanvantari, Sushruta, and Nagarjuna have not been clearly established as historic personages. From internal evidence it seems that the original *Sushruta* was compiled between the late sixth and early fifth centuries BCE. The *Sushruta* has 120 chapters in sections that include general principles, origins and causes of (sixteen types of) diseases, anatomy and sites for venesection (removing parts of arteries or veins), various surgical problems such as abscesses, and rites and rituals of surgery, poisoning (including animal bites and snake venom), and an appendix that discusses diverse medical and surgical problems.

Mainly though not exclusively concerned with surgical matters, the *Sushruta* details 100 instruments of six different types (as well as the most important instrument—the surgeon's hand). Most equipment resembles surgical instruments in use today. The text discusses the operation and the pre- and postoperative phases. It describes the management of wounds and abscesses in great detail and also the choice and use of caustics, leeches, and thermal cauterization (using a heated agent to sear tissue). The surgical trainee is charged to dissect human cadavers and to practice various surgical acts on appropriate inert material such as animal carcasses or gourds before operating on human patients.

The descriptions of many operations, such as those for piles, fistulae, perianal abscesses, and bladder stones, are detailed, explicit, and anatomically accurate. Surgical treatment of head and neck conditions is extensively described, and Sushrutian plastic-surgery techniques for torn earlobes and disfigured noses were known in Europe in the early nineteenth century, as British physicians of the East India Company observed them and brought them back to the West.

***The* Astangahrdaya** The *Astangahrdaya* has six sections—general principles, pregnancy and development of the fetus, the causes of disease and symptoms, treatment methods, the use of emetics, purgatives, and enemas, and an appendix that discusses diverse groups of diseases. Many diseases described in the Ayurveda may be clearly recognized today, though a number overlap and are ambiguous.

***The* Madhavanidana *and the* Madhavachikitsa** Another important Ayurvedic author is Madhavakar (dated somewhere between the sixth through ninth centuries), who wrote two texts: The *Madhavanidana* and the *Madhavachikitsa*. The *Madhavanidana*, which is better known, describes the causes of diseases and their symptoms, complications, and prognostic characters signifying lethality. The text's sixty-six chapters are arranged differently from the *Charaka* and the *Sushruta*, even though much of the material is borrowed from them. Madhavakar adds some new disease entities and enlarges on some entities described in the *Charaka* and *Sushruta*. The *Madhavachikitsa* deals with treatment of most (but not all) of the various diseases described in the *Madhavanidanam*.

Government Provisions for Medical Practice and the Spread of Ayurvedic Medicine

Both state licensing of trained medical and surgical practitioners and specialization in particular branches of medicine existed in ancient India. The edicts of Asoka (c. 265–238 BCE) show that the state provided treatment of sick people and animals and that shelters (resembling hospitals) existed.

There are striking parallels between the Greek (Hippocratic) system and Ayurveda. The Greeks and the Indo-Gangetic Indians had extensive cross-communication even before Alexander of Macedon's failed attempt to conquer India in 323 BCE. The diffusion of medical ideas probably went in both directions, perhaps with doctors from both Greece and India meeting in the Persian court and exchanging information; the Indian system was by no means a copy of the Greek. The monks who spread Buddhism to Southeast Asia, Sri Lanka, the East Indian islands, China, Japan, and Korea took with them the Ayurvedic medical methods (Buddhism proscribed the shedding of blood—hence surgical acts were forbidden). From the seventh century onward, emergent Islam recognized the excellence of Ayurvedic medicine. Islamic rulers had Indian physicians in their courts and had Indian texts translated into Arabic. With the Muslim conquest of northern India the two systems became even more closely associated.

Ayurveda in Modern Times

Ayurvedic medicine is still extensively practiced in India. It has changed much from its original form under the influence of later Islamic and Western medical systems. Ayurvedic treatment is less expensive and in many instances as effective as Western medical treatment. In India Ayurvedic practitioners are available in remote parts of the country, while Western-style medical doctors may not be. As a recognized medical discipline, there are national and state regulatory agencies, and a number of good Ayurvedic medical schools exist. Since India's independence, considerable efforts have gone into standardizing the medications prescribed in the Ayurveda, and the pharmacological properties of Ayurvedic medications are being scientifically studied. Ayurvedic surgery, however, has been completely lost, partly because surgery played a minor role in Islamic medicine, which was favored by the Muslim rulers of most of India from the eleventh century onward.

The details of the Hindu system of medicine are relatively little known in the Western world though interest in alternative medical therapies, including Ayurveda, is growing. Since 1997 the U.S. National Institutes of Health Office of Alternative Medicine, established by the U.S. Congress in 1992, has been studying various alternative therapies, including Ayurveda, with the intention of providing scientific evaluation of the effectiveness of the treatments.

Ranès C. Chakravorty

Further Reading

Gupta, A., ed. (1980) *Astangahrdayam* with *Vidyotini Tika.* 7th ed. Varanasi, India: Chaukhamba Sanskrit Sansthan.

Sastri, S., ed. (1975) *Madhavanidanam* (with *Madhukosh* and *Vidyotini tika*). 2 vols. 4th ed. Varanasi, India: Chaukhamba Sanskrit Sansthan.

Sharma, P. V., ed. (1992) *History of Medicine in India (From Antiquity to 1000 A.D.).* New Delhi. Indian National Science Academy.

Shastri, K. A. (1972) *Sushrutasamhita.* 2 vols. 3d ed. Varanasi, India: Chaukhamba Sanskrit Sansthan.

Zimmerman, Francis. (1988) *The Jungle and the Aroma of Meats.* Berkeley and Los Angeles: University of California Press.

MEDICINE, TRADITIONAL—CENTRAL ASIA

Since the implosion of the Soviet Union in 1991, health care and pharmaceutical industries in the Central Asian states of Kazakhstan, Kyrgyzstan, Tajikistan, Turkmenistan, and Uzbekistan have collapsed. The Semashko model of health organization, named after the first minister of health in Soviet Russia, featured total state authority and control; significant centralization of administration, planning, and financing; and free-of-charge medical assistance at the point of delivery. Now health care providers receive very low salaries, resulting in poor motivation and morale. Malpractice and substantial under-the-counter payments are widespread, causing public pessimism and distrust of hospitals, clinics, and pharmacies in both rural and urban settings.

With the collapse of centralized health care, citizens of the Central Asian states are increasingly turning to traditional or folk medicines to cure common colds, minor infections, and other ailments. Centers for the study and understanding of folk medicine are opening throughout Central Asia. The centers serve as teaching clinics where patients seek alternative medical treatments from folk healers and their apprentices. Sufferers also tap into Central Asia's rich medicinal texts, both modern and historical, which focus on the local flora and fauna as remedies for ills. These books are being published at increasing rates for the use of clinics or medical cooperatives in Central Asian cities.

Heritage of Central Asian Traditional Medicine

Traditional medicine in Central Asia draws on a rich and diverse heritage, bringing together spiritual and empirical elements. Bridging Europe and Asia, Central Asia has been exposed to medical knowledge from a variety of regions near and far. Closely allied with popular religious beliefs, spiritual medicine reflected both pre-Islamic shamanist traditions and Islamic practices before the Soviet period. Shamans and mullahs served as medical practitioners by fighting to expel the evil spirits that Central Asian folk believed lay at the root of disease. Folk doctors, for their part, relied on observable phenomena and treated ailments by using locally available plant and animal products. Despite Soviet rule, knowledge accumulated over hundreds of years passed from generation to generation, enhanced by information about remedies that had met with success in China, Tibet, India, and the Near East. These studies are manifested in current remedies. Central Asians saw folk doctors not in opposition to shamans and mullahs, but as members of allied medical fields.

Animal Remedies

Before the Soviets came to power, Central Asians used not only herbs but also animals in traditional medicine. For example, to treat syphilis Kazakhs burned the entire skeleton of a wolf and ground the ashes into a powder, which was applied to the patient's sores. In cases of fever Kazakhs rubbed sheep liver on the patient's body or beat him or her with the lungs of a sheep or goat. To treat the common cold, the patient was placed in a tub filled with hot water and sheep entrails, which were supposed to promote sweating the illness out of the person's system. Central Asians treated cutaneous anthrax, a natural infectious disease characterized by skin ulcerations, by tying a string around the leg of a live frog, fastening the frog to the patient, and placing it directly on the sores. In a few minutes the frog supposedly suffocated, and its stomach turned black. The process was then repeated with four or five more frogs, after which the wound was rubbed with oil. Allegedly, after several days, the sores disappeared altogether. Bridging both the Soviet era and the present, perhaps the animal product most widely used in traditional medicine is koumiss, or fermented mare's milk. In the Central Asian nomadic cultures, koumiss is readily available as an effective measure to maintain good health and as a successful treatment for a variety of illnesses, such as alleviating colds and the flu.

Plant Remedies

Central Asian herbal medicine is allopathic, not homeopathic. Homeopathy treats diseases by using herbs that would induce in a healthy person symptoms similar to those the disorder causes in the sick person; allopathy induces effects opposed to the symptoms. Plant remedies are typically prepared by brewing a tea made from dried herbs and roots gathered in the mountains and plains. Mint is a frequently used ingredient to soothe the mouth and throat. Central Asians also distill herbs and roots in water or koumiss and distribute the result in ointment form. These herbal solutions are used to treat, among other things, fevers, diarrhea, headaches, psychological afflictions and STDs, namely syphilis. Central Asians use strong black tea to treat headaches, a remedy that is effective because caffeine constricts blood vessels, thereby alleviating pain. For swellings, the ground roots of wild nettles are placed directly on the inflammation. A mild narcotic used to treat the common cold, *nasybai*, is administered under the tongue in a form akin to chewing tobacco. Central Asians use opium and *nasybai* as painkillers.

Government's Role in Traditional Medicine

The Central Asian governments support traditional medicine as a supplement, not a replacement, for modern medicine. Groups such as Avicenna, named after the famous Islamic medical scholar Ibn Sina (980–1037), promote clinics and publish journals on how to use traditional medicines to encourage good physical and mental health. In Central Asia's scientific laboratories, with government encouragement scientists are completing clinical trials of traditional medicinal preparations. Tinctures, ointments, granules, and powders, made from local herbal raw materials, are being developed. The new medicines include healing remedies (bentonite and iodine powder, tincture of Japanese *safara*), and antidiabetic preparations (beans and vigna granules). Central Asians also use minerals such as iodine-sulfuric powder to get rid of skin diseases. Overall, Central Asians use traditional medicines in response to their growing inability to manufacture modern pharmaceuticals.

Theodore Karasik

Further Reading

Abdi, W. H., M.S. Asimov, and A.K. Bag (1990) *Interaction between Indian and Central Asian Science and Technology*. Vols. 1 and 2. New Delhi: Indian National Science Academy.

Elgood, Cyril. (1979) *A Medical History of Persia and the Eastern Caliphate*. Amsterdam: APA-Philo Press.

Hoizey, Dominique, and Marie-Joseph Hoizey. (1993) *A History of Chinese Medicine*. Vancouver, Canada: University of British Columbia Press.

Kamal, Hasan. (1975) *Encyclopaedia of Islamic Medicine*. Cairo, Egypt: General Egyptian Book Organization.

Karryev, M. O. (1991) *Farmakokhimiia lekarstvennykh rastenii Turkmenistana* (Pharmo-Chemical Medicines of Turkmenistan's Plants). Ashkhabad, Turkmenistan: Bylym.

Michaels, Paula. (1998) "Medical Traditions, Kazak Women, and Soviet Medical Politics to 1941." *Nationalities Papers* 26, 3: 493–509.

Rahman, Fazlur. (1998) *Health and Medicine in the Islamic Tradition*. Chicago: ABC International Group.

Ullman, Manfred. (1997) *Islamic Medicine*. Edinburgh, U.K.: Edinburgh University Press.

Yanjuan, Wang, Ying Huang, and Richard R. Pearce. (1997) *Sun Zi's Art of War and Health Care*. Beijing: New World Press.

MEDICINE, TRADITIONAL — CHINA

Traditional Chinese medicine (TCM) has a long history. More than two thousand years ago the earliest of the extant medical classics, the *Huangdi nei jing* (Yellow Emperor's Canon of Medicine), also called the *Canon of Acupuncture*, set forth the medical knowledge of China. It would be neither astounding nor impossible to compare the ancient *Canon of Medicine* with recent works compiled in accordance with the standards of contemporary scientific medicine. In fact, we can regard contemporary medicine as inspired by the Chinese *Canon of Medicine.* While both Hippocrates and the *Canon of Medicine* represent the same monumental break from previous magical or supernatural healing systems, only the *Canon of Medicine* still holds both the prestige of antiquity and scientific interest in the world's largest health system, which serves nearly 25 percent of the world's population. The principles of TCM are still taught to students in all twenty-six colleges and thirty academies of TCM throughout China today.

The Basic Principles of TCM

The basic principles of TCM are the theory of yin and yang, the five elements, viscera, *qi* (life force), blood and body fluids, and the theory of the channels and collaterals.

A significant difference between TCM and Western medicine is the TCM mandate to focus on the entire body. A symptom expressed in one part of the body must be seen in its relationship to the whole body. While the Western physician starts with a symptom and then searches for the underlying mechanism or cause for that specific disorder, the TCM physician concentrates on the complete physiological and psychological aspects of the patient and looks for the body's pattern of disharmony to provide the basis for treatment. In terms of clinical understanding, while the Western medicine physician asks "What X is causing Y?" the TCM physician asks "What is the relationship between X and Y?"

Yin and Yang

Yin and yang were originally part of ancient Chinese philosophy: They represent the dynamic complementarity of paired opposites, such as hot and cold, dry and moist, male and female. The side of a mountain that faces the sun, for instance, is yang, and the side not facing the sun is yin. Yin and yang are embodied in every aspect of TCM's theoretical system. They are used to explain the tissues and structures, physiology, and pathology of the human body, and they also direct the clinical diagnosis and treatment.

The property, flavor, and function of Chinese medicinal herbs are summarized in the light of the yin and yang theory, which forms the basis for the clinical application of Chinese medicinal herbs. This is the reason why this theory is still taught in the colleges of TCM, even though it seems to be obsolete in comparison with the principles of Western medicine. Without a thorough understanding of the yin and yang theory, one cannot learn how to use Chinese medicinal herbs for clinical purposes correctly.

The Five Elements

Initially, the Chinese distinguished five kinds of substance in the world (wood, fire, earth, metal, and water) that were indispensable in the daily life of humankind. Subsequently, a mutual genesis and destruction relationship was theorized to explain the whole material world. The tissues and organs, as well as the emotions, of a person can be classified in the light of the theory of the five elements. For instance, the liver is wood, heart fire, spleen earth, lung metal, and kidney water. Furthermore, the seasons of the year; environmental factors such as wind, heat, dampness, dryness, and cold; color, such as blue, red, yellow, white, and black; taste, such as bitter, sour, sweet, and salty; and the orientations of east, south, west, and north can all be classified in the light of the five elements. For an example, spring is wood, summer fire, late summer earth, autumn metal, and winter water. This is the reason why an autumn wind is called the "golden wind" in Chinese.

The Viscera and Bowels

In TCM the internal organs of the human body are divided into three groups: five viscera, six bowels (that is, organs that are hollow on the inside), and extraordinary organs. The five viscera are the heart, liver, spleen, lungs, and kidneys. Their common features are to preserve the vital substances of the human body. The six bowels are the gallbladder, stomach, large intestine, small intestine, urinary bladder, and the "triple warmer" *(sanjiao).* They have the common function of transmitting and digesting water and food. The extraordinary organs are the brain, bone, bone marrow, blood vessels, gallbladder (which is both an extraordinary organ and a bowel), and in women, the uterus. Although they are also called bowels, their functions are different from those of the six bowels previously mentioned.

The term "triple warmer" is peculiar to TCM. It is a collective term for the upper, middle, and lower warmers, which together form an organ of energy

FROM TRADITIONAL TO MODERN

China's health needs are served by a mix of hospitals ranging from those that practice traditional medicine to those that practice a mix of traditional and modern to the newest that offer Western medicine in modern facilities. The desire for modern facilities is a 1990s development tied to the privatization of the Chinese economy and the presence of many Westerners in major Chinese cities. The Chinese government has been reluctant to support such ventures, but one such hospital is Beijing United Family Hospital, opened in 1997 through the efforts of Roberta Lipson, an American who has worked in China since 1979. In 2001 the hospital continues to serve mainly Westerners, but is engaged in a marketing campaign to attract young, middle-class Chinese families who can afford its services. The hospital has been allowed by the government because it hopes to learn and use the Western medical management practices used there.

Source: Yasmin Ghahremani. "China's Model Hospital." *Asia Week* (16 November): 40–41.

transfer. Generally, it is recognized that "triple warmer" is a large bowel containing all the internal organs. The triple warmer is also used to anatomically locate the body parts. The upper warmer is that portion of the body cavity above the diaphragm that houses the heart and the two lungs. The middle warmer is the portion between the diaphragm and the umbilicus that houses the spleen and the stomach. The lower warmer is the portion below the umbilicus that houses the liver, the kidneys, the urinary bladder, the intestines, and the uterus. Generally speaking, the physiological functions of the triple warmer control the activities of the *qi* of the human body.

Qi, Blood, and Body Fluids

TCM believes that the *qi*, blood, and body fluids are the basic components of the body and maintain the life activities of the human body. The energy needed by the viscera and bowels, channels and collaterals, tissues, and other organs for performing their physiological functions come from *qi*.

Qi in TCM refers both to the vital substance composing the human body and maintaining its life activities, and to the physiological functions of the viscera, bowels, and channels and collaterals. *Qi* is important for the physiological functions of these viscera and bowels. If considered within the yin and yang theory, *qi* is yang and blood is yin; blood is the physical manifestation of *qi*.

The Channels and Collaterals

"Channel" *(jing)* means "route." Channels are the main pathways running lengthwise through the body, through which *qi* flows. "Collateral" *(luo)* means "net," and the collaterals are branches of a channel in the system. The channels and collaterals are distributed over the whole body and are linked with each other and connect the superficial, interior, upper, and lower portions of the human body, making the body an organic whole.

Historic Development of TCM

The legendary Shen Nung was considered the father of agriculture and herbal therapy, and Huangdi (the mythical Yellow Emperor, who was born, according to legend, in 2704 BCE) was considered the creator of ritual and of medicine and the compiler of the *Nei jing* (Canon of Medicine). The Warring States period (475–221 BCE) saw the first corporation of doctors *(yi)* independent of priests and magicians *(wu)*. This body's first known representative was Bian Que (430–350 BCE), who already knew the pulse rate as a basis for diagnosis and prognosis. The authorship of the *Nan jing* (The Classic of Difficulties) has been attributed to him.

Zhang Zhongjing, the Chinese Hippocrates, was the codifier of Chinese symptomology and therapeutics. Born in 158 BCE, in Nanyang, Henan Province, Zhang compiled an authoritative work entitled *Shanghan Lun* (Treatise on Fevers). While the Canon of

Medicine listed only twelve prescriptions and five forms of drugs (pills, powders, pellets, tinctures, and decoctions), Zhang's work listed 370 prescriptions and a greater variety of forms, including emulsions. His prescriptions for dysentery, encephalitis B, pneumonia, and hepatitis are still applicable today.

Hua Tuo (?–208 CE) was the great surgeon of the Han dynasty (206 BCE–220 CE). His most important discoveries were in the field of anesthetics and the art of abdominal section. The Chinese people also owe the practice of hydrotherapy to Hua Tuo. Ge Hong (284–364 CE) was one of Taoism's greatest alchemists and pathologists. His medical handbook covered such diverse ailments as infectious and parasitic diseases and neurological disorders. The first monograph on surgery was a modest collection of procedures by Gong Qingxuan (d. 208 CE). Early surgery focused on the treatment of carbuncles and ulcers, which upper-class patients suffered from.

State-sponsored medical schools started in China in 443 CE, but it was not until 581, at the beginning of the Sui dynasty (581–618 CE), that the government opened an Imperial Medical Academy, which was expanded in 624, during the Tang dynasty (618–907 CE).

In 610 CE, Chao Yuanfang, together with others, compiled the book *Zhou bing yuan ho lun* (General Treatise on the Causes and Symptom of Diseases), which is the earliest extant classic on etiology in China. Its fifty volumes are divided into sixty-seven categories, under which are listed 1,700 syndromes. It details the pathology, signs, and symptoms of various diseases in internal medicine, surgery, gynecology, and pediatrics as well as describing diseases of the five sense organs.

Sun Simiao (581–682 CE), a famous Tang-dynasty medical man, wrote two books: *Ji bei qian jing tao fang* (Prescriptions Worth a Thousand Gold Pieces for Emergencies) and *Qian jing yao fang* (A Supplement to the Essential Prescriptions Worth a Thousand Gold Pieces). These two books deal with acupuncture and moxibustion (the use of moxa, or *Artemisia vulgaris*, as a cautery by igniting it close to the skin), diet therapy, preventative care, health preservation, and so on.

In the Song dynasty (960–1279 CE), more attention was paid to educating doctors in the principles of TCM. The Imperial Medical Bureau was set up and courses for students included "Plain Questions Classic on Medical Problems" and "Treatise on Febrile Diseases." In 1026 CE Wang Weiyi designed two life-size bronze figures and had them cast for use in teaching and in examining students learning acupuncture and moxibustion. When used for the purpose of testing, the bronze figures were filled with water and coated with beeswax by the examiner ahead of time. If a candidate spotted and punctured the right acupoint, water would issue from it.

During the Jin dynasty (1125–1234) and the Yuan dynasty (1279–1368), the four famous medical schools appeared, each with its own special features in the diagnosis and treatment of various disorders. They were the School of Cold and Cool, represented by Liu Wansu (1120–1200); the School of Attacking or Purging, headed by Zhang Congzheng (1156–1228); the School of Injuries of the Spleen and Stomach, headed by Li Dongyuan (1180–1251); and the School of Nourishing the Earth, founded by Zhu Zhenheng (1281–1358).

The only great scientific work written in the sixteenth century uninfluenced by Western scientific thought is the *Ben cao gang mu* (Great Herbal) of Li Shizhen (1518–1593) during the Ming dynasty (1368–1644). The Great Herbal listed 1,892 medicines and more than ten thousand prescriptions. It took Li twenty-seven years to accomplish and is a great contribution to the development of pharmacology both in China and throughout the world. Besides being a great pathological and therapeutic work, it is a treatise on natural history, giving a classification of mineral, vegetable, and animal products. To complete the encyclopedia, there are chapters on chemical and industrial technology and geographical, historical, dietetic, and culinary data, as well as other information. It has been translated into all the languages of East Asia and the principal Western languages.

To put these developments into historical context, Harvey published on the circulation of blood in 1682 CE but was anticipated in Europe by Servenus (1546) and others who had read the Arab studies of al-Nafis (1228). Circadian rhythms and the science of endocrinology (including hormone therapy) were discussed in the second-century BCE Chinese texts, 2,200 years before their acceptance in the West. In attempting to identify and control diabetes, the Chinese were ahead of the Europeans for nearly a thousand years, although they never connected the disease with the pancreas. Immunology developed in China in the tenth century CE, including inoculation for smallpox, which did not occur in Europe until the eighteenth century.

Wang Qingren (1768–1831 CE), a physician of the Qing dynasty (1644–1912), wrote Corrections on the Errors of Medical Works. He corrected the errors in autopsy in ancient medical books, emphasized the importance of autopsy, and developed the theory that blood stasis would result in disease.

TCM has undergone its ups and downs in official policy over the last century. In the early years of the Republic (from 1911/1912), the emphasis officially was on Western medicine. President Sun Yat-sen (1866–1925) was a Western-trained physician, and the bias of his government was definitely toward Western medicine. However, the vast majority of the Chinese people continued to go on much as they did before in seeking treatment from TCM practitioners. The birth of the People's Republic (1949) brought an official revival of TCM. Veteran TCM practitioners started producing texts under government auspices in the 1950s. By the time of the Cultural Revolution (1966–1976), when the official emphasis in general health care shifted from Western medicine to TCM, the body of written knowledge was sufficient to be put to work in the rapid training of "barefoot doctors" with a manual describing TCM remedies for major health situations and problems.

Contemporary Development of TCM

In the twentieth century, with the popularization of Western medicine in China, a new situation has arisen in which TCM and Western medicine are developing side by side. Chinese medical workers have come to realize that TCM and Western medicine each have their own advantages. Efforts have been made to combine the two schools and to put forward a series to assimilate the two schools in theory and practice. Much of this effort has come since the end of the Cultural Revolution, when many prominent Western medicine specialists returned from their banishment to manual labor in the countryside and were assigned to TCM institutions. Their task was to undertake basic and clinical research, using modern rigorous methods, to determine the efficacy of TCM treatments.

TCM is now developing rapidly and is widely being practiced in China. New technological devices, such as lasers, have been incorporated in 2,000-year-old methods. In 1986 the State Council of China created a State Administrative Bureau of TCM and Pharmacy. It controls TCM and Chinese medical materials, as well as the step-by-step integration of TCM and Western medicine. There are now more than 340,000 TCM doctors; 1,500 hospitals of TCM, with a total of 100,000 beds; and 26 colleges and 30 academies of TCM in China.

Chen Bao-xing and Garé LeCompte

See also: **Acupuncture; Five Phases.**

Further Reading

Geng Junying, and Su Zhilong. (1990) *Practical Traditional Chinese Medicine & Pharmacology: Acupuncture and Moxibustion.* Beijing: New World Press.

———. (1990) *Practical Traditional Chinese Medicine & Pharmacology: Basic Theories and Principles.* Beijing: New World Press.

Horn, Joshua S. (1969) *Away with All Pests: An English Surgeon in People's China.* New York: Monthly Review Press.

Huang Jianping. (1990) *Methodology of Traditional Chinese Medicine.* Beijing: New World Press.

Huard, Peter, and Wong Ming. (1968) *Chinese Medicine.* New York: World University Library, McGraw-Hill.

Institute of Traditional Chinese Medicine of Hunan Province. (1985) *A Barefoot Doctor's Manual.* New York: Grammercy Publishing Company. (Originally translated and published in English in 1975 by the National Institutes of Health, U.S. Public Health Service, U.S. Department of Health, Education, and Welfare as DHEW Publication No. (NIH) 75-695).

Kaptchuk, Ted J. (1983) *Chinese Medicine: The Web That Has No Weaver.* London: Rider & Company.

Needham, Joseph. (1969) *The Grand Titration: Science and Society in the East and West.* London: George Allen & Unwin.

Porkert, Manfred, with Christian Ullmann. (1982) *Chinese Medicine.* New York: Henry Holt & Company.

State Administration for Traditional Chinese Medicine. (1992) *Traditional Chinese Medicine and Pharmacology: A Textbook for Foreign Students at Colleges of Traditional Chinese Medicine.* Beijing: New World Press.

Zhang Enqin. (1990) *Basic Theory of Traditional Chinese Medicine.* Shanghai: Publishing House of the Shanghai College of Traditional Chinese Medicine.

MEDICINE, TRADITIONAL — WEST ASIA

West Asia was (and still is) a heterogeneous area in terms of topography, climate, and culture, which perhaps explains its pluralism—even syncretism—in the area of traditional medicine, on both the intellectual and practical levels. Since the middle of the seventh century CE, West Asia has been predominantly Muslim, although Anatolia, or Asia Minor, became Muslim only during the eleventh to the thirteenth centuries. However, many non-Muslims—various Christian sects, Jews, Zoroastrians, and others—have kept their original faiths. Because medicine is always associated with beliefs about God, nature, and human beings' place in the world, it is imbued with religious, cultural, and social values, and these values may differ for people of different faiths.

Since the end of the eighteenth century, major political and socioeconomic transformations have affected health care in Western Asia, and traditional medicine now occupies only a peripheral position. In the past, however, there were three main medical traditions in West Asia, each of which explained the nature of health, the causes of illness, the remedies and other curing techniques used by healers, and the proper care for sick people according to its own worldview. These three major systems were humoralistic medicine, popular or folkloristic medicine, and religious medicine.

Humoralistic Medicine

Humoralistic medicine was the tradition that Muslim societies inherited from the past, particularly from the Greek physicians Hippocrates, the father of medicine (c. 460–c. 377 BCE), and Galen (129–c. 199 CE). This tradition was based in cities and princely courts, where it flourished under the patronage of rulers, high officials, and military dignitaries. Humoralism was based on the assumption that all things were composed of the four elements of fire, earth, air, and water. Each element embodied two of the four qualities of hot, cold, dry, and wet. The human body consisted of four fluids, or humors—blood, phlegm, black bile, and yellow bile—each corresponding to one of the elements. Humoralism stressed the importance of a strict regimen suitable for each individual's lifestyle and environment.

Hence a humoral practitioner had to examine his patient closely by checking the patient's pulse, inspecting the urine, and questioning the patient about the ailment. After diagnosing the problem, the healer would probably first prescribe a suitable diet. If a medical diet did not solve the problem, the doctor would treat the patient with a pharmacopoeia, mostly with botanical ingredients. If this harsher treatment failed, the physician would choose a still harsher course—a simple surgical procedure.

Although Muslim physicians drew on this tradition, they expanded it considerably in all branches of medicine and pharmacy. A famous representative of this school was Ibn Sina (980–1037), known in Europe as Avicenna. His *Qanun* (or Canon of Medicine), one of his almost two hundred literary works, was a standard medical text well into the eighteenth century in Asia as well as Europe.

Popular or Folkloristic Medicine

Popular or folkloristic medicine includes several systems of indigenous medicine practiced in West Asia for hundreds of years. Whereas other medical systems required would-be physicians to study written texts with teachers, to apprentice themselves to masters, or to teach themselves, folkloristic medicine was based on oral traditions and was usually taught via informal apprenticeship. In contrast to urban-based humoralism, popular medicine—though practiced in towns as well—was more common in the countryside. The therapeutical aspect of popular medicine includes practical knowledge about medical herbs and includes procedures that may also appear in humoralism, such as bloodletting and cauterization.

Religious Medicine

Religious medicine refers to medical theory sanctioned by religious figures. Foremost in this area is prophetic medicine (in Arabic, *Tibb Nabawi)*, as in Muhammad's sayings that concerned medical questions. For instance, there are aphorisms of Muhammad dealing with hygiene, with the care of a sick person and his or her family, and with recipes for treatment. For Shiʿite Muslims, the role of Muhammad as healer was less important; they invested their religious leaders (imams) with unique therapeutic skills as part of their supernatural nature and sought treatment from them.

Religious medicine also includes medical rites and practices connected with living and dead saints. Saints are often endowed with extraordinary healing powers. Religious medicine may even refer to a profound belief in the healing capacities of objects like trees, grass, stones, water, earth, tombs, oil, soil, and even saliva, urine, and the excrement of certain animals. The genre of religious medicine incorporates both magical procedures and herbal remedies familiar in humoral and folkloristic medicine as well, but unique to religious medicine is the connection of healing with religious figures, mainly dead ones.

The belief in the healing power of the saints still exists in Western Asia. Everything that comes in contact with a saint or his or her shrine may receive some of the saint's healing powers. Thus objects associated with a saint's shrine may be used for curing and protection; acts performed at a shrine may have the same beneficial effects. For instance, Palestinian Muslims believe that dates brought from Mecca cause children to speak soon and with a sweet voice.

Characteristics of the West Asian Traditional Medical System

Thus traditional West Asian medicine was decentralized; no common doctrine united all its varieties. Nevertheless there was much overlapping in theories and techniques. For example, phlebotomy (bloodletting) and cauterization (burning to destroy tissue) were popular practices among healers in all medical traditions. Cauterization was such a common technique that European travelers in the Ottoman empire commented on the phenomenon of people treating themselves, including cauterizing themselves to treat a host of problems, such as headaches, skin rashes, leprosy, abscesses, and hemorrhoids. Sometimes a practice described in humoralistic treatises was adopted into popular medicine, but after several generations in oral and popular tradition, its roots in the learned past were forgotten.

In West Asia, traditional medicine has become marginal and is not practiced in state-run medical establishments or taught in universities. Those who aspire to a career in the medical establishment, whether at the medical, scientific, or administrative level, can achieve their aim only with knowledge and practice in Western biomedicine, which originated in Europe.

Traditional medical beliefs and practices are, however, still a living tradition in West Asia, despite the dominance of Western medicine. For example, humoralism, though marginalized, has survived; a Persian medical book of the 1950s, meant for contemporary practice, was based on Avicenna. (Humoralism is however much more alive in parts of South Asia, such as India and Pakistan, where it is widely taught and practiced under the name of *yunani tibb*, "Greek medicine.") And throughout Turkey, bazaars sell herbs for pharmaceutical purposes (drugs and poisons), as well as condiments for cooking, scents for perfume, and dyes. Furthermore, cauterization as a medical technique can still be observed in some rural regions in Turkey and the Arab world.

And in recent decades traditional medicine has enjoyed something of a revival. Disenchantment with Western values and Western medicine and the wish to defend Muslim values against Western morality have caused people to return to traditional practices, now known as complementary or alternative medicine (CAM). CAM has even won respect from advocates of biomedicine. Some hospitals try to take measures (or claim to be doing so) toward integrating aspects of CAM into the formal establishment, for instance by introducing optional CAM treatments into Western-type medical treatment.

Miri Shefer

Further Reading

Dols, Michael W. (1984) *Medieval Islamic Medicine: Ibn Ridwan's Treatise "On the Prevention of Bodily Ills in Egypt."* Berkeley and Los Angeles: University of California Press.

Elgood, Cyril. (1951) *A Medical History of Persia and the Eastern Caliphate from the Earliest Times until the Year A.D. 1932.* Cambridge, U.K.: Cambridge University Press.

———. (1970) *Safavid Medical Practice or The Practice of Medicine, Surgery, and Gynaecology in Persia between 1500 A.D. and 1750 A.D.* London: Luzac.

Karmi, Ghada. (1985). "The Colonisation of Traditional Arabic Medicine." In *Patients and Practitioners: Lay Perceptions of Medicine in Pre-Industrial Society*, edited by Roy Porter. Cambridge, U.K.: Cambridge University Press, 315–339.

Ullman, Manfred. (1978) *Islamic Medicine*. Edinburgh, U.K.: Edinburgh University Press.

———. (1992) *Majnun: The Madman in Medieval Islamic Society*. Oxford: Clarendon Press.

MEDICINE, UNANI

Unani medicine, also known as *yunani tibb* or Greco-Islamic medicine, is a therapeutic system used in South and Southwest Asia that developed through the interaction of ancient Greek with some Arab and, perhaps, Ayurvedic medical and pharmaceutical principles. The origin of Greco-Islamic medicine can be traced to Hippocrates (c. 460–c. 377 BCE), Galen (129–c. 199 CE), and Ibn Sina (Avicenna, 980–1037 CE).

The Galenic Medical System

Galen (129–c.199 CE), a philosopher and physician of Pergamum, an ancient Greek kingdom in Asia Minor, was the key figure in the transmittal of the earlier ideas about the four humors—blood, mucus, yellow bile, and black bile—formulated by the Greek Hippocratic school, to medieval Arab scholars, who in turn shared their understanding with Persian and Indian physicians. In essence, one can say that the principles of Islamic medicine were totally Galen's. It was in Galen's book *On the Nature of Man* (c. 180 CE) that the theory of four humors was first laid out in logical detail. They were believed to combine with four primary qualities—warmth, cold, moisture, and dryness—and a person was healthy only if the four humors and their associated qualities were in balance. An imbalance had to be rectified through diet or drugs.

This was to become a dominant theory not only in the Muslim Middle East but also in Christian Europe, where it was accepted until the end of the Renaissance and the discoveries that followed the invention of the microscope. It was an appealing theory because it offered an apparently convincing presentation that put humanity in relation to the macrocosm. In doing so a link was made between physiology and astrology: Islam, Christianity, and medieval Judaism all taught that the universe was divinely created, had a regular procession of stars and seasons, and that this was paralleled in the divinely created human, with his regular system of four humors. Many medieval scholars in fact pointed to the parallels between the four humors, the planets, and the seasons as though there were some overarching sympathy between them. Galen's own ideas about all this were very logical—if one accepted his premises—and they were further improved on by Ibn Sina, an Islamic philosopher and scientist.

Arab and Ayurvedic Influences

Galen's teaching was summarized by Husain ibn Ishaq (809–873 CE) and was thereafter repeated by subsequent writers on Arabic medicine, thereby giving it a certain internal consistency.

More specifically,

> Islamic cosmology was built up from the Ptolemaic conception of concentric spheres, the Aristotelian understanding of the elements fire, water, earth, and air, and the Plotinian view of the emanations of pure intelligences and souls. These ideas were joined in a view of nature as a hierarchy of being that could be analyzed as a series of oppositions and correspondences. Analogical reasoning treated the universe as macrocosm perfectly reflected in the human microcosm. These Greek elements were combined with intense Islamic monotheism, elements of Qur'anic cosmology, mystical practices, pilgrimage and shrine traditions, and with the Middle Eastern Hermetic or wisdom *(hikmat)* tradition.
>
> *(Good and Good 1992: 259)*

Good and Good are not arguing

> that bits and pieces of traditional Greco-Islamic medicine persist in discrete popular beliefs about sexuality or physiology or popular cures, but that for important segments of the Islamic world, the classical epistemology still provides the conditions for meaningful adherence to seemingly diverse practices and beliefs, and that a reading of medical practices from the perspective of the classical cosmology and episteme makes them comprehensible.
>
> *(Good and Good 1992: 261)*

Nonetheless, when the Galenic medical system reached the Middle East it by no means entered a medical vacuum. The practices of the earlier Egyptians, Persians, Israelites, Romans, and others remained in use, and Bedouin folk medicine was attested to in the Qur'an too.

Seven centuries after Galen's death, the major center for the practice and development of Greco-Arab medicine was Baghdad. Medical specialists there were not unwilling to learn from India as well as ancient Greece, and indeed many had themselves come from Persia, Syria, and other countries. Even prior to the establishment of Islam, Burzuya (flourished c. 531 CE), a court physician to the Persian emperor, had visited India to study medical practice and bring back Sanskrit medical texts as well as some Indian physicians. Later, in Baghdad, an invitation was issued to a Hindu therapist known in Arabic sources as Manka to come and treat the famed caliph Harun ar-Rashid (c. 766–809). Being successful in this, Manka made his mark on Islamic society in the famous hospital of the Barmecides and was followed by numerous other Indian medical men who worked as therapists and translators of the Sanskrit texts during their stay in Baghdad. One chief minister, Yahiya-bin-Khalid Barmaki, also sent some Arab scholars to India to learn more about the Ayurvedic system.

The Arab component in the Unani system was derived, however, from classical Greek medicine in the main, as filtered through some 500 known texts of Galen, hence the name (*Unani*, meaning "Ionian" in Arabic, came to mean "foreign" in Indian languages). It was not a case of studying under Greek masters, but rather of translating the classical Greek and Syriac texts, already many centuries old, into Arabic. This was an important activity, which employed many people in Baghdad and elsewhere.

The Unani therapist, normally a Muslim, is generally called a *hakim* (learned man), in contrast to the Hindu therapist, who is known as a *vaid.* But there are also midwives, bonesetters, people who sell herbs, and other kinds of medical specialists. Despite the wide availability of hospitals practicing scientific medicine today, the Unani system survives in some South Asian towns and in some parts of Southeast and Western Asia too. In medieval times Arab hospitals practicing this type of medicine were the best in the world.

Paul Hockings

See also: **Medicine, Ayurvedic; Medicine, Traditional—West Asia**

Further Reading

Bürgel, J. Christoph. (1976) "Secular and Religious Features of Medieval Arabic Medicine." In *Asian Medical Systems: A Comparative Study*, edited by Charles Leslie. Berkeley and Los Angeles: University of California Press, 44–62.

Conrad, Lawrence I. (1993) "Arab-Islamic Medicine." In *Companion Encyclopedia of the History of Medicine*, edited by W. F. Bynum and Roy Porter. New York: Routledge, 1: 676–727.

Good, Byron, and Mary-Jo DelVecchio Good. (1992) "The Comparative Study of Greco-Islamic Medicine: The Integration of Medical Knowledge into Local Symbolic Contexts." In *Paths to Asian Medical Knowledge*, edited by Charles Leslie and Allan Young. Berkeley and Los Angeles: University of California Press, 257–271.

MEGAWATI SUKARNOPUTRI (b. 1947),

President of the Republic of Indonesia. Megawati Sukarnoputri is the daughter of Indonesia's founder

Megawati Sukarnoputri at a rally in February 2000 at which party members endorsed her for president. (AFP/CORBIS)

and first president, Sukarno (1901–1970), who ruled in Indonesia from 1949 to 1965. She attended two universities but never earned a degree. Though born in Java and raised as a Muslim, Megawati lived in Bali where she built up a large base of political support amongst the Hindu and Christian communities of the outer islands. Megawati became a prominent figure in Indonesia, when in 1995 she won control of the Christian-nationalist Indonesian Democratic Party (PDI), one of three legal parties under the regime of Suharto (b. 1921), 1965–1998. For many years Megawati accepted the status quo imposed by Suharto's New Order regime. She started to become critical of the Suharto regime in 1994–1995, accusing it of rampant nepotism and corruption. Angered at her outspokenness, in June 1996 a government-backed faction of the PDI ousted her from the party's leadership in an extraordinary party congress. The regime's heavy-handed tactics backfired and triggered mass demonstrations in Jakarta that ultimately led to Suharto's resignation in May 1998.

Owing to her political pedigree, Megawati became a symbol of opposition to the regime. Megawati established a new party, the Indonesia Struggle for Democracy Party (PDI-P) in 1998. The party won the most seats in the June 1999 election, but did not achieve an outright majority. Megawati was outmaneuvered, and a coalition of Islamic parties instead elected Abdurrahman Wahid (b. 1940), a moderate Islamic cleric and the head of Indonesia's largest Muslim organization, the Nahdlatul Ulama. In a power-sharing agreement, Megawati became vice president. Following Wahid's impeachment for incompetence and economic mismanagement in August 2001, Megawati became Indonesia's fifth president. Megawati has been under attack from the Muslim-oriented parties and publicly criticized for her lack of decisive leadership in the midst of an ongoing economic crisis.

Megawati was the first Muslim leader to visit the United States following the 11 September 2001 attacks, and while she condemned all terrorist acts, she was also very critical of the U.S. military campaign in Afghanistan.

Zachary Abuza

Further Reading

Schwartz, Adam. (1999) *A Nation in Waiting: Indonesia's Search for Stability*. 2d ed. Boulder, CO: Westview Press.

MEGHALAYA (2001 est. pop. 2.3 million). The state of Meghalaya (Sanskrit "Abode of the Clouds"), with an area of 22,429 square kilometers, lies on a mountainous plateau of great beauty in the northeast corner of India. Meghalaya is known as home to two of the rainiest places on earth, the towns of Cherrapunji and Mawsynram. Its hill people trace their origin to pre-Aryan times. The British largely left them alone, and the Indian constitution protected them.

Although Assamese was introduced as the official language in 1960, the predominantly Christian state of Meghalaya possesses a landscape and ethnicity strikingly different from neighboring Assam. Formerly part of Assam state, inhabitants began agitating for autonomy, which led to Meghalaya statehood in 1972. Eighty percent of the population is made up of the Khasi, Garo, and Jaintia peoples, all of whom are matrilineal and matrilocal. Most live in thousands of rural villages. The Khasis, dominating the central area of the state, belong to the Mon-Khmer linguistic group; they also share ancestry with the Mundas of north-central India and the Jaintias, in the east of the state around Jawai. The Garos are of Tibeto-Burman origin; most came by way of East Pakistan, later Bangladesh.

Farming engages 70 percent of the population. Crops include rice, millet, and corn (maize). Almost all of India's sillimanite (a source of high-grade ceramic clay) is produced in Meghalaya. The state has abundant mineral resources, mostly untapped. Industries include furniture making, iron and steel fabrication, tailoring, and knitting. The literacy rate is 49 percent, and the language of instruction is English.

Since the first appearance of Christian missionaries in 1842, the division between Christian and non-Christian has had political repercussions, with continuous episodes of violence and intrigue through the years. Yet, all united in a peaceful, successful struggle for statehood. Since 1972, however, the willingness of matrilineal people to accept outsiders has been sorely tested by migrants who came to dominate local trade and business.

Often compared to Scotland, a source of inspiration to poets and painters, Meghalaya offers an ideal retreat with sylvan surroundings, misty heights, terraced slopes, breathtaking waterfalls, and luxurious vegetation. Great stone monoliths were erected to the old kings in the Khasi and Jaintia hills, as well as in sacred forest groves.

C. Roger Davis

Further Reading

Gurdon, P. R. T. (1975) *The Khasis.* Delhi: Cosmos Publications.

Playfair, A. (1975) *The Garos.* Gauhati, India: United Publishers.

MEI LANFANG

MEI LANFANG (1894–1961), Chinese theatrical performer. Mei Lanfang was a Chinese theatrical performer born in Taizhou, Jiangsu Province, who achieved international recognition for his performances in women's roles. Born to a family of noted opera singers, Mei began studying at the Peking Opera when he was eight years old, making his stage debut at twelve. At the age of fourteen, he joined the Xiliancheng Opera Company and gained a national reputation after a series of performances in Shanghai and elsewhere in China. Mei introduced Peking Opera to foreign audiences when he toured Japan in 1919 and 1924, the United States in 1930, and the Soviet Union in 1932 and 1935. In 1937 he ceased performing and moved to Hong Kong after the outbreak of the Sino-Japanese War in protest of the Japanese invasion. He later returned to China and performed in films and on stage from 1946 until his death. He played more than 100 different characters, one of the most famous being the "Flower-shattering Diva." His distinctive style of dance became known as the "Mei Lanfang School." A remarkably charismatic and modest character, he is remembered as one of the greatest performers in Chinese history.

Daniel Oakman

Further Reading

Mackerras, Colin. (1997) *Peking Opera.* New York: Oxford University Press.

Wu Zuguang. (1981) *Peking Opera and Mei Lanfang.* Beijing: New World Press.

MEIJI PERIOD

MEIJI PERIOD (1868–1912). Meiji, which means "enlightened rule," is the name officially bestowed upon the reign of the sixteen-year-old emperor, Mutsuhito (1852–1912), on 8 September 1868. It is customary, however, to date the Meiji period from 3 January of that year, when he proclaimed the restoration of imperial rule and the abolition of the Tokugawa *bakufu* (military government) that had governed Japan for more than 250 years.

For most of the Tokugawa period (1600/1603–1868) the emperor was a forlorn political and cultural figure, isolated in the imperial capital, Kyoto, and overshadowed by the powerful Tokugawa shogun and his advisors, who claimed to rule in the emperor's name from the castle town of Edo. As discontent with the *bakufu* grew during the eighteenth century, however, some reform-minded critics began to invoke the emperor as an alternate, indeed preeminent, source of political authority. Even so, until the mid-nineteenth century, most of these reformers assumed that revitalizing the *bakufu* was key to resolving the domestic economic and social

JAPAN—HISTORICAL PERIODS

Jomon period (14,500–300 BCE)
Yayoi culture (300 BCE–300 CE)
Yamato State (300–552 CE)
Kofun period (300–710 CE)
Nara period (710–794 CE)
Heian period (794–1185)
Kamakura period (Kamakura Shogunate) (1185–1333)
Muromachi period (1333–1573)
Momoyama period (1573–1600)
Tokugawa or Edo period (Tokugawa Shogunate) (1600/1603–1868)
Meiji period (1868–1912)
Taisho period (1912–1926)
Showa period (1926–1989)
Allied Occupation (1945–1952)
Heisei period (1989–present)

problems that plagued the country. It was not until the 1850s, when the *bakufu* appeared to contravene the emperor's wishes by capitulating to the unequal treaty demands put forward by the United States and other Western trading powers, that plots to topple the *bakufu* began in earnest.

The Charter Oath

The Meiji period became synonymous with the modernization of Japan long before the death of Mutsuhito (known posthumously as Emperor Meiji) brought it to a close on 30 June 1912. That characterization is still widely accepted today. However, in light of his government's response to various dilemmas that accompanied its reforms, there is less agreement over the legacy of the Meiji period for twentieth-century Japan. Some of those dilemmas may be traced back to the provisions contained in the Charter Oath of Five Articles, which the emperor issued on 6 April 1868. The purpose of this imperial declaration was to reassure both the feudal domains and the Western powers of the aims of the new government. The irony is that those who drafted the Charter Oath were in no position to state with certainty what those aims were.

To begin with, neither the composition nor the structure of the new government had been determined. And to complicate matters, the loyalists who had joined together to overthrow the Tokugawa *bakufu* in the name of the emperor were drawn from disparate groups and motivated by competing interests. They included court nobles, daimyo (clan lords) from powerful domains like Satsuma and Choshu, and lower-ranking samurai in charge of administrative and military affairs within their domains.

The future of the new government was also uncertain because it lacked any military or economic power apart from that which the domains backing it were willing to put at its disposal. Fortunately, their support was sufficient to prosecute the civil war (Boshin War) against the pro-Tokugawa resistance, elements of which held out until June 1869. Few, however, believed that this coalition would last indefinitely.

The Charter Oath can thus be seen as a response to these uncertainties. Eager to reach across the class divisions and sectional loyalties that were mainstays of the Tokugawa political economy, drafters of the Charter Oath resorted to broadly worded assurances that: all classes were to unite in promoting the nation's economy and welfare; an assembly would be established and matters of state would be decided by public discussion; all classes would be allowed to fulfill their just aspirations, so as to avoid discontent; base customs of the past would be abandoned, and all actions would conform to universally recognized principles of justice; and knowledge would be sought throughout the world to strengthen the foundations of imperial rule. The wording of the articles may have delayed, but could not prevent, clashes over differing interpretations of them and disagreements over the government's ensuing policies.

As Article One makes clear, the first order of business was to unite the people behind the new government by articulating a common national identity and sense of purpose. The biggest potential threat to government authority and national unity lay with the more than two hundred daimyo who still ruled over their own domains with the help of their samurai vassals. To set an example which they hoped others would follow, the four daimyo who had backed the overthrow of the Tokugawa *bakufu* agreed to surrender their domain registers to the Meiji emperor in 1869. (By this time, the seat of the new government had been transferred to Edo, which was renamed Tokyo, or "eastern capital.") During the next two years other daimyo followed suit. In return, the government assumed the income and debts of the domains, and granted each daimyo a guaranteed stipend and nobility status. Some former daimyo also assumed the title of governor under a new system of prefectures that was established at the same time.

Disenfranchised Samurai

The samurai below them did not fare as well. The modest stipends they had received from the daimyo were taken over by the government. In 1873, however, the government moved to reduce this enormous drain on the treasury by taxing the stipend. Later, in August 1876, it announced that the annual stipend would be commuted to a lump sum payable in government bonds. Adding to the difficulties the samurai faced were concurrent policies that effectively stripped them of their privileged social standing. By 1872, all samurai were reclassified as either former samurai *(shizoku)* or commoners *(heimin)*. The Conscription Law of 1873 meant that military service was no longer their exclusive preserve. Even their right to wear swords was abolished.

As a result of these policies, some 400,000 former samurai experienced a loss of income, employment, and dignity. While some learned to capitalize on their superior education and administrative experience to occupy prominent positions in the political, economic, and social life of Meiji Japan, others experienced only frustration. Fearing a backlash, the government adopted a variety of rehabilitation measures during the 1870s, including grants to engage in commerce or agriculture. These measures were only partially successful, however, and failed to prevent disgruntled members of the *shizoku* class from organizing against the government. Some dusted off their swords and resorted to armed conflict. Significantly, the most famous of these incidents—the Saga Rebellion of 1874 and the Satsuma Rebellion of 1877—were each led by one-time members of the Meiji government, Eto Shimpei and Saigo Takamori, respectively, who had resigned due to disagreements over the new regime's foreign policy and its treatment of the samurai. Their defeat at the hands of the better-trained and equipped conscript army marked the demise of the samurai as a hereditary military class and ruling elite.

Other former samurai mounted a more cunning assault on the government by turning Article Two of the Charter Oath to their advantage. Ironically, this campaign, too, was led by a disillusioned member of the Meiji government, Itagaki Taisuke (1837–1919), who had resigned in 1873, along with Eto and Saigo. For Itagaki, who hailed from Tosa, an additional source of frustration was the near monopoly over key government posts enjoyed by former samurai from Satsuma and Choshu, which had led the loyalist forces against the Tokugawa *bakufu*. Instead of a sword, Itagaki used the power of the pen to petition the government in 1874 for an elected assembly, thereby launching the Freedom and People's Rights Movement *(jiyu minken undo)*. Over the next seven years he continued to press his case by organizing a series of political parties, culminating with the Liberal Party (Jiyuto) in 1881.

Peasants and Merchants

The nationwide prominence enjoyed by the Liberal Party and, by extension, the Freedom and People's Rights Movement as a whole, was due as much to the support of merchants, peasants, and laborers as it was to former samurai. They saw government compliance with Article Two of the Charter Oath as a way to press for compliance with Article Three. In the case of the merchant class, which had ranked at the bottom of the Tokugawa social order (below the samurai, peasants, and artisans), Article Three meant "fulfilling their just aspirations" for public recognition and for a voice in public affairs commensurate with their economic influence.

For peasants, who constituted 80 percent of the population, Article Three meant pursuing their traditional livelihoods with a minimum of government interference and exploitation. During the Tokugawa period, most land was nominally owned by the shogun or daimyo, although registered farmers did exercise certain rights over their individual plots. Peasants who worked the land normally relinquished 40 to 50 percent of their harvest as a land tax, which the daimyo used to pay the stipends of their samurai vassals and meet other expenses. However, as those expenses grew, and as more samurai and daimyo fell into debt to the rising merchant class, peasants could be forced to turn over as much as 70 percent of their crops and to endure miscellaneous taxes on doors, windows, female children, cloth, sake, and so forth. They were also called upon to provide corvée labor, and were the target of sumptuary laws exhorting them to produce more and consume less. Little wonder that in lean years peasants would petition for reductions in these obligations, or that when petitions failed, they turned to mass demonstrations and even riots. Between 1590 and 1867, there were over 2,800 peasant disturbances, most of them occurring during the latter half of the Tokugawa period. Some peasants eventually fell into debt, lost control of their land to other farmers or to absentee landlords living in rural towns, and were reduced to tenant status.

Whatever hopes the peasants might have had for a revival of benevolent rule following the Meiji Restoration were soon dampened by new demands placed upon them by the new government. Anxious to create a unified, centralized tax system that could provide a regular, stable source of revenue, the government in 1872 removed the ban on the sale, purchase, and mortgage of land. The following year it authorized a nationwide survey to determine ownership and value of land that would serve as the basis for reform of the land tax. Henceforth, the annual tax would be assessed against the value of the land rather than the crop yield, it would be payable in cash, rather than in kind, and it would be levied on the individual landowner rather than on the village unit. The tax rate was originally set at 3 percent; later a 1 percent supplement for local government was added. The new system was greeted by violent resistance, prompting the government to reduce the rate to 2.5 percent (local supplement 0.5 percent). Even so, many farmers paid as much as one-third of their harvest in tax, and tenancy rates continued to climb, rising from 20 percent of cultivated land at the time of the Restoration to 45 percent by 1907. The land tax accounted for 80 to 90 percent of total government revenue through the 1880s, declining to 20 percent by 1902 as other sources of revenue were found.

Peasant resentment against the Meiji government was also fueled by the Conscription Law and by the Fundamental Code of Education of 1872. The former required that all men aged twenty serve in the military for three years, followed by another four years in the reserve. This robbed farm households of badly needed labor. So, in its own way, did the Fundamental Code of Education, which—for the first time in the country's history—made primary education compulsory for all boys and girls. Adding to their burden was the expectation that the costs of school construction, teachers' salaries, tuition, textbooks, and so forth would be borne by local governments and families.

The Freedom and People's Rights Movement

To these disaffected elements of Meiji society, the Freedom and People's Rights Movement provided a platform to vent their anger over the government's new laws, as well as to insist that the promises made in Articles Two and Three of the Charter Oath be extended to everyone. Ironically, the government itself helped make this grassroots campaign possible through its articulation of Articles Four and Five. On one hand, its pledge to abandon outmoded customs and embrace universally recognized principles of justice could be cited by government opponents to justify their demand for a representative assembly like those found in "civilized" Western countries. On the other hand, its exhortation to seek knowledge throughout the world, coupled with its ambitious compulsory education policies, encouraged the populace to learn from the West and gave them an essential tool, literacy, with which to do so.

Ultimately, the Freedom and People's Rights Movement did help persuade the Meiji government to issue an imperial edict, in October 1881, announcing that Japan would have a constitution before the end of the decade. The Meiji oligarchy, however, still dominated by the Sat-Cho (Satsuma-Choshu) clique, reserved for itself the exclusive right to draft this document. It also moved to discourage further grassroots political activity. Even before the edict was issued, the government had taken steps in this direction. For example, the 1875 Libel Law and Newspaper Regulations sought to limit the role of the press in the Freedom and People's Rights Movement by stipulating harsh punishment for anyone advocating a change in government or criticizing legislation. And the Public Meetings Regulations, announced in 1880, required that political societies and public meetings be registered in advance with the police, and prohibited teachers, students, soldiers, sailors, and police officers from participating in them.

In conjunction with its promise of a constitution, the government renewed its determination to thwart further challenges to its authority. The 1881 edict carried a warning that anyone who "may advocate sudden and violent changes, thus disturbing the peace of Our realm, will fall under Our displeasure." This was followed by a series of revisions that strengthened the Public Meetings Regulations and the Newspaper Regulations. Finally, in December 1887, the government abruptly issued the Peace Preservation Ordinance that outlawed secret societies or meetings and gave the police authority to ban any mass meeting and the circulation of "dangerous" literature. The ordinance also allowed the Home Ministry to expel all those judged to be plotting or inciting a disturbance, or to be a danger to public peace, from within a seven-mile radius of the imperial palace in Tokyo, which had become a rallying point for advocates who sought to air their grievances directly before the emperor.

The Meiji Constitution

The task of drafting the new constitution was assumed by Ito Hirobumi (1841–1909), a former Choshu samurai. After examining the constitutions of different Western countries, Ito concluded that the Prussian constitution was the most appropriate model for Japan to follow. Ito's opinion was opposed by his chief rival, Okuma Shigenobu (1838–1922), a former samurai from Saga domain, who favored the British system. Okuma's ouster from the government shortly before the imperial edict promising a constitution cleared the way for Ito to proceed with the help of Prussian advisors, who were among the more than three thousand Western experts employed at different times during the Meiji period to help guide Japan's multifaceted drive to modernize.

The product of their labor, the Meiji Constitution, was formally announced on 11 February 1889. It remained in effect from November 1890 through the end of World War II. Whether the Meiji Constitution represents the fulfillment, or a betrayal, of the Charter Oath that was issued two decades earlier continues to be a matter for debate. Many features of the constitution appear to mark a calculated, conservative retreat from the spirit, if not the letter, of the Charter Oath. Presented as a "gift" from the emperor to his subjects, and immune from any amendments other than those initiated by the emperor, the constitution was an important "matter of state" that was never "decided by public discussion" as provided for in Article Two of the Charter Oath. (So anxious was the government to avoid public scrutiny of the document that it suppressed all the radical journals at the time the constitution was announced and warned the rest not to comment unfavorably.) While the other component of Article Two, promising the establishment of an assembly, was provided for in the constitution, the composition and powers of that body fell short of what many in the Freedom and People's Rights Movement had demanded. Only members of the Lower House of the bicameral Diet were to be elected by popular vote. (Until the universal male suffrage law was passed by the Diet in 1925, eligibility to vote was based upon income tax rates, which favored the more affluent classes. Japanese women did not get the vote until after World War II.) Seats in the Upper House were to be appointed from members of the peerage, an institution whose very existence seems at odds with the Charter Oath's attempt to de-emphasize class distinctions. The powers of the Diet were subordinate to those of the emperor, who was declared "sacred and inviolable" and in whom was vested "the rights of sovereignty." The emperor held supreme command of the army and navy, declared war and concluded treaties, and could even issue emergency ordinances when the Diet was not in session. The Diet's influence was further circumscribed by the autonomy granted to the Cabinet, Privy Council, and the military, none of which were responsible to the Diet.

Chapter Two of the constitution, which described the rights and duties of subjects, also appears, at best, as a qualified endorsement of Article Three of the Charter Oath. Its list of rights included freedom of religious belief, freedom of expression, and the right to privacy. Yet, in each case, these rights could be limited by law.

In October 1890, the government introduced one more tool in its campaign to regulate public behavior before the constitution went into effect the following month. The Imperial Rescript on Education set forth ethical precepts that harnessed traditional Confucian virtues to the needs of the modern nation-state. In essence, it called for subordination of the individual through service and sacrifice to one's immediate family, to society at large, and ultimately, to the family-state headed by the emperor. During school ceremonies pupils were required to recite the words to the Rescript and bow before a copy of it, which hung alongside the emperor's portrait in every school.

Emperor Mutsuhito, who ruled Japan from 1852 to 1912. (BETTMANN/CORBIS)

Promulgation of the Imperial Rescript on Education marks the culmination of a conservative educational trend that began in the early 1880s, coinciding with the government's growing political conservatism. At this time, too, the school system was reorganized to better address the needs of business and industry, which the government had been promoting through slogans such as "rich country, strong military" and, more importantly, through a series of ambitious policies.

The Industrial Era

Historians remain divided over whether Japan's phenomenal record of industrialization and commercial development during the Meiji period was due more to government initiative or to private-sector support. Increasingly, they emphasize the role of the former during the years prior to 1885, and the role of the latter thereafter. The government took the lead in developing the necessary infrastructure, including a centralized administrative apparatus with vast regulatory powers, as well as communications (postal system, telegraph), transportation (roads, railroads, shipping), and banking and finance infrastructure, and a meritocratic school system to assure a constant pool of human capital for government and industry alike. The role of government did not end there, however. It sent students abroad to acquire knowledge of key industries such as silk. It also used public funds to construct model shipbuilding facilities, cotton and silk factories, steam-powered factories for the production of glass, cement, bricks, and so forth, in order to showcase the latest Western technology and manufacturing processes. During the early 1880s, in tandem with the deflationary policies instituted by Finance Minister Matsukata Masayoshi, these model facilities were then sold off, at bargain prices, to enterprising Japanese (many with friendly ties to government officials). By this time, private entrepreneurs and private capital were primed to move aggressively into various light industries catering to the foreign and domestic markets. Many of these entrepreneurs emerged from the wealthy peasant class, whose experience in village leadership positions and in rural cottage industries dated back to the Tokugawa period.

One of the best-known success stories during this phase of Japan's industrialization is the textile industry. Silk, which had been a luxury item during the Tokugawa period, gained new importance as an export item once trade was opened with the West. The first modern silk filature was established in 1870 under the direction of a Swiss expert. The government followed two years later with its own model plant. Other plants soon followed, so that raw silk production in Japan jumped from 2.3 million pounds in 1868 to 10.2 million pounds in 1893, accounting for 42 percent of Japan's exports. By 1897, 24 percent of the world's raw silk was produced in Japan; by 1909 that figure had climbed to 34 percent. The chief market for Japanese silk was the United States, which purchased 28.6 percent of Japan's silk exports from 1907 to 1908.

The cotton-textile industry got off to a slower start due to foreign competition, but by 1899 Japan's cotton production reached 355 million pounds of yarn. By 1913 it had risen to 672 million pounds, which accounted for one-fourth of the world's cotton-yarn exports.

This growth did not come without cost or risk, however. In the short term, the rapid growth and productivity of the textile industry was achieved through the blatant exploitation of unskilled workers, mostly young, unmarried women from poor farm families, who were compelled to work long hours in unhealthy conditions for low wages. In the longer term, Japan's growing dependence upon overseas trade made it more vulnerable to the vicissitudes of the global market, a fact that would become painfully clear in coming years and would play a part in domestic and international politics.

War with China and Russia

The principal catalyst for Japan's expansion into heavy industry was the need to equip the Japanese army and navy to fight two foreign wars within a decade. Both wars are replete with irony. Fueling Meiji Japan's drive to modernize was her determination to avoid the fate of China and other countries that had been reduced to colonial or semicolonial status by the Western powers. The unequal treaties that Japan had been obliged to sign in the 1850s, granting extraterritoriality and tariff-setting powers to the Western cosigners, served as continual reminders of what was at stake. And yet, no sooner had Japan succeeded in revising these treaties in 1894 than she attacked China, ostensibly in order to free neighboring Korea from Chinese interference. Japan's victory in the Sino-Japanese War of 1894–1895 not only cleared the way for Japanese influence to supplant China's on the Korean Peninsula, but established Japan as a colonial power in her own right, through the acquisition of Formosa (modern Taiwan) from China. It also set the stage for the Russo-Japanese War of 1904–1905, which was launched in order to protect Japan's new strategic "line of advantage" through the Korean Peninsula and southern Manchuria from Russian encroachment. The Portsmouth Treaty of 1905, which ended the conflict, granted Japan southern Sakhalin Island, and, by recognizing Japan's dominant interests in Korea, paved the way for Japan's uncontested annexation of Korea in 1910. In the end, however, neither these victories, nor Japan's colonial possessions, nor her hard-won stature as a modern economic and military power, could assuage the government's preoccupation with potential threats to the nation's security, both from within and from without. Furthermore, these victories enhanced the prestige of the military and its capacity to influence foreign and domestic policy in years to come.

Mark E. Lincicome

See also: **Russo-Japanese War; Sino-Japanese War; Taisho Period; Tokugawa Period.**

Further Reading

Beasley, W.G. (1987) *Japanese Imperialism, 1894–1945*. Oxford: Clarendon Press.

———. (1995) *The Rise of Modern Japan: Political, Economic and Social Change Since 1850.* 2d ed. New York: St. Martin's Press.

Bowen, Roger W. (1980) *Rebellion and Democracy in Meiji Japan: A Study of the Commoners in the Popular Rights Movement.* Berkeley and Los Angeles: University of California Press.

Braisted, William Reynolds, trans. (1976) *Meiroku Zasshi: Journal of the Japanese Enlightenment.* Tokyo: University of Tokyo Press.

Fujitani, T. (1996) *Splendid Monarchy: Power and Pageantry in Modern Japan.* Berkeley and Los Angeles: University of California Press.

Gluck, Carol. (1985) *Japan's Modern Myths: Ideology in the Late Meiji Period.* Princeton, NJ: Princeton University Press.

Hane, Mikiso. (1982) *Peasants, Rebels, and Outcastes: The Underside of Modern Japan.* New York: Pantheon Books.

Hardacre, Helen, ed. (1997). *New Directions in the Study of Meiji Japan.* Leiden, The Netherlands: Brill.

———. (1989) *Shinto and the State, 1868–1988.* Princeton, NJ: Princeton University Press.

Huffman, James L. (1997) *Creating a Public: People and Press in Meiji Japan.* Honolulu: University of Hawaii Press.

Hunter, Janet E., compiler. (1984) *Concise Dictionary of Modern Japanese History.* Berkeley and Los Angeles: University of California Press.

Irokawa Daikichi. (1985) *The Culture of the Meiji Period.* Princeton, NJ: Princeton University Press.

Jansen, Marius B., ed. (1995) *The Emergence of Meiji Japan.* Cambridge, U.K.: Cambridge University Press.

Jansen, Marius B. and Gilbert Rozman, eds. (1986) *Japan in Transition: From Tokugawa to Meiji.* Princeton, NJ: Princeton University Press.

Ketelaar, James Edward. (1990) *Of Heretics and Martyrs in Meiji Japan: Buddhism and Its Persecution.* Princeton, NJ: Princeton University Press.

Kinmonth, Earl H. (1981) *The Self-Made Man in Meiji Japanese Thought: From Samurai to Salary Man.* Berkeley and Los Angeles: University of California Press.

Lincicome, Mark E. (1995) *Principle, Praxis, and the Politics of Educational Reform in Meiji Japan.* Honolulu: University of Hawaii Press.

Marshall, Byron K. (1994) *Learning to be Modern: Japanese Political Discourse on Education.* Boulder, CO: Westview Press.

Pyle, Kenneth B. (1996) *The Making of Modern Japan.* 2d ed. Lexington, MA: D. C. Heath.

Sievers, Sharon L. (1983) *Flowers in Salt: The Beginnings of Feminist Consciousness in Modern Japan.* Stanford, CA: Stanford University Press.

Walthall, Anne. (1998) *The Weak Body of a Useless Woman: Matsuo Taseko and the Meiji Restoration.* Chicago: University of Chicago Press.

Westney, Eleanor. (1987) *Imitation and Innovation: The Transfer of Western Organizational Patterns to Meiji Japan.* Cambridge, MA: Harvard University Press.

MEKONG PROJECT The Mekong is one of the great rivers of the world; it flows from the mountains of Tibet through China, Myanmar, Laos, Cambodia, Thailand, and Vietnam. It acts as a means of transportation and communications, provider of sustenance, and potentially as provider of hydroelectric power. Changing the nature or scale of the Mekong is likely to have a significant impact upon the lives of 200 million people. Since so much of the river basin region is undeveloped and densely forested, much of the river's course is yet to be fully mapped. It is, therefore, difficult to be certain about the economic and social impact of changes in the condition of the river.

Understanding this, regional governments have made efforts to cooperate to develop not just the Mekong River but also the riparian areas of the greater Mekong subregion, with plans encompassing the development of road and rail links, trade agreements, and human resources, as well as the physical potential of the river. The first attempt at cooperation was made in 1957, and subsequent attempts, first through the U.N. and later mostly under the auspices of the Asian Development Bank, have survived such divisive and debilitating events as the Vietnam War (1954–1975), the Communist victories in Vietnam and Laos, military coups in Thailand, the Sino-Vietnam War, and the decades-long political instability in Cambodia.

Difficulties in developing plans include not just continued political differences but also inaccessible terrain and the prevalence of illicit activities such as smuggling and drug trafficking. Nevertheless, the persistence with which discussions have continued, together with the willingness of regional partners to invest heavily in the plan, suggests that significant progress will eventually be made.

John Walsh

Further Reading

Bakker, Karen. (1999) "The Politics of Hydropower: Developing the Mekong." *Political Geography* 18: 209–232.

Thailand Development Research Institute. (1997) *Towards Public Participation in Mekong River Basin Development.* Bangkok, Thailand: Thailand Development Research Institute.

MEKONG RIVER AND DELTA The Mekong, the twelfth longest river in the world, shapes both the land and the politics of the Greater Mekong subregion. Known as the Lancangjiang or "turbulent river" near its beginnings in China's Yunnan Province, the Mekong originates 5,467 meters high in the Himalayan ranges of the Tibetan plateau. From there, it flows 4,425 kilometers southeast through the rain forests of Xishuangbanna in China, Myanmar, Thailand, the Lao People's Democratic Republic, and Cambodia.

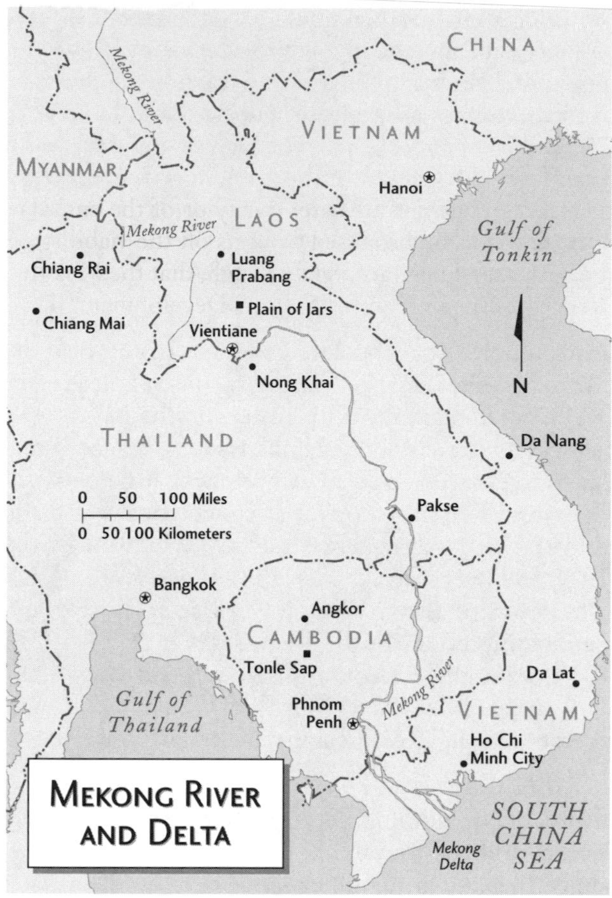

The Mekong River moves south past the Khone Falls on the Laos-Cambodia border. The area surrounding the Khone Falls, considered the Mekong River's most amazing natural wonder, contains some 4,000 small islands (Si Phan Don), Irrawaddy water dolphins, and giant catfish. The amazing rapids and waterfalls became an obstacle for the French whose dream it was to navigate the river, which they hoped would become the transportation gateway to China.

From the Khone Falls, the river then continues south for nearly 500 kilometers past Tonle Sap or "Great Lake," the largest freshwater lake in Southeast Asia, and moves toward Phnom Penh, the capital of Cambodia. At Phnom Penh, with its alternative arms, the Basak River from the south and the Tonle Sap River from the northwest, the Mekong proceeds further southeastward toward Vietnam and the Mekong Delta, a distinctly flat area also known as the Mekong Plain, before emptying into the South China Sea. In Vietnam it is known as the Cuu Long (Nine Dragons) because there the river splits into several rivers. The Tonle Sap acts as a buffer against Mekong River system floods and the source of beneficial dry-season flows. During the rainy season (July–October), the Mekong and Basak Rivers swell with water to the point that the delta cannot handle the enormous volume. At this point, instead of overflowing their banks, the floodwaters force the Tonle Sap River to reverse its flow and to enter the Tonle Sap or Great Lake, increasing its size from approximately 2,600 square kilometers to 10,000 square kilometers, and raising the water level by an average of seven meters. When the floods subside, water begins rushing out of Tonle Sap, increasing mainstream flows by 16 percent and thus helping to reduce saltwater intrusion in the lower Mekong Delta in Vietnam. This particular trait makes the Tonle Sap River the only "river with return" in the world.

Because the Tonle Sap and the Mekong Rivers reverse direction seasonally, they are vital for Cambodia, producing 100,000 tons of fish per year and 80 percent of the protein consumed within the country. The delta is equally critical for Vietnam, enabling it to produce and harvest 14 million tons of rice each year, of which 4 million tons are exported, making Vietnam the second-largest rice-exporting country in the world. Consequently, Tonle Sap Lake and the Mekong Delta are life-supporting organs for the Cambodian and Vietnamese economies.

With a 790,000-square-kilometer catchment area, the Mekong is reputedly the world's second richest in terms of biota, carrying 475 billion cubic meters of runoff and 250 million tons of sediment each year during the monsoon season from Yunnan Province to the Mekong Delta or Cuu Long (Nine Dragons). These nutrients provide irrigation for the region's myriad rice fields and a livelihood for the approximately 60 million residents of the Mekong Basin, including almost all of the Lao People's Democratic Republic and Cambodia, one-third of Thailand, and one-fourth of Vietnam.

Primarily fishers and farmers, the inhabitants of communities along the Mekong River and Delta have survived the natural floods for thousands of years, dependent on the river and the annual flood-drought cycle for their existence. Fully aware that any change in the river flow or sediment load will trigger immediate impacts on their environment and undermine their food security, the people who live along the Mekong rely on the large volume of floodwater to leach, flush, and control acid in their soils. On the banks of the mighty Great Lake and the Tonle Sap and Mekong Rivers, the Khmer people have celebrated the changing river flow for more than two hundred years. Likewise, the residents of the lower delta have learned to tolerate the floods and appreciate the many benefits associated with the floods: the nutrient-rich sediment and the water for their paddies, and the feeding and

THE TWELFTH-LONGEST RIVER

The Mekong River is the twelfth-longest in the world and flows through six nations—China, Myanmar, Thailand, Laos, Cambodia, and Vietnam—before emptying into the South China Sea.

spawning ground for their fish in the seasonally flooded forests.

In addition to the direct socioeconomic and ecological benefits to humans, the Mekong River system provides essential support for a diverse range of animals and plants. Among the endangered wildlife species that inhabit the riverine forests are leopards, tigers, and the near-extinct *ko prey* or jungle cow, which was named the national animal of Cambodia in 1963. In addition, elephants still roam the hills of the Mekong subregion, while monkeys and snakes abound in its forests and mountains. Yet, the Mekong's hydrologic cycle and ecological processes are now threatened by increasing pollution, deforestation, and several massive upstream developments, including a total of twenty-three dams between Yunnan Province and Cambodia. Among the projects already under way are a total of 37,000 megawatts of hydropower projects in China and the Lao PDR and 8,800 cubic meters of water diversions in Thailand. In 1994, the Mittaphap (Friendship) Bridge was also completed between the town of Nong Khai in northeastern Thailand and one of the outlying districts of Vientiane municipality, which includes Laos's capital city of Vientiane some twenty kilometers up the river. The first span ever constructed across the entire river, it signaled a new era of cooperation between two Mekong neighbors. Collectively, these activities are intended to use the power of the Mekong to produce energy for industry in Yunnan, to support agricultural production in northeastern Thailand, and to produce an economic windfall for the national government of Laos. Farther downstream, the inhabitants of the Mekong Delta have been promised that they will benefit from control of the floods and the possible initiation of cruise tourism between Ho Chi Minh City in southern Vietnam and Phnom Penh. Still, there is great concern that, if these development projects are completed, the vibrant Tonle Sap fisheries would be diminished, the Mekong Delta would turn into an acid plain, the groundwater would be diluted by the intrusion of salt water, and the coast would be inundated by the South China Sea. Furthermore, due to the multiple uses of the Mekong, all types of waste are discharged into the water. As a consequence, the water quality has become very poor over the years, adversely affecting both the human environment and the natural. As of July 2001, however, no government agencies or international organizations have undertaken an analysis either of changes in water purity or of the cumulative effects of the proposed projects on the viability of the Mekong. There are signs, though, that the Mekong River Commission and the Asian Development Bank will do so in the near future.

Greg Ringer

Further Reading

Barker, Randolph, Robert W. Herdt, and Beth Rose. (1985) *The Rice Economy of Asia*. Washington, DC: Resources for the Future.

Brown, Frederick Z., and David G. Timberman. (1998) *Cambodia and the International Community: The Quest for Peace, Development, and Democracy*. Singapore: Asia Society.

Chandler, David P. (2000) *A History of Cambodia*. 3rd ed. Boulder, CO: Westview Press.

Dutt, Ashok, ed. (1985) *Southeast Asia: Realm of Contrasts*. Boulder, CO: Westview Press.

Hoskin, John, and Allen W. Hopkins. (1991) *The Mekong: A River and Its People*. Bangkok, Thailand: Post Publishing Company.

Pham, Long P. (1998) *The Existing Challenges and Future Dangers to the Tonle Sap and the Mekong Delta*. Bangkok, Thailand: Mekong Forum.

Ringer, Greg, ed. (1998) *Destinations: Cultural Landscapes of Tourism*. New York: Routledge.

Ringer, Greg. (2000) "Tourism in Cambodia, Laos and Myanmar: From Terrorism to Tourism?" In *Tourism in South and Southeast Asia: Issues and Cases*, edited by C. Michael Hall and Stephen Page. Oxford: Butterworth-Heinemann, 178–94.

Stensholt, Bob, ed. (1997) *Developing the Mekong Subregion*. Clayton, Australia: Monash Asia Institute.

MELAKA (2002 est. pop. 635,000). The state of Melaka (or Malacca in English) is located on the southwest corner of Peninsular Malaysia. Covering some 1,600 square kilometers in area, the state is primarily low-lying with its western coastline fronting the Straits of Malacca. Its principal economic activities once revolved around agriculture and commerce, but since the late 1980s, the tourism and industrial sectors have overtaken them in importance. The Melaka State Development Corporation is the quasi-state agency tasked with developing, coordinating, and promoting industry, tourism, and housing activities in the state.

The capital of the state is also called Melaka. A historic coastal city in western Peninsular Malaysia, it is

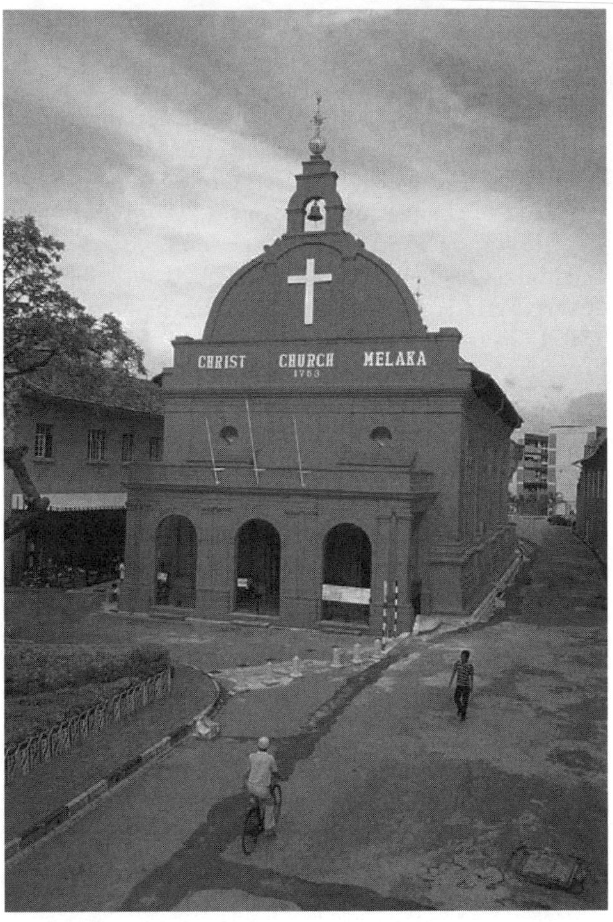

The Red Brick Christ Church built in Melaka in 1753. (NIK WHEELER/CORBIS)

about 140 kilometers south of Kuala Lumpur, Malaysia's capital. Melaka city is a major tourist attraction, which the state tourism board advertises as "the place where it all began." The city boasts of having some of the country's oldest extant heritage buildings (mosques, temples, churches, colonial buildings etc.), as well as long-standing cultural enclaves of Baba-Nyonyas (Straits-born Chinese), Chitty Melaka (Straits-born Indians), and Portuguese Eurasians.

Seng-Guan Yeoh

Further Reading

Hoyt, Sarnia Hayes. (1993) *Old Malacca*. Kuala Lumpur, Malaysia: Oxford University Press.

Nik Hassan Shuhaimi and Nik Abdul Rahman, eds. (1998). *The Encyclopedia of Malaysia*. Vol. 4: *Early History*. Singapore: Archipelago Press.

MELAKA SULTANATE The history of the town of Melaka is full of the glorious past of Malaysia. Melaka probably was established in the thirteenth century as a small fishing village occupied by the Orang Laut (seafaring Malays). Its humble existence then as a collection of mud huts and dugouts is thought to have spared it the fate of Palembang in Sumatra and Singapore in the mid-fourteenth century: both were razed and their inhabitants massacred by the Javanese kingdom of Majapahit, the greatest local power of the time.

Thus, Melaka became the refuge for people who escaped from Singapore and Palembang. At the beginning of the fifteenth century, the township that had begun as a fishing village had become a cosmopolitan trading center with a walled cluster of huts upon the hill overlooking the harbor. Currency dealt in was tin, and the trade was in tin, resin, and jungle produce. The population was little more than a few thousand. The local chief was Hindu by faith and bore the Indian title of *permaisura* (king).

According to the *Malay Annals* that chronicle the courtlier version of the foundation of Melaka, the fugitive king of Singapore, Iskandar Shah, rested in the shadow of a tree at the mouth of the River Bertam. When he asked the name of the tree, he was told it was "Melaka." The king liked the name of the tree and the place and so decided to settle there. This king secured his power by paying visits to China to gain recognition and by converting to Islam. Malay tradition has chronicled the name of the first Muslim ruler of Melaka as Muhammad Shah. Another legend claims that this fugitive king from Singapore was Parameswara, one of the petty princes of a vassal state of the Majapahit empire who had thrown off his allegiance and was forced to flee. He took refuge in Singapore and subsequently assassinated the ruler. Parameswara ruled Singapore for five years before being overthrown by dissatisfied natives and forced to flee until he reached the mouth of the Melaka River.

Muhammad Shah died about 1414 CE and was succeeded by his son, Iskandar Shah. The son reigned for the next ten years and continued to visit China as well as pay tribute to the emperor. During his reign, Melaka continued to be a trading center in the region.

The line of trader princes ended with the ascension to the sultanate of Raja Kasim, who took the title of Mudzafar Shah. This first sultan stopped attending to trade, sent envoys to China, and did not go in person. Instead, he levied tolls on the trade in the port to wage war against little hamlets on the coast and eventually inland. Sultan Mudzafar Shah is believed to have conquered the territories of what are now neighboring states of Pahang, Kampar in Perak, Siak, and Indragiri. Thus was created the new Melaka. This was the golden age of the Melaka sultanate when its rulers reigned over territories to the north, south, and east of the port of Melaka. By then, the township of Melaka had seen settlements spring up in abundance—Javanese, Tamils, and Burmese traders had all set up quarters.

Sultan Mudzafar Shah died in 1459 CE and was succeeded by his son, Raja Abdullah, who assumed the title of Sultan Mansur Shah. The reign of this ruler has been regarded as the most glorious of the Melaka sultanate because of the conquests achieved and the legendary heroes produced during this period. By 1460 CE, Melaka had been transformed from a primitive and semiaboriginal village, when it had been a fringe of houses along the sea and riverfronts backed by orchards and rice fields. At the height of its glory in 1460, it was a bustling cosmopolitan seaport town. Chronicles describe the government as stern, severe, and corrupt. Historians describe the Melaka sultanate as a city of the strong where no weak citizen would be free. So all sought patrons, the mightier the better, in the belief that it is safer to pay blackmail to one robber than to many. Every law but one was broken daily; that one law was that no man might raise his hand against his king. Heroes of Malay chronicles belonged to this period of the Melaka sultanate, among them Hang Tuah and Hang Jebat.

The policy of war and conquest begun by Sultan Mudzafar Shah and his son, Mansur Shah, was fatal for a small trading station like Melaka because it placed severe burdens on its merchants, who had to finance the war campaigns. When the Portuguese sailed into Melaka in 1509, they found a town of foreign settlers who were willing to rise in revolt against their Malay masters. The first foray by the Portuguese was resisted by the Malays in Melaka. But the second, which was led by Viceroy d'Albuquerque in 1511, resulted in Melaka being seized by the Portuguese and the sultan fleeing to Pagoh, from which he was also forced to flee eventually. Sultan Mahmud Shah was the last of the Melaka rulers. The sultanate of Melaka, which in 1500 had ruled much of the Malay Peninsula from Kedah to Patani and the Lingga Archipelago, had lasted less than one hundred years.

Kog Yue Choong

Further Reading

Harrison, Brian. (1954) *Southeast Asia: A Short History*. London: Macmillan.

Wilkinson, R. J. (1923) *A History of the Peninsular Malays with Chapters on Perak and Selangor*. Singapore: Kelly and Walsh.

MENCIUS (c. 371–c. 289 BCE), Confucian philosopher. The influence of Mencius in defining ancient Confucianism is second only to that of Confucius

This classic portrait of Mencius dates to the eighteenth century. (ARCHIVO ICONOGRAFICO, S.A./CORBIS)

(551–479 BCE). The *Records of the Historian (Shiji)* of the second century BCE tells us that Meng Ke (Mencius) was from the state of Zou, which neighbored the state of Lu. He studied with a disciple of Confucius's grandson, Zisi (492–431 BCE). Like Confucius, Mencius traveled to various states looking for a worthy ruler. He held a minor post without any authority as guest minister or teacher under King Xuan of Qi (319–301 BCE). Unable to influence the political climate, he retired with Wan Zhang (flourished fourth century BCE) and other disciples to write the book of philosophy known as the *Mencius*.

The *Book of Mencius* is one of the *Four Books*. After the Tang dynasty (618–907 CE), the *Mencius* eclipsed the *Xunzi*. Unlike the *Analects (Lunyu)*, the *Mencius* contains developed prose essays and detailed arguments. In keeping with most ancient Chinese texts, the *Mencius* employs arguments based on an appeal to the authority of the sage rulers of antiquity. It also makes regular use of argument by analogy.

Mencius believed that a person's moral integrity is a matter of the heart-mind *(xin)*. The emphasis on the inner quality of a person's moral life marked a change from Confucius, who clearly delineated the inner from the outer. Person-to-person care or humanity *(ren)* remained the core value, the innermost quality of the heart-mind, and first among the four cardinal virtues. For Confucius, *ren* meant everything noble in the well-bred person, disinterested concern for oth-

THE WISDOM OF MENCIUS

1. Mencius said, The people are the most important element in a nation; the spirits of the land and grain are the next, the sovereign is the lightest.

2. Therefore to gain the peasantry is the way to become sovereign; to gain the sovereign is the way to become a prince of a state; to gain the prince of state is the way to become a great officer.

The Works of Mencius, Bk. VII, Pt. II, Ch. 14

Source: William H. McNeill. (1970) *Classical China.* New York: Oxford University Press, 64.

ers, and other subtle qualities. For Mencius, *ren* meant simply benevolence. According to Mencius, the other virtues such as rightness *(yi)*, ritual action *(li)*, and moral wisdom *(zhi)* are also qualities of one's heart-mind. In contract to Confucius's general and vague teachings, Mencius's design for humane rulership is practical and effective. Mencius advocated abating punishments, reducing taxes, improving crop yields, and ensuring that the people are trained in moral cultivation. Mencius explicated the notion that human character is basically good, an idea that is only implied in the *Analects.*

Mencius was rediscovered in the Song dynasty (960–1279) by the Neo-Confucians, especially Zhu Xi (1130–1200). As Neo-Confucianism spread across East Asia, the Koreans and Japanese were reintroduced to Mencius's teachings. Emphasis on the inner quality of the heart-mind, the four cardinal virtues, use of education to develop a person's inner nature, and the practice of humane government are characteristics of Chinese, Korean, and Japanese Neo-Confucianism that were originally derived from the ideas of Mencius. It is not an exaggeration to say that East Asian culture was shaped by the Kong-Meng (Confucius and Mencius) teachings.

James D. Sellmann

Further Reading

Allan, Sarah. (1997) *The Way of Water and Sprouts of Virtue.* Albany: State University of New York Press.

Ames, Roger T. (1991) "The Mencian Conception of Ren Xing: Does It Mean Human Nature?" In *Chinese Texts and Philosophical Contexts,* edited by Henry Rosemont. La Salle, IL: Open Court, 143–178.

Chan, Wing-tsit. (1963) *A Source Book in Chinese Philosophy.* Princeton, NJ: Princeton University Press.

Fung, Yu-lan. (1952) *History of Chinese Philosophy.* Vol. 1. Trans. by Derk Bodde. Princeton, NJ: Princeton University Press.

Graham, Angus C. (1986) "The Background of the Mencian Theory of Human Nature." In *Studies in Chinese Philosophy and Philosophical Literature.* Singapore: Institute of East Asian Philosophies, 7–66.

——— (1989) *Disputers of the Tao.* La Salle, IL: Open Court.

Hsiao, Kung-chuan. (1979) *A History of Chinese Political Thought.* Trans. by Frederick Mote. Princeton, NJ: Princeton University Press.

Lau, D. C., trans. (1970) *Mencius.* Middlesex, U.K.: Penguin Books.

Legge, James, trans. (1960) *The Chinese Classics.* 5 vols. Hong Kong: University of Hong Kong.

Munro, Donald J. (1969) *Concept of Man in Early China.* Stanford, CA: Stanford University Press.

Nivison, David S. (1996) *The Ways of Confucianism: Investigations in Chinese Philosophy.* Edited by Bryan W. Van Norden. Chicago: Open Court.

Richards, I. A. (1932) *Mencius on the Mind.* London: Routledge.

Waley, Arthur. (1956) *Three Ways of Thought in Ancient China.* Garden City, NY: Doubleday Anchor Books.

MENDERES, ADNAN (1899–1961), Turkish politician, prime minister. Adnan Menderes was born in Aydin in western Turkey, the son of a wealthy landowner. He entered politics in 1930, joining the Free Party, which was later shut down. Menderes then pursued his political career in the only legal party, the Republican People's Party (RPP), until his expulsion in 1945. He and three others founded the opposition Democrat Party (DP) in 1946. Due to his popularity among the masses during the time that the DP was the opposition party (1946–1950), he became prime minister in the DP's landslide victory in the 1950 elections.

Menderes criticized the RPP's etatist policies and instead promised a liberal program highlighting democracy, free enterprise, and conservative values. Although he was successful in his efforts at economic and structural transformation in the early 1950s, he failed to establish a democratic atmosphere and took authoritarian measures against the opposition. Nevertheless, the DP won the 1954 and 1957 elections by an overwhelming majority, especially thanks to the peasants' alliance. After the mid-1950s, Menderes's legitimacy began to decline in the eyes of elites, and a military coup in 1960 overthrew his government. Menderes was hanged in 1961.

Yilmaz Çolak

Further Reading

Karpat, Kemal H. (1959) *Turkey's Politics: The Transition to a Multi-Party System*. Princeton, NJ: Princeton University Press.

Shmuelevitz, Aryeh. (1990) "Adnan Menderes." In *Political Leaders of the Contemporary Middle East and North Africa*. New York: Greenwood Press, 332–340.

MENDU A form of operatic folk-drama popular in Malay-speaking Sumatra, especially in Riau Province. Obscure in origin, it is thought to have developed in the nineteenth century as an offshoot of the Malay *bangsawan*, though there are traces of Chinese influence as well. *Mendu* performances tend toward the rustic: accompanying music is usually performed on violin, gong, and drums; much of the dialogue is improvised; and the characters are largely set stereotypes. The performing area is partly covered by a temporary roof, but is otherwise left open. Comedy, which is usually rather crude, figures importantly, as does dance. The original *mendu* repertory consisted of one story—the *Dewa Mendu*—though recently elements of other Indonesian epic cycles, such as the *Panji* tales and the *Ramayana*, along with Malaysian *bangsawan* plot lines, have had an impact. *Mendu* performances take place at night and sometimes last many nights in a row. With no scripts, great value is placed on the actors' ability to improvise, which is helped by the stereotyping of roles and plots.

Tim Byard-Jones

Further Reading

Yousouf, Ghulam-Sarwar. (1994) *Dictionary of Traditional South-East Asian Theatre*. Kuala Lumpur, Malaysia: Oxford University Press.

MERSIN (2000 est. pop. 1.8 million). Mersin means "myrtle" in Turkish, and the city took its name from this tree. In 1852, when it was first incorporated, Mersin was inhabited by a cosmopolitan mixture of Turks, Greeks, and Armenians. In the 1950s it was designated as a strategic access harbor for the fertile floodplain of the Euphrates River and a transshipment point on the eastern Mediterranean. However, successive governments placed increasing emphasis on and directed capital to the GAP (Southeast Anatolian) project to harness the Tigris and Euphrates Rivers and Mersin slipped into a social and economic vacuum. Too new a city to benefit from the well-structured Ottoman civic administration that gave stability to other Turkish cities and towns, Mersin easily adapted to alternative cultures. By 1999 most of the projected advantages had not come to fruition.

In 1989 the government made an effort to settle nomadic peoples from the surrounding plains (*yürüks*) in Mersin. Much of their pasture land had been reclaimed and their traditional seasonal livelihood curtailed due to ethnic clashes between Turkish government forces and rebel Kurdish insurgents. However most of the resettled population could not adapt to city life and soon found easier alternatives outside the law.

Suzanne Swan

Further Reading

Dalrymple, William. (1990) *In Xanadu*. London: Flamingo Books.

MIAO—CHINA The Miao (the Chinese character means "young plant"), also known as the Hmong or Meo, are an ethnic group that originated in China. This article deals only with the Miao in China, as the Miao elsewhere generally call themselves and are called Hmong. The fifth-largest ethnic group in China, the Miao numbered 7.4 million in 1990 and inhabited the southern provinces of Guizhou, Hunan, Yunnan, Sichuan, Guangxi, Hubei, and Guangdong.

Miao Language and Writing

The Miao language belongs to the Miao branch of the Miao-Yao subfamily of the Sino-Tibetan family. Due to a long history of migration and dispersed settlements in isolated mountainous areas, the language has developed into scores of dialects, many of them mutually unintelligible. Based on linguistic characteristics and extents of intelligibility, these dialects are identified in three dialect areas: the Western Hunan (or Eastern), Eastern Guizhou (or Central), and Sichuan-Guizhou-Yunnan (or Western) Dialect Areas.

The Miao language was once a spoken language with no written form. At the present time, romanized writing systems for four of the dialects are used among the Miao in China; in 1956, linguists working with native speakers created some of these systems and worked out the others by reforming the existing writing systems.

Various Miao Groups

During their long history, the Miao in different areas acquired distinct ethnic markers, visible traits that distinguished one group from another. For instance, for referential convenience, neighboring ethnic groups used the color of female costume to discriminate one subgroup of the Miao from another. Thus, those Miao in western Hunan are called Red Miao, those in southeastern Guizhou Black Miao, and those in northwestern

Guizhou and northeastern Yunnan Big Flowery Miao. Other well-known modified names include White Miao, Small Flowery Miao, and Green or Blue Miao. As a result of the government-directed Ethnic Identification Project of the 1950s, all the subgroups living in different areas of China were granted the unified name "Miao" and became one of the fifty-six officially recognized ethnic groups in mainland China.

Many Hmong living outside China think that the appellation "Miao" carries a derogatory connotation or simply means "barbarian" in Chinese. It is true that in history all ethnic minorities were regarded as "barbarian" by Chinese speakers and that the term "Miao" was often used together with *man*, a generic term for "southern barbarians." It is also true that in some southern Chinese subdialects *miao* could be used as an adjective describing someone's stubbornness or fierceness. It is important, however, to note that the name Miao in itself is by no means derogatory. The word in Chinese means "young plant" or "offspring." As the name of an ethnic group, it existed long before the "civilized" were differentiated from the "barbarian." Miao is also a surname among the Han, the dominant ethnic group of China.

Miao Culture

The Miao have an extremely rich oral tradition, complete with mythologies, legends, ethnohistory, poems, dramas, operas, and antiphonal songs. In the copious Chinese historical literature, the recorded history of the Miao is as long as that of any other group in the Chinese world. Although written from an apparently biased perspective, Chinese literature contains useful records on Miao ethnic origin, migration, customs, social structure, economic activities, technical achievements, and relations with the state and other ethnic groups. By all accounts, the Miao are one of the few groups in human history that have demonstrated the highest level of ethnic adherence and tenacity.

The Miao have a patrilineal descent system (tracing descent through the father's line) and a patronymic linkage system (a practice in which part of the son's personal name comes from that of his father). Most young people enjoy free marriage, but arranged marriage is also practiced in some areas. Especially in western Hunan and Guizhou, cross-cousin marriage (a preferential rule requiring that one should marry one's cross-cousin—mother's brother's child or father's sister's child—if such a person is available) is popular. Levirate (the custom whereby a man marries the widow of his deceased brother) is practiced in many areas. To a lesser degree, sororate (the custom whereby, when a man's wife dies or is found barren, her unmarried sister is given to him as a wife) is found among the Miao in Yunnan. Quite a few Miao in Guizhou also practice delayed-transfer marriage (a custom in which the newlywed bride does not live with her husband until two or three years after the wedding day). Beyond the household level, kinfolk are organized into lineages, subclans, and clans. A position in the kinship network and a role in the ritual system of ancestral worship are of utmost importance in defining the social status of a Miao.

In addition to ancestral worship, the Miao believe in animism (endowing inanimate objects and natural forces with life) and shamanism. Christianity has influenced the religious life of some Miao in Guizhou, Yunnan, and Sichuan since the nineteenth century.

Agriculture has been the traditional means of subsistence for the Miao, supplemented with fishing, hunting, and handicrafts. The Miao batik cloth, a tourist favorite, has a history of over one thousand years. Education has been rapidly developed in the Miao areas in recent decades. Today, in China as well as the Western diasporas, the Miao have their own teachers, lawyers, medical doctors, scientists, and engineers.

Chuan-kang Shih

Further Reading

Diamond, Norma. (1995) "Defining the Miao: Ming, Qing, and Contemporary Views." In *Cultural Encounters on China's Ethnic Frontiers*, edited by Stevan Harrell. Seattle: University of Washington Press.

Jenks, Robert D. (1994) *Insurgency and Social Disorder in Guizhou: The "Miao" Rebellion, 1854–1873.* Honolulu: University of Hawaii Press.

Lyman, Thomas A. (1979) *Grammar of Mong Njua (Green Miao): A Descriptive Linguistic Study*. Sattley, CA: Blue Oak Press.

Schein, Louisa. (2000) *Minority Rules: The Miao and the Feminine in China's Politics.* Durham, NC: Duke University Press.

MID-AUTUMN FESTIVAL The fifteenth day of the eighth month of the lunar calendar is an important family reunion day for Chinese throughout the world. On that day, family members gather for the evening meal and afterward move outdoors to enjoy the full moon. The perfectly round and bright moon (*yueyuan*) signifies the complete togetherness (*tuanyuan*) of the family. Those who are away from their families during the festival feel depressed for missing such an opportunity.

Two food items are closely associated with this festival. The "moon cake" is a baked cake with a flour shell surrounding sweet bean paste stuffing. A pomelo is a citrus fruit that ripens in southern China around mid-autumn. Both food items are round, like the moon, and further strengthen the importance of family unification.

Popular folklore holds that Emperor Zhu Yuanzhang, founder of the Ming dynasty (1368–1644 CE), invented the moon cake. According to the story, the cakes Zhu made contained a secret message encouraging the people to revolt against the occupying Mongols on the fifteenth day of the eighth month. The current festival probably derives from the harvest celebration in northern China, which later mixed with the Yao tribe's lunar New Year festival.

Huang Shu-min

Further Reading

Bodde, Derk. (1975) *Festivals in Classical China: New Year and Other Annual Observances during the Han Dynasty, 206 BC–AD 220.* Princeton, NJ: Princeton University Press.

Chin, Yin-lien C., Yetta S. Center, and Mildred Ross (1989) *Chinese Folktales: An Anthology*. Armonk, NY: North Castle Books.

Eberhard, Wolfram (1958) *Chinese Festivals.* London: Abelard-Schuman.

———. (1968) *The Local Cultures of South and East China.* Leiden, Netherlands: E. J. Brill.

MIE (2001 est. pop. 1.9 million). Mie Prefecture is situated in the central region of Japan's island of Honshu, where it occupies an area of 5,778 square kilometers. Its primary geographical features are the Kii Peninsula, of which it is the eastern part, low mountains separating the coastal Ise Plain and the central Ueno Basin, and densely forested southern mountains. Mie is bordered by Ise Bay and the Kumano Sea, and by Wakayama, Nara, Kyoto, Shiga, Gifu, and Aichi Prefectures. Once comprising the provinces of Ise, Shima, and Iga, Mie assumed its present name and borders in 1876.

The prefecture's capital city is Tsu, formerly named Anotsu. Once a thriving port, it evolved into an Edo period (1600/1603–1868) post station town along the route to Ise Shrine, while continuing as the castle town of the Todo family. In the early 2000s, Mie is dominated by the shipbuilding, electrical machinery, and textile industries, while agriculture and fishing remain important. Its attractions include the temple Senshuji and the ruins of Tsu Castle. The prefecture's other important cities are Yokkaichi, Ise, Matsusaka, Suzuka, and Kuwana.

Prehistoric archaeological remains and many Kofun tombs indicate early settlement of Mie Prefecture. The erection of the Ise Shrine, devoted to the mythical ancestors of the Imperial family and long the nation's principal Shinto pilgrimage destination, as early as the third century contributed to the region's rapid growth. The provinces then were ruled by a series of feudal lords.

Mie's prime agricultural land produces rice, vegetables, and fruit, along with tea and tobacco. Matsusaka produces highly prized beef, while forestry is pursued in the south. Toba, once an Ise pilgrimage port, is the site of the nation's first cultured pearl beds. The older textile and ceramics industries, along with modern heavy industries, are concentrated in the north. The prefecture's attractions include coastal Ise-Shima National Park and mountainous Yoshino-Kumano National Park. Ueno, known for its famous Iga ware ceramics, is notable as the birthplace of haiku poet Matsuo Basho (1644–1694).

E. L. S. Weber

Further Reading

"Mie Prefecture."(1993) *Japan: An Illustrated Encyclopedia.* Tokyo: Kodansha.

MILETUS Miletus, a major Greek colony in Asia Minor, was established on a site known to the Hittites as Millawanda. The city was founded as a Mycenaean (early Greek) colony on the estuary of the Maeander (now Menderes) River, south of Izmir. After the fall of ancient Ilium, or Troy, around 1200 BCE, a fresh influx of Greeks made Miletus the foremost center in Ionia. The city enjoyed four harbors, and the inhabitants grew wealthy through sea trade; the city was famed for the fine textiles produced there. As the population expanded, colonists set out from Miletus to found many new colonies, from Egypt to the Black Sea, including Byzantium (later Constantinople).

In the seventh century BCE an ancient shrine at Didyma, twenty kilometers south of Miletus, was rededicated to Apollo, and the temple, although never finished, became one of the major oracles of ancient Greece. Visitors to Didyma, as well as Miletus's economic growth, stimulated the age of Ionian enlightenment, and Miletus became a center of philosophy and learning.

Thales of Miletus (c. 625–c. 547 BCE) taught that everything was made of water. Thales' disciple, Anaximander of Miletus (610–c. 547 BCE), was said to have discovered the obliquity of the ecliptic; Anaximenes of Miletus (c. 545 BCE) thought that air was the basic element from which everything was made. Hecataeus of

The eastern analemma of the Theater of Miletus, originally built in the fourth century BCE. (ROGER WOOD/CORBIS)

Miletus (sixth–fifth centuries BCE) wrote an account of his extensive travels, which Herodotus and other Greek travelers used. The architect Hippodamus of Miletus (fifth century BCE) invented the notion of city planning and designed the first town plans based on grid patterns. Aspasia (c. 470–410 BCE) was born in Miletus but traveled to Athens, where, famed for her beauty and intelligence, she became the lover of Pericles.

The kings of neighboring Lydia had led incursions against Miletus, but the city remained free until Croesus (d. c. 546 BCE), the last king of Lydia, conquered it. When Lydia fell to the Persians in the sixth century BCE, Miletus came under Achaemenid rule, but the city led neighboring cities in the so-called Ionian revolt against Persia around 500 BCE. The Ionian cities, however, could not defeat the powerful Persians. In the conflict Miletus lost eighty ships, the city was captured and burned, and the inhabitants enslaved.

Miletus was rebuilt on a new site, but its former glory was never recaptured. Alexander of Macedon besieged Miletus in 334 BCE, and a naval blockade forced its surrender. After his death the city changed hands among his generals, passed to the cultured Attalid dynasty based in Pergamon, and then in 133 BCE, became nominally free under Rome.

The Romans rebuilt the public buildings, but the harbor silted up with malarial marshes. The abolition of the oracle in favor of Christianity in 385 CE confirmed Miletus's decline; her last famous citizen was Isodorus, who built the great Saint Sophia cathedral in Constantinople. Under Turkish rule a caravansaray (trading inn) and a *madrasah* (religious school) temporarily revived the city.

The Site

German archaeologists have been excavating the site of Miletus for a century, and many finds are in Berlin or Istanbul. The theater, once on the water's edge, is the most striking monument, romantic when filled with wild irises in spring. The sacred way to Didyma, lined with an Ionic portico one hundred meters long, and a restored stoa, or colonnade, ran from the Lion Harbor. Places of worship included a temple to Athena (third century BCE), the Delphinion dedicated to Apollo (sixth century BCE), a synagogue from the late Roman period, two Byzantine churches (sixth century CE), and the delightfully marbled fifteenth-century mosque of Ilyas Bey in a shady grove.

Kate Clow

Further Reading

Akurgal, Ekrem. (1969) *Ancient Civilizations and Ruins of Turkey*. Ankara, Turkey: Haslet Kitabevi.

Darke, Diana. (1989) *Discovery Guide to Aegean and Mediterranean Turkey*. London: Michael Haag.

MILITARY, INDONESIA Despite a credibility sullied by its close association with deposed Indonesian president Suharto (served 1966–1998), the Indonesian military continues to play a critical role in Indonesian history and sociopolitical and economic life. It traces its origins to the paramilitary forces set up by the Japanese in 1943–1945 and the Dutch colonial army. Originally known as Angkatan Bersenjata Indonesia (ABRI), the Indonesian military, which included the police, was the vanguard of the revolutionary independence struggle against the Dutch. After the downfall of the Suharto regime, ABRI was reorganized and renamed Tentera Nasional Indonesia (TNI). The 300,000-strong TNI still regards itself as the sole guardian and savior of Indonesian unity. Inspired by Javanese cultural nationalism, TNI remains staunchly anticommunist but has been increasingly accommodating to the rise of political Islam.

ABRI's central role hinged on *dwifungsi* (dual function), which was conceived during the political and economic turmoil and the failure of parliamentary democracy in the 1950s. Given legislative mandate in 1982, *dwifungsi* encapsulated the military's dual role as an external defense force with internal sociopolitical roles and was given effect by its being allocated parliamentary seats. Operationally, *dwifungsi* is manifest in ABRI's territorial function *(kekaryaan)*, in which active and retired officers dominate civilian administrations from provincial down to village levels. This enabled Suharto to extend his power base both laterally and vertically in the aftermath of the abortive 1965 coup, in which the Communist Party of Indonesia was implicated. *Dwifungsi* was discredited after May 1998, but TNI remains relevant in holding the fragile Indonesian state together. TNI's current parliamentary representation has been whittled to thirty-eight seats from one hundred.

Although there is strong political and societal pressure for TNI to subordinate itself to civilian control and confine itself to a purely external defense, military reforms have been tentative. Tension persists between reformists and conservatives, and the *dwifungsi*-guardian doctrinal mindsets resonate within the rank and file. The police have been separated from the military command, but the military still meets many internal security needs, especially those related to the secessionist tendencies in Aceh and West Papua. In the face of large budget cuts, the military retains significant business interests as a means of generating funds for operational needs and the welfare of the soldiers and their families. The pursuit of accountability and justice for the military's and militia groups' human rights abuses have floundered on political expediency and deal-making. The military reforms are doomed to failure unless buttressed by governmental efforts to combat pervasive corruption, decentralize power, and promote the rule of law.

The post-Suharto transition demonstrates that the Indonesian political leadership still needs TNI's support for the government to be able to assert some form of governance. TNI is the only viable institution that can restore stability across the vast multiethnic, multireligious Indonesian archipelago and safeguard any administration. TNI will continue to remain on the political center stage, and the possibility of a resurgent military in Indonesia cannot be foreclosed.

Eugene K. B. Tan

Further Reading

Crouch, Harold. (1988) *The Army and Politics in Indonesia*. Ithaca, NY: Cornell University Press.

Kahin, George M. (1952) *Nationalism and Revolution in Indonesia*. Ithaca, NY: Cornell University Press.

Kammen, Douglas, and Siddharth Chandra. (1999) *A Tour of Duty: Changing Patterns of Military Politics in Indonesia in the 1990s*. Ithaca, NY: Southeast Asia Program Publications, Cornell University Press.

Lowry, Robert. (1996) *The Armed Forces of Indonesia*. St. Leonards, Australia: Allen & Unwin.

Schwarz, Adam. (1999) *A Nation in Waiting: Indonesia's Search for Stability*. St. Leonards, Australia: Allen & Unwin.

MIN

MIN Min is a geographic short term for Fujian Province in China. It has been used as a linguistic term by Chinese dialectologists to refer to the Min dialects for decades. Among the seven major Chinese languages (Mandarin, Wu, Yue, Gan, Hakka, Min, and Xiang), the Min dialect group is the most complicated and divergent of all. Fujian is a mountainous province with very few navigable rivers and not much arable land. The topography has contributed both to the heterogeneity of the dialects and also to migration to other parts of China and overseas.

Prior to the 1960s, when dialect data was scant, the Min dialect group was divided roughly into two subgroups: Minbei (Northern Min) and Minnan (Southern Min). Studies in the 1990s have shown that there are at least six Min subdialect groups: Mindong (Eastern Min), Minbei (Northern Min), Minzhong (Central Min), Minnan (Southern Min), Puxian, and Shaoning. (See Table 1.) Most of these subdialects are mutually unintelligible.

A Mindong Dialect: Fuzhou

The Fuzhou dialect is a characteristic Mindong dialect whose speakers number over 1 million and are found not only in Fuzhou, but also in Southeast Asian communities.

Fuzhou has fourteen initial consonants *(p, p', m, t, t', n, l, ts, ts', s, k, k', ng, x)*, seven vowels *(i, u, y, a, ɛ, œ, o)*, seven tones, and just one paired-consonant ending: *-ng/-q*. The velar nasal *ng* may occur alone and forms a syllabic nasal.

As with other Chinese dialects, the Fuzhou dialect exhibits differences in literary and colloquial readings for some lexical items, but this is true for a smaller

TABLE 1

Speakers of Min Dialect Subgroups

Min Dialect Group	Number of Speakers
Minnan group	34.7 million
Mindong group	7.5 million
Puxian group	2.3 million
Minbei group	2.2 million
Shaoning group	745,000
Minzhong group	683,000

SOURCE: Zhang Zhensheng (1989: 54–59.)

number of lexical items than is the case in Minnan (Southern Min).

The Fuzhou dialect has a very unique sound sandhi (*sandhi* is a term used to describe changes in the sounds of adjacent words) phenomenon, which is rarely found in other Chinese dialects. In words that consist of two syllables, not only does the tone of the first syllable undergo tonal value change, but also the consonant initial of the second syllable undergoes an assimilation change according to the articulation of the coda (syllable ending) of the preceding syllable. For example, the word for "movie" is composed of two syllables. The first, *tieng*^{6}, means "electric." The second, *ing*^{3}, means "shadow." Together they create the compound word *tieng*^{2} *nging*^{3}, whose first-syllable tone and second-syllable consonant initial have changed.

Sometimes not only the consonants but also the main vowels of the second syllables undergo sound sandhi and become different vowels or diphthongs.

Fuzhou also shows some grammatical features that differ from Mandarin (China's national language). For example, in Fuzhou, for animal terms with a gender modifier, the gender modifier follows the head noun. That is, "male dog" is pronounced *k'eing*^{6} *xyng*^{3} (dog-male), while in Mandarin the gender modifier precedes the head noun: *xiong*^{2} *gou*^{3} (male-dog). This feature is shared by other Min dialects and other southern Chinese dialect groups such as Yue and Hakka. Another example is the presence of a perfective aspect marker to indicate completed action. The phrase "I have seen" is in Fuzhou *nguai*^{3} *ou*^{6} *k'ang*^{2} ("I have seen"), while in Mandarin it is *wo*^{3} *kan*^{4} *le* ("I see [*aspect*]"), where [*aspect*] is a verbal category indicating an action is viewed as completed or in progress.

A Minnan Dialect: Amoy

Native speakers of Minnan dialects are found not only in Fujian province but also in the Chinese provinces of Taiwan, Guangdong, Hainan Island, Zhejian, Jiangxi, Guangxi, and Sichuan. Overseas, Minnan speakers are also found in the Chinese communities of the Philippines, Myanmar (Burma), Thailand, Malaysia, Indonesia, and Singapore. There are over 30 million speakers of Minnan dialects; Amoy, which is spoken by more than 510,000 people, is representative of the group.

In every Chinese dialect, there is the phenomenon of literary and colloquial readings of characters. The Amoy dialect is well known for having the most characters with both literary and colloquial readings. The literary form is used only in reading the written language and when using a person's formal name, while the colloquial form is used in all other oral communications. The difference between the literary and colloquial pronunciation is so great that they can be treated as two parallel phonological systems. For example, in literary Amoy the word *blood* is pronounced *hiat*^{7}, while in colloquial Amoy it is pronounced *hui*^{7}.

Both literary and colloquial Amoy have six oral vowels (*i, e, a, u, o,* and *Ô*), but in colloquial Amoy there are an additional five nasalized vowels (i^{n}, e^{n}, a^{n}, u^{n}, $\hat{O}^{n}$). In literary Amoy, there are sixteen consonants (*p, p', b, m, t, t', l, n, ts, ts', s, k, k', g, h,* and *ng*); colloquial Amoy has one more consonant, the glottal stop, *q*, which only occurs in syllable final position. The stops *p, t, k* and their counterpart nasals *m, n, ng* can occur both in the syllable initial and final positions, while the other consonants can only occur in initial positions. The nasals *m* and *ng* may occur alone as syllabic syllables.

Amoy dialect has seven basic tones. In both literary and colloquial Amoy, whenever a compound word or a phrase consists of two or more syllables, the syllables preceding the last one must undergo tone sandhi, except when the last syllable is an atonic (or enclitic) word. For example, the word for "soy sauce" is the combination of *tau*^{6}, meaning "bean," with *iu*^{2}, meaning "oil." The compound word is pronounced *tau*^{5} *iu*^{2}.

Some of the same grammatical features that set Fuzhou apart from Mandarin are also characteristic of Amoy. For instance, like Fuzhou, Amoy's gender markers for animals follow rather than precede the animal; word order in some compound words is also reversed. For instance, in Amoy "guest" is *lang*^{6} *k'eq*^{7} (people-guest), whereas in Mandarin it is *ke*^{4} *ren*^{2} (guest-people). Amoy also uses a prefective marker to show completed action.

A Minbei Dialect: Jian'ou

Jian'ou dialect is a representative subdialect of the Minbei (Northern Min) dialect group. It is spoken in the northern part of Fujian Province. Its native speakers number more than 437,000. It has fourteen initial consonants (*p, p', m, t, t', n, l, ts, ts', s, k, k', x, ng*), nine vowels (*i, u, y, e, ɛ, œ, a, o, Ô*), six tones, and one consonant ending (*-ng*). Because of its adjacency to Mindong dialect area, it shares some phonological features with Fuzhou. For example, they both have rounded front vowels (*y, œ*), more diphthong main vowels, and only one nasal ending (*-ng*).

A Minzhong Dialect: Yong'an

Yong'an is a representative subdialect of the Minzhong (Central Min) dialect group, which is surrounded by Minbei to its north, Mindong to its east, Minnan to its south, and Hakka dialect to its west. It possesses both Min and Hakka dialect features. Native speakers of Yong'an number around 265,000. It has sixteen initial consonants (*p, p', m, t, t', n/l, ts, ts', s, tš, tš', š, k, k', x, ng*), ten oral vowels (*i, Ï, u, û, y, e, ø, a, o, â*), four nasalized vowels (*ĩ, õ, ã, ũ*), and six tones. It has two consonant endings, bilabial nasal *-m* and velar nasal *-ng*. The bilabial nasal *m* can occur alone as a syllabic syllable.

A Puxian Dialect: Putian

Puxian dialect is spoken between Mindong and Minnan. Thus it shares some linguistic features both with Mindong and Minnan. Putian is a representative of this dialect group. Its native speakers number almost 1.5 million. It has fourteen initial consonants (*p, p', m, t, t', n, l, L* [voiceless *l*] , *ts, ts', k, k', h, ng*), eleven vowels (*i, u, y, e, ε, ø, œ, a, o, Ô, A*), and six tones. There are two consonant endings, velar nasal *-ng* and glottal stop *-q*. The velar nasal can occur alone as a syllabic syllable. Putian has sound sandhi that is similar to Mindong and a colloquial and literary system similar to that of Minnan dialect.

A Shaoning Dialect: Shaowu

Shaoning dialect is spoken in the northwest part of Fujian Province. Shaowu is a representative of this dialect group. Its native speakers number just over 258,000. It is adjacent to Minbei to its east and Gan dialect (in Jiangxi Province) to its west, and to the area of the Hakka dialect group to its south. Its status has been a very controversial topic for years. Some scholars claim that Shaowu is a Min dialect, while others claim it is a Hakka dialect. Currently, based on the historical sound changes and dialect specific lexicon, it is considered as a hybrid dialect, a mixture of Min and Hakka-Gan. Shaowu has nineteen initial consonants (*p, p', m, f, v, t, t', n, l, ts, ts', s, tš, tš', š, k, k', x, ng*), eight vowels (*i, Ï, u, û, y, a, o, ë*), and six tones. It has two consonant endings: an alveolar nasal *-n* and velar nasal *-ng*. The velar nasal can occur alone as a syllabic syllable.

Margaret Mian Yan

Further Reading

Chang Kuang-yu. (1996) *Min-ke fangyan shigao* (A History of Min and Hakka Dialects). Taipei: Guoli Bianyiguan.

Chang Kun. (1984) "Lun bijiao Min fangyan" (Comparative Min Phonology). *The Bulletin of the Institute of History and Philology* 55, 3: 415–458.

Li Fang-kuei (1973) "Languages and Dialects." *Journal of Chinese Linguistics* 1,1: 1–13.

Norman, Jerry. (1973) "Tonal Development in Min." *Journal of Chinese Linguistics* 1, 2: 22–38.

———. (1988) *Chinese*. Cambridge, U.K.: Cambridge University Press.

Pan Maoding, Li Rulong, Liang Yuzhang, Zhang Shengyu, and Chen Zhangtai. (1963) "Fujian Hanyu fangyan fenqu lueshuo" (A Brief Account of the Geographical Distribution of the Fujian Dialects). *Zhongguo Yuwen* 6: 475–495.

Ramsey, S. Robert. (1987) *The Languages of China*. Princeton, NJ: Princeton University Press.

Ting Pang-hsin, ed. (1999) *Contemporary Studies on the Min Dialects*. Journal of Chinese Linguistics Monograph Series, no. 14. Berkeley, CA: Journal of Chinese Linguistics.

Wang, William S.-Y. ed. (1991) *Languages and Dialects of China*. Journal of Chinese Linguistics Monograph Series, no. 3. Berkeley, CA: Journal of Chinese Linguistics.

Yan, Margaret Mian. (1994) "Historical Sound Changes as Criteria for the Classification of the Fujian Dialects." In *Taiwan yu Fujian shehui wenhua yanjiu lunwenji* (Monograph on the Studies on the Societies and Cultures of Taiwan and Fujian), edited by Chuang Ying-chang and Pan Ying-hai. Taipei: Institute of Ethnology, Academia Sinica, 257–284.

Yuan Jiahua et al. (1960) *Hanyu fangyan gaiyao* (An Outline of the Chinese Dialects). Beijing: Wenzi Gaige Chubanshe.

Zhan Bohui. (1991) *Xiandai Hanyu fangyan* (Modern Chinese Dialects). Taipei: Xinxueshi Wenjiao Chuban Zhongxin.

Zhang Zhensheng. (1989) "Minyu de fenbu yu renkou" (The Distribution and Population of Min Dialects). *Fangyan* 1: 54–59.

MINARET Although the origin and early function(s) of the minaret have not been clearly identified, the structure was used as a high platform by muezzins (Muslim criers) to call worshipers to daily prayer. During the life of Muhammad (c. 570–632) worshipers at Medina were called to prayer from a rooftop, perhaps in imitation of the Jewish practice of blowing the shofar or ram's horn or the Christian practice of ringing a clapper.

Later, however, as Islamic architecture began to flourish, minarets became an integral part of the design of major mosques and were constructed at the corners of mosque courtyards or were built as free-standing towers. Apart from their use by the muezzins, minarets became convenient locators of mosques from relatively long distances, for travelers and new residents seeking places of worship.

The first minaret was said to have been constructed in Basra in present-day Iraq around 665. Later, the caliph Muʿawuyah I (c. 602–680) issued a decree for the addition of minarets to various mosques in Egypt and elsewhere in his domain. Constructed of stone, these early minarets also came to symbolize the power of the expanding Arab empire and of Islam as a religion. The Umayyad mosque in Damascus, built between 705 and 715, is an early preserved example; the mosque was constructed over a Christian church.

Over the centuries the structural design of minarets became much more elaborate and grandiose, reaching heights of over thirty meters and more. An unusual free-standing minaret in spiral form, at Samarra in modern Iraq, was built between 848 and 852. Particularly elaborate and imposing were those built by the Ottoman sultans: the Suleimanlye mosque in Istanbul, built by the famous architect Sinan around 1550, displayed a pair of minarets with heights in excess of sixty meters.

Merdhad Haghayeghi

Further Reading

Creswell, K. A. C. (1926) "The Evolution of the Minaret, with Special Reference to Egypt." *Burlington Magazine* 48:134–140, 252–259, 290–298.

Mohammad, G. R. (1964) "The Minaret and Its Relationship to the Mosque in Early Islam." 2 vols. Ph.D. thesis, University of Edinburgh.

MINDANAO (2002 est. pop. 13.8 million). Mindanao is the second-largest island (after Luzon) in the Philippines and home to most of the Philippine Muslim population. It is located in the southern Philippines, south of the islands of Negros, Cebu, and Leyte and north of the Sulu archipelago. It covers 36,536 square miles and has a long and irregular coastline. The island is divided administratively into the northern (2002 estimated population 2.9 million), southern (5.4 million), central (2.7 million), western (3.2 million) and Muslim (2.6 million) regions. The major cities are Davao (estimated population 874,000) and Tagum (estimated population 107,000) in the south, Cagayan (estimated population 426,000) in the north, Cotabato (estimated population 171,000) in the center, and Zamboanga (estimated population 153,000) in the west. Mt. Apo, the Philippines' highest peak at 2,954 meters and an active volcano, is located on the island.

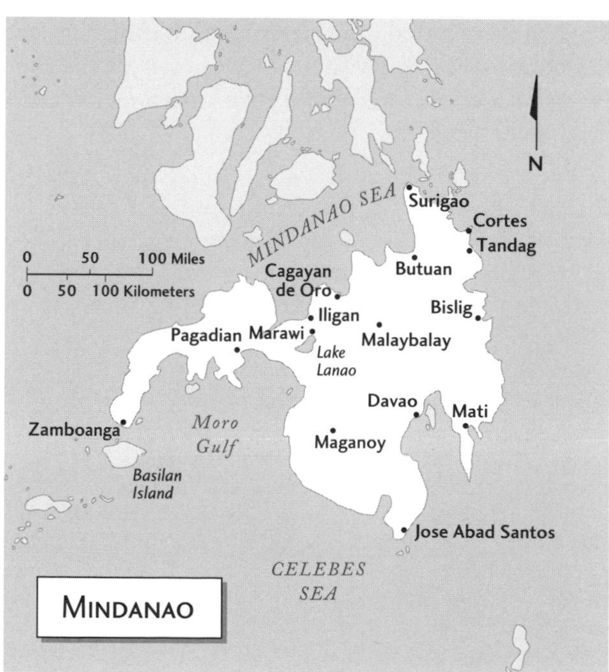

The region was first settled by peoples migrating north from what is now Indonesia and Malaysia. Islam was introduced in the fourteenth century and until the middle of the twentieth century, Muslims formed the majority of Mindanao's population. The three major Muslim ethnic groups on the island are the Maranao, Maguindanao, and Sangill. Massive migration from the north beginning early in the twentieth century and accelerating rapidly after World War II, when settlers were given free land, has made the Muslims a minority (less than 20 percent of Mindanao's total population in 2002) and the Christians (mainly Roman Catholics) the majority. The island is also home to indigenous peoples, who live in remote areas of the interior. One of these groups, the Tasaday, caused an international stir in 1971 when they were "discovered" and publicized as a lost Stone Age people, a description that proved to be less than accurate.

The Muslim peoples of Mindanao have resisted centralized control since the Spanish first colonized the islands in the sixteenth century, and their resistance continues in 2002 with some Muslim groups advocating political autonomy and others separation from the Philippines.

Mindanao came under centralized control only in the early twentieth century when American influence and financial support allowed for the creation of agricultural colonies in the interior. Settlers from the overcrowded central and northern Philippines cleared much of Mindanao's forests and transformed it to an agricultural and later an industrial region. It now houses major commercial agricultural operations, large cattle ranches, pig farms, and rice fields.

David Levinson

Further Reading

Headland, Thomas N., ed. (1991) *The Tasaday Hoax Controversy: An Assessment of the Evidence*. Washington D.C.: American Anthropological Association.

Majul, Cesar Adib. (1973) *Muslims in the Philippines*. Quezon City, Philippines: University of the Philippines Press.

McCoy, Alfred W., and Ed. C. de Jesus, eds. (1982) *Philippine Social History: Global Trade and Local Transformations*. Honolulu: University Press of Hawaii.

Stewart, James C. (1977) *People of the Flood Plain: The Changing Ecology of Rice Farming in Cotabato, Philippines*. Ann Arbor, MI: University Microfilms.

MINERAL INDUSTRY—MALAYSIA Although Malaysia has a rich variety of mineral resources, only petroleum and tin are of any significance in terms of quality and value of reserves. Gold, coal, iron, antimony, and cinnabar (mercury) have at various periods in the past contributed to the country's economy. Prior to World War II, tin was one of the two mainstays of the economy (the other being rubber); during the postwar era, petroleum assumed prominence, particularly from the 1970s onward.

Tin

Although tin had been known and worked in peninsular Malaysia since the fifth century BCE, it was only in the nineteenth century that production and export became significant to the extent of transforming the socioeconomic landscape. The expanding tin-plate industry in Britain in the early nineteenth century increased the demand for tin, especially for the alluvial tin known as "Straits tin" then produced in peninsular Malaysia. The high demand accelerated production, which led to a reorganization of the tin industry in peninsular Malaysia from the 1820s. Malay chieftains who had in the past directly worked the deposits now leased the mines for a lump sum to Chinese merchants of Melaka and Penang. The direct participation of Chinese entrepreneurs enabled a more systematic exploitation through utilization of more advanced mining methodology and equipment coupled with a large pool of imported labor resources from the southern Chinese provinces of Guangdong and Fujian.

The Chinese dominance of the tin industry persisted from the mid-nineteenth century to the first decade of the twentieth century. The period of intensive mechanization of the industry ushered in European participation in mining and smelting that eventually eclipsed Chinese predominance by the 1930s. The introduction of the mining dredge by European enterprise from the 1910s converted the industry from a labor-intensive enterprise involving hundreds of small producers to a capital-intensive enterprise dominated by a handful of large European mining establishments. The advent of British colonial administration from the mid-1870s contributed to the development and expansion of the industry in the provision of political stability, an efficient transportation network (railway and roads), and clear-cut legislation regulating land, water supply, mining activities, and labor recruitment.

By the 1890s peninsular Malaysia exported more tin than all the other tin producers combined. Competition from Bolivia, Indonesia, Thailand, and, to a lesser extent, China and Nigeria reduced its world market share to 34 percent in the 1920s. The Great Depression of the 1930s ushered in controlled schemes (International Tin Agreement, 1931) and the creation of buffer stocks aimed at maintaining high prices. But the forced reduction in production had adverse socioeconomic implications; hundreds of thousands of Chinese mine workers were repatriated owing to cutbacks and closures of mines.

Low demand and the Allied blockade to shipping coupled with inadequate mining equipment resulted in negligible production during the Japanese occupation (1941–1945). The Korean War (1950–1953) boosted postwar revival of the tin industry. Between 1948 and 1960, a leftist-led insurgency referred to as the "Emergency" erupted in peninsular Malaysia. Despite attempts by leftist guerrillas to disrupt the country's economy through terrorism, overall the tin industry was not affected adversely. The Emergency notwithstanding, production continued to rise throughout the 1950s, overtook prewar peak levels in the early 1960s, and continued rising to the mid-1970s. But as an export commodity tin declined in its share in the Malaysian economy. From the late 1970s there was a depletion of reserves, mounting production costs, and falling world prices, resulting in drastic reductions in production. The industry suffered an irreversible setback when in 1985 the London Metal Exchange suspended all dealings in tin, thereby precipitating the collapse of the International Tin Council's buffer stock. By the 1990s, Malaysia had declined as a major tin producer and exporter; it fell behind Indonesia, Brazil, Peru, Bolivia, and Australia. Established in 1953, the Tin Industry (Research and Development) Board aimed to protect and promote the general interests of the tin industry through research and development and public relations exercises. The Malaysian tin industry during the 1990s was but a shadow of the industry during its heyday more than a century earlier.

Petroleum and Natural Gas

The first oil strike in Malaysia was recorded at Miri, Sarawak, in 1910. Sarawak, then under the Brooke Raj, enjoyed this unexpected boom and petroleum became the chief export earner until 1941. Production at Miri peaked in 1929 and thereafter steadily declined. No new fields were opened until the discovery in the 1970s of oilfields offshore from Sarawak (Bintulu), Sabah (western coast), and Terengganu (Kertih and Tok Arun).

A marble quarry in Langkawi Island, Malaysia, c. 1990. (DAVE G. HOUSER/CORBIS)

Production of these oil fields throughout the 1970s and 1980s witnessed the emergence of Malaysia as a net producer of high-quality, low-sulfur petroleum that is in high demand on the world market. Large reserves of natural gas were also discovered during the 1970s in the same vicinity. Production began in the 1980s.

Petroliam Nasional Berhad (PETRONAS), the national petroleum company of Malaysia (established in 1974), is the major organization responsible to undertake and regulate the exploitation and development of oil and natural gas in the country. Exploration during the 1970s uncovered several rich oil fields as well as large areas of natural gas offshore from Sarawak, Sabah, and Terengganu. The early 1980s witnessed the exploitation of these offshore oil and gas fields. The crude oil is of high quality with low sulfur content and much demanded in the world market. Over the two decades since its inception, PETRONAS had expanded its upstream (exploration and production) activities and at the same diversified into the downstream (refining and marketing) sector, gradually carving out a name for itself in the global market as an oil and gas multinational.

Gold and Other Mining

Peninsular Malaysia has been known for its gold since the second century BCE. Gold was one factor that motivated the British to intervene in Pahang in the 1880s. Reputation notwithstanding, the only viable gold mine was located at Raub, Pahang. Production was moderate but sustained until 1941. As early as the 1820s, Chinese miners had crossed the border to Upper Sarawak from Sambas in southwest Dutch Borneo (Indonesian Kalimantan) to exploit the alluvial gold deposits in and around Bau. By the 1880s the labor-intensive mining methods of the Chinese had given way to more mechanization and the cyanidation process (whereby cyanide was utilized to extract pure gold from the ore, producing an extraction of between 70 and 80 percent) utilized by the British-owned Borneo Company Limited (BCL). Gold production increased significantly from the late 1890s with the domination of the BCL and exports were a mainstay of the Sarawak economy until 1921. The 1920s saw the steady decline in gold production due to exhaustion of old fields and the absence of new deposits.

Sarawak coal from the Simunjan colliery in the Middle Sadong competed with gold during the 1890s as a major earner, although the former mainly sustained local needs. Coal at Labuan was a disappointment and incurred deficits. The Chartered Company of British North Borneo (Sabah) profited modestly from coal production at Tawau during the first three decades of the twentieth century. Likewise in peninsular Malaysia, the Batu Arang collieries in Selangor supplied local requirements in the prewar period. Japanese entrepreneurs worked iron ore in Terengganu and Johor until 1941 without much profitable return. An iron boom in the 1960s in Perak momentarily spurred optimism that this mineral could also provide a good source of revenue, but the boom was short lived. Small amounts of cinnabar were produced in Upper Sarawak (Tegora, Gading) from the 1860s; mercury was last exported from Sarawak in 1909. Between the 1820s and the 1880s, antimony was produced and exported from Bidi and Busau Upper Sarawak. Its exports sustained the early growth of Sarawak under Brooke rule. By the early 1920s, antimony and cinnabar ceased to be important as most of the sources were mined out.

Optimism remains in the oil and gas industry. The various ventures of PETRONAS coupled with the large reserves of petroleum and natural gas in the country offer promising prospects for this sector of the mineral industry of Malaysia. Overall in 2000 the mining sector had a workforce of some 38,000 mostly trained and skilled workers and contributed about 10 per cent to the country's gross domestic product.

Ooi Keat Gin

Further Reading

Allen, George Cyril, and Audrey Gladys Donnithorne. (1954) *Western Enterprise in Indonesia and Malaya: A Study in Economic Development*. London: Allen & Unwin.

Amarjit, Kaur. (1985) *Bridge and Barrier: Transport and Communications in Colonial Malaya, 1870–1957*. Singapore: Oxford University Press.

———. (1990) "Hewers and Haulers: A History of Coal Miners and Coal Mining in Malaya." *Modern Asian Studies* 24, 1: 75–113.

Arief, Sritua, and Raymond Wells. (1985) *A Report on the Malaysian Petroleum Industry*. East Balmain, New South Wales, Australia: Rosecons for the Southeast Asia Research and Development Institute.

Jackson, Robert Nicholas. (1966) *Pickering: Protector of Chinese*. Kuala Lumpur, Malaysia: Oxford University Press.

Jomo, Kwame Sundaram, ed. (1990) *Undermining Tin: The Decline of Malaysian Pre-eminence*. Sydney: Transnational Corporations Research Project, University of Sydney.

Ooi, Keat Gin. (1997) *Of Free Trade and Native Interests: The Brookes and the Economic Development of Sarawak, 1841–1941*. Kuala Lumpur, Malaysia: Oxford University Press.

Sandhu, Kernial Singh. (1969) *Indians in Malaya: Some Aspects of their Immigration and Settlement, 1786–1957*. Cambridge, U.K.: Cambridge University Press.

Wong, Lin Ken. (1965) *The Malayan Tin Industry to 1914: With Special Reference to the States of Perak, Selangor, Negeri Sembilan, and Pahang*. Tucson: University of Arizona Press for the Association of Asian Studies.

Yip, Yat Hoong. (1969) *The Development of the Tin Mining Industry of Malaya*. Kuala Lumpur, Malaysia: University of Malaya Press.

MING DYNASTY The Ming dynasty (1368–1644) is the Chinese dynasty founded by Zhu Yuanzhang (temple name Taizu, reign title Hongwu; 1328–1398, reigned from 1368), the second of only two commoners to become emperor of China. Following the Mongol Yuan dynasty (1271–1368), the Ming marks an era of Chinese cultural restoration. The restoration, however, was by no means a replica of earlier Han Chinese models; it signified a time of reform and redefinition. The Ming reforms, in turn, strongly influenced Chinese government and society for about six hundred years. As the last native dynasty to rule China, the Ming inspired Chinese revolutionaries at the turn of the twentieth century who overthrew the Manchu Qing dynasty (1644–1912) and founded China's first republic.

Political Changes

For the Ming founder Hongwu, the first urgent tasks were to unify the country and to consolidate his regime. During Hongwu's thirty-year reign, Ming authority was gradually extended into Outer Mongolia in the north, Guangdong and Guangxi provinces in the south, Sichuan in the west, Guizhou and Yunnan in the southwest, Hami in the northwest, and Manchuria in the northeast. By 1398, the Ming controlled the whole of modern China and had established tributary relations with neighboring regions.

To consolidate his rule, Hongwu initiated a great enterprise to restore Confucian values throughout the empire. He ordered that Chinese customs replace Mongol practices in such social aspects as marriage, dress code, family relations, social hierarchy, and rituals. To promote the Confucian ideals, Hongwu took a particular interest in education and ordered the establishment of government and private schools throughout the empire. In terms of governmental institutions, while Hongwu followed the patterns of the Tang, the Song, and even the Yuan periods, he introduced remarkable innovations that reshaped Chinese political history. For the central government, in 1380 he abolished the Secretariat, the top echelon of the Ming bureaucracy. The emperor in effect served as his own chief minister and became directly responsible for routine government duties run by the six ministries and other offices. Meanwhile, the Chief Military Commission was divided into five coequal and uncoordinated agencies collectively called Five Chief Military Commissions. At the provincial level, in 1376 Hongwu splintered the Branch Secretariat into three coordinating agencies: administration, surveillance, and military commissions. Hongwu's autocratic nature in governing has been labeled "Ming despotism" by some historians.

The Emperor Yongle (1360–1424, reigned from 1403) relied increasingly on secretarial aides from the Hanlin Academy, which led to the establishment of a new institution, the Grand Secretariat *(neige)*, under Emperor Xuande (1398–1435, reigned from 1425). Managing state affairs between the throne and the rest of the civil bureaucracy, the Grand Secretariat enhanced the efficiency of Ming government; it was formally recognized as a state institution in the late sixteenth century. Yongle also transferred the capital from Nanjing to Beijing in 1421, a move that refocused the Ming political landscape by instituting a dual-capital system. In foreign relations, the expansionist Yongle personally led five expeditions against the Mongols on the northern frontiers; on the last expedition he died. In the south, he had annexed the northern part of Vietnam (1406). Between 1405 and 1421, Yongle had launched six maritime expeditions, chiefly under the command of the Muslim eunuch admiral Zheng He (1371–1433), to demand tribute from rulers abroad.

Zheng He's first voyage included more than 27,800 men and 317 ships; his largest ships measured 400 feet long and had nine masts (by comparison, the USS *Constitution*, built almost four hundred years later, was only 204 feet long). The destinations of these voyages included the near areas of Southeast Asia and distant places such as the Indian Ocean, Arabia, and the east coast of Africa. With the death of Yongle, however, political support for these expeditions withered, and

CHINA—HISTORICAL PERIODS

Xia dynasty (2100–1766 BCE)
Shang dynasty (1766–1045 BCE)
Zhou dynasty (1045–256 BCE)
Western Zhou (1045–771 BCE)
Eastern Zhou (770–221 BCE)
Spring and Autumn period (770–476 BCE)
Warring States period (475–221 BCE)
Qin dynasty (221–206 BCE)
Han dynasty (206 BCE–220 CE)
Three Kingdoms period (220–265 CE)
North and South Dynasties (220–589 CE)
Sui dynasty (581–618 CE)
Tang dynasty (618–907 CE)
Five Dynasties period (907–960 CE)
Song dynasty (960–1279)
Northern Song (960–1126)
Southern Song (1127–1279)
Jurchen Jin dynasty (1125–1234)
Yuan dynasty (1279–1368)
Ming dynasty (1368–1644)
Qing dynasty (1644–1912)
Republican China (1912–1927)
People's Republic of China (1949–present)
Republic of China (1949–present)
Cultural Revolution (1966–1976)

they ended. China was to lose its lead in maritime technology and trade interest to the Western powers.

For nearly a century after Yongle, although the Ming dynasty enjoyed general stability and prosperity, it was occasionally threatened by the Mongols along the northern frontiers. In 1449, during a military campaign led by the Ming eunuch Wang Zhen, Emperor Zhengtong (1427–1464) was captured and held prisoner by the Oirat (western Mongols) at Tumu, Beizhili. The Tumu incident indicated the increasing eunuch influence during mid-Ming times. Other eunuchs who dominated court affairs included Wang Zhi in the 1470s and 1480s and Liu Jin from 1505 to 1510. The Tumu incident forced the Ming to focus on defense against the Mongols, which led to the reconstruction of the Great Wall. Under Emperor Jiajing (1507–1566, reigned from 1522), who strongly patronized Taoist alchemists and withdrew from governmental affairs, the Mongols led by Altan Khan (d. 1583) constantly raided Chinese territory, and Japanese pirates attacked coastal regions.

In order to improve government efficiency and financial administration, the grand secretary Zhang Juzheng (1525–1582) carried out a series of reforms in the late sixteenth century. He achieved several of his goals, centralizing the government, repairing the Grand Canal (a series of ancient waterways that links Beijing with Hangzhou), and limiting corrupt practices in civil-service examinations. By means of the "single whip method of taxation," he made land the single basis of tax obligations and used silver as the value base for tax assessment. After Zhang's death, the Ming government again fell into the hands of eunuchs, the most notorious of whom was Wei Zhongxian (1568–1627). When Emperor Chongzhen (1611–1644, reigned from 1627) tried to restrengthen the Ming, his dynasty was ruined by two major occurrences, peasant rebellions that started in northern Shaanxi and Manchu encroachment from the northeastern frontier. When the peasant troops led by Li Zicheng (1605–1645) entered Beijing in April 1644, the Ming emperor committed suicide. Meanwhile, Ming loyalists on the northeast frontier invited the Manchu forces to help suppress the rebels and restore the dynasty. When the Manchus entered Beijing in June, however, they seized the throne for themselves under the dynastic title of Qing.

Socioeconomic Changes

The Ming founder Hongwu envisioned a world of frugality and simplicity based on agricultural economy. He ordered the compilations of "yellow books" to register the population and "fish-scale books" to record the land. The entire population of about 60 million people was categorized into hereditary households such as peasants, soldiers, artisans, and "mean people" (slaves and prostitutes, for example). Without government permits, residents would not move freely around the country. To define women's roles, the emperor dictated the writing of the *Nujie* (Instructions for Women). At the grassroots level, Ming society was organized into communities *(lijia)*, in which every 110 households formed a basic unit that was made responsible for paying taxes, maintaining order, and promoting morality. The main sources of Ming government revenue were the summer and autumn land taxes and the salt monopoly. To recover the economy devastated by famines and warfare, the early Ming government took a number of measures, including transferring population to damaged regions, reclaiming uncultivated areas, constructing irrigation networks, and afforesting the lands. Without much advancement in technology, agriculture was restored during the late fourteenth century.

By the mid-sixteenth century, while agriculture continued to serve as the backbone of the economy, some industries expanded. In the paper, ceramics, and textile industries, small workshops grew into big enterprises, some of which employed several hundred workers. In Jiangxi, thousands of laborers worked in nearly thirty paper factories. At Jingdezhen (Jiangxi), the porcelain center with a population of 1 million, numerous porcelain kilns produced articles of fine ceramics, particularly high-quality cloisonné. Large textile workshops with more than 100,000 looms made Songjiang (Nanzhili) the big cotton-weaving center. Luxury silks were produced in Hangzhou and Suzhou, and iron factories developed at Cixian (Beizhili).

The last century of the Ming witnessed the development of a new urban and mercantile society, the so-called second commercial revolution. The expansion of transportation and communication networks created the preconditions for the growth of trade and the commercialization of the economy. The number of cities and market towns increased, and a national market emerged in which economically specialized macroregions developed. In many areas, agricultural produce became commercialized, especially the cash crops of cotton, vegetable oils, indigo, sugarcane, and tobacco. In international commerce, overseas trading links multiplied, particularly to areas in Southeast Asia such as Siam and the Philippines. In addition to Arab and Asian traders, Europeans arrived in increasing numbers at Macao and Guangzhou (Canton). From countries such as Japan and Mexico, silver flowed into China.

During the course of commercialization, society underwent dramatic changes. The gentry, the landowners with official ranks or civil-service examination degrees who were exempt from labor taxes, took advantage of the new economic opportunities and invested in commercial enterprises and money-lending activities. About 50 percent of *jinshi*, holders of the highest degree in the civil-service examination system, came from families who had never previously produced such a degree holder, which indicates that the Ming period saw a high level of upward social mobility.

The early Ming hereditary household division began to break up by the first half of the fifteenth century. Merchants gradually enjoyed more and more power and social respectability and often formed close political and economic alliances with scholar-officials. By participating in rural handicraft industries and commercial activities, tenants gained greater freedom from landlord domination; they expressed their dissatisfaction with landlord control through a series of rent revolts. By the late Ming, with the breakdown of the *lijia* system and ineffective government, lineages—social groups that descended from a common ancestor and possessed shared assets—grew stronger, taking care of local affairs.

The introduction of new crops such as peanut, maize, and sweet potato from the Americas led to rapid population growth, which rose to about 150 million toward the end of the dynasty. Women continued to play strong roles both at the imperial court and in ordinary families. While women in general were subordinated to men, many sought their own career opportunities. Instead of being oppressed or silenced, for instance, literate gentrywomen in south China created their own culture by way of reading, writing, teaching, publishing, and forming their own communities.

Cultural and Intellectual Changes

In Ming times, the Neo-Confucianism of the great Song thinker Zhu Xi was fully prescribed as the state orthodoxy. In 1382, Hongwu revived the civil-service examinations, taking Zhu Xi's commentaries as the standard interpretations of the Confucian classics. In 1415, Yongle published *Wujing Sishu daquan* (The Great Compendium of the Five Classics and Four Books) and *Xing li daquan* (The Great Compendium of the Philosophy of Human Nature), which served as the basis for classical studies and continued to be used until the beginning of the eighteenth century. The official ideology, however, was often challenged by other thinkers, the most famous of whom was Wang Shouren (also known as Wang Yangming, 1472–1528). Wang denied the external principle *(li)* of Zhu Xi and argued that principle could be discovered only in one's mind-and-heart. He also advocated the unity of action and innate moral knowledge, or *liangzhi*, the original goodness that should be cultivated so as to achieve sagehood. Wang's teachings strongly influenced philosophical schools in the Ming and those in Japan and Korea. Wang Gen (1483–1541), one of Wang Shouren's followers, founded the Taizhou school of philosophy and preached to the masses that common people's daily necessities were where the Way lay. Another radical philosopher, Li Zhi (1527–1602), attacked traditional morality and extended Wang Shouren's individualism to defend selfishness.

Along with the progress in printing and publishing, popular culture flourished during the Ming. The long novels *Shuihu zhuan* (The Water Margins, fourteenth century), *Sanguozhi yanyi* (The Romance of the Three Kingdoms, 1522), *Xiyouji* (Journey to the West, 1592), and *Jing ping mei* (The Golden Lotus, 1617) mark a milestone in Chinese literary history. Large short-story collections emerged in the late Ming, including *Sanyan* (Three Collections of Stories, 1620–1627) and *Paian jingqi* (Tales That Make One Exclaim in Surprise and Strike the Table, 1628, 1632). More than three hundred different genres of opera developed, which combined drama, music, dance forms, singing, and gorgeous costumes and appealed to both elite and nonelite audiences. Some twelve hundred titles, such as the masterpiece *Mudan ting* (The Peony Pavilion, 1598), are still known.

Ming prosperity was also reflected in the proliferation of practical knowledge and scholarship. Under the imperial patronage, the 11,095-volume *Yongle dadian* (Yongle Encyclopedia), the largest imperial encyclopedia ever compiled, was completed in 1407. In private academies and individual studies, scholars produced huge anthologies of independent books and collections of artifact illustrations. The dictionary *Zihui* (Collection of Characters) by Mei Yingzuo (d. 1615) for the first time classified Chinese characters under 214 radicals (distinctive elements of characters that, in combination, form a complete character), a system that has remained in use up to the present. The imperial prince Zhu Zaiyu (d. 1611), who concentrated on studies of mathematics and musicology, became the first person in the world to formulate the equal temperament in music. Song Yingxing's *Tiangong kaiwu* (The Creations of Nature and Humans, 1637) provided the most comprehensive information on industrial and agricultural technology. Li Shizhen, after sixteen years of arduous work, completed the *Bencao gangmu* (Compendium of Materia Medica, 1602), which contained notes on nearly two thousand medicinal plants and over eleven thousand prescriptions and mentioned for the first time a method of inoculation to prevent smallpox. Having made seventeen trips throughout China in more than twenty years, Xu Hongzu finished his monumental *Xu Xiake youji* (The Travel Diaries of Xu Xiake, 1641), which not only recorded China's geographical features and social customs but for the first time in the world documented karst landforms.

During the Ming, the Chinese increasingly interacted with Europeans, who first appeared in China in 1514. The Europeans came to China not only to trade but also to convert the local people to Catholicism. The Italian Jesuit Matteo Ricci (Li Madou, 1552–1610) was the most successful missionary in China. After he entered Guangdong in 1583, Ricci began his efforts by accommodating to Chinese culture, including speaking Chinese, studying Confucian classics, and wearing Chinese clothes—first Buddhist robes and then a Confucian gown. He also gained trust by introducing Western scientific and technical knowledge and such mechanical curiosities as clocks. By the time of his death in 1610, despite the resistance of some Chinese who accused Christians of corrupting Chinese beliefs and causing political disorder, Jesuit communities were established in many cities, including Beijing, and missionaries served at the imperial court as mathematicians, astronomers, cartographers, interpreters, painters, and musicians. Among the 2,500 Chinese converts, the most famous were three literati: Xu Guangqi (1562–1633), Li Zhizao (d. 1630), and Yang Tingyun (1557–1627). These scholar-officials, together with the missionaries, wrote treatises on Christianity; translated European manuals on mathematics, astronomy, geography, and hydraulics; and established new calendars.

The Ming achievements, including political institutions, economic mechanisms, philosophy, science and technology, and material culture, not only left a strong legacy for future China but also made a powerful impact on other East Asian countries. By the time the Ming fell, however, China's leadership in the world was soon to be challenged by the West.

Jiang Yonglin

Further Reading

Brook, Timothy. (1998) *The Confusions of Pleasure: Commerce and Culture in Ming China*. Berkeley and Los Angeles: University of California Press.

Huang, Ray. (1981) *1587, a Year of No Significance: The Ming Dynasty in Decline*. New Haven, CT: Yale University Press.

Ko, Dorothy. (1994) *Teachers of the Inner Chambers: Women and Culture in Seventeenth-Century China*. Stanford, CA: Stanford University Press.

Mote, F. W. (1999) *Imperial China, 900–1800*. Cambridge, MA: Harvard University Press.

Twitchett, Denis, and Frederick W. Mote, eds. (1988 and 1998) *The Cambridge History of China* 7 and 8: *The Ming Dynasty, 1368–1644*. New York: Cambridge University Press.

MINOBE TATSUKICHI (1873–1948), Japanese constitutional scholar. Minobe Tatsukichi was born in Hyogo Prefecture of Japan in 1873. After graduation from the Department of Law of Tokyo Imperial University in 1897, he entered the Home Ministry. From 1899 to 1902, he studied comparative legal systems in Europe, mainly in Germany. In 1902, he was appointed professor at Tokyo Imperial University and lectured on administrative and constitutional law until his retirement in 1934. He was elected to the House of Counselors of Japan in 1918. Minobe had a liberal interpretation of the Meiji Constitution. He called for party cabinets, universal suffrage, and expansion of civil liberties. He advocated the "emperor as organ of the state" theory *(Tenno kikan setsu)*, which divided experts on constitutional law of Japan. His theories in the 1930s came under criticism from ultranationalists and militarists, and in 1935 his books on constitutions were banned until the end of World War II. Under nationalistic pressure, he was forced to resign from the House of Peers, to which he had been appointed in 1932. He died in 1948. Among his writings are the *Kempo Satsuyo* (Outline of the Constitution, 1923) and the *Nihonkoku Kempo Genron* (Principles of the Japanese Constitution, 1946). Minobe's eldest son, Ryokichi, has been governor of Tokyo.

Nathalie Cavasin

Further Reading

Giffard, Sydney. (1994) *Japan among the Powers 1890–1990.* New Haven, CT: Yale University Press.

Miller, Frank O. (1965) *Minobe Tatsukichi: Interpreter of Constitutionalism in Japan.* Berkeley and Los Angeles: University of California Press.

MITTAPHAP BRIDGE The first bridge ever built across the lower reaches of the Mekong River, the Mittaphap (Friendship) Bridge connects Thailand and Laos. Since Laos is a landlocked nation, the bridge is particularly strategic in helping link it to key Thai Pacific ports. The building of the bridge was a joint venture among the governments of Laos, Thailand, and Australia, with the Australian government funding (A$40 million) the construction of the bridge, which was completed in April 1994. This infrastructure project was an important signal of Australian commitment to the Lao PDR, strengthening Laos's linkages to the market economies of Southeast Asia. A new project will build a rail passage on the bridge to link directly the Lao and Thai capitals.

To celebrate the opening of the bridge, the Thai king came to the Lao PDR, the first time the Thai monarch had left the Kingdom in some thirty years. The bridge is symbolic of growing economic ties between Thailand and Laos.

Private automobiles were initially banned from using the bridge. The bridge is primarily for truck and bus traffic. The rationale for this policy was to prevent a flood of Thai private vehicles from entering the Lao capital of Vientiane, causing potential pollution, congestion, and accidents. More recently this policy has been relaxed and private automobiles can use the bridge, though some red tape and fees are necessary to obtain a border pass for a private vehicle.

Gerald W. Fry

Further Reading

Project Appraisal Services. (1995) *A Study on the Usage and Operations of the Mekong River Friendship Bridge: Final Report. Phase 3: May, 1995 update*. Bangkok, Thailand: Project Appraisal Services.

Smith, P. Selby. (1994) "Australia Builds the Friendship Bridge." *Road & Transport Research* 3, 2: 4–18.

MIYAGI (2002 est. pop. 2.4 million). Miyagi Prefecture is situated in the northern region of Japan's island of Honshu, where it occupies an area of 7,292 square kilometers. Its primary geographical features are the Ou Mountains in the west, an eastern coastal plain, and the Abukuma and Kitakami rivers (in Japanese, Abukumagawa and Kitakamigawa). Miyagi is bordered by the Pacific Ocean and by Iwate, Fukushima, Akita, and Yamagata prefectures. Once part of Mutsu Province, it assumed its present name in 1872 and its present borders in 1876.

Various archaeological remains indicate early habitation of the region. During the Heian period (794–1185), Mutsu Province was ruled by the northern Fujiwara family as a virtually independent kingdom. Later rulers included a series of warlords and the Date family in the Edo period (1600/1603–1868).

The prefecture's capital is Sendai, the northeast's largest city and its cultural, economic and political heart. It grew around Sendai Castle, erected in 1601 by Date Masamune (1567–1636). As the core of Sendai Industrial Zone in the early 2000s, the city supports printing plants and the processors of petrochemicals and foodstuffs. Its cultural amenities include Tohoku University, the Osaki Hachiman Shrine, and the Tanabata Festival. The prefecture's other important cities are Kesennuma, Ishinomaki, Furukawa, and Shiogama.

Home to one of Japan's leading fisheries, Miyagi produces large amounts of mackerel, tuna, and sardines. Agriculture, mainly rice farming, continues as a primary economic activity. The region's industries include pulp and paper processors, and metal and machinery fabricators. Visitors are drawn to one of the vistas known throughout Japan as one of the nation's three most famous: the panorama of Matsushima Bay with some 250 small islands with pine trees and irregularly shaped rocks. Other destinations are Rikuchu Coast National Park and various hot spring resorts, including Narugo, Togatta, and Sakunami.

E. L. S. Weber

Further Reading

"Miyagi Prefecture." (1993) *Japan: An Illustrated Encyclopedia*. Tokyo: Kodansha.

MIYAZAKI (2002 est. pop. 1.2 million). Miyazaki Prefecture is situated in the southeast of Japan's island of Kyushu, where it occupies an area of 7,735 square kilometers. Miyazaki's primary geographical features are the northern Kyushu Mountains and the southern Wanitsuka Mountains, the central coastal Miyazaki Plain, and numerous rivers. It is bordered by the Pacific Ocean and by Oita, Kagoshima, and Kumamoto prefectures. Once known as Hyuga Province, it assumed its present name in 1873 and its present borders in 1883.

The prefecture's capital is Miyazaki city, along the Hyuga Sea. It includes the island of Aoshima, to which it is connected at low tide. Once a farming village, it flourished after being declared the capital in 1873. In the early 2000s, it is home to Miyazaki University, along with various museums. Aoshima is habitat to some 230 species of subtropical plants. The prefecture's other important cities are Miyakonojo, Nobeoka, and Hyuga.

Hundreds of fifth- and sixth-century burial mounds, along with their clay *haniwa* (burial mound) figures, indicate the region was the site of a flourishing early civilization. Ruled for centuries by a series of feudal warlords, it was divided into smaller domains during the Edo period (1600/1603–1868), with the Tokugawa shoguns controlling some parts directly.

Agriculture is the main economic activity. The region produces rice and sweet potatoes, along with mandarin oranges, other fruit, vegetables, and dairy goods for export to other areas of Japan. Miyazaki is relatively undeveloped in industry, although its hydroelectric plants provide power to northern Kyushu. Visitors are drawn by the scenic coastline and mountains, especially in Kirishima-Yaku National Park.

E. L. S. Weber

Further Reading

"Miyazaki Prefecture." (1993) *Japan: An Illustrated Encyclopedia.* Tokyo: Kodansha.

MIZORAM (2001 est. pop. 891,000). A state in northeastern India established in 1987, Mizoram ("land of the highlanders") extends southward to cover an area of 21,081 square kilometers, squeezed between Bangladesh and Myanmar (Burma) and bounded by Tripura, Manipur, and Assam. It was organized to meet the aspirations of the Mizo (Lushai) people, whose secessionist insurgency was not quelled with status as a union territory beginning in 1972.

The Mizos are an egalitarian people without gender or class distinctions, proud of *Tlawmgaihna*, their code of hospitality. The Mizos migrated to this region in the eighteenth century from the Chin hills in Myanmar. The British brought the area under their control in 1891. Almost 95 percent of the people are Christian; whitewashed Christian churches cross the landscape. Only a few animists remain, along with some Buddhists.

When Mizoram's main species of bamboo bloom, they attract hordes of rats that devour crops and bring famine. In 1959 apparent government disregard of this natural crisis called *mautam* sparked the Mizo Famine Front, which became the Mizo National Front (MNF). For some twenty years, the MNF functioned as an armed guerrilla group fighting for secession and independence from an Indian administration viewed as inept and uncaring. In 1967 the government's heavy-handed response to the MNF—rounding up Mizos into guarded villages—only boosted support for the MNF and propelled secessionist fervor that led to statehood. The years following Mizoram statehood in 1987 have been peaceful.

C. Roger Davis

Further Reading

Nag, Chitta Ranjan. (1999) *Post-Colonial Mizo Politics, 1947–1998.* New Delhi: Vikas Publishing House.

MOERDANI, LEONARDUS BENJAMIN (b. 1932), Indonesian military and political figure. Leonardus Benjamin (Benny) Moerdani was the Indonesian Military Commander from 1983 to 1988 and the second most powerful person in the 1980s in Indonesia after Suharto, who ruled from 1966 to 1998. His position as a trusted adviser to Suharto ended in tension because of Moerdani's criticisms of the business interest of Suharto's family in the early 1990s. Born on 2 October 1932 in Cepu, Central Java, Moerdani joined the student army and was wounded in the war of Indonesian independence (1945–1949). His involvement in operations against separatist movements in the 1950s, in "freeing" Irian Barat (West Papua) from the Dutch in 1962, and in the *Konfrontasi* with Malaysia (1963–1966) formed his perception about the importance of Indonesian unity in the face of radical movements. Like many Indonesian officers, Moerdani got his military training—including some in intelligence—in the United States, in 1960–1961.

In the 1970s, together with Lieutenant General Ali Murtopo (1924–1984), Moerdani helped Suharto to maintain political stability in Indonesia. Moerdani proposed a "defense-in-depth" concept, which was a comprehensive defense strategy including physical, ideological, mental, and sociocultural aspects, rather than relying solely on military development. The ASEAN (Association of Southeast Asia Nations) region was seen as a belt of strategic stability. Moerdani played a significant role in advising Suharto to take over East Timor in 1975. After holding many intelligence posts, Moerdani became the Indonesian military's supreme commander from 1983 until 1988, when he was made minister of defense and security. He retired in March 1993.

Abubakar Eby Hara

Further Reading

Pour, Julius. (1993) *Benny Moerdani: Profile of A Soldier Statesman*. Trans. by Tim Scott. Jakarta, Indonesia: Yayasan Kejuangan Panglima Besar Sudirman.

Singh, Bilveer. (1994) *ABRI and the Security of Southeast Asia: The Role and Thinking of General L. Benny Moerdani*. Singapore: Singapore Institute of International Affairs.

MOGAO CAVES The Mogao Caves of China, 492 of which are preserved, were dug in the sandstone cliffs outside the city of Dunhuang, in today's Gansu Province, from 366 CE to the Yuan dynasty (1279–1368). An oasis in a desert, where travelers on the Silk Road stopped to resupply and to rest, Dunhuang served as a workshop for over a thousand years for Chinese and Central Asian arts to mix. As a result, some of the most brilliant artistic creations in Chinese art history, such as the Flying Apsara Musicians, were born in these caves. Of the more than two thousand colorful statues and over forty-five thousand square meters of murals, most depict Buddhist history, legends, and ways of life in China as the nation was interacting via the Silk Road with Central Asia and beyond. Today, Dunhuang is an important center for the study of Buddhism, Buddhist arts, and the Silk Road.

MOGAO CAVES—WORLD HERITAGE SITE

Designated a UNESCO World Heritage Site in 1987, the Mogao Caves are a cultural and artistic testament to a thousand years of Buddhism and the influence of the nearby Silk Route.

In 1900, a Taoist monk, Wang Yuanlu (d. 1931), discovered in a sealed cave over fifty thousand pieces of paintings and handwritten texts dated from the fourth to the fourteenth centuries. The texts were written mainly in Chinese or Tibetan, but some were

The "herd of antelopes" painting in the Mogao Caves near Dunhuang, China. (PIERRE COLOMBEL/CORBIS)

also written in Sanskrit and in a half dozen other languages. Besides a large number of works on Buddhism, Taoism, and Confucianism, the texts also contain historical records, accounting books, court records, literary works, and works on geography, astrology, medicine, mathematics, and so on. These texts, encyclopedic in their scope, provide an unusual source for the study of Chinese religions, history, literature, arts, and daily life. As part of his efforts to raise money to rebuild a nearby monastery, which he renamed Sanqinggong (the Taoist Trinity Palace), Wang sold some of his discoveries to smugglers from Britain, Japan, France, the United States, and Russia. Between 1907 and 1925, Dunhuang witnessed an exodus of some of its most valued relics, which are today still held in Britain, India, France, Russia, Denmark, Sweden, Finland, Germany, Turkey, Japan, the United States, and Korea. The Museum of Dunhuang Hidden Library, located in Sanqinggong, has been open since May 2000 to tell the story of the Dunhuang treasures. The Mogao Caves are a UNESCO World Natural and Cultural Heritage Site.

Jian-Zhong Lin

Further Reading

Gu Weiheng, ed. (1998) *Grotto Art in Dunhuang*. Beijing: China Tourism Press.

Li Guishan, trans. (1998) *Frescoes and Fables: Mural Stories from the Mogao Grottoes in Dunhuang*. Beijing: New World Press.

MOHAMAD, GOENAWAN (b. 1941), Indonesian poet and journalist. Goenawan Mohamad became one of Indonesia's most important poets and a tireless fighter for press freedom. Born 1941 in Batang, Central Java, he was educated locally before he moved to Jakarta, where he studied psychology and philosophy, and began writing for the literary magazine *Sastra* (Literature). In 1967, he helped to establish the daily newspaper *Harian Kami* (Our Daily), and in 1970 the weekly newsmagazine *Expres*, but within a year had been dismissed for his criticism of the government.

In 1971, Mohamad became founder and editor of *Tempo*, Indonesia's most respected newsmagazine. After the Suharto government banned *Tempo* in 1994, he continued to fight for a free and independent press by forming the Alliance of Independent Journalists (AJI) and founding the Institute for the Studies on Free Flow of Information (ISAI). With Suharto resigning in 1998, Mohamad together with a group of journalists relaunched *Tempo*, intending to hold the new government accountable for its actions.

Mohamad is one of Indonesia's most prominent essayists. He has written about identity and change, democracy and freedom, and the meaning of history. In addition to numerous essays, he has published several volumes of poetry. In 1992, Mohamad was named recipient of the distinguished Harvard Nieman Fellowship and, in 1993, was presented the first Professor Teeuw Award. In 1998, he was awarded the International Press Freedom Award.

Frank Feulner

Further Reading

Aveling, Harry, ed. (1975) *Contemporary Indonesian Poetry*. Brisbane, Australia: University of Queensland Press.

Mohamad, Goenawan. (1994). *Sidelines: Thought Pieces from Tempo Magazine*. Jakarta, Indonesia: Lontar.

———. (1988) *The "Cultural Manifesto" Affair: Literature and Politics in Indonesia in the 1960s: A Signatory's View*. Clayton, Australia: Monash University.

MOHENJO-DARO Mohenjo-Daro is an archaeological site in the Larkana District of Sind, in southern Pakistan. Although objects of the prehistoric copper-age civilization known as the Harappan or Indus Civilization had previously been found on the surface near Harappa and by R. D. Banerji at Mohenjo-Daro, it was only with the thorough excavation of Mohenjo-Daro by Sir John Marshall in 1926–1931 that the full dimensions of this civilization began to be recognized. There were numerous levels of occupation at the site, spanning the entire period from about 2700 to 1500 BCE. Its population has been estimated at 35,000. Characteristic features of the civilization known first from this excavation were the practice of city planning, to provide a grid of straight streets and lanes, the ex-

MOHENJO-DARO—WORLD HERITAGE SITE

Included on the UNESCO World Heritage List since 1980, the archaeological site where Mohenjo-Daro—one of the first Indus Valley cities—was discovered has great historical significance. This mud-brick third-millennia BCE city is considered one of the cradles of civilization.

istence of a citadel presumably for the commanders or rulers, use of a large public bath that may well be the prototype of Hindu temple tanks, and a high standard of public hygiene expressed materially in covered drains, latrines in private houses, and a judicious use of public space. Opinion varies as to how the city met its end: Increased salinity of its fields, and a move of the Indus River away from the site, have been proposed as the reasons.

Paul Hockings

Further Reading

Marshall, John H. (1996) *Mohenjo-Daro and the Indus Civilization: Being an Official Account of Archaeological Excavations at Mohenjo-Daro Carried Out by the Government of India between the Years 1922 and 1927*. New Delhi, India: Asian Educational Services.

Wheeler, Mortimer. (1968) *The Indus Civilization*. 3d ed. Cambridge, U.K.: Cambridge University Press.

MON The Mon are descendants of one of the oldest civilizations in southeast Asia. An ethnolinguistic branch of the Mon-Khmer peoples, Mon settlers once inhabited wide areas of lower Myanmar (Burma) and central Thailand from the early centuries CE. The Mon population in Thailand, however, is today much reduced to around 80,000 inhabitants, and it is only in Myanmar that Mon culture has strongly survived.

Both Theravada Buddhism and writing were introduced to Myanmar and Southeast Asia by the early Mons. Settling in the Tenasserim coastal region and the Irrawaddy, Sittang, and Salween river deltas, their communities dominated the surrounding plains for over a thousand years. The traditional Mon emblem, the *hamsa* or sacred goose, can still be found displayed in pagodas and settlements throughout the region, testifying to earlier cultural links with India, where the *hamsa* is the mythical mount of Brahma. Ethnic Burmans, too, who first began to migrate into the area after the ninth century CE, called the Mon "Talaing," which is believed to refer to a site in eastern India.

In the eleventh century, the Mon principalities at Thaton and Pegu (Hamsawati, Bago) were overrun by Burman rulers who subsequently assimilated many aspects of Mon learning and culture. Following the fall of Pagan to the Mongols in 1287, however, the independent Mon kingdoms revived. A long power struggle then continued between various Mon and Burman rulers until 1757, when the Burman king Alaungpaya (reigned 1752–1760) quashed the last great Mon rebellion, led by Smin Dhaw, at Pegu.

Under British influence and rule (1824–1948), Mon culture declined rapidly, hastened by immigration and assimilation by ethnic majority Burmans. It was only in southeastern Myanmar, in rural districts around Thaton, Moulmein (Mawlamyine), Thanbyuzayat, Ye, and the Thai border, that Mon was still widely spoken. In modern-day Myanmar, although many citizens still claim Mon ancestry, the number of Mon speakers probably does not exceed one million in the whole country.

At Myanmar's independence in 1948, a Mon nationalist movement took up arms, working closely with Karen insurgent forces in neighboring areas. In 1959, the New Mon State Party (NMSP) was formed by the veteran nationalist leader Nai Shwe Kyin, and this party continued armed struggle even after a Mon State was eventually demarcated in 1974, within the union, on the country's political map.

In 1988, the NMSP received a major boost when hundreds of students joined the party after the suppression of pro-democracy protests by the Burmese army. Mon candidates were also elected in the 1990 general election and, during the following decade, there was an upsurge of interest in Mon culture and language, which was supported by Buddhist monks. Fierce fighting broke out with the Burmese army, in which many Mon villagers were displaced from their homes before the NMSP agreed to a cease-fire with the State Law and Order Restoration Council government in 1995 and set up offices in the towns. In a change of policy, the NMSP pledged to promote the Mon cause through aboveground means. However political problems persisted, and the NMSP and Mon nationalist movement were also weakened by internal splits.

Martin Smith

Further Reading

Bauer, Christian. (1984) *A Guide to Mon Studies*. Clayton, Australia: Monash University Centre.

———. (1990) "Language and Ethnicity: The Mon in Burma and Thailand." In *Ethnic Groups across National Boundaries in Mainland Southeast Asia*, edited by Gehan Wijeyewardene. Singapore: Institute of Southeast Asian Studies.

Guillon, Emmanuel. (1999) *The Mons: A Civilization in Southeast Asia*. Bangkok, Thailand: The Siam Society.

Halliday, Robert. (1917) *The Talaings*. Rangoon, Burma: Superintendent, Government Printing.

Smith, Martin. (1999) *Burma: Insurgency and the Politics of Ethnicity*. 2d ed. London: Zed Books.

Smithies, Michael, ed. (1986) *The Mons: Collected Articles from the Journal of the Siam Society*. Bangkok, Thailand: The Siam Society.

South, Ashley. (2002) *Mon Nationalism and Civil War in Burma: The Golden Sheldrake*. London: Curzon.

MON STATE (1992 est. pop. 2.1 million). A Mon State was created on the modern political map of Myanmar (Burma) for the first time in 1974, during the rule of the Burma Socialist Program Party. Previously, there had been no political recognition, as such, in modern history of the Mon people who once predominated throughout much of southern Burma and neighboring Thailand. An elongated territory in shape, the Mon State covers 12,297 square kilometers (4,748 square miles) in area and extends for 320 kilometers (200 miles) down the Andaman shoreline. The coastal region on the west of the state is characterized by wetlands, islands, and creeks, while the interior consists mostly of hills and forests. To the north lies the Pegu (Bago) Division, to the south lies the Tenasserim (Tanintharyi) Division, and to the east lies the Karen (Kayin) State, with which local politics and business are closely interlinked.

The capital of the state is Moulmein (Mawlamyine), which is Myanmar's third largest city. Located on the Salween River estuary, it was an important seaport and administrative center under British rule (1826–1948). However, its commercial role declined under the isolationist policies of General Ne Win's (b. 1911) Burma Socialist Program Party between 1962 and 1988. Other important towns in the state include Kyaikto, Bilin, Thaton, Mudon, Thanbyuzayat, and Ye, all of which lie along the main road and rail links running parallel to the coast.

The ethnic composition of the state reflects its location on the gateway between central and southeast Myanmar. Exact statistics are disputed, but in the 1990s the population was estimated by the government at just over 2 million, of whom 780,000 were classified as ethnic Mons, 760,000 as Burmans (including Tavoyans), over 300,000 as Karens (including 60,000 Paos), and the rest as a variety of nationalities, including Indians and Chinese who inhabit the main urban areas.

Historically, the state has been the main producer of rubber in Myanmar. Other important crops are rice, groundnuts, pulses, sugarcane, coconuts, betel nuts, durians, mangosteens, and other fruits that grow abundantly in the tropical climate. The major manufacturing plant is the Sittang Pulp and Paper Mill. There also is a sugar mill at Bilin, rubber factory at Thanbyuzayat, and smaller textile and ceramics industries in the state.

Following the 1995 ceasefire by the military government with the armed opposition New Mon State Party, various plans were mooted to develop the territory, parts of which were opened up to tourists. In addition to Moulmein, destinations include the ancient towns of Thaton and Martaban as well as the famed Kyaiktiyo pagoda, which is perched on a mountain outcrop in the north of the state. Various bridge- and road-building projects were also introduced to try to improve infrastructural links with adjoining states and divisions as well as with Thailand. In addition, local and Thai fishing concessions were increased in the Andaman Sea, leading to fears of depletion of a once plentiful resource through overfishing. During 1999–2002, sporadic fighting also occurred with government forces in southern parts of the state where Karen and Mon dissident groups were still active, leading to continuing Burmese army operations in rural areas.

Martin Smith

Further Reading

Bunge, Frederica M., ed. (1983) *Burma: A Country Study.* Washington, DC: American University Foreign Area Studies, Government Printing Office.

Human Rights Watch Asia. (1994) *The Mon: Persecuted in Burma, Forced Back from Thailand.* New York: Human Rights Watch.

South, Ashley. (2002) *Mon Nationalism and Civil War in Burma: The Golden Sheldrake.* London: Curzon.

Tinker, Hugh. (1967) *The Union of Burma: A Study of the First Years of Independence.* Oxford: Oxford University Press.

MONG TAI ARMY The Mong Tai Army ("Shan Land" army) was a Shan (Tai) insurgent force brought together in the mid-1980s by the controversial ethnic minority leader Khun Sa (Chan Shi-fu). Doubts have often been raised about his true motivations. An ethnic Shan-Chinese from Loimaw (Myanmar/Burma), Khun Sa (b. 1934) first entered the complex world of Shan narcopolitics in the early 1960s. Like a number of insurgent leaders at that time, he briefly crossed over to the government side in 1965 to form a local home-guard militia of a kind then used by the Burmese army, and which were known in Burmese as "Ka Kwe Ye." Subsequently, his involvement in narcotics came to international attention in 1967 when his Loimaw militia fought a fierce battle with Chinese Guomindang troops along the Shan-Lao-Thai borderline for control of the Golden Triangle opium trade. Like the Guomindang, Khun Sa's force survived through anti-communist credentials and black market dealings with influential figures in Shan State and neighboring countries, especially Thailand.

In 1970 Khun Sa was arrested by the Burmese army. However, he was quietly released in 1976 after the kidnapping of two Russian doctors by his followers. He then rebuilt his force, renamed the Shan United Army, from a new stronghold at Ban Hin Taek on the Thai side of the border. In 1982, the SUA was forcibly ousted by the Thai army, which was responding to international criticisms, but Khun Sa was able to reestablish his networks inside Shan State by seizing territory from rival Pao, Lahu, and other insurgent forces.

In 1984, Khun Sa appeared to gain new credibility when he formed the Tailand (or Shanland) Revolutionary Council in alliance with the Shan United Revolutionary Army, headed by Gon Jerng (Mo Heing), and also breakaway units from another Shan insurgent force, the Shan State Army. For a brief period, Khun Sa prospered. The armed wing of this new alliance, known as the Mong Tai Army (MTA), grew into a well-armed force, 15,000 strong, which, on Khun Sa's own admittance, was largely financed from the opium trade.

Following the assumption of power in Burma by the State Law and Order Restoration Council in 1988, the MTA for the first time began to fight pitched battles with the Burmese army as well as the newly formed United Wa State Party, which tried to enter MTA territory in the east.

Controversy, however, was never far away. Eventually, in failing health and wanted in the United States on drug trafficking charges, Khun Sa surrendered to the Burmese army in January 1996 at his headquarters in Homong. This precipitated the MTA's collapse. Most of the MTA troops laid down their arms and went back to their villages, but around 3,000 refused, resurrecting the former Shan United Revolutionary Army (subsequently known as Shan State Army [South]) in southwestern Shan State. Khun Sa, meanwhile, went into retirement in Yangon, where his family engaged in business.

Martin Smith

Further Reading

Maung Pho Shoke. (1999) *Why Did U Khun Sa's MTA Exchange Arms for Peace?* Yangon, Myanmar: U Aung Zaw.

McCoy, Alfred. (1972) *The Politics of Heroin in Southeast Asia*. New York: Harper Torchbooks.

Smith, Martin. (1999) *Burma: Insurgency and the Politics of Ethnicity*. 2d ed. London: Zed Books.

Tzang Yawnghwe, Chao. (1987) *The Shan of Burma: Memoirs of a Shan Exile*. Singapore: Institute of Southeast Asian Studies.

MONGKUT, KING

MONGKUT, KING (1804–1868), Ruler of Thailand. King Mongkut (reigned 1851–1868) of Thailand is remembered for his policies of modernization and for preserving his country's independence. He was the son of King Rama II (reigned 1809–1824). Mongkut donned the garb of a Buddhist monk at the age of nineteen and led the life of an ascetic until his coronation. He devoted his time to studying Western science and humanities as well as to studying Buddhism. Well-versed in European affairs, he learned Latin and English. He ascended the throne in 1851 as Rama IV after the death of his half brother Rama III (reigned 1824–1851).

In 1855, he signed an unequal treaty of friendship and commerce with Britain, followed by similar treaties with France, the United States, Prussia, Portugal, and other nations. The unequal treaties provided the Europeans with most favored nation status; they limited Thai tariff control; and they allowed extraterritoriality, which meant that foreigners were not subject to Thai laws and enjoyed special privileges. Thailand also surrendered its claim on parts of Cambodia to the east of the Mekong River to France in 1867.

An undated portrait of Mongkut when he was Crown Prince of Siam (Thailand). (BETTMANN/CORBIS)

By relating to Britain and France and playing them off against each other, Mongkut retained the country's independence from colonialism. He initiated reforms in education and health, encouraging medical work of missionaries, teaching his sons English and liberal arts, establishing a royal mint, relaxing court rituals, and publishing an official gazette. He also established the Buddhist sect called *dhammayutika*, which rationalized Buddhism and remains the center of Thai Buddhism. Anna Leonowens was the English governess of his children, whose story is told in the movie *The King and I*, which is still banned in Thailand for distorting Thai history and patronizing Mongkut to the point of ridicule. The motion picture *Anna and the King* (1999) generated further controversy in Thailand. The Thai Censor Board ruled that Thais should not see the movie, which misrepresents the monarchy and exaggerates the extent of impact of Anna on Mongkut. An avid astronomer, Mongkut invited the courtiers and foreign community to Thailand to observe the solar eclipse in 1868 in malaria-infested Sam Roi Yod. Stricken with the disease, he died soon afterward.

Patit Paban Mishra

Further Reading

Cady, John F. (1976) *Southeast Asia: Its Historical Development*. New Delhi: Tata McGraw-Hill.

Moffat, Abbot Low. (1961) *Mongkut, the King of Siam*. Ithaca, NY, Cornell University Press.

Sardesai, D. R. (1981) *Southeast Asia: Past and Present*. New Delhi: Vikas.

Warren, William. (1993) "Who Was Anna Leonowens?" In *Travelers' Tales Thailand*, edited by James O'Reilly and Larry Habegger. San Francisco: Travelers' Tales, Inc.

MONGOL EMPIRE

MONGOL EMPIRE During the thirteenth century, the Mongols created a vast empire that covered Central Asia, China, and much of the Middle East and Eastern Europe. Their armies threatened Japan, Southeast Asia, and Central Europe. Mongol military strength was based on the extraordinary mobility of their horsemen, tight military discipline, excellent communications, and the ruthlessness and superior leadership of Genghis Khan and others. Under the Mongols, much of Eurasia was united under a single government that encouraged trade and communications to an unprecedented degree. The Mongol empire, however, was relatively short-lived. In the 1260s, the realm split into four subempires in China, Central Asia, Russia, and Persia.

Genghis Khan

The emergence of the Mongols as a great power stemmed initially from the rise of Temujin (c. 1162–1227) as a war leader. Temujin's charismatic personality and his reputation for treating his followers justly enabled him to create an army that first established his dominance among the Mongols then won him victory after victory over neighboring tribes, notably the Keraits and the Naimans. By 1206, his dominance over the Inner Asian nomadic tribes was complete and he took the title Genghis ("Ocean" or "Universal") Khan.

Genghis Khan then demanded tribute from settled kingdoms to the south and west, and he sent armies to subdue those rulers who refused to submit. Mongol troops attacked the states of Jin and Xi Xia in what is now China, capturing Khanbalig (now Beijing) in 1215. The Uighur state of Kara Kitai fell in 1218. In that year, the ruler of Khorezm refused to punish a local governor who had executed all the members of a Mongol diplomatic delegation on suspicion of espionage. Mongols armies attacked Khorezm in 1219 and took a terrible revenge for the diplomatic incident, systematically destroying the kingdom's cities and massacring their inhabitants. The campaign reached as far as northern India and southern Russia and concluded only in 1222.

Genghis Khan's military success rested partly on the traditional skills of the Mongols in horsemanship and archery, but the Mongol armies were consistently innovative, developing new techniques to cope with siege warfare and warfare in mountainous or swampy country. Mongol generals were willing to recruit troops from among subject peoples, especially the Turkic peoples of Central Asia, and to learn new techniques from their enemies. Rapid communications across long distances enabled Mongol armies to coordinate their movements, while a system of whistling arrows facilitated communications during the turmoil of battle. Genghis Khan also paid great attention to cultivating the loyalty of his followers. He was generous in recognizing and rewarding those who supported him capably, and he promoted his followers largely according to their loyalty and ability. On the other hand, he was ruthless in suppressing disloyalty. After the subject king of Xi Xia refused to join the campaign against Khorezm, Genghis Khan launched a campaign against his kingdom that resulted in Xi Xia's complete destruction.

The existence of a single empire, administered from Karakorum in northern Mongolia and stretching from the Pacific Ocean to the Black Sea, facilitated trade between East Asia and the West enormously and contributed to prosperity well beyond the Mongol territories. With trade, too, came the easier movement of religious ideas and culture. In contrast with many other empires, the Mongol empire tolerated all religious beliefs and practices.

Conquests Following the Death of Genghis Khan

When Genghis Khan died in 1227, his empire was divided between his four sons. The eldest son, Jochi (1180–1227), received the lands far to the west in Russia while Ogodei (1186–1241) and Chagatai (d. 1241) obtained the lands in Persia and Central Asia. In Mongolian tradition, the youngest son should be the "keeper of the hearth" and inherit his father's home, so Genghis Khan's youngest, Tolui (1190–1232), received Mongolia proper and the Mongol realm in northern China. In 1229, Ogodei was elected Great Khan to replace Genghis Khan. The military campaigns of expansion continued.

In 1229, Mongol armies attacked the Persians and Cumans (Kipchaks) in the west and began a campaign of expansion that spread first to Georgia and Armenia and then to Russia. Moscow fell in 1238 and Kiev in 1240. In April 1241, the divided Mongol army defeated both the combined forces of the German and Polish aristocracy at Liegnitz and the Hungarian army at Mohi. The lumbering European knights in their heavy armor proved to be no match for the mobile, lightly armed Mongol forces. The invaders seemed likely to sweep through Europe, but Ogodei's death in 1241 obliged the Mongol armies to return home to take part in the election of a new Great Khan.

Meanwhile Tolui had destroyed the northern Chinese state of Jin in a campaign from 1230 to 1234. His successors attacked the Southern Song empire in 1237, beginning a protracted military campaign that ended only in 1279. In order to encircle the Song forces, Mongol armies captured the Southeast Asian kingdom known now as Nanzhao in modern Yunnan in 1253 and invaded Vietnam in 1257.

Khubilai Khan and the Establishment of the Chinese Yuan Dynasty

The campaign against the Song was led by Khubilai Khan (1215–1294), a grandson of Genghis Khan who declared himself Great Khan in 1260 and set up a new capital at Shangdu (Xanadu) in today's Inner Mongolia. Khubilai's claim to be Great Khan was not accepted by other Mongol leaders, however, and from 1260, the four subempires established on the death of Genghis Khan effectively became independent of each other. The Il-khans in Persia did continue to acknowledge Khubilai Khan as great khan, and this is the origin of their name: *Il* meaning "lesser" or "subordinate." Khubilai Khan later moved his capital from Shangdu and to Khanbalig, and he made increasing use of Chinese officials and administrative structures in ruling China. In 1271, he adopted the Chinese name Yuan for his dynasty. Khubilai also sent armies by sea to conquer Japan (1274, 1281), Champa (1281), and Java (1292), but all these expeditions failed because of difficult climatic conditions and effective local resistance.

The Golden Horde

Far to the west in Russia, the descendents of Jochi controlled an area stretching from Lake Balkhash and the Aral Sea to the lower reaches of the Volga River, and collected tribute from the petty Russian states further north. The wealth of their capital on the Volga, Sarai, led them to be called the "Golden Horde." During the second half of the thirteenth century, most of these Mongols converted to Islam. Their power fragmented and declined during the fourteen century with the rise of Christian Muscovy and Lithuania, and their influence in Russia ended in 1480. The last major khanates, Kazan, east of Moscow, and Astrakhan, in southeast Russia near the Caspian Sea, fell to Ivan IV in 1552 and 1556.

The Il-Khans

The Mongol presence in the Middle East was more unstable. In 1258, Mongol armies under the Il-Khan Hulegu, an elder brother of Khubilai, captured Baghdad, the political center of the Muslim world, but they were decisively defeated by Muslim Mamluk forces from Egypt at Ayn Jalut in Palestine in 1260. From its base on the Iranian plateau, the Il-khanate became deeply involved in the complex religious politics of the Middle East, generally siding with local Christian states against the Muslims and even fighting the Muslim Golden Horde. The Il-Khan Mahmud Ghazan (1271–1304) converted to Islam in the late thirteenth century and named himself sultan, but the Il-khanate collapsed in the middle of the fourteenth century.

The Chagatai Khanate

The khanate of Chagatai in Central Asia prospered initially, but the great trading cities of the south, Samarqand and Bukhara, grew more independent. Samarqand revolted in 1356 and became the capital of Timur (Tamerlane) in the fourteenth century. Mongol rulers of Chagatai khanate were increasingly displaced by a Turkic military elite. By the second half of the fourteenth century, the Chagatai khanate had disintegrated into several rival states.

Legacy of the Mongol Empire

Although the Mongol conquests were enormously destructive, Mongol rule was generally benevolent, supporting trade, efficient administration, and freedom of religion. The empire fragmented because of rivalry between the descendents of Genghis Khan and then declined as Mongol rulers absorbed the local cultures they had conquered. Even in the twenty-first century, memories of the Mongol conquests influenced Russian and Chinese perceptions of national security and provided the main imagery for Mongol national identity.

Li Narangoa and Robert Cribb

Further Reading

Christian, David. (1998) *A History of Russia, Central Asia, and Mongolia*. Vol. 1. Oxford: Blackwell.

Grousset, Rene. (1970) *The Empire of the Steppes: A History of Central Asia*. New Brunswick, NJ: Rutgers University Press.

Soucek, Svat. (2000) *A History of Inner Asia*. Cambridge, U.K.: Cambridge University Press.

MONGOLIA—PROFILE

MONGOLIA—PROFILE (2001 pop. 2.7 million). Mongolia refers to the region in east central Asia where Mongolian ethnic groups rose to power in the thirteenth century. Today it includes the independent Republic of Mongolia (formerly Outer Mongolia), the Chinese autonomous region of Nei Monggol (formerly Inner Mongolia), and the Tuva Republic of Russia (once part of Outer Mongolia). Genghis Khan (c. 1162–1227), the first ruler of the Mongols, unified rival groups under his leadership to form an empire, which his successors expanded to cover the territory from China to eastern Europe.

The Mongol empire was short lived, however, and collapsed largely because of internal struggles late in the thirteenth century. It was replaced successively by kingdoms ruled by Genghis Khan's successors; by the kingdom of the Turkic Timur (1336–1405) in western Asia; by the Ming dynasty (1368–1644) of China; and finally by the Manchus (Qing dynasty, 1644–1912) of China. China maintained control over Mongolia until 1911, when part of Outer Mongolia broke away to form Tannu Tuva (which eventually became part of the Soviet Union until 1991, then the Tuva Republic within Russia, and finally a republic of the Russian Federation); Russia helped the rest of Outer Mongolia become independent from China in the same year. The region fell under Chinese rule again under treaties of 1913 and 1915.

The Soviet army helped expel the Chinese in 1921, after which the Mongolian People's Republic was formed; the same region became simply Mongolia in 1992, after the collapse of the Soviet Union. Nei Monggol (Inner Mongolia) became an autonomous region of China after World War II.

Geography and Natural Resources

Mongolia is a landlocked state with an area of 1.565 million square kilometers; it is the seventeenth-largest state in the world. It is situated between Russia in the north and China in the south. Mongolia has mountain ranges in the west, plains or grasslands in most parts of the south and east, and the Gobi Desert in the southeast. Rivers are mainly in the north. The Selenge River drains into Lake Baikal in Russia. Only 1 percent of Mongolia is arable land. Ten percent is forest and woodland, 79 percent meadows and pastures, and the remaining part semidesert. However, Mongolia is considered the largest source of undeveloped natural resources in the world; these resources include oil, coal, copper, molybdenum, tungsten, phosphate, tin, nickel, zinc, wolfram, fluorspar, and gold.

People

The population of Mongolia is 90 percent Mongol, 4 percent Kazakh, 2 percent Chinese, 2 percent Russian, and 2 percent other (including the pastoral Turkic-speaking Muslim people who live in extreme western Mongolia). In 1586, Tibetan Buddhism became the Mongolian state religion. Today, 94 percent of Mongolians practice Tibetan Buddhism, and 6 percent practice Islam or shamanism. The 1992 constitution provides for the separation of church and state. Christian missionaries have emerged in Mongolia in recent years.

Administration

Mongolia has three municipalities—Ulaanbaatar (the capital), Darhan, and Erdenet—and eighteen provinces (*aymags*), which are subdivided into 334 districts or counties (*suums*).

History

In 1206, Temujin, the chief of a Mongol tribe, united all eighty-one rival groups and was crowned as Genghis Khan ("universal ruler"). The Mongolian empire achieved its conquests of one-third of the known world with an invincible combination of Mongolian cavalry and recruited foot soldiers, using novel methods of military strategy and battle tactics and with superior weapons. Mongols controlled Russia during the period of the Golden Horde (1240–1480) and ruled China during the Yuan dynasty (1279–1368). In 1368, the Chinese established the Ming dynasty and drove the Mongols from today's Beijing to the north.

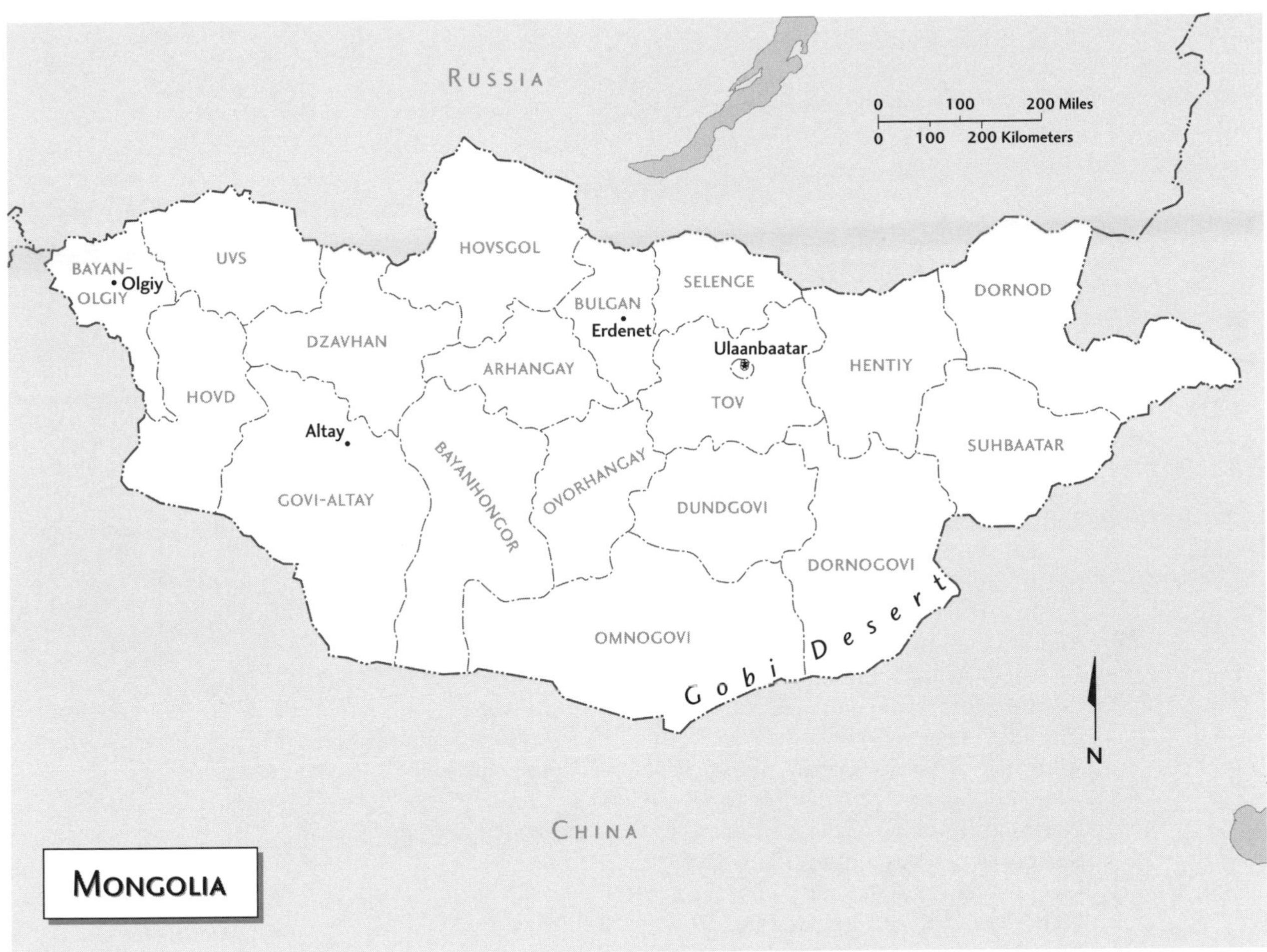

During the next two centuries, Sino-Mongolian relations alternated between war and trade. Under the Manchu rule of the Qing dynasty, Mongolia became part of China (1691–1911). When the Qing dynasty was overthrown by the Chinese, Mongolia declared independence. The national government of Republican China (1912–1917) claimed Mongolia as Chinese territory and launched a military expedition that occupied Mongolia for three years (1919–1921).

With the support of the Soviet Union, Mongolia declared its independence on 13 March 1921 and declared the People's Republic of Mongolia on 24 November 1924, but China did not recognize the new state. A thirty-year Treaty of Friendship and Alliance between the Soviet Union and China was signed on 15 August 1945, which stipulated that China must grant Mongolia a plebiscite to decide the question of independence. The result of the plebiscite, held on 20 October 1945, was a 100-percent vote for independence; China recognized the independence of Mongolia on 5 January 1946, dependent on the Soviet Union's obligation in the 1945 Treaty to recognize the national government of Republican China as the only legal government of China. However, when the People's Republic of China was established on 1 October 1949, the Soviet Union extended it diplomatic recognition, terminating its diplomatic relations with Republican China the following day.

Republican China appealed the Soviet violation of the 1945 Sino-Soviet Treaty to the United Nations (U.N.), which adopted a resolution stating that the USSR had failed to fulfill its 1945 Treaty of Friendship and Alliance with Republican China. Based on the U.N. resolution, Republican China voided the treaty and, therefore, the independence of Mongolia. The Republic of China (Taiwan) still claims Mongolia as Chinese territory. The People's Republic of China, on the other hand, recognized Mongolia's independence on 14 February 1950 without any conditions.

Political Development

The political development of modern Mongolia since 1924 can be divided into three periods. During 1924–1989, Mongolia was under the control of the

MONGOLIA

Country name: Mongolia
Area: 1.565 million sq km
Population: 2,654,999 (July 2001 est.)
Population growth rate: 1.47% (2001 est.)
Birth rate: 21.8 births/1,000 population (2001 est.)
Death rate: 7.1 deaths/1,000 population (2001 est.)
Net migration rate: 0 migrant(s)/1,000 population (2001 est.)
Sex ratio: 1 male(s)/female (2001 est.)
Infant mortality rate: 53.5 deaths/1,000 live births (2001 est.)
Life expectancy at birth—total population: 64.26 years, male: 62.14 years, female: 66.5 years (2001 est.)
Major religions: Tibetan Buddhist Lamaism; Islam (primarily in the southwest), Shamanism, and Christianity
Major languages: Khalkha (Mongol), Turkic, Russian
Literacy—total population: 97%, male: 98%, female: 97.5% (2000)
Government type: parliamentary
Capital: Ulaanbaatar
Administrative divisions: 18 provinces and 3 municipalities
Independence: 11 July 1921 (from China)
National holiday: Independence Day/Revolution Day, 11 July (1921)
Suffrage: 18 years of age; universal
GDP—real growth rate: -1% (2000 est.)
GDP—per capita: (purchasing power parity): $1,780 (2000 est.)
Population below poverty line: 40% (2000 est.)
Exports: $454.3 million (f.o.b., 1999)
Imports: $510.7 million (c.i.f., 1999)
Currency: togrog/tugrik (MNT)

Source: Central Intelligence Agency. (2001) *The World Book Factbook* 2001. Retrieved 5th March 2002, from http://www.cia.gov/cia/publications/factbook.

Soviet Union, on which it modeled its political and economic systems. It was under Communist party control and followed the Soviet Union's guidance in foreign policy.

During 1989–1991, Mongolia, reflecting changes in the Soviet Union under Mikhail Gorbachev (b. 1931), changed from strict Communist rule to a more liberal Communist regime and then to a total withdrawal from Communism. During 1990–1992, Mongolia instituted political reforms to move from a single-party to a multiparty system and to hold elections for legislature and president.

After the adoption and implementation of a new constitution on 12 February 1992, Mongolia entered an era of democracy. The Communist label of "People's" was dropped from the state's name, which became simply "Mongolia." Single-party rule ended, and numerous parties emerged. The first Mongolian legislature, the State Great Hural (parliament), was elected by popular vote on 8 June 1992. Among the seventy-six members, seventy-one were members of the Mongolia People's Revolutionary Party (MPRP; the former Communist Party), and the others were from minority parties. On 6 June 1993, the first presidential election was held, by popular vote rather than by the legislature as before. Before the adoption of the 1992 constitution, the president had been Parisalmaagiyn Orchirbat (b. 1942), a member of MPRP. However, in the 1993 presidential election, MPRP did not nominate the incumbent. Orchirbat was elected as a nominee of an opposition party. In June 1997,

Natsagiin Bagabandi (b. 1950) was elected president with a 60.8 percent popular vote for a four-year term of office, and four years later was reelected for a second term.

State Structure

The highest organ of state power is the State Great Hural, which is vested with supreme legislative power. It is unicameral and consists of seventy-six members, elected for a term of four years. The parliament has the exclusive right to enact laws or make amendments to them; to determine the basis of the state's domestic and foreign policies; to pass laws recognizing the full powers of the president after his or her election, and to relieve or remove the president; to appoint, replace, or remove the prime minister and members of the government; and to define the state's financial, credit, tax, and monetary policies, among other duties.

The president is the head of state and the embodiment of the unity of the people. The president enjoys such prerogatives as the veto, partial or whole, of laws and other decisions adopted by the parliament. The veto may be overridden by a two-thirds vote of parliament members present and voting. The president nominates to the parliament the candidate for prime minister, in consultation with the majority party or parties in the parliament, and proposes to the parliament to dissolve the government. The president heads the National Security Council of Mongolia and is the commander-in-chief of the armed forces.

External Relations and National Security

When Mongolia served as a buffer state between China and Russia during the Cold War, the country participated in the defense system of the Warsaw-Pact states by acting as the eastern frontier. When Soviet troops withdrew from Mongolia, the country adopted a neutral, nonaligned, non-nuclear stance. Mongolia has developed a balanced relationship with its two neighbors, Russia and China. This is, on the one hand, made possible through the cessation of military confrontation between both neighbors as well as their refraining from striving for military influence in Mongolia. On the other hand, Mongolia is not only bound to seek influential partners in the Asia-Pacific region but also determined to develop a strategy serving the country as well as fostering regional security and stability. Mongolia signed treaties of friendly relations and cooperation with the Russian Federation in January 1993 and with China in April 1994.

In developing its relations with other countries, Mongolia has conducted foreign policy based on universally recognized principles and norms of international law as defined in the U.N. charter, including mutual respect for one another's sovereignty, territorial integrity, and inviolability of frontiers; right of self-determination; noninterference in internal affairs; nonuse of force and settlement of disputes by peaceful means; respect for human rights and freedoms; and mutually beneficial cooperation.

Mongolia does not interfere in the disputes between its two neighboring countries unless the disputes affect Mongolia's national interests. Mongolia refrains from joining any military alliance or grouping, does not allow its territory or airspace to be used against any other country, and does not permit the stationing of foreign troops or weapons, including nuclear or any other weapons of mass destruction, in its territory.

Mongolia has supported the development of nuclear-weapons-free zones and initiated and successfully created such a zone in Mongolia itself, as declared by parliamentary resolution in 1992. This resolution was supported by the entire nonaligned movement (114 members) and the U.N. Security Council, and was adopted as a resolution of the U.N. General Assembly. Mongolia is now a member of thirty-one international organizations, including the World Trade Organization, INTERPOL, and the World Health Organization.

Teh-kuang Chang

Further Reading

Akiner, Shirin, ed. (1991) *Mongolia Today.* London and New York: Kegan Paul International.

Batbaiar, Tsedendambya. (1996) *Modern Mongolia: A Concise History.* Ulaanbaatar, Mongolia: Offset Printing, Mongolian Center for Scientific and Technological Information.

Bawden, Charles R. (1968) *The Modern History of Mongolia.* New York: Praeger.

Dupuy, Trevor N., et al. (1970) *Area Handbook for Mongolia.* Prepared for the American University by Historical Evaluation and Research Organization. Washington, DC: U.S. Government Printing Office.

Lattimore, Owen. (1962) *Nomads and Commissars: Mongolia Revisited.* New York: Oxford University Press.

Onon, Urgunge, and Derrick Pritchatt. (1989) *Asia's First Modern Revolution: Mongolia Proclaims Its Independence in 1911.* Leiden and New York: E. J. Brill.

MONGOLIA—ECONOMIC SYSTEM

Like most developing countries, Mongolia has two economies. There is a traditional one, consisting of what Mongols have practiced for centuries. There is also a modern one that is primarily for export.

The Traditional Economy

Mongolia's traditional economy is based on animal husbandry, with the mixture of animals herded varying from one part of Mongolia to another. Sheep, herded from horseback, are found everywhere and are almost always mixed with goats. Cattle are herded in the north while camels are found in the northwest, west, and in the Gobi Desert. Since natural fodder, the basis of most Mongolian herding, is limited, continual movement of herds is usually necessary. Various patterns of movement exist, most commonly from low ground in the spring to high ground in summer and then back again in the autumn. Movement along rivers follows this pattern. Where there is little high ground, principally in the Gobi, movement is circular. Most movement takes place during spring and autumn, while summer and particularly winter pastures tend to be stationary. Traditionally, winter campgrounds were out in the steppe, but in the twentieth century, they moved adjacent to the suburbs of numerous small settlements in the Gobi and elsewhere. This affords a more comfortable life for the herdsmen and their families, possible access to stored fodder during the most difficult times, and a more or less regular exposure of their children to formal education during at least part of the year.

Mongolian sheep are not large, usually about a meal's worth for a large family (and there is little means for storing more meat than that). Their wool is largely worthless for commercial purposes. Better varieties of sheep with better wool were introduced during the Communist era (1921–1989), but herding them has not always proven practical under Mongolian conditions, where special feeds required by some breeds are rarely available, and where long, lush wool is likely to end up entangling the sheep in thorny desert vegetation. What wool there is goes mostly for clothing and for felt that is used as the outer covering of Mongol housing, known as *ger* (yurts). Mongols do not weave as a rule, although there is some card weaving of belt fittings for *ger*, and there has been a carpet industry for several decades. Sheep hides are used locally for clothing and have been exported, but the external market for them is limited since most production is of poor quality. In addition to their meat, ewes produce milk, usually consumed in fermented form. Most of the milk is consumed locally.

The products of the goat are similar to those of the sheep except that goats tend to be larger and produce cashmere, once a major Mongolian export but less so after the late-twentieth-century collapse in world prices. Camel down is exported by Mongols, while camel meat is eaten locally, although camels are generally too valuable to slaughter as food. Both camel and mare's milk are fermented into beverages. The latter, known in English as koumiss, is the preferred Mongolian beverage, while the former is also happily consumed wherever it is available. Neither product is exported. Among Mongolia's livestock, cattle are probably the most valuable for export, but most are raised in geographically limited areas of Mongolia, where rain is sufficient and grass is lush enough to support the cattle. Beef has become an export of growing importance in the last ten years, while leather and cow hides have been important exports since the 1930s. Cow's milk is used like other livestock milks, mostly in fermented forms. Beef is a common food only in areas where cattle are raised.

Thus, except for a small number of products for which there is a demand and which Mongolia can produce for export, the country's traditional economy is largely for subsistence. Mongolia's traditional economy also suffers from its vulnerability to natural disasters such as winter storms when the ground freezes solid and the livestock cannot eat plants under the snow, which can reduce herds to minimal levels almost overnight, and the continued problem of disease epidemics. When livestock numbers plummet, the effect ripples through the rest of the economy and can quickly counterbalance economic gains achieved in more modern sectors. Before the heavy losses of the winter of 1999–2000, Mongolia had almost 33 million head of livestock, mostly sheep (14.6 million) and goats (11.0 million) but also cattle (3.7 million) and horses (3.0 million), as well as a much smaller number of camels (356,400).

Agriculture is practiced to a limited extent in Mongolia, focusing principally on wheat and potatoes, along with a few hardy vegetables. There is some irrigation, but by and large the climate limits agricultural production and soils are usually not rich enough to sustain high yields. In part this is a reflection of severe environmental damage dating back to the Communist era, when production was stressed regardless of the environmental cost.

The Modern Economy and Its Limits

Most important within Mongolia's modern economy is a large mining sector, and since Mongolia has substantial mineral resources, most still unexploited, this sector will continue to grow. There is also a manufacturing sector, mostly based in Ulaanbaatar, Mongolia's capital, producing both for increasingly sophisticated domestic consumption and for export. In addition, there is a large trade and services sector that includes a well-established tourism industry, big-game hunting services for foreigners, and site services for filmmakers.

Mongolia's modern economy faces severe restrictions, the most important one being an inadequate transportation network. The main railroad, less than 2,000 kilometers long, runs north-south, from Russia to China. There are branches to the Nalayh coal fields and into north central Mongolia and the Erdenet mining region. There are railroads in eastern Mongolia, but most are narrow-gauge and were created to support long-gone Soviet forces. Upkeep is poor. They are linked only to Russia's railroads, and not to Mongolia's other rail lines. The modern highway system, consisting of only 1,300 kilometers, is even more limited than rail lines, and new construction is minimal.

Mongolia's modern economic sector must have access to world markets to prosper, but because of poor transportation, development is more or less limited to the north-south rail corridor, its few branches, and a few other points hooked into the Russian road net. The principal areas covered are Bayan-Olgiy *aimag* (province) and parts of eastern Mongolia. Elsewhere, there are only dirt roads at best; at worst, areas are accessible only by horse or camel or by all-terrain vehicle.

Given Mongolia's limited population and resources, these transportation problems will persist indefinitely. As a consequence, most of Mongolia's mineral riches will remain inaccessible. The most important of these resources, mined at some two hundred locations, are coal, copper, gold (3,473 kilograms of the latter were mined during the first six months of 2000), molybdenum, tin, tungsten, and fluorspar. In the 1990s, production of petroleum and diamonds also began. Also present and sometimes exploited in small quantities are phosphates, nickel, zinc, wolfram, uranium, iron, and silver. Most of the minerals mined are also processed in Mongolia; mineral processing constitutes a major portion of the country's heavy industry. Copper, molybdenum, and fluorspar together account for 60 percent of Mongolia's export income.

After a number of late-twentieth-century shocks, above all the sudden end of Soviet aid (equal to 30 percent of Mongolia's gross national product) in 1990, Mongolia's economy has been stabilizing. That in large part is thanks to international help, including aid from the World Bank and International Monetary Fund, which have played an active role not only in financing Mongolian development but in regularizing the Mongolian banking system and bringing it up to international standards. The old, traditional economy remains weak, but with improvements in Mongolia's infrastructure, exports should grow. That will enhance Mongolia's ability to survive hard times such as the difficult 1999–2000 winter, which resulted in outright starvation in some parts of the country.

Paul D. Buell

Further Reading

Sanders, Alan J. K. (1996) *Historical Dictionary of Mongolia*. Lanham, MD: Scarecrow Press.

Mongolian Central Bank. (2001) Numerous economic documents. Retrieved 3 December 2001, from: http://www.mongolbank.mn/english/index.html.

MONGOLIA—EDUCATION SYSTEM

In the past one hundred years, Mongolia's education system has changed in tandem with its dramatic social and political transformations. At the beginning of the twentieth century, a Buddhist theocracy governed what is now Mongolia, and consequently most formal education took place in a system of monasteries that covered Mongolia's territory. These centers of learning not only provided basic religious training, but also offered higher education in topics as diverse as logic, medicine, and the arts. Though sophisticated, the education system was not universal, and no more than 10 percent of the adult population achieved literacy.

This situation changed in the 1920s, when a new one-party government with close ties to the Soviet Union took control of the country. This new government gradually dismantled the religious monastery system and instituted its own system of universal education based on a Russian model. The model excelled in many respects.

In 1989, however, the situation changed again, when the Mongolian government shifted to a multiparty system, loosened its economic ties with Russia, and began the transition to a market economy. These changes had immediate effects on the existing school system, although by 1990, Mongolia could boast a highly educated public with an adult literacy rate of 96 percent. Educational funding has been cut, attendance levels have decreased, and in response to the perceived decline in the quality of public schools, private schools have begun to emerge as educational options. Through these various political changes, Mongolian educational systems have had to overcome common obstacles—a substantial mobile pastoralist population, a transportation system depending on unpaved roads, and the lowest population density on the planet—to reach the minds of individual Mongolians.

Prerevolutionary Education

At the beginning of the twentieth century, a Tibetan Buddhist theocracy had governed the territory of Mongolia for nearly three hundred years. By 1900, nearly 1,700 monasteries checkered Mongolia's territory and served as clinics, courts, markets, centers for the arts, and schools for the local population. Novice monks were trained in the basics of Buddhist religion, while a few select students advanced to higher degrees in the educational system. Generally, the largest monasteries contained four academic colleges—Buddhist studies and debate, Buddhist tantrology (study of a difficult regime of psychophysical exercises meant to speed the practitioner to a perfected state of a Buddha), Tibetan medical science, and Buddhist astrology, which included subjects such as divination, mathematics, and rhetoric. Depending on the discipline, a student might require twenty years to attain the highest degree.

Although nearly one in five Mongolians was counted as a monk in 1921, many Mongolians did not pass through monastery schools. In larger settlements, the government established schools that trained youth to enter the country's small secular bureaucracy. In western Mongolia, for example, a school was established in 1761 to train pupils in the Mongolian, Manchu, and Tibetan languages. In addition to formal schooling, a great deal of education took place in the home and community. Children learned the knowledge necessary for herding from their parents, and occasionally parents invited monks to their home to read scriptures and teach their children short lessons. In addition, skilled craftspeople passed the knowledge of blacksmithing, woodworking, felting, and folk medicine to apprentices outside the monastery system.

The Push for Universal Education

Although the formal education system in prerevolutionary times managed to educate advanced Buddhist scholars and bureaucrats, only a small proportion of the population learned how to read. In the 1920s, this situation began to change as a new one-party secular government supported largely by the nascent Soviet Union pushed to modernize the country according to the Soviet model. Along with this modernization effort came the goal of universal education. By 1934, the government had built fifty-nine state elementary schools, and five years later, the number of state primary schools had grown to ninety-three. Communities and parents, fearing the loss of educational opportunities with the dissolution of the monastic system, had also established more than one hundred voluntary schools, which were taken over by the state in 1939. Still, according to the scholar Charles Bawden (1968: 380), by 1940, only 11 percent of children were being taught in schools of any sort, and the literacy rate for individuals eight years and over was no more than 20 percent.

While the government was building state schools and working toward higher literacy rates, it was also dismantling monasteries; after a series of purges in the 1930s, nearly all monasteries had been abandoned or destroyed. Throughout the middle of the twentieth century, the Mongolian government continued to promote basic literacy. By 1965, all Mongolians were guaranteed four years of education, and the eight-year general-education and labor-polytechnic school system proposed in the same year eventually led to eight years of free education for all Mongolians.

In the 1940s, Mongolia's government began to complement its secondary school network with a system of higher education. In 1942, the Mongolian State University was established in the capital city of Ulaanbaatar as the state's first nationally funded institute for higher education. It was modeled after universities in Russia and had three departments—pedagogy, medicine, and veterinary medicine. Within a decade, the university was establishing semiautonomous research teaching institutes—the State Pedagogical Institute in 1951, the Agricultural Institute in 1958, and the Medical Institute in 1961. During this time, Mongolia began to form academic exchanges with the Soviet Union and other Communist countries, and many Mongolians began to travel to Moscow and eastern Europe for advanced training in the arts and sciences.

Education Today

By 1990, the state schools offered ten years of free education throughout the Mongolian countryside. To fulfill the goal of education for all, children of nomadic families were sent to central settlements and provided with free boarding. Although most education took place in the Mongolian language, Russian was generally required as a second language, and several prestigious schools in larger cities conducted classes exclusively in Russian. After secondary school, students who passed admissions exams were granted free access to higher education in Ulaanbaatar or several other Mongolian cities. The best students were given the option of continuing their studies in the Soviet Union or in other cooperating countries in Europe.

Several indicators attest to the quality and coverage that the Mongolian education system had attained by 1990. Primary school enrollment was nearly universal at 98 percent, while 85 percent of students progressed to secondary school and 15 percent to higher education. Due to this high degree of coverage, the adult literacy rate had reached 96 percent. In 1989, there were 615 state schools, and 14.5 percent of pupils, mostly from herding families, lived in dormitory accommodations.

As Mongolia's economy worsened in the 1990s, the education system experienced several difficulties. Government budget constraints led to decreased funding for schools, while increased fuel costs took money away from teaching to the necessary task of heating classrooms in winter. Attendance has fallen, especially in the countryside, where families frequently keep their children at home to help with herding. To compensate for reduced budgets for higher education, a student fee structure was introduced in 1993, whereby student-paid tuition was expected to cover the full cost of teachers' salaries. Many students who would have had free higher education before 1993 are now unable to pay the tuition for a bachelor's degree. Meanwhile, in 1991, the Mongolian parliament authorized the first private higher-education institutions, which by 1997 had enrolled about 30 percent of the country's 36,000 full-time college students. Despite these changes, many Mongolians still maintain a deep respect and concern for education and will probably work to maintain the advances they achieved in the last century.

Daniel Hruschka

Further Reading

Bawden, Charles R. (1968) *The Modern History of Mongolia.* London: Weidenfeld & Nicolson.

Jagchid, Sechin, and Paul Hyer. (1979) *Mongolia's Culture and Society.* Boulder, CO: Westview Press.

Weidman, John C., Regsurengiin Bat-Erdene, John L. Yeager, Javzan Sukhbaatar, Tsendjav Jargalmaa, and Suren Davaa. (1998) "Mongolian Higher Education in Transition: Planning and Responding under Conditions of Rapid Change." *Tertium Comparationis* 4, 2.

MONGOLIA—HISTORY

Mongolia has two histories, one before the Mongols emerged as a distinct people, and one after. Before the Mongols, the area of today's Mongolia was host to a variety of cultures, some directly ancestral to the Mongols, some not. They included hunter-gatherers, farmers, even fishermen, and from the second half of the first millennium BCE, various groups of pastoral nomads. Such groups introduced those cultural elements that were to typify the area subsequently: an extremely mobile way of life based on the horse; extensive herding, usually of sheep, but also of goats, cattle, and later, camels; the *ger* (yurt), the basis of steppe mobility; and probably koumiss drinking and much of the shared intellectual culture of the area as well. Most famous among the pastoral groups were the Xsiongnu, competitors of the Chinese Han dynasty (206 BCE–220 CE); the Xianbei, proto-Mongols and very active in China; the Rouran, with whom the European Avars may be connected; and various Turkic-speaking groups from whom the Mongols borrowed much, including their script.

The Mongols as such first appeared in the ninth century CE, initially under the control of others, including the Khitan, founders of the Liao dynasty (907–1125), and the Jurchen, the Tungus-speaking successors to the Liao and founders of the Jurchen Jin dynasty (1125–1234). Although sedentary, the Jurchen followed the example of the Khitan in maintaining a presence deep into the steppe, using steppe groups as allies.

Among them seems to have been the young Mongol chieftain Temujin (c. 1162–1227), later Genghis Khan. In his time the Mongols, confined to an area consisting of modern central and eastern Mongolia and adjacent parts of Siberia, were divided into competing herding units of varying sizes. These herding units, in turn, were loosely associated with one another through elite kinship links and were identified with peoples and even confederations, all with hereditary leaderships. Other than this, higher political organization was entirely lacking, thus the importance of the military organization imposed on the Mongols by the Jurchen Jin dynasty.

After an inauspicious start (his father, a minor chieftain, was poisoned, and Temujin's mother and siblings were abandoned on the steppe), Temujin gradually gained power, at first with the support only of his father-in-law, then as an ally of the Jurchen Jin dynasty, and finally on his own, at last uniting most of the steppe under his banner. In recognition of this fact he was elected Genghis Khan (Universal Khan) by his supporters in 1206, marking the formal beginning of the Mongolian empire.

The Growth of the Mongol Empire

Mongol expansion had begun even before, in 1205, with raids on the Xi Xia kingdom. By 1209, Mongol scouts had penetrated today's northern Kazakhstan and Turkistan, subduing the Uighurs. Raids began on Jurchen Jin China in 1211, and by 1214 the Mongols were powerful enough to besiege the Jin capital, Zhongdu, near the site of modern Beijing. Alarmed by this advance, the Jin court fled south in 1215, leaving its capital and much of northern China to the Mongols. Expansion westward began shortly thereafter,

KEY EVENTS IN MONGOLIA'S HISTORY

9th century CE The Mongols first appear as a distinct people.
1206 Genghis Khan unites Mongol tribes, marking the beginning of the Mongolian empire.
1223 Mongol expansion has reached Russia.
1229–1241 During the reign of Ogodei the empire expands farther into China and west into Europe.
1259 The empire is racked by civil war with the empire divided among several rulers.
1279–1368 The Mongol Yuan dynasty rules in China.
14th–16th century The Mongolian dark age of internal chaos and invasion from Siberia.
1578 Mongolia emerges from the dark age with the restoration of Buddhism.
1644–1911 The Qing (Manchu) dynasty in China extends its control into Mongolia.
1911–1921 Mongolia is saved from virtual extinction by the fall of the Manchus in China and it declares independence.
1924 Mongolia comes under Soviet control.
1920s–1930s Mongolia is transformed into a Soviet republic.
1992 With the collapse of the Soviet Union, Mongolia becomes an independent nation.
1990s Mongolia receives much financial investment from the West.
2000 Reformed Communists are victorious in national elections.

initially directed at what is now Chinese Turkistan, and then at western Turkistan and Khwarizm. The Khwarizm empire collapsed almost overnight in the face of a determined Mongol onslaught. The Mongols continued on into Iran and in 1223 appeared in Russia for the first time. The foundations of a world empire had been laid.

Genghis Khan died in 1227 after completing the conquest of the Xi Xia kingdom. After a short interregnum, his second son, Ogodei (1185–1241), was elected khan in 1229. Ogodei continued his father's work both in China, where he completed the conquest of the Jin in 1234 and began Mongol attacks on the Song dynasty, and in the west. Under Ogodei, Mongol armies conquered Russia and advanced to the suburbs of Vienna.

After Ogodei's death in 1241 came another interregnum, after which his son Guyuk (reigned 1245–1247) was elected his successor. But Guyuk did not long survive his accession, probably succumbing to poison. After yet another interregnum, during which intense political maneuvering delayed election of a new khan for some years, Mongke (reigned 1251–1259), the eldest son of Genghis Khan's youngest son, came to the throne.

By this time, internal political pressures were tearing the Mongolian empire apart. Guyuk, for example, appears to have been on the verge of open warfare with Batu (d. 1255?), the son of Genghis Khan's eldest son and ruler of the Golden Horde in Russia. Mongke, who enjoyed Batu's support, unleashed a great purge against the house of Ogodei that further exacerbated tensions.

In spite of these tensions, Mongke was able to consolidate his power and continue Mongolian expansion. With the help of his younger brother, Khubilai (1215–1294), he strengthened Mongol rule in north China and began an advance to outflank the Song. Mongke sent his younger brother, Hule'u (d. 1265), to Iran to continue the advance into the Middle East. Batu continued to rule in Russia, while the descendants of another son of Genghis Khan held much of western Turkistan.

Under Mongke, Mongolia was a hotbed of international exchange centered on the new Mongolian capital of Karakorum. Numerous descriptions of the city survive, thanks to its many foreign visitors. Perhaps the most famous descriptions are those of Mongke's great hall for feasting and drinking, with its semiautomated beverage fountain, set to spout various fermented beverages at the sound of a trumpet. Visitors from France rubbed elbows with Chinese, Tibetans, Persians, Khwarizmians, Uighurs, and of course Mongols.

Decline, Renewal, and Decline

The death of Mongke in 1259 unleashed a civil war. Khubilai eventually won, but his election as khan was recognized outside China and Mongolia only by Hule'u in Iran. The Golden Horde now went its own way and even fought a war with Mongol Iran. Another claimant to universal rule soon emerged in the form of Khaidu (d. 1303), a descendent of Ogodei, who waged war against Khubilai and his house for many decades. Also splitting the Mongols was the conversion of those in the east to Buddhism and almost all others to Islam.

Khubilai continued to assert his control over Mongolia, but his power base was in China, not Mongolia, which increasingly became a backwater. Mongolia had already been depopulated by the very process of expansion. Increasingly, the Mongols living there became impoverished, and later Mongol rulers in China even had to buy back Mongol slaves from Chinese and other owners.

When the Mongol Yuan dynasty of China fell in 1368, the ruling house sought to return to the steppe with its remaining supporters, but many had to stay behind because they were cut off by Chinese rebels. Although the so-called Northern Yuan put up a serious resistance, Mongolia could no longer support conquest or even a court. The area quickly fell into a chaotic Mongolian dark age that persisted until the sixteenth century. Much of Mongolia itself came under the rule of Oirat invaders from Siberia. Only on the fringes of the steppe, in what is now Inner Mongolia, did Mongolian literacy and Buddhism continue to exist.

Mongolian recovery is traditionally dated to the invitation extended by Altan Khan (1507–1583) in 1578 to the head of the Tibetan dGe-Lugs-pa Buddhist order to come to Mongolia and restore Buddhism. Altan Khan granted the Tibetan prelate the title Dalai Lama and recognized his superior religious authority. In exchange, Altan Khan became the secular protector of the religion, thereby reestablishing a relationship that had once existed under Khubilai between the khan and the Sa-sKya bLa-ma aPhags-pa (1235–1280), Khubilai's principal Tibetan ally and religious co-head of state.

Mongolia continued to flourish for most of the next century and was able to field armies that threatened even China. During this period, a Mongolian literary golden age emerged, and a restored Buddhism once again became the dominant religion of Mongolia. The many new monasteries that arose often served the role of urban centers in traditionally nomadic Mongolia; this was true of the cluster of monasteries and temples that grew into the current capital of Ulaanbaatar.

In Mongolia, the dominant ethnic group was the Khalkha. Other groups of Mongols lived in what is now Inner Mongolia and in that portion of Siberia later known as Buryatia. Therefore, Mongolians lived over a far larger area in the seventeenth century than they had five hundred years before. In addition, a large part of the West, principally northern Turkistan and south Russia to the Volga, had been conquered by the descendants of the Oirat, the Dzunghars, and other Western Mongols.

The era of Mongol renewal came to an end in the seventeenth and early eighteenth centuries as the Manchus (founders of the Chinese Qing dynasty, 1644–1911) extended their influence to Mongolia. Mongolia was more effectively conquered by the Manchus than by any previous conquerors, thanks to the Manchu use of firearms, mostly traditional Chinese but including some supplied by the Jesuits.

Although the Buddhist religion of Mongolia was protected by the Manchus, who also respected the authority of the Dalai Lama, the Mongols completely lost their independence and freedom. Mongolia's problems worsened considerably with the appearance of Chinese colonists in the nineteenth century along with growing Russian influence. Mongolia's population was impoverished, diseased, and in decline, with little hope for the future. Only the collapse of Manchu rule in China in 1911 saved Mongolia.

The Communist and Post-Communist Periods

Mongolia was among various parts of the former Qing empire declaring independence in 1911, but not all of Mongolia could be united under the Autonomous Regime that followed, since Inner Mongolia and the Ordos desert region remained under Chinese control, while the Russians continued to hold sway over Buryatia. Between 1911 and 1921 Mongolia was technically a republic, but was actually under the close control of the Jebtsun Damba Khutukhtu of Urga (Ulaanbaatar), Mongolia's principal incarnating lama. When his regime proved unable to resist the forces of Chinese warlords and White Russian armies, the new Soviet regime of Russia sponsored an uprising by a small group of revolutionaries, including Sukhebaatar (1893–1923), later a national hero. The rebels took advantage of popular discontent with the White Russians and others to establish a Communist regime, at first theoretically still subject to the authority of the still popular Jebtsun Damba Khutukhtu, but after his death in 1924 subject only to the orders of the Comintern.

The seventy years of Communist rule were difficult times for Mongolia, but they brought gains as well. The principal difficulties resulted from the so-called leftist deviations of the late 1920s and 1930s that attempted to impose collectivization and that led to rebellion in Mongolia, as in the Soviet Union itself. At one point, the Mongolian Communist regime had all but lost control of the country and had to have its power reestablished with Soviet military help. The Communist regime in Mongolia was also threatened by events in Inner Mongolia, where the Japanese sponsored a limited Inner Mongolian autonomy under nationalist leader Teh Wang, who could present himself as an alternative to Moscow.

On the credit side, the Communist government built up Mongolia's infrastructure, including its first railways and modern highways, the first widespread system of public schools in Mongolian history, as well as a modern but limited health care system. Under the Mongolian dictator Marshal Horloogiyn Choybalsan (1895–1952), the steep decline in Mongolia's living conditions and population was finally arrested. Under Choybalsan's successor Yumjaagiyn Tsedenbel (1916–1991), who held power until 1984, a certain amount of prosperity was achieved. Mongolia, however, was still forced to subordinate its interests to those of Soviet Russia as when, during and before World War II, the Mongols actively fought against the Japanese.

The era of perestroika, followed by the fall of Communism in Mongolia, has meant very rapid change, not all of it favorable for the Mongols. Since the late 1980s, Mongolia has been increasingly on its own economically and has not always been able to cope under this circumstance. Under Communism, the Soviet Union supplied goods at low cost, albeit of poor quality, in exchange for Mongolian minerals and food. Since the dissolution of the Soviet Union in 1991, these goods have had to be bought elsewhere with scarce hard currency. Mongolia's difficulty has been that its traditional exports, such as mutton, are not in great demand, while on the other hand the nation must import much of its food, most industrial goods, and all of its technology. This situation began to change in the late 1990s, after a decade of intensive Western capital investment in Mongolia, much of it sponsored by the World Bank and the International Monetary Fund, which has created new or modernized sources of hard-currency income. Mongolia has also established new industries to reduce its dependence upon foreign sources of manufacture and raw materials. The Mongols have even begun producing and refining oil.

Problems remain, however, and the vast livestock losses of the winter of 1999–2000 have shown the continued weakness of the traditional economy upon which most Mongol income is still based. Mongolia also lacks the highly skilled experts needed to make its new economy work well, although the demographic flood (baby boom) of the Tsedenbel years has now translated into a potentially large labor force for the future. Barring a Chinese invasion, which could happen because Beijing has never reconciled itself to the "loss" of Mongolia, Mongolia's future seems bright, even under the reformed Communists reelected in a landslide in the elections of 2000. More clouded is the fate of those Mongols living outside Mongolia, but relations with the Buryats, with whom the Mongols share a strong Lamaist tradition, remain strong, and the collapse of the Russian Federation seems a strong possibility, in which case the Buryats might federate with Mongolia.

Perhaps the best sign of a potentially bright future for Mongolia is its return to the most important cultural values of the past. Not only is Buddhism undergoing a major revival, along with associated elements of Tibetan culture, once so important for the Mongols, but even shamans are practicing openly once again. In 2000, the president of Kalmykia came to Ulaanbaatar to participate in an official offering to the spirit of Genghis Khan. Since he is the one universal Mongolian symbol, such a celebration clearly marks the intention of the Mongols to reclaim their nationalism and past heritage.

Paul D. Buell

Further Reading

Allsen, Thomas T. (1987) *Mongol Imperialism: The Policies of the Gran Qan Möngke in China, Russia, and the Islamic Lands, 1251-1259.* Berkeley and Los Angeles: University of California Press.

Bawden, C. R. (1989) *The Modern History of Mongolia.* London: Kegan Paul International.

Buell, Paul D. (1994) "Chinqai (1169–1252): Architect of Mongolian Empire." In *Opuscula Altaica, Essays Presented in Honor of Henry Schwarz,* edited by Edward H. Kaplan and Donald W. Whisenhunt. Studies on East Asia, no. 19. Bellingham, WA: Center for East Asian Studies, 168–186.

———. (1992) "Early Mongol Expansion in Western Siberia and Turkestan (1207–1219): A Reconstruction." *Central Asiatic Journal* 36, 1–2: 1–32.

———. (1979) "The Role of the Sino-Mongolian Frontier Zone in the Rise of Cinggis-qan." In *Studies on Mongolia: Proceedings of the First North American Conference on Mongolian Studies*, edited by H. G. Schwarz. Bellingham, WA: Center for East Asian Studies, 63–76.

———, and Eugene N. Anderson. (2000) *A Soup for the Qan: Chinese Dietary Medicine of the Mongol Era As Seen in Hu Szu-hui's Yin-shan Cheng-yao*. London: Kegan Paul International.

Heissig, Walter. (1966) *A Lost Civilization: The Mongols Rediscovered*. Trans. by D. J. S. Thomson. London: Thames and Hudson.

Jagchid, Sechen. (1999) *The Last Mongol Prince: The Life and Times of Demchugdongrob, 1902–1966*. Studies on East Asia, no. 21. Bellingham, WA: Center for East Asian Studies.

Jagchid, Sechen, and Paul Hyer. (1979) *Mongolia's Culture and Society*. Boulder, CO: Westview.

Rachewiltz, Igor de, Chan Hok-lam, Hsiao Ch'I-ch'ing, and Peter W. Geier, eds. (1993) *In the Service of the Khan: Eminent Personalities of the Early Mongol-Yuan Period (1200–1300)*. Wiesbaden, Germany: Harrassowitz.

Ratchnevsky, Paul. (1991) *Genghis Khan, His Life and Legacy*. Trans. by Thomas Nivison Haining. Oxford: Blackwell.

Rossabi, Morris. (1988) *Khubilai Khan: His Life and Times*. Berkeley and Los Angeles: University of California Press.

Rupen, Robert A. (1964) *Mongols of the Twentieth Century*. Indiana University Uralic and Altaic Series, no. 37. Bloomington, IN: Indiana University Press.

Sanders, Alan J. K. (1996) *Historical Dictionary of Mongolia*. Lanham, MD: Scarecrow Press.

Shirendev, Bazaryn. (1997) *Through the Ocean Waves, The Autobiography of Bazaryn Shirendev*. Trans. by Temujin Onon. East Asian Research Aids and Translations, no. 6. Bellingham, WA: Center for East Asian Studies.

MONGOLIA—HUMAN RIGHTS

Despite the association of Mongolia with its formidable thirteenth leader, Ghengis Khan, citizens of modern Mongolia are not subject to wild military excesses. But while Mongolia's record on traditional civil and political rights is impressive, widespread poverty, inadequate health care, the collapse of education, unemployment, and other shortcomings in the area of socioeconomic rights represent challenges.

The U.S. Department of State, Amnesty International, Human Rights Watch, and the United Nations High Commissioner for Human Rights (UNHCHR) have been closely involved with human rights issues in Mongolia. These issues include civil and political, socioeconomic, and religious rights, along with rights of minorities, women, children, prisoners, and refugees. Touching upon the subject of refugees necessitates a brief digression into an area of serious concern: the human rights situation in Inner Mongolia, the half of Mongolia that remains an "autonomous" province in China. Inner Mongolia is home to an estimated 3 million Mongols, more than the 2.3 million of "Outer" Mongolia, the independent and sovereign country known as Mongolia.

International Assessment of Mongolia's Human Rights Situation

Amnesty International has three primary concerns in Mongolia: (1) the application of the death penalty; (2) the death of prisoners by starvation, according to reports from the period 1995–1997; and (3) the failure to allow conscientious objectors, primarily Buddhist monks, either exemption from the compulsory one year of military service required of males from ages eighteen to twenty-six or alternative civilian service. The U.S. Department of State's reports on human rights from 1996 through 1999 list the following concerns: (1) poor prison conditions, with improvements after a prison reform program introduced in 1997, and credible reports of police and prison brutality; (2) the unsolved murder of the minister for infrastructure, a leader of the 1990 democratic movement, which may have been politically motivated; (3) allegations of court corruption hindering the ability to receive a fair trial; (4) attempts, albeit limited, by the government to manipulate the media; (5) violence against women and the existence of homeless street children, with a progressive decrease in the latter but an increase in the former, with evidence of sex trafficking.

The UNHCHR has been involved in human rights projects in Mongolia since 1991. According to the UNHCHR, problems include rights violations in the penal system, poverty, the decreasing quantity and quality of basic social services, increasing gender disparities, the existence of street children, and the threat of HIV-AIDS.

In compliance with international human rights law, Mongolia, like all other states that are party to international law, periodically reports to the Human Rights Committee of the United Nations High Commissioner for Human Rights. On 31 March 2000, the committee at its sixty-eighth session recommended—concerning article 40 of the International Covenant on Civil and Political Rights—that Mongolia clarify domestic law to ensure that the covenant shall have precedence over domestic law. Also, the committee requested more information on the status of women, trafficking in women, prisoners, and any potential threats to the independence and impartiality of the judiciary. In addition, the committee urged Mongolia to

PREAMBLE TO THE CONSTITUTION OF 1992—MONGOLIA

The issue of human rights was in the forefront of the Constitution of 1992.

We, the people of Mongolia:

Strengthening the independence and sovereignty of the nation,

Cherishing human rights and freedoms, justice, and national unity,

Inheriting the traditions of national statehood, history, and culture,

Respecting the accomplishments of human civilization,

And aspiring toward the supreme objective of building a

humane, civil and democratic society in the country

Hereby proclaim the Constitution of Mongolia.

Source: International Constitutional Law. Retrieved 11 March 2002, from: http://www.uni-wuerzburg.de/law.

abolish the death penalty and improve prison conditions. The 17 March 1999 meeting of the Committee on the Elimination of Racial Discrimination considered Mongolia's compliance with the International Covenant on the Elimination of All Forms of Racial Discrimination. The committee remained concerned about street children and rural health care. In addition, the committee noted that, in the early 1990s, reports had circulated of Chinese citizens being expelled from Mongolia, but that the situation had "stabilized." Although the U.N. considered these expulsions racial discrimination, the Chinese citizens at issue may have been ethnic Mongols from Inner Mongolia. In this case, these "forced expulsions" may represent forced repatriation of Inner Mongols. Forced repatriation of Inner Mongolian refugees would represent a serious violation of human rights.

Human Rights Provisions in Mongolian Law

The Mongolian government has made a clear commitment to human rights, unlike any other former Soviet republic or Soviet bloc country. The Mongolian constitution, adopted in January 1992, upholds universal human rights principles and provides for special protection of human rights standards. The UNHCHR reports that the constitution "has integrated international human-rights standards and is key to the promotion and protection of human rights in the country" (UNHCHR 1998: 2). The Mongolian government is characterized by separate legislative, judiciary, and executive powers. Both the U.S. Department of State and the UNHCHR's 1998 Memorandum of Understanding document in detail the Mongolian government's structural commitments to human rights. The Mongolian parliament has a Human Rights Committee. A draft law for the establishment of a national commission on human rights was under parliamentary review in 2001. Beginning in 1994, legislative reform and restructuring of the independent judiciary was carried out with the technical assistance of the UNHCHR. This included, but was not limited to, reform of the criminal code and a national program for human rights education. Regarding freedom of the media and of speech, Mongolia had over 940 registered newspapers, 195 magazines, and twenty-two registered political parties in 2000. Despite the criticism it has received for upholding the death penalty, Mongolia has reduced the number of capital crimes from eighteen in 1994 to four in 2000. Finally, Mongolia has ratified almost all of the significant international human rights instruments, with the notable exception of the 1951 Status on the Convention of Refugees.

Inner Mongolia

Grave human rights violations exist to the south of Mongolia among the ethnic Mongolian population living under Chinese rule in the so-called Inner Mongolian Autonomous Region (IMAR), also referred to as

Southern Mongolia. Recent Amnesty International and Human Rights Watch reports dealing with Mongolia actually relate largely to the Chinese government crackdown that has persisted over the decades on ethnic Mongolians in Inner Mongolia. Mongols in China have suffered severe human rights violations for decades. Some of the more brutal episodes occurred during the Hundred Flowers Bloom campaign of 1957, the Han assimilation movements of 1958–1960 and 1966–1976, the Great Leap Forward of 1959–1965, and the Cultural Revolution of the 1970s. Estimates of the overall ethnic minority death toll in China are as high as 6.2 million. The Great Leap Forward in Inner Mongolia brought not only massive human rights violations but also intensive desertification, an ecological disaster. The Chinese government continues to employ a planned policy of assimilation in Inner Mongolia by relocating Han Chinese there to dilute the minority population. Escapees from Inner Mongolia have set up an Inner Mongolian League for the Defense of Human Rights, with chapters in the United States, Germany, the United Kingdom, and France.

Outlook for the Future

Civil and political human rights problems in Mongolia are no greater than those in the United States, where domestic violence, child abuse, the application of the death penalty, and problems with police violence, among other things, commonly raise accusations by other nations of human rights violations. However, spiraling levels of socioeconomic collapse, correlated to increased levels of foreign assistance, hold the potential to damage Mongolia's hitherto outstanding record. A corporate-governmental human rights partnership, the so-called "fourth generation" of human rights, has the potential to help Mongolia become a successful model for twenty-first-century human rights protection and promotion.

L. M. Handrahan

Further Reading

Amnesty International Annual Report. (1992) "China Section." New York: Amnesty International.

Amnesty International Report. (1995) "Mongolia Prison Inmates Starve to Death." Retrieved 23 May 2001, from: http://www.amnesty.org/ailib/aipub/1995/ASA/300295.ASA.txt.

Bawden, C. R. (1968) *The Modern History of Mongolia*. London: Weidenfeld and Nicolson.

Dikötter, Frank. (1992) *The Discourse of Race in Modern China*. Stanford, CA: Stanford University Press.

Gurr, Ted. (1993) *Minorities at Risk: A Global View of Ethnopolitical Conflicts*. Washington, DC: United States Institute for Peace Press.

Human Rights Watch. (1998) "Clinton: A Letter from the Wife of an Imprisoned Inner Mongolian." Retrieved 23 May 2001, from: http://www.hrw.org/hrw/campaigns/china-98/mong-let.htm.

Human Rights Watch. (1992) "Continuing Crackdown in Inner Mongolia." New York: Human Rights Watch.

Lattimore, Owen. (1955) *Nationalism and Revolution in Mongolia*. New York: E. J. Brill.

Li Ung Bing. (1914) *Outlines of Chinese History*. Shanghai: The Commercial Press Ltd.

Mullin, Chris. "Minority Rights Group Report No. 49: The Tibetans." London: The Minority Rights Group Ltd.

Murphy, George G. S. (1966) *Soviet Mongolia*. Berkeley and Los Angeles: University of California Press.

Nekrich, Aleksandr M. (1978) *The Punished Peoples*. New York, W. W. Norton.

Rummel, R. J. (1991) *China's Bloody Century: Genocide and Mass Murder Since 1900*. New Brunswick, NJ: Transaction Publishers.

Tsengelt, G. (1993) "The Nationality Question in Inner Mongolia and the Ethnic Opposition." Indiana University Lecture Series.

United Nations Children's Fund (UNICEF). (2000). "United Nations in Mongolia." Retrieved 23 May 2001, from: http://www.un-mongolia.mn/unicef.

United Nations High Commissioner for Human Rights (UNHCHR). (1998) "Memorandum of Understanding." Retrieved 23 May 2001, from: http://www.un-mongolia.mn/unhchr/mouhr-eng.htm

U.S. Department of State. (1996–1999) "Country Report on Human Rights Practices." Retrieved 23 May 2001, from: http://www.usis.usemb.se/human/index.html.

MONGOLIA—POLITICAL SYSTEM

MONGOLIA—POLITICAL SYSTEM Mongolia has a rich history of state development. By 1203 Genghis Khan (1162–1227) had united nomadic tribes in Central Asia and established a Mongolian empire that extended from the Yellow Sea to the Mediterranean. To administer this empire, he and his successors created an effective working governmental structure, which dealt with key issues such as war and peace, administration, taxes, and trade, civil, and criminal matters. Despite this administrative tradition, Mongolia's modern political system has changed dramatically.

Following a peaceful democratic revolution in 1989, Mongolia adopted its fourth constitution (1992), under which the government is based on the principle of separation of powers. The major three branches of government, both centrally and locally, are the legislature, executive, and judiciary. Political parties are key players in the governance of country.

Legislature: State Great Hural

Mongolia's parliament is called the State Great Hural (SGH); it passes laws and sends them to the president, who may sign them into law or veto them

CONSTITUTION OF 1992—MONGOLIA

Mongolia's 1992 Constitution is the nation's fourth, the successor to the Constitutions of 1924, 1940, and 1960, which were enacted in the Communist period from 1921–1989. The Constitution, adopted by the 12th People's Great Hural (Ih Hural) in January 1992, rejected Communism and embraced a hybrid form of parliamentary and representative democracy. It is commonly called the "democratic" Constitution.

Legislative power is assigned to a seventy-six-member multiparty, single-chambered Parliament (Ih Hural). Representatives are chosen for four-year terms through direct free elections. It established a Prime Minister who selects a cabinet, the members of which must be approved by the Parliament, and a President, also elected to a four-year term, who is head of state. It created an independent judiciary with a Supreme Court and a Constitutional Court empowered to supervise implementation of the Constitution, solve disputes, and guarantee the strict observance of the Constitution.

Alicia J. Campi

Source: Alan J. K. Sanders. (1996) *Historical Dictionary of Mongolia.* London: The Scarecrow Press, Inc.

within ten days. The president's veto can be overridden by a two-thirds vote of members of the SGH. The SGH establishes ministries and agencies, appoints and removes the prime minister and other ministers, approves the state budget for all government institutions, and certifies presidential elections. It is authorized to ratify and reject international agreements, establish and sever diplomatic relations with foreign states, determine the basis of the domestic and foreign policies of the state, hold national referendums, and declare a state of emergency or a state of war. The current SGH, the third since the 1992 Constitution, was elected in July 2000. The public elects the members of the SGH by direct vote for four-year terms. It has one chamber, with seventy-six members, and it holds spring and autumn sessions, each for seventy-five days.

Executive: President and Government

The president, who is elected to a four-year term by direct and secret ballot, must be a Mongolian native citizen, at least forty-five years of age, and with permanent residency in Mongolia of at least five years. The Constitution limits presidents to two terms in office. A political party that has a seat in the SGH has the authority to nominate candidates. The Constitution did not provide for a vice president. In the absence of the president, the speaker of the SGH presides. Constitutional law professionals consider the presidency in Mongolia to be a weak and ceremonial institution. However, the Constitution does give the president the power to veto a law or act passed by the SGH as well as the right to appeal legislative decisions to the Constitutional Court, the power to nominate the prime minister for appointment by the SGH, the power to grant pardons, and the power to appoint and recall heads of plenipotentiary missions to foreign countries The president also functions as the commander in chief of the armed forces and has the sole power to appoint all judges. In 1999 the president rejected the nominee for the chief judgeship and months later approved another candidate.

The SGH appoints all government ministers; they serve four-year terms and report to the legislature. The SGH is empowered to recall the prime minister, which results in the resignation of the entire cabinet. The president nominates only the prime minister, who proposes all other ministers. Therefore, the government is more dependent on the SGH than on the president. The Constitution did not provide the government an effective mechanism for interaction with the SGH, however. In disagreements between the legislature and executive, the president can use his veto power. This power is not as effective as in the United States, however, because a veto is possible only if the president and prime minister are from one political party and have reached agreement on the disputed issue. There are eleven ministries, but each government is authorized to form its own structure.

Judiciary: Supreme Court and Constitutional Court

Judicial power is divided between the Supreme and Constitutional Courts, two independent bodies that have different jurisdictions and play different roles. The Constitution says judges shall be independent and laws are supreme, and no one, including the president, members of the SGH, or the government, may interfere with the judicial power. The president appoints all judges. The Constitution does not provide a fixed term for judges or establish impeachment procedures. The Supreme Court lacks the power of judicial review, and on 25 April 2000 the United Nations Human Rights Committee requested that Mongolia provide more information on independence and impartiality of the judiciary and due process of law. The Supreme Court is struggling to attain judicial independence, and the courts are slowly moving toward reform.

The courts' jurisdiction is limited to hearing ordinary criminal, civil, and administrative cases. There are thirty-nine trial and twenty-two appeals courts and one Supreme Court. Seventeen of a total of 360 judges sit on the Supreme Court, which has criminal and civil divisions. The Supreme Court makes formal interpretation of all laws, except the Constitution. Its opinions are binding and final. While judges hold office, their party membership is suspended.

The Constitutional Court is the only institution authorized to handle constitutional matters. The SGH appoints nine members of the court for six-year terms. The court members elect its chairman. The court acts independently, confronting laws and acts passed by legislature, and settling disagreements between government institutions. In November 2000 the Constitutional Court ruled that the First Amendment to the Constitution (allowing a member of parliament to hold two positions in government at the same time), which the State Great Hural passed in December 1999 was unconstitutional because it violated an amendment procedure provided in the Constitution. The legislature, the government, and some people were not happy with this opinion, but they abided by the ruling.

Local Government

There are twenty two *aimags* (rural provinces) in Mongolia. The government appoints the mayor of each *aimag*, who functions as its chief executive. The Citizens Representative Hural, elected by the local people, supervises the mayor. Each *aimag* has a local court. Ulaanbaatar, Mongolia's capital, has its own governing body headed by the city's mayor.

Political Parties

There are twenty-one registered political parties in Mongolia. Only three major parties, the Mongolian People's Revolutionary Party (MPRP), the Mongolian National Democratic Party (MNDP), and the Mongolian Social Democratic Party (MSDP), play key roles. The MPRP, the former Communist party, ruled the nation for seventy years in a one-party system until 1989. The MPRP's leaders state that the party has been reformed and is now committed to social-democratic principles. The MNDP and MSDP are young, influential democratic parties. They created the Democratic Coalition to run for the 1996 parliamentary elections and won the majority of seats in the legislature. However, this coalition failed to keep the confidence of people during its four years in power, and the public favored the MPRP in the parliamentary elections in July 2000.

Mongolia's Political Achievement

The most important achievement for Mongolia in last ten years has been that, despite some internal controversies between the government branches, it has been able to institute and develop a democratic form of government with the essential attributes of checks and balances. Each branch acts independently, but overlapping powers enable each to contribute to the nation's successful transition from a centralized economy to a free market economy and from one-party dictatorship system to a multiparty system and democracy. Even though different political parties have gained majorities in the legislature, over the years the government has retained its leadership and strong commitment to democracy and human rights in Mongolia.

Gombosurengiin Ganzorig

Further Reading

Amarsnaa, Jugneegyn. (2000). *Human Rights.* Ulaanbaatar, Mongolia: Mongolian University Press.

Batbayar, D. (2000). "We Are Reborn as New Politician-Thinkers with Consciences." *Zuunii Medee* (6 December).

Berger, Patricia, and Teresa Tse Bartolomew. (1995) *Mongolia: The Legacy of Chinggis Khan.* San Francisco: Asian Art Museum of San Francisco.

Constitution of Mongolia. (1992) Ulaanbaatar, Mongolia: Shuvuun Saaral.

Ginsburg, Tom, and Gombosuren Ganzorig. (1996) "Constitutional Reform and Human Rights." In *Mongolia in*

Transition, edited by Ole Bruun and Ole Odgaar. Richmond, U.K.: Curzon Press.

Henning, Haslund. ([1935] 1992) *Men and Gods in Mongolia*. Reprint ed. Stelle, IL: Adventures Unlimited Press.

Jantsan, Suuriin. (1999) *Judicial Powers*. Ulaanbaatar, Mongolia: Chandmana Erdene Law School.

Laws on Constitutional Court of Mongolia. (1998) Ulaanbaatar, Mongolia: Soembo Co.

Shirin Akiner. (1991) *Mongolia Today*. New York: Kegan Paul International.

MONGOLIA-CHINA-RUSSIA RELATIONS Ever since Russia pushed into the Far East and China extended its domination north of the Great Wall, Mongolia has been one arena of the "Great Game" in the struggle for empire between Russia and China. The Jebtsundamba Khutukhtu (1874–1924), Mongolia's leader at the time, characterized Mongolia's geopolitical position as a "critical condition, like piled up eggs, in the midst of neighboring nations." Russians have historically regarded Mongolia as a buffer state, while the Chinese have viewed Mongolia as historically part of China. After the fall of the Manchu dynasty in 1911, Mongolia asserted, and has since preserved, its independence as a nation in the midst of two hegemonic powers. Russian policy initially sought to preserve Mongolian autonomy from China but did not support Mongolian independence, in order to maintain Russia-China relations and not alarm Japan. After 1917 the Soviet Union did eventually support Mongolian independence but was not firm in this support. China, however, persistently attempted to absorb Mongolia into the new Chinese nation-state.

The 1911 Chinese Revolution and Mongolian Independence

Following the October 1911 Chinese revolution, the Mongolians declared independence in December 1911 and proclaimed the Jebtsundamba Khutukhtu leader of an independent Mongolian nation. Mongolia had enjoyed a special relationship with the Manchu court, and the Mongolians believed that Mongolia was not an integral part of China. At the time, the Chinese maintained that Mongolia was an integral part of China, but it did not have the military strength to force the integration of Mongolia into the new Chinese republic.

Within Russia's czarist government, policy toward Mongolia was also being debated. Russia had not recognized Mongolia's independence, but it was providing Urga, as the Mongolian capital, Ulaanbaatar, then was called, significant political, financial, and military support. In Russo-Japanese negotiations as early as 1907, the Russians considered dividing Mongolia into outer and inner zones, with Russian and Japanese spheres of influence respectively. The period from 1911 to 1915 was one in which Russia, Mongolia, and China engaged in convoluted negotiations, including frequent secret bilateral talks, and military posturing that eventually led to a June 1915 tripartite agreement that afforded the broadest possible "autonomy" for outer Mongolia at the time and paved the way for its eventual total independence from China. The agreements included provisions on trade, taxes, and other matters but no boundary agreement. However, a neutral zone between outer and inner Mongolia was established.

Following the 1917 Russian Revolution, China rejected the tripartite agreement, and under pressure from Beijing, the Jebtsundamba Khutukhtu petitioned for the abolition of Mongolia's autonomy in November 1919, with which China gladly complied. The reassertion of Chinese control did not last long, however. Mongolia became a battlefield in the Russian civil war and the White Russians drove the Chinese from Urga in 1921—only to be defeated themselves at the hands of the Bolsheviks.

Establishment of the Mongolian People's Republic

With the blessings of the Jebtsundamba Khutukhtu and the support of the Soviet Union, Mongolian revolutionaries established a Marxist regime in Urga in 1921. But the Soviet Union, like czarist Russia, still viewed Mongolia as a bargaining chip in its relations with China. In May 1924 the Soviet Union recognized China's "full sovereignty" over outer Mongolia. However, a month later, following the death of the Jebtsundamba Khutukhtu, Mongolia declared its independence as the Mongolian People's Republic (MPR). China's internal problems prevented it from reasserting control; the most it could do was protest the Soviet-Mongolian agreements.

Mongolian independence was bolstered two decades later at the Yalta Conference when the Allies agreed that the status quo in Mongolia be preserved following the war. Following a plebiscite in Mongolia that overwhelmingly supported independence, the Nationalist Chinese government grudgingly agreed to recognize Mongolia's independence in 1946.

Communist China's Quest for Influence

Chinese Communists were also reluctant to acknowledge Mongolian independence and harbored irredentist sentiments. While in Moscow in February 1950, Chinese leader Mao Zedong (1893–1976) raised the issue with Stalin. Although Mao expressed his desire for the eventual "reunion" of Mongolia with China, he did not allow his irredentist dreams to prevent the conclusion of a Sino-Soviet treaty. The MPR and the Soviet Union were apprehensive about China's ambitions in Mongolia and insisted on a Chinese declaration acknowledging Mongolian independence.

Despite that declaration, China raised the issue again in October 1954 during the first trip of Soviet leader Nikita Khrushchev (1894–1971) to China after the death of Joseph Stalin. Under intense pressure from Mao, Chinese premier Zhou Enlai (1898–1976) reluctantly broached the issue with Khrushchev. Khrushchev, according to his memoirs, declined to speak for Mongolia but did not voice strong opposition. Although the Soviets may have refused to reconsider the status of the MPR, subsequent developments in Russian-Mongolian-Chinese tripartite relations give credence to suggestions that the Soviets acquiesced to China's demand to assume a dominant role in Mongolia.

As Sino-Soviet relations deteriorated in the late 1950s, Soviet complacency over Chinese ambitions in Mongolia turned to alarm. The Soviets responded to the Chinese challenge. Mongolia was caught in the middle of the Sino-Soviet dispute. Ulaanbaatar's initial wish was to remain neutral, and a high-level official commented that the dispute would not influence Mongolia's relations with the People's Republic of China (PRC) or the Soviet Union. But its precarious geopolitical circumstances made it impossible to remain neutral for long. Following the open split between the USSR and PRC after the October 1961 Twenty-second Communist Party of the Soviet Union (CPSU) Congress, Mongolia adopted a pro-Soviet position. In June 1962 Mongolia was the first Asian state to become a full member of the Council on Mutual Economic Assistance (COMECON). This was a clear indication that the MPR had decided to closely cooperate with the USSR to the exclusion of China.

Beijing appealed to Mongolian nationalism in its bid to gain influence in Ulaanbaatar. During the commemoration of the 800th anniversary of Genghis Khan's birth in 1962, the Mongolians dedicated a statue at a location believed to be his birthplace. The PRC also celebrated the event and supported the MPR festivities. Beijing, with both nationalistic and racist overtones, portrayed Genghis Khan as a positive "cultural force." Not surprisingly, the Soviets criticized the celebrations. They characterized Genghis Khan as a reactionary "who had overrun, looted, and burned most of what was then Russia" and said his "bloody invasions" were a "great historical tragedy."

The Present Situation

On 16 December 1962, China announced that MPR leader Tsedenbal (1916–1991) would travel to Beijing to sign an agreement to settle the boundary. After demarcating the boundary, a treaty was signed in Ulaanbaatar on 2 July 1964. This boundary agreement closed a long chapter in Sino-Mongolian relations. Despite the boundary treaty, China and Mongolia remain extremely sensitive about their historical relationship. The triangular Mongolian-Russian-Chinese relationship is entering a new period of flux and possible instability. Democratic Mongolia could emerge as the focal point for a reinvigorated pan-Mongolian nationalism that would surely alarm Russia and China. Russia also needs Mongolia as a buffer state to shield it from an awakening Chinese dragon that is becoming an economic and military power. And apparently the legacy of the Chinese empire lingers in the minds of Chinese. In 1992 China's State Security Ministry revived the specter of Chinese irredentism when it issued a statement saying that: "As of now, the Mongolian region comprises three parts that belong to three countries"—the Russian regions of Tuva and Buryatia, Mongolia, and the Inner Mongolian Autonomous Region—but "the Mongolian region has from ancient times been Chinese territory."

Eric Hyer

See also: **Great Game; Mongol Empire; Trans-Mongolian Railway**

Further Reading

Bawden, Charles R. (1989) *The Modern History of Mongolia.* New York: Routledge.

Ewing, Thomas. (1980) *Between the Hammer and the Anvil: Chinese and Russian Policies in Outer Mongolia, 1911–1921.* Bloomington: Indiana University, Research Institute for Inner Asian Studies.

Friters, Girard M. (1974) *Outer Mongolia and its International Position.* New York: Octagon Books.

Grousset, Rene. (1989) *The Empire of the Steppes: A History of Central Asia.* Piscataway, NJ: Rutgers University Press.

Rupen, Robert A. (1966) *The Mongolian People's Republic.* Stanford, CA: Stanford University Press.

Sandag, Shagdariin, and Harry H. Kendall. (2000) *Poisoned Arrows: The Stalin-Choibalsan Mongolian Massacres, 1921–1941.* Boulder, CO: Westview Press.

Soucek, Svat. (2000) *A History of Inner Asia.* New York: Cambridge University Press.

MONGOLIA–SOVIET UNION RELATIONS The Soviet Union's relations with Mongolia, from the Bolshevik Revolution of 1917 until the collapse of the Soviet Union in 1991, were driven by the Kremlin's perceived need to secure its eastern borders against military aggression by Japan before World War II and by Maoist China afterward. To this end, Soviet leader Joseph Stalin (1879–1953) used Mongolia as a pseudoindependent buffer state that could be manipulated from the Kremlin. Using methods similar to those used in Eastern Europe, the Soviet Union conducted secret diplomacy with China to assure the Kremlin a monopoly of influence in Mongolia. A secondary motivating force was the promotion of international communism, but in Mongolia's case, ideology was wielded to exert economic pressure to achieve a military-strategic goal.

Mongolia, wedged between the Soviet and Chinese giants, sought (at times unsuccessfully) to maintain its independence from both. The Mongolians had enjoyed good relations with czarist governments for a century and saw the Russians as friends who could protect them from the Chinese. The collapse of the Qing dynasty (1644–1912) in China enabled Mongolia to achieve autonomy after nearly three centuries of Chinese rule. A new theocratic government headed by the Bogdo Khan—the eighth Jebtsundamba Khutukhtu, or "living Buddha"—proved itself too weak to govern, and in 1921 two groups of revolutionists, one headed by Dogsomyn Bodoo (1895–1922) and the other by Soliyn Danzan (1884–1924), joined forces to form the Mongolian People's Party and a provisional government.

The revolutionaries were confronted on the one hand by Chinese troops attempting to annul Mongolian autonomy and on the other by White Russian (anti-Communist) forces whom the Red Army had forced out of Siberia. The White Russians gained temporary acceptance by dispersing the Chinese, but they antagonized the Mongolians by committing even worse atrocities.

The Mongolian revolutionaries, sympathetic with the new Communist ideology and desperate to rid themselves of the marauding White Russians, sent seven of their more prominent members to the city of Irkutsk, which was close to the Mongolian border, to seek Soviet military and financial assistance. They sought not only military aid but also assistance in areas covering even the most basic governmental functions.

During the coming two decades these seven members figured prominently in Mongolian political affairs. Besides Bodoo and Danzan, the more noteworthy were Horloogiyn Choybalsan (1895–1952) and Namdini Sukhe Baatar (1893–1923). Choybalsan would eventually become the Stalinist dictator of a communist Mongolia. Sukhe Baatar, who had received Russian military training, would die an early and mysterious death but would be elevated to the position of a godlike national hero.

The Advent of Soviet Advisers

Soviet and Comintern (Communist International) advisers who accompanied the Red Army included many ethnic Mongolian Buryats from the Soviet Autonomous Republic of Buryatia who spoke both Russian and Mongolian and were generally better educated than their Kalkha Mongolian counterparts. Quickly inserting themselves at virtually every level of the new Mongolian government, they used their influence to make it a carbon copy of Moscow's Bolshevist regime. The most insidious of these institutional transplants was the Mongolian KGB, installed in the Ministry of Internal Security, which became as pervasive in Mongolian life as the Soviet KGB was in the USSR. Soon the advisers had assumed so many responsibilities that it became painfully evident that the Mongolians had lost control.

Among the Mongolians themselves there were many differences. Under Bodoo's leadership, an "Oath of Accord" was reached in July 1921 that provided for a parliamentary regime under a limited monarchy. Bogdo Khan became titular head of state, and Bodoo became prime minister and foreign minister.

Danzan's group accepted the limited monarchy, but conflicts ensued over organizational methods and economic development strategies. Bodoo and Danzan were both patriotic leaders who wanted relations with the Soviets but also wanted national independence. Without Soviet interference the Mongolians might have been able to work out their differences, but that did not happen.

At the time, Japan was flexing its newfound muscle in nearby Manchuria. In China, Sun Yat-sen (1866–1925) and Chiang Kai-shek (1887–1975) were trying to eliminate warlordism and establish control under the Guomindang (Chinese Nationalist Party). One objective was restoration of Chinese rule in Mongolia. Stalin assured the Mongolians that the USSR would protect their borders against foreign aggression, but his price was a government responsive to control from Moscow. To achieve this, his agents exploited the Mongolian disagreements by sowing discord, intrigue, and suspicion, including false accusations of spying for foreign powers, especially Japan.

Bodoo, aged twenty-seven, and twelve of his associates, unwilling to go along with the Kremlin's policies, were accused of counterrevolutionary activities, tortured into falsified confessions by Soviet KGB agents, and shot without a trial.

Mongolia's Conversion to a Communist Government

In March 1924, the Bogdo Khan died unexpectedly. Just how and why have never been established, but the Soviets took the opportunity to pressure the Great Hural (Mongolia's national legislature) into declaring Mongolia a Soviet-style republic. In August of that year, the Mongolian People's Party held its Third National Congress. Danzan was elected chairman. In the course of the discussions he asserted that Mongolia should retain its independence from the Soviet Union and asked for a significant reduction of Soviet advisers. He had previously antagonized Choybalsan, then head of the Revolutionary Youth League, by opposing the excessive powers exercised by that group. At the request of El'bekdorji Rinchino (1885–1937), the Buryat Comintern representative, Choybalsan summoned the league's death squad. Members of the squad dragged Danzan out of the meeting and shot him on the spot.

During the remainder of the Third National Congress no Mongolian raised his voice against the Russians. The Congress adopted the Soviet-mandated noncapitalist path to development, declared Mongolia to be a people's republic, and established a single-party system called the Mongolian People's Revolutionary Party (MPRP), which would be the Kremlin's weapon in conducting its dictatorial policy in Mongolia.

The Mongolians, intimidated but not completely cowed, saw they had little choice but to go along with the Kremlin's policies. They were forced to cut off all foreign commercial ties except with the Soviet Union. Mongolian students who had been sent to Western Europe were brought home, and anyone wanting to study abroad had to do so in the Soviet Union. Later, Mongolia's ancient script was abandoned in favor of the Cyrillic alphabet, cutting off the nation's ties with the past.

In 1929, MPRP leftists with their Comintern advisers, determined to push ahead in converting Mongolia into a socialist state, gave Choybalsan responsibility for collectivizing Mongolia's livestock industry. He went at it with a vengeance, confiscating the property of monasteries and temples and expropriating the possessions of high seculars, known as feudals. It was an utter disaster. For centuries, nomadic Mongolian herders had moved their cattle, horses, and sheep as necessary for grazing. Collectivization reduced livestock herds by a third and brought untold misery to Mongolian herdsmen, who revolted. Red Army troops who had ostensibly been withdrawn in 1925 had to be brought back to quell the revolt. This time the troops stayed on. Stalin told Soviet representatives in Mongolia to blame the revolt on Chinese spies and shoot those who continued to resist. In 1932, the MPRP conceded that collectivization had failed and called it off. Choybalsan, MPRP leftists, and Soviet advisers found scapegoats for their own mistakes among rightists, who paid with their lives.

Attacks on Religion

Moscow was determined to beef up the Mongolian army so it could play a greater part in the nation's role as a buffer state. However, a high percentage of young Mongolian males traditionally joined religious orders, where they were exempt from military service. With the growing threat of a Japanese invasion, outlawing religion and shutting down the monasteries were ways to provide men for Mongolia's armed forces. Moscow ordered a brutal religious crackdown. At first Mongolians, who held great reverence for their lamas (Buddhist monks), resisted Soviet pressure; but eventually through persistent, vitriolic antireligious campaigns, the Soviets won out. Tens of thousands of lamas were either shot or escaped into exile in Inner Mongolia. Their monasteries were demolished or devastated.

The Soviets saw this antireligious policy vindicated in July 1939 when the Japanese attempted to invade Mongolia at Nomonkhan on the Khalkhiin River. The Japanese aim was the establishment of an anti-Soviet state that would include Inner and Outer Mongolia and the Soviet Autonomous Republic of Buryatia. The invaders were defeated with great losses by combined Russian and Mongolian forces under Marshal Georgy Zhukov (1896–1974). In 1941, a truce defined the Mongolian border with Manchuria. Rather than attempt another invasion, the Japanese turned their attention toward the Pacific.

Mongolia under Choybalsan

Efforts by Mongolian leaders to resist Soviet control of the nation's internal and external affairs invariably ended up in personal disaster. In 1936, Prime Minister Peljidiyn Genden (1895–1937), who had gotten into an argument with Stalin about Communist treatment of the lamas, was given a year's vacation, then arrested, convicted of treason by a Soviet court, and shot the same day. Of the seven revolutionaries who had originally arranged for Soviet assistance in getting rid of the White Russians, all except Choybalsan met their fate in a similar fashion. Leaders were summoned to Moscow for consultation only to be poisoned en route or imprisoned, condemned to death by the Soviet judiciary, and shot. Post-Soviet figures indicate that thirty-two of Mongolia's political leaders were executed in Moscow. Virtually all have since been exonerated of any crime and rehabilitated.

Choybalsan was educated at a school for Russian translators, studied at a military academy in Moscow, and spoke fluent Russian. During a conference in Moscow in the early 1930s, he seems to have caught Stalin's eye and moved steadily upward in the Mongolian hierarchy. In the process he played a suspicious role in a number of fabricated political affairs that resulted in mass executions of more than 10 percent of Mongolia's population of 900,000.

It was evident that Stalin had found his man in Choybalsan, one prepared to follow orders without question and wipe out all opposition. With Stalin's assistance, Choybalsan moved swiftly up the political ladder, each rung marked by execution of his rivals. In 1939, he become prime minister, created his own Stalinist cult of personality, and reigned supreme over Mongolia for the remainder of his life.

With Choybalsan in power, Soviet control of Mongolia was consolidated. Mongolia supported the USSR throughout World War II, providing the Red Army with livestock, raw materials, food, and clothing. Mongolia did not enter World War II as a combatant until the very end, when it served the Soviet Union as a base to move swiftly against the Japanese in Manchuria and to capitalize on Japan's defeat.

On 5 January 1946, China recognized Mongolian independence with the existing boundaries, thus fulfilling Moscow's goal of an independent buffer state under its complete control. After the Communist takeover in China in 1949, a brief period of Moscow-Beijing cooperation brought thousands of Chinese workers to Mongolia for construction projects. With the Sino-Soviet split, however, the workers were sent home. As the Sino-Soviet split grew, Mongolia became an armed camp with Chinese and Soviet troops poised against each along the Sino-Mongolian border, where they remained until the Sino-Soviet rapprochement in the mid-1980s.

In 1952, Choybalsan died in Moscow of liver cancer. He was succeeded by his secretary, Yumjaagiyn Tsedenbal (1916–1991), who continued the close relationship with the Soviet Union. In 1962, Mongolia joined COMECON (Council for Mutual Economic Assistance) and was integrated into the Soviet economic-political-strategic system. Under Tsedenbal, however, Mongolia's economy stagnated; in 1984, at the behest of the Communist Party of the Soviet Union, he was ousted from his position as MPRP secretary general and replaced by Prime Minister Jambyn Batmon (1926–1997), a Moscow-trained economist.

In 1989, after conversations with Soviet Premier Mikhail Gorbachev (b. 1931), Batmon introduced the concept of perestroika (openness) to Mongolia, bringing into the open a deluge of MPRP falsifications that had occurred during the Choybalsan and Tsedenbal regimes. Concurrently, the USSR, on the verge of collapse itself, cut off all economic support to Mongolia and withdrew the last remaining Soviet troops.

Relations between Russia and Mongolia after the Collapse of the Soviet Union

In 1990, a group of fewer than twenty young Mongolian intellectuals led a democratic revolution that brought about free elections and voted out a Communist government for the first time in history, thus casting off the Soviet yoke that had held the country in bondage for seventy years. In 1992, a new, fully democratic constitution went into effect.

In its newfound independence, Mongolia has joined the world's market economy; sympathetic foreign nations (including the United States) and nongovernmental organizations such as the Asia Foundation in San Francisco are lending a hand to help build democratic institutions. An ardent desire to embrace the West has united Mongolians.

Although the overall Soviet presence in Mongolia was distinctly negative, there were positive aspects, especially in raising the literacy rate to 90 percent from 10 percent in the early 1920s. As Mongolian Professor Shagdariin Sandag (Sandag and Kendall 2000: xvii) wrote:

> The Kremlin's expansionist policies also brought to Mongolia many Soviet specialists—medical doctors, scientists and ordinary Russians—who worked honestly and hard to introduce modern methods into our society. If their achievements were limited it was through no fault of their own but because of the comparative backwardness of Soviet technology and hegemonic Kremlin policy.

Harry H. Kendall

Further Reading

Batbayar, Tsedendamdyn. (1996) *Modern Mongolia: A Concise History*. Ulaanbaatar, Mongolia: Mongolian Center for Scientific and Technological Studies.

Bawden, Charles R. (1989) *The Modern History of Mongolia*. 2d ed. New York: Kegan Paul International.

Rupen, Robert A. (1979) *How Mongolia Is Really Ruled: A Political History of the Mongolian People's Republic 1900–1978*. Stanford, CA: Hoover Institution Press.

———. (1964) *Mongols of the Twentieth Century*. Bloomington: Indiana University Press.

Sandag, Shagdariin, and Harry H. Kendall. (2000) *Poisoned Arrows: The Stalin-Choibalsan Mongolian Massacres, 1921–1941.* Boulder, CO: Westview Press.
Sanders, Alan J. K. (1996) *Historical Dictionary of Mongolia.* Lanham, MD: Scarecrow Press.
———. (1987) *Mongolia, Economics, Politics and Society.* Boulder, CO: Lynne Reinner.

MONGOLIAN LANGUAGES

The Mongolian (or Mongolic) languages form a group of genetically related languages, spoken mostly in Mongolia, northern China, and some regions of Russia.

The family is generally subdivided into three groups—Central (or Eastern), Northern, and Western Mongolian. Some languages, especially those spoken in China, are commonly referred to as "isolated" within the family, though their taxonomic subdivision continues to be debated.

Central Mongolian

The most important language of the Central or Eastern Mongolian group is the official language of the Republic of Mongolia, generally called Mongolian (also known as Khalkha, after the prestige dialect; other important dialects in Outer Mongolia are Dariganga and Ujumuchin). It is spoken by 2.5 million people and written in Cyrillic script, although attempts to revert to the traditional Uighur script continue in Outer Mongolia. In the Inner Mongolian Autonomous Region, the language has always been written in the Uighur script, and the linguistic norm is largely based on the Chakhar dialect. Other important dialects of Inner Mongolia include Kharchin, Khorchin, Urat, and the somewhat divergent Ordos dialect, which is sometimes treated as a separate East Mongolian language.

Western and Northern Mongolian

In 1648, the Buddhist cleric Jaya Pandita developed the *todo üseg* ("clear script"), a modification of the Uighur script designed to write Oirat, or Western Mongolian. Oirat dialects are still spoken in western Mongolia and Xinjiang. In Russia, the Kalmyk language has around 130,000 speakers in the Kalmyk Republic on the lower Volga. The Northern Mongolian group is formed by Buryat and its dialects and is spoken in the Buryat Republic in Southern Siberia, where it has around 300,000 speakers and a Cyrillic-based written language.

Mongolian Languages in China

Dagur (about 40,000 speakers) is spoken in the Chinese province of Heilongjiang, Inner Mongolia, and an enclave in Xinjiang, where Dagurs were relocated in the eighteenth century. Another language of the Chinese northeast is Khamnigan, spoken in the

THE MONGOLIAN LANGUAGE THROUGH TIME

The following extracts trace the Mongolian language through time, telling the story of Chinggis (Genghis) Khan's birth in (1) the thirteenth-century Chinese-script version of the *Secret History of the Mongols*, (2) the Uighur-script chronicle *Altan Tobci* ("Golden Summary"), written by *Lubsandanjin* in 1655, and (3) a translation of the *Secret History* into modern Cyrillic-script Khalkha.

(1) Onan-nu deli'ün boldaq-a büküi-tür jöb tende cinggis-qahan töreju'üi; töreküi-tür bara'un qar-tur-iyan si'a-yin tedüi nödün qatqun töreju'üi.
(2) Onan-u deligün-boldag-a büküi-tür (. . .) Cinggis qagan töröbe; töröküi-tür-iyen baragun gar-tur-iyan shagay-yin tedüi qara nöjin-i adqun töröbe.
(3) Onony Delüün boldog gedeg gazar Chingis xaanyg törüülzhee. Chingis töröxdöö baruun gart shagayn chinee nözh atgan, törzhee.

Translation of (1): "When they were in Deli'ün boldaq, on the river Onan, Chinggis Khan was born; when he was born, he held a clump of blood, the size of a knuckle, in his right hand."

Source: Stefan Georg

Hulun Buir region of Inner Mongolia. Dagur and Khamnigan are probably the two most archaic modern languages of the family. A number of Mongolian languages are spoken in the Qinghai-Gansu border region. The language of the Tu nationality, formerly referred to as Monguor, is now separated into its two major variants, Huzhu Mongghul and Minhe Mangghuer. The Tu nationality numbers approximately 150,000 people. Baoan (Bonan) has around 10,000 speakers in Gansu, and Dongxiang, more properly Santa, also in Gansu, has 240,000 speakers. Along with Turkic and Tibetan-speaking groups, the linguistically complex group of the Yugur, also known as Sir-a (or yellow) Yugur, includes around 1,500 speakers of a Mongolian language, Jegün (Eastern) Yugur. In some remote pockets of northwestern Afghanistan, the Moghol language survived well into the twentieth century, but nothing is known about its fate after the Soviet invasion of Afghanistan in 1979.

For Huzhu Mongghul, Dongxiang, and Dagur, Latin-script-based orthographies have been developed and introduced into national schools. Written Mongolian, the language of most Mongolian documents before the twentieth century, is generally viewed as close, but certainly not identical, to the common ancestor of all these languages, Proto-Mongolian. The first Written Mongolian documents date from the thirteenth century. Though the very first undoubtedly Mongolian text is a short inscription in Uighur script dating from 1227, the better part of early Mongolian writing has come down to us in different scripts. The longest of these early documents is *Monggol-un ni'uca tobciyan* (Secret History of the Mongols). A dynastic history of the descendants of Genghis Khan with elements reminiscent of epic poetry, it is only preserved in Chinese characters, designed to be read according to their phonetic values. Another important Sino-Mongolian document is the Mongolian part of the *Hua-i I-yu*, a Sino-Xenic glossary compiled in 1389.

In 1269, the Yuan emperor Khubilai Khan ordered the Buddhist cleric hPhags-Pa (1235–1280) to design a universal script for all languages of the empire. This so-called quadratic script *(dörbeljin üseg)*, based on the Tibetan script, was short-lived, but some Mongolian documents written in it survive. A few Mongolian documents have been written in Arabic script, and some Mongolian words are preserved in Armenian and Georgian medieval documents. Because the language of the Sino-Mongolian and quadratic-script documents shows some peculiarities, which are already to be taken as secondary developments when confronted with more conservative Uighur-script Mongolian, the earliest written documents are often, somewhat paradoxically, said to be written in Middle Mongolian.

From the fourteenth century onward, the written medium for Mongolian is almost exclusively the vertical script, which was originally adopted from the Turkic-speaking Uighurs. After the seventeenth-century conversion of the Mongols to Tibetan Buddhism, a vast amount of canonical Buddhist literature was translated from Tibetan into Mongolian; the language of these translations is generally referred to as Classical Mongolian.

The Khitan confederation, masters of the Liao dynasty in northern China (907–1125), probably spoke an early variant of Mongolian. The highly complex script they used has not been fully deciphered, but based on Khitan glosses in Chinese texts, the Mongolian character of their language seems reasonably clear.

Characteristics of Mongolian Languages

Modern Mongolian languages show all the typological traits that are generally taken as typical for the so-called Altaic languages: vowel harmony; verb-final word order; postpositions; exclusively suffixing, agglutinative morphology; and subordination by nominalization. On the whole, the family is typologically quite homogeneous. Among the more visible differences between them are the different ways the languages treat the problem of verbal concord. While the Central Mongolian languages do not show any verbal concord, the peripheral Northern and Western Mongolian languages (e.g. Kalmyk and Buryat), have developed a system of differentiating subject person by developing verbal suffixes from subject pronouns. Mongghul, Mangghuer, and Baoan have copied an intricate system of concord from Tibetan, which, together with numerous other features of their sound-structure, makes these southernmost Mongolian languages the least typical representatives of the family.

Stefan Georg

Further Reading

Beffa, Marie-Lise, and Roberte Hamayon. (1975) *Eléments de grammaire mongole*. Paris: Dunod.

Janhunen, Juha, ed. (forthcoming) *The Mongolic Languages*. Richmond, U.K.: Curzon.

Poppe, Nicholas. (1954) *Grammar of Written Mongolian*. Wiesbaden, Germany: Harrassowitz.

———. (1955) *Introduction to Mongolian Comparative Studies*. Helsinki, Finland: Finno-Ugrian Society.

———. (1970) *Mongolian Language Handbook*. Washington, DC: Center for Applied Linguistics.

MONGOLIAN SOCIAL DEMOCRATIC PARTY The Mongolian Social Democratic Party (MSDP) developed out of the Mongolian Social Democratic Movement (MSDM) led by R. Gonchigdorj (later vice president of Mongolia) at the end of the Communist era in Mongolia (1989). The party assumed legal status in May 1990, and Bat-Erdeniyn Batbayar was elected chairman. The MSDP is a consultative member of the Socialist International, an international federation of communist parties. It joined the coalition of democratic forces in the July 1990 elections and won 4 of the then 430 seats in the parliament. The MSDM and MSDP merged in September 1991. During the 1990s the party's platform represented western European-style social democracy and neutrality.

In the June 1996 elections, the MSDP joined in a coalition with the Mongolian National Democratic Party (MNDP) to form the Democratic Union. It won an upset victory by capturing fifty of seventy-six seats in the revamped parliament and formed the first non-Communist government in Mongolia in seventy-five years. During its four-year tenure, the Union attempted to carry out a detailed plan for radical democratic reform and privatization of the remaining large state enterprises. However, the collapse of the traditional export market, corruption, and political splintering within the Democratic Union led to four years of political instability and four Union prime ministers. In July 2000 the union decisively lost to the former communist party, the Mongolian People's Revolutionary Party (MPRP). In response to this defeat, on 6 December 2000, the MSDP, led by Batbayar, merged with five other political parties, including the MNDP, to form the Mongolian Democratic Party.

Alicia J. Campi

Further Reading

Sanders, Alan J. K. *Historical Dictionary of Mongolia.* Lanham, MD: Scarecrow Press.

MONGOLIAN WRESTLING. See **Buh.**

MONGOLS The Mongols first appear in Chinese sources at the end of the Tang dynasty (618–907), but must have been a linguistically distinct people long before then, since the Mongolian language—actually a set of closely related dialects—had already had a long history by the time it was first written down in the thirteenth century. It is a branch of the Altaic family and is related to the Turkic and Tungus languages and more distantly to Korean and Japanese. Its closest ancient relatives, including Kitan, are all now extinct.

At the time that they were first noticed by the Chinese, the Mongols lived somewhat to the north of the present territories of the Mongols in what is now Mongol Buriyatia, around Lake Baikal. Other Mongols today live throughout the territories of the Mongolian People's Republic, in Inner Mongolia (part of China), in Manchuria, and in various northern Chinese provinces, including Qinghai and Xinjiang, and along the lower Volga, where they took up residence in the eighteenth century. Recent migrations of Mongols have been to South Korea, where there are now 17,000, mostly illegal, and as far afield as Israel.

Traditional Mongol Life

By the time of Temüjin (d. 1227), the later Genghis Khan, the Mongols had moved considerably to the south and were centered about the Onon and Kerlen rivers, in what is now the north-central part of the Mongolian People's Republic. Although it has been suggested that they were originally hunters and gatherers, they were, by this time, full pastoral nomads. Their way of life, based upon sheep, goats, a few cattle, and occasionally camels, herded from horseback, involved movement in a set pattern, usually from low-lying areas in the spring to mountain pastures in the summer, and then back to the low-lying pastures in the autumn and for the winter months. A variation was movement along river valleys, from upstream as the year grew warmer, and then the return in the autumn. Later, as the Mongols moved into arid regions in the south, another pattern developed of circular movement over essentially flat terrain, to prevent exhaustion of limited local fodder and water resources. The products of this life were some meat, a relatively rare food, and dairy products, eaten in a fermented form by preference. This monotonous diet could be supplemented by game and by gathered foods. There was also some fishing. Herds also produced hides and wool and hair for felting and rope making. There was no weaving.

The early Mongols lived in tents called *ger* (yurts), comprising a wooden latticework, usually with a wooden door and sometimes a wooden base, over which layers of felt, waterproofed with various substances, including animal and dairy-product fats, were thrown for protection from the weather. A smoke hole at the top could be closed when required. Generally, these tents were taken down or put up at each campsite and were intended to be highly mobile. Sometimes

A Mongol woman and her son ride a horse on the grassy plain of Mongolia in the early 1960s. (DEAN CONGER/CORBIS)

they were left mounted permanently on carts, some quite large; these carts also had square cabs in which Mongols could live. They also sometimes lived in smaller, temporary tents, but *ger* were the norm.

In addition to animals and tents, also a key part of Mongol nomadic life were articles of daily life, including wooden cradles, large wooden stirring spoons, equipment for processing hides, horse and ox harness, and lassos on poles for capturing horses. Mongol clothing was most commonly of trade textiles (woven cloth obtained through trade), with fur linings and various stuffing, but could also be furs or even felt, as needed. Boots were pressed felt or leather. The traditional robe, or *deel*, buttoned to the left and was held together below by a leather belt with various trappings. Hats were usually of fur with earmuffs attached. For warfare an armor was made, both for men and horses, by stitching hardened leather plates onto a leather or quilted base. Metal was rarely used, except for helmets. The preferred weapon was the compound bow, and occasionally the lance, but some Mongols used swords as well.

Mongol Expansion and Empire

In the early thirteenth century there were less than a million Mongols. They were characterized by a high birth rate, and as conditions improved, a low death rate. This meant that they were capable of expanding their numbers rapidly as new nomadic territories became available. This is what happened, and the wars of Genghis Khan and his successors were as much migrations as they were conquests. The Mongols poured into what is now Inner Mongolia as the conquest of China proceeded. They also moved west into Turkistan, and even into Iran and Azerbaijan. In most of these areas, Mongols amalgamated with other nomadic groups already present, a process complete by the late thirteenth century, when the Mongols disappeared as an ethnic group in the west, although Mongolian dynasties continued to rule there. In the east it was generally the Mongols who did the absorbing, principally of local Kitan tribesmen, and Inner Mongolia, first invaded by the Mongols in the early thirteenth century, has remained at least partially Mongolian since.

Later Mongols penetrated other parts of China, including Yunnan, then outlying territory, and placed small garrisons throughout the former Song domains conquered in 1279. Most of these garrisons were lost in 1368 when Toghan Timur (reigned 1333–1370), the last Mongol emperor of the successor khanate of China, went back to the steppe, where he died two years later.

The years of empire (in Mongolia, from 1206 to 1370) were a demographic disaster for the Mongols. Although they had gained Inner Mongolia, Mongolia had become depleted of Mongols due to migration, wars in Central Asia, and a general impoverishment of an exhausted Mongolian homeland that led to Mongols even being sold as slaves to replay Chinese debtors. Into this vacuum came a Siberian branch of the Mongols, the Oirat, who had only recently become full nomads. The Oirat raided the Chinese Ming dynasty (1368–1644) and at one point captured the emperor. Elsewhere, on the fringes of the steppe, other Mongol groups, led by members of the house of Genghis Khan, alternatively fought and allied with the Chinese. Most of these groups came under the control of China's Manchu-ruled Qing dynasty (1644–1912), which also conquered most of Mongolia in the late seventeenth century. Only various groups of Oirats living in the far west remained outside China's control, and with these the Qing waged a long series of wars. The Qing subdued most of them in the eighteenth century and forced others to migrate, ultimately to the Volga, where they became the modern

Kalmyks. The Mongols of Siberia, in the meantime, had come under Russian control.

In the nineteenth century, Mongolia was thrown open to the Chinese subjects of the Manchu, who used their clout to reduce most Mongols to utter poverty. By this time the Mongols had been reconverted to Tibetan Buddhism. (The first conversion had occurred during Mongol rule of China, 1279–1368.) This conversion led to the appearance of a religious feudalism paralleling the traditional feudalism of the secular princes supported by the Manchu. The effective head of Mongolia at the time was the Urga Hutughtu, or incarnating Lama of Urga, as the present-day Ulaanbaatar was then known.

The Mongols in the Nineteenth Century

During the nineteenth century Mongolian life remained much as it had been in the era of Genghis Khan and after, except that Mongolia was now dotted with monastic communities that provided the semblance of an urban—or at least town—life, with attendant commercial and manufacturing activities. The religious community also contributed to Mongolia educationally, giving rise to a relatively high literacy rate. Buddhism brought with it the Tibetan language, which not only brought Mongolia into contact with Tibet, the origins of its Buddhism, but with the literary and cultural traditions of India, since most of the great Indian classics had been translated into Tibetan and thus became accessible to educated Mongols. Mongolia, as a consequence, has its own Indian-based medical system that is quite unlike that of China and a literature that is, even today, heavily influenced by Sanskrit classics.

Another of the differences between Mongolian life in the nineteenth century and earlier centuries was the habit of tea drinking. Tea had appeared earlier, but did not catch on until the fourteenth century at the earliest, since which time it has become a national way of life. Mongolian tea is made by long boiling of a pressed brick of tea in milk, to produce a very strong tea but one in which the tannin is counteracted by the milk, making the beverage more drinkable. The Mongols also adopted *tsampa* from the Tibetans. To make *tsampa*, barley or other grains are put into hot buttered tea to combine breakfast and beverage. In the nineteenth century Mongolia also gained access to more distilled alcoholic beverages. Distilled alcoholic drinks had been well known to the elite in the fourteenth century, but the period after empire saw a proliferation of portable distillation equipment. Consequently, almost everyone had some access to distilled liquors, although koumiss, fermented mare's milk or camel milk, remained the beverage of choice. Nineteenth-century Mongols also seem to have had access to a wider range of textiles, thanks to Chinese merchants, and metal implements of everyday life became ubiquitous in the period too, thanks to the same source, although the Tibetans produced such things too.

The Mongols in the Twentieth Century

As the Qing dynasty collapsed in 1911, the Mongols of Outer Mongolia, as it was called by the Qing government, declared their independence, ultimately coming under Soviet control (1921–1991). At first Soviet rule constituted another era of demographic disaster, thanks to Mongolian revolutions against their rule, forced collectivization, and the suppression of Buddhism. Venereal disease and alcoholism were also problems. The Mongols appeared to be becoming extinct, but by the 1950s the population had stabilized, and in the 1960s and 1970s truly rapid growth began. The Mongols of Inner Mongolia also went into decline about the same time, for some of the same reasons. Inner Mongolia was heavily penetrated by Chinese merchants who were anxious to exploit the Mongols and who were followed by Chinese settlers, who deprived the Mongols of the pastures they needed to live. Inner Mongolia also had its own "feudalists," both secular and religious. The region played an important role in China's warlord era of the 1920s and 1930s (stretching into the 1940s in places) and was of interest to the Japanese. Japanese alliances with Mongol princes later created major problems for local Mongols when the Chinese began reasserting their power.

Other Mongols, principally those in Russia, enjoyed a somewhat better life but were heavily pressured to assimilate, which had the opposite effect of causing them to reassert their ethnic identity. Among the Buriyats, for example, shamanism, which was nearly extinct in the mid-nineteenth century, underwent a major revival despite Soviet-era persecution. The revival continues even now.

The Mongols in the Twenty-first Century

Today, the single largest group of Mongols is found in the Mongolian People's Republic, where the demographic decline of the early Soviet period has long been reversed. There are more Mongols there today than at any time in their history, more than 2.4 million, according to a 2001 estimate. No longer are the Mongols totally an agrarian people, living a traditional nomadic life. At least half the country now is involved in industry, particularly mineral extraction, including oil, and for the first time in its history, Mongolia has its own large urban conglomerate, Ulaanbaatar. It had an estimated population of 782,000 in early 2001, but the actual figure is considerably larger when the capital's floating population is counted in. Although the other major centers, Darhan and Erdenet, are much smaller (populations under 100,000, although growing), these are still huge urban complexes by the standards of interior Central Asia and Mongolia.

Elsewhere it is hard to get a fix on numbers of Mongols. As recently as 1992, a total of 3.6 million Mongols was claimed for Inner Mongolia, but most are highly assimilated and Mongol in name only. Probably less than half speak Mongolian at all. Hundreds of thousands of Mongols are claimed by the Chinese for Manchuria and other parts of China but most are even more assimilated than those of Inner Mongolia. Probably there are not more than 2 million Mongols in China, with mother tongue being the distinguishing criterion.

The same problems arise in estimating the number of Buriyats and Kalmyks. There are an estimated 350,000 Buriyats living in the Russian Buriyat Republic, about 35 percent of its total population. A few more Buriyats live in adjacent regions of Russia as well. Kalmyks number perhaps 150,000, about 45 percent of the population of the Kalmyk Republic on the lower Volga. The language retention rate in Russia is probably higher than in China, but the same forces of assimilation apply. Nowhere but in the Mongolian People's Republic are the Mongols a majority.

A major issue separating the Mongolian groups is script. The Mongols of the Mongolian People's Republic use the Cyrillic script, with a few extra letters, as do the Buriyats and Kalmyks, with variations. By contrast, the Mongols of China still use the vertical Uighur script, which is highly ambiguous and uses an archaic spelling that was out of date when the script was first adapted to write Mongolian in the thirteenth century. Although the Mongolian script is used as a second script by other Mongolian groups, written language is a major dividing force between the former Outer and Inner Mongolia. In addition, while the Buriyats and Kalmyks have actively sought to promote Mongolian unity by establishing contacts amongst themselves and with the People's Republic, this path is largely closed to the Mongols of Inner Mongolia, who are jealously guarded by the Chinese to prevent the development of Mongolian nationalism there. It exists nonetheless.

Thus, as a conservative estimate, there are at least 4 million Mongols in the world today. The most important Mongolian language is Mongolian, of which Khalkha, the official language of the Mongolian People's Republic, spoken as a native language by at least 89 percent of its population, is its most important representative. Most other Mongolian languages are dialects of Mongolian, including Chakhar, and Horchin, spoken in Inner Mongolia and other places in China. Differences are small.

Elsewhere, Buriyat, which exists in several dialects, is its own language, although still relatively close to Mongolian, as is Kalmyk, thanks to the presence in Mongolia of other Western Mongolian or Oirat groups that maintain a close connection with Khalkha. The differences between the Mongolian languages are principally in loan words, Buriyat and Kalmyk having more Turkic or, in the case of Buriyat, Siberian vocabulary. Both languages share a Tibetan Buddhist influence with the other Mongolian languages and dialects and, in the case of Khalkha, the other People's Republic languages, Buriyat and Kalmyk, substantial Russian influence. In Inner Mongolia the major foreign influence is Chinese.

Paul D. Buell

Further Reading

Buell, Paul D. (forthcoming) *Historical Dictionary of the Mongol World Empire*. Lanham, MD: Scarecrow Press.

Jane's Information Group. (2002) *Jane's Sentinel Security Assessment: China and Northeast Asia.* Retrieved 10 April 2002 from: http://www.janes.com.

Sanders, Alan J. K. (1996) *Historical Dictionary of Mongolia.* Lanham, MD: Scarecrow Press.

MONGOOSE The mongoose is a small carnivorous mammal belonging to the family Herpestidae and is native to Asia, Africa, and southern Europe. In Asia it is found across the Indian subcontinent and from southern China to Polynesia. There are more than thirty species of mongoose, differing in size, behavior, and habitat. Most widespread are the Indian gray, or common, mongoose *(Herpestes edwardsi)*, immortalized in Rudyard Kipling's *Jungle Book* tale "Riki-Tikki-Tavi," and the small Indian mongoose *(Herpestes auaropunctatus)*. Among the rarer mongooses is the crab-eating mongoose *(Herpestes urva)*, which is found in Taiwan.

Mongooses are sleek, furry animals, varying in coloring from gray through brown to black. They have a long body and tail, short legs, small round ears, and sharp teeth and claws. They typically measure about two feet in length; however, the crab-eating mongoose measures over three feet. Mongooses live in burrows, are territorial, and frequently solitary. They live to about ten years of age and produce litters of one to four young.

Fierce predators, mongooses will attack and kill large venomous snakes such as the cobra, succeeding due to their remarkable speed and agility and thick protective fur. They are not immune to snake venom, but may be resistant to it. In Asia, mongooses' greatest enemies are snakes, but they are also hunted by birds of prey and larger mammals. Mongooses also hunt small rodents, birds, and reptiles and forage for insects, eggs, and fruit. Mongooses are easily tamed, and their usefulness in keeping houses free from vermin means that they are often kept as pets.

In order to control rats, mongooses have been introduced to areas such as Hawaii and the Caribbean, where they have few natural predators. However, they are destructive to poultry and native bird life and are often considered a pest.

Lucy D. Moss

Further Reading

Hinton, H. E., and A. M. Dunn. (1967) *Mongooses: Their Natural History and Behaviour*. Berkeley and Los Angeles: University of California Press.

Kipling, Rudyard. (1997) *Rikki-Tikki-Tavi*. New York: William Morrow.

Macdonald, David. (1992) *The Velvet Claw: A Natural History of the Carnivores*. London: BBC Books.

MON-KHMER LANGUAGES

MON-KHMER LANGUAGES Mon-Khmer is a language family of mainland Southeast Asia that includes the national languages Cambodian (Khmer) and Vietnamese and more than a hundred minority languages spoken in Vietnam, Cambodia, Laos, Thailand, Myanmar (Burma), India, and China.

In the past some Mon-Khmer languages were more important than they are today. For example, in the first century CE the Khmer and the Mon had substantial kingdoms that covered much of what is today Thailand, Myanmar, and Laos as well as Cambodia. Today Mon is only spoken by minorities in Thailand and Myanmar, and is no longer an important written language. Khmer remains the written standard in Cambodia, surviving as the national language.

Many lesser-known Mon-Khmer languages have never been written down, while for some of these languages writing systems have been developed, but are not in widespread use. An exception is Khasi, spoken in Assam (Maghalay State, India) by several hundred thousand people, where a written standard enjoys everyday use.

Being generally dominated by other cultures, Mon-Khmer speakers are commonly multilingual in their own and neighboring or national languages. As such they tend to borrow a lot of words and even grammar. The most extreme example of this is possibly Vietnamese, which was under strong Chinese influence for over a thousand years. The Chinese component in Vietnamese is so great that it is not unusual for more than half of the words in a Vietnamese text to be of Chinese origin. The resemblance to Chinese is further heightened by the historical shift toward monosyllabic word structure and the use of tones.

Typical Mon-Khmer languages are characterized by subject-verb-object word order, by simple word shape with fixed word-final stress, no tones, extensive use of prefixes and infixes but not suffixes, noun classifiers, and serial verb construction.

While the word structures can be very simple, the sound systems can be rather complicated. Normally there are both voiced and voiceless consonants, including partly voiceless nasals, liquids (*r* and *l* sounds), and glides (*w* and *y*). Consonants may also have a laryngeal setting, which may be realized as a glottalized or creaky voice. The vowel inventories are among the largest in the world—most having distinctively short and long vowels and diphthonged vowels. Some even have a "register" distinction between plain and breathy or creaky vowels. In this way some Mon-Khmer languages have developed more than thirty or even forty distinct vowels.

Despite these structural similarities, Mon-Khmer languages vary considerably in their lexicons, so that even simple equivalent sentences are made with very different sounding words, e.g.,

	"Where are you going?"			
Chrau	biː	maːj	saːʔ	
Jruq	ʌːj	saw	maː	rɛʔ
Khmer	loːk	tow	naː	
Vietnamese	ʔaɲ	di	dĕw	dĕj
Khmu	jɛ̀ʔ	jɔ̀h	mə́h	
Mlabri	mɛh	ɟak	ginɛŋ	

	"I am very sick"		
Chrau	ʔaːɲ	ɟiː	maˇʔ
Jruq	ʔaj	ɟiʔ	ʔmat ʔmaːt
Khmer	kɲom	cɨː	nah
Vietnamese	tǒ'i	bı	laˇm
Khmu	ʔo'ʔ	ʔa'h	saŋcu'ʔ saŋkı'ːn
Mlabri	ʔoh	cʰoʔ	reːw

The term Mon-Khmer is sometimes used interchangeably with Austroasiatic. More usually Mon-Khmer is used by specialists to refer to a subgrouping of Austroasiatic languages. The common view regards Austroasiatic as consisting of two branches, Munda languages (spoken in India) and Mon-Khmer languages, consisting of at least ten subbranches. However, the question of whether there really is a Mon-Khmer family, as opposed to Austroasiatic, and what languages belong in it, is far from clear, and views changed many times in the course of the twentieth century. In 1926 Prater Wilhelm Schmidt suggested the following:

Austroasiatic

1) Malaccan (Aslian)
2) Central (Khasi, Palaung-Wa, Nicobar)
3) Mon-Khmer (Mon, Khmer, Bahnar, Jakun) and Munda
4) Chamic

At the time the position of Vietnamese was disputed, with some scholars preferring to classify it with Chinese and Thai, due to the presence of tones. In 1942 Thomas Sebeok suggested the grouping of all of the above languages, except for Munda, in one Mon-Khmer family, establishing the view that has dominated thinking until the present day.

In several papers in the early 1950s, André-Georges Haudricourt showed that Vietnamese developed tones independently and is related to Cambodian rather than Chinese or Thai. At about the same time it also became apparent that the Chamic languages of Vietnam are rather closely related to Malay, and therefore are classified as Austronesian rather than Mon-Khmer. The confusion had arisen because Chamic languages had been in intimate contact with Mon-Khmer languages such as Bahnar and Katu for such a long time that they had borrowed many words and even changed the form of Malay words to resemble Mon-Khmer words.

In the 1960s David Thomas and Robert Headley applied statistical methods to new data, classifying the Pearic, Khmer, Bahnaric, Katuic, Khumic, Monic, Palaungic, Khasi, and Viet-Muong as Mon-Khmer.

Thomas and Headley did not include Nicobarese or Aslian languages in their Mon-Khmer classification. In 1974 Gérard Diffloth suggested the division of these nine groups, plus Nicobarese and Aslian, into three branches based on apparent lexical innovations:

North Mon-Khmer

Khmuic
Palaungic
Khasi

East Mon-Khmer

Khmeric
Pearic
Bahnaric
Katuic
Viet-Muong

South Mon-Khmer

Nicobaric
Aslian
Monic

More recently Ilia Peiros, using statistical methods, found no basis for a distinction between Mon-Khmer and Austroasiatic, and proposed the following six branches (without considering Nicobarese):

Central

Bahnaric
Katuic
Aslian
Monic

Vietic

Northern

Palaung-Wa
Khmuic

Khmer

Khasi

Munda

Today many Mon-Khmer languages are endangered; that is, they have fewer than two thousand speakers and are no longer being spoken by the youngest generation, who learn only national languages in school. This is a direct consequence of economic development and globalization, as swidden farming (shifting cultivation of the forest) is being replaced by sedentary farming of cash crops. Fortunately there are various field linguists working to record and preserve these endangered languages before it is too late.

Paul Sidwell and Pascale Jacq

Further Reading

Binh Nhu Ngo. (1999) *Elementary Vietnamese*. Boston: Tuttle.

Diffloth, Gérard. (1974) "Austro-Asiatic Languages." *Encyclopædia Britannica*. 15th ed. Chicago: Encyclopedia Brittanica, 480–484.

Haudricourt, André-Georges. (1954) "De l'origine des tons en viêtnamien." *Journal Asiatique* 242: 69–82.

Huffman, Franklin, Charan Promchan, and Chhom-Rak Thong Lambert. (1970) *Modern Spoken Cambodian*. New Haven, CT: Yale University Press.

Peiros, Ilia. (1998) *Comparative Linguistics in Southeast Asia*. Canberra, Australia: Australian National University.

Rischel, Jørgen. (1995) *Minor Mlabri: A Hunter-Gatherer Language of Northern Indochina*. Copenhagen, Denmark: Museum Tusculanum Press.

Schmidt, Prater Wilhelm. (1926) *Die Sprachfamilien und Sprachenkreise der Erde*. 2 vols. Heidelberg, Germany: Carl Winter.

Sebeok, Thomas. (1942) "An Examination of the Austro-Asiatic Language Family." *Language* 18,3: 206–217.

Smith, Kenneth. (1979) *Sedang Grammar*. Pacific Linguistics, no. B-50. Canberra, Australia: Australian National University.

Suwilai Premsrirat. (1989) *Khmu: A Minority Language of Thailand*. Pacific Linguistics, no. A-75. Canberra, Australia: Australian National University.

Thomas, David. (1971) *Chrau Grammar*. Oceanic Linguistics Special Publication, no. 7. Honolulu: University of Hawaii Press.

Thomas, David, and Robert Headley. (1970) "More on Mon-Khmer Sub-Groupings." *Lingua* 25: 398–418.

MONSOONS Derived from the Arabic word *mausim* ("season"), monsoons refer to markedly seasonal winds. The Southeast Asian monsoons are part of the Asian monsoon and are characteristically seasonal with local variations due to the influence of islands and geographic relief of the continent. They

MONSOONS, DEATH, AND DISEASE

In villages in South Asia the monsoon is the source of water for the crops but, whether it arrives on time or late or not at all, it is also a source of disease and death, as indicated by this account from a missionary among the Tamil people in South India in the late nineteenth century.

> A monsoon that fails to arrive or comes late results, surely and inevitably, in the most dreadful famine, especially in the higher regions not touched by the rivers, which are altogether dependent on the northeast monsoon. This happened, for example, in 1877 where in the district of the small kingdom of Mysore north of Koimbatur, in a six-month period, 150,000 cattle and sheep succumbed for lack of fodder. . . . An official from Mysore who did all he could to prevent famine in his district . . . wrote at the time: "In this *taluk* of my district 1500 persons died last month, and in the last few days I saw what I had never seen before, moving skeletons, skeletons too weak to walk or even speak, and human corpses lying by the wayside eaten away by dogs."
>
> The more indigent natives find the arrival of the monsoon and the temperature change less agreeable than do the Europeans living in the country. Because of their scant clothing and the poor state of their dwellings which give them little protection against inclement weather, they are obliged to suffer a great deal from bad weather, and actually the death rate among them is greater in November than in any other month. One therefore never hears the gruesome sound of the long death-horns more often, never are the devil's temples, large and small, decorated as they are in the "calamity month" as November is called, when in the villages of the pariahs [untouchables] the piled-up refuse starts to ferment, making them centers of epidemics.
>
> *Source:* Hans Gehring. (1899) *South India: The Tamil People and Their Country*. Gütersloh, Germany: Druck und Verlag von C. Bertelsmann, 28–29, 31.

have a significant impact on the region's human life and economic activities.

Seasonality

The northeast monsoon occurs from about December to March, starting as a cold and dry continental air mass moving in Asia. It picks up moisture over the South China Sea, bringing rain to the coastal areas of Vietnam, the eastern side of the Malay Peninsula, and large parts of Indonesia. The southwest monsoon, from June to September, is a continuation of the southeasterly wind from the southern hemisphere. In east Java this is usually called the east monsoon or dry monsoon, as it brings rather dry air masses but also rain to almost all parts of the Philippines and the Myanmar/Burma-Thai west coast and decreases toward the interior. Nearer to the equator, the two monsoons are very similar.

March-May and September-November are the intermonsoon periods, when winds are variable and weak, and rainfall is influenced by local factors. The large number of islands, the relief, and exposure to the prevailing wind create a large variety of local climates. Local land or sea breezes may reinforce or detract from prevailing winds, leading to increased rainfall on the windward side and increased sea surface roughness.

Impacts

Early traders from Arabia, India, China, and Europe learned to use the monsoons for navigation in their quest for and trade in spices. Seafaring people in the region today employ the winds extensively. For example, sea Bajaus off southeastern Sabah navigate and fish according to an annual succession of four major wind seasons, which correspond roughly to the monsoon seasons. The seasonality of the monsoons plays an essential role in agriculture. The onset of rainfall is crucial for agricultural production, but water control is necessary, especially for growing rice in irrigated fields. The dry period is ideal for crop ripening, and a prolonged rainy period reduces the yield or quality of crops.

In recent years the Asian monsoon system seems related to sea surface temperature anomalies in the Pacific Ocean (a phenomenon called El Niño Southern Oscillation). El Niño events or warmer-than-usual sea temperatures in the Pacific Ocean are associated with drier-than-usual conditions and resulting increased forest fires in Southeast Asia; these can pose a serious problem for agricultural production and food security.

Wong Poh Poh

Further Reading

McGregor, Glenn R., and Simon Nieuwolt. (1998) *Tropical Climatology*. 2d ed. Chichester, U.K.: Wiley.

Sather, Clifford. (1997) *The Bajau Laut: Adaptation, History, and Fate in a Maritime Fishing Society of South-eastern Sabah*. Kuala Lumpur, Malaysia: Oxford University Press.

MONTAGU-CHELMSFORD REFORMS

The 1919 Constitutional Act introduced into India by Edwin Montagu, who served as secretary of state for India from 1917 to 1922, and Lord Chelmsford, who served as viceroy in India from 1916 to 1921, was popularly known as the Montagu-Chelmsford Reforms. These reforms were part of a due process of a constitutional revision instituted ten years after the Morley-Minto Reforms of 1909. However, they were rendered more urgent by India's unprecedented support for England during World War I and the growing demands for political reform being made by Indian nationalists.

One of Montagu's first acts as secretary of state was to make a clear statement of the government's position on increasing the presence of Indians in every branch of the administration and gradually developing India toward self-government within the British empire, a position that had broad cross-party support and that had been drafted by the former viceroy, Lord Curzon. In the winter of 1917–1918, Montagu undertook an extensive tour of India to ascertain public opinion at first hand and to formulate with Chelmsford a concrete scheme for constitutional reform.

The resulting Montagu-Chelmsford Report of 1918 formed the basis of the Government of India Act of 1919. This introduced a system known as dyarchy, or dual government, under which there was to be a devolution of power and responsibility in the executive and legislative spheres to Indian administrators elected on a restricted franchise at the provincial level. Subjects "transferred" to Indian ministers included education, agriculture, and local self-government, although a series of "reserved" subjects, such as irrigation, police, the press, finance, and justice, were retained under British control. Reserve powers were also vested in the governors and the viceroy, and the central government retained its overriding powers. Although the reforms received only a lukewarm reception and fell short of Indian nationalist demands, they did represent a major landmark on the road to the complete devolution of constitutional power by the British in India.

Chandrika Kaul

Further Reading

Robb, Peter. G. (1976) *The Government of India and Reform, 1916–21*. Oxford, U.K. Oxford University Press.

Rumbold, A. (1979) *Watershed in India.* London: Athlone Press.

MOON, SUN MYUNG. See **Unification Church.**

MORI ARINORI

MORI ARINORI (1847–1889), Meiji government official, reformer. A prominent Meiji government official and outspoken reformer, Mori Arinori (also Mori Yurei) remains as controversial among today's historians as he was in his own day. Born in Kagoshima to a Satsuma samurai family on 23 August 1847, Mori spent nearly a quarter of his life as a resident in the West. His time in the West was divided into three periods: 1865–1868, when he studied in Europe and sojourned in America (where he became associated with Thomas Lake Harris's religious community, Brotherhood of the New Life); 1871–1873 as *chargé d'affaires* in Washington, DC; and 1880–1884 as minister to Great Britain. During this period, his reputation as a *Nihon no unda seiyojin* (a Westerner born of Japan) was spawned by his precocious proposal in 1869 to abolish sword-wearing, which briefly forced him out of the government; by his proposal in 1873 to adopt the English language in place of Japanese; by the Meiji Six Society (Meirokusha), which he helped organize in 1873 to promote Western-inspired "civilization and enlightenment" through monthly lecture meetings and a published journal; and by his first marriage to Hirose Tsuneko, daughter of a Shizuoka samurai family, in a Western-style civil ceremony in 1875.

After sixteen years in the Foreign Ministry, Mori was appointed minister of education in 1885. Some historians and critics view Mori's reorganization of the school system, his expansion of the Ministry of Education's role in producing and inspecting textbooks, and his introduction of military drill (*heishiki taiso*) into the curriculum as catalysts for a host of educational problems in twentieth-century Japan: elitism, credentialism, bureaucratism, militarism, and cultural nationalism.

Mori's reputation as a cultural iconoclast may have contributed to his untimely death by a knife-wielding assassin on 11 February 1889, who alleged that Mori had desecrated the sacred Grand Shrine of Ise during an official visit there in December 1887.

Mark Lincicome

Further Reading

Hall, Ivan Parker. (1973) *Mori Arinori.* Cambridge, MA: Harvard University Press.

Lincicome, Mark Elwood. (1995) *Principle, Praxis, and the Politics of Educational Reform in Meiji Japan.* Honolulu: University of Hawaii Press.

Marshall, Byron K. (1994) *Learning to Be Modern: Japanese Political Discourse on Education.* Boulder, CO: Westview Press.

Swale, Alistair. (2000) *The Political Thought of Mori Arinori: A Study in Meiji Conservatism.* Richmond, U.K.: Japan Library.

MORI OGAI

MORI OGAI (1862–1922), Japanese physician and novelist. Intellectual giant and Renaissance man of the Meiji era (1868–1912), Ogai was born Mori Rintaro in Tsuwano (present-day Shimane Prefecture). He excelled in both the arts and sciences as a medical scientist, linguist, translator, critic, and historian. After graduating from medical school, he joined the army and was sent to Germany, where he studied between 1884 and 1888. Ogai served as surgeon general to the Japanese army and continued a productive literary career to the end. Immediately upon returning to Japan, he published an anthology of lyric poetry, *Omokage* (Vestiges, 1889) and his own literary journal. Early novellas such as *Maihime* (Dancing Girl, 1890) show an idealistic romanticism and elements of his own experience in Germany. *Gan* (Wild Goose, 1911–1913), a romantic tale of unrequited love, remains one of the author's most popular works. In his middle period, following the death of Emperor Meiji, he turned to the past and produced many historical works, both fictional and biographical. His late period yielded biographies of doctors of the Edo period. Some of his masterful translations include Andersen's *Improvisatoren*, Goethe's *Faust*, Ibsen's *Ghosts* and *A Doll's House*, Shakespeare's *Macbeth*, and hundreds more.

William Ridgeway

Further Reading

Bowring, Richard John. (1977) *Mori Ogai and the Modernisation of Japanese Culture.* Cambridge, U.K.: Cambridge University Press.

Rimer, John Thomas. (1975) *Mori Ogai.* New York: Twayne Publishers.

MORLEY-MINTO REFORMS

MORLEY-MINTO REFORMS The Indian Councils Act of 1909 also bears the name of the Morley-Minto Reforms after the leading imperial administrators who formulated them—John Morley, the Liberal British secretary of state, and Lord Minto, the Conservative British viceroy to India. However, the application of the reforms was short-lived, since they were considerably overhauled by the Montagu-Chelmsford Report in 1918.

The main features of the reforms included the first formal introduction of the principle of elections to government councils on a very restricted franchise (with details to be worked out in provinces and localities); an increase in additional nonofficial members in the Imperial Legislative Council from sixteen to sixty, with the retention of the official majority; a small increase in powers of discussing the budget; and special provision for the representation of professional classes, the landholders, the Muslims, and European and Indian commerce in elected assemblies. The nomination of an Indian to the Viceroy's Council as well as to the Council of India was also included. (The first appointments—of Ashutosh Mukherjee and S. H. Bilgrami, respectively—proved short-lived.) The scheme of separate electorates for Muslims was a major concession to increasingly vocal demands by the Muslim League. This basis of election on religious grounds was severely criticized by Indian politicians as further evidence of a British policy of divide and rule and as being abhorrent to the principles of parliamentary democracy.

Chandrika Kaul

Further Reading

Gilbert, Martin. (1966) *Servant of India*. London: Longmans.

Koss, Stephen. (1969) *John Morley at the India Office, 1905–10*. New Haven, CT: Yale University Press.

Morley, John. (1917) *Recollections*, Vol. 2. London: Macmillan.

Wolpert, Stanley. (1967) *Morley and India, 1906–1910*. Berkeley and Los Angeles: University of California Press.

MORO ISLAMIC LIBERATION FRONT

The Moro Islamic Liberation Front (MILF) was formed in the Philippines in 1977 as a breakaway from the Moro National Liberation Front (MNLF). Its leader, Hashim Salamat, at the time accused MNLF chairman Nur Misuari of autocratic leadership, Communist sympathies, and corruption. A bid by Salamat to gain recognition from the Organization of Islamic Conference (OIC) for the MILF as the leading Moro organization failed. When in 1986–1987 the Philippine government negotiated with the MNLF over the creation of an Autonomous Region of Muslim Mindanao (ARMM), the MILF was not a party to the talks, and again in the 1990s it did not participate in the negotiations that culminated in the 1996 Peace Agreement. The MILF thus became the leader of the armed struggle for a separate Moro nation. Under the Ramos and Estrada presidencies several attempts were made to negotiate with the MILF, and there appears to have been a tacit acceptance of the MILF's spheres of influence around its headquarters, Camp Abubakr, and other bases in western Mindanao. In 2000, however, a series of clashes between the MILF and government forces resulted in President Estrada's declaring "all-out war" on the MILF. The Armed Forces of the Philippines subsequently overran the MILF bases and a number of MILF fighters reportedly surrendered. In 2001, under the administration of President Gloria Macapagal-Arroyo, new attempts to negotiate a peace settlement appeared to be achieving some success, notably in August 2001with the signing of the Kuala Lumpur Agreement on the Guidelines for the Implementation of the Agreement on the General Cessation of Hostilities between the Government of the Republic of the Philippines and the MILF.

Ronald J. May

Further Reading

Salamat, Hashim. (1985) *The Bangsamoro Mujahid: His Objectives and Responsibilities*. Mindanao, Philippines: Bangsamoro Publications.

Vitug, Marites, and Glenda M. Gloria. (2000) *Under the Crescent Moon: Rebellion in Mindanao*. Quezon City, Philippines: Ateneo Center for Social Policy and Public Affairs, and Institute for Popular Democracy.

MORO NATIONAL LIBERATION FRONT

The Moro National Liberation Front (MNLF) was created around 1971 from a group of young Philippine Muslims who had undergone guerrilla training in Malaysia. It became the leading political organization in the Muslim insurgency against the Philippine government. The MNLF, under the leadership of Nur Misuari, demanded a separate *Bangsa* Moro (Moro nation) in the traditional Muslim heartland of Mindanao-Sulu-Palawan and also opposed traditional feudal structures within Philippine Muslim society. It had a military wing, the Bangsa Moro Army (BMA). The MNLF gained the support of the Organization of Islamic Conference (OIC) and financial backing from Libya and other Islamic countries.

In 1976, the MNLF signed a cease-fire and an agreement with the Philippine government in Tripoli, Libya. Under the Tripoli Agreement, the Philippine government accepted thirteen provinces in Mindanao-Sulu-Palawan as a prospective area of Muslim autonomy. Attempts to implement the agreement broke down, however, when the Philippine government insisted on a plebiscite on the autonomy arrangements in the thirteen provinces (only five of which had a Muslim majority by the 1970s), and each side accused the other of cease-fire violations.

In 1977, splits occurred within the MNLF over issues of strategy, personality, and ideological orientation; the splits also followed major ethnolinguistic

An MNLF soldier awaits orders on Jolo Island in the southern Philippines in May 2000. (REUTERS NEWMEDIA INC./CORBIS)

divisions in Philippine Muslim society. While Misuari remained as the recognized leader of the MNLF, a faction led by Hashim Salamat, a religious leader from Maguindanao, broke away to form the Moro Islamic Liberation Front (MILF), and a second, predominantly Maranao, faction led by Dimas Pundato formed the MNLF-Reformist Group.

The armed conflict was scaled down by the late 1970s, following the splits in the movement and with a number of MNLF fighters surrendering to the government under amnesty programs. In 1986, talks initiated between the incoming president, Corazon Aquino, and Misuari culminated in provisions in the 1987 constitution for an Autonomous Region of Muslim Mindanao (ARMM). Disputes again arose over the issue of a referendum to determine which provinces and cities would join the ARMM; the MNLF boycotted the poll, and Misuari returned overseas. In 1992, however, negotiations were revived under President Fidel Ramos, and in 1996, with the mediation of the OIC, a peace agreement was signed between the MNLF and the Philippine government. It provided for the creation of a Special Zone of Peace and Development in the (now) fourteen provinces and nine cities specified in the Tripoli Agreement, and for a Southern Philippines Council for Peace and Development, with limited autonomous powers, headed by Misuari. Provision was also made for the integration of former BMA fighters into the Armed Forces of the Philippines and the Philippine National Constabulary. Misuari was elected governor of the ARMM in 1996. The breakaway MILF, however, continued the insurgency. In August 2001, there were reports of a rapprochement between the MNLF and the MILF, but there were also factional cleavages within the MNLF, notably in August 2001 with the signing of the Kuala Lumpur Agreement on the Guidelines for the Implementation of the Agreement on the General Cessation of Hostilities between the Government of the Republic of the Philippines and the MILF.

Ronald J. May

Further Reading

Che Man, Wan Kadir bin. (1990) *Muslim Separatism: The Muslims of Southern Philippines and the Malays of Southern Thailand*. Singapore: Oxford University Press.

May, Ronald J. (1989) "The Moro Movement in Southern Philippines." In *Politics of the Future: The Role of Social Movements*, edited by C. Jennett and R. G. Stewart. Melbourne, Australia: Macmillan, 321–329.

Salamat, Hashim. (1985) *The Bangsamoro Mujahid: His Objectives and Responsibilities*. Mindanao, Philippines: Bangsamoro Publications.

MOSO

MOSO The Moso, also known as the Mosuo, Na, or Naze, are a Chinese minority ethnic group living on the border of the southwestern provinces of Yunnan and Sichuan. No census data of the Moso are published as they are officially classified as a subgroup of the Naxi, a large ethnic minority in China. The Moso population is estimated to be around forty thousand.

The Moso practice matrilineal descent (tracing descent through the mother's line) and have a unique visiting sexual system called *tisese* and grand households that usually do not consist of a husband and a wife. Women, not men, are at the center of Moso culture.

Tisese ("walking back and forth") among the Moso differs from marriage in that it is noncontractual, nonobligatory, and nonexclusive. Commonly, the two partners in a *tisese* relationship work and consume in their own matrilineal households, respectively (or separately). The man visits the woman in the evening, stays with her overnight, and goes back to his mother's household the next morning. Children born to such a union belong to the household in which they were born, usually the mother's household. Because Moso culture has been changing rapidly in recent decades, the nonexclusive and nonobligatory features of *tisese* are disappearing.

Chuan-kang Shih

Further Reading

Hua Cai. (2001) *A Society without Fathers or Husbands: The Na of China*. Trans. by Asti Hustvedt. New York: Zone Books; Cambridge, MA: distributed by MIT Press.

Oppitz, Michael, and Elisabeth Hsu, eds. (1998) *Naxi and Moso Ethnography: Kin, Rites, Pictographs*. Zurich, Switzerland: Völkerkundemuseum Zürich.

Shih, Chuan-kang. (forthcoming) *Quest for Harmony: The Moso Systems of Sexual Union and Household Organization.* Stanford, CA: Stanford University Press.

———. (1993) "The Yongning Moso: Sexual Union, Household Organization, Gender, and Ethnicity in a Matrilineal Duolocal Society in Southwest China." Ph.D. diss., Stanford University.

Weng, Naiqun. (1993) "The Mother House: The Symbolism and Practice of Gender among the Naze in Southwest China." Ph.D. diss., University of Rochester.

MOSUL (2002 pop. 1.7 million). Mosul, the second-largest city in modern Iraq, is located on the west bank of the Tigris River opposite the ruins of ancient Nineveh, a capital of the Assyrian empire. Mosul came under Sasanid rule in the second century CE, when it was the site of an important bishopric. Incorporated into the Muslim empire in 641, it became a garrison town and subsequently a provincial capital under the Umayyad and Abbasid dynasties (seventh–thirteenth centuries). It was generally spared the devastation the Mongols visited on many neighboring cities in the thirteenth and fourteenth centuries. Unlike most other Iraqi cities, much of Mosul's historic center remains intact.

Medieval travelers praised the beauty of the city and the fertility of its surroundings; most of its buildings were constructed of stone, and it had a thriving market center and many baths and mosques. The city was incorporated into the Ottoman empire in 1535, although it was ruled almost continuously by a local family, the Jalilis, for much of the eighteenth and nineteenth centuries. In late Ottoman times there were substantial Christian and Jewish communities in the city.

HATRA—WORLD HERITAGE SITE

Hatra, a major citadel in the ancient Parthian empire, was designated a UNESCO World Heritage Site in 1985. Hatra—southwest of Mosul, Iraq—combined Greco-Roman architecture with Eastern influences in its temples and fended off two Roman invasions in 116 and 198 CE.

Mosul's commercial importance ("muslin" is a corruption of the city's name) began to wane with the decline of the overland trade routes following the opening of the Suez Canal in 1869, and with the city's incorporation into the modern state of Iraq in 1920 and its general subordination to the new capital, Baghdad. Located close to Iraq's northern oil fields, Mosul is the largest city in the region with important textile, cement, and food-processing industries.

Peter Sluglett

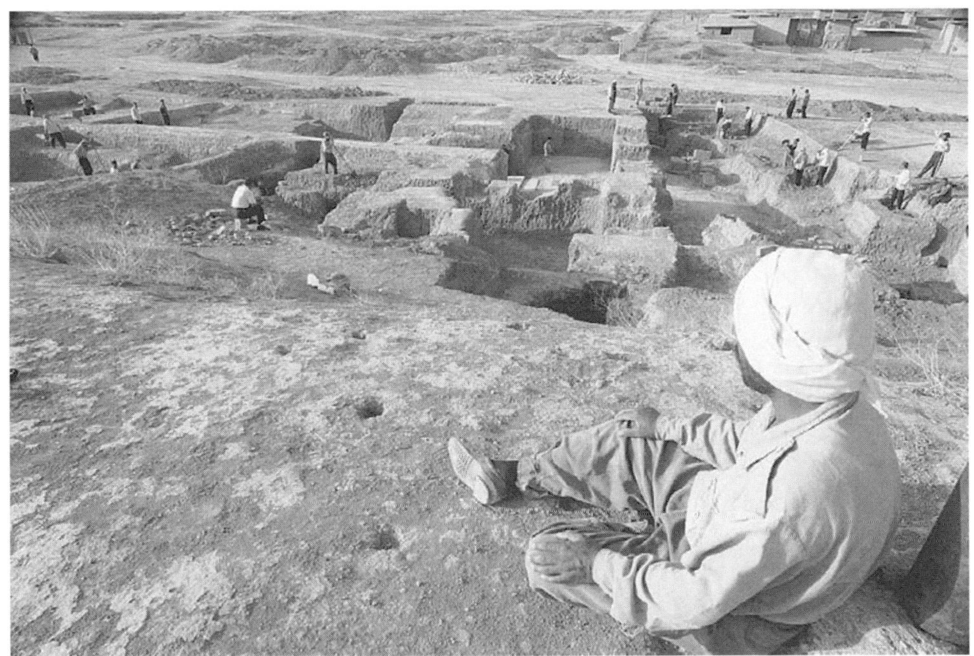

The ruins of an Assyrian temple dating to the eighth century BCE unearthed 35 kilometers south of Mosul by archaeologists. (AFP/CORBIS)

Further Reading

Batatu, Hanna. (1978) *The Old Social Classes and the Revolutionary Movements of Iraq: A Study of Iraq's Old Landed and Commercial Classes and of Its Communists, Ba'thists, and Free Officers*. Princeton, NJ: Princeton University Press.

Khoury, Dina. (1997) *State and Provincial Society in the Early Modern Ottoman Empire: Mosul, 1540–1834*. Cambridge, U.K.: Cambridge University Press.

Shields, Sarah. (2000) *Mosul before Iraq: Like Bees Making Five-Sided Cells*. Albany: State University of New York Press.

MOTHERLAND. See **Turkey—Political System.**

MOTOORI NORINAGA (1730–1801), Japanese scholar. Considered one of Japan's greatest scholars, Motoori Norinaga was born in Ise Province near the Grand Shrine of Ise. In 1752, he went to Kyoto to study Chinese classics and medicine, and during this time he read classical literary works from the Heian period. Toward the end of his studies, he published *Ashiwake obune*, in which he set forth his theory of classical *waka* (Japanese poems in thirty-one syllables). Returning to Ise in 1757, he established himself as a physician and also commenced a series of lectures on *Genji monogatari (The Tale of Genji)*, *Tosa Diary*, and the *Manyoshu (Collection of Ten Thousand Leaves)*. He subsequently published *Shibun yoryo*, a study of *Genji monogatari*, and *Isonokami sasamegoto*, a study of *waka*. In both works his interpretations focused on *mono no aware* (sensitivity to the transience of things). In Kyoto, Norinaga had become familiar with the works of *kokugaku* (national learning) movement founder Keichu (1640–1701). The *kokugaku* movement studied ancient Japanese texts in order to rediscover the native values of Japan prior to the introduction of Buddhism and Confucianism from China. It was not until he returned to Matsuzaka that Motoori became acquainted with the erudite *kokugaku* scholar Kamo no Mabuchi (1697–1769). A single meeting with him convinced Motoori that it was essential to study the earliest of the Japanese classics, the *Kojiki* (Record of Ancient Matters, c. 712). He then turned his attention to philology, Japanese mythology, and political philosophy. In 1796, he published an exhaustive interpretation of *Genji monogatari* and, in 1798, completed his lifework, *Kojiki den*, a comprehensive study of the *Kojiki*. Motoori's writings had significant impact on later generations of scholars in terms of methodology and nationalistic ideology.

James M. Vardaman, Jr.

Further Reading

Keene, Donald. (1976) *World within Walls: Japanese Literature of the Pre-Modern Era, 1600–1867*. Tokyo: Tuttle.

Matsumoto, Shigeru. (1970) *Motoori Norinaga*. Cambridge, MA: Harvard University Press.

MOULMEIN (1995 pop. 250,000). Moulmein is an important port city in southeastern Myanmar (Burma). It is located at the mouth of the Salween River on the Bay of Martaban. The name "Moulmein" is a Western colonial version of the indigenous name for the town (pronounced Mow-la-myine), and since 1989 "Mawlamyaing" (sometimes "Mawlamyine") has officially replaced the colonial version. Moulmein is one of Myanmar's largest cities with about a quarter of a million people, largely of Mon heritage.

As an independent state, Moulmein was a tributary of the Thai kingdom of Ayutthaya from the fourteenth century until 1765, when it fell under Burmese control. The British took Moulmein as part of the province of Tenasserim in the First Anglo-Burmese War (1824–1826), and from 1827 until 1852 Moulmein was the colonial capital of the British province of Tenasserim. After 1852, Moulmein remained the administrative center of Amherst District and Tenasserim Division for the remainder of British rule. Under British rule, the extraction of timber from the area's substantial teak reserves and the local shipbuilding industry helped to turn the town of Moulmein into an important port for the eastern Bay of Bengal. Today, Moulmein is the capital of Mon State.

Michael Walter Charney

Further Reading

Cady, John F. (1958) *A History of Modern Burma*. Ithaca, NY: Cornell University Press.

Harvey, G. E. ([1925] 1967) *History of Burma: From the Earliest Times to 10 March 1824—The Beginning of the English Conquest*. Reprint ed. London: Frank Cass.

MOUNTAINEERING There are more mountains in Asia than in any other continent. Mountains form a backbone to Asia, snaking across the continent from the mountains of eastern Turkey and the Caucasus lying on the border between Europe and Asia, through Iran and Iraq to Afghanistan where they divide at the Hindu Kush. To the north, the link extends through the Pamirs, Tian Shan, and the Altai Mountains, through Mongolia, to divide again, ending at the Kamchatka and Korean peninsulas and offshore in the Japanese Alps. To the south, the

MOUNTAINEERING—TWO VIEWS

Tourists who climb the mountains of the Himalayas describe the mountains as beautiful, awesome, breathtaking, and mysterious. The Sherpa people who live there and often serve as guides have a much different view.

Although it is the environment of the Khumbu that attracts Western tourists, their perception of that environment, ironically, is fundamentally incompatible with that of the Sherpas. The most general Sherpa term for beautiful (lemu) can apply to the physical features as well as the personal qualities of human beings, both men and women. It can also apply to inanimate objects and to the environment as a whole. But while a field or forest might be lemu, the giant snow peaks towering in every direction over Khumbu are never considered lemu. Their lack of color (their whiteness) is seen as uninteresting (though religiously significant)—not a surprising judgment in view of the Sherpa preference for vivid colors evident in such disparate contexts as religious paintings and women's aprons. A snow peak elsewhere might be admired for its shape, and Pertemba, one of the foremost Sherpa sardars of his time, says that one of the pleasures he derives from climbing is the beauty of the different views from high on a mountain. But generally familiarity has bred indifference rather than awe, and the shape of the Khumbu snow and ice peaks is just too boring to be considered lemu. Even the dramatic setting of Tengboche Monastery is said to have been selected without regard to its beauty. It was chosen by name, sight unseen, because the footprints of Lama Sangwa Dorje, a seminal figure in Sherpa history who was born about 350 years ago, had been embedded in rock when he stopped there.

Source: James F. Fisher. (1990) *Sherpas: Reflections on Change on Himalayan Nepal.* Berkeley: University of California Press, 127–129.

chain extends through the Karakoram and the high Himalayas before fanning out into China, Myanmar, and the Malay Peninsula, and offshore into Sumatra.

Mountaineering as we know it, involving adventure, conquest, and recorded ascents, is usually considered to be a Western development, coming to Asia during the period of late colonialism in the latter part of the nineteenth century. There were earlier ascents of sacred mountains, however, and it should not be assumed that only late Victorians had a spirit of adventure. All first ascents should be noted as first recorded ascents.

Present-day mountaineering in Asia may range from rock climbing in Hong Kong and Vietnam, to tourist ascents of Mt. Fuji in Japan, to pilgrimages that complete the circuit of Kailas in Tibet, to archaeological ascents of Mount Ararat in Turkey. But the main focus is on the Karakoram and Himalayas, and especially on the fourteen peaks that exceed 8,000 meters in height. After the Caucasus, these mountains became the prime focus of exploration by mountaineers in the late nineteenth and early twentieth centuries. Several peaks up to 7,000 meters received their first recorded ascents during this period of exploration and discovery of the highest mountains in the world.

Between the two World Wars, national expeditions from Western nations focused on making the first ascents of these mountains, with the Germans concentrating on Nanga Parbat (8,126 meters) and the British on Everest (also known as Chomolungma or Sagarmatha, 8,848 meters). These national expeditions continued after World War II, with technological developments resulting from war leading to the first successes—Annapurna (8,078 meters) by the French in 1950; Nanga Parbat by the Germans and Everest by the British, both in 1953; K2 (the second highest

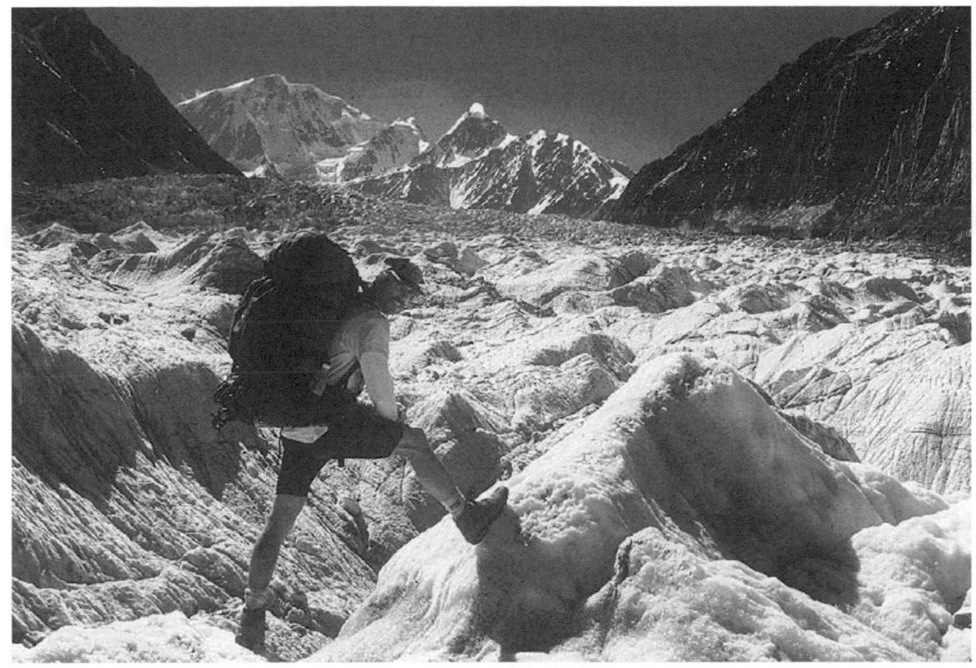

A climber on Passu Glacier in Passu, Hunza, Pakistan, in 1996. (STEPHEN G. DONALDSON PHOTOGRAPHY)

mountain in the world, 8,611 meters) by the Italians in 1954; and Kanchenjunga (the third highest mountain in the world, 8,586 meters) by the British in 1955.

National expeditions continued for the remainder of the twentieth century, with particular emphasis by nations wishing to join the Everest club. The character of Himalayan mountaineering began to change once the major peaks had all received first ascents, and smaller self-contained expeditions that explored alternative routes to the summits became more common. Since the 1980s and 1990s, commercial or charitable interests have sponsored an increasing number of Himalayan mountaineering expeditions.

Although Asians have probably always climbed their own mountains, Western-style recorded ascents have been carried out by Indians and Pakistanis. Mountaineering is well established in Japan and Korea, and the Sherpa people of Nepal are guides to the world's highest mountains.

Peter Donnelly

Further Reading

Cleare, John. (1979) *The World Guide to Mountains and Mountaineering*. New York: Mayflower Books.

Neate, W. R. (1978) *Mountaineering and Its Literature*. Cumbria, U.K.: Cicerone Press.

Pyatt, Edward. (1980) *The Guinness Book of Mountains and Mountaineering*. London: Guinness Superlatives, Ltd.

Unsworth, Walt. (1982) *Everest*. Harmondsworth, U.K.: Penguin.

———. (1992) *Encyclopaedia of Mountaineering*. London: Hodder & Stoughton.

MOXIBUSTION

Moxibustion, as an ancient healing art of traditional Chinese medicine (TCM), cannot be separated from acupuncture. By definition, moxibustion means the use of *moxa* (a Japanese term for *Artemisia vulgaris)* as a cautery by igniting it close to the skin. *Moxa* is a soft, woolly mass prepared from the young leaves of various wormwoods of Eastern Asia, called Artemisia argyl, or Chinese mugwort leaf *(Artemisia folium)*.

Moxibustion treatment is performed with *moxa* rolls or sticks, which, after being ignited, can be held by the doctor's hand at a distance of three centimeters or so away from the selected acupuncture points for ten to fifteen minutes, resulting in a *moxa* cauterization effect. Moxibustion, therefore, can also be defined as burning herbs to stimulate the acupuncture points. With special indications such as acute abdominal pain due to cold, facial muscle atrophy of unknown etiology, and so forth, a thin, small slice of ginger as an insulator can be put at the site of the acupoint between the ignited *moxa* roll and the skin. The patient may feel a sense of heat at the acupoint. Alternatively, the patient may be given acupuncture first, and then

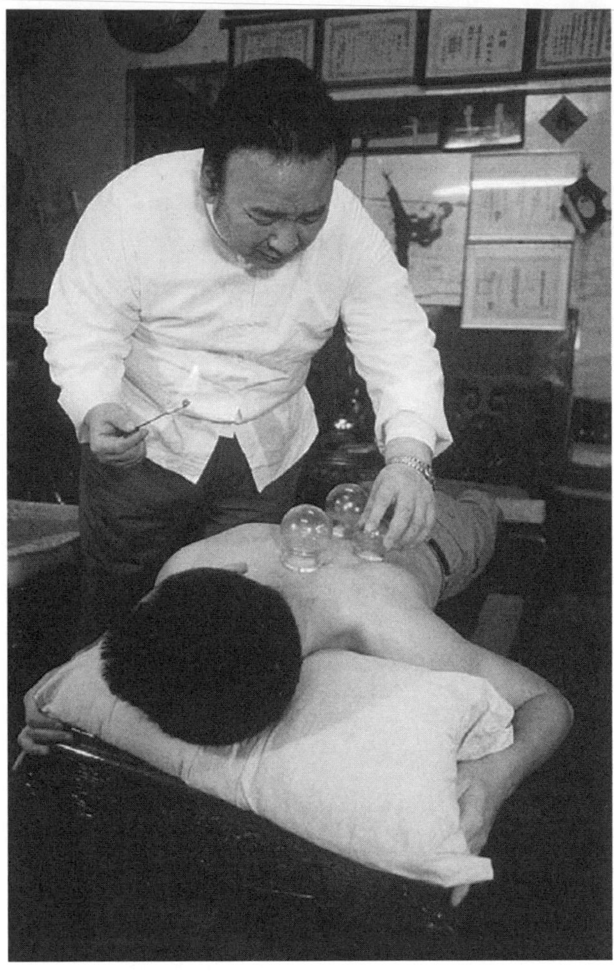

A traditional Chinese doctor applies suction glasses to the back of a patient in Taipei, Taiwan. (NIK WHEELER/CORBIS)

the *moxa* rolls cut into small cylinders are ignited and applied to the ends of the acupuncture needles. The theory and principles of channels and collaterals must be first learned to master the art of both moxibustion and acupuncture.

The concept of administering moxibustion (or moxibustion plus acupuncture) is based on providing heat stimulation at the acupuncture points along the channels and collaterals. The effects are twofold. One is local hyperthermia therapy, and the other is the effect on remote organs along the channels and collaterals. The selection of the moxibustion and acupoints is done according to the indications of the special disorder.

Today, moxibustion and acupuncture are practiced in departments of TCM or, in many Chinese hospitals, by integrating TCM with Western medicine. Study has concluded that serious or severe adverse events are rare in the standard practice of moxibustion and acupuncture.

Chen Bao-xing and Garé LeCompte

Further Reading

Geng Junying and Su Zhihong. (1991) *Practical Traditional Chinese Medicine and Pharmacology: Acupuncture and Moxibustion*. Beijing: New World Press.

Yamashita H., H. Tsukayama, Y. Tanno, and K. Nishijo. (1999) "Adverse Events in Acupuncture and Moxibustion Treatment: A Six-Year Survey at a National Clinic in Japan." *Journal of Alternative and Complementary Medicine* 5, 3 (June): 229–236.

Zhang Enqin. (1990) *Chinese Acupuncture and Moxibustion*. Shanghai: Publishing House of the Shanghai College of Traditional Chinese Medicine.

MOZI (flourished 479–438 BCE), Chinese philosopher. Master Mo (Mozi) may have been a native of the state of either Song or Lu in China. He was a high official in Song. Because he is believed to have been an artisan and because of the practical nature of his philosophy and the many images and analogies drawn from the technical crafts, it is believed that Mozi came from the lower classes. King Hui of Chu (488–432 BCE) refused to grant Mozi an audience supposedly because of his low status. Some claim that Mozi studied Confucius's teachings when he was young; his essays clearly attack the major tenants of Confucianism. Ancient texts do not present Mozi in debate with Confucian scholars; rather he debated with the artisan Gongshu Ban regarding his wall-scaling ladder. Mozi convinced the king of Chu not to employ the ladder militarily against Song, which represents his values of loving everybody and defending the underdog.

The text of Mozi clearly and sharply attacked Confucian values. Mozi and his followers opposed the extravagant use of music and rituals. They especially opposed elaborate funeral ceremonies that were an important part of Confucian ancestor veneration. The Mohists advocated a utilitarian approach and rejected elaborate court music, ritual, and funerals because state resources were wasted on these activities when those resources could benefit the people. They also repudiated offensive warfare. Mozi rejected the Confucian concept of *ming* (destiny), and his text makes no mention of the aristocratic Confucian distinction between the "prince of virtue" or gentleman and the "petty person." Mozi especially spurned the Confucian clan value of graded love, advocating *jianai* (love for everyone). His idea of love for everyone was possibly derived from the Confucian ideal of *shu* (empathy). Love for everyone is based on treating other states, families, and persons as if they were one's own. Mozi's idea of love for everyone is not correctly translated as universal love because *jian* implies "for each," not "for all," and love in this context is moral concern, not deep emotional affection. Mozi considered concern for everyone to be the unifying principle of morality. For later Mohists, love for everyone entailed a notion of moral equality but not social equality.

During the fourth and third centuries BCE the Mohist school was well organized under a grand master. By the end of that period the school split into three sects that denounced each other as heretics. The three sects differed in interpretation of the teachings of Mozi. There were the purists, the compromisers, and the reactionaries. Mohists who took office were expected to donate funds to the organization, and the grand master could remove them from office. The sects taught ten basic principles contained in the ten core essays of the Mozi, namely, Elevation of the Worthy; Conforming Upwards; Concern for Everyone; Rejection of Aggression; Thrift in Utilization; Thrift in Funerals; Heaven's Intent; Elucidating Ghosts; Rejection of Music; and Rejection of Destiny. Many chapters have three versions, which are probably derived from the three sects.

Mohist doctrines were new. So they had to argue on their own behalf, which began systematic debate in ancient China. The expressions "to argue out alternatives" and "to distinguish" or "rational discourse" are first used in the Mozi. The Mozi also proposes that the correctness of an idea does not depend on the person who thought it. Where the Confucians expect thinkers to both talk about and exemplify the way, Mohists discuss ideas based on their own merits regardless of who presents them.

Mozi delineated three criteria to evaluate arguments: the roots, evidence, and use. A position is accepted if one can trace its roots to practices of the ancient sages. It is assented to if it is in accord with the understanding of the masses and if, when applied in the administration of the state or in punishing of wrongdoers, it brings benefit to the people. The practical and utilitarian focus of Mozi's philosophy is notable. Mozi is unique among ancient moralists in the belief that if an idea or practice has been handed down from the ancient sages but does not benefit the people, then he rejects it. Utilitarianism is the basis of many of his criticisms of Confucianism.

James D. Sellmann

Further Reading

Chan Wing-tsit. (1963) *A Source Book in Chinese Philosophy*. Princeton, NJ: Princeton University Press.

Fung Yu-lan. (1952) *History of Chinese Philosophy*. Vol. 1. Trans. by Derk Bodde. Princeton, NJ: Princeton University Press.

Graham, Angus C. (1978) *Later Mohist Logic, Ethics and Science*. Hong Kong: Chinese University Press; London: School of Oriental and African Studies.

———. (1989) *Disputers of the Tao*. La Salle, IL: Open Court.

Hsiao Kung-chuan. (1979) *A History of Chinese Political Thought*. Trans. by Frederick Mote. Princeton, NJ: Princeton University Press.

Mei Yi-pao. (1980) *The Works of Motze*. Taipei, Taiwan: Confucius Publishing.

Watson, Burton, trans. (1967) *The Basic Writings of Mo Tzu, Hsun Tzu, and Han Fei Tzu*. New York: Columbia University Press.

MUANG

MUANG *Muang* (also *mong, meng, muang, muong, meuang*) is a key concept of sociopolitical organization and interpretation of the universe in Tai societies; that is, in societies in which a language in the Tai language family is spoken. The term *muang* is known in all Tai languages and can refer to:

1. a municipality that is a political and ritual center;
2. a sociopolitical unit ("small state" or "chiefdom") consolidated from a number of *baan* (village communities), with an economy based on wet-rice production using the *muang-faai* (canal-weir) irrigation system;
3. a larger political unit that integrated traditional forms of *muang* administration and the Indian mandala concept of the centralized state (concentration of political, religious and spiritual power in the center, which is the seat of a sacred ruler known as devaraja), such as the Tai Buddhist kingdoms of Sukhothai (thirteenth–fourteenth century), Laan Naa (thirteenth–twentieth century), Laan Saang (fourteenth–seventeenth century), Ayutthaya (fourteenth–eighteenth century), and modern nation states; and
4. the traditional Tai understanding of the universe, which consists of numbers of *muang* of worldly as well as supernatural and heavenly nature, all underlying a specific cosmic order or universal law, which determines human ritual life, customary law, the moral order, and behavior.

History

Pre-Buddhist Tai societies were organized principally in so-called *baan-muang* systems. *Baan* (a group of extended families) often but not necessarily were bound together by kinship relations. A *baan* occupied a certain territory *(din baan)* that traditionally included cultivated land, sacred forests, wild forests, and watercourses. Because they were wet-rice-growing societies, Tai *baan* could not have sustained themselves in isolation: the water irrigation necessary for wet-rice cultivation demanded the cooperation of several *baan* communities in the same watershed area. The cooperation of *baan* in irrigation groups probably was the primary reason for founding *muang*, that is, a group of several *baan* managing one common irrigation system, and generally worshiping the same territorial guardian spirit and spirit of the main weir.

Wyatt observes that the *muang* was the primary unit of social and political organization above the village level. He says, "When it is used in ancient chronicles to refer to a principality, it can mean both the town located at the hub of a network of interrelated villages and also the totality of town and villages which was ruled by a single chau, 'lord'" (Wyatt 1984: 7).

The inner structure of a *muang* was characterized by a decentralized administration and a hierarchical order, at the top of which was *muang luang*, the municipality in which the *chau muang* ("chief/lord of the *muang*" resided. The *chau* fulfilled not only the function of a political leader but also the role of the head of administration, and, in time of war, he or she had to organize mutual defense. For this protection, the *baan* rendered labor service or paid quantities of local produce in return. This was a mutually beneficial relationship, supported by the belief that the *chau* was provided with sacred power from the *muang* ancestors. The *chau* did not, however, have the status of a *devaraja* (god-king), a concept that was introduced only with the process of Indianization in the eleventh to fourteenth century, and his power was not that of an absolute monarch. Besides the *chau*, there existed a council of elders elected by several *baan*. This council made decisions regarding irrigation and administration, as well as regarding legal and religious affairs.

The political structure of *muang* has led scholars such as Bruneau to characterize it as rural democracy. Furthermore, the traditional Tai *muang* accommodated the non-Tai populace without affecting those groups' traditional community structure, and established diplomatic and tributary relationships with neighboring states (Khmer, Mon, Vietnamese, Chinese) to maintain inner stability as well as a political balance with external powers.

On the economic front, the *muang* could mobilizc manpower efficiently in a large region, which ensured economic stability. There were enough natural resources and technologies were not so highly developed; therefore manpower was most important for economic stability. The economic surplus was mainly used for ritual purposes and the maintenance of friendly relationships with neighboring powers; it was also invested in articles of value, such as gold, silver, precious stones, and in the establishment of communal utilities. The surplus generally was not, however, used for building ritual-political prestige objects, as it was the case in the Khmer and Mon empires.

From *Muang* to Mandala

Under the influence of the Indianized Mon and Khmer, the Tai *chau muang* adopted not only Buddhism but also Indian concepts of the state, such as the mandala concept. They sought to make their *muang* into Buddhist kingdoms *(raja-anachak)* by unifying a number of *muang* with which they had kinship or friendly relations, or by occupying and subjugating weaker *muang*. The strength of the early Tai kingdoms that appeared suddenly in the thirteenth and fourteenth centuries probably can be explained through the integration of the traditional practice of decentralized administration and the Indian ideology of the centralized state. In other words, the ruler formally had the status of a *devaraja*, but, in practice, the several *muang* forming a kingdom were relatively autonomous in inner affairs and in maintaining relations with other *muang*. Except for Ayutthaya and the later Siam, where the *muang* administration system was radically transformed into the sakdina system(classification of the society according to the possession of rice fields), the practice of integrating both the traditional *muang* administration and the mandala ideology of the centralized state was preserved among the Tai peoples until the beginning of European colonization in the nineteenth century.

Oliver Raendchen

Further Reading

Bruneau, Michel. (1968) "Irrigation traditionelle et moderne dans le nord de la Thailande: l'example du Bassin de Chiengmai." In *Communication à l'Association des Géographes Français:* 1–12.

Cam Trong. (1978) *Nguoi Thai o Tay Bac Viet Nam* (The Tai peoples of Vietnam). Hanoi, Vietnam: Nha Xuat Ban Khoa Hoc Xa Hoi.

Coedes, George. (1996) *The Indianized States of Southeast Asia.* 3rd ed., edited by Walter F. Vella. Honolulu: University of Hawaii Press.

Davis, Richard B. (1984) *Muang Metaphysics: A Study of Northern Thai Myth and Ritual.* Studies in Thai Anthropology, no. 1. Bangkok, Thailand: Pandora.

Keyes, Charles F. (1987) *Thailand: Buddhist Kingdom as Modern Nation State.* Boulder, CO: Westview Press.

Lemoine, Jacques. (1997) "Féodalité Tai chez les Lü des Sipsong Panna et les Tai Blancs, Noirs et Rouges du Nord Ouest du Viêt-Nam." *Péninsule* 35, 2.

Matras-Guin, Jacqueline, and Christian Taillard, eds. (1992) *Habitations et habitat d'Asie du Sud-Est continentale: Pratiques et représentations de l'espace.* Paris: L'Harmattan.

Raendchen, Oliver, and Jana Raendchen, eds. (1998) "Baan-müang: Administration and Ritual." Thematic issue. *Tai Culture: International Review on Tai Cultural Studies* 3, 2.

Surarerks, Vanpen. (1986) *Historical Development and Management of Irrigation Systems in Northern Thailand.* Chiang Mai, Thailand: Chiang Mai University.

Turton, Andrew, ed. (2000) *Civility and Savagery: Social Identity in Tai States.* Richmond, U.K.: Curzon.

Wijeyewardene, Gehan. (1986) *Place and Emotion in Northern Thai Ritual Behaviour.* Studies in Thai Anthropology, no. 2. Bangkok, Thailand: Pandora.

Wijeyewardene, Gehan, and E. C. Chapman, eds. (1993) *Patterns and Illusions: Thai History and Thought.* 2d ed. Singapore: Institute of Southeast Asian Studies.

Wyatt, David Kent. (1984) *Thailand: A Short History.* New Haven, CT: Yale University Press.

MUAY THAI Thai boxing *(muay Thai)* or kickboxing, as it is widely known outside Asia, is one of the several Asian martial arts that in the twentieth century enjoyed considerable popularity in the West. Thai boxing is believed to have developed in medieval Thailand, a time when wars between rival states were waged with bow and arrow, swords, pikes, and hand-to-hand combat involving the arms and legs, knees and elbows. Kickboxing was a component of military training and gained prominence during the reign of King Naresuan in 1560 CE. According to legend, Naresuan was taken prisoner during one of the many wars with neighboring Burma. He was given the opportunity to win his freedom by defeating Burma's best warriors in hand-to-hand combat. Using Thai boxing, he easily defeated all his opponents and was set free. Upon returning to Thailand, he established Thai boxing (then called Siamese boxing) as the national sport.

Thai boxing reached its greatest popularity in the eighteenth century during the reign of Pra Chao Sua when participants came from a broad spectrum of social classes and it was a regular form of entertainment featured at festivals.

In the twentieth century, the rules and equipment were systematized, arenas were built in every province, and the sport has been promoted as a Thai national treasure and then exported to many other nations. Kickboxing is now popular internationally and there are national associations in the United States and Canada and many European nations. In its modern form, the sport is much like boxing, except that the feet and legs may be used as weapons. In Thailand, there are fifteen weight categories ranging from mini-flyweight (48 kilograms or less) to heavyweight (80 kilograms or more). While the sport originally required the use of bare or leather- or hemp-covered knuckles, participants now use regulation-weight boxing gloves but remain barefoot.

Muay Thai bouts take place in a raised square ring with a canvas surface and four ropes along each side. In addition to the boxers and the referee in the ring, at ringside are the handlers, judges, medical personnel, a timekeeper, a mediator, and other officials. Boxers wear red or blue boxing shorts and gloves. A sacred cord known as a *mongkol* may be worn around the head only during the prefight ritual, while amulets may be wrapped around biceps or waist if completely covered by cloth. In traditional matches, boxers pay respect to their teachers through a prayer ritual accompanied by Thai musical instruments: the *pi* (Java pipe), *glawng chana* (drum), and *ching* (cymbals). These instruments are also played during the bout but not during the rest periods. A bout lasts no more than five rounds, each three minutes long, with a two-minute rest period between rounds. The objective is to hit or kick one's opponent with the hand, foot, knee, or elbow so as to injure him, knock him out, or win points from the referee and judges. A bout is won by knockout, technical knockout, decision, or foul and can also end in a draw.

There are two major muay Thai venues in Bangkok (Ratchadamnoen Stadium and Lumpini Stadium) and one in Samut Prakarn (Sam Rong Stadium) and smaller stadiums in every province, with bouts two or three nights a week.

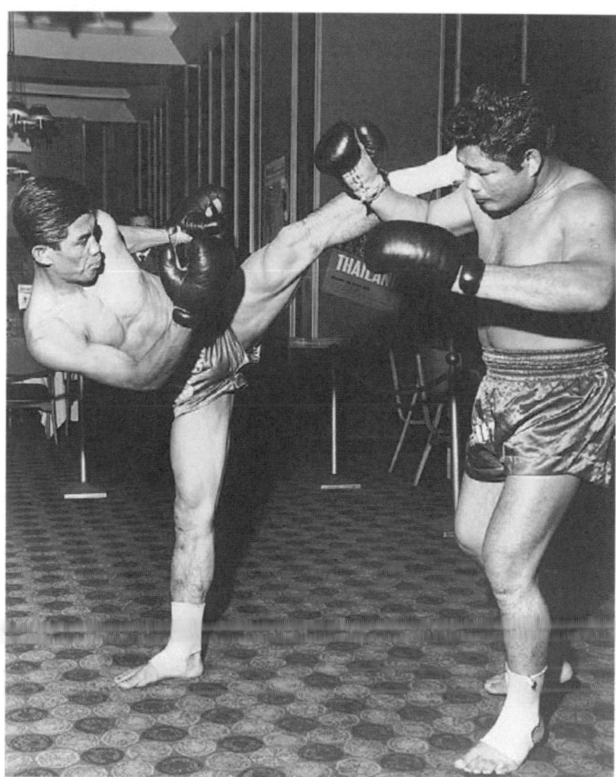

Thai boxers in the early 1970s. (HULTON-DEUTSCH COLLECTION/CORBIS)

Related to muay Thai is the martial art of *krabi-krabong*, which is based on the use of swords, spears, and axes. Unlike muay Thai, it has not emerged as a modern sport but instead has become a form of performance ritual in which participants act out a script accompanied by traditional Thai music.

David Levinson

Further Reading

Tourism Authority of Thailand. (2000) *A Traveller's Guide to Thailand*. Bangkok, Thailand: Tourism Authority of Thailand.

Wagner, Eric A. (1989) *Sport in Asia and Africa: A Comparative Handbook*. New York: Greenwood Press.

QUTB MINAR—WORLD HERITAGE SITE

The construction of this minaret in Delhi, India, began in 1193 and symbolized the dominance of the new Mughal empire over the last Hindu armies. A staggering 72.5-meters high, the Qutb Minar and its surrounding buildings—Mughal masterpieces in their own right—were designated a World Heritage Site in 1993.

MUGHAL EMPIRE

MUGHAL EMPIRE The Mughal empire (also known as the Moghul, Mongol, or Mongolian empire) was a large empire of the Indian subcontinent, controlled by a Muslim dynasty of central Asian origin from 1526 to 1857. It included, at its peak, much of present-day Pakistan, parts of Afghanistan, and most of northern, eastern, and central India.

It was established by Babur—Zahir-ud-Din Muhammad—(1483–1530), a descendant of the Turkic conqueror Timur (Tamerlane) and of Chagatai, second son of the Mongol ruler Chinggis Khan; hence the association with the Mongols. Babur's successor Humayun—Nasin-ud-Din Muhammad—(1508–1556) ruled briefly (1530–1543, 1555–1556) before facing Sher Shah's revolt and then living in exile in Safavid Iran for twelve years. The brief reestablishment of Mughal power on his return was abruptly halted by his death in 1556. The empire's high point came during the rule of Akbar—Abu-ul-Fath Jalal-ud-Din Muhammad Akbar—(1542–1605), who transformed the kingdom into a vast empire stretching from Kabul to the Deccan. Imperial administrative reforms and artistic patronage continued under his successors Jahangir (1569–1627) and Shah Jahan (1592–1666). The rule of the next successor, Aurangzeb—Alamgir or Muhi-ed-Din Muhammad—(1618–1707), however, was marked by a significant increase in Islamic orthodoxy, causing a substantial decline in artistic production and patronage. In contrast to the consolidated nature of the ear-

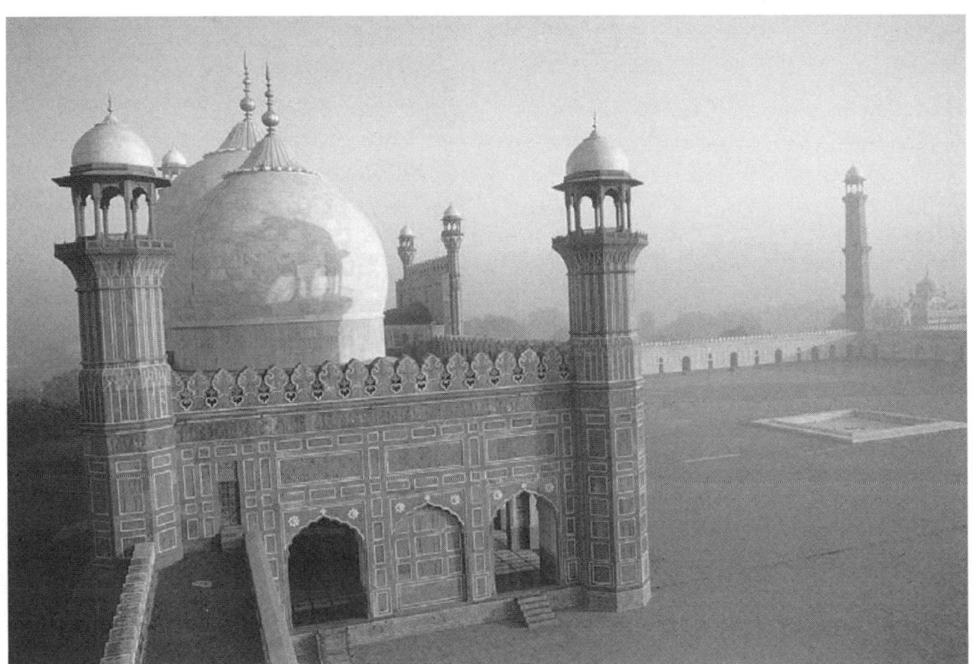

A mosque in Lahore, Pakistan, built during the Mughal empire. (CHRISTINE OSBORNE/CORBIS)

FATEHPUR—WORLD HERITAGE SITE

Fatehpur Sikri in Agra, India, became a UNESCO World Heritage Site in 1986. It was built as a capital city for the Mughal empire and contains the enormous Jama Masjid Mosque. Occupied for only ten years, this architectural gem was abandoned when the city ran out of water.

lier period, political instability and disintegration characterized the rule of the later Mughals until the empire finally dissolved in 1857. Factions such as the Hyderabad Nizams, and the Nawabs of Murshidabad and Lucknow, began gradually to break away. The Marathas made significant inroads in the region of Central India, while the British expanded their holdings in Bengal. Finally, the Sikhs emerged as a major militant force in Punjab. The biggest blow to the empire came with Nadir Shah's attack on the Mughal capital at Shahjahanbad (modern-day Delhi) in 1739. Not only did this result in rampant destruction and loss of life, it also put an end to the political and cultural dominance of the Mughals over India. The empire survived in a much-reduced form until the Indian Revolt of 1857, when the last Mughal emperor, Bahadur Shah Zafar (1775–1862), was captured by the British and exiled in Rangoon, Burma.

Manu Sobti

Further Reading

Bérinstain, Valérie. (1998) *India and the Mughal Dynasty.* New York: Abrams.

Habib, Irfan. (1982) *An Atlas of the Mughal Empire.* New York: Oxford University Press.

Koch, Ebba. (1991) *Mughal Architecture.* Munich: Prestel-Verlag.

Richards, J. F. (1993) *The Mughal Empire.* New York: Cambridge University Press.

Streusand, Douglas E. (1989) *The Formation of the Mughal Empire.* New York: Oxford University Press.

MUHAJIR *Muhajir* is an Arabic term designating a person who has gone on a hajj (the pilgrimage to Mecca, which is mandatory for all Muslims at least once in their lifetime).This term also gained a political overtone when it was applied to the millions of Muslim migrants who crossed the border into Pakistan from India in 1947. The British created Pakistan in 1947 as a homeland for Indian Muslims by separating parts of the Punjab and the Sind from India. This led to much bloodshed on both sides as Hindus and Muslims clashed in communal riots.

These migrants, or *muhajirs*, have faced constant discrimination from those who are native to the region and did not need to migrate. This ill will has led to frequent violent outbursts between *mujahirs* and non-*muhajirs*, with outright rioting in Sind Province in 1986–1987, when the *muhajir* political party, the MQM (Muhajir Qawmi Mahaz, the Muhajir's People Movement), gained political prominence. The MQM, under its leader Altaf Hussain, sought equal employment opportunities for people of *muhajir* descent. The political weight of the MQM was felt in the 1988 elections when it became the third-largest party in the Pakistani Assembly. The tensions continued until 1992, when the army moved to crush the MQM. The result was that the entire *muhajir* community bore the brunt of this violence because it was deemed guilty by association. From 1985 onward, the *muhajir* identity was politicized.

Nirmal Dass

Further Reading

Jamal, Rashid. (1998) *Muhajirs of Pakistan: Plight and Struggle for Survival.* Karachi, Pakistan: Loh-e-Abad Publication.

Verkaaik, Oskar. (1994) *A People of Migrants: Ethnicity, State, and Religion in Karachi.* Amsterdam: VU University Press.

MUHAJIR QAWMI MOVEMENT The Muhajir Qawmi Movement (MQM), an immigrant-rights organization, is based in Karachi, Pakistan, where the *muhajirs*, or immigrants, mostly Urdu speaking, came from India as a consequence of the partition of the subcontinent on 14–15 August 1947. In 1984, they started a *qawmi*, or national movement, for more political autonomy and economic opportunities in response to what they perceived as a continuous pattern of discrimination. The national government believed these demands were at the expense of the other ethnic groups such as the Punjabis, Pathans, and Baluchis, and, especially, the Sindis, of Sind Province, the capital of which is Karachi. Violence between ethnic and Sunni-Shi'a sectarian groups has plagued Karachi ever since. Pakistan military and rangers have been fighting the MQM armed activists, with drive-by shootings, execution-style murders, counter killings, and torture during police custody alleged by both sides. The government of Pakistan accuses India of supporting the MQM. Several attempts at resolving the worsening situation have failed. On 27 July

1997, the Muhajir Qawmi Movement was reorganized and transformed into the Mutthida Quami ("united national") Movement, with the same initials, under the new leadership of Altaf Hussain. Hussain, who is wanted in Pakistan under criminal charges, lives in exile in England, where he received British citizenship in February 2001.

Abdul Karim Khan

Further Reading

Jafri, A. B. S. (1996) *Behind the Killing Fields of Karachi: A City Refuses to Surrender*. Karachi, Pakistan: Royal Book Co.

Verkaaik, Oskar. (1994). *A People of Migrants: Ethnicity, State, and Religion in Karachi*. Amsterdam, Netherlands: VU University Press.

MUHAMMADIYAH The Muhammadiyah was established on 18 November 1912 in Yogyakarta, Java, Indonesia, by K. H. Ahmad Dahlan (1868–1923), as a socioreligious organization aimed at adapting Islamic teachings to modern life. It is considered the largest educational and social movement in Southeast Asia. It is said to be inspired by the Egyptian reform movement of Muhammad ʿAbduh (1849–1905), which professed a rational approach to Islamization. Its activities are multifaceted, encompassing religious education, social welfare (running of orphanages and hospitals), and promotion of economic development.

From the Muhammadiyah perspective, Islamic ideology advocates the abolition of TBC: *Tachyul* (myths), *Bidʿah* (religious innovations), and *Churafat* (superstitions). According to the Muhammadiyah's teachings, TBC, also the acronym for tuberculosis, needs to be eradicated like the deadly disease. Relics of local pre-Islamic religious practices and the weakening of "pure" Islamic values are perceived as obstacles to progress.

The Muhammadiyah, like the Christian missionaries before it, considered education as the way to progress. It set up modern schools to teach Dutch, English, and the sciences. The organization runs over a thousand schools from kindergarten to university level, across Indonesia.

The organization was criticized by radical Indonesian nationalists for accepting government funding for its schools, and for alleged cooperation with the Dutch colonial rulers. As well, as a "modernist" organization, the Muhammadiyah is persistently challenged by the Nahdlatul Ulama (NU), a "traditional" socioreligious organization in Indonesia. The Muhammadiyah publishes many educational books and other publications.

It has set up hospitals, clinics, maternity centers, and nursing schools in major cities, towns, and rural areas. It has autonomous wings for youth, for school and university students, and for women. The latter, the ʿAisyiyah, is the largest Muslim women's organization in the world. The Muhammadiyah also runs poorhouses, labor unions, cooperatives, and factories. It is praised for efficiency, leadership, and good management. Many of its organizers and members are volunteers as well as donors.

The Muhammadiyah claims 30 million followers, including sympathizers, mainly from middle-class and urban backgrounds. It has branches and followers in other Southeast Asian countries, making it one of the few transnational movements in the region. The Muhammadiyah has been compared by many to the Protestant movement. Its former head, Dr. M. Amien Rais, president of the Muhammadiyah-supported National Mandate Party (Partai Amanat Nasional), was chosen in October 1999 to be speaker of the People's Consultative Assembly (Majlis Permusyawaratan Rakyat), the highest state political institution in Indonesia.

Andi Faisal Bakti

Further Reading

Alfian. (1989) *Muhammadiyah: The Political Behavior of a Muslim Modernist Organization under Dutch Colonialism*. Yogyakarta, Indonesia: Gadjah Mada University Press.

Jainuri, Ahmad. (1997) "The Formation of the Muhammadiyah's Ideology 1912–1942." Ph.D. diss., McGill University.

Noer, Deliar. (1973) *The Modernist Muslim Movement in Indonesia, 1900–1942*. Singapore: Oxford University Press.

Peacock, James L. (1978) *Purifying the Faith: The Muhammadijah Movement in Indonesian Islam*. Menlo Park, CA: Benjamin/Cummings.

Shihab, M. Alwi. (1995) "The Muhammadiyah Movement and Its Controversy with Christian Missionaries in Indonesia." Ph.D. diss., Temple University.

MUJAHIDEEN The word "mujahideen" is Arabic for "warriors of god," or "holy warriors," which is the term most recently applied to the Afghani Muslim militia. In the 1980s the mujahideen were organized in response to the Soviet invasion of Afghanistan. Members were mostly drawn from tribes and villagers. Reportedly, many mujahideen members were among those Afghans who lost family and friends during the Soviet invasion. However, the mujahideen also included some Muslim foreign forces who stood alongside Afghans in the struggle against atheist Communist Russians. The mujahideen were mainly organized by tribal leaders, although the leadership also included some people from the cities.

During the decade between 1979 and 1989, the mujahideen were able to challenge the Soviet army despite their limited forces, which were estimated at between 80,000 and 150,000. This resistance group received military support from both American and Pakistani secret intelligence agencies and financial assistance from the United States and Saudi Arabia, both of which hoped to destabilize Soviet influence in the region and contain Communism. Against all odds, the mujahideen were victorious, and Afghanistan was proclaimed an Islamic state in April 1992. Once the war was over, however, conflicts developed among the various factions of the mujahideen, creating an explosive political environment in Afghanistan, and the mujahideen's activities spilled over into other areas of the Central Asian region.

Houman A. Sadri

Further Reading

Cordovez, Diego. (1995) *Out of Afghanistan: The Inside Story of the Soviet Withdrawal.* New York: Oxford University Press.

Jalali, Ali Ahmad. (1999) *The Other Side of the Mountain: Mujahideen Tactics in the Soviet-Afghan War.* Quantico, VA: U.S. Marine Corps, Studies and Analysis Division.

Kakar, M. Hassan. (1995) *Afghanistan: The Soviet Invasion and the Afghan Response, 1979–1982.* Berkeley and Los Angeles: University of California Press.

Mialey, William. (1998) *Fundamentalism Reborn? Afghanistan and the Taliban.* New York: New York University Press.

Rai, Rasul Bux. (1994) *War without Winners: Afghanistan's Uncertain Transition after the Cold War.* New York: Oxford University Press.

MULTAN (1998 pop. 1.2 million). A major city in Pakistan, Multan serves as the commercial and cultural center for southern Punjab Province. It was first mentioned in written sources as the place (identified as Malli) where Alexander (d. 323 BCE) was grievously injured during his campaigns in India. Multan was the site of an important Hindu temple at the time of the Arab Muslim invasion in 712 and gained significance as a commercial and administrative hub in subsequent centuries. Muslim rulers left the temple intact (and benefited from its revenues) until approximately the eleventh century. The city was a major western outpost during the Delhi Sultanate and Mughal periods (thirteenth to eighteenth centuries), though it was subject to invasions from the west. The Sikhs under Ranjit Singh (reigned 1801–1839) captured the city in 1818 but lost it to the expanding British Indian empire in 1848. Since the creation of Pakistan in 1947, Multan has been an important commercial market for crops such as cotton, wheat, and mangoes, and the city's hospitals, university, and medical college serve as a resource for the surrounding region.

Multan was one of the earliest centers of Islamic culture in India. Baha' al-Din Zakariyya (d. 1262 or 1267), whose mausoleum lies in the inner city, established the Suhravardi Sufi order from his seat in Multan. The city was also host to important Ismaili missionaries in the thirteenth and fourteenth centuries, including Pir Shams al-Din Sabzavari (d. c. 1300), whose tomb is still an important site. The tomb of Shah Rukn al-Din 'Alam (built c. 1315) is the finest example of local architecture and was originally built by the king for himself. Multan is famous today for its distinctive blue and white tilework and handicrafts made with camel skin. The city is also the literary and cultural center for people speaking Punjab's Siraiki dialect.

Shahzad Bashir

Further Reading

Dashti, Humaira Faiz. (1998) *Multan, A Province of the Mughal Empire, 1525–1751.* Karachi, Pakistan: Royal Book Co.

Khan, Ahmad Nabi. (1983) *Multan: History and Architecture.* Islamabad, Pakistan: Institute of Islamic History, Culture & Civilization, Islamic University.

Maclean, Derryl N. (1989) *Religion and Society in Arab Sind.* Leiden, Netherlands: E. J. Brill.

Raza, M. Hanif. (1988) *Multan: Past and Present.* Islamabad, Pakistan: Colorpix.

MUMBAI (2002 est. pop. 12.1 million). Bombay, renamed Mumbai in June 1981, is on the western coast of India. Endowed with a natural harbor and a wide bay facing Africa and East Asia, the city is partly on Bombay Island and other smaller islands in the harbor (originally seven main islands comprised Bombay; in 1784 these were merged through land reclamation), and the archipelago is a natural shipping and trading center. Around the third century BCE, fishermen living here worshiped the goddess Mumba Devi, after whom the city is named.

From the ninth to thirteenth centuries, the Arabian Sea (the part of the Indian Ocean between Arabia and India) played an integral role in world commerce, and heavy freight traffic occurred between Aden, Calicut, Cambay, and cities on the west coast of Africa. The caves of Elephanta (a small island in the harbor) and part of the Walkeshwar temple complex that was built at this time indicate that Elephanta belonged to the

BOMBAY IN THE 1800s

"Every family visiting Bombay, must feel the great inconvenience of there being neither a hotel, or other place of public accommodation, at which they can put up, in the event of their not possessing an acquaintance, whose hospitality they may venture to claim; and this position, however awkward and perplexing, is one in which individuals are commonly placed, who have long been residents at a distance from the Presidency. The Victoria Hotel solicits the patronage of travellers; but, as it is situated in the very dirtiest and very narrowest street of the fort, the additional annoyances of flights of mosquitoes, a billiard table, a coffee and a tap room, place it without the pale of respectable support. The Sanitarium affords shelter to invalids, and is delightfully situated, where the smooth sands and fine sea-breeze render it a tempting locality for the convalescent; but the rooms are far too small for family accommodation. In this dilemma, visitors usually pitch tents on the esplanade; and if in the hot season, cause them to be *chuppered in*, as the phrase is, or a false roof erected with bamboos and date leaves, to secure them equally from the intense heat of the midday sun, and the evil effects of the evening dews."

Source: Mrs. Thomas Postans. (1839) *Western India in 1838*, as quoted in *The Sahibs* (1948), edited by Hilton Brown. London: William Hodge & Co., 79–80.

Silhara dynasty, ruled by the sultan of Gujarat in western India. The mosque in Mahim in the northern part of Bombay also dates to this period.

In 1534, Bahadur Shah of Gujarat was forced to cede the islands of Bombay to the Portuguese. Saint Andrew's church in Bandra, a suburb of modern Mumbai, dates from this period. In 1661, Catherine of Braganza (1638–1705) brought the islands to Charles II (1630–1685) of England as part of her dowry. The British East India Company received them from the crown in 1668, built the city, and moved its main holdings to Bombay from Surat, a city to its north. Gerald Aungier (d. c. 1677), the second governor of the city (1672–1675), capitalized on the Mughal empire's lack of interest in developing its naval strength and developed the islands into a center of commerce. Skilled workers and traders—Parsis (Zoroastrians), Bhoras (a branch of the Ismaili sect of Shi'a Islam), Jews, and *bania*s (a Hindu merchant caste) from Surat and Diu, northwest of Bombay—migrated to Bombay. The population increased from 10,000 in 1661 to an unprecedented 60,000 in 1675. The influx of skilled workers continued with the migration of goldsmiths, ironsmiths, and weavers who came from Gujarat. The Hornby Vellard refers to the landmass created by the merging of the seven islands of Bombay. The Mahim Causeway (1845) was another British engineering feat. In 1853, a thirty-five-kilometer-long railway line between Thana, a suburb of the city, and Bombay was inaugurated, the first of its kind in India, and in 1854 the first cotton mill was founded, drawing large-scale migration of Marathi workers from south-central India.

After the First War of Indian Independence in 1857, Bombay came under the control of the crown, as the East India Company was accused of misman-

ELEPHANTA CAVES—WORLD HERITAGE SITE

Designated a UNESCO World Heritage Site in 1987, the "city of caves" is home to many fabulous bas-relief limestone carvings dedicated to the Hindu god Siva. The Elephanta Caves are located on a small island just off the Indian city of Mumbai.

agement. Increased commercial enterprise necessitated improved communication within the country, and imperial Bombay evolved in the nineteenth and twentieth centuries. Bombay played a key role in the Indian independence movement. The business capital of India and the nerve center of India's economy, Mumbai today boasts the largest and busiest port of India and has the country's largest stock exchange, the third largest in the world. The gigantic Indian film industry, Bollywood, is located in Mumbai and churns out hundreds of Hindi films yearly.

Kokila Ravi

Further Reading

Enthoven, Reginald Edward. (1924) *The Folklore of Bombay*. Oxford, U.K.: Clarendon Press.

Gupchup, Vijaya V. (1993) *Bombay: Social Change, 1813–1857*. Mumbai, India: Popular Book Depot.

Moraes, Dom F. (1979) *Bombay*. Time-Life Books. Amsterdam, Netherlands: Time-Life.

Patel, Sujata, and Alice Thorner, eds. (1995) *Bombay: Metaphor for Modern India*. Mumbai, India: Oxford University Press.

Rohatgi, Pauline, Pheroza Godrej, and Rahul Mehrotra, eds. (1997) *Bombay to Mumbai: Changing Perspectives*. Mumbai, India: Marg.

Subramanian, Lakshmi. (1996) *Indigenous Capital and Imperial Expansion: Bombay, Surat, and the West Coast*. Delhi: Oxford University Press.

Tindall, Gilliam. (1982) *City of Gold: The Biography of Bombay*. London: Templesmith.

MUNDA LANGUAGES

Munda languages, which belong to the Austroasiatic language group, are spoken by about 9 million people in northern and central India. Friedrich von Max Müller (1823–1900) first clearly distinguished the family from the Dravidian language family. Some scholars divide the languages into two subfamilies: the North Munda (spoken in the Chota Nagpur plateau of Jharkhand, Orissa, and Bengal), including Satali, Korku, Mundari, Bhumij, and Ho; and the South Munda (spoken in central Orissa and along the border between Andhra Pradesh and Orissa). South Munda is further divided into Central Munda, including Kharia and Juang, and Koraput Munda, including Gutob, Remo, Savara, Juray, and Gorum.

North Munda languages, the more important of the two groups, are spoken by about nine-tenths of Munda speakers. Of these, Santali is the chief language. The Mundari and Ho languages rank next in the number of speakers, followed by Korku and Soara. The remaining Munda languages are spoken by small isolated groups and are little known.

General Characteristics

The Munda languages are polysyllabic and differ from other Austroasiatic languages in their word formation and sentence structure. The structure of the Munda languages is quite different from that of any language in the Indo-European group. In many ways it is simpler and calls for far less memory than Indo-European languages do.

Munda languages characteristically have three numbers (singular, dual, and plural), two classes (animate and inanimate) for nouns, and the use of either suffixes or auxiliaries for indicating tenses of verb forms. Munda languages possess nothing corresponding to the cases of direct and indirect objects. These relations find their expression in the verb.

In Munda sound systems, consonant sequences are infrequent, except in the middle of a word. Hard and soft consonants are freely used, and both classes can be aspirated. Another characteristic feature of the Munda languages is the presence of semiconsonants. Except in Korku, in which syllables show a distinction between high and low tone, accent is even in the Munda languages. Words are formed from bases or other words through reduplication or by adding affixes. The most important method of modifying a root is by the insertion of infixes. The Munda languages possess a rich stock of words denoting individual things and ideas but are poor in general and abstract terms.

Santali

Santali is the most important of the Munda languages. Santali is spoken over a vast region extending from the south of Bhagalpur and Monghyr in Bihar to Birbhum and west of Burdwan in West Bengal; almost the whole of Bankura; western Midnapore; the greater part of Mayurbhanj and northeast of Keonjhar in Orissa; and Seraikela, Kharsawan, Manbhum, and the Sonthal Parganas in Jharkhand. There are further scattered settlements in the southwest of Murshidabad; in the central part of Twenty-Four Parganas; in the jungles of south Dinajpur; and in the adjoining tracts of Malda, Rajshahi, Bogra, and southwest Rangpur. However, Santali is the principal language only in the Santal Parganas. Elsewhere minor Munda languages coexist with Santali.

Santali has only two dialects, Karmali and Mahle, and these do not differ much from the standard form of speech. The language, particularly the vocabulary, has been to an extent influenced by neighboring Aryan languages, notably Hindi, Bengali, and Oriya. The purest form of Santali is spoken in the north, especially in the Santal Parganas and in Manbhum. The dialect spoken in Midnapore, Balasore, and Singhbhum is more mixed and shows evidence of Aryan influence.

Santali has a richly developed system of vowels, which are long as well as short. A set of Santali vowels called neutral is apparently due to the influence of an *i* or *u* in the preceding or following syllable. There is a tendency to make the sound of vowels in consecutive syllables approach each other. Santali possesses the same set of consonants as Hindi: four gutturals, four palatals (consonants formed with the front of the tongue behind the lowered tip near or behind the hard palate), four dentals (consonants articulated with the tip or blade of the tongue against or near the upper front teeth), and four labials (consonants that derive their tones by the impact of air current on the lip), with the corresponding nasals (consonants uttered through the nose with the mouth passage occluded). In addition to the sounds *y*, *r*, *l*, *v*, *w*, *s*, and *h*, there are four semiconsonants *k'*, *ch'*, *t'*, *p'*, during the plosion of which contact is released before the breath comes out, and in this way an abrupt sound is produced.

Santali makes use of numerous affixes of various kinds: prefixes, infixes, and suffixes. Most of them play a role in what corresponds to the inflectional system of Indo-European languages. An infix *-k'-* is used to form intensives from verbs. Distributives are formed from some numerals beginning with vowels. An infix *-p-* is used to form collective nouns and reciprocal verbs. It is thus added to *manjhi* (headman) to form the collective *mapanjhi* (a group of village headmen). Similarly, the infix *-n-* is used to form collective numerals and *-t-* to form nouns from verbs.

In Santali every word can perform the function of a verb, and every verb form can, according to circumstances, be considered a noun, adjective, or verb. The relation of one verb to another in a sentence is indicated by means of particles, the original meaning of which can no longer be ascertained.

There are two classes of nouns in Santali, one denoting animate objects and the other all inanimate objects. Gender plays no role in the inflexion of nouns but is indicated by using different words or by prefixing certain words meaning male and female. There are three numbers: singular, dual, and plural. The suffix of the dual is *-kin* and that of the plural *-ko*. The suffix of the plural, however, is often dispensed with, and the base is used as a collective singular. Real cases, which denote the relation of the noun to the verb, do not exist in Santali. The verb indicates direct and indirect objects, and there is therefore no dative or accusative case. Local and causal relations are indicated by means of postpositions rather than by prepositions.

Adjectives do not change for gender and number. It is often simply a matter of convenience which word is considered a noun and which an adjective. Postpositions after the compared noun are used to indicate comparisons. Pronouns are, generally speaking, inflected like nouns in number and case. Personal pronouns have separate forms for dual and plural. The first-person pronoun, moreover, has two forms each in the dual and the plural, one excluding and one including the person addressed. Demonstrative pronouns are used as personal pronouns of the third person. There is also a pronoun meaning "self," which can be considered a third-person personal pronoun. There are no honorific pronouns; most people are addressed with the pronoun *am* (thou).

Santali possesses a rich variety of demonstrative pronouns, which have different forms according to whether they refer to animate or inanimate objects. The former group ends in *i* (singular), *kin* (dual number), and *ko* (plural) when referring to inanimate objects. When referring to animate objects, the pronoun ends in *a* (singular), *akin* (dual), and *ako* (plural). Thus, "this animal" translates as *nui* and "this thing" as *noa*. There are no relative pronouns; verbal adjectives are used instead.

The verb is the most characteristic feature of Santali grammar. Various tenses are formed by agglutination, that is, by suffixing certain elements to the unchanged root. To indicate that an action has really taken place, the categorical *a* is added to the root. This changes the inflectional base to a finite tense. A verb's indirect or direct object is indicated by means of pronominal infixes. Santali verbs have separate forms for active voice, passive or direct middle voice, and indirect middle voice. The root of the verb remains unchanged through all tenses. It can be modified in two ways to form the base of a separate conjugation. These two forms are conjugated throughout all tenses. The root can simply be repeated, the resulting double base denoting repeated or intensified action. Thus, *dal* ("strike") means "strike repeatedly or hard" as *dal-dal*. If the verb begins with a vowel, the infix *k'* is used instead of reduplication.

Verbs do not change according to person. For animates, the person of the subject is indicated through pronominal suffixes, which are added to the word immediately preceding the verb. If a sentence consists of only a verb, the suffix is added after the categorical *a*. Suffixes of times have two forms, one denoting active and the other passive and middle. The former ends in *t'* and the latter in *n*. Actions in the past are denoted by two infixes, *-ke* and *-le*. The former is used only in the active voice with a direct object. The infix *-le* denotes an action performed in the more remote past. It is used both in the active voice with a direct object and in the passive. Compound tenses are formed by inserting auxiliaries between the inflectional base and *a*. Usually the negative particle is a prefix *ban*. In the case of pronominal suffixes the final *n* is dropped.

Mundari

Mundari is the language spoken by the Munda tribe concentrated in the southern and western parts of the Ranchi district, Palamau, and southeast Hazaribagh, all in the state of Jharkhand in India. Mundari is also spoken along with Ho in north Singhbhum and in the Bamra and Sambalpur districts in Orissa and the neighboring districts of Madhya Pradesh. Emigrants, moreover, have carried the language to districts of Bengal and Assam. In Mundari there are a great number of Aryan roots, many belonging to Sanskrit and other related Indian languages.

Mundari and Santali have much in common. The laws of harmonic sequence are the same in Mundari as in Santali. In the pronunciation of semiconsonants there appears to be a tendency to exhale the current of air through the nose instead of through the mouth. In pronouncing the dental semiconsonants a greater part of the tongue strikes against the palate in Mundari than in Santali. The semiconsonants have the same tendency to develop into soft consonants in both languages.

Genders and numbers are the same in Mundari and Santali. However, in Sambalpur and Bamra, where the Aryan influence is the strongest, the dual and the plural are sometimes confused. The case suffixes, again, are mainly the same in both languages. Outside the Ranchi district the Aryan suffix *-ke* is often used for the dative and accusative. In Mundari, adjectives usually end in *-n* (*bugi-n* = good). Personal pronouns are similar to Santali forms, though Mundari does not seem to possess the rich variety of demonstrative pronouns that Santali has.

The inflection of verbs is mainly the same as in Santali, and the pronominal infixes play the same role. The categorical *a* is dropped after the pronominal infix *-ak'-*. The pronominal infixes too have the same role in Mundari and Santali, and the conjugational bases are similarly formed.

There are, however, certain differences between the Mundari and Santali languages. Usually the future and past tenses of reservative (continuative) forms begin with *t* in Mundari, whereas in Santali they begin with *k*. Although the perfect is formed as in Santali, the infixes of the direct and indirect objects are not distinguished. In Mundari, the negative particles are *ka* and *alo*.

An interesting characteristic of Mundari is the use of distinct words for forms or modes of activity, which are denoted in other languages by a single common verb or abstract noun.

Ho

Ho is spoken by the people of the Ho tribe in Singhbhum, Kharsawan, and Seraikela districts of Jharkhand and the adjoining districts of Mayurbhanj, Keonjhar, and Gangpur in Orissa.

In common with other Munda languages, Ho also has unchangeable primary roots, which can be used for nouns, verbs, or adjectives. There are three numbers, singular, dual, and plural. Ho makes a distinction between animate and inanimate beings. There is no declension of nouns, the root remains static, and various postpositions are affixed in cases where in some other language the nouns would be declined. Nouns can be formed from roots that have a primary verb function by adding the nominalizing infix, *-n-*. An *-n-* is infixed after the first vowel of a word, and the vowel then is repeated. Nouns can also be formed from participal forms and adjectival roots.

The Ho language so closely resembles the Mundari language that these two languages can practically be considered dialects of the same language rather than two separate languages. Nevertheless, many hundreds of words in Ho are not used in Mundari and vice versa. Moreover, although both languages may contain the same word, its meaning may vary in nuance. To some extent, the Ho spoken in the northern part of Singhbhum more closely resembles Mundari than the Ho spoken in Kolhan, the central part of Singhbhum.

An important difference between the two languages is the treatment of the hard *r*. It is retained in Mundari, but dropped in Ho. Thus, the Mundari *kora* (a boy) becomes *koa* in Ho. While semiconsonants are treated as in Mundari, the final *t'* of verbal tenses becomes *d*, or it is retained by sounding very weakly. Ho nasalizes the vowel in some Mundari words ending in the letter *l* or *r*. Because Ho words can never have *h* in the middle of a word, words that have an *h* in the middle in Mundari drop the *h* in Ho, and the adjoining vowels form one vowel. Thus, *sahatin* ("endure" or "persevere") in Munda is *satin* in Ho.

Relationship to Other Languages

Several Aryanized tribes in northern India are believed to have spoken a dialect of Munda. Traces of the old Munda element are still extant in some Tibeto-Burmese dialects spoken in the Himalayas. In India proper, the Munda languages form an isolated philological group. It is surmised that Munda languages were once widely spoken in central India and probably also in the Gangetic valley.

While it is no longer possible to determine the extent to which Munda languages influenced the other linguistic families of India, scholars have pointed to the existence of a Munda element in Dravidian grammar. Around one hundred Sanskrit and Prakrit words have been shown to be derived from the Proto-Munda branch of the Austroasiatic source. The term "Proto-Munda" indicates that the Munda languages had departed considerably from the Austroasiatic language type as early as the Vedic period (seventh–fifth centuries BCE) in a process of Dravidization of the Munda tongues. A considerable amount (say some 40 percent) of the New Indo-Aryan vocabulary is borrowed from Munda, either via Sanskrit (and Prakrit), or via Prakrit alone, or directly from Munda; wide-branched and seemingly native word-families of South Dravidian are of Proto-Munda origin.

Sanjukta Das Gupta

Further Reading

Bodding, P. O. (1995) *A Santal Dictionary*. Vols. 1–5. New Delhi: Gyan Publishing House.

Deeney, J. (1975) *Ho Grammar and Vocabulary*. Chaibasa, India: Xavier Ho Publications.

———. (1991) *An Introduction to the Ho Language*. Chaibasa, India: Xavier Ho Publications.

Hoffmann, John Baptist. (2001) *Mundari Grammar and Exercises*. New Delhi: Gyan Publishing House.

Mitra, Parimal Chandra. (1991) *Santhali: A Universal Heritage*. Calcutta, India: Firma KLM Private, Ltd.

Ramaswami, N. (1992) *Bhumij Grammar*. Mysore, India: Central Institute of Indian Languages.

Sinha, N. K. (1975) *Mundari Grammar*. Mysore, India: Central Institute of Indian Languages.

Zide, Norman N. (1969) "Munda and Non-Munda Austroasiatic Languages." In *Current Trends in Linguistics 5: Linguistics in South Asia*, edited by Thiams A. Sebeck et al. The Hague, Netherlands, and Paris: Mouton, 411–430.

MURASAKI SHIKIBU (973?–1014?), Japanese writer. Murasaki Shikibu wrote the undisputed masterpiece of Japanese literature *Genji monogatari* (*The Tale of Genji*, 1001?–1014?). This monumental prose work, interspersed with 795 short poems, takes place at the imperial court. Although much of the author's life remains a mystery, some facts can be gleaned from remarks by her contemporaries, her memoirs (c. 1010), and her poetry collection (1014?). The author's actual name is unknown. "Murasaki Shikibu" is a sobriquet made from "Murasaki," the name of the favorite wife of the eponymous hero of *Genji*, and "Shikibu," an office once held by her father Fujiwara Tametoki (945–1020) and her brother Nobunori (980?–1011). Although Murasaki Shikibu came from the powerful northern branch of the Fujiwara clan, her lineage had fallen to the level of provincial governor. As a writer she followed the path of her paternal relatives, many of whom were distinguished poets.

In 998, Murasaki married Fujiwara Nobutaka (950?–1001), a second cousin. She bore him one daughter, Kenshi (999–1083). Murasaki began writing soon after her husband's unexpected death in 1001. Her genius was immediately recognized, and she was summoned to the imperial court as a tutor to Empress Shoshi (Joto Mon'in, 988–1074), daughter of the brilliant statesman Fujiwara Michinaga (966–1027).

Doris G. Bargen

The illustrated diary of Lady Murasaki dating to c. 1185–1333. (SAKAMOTO PHOTO RESEARCH LABORATORY/CORBIS)

Further Reading

Bargen, Doris G. (1997) *A Woman's Weapon: Spirit Possession in The Tale of Genji.* Honolulu: University of Hawaii Press.

Bowring, Richard, trans. (1982) *Murasaki Shikibu: Her Diary and Poetic Memoirs.* Princeton, NJ: Princeton University Press.

Dalby, Liza. (2000) *The Tale of Murasaki: A Novel.* New York: Doubleday.

Field, Norma. (1987) *The Splendor of Longing in* The Tale of Genji. Princeton, NJ: Princeton University Press.

Morris, Ivan. (1964) *The World of the Shining Prince: Court Life in Ancient Japan.* Oxford, U.K.: Oxford University Press.

Seidensticker, Edward G., trans. (1976) *The Tale of Genji.* New York: Knopf.

Shirane, Haruo. (1987) *The Bridge of Dreams: A Poetics of* The Tale of Genji. Stanford, CA: Stanford University Press.

Tyler, Royall, trans. (2001) *The Tale of Genji.* New York: Viking Penguin.

MURGAB RIVER The Murgab River (also called the Murghob or Murghab in Tajik) is 978 kilometers long with a basin area of around 50,000 square kilometers. The river, which forms a part of the Afghanistan-Turkmenistan border, flows from the mountains of northeast Afghanistan through a narrow valley between the Bandi-Turkistan and Safad-Koh ranges into Turkmenistan's Merv oasis, then disappears in the Kara Kum desert. The river's highest flow is from March to July, as snow melts in the high mountains of Afghanistan, and its lowest in November and December.

The Murgab is one of the most important sources of drinking and irrigation water for southern Turkmenistan. Great cities flourished along the river for centuries. Merv (ancient Margiana), one of the oldest ancient cities in Central Asia, is situated on the Murgab in the large oasis of the Kara Kum desert. Probably founded in the third century BCE, the city became an important regional economic and trading center. From 1118 to 1157 it was the capital of the Seljuk empire. During the Soviet era six reservoirs were built on Turkmenistan's part of the Murgab River, and water was excessively used for irrigation of cotton fields. The overexploitation of the water resources in this extremely dry region led to salinization of some areas around the Murgab in the 1970s and 1980s. In the 1990s the situation became even worse when southern Turkmenistan experienced several years of severe drought. There were reports that the river completely dried out and water shortage affected many districts of Turkmenistan.

Rafis Abazov

Further Reading

Atamamedov, N., ed. (1984) *Entsiklopedia: Turkmenskaia Sovetskaia Sotsialisticheskaia Respublika* (Encyclopedia: Turkmen Soviet Socialist Republic). Ashkhabad, USSR: Glavnaia redaktsia Turkmenskoi Sovetskoi entsiklopedii.

Kobori, Iwao, and Michael Glantz, eds. (1998) *Central Eurasian Water Crisis: Caspian, Aral, and Dead Seas.* Tokyo: United Nations University.

Micklin, Philip. (2001) *Managing Water in Central Asia.* London: Royal Institute of International Affairs.

MUROMACHI PERIOD The Muromachi period (1333–1573) in Japanese history was named after the location in northeastern Kyoto of the offices of the military government, or shogunate, of the Ashikaga line of the warrior rulers (shoguns). The shogunate was founded in 1336 by Ashikaga Takauji (1303–1358) after the overthrow of the Kamakura shogunate in 1333 and the failure of a brief attempt by Emperor Godaigo (1228–1339) to revive direct imperial rule between the years 1333 and 1336.

The Muromachi period (also known as the Ashikaga period) was one of the most tumultuous ages in the history of Japan. The Ashikaga shoguns, at their peak in the late fourteenth and early fifteenth centuries, controlled only a part of Japan. During the last hundred years of Muromachi, also known as the Sengoku

JAPAN—HISTORICAL PERIODS

Jomon period (14,500–300 BCE)
Yayoi culture (300 BCE–300 CE)
Yamato State (300–552 CE)
Kofun period (300–710 CE)
Nara period (710–794 CE)
Heian period (794–1185)
Kamakura period (Kamakura Shogunate) (1185– 1333)
Muromachi period (1333–1573)
Momoyama period (1573–1600)
Tokugawa or Edo period (Tokugawa Shogunate) (1600/1603–1868)
Meiji period (1868–1912)
Taisho period (1912–1926)
Showa period (1926–1989)
Allied Occupation (1945–1952)
Heisei period (1989–present)

Temple of Ginkaku-ji, the Silver Pavilion, in Kyoto. (ARCHIVO ICONOGRAFICO S.A./CORBIS)

age, Japan had no effective central government. Emperors had long been figureheads, and the Ashikaga shogunate controlled little more than Kyoto and its environs. Toward the end of the Muromachi period, however, independent territorial domains ruled by warrior chieftains called daimyo appeared throughout the country, and from about 1560 on, these domains were unified by a series of warlords whose triumphs led finally to two and a half centuries of peace under the Tokugawa shogunate (1600/1603–1868).

Although much of the Muromachi period was unquestionably a dark age, it was also a time of cultural achievement. Pure Land (Jodo) and Zen Buddhism flourished, and arts such as Noh drama, tea ceremony, monochrome ink painting, landscape dry gardening, and flower arrangement were primarily the products of Muromachi culture. While the Ashikaga shoguns were generally ineffective rulers, collectively they were superb patrons of the arts. The patronage derived in part from sending missions to China that returned to Japan with vital ideas in philosophy and religion, new styles of art, and countless objects of art and craft. Through the patronage of the Ashikaga shoguns, China exerted great influence over the shaping of Muromachi culture.

The Muromachi period is also remembered as the time when Europeans first visited Japan. Portuguese traders arrived in 1543 and were followed in the ensuing half-century by the Spanish, Dutch, and English. The Catholic countries Portugal and Spain also brought Christian missionaries, who launched vigorous campaigns to convert the Japanese. Eventually, Japan rejected Christianity and in the early seventeenth century commenced a persecution against the foreign religion that was a major factor in shaping the policy of national seclusion by the Tokugawa shogunate from the 1630s.

Paul Varley

Further Reading

Hall, John W., and Takeshi Toyoda, eds. (1977) *Japan in the Muromachi Age*. Berkeley and Los Angeles: University of California Press.

Sansom, George. (1961) *A History of Japan, 1334–1615*. Stanford, CA: Stanford University Press.

MUSHARRAF, PERVEZ (b. 1943), president of Pakistan. Pervez Musharraf was born in Delhi on 11 August 1943. Following the founding of Pakistan in 1947, his family moved to Karachi. His father was a career diplomat and his mother, a homemaker, also worked for the International Labour Organization. He was educated at Christian schools in Pakistan and Turkey, where he lived from 1949 to 1956 when his father was stationed there. Following graduation from the Pakistani Military Academy in 1961, he pursued a career in the army, serving as a commando and in various staff and instructional positions. In 1998 he was promoted to the rank of general and appointed chief of army staff. The following year he was appointed chairman of the Joint Chiefs of Staff Committee.

In October 1999, following a disagreement with Prime Minister Nawaz Sharif (b. 1949) over Sharif's policies, Musharraf seized power in a bloodless coup and on 12 October had himself appointed chief executive of Pakistan. On 20 June 2001 he appointed himself president of Pakistan. He continued to hold his previous posts of chief of army staff and chairman of the Joint Chiefs of Staff Committee. Although his taking of power disrupted the movement toward democracy in Pakistan, Musharraf promised a return to civilian rule in October 2002. He is viewed by other world leaders as a moderate, and following the 11 September terrorist attack on the United States become a strong ally of the United States. Despite criticism in Pakistan, he assisted the United States in the invasion of neighboring Afghanistan and cracked down on Muslim terrorists in Pakistan.

David Levinson

Further Reading

Chadda, Maya. (2000) *Building Democracy in South Asia: India, Nepal, Pakistan*. Boulder, CO: Lynne Rienner Publishers.

MUSIC—BANGLADESH Before the end of British rule in India in 1947, the land that is now Bangladesh formed an eastern subdivision of the region known as Bengal. Consequently Bangladeshis and their West Bengali neighbors in India share most of their cultural heritage, language, and ancient history.

In 1947 western Bengal, with its majority population of Hindus, became part of India, while eastern Bengal, with its largely Muslim population, became the eastern "wing" of the nation of Pakistan. In 1971 Bangladesh (Bengal-land) became independent from Pakistan. In the twenty-first century Bangladeshi culture continued to be predominantly Islamic, but its roots remained embedded in its Hindu and Buddhist past.

Ancient Song Forms

Although no transcriptions exist of Bengali music prior to the nineteenth century it is possible to delineate particular forms of vocal music from the texts of ancient Bengali poems and from melodies preserved through oral transmission. Twelfth-century Buddhist poems called *charya-giti* (religious observance songs) and the thirteenth-century *Gitagovinda* (Songs of the Cowherder), a cycle of songs by the poet Jayadeva, bear the names of the specific melodic modes assigned to each song. Hindu and Buddhist kings in Bengal commissioned poets to compose *raso*, epic poems, in their honor, which were chanted by the poet-composers themselves. These royal patrons also commissioned poets to render into Bengali verse the great Sanskrit epics from Indo-Aryan literature, such as the *Mahabharata*, the *Ramayana*, and other *mahakabya* ("great poems"). The poetic meter employed in the Bengali versions of these epics is reflected in present-day Bengali folk ballads. By analogy, it is likely that the melodies of ballads heard in the twenty-first century are descendants of *raso* and *mahakabya* minstrel songs.

By the sixteenth century the flowering of various Hindu and Islamic cults, each possessing its own kind of songs, had enriched Bengali music. The Hindu Vaishnava sect developed *kirtan* (songs of praise) that focused on the god Krishna. During Turkic and Mughal rule Muslim Sufi missionaries from the Middle East introduced their genres of spiritual songs. By the eighteenth century mendicant minstrels called Bauls combined Vaishnava and Sufi themes with their own spiritual ones. Other Bengali cults composed ballads honoring the exploits of local deities and hero-saints.

Classical Forms

South Asian musicologists generally divide Indian music into classical (or art) and folk forms. Indian classical music developed prior to Sarangadeva's thirteenth-century treatise *Sangita-ratnakara* (The Music Mine of Jewels), in which over two hundred melodic models called ragas (coloring agents) are identified by name. During Mughal rule the raga system of Indian music developed fully.

Indian classical music is primarily a solo improvisation based on a specific raga chosen from the several hundreds passed down from master musicians to their disciples. The composer-soloist generally begins with a melodic improvisation in free rhythm called an *alap* (conversation) followed by an improvisation structured to fit a particular *tala* (rhythmic pattern) selected from over one hundred types.

Folk Forms

Bangladeshi folk music belongs to the region's agrarian communities, whose education was acquired mainly through oral transmission, especially through songs. The three main branches of Bangladeshi folk songs are described below.

Mystical Songs The mystical texts of the Vaishnava, Sufi, and other Bengali sects comprise the most melodically arresting Bangladeshi folk songs. These are sung informally in family or neighborhood gatherings or more formally as part of religious festivals or ceremonies. Their poetry generally expresses a longing for union with a divine being, often portrayed as the longing of Radha for the god Krishna. Popular songs include the ecstatic songs of Bauls and Sufi *darbesh* (dervishes), the Muslim *murshidi* and *marfati* (spiritual guides) songs, and the fluid melodies of *bhatiali* (boat rowers' songs) and *bhaowaiya* (cart drivers' songs).

Minstrels who perform mystical songs often begin with a few short phrases in the *alap* form before embarking on the main verses. The melodies of mystical songs encompass and sometimes surpass a tonal range of an octave. Set to lively rhythmic beats, they trace a graceful contour.

Narrative Songs In Bengal, especially during the nineteenth century, lengthy narrative songs, variously known as *panchali* (narratives), *punthigan* (manuscript songs), and *palagan* (drama songs) among other classifications, flourished in the countryside as mass entertainment. They are similar in structure to Bengali literary epics, and their performance requires a talented minstrel called a *bayati* (verse maker) or *mulgayen* (chief singer) trained as a master poet-composer.

Epic ballads glorifying local deities and hero-saints are known as *vijay* (triumph songs), *mangala* (blessing songs), and *ghazigan* (warrior-saint songs). *Jarigan* (songs of grief) comprise a treasury of dramatic stories based on Muslim lore performed by a *bayati* with a chorus of *dohar* (refrain singers) and an instrumental ensemble. Audiences numbering in the thousands once attended sessions of *kabigan* (poet songs), competitions in extempore singing about epic or topical themes. The melodies of these narrative songs are characteristically syllabic (one tone per syllable) to render the text clearly, but expert minstrels often dramatize their singing with melodic elaboration, departing freely from the verbal structure of the text.

Occasional Songs Many Bangladeshi folk songs are associated with particular social occasions or occupations. These include cradle songs; satires performed at weddings; seasonal songs; melodies to accompany harvesting, house construction, and boat racing; and the songs of snake charmers, dirges, and many others. Rural theatrical productions called *jatra* include popular song and dance music or pieces composed for a particular drama. Some occasional songs may be accompanied by group dancing, especially in Bangladeshi tribal communities. The melodies of occasional songs tend to be syllabic, lending themselves to congregational as well as solo singing.

Semiclassical Forms

Many Bangladeshi rural songs are so poetically and musically sophisticated that they transcend the folk category. In addition, a large number of Bangladeshi songs display a strong affinity to classical raga music yet are too verse-bound to allow the improvisational scope of classical music. Therefore an intermediary semiclassical category of Bengali music encompasses the large number of Bangladeshi musical compositions that straddle the folk and classical categories.

For example, *kirtan* songs, such as composed by the Vaishnava saint Sri Krishna Caitanya (Chaitanya) (1486–1533), employ classical raga melodies, *tala* rhythmic patterns, and the *dhrupad* (fixed verse) configuration of South Indian classical compositions. The aesthetic refinement of mystical songs by such famous Baul minstrels as Lalan Shah (c. 1792–c. 1890) place them in the semiclassical category. Likewise, Hindu hymns called *bhajan*s (devotional songs), Persian-style love songs called *ghazal*, and Sufi spiritual songs called *qawwali* are semiclassical by virtue of the poetic and musical artistry required for their performance.

During the late nineteenth century and the early twentieth century Bengali urban poet-composers, such as Rabindranath Tagore (1861–1941) and Qazi Nazrul Islam (1899–1976), composed songs in their own personal styles that innovatively blended Bengali classical, folk, and "modern" influences. Learning to sing *rabindra-sangit* (Rabindranath Tagore songs) or *nazrul-git* (Nazrul Islam songs) is part of a young Bangladeshi's formal education, and these songs usually appear in the programs of Bangladeshi state or social functions.

New Trends

During the twentieth century, music from around the world affected traditional forms of Bangladeshi music and influenced the development of new forms. By the 1960s Bangladeshi instrumental ensembles included such nontraditional instruments as saxophones and Hawaiian-style guitars. Electric guitars became popular, and commercial recordings and films included electronically modulated music.

By the twenty-first century, simple harmonization often accompanied song melodies, especially in film songs and urban versions of folksongs. However, pure melody continues to be the main component of Bangladeshi musical expression. The melodies of Bangladeshi folksongs, especially Baul, *bhatiyali*, and *bhaowaiya* songs, remain sources of inspiration for classical compositions and popular songs.

Mary Frances Dunham

See also: **Bhakti; Jatra; Music—India**

Further Reading

Capwell, Charles. (1986) *The Music of the Bauls of Bengal*. Kent, OH: Kent State University Press. Includes a sound cassette.

Dunham, Mary Frances. (1997) *Jarigan: Muslim Epic Songs of Bangladesh*. Dhaka, Bangladesh: University Press, Ltd. Includes a sound cassette.

Ghosh, J. C. (1948) *Bengali Literature*. London: Oxford University Press.

Ray, Sukumar. (1988) *Folk Music of Eastern India with Special Reference to Bengal*. Calcutta, India: Naya Prakash.

Saaduddin, Abul H. (1980) "Bangladesh." In *The New Grove Dictionary of Music and Musicians*, edited by Stanley Sadie. London: Macmillan, 110–116.

Shankar, Ravi. (1968) *My Music, My Life*. New York: Simon & Schuster.

Recordings

Abbasuddin. *Abbasuddin Sings Folk Songs of Bengal*. Gramophone Company of India ELRZ.12.

Chowdhury, Nirmalendu, et al. *Folk Songs of Bengal*. Gramophone Company of India, vol. 1 (ECLP-2256), vol. 2 (ECLP-2336), vol. 3 (ECLP-2403). 33 1/3 RPM record.

Goswami, Karunamaya. (1995) *History of Bengali Music in Sound*. LOSAUK. Ten audio cassettes with a booklet.

MUSIC—CENTRAL ASIA Central Asian music, that is, the music of the former Soviet states of Uzbekistan, Tajikistan, Kazakhstan, Kyrgyzstan, and Turkmenistan, is based on the interaction of nomadic and sedentary cultures and on the blending of the region's Persian and Turkic cultures and languages. Central Asian music has close links with the music of the bordering regions of northern Afghanistan and Xinjiang (an autonomous region in western China) and more broadly with the music of Iran, Azerbaijan, and Turkey.

The construction of national musical canons, begun in the early twentieth century under the Soviets and continuing in the new Central Asian states today, cuts across a complex historical picture of exchange, coexistence, and blending. For example, Jewish professional musicians (Uzbek *sazande*) of Bukhara in Uzbekistan used to sing bilingual Tajik-Uzbek love songs *(ghazal)*. These Jewish musicians have now largely emigrated to Israel or the United States.

In the twentieth and twenty-first centuries conservatory-trained professional musicians in Central Asian towns and cities largely replaced musicians who trained by apprenticing to a master *(ustad)*, but the practice of handing on musical skills in the family continues. The use of written scores has partly supplanted the old system of oral transmission. Probably the most numerous professional musicians today are the wedding singers and pop singers, whose cassette recordings now enliven the teahouses and restaurants of Central Asian towns, formerly contexts for live musical performances.

Performances of Folk Music

Along with informal gatherings (*gap* in Tajik and Uzbek, *meshrep* in Uighur) where music is commonly played for entertainment, weddings are perhaps the major contexts for musical performance throughout Central Asia. Singers and instrumentalists are employed to play a range of music from classical to popular songs at wedding banquets, while kettledrum-and-shawm bands *(naghra-sunay)* escort the groom on his way to fetch the bride. These bands also play at religious festivals, especially Qurban and the end of Ramadan. In Sunni Central Asia there is little concern about the Islamic proscriptions against music common elsewhere in the Islamic world; indeed, music is an integral part of religious life and is thought to form a link between the sacred and the secular.

Storytellers sing tales from the Qur'an during Ramadan and on pilgrimages *(mazar)*. Musicians may also be mullahs or wandering holy men *(ashiq)*. Sufi influence in particular pervades music and thought. Music is found in the chants *(zikr)* and sometimes in the instrumental music of Sufi ceremonies. In the nineteenth-century *Tarikhi Muziqiyun* (History of Musicians) by Mujiz, one of the few surviving historical documents on Central Asian music, stories linking music and ecstatic trance abound. In the tale of the master musician Balkhi, for example, a nightingale perched on Balkhi's *tanbur* (long-necked lute) as he sang, and the people at the festival shouted, wept, and rolled about.

Maqam

Song lyrics are also deeply imbued with Sufi thought, especially in *maqam*, the most prestigious genre of Central Asian music. In Central Asia, the term *maqam* refers to a series of large-scale musical suites, including sung poetry, popular stories, and dance music. As with songs and instrumental pieces, *maqam* are associated with specific regions; there are, for example, the Bukharan Shashmaqam, the Khokand Chaharmaqam, and the Kashgar Muqam. A scholarly debate has raged over whether Central Asian *maqam* are a local variation of a Near Eastern form (as evidenced by the Arab-Persian terminology associated with them) or the continuation of ancient Central Asian traditions carried to the Chinese imperial court and thence to Japan. It is probably more helpful to think of Central Asian *maqam* as arising from a fusion of these two sources.

Each instrumental or vocal piece in a *maqam* derives from a rhythm *(usul)*, which is marked by the frame drum; "limping" irregular rhythms *(aksak/lang)* are common. Pieces with the same names appear in different *maqam*, but their melodies vary depending on the modal characteristics of each *maqam;* thus the term *maqam* in Central Asia to some extent denotes the idea of mode, as it does in Arab-Turkish traditions.

Much use is made of ornamentation, shifting, or leaning on the notes to produce subtle effects. Central Asian *maqam* have not traditionally been improvised in performance, but are rather precomposed; that is, a personal interpretation is developed and fixed in memory.

Many instruments are used for playing *maqam*, especially the long-necked lutes, such as the *tanbur* with three metal strings. The bowed lute *(sato/satar)*, with up to twelve sympathetic strings, is particularly linked to *maqam;* thought of as a noble instrument, it is often played by older men. The frame drum *(dayera dap)* is also an important instrument for *maqam*, as it forms the rhythmic basis; often associated with women and religious beggars, it is sometimes thought to have magical powers. The Kashgar *rawap* is a small lute with five metal strings. A virtuosic instrument, it is usually found in an accompanying role, as is the *ghijak* spike fiddle with its four metal strings, related to the Iranian *kemenche*, but now tuned to resemble the violin. The *dutar* lute, strung with two silk strings, is the most common instrument among the Uzbeks and Uighurs, found in almost every home and played by men, women, and children alike, often to accompany songs.

Nomadic Peoples

Among the nomadic peoples of the region, the main musicians are poet-bards, like the Kazak *akhun* or the Uzbek *bakhshi.* Among some peoples a special class of bards sing long, heroic epic tales, such as the Kyrgyz *Manas* epic. There is a great deal of interchange between these bards and the shamanic ritual healers who are still common across the region. Bards are often said to learn their epics from spirits in their dreams, and their performances are also thought to have healing powers. The bards usually accompany themselves on plucked lutes (like the *dombra*) or fiddles (such as the three-stringed *qobuz*).

Rachel Harris

Further Reading

Beliaev, V. M. (1975) *Central Asian Music.* Trans. and ed. by Mark Slobin and Greta Slobin. Middletown, CT: Wesleyan University Press.

During, Jean. (1993) *Asie Centrale: Les Maitres de dotar* (Central Asia: Masters of the Dotar). Recording, AIMP 26.

During, Jean, and Theodore Levin. (1993) *Asie Centrale: Traditions classiques* (Central Asia: Classical Traditions). Recording, Radio France, Ocora.

Levin, Theodore. (1996) *The Hundred Thousand Fools of God: Musical Travels in Central Asia.* Bloomington and Indianapolis: Indiana University Press.

Levin, Theodore, and O. Matyakubov. (1991) *Bukhara: Musical Crossroads of Asia.* Folkways recording SF40050.

Slobin, Mark. (1969) *Kirghiz Instrumental Music.* New York: Society for Asian Music.

———. (1976) *Music in the Culture of Northern Afghanistan.* Tucson: University of Arizona Press.

———. (1977) *Music of Central Asia and of the Volga-Ural Peoples.* Bloomington: Indiana University Asian Studies Research Unit.

MUSIC—CHINA In Chinese music, a great deal of variety is achieved on the basis of a small musical repertoire through variation techniques. Metric variation is common in instrumental and opera music, whereby a skeletal melody is augmented or diminished metrically and performed with an accordingly greater or lesser degree of ornamentation.

China's diverse musical traditions and regional styles should be seen as part of the wider picture of music in Asia. Although politically part of China, Tibet and Xinjiang lie outside the scope of this entry, but their music was influential. Many instruments and musical genres, like the drum and shawm (a woodwind instrument) bands *(guchui)*, the *pipa* (a four-string plucked lute), and the *yangqin* (a hammer dulcimer) were brought to China from the Near East and Central Asia. In turn, Chinese music has influenced the music of Japan and Korea.

Much Chinese music is linked to ritual contexts, from the Confucian rituals of the imperial court to those of village weddings, funerals, and festivals. This ritual basis shaped the aesthetics of Chinese music, whose emphasis on harmony, restraint, and conformity to tradition is linked to the need for correct, nondeviating observance of ritual. Variation and reinterpretation of existing melodies are prized over creation of the new. However, there are also dynamic, extrovert traditions, especially in northern China.

Characteristics of Chinese Music and Chinese Musicians

Chinese music is divided into fine *(xi)* and coarse *(cu)*, civil *(wen)* and martial *(wu)* music. Professional musicians in China, like the drum and shawm bands or the opera troupes, were traditionally low class and disdained, whereas the gentleman amateur musician had much higher status. Likewise it was considered shameful for women to play music in public; few traditional genres are performed by women, though some are valued, like the southern narrative song genre of *nanguan.*

The ritual music of the imperial court was imbued with complex Confucian theories that linked musical sound to the stability of the empire and the turning of the seasons. This music was lost at the beginning of the twentieth century with the abdication of the last emperor, but court entertainment music has been partially preserved in the beautiful instrumental traditions of Buddhist temples and village ritual ensembles.

More widespread are the amateur silk and bamboo instrumental ensembles often found in urban teahouses. They are named for the silk strings of the *erhu* (a two-stringed fiddle) and *sanxian* (a three-stringed lute) and the bamboo of the *dizi* (a transverse flute). Percussion ensembles of gongs, cymbals, and drum are also widespread, as are the drum and shawm bands. Each region has its own repertoire and style.

Musical Notation and Meter

The most common traditional musical notation *(gongchepu)* uses symbols based on the heptatonic (seven-tone) scale. Although Chinese music is basically pentatonic (five tones), the neutral fourth and seventh of the scale are used as passing notes and for modulation. Notation serves as a basic guide, recording only the skeletal notes *(guganyin)* of a melody. In performance, this skeleton is fleshed out by adding decoration *(jiahua)*. Each musical instrument ornaments the skeletal notes in its own way, creating a delicate variety of sounds.

Meter is marked by *banyan* (beats and "eyes," or rests), based on the beats of the *ban* (wood clappers). Many of these skeletal melodies are drawn from a stock of labeled (titled) melodies *(qupai)*, found in varying forms in instrumental music and narrative song and opera genres across China. The titles or labels of these melodies are drawn from the Song dynasty (960–1279) poetry of the ninth and tenth centuries, and the melodies themselves can be traced back to the Yuan dynasty (1279–1368).

Opera

Labeled melodies also make up an important part of the opera repertoire. We may think of a musical spectrum ranging from solo narrative songs, accompanied by percussion or *sanxian* lute, to the high opera forms, such as those of the Beijing Opera. There are numerous regional styles, but they all draw on the same stock of melodies and stories taken from popular novels.

Traditionally, all-male professional troupes performed at rural temple fairs or public theaters in towns. In more complex genres, stock characters are used, with fixed conventions of costume and makeup, such as the painted faces of the warrior *(hualian)*, clown *(chou)*, and woman warrior *(wudan)*. Labeled melodies are adapted to fit the words of the arias, which are interspersed with heightened speech. A drummer serves as conductor, directing the actors' movements and leading a percussion ensemble that accompanies the dramatic action. Set percussion patterns represent different characters and different dramatic situations.

Folk Songs

A separate vocal genre is that of rural folk songs, often called mountain songs *(shan'ge)*. Again there is great regional variation; folk song is strongly tied to locality. The most beautiful are thought to be the songs of northwest China, especially the bitter songs *(suanqu'er)* of the boat pullers on the Huang (Yellow) River and the camel drivers on the Silk Road.

Big folk-song festivals are held in the northwest, linked to the temple fairs, where men and women gather in groups to sing improvised, often crude sexual lyrics. Such occasions lie outside the normally strict Confucian morality of village life.

Guqin Music

Another unique musical tradition is that of the *guqin* (a seven-stringed zither). This instrument—the ancient, indigenous gentleman-scholar's zither, played for personal refinement and meditation—has come to be emblematic of Chinese music. Its tunes are thought to be programmatic (they describe a scene or story), and much traditional literature is devoted to tales of disciples who perfectly understood the mood and images their master's playing evoked. The *guqin* has its own special complex notation, and its performance traditionally involves an element of historical research: interpretation and reworking of centuries-old scores and their commentaries, themselves based on still earlier notations.

Modernization and Westernization of Music

All of these traditional genres still thrive in contemporary China, but Chinese music also underwent much change in the twentieth century in terms of modernization and Westernization, through the introduction of new instruments, theories, and attitudes and the implementation of a musical schooling system and professional troupes and orchestras.

The Communist revolution in 1949 brought with it attacks on traditional culture along with extensive reworking of folk music to produce revolutionary folk songs and model operas *(yangbanxi)*, which the Communist cultural authorities use to instruct people through revolutionary models. After the excesses of the Cultural Revolution, the loosening of social controls in the 1980s brought about a great revival of traditional music alongside its old ritual contexts. It has also permitted the swift rise of a big pop- and rock-music industry promoted on television and through the ubiquitous karaoke bars. Several modern Chinese composers have also achieved international recognition with works that draw in part on Chinese traditions.

Rachel Harris

Further Reading

Jones, Andrew. (1992) *Like a Knife: Ideology and Genre in Contemporary Chinese Music.* Cornell East Asia Series 57. Ithaca, NY: Cornell University Press.

Jones, Stephen. (1995). *Folk Music of China: Living Instrumental Traditions.* Oxford, U.K.: Clarendon Press.

Kraus, Richard. (1989) *Pianos and Politics in China: Middle-Class Ambitions and the Struggle over Western Music.* New York and Oxford: Oxford University Press.

Schimmelpenninck, Antoinette. (1997) *Chinese Folk Songs and Folk Singers: Shan'ge Traditions in Southern Jiangsu.* Leiden, Netherlands: Chime Foundation.

Stock, Jonathan. (1996) *Musical Creativity in Twentieth-Century China: Abing, His Music, and Its Changing Meanings.*

Eastman Studies in Music, no. 6. Rochester, NY: University of Rochester Press.

Wichmann, Elizabeth. (1991) *Listening to Theatre: The Aural Dimension of Beijing Opera.* Honolulu: University of Hawaii Press.

Witzleben, J. Lawrence. (1995) *Silk-and-Bamboo: Jiangnan sizhu in Shanghai.* Kent, OH: Kent State University Press.

Yung, Bell. (1989) *Cantonese Opera: Performance as Creative Process.* Cambridge Studies in Ethnomusicology. Cambridge, U.K.: Cambridge University Press.

Yung, Bell, Evelyn Rawski, and Rubie Watson, eds. (1996) *Harmony & Counterpoint: Ritual Music in Chinese Context.* Stanford, CA: Stanford University Press.

MUSIC—EAST ASIA, RYUKYUAN The Ryukyu Islands, the largest of which is Okinawa, form the long archipelago situated to the south of the Japanese mainland. Until the late nineteenth century this group of islands was an independent kingdom that maintained strong links with both China and Japan. This unique environment allowed the arts of the kingdom, especially music, to develop in a special way, incorporating traditional Chinese and Japanese elements. Some of the plots of formal Ryukyuan drama are influenced by Noh, a traditional form of Japanese dance-drama.

Essentially, the music of the Ryukyu chain can be divided into two broad categories: court and folk music. With court music, the primary form is further divided into formal songs accompanied by the music of a *sanshin* (three-stringed lute with snakeskin) and dance repertoire. The dance category itself is further divided into subcategories in terms of style (for the old, for the young, for men, for women) and folk derivation. Court music and dance have also been adopted into a formal drama type, known as *kumiodori*, in which song, music, and dance are integrated into a carefully structured artistic framework.

Over the centuries, Ryukyuan folk song and dance have been adapted to different circumstances and evolved into a variety of styles—religious rituals, secular entertainment, love songs, lullabies, epic poem-songs, and the like—which do not necessarily incorporate the *sanshin*. Ryukyuan classical music is still listened to and performed by a large number of people in Okinawa. In addition, it has been accepted widely in mainland Japan as a kind of exotic music since the 1980s. Based on traditional elements, a new style of Okinawan pop music, enjoyed by Okinawans and mainland Japanese, has been created by younger generations of Okinawans.

Naoko Terauchi

Further Reading

Nippon Hoso Kyokai, ed. (1993) *Nippon Min'yo Taikan (Okinawa-Amami): Amami Shoto-hen* (A Survey of Japanese Folksongs [Okinawa–Amami Islands]: Amami Islands Volume). Tokyo: Nippon Hoso Shuppan Kyokai.

———. (1991) *Nippon Min'yo Taikan (Okinawa-Amami): Okinawa Shoto-hen* (A Survey of Japanese Folksongs [Okinawa–Amami Islands]: Okinawa Islands Volume): Tokyo: Nippon Hoso Shuppan Kyokai.

———. (1990) *Nippon Min'yo Taikan (Okinawa-Amami): Miyako Shoto-hen* (A Survey of Japanese Folksongs [Okinawa–Amami Islands]: Miyako Islands Volume). Tokyo: Nippon Hoso Shuppan Kyokai.

———. (1989) *Nippon Min'yo Taikan (Okinawa-Amami): Yaeyama Shoto-hen* (A Survey of Japanese Folksongs [Okinawa–Amami Islands]: Yaeyama Islands Volume). Tokyo: Nippon Hoso Shuppan Kyokai.

MUSIC—INDIA Indian music is one of the dominant forms of Asian music. Its influence extends beyond the subcontinent into China and the Far East and through Iran, Iraq, and Turkey to Greece. It preserves the oldest tradition of playing a monophonic melodic line untouched by the use of vertical harmony and tempered scale. It has an extremely complicated and varied system of rhythmic cycles, and it is based on the ancient concept that the human voice is the foremost expression of musical emotion, and therefore all instruments should imitate and accompany the voice. Consequently, lyrics and literary content are preserved as a major feature of the music; however, there is not a written notational score to be followed while performing. Except for the lyrics, most of the structure and score of the music is created by the performer during performance, along certain traditionally accepted norms.

Historical-Cultural Roots

The earliest-known Indian music consists of Vedic mantras or chants (of the first millennium BCE, or even earlier), in ancient Sanskrit verses, employed in the religious rites of sacrifice offered to the gods. These chants were tritonal in the Rig Veda but later employed seven notes in descending order in the Sama Veda. Descriptions of nonritual music of that time do not survive, but some later texts—for example, the *Nardiyashiksha*—do clarify the differences between Vedic chants and non-Vedic music.

A more detailed description of secular music is found, in the classical period, in the great work of theater theory, the *Natya sastra* (fifth century BCE), by Bharata Muni. This work contains an extensive musicological account of the grammar and practice of Indian music that prevailed in ancient India until medieval times. Music is called *gandharva* in the *Natya sastra*, after the region of Gandhara (modern Kandahar in Afghanistan), which is believed to have been a great center of music in the past. In the *Natya sastra*, certain celestial musicians were called Gandharvas. It has been suggested that the Greek *Kentauros* ("centaur"), also adept in the arts, is a version of the Gandharva, indicating old musical links between Greek Ionia and western India.

During the age of the formulation of the *Natya sastra*, certain melodic tunes, called the *jatis*, were in vogue throughout India. *Jatis* were used to formulate scale-groups (*gramas*), scales (*murcchanas*), notes (*svaras*), and note intervals or microtones (*shrutis*). The Indian septet was not made up of tetrachords as was the Greek septet, but instead consisted of two trichords. *Shadja*, *rishabha*, and *gandhara* made up one trichord, while *pancama*, *dhaivata*, and *nishada* made up the other. The trichords were placed on either side of the middle note, called *madhyama*. In short signs, or symbols that denote the name of a note by the first two letters of the full name of the note (for example, *sa* used to denote *sadja)*, the notes could be indicated as: *sa*, *ri*, *ga*, *ma*, *pa*, *dha*, *ni*.

A sequence of any seven notes was called a *murcchana*. Unlike present-day universal practice, the first note of the septet (or scale) was not always the tonic, that is, *sa* or "do." Any note of a *murcchana* could be the tonic. In their so-called natural positions in a septet, *shadja* and *madhyama* made a consonance of a fourth, as did *madhayama* and *nishada*. *Shadja* and *pancama* made a consonance of a fifth. This septet also was the first *murcchana* of the *shadjagrama*. By placing the tonic on one note at a time, that is, for the first *murcchana* at *sa*, for the second at *ri*, and so on, seven *murcchanas* could be obtained. This scale-group was called the *shadjagrama* and its seven pure *murcchanas*.

The other generic scale, called the *madhyamagrama*, was formulated in the following manner: in the fourth *murcchana* of the *shadjagrama*—that is, the scale *ma*, *pa*, *dha*, *ni*, *sa*, *ri*, *ga*—an alteration was made. A consonance of a fourth was created between *pa* and *ri* (which means that *pa* was lowered slightly, by a diesis [Pythagorean]), thus changing the scale. Then seven *murcchanas* were obtained by placing the tonic on each of the seven notes. Thus, the scale-group of the *madhyamagrama* and its seven pure *murcchanas* had a consonance of a fifth between *pa* and *ri* notes. In other words, all scales that had a consonance of a fifth between *sa* and *pa* were categorized in the *shadjagrama*, and all scales in which there was a consonance of a fifth between *pa* and *ri* were categorized in the *madhyamagrama*. *Sadjagrama* contained seven *jatis*—namely, *shadji*, *arshabhi*, *dhaivati*, *naisadi*, *sadjodicyava*, *sadjakaisiki*, and *shadjamadhya*. *Madhyamagrama* contained eleven *jatis*—namely, *gandhari*, *madhyama*, *gandharodicyava*, *pancami*, *gandharapancami*, *raktagandhari*, *madhyam-odicyava*, *nandayanti*, *andhri*, *karmaravi*, and *kaisiki*.

All the prevalent tunes of the times—that is, the *jatis*—were put into either *grama*, and, by further flattening or sharpening of *ga* and *ni* more variations were made. The *Natyashastra* has classified eighteen *jatis*, seven as pure and eleven as hybrid. The pure could make 146 modified forms. The hybrid also had many variations. A third *grama*, called *gandharvagrama*, was said to have gone out of use very early.

It should be noted that there was no concept of a fixed pitch for the notes in ancient India, and this is still the case in present-day Indian music. The tonic shifts from one note to another to create a different *murcchana*, but the actual tuning of the harp, which always accompanies the singer, is not altered so drastically.

The fundamental concepts needed to expand on a melodic structure were well formulated by the time of the *Natyashastra*, and they continue to be practiced, albeit with a change of names. The ten characteristics of a *jati* that gave shape to its presentation continued to do so in a raga in modern times. *Amsha* was the most dominating note of the melody and also was the tonic. *Graha* was the note with which an exposition was begun, and *nyasa* was the note to which the performer returned each time on the completion of a melodic phrase. *Apanyasa* was the note that was auxiliary to *nyasa*. *Tara* was the upper register and *mandra* the lower. When only six of the seven notes of the scale were used for a melody, this was called *shadava*, and when five notes were used, it was called *audava*. Abundant usage of certain notes was called *bahutva*, and sparing usage was *alpatva*. Nowadays, *amsha*, *graha*, *nyasa*, and *apanyasa* are practiced, but vernacular terms are used.

From the descriptions of these and related concepts, it seems that the *jatis* were sung pretty much as the ragas are in modern times. The preliminary wordless expansion of the melody, called *alapana*, was made by the singer or player, and then compositions to the accompaniment of the drums were rendered. The embellishments were also similar to those used at present. There is, however, no clear indication that any instrument or set of voices produced the tonic and its consonant as a constant drone in the way that the modern tamboura (a lutelike instrument) does for Indian music at the beginning of the twenty-first century.

HARMONIUM

Originally of European origin, the harmonium *(peti,* or *baja),* began to be implemented into Indian music during the nineteenth century. The overall shape of the instrument is that of a box. Running along the top of the box is a row of keys, or *chabi,* similar to that of a piano. An instrument without a keyboard but similar to a harmonium is called a *surpeti* and is used to generate an underlying drone. Inside the harmonium is a flat wooden reed board with several holes, although there are styles where the board is not flat. The instrument can have up to three banks of reeds, in which case it is called a triple-reed harmonium. Reeds of brass cover these holes. The reeds vibrate as air passes over them, and this air is forced through the instrument when the musician pumps the bellows. The external bellows are worked by the musician, who pumps air into the internal bellows, which acts as a reservoir for the air pushing against a spring and forcing the air over the reeds. The control of the airflow through various reed chambers is managed by main stops. Drone stops control the flow of the air over the unkeyed reeds.

Stacey Fox

Another distinct feature of Indian musical theory, the relationship between melodies and emotions like fear, pity, courage, erotic desire, and so on, also was postulated in this period of the compilation of the *Natya sastra.* Specific notes were believed to arouse specific emotions, and a system of their use in melodies was explained in the *Natya sastra.*

In ancient times, the analysis of notes and their intervals was facilitated by harps (*vinas*). The system of Vedic chants was kept insulated from the musical system of *gramas* and *jatis*, and no interaction was allowed between the two. No Vedic verse would be sung in a secular scale; neither would a non-Vedic text be sung in the Vedic tones. This separation was maintained until the final decade of the twentieth century. The *gandharva* system was used for all spiritual, ritual, liturgical, theatrical, aesthetic, and social needs, and a wide variety of instruments (strings, pipes, drums, and cymbals) were used.

Secular Uses of Music

In addition to its use in ritual practices, music was used widely in ancient Indian theater, dance, and poetic compositions, in many languages. Besides Sanskrit, a large number of languages—among them, Pali, Magadhi, Avanti, Shaurseni, and Tamil—were used for all these purposes. A variety of songs (*gitas*, *prabandhas*) from throughout the country are recorded in literary works dating from 500 BCE to 900 CE. All ancient string instruments were harplike, similar to the kithara. The zither also was known but was used very sparingly. From the second century CE, records show that music acquired a central place in the temples and monasteries, or ashrams. Music also was patronized at the royal courts and the numerous courtesan houses.

By the sixth century CE, the older system of *grama-jati* expanded into a system of mixing scales to create melodies, called the *grama*-ragas and *bhasha*-ragas. The ancient *jatis* came to be reserved for more esoteric music for spiritual worship, of which not many examples survive. After a few centuries, the ragas emerged as basic scales, without the *gramas* and *murcchana* classifications.

Medieval Transition

With the Turkic invasion of India (early twelfth century) and the establishment of Islamic governments in most parts of the country, a major change in the performing arts occurred. As a consequence of the puritanical denunciation of music by the Islamic clergy, music was patronized by royalty only as a deviation from Islamic beliefs. Indian dancing and its music, which were either temple worship or theatrical repertoire (mostly centered on Hindu myths) had neither any place in the royal courts nor could be funded by the Islamic rulers, who often were fanatic iconoclasts. The fury of temple destruction that raged for nearly four centuries in most parts of India (except in the far south) rendered homeless all the arts supported at temple complexes, theaters, and courtesan houses. Only the concert repertoire of vocal and instrumental music, presented largely as chamber music, could be patronized by those rulers who could afford to disregard the censure of their clergy. This was the genre of music that survived and even flourished and that drew performers of other genres. It also was a point of contact with musicians from Iran and other Southwest Asian nations. In addition to the royal courts, Indian musicians found the many sects *(silsilas)* of Sufi saints and their camps *(dargahs)* to be sites where music was valued as a legitimate method of worship. But such places, although they could furnish an audience, provided less material patronage. Vernacular songs for ecstatic dancing *(samah)* and in praise of the Prophet and his sayings *(qawali)* were cultivated and acquired great popularity.

Indian musicians thus turned in a big way to the Hindu monastic centers (ashrams) of saints and mendicants, usually located outside towns and villages. For the average Hindu devotee, ashrams were replacements for the great temple complexes as spaces of spiritual, cultural, and aesthetic activity. The music that developed there, however, was largely devotional, hymnal, and otherworldly and supported the great flowering of devotional poetry in the vernacular. In northern India, earlier vernacular compositions, called *prabandhas*, first were replaced by new compositions in Brijbhashas Hindi, called *dhruvapadas*, and, later, by *khayals*, *thumris*, *dadras*, and so on. In the south, devotional vernacular compositions also were abundant and were known as *kritis*, *varnams*, *pallavis*, *jawalis*, and so on. They all are in praise of the gods—such as Krishna, Rama, Siva, and Devi—and the power of Nada (sound as a cosmic principle) and yogic consciousness. This music that was cultivated in the ashrams was also patronized at both Islamic and Hindu royal courts.

Around the fourteenth century, a major shift occurred in the musical grammar of India. The *grama-murcchana* system, which defined the shifting of the tonic from one note to another, was abandoned, and a new system evolved, which was called the *mela*. In this system, the tonic was fixed on the first note of the septet, the *sa*. Instead of allowing a modification in the position of all seven notes, as in the earlier system, five notes were added to the septet—that is, flat *ri*, sharp *ga*, sharp *ma*, flat *dha*, and sharp *ni*—to make a series of twelve notes. *Sa* and *pa*, a consonance of a fifth, were unchanging notes. This is first stated by Lochana in the *Ragatarangini* (c. fifteenth century CE). The development of fretted zithers and the impact of the Persian *maqam* system (a system of scales in which seven sharp and five flat notes made a sequence of twelve notes in a given octave) is said to be the major cause of this change. The *mela* system is called *thaat* in northern India.

Around the same time, Indian music acquired some diverse and distinctive characteristics, exemplified in a division between north and south. In the north, most lyrics for classical music were composed in Brijbhasha Hindi; in the south, they were composed in Telugu. Differences in stylistic renderings, names of the ragas, beats, use of instruments, nature of embellishments, methods of training, and modes of performance also contributed to the different identities. Northern music (also called Hindustani) still concentrates on the expansion of the melodic structure through *alapana* and improvisation, a progression of rhythm from slow to fast, and the work of the lead performer. Its compositions are also on erotic themes, descriptive of seasonal and natural beauty, in addition to hymnal themes. Southern music (also called Karnataka) has reduced *alapana*, better preserved lyrical composition, dominance of the middle beat, emphasis on group work, and greater rhythmic variety. The content of Karnataka lyrics is nearly always religious. *Malkaus*, *Todi*, *Kalyana*, *Jaijaiwanti*, *Bihag*, and *Piloo* are some of the popular Hindustani ragas, and *Kalyani*, *Hindolam*, *Sauviri*, *Malayamarutam*, and *Bhoop* are some of the Karnataka ones.

Music in India at the End of the Twentieth Century

The variety of music performed in India is still staggeringly large. From the thousands-of-years-old chanting of the Sanskrit mantras of the four Vedas to the latest film-hit songs, there are tribal and ritual songs of marriage, birth, naming, clothing, bathing, leaving home, and death, in dozens of languages and dialects across the subcontinent. The traditions of Hindustani and Karnataka are moving closer toward a healthy interchange. For three decades after independence from British rule (1947), classical music was a major source of encouraging national pride both at home and abroad.

In spite of its archaic features, Indian music has adapted with ease to modern technical innovations, from the microphone to the microchip, without adversely altering any of its content. The technological revolution actually helped spread music within India and throughout the world and helped it influence the music of many other nations.

The process of notating and printing lyrics, historically orally handed down, began in the early twentieth century. This was followed by performances of folk and classical music in modern concert halls and on the radio. Artists recorded works on gramophone records as early as in the West. The Indian film industry consolidated the immense variety of music from all parts of India and transmitted it to the global listener. Through films, Indian music is a major influence on countries and regions such as Iran, Iraq, Turkey, the Persian Gulf, and the states of Central Asia. In spite of the emergence of global pop, Indian music has succeeded in maintaining its very distinct identity and independence from Western music. Its classical performers have taken it live to all corners of the world, and recordings can be found increasingly in private collections.

Bharat Gupt

Further Reading

Bharatakosa: A Dictionary of Technical Terms with Definitions Collected from the Works on Music and Dramaturgy by Bharata and Others. (1951) Compiled by M. Ramakrishna Kavi. Tirupati, India: Tirupati Devasthanam.

Bharatamuni. (1956–1964) *Natya sastram,* with *Abhinahavabhi.* Ed. by Ramakrishna Kavi. 4 vols. Gaekwad's Oriental Series. Baroda, India: Oriental Institute.

Gaston, A. (1997) *Krishna's Musicians.* Delhi: Manohar.

Gupt, Bharat. (1994) *Dramatic Concepts: Greek and Indian: A Study of Poetics and the Natya sastra.* Delhi: D. K. Printworld.

———. (1996) *Natyasastra: Ancient Scales of Indian Music.* Sanjivanam commentary by Acarya Brihaspati. Intro. and trans. by Bharat Gupt. Delhi: Brahaspati.

MUSIC—INDIA, DEVOTIONAL

"Devotional music" is a term used most frequently for the religious music of Hinduism and any other religion of Asian origin. Christianity and Islam also have developed some indigenous traditions of spiritual music, but as Hinduism (or the Vedic religion, as it is sometimes called) has a vast ambit of ritualistic prayer, nearly all devotional music currently prevalent in India is nurtured under its impact.

In India, the intense personal relationship of the individual devotee to God has been a major philosophy of liberation for fifteen hundred years. In this system of belief, God may be imagined as a lover, mother, child, master, or friend, and devotion to God in any of these forms should be expressed as a song. Use of poetry, music, and dance has been considered one of the most natural methods of worship in sanctuaries, temples, and personal idolatory. The code of ethics called the Yajnavalkya Smriti (from approximately the third century BCE) states, "One who knows the secrets of the harp, of musical scales like jatis, their microtonal tones and of rhythms, walks along the path of liberation." Censure and suspicion of music as an instigator of base desires and, hence, ungodly have hardly ever been the view of any sect of Indian origin.

Monks use cymbals and chant in prayer at a Buddhist temple in Swayambhunath, Nepal. (EARL & NAZIMA KOWALL/CORBIS)

The hymns of the Rig Veda (scholars date these either from the fifth or second millennium BCE) for the Vedic gods like Indra, Agni, Varuna, and Mitra are the earliest extant example of devotional music. These were fine poetry recited with to three tones. But the Samavedic tradition, which was called *gana* (song), expanded the number of notes used to seven, thereby utilizing a musical scale. It also is known that sometimes harps were employed for accompaniment. The nature of this devotion was more communal than individual.

In the post-Vedic phase, most evident from the third century BCE, hymns in classical Sanskrit and other vernaculars were composed for gods like Shiva, Vasudeva, Parvati, Brahma, and Kamadeva and sung in temples, theaters, and in social rituals. The great temple complexes that were built from the second century BCE to the sixteenth century CE maintained a big retinue of dancers and musicians who performed several times in a day before the deity. Often composer-poets also were employed to make new compositions for the musicians.

Even the nonidolatrous sects like Buddhism and Jainism, while avoiding the personal praise of Buddha or Mahavira as God, nevertheless developed a devotional music that consisted of intricate chants and mantras with which their caves and monasteries resounded. Buddhist chants such as "Buddham Sharanam Gacchami" were modeled after the three-tone Rig Vedic chants.

The great age of devotional music in India, however, began around the seventh century, with the so-called philosophy of personal and individual *bhakti* (devotion). This sect had two broad divisions: those who worshiped God as incarnation and those who contemplated on him as the formless source of creation, preservation, and destruction. For the former, the life deeds of incarnations like Krishna or Rama were a *lila* (divine play), to be sung for liberation. The saint poets of this sect—Jayadeva, Surdas, Tulsidas, Mira, Rasakhan, Kamban, Potanna, Tyagaraja, and many others—always set their poetry to music. Singing was the chief mode of worship whether done individually in isolation or in community of the faithful. For the latter, the formless God was to be contemplated by calling/singing his name. Music was the most desirable means of devotion during this phase of religious approach, which lasted for eight centuries. Traditional music of India bears the stamp of this great religious movement to this day.

Bharat Gupt

Further Reading

Gautam, M. R. (1980) *The Musical Heritage of India.* Delhi: Abhinav Publications.

Roy Chaudhury, H. C. (1962) *Materials for the Study of the Early History of the Vaisnava Sect.* Calcutta, India.

Swami Prajnananda. (1965) *A Historical Study of Indian Music.* Calcutta, India: Anandadhara Publications.

MUSIC—INDONESIA

The thousands of islands in Indonesia have been home to its mainly Malayo-Polynesian ethnic groups and musical practices since prehistoric times. The broadly similar musical instruments, performance practices, and music-generating concepts throughout the archipelago are partly due to use of the Malay lingua franca and constant sea and land contact over the millennia.

Culturally, the ethnic groups can be classified as uplanders and lowlanders. Uplanders (for example, the Torajans of South Sulawesi, the Dani in Papua, and the Batak, Kerinci, and Basemah of the mountainous backbone of Sumatra) speak diverse local languages and are mostly nomadic or seminomadic hunters and gatherers who adhere to ancestral and nature-venerating (animist) beliefs and practices, or, from the seventeenth century, to a blend of Christianity and animism. Each performs ritual-associated songs (for healing, lamenting, soothing, war making, celebrating life events, and so forth) and self-expressive songs (for example, for love, courting, raising one's morale while in the forest), often playing portable musical instruments (for example, flutes, Jew's harps, and drums).

Lowlanders, who are mainly Muslim wet-rice farmers, gardeners, and fishers, have a great trading and seafaring culture. Each group has its own instrumental ensembles and vocal styles, and many have their own music-theatrical traditions. Examples include Javanese *wayang* (shadow puppet theater), magical songs, such as solo *kapri* songs of coastal northwestern Sumatra, and many Muslim-associated forms. Some minority Chinese, Arab, Indian, and other immigrant communities practice musical forms from their cultural heritage or practice syncretic forms. As the reliefs on the eighth-century Buddhist Borobudur and the ninth-century Hindu Prambanan temples in lowland Java indicate, musical ensembles comprising gongs, drums, xylophones, and flutes already existed during the period 400–900 CE; their aesthetic remains Hindu-Buddhist. In southern Sumatra, the Srivijaya empire (flourished from the seventh through the eighth centuries) brought Buddhism to various areas, whereas in central Java the Majapahit empire (1200–1500) continued the Hindu tradition, giving way from around the 1400s to Islam, with communities in Java, Sumatra, Kalimantan, the Moluccas, and beyond being governed by sultanates. The main surviving musical expressions of Hinduism today are the gamelan (Indonesian percussion orchestra) ensembles and vocal music of Java, West Java, and Bali. Associated with Hindu-Balinese religious functions and theater forms, the latter have been performed for centuries at temple festivals, street processions, cremations, and other life-event ceremonies.

Music and the Natural Environment

That music everywhere reflects the natural environment is widely apparent, as in Javanese *gara-gara* gamelan music, which depicts natural turbulences during the middle section of the Javanese *wayang* or *wayang orang* (human theater) night. The materials of which the puppets, theatrical properties, and musical instruments are made—mainly leather, bronze, iron, wood, and bamboo—are determined by local flora, fauna, and metals, while traditional farming and socioreligious practices provide the contexts for their artistic usage. Bronze, known to have been made in mainland Southeast Asia from about 3000 BCE, was brought to Indonesia during the period 300–200 BCE; remnants of bronze Dong-son era (400 BCE–200 CE) "kettledrums" have been found in Java, Sumatra, and the Moluccas. Around 200–100 BCE, bronze gongs are thought to have been made in Java and other islands, ranging from large hanging gongs to gong chimes and bronze metallophones. Gongs of various alloys and sizes are still made, for example, for iron gamelans in central Java and for the brass *talempong* (gong chime and drum) ensembles used in Minangkabau (on the western coast of the central portion of Sumatra). Varieties of bamboo and wood found ubiquitously are used to make tuned slabs of keys for trough, leg, and frame xylophones and many kinds of plucked lutes, flutes, oboes, mouth organs, board and tube zithers, Jew's harps, bullroarers, slit drums, shaken idiophones (an instrument that is naturally sonorous and that may be shaken, struck, plucked, or rubbed), and stamping poles. Conical, truncated conical, cylindrical, hourglass-shaped, and other shaped wooden drums with buffalo or goat skins occur in many sizes, producing various drum timbres when beaten with hands, fingers, or sticks.

Ensemble Music

Ensembles minimally comprise drums, gongs, and an optional melodic instrument or voice. The gamelans of Java and Bali combine various sizes of drums, gongs, metallophones, xylophones, cymbals, zithers, plucked lutes, bowed strings, and solo or group vocal parts, or both. Textures usually comprise layers of musical parts (stratification), each performed idiomatically for the particular instrument or human voice and combining to produce composite rhythms and melodies in binary meter by sharing (interlocking, or colotomic) parts. Mostly tuned in pentatonic (five-tone) *slendro* and heptatonic (seven-tone) *pelog* occurring in several modes *(pathet)* (Javanese terms), they feature (1) a rhythmic, tempo-controlling drumming part, (2) a repeated fixed melody at walking pace on the slab metallophones, (3) slower-moving interlocking parts on the hanging and horizontal bossed gongs, and (4) more densely ornamented parts on the gong chimes, softer metallophones, spike fiddle, flute, and vocal parts. Interlocking also governs the practice of many other ensembles, including *gender wayang* quartets in a Balinese shadow play, the long wooden pole-beating on stones in Minangkabau, and the thunderous *gordang sembilan* (nine-drum ensemble) played with gongs, cymbals, and oboe in Mandailing (just above Minangkabau on Sumatra). In addition, strict- or free-meter narrative story-telling, histories, or genealogies, with or without instrumental accompaniment, are performed, as are ritual songs of love and courting, laments, lullabies, magical shamans' songs, songs for and by children, and work songs.

Popular Music

Kroncong music (which originated via sixteenth-century contact with Portuguese traders and features vocal soloists, string instruments, and flute) and *orkes Melayu* ("Malay band," which originated in the early twentieth century and includes vocalists, strings or harmonium, and drums) still accompany couples dancing and also serve as progenitors of modern popular forms. Thus *dangdut*, Indonesia's main contribution to the world's popular music from the 1970s, developed from *orkes Melayu*, combining Indonesian texts and styles with electrified Western rock and pop and featuring a distinctive rhythm often heard in Indian film music. Other popular forms adopted since the introduction of radio, television, and cassette technology and consumed by all social classes contribute to the lucrative domestic and foreign commodity industry, including the indigenous Sundanese popular genre *jaipongan* (with a female singer-dancer and small gamelan) and various fusions of regional and Western popular elements that express youthful rebellion, social criticism, and love themes. Meanwhile, from the 1970s, avant-garde composers created new music, largely based on traditional forms, for specialized audiences.

Margaret J. Kartomi

Further Reading

Becker, Judith. (1980) *Traditional Music in Modern Java: Gamelan in a Changing Society*. Honolulu: University of Hawaii Press.

Becker, Judith, and Alan Feinstein, eds. (1984, 1987, 1988) *Karawitan: Source Readings in Javanese Gamelan and Vocal Music*. Ann Arbor: Center for South and Southeast Asian Studies, University of Michigan.

Frederick, William H. (1982) "Rhoma Irama and the *Dangdut* Style: Aspects of Contemporary Indonesian Popular Culture." *Indonesia* 34: 103–130.

Kartomi, Margaret. (1998) "Sumatra," "Sulawesi," and "Maluku." In *The Garland Encyclopedia of World Music: Southeast Asia*, edited by Terry E. Miller and Sean Williams. New York: Garland Publishing, 598–629, 804–811, 812–822.

Kunst, Jaap. (1973) *Music in Java: Its History, Its Theory, and Its Technique*. The Hague, Netherlands: Martinus Nijhoff.

McPhee, Colin. (1966) *Music in Bali: A Study in Form and Instrumental Organization in Balinese Orchestral Music*. New Haven, CT: Yale University Press.

Sutton, R. Anderson. (1991) *Traditions of Gamelan Music in Java: Musical Pluralism and Regional Identity*. Cambridge, MA: Cambridge University Press.

Sutton, R. Anderson, Endo Suanda, and Sean Williams. (1998) "Java." In *The Garland Encyclopedia of World Music: Southeast Asia*, edited by Terry E. Miller and Sean Williams. New York: Garland Publishing, 630–728.

Tenzer, Michael. (1991) *Balinese Music*. Singapore: Periplus Editions.

MUSIC—JAPAN Japan's long history of cultural influence from the continent, alternating with independent development and adaptation to suit indigenous aesthetics, has resulted in a rich and varied

A drummer in traditional costume plays the kakko, a drum beaten with two sticks to keep time, which leads other instruments. (BETTMANN/CORBIS)

musical culture reflecting the country's geographical location at the terminus of the Silk Road.

Several major characteristics typify the traditional music of Japan, many of which are common to other counties in Asia. With the exception of gagaku (court music), traditional music is monophonic, focusing on subtleties of tone, timbre, and rhythm rather than on harmony. Melody is based on the twelve-tone unequal-tempered tone system, within which three types of scales can be identified: two five-tone scales, used in koto, *shamisen*, and folk music; a seven-tone scale, used in gagaku; and a tone system based on the tetrachord, used in *shomyo* (Buddhist chanting) and Noh drama. Melodic line is often based on the arrangement of recognizable melodic patterns. The range of timbre in traditional music is narrow, limited to plucked strings, bamboo wind instruments, and barrel and hourglass drums of differing sizes. Consequently, subtleties of timbre among Japanese instruments are highly refined. Each musical genre has developed its own notation system, with little overlap. As in many other Asian countries, much of Japanese music has been created in combination with literature, theater, and dance.

Gagaku

Gagaku, literally "elegant music," is the oldest surviving musical form in Japan. Gagaku refers to purely instrumental music as well as to music that accompanies the court dance called *bugaku*. Originally imported from Korea, China, and China's various vassal states during the Nara period (710–794), gagaku was fostered by the imperial court and served as ceremonial music at rituals and festivals and as a pastime for aristocratic nobles. It reached its peak of popularity in the tenth century, but lost favor in the Kamakura period (1185–1333), when the power and prestige of the court aristocracy waned in favor of the new, rising military class.

By the beginning of the Tokugawa period (1600/1603–1868), only fragmentary gagaku groups remained. The first shogun, Tokugawa Ieyasu (1543–1616), consolidated the remaining gagaku ensembles into two groups, thus maintaining the tradition, though with a limited repertory. In 1955, gagaku was designated an important national treasure by the Japanese government.

Both music and dance gagaku are divided into compositions of the left (Chinese, Indian, and Japanese origin) and right (Korean or Manchurian origin); there are slight variations in the instrumental ensembles for each side. Though the ensemble consists of strings, percussion, and winds, these areas of sound remain distinct, with the winds (*hichiriki, ryuteki*) serving as the melodic instruments, and the stringed instruments *(gakuso, biwa)* and drums marking time units with stereotyped patterns.

Biwa Music

With the rise of the military class in the late twelfth century, the *biwa*, a four-stringed lute plucked with a large plectrum, was used by blind musicians to accompany tales of the rise and fall of great warriors of the Heike clan. Though poetry had long been sung in court-music traditions, this new *biwa* music marked the beginning of a narrative musical tradition. The idea of narrative music was important in the development of Noh theater in the fourteenth century, as well as in developments in *shamisen* music beginning in the sixteenth century.

Noh Music

Noh music consists of solo speech and singing by actors, unison singing by a chorus of seven to ten, and an instrumental ensemble. The transverse bamboo flute *(nokan)* plays melodies independent of the vocal line, while the rhythm of the percussive instruments—shoulder drum *(kotsuzumi)*, hip drum *(otsuzumi)*, and stick drum *(taiko)*—is based on an eight-beat structure matched to the text in one of several clearly defined rhythmic modes. The tone system of Noh, which was influenced by the *shomyo* Buddhist chant, is constructed around three main nuclear tones: high, middle, and low, each separated by an interval of a perfect fourth, with additional important tones a perfect fifth above the high tone and a perfect fourth below the low tone.

Shamisen Music

As urban centers grew in the Tokugawa period, commercial theatrical forms and musical forms within the lively licensed quarters (where theaters and houses of prostitution were permitted) rapidly developed. Central to these developments was the *shamisen*, a three-stringed banjolike lute descended from the Chinese *sanxian*. It first arrived in Japan via the Ryukyu Islands (Okinawa) around 1562 and underwent several transformations, including the addition of *sawari*, a buzzing sound incorporated into the vibration of the first (lowest) string, and the borrowing of the large plectrum used to play the *biwa*.

Over the next three centuries, various genres of *shamisen* music developed: the heavy-sounding narrative of *gidayu* in puppet drama (Bunraku); lyrical *nagauta* in Kabuki (traditional dramas with dance and singing); and the versatile narrative genres of *tokiwazu-bushi*, *kiyomoto-bushi*, *kato-bushi*, *shinnai-bushi*, and others, which were heard in the licensed districts as well as on the Kabuki stage. Each genre is distinguished by subtle differences in timbre, achieved by varying the body size of the *shamisen*, thickness of the neck and strings, height of the bridge; size, composition, and attack of the plectrum; pitch range of the vocal line, and stereotyped patterns of the instrumental and vocal lines.

Koto Music

During this same period, new styles of music developed for the koto, a thirteen-string zither originally found in the gagaku ensemble. Yatsuhashi Kengyo (1614–1685), and later Ikuta Kengyo (1656–1715), created new tunings, solo compositions for koto, and compositions for *sankyoku*, a trio consisting of koto, *shamisen*, and *shakuhachi* (a long end-blown bamboo flute).

Influences of Western Music

The Meiji period (1868–1912) was a time of rapid modernization, with overwhelming influence from the West. Education policies emphasized the need to study Western music. The imperial army and navy had military bands that performed the first public concerts, introducing popular Western music and in turn greatly influencing the popular songs of Japan. Christian hymns brought by missionaries shaped the composition of children's songs taught as part of the new elementary school music curriculum. The Tokyo Music School (now Tokyo University of Fine Arts and Music), established in 1887, offered the first Western music conservatory training in Japan. Composers such as Miyage Michio (1895–1956) introduced the diachronic scale to koto music and fused Western and Japanese music traditions in orchestral compositions for thirteen-string and newly designed seventeen-string bass koto. One of Miyage's most famous compositions, *Haru no Umi* (The Spring Sea, 1929) remains a perennial favorite at New Year's time.

Music in Japan Today

Today Japan boasts over twenty professional symphony orchestras and has nurtured internationally known talents such as Toru Takemitsu (1930–1996), a composer of more than one hundred works for piano and chamber and symphony orchestra, and Seiji Ozawa (b. 1935), conductor of the Boston Symphony for nearly thirty years. One notable phenomenon that spread from Japan throughout Asia, Europe, and the Americas is the popular pastime of singing karaoke, literally "empty" *(kara)* "orchestra" (*oke*, in abbreviated form). Urban areas also boast hundreds of pop, rock, blues, jazz, and world beat bands that play in countless bars and "live houses" throughout the cities.

For many Japanese, Western music—classical and popular—is more familiar than are traditional Japanese music genres. Music education policies, a legacy of the Meiji period, include Western music in school curricula, but place traditional musical genres outside the formal education system, to be sustained by an apprentice system. Nevertheless, all of these musical worlds thrive side by side, and on any given day in

Japan one may experience everything from ancient gagaku to modern electronic music.

Julie A. Iezzi

Further Reading

Harich-Schneider, Eta. (1973) *A History of Japanese Music*. London: Oxford University Press.

Kishibe Shigeo. (1966) *The Traditional Music of Japan*. Tokyo: Kokusai Bunka Shinkokai.

Komiya Toyotaka. (1956) *Japanese Music and Drama in the Meiji Era*. Trans. by Edward Seidensticker and Donald Keene. Tokyo: Obunsha.

Malm, William P. (1963) *Nagauta, The Heart of Kabuki Music*. Rutland, VT: Charles E. Tuttle.

———. (2000) *Traditional Japanese Music and Musical Instruments*. Tokyo: Kodansha International.

MUSIC—KOREA On the surface, Korean musical culture shares many similarities with the musical cultures of China and Japan. The evidence includes notations, instruments, repertory, and so on. However, certain deep underlying aesthetic concepts distinguish Korean traditional music from its neighbors. The personal performance style, which incorporates a high degree of individualistic and creative variation and improvisation, sometimes beyond all prediction and anticipation, has resulted in a musical environment in which individual creativity, not rigid imitation, is the norm. Adherence to a standardized performance practice was not a convention in Korean traditional music. The resultant differences from such a diverse performance practice have often given rise to arguments regarding the authenticity of the performance. This kind of musical discourse further strengthens the notion that the open-ended nature of musical style is indeed an important characteristic of Korean music. It has brought about a rich variety of styles. The continuity of traditional musical practice in contemporary society is apparent in the realm of neotraditional music and popular song. However, the overwhelming influence of Western music, the impact of cultural policy-making, and the desire for globalization are all detrimental influences on Korean traditional music and musical aesthetics.

Historical Situation

The music history of Korea up to the early twentieth century is characterized by gradual evolution over time rather than by drastic reform in the process of transmission. Most of the long-lasting indigenous repertories have been transmitted and preserved without pronounced reform, although many of their origins are unknown. Imported repertories, mostly from China, existed alongside indigenous music without either repertory influencing the other significantly. This is true to such a degree that some repertories and instruments that have been lost in China, such as Chinese court ritual music and court banquet music (which were introduced into Korea in the twelfth century), are still being performed in Korea. It is also interesting to note the respect with which the Korean court treated the instruments used in Chinese court ritual music: These instruments were never secularized or modified in Korea, while some of them became folk instruments in China.

Contemporary Situation

The present musical landscape in South Korea is diverse and lively. While other countries lament the loss of their traditional music, in South Korea concert halls hosting traditional music performances are usually packed. Ever since the introduction of Western classical music to Korea in the late nineteenth century, Korean traditional music has been identified as *kugak* ("national music"), reserving the term *umak* ("music") or *yangak* ("Western music") for Western classical music.

Traditional Instruments

Korean musical instruments have two distinctive characteristics: the ability to produce pitch variants during performance and the ability to produce a some-

A group of traveling musicians with drums and tambourines in central Korea in 1946. (HORACE BRISTOL/CORBIS)

what raspy, buzzing, or rattling sound quality. Thus, the *komungo* (plucked zither), *haegum* (two-stringed fiddle), *p'iri* (reed pipe), and *taegum* (large flute) play important roles in traditional music. Such Chinese instruments as the *ajaeng* (bowed zither) satisfied these requirements and were adopted for indigenous music with slight modification. Even some major indigenous instruments such as the *komungo* and *taegum* have gone through a certain degree of modification to emphasize the foregoing requisite qualities. Conversely, instruments with fixed tuning such as the *yanggum* (dulcimer), or with a polished sound such as the *tanso* (short vertical flute) are not considered important in Korean traditional music.

Characteristics of Korean Music

The most important aspect of style in Korean music is flexibility, which permits personal deviation, variation, and improvisation during performance. The extent to which improvisation is taken depends on the performer and ranges from a mere ornamental deviation, as often occurs in court music, to full-blown improvisation, as occurs in such folk forms as *sinawi* (improvised instrumental ensemble), *sanjo* (solo instrumental music), and *p'ansori* (one-person musical story-telling). These three genres all originated in the southern part of Korea, and their history is related to shaman rituals of the region. Together with the *samulnori*-type of music, the post-1970 percussion quartet utilizing folk rhythms, they are the most popular folk music in South Korea today.

The improvisational aspects of the *sanjo* have gradually been disappearing with the constraints of modern performance, however. For example, the limited duration of performance in the mass media and the teaching of *sanjo* from transcription since the 1960s have contributed to a decline in improvisation in *sanjo*. Teaching from transcription in particular has led to standardization of this once flexible style of music.

The texture of Korean music is basically monophonic, and most ensemble music is organized lineally. Unlike in Western music, in which the sound is formed by the vertical build-up of harmony, in Korean ensemble music each part is supposed to be heard individually. Sometimes, the parts may take off in quite different directions momentarily, resulting in melodic contrasts, and then meet at the same melodic line.

Most of the rhythms of Korean traditional music are based on triple time, or groups of three beats. The characteristic detail of Korean triple time is that the third beat is either articulated or accented, drawing more attention than the first beat. Duple time does exist in traditional music, but it is very rare. In folk music duple meter is always combined with triple meter, forming a lengthy asymmetric rhythm. Asymmetric rhythms abound in regional *p'ungmul* (rural outdoor band music and dance) and shamanic ritual music. The length of these rhythms or rhythmic cycles may range from five beats (duple plus triple) to as long as thirty-six beats. When the rhythm is actually played by drums or gongs, the details of strokes vary considerably for each repetition to suit the melodic rhythm or to express rhythmic virtuosity.

Lee Byongwon

Further Reading

Korean National Academy of Arts. (1973) *Survey of Korean Arts: Traditional Music.* Seoul: Korean National Academy of Arts.

Lee, Byong Won. (1980) "Korea." In *The New Grove Dictionary of Music and Musicians*, edited by Stanley Sadie. London: Macmillan.

———. (1997) *Styles and Esthetics in Korean Traditional Music.* Seoul: National Center for Korean Traditional Performing Arts.

MUSIC—LAOS, FOLK

Legends state that the origin of Lao folk music comes from nature, such as the wind blowing through bamboo groves and the melodic songs of birds. Lao folk music is based on a tempered heptatonic scale, or a division of the octave into seven equal parts. It is also polyphonic and has been influenced by the music traditions of the Khmer kingdoms of Cambodia. Dancing *(fawn)* usually accompanies the playing of folk music at festivals or ceremonies.

The *khaen* is the foundation of Lao folk music. The *khaen* is an open reed instrument made from two rows of eight to nine hollow bamboo pipes held together in a wood support. Each pipe contains a metal reed. The *khaen* can be played as a solo instrument but usually serves as an accompaniment to folk songs called *lam.* The subjects of the folk songs are love and courtship, religious themes, and adventurous tales and legends. There are approximately twenty schools of *lam* folk music—classified by their geographical origins—such as Lam Saravan, Lam Siphandone, Lam Khon Savan, Lam Mahaxay, Lam Ban Sok, and Lam Muang Luang. Subject matter, the number of singers, and poetic form are the basis for other *lam* classifications. The style of the folk music also depends on whether the *khaen* is played alone or with other instruments such as the *pin*, a two- or three-stringed instrument played like a mandolin, or *saw*, a type of fiddle.

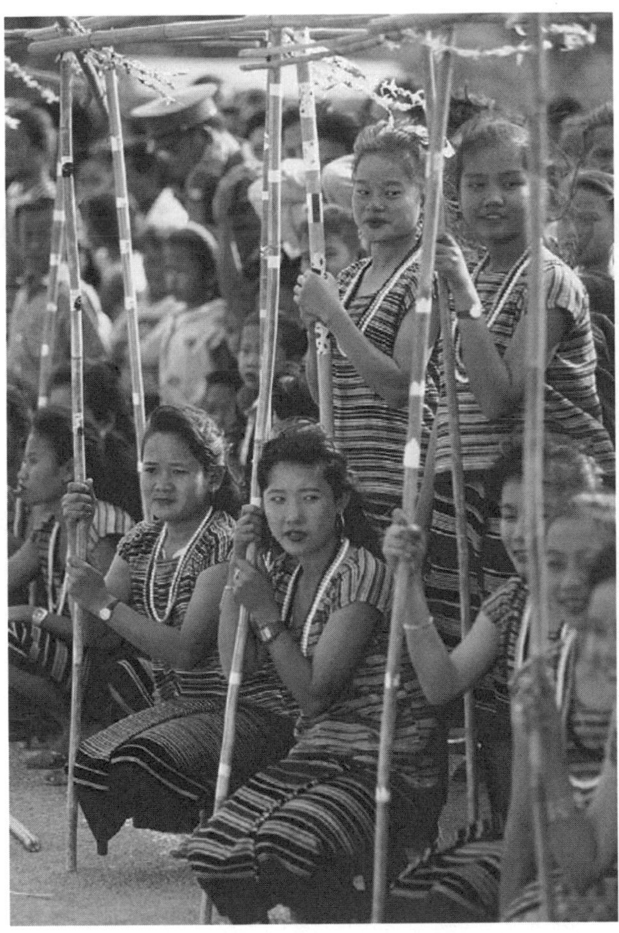

Women with traditional musical instruments in Vientiane, Laos. (NIK WHEELER/CORBIS)

An expert *khaen* player is a *maw khaen*, and an expert folk singer is called a *maw lam*. Both men and women can be expert singers and usually sing in pairs *(lam khu)* at important events such as festivals. Lao folk singing requires improvisation since each singer attempts to outwit the other in songs of courtship, for example. The singers' improvisation must follow rules of versification and the general tempo of the music. The singing jousts continue late into the night and may last for hours. Both the *maw lam* and *maw khaen* also perform at weddings and other festive occasions. A folk music performance is a community event, uniting village members in a relaxed atmosphere.

The popularity of the *khaen* and folk music in general has decreased due to exposure to other forms of entertainment such as television and radio. Music of both Lao and Thai pop bands using electrical instruments is available throughout the country. However, the Lao government has named the *khaen* the national musical instrument. Lao expatriates living in the United States and France, for example, continue the tradition of *khaen* playing and folk singing. Nouthong Phimivilayphone is a *khaen* player producing Lao folk music in France for an international audience. Lao folk music presently coexists with other types of music and will persevere due to its importance to Lao identity and ideas of nationhood. A Lao proverb states that a Lao person eats sticky rice and fermented fish and plays the *khaen*.

Linda McIntosh

Further Reading

Miller, Terry E. (1985) *Traditional Music of Laos: Khaen Playing and Mawlam Singing in Northeast Thailand*. Westport, CT: Greenwood Press.

Phraxayavong, Viliam. (2001) "The Khene: Lao National Musical Instrument and Its Role in Lao Culture." Retrieved 12 December 2001, from: http://www.global.lao.net/laostudy/khene.htm.

MUSIC—TURKEY Turkish music has several distinctive styles, some of which originated as early as Ottoman times. During the Ottoman empire (1453–1922), there were two categories of music: court and folk. Today, traditional court music is commonly called Turkish classical music or Turkish art music. This tradition reflects combinations of Turkish, Arabic, Persian, and Byzantine styles and motifs, and it developed a rich repertoire during the centuries of Ottoman rule. Sultans brought popular musicians and composers from all over the world to their courts, where they were employed as state musicians. Schools in the palace were also devoted to training musicians. Turkish classical music incorporates a wide array of musical instruments, most commonly Turkish varieties of lutes, woodwinds, flutes, violins, and zithers.

Turkish folk music, originally village music, includes dance tunes, folk songs, even lullabies. Each region of Turkey has its distinctive musical styles and instruments. The most commonly used folk music instruments include drum, shawm, *saz* (a long-necked lute), vase drum, reed pipe, and flute.

In addition to these two traditional styles, contemporary Turkish music includes both new musical genres and subgenres of traditional Turkish classical and folk traditions. Among these new forms is *fasil* music, a nightclub version of classical Turkish music with distinctive forms, styles, instruments, and atmosphere. *Fasil* music is heavily influenced by Gypsy/Roma musical traditions. Among its best-known performers are Mustafa Kandirali and Kadri Sencalar.

Another new musical category is Turkish popular music, which combines Turkish folk songs, Arabic music, and other styles. Due to its resemblance to Arabic

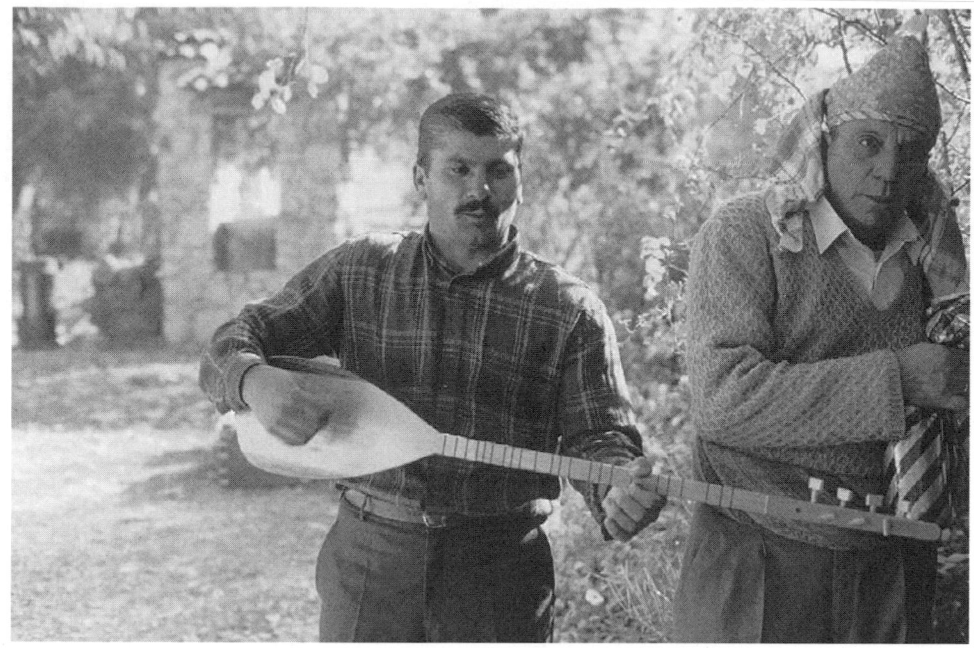

Man playing the *saz* near Kusadasi, Turkey. (WOLFGANG KAEHLER/CORBIS)

music, some people call it "arabesk." The main lyrical themes of Turkish popular music are complaints about life and expressions of remorse and loneliness. This genre, which emerged in the 1960s, a period of rapid urbanization and mass migration in Turkey, conveys popular sentiments about adjustments to big-city life and shared disappointments. Ibrahim Tatlises, Ferdi Tayfur, and Orhan Gencebay are the most prominent musicians in this category.

Like popular music, another new type, Turkish protest music, also employs folk music forms. Its lyrics, deriving from ordinary people's struggles, are heavily politicized. The best-known protest music singers are Ahmet Kaya and Zulfu Livaneli.

Turkish music also includes less commonly practiced musical traditions, such as Sufi music and Janissary music. Sufi music is mostly associated with followers of both the Mevlevi (whirling dervishes) and Bektashi orders of Sufism. Janissary music is the historic military music used by Ottoman armies, which influenced some European composers.

Styles of Western music have also been influential in contemporary Turkish society. During the early years of the Turkish republic, Western music gained recognition as the state encouraged its appreciation over Turkish classical music, which was regarded as distinctly Ottoman. Western styles continue to play important roles in current Turkish pop music.

Emine O. Evered

Further Reading

Bartok, Bela. (1976) *Turkish Folk Music from Asia Minor.* Edited by Benjamin Suchoff. Princeton, NJ: Princeton University Press.

Stokes, Martin. (1992) *The Arabesk Debate: Music and Musicians in Modern Turkey.* Oxford, U.K.: Clarendon Press.

MUSIC—WEST ASIA

The territories of West Asia share a centuries-old history that expresses itself in the traditional music of the region, in voice and instrumental forms. Amateur musicians are often found playing at social gatherings and communal gathering places (*mudhifs*).

Song

Song is used at celebratory social festivals as well as at funerals, where it is used to mourn the dead. Sung plays known as *ta'ziyah* and *rowzeh* are based on the life of the Shi'ite marytr Imam Husayn and his family and are performed throughout Iran. In *ta'ziyah* plays, singing is used by the good characters only; the evil characters do not sing their lines. The *rowzeh* is performed by a special singer at devotional gatherings and is an extended poetic narrative. Work songs are used to motivate and add interest to fishing, hunting, and farming, and there are even songs for exercise workouts.

In Arabic vocal music the text is strongly related to the music. One of the oldest traditions is that of the *qasida*. In classical vocal form it utilizes sung poetry or a classical ode. Frequently there can be more than one hundred lines to the poem. The folk version of this form is also called *qasida*, but the language used in the text is more colloquial. The *qasida* is one of three vocal poetic styles of the Iraqi *maqam*. The other two are the *takhims* and *mawwal* (also known as *zheiri*). Iranian poetic singing often uses text from Firdawsi's *Shahnameh* ("Book of Kings").

Sufi Music

There are various Sufi (Islamic mystic) sects throughout West Asia. *Tasavvuf* (Sufi) music is music composed as part of the Sufi searching and celebration of the unification of existence. Images of whirling dervishes of the Mawlawi order (Mevlevi in Turkish, named for their founder Mawlana Rumi), with their camel hair hats and white wool robes flowing as they spin to achieve connection with God and the universe, come to mind as one listens to the otherworldly mystical sounds of Sufi music. Various instrumental combinations are used along with the voice in *tasavvuf* music. The *ney* (flute) is the most common instrument used, along with the *kudum*, a double drum played with two sticks.

Qur'anic Recitation

Due to the overwhelming influence of Islam in West Asia, Islamic religious chanting is part of the daily lifestyle. *Qira'a* (qur'anic recitation) differs from the *maqam* style of singing. Religious chanting performed in mosques is not considered to be singing. Often performed as a solo, the aim of the chanting is not to create beautiful music, but to focus the worshipers on the words of the *Qur'an*.

Frame Drums

Many of the instruments found in West Asia have common origins. Nowhere is this more obvious than with percussion instruments, the most common being the frame-drum family.

Frame drums are among the most prevalent instruments in West Asia. The *tar*, *duff*, and *bandir* are the most common names for such drums. The frame itself is of a circular shape, commonly made out of wood with a goat- or calfskin stretched across one side of the frame. The percussionist utilizes the whole surface of the membrane stretched across the frame of the drum. Finger snaps, strokes, and palms are used to produce various tones and textures from the membrane. In some instances jingles and beads may be added to the frame to produce extra sound when the instrument is struck.

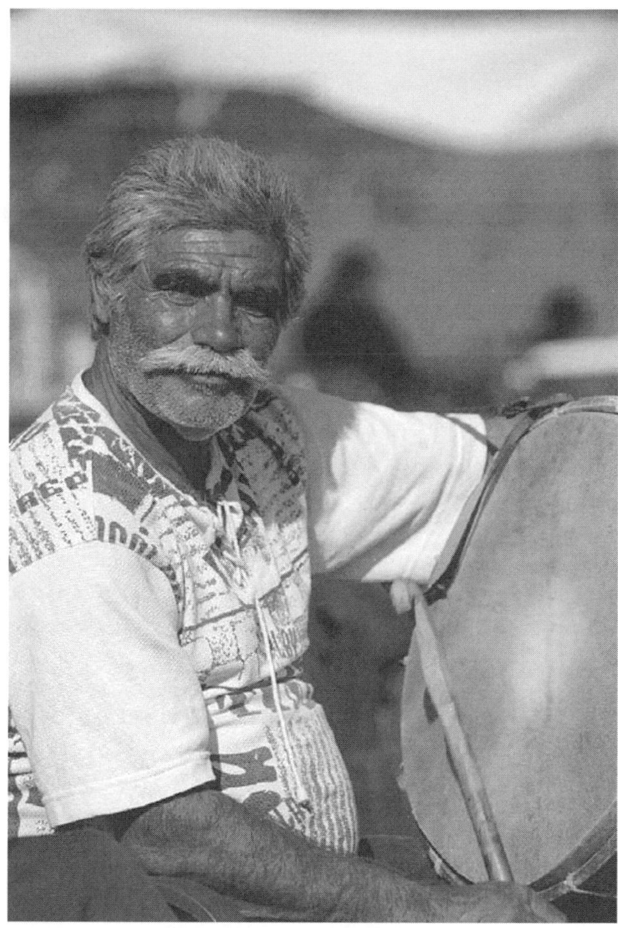

An orchestra drummer at a wrestling tournament in Finike, Turkey, in 1999. (NIK WHEELER/CORBIS)

The *darbukka* is a vase-shaped drum made from clay, wood, or metal, with a single goat- or calfskin head at the top of the vase shape. The *darbukka* has a much higher pitch than the *tar*. Like the frame drum, palms and fingers are used to produce sound. Tones may also be raised and lowered by placing one hand inside the drum and moving it back and forth across the length of the instrument while the player uses the other hand to strike the membrane. The third most common type of drum, *the dawul*, *tabl*, or *tabl baladi*, is a double-headed wooden cylindrical drum that is struck with beaters. This instrument hangs from the percussionist's shoulder by a strap and uses muted and open strokes.

The kettledrums of today's contemporary symphony orchestras can trace their roots back to the *tasat* or *naqqarat*. A pair of drums, one large and one smaller, were mounted on either side of a camel and were struck with a beater during long pilgrimages.

Many contemporary hand drums manufactured today use a synthetic fiber for the head in place of traditional animal skins. This limits the effect of climate changes on the drum head during performance. Often metallic cymbals are added to the percussion playing, including *sunuj* or *sajat*, finger cymbals used by dancers, and *kasat*, cymbals used in religious rituals, including those of the dervishes in Turkey. The Turkish Janissary band crescent, a long pole with various jingles, nicknamed "jingling Johnny," was integrated into Western European music by composers such as Mozart, Beethoven, and Berlioz.

Blown Instruments

Another very common instrument found throughout West Asia is the *ney*. An end-blown flute, the *ney* is made from wood or bamboo, with contemporary versions crafted from copper or PVC pipe. Wind instruments that require a reed to produce sound include the shawm, *zurna*, *ghatyta*, and *zamr*, the latter three known as double-reed instruments. Single-reed instruments with two pipes are the *jift*, *zummara*, and *mijwiz*. Also double-piped is the *duzele* or *qooshmeh*, a double clarinet. The *jirba* or *hibban* is West Asia's version of bagpipes. The *mashura*, a single-reed, double pipe, produces a drone as well as melodic tones. The *karna* is a trumpetlike instrument that has a long wooden body with a detachable lower section made of brass or copper.

Stringed Instruments

Used to accompany the voices of poets, the *rabab* or *rebab* is a one-stringed, bowed instrument shaped like a box guitar. The frame is made of wood covered with animal skin front and back, with the one string made from horsehair. Three to four strings are incorporated on the *kamancheh*, or spike fiddle, which is also bowed. There are also many lutelike instruments, including the *ud* and the long-necked *tanbur* and *saz*. The *santur* is a dulcimer-style instrument played with soft felt and wood hammers. A harp-style instrument used in coffee houses and to accompany dances is the *simsimiyah* or *tunbur*.

Contemporary West Asian Music

Especially in Turkey, the music scene since the 1960s has seen the emergence of polyphonic music in the compositions of artists such as Kamran Ince, Aydin Esen, and Fazil Say. Their works combine traditional Turkish music with Western musical approaches, including pop and jazz. In addition, Western pop music is especially popular with young people.

Stacey Fox

Further Reading

H. G. Farmer. (1940) *The Sources of Arabian Music*. Beardson.

Rovsing, Poul, and Ulrich Wegner. (2001) "Arabian Gulf." In *New Grove Dictionary of Music and Musicians*, 2d ed., edited by Stanley Sadie. London: Macmillan Reference.

Wright, Owen. (2001) "Arab Music, Introduction." In *New Grove Dictionary of Music and Musicians*, 2d ed., edited by Stanley Sadie. London: Macmillan Reference.

MUSLIM LAW.

See **Shari'a.**

MUSLIM LEAGUE

As a political association representing Muslims in India, the Muslim League's origins can be traced to such organizations as the Muhammedan Association (1856), the Muhammedan Literary Society (1863), the All India Muhammedan Education Conference (1886), and the Mohammedan Anglo-Oriental Defense Association (1893). On 1 October 1906, thirty-five leading Muslims, headed by the Aga Khan, called on the British viceroy in India, Lord Minto, in Simla with a petition emphasizing the distinctiveness of the Muslims as a community and requesting special reservations in constitutional and economic terms. The Simla Deputation formed the basis of the Muslim League Party, which was formed on 30 December 1906. Its professed aims were to promote loyalty to the British government among Muslims, to protect and advance political rights and interests of the Muslims and represent their interests to the government, and to prevent the growth of hostility among Muslims toward other communities in India.

In practice, the League and the Indian National Congress Party cooperated fitfully—most dramatically between 1916 and 1922. But for the most part, its activities involved an increasing separation of interests, with the interwar years seeing a major increase in communal violence in the subcontinent. The league had to compete with other Muslim parties, and its claims to represent all Indian Muslims were not borne out at elections until 1937. Its fortunes, however, were dramatically transformed from the late 1930s under the leadership of Mohammed Ali Jinnah (1876–1948), and it won the greatest share of Muslim votes during elections to the Indian legislatures in 1946. Under Jinnah, the league successfully secured the formation of the separate Islamic state of Pakistan on 14 August 1947, after the British partitioned India along religious lines.

Chandrika Kaul

Further Reading

Bahadur, Lal. (1954) *The Muslim League*. Agra, India: Agra Book Store.

A SEPARATE HOMELAND FOR MUSLIMS IN SOUTH ASIA

At the March 1940 meeting of the Muslim League in Lahore, League leader Ali Jinnah issued a statement demanding a separate homeland for Muslims. The opening of the statement below establishes the large-scale presence of Muslims in parts of India.

> As far as our internal position is concerned we have also been examining it and, you know, there are several schemes which have been sent by various well-informed constitutionalists and others who take interest in the problem of India's future constitution, and we have also appointed a sub-committee to examine the details of the schemes that have come in so far. But one thing is quite clear. It has always been taken for granted mistakenly that the Mussulmans are a Minority and of course we have got used to it for such a long time that these settled notions sometimes are very difficult to remove. The Mussulmans are not a Minority. The Mussulmans are a nation by any definition. The British and particularly the Congress proceed on the basis, 'Well, you are a Minority after all, what do you want?' 'What else do the Minorities want?' Just as Baba Rajendra Prasad said. But surely the Mussulmans are not a Minority. We find that even according to the British map of India we occupy large parts of this country, where the Mussulmans are in a majority—such as Benga, the Punjab, North-West Frontier Province, Sind and Baluchistan.

Source: Jagdish Saran Sharma. (1965) *India's Struggle for Freedom: Select Documents and Sources*. Vol. 2. Delhi: S. Chand & Co., 521–522.

Rajput, A. B. (1948) *Muslim League Yesterday and Today*. Lahore, Pakistan: M. Ashraf.

MUSLIM PEOPLES IN CHINA Islam appeared in China simultaneous with the seventh-century advance of Muslim armies into Central Asia and has flourished there since. Initially, Islamic communities were concentrated in the large Chinese cities of the interior that were connected to the Silk Road. Soon Islamic communities also appeared in the maritime communities of the southeast and south as Muslim traders replaced non-Muslim Persians and others who had long frequented the route. By Song-dynasty times (960–1279), a few Middle Eastern families who had settled along the route had become so powerful that virtually the entire Song overseas trading system was in their hands.

This influence continued under the Mongols, who encouraged Muslim migration. Among the new areas opened to Muslim influence by the Mongols was Yunnan Province, where Muslim influence remains strong (and Mongols continue to live). The Mongol court itself was also heavily Islamicized, with Persian possibly spoken as widely as Mongolian. Evidence of the extent of Islamic influence is the many Iraqi, Persian, and Uighur dishes of the Mongol imperial dietary *Yinshan zhengyao* ("Proper and Essential Things for the Emperor's Food and Drink"). "Muslim" recipes are found in other sources as well, indicating popularity outside court circles. Mongol court medicine was also heavily Islamicized with what was apparently its own school of Islamic medicine, as witnessed by the surviving chapters of the encyclopedic *Huihui yaofang* (Muslim Medicinal Recipes), which was unique in its Arabic-script entries.

ARE CHINESE MUSLIMS CLEANER?

This extract from an early-twentieth-century traveler's report contains a persistent stereotype about Muslim and the Chinese—that Muslims in China are cleaner than the Chinese. Even in modern-day tour books, there is the advice that Muslim restaurants in China are cleaner than Chinese ones.

> It is recognized that a Mohammedan [Muslim] Chinese is cleaner than a pagan Chinese. Even with a Mohammedan Chinese, however, cleanliness has nothing to do with godliness—only with churchliness. Now it is one of the sundering differences between the Asiatic and the European. If a man says to you, 'Of course his house (or his tent) is cleaner than mine; he is a Mohammedan,' you know that you are indisputably listening to an Asiatic. It does not matter what type of Asiatic he may be or what kind of European you are; the broad difference is there. Only the Asiatic is inherently unable to detect that different ways of life are admirable or imitable or attainable in different degrees. His way of life is to him something to be accepted.
>
> *Source:* Owen Lattimore. (1929) *The Desert Road to Tirkestan.* Boston: Little, Brown and Company, 225.

Large Muslim populations persisted in China after Yuan-dynasty times (1279–1368) and continued to flourish. One famous Ming-dynasty Muslim was Admiral Ma Zhenghe (1371–1433), the great explorer. During Qing-dynasty times (1644–1912), Chinese Muslims became famous because of the large-scale "Muslim" rebellions in Yunnan, Turkistan, and the Chinese northwest. Repercussions from these uprisings continue into the twenty-first century. Today, Huihui (Muslim) populations exist throughout China, where they constitute a large minority. Their numbers continue to grow, as does their influence on Chinese society. Among China's Muslims, the Uighurs of Turkistan are a particular problem for the current Chinese regime, in large part because the Uighurs do not consider themselves Chinese and look more to Turkic Central Asia than to China. Although the primary issue is political and not religious, religious influences from the outside in an era of Muslim renaissance cannot help but create new feelings of solidarity with Muslims everywhere, not just those in China.

Paul D. Buell

Further Reading

Buell, Paul D. (1999) "Mongolian Empire and Turkicization: The Evidence of Food and Foodways." In *The Mongol Empire and Its Legacy*, edited by Reuven Amitain Preiss. Amsterdam, Netherlands: E. J. Brill, 200–223.

Gladney, Dru C. (1996) *Muslim Chinese: Ethnic Nationalism in the People's Republic.* Harvard East Asian Monographs, 149. Cambridge, MA: Harvard University Press.

MUSLIM RELIGIOUS BOARD OF CENTRAL ASIA Established by Stalin as one of the four Spiritual Directorates to oversee religious affairs in the Soviet Union, the Muslim Religious Board of Central Asia and Kazakhstan began its activities in 1941. Stalin's decision to establish these religious institutions was motivated by the need to generate support for his war efforts and thereby to increase the country's military might in the face of advancing German forces during World War II.

The first Muslim clergy to lead the resumption of religious activities under the auspices of the Soviet authority in Central Asia were Ishon Babakhan Ibn al-Majid Khan and Zia al-din Babakhanov. Appointed mufti and vice-chairman of the Board, both men were instrumental in keeping Soviet leaders informed of the extent of religious activities in the region. After the war and as the status of the Soviet Union rose around the globe, Stalin chose to use the Spiritual Directorates as a foreign-policy tool to establish closer ties with the Middle Eastern countries.

In the 1960s and 1970s under the direct supervision of the Board, a limited public theological training was resumed in Central Asia, and students were dispatched to receive religious training in selected Islamic countries. The Board's headquarters were in Tashkent, Uzbekistan, but each Central Asian republic was assigned a mufti or *kazi* to monitor the activities of Muslims.

With the breakup of the Soviet Union and the perceived threat of an Islamic revival, Kazakhstan became the first republic in Central Asia to withdraw from the Board and to establish an independent directorate. Later other republics followed suit, and the Board was fully dismantled in 1994.

Mehrdad Haghayeghi

Further Reading

Bennigsen, Alexandre, and S. Enders Wimbush. (1986) *Muslims of the Soviet Empire: A Guide*. Bloomington: Indiana University Press.

Caroe, Olaf. (1967) *The Turks of Central Asia and Stalinism*. London: Macmillan.

Haghayeghi, Mehrdad. (1996) *Islam and Politics in Central Asia*. New York: St. Martin's Press.

Kolarz, Walter. (1961) *Religion in the Soviet Union*. New York: St. Martin's Press.

Marshall, Richard. (1971) *Aspects of Religion in the Soviet Union, 1917–1967*. Chicago: University of Chicago Press.

MUSLIM SAINTS

MUSLIM SAINTS In Islam, saints are men and women whose perceived close relationship with God endows them with charismatic powers and makes them intercessors between ordinary human beings and the divine. Most commonly known as friends *(awliya'*, singular: *wali)* of God, Muslim saints acquire their designation through either genealogical distinction or social processes in which they become renowned as bearers of spiritual power *(baraka)*, which they can use to grant wishes and alleviate suffering. There is no formal process of sanctification in Islam, and most of the celebrated saints acquired their reputations from their activities during their lifetimes or posthumously through the development of literary and popular hagiographic traditions. The characteristics ascribed to saints and the historical evolution of hagiographic traditions vary widely between Muslim societies and sects, though the phenomenon as a whole is nearly ubiquitous in Islamic religious life throughout Asia and beyond.

Shi'ite Saints

Foremost among saints known for their genealogical charisma are descendants of the Prophet Muhammad, particularly those accepted as imams or holy men by the various Shi'ite sects. The imams' spiritual properties are seen as deriving from their ancestry, linking them to Muhammad through his daughter Fatimah. Over the course of history, significant population centers have sprung up around the shrines of these saints, including the city of Najaf in southern Iraq, which contains the shrine of the first imam 'Ali (d. 661), and the Iranian cities of Mashhad and Qom, centered around the shrines of the eighth imam, 'Ali ar-Rida (d. 818), and his sister Fatimah Ma'sumeh (d. c. 815), respectively. Numerous other shrines of the imams' relatives are to be found throughout areas in which the majority of the population are Twelver Shi'a (that is, they venerate twelve historical imams); these shrines serve as focal points of local religious practice. Similarly, members of another branch of Shi'a Islam venerate separate lines of imams as saints, with the Nizari subsect carrying the tradition to the current living imam, the Agha Khan.

Sufi Saints

Considerably more numerous than the Shi'ite saints are those Sufis whom multitudes of Muslims regard as saints because of their reputations as spiritual guides, workers of miracles, and important historical figures in the establishment of Islamic communities. Most of these saints belong to the Sunni sect of Islam. The first Sufis seen as saints by later generations lived as early as the eighth century, though Sufism became the predominant religious paradigm throughout Islamic lands only in the later medieval period, 1300–1700.

Sufi practice most often centers around religious guides *(shaykh/pir)*, who interpret their devotees' spiritual experiences and initiate them into religious paths by teaching specific liturgical practices *(dhikr*, or "recollection" of God's name). Such guides occur at all levels in society, becoming acknowledged as saints in small groups, in particular localities, or across regions. Saints' reputations depend on their perceived mastery of esoteric knowledge, which allows them to apprehend matters through extrasensory means and to grant material and spiritual benefits such as cures for illnesses and progress on the spiritual path. Miraculous deeds and knowledge of the unseen spiritual world are particular markers of saintly status as witnessed in both the reputations of local saints and the hagiographies of the most famous.

Along with their personal capabilities, Sufi saints often derive their legitimacy through initiation into voluntary sociointellectual associations known as Sufi orders *(turuq*, singular: *tariqa)*, which are based on chains of transmission of religious knowledge going

Devotees of the Muslim saint Hazrat Shah Abdul Latif Barri Imam dance at his shrine on the outskirts of Islamabad, Pakistan, in May 2001. (AFP/CORBIS)

back to earlier famous saints and great Islamic figures such as Muhammad and 'Ali. Most prominent among such orders in Islamic Asia are Naqshbandiyya, Qadiriyya, Chishtiyya, Suhrawardiyya, Kubrawiyya, and Bektashiyya. There are numerous other orders and suborders named after earlier saints, including antinomian groups (groups that reject established morality) such as the Qalandars and Haydaris, who deliberately flaunt conventional norms such as the prohibition on intoxicants as a way of showing complete rejection of ordinary social life and total devotion to God. Amid all the variety of traditions and behavior, the efficacy of Sufi saints' powers depends on their perceived closeness to God, encapsulated in the concepts of passing away *(fana')* from their confined earthly existence and subsisting *(baqa')* in divine reality. The saints are earthly mediators of God's powers and are seen by their devotees as indispensable intermediaries without whom the cosmos would cease to function normally.

Social, Political, and Economic Roles

In addition to having spiritual significance, saints, their shrines, and their genealogical and pedagogical lineages have played crucial roles in the development of Islamic social history. Throughout Asia, "natural" communities, such as tribes and castes, often trace their conversion to Islam to the proselytization and miraculous works of Sufi saints. Actual events associated with such conversions are usually embellished into elaborate hagiographies in which particular saints may become the center of communal identity. Hagiographic traditions are, therefore, major sources for the social history of Islamic communities throughout Asia.

Shrines of important saints also act as stimuli for economic activity in various regions, and most major cities in Central and Southern Asia with large Muslim populations fall under the spiritual domain of patron saints, whose presence continues to be felt long after their death through the powers of their monuments and the activities of their descendants and disciples. Examples of such powerful saints' monuments include the shrine complexes of Ahmad Yasawi (Kazakhstan), Baha al-Din Naqshband (Uzbekistan), Data Ganj Bakhsh (Pakistan), Nizam al-Din Awliya and Muin al-Din Chishti (India), and Jatal al-Din Rumi and Haji Bektash Vali (Turkey).

The social significance of sanctification of space is evident also in cases where saints' posthumous presence can be "discovered" through spiritual auguries at crucial historical moments to legitimate sociopolitical activity. The most famous examples of this pattern are the discovery of the grave of Muhammad's companion Abu Ayyub Ansari (Turkish: Eyup) in Istanbul at the time of the Ottoman conquest of the city in 1453, and the development of the city of Mazar-e Sharif in northern Afghanistan after the alleged discovery of the grave of ʿAli at the site in 1480. Because of their role in social and economic life, saints and their descendants have in the past also exercised considerable political influence by becoming the spiritual patrons of ruling dynasties. The Iranian Safavid dynasty (1501–1722) was a saintly lineage that transformed itself into a ruling house. In modern times, descendants of powerful saintly lineages, such as the Pir Pagaros of Sind, Pakistan, have exercised considerable political influence at the national level, either directly or through their disciples.

To understand the religious and social spheres of life in Islamic communities in Asia, one must understand Muslim saints and their followers. Local traditions and patterns of historical development should be given careful consideration when drawing conclusions about the roles ascribed to dead or living saints in any particular region. However, at the most general level, for Muslims, saints are the extraordinary beings who convey sacred power between the divine realm and earthly human existence.

Shahzad Bashir

Further Reading

Ansari, Sarah. (1992) *Sufi Saints and State Power: The Pirs of Sind, 1843–1947*. Cambridge, U.K.: Cambridge University Press.

Currie, P. M. (1989) *The Shrine and Cult of Muʿin al-Din Chishti of Ajmer*. Delhi: Oxford University Press.

Daftary, Farhad. (1990) *The Ismaʿilis: Their History and Doctrines*. Cambridge, U.K.: Cambridge University Press.

Deweese, Devin A. (1994) *Islamization and Native Religion in the Golden Horde: Baba Tukles and Conversion to Islam in Historical and Epic Tradition*. University Park: Pennsylvania State University Press.

Eaton, Richard Maxwell. (1978) *Sufis of Bijapur, 1300–1700: Social Roles of Sufis in Medieval India*. Princeton, NJ: Princeton University Press.

Ernst, Carl W. (1992) *Eternal Garden: Mysticism, History, and Politics at a South Asian Sufi Center*. Albany: State University of New York Press.

———. (1997) *The Shambhala Guide to Sufism*. Boston: Shambhala.

Ewing, Katherine. (1997) *Arguing Sainthood: Modernity, Psychoanalysis, and Islam*. Durham, NC: Duke University Press.

Frembgen, Jürgen Wasim. (1998) "Saints in Modern Devotional Poster-Portraits: Meanings and Uses of Popular Religious Folk Art in Pakistan." *Res* (Cambridge, MA) 34 (autumn): 184–191.

Karamustafa, Ahmet. (1994) *God's Unruly Friends: Dervish Groups in the Islamic Later Medieval Period, 1200–1550*. Salt Lake City: University of Utah Press.

McChesney, R. D. (1991) *Waqf in Central Asia: Four Hundred Years in the History of a Muslim Shrine, 1480–1889*. Princeton, NJ: Princeton University Press.

Momen, Moojan. (1985) *An Introduction to Shi ʿi Islam: The History and Doctrines of Twelver Shiʿism*. New Haven, CT: Yale University Press.

Nakash, Yitzhak. (1994) *The Shiʿis of Iraq*. Princeton, NJ: Princeton University Press.

Sadeghi, Zohreh. (1996) *Fatima von Qum: Ein Beispiel für die Verehrung heiliger Frauen im Volksglauben der Zwölfer-Schia*. Berlin: K. Schwarz.

Smith, Grace Martin, and Carl Ernst. (1993) *Manifestations of Sainthood in Islam*. Istanbul, Turkey: Isis Press.

Troll, Christian W., ed. (1989) *Muslim Shrines in India: Their Character, History, and Significance*. Delhi: Oxford University Press.

Werbner, Pnina, and Helene Basu, eds. (1998) *Embodying Charisma: Modernity, Locality, and Performance of Emotion in Sufi Cults*. London and New York: Routledge.

Woodward, Mark. (1989) *Islam in Java: Normative Piety and Mysticism in the Sultanate of Yogyakarta*. Tucson: University of Arizona Press.

MUSLIMS, SHIʿITE

MUSLIMS, SHIʿITE Shiʿite Muslims make up the second largest sect of the Islamic community after the Sunni Muslims, and they are the predominant Muslim population in Azerbaijan, Bahrain, Iraq, and Iran. There are also significant Shiʿite minorities in India and Pakistan and in several Arab states. Today there are approximately one hundred million Shiʿites worldwide; they account for approximately 10 percent of the world's Muslim population.

Emergence of the Shiʿite Community

When the Prophet Muhammad died in 632 CE, the Muslim community erupted into disputes about his successor. Soon a split occurred over the criteria for the legitimate ruler. A powerful coalition of leaders chose Abu Bakr, one of Muhammad's uncles and disciples, as caliph or successor, against the objections of those who believed Muhammad's cousin and son-in-law, ʿAli ibn Abi Talib, should have been chosen. The former are known as Sunni Muslims, while the latter are known as Shiʿite Muslims.

Abu Bakr was succeeded by ʿUmar and then by ʿUthman. When ʿUthman was assassinated, ʿAli was finally made caliph, but a relative of ʿUthman, Muʿawiya, who was also the governor of Damascus and one of the last companions of Muhammad, contested his rule, charging that ʿAli had been responsible for ʿUthman's death. The ensuing conflict ended with a truce of sorts; Muʿawiya ruled in Syria, Egypt, and northern Mesopotamia, and Ali ruled over the Arabian Peninsula and the east. When ʿAli was assassinated in 661, Muʿawiya quickly seized control of ʿAli's region, naming his family, the Umayyads, the ruling family. The Umayyad dynasty ruled the Islamic world from 661 to 750.

ʿAli and His Descendants in Shiʿite Belief

The Shiʿite Muslims believed that ʿAli was the first imam (spiritual leader) and that his descendants were the only rightful leaders of the Islamic community. They considered imams spiritual and physical beings with the duty and right to rule the community after the Prophet. ʿAli's son Hasan became the second imam, and Hasan's brother Husayn became the third imam when Hasan was poisoned in 670. Ten years later Husayn and most of his family were killed by the Umayyads, leaving only his son Zayn al ʿAbidin to carry on as the fourth imam. Zayn al ʿAbidin's son Yahya became the fifth imam. The attack on Husayn and his family outraged the public, already tired of many policies of the Umayyads. Eventually, in 750, the Umayyads were replaced by the Abbasids, a Hashimite family that was a branch of the Prophet's own clan. During the Abbasid era (750–1258) the Shiʿites grew in number, since they were not systematically persecuted.

Seveners and Twelvers Sects in Shiʿite Belief

Jaʿfar al-Sadiq was the sixth imam, and he had two sons, Ismaʿil and Musa. Once again, a dispute over leadership occurred among Muslims, but this time among the Shiʿite Muslims. Ismaʿil was initially named to succeed Jaʿfar, who later named Musa as successor. However, one group of people followed Ismaʿil, believed him to be seventh imam, and thought that the line of imams ended with him. These Shiʿite Muslims are called the Seveners or Ismailis.

Others, however, believed Musa was the seventh imam and followed his lineage until the twelfth imam, Madhi, who disappeared as a child in the city of Samarra in 873; this disappearance is also referred to as an occultation or absenting from the earth. According to the Twelvers sect of Shiʿite Muslims, the rulers of Islam must reign in the name of the twelfth imam, Madhi, the one who vanished. This sect is known as Twelvers because it honors the twelve imams.

The Twelvers believe that Mahdi will return one day to bring salvation and a new era of peace and prosperity to the world. The sect of Seveners also believes in the imam's returning to usher in a new era of peace and prosperity, except that the imam will be Ismaʿil.

For both sects the ideal government is run by clerics well versed in Islamic law and philosophy. Originally this idea was interpreted to mean that Islamic religious leaders would play a role in guiding and advising governments to adhere to Islamic principles. Over the years, however, others decided that Islamic religious leaders should actually run the government. The concept of *vilayet-i faqih*, or the rule of religious jurisprudence, was fully articulated and explained by Ayatollah Khomeini (1900–1989) in his book *Hukkkumet-i Islami* (Islamic Government), and he preached these views to the masses. *Vilayet-i faqih* was finally made a political reality when Ayatollah Khomeini proclaimed Iran an Islamic republic in 1979.

Spread of Shiʿism

By the end of the ninth century Shiʿite believers grew in number. The Seveners were strong in North Africa due to the affiliation of the Fatimid dynasty (909–1171), which ruled not only in North Africa but also in Egypt, Syria, and Hijaz. The Fatimids had hoped to firmly establish their religion in Egypt, but met with little success as the Sunni Muslims there resisted strongly. In another part of the Islamic community, the Buyid dynasty (c. 945–1055) subscribed to the teachings of the Twelvers. This dynasty was unable to convert most of its subjects, but helped spread Shiʿism by protecting its followers and commemorating Husayn's murder.

The Twelvers received a tremendous boost when the Safavid dynasty (1502–1736) of Iran named Shiʿism its state religion. By the time the Safavid dynasty fell, most Iranians had converted to Shiʿism, which is still their belief today.

Shiʿite clerics are trained in Islamic seminaries. Qum and Mashhad in Iran are currently prominent centers of Shiʿite teaching. A cleric's standing in the Islamic community is determined by his religious education and how he applies his knowledge to his people and to the government. The highest level of acclaim to be achieved is considered to be the title "ayatollah." Those clerics who do not achieve such prominence either teach the message of Islam to villagers or serve in an administrative capacity at mosques or seminaries.

Houman A. Sadri

Further Reading

Algar, Hamid. (1991) "Religious Forces in Twentieth-Century Iran." In *The Cambridge History of Iran*, edited by Peter Avery, Gavin Hambly, and Charles Melville. Cambridge, U.K.: Cambridge University Press, 7:732–764.

Khomeini, Ruhollah. (1981) *Islam and Revolution: Writings and Declarations of Imam Khomeini.* Translated and annotated by Hamid Algar. Berkeley, CA: Mizan Press.

Sachedina, Abdulaziz A. (1988) *The Just Ruler in Shiite Islam.* New York: Oxford University Press.

MUSLIMS, SUNNI Sunni Islam is practiced by the majority (90 percent) of Muslims, with large communities in western Asia, the Indian subcontinent, the Caucasus, Central Asia, China, and Southeast Asia. The word "Sunni" derives from the Arabic word "Sunnah," which generally means "customary practices" and refers to the oral traditions (hadiths) of what the Prophet Muhammad said or did. Sunni Muslims regard these traditions and the Qur'an as forming the basis of their religious knowledge. The Sunnis are distinguished from the Shiʿites, the partisans of Muhammad's son-in-law, ʿAli.

The experience of Sunni Muslims in Asia during the modern period has largely depended on how these groups have responded to the twin forces of European colonial and Asian territorial expansion and the emergence of modernity. Each of these forces has influenced the organizational structure of Sunni communities, reshaped the theological goals of Sunni Islam, and influenced the role that Sunni Islam plays in modern national identities and political movements. The position of Sunni Muslim women in Asia varies according to several regional and political factors.

Western Asia

In western Asia, Sunni Muslims are predominantly Arab and live in Iraq, Israel, and the borders of former British Mandate Palestine (1923–1948), Jordan, Lebanon, Syria, Yemen, Saudi Arabia, and the states of the Persian Gulf region. During the latter part of the nineteenth century, some Arabs called for a revival of Sunni Islamic thought as a response to the penetration of European culture and its increasing political influence in the region. They advocated returning to the fundamental sources of their faith, the Qur'an and the early traditions, and abolishing popular religious practices, such as the ritual visitation to saints' tombs. This reform movement would inspire other Sunni communities throughout Asia, particularly those that came under European colonial rule.

After World War I, Britain and France occupied the region and founded many of the modern Arab nations, although these nations did not achieve independence until after World War II. Although many of these nations stress an Arab cultural identity, Islam continues to serve as a powerful idiom for nationalist rhetoric and as an alternative to state ideology, as the increasing influence of Islamic groups in contemporary politics attests. Whereas some nations, such as Syria, Iraq, and Jordan, have adopted secular penal and civilian legal codes to work alongside Islamic law, Saudi Arabia and Kuwait continue to impose strict versions of Islam in law and government.

Indian Subcontinent

Sunni Muslims form the majority of the population in Pakistan and Bangladesh and comprise a large minority in India. After the breakup of the Islamic Mughal empire and the imposition of British rule in India in the nineteenth century, Sunni theologians and intellectuals in India adopted the reform ideals emerging from the Arab lands, believing that religious revivalism could help their communities confront British colonialism.

Eventually, the British encouraged the Sunni Muslim community of India to identify itself as a group distinct from the larger Hindu population, which led to calls for the creation of a separate Muslim state. Pakistan emerged as a state in 1947 for the Muslims of India, and although it has remained heavily Islamic in national character, it is not officially a Muslim nation. The eastern part of Pakistan, Bangladesh, was established as a separate nation in 1972 and remains a secular nation more focused on national than Islamic identity. In India, communal hostilities continue to mar relations between Sunnis, Shiʿites, and Hindus.

Central Asia, the Caucasus, and China

Sunni Muslims in Central Asia, the Caucasus, and China live within the former Soviet republics of Azerbaijan, Kazakhstan, Kyrgyzstan, Tajikistan, Turkmenistan, and Uzbekistan, as well as in Afghanistan and China. By the late nineteenth century, most Muslims in these regions had come under either Russian or Chinese rule. Because these areas are contiguous to the imperial homeland of Russia and China, a unique problem emerged; some Muslims became a minority population who had to defend against assimilation into the culture of the ruling powers.

The czarist Russian empire coopted local religious leaders like the ulama (scholars of Islam) to govern these areas, even though most Muslims favored the spiritual leadership of Sufis (Muslim mystics). Performing ritual pilgrimages and attending Sufi celebrations became expressions of Sunni Muslim opposition to Russian, and later Soviet, rule. In the post-Soviet era, Sunni Islamic groups compete for power with large non-Sunni populations, such as Russians,

Shiʿites, Armenian Christians, and various Turkic groups.

Two groups represent the divergent experiences of Sunni Muslims in China. The Hui in Han Province speak Chinese but observe most Islamic practices, whereas nonassimilated Inner Asian people, such as the Kazakhs and the Uighurs, speak Turkic languages and maintain a distinctive non-Chinese identity.

Southeast Asia

In Malaya and Indonesia, Sunni Muslim populations faced the same difficulties that colonialism posed to Muslims in other parts of Asia. By the mid-nineteenth century, Holland and Britain had established their imperial rule in Southeast Asia. Islamic revivalism quickly emerged as a powerful ideological force against European colonialism, and by the 1920s the port towns of Java, Malaya, and Sumatra acted as centers of Islamic activism and reservoirs of Islamic modernist thought emanating from other parts of the Muslim world.

Indonesia achieved independence in 1945. Although not officially proclaimed an Islamic nation, it is nonetheless the world's most populous Islamic nation. The Ministry of Religion regulates Islamic education and courts. Malaya became independent in 1957; it maintains strong central control over the administration of religious affairs, a system introduced during British rule.

Women

The position of Sunni Muslim women in modern Asian societies depends on such factors as the nations in which they reside, their socioeconomic positions, and the degree of formal education that they hold. Whereas women in Yemen and Afghanistan have difficulty pursuing activities outside the household, women in Jordan, Syria, and Pakistan remain active in the public sphere and have fought for political and legal changes, although the rise of militant and conservative Islamic groups hinders these advancements. Many women traditionally professed their faith by attending religious festivals, visiting the tombs of saints, and praying at shrines, although the imposition of modern state control over religious life has curtailed these practices.

Sunni Muslims have been forced to reformulate their beliefs to meet the challenges posed by the expansion of European and Asian nations. Religious revivalism evolved as a response to these challenges of the modern age, but the greatest legacy of this history may have been the control that hierarchical religious authorities (that is, ulama) and state forces acquired over religious affairs.

Awad Eddie Halabi

Further Reading

Ahmed, Laila. (1992) *Women and Gender in Islam.* New Haven, CT: Yale University Press.
Lapidus, Ira. (1991) *A History of Islamic Societies.* Cambridge, U.K.: Cambridge University Press.
Madan, T., ed. (1976) *Muslim Communities of South Asia.* New Delhi: Vikas Publishing House.

MUTINY, INDIAN

MUTINY, INDIAN. The Mutiny or Sepoy rebellion (1857–1858), or, as it is often referred to in contemporary India or Pakistan, the War for Indpendence, changed the shape of the British empire. Before the Mutiny, British India was ruled through a chartered business corporation, the East India Company, under the fiction that they were the proxies of native princes. After the struggle, that fiction was laid to rest.

The Rebellion

The thirteen-month rebellion traditionally has been blamed on the East India Company army's issue of the Enfield rifle. To load the gun, the Sepoys—Indian soldiers in the British army—had to bite off the ends of a lubricated cartridge. The soldiers felt they were greased with beef and swine fat—anathema to Hindu and Muslim alike. But most contemporary historians now feel this was only one of many causes.

It probably was more important that the state of Oudh, from which many of the native soldiers derived, had recently been annexed by the British. This produced political resentments among the Indian soldiers. Furthermore, in consolidating the British supremacy in India, the company forced a radical and rapid Westernization on traditional society that was a major cause of the troubles.

The Mutiny broke out first in the Bengal army. At Meerut, several Sepoys received severe punishment for refusing to use the Enfield cartridge in April 1857. In reaction, native soldiers began to shoot their European officers, after which the mutineers marched on Delhi, at that time bereft of English defenders. The local Indian troops joined the insurgents in restoring the aged Mughal emperor Bahadur Shah II (1775–1862) to the throne of his ancestors.

Europeans and Indian Christians were butchered—some quite horribly. But company troops also committed atrocities. Disturbances also spread to Cawnpore and Lucknow. When the British retook these cities, the punishment also was severe for the perpetrators.

Aftermath

After the Mutiny, British India became a Crown possession, and Victoria was granted the title of Queen Empress of India. Military and civil reorganization was instituted. The British army came to depend heavily on their loyal native troops—especially the Sikhs and the Gurkhas. India was governed by parliamentary law, directly from London. Within India, a more professional civil service developed, which became one of the best in the world. Governmental sponsorship of Westernization slowed down. The Indian middle classes realized a violent revolution was not viable. This influenced the tactics of the later Indian Nationalist struggle.

Geoffrey Cook

Further Reading

Chaudhauri, S. B. (1965) *Theories of the Indian Mutiny, 1857–1859.* Calcutta: World Press.

Forrest, G. W. (1904–1912) *A History of the Indian Mutiny.* 3 vols. London: W. Blackwood and Sons.

Hibbert, Christopher. (1978) *The Great Mutiny in India, 1857.* London: Allen Lane.

Kaye, J. W., and G. B. Malleson. (1897–1898) *Kaye's and Malleson's History of the Indian Mutiny of 1857–1858.* 6 vols. London: W. H. Allen.

Metcalf, Thomas. (1964) *Aftermath of Revolt: 1857–1870.* Princeton, NJ: Princeton University Press.

Stokes, Eric. (1986) *The Peasant Armed.* Oxford: Oxford University Press.

MYANMAR—PROFILE

(2000 est. pop. 41.7 million). Myanmar, officially the Union of Myanmar (also known as Burma), is located in Southeast Asia, bordered by Bangladesh on the west, India on the northwest, China on the northeast, and Laos and Thailand on the east. The country has a land area of 678,500 square kilometers, and it is the second largest country in area in the Association of Southeast Asian Nations (ASEAN), after Indonesia.

Climate and Topography

Myanmar's landscape is diverse. It includes mountain ranges in the north, northeast, and northwest; large hilly plateaus and river valleys in the central regions; and twisted coasts with numerous river deltas and small islands in the south and southwest. Most of the country lies in the tropics, with temperatures reaching 38° C between May and October and falling to 20° C between December and February.

Population

Myanmar is a predominantly rural country, with only around 28 percent of the population living in cities and towns, up from 19 percent in 1960. The country's capital, Yangon (Rangoon), is home to about 4 million people (2001), up from approximately 2.5 million in 1983. The country's population is relatively young, with 30 percent below the age of fourteen and only 5 percent older than sixty-five. At present, Myanmar has one of Southeast Asia's lowest population growth rates—.64 percent—and a net annual migration rate of –1.85 migrants per 1,000 people.

It is very difficult to project the dynamics of population growth because of Myanmar's international isolation, high emigration rate, and very high infant mortality rate of 75.3 deaths per 1,000 live births (2000). Myanmar's officials estimate that current population

MYANMAR (BURMA)

Country name: Union of Myanmar (Union of Burma)
Area: 678,500 sq km
Population: 41,734,853 (July 2000 est.)
Population growth rate: 0.64% (2000 est.)
Birth rate: 20.61 births/1,000 population (2000 est.)
Death rate: 12.35 deaths/1,000 population (2000 est.)
Net migration rate: −1.85 migrants/1,000 population (2000 est.)
Sex ratio, total population: 0.99 males/female (2000 est.)
Infant mortality rate: 75.3 deaths/1,000 live births (2002 est.)
Life expectancy at birth, total population: 54.91 years; male, 53.6 years; female, 56.29 years (2000 est.)
Major religions: Buddhism, Christianity, Islam
Major languages: Burmese
Literacy, total population: 83.1%; male, 88.7%; female, 77.7% (1995 est.)
Government type: military regime
Capital: Yangon (Rangoon)
Administrative divisions: 7 divisions and 7 states
Independence: 4 January 1948 (from U.K.)
National holiday: Independence Day, 4 January (1948)
Suffrage: 18 years of age; universal
GDP—real growth rate: 4.6% (1999 est.)
GDP—per capita (purchasing power parity): $1,200 (1999 est.)
Population below poverty line: 23% (1997 est.)
Exports: $1.2 billion (1998)
Imports: $2.5 billion (1998)
Currency: kyat (K)

Source: Central Intelligence Agency. (2001) *The World Book Factbook* 2001. Retrieved 5 March 2002, from: http://www.cia.gov/cia/publications/factbook.

might double within the next forty years. Myanmar has one of the lowest population densities among the member nations of ASEAN, standing at 61 people per square kilometer. However, the areas around the three major cities of Yangon, Mandalay, and Moulmein are overcrowded, with large numbers of young people arriving from rural areas in search of jobs and new opportunities.

Myanmar is a multiethnic country with a very diverse population. Burmans make up 68 percent of the population, Shans make up 9 percent, Karen 7 percent, Rakhine 4 percent, Chinese 3 percent, Mon 2 percent, Indians 2 percent, and various other small groups make up the remaining 7 percent. Historically, the country brought together different ethnic groups, including small tribal groups on its border with Thailand and Laos. During British rule (1885–1948), many Indian and Chinese immigrants settled in the country. During the twentieth century, the ethnic structure remained relatively stable, although many urban Indians and Chinese left Myanmar at the outbreak of World War II; many also left in the 1960s. Due to harsh economic conditions in the 1980s and 1990s, many people left Myanmar for neighboring countries, either temporarily or permanently but often illegally, in search of jobs and better living prospects. According to an Economic Intelligence Unit report, there are an estimated 1 million illegal migrant workers in Thailand, the majority of them from Myanmar.

The Burmese language (the country's officials call it the Myanmar language), which belongs to the Sino-Tibetan group of languages, is the official language of the state. It is spoken by the majority of the population. Around 15 percent of the population speak Shan

MYANMA(R)—BAMA(R) RENAMING

Burmans constitute a majority and have dominated the military and the civil service since national independence. In English, "Burman" has mostly been used in reference to the dominant ethnic group (though at times confusingly it has also been used to mean "all the indigenous inhabitants of Burma together with permanent residents of alien origin who have come to regard themselves as natives of the country" Furnivall 1957:11). On 18 June 1989, not tolerating "foreign" pronunciation, the SLORC [State Law and Order Restoration Council] announced the Adaptation of Expressions Law, substituting references to "Burman" in non-Burmese languages with "Bama(r)," and "Burmese" and "Burma" with "Myanma(r)," thus enforcing ethnic referencing for the country in its own mother tongue upon foreign languages, effectively making "Burman," "Burmese" and "Burma" redundant.

Though in doing so it hopes to clarify the distinction between the dominant ethnic group and the nation-state, it has in fact made the situation more complicated. In the 1930s, the Thahkins used Bama(r), not Myanma(r), as a term for the country as a whole, including the Burmans, and it continues to be used in this way in the Burmese language even today.

Also, it makes little sense to redefine Bama(r) as a limited ethnic category while the mother tongue should be designated as Myanma(r). Bama(r) and Myanma(r) overlap in meaning to such an extent even today, as evident from most Burmese dictionaries, that this change has not put non-Burman ethnic groups at ease. Unlike Indonesia, where the national language is not tied to the native language of the dominant ethnic group, the Myanma(r) language is closely tied to ethnic identity of the Bama(r) native speakers.

Furthermore, imposition upon minority groups of Burmanized terminology of the country, but more particularly of the way many of their own ethnic place-names were changed without consultation (the law renamed ethnic place-names according to Burmese pronunciation also, but the Committee deciding upon the renaming contained no representatives from the ethnic groups).

Though the usage implemented by this law was accepted by the United Nations and is now in everyday use throughout Asia, in Europe and in the USA "Myanma(r)" has not gained widespread acceptance and "Burma"/"Burmese" continue to be widely preferred. To compound confusion, "Burmese" is also rarely used in English in the sense of "Burman," i.e., as an ethnic or racial term (e.g., Furnivall 1957:11). But such confusion is no different from the Burmese language itself, where Myanma(r) continues to be referred to in formal or literary reference to Bama(r) ("Burman"), suggesting a less impartial idea of the country and ethnicity than the authorities put forth.

Gustaaf Houtman

Source: J. S. Furnivall. (1957) *An Introduction to the Political Economy of Burma.* 3rd ed. Rangoon, Burma: People's Literature Committee & House.

and Karen. English is spoken mainly in large cities and among most educated social groups.

Around 89 percent of the population are Buddhists. The remaining 11 percent are Muslims, Christians, and animists. Some of the indigenous people in the hill areas, who followed various types of shamanistic rituals in the precolonial era, were converted to Christianity in the nineteenth and twentieth centuries.

Political History

The first unified Burma state was established in the middle of the eleventh century at Pagan in upper Burma. It was conquered by the Mongols under Kublai Khan at the end of the thirteenth century. A new dynasty emerged in the sixteenth century in central Burma. During the 1600s and 1700s, the Burmese were increasingly involved in trade, including rice, tea, and opium, with British, Dutch, and French merchants.

Burma (the name was changed to Myanmar in 1989) came under British control in 1886 after three Anglo-Burmese wars. The British moved the capital from Mandalay to Rangoon (now Yangon), which became one of the largest ports in Burma. The British struggled to retain control over the country during World War II, and it became a battlefield for the Allies and the Japanese army. In 1945 Japan was defeated, but the Burmese demanded independence. Under the leadership of the popular leaders Aung San (1914?–1947) and U Nu (1907–1995), the pro-independence Anti-Fascist People's Freedom League won the April 1947 elections. Burma declared its independence from British rule on 4 January 1948, forming the Union of Burma. The first constitution was adopted in 1948; however, the civil government was overthrown by the military in 1962. In 1974, a new constitution was adopted that significantly changed many ideas of the previous constitution and declared the country a one-party socialist state. The Lanzin Party (Burma Socialist Programme Party) introduced the so-called Burmese Way to Socialism, based on a mixture of Buddhism, Marxism, nationalism, and political isolation.

Military rule was undermined by widespread dissatisfaction with poverty and economic mismanagement, leading finally to mass protests. In March 1988, widespread demonstrations began in the capital, Yangon. In August 1988, government troops used force and opened fire against demonstrators, killing thousands of civilians. After some changes in the military junta, the State Law and Order Restoration Council (SLORC) was formed, abandoning the one-party system and promising free, multiparty elections. In May 1990, the National League for Democracy (NLD), led by Aung San Suu Kyi (the daughter of Aung San; b. 1945), won the general elections for the Pyithu Hluttaw (Parliament) by a landslide, but the junta refused to accept the results. Many opposition pro-democracy leaders were arrested or isolated under house arrest. In 1997, the SLORC was dissolved and replaced by the State Peace and Development Council, which promised to produce a new constitution. In the first years of the twenty-first century, the military junta faced growing pressure from the pro-democracy political parties, led by the NLD, from political groups in exile, from various ethnic groups and their armed units, and increasingly from the international community.

Economy

Myanmar experienced slow economic growth after World War II, as political instability and military coups negatively affected the country's economic development. Agriculture is the main pillar of the economy: peasants cultivate rice, corn, peanuts, tobacco, oilseeds, and sugarcane. During the second half of the twentieth century, Myanmar became the world's largest source of illicit opium. According to the World Bank, the agricultural sector contributes about 53 percent of the gross domestic product (GDP) and provides employment for 65 percent of the workforce; services contribute around 25 percent; and industry contributes 10 percent, providing employment for 10 percent of the workforce (1998). According to the World Bank, between 1989 and 1999, the average annual GDP growth was around 6 percent, with industrial production growing at an annual average of almost 10 percent and exports of goods and services at an annual average of 8 percent, albeit from a very low base. From 1962 until 1988, the government enforced centralized control over all the sectors of economy, nationalizing most large- and medium-sized enterprises. Since the late 1980s, the Myanmar government has been conducting a policy of economic liberalization and deregulation, encouraging the private sector and foreign investments. However, these efforts were undermined by the international boycott due to the poor human rights record in the country. Myanmar remains one of the world's poorest countries, with an estimated purchasing power parity at around $1,200. In 2000, the United Nations Development Programme's Human Development Index put Myanmar in 125th place, behind Gabon and Morocco but ahead of Iraq and Lesotho.

Rafis Abazov

Further Reading

Aung San Suu Kyi. (1995) *Freedom from Fear.* New York: Penguin Books.

Becka, Jan. (1995) *Historical Dictionary of Myanmar*. Lanham, MD, and London: Scarecrow Press.
Central Statistical Organisation. (various years) *Statistical Yearbook*. Yangon, Myanmar: Central Statistical Organisation.
International Monetary Fund. (1997) *Myanmar: Recent Economic Developments*. Washington, DC: IMF.
Lintner, Bertil. (1994) *Burma in Revolt: Opium and Insurgency since 1948*. Boulder, CO: Westview Press.
Maung, Mya. (1998) *The Burma Road to Capitalism: Economic Growth versus Democracy*. Westport, CT: Praeger.
The Myanmar Times. (weekly in English) Retrieved October 2001, from: http://www.myanmar.com/myanmartimes/.
Open Society Institute. (2000). "The Open Society's Burma Project." Retrieved October 2001, from: http://www.soros.org/burma.
Saw Myat Yin. (2001) *Myanmar (Cultures of the World Series)*. New York: Benchmark Books.
Smith, Martin. (1991) *Burma: Insurgency and the Politics of Ethnicity*. London: Zed Books.
Steinberg, David. (2001) *Burma, the State of Myanmar*. Washington, DC: Georgetown University Press.
World Bank. (1995) *Myanmar: Policies for Sustaining Economic Reform*. Washington, DC: World Bank.

MYANMAR—ECONOMIC SYSTEM

Reflecting both its history as an exporter of raw agricultural produce and as a country that has for decades isolated itself from the world economy, the economy of Myanmar (Burma before 1989) is largely agricultural. After the seventeenth century and prior to British colonial rule, rice exports were usually forbidden by the Burmese royal court due to fears of chronic domestic famine. Some rice exports were allowed in the early nineteenth century in an effort to gain firearms and Indian textiles. In general, however, Burma's strong early modern domestic economy was self-sufficient in textiles, ceramics, and other goods. Upper Burma, the chief rice-cultivation center of the country, remained Burma's demographic and economic center.

British expansion in Burma changed the overall Burmese economy. After the First Anglo-Burmese War (1824–1826), the British opened up the province of Arakan (now Rakhine) to rice merchants, and rice exports increased so rapidly that by the late 1850s Akyab (now Sittwe), the chief port of Arakan, was the world's foremost rice-exporting port. Increased agricultural cultivation and the emergent colonial port economy at Akyab led the British to encourage large-scale labor immigration from northeastern India. Tenasserim, meanwhile, depended more upon teak logging, shipbuilding, and tin mining. After the Second Anglo-Burmese War (1852), the British annexed Burma's chief port, Rangoon (now Yangon), and the whole of sparsely populated but fertile lower Burma. Rangoon soon overshadowed Akyab as a rice-export center, and large-scale Indian and Chinese immigration turned Rangoon into a city where the immigrant population formed the majority. Indians and Chinese became the commercial middlemen of colonial Burma, dominating steam mills and urban businesses, as well as the sources of credit to Burma's poor agriculturists. The quickly expanding colonial economy led to large-scale immigration into the south from the neighboring kingdom of Burma in the north, especially into agricultural areas. British economic development was focused on timber extraction and rice agriculture.

Starting at the beginning of World War II, Burma began a long trek toward impoverishment. Small-scale industrial enterprises and Burma's transportation infrastructure were destroyed in the war, especially by the British in their flight from the Japanese. Ethnic hostilities directed by poor Burmese toward Indian moneylenders and Chinese commercial elites also fundamentally disrupted the colonial economy. The Burmese independence struggle that began before Japanese occupiers left Burma at the close of World War II left little time for economic revitalization.

Independent Burma to 1993

In the early 1950s, Burma benefited from soaring demand for its rice exports due to the Korean War. Afterward, growing ethnic rebellions and a Communist insurgency destabilized the government and the economy and led to the seizure of power by the military in 1962. Economic decline followed.

Under the regime of Ne Win (b. 1911), from 1962 to 1988, Burma followed the "Burmese Way to Socialism." Industries, both domestic- and foreign owned, were nationalized. Industrial development was directed to reduce expensive foreign imports by manufacturing goods at home. These were state enterprises, owned by the Burmese government, and included automotive and tractor-assembly plants, ceramic and glass factories, and electric-appliance assembly plants. In a political move directed at those among the country's middle and upper classes who were opposed to the regime, Ne Win invalidated a range of large-denomination Burmese banknotes, suddenly impoverishing many of Burma's wealthiest consumers.

Burma's severe economic problems provided the context for the pro-democracy student riots in 1988 and the end of the Ne Win regime. From 1988 until 1993, the State Law and Order Restoration Council (SLORC) regime sought to reverse Myanmar's economic troubles and began limited economic liberalization policies. In

December 1988, the SLORC also established a secure legal basis for foreign investment with a new investment law, derived from the commercial law of the British colonial period in Burma. Although the SLORC was replaced by the State Peace and Development Council (SPDC) in November 1997, this was essentially a name change accompanied by a reshuffling of ministers, and little real change has taken place in economic policies (or in government policies in general).

Myanmar's Agricultural Sector

Myanmar's agricultural sector (including fishing, forestry, and animal husbandry) employs about 63 percent of the country's labor force and makes up 60 percent of the country's economy (2000–2001). Myanmar's chief agricultural products include rice, corn, oilseed, legumes, and sugar. The government officially owns all land and forcibly procures a portion of paddy rice at an artificially low price (as low as one-fifth of the market price) as an unofficial tax. Recently this policy has been extended to other crops, including beans and legumes, in an effort to gain foreign-exchange earnings.

From 1962, when the military regime took over, until 1992, rice exports steadily dropped, especially in the period after 1987–1988. From 1992 to 1993, the SLORC regime was able to achieve an increase in rice exports due to expansion of supply. This was achieved by the introduction of multiple cropping (up to three crops per year), introduced to rural farmers by government specialists. Moderate increases in yield and in area under cultivation, as well as private efforts to use pumped water during the dry season, have also aided this growth. Paddy cultivation has been supplemented by the extension of bean and legume crops by the government to increase export earnings.

Industry and Raw Materials

Compared with most Asian countries, contemporary Myanmar has a very underdeveloped industrial sector. The industrial sector accounts for only about 10–11 percent of the gross domestic product (GDP; manufacturing produced 8.8 percent of the GDP in 1991–1992), far below many other countries in Southeast Asia, and this sector employs only about 10 percent of Myanmar's labor force. Eighty-five percent of Myanmar's industrial output is devoted to food and beverage processing, and only 10 percent is focused on manufacturing. As a result, Myanmar has to import most manufactured goods. Myanmar's chief industries are devoted to the processing of agricultural products and raw materials (wood, copper, iron, tin, and tungsten) and the production of fertilizer, footwear, pharmaceuticals, and textiles.

A major transition has begun in the industrial sector since the 1980s. During the Ne Win period, for example, consumer demand for small manufactured goods was met by the emergence of cottage industries. Due to the growth of a large black market and cheap supplies of these goods from neighboring countries, including China, India, and Thailand, the survival of these cottage industries is increasingly threatened. Under the SLORC, however, economic liberalization and the encouragement of foreign investment, including special privileges, led to moderate foreign investment in Myanmar's industrial sector, although that sector is still dominated by mismanaged and inefficient state industries originally established under the Ne Win regime. Pressure from foreign imports, including the black market, downsizing due to reduced availability of hard foreign currency (and thus inability to purchase expensive foreign raw materials), and the weight of an inefficient labor force continue to plague the government-owned portion of the industrial sector under the SPDC.

Myanmar's raw-materials production includes the extraction of natural fuels, precious metals, and minerals. In 1993–1994, Myanmar produced approximately 689 million liters of petroleum, 138 million liters of natural gas, 29 thousand metric tons of coal, and smaller amounts of lead, silver, and tin. Oil, silver, minerals, paraffin wax, and gems figure prominently as exports. Mining, however, produces only a fraction of the country's GDP (just over 1 percent in 2000–2001).

Foreign Trade, Investment, Loans, and the Black Market

Myanmar's chief exports and imports continue to be dominated by inefficient state-run enterprises, despite limited privatization under the SLORC/SPDC regime. Myanmar's largest exports, such as rice and teak, remain government monopolies. In addition to rice and teak (the latter is exported almost exclusively to the rest of Asia), limited supplies of rubber are also exported. In the 1990s, the government also successfully promoted exports of beans and legumes, the latter largely derived from state requisitioning from rural farmers. Myanmar's exports go mainly to India, Singapore, China (including Hong Kong), Thailand, and Japan. In 1993–1994, 241,000 metric tons of Myanmar's largest export, rice, was distributed as follows: Africa, 34,000 metric tons; Sri Lanka, 32,000 metric tons; Singapore, 13,000 metric tons; Western Europe, 10,000 metric tons; India, 3,000 metric tons; the Middle East, 2,000 metric tons; and the rest of the world, 146,000 metric tons.

Weak domestic economic development requires Myanmar to import substantially. Myanmar's chief imports include construction materials, food products, and machinery. Myanmar's imports come chiefly from Singapore, Japan, China (including Hong Kong), Thailand, and Malaysia.

Foreign direct investment (FDI) in Myanmar is guided by a new investment law and is overseen by the Myanmar Investment Commission. By the beginning of 1997, Myanmar had 244 approved FDI projects worth just over $6 billion, although only a quarter of these projects actually reached fruition. The largest sources of FDI were, in order, Great Britain, Singapore, Thailand, France, the United States, Malaysia, Indonesia, and Japan and were largely directed into oil and gas extraction and the hotel and tourism industry. Although the military regime hoped that increased support for tourism would help raise hard foreign-currency earnings, successful campaigning on the part of antigovernment groups for a tourist boycott of Myanmar has kept tourism at a minimal level.

Low FDI (relative to countries in comparable stages of development) is due directly and indirectly to Myanmar's government policies. The invalidation of the 1990 elections, the suppression of the National League for Democracy (NLD), the NLD's calls for an end to foreign investment to force the regime to come to the bargaining table, and reports of various other human-rights abuses (including torture of political opponents and forced unpaid labor of rural peasants on government transportation projects) have led many foreign governments and international bodies to initiate economic sanctions against the country. Myanmar's policies regarding foreign investment are also at fault, especially regulations that require foreign companies to partner with investors in Myanmar, with the domestic share calculated at an exorbitantly high rate of exchange. The generally poor, underdeveloped economy also offers little attraction for foreign investment except for raw materials such as oil, teak, and agricultural produce. Heavy foreign investment in hotels, restaurants, and other aspects of the tourist industry in Myanmar has also not provided the expected profits, and many large hotels experience very low occupancy levels.

A poorly run economy, low foreign-exchange earnings, and high military spending have resulted in large government deficits that have led to heavy foreign borrowing. Myanmar's case became so severe that in 1995 Japan, one of Myanmar's largest foreign lenders, changed its loans to Myanmar into grants. Myanmar has fallen seriously behind on its International Monetary Fund repayments and has stopped making payments on multilateral loans altogether. Loans from Thailand, China, and private lenders await repayment from the profits gained by a new gas pipeline.

Remittances by nationals working abroad keep a large supply of foreign exchange coming into Myanmar. There are from 800,000 to 1 million Burmese who work legally and illegally in Thailand, ten to twenty thousand in Singapore, forty thousand Burmese registered seamen, and Burmese abroad elsewhere.

The black market, including illegal imports and exports, private trading, private currency exchange, and the drug trade, may equal or exceed the formal economy in size. Myanmar is the world's largest producer of opium used illicitly. Some of the items exported illegally from Myanmar include jade and gems, animals, rice, and teak. Furthermore, irregular amounts of palm-leaf manuscripts, Buddha images, and other cultural items forbidden for export by the government also support the black market.

Communication, Transportation, and Education Infrastructure

Myanmar's communications sector, which is controlled by the government, is among the least developed in the world. In addition to government restrictions on access to fax machines, computer modems, and satellite dishes and prohibition of private access to the Internet, Myanmar possesses few telephones. In 1995, the whole country had only about 190,000 telephones (140,000 in 1993) for a population estimated at 52 million (2002 est.).

The poor state of Myanmar's transportation infrastructure is a major inhibitor to economic development. In 1996–1997, the transportation sector accounted for only 4 percent of the country's GDP and about 4 percent of employment. Road mileage has grown at a snail's pace, from 22,934 kilometers of roads in 1984 to 26,434 kilometers in 1993, even though the number of cars in Myanmar during the same period doubled from about 1 million in 1984 to just below 2 million in 1993. Myanmar has only about 0.11 kilometers of roads per square mile. Although railway mileage has increased over the same decade at a rate of 3.4 percent per year, aging rolling stock is causing a net decline in use. In 1986, for example, the country had 4,437 kilometers of railways, which increased to 4,966 kilometers by 1993. During the same period, the number of locomotives declined from 384 in 1986 to only 311 by 1993. Public works and transportation systems are notorious for being developed now with the use of armed-forces labor and forced labor of villagers. Gasoline is rationed, with a daily limit of several liters.

A man crosses a bridge over a rice field in Myanmar in 1996. (RICHARD BICKEL/CORBIS)

One of the biggest problems facing the Myanmar economy is the impact of poor education policies, including reduction in government spending on education, extremely low matriculation rates, and the repeated closure of universities for years at a time from a fear of student activism. The government's claimed national literacy rate of 80 percent is questionable. Although most children attend primary school until the age of ten years, most also drop out of school before entering the fifth grade. Some major reasons for this include, in rural areas, the low school to village ratio (about one school per twenty-five villages in some areas) and thus low teacher to student ratios and, in urban areas, rising school fees and other costs related to attending school. The quality and supply of instructional materials are also extremely limited. Government spending on education as a percentage of the GDP has dropped each year since a peak in 1990–1991.

After student demonstrations in 1996 and again in August 1998 on the tenth anniversary of the 1988 prodemocracy uprising, the government kept the universities in Myanmar closed until very recently. Current government efforts have been directed at shifting technical training to regional campuses and severely reducing the scope and enrollment at the University of Yangon in an effort to reduce the potential for student political activities. This is creating a serious shortage in professionals and technicians necessary to develop the economy. In recognition of this, the government has recently begun to decentralize technical and college education, in order to remove students from the locale of the central government by shifting them to various outlying technical colleges, such as that in Sittwe.

Chief Hindrances to Economic Growth

A major hindrance to economic growth is high military spending. Security problems facing the nation in the past, such as the armed rebellion of the Communist Party of Burma (1948–1989), independent druglord armies, and ethnic insurgencies, have largely been eliminated today. Defense spending has increased, however, to maintain stability after the regime invalidated the democratic elections of 1990, which it lost. Military spending has increased to about a third of government spending (31.6 percent in 1997–1998). Myanmar yearly runs a serious fiscal deficit. Increasing the money supply to meet this deficit has resulted in a high rate of inflation of 20–50 percent per year. Although income has also increased, real income growth for everyone has not kept pace with inflation, and thus the average citizen is getting poorer.

Despite significant economic liberalization after the imposition of the SLORC government, holdovers from the socialist policies of the Ne Win regime continue to monopolize most (especially heavy) industries and chief exports (especially rice) and dominate key sectors of the economy under the SPDC.

Michael Walter Charney

See also: **Communist Party of Burma; Myanmar—History; Myanmar—Human Rights; Myanmar—Political System; Ne Win, U; Rakhine State; State Law and Order Restoration Council—Myanmar**

Further Reading

Adas, Michael. (1974) *The Burma Delta: Economic Development and Social Change on an Asian Frontier, 1852–1941.* Madison: University of Wisconsin Press.

Andrus, J. Russell. (1947) *Burmese Economic Life.* Foreword by J. S. Furnivall. Stanford, CA: Stanford University Press.

Brown, Ian. (1997) *Economic Change in South-East Asia, c. 1830–1980.* Oxford, U.K.: Oxford University Press.

Cheng Siok-Hwa. (1968) *The Rice Industry of Burma, 1852–1940.* Kuala Lumpur, Malaysia: University of Malaya Press.

Ghosh, Anjali. (1989) *Burma: A Case of Aborted Development.* Calcutta, India: Papyrus.

Hill, Hall, and Sisira Jayasuriya. (1986) *An Inward-Looking Economy in Transition: Economic Development in Burma since the 1960s.* Singapore: Institute of Southeast Asian Studies.

Khin Maung, M. I. (1997) *The Myanmar Labour Force: Growth and Change, 1973–83.* Singapore: Institute of Southeast Asian Studies.

Khin Maung Kyi, Ronald Findlay, Sundrum Mya Maung, Myo Nyunt, Zaw Oo, et al. (2000) *A Vision and a Strategy: Economic Development of Burma.* Stockholm, Sweden: Olof Palme International Center.

Mya Than, and Joseph L. H. Tan. 1990. *Myanmar Dilemmas and Options: The Challenge of Economic Transition in the 1990s.* Singapore: Institute of Southeast Asian Studies.

Saito, Teruko, and Lee Kin Kiong. (1999) *Statistics on the Burmese Economy: The 19th and 20th Centuries.* Singapore: Institute of Southeast Asian Studies.

United States State Department, Embassy of Burma. (2002) *Country Commercial Guides: Burma.* Retrieved 10 January 2002, from: http://www2.usatrade.gov/Website/CCG.nsf/CCGurt/CCG-BURMA2002-CH-2-0045F7E4.

MYANMAR—EDUCATION SYSTEM

The Burmese have always had a great respect for education and a relatively high literacy rate. However, there are serious deficiencies in the education system deriving from the years of isolation during the period of Ne Win's military socialist rule (1962–1988) and, since then, from the repeated closure of schools and universities by the ruling State Law and Order Restoration Council (renamed State Peace and Development Council in 1997, SLORC/SPDC). Decades of military rule and a preoccupation with curbing dissent have resulted in a tightly controlled education system with teachers and students required to sign declarations of noninvolvement in politics to the government and kept under close surveillance by military intelligence.

Structure

Myanmar's (Burma's) educational system is supervised and coordinated by the Myanmar Education Committee set up in 1991 and headed by Secretary-One of the State Peace and Development Council, which requires the Ministry of Education to implement policies set by the state. The Ministry of Education is made up of the Minister's Office and five departments: Higher Education, Basic Education, Myanmar Language Commission, Myanmar Board of Examinations, and Myanmar Educational Research Bureau. The Minister's Office supervises the implementation of educational programs and is responsible for fiscal planning within the ministry. The Department of Higher Education is responsible for universities and colleges, and several affiliated bodies (among them the universities' central library, the Historical Research Institute, the universities' press, and the translations and publications departments). Yangon Institute of Technology (founded 1964), the Mandalay Institute of Technology (1991), the Yangon Institute of Computer Science and Technology (1971), and the Mandalay Institute of Computer Science and Technology (1997) became part of a Department of Advanced Science and Technology, under a new Ministry of Science and Technology that took over responsibility for the former Department of Technical, Agricultural, and Vocational Education from the Ministry of Education. Forestry, agriculture, and veterinary science institutes are located at Yezin in central Myanmar. The Ministry of Health is responsible for medical education at institutes of medicine, dentistry, and nursing. Military medical and engineering universities and schools for military personnel are run by the Ministry of Defence.

Historical Perspective

Education in the precolonial period was largely confined to Buddhist monastic schools, which taught reading, writing, and arithmetic and, through recitation and instruction in Buddhist texts, imparted the essential principles of the Buddhist religion and ethics that inform much of Burmese culture and society. This system ensured a high literacy rate for Burmese Buddhist boys who, to this day, nearly all enter the monastery as novice monks at some time between the ages of seven and sixteen. Education for girls in the precolonial period was much more limited, but some private lay schools existed to supplement monastic education. In the eighteenth and nineteenth centuries some Burmese monarchs, perceiving the need for training in secular and practical skills, allowed Catholic and other Christian missionaries to establish a small number of schools.

However, it was only after the British annexation of Arakan and Tenasserim in 1826 that Christian mission schools became firmly established, with the American Baptist Missionary Society becoming most active, particularly among the Karen. In 1852, Lower Burma came under British rule, and at first attempts were made to introduce a more modern and practical curriculum through the existing monastic schools. An Education Syndicate was set up in 1881 to regulate the curriculum and standard of instruction.

Under British colonial rule a secular form of education was introduced to Burma in the nineteenth century. By the early 1900s, lay schools began to outnumber monastery schools, and three types of schools, differentiated according to the language of instruction, had evolved: vernacular schools that taught in Burmese (or one of the recognized minority languages), bilingual Anglo-vernacular schools, and English (missionary, private, and government) schools. The majority of the population attended vernacular schools, but education in Anglo-vernacular and English schools was highly prized as a means of gaining employment in the colonial administration. Higher educational opportunities were extremely limited. Before 1920 there were only two colleges in Burma, Rangoon College, founded in 1880 (renamed Government College in 1904), and Baptist College, founded by the American Baptist Mission in 1894 (renamed Judson College in 1918, and University College in 1920). Both were affiliated with Calcutta University and by 1920, when the two colleges became the nucleus of the new University of Rangoon, only about 400 Burmese had attained an Indian degree. In 1930 Rangoon's Teachers' Training College and Medical College became constituent colleges of the University of Rangoon, as did the Agricultural College and Research Institute at Mandalay in 1938. Mandalay's Intermediate College, founded in 1925, was raised to degree status in 1948 and became a separate university only in 1958.

The University of Rangoon, as originally conceived, was regarded by Burmese nationalists as imperialist and elitist, open only to the most affluent and privileged. Its foundation on 1 December 1920 provoked a mass student boycott that attracted much popular support and inaugurated student involvement in national politics—a link of lasting significance in the history of Burma's struggle for independence from colonial rule and, later, in the democracy movement since 1988. The university boycott of 1920 (commemorated as National Day) gave birth to the national education movement that established a (short-lived) independent national college and more than a hundred national schools that made education more accessible and promoted patriotism. The 1930s saw the rise of the Do Bama Asiayone ("We Burmans" Association), which attracted radical young students who turned the Rangoon University Students' Union into a highly politicized body that organized student strikes in 1936 and 1938.

Independent Burma

Since independence in 1948, efforts were made to improve access to basic education and to centralize control of the education system. In 1952, U Nu's government launched an ambitious educational plan that aimed to provide free education in state schools from primary to university level, introduced more technical and practical subjects to middle and high schools and, in order to support Burmese as the medium of instruction, sought to provide modern textbooks in the vernacular. English remained the medium of instruction in private schools and at the university level. Following Ne Win's military coup in 1962, all schools were nationalized, universities and colleges placed under direct government control, and the students' union building was dynamited by the army. The educational system was reorganized to give priority to the inculcation of socialist values and to the teaching of science. Burmese was made the medium of instruction at all levels, including university. Although many new schools were opened in the socialist period and vigorous illiteracy eradication programs undertaken, educational standards declined and social inequalities increased. Middle-school examinations at age fourteen separated students into sciences and arts streams, while school-leaving examinations at age sixteen determined which subjects could be studied at university, with places in medical school reserved for those with the highest pass marks, down through a descending scale that ranked arts subjects lowest. A further form of discrimination barred many of Indian and Chinese origin from studying medicine and technical subjects at university. Indigenous minority peoples had limited resources. Student demonstrations in the 1970s prompted the authorities to decentralize university education by establishing seventeen regional colleges and, in 1974–1976, "distance learning" programs. English language skills, taught from age ten onward, declined greatly in the socialist period, and disadvantaged students at the university level (where English was reintroduced as the medium of instruction in 1981). In urban areas, private tuition classes proliferated. Families of students sent abroad as state scholars had to act as guarantors, paying huge financial penalties if the student failed to return to Burma. In 1986–1987, 41 percent of higher education enrollment

Children, some dressed in army clothing, learning Chinese at a school in the Golden Triangle region of Myanmar. (CHRISTOPHE LOVINY/CORBIS)

was in correspondence courses. More recently, decentralized and distance education has greatly increased.

Outlook

Since 1962, the Burmese education system has suffered from underinvestment and the subordination of educational standards and academic freedom to political indoctrination, rigorous control, and corruption. This process has greatly intensified since 1988 under the military regime of SLORC/SPDC. In 1990–1992 the Ministry of Education, in conjunction with the United Nations Development Programme (UNDP) and UNESCO, conducted an education sector survey with the objective of identifying education needs and goals. In 2000–2001 a Four Year Plan for Promotion of Education was launched to improve the "efficiency of the basic education sector." A 1995 UNICEF report noted that 39 percent of children never enrolled in primary school, that 34 percent dropped out, and that of the 27 percent who completed primary education, less than 2 percent completed secondary education. Myanmar continues to devote a disproportionately high amount of public expenditure to the armed forces, with low allocations (1.1 percent of GDP in 1995) going to education.

Patricia M. Herbert

Further Reading

Aye Kyaw. (1993) *The Voice of Young Burma*. Ithaca, NY: Cornell University Press, Southeast Asia Program.

Kaung, U. (1963) "A Survey of the History of Education in Burma before the British Conquest and After." *Journal of the Burma Research Society* 46, 2: 1–124.

Khin Maung Kyi, Ronald Findlay, R. M. Sundram, et al. (2000) *A Vision and a Strategy: Economic Development of Burma*. Stockholm, Sweden: Olof Palme International Center.

Nyi Nyi. (1964) "The Development of University Education in Burma." *Journal of the Burma Research Society* 47, 1:11–76.

Ono, Toru. (1981) "The Development of Education in Burma." *East Asian Cultural Studies* 20: 107–133.

Smith, Martin. (1995) "Burma (Myanmar)." In *Academic Freedom 3: Education and Human Rights*, edited by John Daniel, Nigel Hartley, and Yves Lador. London: Zed Books, 92–107.

MYANMAR—FOREIGN RELATIONS

MYANMAR—FOREIGN RELATIONS The physical geography of Myanmar (as Burma has been known since 1989) has played an important role in the history of its foreign relations. Dividing western and central Myanmar is the Arakan Yoma mountain range, which meant that until 1785 there were essentially two "Burmas," each with its own sphere of foreign relations. The Irrawaddy Valley, for example, has with a few exceptions maintained chiefly overland relations with bordering Thailand in the east, China in the north, the numerous small Shan states between, and Assam and Manipur to the northwest. Arakan (now Rakhine), however, had few overland relations, and its long coastline meant that its foreign relations, historically, have been maritime ones, with eastern Bengal (today Bangladesh) in the north, India in the west, and Sri Lanka to the southwest. The Arakan Yoma was a barrier to Arakan's relationship with the Irrawaddy Valley, and thus relationships between the two Burmas were minimal except during a few important episodes discussed below. Furthermore, for much of its precolonial history, the Irrawaddy Valley itself was divided into numerous Burmese, Mon, Shan, and other kingdoms that maintained a myriad of interstate relationships.

The Burmese perceived the world as a series of circles with the king at the center and rings of decreasingly powerful rulers, attracted into orbit by the central ruler's superior store of charismatic power, around that center. In precolonial Burmese perceptions, political borders were not hard, fixed, and absolute, but soft, flexible, and relative. (This perception would later bring the Burmese to blows with the British.)

In practice, the rulers of this system were bonded by intermarriages. Burmese foreign relations typically involved the presentation of the daughters or sisters of vassal rulers to the king or the exchange of high-ranking princesses with other important kings, the exchange of presents, and, depending upon the kind of relationship (overlord-vassal), the exchange of royal regalia. These relationships frequently soured when the overlord appeared weak or a vassal did not send tribute. Sometimes, as in the case of Imtaw Syan in 1165, a foreign ruler might dispatch assassins to kill a Burmese ruler who had offended him.

Early Period (to 1751)

Although Chinese accounts of Burma in the eighth century indicate foreign political interactions, reliable records of Burma's foreign relations emerge in the Pagan period (eleventh–thirteenth centuries), during which time Burma maintained significant relationships with courts in Sri Lanka and China. Much of the relationship with Sri Lanka, a Theravada Buddhist country like Burma, was religious in nature. In the mid-twelfth century, however, increasingly powerful Pagan made a bid to take control of the northern Kra Isthmus and thus deny Sri Lanka access to Cambodian trade, which Pagan wanted for itself. Although Sri Lankan chronicles claimed that Sri Lanka conquered Pagan in retaliation, it is clear only that a pro-Sri Lankan faction emerged in the Pagan royal court. Sri Lankan political influence thereafter became an important characteristic of Pagan.

The exact nature of Burma's relationship with China during this period is unclear, as Burma and China were separated by the enigmatic Tai kingdom of Nanchao. In the late thirteenth century, however, China and Burma came into direct relations, due to the Mongol conquest of China and the Mongol-established Yuan dynasty that ruled over China in the thirteenth and fourteenth centuries. In 1253, the Mongols took Nanchao and demanded that Burma become tributary but were refused; in 1277, the Yuan defeated the Burmese in battle but then withdrew; in 1283, Yuan armies took Bhamo in northeastern Burma; and in 1287, Yuan armies took the capital of Pagan itself, playing a significant role in the demise of the Pagan state in the decades thereafter. After 1298, the so-called three Shan brothers, who in reality were apparently of uncertain ethnicity, led Burma's early post-Pagan states. In 1301, they successfully resisted another invasion of Burma by China. Subsequently, the three brothers entered into tributary relationships with China, thereby gaining Chinese recognition and discouraging the involvement of China in Burma's affairs. Although Chinese overlordship was directly imposed over upper Burma again in the mid-fifteenth century, the interest of China's Ming dynasty (1368–1644) in Burma was short-lived.

The western Burmese state of Arakan (now Rakhine), politically separate from the kingdom of Pagan, maintained a separate sphere of foreign relations. Unlike Pagan, Arakan's relationships were chiefly with India, and there appears to have been no interaction with China, of whose tributary system Arakan was not a part. As a result of its presence on the Bay of Bengal and simultaneous interaction with Muslim, Hindu, and Theravada Buddhist courts, cultural influences, political institutions, and representations, Arakan's economic relationships differed substantially from those of Pagan and the successor states of Sagaing, Pinya, and Inwa in the Irrawaddy Valley. On the one hand, Arakanese rulers adopted Islamic titles and coinage and catered to Muslim merchants. Evidence also suggests that Arakan was part of Bengal's tributary system in the fourteenth and fifteenth centuries. On the other hand, Arakan maintained long-term exchanges of Buddhist monks and texts with Sri Lanka. Relations between Arakan and Inwa were assuaged in the mid-fifteenth century during a meeting between the Inwa and Arakanese kings in which they agreed that each should rule one side of the Arakan Yoma mountains separating western and central Burma.

Burma's foreign relations became more far-flung in the sixteenth century. During this century, the First Toungoo dynasty established a vast Burmese empire by devouring the various independent Burmese states that had emerged with the decline of Pagan and by then moving to conquer most of Lan Xang (Laos) and Siam (Thailand). These campaigns were made possible by the growth of maritime trade connections, many of which were with the Muslim trading world and the Portuguese. Both of these sources also supplied First Toungoo dynastic rulers with firearms and introduced a gunpowder revolution to Burmese warfare. The First Toungoo empire, however, stretched too far and too quickly for Burma's resources and declined rapidly in the 1590s, followed by the political redisintegration of Burma.

Arakanese expansion took advantage of the First Toungoo dynasty's misfortunes and not only helped to destroy the capital of Pegu in 1599, but also took control of lower Burma (1599–1603), isolating the restored kingdom of Inwa from maritime commerce and foreign relationships. Portuguese blockades (1603–1617) of the lower Burmese and Arakanese coasts, however, encouraged Arakan's rapid decline, and Inwa once again regained access to the maritime world.

The Restored Toungoo dynasty (1597–1752) experienced a relatively unbroken era of peaceful relations with its neighbors. In 1635, this dynasty, which had reestablished itself at Pegu, withdrew its capital back to Inwa, suggesting the growing prosperity of upper Burma's domestic economy over the course of the seventeenth and early eighteenth centuries. Especially important was the growing trade interaction with China, in which political reconsolidation and long-term stability under the Qing dynasty (1644–1912) encouraged increasing trade between China and Burma. The revival of Asian maritime trade in the eighteenth century, and the arrival of British and French traders, bringing supplies of ships, arms, and munitions to the lower Burmese coasts, appears to have played a role in stimulating the Mon rebellion (1740–1759) that brought the demise of the Restored Toungoo dynasty, marked by the Mon sacking of Inwa in 1752.

Konbaung Dynasty and British Burma (1752–1947)

Burmese foreign relations under the kings of the Konbaung dynasty (1752–1886) were marked by arrogance on the part of Burmese kings, especially Alaungpaya (1714–1760, reigned 1752–1760), who once boasted that he might conquer England. Konbaung rulers faced serious challenges in their relationships mainly with the Qing dynasty of China. Numerous invasions (1765–1769) by Chinese armies were met by strong Burmese resistance and Chinese defeat. By the end of the eighteenth century, however, as is clear from Michael Symes's account of his 1798 visit to the Burmese regime, the Chinese and the Burmese were on very good terms and shared an intimacy that the British lacked in their relations with the Burmese court. Special Burmese ministers also catered to the needs of the Chinese living in Burma, and some Burmese ministers in the royal court were known for their fluency in Chinese.

The Burmese brought much of Siam under their control, temporarily, again in 1766, after their destruction of the Siamese capital of Ayutthaya. Konbaung expansionism, however, also brought Burma into hostile relations with British power, which itself was expanding in Bengal and the Strait of Malacca in the late eighteenth century. In the 1780s, Konbaung armies, on the pretext of protecting the Buddhist religion, invaded and annexed Assam and Arakan. From 1785, Burma shared a political frontier with British possessions. Disagreements over what political borders meant emerged two decades later. An Arakanese rebel, Chan Byan, took advantage of the British presence to launch attacks into Burmese Arakan from British India. Burmese punitive missions likewise crossed into British territory to capture the rebels, violating British understandings of territorial sovereignty. During the First Anglo-Burmese War (1824–1826) that followed, the Burmese were soundly defeated, and in the Treaty of Yandabo (1826) that brought the war to a close, Burma surrendered the provinces of Assam, Arakan, and Tenasserim, all of which were annexed by the British. Another war in 1852, the Second Anglo-Burmese War, led to the transfer of all of lower Burma to the British.

The heyday of late Konbaung foreign relations came with the rule of Mindon Min (1814–1878) after the Second Anglo-Burmese War. Likened to the visionary and capable Thai ruler Mongkut (1804–1868), Mindon Min embarked on an ambitious campaign to advance Burma militarily, technologically, and politically (in terms of foreign relations). Dozens of European specialists in all areas of administration and technology were hired to accomplish these goals. Mindon Min also tried, but failed, to prevent Britain from choking off Burma's access to the outside world. He sought to accomplish this by establishing good foreign relations with rival European and other powers, sending diplomatic missions to the United States, Italy, France, and China. From 1852 until 1885, however, while upper Burma became impoverished, British Burma, in command of the fertile lower delta and thousands of Burmese immigrants, prospered. Ultimately, independent Burma was brought to an end by the annexation of upper Burma by the British in the Third Anglo-Burmese War (1885).

Prior to the outbreak of World War II in the Pacific, Japanese military planners had gathered thirty student leaders, known popularly as the Thirty Comrades, from the anticolonial Thakin movement of the 1930s and trained them militarily on Hainan. In 1942, when Japanese armies occupied British Burma, they were accompanied by the Thirty Comrades, with Aung San (1914?–1947) as the head of the Burma Independence Army. In 1942, in order to enhance local support for the Japanese army and to help slow the return of Allied forces, Japan sponsored the Provisional Government of Baw Maw, which in 1943 became "independent" and declared itself an ally of Japan. In 1943, a Burma National Army was established under Aung San. In 1944, as Japan seemed destined to lose the war, this army joined the Anti-Fascist People's Freedom League, founded by Aung San and Than Tun (1911–1968), and turned against the Japanese on 28 March 1945.

Having mobilized Burmese nationalists and armed them, British rule could enjoy only a brief and superficial return from 1945 until 1947, during which period it became clear that Britain's days in Burma were over. Although the independence leader and his

THE TREATY OF YANDABO

During the First Anglo-Burmese War (1824–1826) the Burmese were soundly defeated and in the Treaty of Yandabo of 1826 extracted below, Burma surrendered the provinces of Assam, Arakan, and Tenasserim to the British.

> Article I. There shall be perpetual peace and friendship between the honourable Company on the one part, and His Majesty the King of Ava on the other.
>
> Article II. His Majesty the King of Ava renounces all claims upon and will abstain from all future interference with, the principality of Assam and its dependencies, and also with the contiguous petty states of Cachar and Iyntia. With regard to Munnipore, it is stipulated that, should Gumbheer Singh desire to return to that country, he shall be recognized by the King of Ava as Rajah thereof.
>
> Article III. To prevent all future disputes respecting the boundary line between the two great nations, the British government will retain the conquered provinces of Arracan, Ramree, Cheduba and Sandowey, and His Majesty the King of Ava cedes all right thereto. The Annonpeeteetonmien, or Arracan mountains, (known in Arracan by the name of Yeornabourg or Pokhengloung Range) will henceforth form the boundary between the two great nations on that side. Any doubts regarding the said line of demarcation will be settled by commissioners appointed by the respective governments for that purpose, such commissioners from both powers to be of suitable and corresponding rank.
>
> Article IV. His Majesty the King of Ava cedes to the British government the conquered provinces of Yeh, Tavoy and Mergui and Tenasserim, with the islands and dependencies thereto appertaining taking the Saluen [Salween] river as the line of demarcation on that frontier. Any doubts regarding their boundaries will be settled as specified in the concluding part of Article III.
>
> Article V. In proof of the sincere disposition of the Burmese government to maintain the relations of peace and amity between the two nations, and as part indemnification to the British government for the expenses of the war, His Majesty the King of Ava agrees to pay the sum of one *crore* [10,000,000] of rupies.

Source: George F. de Martens. (1828) *Nouveau Recueil de Traites . . . des Puissances et Etats de l'Europe depuis 1808 jusqu'a Present.* Gottingen, Germany: n.p., 894.

cabinet were assassinated in 1947, Burma was granted independence in 1948.

Contemporary Period (1948 to the Present)

In the overall context of the Cold War, Burma's foreign relationships began to change in the early 1950s because of changes in the international market for Burma's chief export, rice. Burma had been, under colonial rule, the world's largest exporter of rice. During the Korean War, the demand for Burmese rice, and the price made for it, underwent a tremendous but short-lived boom. When the fighting in Korea stopped, Asia's former purchasers of Burmese rice had already begun to replace Burmese imports with homegrown varieties or with accelerating U.S. rice exports. Burma was thus forced to turn to the Soviet Union and China, both of which began to supply aid and began to buy up Burmese rice. This led to Burma's realignment not to the Sino-Soviet bloc per se, but to a neutral position between it and the United States.

After independence, Burma's internal problems overshadowed foreign relations for almost fifteen years. First, Karen, Arakanese, Mon, Shan, and other separatist groups contributed to domestic political instability. Second, in 1950, Chinese nationalist armies, cut off from escape to Taiwan by Communist forces, crossed the border and remained in northeastern Burma during the following decades, taking control of parts of local opium production and trade and ruling as warlords in areas inside the Burmese border. Third, from 1948 until the late 1980s, Communist bloc countries sponsored a significant Communist insurgency, also strongest in border areas. All of these developments proved too much for the government of U Nu (1907–1995), then in power. By the end of 1958, U Nu's civilian government permitted the Burmese military to take control of the country temporarily to prevent political fragmentation (1958–1960); permanent military rule was established in a coup in 1962.

Military rule in Burma has been the chief factor isolating Burma politically and economically from the outside world. Despite significant foreign aid from countries such as Japan, the regime of Ne Win (b. 1911) proved unable to modernize the Burmese economy. Ultimately, Ne Win's regime was replaced by the State Law and Order Restoration Council in 1988, as a result of an economic crisis and massive student protests. The new military regime refused to surrender the government to the National League for Democracy (NLD), which in 1990 won elections by a landslide. For this reason and in response to the military's violent suppression of student protests, the regime grew even more isolated from the rest of the world, becoming the target of international sanctions led by the United States.

Since the mid-1990s, Myanmar has begun to take a more aggressive role in regaining access to the outside world and has been supported by the Association of Southeast Asian Nations (ASEAN), an organization that Myanmar joined in 1997. At the same time, the collapse of the insurgency led by the Communist Party of Burma in the late 1980s made it easier for Myanmar to interact more with China. China is now one of Myanmar's most significant trading partners, and it appears that China has a growing military influence in

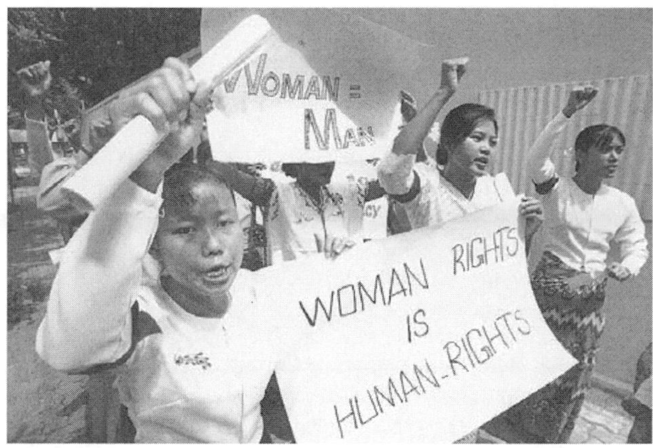

Exiled Myanmar women protest outside the Myanmar embassy in Bangkok, Thailand, on 19 June 1999, to mark the "Women of Burma Day" and to call for democratic rule in Myanmar. (AFP/CORBIS)

the country, becoming a major source of munitions and weaponry for the Burmese military. Despite U.S.-led sanctions, the government has also cooperated with the U.S. Drug Enforcement Agency, as Myanmar's drug trade was a major source of revenue for some of Myanmar's insurgencies. Meanwhile, Burmese antigovernment groups abroad have successfully maintained pressure on local and national governments and business groups to support sanctions and to keep up awareness of continued military rule and the government's prevention of the NLD from taking power. Alongside the support for a boycott of Myanmar among antigovernment groups and Western regimes, encouraged by Aung San Suu Kyi, many Asian states, particularly those of ASEAN, have favored a policy of constructive engagement, in which slow change in Myanmar would be encouraged through stronger ties and interactions with the outside world.

Foreign Relations in the Twenty-first Century

It is difficult to speculate on the future of Myanmar's foreign relations. There have been indications, however, that the military regime is willing to form a new government with some role for Aung San Suu Kyi and the NLD. Should this occur, it would probably soften the stance of many Western states and open the doors further for a stronger role for Myanmar in ASEAN and in a relationship with Japan. Such a development would help balance the increasing Chinese influence in Myanmar.

Michael Walter Charney

See also: **Anti-Fascist People's Freedom League—Myanmar; Communist Party of Burma; Myanmar—Human Rights; Ne Win, U; Nu, U; Pagan; Pegu;**

Rakhine State; Rohingya; State Law and Order Restoration Council—Myanmar

Further Reading

Aung San Suu Kyi. (1991) *Freedom from Fear and Other Writings*. Edited by Michael Aris. London: Penguin Books.

Aung-Thwin, Michael. (1998) *Myth and History in the Historiography of Early Burma: Paradigms, Primary Sources, and Prejudices*. Athens: Ohio University Center for International Studies.

Blackburn, Terence R. (2000) *The British Humiliation of Burma*. Bangkok, Thailand: Orchid Press.

Cady, John F. (1976) *The United States and Burma*. Cambridge, MA: Harvard University Press.

Carey, Peter, ed. (1997) *Burma: The Challenge of Change in a Divided Society*. London: Macmillan.

Charney, Michael W. (2000) "A Reinvestigation of Konbaung-Era Burman Historiography on the Beginnings of the Relationship between Arakan and Ava (Upper Burma)." *Journal of Asian History* 34, 1: 53–68.

Fink, Christina. (2001) *Living in Silence: Burma under Military Rule*. Bangkok, Thailand: White Lotus.

Hall, D. G. E. (1945) *Europe and Burma: A Study of European Relations with Burma to the Annexation of Thibaw's Kingdom, 1886*. Oxford, U.K.: Oxford University Press.

Houtman, Gustaaf. (1999) *Mental Culture in Burmese Crisis Politics: Aung San Suu Kyi and the National League for Democracy*. Tokyo: Tokyo University of Foreign Studies, Institute for the Study of Languages and Cultures of Asia and Africa.

Koenig, William J. (1990) *The Burmese Polity, 1752–1819: Politics, Administration, and Social Organization in the Early Kon-baung Period*. Ann Arbor: University of Michigan Center for South and Southeast Asian Studies.

Lieberman, Victor B. (1984) *Burmese Administrative Cycles: Anarchy and Conquest, c. 1580–1760*. Princeton, NJ: Princeton University Press.

Lintner, Bertil. (1994) *Burma and Revolt: Opium and Insurgency since 1948*. Boulder, CO: Westview Press.

Mya Maung. (1992) *Totalitarianism in Burma: Prospects for Economic Development*. New York: Paragon House.

Silverstein, Josef. (1989) *Independent Burma at Forty Years: Six Assessments*. Ithaca, NY: Cornell University Press.

Smith, Martin. (1999) *Burma: Insurgency and the Politics of Ethnicity*. London: Zed Books.

Steinberg, David I. (1982) *Burma: A Socialist Nation of Southeast Asia*. Boulder, CO: Westview Press.

Taylor, Robert H. (1987) *The State in Burma*. London: C. Hurst.

———, ed. (2000) *Burma: Political Economy under Military Rule*. London: C. Hurst.

Trager, Frank. (1966) *Burma: From Kingdom to Republic*. Westport, CT: Greenwood Press.

MYANMAR—HISTORY Myanmar (Burma) has been the home of some of the most powerful Southeast Asian states. Prior to 1000 CE, the lands that would become Myanmar were populated by the Mon people, who migrated westward from the Mekong Valley into southeastern Burma, and the Pyu, a Tibeto-Burman–speaking people, who entered upper Burma in the later centuries of the first millennium BCE, although neither group established large-scale unified kingdoms. Both the Pyu and the Mon were Buddhists, and early Chinese records suggest that their major settlements centered on large images of the Buddha. Important Pyu city-states included Beikthano, Halin, and Sriksetra, while important Mon city-states included Thaton, which survived until 1058.

In the first half of the ninth century, the Nanchao kingdom exerted some influence over upper Burma, but Nanchao influence declined from the 860s. In the ninth century, the Burmans, whose origins are obscure, appeared and came to dominate both the Irrawaddy Valley and northern Arakan (now Rakhine) by the tenth century.

Classical Period

Classical Burmese civilization was centered chiefly at Pagan. In the eleventh century, Pagan emerged under Anawrahta (reigned 1044–1077) and Kyanzittha (reigned 1084–1112) as a major kingdom based upon irrigated wet-rice agriculture in the dry middle zone of Burma. Territorially, these kings unified under their rule the entire Irrawaddy Valley from the Shan Hills to the Bay of Bengal in the south and possibly the Arakan littoral to the west of the Arakan Yoma mountain range.

Pagan society was Theravada Buddhist, and its economy depended upon the emergence of Buddhist religious institutions to which landholding elites and the king donated land and wealth in the hope of accumulating merit. Pagan kings, whose role in relation to the Buddhist *sasana* (religion) was reflected in the place of Thakya (king of the *nats* and the Burmese version of Hinduism's Indra) as protector of Buddhism, were the guardians and chief patrons of the Buddhist religion in Pagan society. Land and slaves donated to the *sangha* (Buddhist monkhood) and monastic estates were tax-free and granted in perpetuity (so long as the monastery in question was not deemed corrupt). Also during the Pagan period, religious inscriptions underwent a transition from the Mon to the Burmese language, indicating the cultural ascendance of the Burmans.

Pagan declined and fell in the late thirteenth and early fourteenth centuries due to long-term and short-term crises. The internal mechanism of Pagan society and economy—for example, tax-free land donations to the Buddhist monkhood—gradually robbed the state of taxable agricultural lands, its chief resource base. Although Pagan rulers could theoretically have de-

KEY EVENTS IN MYANMAR HISTORY

c. 1000 CE Myanmar is home to the Mon and Pyu peoples.
9th century The Burmans appear and dominate the Irrawaddy Valley.
11th–14th centuries Period of classical Burmese civilization centered at Pagan.
14th century Pagan declines and new centers of power are located at Pinya, Sagaing, and Ava.
1531–1599 First Toungoo dynasty reunites the Irrawaddy Valley.
1597–1752 Restored Toungoo dynasty again reunites the Irrawaddy Valley.
1752–1885 Period of the Konbaung dynasty and Burmese expansion.
1824–1826 First Anglo-Burmese War.
1852 Second Anglo-Burmese War.
1885 Third Anglo-Burmese War.
1900s Early in century, Burmese nationalism emerges.
1920–1921 Students hold a politically motivated strike.
1930–1931 The Saya Sun Rebellion.
1936 Students strike against British rule.
1937 Burma is separated from India.
1942–1945 Period of Japanese occupation.
1948 Burma becomes independent.
1962 A military coup places Ne Win in power.
1974 A new constitution formally ends military rule, but the military and its allies remain in power.
1988–1989 The military government severely represses and public protests, establishes SLORC and imprisons opposition leader Aung San Suu Kyi.
1990 The government ignores election victory by the opposition National League for Democracy.
1995 Aung San Suu Kyi is released from house arrest.

clared the *sangha* corrupt and thereby regathered the donated land, such an action was difficult in practice, due to collusion between powerful elites and monastic establishments. As a result, as monastic estates became resource-rich, kings became resource-poor, effectively reducing the ability of the court to hold the kingdom together and to defend it against external enemies. As for the additional short-term causes of Pagan's collapse, colonial historiography pointed to a supposed sack of the city of Pagan in 1287 by Mongol-led Chinese armies and to the usurpation of power in upper Burma afterward by the three so-called Shan brothers. Recent research, however, has questioned whether Pagan actually did decline as early as is supposed, whether the Chinese actually sacked the town, and whether the "three Shan brothers" were Shan, although neither the colonial nor the revisionist arguments are completely supported by clear evidence. It is certain, however, that by the mid-fourteenth century new political and economic centers had emerged in upper Burma at Pinya, Sagaing, and Ava (founded in 1364) and that Pagan had ceased to be the epicenter of Burmese civilization and power. Furthermore, what had been the mighty kingdom of Pagan was in disarray outside upper Burma as well: a Mon kingdom reemerged at Martaban in 1287, and lower Burma broke away, isolating upper Burma from the sea. The kingdom of Arakan may have broken away as early as the 1240s.

Early Modern Period

The growth in maritime-trade revenues in the fifteenth and sixteenth centuries and improvements in firearm technologies (including the replacement of Muslim Indian firearms by Portuguese weaponry and mercenaries in the sixteenth century) aided emergent kingdoms in coastal Burma (and elsewhere in Asia) vis-à-vis interior areas with little or no access to the sea. As a result, the First Toungoo dynasty (1531–1599) in lower Burma succeeded in reunifying the Irrawaddy Valley under one kingdom based at Pegu and bringing Thailand and areas of Laos under Burmese rule. This dynasty collapsed almost as quickly as it emerged, however, as continual warfare had drained lower Burma of its manpower reserves, resulting in the rebellion of outlying political centers and the siege and fall of the capital of Pegu in 1598–1599.

The Restored Toungoo dynasty (1597–1752), based at Ava after 1635, succeeded the First Toungoo dynasty and brought the Irrawaddy Valley under its control. Under this dynasty, Burmese literature and historiography blossomed, resulting in the great chronicle composed by U Kala in the 1710s. Economic problems, however, brought a rebellion in lower Burma in 1740, which resulted in a new emergent kingdom centered at Pegu and the fall of the capital of Ava in 1752. Although this conflict (1740–1756) has been portrayed both in contemporaneous accounts and in some secondary literature as an ethnic struggle between Burmans in the north and Mon in the south, this view is probably too simplistic; members of both ethnic groups fought on both sides. After the capture of the Avan court, a local official's son, Alaungpaya (1714–1760), led a counterrebellion that resulted in the fall of Pegu, the establishment of the Konbaung dynasty (1752–1885), and the conquest again of Thailand (1767) under one of Alaungpaya's successors. Under King Bodawpaya (reigned 1782–1819), Arakan (1785) and Assam (1812) were also brought under Burmese rule.

Nineteenth and Early Twentieth Centuries

The Konbaung dynasty declined in the nineteenth century for a number of reasons. Overexpansion into Arakan and Assam brought new troubles, especially on the part of local rebels. Economic factors also played a substantial role. Immediate troubles, however, resulted from border disagreements with the British in Bengal. Cultural differences in the understandings of territorial borders and national sovereignty resulted in the First Anglo-Burmese War (1824–1826), which the Burmese lost. By the Treaty of Yandabo (1826), Burma signed away the provinces of Arakan, Assam, and Tenasserim to British rule. Further misunderstandings resulted in the Second Anglo-Burmese War (1852) and in the annexation by the British of the whole of lower Burma, cutting upper Burma off from access to the sea.

In the midst of the problems with the British, the rise of the reform-minded king Mindon Min (1814–1878) led to a new approach to the encroaching West. Mindon Min wholeheartedly embraced Western technologies and Western-trained personnel and instigated serious economic reforms and institutional changes. The Third Anglo-Burmese War (1885) resulted in the deposition of King Thibaw (reigned 1878–1885), the last Burmese king, and the annexation of upper Burma by the British. Indigenous resistance to the imposition of British rule continued until the mid-1890s.

Under British rule, Burma was a province of India until 1937, when the Government of Burma Act of 1935 separated Burma from India. Under the terms of this act, the Burmese in 1936 elected a parliament that from March 1937 partly administered most of Burma, while ethnic minority areas, termed Scheduled Areas, were administered by a British governor. The British governor also remained in control of Burma's external relations, its defense, and monetary policies.

Colonial Burma developed a colonial export economy largely based upon the export of rice and teak. During colonial rule, Burma emerged as the world's largest rice exporter. Colonial ports grew rapidly and became the chief political and economic centers of the country, especially Rangoon (now Yangon), which had served as the colonial capital since the 1850s. The monetization of the economy and the commercialization of rural social relations led to dependence upon agricultural loans and Chettyar (Indian) moneylenders and Chinese merchants. Immigrant Indian labor also filled many of Burma's major cities; in the nineteenth century, the Burmese were a minority in the city of Rangoon.

The dissolution of the Buddhist monarchy, the immigration of large numbers of Muslim agriculturalists to Arakan and Muslim Indian laborers to lower Burma, and a colonial regime that tended to favor Muslims as a minority in Burma caused friction between Buddhist and Muslim communities in Burma. The appearance of mutually antagonistic literature, including a book by the Muslim writer Shwe Hpi critical of the Buddhist religion, helped spark violence, including the anti-Indian riots of 1938. Furthermore, the land crisis, in which Chittagonian immigrants and Arakanese migrants competed for agricultural land in Arakan, and the emergence of religious communalism as a major factor in rural solidarity and collective action, drew clearer lines between Buddhists and Muslims in Burma.

In addition to religious communal violence, Burmese attempts to promote Buddhism as Burma's religion nurtured the beginnings of the nationalist movement in Burma. In 1906, the Young Men's Buddhist Association was founded in Rangoon. Another organization, the All Burma Council of Young Monks Association, acted as a cover for some who became monks to engage in political activities without the in-

MOVING TOWARD AN INDEPENDENT BURMA

On 22 December 1932 the Burma Legislative Council passed the following resolution advocating policies that would lead to separation from India and which were based on the emerging Burmese nationalism of the time.

(1) That this council opposes the separation of Burma from India on the basis of the Constitution for a separated Burma outlined in the statement of the Prime Minister made at the Burma Round Table Conference on the 12th January, 1932.

(2) That this Council emphatically opposes the unconditional and permanent federation of Burma with India.

(3) This Council will continue to oppose the separation of Burma from India until Burma is granted a Constitution on the following basis:

(a) The future Constitution of Burma shall provide for the immediate transfer to popular control of at least the same measure of responsibility and the same subjects and powers as will be transferred to popular control in the Indian Federation, both at the Centre and in the Provinces.

(b) The subjects and powers reserved to the Governor shall be only for a period of transition and such Reserved powers shall be framed and exercised in accordance with recognized constitutional practice and shall in no way prejudice the advance of Burma through the new Constitution to full responsibility for her own Government within a reasonable period and the new Constitution for Burma shall further prescribe the manner in which or the time when the said Reserved subjects and powers are to be transferred to popular control on the basis of full responsibility.

In the event of failure to obtain a definite pronouncement from His Majesty's Government that Burma, if and when separated from India, will be granted the aforesaid Constitution, this Council proposes that Burma shall enter the Indian Federation with at least the following terms:

(a) Burma shall have the right to secede from the Indian Federation which it may exercise through its Legislature.

(b) There shall be such financial adjustments between Burma and India as may be required by Burma's peculiar local conditions and other circumstances.

(c) The division of central and provincial subjects in the proposed Indian Federation shall be reconsidered with reference to Burma with a view to provincialization of additional subjects, special regard being had to Burma's geographical position and its peculiar needs and conditions, and further Burma shall be afforded all necessary facilities for acquiring administrative experience and knowledge of the Reserved and Federal subjects.

That in view of the statement made by the Hon'ble Leader of the House on the 16th December 1932, in paragraph 3 of the passage explaining the position of His Majesty's Government that His Majesty's Government have always contemplated that an opportunity should be given to representatives of Burma to express further views on the provisions of the Constitution outlined before they are finally enacted, this Council expresses its deep satisfaction and gratitude and urges that a conference will be called at an early date for the purpose of determining the future constitution of Burma either as a separate unit on the aforesaid basis or as a unit in the Indian Federation with the aforesaid terms.

Source: Jagdish Saran Sharma. (1965) *India's Struggle for Freedom: Select Documents and Sources*. Vol. II. Delhi: S. Chand & Co., 214–215.

terference of the police, because monks were, by their vows, not to involve themselves in politics.

University students provided some of the early leadership for the nationalist movement. Their first strike (1920–1921) was held at the University of Rangoon. Many of these students demanded to be referred to as *thakin*, the Burmese word for "master," to stress that they considered themselves the equals of the British colonialists. In 1935, the Thakins organized a political party called the Dobama Asiayone or We

Burmans Society by uniting two smaller Thakin political organizations formed in 1930–1931. In 1936, a more serious strike in Rangoon University and in the schools was led by Thakin Aung San (1914?–1947), the president of the All Burma Student Movement.

The 1930s also witnessed other approaches to Burmese nationalism, including that of Saya San, a charismatic ex-monk. He led a rebellion known as the Saya San Rebellion (1930–1931), which drew upon traditional Burmese political culture and attempted to establish Saya San as king of Burma in December 1930. The British military police quickly captured and destroyed the jungle capital and throne of the would-be kingdom, apprehending Saya San in August 1931; resistance continued until April 1932, when the last of the major contingents of rebels was suppressed. Defended by the famous anti-British Mon lawyer Ba Maw (1893–1977), Saya San was convicted of treason and executed on 28 November 1931.

World War II and Independence

Burmese nationalists were frustrated by 1940 and sought foreign help, including a secret but failed trip to China by Thakin Aung San (general secretary to the Dobama Asiayone in the late 1930s), to gain the help of the Chinese Communist Party. A better opportunity emerged in December 1941 with Japanese invasions of European colonies in Southeast Asia. Prior to their invasion of Burma, the Japanese gathered thirty Thakins (the "Thirty Comrades"), gave them military training on Hainan Island, and used them as the core of the Burma Independence Army that aided in the invasion of Burma in 1942. The Japanese occupied Burma from 1942 until 1945.

The Japanese invasion and occupation had an enormous negative impact upon the Burmese economy well into the postwar period. Many members of the commercial elites, including British, Chinese, and Indians, fled or were forced out of Burma in advance of the Japanese arrival. Furthermore, in order to deny resources to the Japanese, the British destroyed much of Burma's transportation infrastructure (and thus economic infrastructure in an export-based economy), including the steamships of the Irrawaddy Flotilla Company, which were scuttled. Allied bombing and combat within Burma also caused much destruction.

A Japanese puppet regime declared independence under Ba Maw in August 1943, but had little popular support. Resistance to the Japanese was led toward the end of the war by the Anti-Fascist People's Freedom League (AFPFL), which was founded in August 1944. In March 1945, when Japan appeared certain to lose the war, the AFPFL, led by Aung San, launched a rebellion against the Japanese.

After the surrender of Japanese forces in August 1945, Aung San and the AFPFL resisted the reintroduction of British colonial rule, and in January 1947, Aung San and the British signed an agreement on the transfer of power in Burma. On 19 July 1947, Aung San and some of the ministers of the interim government were gunned down by assassins. Aung San was succeeded by a fellow AFPFL leader, Thakin U Nu (1907–1995). Finally, on 4 January 1948, Burma declared its independence from British rule.

U Nu's government, which led the Union of Burma throughout most of the first fifteen years of Burma's independence, faced continual problems with which it was largely unable to cope. A Communist insurgency, separatist movements, and a bid by Karen nationalists to seize lower Burma led to U Nu's resignation in 1958 and the request for the army's commander-in-chief, Ne Win (b. 1911), to establish a caretaker military regime. Elections held in 1960 returned U Nu and his party back to power, but continued ethnic hostilities led to a military coup in 1962 led by Ne Win.

The Ne Win regime legitimated military rule as an indigenous alternative to the problems of Western parliamentary democracy. Ne Win's "Burmese Way to Socialism" was institutionalized by the 1964 establishment of the Burma Socialist Programme Party (BSPP) as the sole legal political party in Burma. A new constitution and elections in 1974 formally ended military rule, but the military and connected elites retained de facto control.

Under military rule, economic mismanagement and corruption were rife and resulted in the reversal of Burma's economic development. Burma went from being the world's largest exporter of rice to being an importer of rice. In 1987, the United Nations declared Burma one of the world's least developed nations. In the same year, demonetization without compensation, including the invalidation of all large-*kyat* banknotes, eliminated the savings of Burma's upper and middle classes.

The year 1988 witnessed a series of crises for the military regime. Following Ne Win's formal resignation as chairman of the BSPP on 23 July 1988, a pro-democracy movement was sparked, leading to a mass uprising on 8 August 1988 (known as 8-8-88) in Rangoon. It soon spread to other areas of the country. A military crackdown led to the killing of thousands of Burmese. Aung San Suu Kyi (b. 1945), the daughter of Aung San, came to the forefront of the pro-democracy movement and called for the establishment of a democratic government. Unable to stem opposition, the military launched a coup on 18 September 1988, declaring the State Law and Order Restoration Council (SLORC), imposing martial law, and placing Aung San Suu Kyi under house arrest in July 1989. The new regime also changed the country's anglicized placenames to new ones that more closely followed indigenous pronunciations, substituting Myanmar for Burma, Yangon for Rangoon, Bago for Pegu, and so on. (Many foreigners and Burmese refugees, however, do not recognize the new names.) The overly confident SLORC allowed parliamentary elections in May 1990, although after the National League for Democracy (NLD), led by the detained Aung San Suu Kyi, won over 80 percent of the seats, the election results were ignored.

The military's suppression of the NLD was followed by international sanctions against the military regime and the award of the 1991 Nobel Peace Prize to Aung San Suu Kyi. In order to change its image, the military reshuffled its government, changed its name from State Law and Order Restoration Council to State Peace and Development Council, and officially released Aung San Suu Kyi from house arrest on 10 July 1995, although her activities in Myanmar are severely restricted by the government. These cosmetic changes, however, have not reversed negative international reactions to the junta's activities.

Michael Walter Charney

See also: **Anti-Fascist People's Freedom League—Myanmar; Aung San; Aung San Suu Kyi; Burma Independence Army; National League for Democracy—Myanmar; Ne Win, U; Nu, U; State Law and Order Restoration Council—Myanmar; Thakins**

Further Reading

Adas, Michael. (1974) *The Burma Delta: Economic Development and Social Change on an Asian Frontier, 1852–1941.* Madison: University of Wisconsin Press.

Aung-Thwin, Michael. (1985) *Pagan: The Origins of Modern Burma.* Honolulu: University of Hawaii Press.

———. (1998) *Myth & History in the Historiography of Early Burma: Paradigms, Primary Sources, and Prejudices.* Athens: Ohio University Center for International Studies.

Blackburn, Terrence R. (2000) *The British Humiliation of Burma.* Bangkok, Thailand: White Orchid Press.

Cady, John F. (1958) *A History of Modern Burma.* Ithaca, NY: Cornell University Press.

Charney, Michael W. (1998) "Crisis and Reformation in a Maritime Kingdom of Southeast Asia: Forces of Instability and Political Disintegration in Western Burma (Arakan): 1603–1701." *Journal of the Economic and Social History of the Orient* 41, 2: 185–219.

Harvey, G. E. ([1925] 1967) *History of Burma: From the Earliest Times to 10 March 1824, The Beginning of the English Conquest.* Reprint. London: Frank Cass.

Koenig, William J. (1990) *The Burmese Polity, 1752–1819: Politics, Administration, and Social Organization in the Early Kon-baung Period.* Ann Arbor: University of Michigan Center for South and Southeast Asian Studies.

Lieberman, Victor B. (1984) *Burmese Administrative Cycles: Anarchy and Conquest, c. 1580–1760.* Princeton, NJ: Princeton University Press.

———. (1987) "Reinterpreting Burmese History." *Comparative Studies in Society and History* 29: 162–194.

———. (1991) "Secular Trends in Burmese Economic History, c. 1350–1830, and Their Implications for State Formation." *Modern Asian Studies* 25: 1–31.

Mendelson, E. Michael. (1975) *Sangha and State in Burma: A Study of Monastic Sectarianism and Leadership.* Ed. by John P. Ferguson. Ithaca, NY: Cornell University Press.

Smith, Martin J. (1991) *Burma: Insurgency and the Politics of Ethnicity.* London: Zed Books.

Taylor, Robert H. (1987) *The State in Burma.* London: C. Hurst.

MYANMAR—HUMAN RIGHTS

Since Myanmar's independence from Great Britain in 1948 (at which time Myanmar was still known as Burma), the issue of human rights has become one of the most contentious in its modern-day politics and evolution. Many of the most serious human-rights violations—notably extrajudicial executions and the forced relocation of civilian populations—have developed against the backdrop of the country's long-standing insurgencies. Reflecting this legacy, at the beginning of the twenty-first century Myanmar remained one of the most militarized countries in Asia. Under the ruling State Peace and Development Council (SPDC), Myanmar entered its fifth decade of military rule, over twenty ethnic opposition groups maintained arms and territory, and, despite a growing number of cease-fires, fighting was continuing in several border areas.

Such conflict and loss of life highlighted the longstanding impasse in Myanmar's politics. But by the 1990s, concern over human-rights abuses and the scale of humanitarian suffering had also spread to the international stage. In particular, great hopes of peaceful transition had been engendered by the landslide victory of Aung San Suu Kyi's National League for Democracy (NLD) in the 1990 general election, Myanmar's first in three decades. However, the new century began with the reform process still deadlocked and an estimated 1,800 political prisoners held in the country's jails. This led to frequent condemnations of humanrights abuses in Myanmar by Amnesty International and other international organizations as well as critical investigations of governmental practices by both the International Labor Organization (ILO) and United Nations (U.N.) Commission on Human Rights.

Human Rights from 1948 to 1988

During the democratic era (1948–1962), in contrast, the country had enjoyed the reputation for one of the most free presses in Asia. Despite the countrywide insurgencies, there was relative freedom of movement and expression, and parliamentary elections were held on three occasions (in 1950, 1955, and 1960). It was nevertheless during the parliamentary era that a number of restrictive practices were first introduced, including the 1950 Emergency Provisions Act, which provides long jail terms for anyone suspected of circulating reports "disloyal to the state."

Many of these restrictions were widely used during General Ne Win's "Military Caretaker" administration (1958–1960), during which time a number of newspapers were shut down and many civilians detained for alleged pro-Communist or proinsurgent sympathies. The climate of repression escalated under Ne Win's Burma Socialist Programme Party (BSPP) government (1962–1988). Following the 1962 coup, Prime Minister U Nu and hundreds of political, ethnic, and trade union leaders were detained as Ne Win set about imposing a one-party system of government. The new intolerance was demonstrated in July 1962 when protests were ended at Rangoon University by troops blowing up the student union building. At least sixteen demonstrators were killed and many more wounded.

The sovereignty of the BSPP in a one-party state was enshrined in the 1974 constitution (Article 11), and this was backed up by a series of new laws controlling many aspects of national life. The most frequently invoked of these were the 1962 Printers and Publishers Registration Law and the 1975 State Protection Law. In addition, certain rights to freedom of association, expression, and religion were permitted under the constitution, but it was cautioned that they must not be "contrary to the interests of the working people and socialism."

Governed by such regulations, for twenty-six years the country disappeared from the outside world under a security blanket. Independent trade unions and media were banned, and restrictions were imposed on Buddhist monks, Christian churches, and other nongovernmental groups. Particular grievances were felt in many ethnic minority communities where the "Burmese Way to Socialism" was widely perceived as a cloak for "Burmanization" (policies favoring the Burman ethnic group). Publication in ethnic minority languages was curtailed by censorship boards, and the teaching of minority languages virtually disappeared from schools. Even the learning of English was restricted by the BSPP until the early 1980s.

However, it was in Burma's war zones that many of the most serious abuses against the United Nations Charter and Universal Declaration of Human Rights continued to occur. Summary arrests, torture, and extrajudicial executions were reported on all sides as military operations were intensified against a variety of political and ethnic insurgent groups. Under the BSPP, there was a marked toughening in tactics. Especially notorious were forced labor and the "Four Cuts" campaign, a counterinsurgency operation first introduced in the Irrawaddy Delta region in the 1960s under which large areas were declared "free fire" zones; in effect, villagers must move or risk being shot on sight. Subsequently, this tactic was employed in many other parts of the country, internally displacing hundreds of thousands of civilians in what the government called its version of "people's war."

Human Rights from 1988 to the Present

With Ne Win's resignation and the collapse of the BSPP, a new era of military government began in 1988 under the State Law and Order Restoration Council (SLORC) and its successor, the SPDC. Several thousand lives are reported to have been lost (if war-zone casualties are included) in the political violence and repression of that year, which witnessed Ne Win loyalists suppressing mass pro-democracy demonstrations across the country.

Upon assuming power, military officers promised to usher in a new system of "open door" and "multiparty democracy" once law and order had been restored. In line with these objectives, the 1990 general election was held, which was won by the NLD. In addition, in 1989 the military government introduced a new cease-fire policy that gathered momentum over the next decade to include the majority of armed ethnic opposition forces in the country.

Nevertheless, domestic and international concerns over the human-rights situation only continued to grow. After the NLD's landslide victory in the election, the SLORC-SPDC did not hand over power. Ruling through an amalgam of existing laws and new martial-law decrees, they cast the security net even wider. Among the most commonly employed laws restricting freedom of expression and movement were the 1908 Unlawful Association Act, the 1950 Emergency

STUDENTS FOR PEACE AND FREEDOM

In Myanmar, students have been in the forefront of the movement for democracy. The following poem is from a collection published as *Battle for Peace* by the Revolutionary Students (Burma) in 1992.

The Hands of History
(Never think of drifting downstream,
But always determined to go upstream,
To break free.
As true youths,
Our spirits are as high as the sky.
We'll march on boldly,
Along the rough and thorny road.)
Don't let your smile go,
Holding hand in hand together,
Let us be united.
There will never be a permanent defeat.
For the blood in our hearts
Is still radiantly red.
Our hands that make the history
Are ready for the sake of freedom.
At this moment of our lifetime,
Students, let us be united.

Provisions Law, the 1962 Printers and Publishers Law, and the 1975 State Protection Law as well as SLORC Order 2/88 under which public meetings of more than five people were banned. A new Computer Science and Development Law in 1996 also provided jail terms for anyone using modems without permission.

In the process of this clampdown, thousands of citizens were detained, including over 100 members of parliament-elect, and Aung San Suu Kyi, who was held under house arrest between 1989 and 1995. Many prodemocracy activists also received long prison terms, including the student leader Min Ko Naing, the comedians Zargana and U Pa Pa Lay, and the women writers Ma Thida and Daw San San Nweh. At least twenty political prisoners were also reported by Amnesty International to have died in jail, including Maung Thawka, chairman of Burma's Writers Association, and U Maung Ko, the NLD workers' leader.

In the ethnic war zones, meanwhile, the loss of life largely ended in areas where cease-fires had been agreed, and greater freedom of movement was allowed. In other areas, fighting still continued, with ongoing reports of extrajudicial executions, forced relocations, and the flight of refugees into neighboring Thailand, India, and Bangladesh. As in other parts of the country, a particular issue of human-rights controversy was the use of forced labor by government troops, especially for construction and the portering of goods.

Concerned by such reports and the continuing political detentions, the international community has kept the pressure on Myanmar to engage in human-rights reform. Generally, Western governments and campaign groups have followed tactics of boycotts and isolation of the military government, while neighboring Asian governments have preferred talking with the regime in a policy known as "constructive engagement." In particular, a U.N. special rapporteur on human rights to Myanmar was appointed in 1992; the rapporteur continued to produce annual reports documenting the human-rights situation, and in 2000 the International Labor Organization (ILO) called for sanctions to be considered, the first time it had called for such actions against a member state.

In consequence, human rights became a major issue in discussions of political reform in Myanmar. Although the deadlock remained, there was evidence that such pressures did produce some results as the 1990s progressed. Under the SLORC-SPDC government, the Geneva Conventions and the U.N. Convention on the Rights of the Child were ratified, and greater access was allowed to international aid organizations. In 1999, the International Committee of the Red Cross was permitted to begin visiting political prisoners, and the following year human-rights training classes for government officials began under Australian sponsorship. In 2001, the ILO also gained permission to begin an in-country investigation into labor practices, subsequently producing a critical report.

However, for most observers, the question remained whether such measures were translated into real human-rights protection in the field. After 1992, martial law was lifted, but the universities continued to be closed at the first sign of protest (including 1996–2000), while mass roundups of NLD supporters occurred on several occasions in the late 1990s to prevent party meetings. As a result, many leading democracy activists remained in jail or detention.

Only in 2001 were there indications of a change in atmosphere as the dialogue between Aung San Suu Kyi and SPDC officials increased. Release of political prisoners was begun, including Daw San San Nweh, U Pa Pa Lay, and the veteran Rakhine leader and MP-elect, Saw Mra Aung. A go-between in these talks was Razali Ismail, the special representative of the U.N. secretary-general, who had been mandated to encourage "tripartite" dialogue between the three main groups in Burmese politics: the military government, the NLD, and the diverse ethnic minority groups.

The outcome remains uncertain, but it is now widely accepted that the issue of human-rights reform is critical if Myanmar's long-standing political crisis is to be resolved.

Martin Smith

Further Reading

Allott, Anna. (1993) *Inked Over, Ripped Out*. New York: Pen America Center.

Amnesty International. (1992) *Myanmar: "No Law at All": Human Rights Violations under Military Rule*. London: Amnesty International.

———. (2001) *Myanmar: Prisoners of Political Repression*. London: Amnesty International.

Article 19. (1996) *Fatal Silence? Freedom of Expression and the Right to Health in Burma*. London: Article 19.

Fink, Christina. (2001) *Living Silence: Burma under Military Rule*. New York: Zed Books.

Smith, Martin. (1994) *Ethnic Groups in Burma: Development, Democracy and Human Rights*. London: Anti-Slavery International.

U.N. Commission on Human Rights. (1998) *Situation of Human Rights in Myanmar: Report of Special Rapporteur, Mr. Rajsoomer Lallah*. Geneva, Switzerland: U.N. Commission on Human Rights.

MYANMAR—POLITICAL SYSTEM

The political system of Myanmar (Burma until 1989) has been in a state of continual change since precolonial times. From the eleventh century CE until the British annexation during the nineteenth century, power in lowland areas was concentrated in city kingdoms presided over by various ethnic Burman, Mon, Shan, and Rakhine monarchs and their royal courts. Among the most famous were Pegu, Pagan, Ava, Shwebo, Mandalay, and Mrohaung (Mrauk-U). These principalities were often polyethnic and often shared many aspects of Buddhist tradition and belief. But the rulers and cultures generally retained distinctive characteristics of the Burman, Mon, Shan, or Rakhine peoples who predominated in different areas.

These four ethnic families formed large communities, mostly practicing wet-rice cultivation in the plains. Across the centuries, bitter wars of conquest occurred as dynasties rose and fell, leaving a legacy of conflict in Myanmar's ethno-political traditions that has never been fully addressed. In particular, it was three great Burman monarchs, Anawrahta (d. 1077), Bayinnaung (d. 1581), and Alaungpaya (1714–1760), living seven hundred years apart, who extended central authority to borders approximating those of modern Myanmar.

Meanwhile, in the vast horseshoe of mountains that surrounds the Irrawaddy plains, very different forms of political governance evolved. Until the British annexation in the nineteenth century, such peoples as the Chin, Kachin, Karen, and Wa were mostly animists or traditional spirit-worshipers, practicing swidden (slash-and-burn) dry-rice cultivation and living in small settlements. Here political life was mostly organized at the village or village circle level under traditional rulers. Intervillage raiding was a common feature of life in the hills. But, although chiefs often paid tribute to rulers of the lowland kingdoms, most communities remained largely independent of any central authority.

Such differences between lowland and highland peoples were amplified under British colonial rule. In 1886, the Burman monarchy was abolished and the nation incorporated as a province of the British Indian empire, from which it was separated only in 1937. In the meantime, a two-tier system of administration was built for the country: Ministerial Burma, inhabited largely by the Burman majority, and the Frontier Areas, where most ethnic minority groups live. In Ministerial Burma, a degree of democratic home rule was introduced in the 1920s as well as reserved seats in Parliament for certain ethnic groups, including the Karen, Indians, and Chinese. By contrast, in the Frontier Areas the British governor maintained overall control, but local authority was left in the hands of traditional rulers.

The result was that two different administrative systems emerged, reflecting a diversity of political cultures and values. Economic life was equally distinct, and only at independence in 1948 was an attempt made to forge the nation into a new political union on the basis of equal rights for all.

The Postindependence Era

Since independence from Great Britain, Myanmar has struggled to achieve a stable political identity. There have been three major political eras, each significantly different.

The first era was the democratic period from 1948 to 1962. Although the term "federal" was not actually used, the first constitution (1947) was federal in intention. Reflecting ethnic differences, the country was to have a bicameral legislature, with both a 125-seat Chamber of Nationalities and a 250-seat Chamber of Deputies. However, there were many inconsistencies. Only four ethnic groups were granted nationality states: the Kachin, Karen, Shan, and Karenni, the latter two of which were left under the authority of their traditional *sawbwa*s (princes) and granted the additional right of secession after a ten-year period. The Chin, in contrast, were accorded only a Special Division, whereas such ethnic groups as the Rakhine, Mon, and Pao were given no political recognition at all.

Dissatisfaction was not confined to ethnic groups. The Anti-Fascist People's Freedom League (AFPFL) government of Prime Minister U Nu (1907–1995) was also challenged by the insurrection of the Communist Party of Burma after March 1948. As a result, the era of parliamentary government was characterized by insurgency and political violence. Democratic institutions, including a free press, trade unions, and independent judiciary, did appear to take root, but the politics of government in Rangoon (now Yangon) was frequently dominated by factionalism within the ruling AFPFL, which won both the general elections in 1951–1952 and 1955. Significantly, too, despite the socialist leanings of the AFPFL, principal political opposition in parliament also came from pro-Marxist organizations, notably the Burma Workers and Peasants Party.

During 1958–1960, democratic government was briefly suspended during the emergency "Military Caretaker" administration of the armed forces chief, General Ne Win (b. 1911). Parliamentary rule was restored following the 1960 election, which was again won by U Nu. However, in March 1962, against a backdrop of continuing political and ethnic uncertainty, Ne Win seized power in a military coup. The short-lived era of democracy was brought to an abrupt halt.

Ne Win's military government (1962–1988) marked the second major era in modern Burmese politics. Initially ruling through a military revolutionary council and network of local security and administrative councils, the government was superseded by the Burma Socialist Programme Party (BSPP), of which Ne Win was appointed chairman. This, however, never disguised the underlying character of military rule. The ideology of Ne Win's "Burmese Way to Socialism" was detailed in a brief 1963 book, *The System of Correlation of Man and His Environment*, which was an idiosyncratic blend of Buddhist, Marxist, and nationalist principles. It was never elaborated on.

One-Party State

Under Ne Win's rule, Burma became a one-party state. Independent parties, trade unions, and media organizations were closed, opponents imprisoned, the economy nationalized, and virtually all foreign visitors, including business people and missionaries, expelled as the country retreated from world affairs for a quarter of a century.

In 1974, a new constitution was introduced after a much-disputed national referendum. A new symmetry was created on Burma's political map by the demarcation of seven "divisions," dominated by the Burman majority, and seven ethnic minority "states." A national People's Assembly was also created and efforts made to form mass workers' and peasants' bodies to support the BSPP. However, virtually all senior posts in government were held by serving or retired military officers, so it is doubtful how far the BSPP government was ever truly established. Underground revolt continued throughout Ne Win's rule. Worker and student protests in the cities in the mid-1970s were quickly crushed, but in the borderlands such well-armed groups as the Communist Party of Burma, Karen National Union (KNU), and Kachin Independence Organization remained highly active, administering large territories of their own. Even deposed Prime Minister U Nu took up arms for a brief period in the late 1960s through the creation of the insurgent Parliamentary Democracy Party, which allied with the KNU and other ethnic opposition groups.

In 1988, Ne Win resigned and the BSPP collapsed during the nation's short-lived "democracy summer." This heralded the third major political era in the country's politics. Repeating a twentieth-century pattern, students and Buddhist monks again played a leading

MYANMAR—THE TRUTH

The following two extracts provide very different takes on the human rights situation in Myanmar. The first is an analysis of the announcements issued by the National League for Democracy by the Office of Strategic Studies, Ministry of Defense of Myanmar. The second is a report by Amnesty International.

The Truth

An analysis of the Announcements Issued by the National League for Democracy

The National League for Democracy has issued many announcements alleging that the government has been violating human rights in the country. It has been sending announcements to foreign embassies and broadcasting stations such as VOA [Voice of America], BBC [British Broadcasting Corporation], RFA [Radio Free Asia?], etc.

These announcements were not issued with the honest aim of submitting constructive suggestions to the government. The announcements are based on false news and utilized as tools to attack the government politically by exaggerating the weaknesses of some local authorities in the execution of their duties in the remote areas.

Most of the facts of thc NLD announcements are found to be based, not on actual incidents after a systematic inquiry, but on rumors and reports of some NLD members. The NLD is issuing such random announcements with no credibility. It sends these false reports to foreign governments as to the world at large via powerful broadcasting stations. As a result, the Government's admirable and noteworthy endeavors for developing the country have been greatly misunderstood by governments and people of some nations, and our country has been wrongly assumed to be a nation with poor human rights norms and practices.

Source: Consulate of Myanmar in Hong Kong. Retrieved 8 March 2002, from: http://www.myanmar-information.net/truth/truth-1.pdf.

Torture has become an institution in Myanmar, used throughout the country on a regular basis, Amnesty International said today in a new report. Police and the army continue to use torture to extract information, punish, humiliate and control the population.

"Torture is employed as an instrument by the authorities to keep the population living in a state of fear," the organization said.

The victims of torture in Myanmar are political activists, criminal prisoners and members of ethnic minorities. Torture has been reported for over four decades yet the methods of torture have remained constant.

Torture techniques include: the "iron road," rolling an iron up and down the shins until the skin peels off; "the helicopter," being suspended from the ceiling and spun around while being beaten; "*Taik Peik*," spending weeks or months in tiny brick cells with little air or light; "*ponsan*," being forced to maintain difficult positions for prolonged periods.

Political prisoners, believed to number around 1,700, are at risk of torture during the initial phases of detention. Activists from the National League for Democracy (NLD), the party which overwhelmingly won the 1990 elections, are frequently the targets of torture and ill-treatment. Hundreds of its members are imprisoned and tens of thousands have been forced to resign from the party.

Student activists who have been at the forefront of the pro-democracy movement are also often tortured in detention. Freedom of expression and assembly is almost completely denied to all.

One 23-year-old former political activist was arrested twice during the 1990s, the first time when he was just 14. After his second arrest he was forced to stand on his tiptoes with a pin under his heel and kneel on sharp stones for prolonged periods. At Military Intelligence 12 headquarters he was also subjected to the "*ponsan*" technique. He told Amnesty International

CONTINUED ON NEXT PAGE

CONTINUED FROM PREVIOUS PAGE

that he was interrogated non-stop by rotating teams of Military Intelligence personnel. He said "MI quarrelled amongst themselves—they were afraid I was going to die on them."

Hundreds, perhaps thousands of criminal prisoners have died in labour camps where they are forced to work under torturous conditions building roads and breaking up stones. The authorities openly admit that "the debt of crime will be repaid with sweat."

Members of ethnic groups such as the Shan, Karen and Karenni, who live in areas of conflict, are seized, interrogated and tortured to extract information on the whereabouts of armed ethnic minority groups. Men, women and children also face torture when they are taken by the Myanmar Army and forced to carry heavy supplies as porters for days or weeks at a time or forced to work on construction projects such as roads, railways and dams.

A Karenni Christian farmer from Kayah state was arrested by the army and accused of working for an armed opposition group after a battle in February 2000. He reported; "Three soldiers beat me with rifle butts on my head and punched my face. I got cut on my head and blood was running down from my nose. When I fell down, they kicked me with military boots. My hearing is still bad . . ." He was forced to accompany troops as a guide for one week during which time he was beaten every day with sticks and tied with a rope. He finally escaped, and after returning to his village he hid with his family in the jungle for two weeks before fleeing to Thailand.

Women who are taken as porters are vulnerable to rape by soldiers. Amnesty International was told about the rape and murder of a 12-year-old girl, Naw Po Thu, in October 1998. She was allegedly raped by a major and managed to escape, but was recaptured, raped again and then shot dead through the vagina. The major gave the girl's family one sack of rice, a measure of sugar, a tin of condensed milk and a small amount of money as compensation. "Torture is used in a variety of settings in Myanmar but the objectives are always the same—repression and control," the organization said.

The military government denies torture exists, stating that it is illegal in domestic law. Amnesty International urges the Myanmar government to issue clear orders to all security forces to adhere to this law and immediately stop the practice of torture. It should also investigate all allegations of torture, bring perpetrators to justice, and prohibit incommunicado detention which facilitates the practice.

Source: Amnesty International. Retrieved 8 March 2002, from: http://web.amnesty.org/ai.nsf/Index/ASA160262000?OpenDocument&of=COUNTRIES\MYANMAR.

role in organizing popular protests. However, in September 1988, following the suppression of prodemocracy demonstrations, governmental power was reassumed by Ne Win loyalists under a new name: the State Law and Order Restoration Council (SLORC). In November 1997, the SLORC was renamed the State Peace and Development Council (SPDC), but it remained essentially a military government, headed by leading officers, including Generals Than Shwe, Maung Aye, and Khin Nyunt.

Unlike the BSPP, the SLORC/SPDC never announced a political manifesto of intentions other than to act as an interim government during a period of transition to a so-called open-door, market-oriented, and multiparty democracy. In line with these statements, democratic political parties were initially permitted to form, and in 1990 a general election was held and overwhelmingly won by the National League for Democracy (NLD) and twenty-six other parties, most of which represented ethnic groups. The military government's favored party, the National Unity Party, which had succeeded the BSPP, won just ten seats. The SLORC/SPDC, however, never accepted the result as a vote for government and continued to arrest opposition leaders, including Aung San Suu Kyi (b. 1945), the daughter of the nationalist leader Aung San, who was held under house arrest during 1989–1995.

Instead of transferring power, the Myanmar armed forces continued to govern under existing laws as well as martial-law decrees through a nationwide system of local military-dominated councils that echoed the security and administrative councils of the BSPP era. Claiming legitimacy through its national security role, the SLORC/SPDC defined national politics as the his-

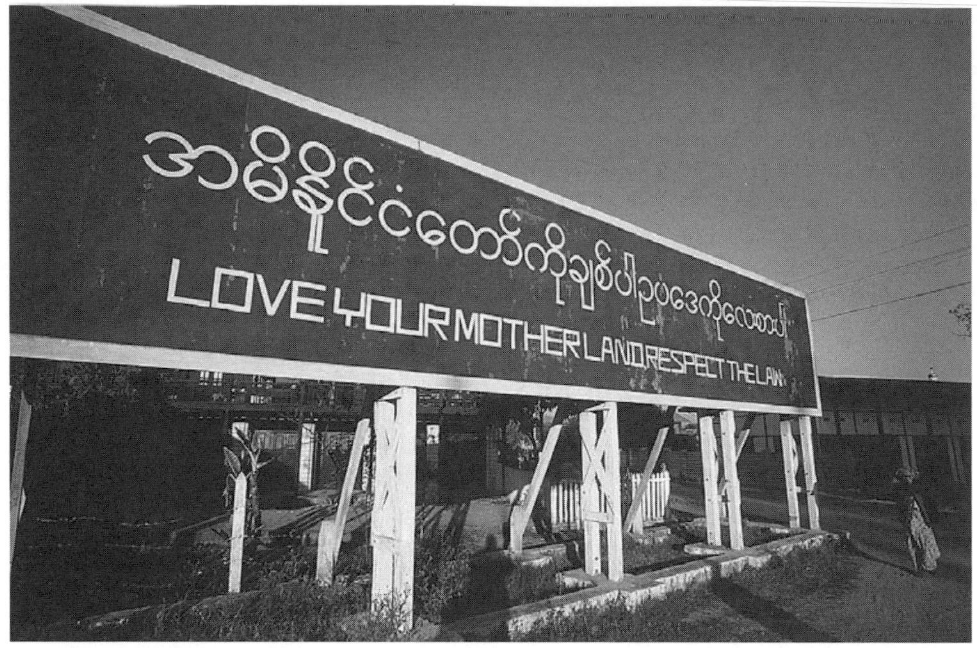

This Myanmar government billboard in Nyaunghwe in 1996 seeks to promote national unity by proclaiming "Love Your Motherland, Respect the Law" in Burmese and English. (RICHARD BICKEL/CORBIS)

toric duty of the Myanmar armed forces, as opposed to the so-called party politics of opposition groups. The SLORC/SPDC also introduced a number of policy changes from the BSPP era, including declaring cease-fires with armed ethnic opposition groups and ending Myanmar's international isolation. In particular, in 1997 Myanmar joined the Association of Southeast Asian Nations (ASEAN), allying with member states such as Thailand and the Philippines, which had already undergone transition from military to democratic rule.

The reform process, however, remained deadlocked. In 1993, the SLORC created a hand-picked national convention that began drawing up the nation's new constitution. As its first guiding principle, the leading role of the Myanmar armed forces in national political life had to be endorsed. Moreover, although the creation of new self-administered zones was promised for ethnic groups such as the Wa, Naga, and Pao, the intention to continue military dominance in political structures remained clear.

A new People's Assembly *(hluttaw)* would be established with two chambers: a House of Representatives elected on a population basis and a House of Nationalities, representing the states and divisions. But 25 percent of seats in both bodies would have to be reserved for military candidates. Myanmar's future president would also have to have military experience, and the determination to continue military government was signaled by the 1993 formation of the mass Union Solidarity and Development Association, which many observers expected would be converted into a political party.

In late 2000, secret talks began between the SPDC and NLD leader Aung San Suu Kyi, who was under virtual house arrest. These talks continued intermittently into 2002 and were encouraged by Razali Ismail, the special representative of the U.N. secretary-general, who also met with ethnic minority leaders in a bid to encourage "tripartite" dialogue between the military government, NLD, and ethnic nationality groups. But political reform and transition still appeared to be a long-term process.

Martin Smith

See also: **Anti-Fascist People's Freedom League—Myanmar; Communist Party of Burma; Kachin Independence Organization; Karen National Union; National League for Democracy—Myanmar; Ne Win, U; Nu, U**

Further Reading

Aung-Thwin, Michael. (1984) "Hierarchy and Order in Pre-Colonial Burma." *Journal of Southeast Asian Studies* 15, 2: 224–232.

Carey, Peter, ed. (1997) *Burma: The Challenge of Change in a Divided Society*. Basingstoke, U.K.: Macmillan Press.
Houtman, Gustaaf. (1999) *Mental Culture in Burmese Crisis Politics: Aung San Suu Kyi and the National League for Democracy*. Tokyo: Tokyo University of Foreign Studies, Institute for the Study of Languages and Cultures of Asia and Africa.
Naw, Angelene. (2001) *Aung San and the Struggle for Burmese Independence*. Chiang Mai, Thailand: Silkworm Books.
Ni Ni Myint, Daw. (1983) *Burma's Struggle against British Imperialism, 1885–1895*. Yangon, Myanmar: Universities Press.
Silverstein, Josef. (1977) *Burma: Military Rule and the Politics of Stagnation*. Ithaca, NY: Cornell University Press.
———. (1980) *Burmese Politics: The Dilemma of National Unity*. New Brunswick, NJ: Rutgers University Press.
Smith, Martin. (1999) *Burma: Insurgency and the Politics of Ethnicity*. 2d ed. London: Zed Books.
Taylor, Robert. (1987) *The State in Burma*. London: C. Hurst.
Thant Myint-U. (2001) *The Making of Modern Burma*. Cambridge, U.K.: Cambridge University Press.
Tinker, Hugh. (1967) *The Union of Burma: A Study of the First Years of Independence*. Oxford, U.K.: Oxford University Press.
Woodman, Dorothy. (1962) *The Making of Burma*. London: Cresset Press.

MYSORE (2001 est. pop. 742,000). Mysore, which is the headquarters of Mysore district in the state of Karnataka, is one of the key cities in South India. The city is approximately 140 kilometers from the state capital, Bangalore. Known for its pleasant climate throughout the year, Mysore is famous for its distinctive history and culture. The city derives its name from the mythic episode of the killing of the buffalo-headed demon, Mahishasura, by the royal deity of Mysore province, Chamundeshwari. The temple that is dedicated to the deity sits atop the Chamundi Hill and is an important landmark of the city.

Historically, Mysore has been associated with some of the most important ruling dynasties of India, from the Gangas in the fourth century CE to the Wodeyars of the British era in the nineteenth century. Because of the sustained interest of the Wodeyar kings in art, music, architecture, education, and business, Mysore became a hub of cultural and commercial activities in the south. To this day, it retains its reputation as a place providing fine specimens of silk, sandalwood, and oil. The many palaces dotting the city, chief among which is Mysore Palace, lend an Old World charm to the area. For a ten-day period every year during September and October, the city celebrates the Dasehra Festival, which celebrates the victory of good over evil, with unfailing zeal and splendor. Unlike other Indian cities, which have fallen into routine decay, Mysore still exudes a quaint charm.

Ram Shankar Nanda

Further Reading

Swami Sivapriyananda. (1995) *Mysore Royal Dasara*. Delhi: Abhinav Publications.

NABIEV, RAKHMON (1930–1993), Tajik politician. Rakhmon Nabiev led the Tajikistan Soviet Socialist Republic from 1982 to 1985 as the First Secretary of the Communist Party, and in 1991 he became the first president of independent Tajikistan. Born in Shaihburkhan (a remote northern province of the republic) in 1930, Nabiev was appointed chairman of the Tajikistan Council of Ministers in 1973. He assumed leadership of the country in 1982 but in 1986 was unexpectedly removed from his post.

In 1991 on the eve of the Soviet Union's dissolution, Nabiev was invited to become the chairman of the Tajikistani Parliament. In November 1991 as a Communist candidate he won the first presidential election in the history of Tajikistan, contesting a representative of the united front of democratic and Islamic opposition. Nabiev belonged to the cohort of leaders who rose to power mainly because of their faithful support of Soviet policies. His own policies as president led to a devastating seven-year civil war and to the rise of regionalism; he failed to relinquish his Communist ideology, to comprehend the importance of nationalism and Islamic symbols in post-Soviet state building, and to abandon his reliance on regional patronage rather than on the policy of national reconciliation. He was forced to resign at gunpoint in September 1992 and died at his home from a heart attack in April 1993.

Rafis Abazov

Further Reading

Akbarzadeh, Shahram. (1996) "Why Did Nationalism Fail in Tajikistan?" *Europe-Asia Studies* 48, 1 (November): 1,105–1,129.

Djalili, Mohammad-Reza, Frédéric Grare, and Shirin Akiner, eds. (1997) *Tajikistan: The Trials of Independence.* New York: St. Martin's Press.

NAGALAND (2001 est. pop. 2 million). Since 1963 a state in India's northeastern corner bordering Myanmar (Burma), Nagaland has an area of 15,579 square kilometers and is inhabited by sixteen major and twenty minor ethnic groups, all called Nagas. Most are fiercely independent, each with their own dialect, customs, and culture; most live in politically sensitive areas all but closed to foreigners, in the starkly remote terrain of villages high on the mountain ridges of the Naga Hills, at the extremity of the subcontinent. Only in reaction to external encroachment—by the British, Christians, Japanese, the Indian government—did the Nagas gain a sense of common identity. After Indian independence in 1947, the Nagas did not wish to join the Indian Union, but in 1960 an agreement led to statehood. In 1975 Nagaland agreed to accept the Indian constitution and surrender arms, but clashes continued, and in 1995 India declared Nagaland a disturbed area. In 1997 a cease-fire agreement was announced, but conflict continues.

Rice is cultivated on terraced fields. Nearly all villages are electrified. Industrialization is in its infancy. Weaving is traditional among women. War dances in colorful costumes form the distinctive art of Nagaland at festivals, marriages, and harvests.

C. Roger Davis

Further Reading

Bower, Ursula Graham. (1952) *Naga Path.* London: John Murray.

Jacobs, Julian. (1999) *Nagas: Hill Peoples in Northeast Asia.* Columbia, MO: South Asia Books.

NAGANO (2002 est. pop. 2.2 million). Nagano Prefecture is situated in the central region of Japan's island of Honshu, where it occupies an area of 13,585 square kilometers. Its primary geographical features are the Hida, Kiso, Akaishi, and Mikuni mountain ranges. Among its many rivers are the Chikumagawa, Himekawa, Kisogawa, and Tenryugawa. Landlocked Nagano is bordered by Niigata, Gumma, Saitama, Yamanashi, Shizuoka, Aichi, Gifu, and Toyama prefectures. Once known as Shinano Province, it assumed its present name in 1871 and its present borders in 1876.

The prefecture's capital is Nagano city in the north. It was founded in the Kamakura period (1185–1333) as the Buddhist temple town of Zenkoji; today its temple complex remains one of the nation's most popular Buddhist pilgrimage sites. During the Edo period (1600/1603–1868), Nagano city evolved into a market center and a highway post station. Today it is home to Shinshu University and to such commercial enterprises as printers, publishers, electrical machinery manufacturers, and food processors. As host of the XVIII Winter Olympics in 1998, the city was connected by bullet train to Tokyo. The prefecture's other important cities are Matsumoto, Ueda, and Iida.

Historically, the region was at the crossroads of several primary routes between western and eastern Honshu. Various warrior clans, including the Uesugi and Takeda, ruled the province for centuries. During the Edo period, it was divided into many small domains.

Once a center of silk production, the prefecture remains a major source of rice, apples, yams, and dairy products. Its larger and more recent industries are metals processing, machinery fabrication, and woodworking. Visitors are drawn to Matsumoto, gateway to the Japan Alps, one-time Nara period (710–794 CE) provincial capital, and the site of Matsumoto castle, built in 1597. Other attractions are the scenic mountains and lakes, located in four national and three quasi-national parks.

E. L. S. Weber

Further Reading

Tamanoi, Mariko A. (1998) *Under the Shadow of Nationalism: Politics and Poetics of Rural Japanese Women*. Honolulu: University of Hawaii Press.

NAGARJUNA (flourished c. 150–250 CE), Buddhist philosopher. Nagarjuna, whose influence persists in modern-day Buddhism, is thought to have been born to a Brahman family in India. Although he is a historical figure, details of his life are drawn primarily from legends. It is generally believed that his parents urged him to go on a pilgrimage, and that he then made his way to the famous Buddhist university of Nalanda, where a monk urged him to adopt the monastic life.

According to one legend, the boy Nagarjuna, after studying the four Vedas (the earliest Hindu scriptures), took to worldly pleasures. He mastered the technique of making himself invisible and frequently broke into peoples' homes. Eventually, his offenses were discovered, and he nearly had to atone for them with his life. Subsequently, he became a devout Buddhist and an adept of Buddhist philosophy.

Nagarjuna's ethical system, popularly known as Madhyamika (The Middle Way), attempted to dispel erroneous interpretations of Buddhist doctrine relating to the philosophical concept of reality. His dialectic approach, which takes a middle course, led to the theory of *sunyata*, or Emptiness. This theory holds that all things are nonessential by nature. Furthermore, Nagarjuna's philosophical precept of *pratityasamutpada*, or dependent origination, emphasizes that devoid of their inherent qualities, all things are interdependent. Nagarjuna believed that everything was formed of one substance.

Nagarjuna's philosophy represented neither an orthodox expression of early Buddhism nor a total negation of it. Without conforming stringently to the original tenets of Buddhism, Nagarjuna proceeded exclusively from the principles established in the Buddhist canon and arrived at unique conclusions based on a deductive method that the founder of Buddhism would have approved of.

Nagarjuna also pioneered the renaissance of Sanskrit learning among Indian Buddhists. At the same time, he can be credited with refining the analytical method of inquiry developed by the historical Buddha. Thus, Nagarjuna's intellectual feats assume a significance as profound as the doctrine propounded by Buddha himself.

Rajsekhar Basu

Further Reading

Fatone, Vincente. (1981) *The Philosophy of Nagarjuna*.Trans. from the Spanish by Dr. Prithipaul. Delhi: Motilal Banarasidass.

Ghosh, Ramendranath. (1987) *The Dialectics of Nagarjuna*. Allahabad, India: Vohra.

NAGAS The Nagas (with an estimated population of 3.5 million in 2000) are a group of tribes inhabiting Arunachal Pradesh, Assam, Manipur, and Nagaland states in northeast India and neighboring areas of Myanmar (Burma). The 1971 census conducted by the Republic of India identified sixteen major Naga communities, namely the Angami, Ao, Chakhesang, Chang, Chirr, Khiamngan, Konyak, Lohta, Makware, Phom, Rengma, Sangtam, Sema, Tikhir, Yimchunger, and Zeliang. Of Mongoloid stock, Nagas probably migrated to northeast India from central China. Every Naga tribe speaks its own language, and sixty spoken dialects have been identified. All Naga languages belong to the Tibeto-Burmese branch of the Sino-Tibetan language family.

Naga tribes have their own distinctive shawls. The older people of some communities of eastern Nagaland have elaborate tattoo marks. Among different Naga tribes, the forms of government, polity, and modes of law enforcement vary. Southern Nagas, such as Angami and Chakhesang, still practice tribal democracy at the village level, while despotic chieftainship prevails among the Konyak and the Sema.

Nagas traditionally believed in a benevolent female Supreme Creator, Kenopfu. Significant religious functionaries included the *kemovo*, who directed public ceremonies, and the *zhevo*, who performed personal rituals. Nagas today are overwhelmingly Christians (92.97 percent in the 1981 census). The American Baptist mission has been particularly active in the region since the nineteenth century. Nevertheless, Nagas continue to observe traditional life-cycle rituals, cosmological dogma, and tribal religious beliefs.

Literacy among Nagas is higher than other tribal groups in India and varies between 45.58 percent (according to the 1981 census) among Angamis and 64.10 percent among Aos. They practice shifting cultivation *(jhum)* and terraced agriculture, growing crops both for trade and their own consumption. With education, many have taken to trade, government services, and other professions.

Traditional village councils continue to play a crucial role in their social life. Tribal polity and chieftainship have not been disturbed to any great extent. Postindependence statutory *panchayats* (councils) generally deal with development activities. The Village Development Board (VDB) conducts the development process at the grassroots level.

At India's independence in 1947, the Nagas were unwilling to accept New Delhi's rule and demanded independence. In 1955 the Naga secessionist movement developed and was suppressed by the Indian security forces. The creation of Nagaland as a fully fledged state of the Indian Union in 1963 failed to meet the demands of the extremists, and the dream of independence persists. Recently, several insurgent groups have coordinated their activities under the banner of the Nationalist Socialist Council of Nagaland (NSCN), and sporadic acts of violence continue.

Sanjukta Das Gupta

Further Reading

Hodson, T. C. (1911) *The Naga Tribes of Manipur.* London: Macmillan.

Yomuo, Asoso. (1984) *The Rising Nagas: Historical and Political Study.* Delhi: Manas Publications.

NAGASAKI (2001 est. pop. 430,000). Nagasaki is a seaport town on the west coast of Kyushu, Japan. Originally a tiny fishing village, Nagasaki first gained prominence with the establishment of its port by the Portuguese in 1571. It served as an active entrepôt of foreign trade and a haven for Christians until *bakufu* (shogunate) policies placed restrictive controls on trade and virtually eliminated Christianity. During the Edo period (1600/1603–1868), Nagasaki became Japan's primary source of contact with the outside world through its Chinese and Dutch settlements—the latter situated on the man-made island of Dejima in Nagasaki Harbor. In the second half of the nineteenth century, Nagasaki was designated one of Japan's foreign settlements and its streets were crowded with Western sailors, merchants, and missionaries. Nagasaki began to lose its international importance after the Russo-Japanese War and did not reenter the world stage until the catastrophic atomic bombing of the city by American military forces on 9 August 1945, in which more than 75,000 residents were killed.

Today, Mitsubishi Shipyards provides the principal economic impetus for Nagasaki. The city also relies heavily on tourism, and major tourist sites include Chinese temples and stone bridges, the Suwa Shrine (the home of the annual Kunchi Festival), Siebold Museum, Oura Catholic Church, Glover Garden, Dejima Museum, Monument of the Twenty-Six Saints, Urakami Cathedral, the Peace Park, and the Atomic Bomb Museum.

Lane R. Earns

The Nagasaki Gas Works in August 1949, four years after the city was devastated by a United States atomic bomb, effectively ending World War II. (BETTMANN/CORBIS)

Further Reading

Boxer, C. R. (1951) *The Christian Century in Japan, 1549–1650*. Berkeley and Los Angeles: University of California Press.

Kaempfer, Engelbert. (1999) *Kaempfer's Japan: Tokugawa Culture Observed*, edited by Beatrice M. Bodart-Bailey. Honolulu: University of Hawaii Press.

Paske-Smith, M. (1968) *Western Barbarians in Japan and Formosa, 1603–1868*. New York: Paragon Book Reprint.

NAGAUTA *Nagauta* (long poems or songs) is the dominant musical form for the Kabuki theatre and depicts the various poetic descriptions of the dance and scenes. The early dances of Kabuki were accompanied by *kouta* (short songs). *Nagauta* developed during the Genroku period (1688–1703) and was further refined with the introduction of highly skilled shamisen players. In 1727, in Edo (the old name for Tokyo), a style called Edo Nagauta was born. These pieces were composed of short lyrical sections strung together. *Nagauta* further developed with the addition of other forms and instruments in later periods. This layering of genres and instruments makes *nagauta* a highly refined and versatile form. While *nagauta* is vital to Kabuki, it stands on its own as a musical genre and is well suited to independent performances. The main line of *nagauta* performers began with Kineya Rokuzaemon; it is now in its fifteenth generation.

Nagauta is categorized in five forms: Noh, which draws upon sophisticated structures found within Noh plays as far back as the fourteenth century; *kumiuta*, which developed from the tradition of grouping together a series of poems set to music, popular in the late seventeenth century; joruri, which was influenced by *gidayubushi* narrative recitation of the joruri (Bunraku) puppet theatre; Kabuki music, which is suitable accompaniment for dancing; and mixed forms, which contain an assortment of dance borrowed from the other forms.

Nagauta is a lyrical form that consists of four to nine singers, four to nine shamisen, and a Noh ensemble (one to three hip drums, one stick drum, and one flute). As an orchestra, the ensemble is called the *shibyoshi* (four rhythms). The *nagauta* ensemble is most often associated with the *geza* room. When the *nagauta* shamisen play from the *geza* alone, it is called *aikata;* when accompanied by singing, it is called *ainote*. There are also a number of other instruments played in the *geza;* the number and variety depend on the play being performed. The *nagauta* ensemble may also appear onstage and is then called the *debayashigata*. *Nagauta* musicians and singers sit on a special platform called the *hinadan*. The *geza* ensemble *(hayashigata)* sit on a step below the *hinadan*.

Stacey Fox

Further Reading

Brandon, James R., ed. (1982) *Chushingura: Studies in Kabuki and the Puppet Theater*. Honolulu: University of Hawaii Press.

Brandon, James R., William P. Malm, and Donald H. Shively. (1987) *Studies in Kabuki: Its Acting, Music and Historical Context*. Honolulu: University of Hawaii Press.

Ernst, Earle. (1974) *The Kabuki Theatre*. Honolulu: University of Hawaii Press.

Halford, Aubrey S., and Giovanna Mittalford. (1969) *The Kabuki Guide Handbook: A Guide for Understanding and Appreciation with Summaries of Favorite Plays, Explanatory Notes and Illustrations*. Tokyo: Charles E. Tuttle.

Masakatsu Gunji. (1987) *The Kabuki Guide*. Tokyo: Kodansha.

Raz, Jacob. (1983) *Audience and Actors: A Study of Their Interaction in the Japanese Traditional Theatre*. Leiden, Netherlands: E. J. Brill.

NAHDLATUL ULAMA Established in 1926 in Surabaya, Indonesia, by K. H. Muhammad Hasyim Asy'ari (1871–1947), the Nahdlatul Ulama (NU) is one of the largest socioreligious organizations in the country. It aims at promoting solidarity between traditionalist *ulama* (religious scholars) and their followers from all four classical schools of law of Sunni Islam, particularly the Shafi'i school. Its activities focus on ideology, education, social services, and politics.

Ideologically, NU members see themselves as "people who follow Muhammad's traditions and the Sunni community" *(ahl al-sunnah wa'l jama'ah)*. The stronghold of the NU lies in rural areas, particularly in East Java, as well as in traditional schools *(pesantren)*, where students are taught classical Arabic texts supervised by a *kyai* (religious teacher). The NU owns over six thousand schools, mosques, orphanages, poorhouses, farmer unions, and merchant unions, as well as small industries.

The NU has been politically active since the national struggle leading to Indonesia's independence. It encouraged Indonesian participation in politics under the Dutch rule. During the Japanese occupation, it became a tool for mass mobilization. As a member of Masyumi (Majlis Syura Muslimin Indonesia, a modern comprehensive confederation of Islamic organizations), the NU vowed to wage a holy war, under Japanese guidance, against the Allied forces.

In 1952, the NU became an independent political party rejecting the secularly educated leadership of the Masyumi. In the 1955 elections, the NU received unexpected popular support. While the NU joined other parties in striving for an Islamic state, it was the first Islamic organization to adhere to Suharto's imposition of the Pancasila (five principles), with belief in one God cited as the first principle. Because the NU has changed its position on the Masyumi and other confederations of Islamic organizations a number of times, the NU has been accused of being opportunistic.

The grandson of the founder of NU, Abdurrahman Wahid (b. 1940), himself the founder of the National Awakening Party (Partai Kebangkitan Bangsa—PKB) within the NU, became the first democratically elected Indonesian president (October 1999). The NU claims a membership of 35 million in Indonesia's volatile multicultural society. The organization faces the challenge of protecting the country's unitary ruling system (which might, however, accentuate nationalism) while promoting democracy (which might encourage community revivalism). While Wahid's philosophy has elements of democracy, his actions reflect a Javanese ideal.

Andi Faisal Bakti

Further Reading

Benda, Harry J. (1983) *The Crescent and the Rising Sun: Indonesian Islam under the Japanese Occupation, 1942–1945*. Leiden, Netherlands: Van Hoeve.

Bruinessen, Martin van. (1990) "Indonesia's Ulama and Politics: Caught between Legitimizing the Status Quo and Searching for Alternatives." *Prisma* (English ed.) 49: 52–69.

———. (1991) "The 28th Congress of the Nahdlatul Ulama: Power Struggle and Social Concerns." *Archipel* 41: 185–199.

Noer, Deliar. (1973) *The Modernist Muslim Movement in Indonesia, 1900–1942*. Singapore: Oxford University Press.

Wahid, Abdurrahman. (1986) "The Nahdlatul Ulama and Islam in Present Day Indonesia." In *Islam and Society in Southeast Asia*, edited by Taufik Abdullah and Sharon Siddique. Singapore: Institute of Southeast Asian Studies, 175–185.

NAKASONE YASUHIRO (b. 1918), prime minister of Japan. Probably Japan's best-known politician internationally, Nakasone Yasuhiro was prime minister from November 1982 until November 1987. Most famous for his nationalist and neoconservative views,

Nakasone formed a close friendship with foreign leaders, in particular Ronald Reagan and Margaret Thatcher, sharing their interest in privatization and small government. As prime minister, Nakasone sought to strengthen the U.S.-Japan security relationship and Japan's role in it, both politically and militarily, at one point proclaiming Japan to be an "unsinkable aircraft carrier."

Nakasone was born in May 1918 in Gunma Prefecture, the second son of six children. Graduating from the political science department of Tokyo Imperial University in 1941, Nakasone entered the Ministry of Home Affairs that April and shortly thereafter was assigned to the navy as a paymaster, serving in Taiwan and elsewhere.

After the war, Nakasone resigned from the ministry and was elected to the Diet in 1947 on the Democratic Party ticket. Nakasone ran on an anti–Allied Occupation policy platform. He believed that the reforms of occupational policy undermined traditional Japanese society. Since then, the high-profile Nakasone was elected in every election, despite the fact that his election district, which included a former and future prime minister, was considered one of the most competitive. Nakasone, who served in numerous cabinets and party positions, attempted to break many taboos while in office, such as revising the constitution, urging compulsory use of the Hinomaru flag and *Kimi Ga Yo* anthem in schools, and making official visits to the Yasukuni Shrine for war dead, angering in particular Korea and China.

Robert D. Eldridge

Further Reading

Atsushi Kusano. (1995) "Nakasone Yasuhiro: Daitoryoteki Shusho no Menmoku" (Nakasone Yasuhiro: The Face of a Presidential-like Prime Minister). In *Sengo Nihon no Saishotachi* (The Prime Ministers of Postwar Japan), edited by Watanabe Akio. Tokyo: Chuo Koronsha.

Nakasone Yasuhiro. (1999) *The Making of the New Japan: Reclaiming the Political Mainstream*. Surrey, U.K.: Curzon Press.

NAKHON RATCHASIMA (2002 pop. 210,000). Nakhon Ratchasima city, also known as Khorat, is situated in northeastern Thailand 177 kilometers north of Bangkok. It is located in the second largest province in the nation. Nakhon Ratchasima is the provincial capital and the most affluent city in the region. The city is located on the Mun River and is near the mountain pass connecting this region with the central plains of Thailand.

Established in the seventeenth century, near the ruins of the ancient Khmer dynasty (c. eleventh century), the city was formed by the combining of the settlements of Sema and Khorakpura. The remains of the old city can be seen today in its walls, gates, and moat. It was in 1890 that the city began a period of rapid growth with construction of a rail line from Bangkok. During the U.S. war in Vietnam, Nakhon Ratchasima's Royal Thai Air Force Base served as an operations center for the U.S. military.

Today Nakhon Ratchasima is considered the center of the Khorat Plateau, with government, the provincial economy, and transportation based there. The region is known for copper, livestock, rice, maize, and tobacco. The city remains a rail hub, since the line from Bangkok splits here with lines to Ubon Ratchatani and Nong Khai.

Linda Dailey Paulson

NAKTONG RIVER AND DELTA The Naktong River drains one-fourth of South Korea. Its headwaters lie near Hambeck Mountain at Taebeck City, Kangwon Province, and the river flows across the Southern Plain to the Korea Strait (South Sea). It is the longest river in South Korea, at 523 kilometers (325 miles). The Naktong River has created many deltas. Offshore, Eulsook Island attracts thousands of migratory birds, in addition to resident sea and river birds, because it provides wetland, fish, and grains. Many Korean poets and writers consider the island the most beautiful nature conservancy area in Korea and East Asia. Another delta is the Kimhae Plain, whose rich farmlands made the Kaya civilization (42–562 CE) possible.

During the Korean War (1950–1953) the Naktong River was a bloody boundary of confrontation. U.S. and Allied troops stopped the deepest North Korean Communist advance at the Naktong River at Taegu. North Korea succeeded in crossing the river on 6 August 1950. But U.S. Marines and Army infantrymen counterattacked and prevented a general breakthrough.

Urbanization, industrial development, and population growth along the Naktong River have made water quantity and water quality troublesome since the 1970s. In the 1980s, Dusan Electronics' accidental release of phenol into the river was the first industrial pollution crisis in South Korea. This event helped awaken people to the state of the river. Drinking water in Pusan, the second most populous city in South

Korea located at the mouth of the Naktong River, is in short supply in the dry season. Upstream and downstream cooperation in water resources management was seriously discussed in 2000. Control of point and nonpoint sources of water pollutants has been devised, and a buffer zone between the river and human settlements has been legislated. Sophisticated wastewater treatment systems in urban and rural areas have been installed.

Yearn Hong Choi

Further Reading

Bartz, Patricia M. (1972) *South Korea: A Descriptive Geography*. Oxford, U.K.: Clarendon Press.

Choi, Yearn Hong. (2000) "South Korea's Water Resources Policy for the 21st Century: A Conflicting View." In *Proceedings of the American Society of Civil Engineers—EWRI Conference*. Minneapolis, MN: American Society of Civil Engineers.

———. (1994) "Environmental Management in South Korea: Origin, Policy, Program, Questions." In *Asian Development and Public Policy*, edited by Stuart Nagel. New York: St. Martin's Press.

NAMP'O (2001 est. pop. 645,000). Namp'o (Chinnampo) is a major port and industrial city on the west coast of the Democratic People's Republic of Korea (North Korea). The city is 55 kilometers southwest of Pyongyang and 8 kilometers inland from the sea.

The major industries of Namp'o are steel production, shipbuilding, and farm vehicle production. In 1995, Namp'o became the site of some of the first joint economic ventures between North and South Korea. These ventures were the production of clothing for export.

Namp'o has extensive port facilities, which were augmented in the 1980s by construction of the West Sea Barrage, an 8-kilometer dam that stretches across the Taedong River. This dam, built between 1981 and 1986, includes three locks capable of lifting ships of up to 50,000 tons. It has created a freshwater lake that reaches Namp'o, ending the tidal surge that once disrupted river activities. However, the damming of the river has also led to higher levels of pollution in the river because industrial pollutants are no longer carried out to sea. In 2000, a ten-lane highway between Namp'o and Pyongyang was completed.

Thomas P. Dolan

NAN HAI. See **South China Sea.**

NANGNIM RANGE Mt. Nangnim (Nangnimsan) lies between Huich'on-gun in North P'yongan Province and Yongwon-gun in South P'yongan Province in North Korea. The mountain is 2,184 meters in height. It is the central and highest peak of the Nangnim mountain range that, along with such mountains as Mt. Maengbu, Wagal Peak, and Huisaek Peak, forms the border between the Kwanbuk Area, the land "north of the passes," and the Kwanso Area, the land "west of the passes." The Nangnim mountain range trends north–south and constitutes the border between North P'yongan Province and South Hamgyong Province. The range has an average height of 1,500 meters and stretches for 250 kilometers. The southern edge of the mountain range connects with the Myohyang mountain range that bends into a southwesterly direction.

Richard D. McBride II

Further Reading

McCune, Shannon Boyd-Bailey. (1980) *Views of the Geography of Korea, 1935–1960*. Seoul: Korea Research Center.

NANJING (1997 pop. 2.7 million). The capital of Jiangsu Province in central eastern China, metropolitan Nanjing (Nanking) had a population in 1997 of 5.3 million and the city proper 2.7 million. The city's name, which translates as "southern capital," denotes the important role that it has played in Chinese history. Located on the southern bank of the Chang (Yangtze) River, Nanjing was the capital of the kingdom of Wu (220–280) and several other small local dynasties between the third and sixth centuries, before becoming the capital of the Ming dynasty between 1368 and 1421. The third Ming emperor, Yung Lo (reigned 1403–1424), moved the capital to Beijing, the "northern capital," in the early 1420s.

Nanjing continued to play an important role in the economy and administration of the lower Chang River region during the later Ming and Qing dynasties due to its proximity to both the major river of central China and the Grand Canal that linked the southern region of the empire to the administrative north. During the Taiping rebellion of the mid-nineteenth century, Nanjing rose to prominence as the rebels' capital between 1853 and 1864.

Following the October 1911 revolution, the new president, Sun Yat-sen, proclaimed the birth of the new Republic of China in Nanjing. The city again became the nation's capital under Chiang Kai-shek's

Guomindang between 1927 and 1937. It was captured by the Japanese army in December 1937, which ushered in one of the worst atrocities of the Pacific War, the "Rape of Nanjing." The victorious Japanese armies embarked on an orgy of raping and killing the local civilian population. By the time order was restored six weeks later, between 100,000 and 250,000 Chinese had been killed.

Since the Communist victory in 1949, the city's industrial base has developed to include not only its traditional textile manufacturing, but also iron and steel mills, porcelain manufacturing, and light machinery. The city continues to be an important regional administrative center and transportation hub.

Robert John Perrins

Further Reading

Fogel, Joshua A., ed. (2000) *The Nanjing Massacre in History and Historiography*. Berkeley and Los Angeles: University of California Press.

Hobart, Alice Tisdale, and Florence Wheelock Ayscough. (1929) *Within the Walls of Nanking*. New York: Macmillan.

Mote, F. W. (1977) "The Transformation of Nanking, 1350–1400." In *The City in Late Imperial China*, edited by G. William Skinner. Stanford, CA: Stanford University Press, 101–154.

NANJING MASSACRE The Nanjing Massacre (also known as the Nanking Massacre) refers to the war crimes perpetrated by Japanese troops during their invasion and occupation of Nanjing, China, from December 1937 to February 1938. These crimes included the execution and murder of more than 200,000 defenseless and unarmed Chinese soldiers and civilians, the widespread rape and torture of reportedly about 20,000 women and girls, the dismembering of human bodies—both male and female—and the widespread slaughter of domestic and farm animals. The massacre was not limited to Nanjing, which was then the capital of the Republic of China, but encompassed the line of march of the Japanese general Matsui Iwane's Tenth Army and the Shanghai Expeditionary Force from Hangzhou—the landing site—through Shanghai and into Nanjing.

The bloodletting was contained only after the establishment of the Japanese puppet government of Nanjing in late March 1938. General Matsui was found guilty of committing crimes against humanity by the Tokyo War Crimes Tribunal and was sentenced to hanging.

Although the massacre was well reported by the English-language press, its memory was obscured for some years by the refusal of the Japanese government to admit to the crimes and by the failure of the Chinese government to raise the issue internationally. It was not until the 1980s that the Chinese began a serious study of the massacre. After painstaking research of burial records, documents, and interviews, it was concluded that the event took the lives of nearly 300,000. This figure is significantly larger than the estimate of 200,000 given by the Tokyo War Crimes Tribunal.

Corroboration of these numbers is important because the nationalist movement in Japan is trying to deny the legitimacy of the tribunal. For them, the war was a patriotic and just struggle against Western domination. The Chinese confirm and exaggerate the tribunal's findings with the political intent of convincing Asians that Japan has been and still is a threat to Asian nations. The massacre has inspired artistic representations by both Chinese and Japanese artists, and the International Committee to Study the Nanjing Massacre has commissioned a symphonic requiem entitled *Hun Qiao* (The Bridge of Spirits) to honor and memorialize the victims. The search for the truth and meaningfulness of this massacre will be discussed and remembered in various ways for many decades.

Richard C. Kagan

Further Reading

Brook, Timothy, ed. (1999) *Documents on the Rape of Nanking*. Ann Arbor: University of Michigan Press.

Chad, Meira. (1996) *A Choice of Evils*. London: Orion Publishing.

Chang, Iris. (1997) *The Rape of Nanking: The Forgotten Holocaust of World War Two*. New York: Penguin.

Honda, Katsuichi. (1999) *The Nanjing Massacre: A Japanese Journalist Confronts Japan's National Shame*. Armonk, NY: M. E. Sharpe.

NANYANG TECHNOLOGICAL UNIVERSITY Nanyang Technological University (NTU) of Singapore has its origin in the former Nanyang Technological Institute (NTI), which was set up in August 1981 to provide tertiary education and research in engineering and technology. NTU was established by an act of Parliament on 1 July 1991 when NTI was renamed NTU and empowered to award its own degrees. Its campus is located at the former Nanyang University at Jurong in the western part of the island nation. Nanyang University was founded by the late rubber tycoon and community leader Tan Lark Sye in

1955, and it was merged with the University of Singapore to become the National University of Singapore in 1980.

NTU admitted its first class of students in July 1982. The university is moving rapidly into programs in computer science, computer engineering, software engineering, and systems engineering. Currently the university offers eighteen master's degree programs in engineering, computer science, and technical management via telecommunications technologies.

There have been calls from alumni of Nanyang University to restore the university's former name, but official resistance has been strong. Although new graduates have no memories of the past, graduates are stepping up efforts to restore the glories of the former university.

Khai Leong Ho

Further Reading

Kee, Pookong, and Choi Kwai Keong. (2000) *A Pictorial History of Nantah*. Singapore: Published for the Chinese Heritage Centre by Times Media.

Lu, Sinclair. (1995) *The NTU Story: The Making of a University of Industry and Business*. Singapore: Nanyang Technological University.

NAQSH, JAMIL (b. 1939), Pakistani artist. Jamil Naqsh is known for his romantic compositions of women and pigeons. Born in Kairana, India, he fled to Peshawar, Pakistan, during the Indian partition and then moved to Lahore. At the National College of Art in Lahore, Jamil Naqsh studied painting with the noted miniaturist Ustad Mohammad Sharif, but left after two years without receiving his degree. In 1962, Naqsh held his first exhibition, at the Pakistan Arts Council in Lahore, soon after which he moved to Karachi. Supplementing his income by working in advertising agencies, the artist continued to produce meticulously drafted and beautifully balanced paintings, in both oils and watercolors. In 1989, Naqsh received the President's Pride of Performance Award in recognition of his artistic contributions.

Jamil Naqsh's representations of women alternate between realism and abstraction, in both face and figure. His paintings are either straightforward depictions, or fragmented collages, of the human figure. Although other motifs such as horses and babies appear in his work, Naqsh's women seem the core of his artistic inspiration. Nonetheless, in 1996 Jamil Naqsh exhibited a series of calligraphic works called *Modern Manuscripts*, his interpretation of Arabic script. That year a group of patrons inaugurated the Jamil Naqsh Foundation in Karachi.

Kishwar Rizvi

NAQSHBANDIYA This Sufi order of Islam derives its name from Muhammad b. Muhammad Baha al-Din al-Naqshband (1318–1389), a Tajik from Central Asia. Sufism is the mystical expression of Islam that emphasized above all abstemiousness and self-discipline for the individual. However, the Naqshbandi tradition itself does not regard Baha al-Din as the founder of this Central Asian Sufi order *(tariqa)*. The chain of masters *(silsilat al-tarbiya)* begins rather with Abu Ya'qub Yusuf al-Hamadhani, a Central Asian mystic who died in Merv in 1140. His spiritual successor *(khalifa)*, 'Abd al-Khaliq al-Ghujawani (d. 1220), is responsible for giving this order its specific cast, including the emphasis on silent remembrance of God *(dhikr khafi)*. Baha al-Din is the seventh in this series of masters; he is regarded as the patron saint of the city of Bukhara, seat of a once-powerful Islamic kingdom in present-day Uzbekistan. His mausoleum there has become one of the most important Sufi places of pilgrimage.

With their emphasis on silent rather than vocal *dhikr*, Naqshbandi practices stress quiet, spiritual communion with the divine and inner discipline of the adherent, rather than external, showy rites. The early Naqshbandiya, in accordance with this emphasis on silent *dhikr*, eschewed the music and dance *(sama')* that accompany Sufi practices in some orders, as well as the adoption of distinctive attire and the performance of miraculous feats *(karamat)*. The Naqshbandiya are also known for their adherence to the *shari'a*, the religious law of Islam, and for their distinctive Sunni sympathies.

From Central Asia, the Naqshbandi *tariqa* spread to practically all parts of the Turkish world and the Caucasus by the fifteenth century. Its Sunni allegiance attracted the support of the Ottoman Turks; many Naqshbandis began to migrate from Central Asia to Istanbul and other places and established a number of *tekkes* (Sufi lodges) there. Naqshbandi Sufism also made significant inroads among Kurds and South Asians. By the eighteenth century, the Mujaddadi order of the Naqshbandiya, established by Sheikh Ahmad Sirhindi (d. 1624) of India, had spread to Ottoman Turkey and the Balkans. In the nineteenth century, Mawlana Khalid Baghdadi (d. 1827), a Kurd, established the Khalidi branch of the Naqshbandi order, which shortly thereafter became the principal *tariqa* in

Central Asia and much of Ottoman Turkey as well. In addition to these areas, the Naqshbandi order at the present time also has small pockets of adherents in some parts of the Arab world, Europe, and North America.

Asma Afsaruddin

Further Reading

Algar, Hamid. (1960–) "Nakshbandiyya." In *The Encyclopaedia of Islam.* Vol. 7, edited by H. A. R. Gibb, et al. New ed. Leiden, Netherlands: Brill, 934–937.

Knysh, Alexander D. (2000) *Islamic Mysticism: A Short History.* Leiden, Netherlands: Brill.

Trimingham, J. Spencer. (1971) *The Sufi Orders in Islam.* Oxford, U.K.: Clarendon Press.

NARA (2002 est. pop. 1.5 million). Nara Prefecture is situated in the central region of Japan's island of Honshu. Once the cultural and political heart of ancient Japan, it occupies an area of 3,692 square kilometers. Its primary geographical features are the Ikoma, Kongo, and Kii Mountains; the Yamato Kogen Highland; and the Nara Basin. Its main rivers are the Yoshinogawa, Yamatogawa, and Totsukawa. It is bordered by Kyoto, Mie, Osaka, and Wakayama prefectures. Once known as Yamato Province, it assumed its present name and borders in 1887.

The prefecture's capital is Nara city, named Heijokyo in the Nara period (710–794), when it became Japan's first permanent capital. Designed according to Chinese precepts, it hosted the first great flowering of Japanese literature and art. The imperial court sponsored the spread of Buddhism, and, although the capital moved in 794 to Heian-kyo, some of the world's finest Buddhist monuments remain in Nara.

Archaeological remains of the Jomon (10,000 BCE–300 BCE) and Yayoi (300 BCE–300 CE) cultures indicate that agriculture arrived in Nara Prefecture two thousand years ago. Today the leading crops are rice, vegetables, tea, and persimmons, and forestry remains important. Its traditional products include woodwork, lacquerware, *sumi* (india ink), calligraphy brushes, *washi* paper, and *somen* noodles. More recent industry is devoted to plastics, rubber, electrical machinery, and spinning. The region's attractions, aside from Nara city's historical sites, include the nearby Buddhist temples of Horyuji, Yakushiji, and Toshodaiji. Visitors also are drawn to Yoshino-Kumano National Park.

E. L. S. Weber

Further Reading

"Nara Prefecture." (1993) *Japan: An Illustrated Encyclopedia.* Tokyo: Kodansha.

NARA—WORLD HERITAGE SITE

A UNESCO World Heritage Site since 1998, Nara's Shinto shrines and archaeological site give an unparalleled glimpse into life in eighth-century CE feudal Japan.

NARA PERIOD During the Nara period (710–794), the Japanese imperial central government was unified, strengthened, and developed through religious ritual and the importation of Chinese bureaucratic methods. Drawing from classical Chinese texts, the penal and administrative codes known collectively as *ritsuryo* allowed the central government to control the capital and outlying districts through taxation and a network of officials. This period is named after its capital city of Nara, occupied in 710, which was planned and built according to Chinese architectural principles.

Central authority was further legitimized through Japan's two major religions. Shinto, the native religion, traced the imperial lineage back to the sun goddess Amatesaru. This occurred prior to the Nara period when Amatesaru was adopted as the founding spiritual ancestor of the imperial Yamato clan. During this same earlier period, the sun goddess was also accorded a higher rank than the spiritual ancestors, or *kami*, of all the other Japanese clans. This spiritual shift was gradual, and as Shinto became supported by the state the rulers, in turn, helped shape Shinto beliefs to provide a historic legitimacy to the imperial line.

But it was Buddhism, imported through China and Korea, that received the blessings and support of the state. In part, Buddhist teachings were promoted because they were seen to protect and serve the welfare of the state, and Buddhist priests received official positions and political influence. Just as important, temple building was undertaken with great fervor. The most impressive of these temples is the Todaiji, completed in 752, which houses the massive Universal Buddha Rushana.

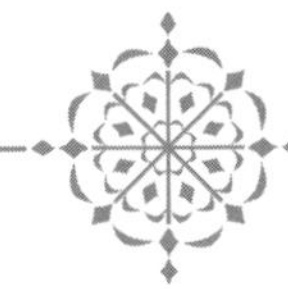

JAPAN—HISTORICAL PERIODS

Jomon culture (10,000–300 BCE)
Yayoi culture (300 BCE–300 CE)
Yamato State (300–552 CE)
Kofun period (300–710 CE)
Nara period (710–794 CE)
Heian period (794–1185)
Kamakura period (Kamakura Shogunate) (1185–1333)
Muromachi period (1333–1573)
Momoyama period (1573–1600)
Tokugawa or Edo period (Tokugawa Shogunate) (1600/1603–1868)
Meiji period (1868–1912)
Taisho period (1912–1926)
Showa period (1926–1989)
Allied occupation (1945–1952)
Heisei period (1989–present)

In addition to these architectural endeavors are the important literary contributions of the Nara period. The first official anthology of poetry, the *Man'yoshu* (Collection of Ten Thousand Leaves, c. 759), dates from this period. Two grand imperial histories were also written. The *Kojiki* (Record of Ancient Matters, c. 712) details ancient history and origin myths, while the *Nihon shoki* (Chronicle of Japan, 720) is generally concerned with more current imperial succession and historic accounts.

The conclusion of the Nara period was marked by an imperial decision to abandon the capital at Nara in favor of constructing a new capital at Heian-kyo, modern-day Kyoto. A motivating factor for this move was probably the growing power and influence of the Buddhist clergy.

While Shinto and Buddhism have generally coexisted in Japan, a notable challenge to the imperial line, often referred to as the Dokyo Incident, arose from a member of the Buddhist clergy. Dokyo (d. 772) was an ambitious priest who gained favor with the female emperor Koken (later called Shotoku, 718–770); he was given titles suggesting that he might succeed Shotoku after her death. Although this immediate crisis of succession passed with little incident, it marked a clear challenge to imperial legitimacy.

Allen Reichert

Further Reading

Bender, Ross. (1979) "The Hachiman Cult and the Dokyo Incident." *Monumenta Nipponica* 34, 2: 125–153.

Brown, Delmer M., ed. (1993) *The Cambridge History of Japan*, Vol. 6: *Ancient Japan*. Cambridge, U.K.: Cambridge University Press.

The Manyoshu. (1965) Trans. by Japanese Classics Translation Committee. New York: Columbia University Press.

Nihongi: Chronicles of Japan from the Earliest Times to A.D. 697. (1975) Trans. by W. G. Aston. Rutland, VT: Charles E. Tuttle.

Piggott, Joan R. (1997) *The Emergence of Japanese Kingship.* Stanford, CA: Stanford University Press.

NARANTSATSRALT, JANLAVYN (b. 1957), former prime minister of Mongolia. Janlavyn Narantsatsralt was born in 1957 in Ulziit somon, Dundgobi Province, Mongolia. After graduating from secondary school there in 1975, he studied in Moscow at the Land Management Institute from 1975 to 1981, obtaining a diploma as a land management engineer/economist. He graduated from the Moscow Administrative Management Institute in 1985. Narantsatsralt also received a master's degree from the Mongolian National University, where he studied land management, in 1992.

In the 1980s, Narantsatsralt worked as chief engineer in the Land Management Institute and from 1989 to 1991 as a research worker at the Mongolian Institute of Land Policy in Ulaanbaatar, the Mongolian capital. In 1991, he became head of Ulaanbaatar's city management and planning department and later served as a city council member, head of the land bureau, and general director of the Institute of Land Policy. A member of the Mongolian National Democratic Party (MNDP), he was elected mayor of Ulaanbaatar in November 1996. After the dismissal of two democratic coalition prime ministers stemming from political in-fighting and rumors of corruption, Narantsatsralt was chosen as a compromise figure by coalition members to become prime minister in December 1998. His candidacy was approved by Mongolian president Bagbandi of the rival Mongolian People's Revolutionary Party (MPRP), which led to Narantsatsralt's installation as the country's nineteenth prime minister since independence in 1911. However, he could only maintain support within the shattered coalition until August 1999, when he lost a vote of confidence. In the July 2000 parliamentary elections, Narantsatsralt was one of only four democratic coalition candidates to win seats in the seventy-six-member Mongolian parliament during the MPRP landslide. Thus, his position as a leader within the democratic coalition movement grew in stature, leading to his election in December 2000 as deputy head of a new party, the Mongolian Democratic Party.

Alicia J. Campi

NARAYAN, R. K. (1906–2001), Indian novelist. Rasipuram Krishnaswami Narayan (professionally R. K. Narayan) was one of India's leading novelists throughout the latter half of the twentieth century. He was born of Tamil Brahman parents in Madras in 1906, but long lived in Mysore City, Karnataka. It is in the latter area that all of his delightful English-language novels are set. His work has been more widely published outside India than that of any of his Indian contemporaries (with the possible exceptions of Salman Rushdie and Arundhati Roy). In the early stages of his career, his work was championed by the British novelist Graham Greene. That such an internationally visible writer should only be known for such highly localized novels (most of them are set in the one fictional Mysorean village of Malgudi) is remarkable. The general tone in all his novels is one of wry humor, as in *The Guide* (1958), which shows up the tragicomic aspects of the modern Indian penchant for half-baked metaphysics. His first novel was *Swami and Friends* (1935), and several others of note are *The Man-Eater of Malgudi* (1962), *The Financial Expert*, *The Bachelor of Arts*, *Waiting for the Mahatma*, and *Mr. Sampath*. In addition, Narayan wrote an autobiography, *My Days* (1974), and produced a shortened English prose version of the Mahabharata (1972).

Paul Hockings

Further Reading

Walsh, William. (1971) *R. K. Narayan*. Harlow, U.K.: Longman, for the British Council.

NARMADA DAM CONTROVERSY India's Narmada Valley Project (NVP) involves the construction of 31 major, 135 medium, and 3,000 minor dams on the Narmada River and its tributaries. First proposed in 1946, the NVP covers the Narmada River watershed in the western Indian states of Madhya Pradesh, Gujarat, and Maharashtra. Construction began in 1978, when the Narmada Dam Dispute Tribunal approved a plan resolving water-sharing disputes among these states. The project was to be funded with World Bank assistance, but in 1993, after the World Bank issued a highly critical report, the government of India renounced the loan, refusing to accept any more money from the bank. The controversy has centered on the Sardar Sarovar Project (SSP) in Gujarat and the Narmada Sagar Project (NSP) in Madhya Pradesh. Led by two nongovernmental organizations, ARCH-Vahini and Narmada Bachao Andolan, opponents of the dams have charged that more than one hundred thousand villagers would be displaced by the dams despite rehabilitation plans, which they characterize as wholly inadequate. In addition the opponents question the absence of mandatory environmental impact studies at the time of construction.

Opponents of the dams have staged numerous large-scale protests in New Delhi and at the dam sites, thereby gaining international attention. After preliminary court rulings in 1995 and 1998, construction on the dams was delayed pending the Indian Supreme Court's final decision on the suits against the dams.

Eric A. Strahorn

Further Reading

Drèze, Jean, Meera Samson, and Satyajit Singh, eds. (1997) *The Dam and the Nation: Displacement and Resettlement in the Narmada Valley*. Delhi and New York: Oxford University Press.

Rosencranz, Armin, Shyam Divan, and Martha L. Noble. (1991) *Environmental Law and Policy in India: Cases, Materials, and Statutes*. Mumbai (Bombay), India: N. M. Tripathi.

Roy, Arundhati. (1999) *The Cost of Living*. New York: Modern Library.

Singh, Satyajit. (1997) *Taming the Waters: The Political Economy of Large Dams in India*. Delhi: Oxford University Press.

NARMADA RIVER Narmada (or Narbada, sometimes Nerbudda) River, 1,290 kilometers long, was mentioned by Ptolemy as the Namados. Ancient Sanskrit names for the river included Reva, Samodbhava, and Mekalasuta. Traditionally, the Narmada River formed the boundary between the Dekkan Plateau and what was known as Hindustan, the North Indian plains. It rises in western India in the Maikala Range, on Amarkantak Hill, very close to the source of the Mahanadi, and is the only major Indian river to flow westward into the Arabian Sea, meeting it at Broach (or Bharuch) after crossing all of Madhya Pradesh state and flowing in a straight course between the Satpura and Vindhya Ranges to the Gulf of Khambhai, in eastern Gujarat State.

Navigation is confined to the lower 100 kilometers, and the river has not been used for irrigation purposes. In 1978 a controversial project was launched in the face of massive opposition, to dam the river just inside

Gujarat State, by drowning hundreds of villages in the state of Madhya Pradesh and displacing several million people, thereby creating a new source of power for Gujarat's industries and of irrigation for area farmers. Amid much criticism of the project, the government of India halted the dam construction in 1995. A ruling in 2000 by the Supreme Court of India allowed the project to move forward; however, the public debate over building the dam remains heated.

Paul Hockings

Further Reference

Alvares, Claude, and Ramesh Billory. (1988) *Damming the Narmada: India's Greatest Planned Environmental Disaster*. Penang, India: Third World Network/APPEN.

NATAKA

Nataka was one of the ten genres performed in ancient Indian theater. These ten genres were called the *dasarupakas* (the ten forms) and were *nataka, prakarana, samavakara, dima, vyayoga, ihamriga, utsristikakanka, prahasana, bhana,* and *vithi*. *Nataka* was the most prominent of these, so much so that by modern times the term *nataka* has come to be used for all drama rather than a particular genre.

The primary and most comprehensive text of the ancient Indian dramatic theory, the *Natya Sastra* (c. 450 BCE), describes the ten genres in ample details that have been repeated with minor additions by literary theorists through the ages. These genres, however, can be divided into two groups, one for erotic themes and the other for conflicts. In the first group, some genres, such as the *nataka* and *prakarana*, were meant to depict sensitive and profound love, whereas others, such as *prahasana* and *bhana*, were meant to depict crude sexuality, often making such plays bawdy and satirical. The conflict plays could also be subdivided into two categories. Genres like *samavakara, ihamriga,* and *dima* showed divine combats, whereas *vyayoga* and *utsristikakanka* showed human duels. But *nataka* was the most complete of them all because it dealt with the psychological probings of humans in love and despair.

Nataka dramas were designed to be based on well-known stories from the ancient tales of royal families. The dramas could not be about a contemporary patron, though the playwrights adjusted the ancient tales to reflect their own times. The wealth of royalty, their erotic exploits, and the ensuing cycle of pleasure and suffering were fully depicted. As a result, the *natakas* describe ancient Indian royal lifestyles. The ancient audience looked not so much for new events in the plot as for improvisation in characters and performance style. The hero in *nataka* drama either belonged to a royal family or was a king himself. His love affairs (with royal women only) thus always had a significant political fallout. A typical example of this motif comes from the play *Svapnavasavadattam* (The Dream of Vasavadatta) by Bhasa (flourished second or third century CE). Here the king, Udayan, is led to believe that his beloved wife, Vasavadatta, has died in a fire and that freed of his excessive preoccupation with his love he can work to consolidate his kingdom and defeat his enemies. After the task of political stability is achieved, the wife is brought back, but in the meantime he is made to marry the daughter of an ally. Both women accept the outcome with grace and magnanimity. Strange as it may seem today, not only is the principle of harmonious polygamy affirmed but also a psychological exploration of the hero's profound love for Vasavadatta is combined with examination of a marriage of convenience for social utility. Usually the *nataka* had a happy ending in the sense that it ended with the union of lovers, but to call it a comedy would be a mistake because prolonged separation and suffering were essential. The final union itself was not a triumph of passion but rather an affirmation of just desire unified with public good. Sometimes the final union was only for social benefit, such as to provide an heir to the throne.

Heroes and Heroines

The protagonist in the *nataka* always had an elevated character and was often a connoisseur of the arts. His love was expressed in refined dialogue, both prose and poetry, and his longings through conventional use on stage of songs and paintings. Patience, magnanimity, and gravity of purpose were musts for all heroes and heroines. A supernatural episode was also necessary as part of the plot to indicate the interest of the gods in human affairs and to raise the element of wonder in the play. For example, in *Abhijnanasakuntalam* (The Ring of Sakuntala), a famous play by Kalidasa (flourished fifth century), when the heroine Sakuntala is turned away by the king Dusyanta, she disappears in a whirl of light and is transported far away by her divine mother to the retreat of a sage teacher.

The *nataka* relied heavily upon the presence of a jester *(vidusaka)*, a distinctive feature of ancient theater. The role of the *vidusaka* is rooted in the precept of the *Natya Sastra* that "laughter arises best in an erotic situation." The *vidusaka* was a humorous foil to the moody, melancholic, or impractical longings of the royal hero. But above all, this jester belonged to the tradition of Indian theater that consciously ridiculed the pretensions and hypocrisy of the upper classes, intellectual elite, Brahmans, pundits, scholars, and ascetics. Whereas the dramatic genre called *prahasana* perfected vitriolic satire, *nataka* took the middle way of milder ridicule. The typical *vidusaka* in the *nataka*s was a bosom friend and not a paid court jester. He was usually depicted as a distorted figure, an ugly-faced, dirty-looking, bald Brahman who walked like a crane, looked up and down, and ogled stupidly. He spoke rubbish, ridiculed the hero, or made vulgar comments. In most plays, he was shown as a slothful, sleepy glutton. He never spoke Sanskrit but rather the common language, called *avantika*. In short, he was a caricature of the alert, grave, and scholarly Brahman. But genuine affection and absolute faithfulness to the hero were his most endearing qualities.

A *nataka* consisted of five to ten acts and sometimes contained a subplot that extended its length. It was also recommended that in a *nataka* there should be no more than four to five players at a time on stage. This restriction was imposed to allow the dramatist to concentrate on the characters and their dramatic development. To create memorable and special characters was the dramatist's main challenge. For example, improving upon the story of Sakuntala as found in the epic *Mahabharata*, Kalidasa made his heroine capable of much greater suffering and sacrifice.

Dance and Music

The *nataka* was to be performed with plenty of dance and music, which the other nine dramatic genres used sparingly. For this reason, as compared with modern naturalistic theater of the European kind, the progress of the ancient *nataka* was slow. If an injunction regarding an act in the *Natya Sastra* is taken to mean "to be performed in one day" and not to mean "depiction of the actions of one day," then the playing time for a single act was supposed to be one day. If so, then a single play that nowadays takes only three hours would have taken five to ten days to be performed.

The *nataka* was intended to display all the essential features of the ancient art of theatrical representation, in which were employed not only the verbal medium of dialogue but also gestural communication through highly complicated body language *(angika abhinaya)*, subtle facial expressions, and elaborate costumes. The aim was to create an intense aesthetic experience for the audience through a variety of dramatic emotions that transported the audience to the state of delight and special taste called *rasa*.

With the decline of ancient theater from the eleventh century onward, the *nataka*, like the other nine genres, fell into disuse. In modern times, with the revival of drama, it has been revived as a cross between traditional and modern realistic drama.

Bharat Gupt

Further Reading

Gupt, Bharat. (1994) *Dramatic Concepts: Greek and Indian. A Study of Poetics and the Natyashastra.* Delhi: D. K. Printworld.

Kavi, M. Ramakrishna, ed. (1951) *A Dictionary of Technical Terms with Definitions Collected from the Works on Music and Dramaturgy by Bharata and Others.* Tirupati, India: Tirupati Devasthanam.

Kavi, Ramakrishna, ed. (1956–1964) *Natyasastram with Abhinahavabhi.* 4 vols. Gaekwad's Oriental Series. Baroda, India: Oriental Institute.

Panchal, Govardhan. (1996) *The Theatres of Bharata and Some Aspects of Sanskrit Play-Production.* Delhi: Munshiram Manoharlal.

Sastri, Madhu-sudana. (1971–1981) *Natyasastram with Abhinavabharati and Madhusandani.* 3 vols. Varanasi, India: B. H. U.

Shekhar, Indu. (1997) *Sanskrit Drama, Its Origin and Decline.* Delhi: Munshiram Manoharlal.

Tarlekar, G. H. (1975) *Studies in Natyasastra.* Delhi: Motilal Banarsidas.

NATION-RELIGION-MONARCH

Chat-Sasana-Phramahakasat (Thai for Nation-Religion-Monarch) is a metaphor for national integration and national identity in Thailand. This trinitarian phrase was introduced by King Vajiravudh (Rama VI), who ruled Siam from 1910 to 1925. The trinity Nation-Religion-Monarch was the foundation of Vajiravudh's nationalistic ideas, which were a central theme in Thai politics during that time. Due to the increasing influence of the British and French colonial powers in Southeast Asia and the losses of large territories east of the Mekong that Siam had occupied and controlled until 1893, there was an urgent need to create an ideological basis for unifying the several ethnic groups forming the population of the modern Thai nation-state, in which the ethnic Thai (Siamese)—though forming the political elite—in fact were a minority of only about 25 percent. The other ethnic groups were the Lao in the Northeast (a great number of whom were forced by the Siamese government to resettle from the east bank to the west bank of the Mekong River during the nineteenth century), the Muang or Yuan and the Lu in the North, Malay-speaking groups in the South, Chinese and Vietnamese immigrants, and other ethnic groups of the Tibeto-Burman and Mon-Khmer language families.

Nation-Religion-Monarch was a "trinitarian mystery in which all three elements were inextricably bound together. . . . Allegiance to any one of the three meant loyalty to all three, disloyalty or disobedience or disrespect toward one meant disrespect toward all" (Wyatt 1984: 229). Vajiravudh, who had been educated in England at Sandhurst Military Academy and Oxford University, established a governmental program that was essentially one of Westernization, and his nationalism was a Western import founded on the Hobbesian theory of man being in need of leadership, though traditional Thai values such as loyalty to Buddhism, love for the monarchy, and cultural pride were integrated therein. Historically, the trinity of Buddhism, kingship, and the people was a general concept of the "Buddhist Kingdom" (Tambiah 1978: 111). Vajiravudh himself had published a number of essays, newspaper articles, plays, songs, and poems to make his version of the trinity and his understanding of the nation popular. The idea of Nation-Religion-Monarch also was a central motto for the paramilitary Wild Tiger Corps and the Thai Boy Scout movement, which were created by Vajiravudh. Each of the three elements of the trinity, which commonly are called the "three holy pillars of the Thai state," has a broader meaning that can best be explained only against the background of traditional Thai society and history.

Chat (Nation)

The term *chat*—from the Sanskrit *jati,* meaning a "lifespan" or "circle of rebirths"—traditionally was known to Thai people as "common ancestry" or "common origin." As part of the trinity, the meaning of *chat* was extended to include "nation." In Vajiravudh's works the definition of *chat* started with family line or caste, and went on to a group of people who had originally been relatives and lived together in one place. Herewith, Vajiravudh referred to the supposed common ancestorship of the Tai peoples. The term "Tai" (etymologically meaning "man" or "mankind" in Proto-Tai) was transformed into Thai (by replacing the unaspirated initial consonant of "Tai" with the aspirated consonant beginning the word "Thai"), a term that more and more replaced the name Siamese (Tai Sayam), and then was defined to mean "free." Vajiravudh created the name Thailand ("land of the free"), emphasizing the Siamese success in maintaining independence from European colonialism.

Chat in the context of the trinity is a term having an ethnic as well as a political-historical and cultural dimension. It first refers to the T(h)ai as an ethnic group, but also to Thai citizenship. The term also includes historical aspects, especially the continuity of Thai history and civilization, which were traced 6,000 years back to the Altai, and which reached a first political climax in the kingdom of Nanchao before the first great Tai kingdoms (Muang Mao, Lanna, Sukhothai, Lan Sang, and Ayutthaya) were founded in Southeast Asia. Culturally, *chat* stresses the freedom-loving character of the Thai, as well as common values and sociocultural patterns of all T(h)ai peoples. In addition, the use of a national language—Central Thai—was emphasized. After the 1932 revolution, in which the absolute monarchy was abolished and replaced by a constitutional monarchy, many writings added loyalty to democracy and democratic values when defining the term *chat.*

Sasana (Religion)

Sasana is used synonymously for Theravada Buddhism, the official state religion of Thailand. Buddhism was probably the most important factor supporting the national integration of different groups of the Tai language family, which all followed the same religion. From the thirteenth century on, Theravada Buddhism was favored by the Thai, Lao, and Yuan kings as a means of increasing royal virtue and public welfare and as a way of adding miraculous power to the state. Vajiravudh broadened the meaning of Buddhism and identified it with patriotism and political morality. He continued the reforms of Buddhism and especially of Buddhist education that began with the religious reforms of his predecessors, Mongkut and Chulalongkorn.

The person to be credited with the creation of what today is termed "Thai Buddhism" was Vajiravudh's uncle, Prince Vajiranana, who was Sangharaja (head of the *sangha,* or Buddhist monastic community) from 1910 to 1921, and who worked toward bringing monks of different traditions into a unified national *sangha* in which the reformed Theravada tradition was to be practiced and communicated to the laity in the form of a national institution. The state-controlled *sangha* played an important role in general education, especially in mediating Central Thai as a national language and in communicating Siamese history as a national history that was tied up with Buddhism. Another important function of the *sangha* was (and is) to legitimate the sociopolitical status of the monarch, who was always seen as the protector of *sasana.*

Phramahakasat (Monarch)

Traditionally, the king in Buddhist Tai societies was seen as *dharmaraja* (righteous ruler) and *chakravartin* (wheel-rolling emperor), which meant that he was not only a political but also a religious and moral leader of the people. The king was said to be the patron and supporter of the Buddhist religion, and religion in turn was understood as the special treasure of the kingdom and a marker of its legitimacy. The king was provided with Buddhist symbols that were thought to give the king sacred power.

Vajiravudh's concept of kingship was based on these traditional foundations. He saw kingship as natural to Siam and essential to Siam's progress. Siam's success and continuity in history and its independence from colonial powers were interpreted as the results of wise royal leadership and diplomacy. However, though the emphasis was on traditional values, Vajiravudh also developed new ideas that would promote the monarch as the embodiment of the nation. He presented himself no longer as *devaraja* (god-king) but as a "citizen king" by abandoning certain forms of etiquette and privileges that had underpinned the formal sacredness of the monarch. His new type of kingship, which was emulated by subsequent kings—most notably by the present king, Bhumibol Adulyadej—was characterized by a close linkage between the monarch and the people (nation).

Despite the dissenting voices of some Marxist scholars, who assert that Vajiravudh's nationalism was a "*sakdina* nationalism" (feudal nationalism) that aimed at continuing the old structures of sociopolitical organization and securing for the king the status of absolute monarch, the concept of Nation-Religion-Monarch continues in contemporary Thai politics. Even today, the inseparability of the monarchy from the nation is stressed.

Jana Raendchen and Oliver Raendchen

Further Reading

Fessen, Helmut, and Hans-Dieter Kubitscheck. (1994). *Geschichte Thailands.* (History of Thailand). Bremen Asia Pacific Studies, no. 7. Münster/Hamburg, Germany: Lit Verlag.

Grabowsky, Volker, ed. (1995) *Regions and National Integration in Thailand 1892–1992.* Wiesbaden, Germany: Harrassowitz.

Keyes, Charles F. (1987) *Thailand: Buddhist Kingdom as Modern Nation State.* Boulder, CO.: Westview Press.

Kuhnt-Saptodewo, Sri, Volker Grabowsky, and Martin Grossheim, eds. (1997) *Nationalism and Cultural Revival in Southeast Asia: Perspectives from the Centre and the Region.* Wiesbaden, Germany: Harrassowitz.

Raendchen, Jana. (1997) *Erneuerung durch Tradition. Das Wirken des Vajiranana Varorasa bei der Modernisierung des Thailandischen Allgemeinbildenden Schulwesens.* (*Tradition in Modernity: Vajiranana Varorasa and the Modernization of Education in Thailand.*) SEACOM Studies on Southeast Asia, no. 4. Berlin, Germany: SEACOM.

Reynolds, Craig J. (1991) *National Identity and Its Defenders: Thailand, 1939–1989.* Monash Papers on Southeast Asia, no. 25. Clayton, Australia: Monash University.

Tambiah, Stanley J. (1978) "Sangha and Polity in Modern Thailand: An Overview." In *Religion and Legitimation of Power in Thailand, Laos, and Burma*, edited by Bardwell L. Smith. Chambersburg, PA: Anima Books, 111–133.

Terwiel, Barend Jan. (1983) *A History of Modern Thailand 1767–1942.* St. Lucia, Australia: University of Queensland Press.

Vella, Walter F. (1978) *Chaiyo! King Vajiravudh and the Development of Thai Nationalism.* Honolulu: University Press of Hawaii.

Wyatt, David Kent. (1984) *Thailand: A Short History.* New Haven, CT: Yale University Press.

NATIONAL DAY—CHINA

NATIONAL DAY—CHINA By the autumn of 1949, the Chinese civil war was drawing to a close, the People's Liberation Army of the Chinese Communist Party having defeated the Nationalists led by Chiang Kai-shek (1887–1975). On 1 October 1949 Mao Zedong (1893–1976) stood on the Gate of Heavenly Peace in Tiananmen Square in Beijing to announce the founding of the People's Republic of China. This date subsequently was declared National Day and since then has been a hugely significant date in China's calendar, the celebrations often coinciding with the launch of major new political campaigns. Until the advent of the reform and opening up of China in 1978, military parades in Beijing and other cities took center stage. Although the emphasis of the National Day festival has now shifted toward the holding of civil events, the military played an important role in the lavish fiftieth anniversary celebrations of 1999, which were notable not simply for their extravagance but also for the massive disruption to life in Beijing caused by the extensive security precautions. The National Day festivities now stretch to a weeklong holiday, during which the country's most popular tourist sites are at their busiest.

Julian Ward

Further Reading

Hutchings, Graham. (2000) *Modern China: A Companion to a Rising Power.* London: Penguin.

NATIONAL FRONT FOR THE LIBERATION OF SOUTH VIETNAM During the U.S. War in Vietnam (also known as the Second Indochinese War), in a major move to overthrow the

U.S.-backed Saigon regime in South Vietnam and establish Communist rule throughout the country, the Democratic Republic of Vietnam (DRV) leadership established the National Front for the Liberation of South Vietnam (NFLSV) on 20 December 1960 in Tay Ninh Province. After six years of trying to unify the country through political means, the Vietnamese Communist Party (Lao Dong Party) had concluded that armed violence was the best way to do so.

The NFLSV, usually known as the National Liberation Front (NLF), was typical of most Communist-front organizations. It drew its membership from the South Vietnamese who were anti-Diem—or opposed South Vietnam's government—and anti-American, including Communists and non-Communists alike. For example, Nguyen Huu Tho (1910–1994), a supposed non-Communist, presided over the Communist Party–dominated NLF.

The NLF, known as the Viet Cong by its enemies, was perceived by U.S. policymakers as a purely Hanoi-directed movement. These policymakers argued that if the flow of supplies and troops to the NLF was halted, the southern revolution would die and the Diem regime would remain safe, justifying American involvement in the conflict. Others argued that the conflict in the south was a locally based insurgency and that the NLF was a southern organization that had risen organically from the people opposed to Diem.

Throughout the war the NLF staged assaults through its military arm, the People's Liberation Armed Forces (PLAF), on U.S. and ARVN (Army of the Republic of South Vietnam) forces. The most dramatic of these assaults was the 1968 Tet Offensive. Beginning in 1968, the NFLSV sent representatives to the Paris peace talks, and it played a major role in forming the Provisional Revolutionary Government (PRG), the government-in-waiting during the later stages of the war. At the war's end, only a few NFLSV representatives were incorporated into the new national government of South Vietnam.

Richard B. Verrone

Further Reading

Pike, Douglas. (1966) *Viet Cong: The Organization and Techniques of the National Liberation Front of South Vietnam.* Cambridge, MA: M.I.T. Press.

Tang Truong Nhu. (1985) *A Viet Cong Memoir: An Inside Account of the Vietnam War and Its Aftermath.* New York: Vintage Books.

Thayer, Carlyle A. (1989) *War by Other Means: National Liberation and Revolution in Viet-Nam, 1954–60.* Sydney, Australia: Allen and Unwin.

NATIONAL LEAGUE FOR DEMOCRACY—MYANMAR

NATIONAL LEAGUE FOR DEMOCRACY—MYANMAR The National League for Democracy (NLD) was Myanmar's (Burma's) leading political party during the 1990 elections. It won a landslide victory in the May 1990 elections, the first to be held for thirty years: of the 485 seats, the NLD won 396 (82 percent), the army-backed National Unity Party 10 (2 percent), and others 79 (16 percent). The party was founded on 24 September 1988 by retired Brigadier-General Aung Gyi (chair), retired General Tin Oo (vice chair), and Aung San Suu Kyi (general secretary) in response to the injustices they felt the army was committing against the Burmese people. A systematic campaign against the NLD was initiated before the elections. The State Law and Order Restoration Council (SLORC) imprisoned Tin Oo, placed Aung San Suu Kyi under house arrest, and generally harassed NLD members. SLORC anticipated during the elections that if they would not win, the results would probably be a draw and disagreement would arise among party leaders, in which case there would be a role for the military. They were greatly disappointed with the results.

SLORC refused to convene the parliament and nullified the elections with the excuse that it would not accept an interim government under the 1947 constitution. Legally, parliament would have had to be convened by 27 July 1990, within sixty days of the elections. In anticipation, SLORC issued on 27 July its notorious Notification No. 1/90, stating that only SLORC has the right to exercise legislative, executive, and judicial powers, and that it would not accept a government formed under an interim constitution. The constitution became an excuse for not handing over the reins of government. The Gandhi Hall declaration, resulting from a meeting on 28–29 July 1990 of elected members and the NLD executive committee, called for the authorities to transfer power to the NLD under the 1948 revised constitution before 30 September 1990. At a meeting of 500 elected members of parliament in Mandalay on 29 September, seven were elected to map the action program to implement the Gandhi Hall declaration, resulting in a resolution on 1 October to establish a government in liberated areas inside Burma if necessary. Under severe repression and with the future for democratic government bleak, many members of parliament were forced to escape to the Thai border. Failing to take the reins of government, NLD elected representatives formed the National Coalition Government of the Union of Burma (NCGUB) in Manerplaw (just inside Myanmar on the Thai border) on 18 December 1990. Manerplaw was destroyed a few years later by SLORC, forcing the NCGUB to move inside Thailand. Headed by Dr. Sein Lwin, NCGUB today represents elected government in exile.

In January 1993, the authorities in Myanmar announced a national convention to draft the new constitution. In 1995, after Aung San Suu Kyi's release from house arrest, the NLD demanded to be fully included in the constitution drafting process. SLORC refused and the NLD set out to draft its own constitution, to which the authorities responded by promulgating Law No. 5/96, prohibiting everyone including NLD members and elected representatives from drafting, debating, or even discussing a future constitution outside the national convention.

The NLD has shown considerable ingenuity to survive. U Kyi Maung took over temporary leadership of the NLD to lead the party to electoral victory in 1990 after Aung San Suu Kyi, U Tin Oo, and other senior colleagues had been arrested. U Kyi Maung became vice chair in 1992 but eventually resigned in 1997. Aung Shwe took over as NLD chair in the context of party reorganization in 1992.

In the wake of negotiations that began in October 2000 between General Khin Nyunt and Aung San Suu Kyi, the government-controlled media toned down their criticisms of the NLD, prisoners were released, and the NLD was once again permitted to put up signboards above its offices. This is a hopeful sign, but observers express considerable caution over it.

Gustaaf Houtman

Further Reading

Burma Center Netherlands and Transnational Institute, eds. (2000) *Strengthening Civil Society in Burma: Possibilities and Dilemmas for International NGOs*. Chiang Mai, Thailand: Silkworm Books.

Carey, Peter. (1997) *From Burma to Myanmar: Military Rule and the Struggle for Democracy*. London: Research Institute for the Study of Conflict and Terrorism.

Carey, Peter, ed. (1997) *Burma: The Challenge of Change in a Divided Society*. New York: St. Martin's Press, Inc.

Houtman, Gustaaf. (1999) *Mental Culture in Burmese Crisis Politics: Aung San Suu Kyi and the National League for Democracy*. Tokyo: Institute for the Study of Languages and Cultures of Asia and Africa.

Victor, Barbara. (1998) *The Lady: Aung San Suu Kyi, Nobel Laureate and Burma's Prisoner*. Boston: Faber and Faber.

NATIONAL MINORITIES—CHINA

A 2000 census in China revealed that 106 million people in that country, or about 8.41 percent of the total population, belonged to an ethnic minority. Thus, China is a multiethnic state. The areas populated by the fifty-five national minorities make up about 60 percent of the total Chinese territory, although in most areas the Han Chinese are in the majority. In 1990 the largest minority, the Zhuang, numbered almost 15.5 million people, and the smallest minority, the Lhoba in Tibet, only twenty-three hundred. (See Table 1.)

Except for the Hui, all these nationalities have their own languages, but most Manchu and She (not included in Table 1) use Chinese. Until the late 1940s, nineteen groups still used their own writing. Since the 1950s, new scripts based on the Latin alphabet were created by the Chinese government.

Traditional Perceptions

Against the background of more than two thousand years of Chinese culture, during most of which time a central power held sway, traditional perceptions have shaped the government's conduct toward other people (minorities) and the expectations about how those minorities must behave toward the central power. Imperial China saw itself as the cultural center of the world and its culture as the culture of humanity. The existence of various peoples living in distinct settlement areas was accepted; but heaven had entrusted only one group with rule over the entire human race. This group—the Han Chinese—was considered to inhabit the center of the world, or the Middle Kingdom (Zhongguo), and its emperors were "Sons of Heaven." The Han Chinese, who were farmers, were contemptuous of the non-Chinese peoples around them, who were hunters and gatherers or nomads and were thought to be culturally and technologically inferior.

Confucianism, for centuries the Chinese state ideology, enshrined this contempt of the "barbarians." According to the historian Sima Qian (145?–86? BCE), the barbarians were ignorant of *li*, the proper rules of life, and of *yi*, the duties of life. The Chinese thus understood difference as ignorance of the social structure of relations and of the Confucian rites. They concluded that barbarians were unable to control their emotions, tended to give way to their feelings, and behaved like wild animals.

Nevertheless, Confucianism did not propose annihilating these people; instead, the non-Chinese had to subordinate themselves to the emperor's power and allow themselves to be integrated into Chinese society in a nonviolent fashion. This traditional attitude has

TABLE 1

Chinese Language Groups and Nationalities with More Than 1 Million Population in 1990 Census

Language Group	Nationality	Number of People (in millions)
1. Han Chinese		1,042.5
2. Sino-Thai		
	Zhuang	15.4
	Bouyei	2.5
	Dong	2.5
	Dai	1.0
3. Tibeto-Burmese		
	Yi	6.6
	Tujia	5.7
	Tibetan	4.6
	Bai	1.6
	Hani	1.3
4. Miao-Yao		
	Miao	7.4
	Yao	2.1
5. Turkish		
	Uygur	7.2
	Kazakh	1.1
6. Mongolian		
	Mongol	4.8
7. Tungusic		
	Manchu	9.8
8. Korean		1.9
9. Other		
	Hui	8.6

Note: Nationalities with populations under 1 million people are not included.

SOURCE: China Statistics Press (2001: 93).

weakened since the mid-nineteenth century, partly through Western influence and penetration, but its basic ideas have by no means disappeared.

Nationalities Policies

During the initial years following the foundation of the People's Republic of China in 1949, for the first time in Chinese history the existence of separate nations in the country was acknowledged without reservation. However, incipient steps in the early 1950s toward legal and de facto equality for all later fell victim to the radical political experiments of Mao Zedong (1893–1976). Proliferating incursions into the territory of non-Han peoples and radical interference with their social structures provoked vehement opposition on the part of those peoples, starting even in the 1950s. In some cases, the minorities in the border regions escaped the oppression emanating from Beijing by mass exodus over the borders.

It was during the Great Leap Forward (1958–1960) that a deliberate policy of forced assimilation was first pursued. This policy of absorbing the nationalities into Chinese society brought compulsory restrictions or even bans on the use of national languages, the cultivation of national literatures, and the practice of national rites, customs, and religions; the government used force to eliminate the social structures of the minorities. Not only in Tibet, but also in numerous other regions inhabited by non-Han peoples, popular unrest, culminating in armed uprisings, was quashed by the military. Finally, the Cultural Revolution (1966–1976) brought with it the most extreme form of forced assimilation: physical destruction and cultural annihilation. For all non-Han peoples, even today, this traumatic experience is remembered as the most severe national oppression.

Regional Autonomy

At the beginning of the 1980s, the Chinese leadership saw itself forced to formulate a more moderate policy because of discontent in non-Han areas. The results of the Cultural Revolution had made it clear that the integration of non-Han people had to be achieved, not through force, but through measures that were based on a broad consensus. The constitution of 1982 revalorized the minorities correspondingly, and a 1984 Autonomy Law formally extended to them the widest-reaching freedoms since the founding of the People's Republic.

Central government decisions and directives that did not correspond to the concrete conditions of an autonomous region no longer had to be carried out (but only if the central government agreed); the leading cadres were supposed to come from the autonomous nationalities; the autonomous areas received a larger catalog of rights in respect to planning, economic development, protection, and exploitation of their resources, foreign trade, education, finance, public health, and other sectors.

Most clauses of the Autonomy Law, however, are so vaguely worded that they cannot be implemented on their own. The Autonomy Law makes no reference to an effective system for protecting the autonomy of minorities, and there are no legal measures for implementing the law. The new law did not answer the calls of many minority leaders for broader autonomy. Particularly among the larger nationalities, younger people became radicalized because they no longer expected Beijing to offer any solutions to their problems. In the early 1980s, the non-Han peoples had looked to Beijing, which promised much but had given little.

Growing Lines of Conflict and Prospects

Percentage increases in the economic and educational spheres and the regranting of certain freedoms in the cultural sector ignored the basic problem that the minorities and their cultural identities took second place to the interests of the Han Chinese because of the government's attempts to make the economy roughly equal for all groups ("development") and because of the increasing Sinification of culture. Despite the government's reform policies, the gap in development between the autonomous regions of the non-Han peoples and the Han regions increased. Of the official number of 80 million people living below the poverty line in China in the mid-1990s, about 64 million, or 80 percent, lived in minority areas. Although considerable materials flowed from the center to the minority areas, nearly half of the counties classified as "poor" lie in national minority areas.

Of course, the central government was not solely responsible for this situation. Some ethnic areas are remote regions of refuge, into which non-Han peoples have had to flee before the Han expansion in recent centuries. But it is also clear that since the founding of the People's Republic, no development policy suited to these areas has ever been followed. The reform policies have visibly diminished state oversight, but this has brought no advantages to the minority areas. According to Chinese reports, the center and the provinces have not given many autonomous areas enough credit, subsidies, foreign exchange, and materials.

Hand in hand with dissatisfaction over economic and social deterioration and backwardness goes dissatisfaction over immigration, which is making local nationalities into minorities in their own areas, along with dissatisfaction with constant bureaucratic interference in religious and cultural life, as well as the decades-long destruction of nature and the environment. A new flood of Han Chinese moved into the autonomous regions in recent years; enterprises were established using cheap local resources to produce products that were "exported" to Han areas. But these enterprises brought nothing useful to the local population, only environmental pollution, deforestation, destruction of the landscape, and illnesses.

The increasing consciousness of national identity, especially among the more numerous peoples, expresses itself, among other ways, in rising religiosity. In Tibet the monasteries became the center of resistance because the danger that threatens Tibetan culture is felt most strongly there. In Muslim areas (there may be about 17 million Muslims in China), Islam radicalized itself. Fundamentalist influences from Iran, Pakistan, Turkey, and the new states in Central Asia did not remain without influence. It is not impossible that if the central power weakens, nationalist movements of smaller nationalities will arise, as was the case in the former Soviet Union.

China has promoted some affirmative policies toward non-Han nationalities: recognition of the existence of different ethnic groups, prohibition of discrimination, special laws for minorities in the 1950s and 1980s, aid to minority areas, guarantees of special representation, special benefits in regard to population policy and university entrance examinations, freedom to choose ethnic identity. But the future of minorities in China may be affected not only by positive policies but also by policies and actions that generate conflicts and affect stability.

Thomas Heberer

Further Reading

China Statistics Press. (2001) *China Statistical Yearbook*. Beijing: China Statistics Press.

Gladney, Dru. (1991) *Muslim Chinese*. Cambridge, MA: Harvard University Press.

Harrell, Stevan, ed. (1995) *Cultural Encounters on China's Ethnic Frontiers*. Seattle and London: University of Washington Press.

Heberer, Thomas. (1989) *China and Its National Minorities: Autonomy or Assimilation?* Armonk, NY: M. E. Sharpe.

———. (1984) *Nationalitätenpolitik und Entwicklungspolitik in den Gebieten nationaler Minderheiten in China* (Politics of Nationalities and Development in the Areas of National Minorities in China). Bremen, Germany: Bremer Beiträge zur Geographie und Raumplanung, Universität Bremen.

Mackerras, Colin. (1995) *China's Minority Cultures: Identities and Integration since 1912*. Melbourne, Australia, and New York: Longman and St. Martin's Press.

NATIONAL PEACEKEEPING COUNCIL—THAILAND

The National Peacekeeping Council (NPC) was the military junta headed by General Suchinda Kraprayoon, who briefly administered Thailand following the 23 February 1991 coup that ousted Prime Minister Chatichai Choonhaven. Although the military claims to have staged the coup for the public good in order to stem the rampant corruption of the Chatichai government, the military leadership was concerned about its declining political role in governing. The NPC disbanded parliament and imposed restrictions on the media, but it allowed political parties to continue operating and pledged to restore democracy. The NPC appointed the respected bureaucrat and former businessman Anand Panyarachun interim premier until a new constitution was promulgated.

The NPC's new constitution gave the military substantial political power, including control over the senate and a provision for the appointment of an unelected premier. Despite a pledge to restore politics to civilians, the military established a political party, the Samakkee Tham (United in Virtue). After their candidate was accused by the United States of drug trafficking, coup leader Suchinda successfully contested the March 1992 election. Suchinda became prime minister on 7 April 1992, infuriating students and the middle class, which had been hit hard by the economic repercussions of the coup. After the military brutally crushed demonstrations, Suchinda was forced to resign on 24 May 1992.

Zachary Abuza

See also: **Thailand—Political Parties; Thailand—Political System.**

Further Reading

Fry, Gerald. (1992) "'Saturday Surprise,' the February 23, 1991 Coup in Thailand: The Role of the Military in Politics." Washington, DC: Institute for the Study of Diplomacy, School of Foreign Service, Georgetown University.

———. (1992) "The February 1991 Coup in Thailand: Thailand's Painful Path to Democracy." Washington, DC: Institute for the Study of Diplomacy, School of Foreign Service, Georgetown University.

Murray, David. (1996) *Angels and Devils: Thai Politics from 1991 to September 1992: A Struggle for Democracy?* Bangkok, Thailand: White Orchard Press.

NATIONAL TAIWAN UNIVERSITY

The National Taiwan University is the oldest and the most prestigious university in Taiwan. Its antecedent was the Taihoku (Taipei) Imperial University, founded by the Japanese colonial government in 1928. When the Taihoku University was first established, it had only two colleges with sixty students. It was then expanded to include five colleges with 302 students before the end of World War II.

Following Taiwan's retrocession to Chinese sovereignty in 1945, the Nationalist government resumed the administration of the Taihoku University and renamed it National Taiwan University. Dr. Lo Tsung-lo, a Japan-trained botanist, was appointed by the Ministry of Education as the first president. In the 2000 academic year, the university had in total ten colleges and eighty departments and graduate institutes with a student body of more than 27,000.

Over the past seventy years, the National Taiwan University produced many prominent people in various fields. In political circles, since the 1990s, its graduates gradually replaced politicians trained by universities in the Chinese mainland before 1949 and occupied most of the minister-level positions within the government.

Chang Jui-te

NATIONAL UNITY PARTY—MYANMAR

The National Unity Party (NUP) of Myanmar (Burma) is the successor to the Burma Socialist Programme Party (BSPP) of General Ne Win, which collapsed during the 1988 pro-democracy protests. Although publicized as a change in political direction, the NUP inherited much of its membership and infrastructure from the defunct BSPP. Its leadership consisted of former BSPP functionaries and retired military officers, including the party's founding chairman, U Tha Kyaw.

The NUP was promoted by the ruling State Law and Order Restoration Council (SLORC) in the run-up to the 1990 general election, which it clearly expected the party to win. In the event, the NUP won only ten seats, although its supporters argued that this was an unfair showing for 25 percent of the nationwide vote. Subsequently, NUP officials began attending sessions of the SLORC-convened National Convention, which was assigned the task of drawing up Myanmar's new constitution.

However, after 1993 the role of the NUP appeared to be superseded by the formation of another new body, the Union Solidarity and Development Association. A mass organization with more than 5 million members, the USDA was more often publicized in the state-controlled media than the NUP to try and demonstrate civilian support for the military government. Such moves suggested that the NUP had failed to establish itself as the political face of the Burmese armed forces in the post-BSPP era.

Martin Smith

Further Reading

Diller, Janelle. (1997) "The National Convention: An Impediment to the Restoration of Democracy." In *Burma:*

The Challenge of Change in a Divided Society, edited by Peter Carey. Basingstoke, U.K.: Macmillan, 27–54.

Steinberg, David. (1997) "The Union Solidarity and Development Association: Mobilization and Orthodoxy in Myanmar." *Burma Debate* 4, 1: 4–11.

NATIONAL UNIVERSITY OF SINGAPORE

National University of Singapore (NUS) is a multidisciplinary, publicly funded university. It is Singapore's oldest, biggest, and most comprehensive tertiary educational institution. Its roots go back to 1905, when Singapore's first medical school was established. Its lineage of predecessor institutions includes the University of Malaya (Singapore), Raffles College, the University of Singapore, and Nanyang University. NUS was inaugurated after the University of Singapore merged with Nanyang University.

From the initial seven, the student enrollment at the turn of the century was more than 30,000 undergraduate and graduate students. English being the medium of instruction, more than 20 percent of NUS students come from outside Singapore.

Located on 150 hectares of undulating green on Singapore's west coast, NUS offers courses in business, computing, dentistry, engineering, the humanities, law, medicine, and sciences. NUS is also actively engaged in research and development activities. Collaboration with national research institutes and industry enriches its research culture. With its extensive student and alumni base, NUS graduates have made their mark in all sectors of Singapore's government, economy, and society.

Chiu-Ai Ngooi

Further Reading

"National University of Singapore." (2002) Retrieved 23 May 2001, from: http://www.nus.edu.sg.

Singapore Facts and Pictures. (2001) Singapore: Ministry of Information and the Arts.

NATSAGDORJ, DASHDORJIYN (1906–1937),

Mongolian writer, poet, playwright. Dashdorjiyn Natsagdorj, considered one of the founding fathers of modern Mongolian literature, was born in Tov Province of an impoverished noble family and, due to an absence of formalized education in Mongolia, received much of his early education from a tutor. By 1923, Natsagdorj was a member of the Mongolian People's Revolutionary Party, through which he participated in revolutionary activities as well as in the first theatrical group in Ulaanbaatar, for which he wrote plays and songs. Between 1925 and 1929 Natsagdorj studied in Soviet Russia and Germany. After returning to Mongolia in 1929, he worked for the Mongolian Committee of Science, where his activities included historical research and translating, but he also contributed to Mongolian theater as a playwright.

The 1930s were difficult for Natsagdorj. In 1932, Communist writers accused him of nationalist leanings because his writings emphasized themes of patriotism rather than identifying with the international proletariat, and he was subsequently imprisoned for six months. Then his wife, Pagmadulma, and daughter, Anandaa-Shirii, were sent to Leningrad in 1935 under mysterious circumstances. For the remaining two years of his life, Natsagdorj was deeply depressed. Although reflecting a different era, his opera *Uchirtay Gurvan Tolgoy* (Three Sad Hills) and famous poem "Minii Nutag" (My Homeland) form the cornerstones of modern Mongolian literature.

Timothy M. May

Further Reading

Hangin, John Gombojab. (1967) "Dashdorjiin Natsagdorj." *The Mongolia Society* 6: 15–22.

Sodnom, B. D. (1961) *Natsagdorj zoxioluud* (The Literature of Natsagdorj). Ulaanbaatar, Mongolia: Committee of Mongolian Writers, Mongolian People's Republic Academy of Sciences.

NATSUME SOSEKI (1867–1916),

novelist and scholar. Natsume Soseki was born in Tokyo under the name of Natsume Kinosuke but adopted the pseudonym Natsume Soseki as a writer. Soseki and Mori Rintaro (1862–1922), who wrote under the pen name of Mori Ogai, are widely regarded as the twin titans of modern Japanese literature. Soseki was sent to England as a government student in 1900 and returned to Japan in 1903 to replace Lafcadio Hearn (1850–1904) as lecturer in English Literature at Tokyo Imperial University (now University of Tokyo). With his first novel, *Wagahai wa neko de aru* (I Am a Cat, 1905–1906), a satire on par with Laurence Sterne's *Tristram Shandy*, Soseki made his mark and quickly established himself as a novelist. This work was closely followed by his 1906 works, *Botchan* (Little Master) and *Kusamakura* (Grass Pillow), which was translated and published as *The Three-Cornered World*. He quit teaching in 1907 and joined the newspaper *Asahi shimbun*, in which his next ten novels were serialized, approximately one each year. His later novels, in contrast to his humorous early works, reveal profound psychological insight.

Plagued by deteriorating health and poor marital relations, in his later works Soseki probed the alienation and isolation of the modern intellectual. His final and unfinished novel, *Meian* (Light and Darkness, 1916), the literary critic Eto Jun called one of the few Japanese modern novels that deserves the name of a true modern novel. It shows the possibilities of the Meiji period novel for sharp social commentary.

William Ridgeway

Further Reading

Doi Takeo. (1976) *The Psychological World of Natsume Soseki*. Trans. by William Jefferson Tyler. Cambridge, MA: Harvard University Press.

Iijima Takehisa, and James M. Vardaman, eds. (1987) *The World of Natsume Soseki*. Tokyo: Kinseido.

McClellan, Edwin. (1969) *Two Japanese Novelists: Soseki and Toson*. Chicago: University of Chicago Press.

Yiu, Angela. (1998) *Chaos and Order in the Works of Natsume Soseki*. Honolulu: University of Hawaii Press.

Yu, Beongcheon. (1969) *Natsume Soseki*. New York: Twayne.

NAVA'I , MIR 'ALI SHIR (1441–1501), Uzbekistan poet and cultural and political figure. Mir 'Ali Shir Nava'i (also Navoi, Nawa'i) was born in Herat into a family of scribes and literati; there he became a school companion of Sultan Husayn Bayqara. The young 'Ali Shir left Herat and studied at Samarqand amid political instabilities. Returning in 1469 with the accession of Sultan Husayn, he passed the rest of his life in the Sultan's service, despite periods of disfavor. He had the rank of amir (mir) and held some offices briefly, but in general he avoided official positions. His personal intimacy with Sultan Husayn gave him extraordinary powers, as when he governed Herat in the sultan's absence.

Nava'i 's greatest legacy is in the sphere of culture. He is credited with perfecting Chagatay Turkic as a literary language. His influence as a patron of literature, science, architecture, painting, calligraphy, and music was a vital catalyst in the cultural efflorescence of late-fifteenth-century Herat. A pupil of Naqshbandi Sufism under his friend, the mystic savant Jami (1414–1492), Nava'i used his wealth to endow about 370 mosques, *madrasahs* (Islamic seminaries), and other pious institutions. Nava'i has been revered by Islamic Turkic peoples; the State Library and other institutions in Uzbekistan bear his name.

D. Prior

Further Reading

Barthold, Vasilii V. ([1928] 1962) "Mir 'Ali Shir." In *Four Studies on the History of Central Asia* 3, trans. by Vladimir and Tatiana Minorsky. Leiden, Netherlands: E. J. Brill, 1–72.

Mir 'Ali Shir. (1966) *The Muhakamat al-Lughatain (Judgment of Two Languages)*. Trans. by Robert Devereux. Leiden: E. J. Brill.

[Mir] Alisher Navoii. (1963–1968) *Asarlar: Un besh tomlik* (trans. *Works, in 15 Volumes*), edited by Porso Shamsiev. Tashkent, Uzbekistan: Badiii Adabiët Nashriëti.

NAW ROOZ. See **No-ruz.**

NAZARBAEV, NURSULTAN (b. 1940), president of the Republic of Kazakhstan. Nursultan Nazarbaev was born in the town of Chemolgan. He joined the Communist Party of Kazakhstan (CPKaz) in 1962 while he was studying at the Karaganda (Qaraghandy) Metallurgical Combine in Kazakhstan. Rising through the CPKaz party ranks, Nazarbaev eventually became the first secretary of the Karaganda Oblast (Region) CPKaz Committee. In 1984, he assumed the position of chairman of the Council of Ministers of the Kazakh Soviet Socialist Republic, and, in 1989, first secretary of the CPKaz. In 1990, he was elected president of the Kazakh Socialist Soviet Republic, a position he held when Kazakhstan became an independent republic in December 1991.

Since independence, Nursultan Nazarbaev has maintained his hold on power. A referendum on 30 April 1995 extended his tenure as president until the year 2000. Calling an early election, he won a seven-year term in 10 January 1999 by 82 percent of the vote, with his main rival, Serikbolsyn Abdildin, receiving only 12 percent.

In the late 1990s and early 2000s, Nazarbaev has expanded his presidential powers by decree. He can appoint and dismiss the cabinet and regional officials, dissolve parliament, call referenda, and initiate constitutional amendments. Western governments have been critical of his authoritarian tendencies and human-rights record. However, the energy wealth of Kazakhstan, as well as its strategic location (south of Russia and west of China), ensures that the country will remain of some importance in international affairs.

Roger D. Kangas

Further Reading

Colton, Timothy J., and Robert C. Tucker, eds. (1995) *Patterns in Post-Soviet Leadership*. Boulder, CO: Westview Press.

Cummings, Sally, ed. (2001) *Power and Change in Central Asia*. London: Routledge.
Nazarbaev, Nursultan. (1998) *Kazakhstan—2030*. Almaty, Kazakhstan: Bilim.
Olcott, Martha Brill. (2002) *Kazakhstan: Unfulfilled Promises*. Washington, DC: Carnegie Endowment.

NE WIN, U (b. 1911), dictator of Myanmar. U Ne Win ruled Myanmar (Burma) from 1962, when he took power in a military coup, until his resignation as chairman of the single ruling party, the Burma Socialist Programme Party (BSPP), in July 1988. He is best known for his abolition and suppression of democratic institutions and for undermining the principle of an independent judiciary, culminating in his consolidation of the legislature, executive, and judiciary in 1972.

Known from youth as Shu Maung, he attended University College in Rangoon (now Yangon) from 1929 to 1931, hoping to study medicine. However, uninspired by university life, he failed his exams and did not finish his degree. Supporting the Ba Sein-Tun Oke Thahkin, a right-wing political faction, he ended up opposing more radical university students such as U Nu and Aung San. Among the Thirty Comrades sent to Japan for military training, Shu Maung took the nom de guerre Bo Ne Win on 26 December 1941 at the founding of the Burma Independence Army before it marched into Burma.

At national independence Ne Win served as second commander in chief of the army. He was briefly deputy prime minister and minister of defense and home affairs (1949–1950). When ethnic insurgency became severe, Ne Win was promoted to chief of the army, and, in 1958, he was asked to serve as prime minister in the caretaker government. He stood down after the 1960 elections returned U Nu to power.

General Ne Win U at Arlington National Cemetery in Washington, D.C., in September 1966. (BETTMANN/CORBIS)

On 2 March 1962, Ne Win carried out a coup d'état: he imprisoned U Nu and established the Revolutionary Council, whose original members (excepting one civilian) were drawn from the armed forces. He advocated the "Burmese Way to Socialism," which brought Burma into isolation, supervised by the BSPP, which Ne Win founded in 1962. Forgoing democratic elections and relying on army support, he occupied the most important positions of government and state between 1962 and 1988—chairman of the Revolutionary Council (until 1974) and subsequently president (until 1981, when he relinquished the office to San Yu), chairman of the BSPP (from 1962), and chairman of the BSPP Executive Committee. By his complete control and use of the army, he was able to maintain his control until 1988. Still, his government was plagued by administrative inefficiency.

The gradual decline in the Burmese economy eventually caused Ne Win to devalue the kyat in November 1985 and again in September 1987, which wiped out the savings of the poor. This resulted in major protests and the reassertion of demands for democratic reforms. At an Extraordinary Party Congress in July 1988, Ne Win announced his resignation and called for multiparty elections. Though the May 1990 elections resulted in a landslide victory for the National League for Democracy, power was not transferred, and army personnel with close personal ties to Ne Win continued to hold power in the State Law and Order Restoration Council and subsequent State Peace and Development Council regimes.

Gustaaf Houtman

Further Reading

Badgley, John Herbert, and Jon A. Wiant. (1974) "The Ne Win-BSPP Style of Bama-Lo." In *The Future of Burma in Perspective*, edited by Josef Silverstein. Athens: Ohio University Press.
Everton, John. (1964) "The Ne Win Regime in Burma." *Asia* 2: 1–17.
Maung Maung, Gyi. (1974) "The Crucial Third Dialectic of Burma's Neutralism under U Ne Win." In *The Future of Burma in Perspective*, edited by Josef Silverstein. Athens, OH: Ohio University Press.
Maung Maung, U. (1969) *Burma and General Ne Win*. London: Asia Publishing House.

Silverstein, Josef. (1966) "Burma: Ne Win's Revolution Reconsidered." *Asian Survey* 6, 2: 95–104.
Yawnghwe, Chao Tzang. (1990) "Ne Win's Tatmadaw Dictatorship." M.A. thesis, University of British Columbia.

NEEDHAM, JOSEPH (1900–1995), British expert on Chinese science. Joseph Needham was a prolific twentieth-century writer on Chinese science and technology. He was born in London into a middle-class intellectual family. Educated at the University of Cambridge in England, Needham was already an embryologist of some distinction in 1937, when his interests in the history of science and Chinese civilization prompted his study of Mandarin Chinese. War in Asia took him to China in 1943 to work with Chinese scientists and learn more about China's remarkable scientific traditions.

After returning to Cambridge in 1948, Needham began writing *Science and Civilization in China*, a complete exploration of China's scientific and technological past. At first, Needham thought that his survey might be no more than 800 pages, but he later expanded the work to seven volumes embracing all aspects of Chinese physics, mathematics, chemistry, astronomy, agriculture, and engineering. As he investigated each tradition, Needham uncovered more and more evidence of Chinese contributions in these fields. Joined in his effort by leading Chinese, European, and American experts, *Science and Civilization in China* now includes seventeen volumes with a dozen more in preparation.

Joseph Needham's interest in the history of Chinese science stimulated many Asian scholars to explore and document their own scientific past. The founding of several prominent research institutes and museums in China, Japan, and Korea devoted to Asian science, technology, and medicine are due in part to Needham's enthusiasm and encouragement.

Paul Forage

Further Reading

Needham, Joseph. (1969) *The Grand Titration: Science and Society in East and West*. Toronto: University of Toronto Press.
Needham, Joseph, et al. (1986) *Heavenly Clockwork: The Great Astronomical Clocks of Medieval China*. 2d ed. Cambridge, U.K.: Cambridge University Press.

NEGERI SEMBILAN (2002 est. pop. 874,700). Negeri Sembilan is a state on the west coast of Malaysia. The term "Negeri Sembilan," which means "Nine States" in Malay, historically refers to nine districts or small chieftaincies under the suzerainty of the sultan of Johor from around 1640 to 1760. Negeri Sembilan covers an area of 6,643 square kilometers and has a population approaching 880,000: 53 percent Malay, 30 percent Chinese, 16 percent Indian, and 1 percent other. Its capital is Seremban. Port Dickson, which lies in the district of Pantai Laut, is well known for its beaches and resorts. The features that distinguish Negeri Sembilan from the other states in Malaysia are its architecture—the buffalo horn–shaped roof peaks—and its matrilineal system *(adat perpateh)*, both being legacies of the Minangkabau people.

Historically, the Minangkabau people were from Sumatra. In the eighteenth century, they were attracted to the gold districts of Pahang State and the valleys of what was later known as Negeri Sembilan. When they came, they brought their unique matrilineal system. The coming of the Bugis, a seafaring race, in the early eighteenth century contributed to a decline of Malay power, and the control of the Johor sultanate became less and less effective. The Minangkabau population was reluctant to offer allegiance to the Bugis. The Negeri Sembilan chiefs asked the sultan of Johor to let them have a prince to govern the country and drive out the enemy, but the sultan would not give them a prince. With permission from the sultan of Johor, the chiefs referred to the Minangkabaus in Sumatra. The sultan in Minangkabau gave them one of his sons, Raja Melewar, who became the first *yang di-pertuan besar*, or *yamtuan besar* (ruler), in 1773.

In the 1820s, there were five claimants to the Negeri Sembilan throne. Civil wars led to British intervention in 1874. Before the 1870s, Britain had a policy of noninvolvement in the affairs of the Malay states, although it had extensive trading interests there. In 1895, a British resident, Martin Lister, was appointed for the whole of Negeri Sembilan. The role of the resident was to advise the sultan on how to improve the administration of his state. Although the resident was to have no executive powers, his advice had to be sought and acted upon in all matters other than those relating to Malay religion and customs. It was a system used to exercise British influence over the Malay states. The three general aims were the establishment of law and order, the centralized collection of revenue, and the development of the resources of the states. Lister died in 1897 and was succeeded by E. W. Birch, who effected the union of the Negeri Sembilan states and ended the civil war by the election of Tengku Muhammad as the *yang di-pertuan besar* of the whole state.

In 1896, Negeri Sembilan, together with the states of Selangor, Perak, and Pahang, formed the Federated Malay States. In 1948, the Federated Malay States became part of the Federation of Malaya. The federation gained independence from British colonial rule in 1957. Together with Sabah and Sarawak, the federation formed Malaysia in 1963.

Yik Koon Teh

Further Reading

Andaya, Barbara Watson, and Leonard Y. Andaya. (1982) *A History of Malaysia*. London: Macmillan.

Eliot, Joshua, and Jane Bickersteth, eds. (1995) *Indonesia, Malaysia and Singapore Handbook*. Bath, U.K: Trade and Travel Publications.

Khoo, Kay Kim. (1975) *The Western Malay States 1850–1973*. Kuala Lumpur, Malaysia: Oxford University Press.

Ryan, N. J. (1969) *The Making of Modern Malaysia and Singapore: A History from Earliest Times to 1966*. Kuala Lumpur, Malaysia: Oxford University Press.

Wilkinson, R. J., ed. (1971) *Papers on Malay Subjects*. Kuala Lumpur, Malaysia: Oxford University Press.

Winstedt, Richard O. (1966) *Malaya and Its History*. London: Hutchinson & Co.

———. (1982) *A History of Malaya*. Kuala Lumpur, Malaysia: Marican & Sons.

Jawaharlal Nehru in the 1940s. (CORBIS)

NEHRU, JAWAHARLAL (1889–1964), Indian politician. Jawaharlal Nehru was born 14 November 1889 in Allahabad. His father Motilal Nehru (1861–1931) was a rich lawyer who sent him to England in 1905 for an elite education at Harrow, Cambridge, and London. He returned to India in 1912 and practiced law. In 1917, he joined the Home Rule League.

After the Amritsar massacre in 1919, Nehru was a close associate of Mahatma Gandhi (1869–1948) in the Indian National Congress (INC). Nehru was influenced by Marxist ideas and was cofounder of the Indian branch of the League against Imperialism. Ideologically, he differed from Gandhi in many ways, but Gandhi sponsored him twice for the presidency of the INC in 1929 and 1936, as Gandhi was aware of Nehru's influence on the younger generation.

Nehru's autobiography, published in London in 1936, was widely appreciated as a moving document of the Indian freedom struggle. In August 1946 the Viceroy of India appointed him interim prime minister. He continued as prime minister of independent India. As a passionate parliamentarian, he laid the foundations of India's democracy. Under his leadership the INC won the general elections of 1952, 1957, and 1962. The INC retained a "centrist" position profiting from the polarization of incompatible opposition parties. The Planning Commission, with the prime minister as ex-officio chairman, was established by cabinet resolution in 1950. The Five Year Plans inaugurated by Nehru in this capacity stressed rapid industrialization based on public-sector enterprises. He advocated a "socialist pattern of society" and insisted that the state should control the "commanding heights of the economy."

In his foreign policy Nehru supported both the idea of Afro-Asian solidarity (Bandung Conference, 1955) and the movement of nonaligned nations (Belgrade Conference, 1961). He first met Egyptian prime minister Gamal Abdel Nasser (1918–1970) and Yugoslav leader Josip Broz Tito (1892–1980) in 1954 and joined with them in sponsoring the nonaligned movement. In spite of his commitment to this movement, he also cultivated good relations with the Soviet Union, whose economic achievements he had admired since visiting it for the first time in 1927. He also thought of Communist China as an anti-imperialist power and hoped for peaceful coexistence with it. This hope was shattered by the border war of October 1962 when Chinese troops invaded India. His health broke down after this experience, and he died in May 1964.

Dietmar Rothermund

NEHRU MOVES FOR INDEPENDENCE

At the Indian National Congress in Madras in 1927, Jawaharlal Nehru offered the "Independence Resolution."

> It is my high privilege to place before you the resolution on Independence (Cheers).
>
> The resolution reads thus:
>
> The Congress declares the goal of the Indian people to be complete national independence.
>
> I do not think I can describe this resolution in any better language than that used by the distinguished Ex-President of the Congress, Dr. Annie Besant, in an interview which she gave immediately after the Subject Committee had accepted this resolution. She said that it was a dignified and clear statement of India's goal (Cheers).
>
> No special remarks are necessary from me in commending this resolution for your acceptance specially after the almost complete unanimity with which the Subject Committee approved of it. But I wish to explain very clearly one or two points connected with this resolution. The first thing is that this resolution although it makes clear the goal does not change the present creed of the Congress. If you pass this resolution you declare by a majority. I hope by an overwhelming majority that the Congress is to-day for complete independence. Nonetheless you have the doors of the Congress open to such persons as may not approve of this goal as they perhaps are satisfied with a lesser or a smaller goal. I think that although the door of the Congress is open, there should be no doubt if you approve of this resolution then everybody must say that the majority of the Congressmen today demand complete independence for the country. Now this resolution as placed before you is a very short and simple one. In the Subject Committee the resolution as you may know because the proceedings are quite public was slightly longer and more complicated. But ultimately it was changed to this present formula and this formula was adopted.
>
> I wish to make it clear to you that the adoption of this formula does not in any way change the spirit or the meaning of the resolution. It means what it says. It means complete independence. It means control of the defense forces of the country. It means control over the financial and economic policy of the country. It means control over the relations with the foreign countries. (Hear, Hear). Without these things independence would be a travesty and camouflage.
>
> Thirdly I wish to point out to you lest there be any mistake that this goal which I hope you will adopt today is the immediate goal and not a goal of the far distant future (Cheers). Whether we achieve it today or tomorrow, a year hence or 10 years hence I cannot say. That depends on your strength and the strength of the country.
>
> May I in conclusion express my heartfelt gratitude that the Congress is about to adopt the goal worthy of our country's high destiny and hope that this goal may be reached in the near future (Cheers).
>
> (He then explained the resolution in Hindi.)

Source: Jagdish Saran Sharma. (1965) *India's Struggle for Freedom: Select Documents and Sources*. Vol. II. Delhi: S. Chand & Co., 276–277.

Further Reading

Brecher, Michael. (1959) *Nehru—A Political Biography*. London: Oxford University Press.

Nehru, Jawaharlal. (1936) *Toward Freedom: The Autobiography of Jawaharlal Nehru*. London: Bodley Head.

NEHRU, MOTILAL (1861–1931), Indian politician and nationalist. Motilal Nehru was the father of the first prime minister of independent India, Jawaharlal Nehru. Born in Agra, in north India, in 1861, Motilal was descended from a family of high-caste

Kashmiri Brahmans. He established a legal practice in Allahabad, becoming one of the highest paid and most successful lawyers in India. A product of Western education, he was strong willed, with a steely individualism, widely traveled, and English in manners, dress, and temperament. He took a keen interest in liberal politics and was an outspoken member of the Indian National Congress Party. His interest in Indian nationalism deepened over time and, under the influence of Mohandas Karamchand Gandhi (1869–1948) and his own son, he began to wear traditional Indian clothes. He married twice and had two daughters in addition to his son Jawaharlal.

Nehru took an active part in espousing a strategy of moderation and cooperation with the British regime at the provincial legislative level to achieve constitutional advance, and he played an important role in brokering amity between Hindus and Muslims through the political cooperation of the Congress and the Muslim League embodied in the Lucknow Pact of 1916. He was elected president of the Congress in 1919 and was a member of the Congress Inquiry Committee that investigated the 1919 Amritsar massacre. In 1920 he was general secretary of the Congress, and during the Non-Cooperation Movement (1920–1922), he was imprisoned for six months. Along with C. R. Das, he set up the Swaraj (self-rule) Party in March 1923, which contested the elections to the new legislatures in November of that year, and as a result Motilal won a seat in the Central Legislative Assembly. He believed in the efficacy of working from within the system to further nationalist demands. Elected president of the Congress again in 1928, he formulated the Nehru Report, which was endorsed by the Congress as the formal demand for dominion status with full self-government, giving Britain one year in which to respond before the declaration of a demand for full independence would be made. Though India's independence was to come in 1947, actions of men like Motilal Nehru paved the way for the education of his fellow citizens in the workings of parliamentary government.

Chandrika Kaul

Further Reading

Chablani, S. P. (1961) *Motilal Nehru: Essays and Reflections on His Life and Times.* New Delhi: S. Chand.

Lamb, Beatrice Pitney. (1967) *The Nehrus of India: Three Generations of Leadership.* New York: Macmillan.

NEI MONGGOL (1996 pop. 23.6 million). Bordering on the Mongolian People's Republic and Russia in the north, Nei Monggol, or Inner Mongolia, is China's northern frontier. It is an oblong strip of land, extending from northeast to southwest, with an area of 1.2 million square kilometers. Internally, it borders on Gansu, Ningxia, Shaanxi, Shanxi, Liaoning, Jilin, and Heilongjiang Provinces. It is home to the Mongolian, Han, Hui, Manchu, Daur, and Ewenki peoples.

Nei Monggol, with a temperate continental monsoonal climate, has a cold, long winter with frequent blizzards and a warm, short summer. With its vast stretch of grasslands, it is a major stockbreeding center known for its Sanhe horses, Sanhe oxen, and fine wool sheep. Daxinganling Forest, in Nei Monggol's northeast sector, makes up one-sixth of China's total forest reserve. Apart from wheat, naked oats, millet, sorghum, maize, and rice, a wide range of cash crops is grown, including soybeans, linseed, rapeseed, castor oil plants, and sugar beets. Inner Mongolia holds first place in the country in rare earth metals and niobium and natural soda reserves and second place in coal reserves.

Huhehaote, capital of Nei Monggol, is an ancient city that is located north of the Great Wall. Baotou, another major city in the region, is one of China's major iron- and steel-producing centers.

Di Bai

NEO-CONFUCIANISM "Neo-Confucianism" is the Western term given to a major phase in the development and reformulation of Confucianism beginning in eleventh-century Song-dynasty China. It brought a revival of classical Confucian values, texts, concepts, and practices that were clothed in new language and given new interpretations, reflecting the changed social and cultural conditions of the Song. At the same time, it responded to the philosophical and religious challenges that came from Buddhism and Taoism in the postclassical age of the Zhou and Han dynasties (eleventh century BCE–third century CE).

Many of the contributions of this Confucian revival were summed up, synthesized, and systematized by the late-Song scholar, philosopher, and teacher Zhu Xi (1130–1200), whose teachings and texts became so dominant in East Asia that it was primarily Zhu's "learning" that came later to be identified as Neo-Confucianism. Earlier this teaching had been known variously as the Learning of the Way *(dao xue)*, the Learning of the Sages *(sheng xue)*, the Learning of Principle *(li xue)*, the Learning of Human Nature and Principle *(xingli xue)*, and the Learning of the Mind-and-Heart *(xin xue)*. Each of these names referred to an important aspect of the larger, multifaceted learning that inspired and informed a whole new cultural era in East Asia. Subsequently, this learning came to stand for the established tradition in East Asia, and to twentieth-century modernizers it represented the stolid past from which they sought to break.

MOUNT WUYI—WORLD HERITAGE SITE

Mount Wuyi in southeast China was designated a UNESCO World Heritage Site in 1999 for the outstanding natural beauty and biodiversity of the Nine Bend River, and the cultural and historic importance of its many monasteries. The concentration of religious study and practice in the area led to the Neo-Confucian movement in the eleventh century.

Zhu Xi and the Origins of Neo-Confucianism in China

At its inception Neo-Confucianism arose from a renewed concern for civil government as opposed to warlordism in the late ninth and early tenth centuries. It aimed to achieve "Great Peace and Order" (Taiping) through the establishment of civilized institutions. The pervasive ideal of public service at this stage was expressed by the Song statesman Fan Zhongyan (989–1052) in his characterization of the Confucian ideal of the noble person as "first in worrying about the world's worries and last in enjoying its pleasures" (de Bary and Bloom 1999: 596). Fan, using the rulership ideal of the Confucian thinker Mencius, expressed the kind of active solicitude a king should have placing the welfare of his people first in contrast to the Buddhist bodhisattva who first sought the peace of Nirvana before returning to share it with others.

Along with attempting reforms in the political economy and education, Fan invited the scholar-teacher Hu Yuan (993–1059) to court. Hu Yuan was an educator who emphasized both the principles of classical Confucianism and their practical implementation through specialized studies in law, mathematics, military arts, and water control. Many of Fan Zhongyan's reformist ideals, especially in education and the civil service, were carried forward by the statesman Wang Anshi (1021–1086), who emphasized strong government intervention in the economy and an active development policy to achieve a kind of welfare state. Wang's measures, which claimed the sanction of the Confucian classics, especially the *Zhou li* (Institutes of Zhou), were nevertheless called "New Laws" because of their innovative character. These policies reflected the pervasive spirit of innovation and adaptation in those times, which also fostered and stimulated new philosophical formulations.

In response to the radical challenge of Mahayana Buddhism, several philosophical speculations, which later became incorporated in Zhu Xi's system, aimed to provide a better metaphysical foundation for the new civil order. In contrast to the Buddhist view of impermanence and the insubstantiality of all things, Zhou Dunyi (1017–1073), basing his philosophy on the *Yi jing* (Classic of Changes), characterized the Way *(dao)* as a vital process of creation and re-creation, in which change is marked by growth and renewal, not constant negation. This Way he saw not only as nonfinite and limitless *(wuji)* but also as a route toward the perfecting of the natures of all things *(taiji)*. As an alternative to realizing an ineffable Buddhahood, Zhou proposed the cultivation of sagehood—the perfecting of a spirituality based on human moral and intellectual values.

Another Song thinker whose ideas were incorporated in Zhu Xi's later synthesis was Zhang Zai (1020–1077), who affirmed the psychophysical substance *(qi)* as the vital force in all things and, in his *Xi ming* (Western Inscription), advocated an ethical cultivation aimed at achieving unity with all creation. Two other Song thinkers, Cheng Hao (1032–1085) and Cheng Yi (1033–1077), pursued the idea of cultivating sagehood to achieve the "Humaneness which forms one body with Heaven and Earth and all things" (de Bary and Bloom 1999: 694). The Cheng brothers saw the "one body" as a compound of *qi* and a generic and genetic principle *(li)* inherent in all things, which formed an inner and innate principle for growth. Principle, understood in a moral and rational sense, was to be dealt with in both its unity and diversity. Humaneness stood for the underlying empathetic attraction among all things, while the practice of humaneness was differentiated according to the specific relations of things, such as filiality in relation to parents or rightness in relation to rulers.

Zhu Xi anthologized these and other ideas of his predecessors in a manual of self-cultivation entitled *Jinsi-lu*, which can be translated as both "A Record of Recent Thought" and "Thinking about Things Near-at-Hand." He also wrote commentaries on key classic texts—the *Da Xue* (Great Learning), the *Analects* of Confucius, the text of *Mencius*, and the *Chong yong*

WANG YANG-MING ON INSANITY

There are cases when people see their fathers, sons, or brothers falling into a deep abyss and getting drowned. They cry, crawl, go naked and barefooted, stumble and fall. They hang onto dangerous cliffs and go down to save them. Some gentlemen who see them behave like this talk, laugh, or bow ceremoniously to one another by their side. They consider them to be insane because they have discarded etiquette and taken off their clothing, and because they cry, stumble, and fall as they do. . . . In the case of fathers, sons, and brothers, because of love one will surely feel an ache in his head and a pain in his heart, run desperately until he has lost his breath, and crawl to save them. He even ignores the danger of drowning himself. How much more will he ignore being ridiculed as insane! And how much more will he fail to worry about whether people believe him or not! Alas! It is all right if people say that I am insane. The minds of all people are the same as mine. There are people who are insane. How can I not be so? There are people who have lost their minds. How can I not lose mine?

Source: Chan, tsit-Wing, trans. (1963) *Instructions for Practical Living and Other Neo-Confucian Writings of Wang Yang-ming.* Section 181. New York: Columbia University Press.

(Doctrine of the Mean)—thereafter called the Four Books. The *Chong yong* and the *Da Xue* were chapters excerpted from the classical *Li ji* (Record of Rites). In his important prefaces to these two works, Zhu stressed the need for universal schooling and individual cultivation as the basis for all governance and public morality, combining intellectual investigation with moral judgment to arrive at a state of empathetic understanding of others and of all things. In his preface to the *Chong yong*, he spoke of the succession to or repossession of the Way of the Sages as based on both surviving classic texts and the recognition of basic principles in those texts by informed and insightful minds—emphasizing both textual evidence and public discourse—in contrast to private experience tacitly communicated from mind to mind through Chan (Zen) lineages. Zhu also advocated a method of self-examination and self-control, known as the Method of the Mind, which encouraged the exercise of proper value judgment as the way to achieve unity with others and indeed with all things sharing in the universality of principle and common psychophysical substance.

Further in pursuit of the educational ideal at the core of his philosophy, Zhu prepared another anthology, *Xiao Xue* (The Elementary Learning), which dealt with self-development and with the training of the young in the home and in social relations. *Xiao Xue* and the Four Books became standard texts in the Neo-Confucian curriculum, along with *Zhu Xi jiali* (The Family Ritual of Zhu Xi), Zhu's guide to family rituals simplified from the more complex and demanding rituals found in the ritual classics.

Through these new versions of old texts, Zhu reshaped and repackaged the classical Confucian tradition in a form that could be easily diffused through the new media of printed books (printing having come into wide use in the Song dynasty). In addition, Zhu, as a local official, promulgated guidelines for local schools and academies, for the organization of community compact organizations, and for community granaries. These institutions, in adapted form, became models for village life in much of East Asia. Even his lectures to the emperor on the classics became a standard practice and genre in the courts of China and Korea. Neo-Confucianism as it took shape in the hands of Zhu Xi was not only a systematic philosophy but also a comprehensive social and cultural program.

Since Zhu Xi in his own time was often at odds with the powers at court and his teachings were condemned as heterodox, the successful propagation of his ideas depended upon the independent efforts of his followers in local schools and academies. In the late thirteenth century, the Mongol emperor Kublai Khan (1215–1294) recognized the wide acceptance of Zhu's teachings among Confucian scholars, and he authorized them for official instruction in state schools. Zhu's texts became the basis of the Chinese civil-service examinations in 1314–1315, and they remained such until 1905. Meanwhile, Korean scholars at the Yuan-dynasty (1279–1368) court in China took these teachings back to Korea, where, under the Choson dynasty (1392–1910) they became the official state teaching and the principal form of learning in local academies sponsored by the *yangban* aristocracy.

Apart from its official uses, Neo-Confucianism emphasized scholarly study through broad learning *(boxue)* that was also called discursive learning *(jiang xue)* in lecture and discussion format. It also aimed at learning for oneself and self-cultivation through such practices as quiet sitting. Quiet sitting, though obviously influenced by Chan Buddhist meditation, stressed moral self-examination and cultivation of a spiritual state in which one experienced a sense of unity with Heaven, Earth, and all things.

The degree to which Neo-Confucians engaged in such spiritual exercises or devoted themselves instead to scholarly study or public service varied from school to school and scholar to scholar. Many scholars combined interior reflection with active public engagement. Others, recoiling from prevailing misrule, sought to disengage from official service altogether, so as to nourish and preserve their moral integrity and purity in relative isolation. Hence different strains of thought developed within the same Neo-Confucian frame of reference.

Neo-Confucianism during the Ming and Qing Dynasties

In the Ming dynasty, Wang Yang-ming (1472–1529) focused on the inner springs of moral sensibility to enliven a teaching that he saw as, by that time, too routinized in conduct and too given to book learning and literary embellishments. He encouraged a natural, spontaneous response to the moral promptings of the heart-and-mind (which he called "innate knowledge or knowing"). His contemporary and critic Luo Qinshun (1465–1547) tried to restore the balance in favor of objective learning and normative standards less given to subjective interpretation. Subsequently, the Donglin school also reacted against the moral relativism the more subjective wings of the Wang Yangming school seemed to fall into, but the attempt to rescue the late Ming dynasty from a decline in both intellectual and moral standards did not prevent the fall of the dynasty to the Manchus, who, after their conquest of China, promptly reaffirmed Zhu Xi's teachings as orthodox.

During the Qing dynasty (1644–1912), with Zhu Xi's texts established in the civil-service examinations and Neo-Confucian scholarship actively promoted by the Manchu rulers, the official scene was largely dominated by Neo-Confucianism. On the level of independent scholarly research, however, the resolution of contested philosophical issues brought increasing critical scrutiny of the classics as the basis for authoritative judgments on matters of authenticity and orthodoxy. The school of evidential learning, developed during the seventeenth and eighteenth centuries, excelled in textual criticism that advanced this critical scrutiny. Gu Yanwu (1613–1682) is generally regarded as the leading figure of evidential learning.

This Qing-era critical reexamination also extended to some of the metaphysical elements in Zhu Xi's philosophy of human nature, and the moralistic rigor of the early Zhu Xi school gave way to a view more accepting, and less restrictive of, human desire. Yet the basic curriculum in most schools, whether official or unofficial, remained the texts edited and interpreted by Zhu Xi. The terms of educated discourse and the general frame of intellectual reference, even among his critics, remained within the orbit of Zhu Xi's thought into the late nineteenth century. Also, since Zhu had given much attention to the reform of political and social institutions, the kind of historical scholarship and encyclopedic learning he encouraged continued to manifest itself in statecraft studies, increasingly critical of many dynastic institutions, a critical stance that would have a bearing on the readiness of Qing scholars later to consider new alternatives to established institutions and corrupt practices.

Neo-Confucianism in Korea and Japan

This same wide spectrum of Neo-Confucian activity was to be found in the Choson dynasty in Korea.

The new teaching had already found its way to Korea under the previous Koryo dynasty (918–1392), long dominated by Buddhism, and it inspired a new generation of scholars who subsequently installed Neo-Confucianism as the official ideology of the new Choson regime, incorporating many of its key institutions in a new constitutional order.

Leading Neo-Confucian scholars of this period included Yi Toegye (1502–1570), who emphasized self-cultivation through the inculcation of reverence as a basic virtue and quiet sitting as a form of personal praxis. At the same time, Toegye presented a broad range of scholarly studies similar to those of Zhu Xi and became the paragon of Zhu Xi learning in Korea.

Shortly after Toegye, Yi Yulgok (1536–1584), following the emphasis on empirical studies in the Neo-Confucian line of Luo Qinshun, greatly expanded the range of practical studies in the Zhu Xi school and laid the groundwork for the flowering of *silhak*, or "substantial learning" (also known as "practical learning"), which in the late eighteenth and early nineteenth centuries showed an interest in the Western studies made available through Jesuit missionaries in Beijing. Throughout this period, the Neo-Confucian texts and curriculum remained standard in Korean education and provided the terms of educated discourse.

Chinese Song-dynasty literature, and with it the texts of Zhu Xi, became available in Japan through Japanese Zen monks traveling and trading in China during the thirteenth and fourteenth centuries. For the most part, however, the study of Zhu's works had a low priority until, in the late sixteenth century, the process of Japan's unification and contacts with Korean scholarship gave a new impetus to Neo-Confucian studies, which had a direct relevance to the establishment of a new social order.

Ex-Zen monks like Fujiwara Seika (1561–1619), Hayashi Razan (1583–1657), and Yamazaki Ansai (1618–1682) were prominent among those who promoted Neo-Confucian studies. Razan established his own school under the patronage of Tokugawa Ieyasu (1543–1616), founder of the new Tokugawa shogunate, and Razan's successors enjoyed the hereditary patronage of the shoguns down until the end of the Tokugawa period in 1868, though they did not necessarily keep to a strict Zhu Xi orthodoxy.

Indeed, there was no institution in Tokugawa Japan equivalent to the civil bureaucracies and examination systems in China and Korea that could serve as a standard of official orthodoxy. Instead there was a variety of independent schools exhibiting different lines of study and teaching. Yamazaki Ansai emphasized culture of the mind-and-heart with close adherence to Zhu Xi and the practice of quiet sitting. Kaibara Ekken (1630–1714) popularized Neo-Confucian ethics as shared among different classes and status functions, but he also engaged in a range of empirical, scientific studies of nature. The Mito school emphasized dynastic history and the Confucian concept of loyalty. Townspeople in Osaka supported a local school, the Kaitokudo, teaching Neo-Confucian ethics in a form oriented to the educational level of the merchant class.

Eventually, scholars began to challenge some Song-era developments of Neo-Confucianism as manifestations of the subversive influence of Buddhism rather than true innovations of original Confucian ideals. Yamaga Soko (1622–1685), a military instructor of the samurai class, deplored the contemplative and quietistic tendencies of Song Neo-Confucianism, especially quiet sitting, as unsuited to the life of the samurai. Ito Jinsai (1627–1705) taught a fundamentalist brand of Confucianism, emphasizing the virtue of humaneness as found in the texts of Confucius and Mencius. Ogyu Sorai (1666–1728) insisted that Confucianism could be understood only in the total context of early Chinese history and society shown in the whole corpus of the Chinese classics and that it was applicable to Japan only in the context of Japanese institutions and their historical development. Each of these forms of Confucian revisionism put forward rival claims to a fundamentalism based on new, "literal" readings of classic texts in a contemporary setting; each also was reenacting the origins of Neo-Confucian revisionism in the Song.

Independent schools continued to proliferate in the late Tokugawa period, producing a wide variety of scholarship, some of it oriented toward Japanese tradition and some toward Western learning. Until the imperial restoration and renovation of the Meiji period (1868–1911), the basic texts used in most schools tended to be based on the Neo-Confucian curriculum set by Zhu Xi. Into the late nineteenth century, the intellectual and moral formation of most educated East Asians continued to be based on this Neo-Confucian discourse. Simply put, this common teaching focused on self-cultivation in a social context, with emphasis on the individual development of moral, rational, and affective nature so that the mind-and-heart entered empathetically, through shared principles and practical action, into "one body" with Heaven and Earth and all creation.

Wm. Theodore de Bary

Further Reading

Chan, Wing-tsit, ed. (1986) *Chu Hsi and Neo-Confucianism.* Honolulu: University of Hawaii Press.

de Bary, Wm. Theodore. (1991) *Learning for One's Self.* New York: Columbia University Press.
de Bary, W. T., Donald Keene, George Tanabe, and Paul Varley. (2001) *Sources of Japanese Tradition.* 2d ed. 2 vols. New York: Columbia University Press.
de Bary, W. T., and Irene Bloom, eds. (1999) *Sources of Chinese Tradition.* New York: Columbia University Press.
Fung Yu-lan. (1953) *A History of Chinese Philosophy.* Vol. 2. Princeton, NJ: Princeton University Press.
Lee, Peter H., and Wm. Theodore de Bary. (1997) *Sources of Korean Tradition.* 2d ed. Vol. 1. New York: Columbia University Press.
Yongho Ch'oe, Peter H. Lee, and Wm. Theodore de Bary. (2000) *Sources of Korean Tradition.* 2d ed. Vol. 2. New York: Columbia University Press.

NEPAL—PROFILE (2001 est. pop. 25.3 million). The kingdom of Nepal is a landlocked nation, 140,800 square kilometers in area, surrounded by the Tibetan region of China to the north and India to the east, west, and south. Its capital is Kathmandu. Agriculture is its mainstay, employing over 80 percent of the population although accounting for less than 47 percent of the gross domestic product. The mountainous nature of the nation allows for only about 20 percent of the total land area to be cultivated and also provides the government of Nepal with many challenges in providing basic infrastructure and services to its people. Population pressures on the land have led to deforestation and erosion of soils, causing landslides. With 42 percent of its population living below the poverty line, Nepal is among the poorest and least-developed nations of the world.

Geography

Nepal contains eight of the world's fourteen peaks that are over 8,000 meters in height, the most famous and tallest being Mount Everest (Sagarmatha) at 8,848 meters. Nepal has seventy-five administrative districts and can be divided into three geographical regions.

1. Terai region: This is a fertile plain found along the southern portion of Nepal bordering India. It constitutes close to 23 percent of the nation's area; 40 percent of the Terai region is under cultivation. The subtropical climate and fertile soil make it the grain belt of Nepal. Population pressure and declining productivity of agriculture in the hills have led to migration to the Terai, increasing its population, which as of 1991 constituted 46.7 percent of the total population.

2. Hill region: This is an area ranging in altitude from 610 meters to 4,877 meters, constituting

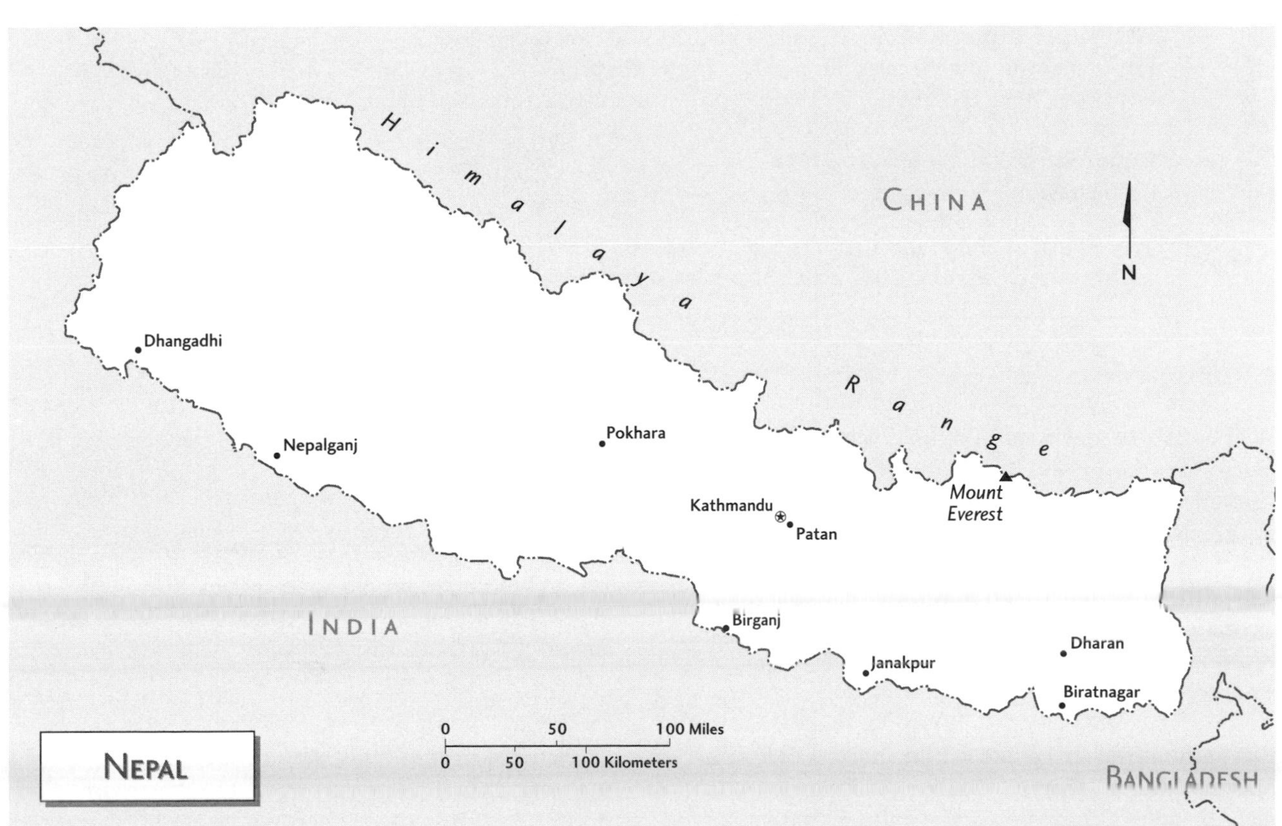

NEPAL

Country name: Kingdom of Nepal
Area: 140,800 sq km
Population: 25,284,463 (July 2001 est.)
Population growth rate: 2.32% (2001 est.)
Birth rate: 33.4 births/1,000 population (2001 est.)
Death rate: 10.22 deaths/1,000 population (2001 est.)
Net migration rate: 0 migrants/1,000 population (2001 est.)
Sex ratio: 1.05 males/female (2001 est.)
Infant mortality rate: 74.14 deaths/1,000 live births (2001 est.)
Life expectancy at birth—total population: 58.22 years; male, 58.65 years; female, 57.77 years (2001 est.)
Major religions: Hinduism, Buddhism, Islam
Major languages: Nepali (official; spoken by 90% of the population), about a dozen other languages and about 30 major dialects; many in government and business also speak English
English literacy—total population: 27.5%; male, 40.9%; female, 14% (1995 est.)
Government type: parliamentary democracy and constitutional monarchy
Capital: Kathmandu
Administrative divisions: 14 zones
Independence: 1768 (unified by Prithvi Narayan Shah)
National holiday: Birthday of King Gyanendra, 7 July (1946)
Suffrage: 18 years of age; universal
GDP—real growth rate: 3.7% (2000 est.)
GDP—per capita (purchasing power parity): $1,360 (2000 est.)
Population below poverty line: 42% (FY95/96 est.)
Exports: $485 million (f.o.b., 1998), but does not include unrecorded border trade with India
Imports: $1.2 billion (f.o.b., 1998)
Currency: Nepalese rupee (NPR)

Source: Central Intelligence Agency. (2001) *The World Book Factbook* 2001. Retrieved 5th March, 2002 from http://www.cia.gov/cia/publications/factbook.

42 percent of the total area but of which only 10 percent is cultivable. The terraced slopes used for farming are a major feature of this region.

3. Mountain region: This area ranges from 4,877 meters to 8,848 meters in altitude, covering one-third of Nepal's area; only 2 percent of the mountain region is cultivable. Due to the high altitude and colder climate, it is sparsely populated and contains a mere 7.3 percent of the total population. The people of this region make a living through raising sheep and yaks, which provide milk, meat, hides, and wool. While the slopes are difficult to cultivate, some of the valleys can support agriculture. Tourism (trekking and mountaineering) is also a growing industry that helps to support the population in this region.

The main crops grown in Nepal are rice, maize, wheat, barley, millet, buckwheat, and a variety of vegetables. The major cash crops are potatoes, oilseed, sugarcane, jute, and tobacco.

People

Nepal is a multiethnic Hindu society, although the majority practices a mixture of Hinduism and Buddhism. Nepali is the official language, but Newari is widespread; many groups have their own languages and customs. Ethnic groups can be divided according to the following language groups:

1. Indo-Aryan language group
   a. Nepali—Brahman, Chhetri, Khas, Thakuri, Kami, Sarki, Damai
   b. Northern Indian (Terai)—Maithali, Bhojpuri, Tharu, Awadi, Rajbanshi
2. Tibeto-Burman language group
   a. Tibeto-Burman—Tamang, Newari, Rai, Limbu, Magar, Gurung, Thakali, Sunuwar
   b. Tibetan—Sherpa, Bhote (Humli, Jumli, etc.)

History

Nepal's history is ancient, but it did not attain unity until 1768, when the Gurkhas, under the leadership of Prithvi Narayan Shah (reigned 1742–1775), were able to capture the Kathmandu Valley, which they used as their capital and base of operations. During the period of Gurkha ascendancy, infighting among aristocratic families was intense; it culminated with one family achieving supremacy by monopolizing the post of prime minister, which became hereditary, and controlling the monarchy by arranging marriages between the royal family and itself. The family took the name Rana (a term signifying strength in battle). The Ranas were supported by the British colonial government in India; they kept the nation independent and isolated from the world until after Indian independence, when the monarchy was reinstated and the *panchayat* system of village government was introduced. The system was multitiered, from the village to the national level, and, in theory, decentralized. In fact, rule was authoritarian and centralized until King Birendra (1945–2001) came to the throne in 1972. The *panchayat* system was dismantled in 1990, but Nepal's bicameral parliamentary system is encountering difficulties in meeting the challenges of fostering Nepal's economic development.

In 1996, inefficient governance and intensifying corruption opened the door for the creation of a Maoist insurgency, which poses a threat to the developing democracy, making the life of citizens uncertain.

In the midst of this uncertainty, on 1 June 2001, ten royal family members, including King Birendra and Queen Aishworya, were killed during dinner in Narayanhiti Royal Palace at Kathmandu. Crown Prince Dipendra (1972–2001) opened fire on his family, allegedly over a dispute with his parents about his choice of a bride, and then shot himself. Prince Dipendra did not die immediately and was declared king the next day, under the regency of King Birendra's younger brother Gyanendra (b. 1946). Gyanendra became king upon the death of Prince Dipendra. It was later found that the crown prince had been under the influence of alcohol and narcotics and had used weapons that he had procured from sources in the army for his gun collection.

Keshav L. Maharjan

Further Reading

ICIMOD. (1997) *Districts of Nepal: Indicators of Development.* Kathmandu, Nepal: ICIMOD.

Nepal Research Associates. (1999) *Nepal District Profile.* Kathmandu, Nepal: Samudayik Printers.

Savada, Andrea Matles. (1991) *Nepal and Bhutan: Country Studies.* Washington, DC: Library of Congress.

Seddon, David. (1988) *Nepal: A State of Poverty.* New Delhi: Vikas Publishing House.

UNDP. (2000) *Human Development Report 2000.* New York: UNDP.

NEPAL—ECONOMIC SYSTEM

In 1951, when the 104-year feudalistic Rana oligarchy came to an end, the Nepal economy was in terrible condition. The revenue base was so narrow, due to the absence of major industries and related infrastructures, that paying for even basic expenditures was impossible. In 1956, under the guidance of the Colombo Plan for Cooperative Economic and Social Development in Asia and the Pacific, Nepal initiated five-year economic plans, which became the focus of the economic system. Development efforts are undertaken on the basis of planned projects. Certain sectors, such as infrastructure and agriculture, are given priority, with the bulk of such expenditures being met by foreign aid in the form of grants and loans.

National Budget

During the autocratic *panchayat* period (1960–1990), the tax base was broadened and revenue was increased. However, national expenditures also increased constantly, and thus the negative balance of the budget widened every year. Foreign aid balanced this deficit and helped to meet development expenditures from the late 1970s. Income from foreign aid often exceeded tax revenues. Despite efforts to develop a market economy after democratization in 1990, the absence of major industry inhibited growth of the fragile revenue base. This, together with a decrease in the grant component of foreign aid, has created a major economic challenge.

Industry

Agriculture is the main industry, absorbing over 90 percent of the labor force between 1951 and 1981 and

Potters display their goods in Potter's Square in Bhaktapur, Nepal, in 1997. (MICHAEL FREEMAN/CORBIS)

80 percent thereafter. In spite of this, agriculture is predominantly subsistence in nature and is the sole source of food for many, with the major food crops being rice, wheat, barley, buckwheat, millet, maize, potatoes and other vegetables, and spices. To some extent it also provides raw materials (jute, tobacco, sugarcane, oilseeds, and cotton) for domestic agricultural industries. However, geographical and other natural constraints coupled with a lack of agricultural infrastructure have prevented agricultural growth since the 1950s, and its share in the gross domestic product has been constantly decreasing.

Nepal began to industrialize during the 1950s by building mills and factories to process jute, rice, oilseed, cotton, and tobacco and to produce sugar, matchsticks, and agricultural tools. Manufacturing industries such as cement, steel, leather, plywood, carpets and other textiles, alcohol, and tea were added in the 1970s. All these industries utilized foreign technologies to provide import substitutes and promote the use of local resources. In the 1980s these industries were reinforced in order to produce export-oriented goods. The carpet industry, later joined by the garment industry, took the lead role in exporting products. However, the use of child labor and environmentally unfriendly dyes made Nepali exports less popular in the 1990s, and the country is now trying hard to overcome these problems. The manufacturing sector as a whole increased its share of gross domestic product from a few percentage points in the early 1970s to 10 percent in the late 1990s.

The service industry, inextricably linked to tourism and comprising trade (primarily merchandise), hotels, and restaurants, has also grown constantly, expanding its share of GDP to more than 10 percent. Tourism, especially trekking and mountaineering, is providing much of Nepal's needed hard currency. The construction, transportation, communication, finance, and social-welfare sectors are growing relative to economic development as a whole. However, utilities (electricity, gas, drinking water) are increasing only at nominal rates and are confined to urbanized and tourist areas. The mining industry, perhaps due to the fragile nature of the geologically young Himalayas, is almost nonexistent. Efforts are being made, with bilateral and international cooperation, to use the potential of hydroelectric power generation.

International Trade

Originally, international trade was conducted solely with India, heavily favoring the latter's trade balance. Whereas the exports from Nepal are crude agricultural (including forestry) products, imports from India consist of manufactured consumer goods, intermediate inputs and machines for Nepal's infant industries, and service goods catering to the demands of tourists and the well-to-do. Trade diversification began in the late 1960s when Nepal started importing consumer goods from other countries, such as China and Japan, and started exporting agricultural products to Singapore and African countries. The volume of trade and the number of trading countries increased further after the 1970s with the import of various goods from different countries, often in line with the aid received from those countries. This period also witnessed a growth in exports of Nepalese carpets, garments, and other locally produced goods to Germany, other European Community countries, and the United States. The lion's share of trade is still with India, with the trade balance persistently against Nepal. The Nepalese economy is virtually dependent upon Indian policies and economic conditions.

The 1999 trade deficit with India was greater than the total of earnings from tourists, foreign aid, peacekeeping operations, Gurkhas serving as British and Indian soldiers, and remittances paid to Nepali migrant laborers in other countries. However, in the same year, Nepal had high proportions of gross capital formation (20 percent) and gross domestic savings (10 percent) to GDP (296.5 billion Nepali rupees, equal to approximately 4.8 billion dollars), and it is hoped that the economy will improve in the near future. Much is expected of the sectors of agriculture, tourism, and hydroelectric power generation.

Keshav Lall Maharjan

Further Reading

Central Bureau of Statistics. (1999) *Statistical Year Book of Nepal.* Kathmandu, Nepal: His Majesty's Government, National Planning Commission.

Dahal, Madan K., et al. (1999) *Development Challenges for Nepal.* Kathmandu, Nepal: Nepal Foundation for Advanced Studies.

Gurung, Harka. (1989) Nepal: *Dimensions of Development.* Kathmandu, Nepal: Mrs. Saroj Gurung.

Integrated Development Systems. (1983) *Foreign Aid and Development in Nepal.* Kathmandu, Nepal: Integrated Development Systems.

Shrestha, Badri Prasad. (1990) *Nepalese Economy in Retrospect and Prospect.* Kathmandu, Nepal: Himalayan Booksellers.

NEPAL—EDUCATION SYSTEM

Nepal is a landlocked country, situated amid the Himalaya Mountains and surrounded by India in the east, west, and south and by China in the north. Civilization has flourished here under Buddhism since the sixth century BCE, in the Kathmandu Valley where the capital city is located. Buddhism was born in present-day Nepal: Its founder, Siddhartha Gautama (c. 563–c. 483 BCE) the Buddha or Enlightened One, was born here in present-day Rummindei.

A teacher conducts class in a school in Solu Khumbu, Nepal, in 1996. (ALISON WRIGHT/CORBIS)

Modern Education in Nepal

Modern education development began in Nepal in 1959, with the dawn of democratic government. Before that, education had been the exclusive prerogative of the ruling elite, while the rest of the population remained largely illiterate. At the start of the modern era, education was available only to the sons of the aristocracy. There were eleven secondary schools in the country, and the literacy rate was below 1 percent. Girls rarely received formal education.

The goal of primary education is to teach children reading, writing, and arithmetic. Secondary education stresses character formation to prepare students to enter higher education. The objective of education is to produce the personnel required for national development.

Primary school begins at six years of age in Grade 1; secondary education consists of lower secondary, Grades 6 and 7, and secondary, Grades 8 to 10. District-level examinations are conducted at the end of primary as well as lower secondary education.

Tribhuvan University provides a two-year proficiency certificate, two-year bachelor's degrees, two-year master's degrees, and doctoral programs in various institutes. Thirty-six privately run liberal arts and commercial colleges offer certificate courses accepted by the university.

Administration of Education

The Ministry of Education is responsible for the administration and supervision of school-level education. Tribhuvan University controls higher education. The Ministry has three divisions: general administration, educational administration, and the program and planning section, each headed by joint secretaries.

Under the Ministry of Education, there are five regional directorates and seventy-five district education offices with which some four hundred school supervisors are affiliated. The schools are controlled by management committees.

Recent Developments in Education

Since education is fundamental to national development, the Ministry of Education formed the Department of Education, which started operations in 2000, with the vital role of providing equal access to education, making quality reforms, improving internal and external efficiency, and making education a development-friendly venture.

For basic and primary education, programs include improvement of access to primary education, school management, and upgrading of teachers' standards at primary level.For increasing women's access to education, programs include increasing female enrollment, encouraging greater numbers of educated women to go into teaching as a profession, increasing the completion rate of primary education of female students, and providing scholarships to female students of various levels. For improving literacy, a campaign has been instituted to eliminate illiteracy.

For improvement in the quality of education, nine primary teacher-training centers have been established under the Primary Education Development Project for developing teaching skills and improving school management. For the development of skilled manpower, the Council for Technical Education and Vocational Training has conducted regular training for basic- and medium-level personnel. For improvement of higher education, the curriculum, textbooks, and education system have been modified. In line with international standards, Tribhuvan University has upgraded the bachelor course from two years to three since the 1997 academic year.

For increasing the number of institutes for higher education, initiatives have been taken to open universities in the five development regions of the country. Similarly, efforts for setting up technical universities, such as the University of Agriculture and Forestry, are also under way.

In the academic year 1999–2000, the total number of schools in the kingdom of Nepal at primary and secondary levels was recorded at 37,397, with the total number of students being 5,286,039 and 142,617, respectively.

By the academic year 2000–2001, 516 schools and institutions were affiliated with the Higher Secondary Education Board. The total number of students enrolled in the higher secondary education system (Grades 11 and 12) in the 1999–2000 academic year was 42,306. There are now five universities in operation, namely, Tribhuvan University, Mahandra Sanskrit University, Kathmandu University, Eastern Regional University, and Pokhara University. In 2000, sixty-one campuses directly under Tribhuvan University and 158 private campuses affiliated with it were in operation. The total number of students at all campuses of the university was estimated at 153,527.

Teh-Kuang Chang

Further Reading

CERID. (1997) *Gender and Secondary Education.* Kathmandu, Nepal: Research Centre for Educational Innovation and Development, Tribhuvan University.

———. (1996) *A Review of the Education Sector in the Eighth Five-Year Plan and the Proposed Approach for Education in the Ninth Five-Year Plan.* Kathmandu, Nepal: Research Centre for Educational Innovation and Development, Tribhuvan University.

Kasuju, P., and S. R. Joshi. (1977) *Educational Prospect in Nepal.* Kathmandu, Nepal: National Education Committee.

Mainali, M. P., J. R. Girt, B. D. Pande, S. R. Mamichhane, and G. S. Pradhan. (1988) *A Study on Secondary Education in Nepal.* Kathmandu, Nepal: Research Centre for Educational Innovation and Development, Tribhuvan University.

Ministry of Education (MOE). (1971) National Education System Plan. Kathmandu, Nepal: Ministry of Education.

Ministry of Education and Culture (MOEC). (1991) *Basic and Primary Education Master Plan.* Kathmandu, Nepal: HMGN Ministry of Education.

———. (1991) *Basic and Primary Education Master Plan, 1991–2001.* Kathmandu, Nepal.

———. (1997). *Basic and Primary Education Master Plan, 1997–2002.* Kathmandu, Nepal.

———. (1997) *Secondary Education Perspective Plan.* Kathmandu, Nepal: HMGN Ministry of Education.

Parajuli, M. N. (1995) *Women Education Programme Monitoring Project.* Kathmandu, Nepal: Women Education Unit, HMG.

Sharma, S. R. (1982) "Education Development and Role of Nonformal Education." In *Non Formal Education in Nepal,* edited by S. R. Sharma, et al. Kathmandu, Nepal: CERID, Tribhuvan University.

Tancock, N. (1999) *Mighty Nepal.* Developments 5. London: Department for International Development.

Thapa, B. K. (1996) "Financing of Education in Nepal." In *Education and Development,* edited by B. R. Shakya, H. R. Bajracharya, B. K. Thapa, and R. Chitrakar. Kathmandu, Nepal: Research Centre for Educational Innovation and Development.

World Bank. (1994) Nepal: *Critical Issues in Secondary Education and Options for Reform.* Report 12243-NEP. Washington, DC: World Bank.

NEPAL—HISTORY

The kingdom of Nepal occupies 140,800 square kilometers of the central mountainous area between the Himalayan crest and the plains of northern India. Not until the late eighteenth century did a unified political and social system emerge in this rugged region. Historically the name Nepal referred to the Kathmandu Valley in the midmontane region, and only in the early nineteenth century was the name applied to the entire country, when the Shah dynasty consolidated the various principalities into a kingdom in the period from 1769 to 1850.

Geophysically Nepal is divided into numerous small, isolated valleys and hills by three ranges running east–west and four major river systems running north–south from the Himalayan crest to the plains. These physical divisions resulted in a strong sense of ethnicity and regionalism that still pervades Nepali society despite the nominally highly centralized polity that emerged under the Shah dynasty and subsequent governments.

Early History

The Kathmandu Valley figures prominently in several ancient Hindu and Buddhist classics going back more than two millennia. Southern Nepal was the birthplace of Siddhartha Gautama (c. 563–483 BCE), known as the Buddha, and thus had a close relationship with the Buddhist sociopolitical system that dominated much of northern India. In the fourth century BCE the Buddha's disciples built several shrines in the valley as well as on Nepal's border with India.

A coherent political system emerged in Kathmandu only in the fourth century CE, when a Hindu Indian dynasty, the Licchavi, established control over the valley, but its authority never extended over most of the hill areas of Nepal. From then on, high-caste Hindu kings ruling over the valley never could extend their territory over the largely non-Hindu, non-Indian tribal communities in the sub-Himalayan region. By 500 CE Nepal's population consisted primarily of tribal communities that had migrated to Nepal from Tibet, China, Southeast Asia, and northeastern India. By 800 CE Nepal was a composite of numerous small ethnic communities scattered throughout the hill area. The most prominent of these was the Newar community, the indigenous community in the Kathmandu Valley, which played an influential role in the social history and economy of Nepal. The Newars developed the trade route from India through Kathmandu to Tibet,

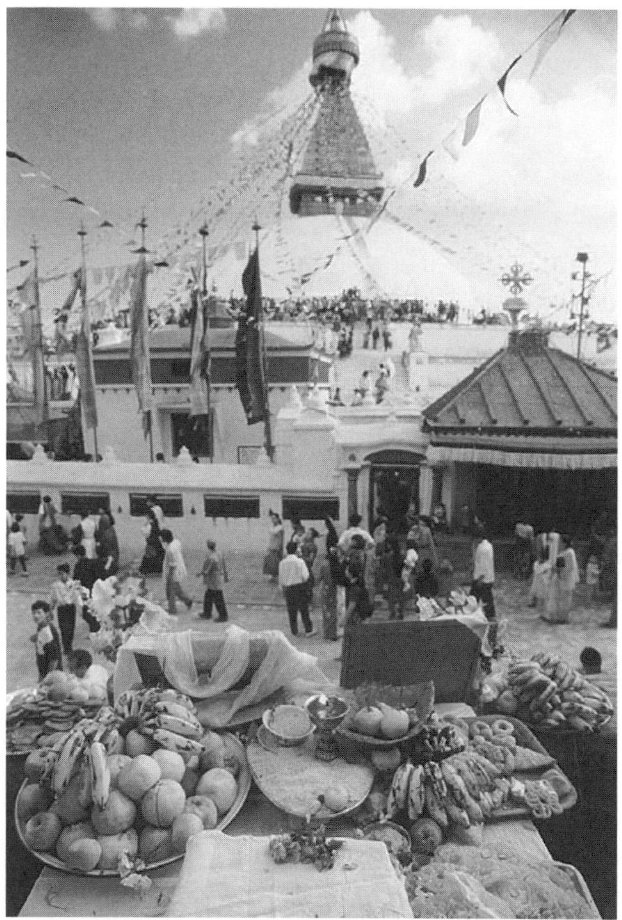

Offerings at Boudanath Stupa in May 1996 for the holiday of Buddha Jayanti, the triple anniversary of the Buddha's birth, enlightenment, and death. (MACDUFF EVERTON/CORBIS)

in the process changing the valley from a remote backwater into the major intellectual and commercial center between south and central Asia.

The Muslim invasions of India in the eleventh century led to major changes in Nepal's population, at least at the elite level, and in the political system. Many high-caste Hindu families in northern India fled to the western hill areas in Nepal, where they gradually established political control. By 1200 over fifty small hill principalities were ruled by these high-caste émigré families. As a result, most of the western Nepal hill areas were effectively Hinduized in sociopolitical terms while retaining a broad range of Buddhist and animist beliefs. This was evident in the *Muluki ains* (legal codes) imposed by some Hindu rulers, which were carefully moderated to include traditional tribal practices.

In the mid-eighteenth century the Shah family dynasty emerged in the western principality of Gurkha. In 1769 Prithvi Narayan Shah (1730–1775) launched a

KEY EVENTS IN NEPAL'S HISTORY

c. 566 BCE The Buddha is born in southern Nepal.
4th century CE The Indian Licchavi dynasty establishes control over the Kathmandu Valley.
800 The Newars are the most prominent of the ethnic groups which inhabit the region.
1200 High-caste Hindu families who had fled the Muslim invasion of India rule over 50 hill principalities in Nepal.
1769–1800 The modern Kingdom of Nepal emerges when the principalities are unified by the Shah dynasty.
1850 The Rana elite family attains the dominant position in the government.
1950 The Ranas are overthrown.
1959 A new constitution is promulgated and elections held.
1960 King Mahendra dismisses the newly elected government.
1962 King Mahendra abolishes the constitution and establishes a monarchy.
1980 A national referendum abolishes political parties.
1990 Political protests lead to the revival of political parties and a new constitution is drafted.
2001 The royal family is massacred by a prince who then kills himself.

vigorous campaign to conquer the Kathmandu Valley. After succeeding, he moved his capital from Gurkha to Kathmandu, brought the India-Kathmandu-Tibet trade route under his control, and gradually extended his power over most of the other hill principalities in western Nepal as well as over the tribal communities in eastern Nepal. By 1800 the Shah dynasty ruled the entire hill area of present-day Nepal as well as some of the adjacent areas in India, Sikkim, and Kumaon.

The Shah dynasty extended its authority by concluding agreements with local leaders in the western hills and with ethnic groups in the east. Regional communities vowed allegiance to the ruler but retained broad self-governing powers. The elite families that came to Kathmandu with the ruler became factionalized by 1800, however, and were involved in internal government conflicts. The king was technically an absolute monarch but in fact had to work with both the Kathmandu elite families and the political leadership in the hill areas. The elite families were dedicated to preserving their families' political and social status, and concepts of nationalism never were an important political factor.

The Rana System

A modified political system emerged in Nepal after 1850 when one elite family, the Ranas, attained a dominant position in the government. Because most other elite leaders had died in a massacre organized by the Ranas, the Ranas managed to relegate the Shah family to the status of a nominal ruling family with no role in the governance of the country, while the Ranas became perpetual prime ministers with broad authoritarian powers.

The Ranas introduced a new system for selecting the head of state, whereby the eldest male in the various branches of the Rana family was elected prime minister. While conspiracies and attempted coups were as much a part of the history of the Rana period as they had been in pre-1850 Nepal, they did not seriously threaten the regime. Only when, in the early 20th century, subunits of the Rana family began struggling among themselves was the system itself endangered. The Rana period saw the gradual institutionalization of government and administrative functions on a national basis, with periodic revisions of the national legal code, reforms in land tenure and taxation systems, and the gradual extension of the authority of the center over the former principalities and hill ethnic communities.

The Rana family controlled Nepal's army through appointments of commanding officers throughout the country. Any rival or elite family or faction was vigorously suppressed, but some members of these rival families were also absorbed into the Rana bureaucracy. The Ranas discouraged the spread of education and thus perpetuated the illiteracy and ignorance of most hill people. Finally, the dynasty maintained a close relationship with the British imperial government in India, allowing the recruitment of many Nepalis into the Gurkha units of the British Indian Army. Their policies worked well for almost one hundred years, until 1945, but began to fall apart in the post–World War II period. The Ranas were overthrown in 1950. After continuing political turmoil in the country, a constitution was agreed upon in 1959, and this led to general elections. However, King Mahendra (1920–1972) remained opposed to parliamentary government, and so in 1960 he dismissed the elected government and in 1962 abolished the constitution. A new one was promulgated that established the monarch as the real authority in Nepal. Mahendra was succeeded by his son Birendra (1945–2001). A national referendum in 1980 supported the idea of a nonparty parliamentary system, and political parties were sidelined. In 1990, however, a coalition of opposition parties demanded political reforms, and strikes and other civil action forced the king to lift the ban on political parties.

At the end of 1990 a new constitution was drafted; it provided for a constitutional monarchy and a multiparty political system. The new government had to struggle with economic stagnation, ecological degradation, political turmoil occasioned by splits in various parties, and a Maoist revolutionary movement.

Then in 2001 came the staggering massacre of the royal family, when a prince opened fire with a machine-gun on them because they were opposing his marriage to a commoner. The prince then committed suicide, the woman in question fled to India, and an uncle of the king, Gyanendra (b. 1947), became the new king of Nepal.

Leo Rose

Political rivals for the office of Premier Sher Bahadur and Shushi Koirala in Kathmandu in July 2001. Bahadur won the election. (AFP/CORBIS)

Further Reading

Bhandari, Dhundiraj. (1958) *Nepal ko aiti vivechana* (Historical Analysis of Nepal). Varanasi, India: Krishna Kumari.

Karan, Pradyumna P. (1960) *Nepal: A Physical and Cultural Geography.* Lexington, KY: University of Kentucky Press.

Pant, Dibyadeb. (1975) *Shah vansa charitan* (An Account of the Shah Dynasty). Varanasi, India: Sangared Vidyalaya Press.

Regmi, Mahesj Chandra. (1999) *Imperial Gorkha.* Delhi: Adroit Publishers.

Stiller, Lugwig S. (1973) *The Rise of the House of Gorkha.* Patna, India: Society of Jesus.

Tucci, Giuseppe. (1962) *Nepal: The Discovery of the Malla.* London: George Allen and Unwin.

Wright, Daniel. (1897) *History of Nepal.* Cambridge, U.K.: Cambridge University Press.

NEPAL—POLITICAL SYSTEM

In the late eighteenth century, the expansion of the Shah dynasty from the hill principality of Gurkha into a large and very diverse nation-state in the central Himalayas with its capital at Kathmandu was the decisive factor in the political development of Nepal. The Shah family rarely exercised effective authority over the many small principalities, Kathmandu-based aristocratic families, and tribal ethnic elites in the hill areas, but there was a central system of government in which the various factions could negotiate and interact. But by 1850 one aristocratic family, the Ranas, emerged as the dominant power in Nepal through its status as the hereditary prime minister under a royal ordinance. The Shah kings retained their royal status but were effectively kept out of governmental functions and were isolated from the political process.

The Rana regime lasted for one century, 1850 to 1950, but some developments in the post–World War II period in South Asia undermined the Rana regime both internally and externally. First, the British Indian Empire that had strongly supported the Ranas ceased to exist in 1947. The new independent Indian government, dominated by the Indian Congress Party, had mixed views on Nepal but generally tended to support Nepal's anti-Rana political parties. Second, a large Nepali migrant community had emerged in northern India with both elite and hill tribal migrants, and these provided the social base for the Nepali Congress Party and other anti-Rana political factions that had their organizational base in India but that gradually extended their activities into Nepal. More divisive, perhaps, were the structural divisions in the contending factions within the Rana family, some of whom sought refuge in India and then established close working relations with the more radical Nepali political parties. Moreover, the Shah ruler, King Tribhuvan (d. 1956), assumed a more public anti-Rana position and, with Indian assistance, moved from Kathmandu to New Delhi, where he developed a close relationship with the Indian government and the various revolutionary Nepali organizations in India.

Serious negotiations between the Ranas, King Tribhuvan, the Nepali Congress, and the Indian government commenced in New Delhi in late 1950, leading to an agreement in 1951 under which the Rana prime minister retained his post but with greatly reduced powers. King Tribhuvan regained royal powers

PREAMBLE TO NEPALESE CONSTITUTION

Adopted 9 Nov 1990

Whereas, We are convinced that the source of sovereign authority of the independent and sovereign Nepal is inherent in the people, and, therefore, We have, from time to time, made known our desire to conduct the government of the country in consonance with the popular will; and Whereas, in keeping with the desire of the Nepalese people expressed through the recent people's movement to bring about constitutional changes, we are further inspired by the objective of securing to the Nepalese people social, political and economic justice long into the future; and Whereas, it is expedient to promulgate and enforce this Constitution, made with the widest possible participation of the Nepalese people, to guarantee basic human rights to every citizen of Nepal; and also to consolidate Adult Franchise, the Parliamentary System of Government, Constitutional Monarchy and the System of Multi Party Democracy by promoting amongst the people of Nepal the spirit of fraternity and the bond of unity on the basis of liberty and equality; and also to establish an independent and competent system of justice with a view to transforming the concept of the Rule of Law into a living reality: Now, Therefore, keeping in view the desire of the people that the State authority and sovereign powers shall, after the commencement of this Constitution, be exercised in accordance with the provisions of this Constitution, I, *King Birendra Bir Bikram Shah Deva*, by virtue of the State authority as exercised by Us, do hereby promulgate and enforce this *Constitution of the Kingdom of Nepal* on the recommendation and advice, and with the consent of the Council of Ministers.

Source: International Court Network. Retrieved 8 March 2002, from: http://www.uni-wuerzburg.de/law/np00000_.html.

and assumed a significant role in the political process. The Nepali Congress emerged as the leading Nepali political faction on the popular level.

The Rana system officially ended in 1951, but it took nearly a decade for a viable alternative system to emerge. King Tribhuvan usually worked closely with the Nepali Congress in an effort to democratize politics in Nepal, but with his death in 1956 the new Shah ruler, King Mahendra (d. 1972) followed a very different path, carefully exploiting the serious divisions within the political parties. Parliamentary elections were held in 1961, and the Nepali Congress gained a majority and formed the first party government. Mahendra then used the broad emergency powers granted to the king in the constitution to dismiss the Congress government and imprison many of the party's leaders, and assumed authoritarian powers that he hoped to make permanent.

For over ten years (1961 to 1972) Mahendra's authoritarian system was the *panchayat* polity, whose objective was the creation of a decentralized administrative system in the districts and villages. But it never really worked, and Nepal was once again as centralized and authoritarian as it had been under the Rana rulers.

With King Mahendra's death in 1972 his son Birendra came to the throne. Educated abroad, Birendra held views on political objectives and on the process of governing that were very different from those of his father, but Mahendra's bureaucratic elite system was so firmly in place that Birendra faced major obstacles in his efforts to introduce some basic reforms. With the emergence of a much-strengthened Nepali Congress Party, and working with the moderate branch of the Nepal Communist Party (NCP), the United Marxist Leftists (UML) launched a major campaign throughout the country in 1989–1990 directed at the overthrow of the *panchayat* system. King Birendra finally reached an agreement with the party leaders, and a new democratic governmental system was established under the 1991 constitution.

A Constitutional Monarchy—At Last

With the broad-based agreement in late 1989 between King Birendra and the NCP-UML coalition, the stage was set for the introduction of a democratic constitutional monarchy. An NCP leader, K. P. Bhattarai, became the interim prime minister until the elections were held. Some feared that the king would not accept this major diminution of his status and power, but in the 1990s Birendra carefully followed the principles of a constitutional monarchy.

In mid-1991, political party leaders wrote a new constitution, under which elections were held a few months later. The NCP won a majority of the parliamentary seats and formed a new government. Bhattarai was shunted aside and G. P. Koirala was asked to form the government, in which most of the ministers were drawn from the hills and terai constituencies.

The Koirala government held office until mid-1994, when further divisions within the party organization led Koirala to resign and call for elections in November 1994. The NCP did poorly in the election, while the UML won a plurality of seats. The UML formed the government, but it lasted only until September 1995, when a censure motion was passed against it by parliament. A three-party coalition assumed office, led by S. P. Deuba, and lasted until March 1997. A new two-party coalition headed by L. B. Chand, the leader of one faction of the Rashtriya Prajantar Party (RPP), was formed with the support of the UML. But Chand resigned on 4 October 1997, and politics remained turbulent for the rest of the 1990s.

All political parties accept the concept of a democratic parliamentary system and constitutional monarchy. The one exception is the ultraradical Maoist wing of the Communist movement in Nepal, which has a base in several western hill districts. The Maoists demand the replacement of the monarchy by a people's republic and do not participate in elections. Their relations with the other parties are hostile and even the UML is denounced as "too conservative." In 1996 the Maoists launched a violent insurrection against the government and the parties. The Maoists, however, lack a substantial support base even in the districts in which they are based, and they also lack external support, even from China, the land of Mao. The Maoists have been a divisive factor in Nepali politics on occasion, but by late 1999 there was broad agreement among the other parties on the need to bring them under control.

In the elections in May 1999 the NCP won a majority (111 of 205 seats), while the UML won 71 seats. The thirty-six other parties won only twenty-three seats and were relegated to the sidelines. Since between them the NCP and the UML hold most of the 205 seats in parliament, some form of two-party system may finally emerge in Nepal. Whether the murder of the royal family by a disaffected prince in 2001 spelled the end of the monarchy remains to be seen.

Leo Rose

Further Reading

Baral, Lok Raj. (1993) *Nepal: Problems of Governance.* New Delhi: Konark Publishers.

Borre, Ole, Sushil R. Panday, and Chitra K. Tiwari. (1994) *Nepalese Political Behavior.* Aarhus, Denmark: Aarhus University Press.

Joshi, Bhuwan Lal, and Leo E. Rose. (1966) *Democratic Innovations in Nepal: A Case Study of Political Acculturation.* Berkeley and Los Angeles: University of California Press.

Khanal, Y. N. (1988) *Essays in Nepal's Foreign Affairs.* Kathmandu, Nepal: Mala Press.

Kumar, Dhruba. (1992) *Nepal's India Policy.* Kathmandu, Nepal: Centre for Nepal and Asian Studies.

Political Science Association of Nepal. (1992) *Political Parties and the Parliamentary Process in Nepal.* Kathmandu, Nepal: Political Science Association of Nepal (POLSAN).

NESIN, AZIZ

NESIN, AZIZ (1915–1995), Turkish writer. Aziz Nesin (Mustafa Nusret Nesin), one of the most important authors and satirists in modern Turkish literature, had a gift for observing the ridiculous in human relationships. His writings exposed intolerance, absurdity, cruelty, and stupidity in all situations of human life and among all types of people.

He was born at Heybeli Ada in Istanbul and lost his mother at an early age. After completing Dar-ul Safaka, a high school for orphans where English was the language of instruction, he entered a military boarding school, which he described as the only institution where poor, penniless children could study free of charge.

He started writing while he was in the army under the alias Aziz Nesin, his father's name. In 1944 he was discharged for allegations of misusing his authority and sentenced to three months' imprisonment. He published *Marko Pasa*, a weekly satirical paper, which survived several closings during its five-year existence because Nesin modified the paper's name ("Marko Pasa" is a nominative idiom referring to someone who listens to other people's complaints and problems—"Tell your troubles to Marko Pasa," people often say.) Nesin was finally imprisoned for five and a half years for his writings. He wrote for different magazines and newspapers under more than a hundred assumed names to evade censorship.

His decision to translate and publish parts of Salman Rushdie's *Satanic Verses* in Turkish drew the anger of Islamic fundamentalists who attempted to kill him in 1993 during the annual commemoration of the death of a sixteenth-century Alevi folk hero in the city of Sivas. Although he escaped, the arson attack at his hotel killed thirty-seven writers, poets, and intellectuals.

In 1972 he founded the Nesin Trust for orphans and transferred all of his copyrights and most of his royalties to it. The foundation, which began operating in 1982, provides education and shelter to four poor children each year until they complete high school or acquire a vocation.

Nesin published over one hundred novels, short stories, and plays. His writings have been translated into twenty-three languages, and his plays have been performed in seven countries. A multiple award winner in various international humor contests, Nesin was elected a member of the PEN Club by Germany in 1985. He died of a heart attack at the age of eighty during a book-signing tour in Cesme, Turkey.

H. Ayla Kiliç

Further Reading

Nesin, Aziz. (1991) *Turkish Stories from Four Decades*. Selected and translated by Louis Mitler. 1st ed. Washington, DC: Three Continents Press.

———. (1995) *Böyle Gelmis Böyle Gitmez* (trans. *Istanbul Boy: That's How It Was but Not How It's Going to Be: The Autobiography of Aziz Nesin*). Trans. by Joseph S. Jacobson. Austin: University of Texas at Austin, Center for Middle Eastern Studies.

NESIN, MUSTAFA NUSRET. See **Nesin, Aziz.**

NETHERLANDS EAST INDIES Netherlands (Dutch) East Indies (Nederlands[ch] Oost-Indie) was the colony covering much of present-day Indonesia. Until the late 1700s, the East Indies Company (VOC) represented Dutch authority in Asia. Headquartered in Batavia (now Jakarta), the VOC had posts and territories that stretched from South Africa to Japan. The Netherlands Indies arose when the Dutch government acquired VOC possessions in 1795 and the bankrupt company's charter lapsed in 1800. The Dutch lost their Asian territories outside the Indonesian archipelago, especially during the Napoleonic Wars, and from 1824 their sphere of influence was confined to present-day Indonesia. In 1830, the Dutch ruled only Java and parts of Sumatra and other islands; they gradually conquered or incorporated the remainder of the archipelago, especially in the 1870–1911 period.

Batavia remained the colony's administrative center, with a governor-general ruling on behalf of the Dutch state. The archipelago was divided into *gewesten* (provinces), generally headed by residents. The lower levels of administration were largely indigenous, either consisting of coopted local elites, such as the *bupati* (regents) on Java, or *zelfbesturen* (native states) with limited autonomy. Nineteenth-century colonial policy was aimed at enriching the Dutch, first through forced cultivation (the Cultivation System—*Cultuurstelsel),* and from 1870 by the Liberal Policy that opened the economy to private enterprise. The 1901 Ethical Policy aimed also to improve local living standards and make education more widely available.

In the twentieth century, the Netherlands Indies gradually became constitutionally distinct from the Netherlands. The Volksraad (People's Council), elected by restricted franchise and with limited legislative powers, was created in 1918; in 1922, the Indies became a *rijksdeel* (part of the realm), formally on par with the Netherlands. There were, however, no official plans for eventual independence or autonomy, despite the demands of a nationalist movement.

The Japanese conquered most of the Indies in 1942, and a colonial government-in-exile was established in Australia. On 6/7 December 1942 (6 December in the Netherlands, 7 December in Indonesia), Queen Wilhelmina promised postwar reforms, but after the 1945 Indonesian revolution the Dutch were able to recover only part of the Indies. The Dutch sought to retain influence by creating a federal system, including the nationalist Indonesian Republic, but military and diplomatic pressure forced them to transfer sovereignty to independent Indonesia in December 1949.

Robert Cribb

Further Reading

de Kat Angelino, A. D. A. (1931) *Colonial Policy:* Vol. 2 of *The Dutch East Indies*. Chicago: University of Chicago Press.

Vandenbosch, Amry. (1942) *The Dutch East Indies: Its Government, Problems, and Politics*. 3d ed. Berkeley and Los Angeles: University of California Press.

NEW ECONOMIC MECHANISM.

See **Chintanakan mai.**

NEW ECONOMIC POLICY—MALAYSIA

The New Economic Policy (NEP) of Malaysia was a set of government actions introduced in 1970 to promote the interests of ethnic Malaysians (*bumiputras*, or "sons of the soil") over those of the nation's other two large ethnic groups: the Chinese and the Indians. The NEP was introduced in the wake of fear over a Communist uprising and widespread ethnic tension that threatened the nation. It aimed to bring social stability by reducing overall poverty and strengthening the economic and social positions of *bumiputras* over the other two groups. This aim has broadly been achieved, and the NEP should therefore be considered a success, even though it has been criticized.

Historical Context

Like many other Southeast Asian nations, Malaysia historically had a comparatively low population density, partly as a result of inaccessible terrain. When the nation was colonized by the British in the late eighteenth century, the labor force was not sufficient for the large-scale processing and manufacturing activities planned to exploit the rich natural resources. Specifically, large-scale tin mining for the canning industry and cultivating rubber trees for the tire industry required larger labor pools. The British imported workers from India to meet the needs of the rubber industry and introduced modern technology to be used by Chinese migrants in the tin mines. This also helped prevent economic power falling into the hands of indigenous people and hence reduced the chance of organized resistance to colonization. Migration from China had been a long-term phenomenon, and trading networks had been established since at least the fifteenth century. Activities supporting these industries, such as retailing and wholesaling, therefore also tended to fall into Indian or Chinese hands. This situation led to the relative impoverishment of the more numerous *bumiputras* and their marginalization in economic terms as they remained largely in rural occupations.

After the Japanese occupation during World War II demonstrated that the European powers were not irresistible, opposition to the colonists grew, and new British settlement plans in 1946 and 1948 were strongly resisted. At the same time, a Communist insurrection, led mainly by Chinese, threatened the security of Malaysia, and the British took strong steps to end it, including the resettlement of 500,000 Chinese in villages that the British controlled. Violence broke out sporadically in subsequent years. When independence was finally granted in 1967, therefore, it was against a background of ethnic tension and division, with both Chinese and *bumiputras* feeling threatened. Tensions were worsened by the creation and strengthening of political parties almost wholly along ethnic lines—a situation that persists.

Riots continued after independence; in 1968 two hundred people were killed in Kuala Lumpur in incidents sparked by fears of excessive ethnic Chinese wealth and power. These incidents convinced the ruling United Malays National Organization (UMNO) that action was necessary not just to settle the emergency but also to institute social and economic reform to prevent a repeat. This is the context in which the NEP was created.

The New Economic Policy

The NEP consisted of a series of linked measures with two specific objectives: reduction of the absolute poverty of the *bumiputras* and an increase in their participation in the economic system. A principal measure to achieve these objectives was the forcible restructuring of corporate equity; that is, overseas firms were required to divest part of their ownership to *bumiputra* interests, primarily through trust companies set up for that purpose. The aim was to achieve 30 percent of corporate ownership by *bumiputras*, 40 percent by other Malaysians, and 30 percent by others. In other words, both Chinese Malaysians and overseas investors were obliged to cede control of parts of their firms to the government-controlled *bumiputra* nominees. The Malaysian government has often intervened in the economy in this way, and although economic success has followed, international investors have lower levels of confidence that their interests will be respected.

At the same time, incentives were offered to *bumiputra* companies to establish themselves and to invest. Preferential opportunities were also provided to *bumiputras* for higher education and for other forms of personal and professional development.

The NEP was put into effect through successive Five-Year Plans, which began with specific goals of redistribution and which gradually adopted goals of growth more generally. The NEP was introduced with a lifetime of twenty years, and, by 1990, when it was replaced by the National Development Plan and other policies, the government had become concerned with more sophisticated maneuvering of an economy engaged in the struggle to be competitive on a global scale and with the needs of a developing, mixed export-led economy in which industry had succeeded agriculture as the main activity.

Assessment

The NEP was an affirmative action plan, and so assessments of its success or failure are subject to the arguments that affect affirmative action programs generally. In its own terms, the NEP was successful: poverty in Malaysia was reduced from 49 percent at the policy's inception to 9 percent at its conclusion in 1990. Many indicators demonstrate that *bumiputra*s have a much greater share of the national wealth and are taking more active senior administrative and executive roles. However, many international businesses complain that *bumiputra* nominees are underqualified and lack motivation. Further, it is clear that inequality of income and opportunities within the ethnic Malay community has increased substantially and that this factor is now one of the most divisive in the nation. This inequality is manifested in the apparently disproportionate access to benefits obtained by a small group associated with the UMNO government—in other words, cronyism. Additionally, in the comparable case of Indonesia, poverty rates were reduced by a greater extent without affirmative action, although it is true that ethnic relations there (as was revealed in the aftermath of the 1997–1998 currency crisis) are still fractured below the surface.

However, the NEP assisted in shaping a modern multicultural society that has achieved splendid rates of economic growth since the early 1970s, even if political development has not fully kept pace. It avoided large-scale outbreaks of ethnic rioting and has retained a considerable degree of economic sovereignty.

John Walsh

Further Reading

Hiebert, Murray. (1999) "Tin Cans and Tyres." *Far Eastern Economic Review* (April 15).

Kok Swee Kheng. (1994) *Malaysia to 2003: From Redistribution to Growth.* London: EIU.

Reid, Anthony. (1999) *Charting the Shape of Early Modern Southeast Asia.* Chiang Mai, Thailand: Silkworm Books.

Unido. (1991) *Malaysia: Sustaining the Industrial Investment Momentum.* Oxford, U.K.: Basil Blackwell.

NEW ECONOMIC ZONES—VIETNAM

After the Communist takeover in South Vietnam in May 1975, the Communist government established New Economic Zones (NEZs). Ostensibly this action was taken to alleviate overcrowding in the cities, whose population swelled with refugees fleeing the war, but the NEZs were inextricably intertwined with the notion of reeducation camps. Although there was no revolutionary reign of terror following the Communist takeover in the south, up to a half-million people, mainly members or supporters of the anti-Communist Republic of Vietnam regime or the Army of the Republic of Vietnam, went through short-term reeducation, while up to 100,000 people were sentenced to long-term reeducation. The reeducation camp programs ran parallel to those of the NEZs.

Though nominally voluntary, hundreds of thousands of people, especially urbanites suspected of disloyalty to the new regime as well as political and common prisoners, were sent to a series of remote camps along Vietnam's isolated border region. There they were subjected to harsh physical labor, including land reclamation and agriculture work, because the zones were supposed to be self-sufficient. Although the zones were hypothetically established before people were sent there, with rudimentary infrastructure, tools, seeds for crops, pumps, and farm equipment, in reality few NEZs were prepared for the influx of urbanites, and the living conditions were exceptionally harsh. The camps had woefully poor infrastructure, including minimal health services and other social programs. The internees were also forced to undergo political indoctrination classes. Unprepared and unskilled at making a living in the harsh rural interior, a large number of urbanites fled Vietnam in what became known as the exodus of the boat people.

Beyond the intent of political reeducation, there was a strong economic rationale for the camps as well. Some 3 million unemployed people lived in urban areas in 1975, and there were huge colonies of squatters' camps on the outskirts of cities, whose infrastructure was crumbling under the extreme demographic pressure. The party's long-term solution was to relocate large numbers of people, including over 1 million from Saigon alone, to the underpopulated regions in the countryside.

NEZs were also part of the Communist government's plan to socialize the southern economy and to serve as district-level agricultural and administrative centers. Increasing food production was one of the government's most essential tasks. To this end, the regime implemented the collectivization of agriculture. The government hoped to achieve the breakdown of private plots and the establishment of communes that could reap economies of scale to increase yields and garner efficiencies by the state's monopolizing trade and commerce. Yet the rapid transformation of the southern economy caused massive dislocations and food shortages, which put more pressure on increasing the NEZs' output. Although the policy of establishing NEZs was abandoned, the government of Vietnam still encourages settlement in remote border areas.

Zachary Abuza

Further Reading

Duiker, William. (1998) *The Communist Road to Power in Vietnam.* Boulder, CO: Westview Press.

Porter, Gareth. (1993) *Vietnam: The Politics of Bureaucratic Socialism.* Ithaca, NY: Cornell University Press.

NEW ORDER General Suharto emerged from the turmoil of the abortive 30 September 1965 coup in Indonesia as the ascendant political player in that country, and he gradually instituted what came to be known as the New Order (Orde Baru). After effectively deposing Sukarno in March 1966, Suharto firmly established his regime, officially being installed as Indonesia's second president in March 1968. His main policies comprised depoliticizing Indonesian society, the dual function *(dwifungsi)* of the military, and economic development. Conducive foreign policy helped restore sociopolitical stability: Indonesia ended its confrontation with Malaysia, rejoined the U.N., and was influential in creating the Association of Southeast Asian Nations (ASEAN) in 1967.

Depoliticization essentially meant the purge of Communism and any criticism of the new regime, accompanied by a reduction of the number of political parties to three in 1973: the United Development Party (PPP), the Indonesian Democratic Party (PDI), and the Joint Secretariat of Functional Groups (GOLKAR)—an allegedly nonpartisan, government-supported organization representing various segments of the nation. Restoration of "social harmony" heavily relied on the dual function of the military, which enabled its members to hold both legislative and executive positions within the political system.

Economic development was facilitated by the foreign investment law of 1967, which attracted foreign investment and aid. The resultant increase in manufacturing and oil and gas production led to the emergence of a middle class increasingly dedicated to conspicuous consumption. The mid-1980s decline in oil prices prompted a shift from oil and commodity exports to the export of manufactured goods and the promotion of tourism.

The government's successful attempts to distribute development more evenly across the archipelago helped abate the separatist feelings of the 1950s. Opposition to Jakarta, however, never fully subsided in Irian Jaya, Aceh, or East Timor (the latter was forcefully integrated into Indonesia in 1975–1976). The country achieved recognition as a developing-world leader and major regional player.

When, in the wake of the 1997 Asian financial crisis, economic activity collapsed, sociopolitical stability deteriorated and with it the legitimacy of the New Order government. Unremitting demonstrations against Suharto's "crony capitalism" prompted his resignation in May 1998. Resurgent political Islam has partially filled the ensuing ideological vacuum.

Martin Ramstedt

Further Reading

Hill, Hal, ed. (1994) *Indonesia's New Order: The Dynamics of Socio-economic Transformation.* St. Leonards, Australia: Allen and Unwin.

Suryadinata, Leo. (1996) *Indonesia's Foreign Policy under Suharto.* Singapore: Times Academic Press.

Vatikiotis, Michael R. J. (1993) *Indonesian Politics under Suharto: The Rise and Fall of the New Order*. London and New York: Routledge.

NEW RICH From the early 1960s until mid-1997, several nations in East and Southeast Asia, including South Korea, Taiwan, Singapore, and Hong Kong, experienced rapid economic growth. They had embarked on industrialization only after World War II, hence they were called newly industrializing economies (NIEs). The relentless industrialization was driven by the state under what could be called authoritarian or semidemocratic governments, with the exception of Hong Kong, then a British colony. These economies were followed by similar developments in Malaysia, Thailand, and Indonesia in the 1970s and 1980s. The often double-digit annual growth rates were so impressive that the World Bank hailed the entire development process as the "Asian miracle." But economic growth came abruptly to a halt in early 1997 as a result of a currency crisis in Thailand, which quickly spread throughout the nations in East and Southeast Asia, at least slowing the rapid growth of the previous thirty-five years.

By then the phenomenal economic growth had spawned a new middle class of entrepreneurs of small- and medium-sized enterprises, state bureaucrats, managers of transnational corporations, and other professionals who, in aggregate, constitute what is now known as Asia's "new rich." The influence of this emergent class in the cultural sphere, both high and

A textile company executive talks on his cellular phone next to his 1930 Citroen in Ho Chi Minh City, Vietnam. (DAVID & PETER TURNLEY/CORBIS)

popular cultures, has significantly changed the everyday life of fellow citizens beyond their own ranks.

Cultures and Lifestyles

The most obvious measure of the new rich is the rapid improvements of their material life and expansion of their culture of consumerism. Homes and bodies are the two spheres of consumption that stand out as emblems of success.

As necessary shelter, the home is a consumer good. However, its size, design, and location are features that signify publicly the economic position, and hence status, of the owner's family. A "typical" design of a new rich home is likely to be a pastiche of design elements borrowed from different architectural traditions: roof of blue Chinese or Japanese tiles, stunted classical Roman or Greek columns, Spanish arched windows combined with elements of local tradition. If the owner is Chinese, the home might be built with due consideration to the dictates of geomancy (feng shui). Such displays of "taste" and "cultivation" often offend those with deeper appreciation of specific aesthetic traditions, namely those born into established wealth.

The home is also a piece of real estate, thus an investment. It is often yet another avenue of earning income or accumulating capital for the new rich. In almost all East and Southeast Asian cities, investment in houses, condominiums, and even commercial properties is common among the new rich. This is especially so in island states such as Singapore and Hong Kong, where land is scarce and limited, causing condominium prices to escalate quickly when the economy is booming. Capital gains from buying and selling of houses outstrip salaries from any forms of employment. The huge borrowing, by both individuals and developers, to invest in the inflated real estate sector gave rise to an "asset bubble" economy, which imploded during the regional crisis, burdening the banks in the region with huge nonperforming loans that caused some to go bankrupt. By the time the economic crisis subsided in mid-1999, every city in the region was dotted with incomplete high-rise buildings waiting for better times.

For the younger professionals and children of new rich parents, bodily adornment is the primary modality for consumption: They wear "designer" clothes and accessories, see and are seen in discos, and eat foreign food in restaurants and wine bars. These are often habits picked up from education abroad. Such highly visible consumption has given rise to public reprobation of the young as being "Westernized" and "decadent" by parents and other moral gatekeepers, including government officials. Older new rich individuals appear to have forgotten their own symbolic consumption.

Politics of the New Rich

The historical conditions from which Asia's new rich emerged are very different from those that gave rise to the bourgeoisie in nineteenth-century Europe. Europe's bourgeoisie came into their own wealth and status independently of the state. They were thus able to play a decisive role in the democratization of European nations. Asia's new rich generally grew out of their respective states' drive for industrial economic growth; thus they are beholden to the state. Consequently, their political stance toward authoritarianism or democracy is ambivalent and varies from nation to nation.

In South Korea in 1987 and Thailand in 1992, for example, the new rich played a decisive role in the political struggles and eventual removal of the respective military regimes. However, in both these instances, greater democratization did not result immediately. It was not until the 1997 regional economic crisis that democratization pressure intensified. In contrast, semidemocratic regimes such as the single-party-dominant states of Singapore and Malaysia continue to be well supported by a majority of the new rich. In general, it may be said that while the new rich would like to have greater political democratization, they are equally, if not more, concerned with the maintenance of social and political peace so as to further their own interests. Ironically, their consumption interests often unwittingly drive them to greater politicization in the cultural spheres; for example, interest in theater and movies requires them to challenge censorship laws and practices. However, such politicization need not necessarily, if ever, lead to challenging the incumbent political elite for state power.

The political ambivalence of Asia's new rich is partly the consequence of its loose social composition, with members occupying different positions in the society and economy, from managers of the state and transnational corporations to owners of small enterprises and independent professionals. Unifying them is their desire to continue to enjoy their enhanced material life, and that desire can lead them to be politically conservative in the face of less-than-democratic regimes.

Chua Beng-Huat

Further Reading

Chua Beng-Huat, ed. (2000) *Consumption in Asia: Lifestyles and Identities.* London: Routledge.

Pinches, Michael, ed. (1999) *Culture and Privilege in Capitalist Asia.* London: Routledge.

Robison, Richard, and David S. Goodman, eds. (1996) *The New Rich in Asia: Mobile Phones, McDonald's and Middle-Class Revolution.* London: Routledge.

NEW YEAR. See **Chinese New Year; No-ruz; Tet.**

NEW ZEALAND-ASIA RELATIONS

Asia, particularly East Asia, has recently become one of New Zealand's most important focuses of trade and diplomatic relationships. This international tie is bound to become even more important in the future. The Asia that New Zealanders generally refer to includes the area from the Indian subcontinent to the Japanese archipelago but excludes Russian Siberia. This region covers the vast area of diverse environmental conditions and the wide range of linguistic, ethnic, and cultural characteristics found in East Asia, Southeast Asia, South Asia, and Central Asia.

Before the arrival of European settlers in New Zealand, the indigenous Maori people apparently had no contact with Asia. It is generally accepted that Polynesians, of whom the Maori represent one subgroup, migrated from Southeast Asia to the islands of the Pacific; the Maori may have arrived in New Zealand around 800 CE. During the nineteenth century, early European settlers (mainly British) in New Zealand had little interest in or contact with Asia other than the importing of tea from China.

In the twenty-first century, New Zealand's relationship with Asia is concentrated on East Asian countries: Japan, Korea, and China, including Hong Kong and Taiwan. Contrasting geographical locations and industrial characteristics of East Asia and New Zealand complement each other. Industrialized East Asia is a good market for New Zealand's agricultural products (which, since New Zealand is in the Southern Hemisphere, can be supplied during East Asia's off season), and New Zealand, for its part, imports diverse manufactured goods from East Asia at relatively low prices. Presently, New Zealand is eager to foster close relationships with Asia based on trade, immigration, and tourism, because much of New Zealand's commodity exports depend on the East Asian market conditions. This enthusiasm is demonstrated in the New Zealand government's launching of the Asia 2000 Foundation as an arm of the Ministry of Foreign Affairs and Trade in 1994. The foundation aims to improve New Zealanders' awareness of Asia and to build beneficial relationships with Asia through making grants and engaging in other business, educational, and cultural activities.

In recent years, there have been dramatic changes in New Zealand's trade, immigration, and diplomatic relationships with Asia.

Trade

In the early to mid-twentieth century, Britain was the guaranteed market for almost all of New Zealand's commodities, at one stage taking more than 90 percent of

New Zealand's exports. New Zealand could rely on her "mother country" and did not have to be concerned with the rest of the world. However, ever since Britain joined the European Community in 1973, New Zealand's exports to Britain have declined. While Britain took 36 percent of New Zealand's exports in 1970, it took only 14 percent in 1980. From 1973, New Zealand realized it could no longer expect Britain to continue to be its principal and guaranteed market and was forced to take an independent road. It therefore looked to formerly unfamiliar parts of the world to set up new diplomatic posts and find new trading partners. At this juncture, New Zealand began to pay special attention to Asia, especially Japan and other East Asian countries. However, replacing Britain's role with another single country was neither desirable nor possible; neither Japan nor the United States was willing to be a guaranteed market for New Zealand in the way that Britain was.

During the 1980s, Britain's role in New Zealand's overseas trade dropped even further, so that in 1985 it imported a mere 9 percent of New Zealand's exports, dropping to become New Zealand's fourth largest market, after Australia, Japan, and the United States. At the same time, New Zealand's exports to East Asia (especially Japan and Korea) were increasing fast. New Zealand's exports to Britain dropped to only 6 or 7 percent in the 1990s, while Japan came to take between 15 and 18 percent of New Zealand's exports from 1985 onward. Japan has been New Zealand's second largest export market since 1970. The most common imports by the Japanese are meat, aluminum, wool, dairy products, and forestry products.

Over the last decade, the South Korean market has grown dramatically to become New Zealand's fifth largest market. New Zealand's exports to Korea grew from a mere NZ$1.6 million in 1970 to more than a billion New Zealand dollars in 1996, which accounted for slightly over 5 percent of New Zealand's exports. These exports consisted of mainly meat, wool, deer antler velvet, and forest products.

China became New Zealand's sixth largest market in 1998–1999, importing NZ$625 million in goods. Closely following China were Hong Kong (NZ$602 million) and Taiwan (NZ$580 million), which ranked as New Zealand's eighth- and ninth-largest export markets in 1998–1999. In total, about 30 percent of New Zealand's exports are currently absorbed by the East Asian market.

In return, New Zealand imports mostly manufactured goods from these East Asian countries. From Japan and Korea, cars and electronic goods are among the main import items, while electronic goods and computers are imported from Taiwan and Hong Kong and various manufactured goods, including textiles and toys, are imported from China.

The main trading countries from Southeast Asia, which makes up about 8 percent of the market for New Zealand's exports, are Malaysia and Singapore. New Zealand's trade relationships with the remaining parts of Asia are only modest.

Immigration

The earliest emigrants from Asia to New Zealand were the Chinese laborers who worked in the Otago gold mines and who numbered more than five thousand by the 1870s. The Chinese were initially welcomed but soon came to experience immigration restrictions and discrimination, which resulted in the majority of these laborers leaving New Zealand. Most present-day Chinese–New Zealanders are recent immigrants. In 1986, New Zealand changed its immigration policy, and Asians didn't face more restrictions than Europeans did.

According to the 1986 New Zealand census, at that time there were about fifty-five thousand Asians, and these identified themselves as mostly Chinese or Indians. However, by the next census in 1991, the Asian population had jumped to ninety-nine thousand, with a much more diverse national background. The adoption of business migration and the general points system (which assesses immigration applicants by awarding them points based on such factors as educational and professional qualifications, work experience, and age) in November 1991 resulted in a dramatic increase of Asian immigration to New Zealand, and the total Asian population reached 140,000 in 1996. By allowing business migration, New Zealand hoped to attract wealthy Asians who would invest funds in New Zealand, thereby boosting the economy.

When the recent immigrants came in the 1990s, they experienced some discrimination by the New Zealanders of European origin, who were rather taken aback by the sudden influx of Asians they thought had arrived to stay. But many of the immigrants, especially those with marketable skills and good financial support, have moved on to a third country, seeking jobs in Australia, the United States, and Canada, or going back to their countries of origin. Nevertheless, emigration from Asia has become an important element in New Zealand-Asia relationships.

Diplomatic Relations

In 1998 New Zealand had fourteen diplomatic and consular posts in Asian countries, and the number of diplomatic representatives in those posts is increasing. This trend closely reflects the strengthening of trade and immigration ties more than political, security, or other bilateral interests. New Zealand has diplomatic posts in Tokyo, Seoul, Beijing, Hong Kong, Hanoi, Manila, Jakarta, Bangkok, Kuala Lumpur, Singapore, and New Delhi.

New Zealand has been active in Asian international organizations. New Zealand is an original dialogue partner of ASEAN (the Association of Southeast Asian Nations) and participates in the ASEAN Regional Forum to discuss and cooperate in regional security issues. New Zealand is also a founding member of the APEC (Asia Pacific Economic Cooperation) forum, and in September 1999 New Zealand hosted a meeting of APEC leaders at Auckland. As New Zealand looks to the future, it increasingly aligns itself with Asia; indeed, in 1996, Prime Minister Jim Bolger even called New Zealand a part of Asia.

Hong-key Yoon

Further Reading

Hooson, D. (1976) "A Lonely Independence: New Zealand's Changing Place in the World." *Professional Geographer* 28, 1: 35–39.

Lissington, M. P. (1972) *New Zealand and Japan 1900–1941*. Wellington, New Zealand: A. R. Shearer.

McKinnon, Malcolm. (1996) *Immigrants and Citizens: New Zealanders and Asian Immigration in Historical Context*. Wellington, New Zealand: Institute of Policy Studies, Victoria University of Wellington.

Statistics New Zealand. (1996) *New Zealand Census of Population and Dwellings: Ethnic Groups*. Wellington, New Zealand: Statistics New Zealand.

———. (1998) *New Zealand Official Yearbook 1998*. Wellington, New Zealand: Statistics New Zealand.

Vasil, Raj, and Hong-key Yoon. (1996) *New Zealanders of Asian Origin*. Wellington, New Zealand: Institute of Policy Studies, Victoria University of Wellington.

NGO DINH DIEM (1901–1963), first president of the first Republic of Vietnam. Born of a well-known Catholic family of central Vietnam, Ngo Dinh Diem (pronounced N-go Dinh Ziem) pursued a Westernized education that, in his time, still preserved some values of the traditional Confucian system. It prepared him for a brilliant career in the royal government of Vietnam, in which he rose to the level of provincial governor at the age of twenty-eight. His career took an advantageous turn in 1933, when the young emperor Bao Dai offered him the position of minister of the interior in the first cabinet of his reign. Following some difference of opinion with either the emperor or

President Ngo Dinh Diem at his desk in Saigon (Ho Chi Minh City) in February 1958. (BETTMANN/CORBIS)

his close collaborators, Diem handed in his resignation a few days later, whereon he was stripped of all his functions and honorific distinctions. Subsequently, the court gave back his medals, without, however, reintegrating him into the government.

Diem acquired a reputation of independence, honesty, and integrity, which increased further when, in 1945, he refused to collaborate with the first government of independent Vietnam headed by Ho Chi Minh because he accused the Communists of the murder of one of his brothers. Diem's hopes of playing a role in public affairs on the side of the French-sponsored anticommunist factions were totally dashed in 1949 when the French chose his nemesis, the former emperor Bao Dai, as the head of the State of Vietnam they built up as the rival to Ho Chi Minh's Democratic Republic of Vietnam (DRV). Disheartened, Ngo Dinh Diem went on a world tour, which ultimately landed him in the United States.

Meanwhile, the State of Vietnam did not live up to expectations: Its government was corrupt to the core, its attraction as a "nationalist" substitute to the DRV was limited, and the war turned from bad to worse. Then followed Dien Bien Phu and the Geneva Conference. The United States put intense pressure on France and Bao Dai to give Diem a chance. He was then appointed prime minister of the State of Vietnam; his government was presented on 7 July 1954, a mere two weeks before the Geneva Accords divided

Vietnam into two temporary administrative zones. With U.S. aid, Diem firmly intended to delete the word "temporary" from the Accords.

After securing total control of the army, Diem unleashed it against the political factions that had been the loyal supporters of Bao Dai: the Cao Dai, Hoa Hao, and Binh Xuyen. He then turned against Bao Dai by organizing a plebiscite in which the people had to choose between Bao Dai and Diem as chief of state. Diem got more than 90 percent of the votes. On 25 October 1955, Diem created the Republic of Vietnam (RVN) and proclaimed himself its first president. A period of authoritarian government ensued, and as popular support dwindled, Diem relied more and more on members of his own family. His terror campaign against suspected Communists and his dictatorial rule alienated even noncommunist dissidents, who, in 1960, with the assistance of the DRV, formed the National Liberation Front of South Vietnam (NLF), the aim of which was the overthrow of Diem's republic and the reunification of Vietnam. The United States stayed firmly behind the Diem regime, which it hoped to make into a bastion of resistance against the expansion of Communism. But in 1963, on a trivial government interdiction against flying the Buddhist flag during the celebration of Buddha's birthday, the Buddhist hierarchy led the Buddhist community of Vietnam in an unprecedented revolt against the Diem government, whom the rebels accused of discrimination and excessive repression. The open Buddhist rebellion combined with the military attacks mounted by the NLF rendered Ngo Dinh Diem's government completely inoperative; the war against Communist subversion in South Vietnam suffered intolerable setbacks.

Washington then allowed the army to mount a coup against Diem on 1 November 1963; the next day, Diem and one of his brothers were killed. Thus ended the first Republic of Vietnam. The people who lived through it used only one short expression to describe it: "What a pity!" They felt that Diem was an honest and strong leader, the only one—compared with his successors—able to resist the interference of foreign powers, despite his connections with his brother Ngo Dinh Nhu and his wife. He appeared to have all the objective conditions to build up a viable alternative to the DRV, but many think he squandered them by a wrong assessment of the needs of his people.

Truong Buu Lam

Further Reading

Halberstam, David. (1965) *The Making of a Quagmire.* New York: Random House.

Warner, Denis A. (1963) *The Last Confucian.* New York: Macmillan.

———. (1971) *The Pentagon Papers: The Defense Department History of the United States Decisionmaking on Vietnam.* 2 vols. Boston: Beacon Press.

NGO DINH NHU (1910–1963), Vietnamese politician. Younger brother of Ngo Dinh Diem (1901–1963), the first president of South Vietnam, and husband of Madame Nhu (b. 1924, formerly Tran Le Xuan), Ngo Dinh Nhu served as an agent against French rule in Vietnam and later at the side of his brother after Diem was elected president in 1955. Known as an exceptional organizer and a poor administrator, Nhu began his national political life in 1953 in Saigon, organizing demonstrations against the Communists and the French and planning the overthrow of the regime of Emperor Bao Dai (1913–1997). He organized the National Union for Independence and Peace, and, with the support of the Binh Xuyen gang of river pirates and the Cao Dai and Hoa Hao religious sects, attempted a premature ouster of Bao Dai that failed. Nhu then organized, in 1954, a coalition called the Front for National Salvation, made up of the political-religious sects, the Catholics, the Dai Viet, and other nationalist groups, which intended to solidify his brother's ascent to the head of a new government while also publicly denouncing the Communists.

In June 1954, in the face of Nhu and Diem's activity, Bao Dai invited Diem to form a new government as prime minister. After his brother was in power, Nhu organized the Revolutionary Personalist Labor Party, an organization made up of small covert security, political, and labor groups that reported on opponents of the Diem regime. Along with Diem, he moved to consolidate power by crushing all opposition, including his former supporters, the Binh Xuyen and the religious sects. While this process was under way, Nhu masterminded the plan to gain the final removal of Bao Dai. He organized a group (the General Assembly of Democratic and Revolutionary Forces of the Nation) in April 1955 to demonstrate against the emperor and call for his abdication. In the wake of this movement, Diem was able to call for national elections to determine the new government, elections which he rigged with Nhu's assistance, and easily won. Again, the brothers attempted to further consolidate power and crush all opposition. The corruption and brutality of the brothers' regime, coupled with the inflammatory statements made by Madame Nhu, eventually caught up with them and led to a 1 November 1963 coup, unopposed by the United States, that saw both Nhu and Diem assassinated.

Richard B. Verrone

Further Reading

Boettcher, Thomas D. (1985) *Vietnam: The Valor and the Sorrow*. Boston: Little, Brown.

Jamieson, Neil L. (1993). *Understanding Vietnam*. Berkeley and Los Angeles: University of California Press.

Karnow, Stanley. (1991) *Vietnam: A History*. New York: Viking.

Tucker, Spencer C., ed. (1998) *Encyclopedia of the Vietnam War*. Oxford, U.K.: Oxford University Press.

NGUYEN CAO KY (b. 1930), Vietnamese political leader. Nguyen Cao Ky was born in Son Tay Province, northwest of Hanoi, in 1930. In 1950 he was drafted into the Vietnamese National Army. He rose to the rank of lieutenant, and in 1953 he volunteered for pilot training. He trained in Algeria and France and graduated in 1954. He eventually was promoted to lieutenant general in the South Vietnamese Air Force.

Ky participated in the 1964 coup that ousted Duong Van Minh from power, and served as prime minister of the Republic of Vietnam between 1965 and 1967. While prime minister, Ky lost much support when he ordered severe repression of Buddhists, whom he believed to be Communist allies. In April 1966, with the help of General William Westmoreland, he led two Army of the Republic of Vietnam battalions against what he believed were Buddhist bases in Da Nang. His actions against the Buddhists led to numerous protests in southern Vietnamese cities.

Premier Nguyen Cao Ky in February 1966. (BETTMANN/CORBIS)

Following the 1967 elections, Nguyen Cao Ky became vice president of South Vietnam. In the 1971 elections he chose not to run against Nguyen Van Thieu. He then faded from the political scene. Despite a public promise never to leave Vietnam, he fled to the United States in April 1975.

Micheline R. Lessard

Further Reading

Duiker, William. (1981) *The Communist Road to Power in Vietnam*. Boulder, CO: Westview Press.

Kahin, George M. (1987) *Intervention: How America Became Involved in Vietnam*. New York: Anchor.

Karnow, Stanley. (1983) *Vietnam: A History*. New York: Viking.

NGUYEN DU (1765–1820), Vietnamese poet. Nguyen Du was a Vietnamese poet and minor court official, widely regarded as the greatest writer in vernacular Vietnamese. Du's epic narrative poem *The Tale of Kieu* is considered the preeminent work of classical Vietnamese literature, and its characters and language have left a profound mark on Vietnamese society and culture. Born to a family of scholars in the northern province of Ha Tinh, Nguyen Du grew up in a time of enormous political and social turmoil during the final years of the Late Le dynasty (1428–1788). When armies of the Tay Son rebellion (1778–1802) overthrew the Le, he, like many other loyal scholars, went into hiding rather than serve the new regime. When the Tay Son were themselves overthrown by the Nguyen dynasty (1802–1955), Du reluctantly lent his support to the new regime serving in a number of minor court positions. In 1813, he accompanied an imperial embassy to the Chinese court, and while there he may have found the literary inspiration for his masterwork.

In *The Tale of Kieu*, Nguyen Du skillfully combined the Vietnamese vernacular with the six-eight rhythm of folk poetry to rework a seventeenth-century Chinese tale into the great Vietnamese epic. *The Tale of Kieu* weaves together a series of encounters involving archetypal characters of Du's age— the filial daughter (Kieu), corrupt officials, pious Buddhist nuns, heroic rebel leaders, and traitorous mandarins—reflecting the social and political turmoil of his time, as well as his own personal tribulations. The work also highlights the plight and status of women in Vietnamese society, and Nguyen Du lauds Kieu's resilience in the face of immense hardships. In addition to *The Tale of Kieu*, Du also produced a substantial body of shorter poetry in both Vietnamese and classical Chinese, including the noted "Funeral Oration to the Ten Types of Wandering Souls," an elegy to the dead of the Tay Son–Nguyen wars.

George E. Dutton

Further Reading

Durand, Maurice, and Nguyen Tran Huan. (1985) *An Introduction to Vietnamese Literature*. Trans. by D. M. Hawke. New York: Columbia University Press.

Mai Quoc Lien. (1996) "Nguyen Du's Poetry in Classical Chinese." *The Vietnam Review* (Autumn–Winter): 15–20.

Nguyen Du. (1983) *The Tale of Kieu: A Bilingual Edition*. Trans. by Huynh Sanh Thong. New Haven, CT: Yale University Press.

———. (1996) *Nguyen Du Toan Tap* (The Complete Works of Nguyen Du). Hanoi, Vietnam: Nha Xuat Ban Van Hoc.

Woodside, Alexander. (1983) "The Historical Background." In *The Tale of Kieu: A Bilingual Edition*, translated by Huynh Sanh Thong. New Haven, CT: Yale University Press.

NGUYEN GIA THIEU (1741–1798), Vietnamese poet. Nguyen Gia Thieu is considered one of Vietnam's foremost classical poets. He was born in Lieu Ngan village in Bac Ninh Province in northern Vietnam of aristocratic parents. His father was Nguyen Gia Cu, also known as the Marquis Dat Vu, and his mother was Princess Quynh Lien. He began his classical studies at the age of five at the Trinh Palace. He worked for a time, though without much enthusiasm, in the Vietnamese civil service, and in 1782 he was made commander of the Hung Hoa troops. Nguyen Gia Thieu chose not to pursue a military career, however, and he retreated to a quiet house in Hanoi (then Thang Long), where he engaged in spiritual study and practices. He was particularly interested in Buddhism and Taoism and both philosophies influenced his poetry. In 1786 he was captured by the Tay Son rebels when they took control of Hanoi. In order not to serve the rebels he feigned insanity. He left a considerable body of poetry in both Chinese and Chu Nom. His most celebrated work is *Cung Oan Ngam Khuc* (sometimes translated as "Lament inside a Harem"), a poem depicting the fate of a beautiful woman living in a royal harem.

Micheline R. Lessard

Further Reading

Huynh Sang Thong. (1979) *The Heritage of Vietnamese Poetry*. New Haven, CT: Yale University Press.

NGUYEN THI MINH KHAI (1910–1941), Vietnamese revolutionary. Nguyen Thi Minh Khai was a leading Vietnamese revolutionary and was rumored to be the wife of Ho Chi Minh (1890–1969). Born in 1910, she attended school in Vinh, where she stood out for her anti-French activism. In 1927, she was recruited into the Tan Viet Party and was quickly promoted through the ranks. Anticipating arrest, she fled to Hong Kong in 1930, where she worked as Ho Chi Minh's assistant in the Comintern's Southern Bureau. She was an alternate to the October 1930 plenary conference that saw the founding of the Indochina Communist Party (ICP). Ho requested permission from the Comintern to marry her, but before a marriage could take place, British police arrested Nguyen on 29 April 1931 on suspicion of involvement in subversive activities. After her release in 1934, she returned to Hong Kong to resume party work and was a member of an ICP delegation to the Comintern's seventh congress in 1935, where she spoke about the exploitation of women in Asia and their revolutionary potential. She returned to Vietnam in 1937 and worked clandestinely in Saigon with Le Hong Phong, whom she later married. Following the ICP leadership's retreat to China in 1940, Khai and her sister, Nguyen Thi Quang Thai, the first wife of Vo Nguyen Giap (one of Ho Chi Minh's closest associates, the founder of the Viet Minh armed forces and minister of defense for the ICP), were ordered to remain in Vietnam to serve as liaisons. Khai was arrested by the French in July 1940. Following interrogation and torture, she was executed on 25 April 1941.

Zachary Abuza

Further Reading

Duiker, William. (2000) *Ho Chi Minh*. New York: Hyperion.

Huynh Kim Khanh. (1986) *Vietnamese Communism, 1925–1945*. Ithaca, NY: Cornell University Press.

NGUYEN VAN THIEU (b. 1923), president of the Republic of Vietnam (1967–1975). A career military officer, Nguyen Van Thieu graduated from Vietnam's National Military Academy in 1949 and the Command and General Staff Office at Ft. Leavenworth, Kansas, in 1957.

Thieu participated in the November 1963 coup that brought down President Ngo Dinh Diem (1901–1963) and served briefly as deputy premier before becoming chief of state in the government of Nguyen Cao Ky (b. 1930) from 1965 to 1967. Thieu defeated Ky in the 1967 presidential election and consolidated political power in the post of the presidency. In a power-sharing arrangement, Ky remained premier, though the post was stripped of much of its power. Ky also became Thieu's vice-presidential running mate. Thieu

Nguyen Van Thieu in 1969. (BETTMANN/CORBIS)

failed to broaden his base of popular support, especially in the countryside, where he was unable to implement meaningful land reform, while urbanites were frustrated by his repression and widespread corruption, and hence he had to rely on an enlarged military to consolidate his power. In 1971, Thieu disqualified his election challengers, including his vice president, Nguyen Cao Ky, while disastrous 1971–1972 offensives against the North Vietnamese during the Vietnam War (1954–1975) weakened his regime.

Because Thieu was unwilling to negotiate with North Vietnam, which demanded his resignation, U.S. Secretary of State Henry Kissinger began meeting secretly with representatives from North Vietnam. Upset with the draft peace agreement, Thieu made twenty-six changes but signed under intense U.S. pressure. Thieu tried to consolidate power after the Paris Peace Accords and went on the offensive, but his forces were no match for the North Vietnamese troops, who occupied much of South Vietnam. On 21 April 1975, days before the Communists took control, Thieu resigned and fled Vietnam; he lives in exile in America.

Zachary Abuza

Further Reading

Young, Marilyn B. (1991) *The Vietnam Wars 1945 1990* New York: HarperCollins.

NHU, MADAME NGO DINH (b. 1924), sister-in-law of President Ngo Dinh Diem. Madame Ngo Dinh Nhu, a notorious and feared member of South Vietnam's presidential family (1955–1963), was born Tran Le Xuan in 1924 to a wealthy family that served the French colonial administration. She married Ngo Dinh Nhu (1910–1963), brother of Ngo Dinh Diem (1901–1963), in 1943 and, upon the latter's ascension to the presidency of South Vietnam (RVN) in 1955, moved into the presidential palace in Saigon with her husband. Because Diem was unmarried, Madame Nhu effectively became the RVN's First Lady and acted as official hostess of the presidential palace. With Diem's office came benefits for the family: Madame Nhu's father served as ambassador to the United States, her mother became an observer at the United Nations, and two of her uncles served as cabinet members. She was criticized for her

Madame Nhu in Washington, D.C., in October 1963. (BETTMANN/CORBIS)

arrogance, caustic remarks, insensitivity, and intolerance. Lashing out at anyone critical of the Diem regime, Madame Nhu was nicknamed "Dragon Lady." For example, when she found out that U.S. Ambassador General J. Lawton Collins (1896–1987) encouraged Diem to oust her, she blamed the United States for assisting factions that sought to topple the Diem government. When Buddhist monks, whom she once called "hooligans in robes" (Karnow 1991: 312), protested the Diem regime through self-immolation, she referred to the protests as "barbecues" and offered to supply gasoline for future demonstrations. While in power, the Catholic Nhu called herself a feminist and formed the Women's Solidarity Movement, yet she issued decrees banning dance, divorce, contraceptives, beauty contests, fortune-telling, gambling, adultery, prostitution, and certain hairdos and music. Her outspokenness against protestors in 1963 helped turn the Kennedy administration against the Diem regime, which in turn led to the coup that toppled the government, resulting in the deaths of her brother-in-law and husband in November of that year.

Richard B. Verrone

Further Reading

Boettcher, Thomas D. (1985) *Vietnam: The Valor and the Sorrow*. Boston: Little, Brown.

Karnow, Stanley. (1991) *Vietnam: A History*. New York: Viking.

Tucker, Spencer C. (1999) *Vietnam*. Lexington: University Press of Kentucky.

———, ed. (1998) *Encyclopedia of the Vietnam War*. Oxford, U.K.: Oxford University Press.

NICHIREN (1222–1282), Japanese Buddhist reformer. Nichiren, a medieval Japanese Buddhist teacher, is regarded as the founder of the Hokke (Lotus) or Nichiren sect. He had entered a monastery in 1233 and then based himself in Kamakura, near Yokohama, preaching among Japan's eastern warriors. Trained in Tendai teachings of the Lotus Sutra and in esoteric Buddhism, Nichiren sought the authentic teachings of the Buddha, taught exclusive faith in the Lotus Sutra as the true Buddhism, and advocated the practice of chanting its *daimoku* or title in the formula, *Namu-myoho-renge-kyo*.

His early writings criticized Pure Land doctrines of otherworldly salvation; later, he also criticized Zen and other Buddhist traditions, asserting that only the Lotus Sutra offered immediate access to Buddhahood in that era. Nichiren saw disasters, including famines, epidemics, and Mongol invasion attempts, as due to collective rejection of the Lotus in favor of "inferior" teachings; spreading faith in the Lotus, however, would bring peace to the land. He incurred persecution, including two sentences of exile, for his attacks on the Buddhist establishment and its patrons in government, but he believed that worldly authority must be defied when it contravened Buddhist truth.

Nichiren's ideal of realizing the Buddha land in the present world has inspired modern followers, who have assimilated it to numerous political and humanitarian agendas. Today nearly forty religious organizations claim association with him, including traditional sects and new religions.

Jacqueline I. Stone

Further Reading

Dolce, Lucia Dora. (2002) "Esoteric Patterns in Nichiren's Interpretation of the Lotus Sutra." Ph.D. diss., University of Leiden.

Habito, Ruben, and Jacqueline I. Stone, eds. (1999) "Revisiting Nichiren." *Japanese Journal of Religious Studies* 26 (fall), 3–4.

Stone, Jacqueline I. (1999) "Nichiren and the New Paradigm." In *Original Enlightenment and the Transformation of Medieval Japanese Buddhism*. Honolulu: University of Hawaii Press, chap. 6.

NIHONGA *Nihonga* (Japanese-style painting) was practiced beginning in the mid-Meiji period (1868–1912) and combines aspects of Western painting such as shading and perspective with traditional Japanese techniques. In 1884, Ernest Fenollosa (1853–1908), an American who taught philosophy and political economy at Tokyo University and the author of the first English-language work on Japanese art *(Epochs of Chinese and Japanese Art)*, along with Okakura Kakuzo (1862–1913), founded the Kangakai (Painting Appreciation Society) to promote traditional Japanese arts. Together, they also established the Tokyo School of Fine Arts, where Japanese-style painting was taught. Fenollosa left Japan for the United States in 1890, and Okakura continued as director until his resignation in 1898, when he went on to found the Japan Fine Arts Academy.

Two artists of the Kangakai were Kano Hogai (1828–1888) and Hashimoto Gaho (1835–1908). Meiji values strongly promoted Western ideals, which created a difficult environment for traditional artists. Such was the case with Hogai, who had great talent and strong connections to the Kano school of painting, but had to resort to means other than painting to make a living. In 1884, Fenollosa had seen his work and asked Hogai to join the Kangakai, where he spent the last years of his life successfully combining Japanese and Western elements in his work. Gaho's situation was similar. After finding it difficult to make a living through his art, Gaho came to the Kangakai at Fenollosa's request, later becoming an instructor of painting at the Tokyo School of Fine Arts and the Japan Fine Arts Academy. Through these appointments, Gaho was able to teach the next generation of Japanese-style painters.

Of Gaho's students, three were particularly important in transmitting *nihonga* ideals of combining elements of Western and Japanese painting: Yokoyama Taikan (1868–1958), Shimomura Kanzan (1873–1930), and Hishida Shunso (1874–1911). All studied together at the Tokyo School of Fine Arts, and all left the school with Okakura to join him at the Japan Fine Arts Academy.

In 1906, the Japan Fine Arts Academy experienced financial difficulties that forced it to be moved from Tokyo to the fishing village of Izura. Despite the Academy's remote location, students remained loyal; following Okakura's death in 1913, it was reorganized under Yokoyama and Shimomura and remains an active institution, holding annual exhibitions of its students' work.

Today, *nihonga* enjoys renewed popularity. Redefined to meet the demands of a twenty-first-century audience, *nihonga* encompasses broader subject matter and styles to include both the traditional and the avant-garde. Higashiyama Kaii (b. 1908) is considered Japan's premier twentieth-century *nihonga* artist. Among his many important commissions are his screens for the Toshodaiji in Nara, a project he began in 1971 and completed in 1982. Characterized by their striking blue-green color, these paintings represent the pinnacle of modern *nihonga* art.

Catherine Pagani

Further Reading

Baekeland, Frederick. (1980) *Imperial Japan: The Art of the Meiji Era (1868–1912).* Ithaca, NY: Herbert F. Johnson Museum of Art.

NIIGATA (2002 est. pop. 2.5 million). Niigata Prefecture is situated in the central region of Japan's island of Honshu, where it occupies an area of 12,579 square kilometers. Its primary geographical features are a mountainous terrain, central plateaus, a coastal plain, and the offshore island of Sado, one of Japan's largest. Niigata is bordered by the Sea of Japan and by Yamagata, Fukushima, Gumma, Nagano, and Toyama prefectures. It assumed its present name in 1871, subsuming the provinces of Echigo and Sado; its present borders were fixed in 1886.

The prefecture's capital is Niigata city, the largest along the Sea of Japan. A leading Edo-period (1600/1603–1868) port, the city was declared an international port in 1858. Home to Niigata University, it is a major industrial center as well. The prefecture's other important cities are Nagaoka, Joetsu, Sanjo, and Kashiwazaki.

In ancient times, Niigata Prefecture was home to the aboriginal Ezo people, whom government soldiers eventually conquered and forced northward. During the Heian period (794–1185), the Uesugi and other warrior families controlled Echigo, which was divided into many domains during the Edo period. At the same time, the Tokugawa shogunate assumed direct control of Sado, where rich lodes of gold and silver had been discovered. Forced labor was used to work the mines, which provided a major source of revenue to the government. Today Sado's unique folk culture of music, dance, Noh drama, and Bun'ya puppet drama makes the island a popular destination.

Niigata Prefecture possesses the nation's largest oil and natural gas reserves. Its heavy industry ranges from petroleum refining to machinery and chemical production. A major rice grower, the prefecture also has flourishing sake brewing, textile, and woodworking companies.

E. L. S. Weber

Further Reading

"Niigata Prefecture." (1993) *Japan: An Illustrated Encyclopedia*. Tokyo: Kodansha.

NIKKYOSO Nikkyoso is the abbreviated name of Nihon Kyoshokuin Kumiai (Japan Teachers' Union). It was formed in 1947, and in its early days the vast majority of school teachers in Japan were participating members. During the 1950s and 1960s, Nikkyoso's left-wing leadership had a confrontational relationship with the Japanese government. The union opposed the government's efforts to reverse somc of the democratic reforms introduced during the Allied occupation (1945–1952). Bitter disputes were fought over the issues of central government control of textbooks, the curriculum, and teacher training and assessment. During this time, Nikkyoso was closely allied with other public sector unions and the Japanese Socialist Party.

By the 1980s, Nikkyoso faced a crisis brought about by declining membership and internal divisions over policy. In 1989, a serious split took place that involved one-third of the members leaving the union and forming a new teachers' union called Zenkyo. After this split, Nikkyoso went on to revise its educational and political policy with a view to working with the government rather than opposing it. Zenkyo, on the other hand, was determined to continue the left-wing struggle against the government and the education bureaucracy.

Robert Aspinall

Further Reading

Aspinall, Robert. (2001) *Teachers' Unions and the Politics of Education in Japan*. Albany, NY: State University of New York Press.

NILGIRI DISTRICT (2001 pop. 765,000). Nilgiri district is an administrative district of 2,549 square kilometers, the most northwesterly district in Tamil Nadu State, India. The area lies at the juncture of the Eastern and the Western Ghats, about 425 kilometers west of Madras City (or Chennai). Two-thirds of the district is a high mountain plateau; one-third is the much lower Wainad Plateau. The highest point in the district is Doddabetta Peak, 2,637 meters in elevation.

The district headquarters is the well-known resort of Ootacamund. Nilgiri district is home to well over a dozen tribal groups, most found only in this area and most having their own distinctive Dravidian language. These groups include the Todas, Kotas, Badagas, Panias, four tribes of Irulas, and seven tribes of Kurumbas. The cultures and economies of these indigenous groups are very distinct and form the basis for complex symbiotic exchange relationships. The district is chiefly important for its exports of tea, but coffee, rubber, cardamom, potatoes, and cabbages are also prominent exports, as is hydroelectric power generated through numerous man-made dams.

Paul Hockings

Further Reading

Hockings, Paul, ed. (1989) *Blue Mountains: The Ethnography and Biogeography of a South Indian Region*. New Delhi: Oxford University Press.

———. (1997). *Blue Mountains Revisited: Cultural Studies on the Nilgiri Hills*. New Delhi: Oxford University Press.

NINGKAN, STEPHEN KALONG (1920–1997), first chief minister of the East Malaysian state of Sarawak. Stephen Kalong Ningkan served as first chief minister of the East Malaysian state of Sarawak between July 1963 and September 1966. Prior to Sarawak's joining the union of Malaya, Singapore, and North Borneo to form the Federation of Malaysia, Sarawak was a British colony. Born in Sarawak of Iban and Chinese ancestry, Ningkan is probably best known for triggering a constitutional crisis when he refused to vacate his office after being dismissed by the Sarawakian governor. Ningkan, as leader of the Council Negri (the state legislature), had purportedly ceased to command the confidence of the majority of the council. With the backing of the federal government in Kuala Lumpur, the governor proceeded to appoint a new chief minister. Ningkan's refusal to vacate his office, resulting in a constitutional impasse that was perceived to threaten the fragile unity of Malaysia, aroused a vigorous reaction from the federal government.

On 14 September 1966, Yang di-Pertuan Agong, Malaysia's head of state, proclaimed a state of emergency in Sarawak on the basis that its security was threatened by the constitutional crisis. Under emergency rule, Parliament was legislatively enabled to exercise further powers, effectively governing Sarawak from the federal capital. Ningkan appealed his dismissal all the way to the Privy Council in London, Malaysia's then final appellate court, but lost his appeal for a declaration that he was still chief minister of Sarawak. A firm believer that Sarawakians were entitled to have full citizenship rights and to participate in Malaysia's national development on a par with the Malays on the Malaya Peninsula, Ningkan slipped into political oblivion after his removal from office.

The constitutional crisis that Ningkan was embroiled in should be seen in the light of the volatile political matrix in Malaysia then. After Malaysia was created through the union of Malaya and Singapore, Sabah, and Sarawak on 16 September 1963, communal tension rose over the core identity of Malaysia. The politically convenient union was short-lived and Singapore left the federation on 9 August 1965. At the federal level, there was concern that Sarawak and Sabah might follow Singapore and secede from Malaysia. The removal of Ningkan, albeit by constitutional means, was an attempt by the federal government in Kuala Lumpur to exercise indirect control by aligning East Malaysian political parties with the United Malays National Organization–dominated coalition at the center.

Eugene K. B. Tan

Further Reading

Means, Gordon P. (1970) *Malaysian Politics*. London: University of London Press.

Milne, Robert Stephen, and Kanagaratnam Jeya Ratnam. (1974) *Malaysia—New States in a New Nation: Political Development of Sarawak and Sabah in Malaysia.* London: Frank Cass.

Roff, Margaret Clark. (1974) *The Politics of Belonging: Political Change in Sabah and Sarawak.* Kuala Lumpur, Malaysia: Oxford University Press.

Von Vorys, Karl. (1975) *Democracy without Consensus: Communalism and Political Stability in Malaysia.* Princeton, NJ: Princeton University Press.

NINGXIA (2002 est. pop. 5.9 million). Ningxia, with the official name of Ningxia Hui Autonomous Region, is located in northwest China and covers an area of 51,800 square kilometers. Ningxia borders on Gansu in the east, south, and west; on Mongolia in the north; and on Inner Mongolia and Shaanxi in the east. It is traversed by the Huang (Yellow) River, which in the middle of the region changes its west–east course and runs north. The larger part of the region consists of loess plateau and its altitude averages 1,000 meters above sea level. The majority of the region's 5.2 million (1996) people live in the fertile Huang River Valley, which lies sheltered by the Helan Mountains. The capital of Yinchuan (population of 559,000 in 1996) is also situated in the valley.

The Ningxia region was carved out of Gansu Province and was accorded provincial status from 1928 to 1954, when it reverted to Gansu, but in 1958 several Hui autonomous districts were combined into one independent region, which is divided into sixteen counties and one banner, the Alashan East Banner, home of a Mongol minority people. The 1.8 million Hui—Chinese Moslems—are concentrated in and around the capital, while several other minority groups are scattered around the region. Irrigated fields along the 320-kilometer-long south to north river valley produce wheat, rice, sugar beets, vegetables, and fruit, and animal husbandry is dominated by sheep. Industries are concentrated around Yinchuan and the second largest city, Shizuishan.

Bent Nielsen

Further Reading

Schran, Peter. (1976) *Guerrilla Economy: The Development of the Shensi-Kansu-Ninghsia Border Region, 1937–1945.* Albany: State University of New York Press.

NINOY. See **Aquino, Benigno.**

NIRAT *Nirat* is a type of Thai poem, often written in *khlong* meter, in which traditionally the poet describes his separation from either a loved one or a familiar place. Typically, sights and sounds on the poet's journey will remind him of the girl he has left behind and evoke a sense of melancholy, which is then expressed through clever punning on the names of places or meanings of the names of places that he passes through.

Famous *nirat* poems include *Khlong Nirat Hariphunchai*, composed in the sixteenth century, in which the poet Si Thep describes his journey from Chiang Mai to Hariphunchai in Lamphun, and *Khlong Kamsuan*, in which the poet Si Prat describes his journey from Ayutthaya to exile in Nakhon Si Thammarat. The most famous of all *nirat* poets is Sunthorn Phu (1786–1855), who broadened the thematic scope of the genre beyond the conventional theme of separation and love-longing, by including reflective, humorous, and philosophical passages. With increasing travel abroad in the nineteenth century, *nirat* poems often became "travel poems," recording the poet's impressions of foreign lands. Particularly famous is *Nirat London* by Mom Rachothai, the interpreter with the Thai mission sent to the court of Queen Victoria in 1857. In this poem, the poet mentions the English ports of Dover and Portsmouth and describes in detail the material sophistication of mid-nineteenth-century Britain, court manners, functions at Windsor Castle, and Queen Victoria herself. Although the *nirat* poem became less popular during the twentieth century, competitions are held to encourage its survival, and prominent poets still occasionally turn their hand to it.

David Smyth

Further Reading

Chitakasem, Manas. (1972) "The Emergence and Development of the *Nirat* Genre of Thai Poetry." *Journal of the Siam Society* 60, 2 (July): 135–168.

Wenk, Klaus. (1986) "Some Remarks about the Life and Works of Sunthon Phu." *Journal of the Siam Society*, 74: 169–198.

NISHIDA KITARO (1870–1945), Japanese philosopher. Japan's most important philosopher of the modern period, Nishida Kitaro was born near Kanazawa in Ishikawa Prefecture and attended Tokyo Imperial University as a student in philosophy. Along with being an excellent student, he intermittently practiced Zen meditation. Graduating in 1884, he returned to Kanazawa, where he grew up, and taught German, mathematics, and philosophy.

Appointed lecturer at Kyoto Imperial University in 1909, Nishida composed the philosophical essays that were published in 1911 as *Zen no kenkyu* (A Study of Good). In this work, Nishida reflected on the nature of Japanese culture within a Western rational framework. His belief in the need to achieve a transcendent state detached from worldly concerns was presented as his philosophy of "pure experience." The book became a bestseller, and Nishida subsequently was awarded a doctorate, appointed full professor, and given tenure. In *Geijutsu to dotoku* (Art and Morality, 1923), Nishida studied moral will and the beautiful as artistic intuition, focusing attention on the experimental ground from which the creativity of the artist and moral decisions of the self arise. In later works, he investigated Japanese culture, the notion of Buddhist "nothingness," and fundamental principles necessary for bridging Eastern and Western ways of thinking. Throughout his philosophy, Buddhism and traditional Eastern concepts remain dominant, yet his efforts to bring Western and Japanese concepts together in a logical framework have had a major impact on Japanese intellectual circles.

Despite bouts of ill health and a series of deaths in the family, Nishida remained at Kyoto University until his retirement, when he moved to Kamakura.

James M. Vardaman, Jr.

Further Reading

Dilworth, David A., Valdo H. Viglielmo, and Agustin Jacinto Zavala, eds. (1998) *Sourcebook for Modern Japanese Philosophy: Selected Documents*. Westport, CT: Greenwood Press.

Nishida Kitaro. (1973) *Art and Morality*. Trans. by David A. Dilworth and Valdo H. Viglielmo. Honolulu: University of Hawaii Press.

Tsunoda Ryusaku, et al. (1958) *Sources of Japanese Tradition*, vol. 2. New York: Columbia University Press.

NITOBE INAZO (1862–1933), educator, writer, public servant. Nitobe Inazo was Japan's best known twentieth-century internationalist. Born in Morioka in northern Japan, he studied at the most prestigious institutions: Sapporo Agricultural College and the University of Tokyo in Japan, Johns Hopkins University in the United States, and several German universities. While abroad, he married Mary Elkington, a Quaker from Philadelphia, and for the rest of his life he remained a steadfast Quaker.

The list of Nitobe's posts constitutes a who's who of elite organizations. Among other positions, he was headmaster of Tokyo's First Higher School (1906–1913), professor at the University of Tokyo (1913–1918), president of Tokyo Women's College (1918–1923), undersecretary general of the League of Nations (1920–1926), a member of the Diet's House of Peers (1926–1933), and Japanese chair of the Institute of Pacific Relations (1929–1933).

His sixteen volumes of writings (a third of them in English) focused on internationalism and ethical development, as well as his technical specialties: agricultural economics and colonial policy. He was acclaimed internationally for *Bushido: The Soul of Japan*, a favorite of U.S. president Theodore Roosevelt, which analyzed the ethical foundations of Japan's modern successes. His best-known work in Japanese, *Shuyo* (Self-cultivation), was reprinted 140 times.

Nitobe's reputation as a pacifist was damaged at the beginning of the 1930s when, in a series of lectures abroad, he tried to explain Japan's expansion into Manchuria. Until the end of his life, however, he defended internationalism and Quaker pacifism.

James L. Huffman

Further Reading

Howes, John F., ed. (1995) *Nitobe Inazo: Japan's Bridge across the Pacific*. Boulder, CO: Westview Press.

Nitobe, Inazo. (1969) *Bushido: The Soul of Japan*. Rutland, VT: Charles E. Tuttle.

NIXON SHOCK In a move that astonished the world, in July 1971 President Nixon announced his intent to visit the People's Republic of China (PRC) in 1972 and hence initiate the normalization of Sino-American relations. Japan, the United States's closest ally in East Asia, was not informed about Nixon's trip prior to its announcement. This situation became known in Japan as the first Nixon "shock," or *shokku*. The ostensible motivation behind Nixon's action was not to isolate Japan, but to warm relations with the PRC, within the context of the bipolar U.S.-USSR Cold War struggle. In Japan, Prime Minister Sato Eisaku, who was given no advance notice of the U.S. policy change vis-à-vis China, privately suggested that the United States was being insensitive to Japan's security position in Asia. Moreover, it seemed to the Japanese public that the United States was, at worse, retreating from its security commitments to Japan or, at best, exploiting the comfortable relationship between the two countries to the point of ignoring Japan's security needs.

The second Nixon *shokku* was the U.S. president's statement that initiated the end of the gold standard, one of the mainstays of the post–World War II world economy. In August 1971 Nixon announced that the United States would no longer exchange dollars for gold. This and related steps denoted the start of a floating exchange rate system by 1973. Nixon also put in place a 10 percent surcharge on all imports. Both moves were designed to improve the position of American exporters who were disadvantaged by an overvalued dollar. Japan, with its high dependence on the U.S. market, suffered more than other U.S. trading partners as the yen appreciated in value, making Japanese products more expensive in the United States and other markets.

Nixon's rapprochement with China and the unilateral termination of the fixed-exchange rate system, coupled with the high cost to Japanese exporters of the new trade policy, raised serious questions about the American commitment to Japan. In large part, Japan's shock with the moves by Nixon was based on the fact that Japanese leaders were not consulted.

Jonathan R. Strand

See also: **Japan-U.S. Relations; Sato Eisaku**

Further Reading

Barnhart, Michael A. (1995) *Japan and the World since 1868.* London: Edward Arnold.

Pyle, Kenneth B. (1992) *The Japanese Question: Power and Promise in a New Era.* Washington, DC: AEI Press.

NIYAZOV, SAPARMURAT (b. 1940), president of Turkmenistan. Born in 1940 in Ashgabat, Saparmurat Niyazov trained as an engineer and rose through the Communist Party ranks, becoming first secretary in 1985. When Turkmenistan gained independence in 1991, he became its president. Occupying his country's highest office since 1985, he is the longest continuously serving leader in the former Soviet Union.

Niyazov claims credit for winning international recognition of his country's neutral status and maintaining internal stability. His economic program is based on plans to export Turkmenistan's natural gas reserves (fourth largest in the world), although he has not resolved the problem of transporting the gas to countries that can pay for it. Meanwhile, his failure to launch market reforms has led the International Monetary Fund to pull out and the European Bank for Reconstruction and Development (EBRD) to threaten a cutoff of lending.

The pace of political reform is even less encouraging. Despite formal adherence to the Helsinki Final Act, Niyazov has stifled social initiative and all individual liberties, isolating his desert kingdom while becoming a virtual demigod and the focus of a Stalinist personality cult in the tightly controlled media. Niyazov has taken the appellation "Turkmenbashi" (Leader of the Turkmen), in apparent imitation of Ataturk, and locales, factories, and institutions bear his name. The rubber-stamp People's Council in December 1999 authorized him, as the country's first president, to rule indefinitely. In May 2001, the World Humanitarian Turkmen Association bestowed on Niyazov the title "Turkmenbashi the Great." Niyazov has also released a virtual bible (the *Rukhname*), which he intends to be the moral guide for his countrymen, thus becoming their spiritual as well as secular leader.

Under Niyazov, political institutions have been stunted. Turkmenistan is the last one-party state in the former Societ bloc. All elections have been farces; no dissent or opposition is tolerated, and schoolchildren must daily recite a poem that includes the line: "At the moment of my betrayal of my motherland, of her sacred banner, of my president, let my breath stop." Turkmen authorities have also targeted religious communities, demolishing a Hare Krishna temple and Seventh-Day Adventist Church in Ashgabat in November 1999 (only Sunni Islam and Russian Orthodoxy are registered).

In 2001, Niyazov isolated Turkmenistan and its people even farther from the rest of the modern world, closing opera and ballet houses and cutting education. Foreigners who want to marry Turkmen citizens must now pay the state $50,000. Niyazov has allowed no potential successor to come to the fore. His style of leadership involves frequent dismissals of ministers and other appointees, often followed by their public humiliation. Foreign dignitaries relate that Niyazov degrades his officials in the presence of visiting delegations. In November 2001, a wave of defections of former high-level officials signaled the first serious rift within Niyazov's elite. Perhaps fearing a coup attempt, Niyazov in March 2002 launched a purge of the security ministries, on which he has hitherto relied.

The international community has come to see Niyazov as an unpredictable megalomaniac who will not allow any reform or tolerate any opinion other than his own. His control of the political system and its coercive apparatus makes unlikely his removal from power, unless discontented underlings conspire successfully to oust him. It is widely assumed that only Saparmurat Niyazov's death will usher in a new era in Turkmenistan.

Michael Ochs

Further Reading

Ochs, Michael. (1997) "Turkmenistan: The Quest for Control and Stability." In *Democratization and Political Participation in Post-Communist Societies*, edited by Karen Dawisha and Bruce Parrott. Cambridge, U.K.: Cambridge University Press.

Ochs, Michael, and Sally N. Cummings. (2001) "Turkmenistan: Saparmurat's Inglorious Isolation." In *Power and Change in Central Asia*, edited by Sally N. Cummings. London: Routledge.

NIZAM AD-DIN AWLIYA' (1238–1325), Muslim saint of India. Nizam ad-Din Awliya'—whose real name was Muhammad bin Ahmad bin 'Ali al-Bukhari al-Bada'uni—was born at Bada'un, India, to a Turkish family who had migrated from Bukhara in today's Uzbekistan. He is one of the most venerated Muslim saints of the Indian subcontinent, his popularity reflected by the Arabic appellative Sultan al-Awliya' (King of the Saints), generally used by Muslims in referring to him.

After having received a traditional education in Arabic and Islamic studies, he went first to Delhi and then in 1257 to Ajudhan (a town on the river Satlej, an affluent of the Indus River), joining the Sufi Chishti (the most influential and popular Indian Islamic mystical order of the time) community led by the Sufi sheikh (master) Farid ad-Din Ganj-i Shakar (d. 1265). Nizam ad-Din soon became his favored disciple, and in 1258 Shakar nominated him as his *khalifa* (spiritual successor), sending him back to Delhi. He settled in the adjacent village of Ghiyaspur and established a Sufi community, which attracted followers from all the social strata, as Nizam ad-Din gained a remarkable reputation among and influence over Indian Muslims. He did not confine his teachings to mysticism but rather also focused on *tafsir* (commentary on the Qur'an), *hadith* (traditions), and literature. Some of his preachings—known as *malzufat*—were written down by his disciples and collected in the work *Fawa'id al-fu'ad* (Things Useful for the Heart), compiled by the poet Hasan Sijzi. Nizam ad-Din's *malzufat* thus became an important vehicle for the diffusion of mystical thought and practices throughout India. Cornerstones of his thought—in accordance with Chishti ideology—were the concepts of *wahdat al-mujud* (unity of being), the rejection of all material attractions, and nonviolence.

Amir-i Khosraw (1253–1325), generally considered the greatest poet of Delhi, was among his disciples. According to popular legend, he became a poet when Nizam ad-Din placed some of his saliva on Amir's tongue; certainly his poems reflect Amir's veneration for his master, and they contributed to the popularity of the saint.

In 1325, Nizam ad-Din died at Ghiyaspur. His tomb rapidly became a shrine for Muslims of the Indian subcontinent; on the anniversary of his death devotees crowd into the tomb and pray to the saint, asking for favors and his intercession.

Riccardo Redaelli

Further Reading

Nizam ad-Din Awliya'. (1995) *Fawa'id al-fu'ad: Spiritual and Literary Discourses of Shaikh Nizamuddin Awila*. Originally compiled by Amir Hasan 'Ala' Sijzi Dehlawi. Trans., with introduction, notes, and historical annotation, by Ziya-ul-Hasan Faruqi. New Delhi: D. K. Printworld.

NOBI *Nobi* were the slaves of premodern Korea. Male slaves (*no*) and female slaves (*pi*) were owned, traded, and inherited, but a distinct feature of Korean slavery was that slaves could own property, including other slaves. The origin of this institution is obscure, but during the Koryo dynasty (918–1392) private estates and slave cultivators increased. During the Choson dynasty (1392–1910) about 30 percent of the population were slaves.

A distinct social status group in which membership was hereditary, *nobi* were divided into public and private slaves. Public slaves (*kong nobi*) were kept in temples, government offices, schools, and posting stations; private slaves (*sa nobi*) were divided into domestic servants and outside resident slaves (*oego nobi*) who worked on distant land owned by the master. The relationship of the latter group to the master was similar to one of tenants to a landlord.

Intermarriage of slaves and commoners was common. According to law, for most of the Choson dynasty the status of the mother decided her children's status, but in practice, if either parent was a slave, the children became slaves as well. The *nobi* population was also perpetuated by poor peasants who sold themselves into slavery. In 1801, public slavery was abolished; in 1886, slave status was abrogated; and in 1894, private slavery was outlawed.

Anders Karlsson

Further Reading

Palais, James. (1996) *Confucian Statecraft and Korean Institutions: Yu Hyongwon and the Late Choson Dynasty*. Seattle: University of Washington Press.

———. (1984) "Slavery and Slave Society in the Koryo Period." *Journal of Korean Studies* 5: 173–190.

Peterson, Mark. (1985) "Slaves and Owners; or Servants and Masters? A Preliminary Examination of Slavery in Traditional Korea." *Transactions of the Royal Asiatic Society, Korea Branch* 60: 31–41.
Unruh, Ellen. (1976) "The Landowning Slave: A Korean Phenomenon." *Korea Journal* 16, 4: 27–34.

NOER, ARIFIN C. (1941–1995), Indonesian playwright, actor, stage director, film director. Born 10 March 1941 in Cirebon, West Java, Arifin is one of a group of modern Indonesian dramatists who present social problems on stage in a variety of dramatic guises. Aside from traditional Indonesian theater, his main influences are Ionesco and Brecht. The influence of traditional Indonesian forms is apparent in his blending of dramatic action with music. Arifin presented most of his works with the theater company Teater Kecil (Small Theater). His most frequently performed work is *Sumur Tanpa Dasar* (The Bottomless Well), first produced in 1964, which blends techniques drawn from theater of the absurd and traditional Indonesian theater, with a strong element of Islamic morality. When the actor, writer, and director W. S. Rendra returned from studying in the United States in 1968, Arifin acted for a time in Rendra's company, and later works show the influence of Rendra's minimalism. Also a celebrated director, he made six films between 1977 and 1991, the best-known of which is *Taksi*. He died 28 May 1995.

Tim Byard-Jones

Further Reading

Noer, Arifin C. (1992) *The Bottomless Well: A Play in Four Acts*. Trans. by Karin Johnson and Bernard Sellato. Jakarta, Indonesia: Lontar Foundation.
———. (1974) *Moths*. Trans. by Harry Aveling. Kuala Lumpur, Malaysia: Dewan Bahasa dan Pustaka.

NOH-KYOGEN Noh is a highly refined Japanese theater form combining drama, dance, music, and poetry. In the latter half of the fourteenth century, the actor and playwright Kanze Kan'ami Kiyotsugu (1333–1384) and his son, Kanze Zeami Motokiyo (1363–1433), moved Noh beyond its popular roots, incorporating the aesthetics of the military elite who patronized the art. This father and son team is responsible for many of the approximately 250 plays in the active repertory today. Plays are in one or two acts, and generally focus on an event in the life of one (usually masked) main character (*shite*), frequently a historical or legendary figure. A secondary character (*waki*), often a traveling priest, serves as a catalyst for the *shite* to reveal his or her story. A seven- to ten-member chorus, seated on the left side of the stage, chants narrative sections and takes over the lines of the *shite* and *waki* at emotional peaks. The actors are male; masks and costumes indicate the sex, age, and mental state of the character being portrayed.

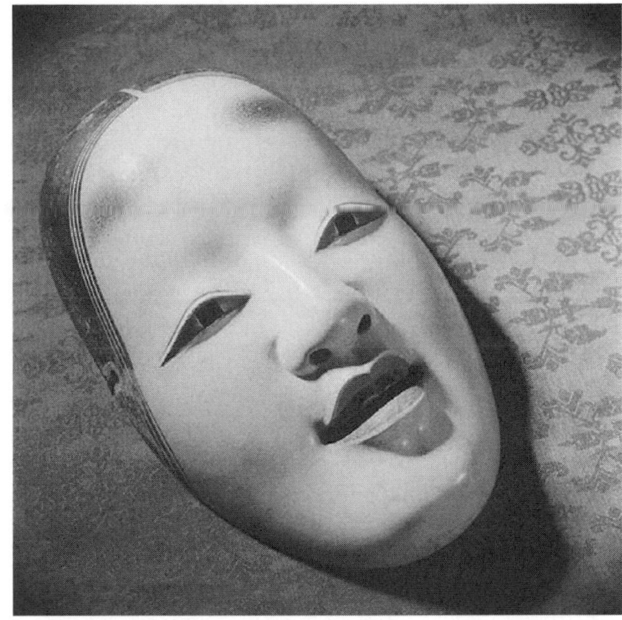

A Noh mask of noble beauty. (HORACE BRISTOL/CORBIS)

Many Noh plays include an interlude, performed by a *kyogen* actor (*kyogen* are comic spoken dialogue plays, performed between Noh plays or independently), which provides background information or summarizes the action of the play in colloquial language. A musical ensemble sits upstage center and accompanies the entire play.

There are 257 *kyogen* plays in the active repertory. They feature stock characters such as masters and conniving servants, tricksters and country bumpkins, inept warrior priests, overbearing wives, humorous demons, and felicitous deities. Unlike the highly literary scripted Noh plays, for hundreds of years *kyogen* plays were improvised based on skeletal outlines; they only began to be written down in the seventeenth century.

Noh and *kyogen* also have many things in common. Both are performed on a Noh stage—a long passageway (*hashigakari*) connecting to a main stage area that is approximately five square meters. The rear wall of the roofed stage depicts a large pine tree, and massive earthenware jars beneath the raised wooden floor amplify sound. A limited number of types of costume pieces, silk in Noh and linen in *kyogen*, are combined in different ways for various characters. Scenery is not used, as setting is created by the words or actions of the actors, and use of props is minimal. Both forms have been passed down from father to son for over six hundred years, are maintained by several important families, and remain vibrant forms of theater today.

Julie A. Iezzi

Further Reading

Bethe, Monica, and Karen Brazell. (1982) *Dance in the Nô Theater*. Ithaca, NY: China-Japan Program, Cornell University.

Komparu Kunio. (1983) *The Noh Theater: Principles and Perspectives*. New York: Weatherhill/Tankosha.

Rimer, Thomas J., and Yamazaki Masakazu, trans. (1984) *On the Art of the Nô Drama*. Princeton, NJ: Princeton University Press.

NOMADIC PASTORALISM—CENTRAL ASIA From around 800 BCE until the sixteenth century, nomadic pastoralists ruled the steppes (grassy plains) that stretch north of the Black Sea, across Kazakhstan, and into the Tian Shan and Altay Mountains of western China, western Mongolia, and southern Siberia. Sometimes called mobile herders, these groups did not, as often believed, freely move when and where they liked. Instead, they followed a yearly route between summer and winter pastures, riding on horseback and driving wagons and carts, moving their vast herds as the seasons dictated. Although some herders did live in villages or towns during the winter, nomadic pastoralism implies a way of life without permanent housing; generally the herders lived in tents or even houses carried on wagons. They were expert horsemen; in some ethnic groups, women rode and fought alongside the men, for mobile herding encouraged an aggressive way of life.

Most pastoralists depended not only on their herds but on booty and tribute that they plundered from surrounding settled folk. City dwellers often considered these people troublesome barbarians or even a threat to civilization, although those who never came in contact with these groups often saw them as enjoying a simple, noble life untouched by corruption and decadence. Remnants of nomadic pastoralism can still be found today in Mongolia and western China.

Definition of Nomadic Pastoralism

Horses had probably been domesticated on the steppes around the beginning of the first millennium BCE, and, thereafter, people began to ride horses while herding their animals. This way of life probably combined pastoralism—herding animals—and farming on the Black Sea steppes, and in the steppes to the east the use of horses allowed herders to enlarge their herds

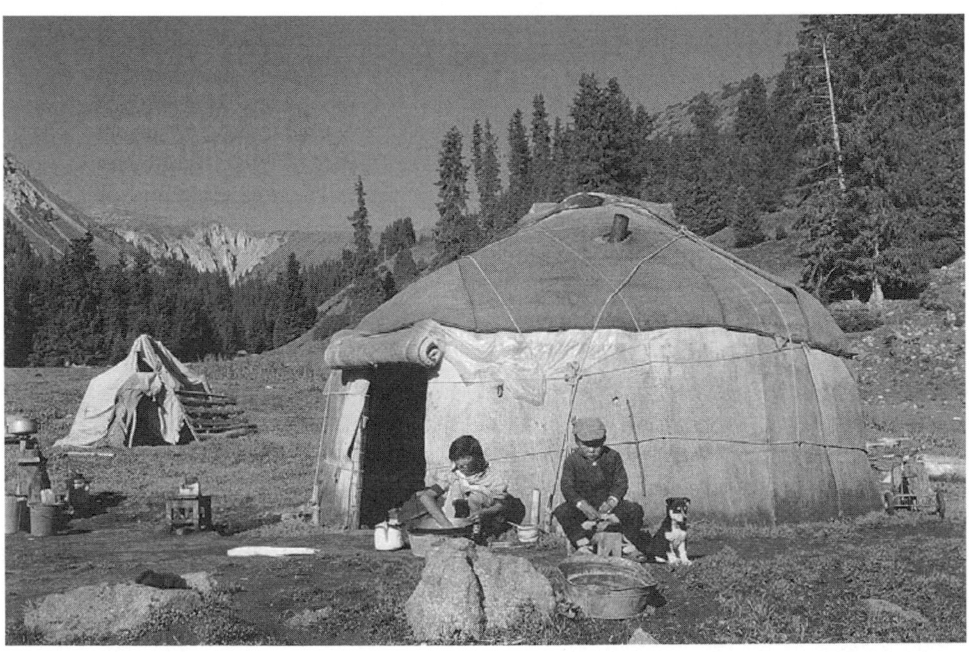

A Kyrgyz family outside its yurt in Djety Oguz, Kyrgyzstan, in 1995. (JANET WISHNETSKY/CORBIS)

by pasturing them over larger areas than would be the case if animals and men traveled on foot and then returned to their homes each evening.

The steppe inhabitants became mobile herders from about the ninth century BCE, tending horses, sheep, goats, camels, or yaks (in the higher elevations), depending on the geographic area, and moving seasonally between pastures, sometimes visiting low-lying pastures in winter and mountainous areas in summer or moving between northerly and southerly regions of the steppes as the seasons changed. They probably depended to a certain extent on neighboring settled groups for agricultural products and wealth in the form of tribute, but this lifestyle was primarily mobile.

Modern nomads today follow a circuitous yearly route, nomadizing from spring to summer to fall pastures while living in portable housing, called yurts (Turkish) or *gers* (Mongolian), and wintering in permanent housing in sheltered river valleys or, in the mountains, below south-facing stone escarpments that absorb and radiate solar heat.

Early Evidence of Nomadic Pastoralism

The Greek historian Herodotus (c. 484–430/420 BCE) chronicled the Scythians, who interacted with the Greeks in the northern Black Sea region, and the Sauromatians, whom he described as descendants of the Amazons and Scythians living on the steppes east of the Scythians. Persian and Chinese Han-dynasty historians provided information on the Saka, the name the Persians used in the fifth century BCE to refer to most of the nomadic groups living to the north of the Persian empire, on the steppes from the Aral Sea to Siberia. These steppe nomads spoke Indo-Iranian languages and were of European type or mixed European-Asiatic type.

Aside from written testimony of the civilized folk around them, these nomads are known from their rich tombs of their chieftains, elaborately constructed, topped by high earthen mounds, and filled with weapons, jewelry, and horse trappings often decorated with gold and silver. The decoration is in the so-called animal style: figures of deer, birds of prey, felines, and other animals.

In the Altay Mountains of Siberia, the fifth- and fourth-century BCE frozen tombs at Pazyryk and Ukok were preserved for more than two thousand years through freezing of the contents after robbers had dug into the graves. Archaeologists discovered sacrificial horses with colorful saddles and bridles, elaborately decorated felt textiles, carved wooden animal figures that had once been overlaid with gold, and embalmed remains of high-ranking personages, some of whom had been tattooed with animal figures. The burials had been robbed of their precious metals; the artifacts that remained suggested that nomadic rulers had accumulated wealth in the form of gifts from settled people and from caravan traders who wanted to appease these fierce warriors. Burial artifacts also indicated that, in addition to chieftains, other high-status pastoral nomads included warriors, priestesses, and warrior priestesses.

Nomads of the Early Middle Ages

Around the third century BCE, powerful confederacies of nomads arose in the eastern steppes. These included the Xiongnu (who caused the Chinese to build the Great Wall of China), and the Yueh Chih. They forced the Saka and other tribes westward and into northern Afghanistan. Simultaneously, the various groups of Sarmatians (descendants of the earlier Sauromatians), who were concentrated on the steppes north of the Aral Sea, also began expanding westward, displacing the Scythians who had dominated the Black Sea steppes. The Sarmatians were known to Greek and Roman sources as raiders and traders; they pillaged settled folk and extracted tribute from caravans that now plied the great Silk Road from Europe to China. Many Sarmatians became mercenary soldiers for the Roman armies; one group of 5,500 was ordered to Britain in the second century CE to guard Hadrian's Wall, where they lived out their years.

The Turks

In the sixth century CE, a mighty political confederacy of Turkic-speaking pastoral nomads arose in the central Altay Mountains. Throughout Eurasia, they marked their burials with commemorative sculptures, and portraits of male warriors and females of high status. Extending the Silk Road, the Turkic nomads traded with the Chinese Tang dynasty (618–907) as well as with Byzantium and the merchants of present-day Iran. Eventually, they spread across Eurasia, and today Turkic-speaking people are the dominant populations in many regions of Eurasia, including Kazakhstan, Kyrgyzstan, Uzbekistan, Bashkortostan, Tatarstan, and modern Turkey.

Genghis Khan and the Mongol Empire

One of the most renowned Central Asian nomads of all time was no doubt Genghis Khan (c. 1162–1227). Born Temujin in Mongolia and possessed of courage, charisma, and iron discipline, he united the Mongol and Turkic tribes into a vast and well-organized confederacy before he began his horrific and bloody conquest to expand Mongol lands. After his death, his descendants continued the Mongol expansion, and, by 1240, had captured Russia. Before long, the Mongols were menacing eastern Europe and arousing fears that they would overrun the Western world. Writings of papal emissaries, royal embassies from France and China, and traders such as Marco Polo (1254–1324) have revealed much about these pastoral nomads, as well as about Westerners' attitudes toward these threatening hordes.

Despite the efforts of foreign missionaries, many elements of shamanism and animism, the original beliefs of the nomads, remained in the Buddhism that was formally adopted as the official Mongol religion during the reign (1251–1259) of Genghis Khan's grandson Mongke at his capital Karakorum and south-central Mongolia.

Genghis Khan's heirs included Mongke, who consolidated the Mongol empire; Khubilai (1215–1294), who established the Mongol-ruled Yuan dynasty in China (1279–1368); Hulegu (c. 1217–1265), who founded the Il-Khanate in Iran; and Batu (d. 1255), who was great khan of the Golden Horde in the territory of present-day Russia. The latter nomadic confederacy was established along the lower Volga River and eventually controlled east–west trade through Central Asia as well as trade with the Vikings who came down the Volga from Scandinavia seeking silver coinage. Little is known of the White Horde further to the west, but it is thought that from its headquarters in Moldova, the Black Plague spread to Europe. After much internal strife over Christianity, shamanism, and Islam, Khan Berke (d. 1267) of the Golden Horde, a confederacy of many tribes, adopted Islam, which remains today the principal religion of the Central Asian Turkic-speaking nomads.

The Mongols remained a force to be reckoned with at least until the sixteenth century, although their empire began to disintegrate during the fifteenth century, partly because the Russian grand dukes battled to free Russia from their overlords. Russian tribute to the Mongols ended in 1480, but not until the sixteenth century was Russia completely free from Mongol overlordship.

Early Modern Pastoral Nomads

Descending from the groups that were successors to the Mongol empire, the Kyrgyz-Kazakhs, as the Kazakhs were known in early Russian texts, were divided into three hordes (Great, Little, and Middle) and nomadized from the Volga River eastward through present-day Kazakhstan in the sixteenth and seventeenth centuries. During the Russian expansion under Peter the Great and subsequent Russian czars, in the eighteenth and nineteenth centuries, the Kazakhs, Naiman, Kyrgyz, and other pastoral nomads were pitted against one another and were frequently displaced. Some took their herds to the Tian Shan range in western China. Others migrated into the Dzungar Basin in present-day Xinjiang Uygur Autonomous Region in western China, but soon Dzungarian nomads began to confiscate their pastures, forcing them to migrate into western Mongolia, where they petitioned the Mongol government for grazing rights in Bayan Olgii *aimag* (province). Mongols in the Chinese Tian Shan migrated west of the Caspian Sea to form the republic of Kalmykia, although some later returned to the mountainous pastures, during the eighteenth and nineteenth centuries, where they remain today, subsequent to their deportation to Siberia during the regime of Soviet leader Joseph Stalin (1879–1953).

Twentieth-Century Nomads under the Soviets

Although imperial Russian expansion had previously created major problems between nomadic tribes, it was Khrushchev's mandate in the 1950s to cultivate the "Virgin Lands" that brought Russian settlers eastward, expanding into the nomads' grazing lands. Sovietization produced a much more violent change. The Soviets forced the pastoralists to abandon their lifestyle and form collective farms, although some managed to nomadize for part of the year. During this period, thousands of native inhabitants of the steppes starved; others migrated into western China, while others eventually became agriculturists.

Pastoral Nomadism Today

In the late twentieth century, only pockets of pastoral Kazakhs and Mongol nomads remained in the Altay Mountains and the Chinese Tian Shan and across Mongolia, living in yurts and *gers* while nomadizing much as the early nomads did 2,500 years ago. Following the demise of the Soviet Union in 1991, thousands of nomadic Mongolian Kazakhs joined their compatriots on collective farms in Kazakhstan, although subsequently a great portion of these returned to Mongolia, preferring pastoral nomadism to agriculture.

Pastoral nomadism as an economic lifestyle, today, as always, is extremely tenuous and has become more fragile as urban migrations and international diasporas, particularly among the younger generations, have further reduced the population of herders. Equally grim is the threat from severe and extremely varying climatic conditions—summer droughts leaving the pastures barren, bitterly cold winds, tremendous summer hailstorms, and deep snows concealing winter grasses—which can cause near-total annihilation of the herds. Without animals, a nomadic pastoral economy must vanish, and with it is lost all traces of the distinctive traits of nomadic culture.

Jeannine Davis-Kimball

Further Reading

Barfield, Thomas J. (1993) *The Nomadic Alternative.* Englewood Cliffs, NJ: Prentice Hall.

———. (1989) *The Perilous Frontier: Nomadic Empires and China.* Cambridge, MA: Basil Blackwell.

Christian, David. (1998) *A History of Russia, Central Asia, and Mongolia: Inner Eurasia from Prehistory to the Mongol Empire.* Vol. 1. Malden, MA: Blackwell Press.

Davis-Kimball, Jeannine, Vladimir A. Bashilov, and Leonid T. Yablonsky, eds. (1995) *Nomads of the Eurasian Steppes in the Early Iron Age.* Berkeley, CA: Zinat Press.

Davis-Kimball, Jeannine, Eileen Murphy, Ludmila Koryakova, and Leonid T. Yablonsky, eds. (2000) *Kurgans, Ritual Sites, and Settlements: Eurasian Bronze and Iron Age.* British Archaeological Research Reports, International Series 870. Oxford, U.K.: Archaeopress.

Frey, Richard N. (1988) *The Heritage of Central Asia: From Antiquity to the Turkish Expansion.* Princeton, NJ: Markus Wiener.

Grousset, René. (1970) *The Empire of the Steppes: A History of Central Asia.* Trans. by Naomi Walford. New York: Barnes and Noble by arrangement with Rutgers University.

Khazanov, Anatoly A. (1994) *Nomads and the Outside World.* Trans. by Julia Crookenden. Madison: University of Wisconsin Press.

NOMADIC PASTORALISM—SOUTH ASIA

Nomadic pastoralism is an economic activity whereby a society that derives its livelihood from herding domesticated animals undertakes seasonal migrations to provide water and pasture for its livestock. Such groups generally occupy lands that are unsuitable for settled agriculture. Thus, in South Asia, nomadic pastoralists are found mainly in the higher foothills of the Himalayas and in the arid hills, plains, and deserts of the subcontinent's northwestern region.

The groups in the Himalayas practice a form of nomadism known as transhumance. The Bhotiya, for example, a people of Tibetan descent found from Ladakh to Bhutan, spend the summer high in the mountains, in villages situated at an elevation between 3,500 and 4,500 meters. They keep goats, cattle, and yak (a bovine adapted to high altitudes). With the onset of winter, the Bhotiya and their herds descend to villages in the lower valleys where they live until the snows melt and they can return to their summer pastures. The Gujars of Kashmir and the Gaddi of Himachal Pradesh have similar patterns of transhumance.

Pastoralist groups in the northwestern areas of South Asia follow a lifestyle more typical of traditional nomads. They herd goats, sheep, camels, and cattle, following well-defined seasonal migration routes in search of grazing and water. They use the products of their animals (wool, meat, milk, hides) for their own consumption as well as to trade for food and other goods they do not produce themselves. The Rabari, sheepherders of Rajasthan and Gujarat; the Gadariya; and the Dhangar are among the nomadic pastoralists of northwestern India. (Other nomads of this area, the Lohars, are unusual in that they are ironworkers rather than pastoralists.)

The Baluchi of western Pakistan represent an extension of the nomadic pastoralism of Central Asia into South Asia. Though historically, culturally, and linguistically related to the peoples located to their west, they find themselves situated within Pakistan's national borders. The Baluchi have resisted, sometimes by force, government attempts to integrate them into modern Pakistani society.

Nomadic pastoralists in South Asia are, in general, seminomadic rather than true nomads, most living in villages for part of the year. They also have well-developed economic and social relationships with surrounding agricultural peoples. Although precise numbers are not readily available, nomadic and seminomadic peoples amount to less than 1 percent of the total population of South Asia. These numbers are steadily declining as nomadic pastoralists face social, environmental, economic, and political pressures to abandon their traditional ways of life.

Deryck O. Lodrick

See also: **Himalaya Range**

Further Reading

Davidson, Robyn. (1996) *Desert Places.* New York: Viking Penguin.

Leshnik, Lawrence Saadia, and Gunther-Dietz Sontheimer, eds. (1975) *Pastoralists and Nomads in South Asia.* Wiesbaden, Germany: Harrassowitz.

THE SEARCH FOR PASTURAGE

The Sherpa people of Nepal are one of the nomadic, or seminomadic peoples, of the mountains of South Asia. As described below, they must move in order to find pastures for their cattle.

Periodic movements from pasture to pasture are an essential element of the Sherpas' cattle economy. Their extent and range, however, varies with the size of herds. The owner of a small herd may base his yak for five months in the year on the main village, move with his animals to higher pastures for another five months and spend perhaps two months at one or two *gunsa*-settlements. A man owning thirty or more yak, on the other hand, may keep them only one month out of twelve in the main village, and take them even during part of the winter to some high *yersa*-settlements.

This system can be demonstrated by tracing the annual movements of the herds of two men of Khumjung: Dorje Ngungdu, who in 1957 owned 8 female yak and 1 bull, and Ang Tandin, who owned 2 male and 32 female yak, 1 female cross-breed and 1 bull.

Dorje Ngungdu kept his cattle in Khumjung from November until March, and during that time the animals grazed as long as possible on the surrounding slopes, and from December onwards were fed on hay and the dried stalks of buckwheat stored in Khumjung. In April his son took the herd to Chermalung, a site near some caves half-way between Teshinga and Lapharma. Dorje Ngungdu had a store of hay in Lapharma, which was then still under snow, and he hired men to carry some of this hay to Chermalung to supplement the meagre food found on the pastures which had only just emerged from that grip of winter. In May the yak were driven to Lapharma, where there was even less grazing, but where they were fed on the hay stored in Dorje's house. By the beginning of June new grass sprouted on the pastures near Khumjung and Dorje's herd, like those of other villagers, was brought down and kept at various *resa*-camps above Teshinga and Khumjung.

In July, however, all cattle had to leave the hill-slopes close to the area of cultivation, and part of Dorje's family moved with the yak to their *yersa*-settlement at Lapharma, where by that time the pastures were covered by a carpet of luscious grass and flowers. After a few weeks herdsmen and herd moved further up to the settlement of Macherma. There Dorje Ngungdu and five other families celebrated the *Yer-chang* rite, which is designed to ensure the well-being of the herds. During the first part of September the yak remained at Macherma, and the grass on the walled-in meadows was cut and dried. When the hay had been safely stored, the herd was driven down to Lapharma and haymaking began there.

Two members of the family stayed with the yak at Lapharma until the middle of October. By that time the harvest in Teshinga had been completed and the cattle could be moved down to this *gunsa*-settlement. In its vicinity there was still ample grazing and when, at the end of October, Khumjung was reopened to the cattle, Dorje brought his yak back to the village, kept them at night in a harvested field next to his house and during the day let them graze on the hill-slopes above the village.

Source: Christoph von Fürer-Haimendorf. (1975) *Himalayan Traders: Life in Highland Nepal.* London: John Murray, 52–53.

NORODOM RANARIDDH. See **Ranariddh, Norodom.**

NORODOM SIHANOUK. See **Sihanouk, Norodom.**

NORTH AND SOUTH KOREAN ECONOMIC VENTURES For almost four decades following the June 1950 outbreak of the Korean War, commercial contacts between the Republic of Korea (ROK, or South Korea) and the Democratic People's Republic of Korea (DPRK, or North Korea) were essentially nonexistent—in fact, purchase of North Korean merchandise was a punishable offense under South Korean security laws. But in October 1988, as part of his strategy of *Nordpolitik*, ROK president Roh Tae Woo unilaterally sanctioned the exchange of commodities between South and North. The following month, the first legal inter-Korean commercial transaction was effected: an import into Pusan of 40 kilograms of North Korean clams (routed via Japan). Though the two states remained (and still remain) formally at war, inter-Korean trade thereby commenced.

According to statistics compiled by the ROK's Ministry of Unification, the cumulative turnover for inter-Korean economic transactions between early 1989 and year-end 2000 exceeded $2.5 billion. Official numbers on inter-Korean trade must be used with some care, however. Seoul maintains that its commerce with the North is domestic rather than international in nature, and thus the ROK does not tabulate that trade in accordance with conventional international trade schema.

By Seoul's reckoning, inter-Korean economic transactions have included nearly $500 million in officially designated "noncommercial exchanges": concessional resource transfers from Seoul to Pyongyang for purposes both humanitarian (e.g., food and medicine for famine relief) and political (e.g., heavy fuel oil and components for light-water nuclear reactors under terms of the October 1994 Washington-Pyongyang "Agreed Framework"). Of the roughly $2 billion in ostensibly commercial transactions, the great preponderance (about $1.6 billion) constituted South Korean purchases of North Korean goods: principally, metals (gold, zinc, iron, copper, lead) and agricultural products, and, increasingly, "processing on commission" work for textiles and electronics. (The latter trade, which entails North Korean import, assembly, and re-export of semifinished South Korean wares on consignment, registered a cumulative total of about $500 million for the years 1992–2000.)

Though the absolute volumes of goods and services exchanged between the two Koreas to date remain rather modest, they figure prominently in Pyongyang's overall trade profile, owing to the DPRK's relatively limited exposure to international trade and finance. Depending upon exactly how one counts, South Korea is currently either North Korea's third-largest trade partner, or possibly even its second largest (after only China).

Up to now, South Korea's *chaebol* (family-controlled business conglomerates) have been the major actors attempting to stimulate North–South commerce. In late 1998, the Hyundai *chaebol* signed an unprecedented six-year, $932-million deal with Pyongyang for permission to ferry South Korean tourists to North Korea's scenic Kumgang Mountain region. This landmark venture, however, was a financial disaster: by early 2001, the Hyundai subsidiary responsible for the project announced it could not continue to meet its scheduled payments to the DPRK.

In sharp contradistinction to the cross-Strait trade in divided China (which has generally been quite lucrative for Taiwanese entrepreneurs operating in China), doing business with the North has so far apparently been unprofitable for most South Korean concerns. The problems encountered by South Korean companies have been both practical (such as the pervasive lack of familiarity in the DPRK with standard market procedures) and ideological (such as Pyongyang's professed determination to shield its socialist society against capitalist "cultural and ideological infiltration"). In November 2000, following the historic June 2000 Pyongyang summit between ROK president Kim Dae Jung and DPRK National Defense Commission chairman Kim Jong Il, North and South Korea initialed four sets of agreements to facilitate inter-Korean business (on investment protection, prevention of double taxation, clearing settlement, and dispute settlement procedures). If actually implemented, such measures would be a step toward a more attractive inter-Korean "business climate."

In theory, increased economic integration could offer great benefits to both Koreas—and could facilitate the transition to an ultimate reunification. As of midyear 2001, South Korean *chaebol* were drafting ambitious plans for mammoth inter-Korean ventures; Hyundai, for example, had signed an agreement to develop a 3.3-million-square-meter industrial complex near the DPRK city of Kaesong. Whether these plans will remain on paper only or, alternatively, will presage a further upswing of North–South ventures remains to be seen, but it seems safe to predict that the future of inter-Korean commerce will be strongly influenced by the degree to which Pyongyang acquiesces in the creation of a more attractive business environment within the DPRK.

Nicholas Eberstadt

Further Reading

Eberstadt, Nicholas. (2000) "Prospects for Inter-Korean Economic Cooperation in the 'Sunshine' Era." *Korea and World Affairs* 24, 4: 537–572.

Hwang, Eui-gak. (1993) *The Korean Economies: A Comparison of North and South*. New York: Oxford University Press.

NORTH ATLANTIC TREATY ORGANIZATION AND TURKEY Cooperation between the United States and the USSR during World War II came to an end soon after the war's end in 1945. The presence of Soviet armies in the center of Europe and Communist infiltration into "popular front" governments brought Albania, Bulgaria, Romania, East Germany, Poland, Hungary, and Czechoslovakia within the sphere of Soviet domination.

The West's fear of German power remained even after military victory, but fear of Communism and the intentions of the Soviet Union quickly became more pressing. Turkey had stayed clear of the war, and its territory was not occupied. But soon after the war ended in Europe, the Soviet government cancelled its nonaggression treaty with Turkey on 19 March 1945, demanded joint defense of the Dardanelles, and extended territorial claims toward three Turkish provinces. Highly alerted, Turkey moved closer to the West.

The Formation of NATO and Turkey's Early Rejections

Relations between the USSR and the West steadily worsened, and on 12 March 1947, U.S. President Harry Truman (1884–1972) made a speech in which he announced the policy of the United States to support "the free peoples who are resisting attempted subjugation by armed minorities or by outside pressure" and extended $400 million in aid to the Greek and Turkish governments to help them resist international Communism. Turkey cordially welcomed the so-called Truman Doctrine, but the $100 million allocated as Turkey's share was not enough to deter the Soviet threat.

In the meantime, Belgium, France, Luxembourg, the Netherlands, and the United Kingdom met in Brussels on 17 March 1948 to sign the Brussels Treaty, by which they pledged themselves to build a common defense system. It soon became apparent, however, that support by other Western states, especially the United States, was necessary in the face of the Soviet Union. Accordingly, the North Atlantic Treaty was signed in Washington on 4 April 1949, by the Brussels Treaty powers and Canada, Denmark, Iceland, Italy, Norway, Portugal, and the United States. The new treaty formed the North Atlantic Treaty Organization (NATO), which basically aimed to collectively defend its members against armed aggression. There was no mention of the Soviet Union, but it was obvious that the treaty was mainly motivated by the Soviet threat.

A Greek soldier participating in a NATO military exercise in Turkey in October 2000. It was the first time in 78 years that Greek soldiers had operated in Turkey. (AFP/CORBIS)

The Turkish government was disappointed that Turkey was not invited to the alliance. But the Truman administration tended to see Turkey as part of the Middle East rather than Europe, and the United Kingdom advanced the idea that, rather than join NATO, Turkey should take part in a British-led Middle Eastern or Mediterranean defense system. Nevertheless, Turkey applied for NATO membership on 11 May 1950, and was rejected. Its second application came just after the outbreak of the Korean War. In parallel with its decision to dispatch 4,500 soldiers to Korea to fight under the U.N. command, Turkey applied once more for NATO membership, on 1 August 1950. Although NATO rejected this application, too, a radical change in U.S. strategy toward European defense occurred beginning in 1951. Dwight Eisenhower (1890–1969), Supreme Allied Commander in Europe (SACEUR), attached great importance to anti-Soviet nations in southern Europe to repel possible Soviet aggression and lobbied President Truman for Turkish and Greek membership. Accordingly, in September 1951 NATO invited both nations to join, and in February 1952, Turkey and Greece became NATO members.

Turkey in NATO

After joining NATO, three-quarters of Turkey's land forces were reserved for NATO purposes under the commander-in-chief of Allied forces, southern Europe (CINCSOUTH), based in Naples, and the air force and navy were assigned to SACEUR. Under a series of agreements with NATO and the United States, important military facilities were built in Turkey, including air bases in Incirlik, Karamursel, Cigli, and Diyarbakir, and radar stations on the Black Sea coast. By an agreement in 1957, the U.S. Air Force stationed tactical nuclear weapons at NATO bases in Turkey. The number of U.S. military personnel in

Turkish territory reached twenty-four thousand in the early 1970s, turning Turkey into "an unsinkable aircraft carrier" for NATO.

Starting in the mid-1960s, a number of substantial developments internationally and in Turkish-American relations deeply affected the Turkish public's views of foreign policy and Turkey's presence in NATO. The Cuban missile crisis of 1962 and its repercussions; a letter from U.S. President Lyndon Johnson (1908–1973) to Premier Ismet Inonu, with which he prevented a Turkish operation in Cyprus in 1964; U.S. pressure on Turkey to stop its poppy cultivation and the "opium poppy crisis" during 1968–1974; concerns about American Peace Corps activities during the 1960s; and a U.S. arms embargo on Turkey between 1975 and 1978 were decisive developments in Turkish-American relations. However, none of these developments caused a radical change in the Turkish government's approach to NATO, and Turkey remained a member.

Turkey and NATO in the Post–Cold War Era

After the Cold War ended with the Soviet Union's collapse in 1991, Turkey supported new strategic concepts of NATO and its enlargement. Turkey also took an active role in NATO's Partnership for Peace (PFP) initiative, which was introduced at the 1994 Brussels summit. The partnership of twenty-seven nations, including former Warsaw Pact (Soviet bloc) members, was designed to expand and intensify political and military cooperation throughout Europe, increase stability, diminish threats to peace, and build strengthened relationships by promoting the spirit of practical cooperation and commitment to democratic principles that underpin NATO. Turkey contributed to the program by establishing a PFP training center in Ankara.

In 1992, NATO began to give support to the Organization for Security and Cooperation in Europe (OSCE) and to the U.N. in peacekeeping operations in the former Yugoslavia. It implemented maritime and air operations in order to maintain the U.N. Security Council's resolutions in the region. After the Dayton Agreement of 1995, NATO continued to give air observation support to the U.N.

In 1998 and 1999, NATO once more engaged in the issue of the former Yugoslavia. In order to deter Serbian forces from occupying Kosovo, contrary to the U.N. Security Council's decisions, NATO conducted heavy air strikes on major Yugoslavian targets, including the capital, Belgrade. This operation, which was implemented without a U.N. Security Council resolution, was highly criticized by Russia, China, and some other nations. Turkey actively participated in both the Yugoslavia and Kosovo operations and dispatched military troops to the region to implement peacekeeping missions under the U.N. resolutions.

Mustafa Aydin and Cagri Erhan

Further Reading

Brenner, Michael. (1995) *NATO and Collective Security*. New York: Macmillan.

Carpenter, Ted. (1995) *The Future of NATO*. London: Frank Cass.

Cook, Don. (1989) *Forging the Alliance, NATO 1945–1950*. London: Secker and Warburg.

Fedder, Edwin H. (1973) *NATO: The Dynamics of Alliance in the Post-War World*. New York: Mead.

Hale, William. (2000) *Turkish Foreign Policy 1774–2000*. London: Frank Cass.

Heller, Francis, and John R. Gillingham. (1992) *NATO: The Founding of the Atlantic Alliance and the Integration in Europe*. London: Macmillan.

NATO. (1996) *NATO at a Glance*. Brussels, Belgium: NATO.

———. (1999) *The North Atlantic Treaty Organization: Facts and Figures*. Leuven, Belgium: NATO.

Papacosma, Victor. (1995) *NATO: In the Post-Cold War Era, Does It Have a Future?* New York: St. Martin's Press.

Rappaport, Armin. (1975) *A History of American Diplomacy*. New York: Macmillan.

NORTH CHOLLA PROVINCE

(1999 est. pop. 2 million). Located in the southwest region of South Korea (Republic of Korea), North Cholla Province (Chollab pukdo) has an area of 8,058 square kilometers. The province's six cities are Chonju (the provincial capital), Chongju, Kunsan, Iri, Kimje, and Namwon. There are also eight counties (*kun*) within the province.

Paekche (18–663 CE), one of the original Three Kingdoms subsumed by Shilla (57–935 CE) and resurrected as Later Paekche (892–936 CE) before its surrender to Koryo (918–1392 CE), was located in the present-day Cholla and Ch'ungch'ong Provinces.

North and South Cholla provinces, collectively called the Honam region, have a rich cultural heritage of folk music and dance. There are numerous Buddhist temples, including the Songgwang temple. Mount Chiri is shared by both North and South Cholla, as well as neighboring North Kyongsang Province.

The fertile soils and comparatively gentle topography enable the region to supply much of the nation's grains and cereals such as rice, barley, and beans. There are fisheries on the coastal region, and the province also has mining operations in gold, silver, lime, and coal. North Cholla is home to many industries, which produce chemicals, paper goods, textiles, apparel, machinery, electronics, and automobiles. The region is also known for its ceramics and pottery.

Jennifer Jung-Kim

Further Reading

Cho, Chung-Kyung, Phyllis Haffner, and Fredric M. Kaplan. (1991) *The Korea Guidebook*. 5th ed. Boston: Houghton Mifflin.

Nilsen, Robert. (1997) *South Korea Handbook*. Chico, CA: Moon Publications.

NORTH CH'UNGCH'ONG PROVINCE

(2000 est. pop. 1.5 million). North Ch'ungch'ong province (Ch'ungch'ong pukdo), in the central region of South Korea (Republic of Korea), has an area of 7,433 square kilometers. The provincial capital is at Ch'ongju, and the other cities in the province are Ch'ungju and Chech'on. There are also eight counties (*kun*).

Present-day North Ch'ungch'ong had been divided among the Three Kingdoms; Paekche (18–663 CE) was located in modern-day Ch'ongju and Poun, while Shilla (57–935 CE) controlled the south, and Koguryo (37 BCE–668 CE) occupied the northeast. Paekche, however, encompassed all of North Ch'ungch'ong from the fourth century until it fell to Shilla in 663.

The region is highly industrialized; its products include chemicals, machinery, electronics, cement, foodstuffs, textiles, and clothing, as well as ceramics and pottery. North Ch'ungch'ong is ideal for agriculture because of the fertile soil provided by the Han and Kum rivers and their numerous tributaries and basins. Primary agricultural products include rice, barley, apples, pears, grapes, red pepper, garlic, ginseng, and tobacco. The province is quite mountainous and is a source for gold, iron, lime, and coal.

Jennifer Jung-Kim

Further Reading

Cho, Chung-Kyung, Phyllis Haffner, and Fredric M. Kaplan. (1991) *The Korea Guidebook*. 5th ed. Boston: Houghton Mifflin.

Nilsen, Robert. (1997) *South Korea Handbook*. Chico, CA: Moon Publications.

NORTH CYPRUS, TURKISH REPUBLIC OF

(1998 est. pop. 188,000). The Turkish Republic of North Cyprus (TRNC) is a self-proclaimed political entity located in the northern part of the island of Cyprus in the eastern Mediterranean. The republic, with an area of 3,355 square kilometers, has not been recognized by any nation except Turkey. The official language is Turkish, and the capital is Lefkosia, also known as Nicosia; the population includes Turkish settlers, a military contingent, and a small number of Greek natives. Although there is no official religion, more than 98 percent of the population identify themselves as Muslims, with Maronites (Syriac Christians) and Orthodox Greeks making up less than 2 percent.

The island of Cyprus has an exceptionally rich history; its first agricultural settlements were as early as 2700 BCE. Cyprus was then dominated in succession by the Egyptians, Phoenicians, Persians, Greeks (the name "Cyprus" is derived from the Greek word for copper), Romans, and Byzantines. The island frequently changed hands in the Middle Ages, boasting such temporary masters as Richard the Lionhearted of England. Venice controlled it for more than a hundred years, losing it to the Ottomans in 1570. Britain began to encroach on Cyprus in the nineteenth century and annexed it outright when the Ottoman empire entered World War I as a German ally.

Cyprus achieved independence from Britain in 1960. Ethnic tensions began to escalate in 1963 as the Greek Cypriot majority clashed with the Turkish minority. Following a Greek nationalist coup attempt in 1974, Turkey launched a military intervention, occupying the northern part of the island. In 1975 self-rule was proclaimed in the north, but only on 15 November 1983 was independence officially proclaimed and the TRNC created. The Greek Cypriots continue to control most of the island and are the only internationally recognized government. Turkey still maintains about 30,000 ground troops in the TRNC, backed by Turkish artillery and local military units. Although a number of attempts have been made by the international community at reconciliation and reunification of the island, little progress has been achieved to date.

The Turkish Republic of Northern Cyprus is a semipresidential democracy, with a president as head of state and a council of ministers composed of a prime minister and ten cabinet members. The current president is Rauf R. Denktash. The legislative power is vested in a unicameral legislative assembly of fifty deputies, elected for a period of five years through universal suffrage. The judiciary is set up as a separate branch.

During the first decade of independence, the TRNC suffered from economic underdevelopment. In the 1970s and 1980s the economy managed a modest recovery, with the gross domestic product growing by 20 percent between 1977 and 1984, although it remains far behind Greek Cyprus. Significant efforts were made to develop manufacturing and tourism, but agriculture remains the dominant sector of the economy and the main export. Turkey and the United Kingdom are the TRNC's most important trading partners, and the republic continues to run a trading deficit. The Turkish lira is legal tender.

Mikhail Zeldovich

Further Reading

Necatigil, Zaim M. (2001) *The Cyprus Question and the Turkish Position in International Law.* 2d ed. Oxford, U.K.: Oxford University Press.

Stefanidis, Ioannis D. (1999) *Isle of Discord: Nationalism, Imperialism and the Making of the Cyprus Problem.* New York: New York University Press.

NORTH HAMGYONG PROVINCE (2002 est. pop. 2.6 million). North Hamgyong Province (Hamgyong pukdo) is located in the northeast corner of North Korea (Democratic People's Republic of Korea). To the north, it borders the Tumen (Tuman) River separating the eastern half of the Korean Peninsula from China (People's Republic of China). North Hamgyong lies on the Sea of Japan. The province also shares a short 16.5-kilometer border with Russia near the city of Vladivistok. It has an area of 18,558 square kilometers.

The provincial capital is at the port city of Ch'ongjin, and the other cities are Kimch'aek, Najin, and Hoeryong. Najin, however, is an autonomous administrative unit and an economic enterprise zone that is independent of the province. There are also thirteen counties (*kun*). Because of its isolated location, the region is not heavily industrialized or agricultural.

About 80 percent of the province is mountainous, accounting for the rich flora and fauna and high average elevation. The Hamgyong mountain range is 340 kilometers long with 7 mountains with peaks higher than 2,000 meters. The province is also the coldest of all the Korean provinces, with the first frost arriving in early October and the snows lasting through late April or early May.

Jennifer Jung-Kim

Further Reading

Cho, Chung-Kyung, Phyllis Haffner, and Fredric M. Kaplan. (1991) *The Korea Guidebook.* 5th ed. Boston: Houghton Mifflin.

Storey, Robert, and Alex English. (2001) *Korea.* 5th ed. Berkeley, CA: Lonely Planet.

NORTH HWANGHAE PROVINCE (2002 est. pop. 1.8 million). North Hwanghae Province (Hwanghae pukdo) lies between South Hwanghae and Kangwon Provinces in North Korea (Democratic People's Republic of Korea). The province's southern border is located partly along the DMZ (demilitarized zone) separating the two Koreas.

North Hwanghae Province is 8,154 square kilometers. The provincial capital is at Sariwon, and the only other city in the province is Songnim. There are fourteen counties (*kun*).

Although the province is said to be mountainous, the region does not have a high average elevation. The highest peak is Mount Haram, with an elevation of 1,485 meters. Only about 1.5 percent of the terrain is higher than 1,000 meters above sea level, and 91.1 percent of the land is below 500 meters in elevation. There are three mountain ranges.

The key manufacturing sectors are smelting, ironworks, cement, and textiles. The main agricultural products are fruits, tobacco, cotton, peanuts, sesame, and mint. There is also an abundance of minerals such as gold, silver, lead, zinc, molybdenum, nickel, and cobalt. Granite, marble, and coal are plentiful as well.

Jennifer Jung-Kim

Further Reading

Cho, Chung-Kyung, Phyllis Haffner, and Fredric M. Kaplan. (1991) *The Korea Guidebook.* 5th ed. Boston: Houghton Mifflin.

Storey, Robert, and Alex English. (2001) *Korea.* 5th ed. Berkeley, CA: Lonely Planet.

NORTH KOREA—PROFILE (2001 est. pop. 22 million). The Democratic People's Republic of Korea (DPRK) is located in the northern part of the Korean Peninsula. It is bordered on the north by China and Russia, and below the thirty-eighth parallel by the Republic of Korea; east and west it borders the sea. Its total area, 120,540 square kilometers, accounts for 55 percent of the Korean Peninsula. It is slightly smaller than the state of Mississippi. Because 80 percent of the country is mountainous—in contrast to the south, the peninsula's agricultural center—the North Korean economy is primarily industrial, including manufacturing, mining, hydroelectric production, and metallurgy.

A large bronze statue of Kim Il Sung, the founder of North Korea, in central P'yongyang in 2000. (REUTERS NEWMEDIA INC./CORBIS)

Its primary rivers, the Yalu and Tumen, are both located in the extreme north. P'yongyang, the capital city, is home to 10 percent of North Korea's population.

Political System

Since its inception in 1948 the DPRK has been governed by a socialist regime headed by the Kim family. Kim Il Sung (1912–1994), secretary general of the Korean Workers' Party (KWP), remained the country's only political leader until his death. By the 1980s, however, he had begun grooming the nation to accept his son as his successor, and within three years of his father's death Kim Jong Il (b. 1941) had succeeded in assuming the three important positions once held by the elder Kim: secretary general of the KWP, head of state, and commander of the armed forces.

University of Chicago professor Bruce Cumings describes the North Korean domestic political structure as "socialist corporatism," a system anchored by three pillars: hierarchy, organic connection (internal connection, the connection with Korean virtue), and family. The core political thought of this corporatism is *juche*, a concept that translates as "self-reliance." In the minds of the North Korean government, *juche* legitimizes the policies of the KWP, especially in relation to South Korea: whereas the latter lacks *juche*, and must rely on a foreign military to maintain its political position, North Korea, having liberated itself from foreign troops in 1958, sees itself as self-reliant, and thus the legitimate political power on the Korean Peninsula.

Within the framework of DPRK foreign relations, *juche* was first practiced to play the Soviet-Chinese rift to North Korea's political and economic advantage. The North Korean government skillfully avoided choosing sides in the conflict, instead securing economic and strategic assistance from both countries. More recently *juche* is apparent in the DPRK's efforts to secure nuclear and missile technology. This technology provides the DPRK with an energy supply, weapons for security, trade items for hard currency, and chips for bargaining.

Economy

Since its inception the North Korean economy has been driven by a series of long-term (five- to ten-year)

NORTH KOREA

Country name: Democratic People's Republic of Korea
Area: 120,540 sq km
Population: 21,968,228 (July 2001 est.)
Population growth rate: 1.22% (2001 est.)
Birth rate: 19.1 births/1,000 population (2001 est.)
Death rate: 6.92 deaths/1,000 population (2001 est.)
Net migration rate: 0 migrants/1,000 population (2001 est.)
Sex ratio—total population: 0.94 males/female (2001 est.)
Infant mortality rate: 23.55 deaths/1,000 live births (2001 est.)
Life expectancy at birth—total population: 71.02 years; male, 68.04 years; female, 74.15 years (2001 est.)
Major religions: Buddhism, Confucianism, Christianity, syncretic Chondogyo (Religion of the Heavenly Way)
Major language: Korean
Literacy—total population: 99%; male, 99%; female, 99% (1990 est.)
Government type: authoritarian socialist; one-man dictatorship
Capital: P'yongyang
Administrative divisions: 9 provinces and 3 special cities
Independence: 15 August 1945 (from Japan)
National holiday: Founding of the Democratic People's Republic of Korea, 9 September (1948)
Suffrage: 17 years of age; universal
GDP—real growth rate: −3% (2000 est.)
GDP—per capita (purchasing power parity): $1,000 (2000 est.)
Population below poverty line: not available
Exports: $520 million (f.o.b., 1999 est.)
Imports: $960 million (c.i.f., 1999 est.)
Currency: North Korean won (KPW)

Source: Central Intelligence Agency. (2001) *The World Factbook* 2001. Retrieved 18 October 2001, from: http://www.cia.gov/cia/publications/factbook.

plans. Until recently the system generally prohibited market-driven economic activity, save for allowing people to sell small amounts of produce from their private plots. Throughout this early period the North Korean government depended on Soviet, Chinese, and (to a much lesser extent) Eastern European assistance for its economic growth. The cheap oil provided by the Soviet Union, in particular, was essential for North Korean economic development. Economic assistance—much less than the United States provided South Korea—helped the DPRK outperform the Republic of Korea in economic production, at least through the early 1970s.

North Korea recovered from the destruction of the Korean War at a faster pace than did its southern neighbor; by the end of the 1950s it had surpassed the industrial and agricultural levels attained before the war. The first three-year plan started just before the Korean War ended; it was succeeded by a series of five-, seven-, and ten-year plans. In 1956 the government felt confident enough in the state's economic circumstances to initiate the *cho'llima* ("flying horse") movement, an effort designed to encourage North Korean workers to make the "superhuman effort" required to rebuild the country without relying on external assistance, according to Suh Dae-Sook (1988).

The fragility of this economic system became evident soon after the United States began to seek amicable relations with the Soviet Union and China. North Korea remained economically strong only as long as the socialist economic network offered preferential prices. The North Korean economy weakened even further in the 1980s when the Soviet Union and China began to demand hard currency in exchange for their products. The end of the Cold War improved relations between the two Communist giants and South Korea, effectively ending much of North Korean economic activity with its traditional allies. In the 1990s flooding exacerbated systemic problems of energy procurement and food distribution, leaving the country's economy in shambles and its people starving.

The DPRK has attempted to cure its economic deficiencies in a number of ways. Since the 1980s it has attempted to attract foreign currency through arms exports, in particular through missile sales to Middle Eastern states such as Syria and Iran. In 1991 it established a special economic zone in the northern area of Rajin-Songbong to encourage foreign investment. More recently the government has relaxed restrictions on private enterprise. Recent trips to China by Kim Jong Il have led some to speculate that the North Korean leader is considering adopting policies similar to those enacted by the Chinese to breathe fresh life into his country's ailing economy.

Culture

North Korea is populated by one of the most homogeneous peoples in the world, unified by language and neo-Confucian ideology, and fortified by what some have called a Kim cult, or Kim Il Sungism. Kim Il Sung's name is used for the national university, national museums, and other public institutions; his face appears throughout the country on murals and monuments. Important landmarks in the former North Korean leader's life, such as his place of birth, serve as the country's national shrines. The general's battles with the Japanese during the period of occupation are legendary; the stories are kept alive in North Korean music, poetry, and national histories.

Current Issues

The 1990s have seen the DPRK struggling to forge congenial relations with its traditional enemies while maintaining state sovereignty. Harsh economic times have forced the state to compromise its position by accepting aid from hostile states, including the Republic of Korea, the United States, and Japan. The development of nuclear and missile technology, while posing a threat to its neighbors, succeeded in bringing the United States to the negotiating table during the Clinton administration. The George W. Bush administration has been less willing to negotiate, however, insisting that North Korea demonstrate efforts to comply with U.S. demands for weapons reduction and verification before agreeing to discuss other issues, such as the DPRK's removal from terrorist lists and a bilateral treaty of normalization.

A trend toward improved relations with the Republic of Korea peaked in June 2000 at the summit held in P'yongyang between Kim Jong Il and South Korea's president, Kim Dae Jung (b. 1925). Since then progress has stalled for a number of reasons, most importantly the Bush administration's hard-line position on negotiations, and Kim Jong Il's apparent reluctance to visit Seoul. Areas that have drawn the two sides to meet include the possibility of reuniting family members separated since the end of the Korean War, and the creation of transportation and communication links across the demilitarized zone.

Internationally, the DPRK has recently secured ties with many European Union states, as well as with countries in East Asia. Relations with Russia and China have strengthened as well, particularly in response to U.S. actions, such as the missile defense program, that allegedly threaten the interests of the three states. Attempts to initiate a DPRK-Japan dialogue have ended with little success, efforts bottlenecked by Japan's colonial legacy and Japan's disapproval of DPRK intrusions on its sovereignty that include the kidnapping of its citizens and a missile firing over its territory.

Mark E. Caprio

Further Reading

Cumings, Bruce. (1997) *Korea's Place in the Sun: A Modern History*. New York: Norton.

Mazarr, Michael J. (1995) *North Korea and the Bomb: A Case Study in Nonproliferation.* New York: St. Martin's Press.

Suh Dae-Sook. (1988) *Kim Il Sung: The North Korean Leader.* New York: Columbia University Press.

NORTH KOREA—ECONOMIC SYSTEM

North Korea occupies about 55 percent of the total land area of the Korean Peninsula—about 123,000 square kilometers. Only 20 percent of North Korea's land is arable, however, and a generally harsh climate restricts the production of arable farming to one crop per year. Most farms are cooperatively owned by each village cooperative unit and small, with an average size of under 2 hectares in the late 1990s. As a result of a sizable loss in population resulting from the Korean War (1950–1953) and from migration to the South, combined with a low fertility rate, North Korea has been a relatively labor-scarce economy; the current population is estimated at around 22 million. The maintenance of a large armed force (with more than 1 million members) has exacerbated the shortage of civilian labor. As a result, the armed forces have frequently been mobilized for work on civilian projects. The labor force in 2000 was estimated at 13 million, of whom some 30 percent were employed in primary industry.

Central Planning

Since the establishment of the North Korean state in 1948, its economic policy has been grounded principally on Karl Marx's hypothesis that the structure of social relations in the economic subsystem exerts a powerful influence upon the subsystems of law, opinion, politics, and ideology. In practice, North Korea's economy has been more centralized, more controlled, and more ideologically orthodox and monocratic than those of any of the world's other socialist states. With its autarchic command and rationing system, the North Korean economy has put great emphasis on social equity and welfare, with equal distribution of food and clothing, free medical care and education from kindergarten to college, and child care provisions.

The means of production are socially owned, and most economic actors are mostly motivated toward political and social objectives. Allowable economic actions are in the hands of the top planning authority, the State Planning Commission, which is entrusted with the formulation, execution, and control of economic plans and policies for the Workers' Party in North Korea, and which behaves in accordance with given resource constraints. The top planning authority, the leader Kim Jong Il, decides which economic actions are allowable and orders the subauthority and the people to undertake them in accordance with the given guidelines. Thus, the market is largely irrelevant in both production and distribution decision making.

The central plan specifies a large number of value aggregates (income and specific quantities of products targeted for accomplishment during a planning period specified in the central plan) and physical inputs and outputs in the economy; in this system, money plays only a passive, accounting role. The structure of the plan is strictly hierarchical, so that the lower levels are formally subordinated to those above. The plans are enforced by rationing the means of production (materials, labor, and capital), by rationing goods and services, and through the administrative allocation of labor and job targets. By and large, competition is limited to efforts at plan fulfillment and overfulfillment, except for a small (legal, semilegal, and illegal) private market for some farm products and services. All enterprises are state owned, but farmers are allowed to own or dispose of the products of small areas of land adjacent to farmhouses, though the land itself is not private.

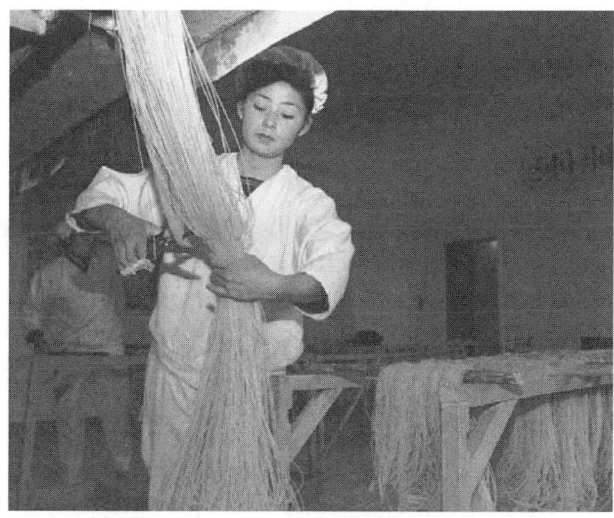

North Korea continues to rely on outside aid to feed its population. Here, a woman cuts noodles at a factory sponsored by the World Vision humanitarian organization in November 2000. (REUTERS NEWMEDIA INC./CORBIS)

The top decision makers or party authorities ration outputs to the needy. Usually priorities of goods distribution go to defense, education, medical care, and consumption, in that order. The share allocated for final household consumption is always marginal, as long as the economy is constrained by severe shortages of food and other necessary goods. The North Korean State Planning Commission has developed its own material incentive systems, which are coupled with basic wages, bonuses, and awards of medals as means of encouraging the fulfillment or overfulfillment of obligatory plan targets, usually defined in percentage growth rates of physical quantities. These incentive systems seemed workable until the mid-1970s, but since then they have broken down, because workers have become unwilling to pursue the goal of overfulfillment. They realize that production levels in one period are the basis for targets in the next period. Unless the rewards and bonuses are large enough to compensate for their increased toil, workers have little reason to increase their efforts. In addition, workers tend to meet only the quantity target without caring about improving the quality of their work.

North Korea's Economic Stagnation during the 1990s

Since 1990, when the Soviet Union began to dissolve, the North Korean economy has shrunk. Continuing bad weather conditions as well as severe energy shortages severely damaged North Korea's agriculture and industrial activities during the 1990s. Per capita gross national income (GNI) dropped from $1,142 in 1990 to $573 in 1998; in 1999, the GNI was $714 and in 2000 $757.

After persistent reports of food-supply problems and rationing for several years, North Korea officially acknowledged that, as a result of damage caused in 1995 and 1996 by the heaviest floods of the century, the country faced serious food shortages. In an unprecedented move that indicated the severity of the situation, North Korea requested and received assistance from various international organizations, developed countries, and South Korea. Prolonged drought in 1997 and floods in 1998 further exacerbated the situation, and millions of North Koreans were threatened by starvation. During the last years of the 1990s, the North Korean populace marginally survived only with humanitarian food aid from South Korea and Western countries. South Korea alone provided North Korea with 150,000 tons of rice in 1995 and 500,000 tons of rice and corn from 1998 to 2000 to mitigate the food crisis.

North Korea's Turnaround

In 1999, the North Korean economy showed a positive growth rate for the first time in ten years. Its gross domestic product (GDP) growth rate was about 6 percent in 1999, a little more than 1 percent in 2000, and an estimated below 1 percent in 2001. North Korea in recent years has also concentrated on land rearrangement and farming improvement programs. It has encouraged farmers to engage in fish farming and to breed grass-eating animals such as rabbits and goats that need no grain fodder, and it has encouraged farm cooperatives and workers to expand the area devoted to potatoes. As a result, grain production increased in 1999 by 40 percent over the previous year to approximately 4 million tons (unpolished basis). Yet North Korea still needed about an additional 1 million tons of food aid from outside to adequately meet its demand in the year 2000.

Energy shortages as well as food shortages have been a drag on the growth of the North Korean economy. Coal output dropped from 33 million metric tons in 1990 to about 19 million metric tons in 1998 due to resource depletion and aged equipment. Electric power output also decreased from about 28 billion kilowatt hours in 1990 to 17 billion kilowatt hours in 1998, while crude oil imports shrank from under 3 million metric tons to 500,000 metric tons during the same period. The growth in the North Korean economy in 1999 and 2000 can be attributed to support from the international community, an increase in grain production, and an improvement in energy supply.

Designating 1999 as the "epochal turning point for constructing a strong, great nation," North Korea achieved a 6 percent annual rate of growth. In 1999, the manufacturing sector grew by almost 9 percent (heavy industry by almost 12 percent and light industry by over 2 percent) as compared with the 3 percent shrinkage of the previous year. The increased supply of energy and raw materials from overseas aid contributed largely to this higher growth. Electricity, gas, and drinking water supply increased by almost 7 percent due to renovation and repair of production facilities (contrasting with the 9 percent decline of the previous year). Thermal electricity and hydroelectricity generation grew by almost 23 percent and less than 1 percent, respectively. The general and housing construction sector grew by 24 percent as compared with an 11 percent decline in 1998. In the service sector, wholesale and retail services rose by 10 percent, transportation by almost 8 percent, and food and lodging by close to 16 percent—but the overall service-sector growth was down almost 2 percent due to a large reduction in administrative services. In 2000, North Korea recorded a less than –2 percent growth in the agriculture and fishery sectors, almost 6 percent growth in mining, and under 1 percent in manufacturing. The overall GDP demonstrated more than 2 percent positive growth following the over 6 percent breaking rate in 1999.

Trade

North Korea's trade declined sharply in 1998, but in 1999 it is estimated to have reached $1.5 billion, a slight increase ($400 million) from the previous year. Trade with Asian states such as China, Japan, Hong Kong, India, and Singapore is increasing, and trade volume with South Korea in 1999 amounted to $333 million (North Korea's imports were $212 million and exports were $122 million), the largest two-way volume since 1989, when indirect trade between the South and North first began. During the first half of 2000, trade with South Korea reached $203 million, compared with $165 million during the corresponding period the previous year. In 1999, total trade with South Korea amounted to $333 million; this figure grew by almost 28 percent to $425 million in 2000. Under Kim Jong Il's guidance, North Korea is retaining its socialist system domestically, but it is cautiously opening the external doors wider, especially with its peninsular partner. At home, North Korea is likely to continue its efforts to raise food production, especially of potatoes and animal protein, while placing renewed emphasis on energy and heavy industry. Externally, it will step up efforts to attract more humanitarian food and medical supplies from the outside world.

North Korea is intent on luring overseas investors as well as South Korean enterprises by offering special economic zones and other attractive incentives. The question is how the regime will successfully isolate the special economic zones so as to shield its own population from capitalist influences. Nevertheless, North Korea is recognizing the need for change, since its earlier strategy of keeping up military tensions in order to extort concessions from the United States, Japan, and South Korea has reached the end of its usefulness. Further signs of this new policy stance were apparent both just before and after the June 2000 P'yongyang summit between North Korea's Kim Jong Il and South Korea's Kim Dae Jung. North Korea grew more eager to discuss establishing diplomatic relations with Italy, Australia, Canada, Sweden, Germany, England, Japan, the United States, and others—in sharp contrast to its policy position before the mid-1990s.

North Korea's Opening Door

In his publication of June 1995 entitled "Giving Priority to Ideological Work Is Essential for the Accomplishment of the Socialist Cause," Kim Jong Il strongly defended socialist ownership and the consolidation and development of a socialist economic system embodying the *juche* (self-reliance) idea, emphatically rejecting the introduction of capitalist methods. But since taking formal command of both the military and the party in September 1998, Kim Jong Il has embarked on a multifaceted transformation of North Korea's economic system and policies, moving gradually toward an open-door policy. This new policy will be a difficult one to reverse. If it works out smoothly and does not face any serious internal resistance, the North Korean economy is expected to continue growing and begin to reduce the serious shortages of basic necessities.

Of course, to revive its economy, North Korea urgently needs to expand economic ties with Western countries as well as South Korea. Internally, the most urgent tasks are expanding land-transport networks and easing energy shortages. If the capacity utilization ratio of North Korea's industries and its energy generation facilities are increased to about the 50 percent level from the current level of 20 to 30 percent, the cost of investment in necessities and fertilizer production would be halved, and the expanded production would significantly ease shortages of food and foreign exchange. North Korea must also overcome persistent shortages in skilled labor, modern equipment, and technology, as well as low levels of investment in infrastructure.

After the Kim-Kim P'yongyang summit of June 2000, the two Koreas agreed to facilitate mutual trade and exchange. As North Korea moves from isolation to engagement, it will attract increasing investment from South Korea and Western countries.

Hurdles to Overcome

A shortage of modern equipment and vehicles and an insufficient energy supply and infrastructure are the main problems facing both land and marine transport. Lacking any known deposits of petroleum and relying increasingly on coal—the production of which has been static— for energy, North Korea has been unable to achieve consistent industrial expansion. In addition, its limited foreign-exchange earnings and relatively small trade volume, the legacy of its longstanding self-reliance policy, have hampered the import of oil and other necessary goods. These are the areas the North Korean regime needs to focus on while it continues to pursue its new open-door policy and begins to introduce market economic factors into its hitherto-isolated socialistic economy.

Hwang Eui-Gak

See also: **Food Crisis—North Korea; Juche; Kim Il Sung; Kim Jong Il**

Further Reading

Bank of Korea. (2000) *North Korea's GDP Estimate for 1999.* Seoul.

Chung, Joseph S. (1974) *The North Korean Economy: Structure and Development.* Stanford, CA: Hoover Institution Press.

Clough, Ralph N. (1960) *Embattled Korea: The Rivalry for International Support.* Boulder, CO: Westview Press.

Hwang, Eui-Gak. (2000) "Beyond the Summit: Deepening Linkages on the Korean Peninsula." Paper presented at the Annual KEI Academic Symposium held at the Paul H. Nitze School of Advanced International Studies, Johns

Hopkins University, Baltimore, MD, 18–19 September 2000.

———. (1993) *The Korean Economies: A Comparison of North and South.* Oxford, U.K.: Clarendon Press.

NORTH KOREA—EDUCATION SYSTEM

North Korea's P'yongyang regime has been single-mindededly dedicated to transforming society, nature, and human beings; the efforts to accomplish these three are known as the three great revolutions. The educational system is charged with the responsibility for *kyoyuk* (instruction in scientific knowledge and technical skills) and *kyoyang* (indoctrination), which transforms North Korean citizens, young and old, male and female, into loyal Communists. The Communist ideology that undergirds the educational theory and practice of transforming human beings from birth to death is articulated in Kim Il Sung's treatise "A Thesis on the Socialist Pedagogy," published 5 September 1977.

Compulsory Education

The present educational system in North Korea has gone through five separate revisions. It now maintains an eleven-year universal, free, and compulsory school system, followed by a higher educational system that covers diverse areas of study and varies in the number of years it requires. The primary and secondary school system starts with one year of kindergarten schooling followed by four years of primary education. This is done at *Inmin hakkyo*, or the people's school. A six-year course of secondary schooling follows, and the institution responsible for this education is called *Kodung chunghakkyo* or the higher middle school. All children in North Korea have the same opportunities for education from kindergarten to higher middle school, but the quality of schooling they receive varies greatly.

Generally speaking, children in P'yongyang have access to the best education available in North Korea. The capital of North Korea is a city where only people chosen for their loyalty to the regime are allowed to live. Provincial cities tend to have better schools than do the agricultural and industrial cooperatives to which North Korean citizens are assigned to work and live. The recent economic hardship in North Korea, however, worked havoc on almost every aspect of education: textbooks and notebooks are said not to be readily available, and children in rural areas lack pencils.

Higher Education

There are different types of higher education. First, there are three major universities: Kim Il Sung University, Kim Ch'aek Technical University, and Koryo Sungkyunkwan University. But in the true sense of the word, there is only one university in North Korea: Kim Il Sung University. It is the only academic institution in the country offering a variety of programs comparable to those of Western universities. The number of years required for graduation is between four and six, depending on the field of study.

Second, there are colleges that instruct students in specialized areas of study such as light industry, chemical engineering, electrical engineering, architectural engineering, transportation, international relations, People's economy, foreign languages, medicine, pharmacy, and horticulture. These colleges generally have a four-year course of study, although some require five years for graduation.

Third, there are teacher-training institutions that are divided into levels. There are *kyowon taehak*, three-year institutions in which elementary schoolteachers are trained, and *sapom taehak*, four-year institutions in which teachers of higher middle school are trained.

Fourth, there are colleges established at various industrial, agricultural, and fishery plants where workers can receive their higher education. These are known as factory colleges, agricultural colleges, and fishery colleges. Besides these institutions of higher learning, there are also technical high schools that offer a three-year course of study in various fields such as automation, printing, railroading, commerce, and building materials.

Students are normally admitted into major colleges and universities primarily on the basis of their *songbun*, or class background (whether one was born into a landlord family, a tenant family, a family that collaborated with Japanese colonialists, or a family who fled to South Korea before or during the Korean War; family background also depends on the degree of loyalty one shows in speech, work, and life attitudes) and *tangsong*, or party loyalty rather than on their academic merits. Students are recommended for higher education by their secondary school principals and teachers, and students with undesirable class background or low party loyalty are usually not given recommendations for further education. Those failing to advance to higher education are given an opportunity to join the military, and those who fail to do so are then assigned to various workplaces such as collective farms or mines. In North Korea today, one's class background and party loyalty are the two most crucial factors that determine one's success.

Hyung-chan Kim

See also: **Three Revolutions Movement**

Further Reading

Henriksen, Thomas, and Jongryn Mo. (1997) *North Korea after Kim Il Sung: Continuity or Change?* Stanford, CA: Hoover Institution Press.

Hunter, Helen-Louise. (1999) *Kim Il-Song's North Korea.* Westport, CT: Greenwood Press.

Hyung-chan Kim. (1969) "Ideology and Indoctrination in the Development of North Korean Education." *Asian Survey* 9, 11: 831–841.

———. (1970) "Teaching Social Studies in North Korean Schools under Communism." *Social Education* 34, 5: 528–533, 542.

———. (1973) "Patterns of Political Socialization in North Korean Schools." *Peabody Journal of Education* 50, 4: 265–275.

———. (1981) "For the Heirs of the Revolution: Current Educational Practices in North Korea." *Social Education* 45, 7: 574–577.

———. (1994) "Towards a New Philosophy of Education for a Unified Korea." *Korea Observer* 25, 2: 261–289.

———. (2000) "Prospect for Social Change in North Korea: Reflections on My Trip to Pyongyang." *Korea and World Affairs* 24, 4: 619–629.

Park, Han S. (1996) *North Korea: Ideology, Politics, and Economy.* New York: Prentice-Hall.

Ryang, Sonia. (1997) *North Koreans in Japan: Language, Ideology, and Identity.* Boulder, CO: Westview Press.

NORTH KOREA—HUMAN RIGHTS

The state of North Korea is likely the worst abuser of human rights in the world today. Like that of his father before him, the regime of Kim Jong Il is a dictatorship that employs widespread fear and repression to control its people.

North Korea is also arguably the world's most restricted and isolated country, and thus it is extremely difficult for the international community to assess its current human-rights situation. The government has allowed a handful of aid workers, religious groups, and some journalists to visit in recent years, but what they are permitted to see is restricted. Although in many cases confirmation is not possible, a wide spectrum of grave human-rights abuses in North Korea has been reported by defectors, refugees, intelligence communities, humanitarian-aid workers, and international nongovernmental organizations.

Abuse of Civil and Political Rights

The North Korean constitution protects many human rights, but this means little in practice. North Koreans are denied freedom of speech, the media, religion, movement, assembly, petition, emigration, and association. They do not have the right to peacefully change their government. Foreign travel is prohibited for nearly all. Workers' rights are not observed, and only government-controlled unions are allowed. The government regularly mobilizes the population for compulsory labor projects in construction. In August of 1997, North Korea became the only country that has ever attempted to withdraw from a key human-rights treaty, the International Covenant on Civil and Political Rights (ICCPR).

The North Korean government also denies civil liberties to foreigners within its borders. Thousands of North Koreans who had Japanese nationality and citizenship voluntarily returned to North Korea in the 1960s and 1970s but are now denied home visits to Japan, despite North Korean government assurances to the contrary. Hundreds of South Koreans, mostly prisoners of war, are thought to be held in unacknowledged detention.

The North Korean government subjects its population to intensive ideological indoctrination and rigid controls in order to promote monolithic unity and loyalty to the state. The cult of personality for "Dear Leader" Kim Jong Il and his family as well as the semimystical ideology of *juche*, or national self-reliance, is systematically fostered through the media, educational institutes, worker and neighborhood associations, and staged marches and rallies. The government has classified the population into groups according to family background and allegiance to the state. One-third of all North Koreans are characterized as "hostile" to the regime and thus face discrimination in access to social services. Tens of thousands of people, including those with perceived disloyalty or physical disabilities, have been forcibly relocated from the capital to the countryside. The state controls all social and cultural aspects of life, permitting only activities that support its goals. It engages in strict censorship and monitors correspondence and telephones. There is a highly organized and pervasive system of informers. Little information reaches North Koreans from the outside world without government consent.

North Korea's judiciary is tightly controlled as well. According to defector and press accounts, the security forces engage in arbitrary detentions, extrajudicial killings, disappearances, public executions, and executions of political prisoners. Capital punishment and seizure of all assets is applicable to those who attempt defection, criticize the regime, listen to foreign broadcasts, write or possess "reactionary" printed matter or letters, or engage in "counterrevolutionary crimes."

Those accused of political offenses can also be sentenced, without due process, to reeducation through labor. Credible but unconfirmed reports suggest that North Korea has imprisoned about 150,000–200,000 people in twelve camps in remote areas. The vast majority of the inmates are reportedly family members of the accused who are guilty by association in the eyes of the state. According to escapee accounts, prisoners are held incommunicado and forced to work for seventeen hours per day. They are denied access to medical services and the right to marry or have children. They are allowed only the barest means of subsistence and are subject to severe mistreatment, including beatings, torture, and public executions. Some human-rights groups estimate that 400,000 North Koreans have already died in such camps.

In the North Korean–run work settlements in the far eastern area of Russia near the border, Amnesty International has documented abuses among the six thousand North Koreans working there. These include harsh living conditions and brutal disciplinary measures, such as physical abuse and torture. North Korea has also established work camps for homeless and orphaned children.

Economic and Social Rights Abuse, Famine, and Displacement

North Korea's government-controlled economy has been in crisis since the fall of the Soviet bloc in 1991, which ended Soviet and Chinese concessional trade and assistance to the country. The failure of collectivist agricultural policies and poor harvests due to bad weather during the 1990s have exacerbated negative growth rates. Widespread starvation has set in, and people have been forced to flee their homes. Petty corruption is thriving, and the nation's medical system has collapsed. Food, clothing, and energy are rationed. Despite this, the regime continues to spend approximately 25 percent of GDP on defense and armaments.

In the wake of massive floods in August 1995, reports of people driven to cannibalism leaked out of the closed state. The North Korean government appealed to the international community for assistance, and relief has since been forthcoming. However, it is estimated by humanitarian agencies that 2 to 3 million people may have died in North Korea of starvation and famine-related illnesses from 1994 to 1998. Acute food shortages continue. Some humanitarian groups have withdrawn from North Korea because they were denied access to affected populations. They have also reported that food is being unfairly distributed along lines of loyalty to the regime.

North Korean guest workers in Russia are overstaying in the country illegally rather than return to their famine-striken homeland. Having surrendered their passports and identification papers to North Korean border guards upon entry to Russia, such workers face hardships due to lack of identification. In search of food, hundreds of thousands of North Koreans are illegally crossing the mountainous border into China. Those who are caught by the authorities of both countries reportedly have their belongings confiscated and are beaten, detained, and later sent to "9-27"camps in North Korea. Established by decree on 27 September 1997 to address the problem of internal displacement resulting from the famine, such camps may hold as many as hundreds of thousands of North Koreans annually. The conditions are reportedly deplorable, with no heat in freezing temperatures, poor sanitation, inadequate food, infectious disease, and high death rates. Detainees are eventually forcibly returned to their villages.

Response to Human-Rights Abuse in North Korea

The North Korean government asserts that human rights are "fully ensured." Violations are "unthinkable," and such allegations are regarded as propaganda forwarded by South Korea and its allies. International and regional human-rights and humanitarian groups stress the need for North Korea to open itself up to visits by independent monitoring groups and improve human-rights practices. Government responses to North Korea's dismal human-rights record have been overshadowed by regional security concerns, such as North Korea's nuclear threat.

The South Korean, Japanese, and U.S. governments have all adopted policies of limited engagement in efforts to coax North Korea into the fold of the international community. Supporters of such a policy argue that without first gaining some leverage in this regard, the international community is unlikely in the long run to be able to influence better respect for human-rights practices in what is viewed as a rogue state. Critics of this approach charge that it only prolongs the life of the oppressive regime, which will never change its draconian practices. They argue that a more direct focus on human-rights concerns in diplomatic efforts toward North Korea is imperative and could even hasten the demise of the dictatorship.

North Korea currently appears to be expanding its official state contacts and, for the first time in more than ten years, in 2000 it submitted an implementation report on the ICCPR to the United Nations.

However, there are unfortunately no signs that the government is improving conditions for its people. In fact, the ongoing restrictions on access and information continues to give rise to concerns that the population is vulnerable to hidden human-rights violations.

Catherine Moller

See also: **Food Crisis—North Korea; Juche**

Further Reading

Amnesty International. (1997) "General Secretary Kim Jong Il Should Consider Human Rights Reforms." London: International Secretariat of Amnesty International.

———. (1999) *Annual Report: Korea (Democratic People's Republic of Korea).* London: International Secretariat of Amnesty International.

Baker, Michael. (2000) "In Camps, North Korea at Its Darkest." *The Christian Science Monitor*, 7 January.

Eberstadt, Nicholas. (1999) *The End of North Korea.* Washington, DC: American Enterprise Institute Press.

Edwards, Catherine. (1999) "Communist Gulag in All Its Horror." *Insight on the News.* Washington, DC: Washington Times Corporation.

Kagan, Richard C., Matthew Oh, and David Weissbrodt. (1988) *Human Rights in the Democratic People's Republic of Korea.* Washington, DC: Asia Watch and the Minnesota Lawyers International Human Rights Committee.

Korean Buddhist Sharing Movement. (1999) "Report on Daily Life and Human Rights of North Korean Food Refugees in China." Retrieved 2 March 2000, from: http://blue.nowcom.net/~kbsm/eng/frame.htm.

Natsios, Andrew. (1999) "The Politics of Famine in North Korea." Retrieved 2 March 2000, from: http://www.usip.org/oc/sr/sr990802/sr990802.html-.

Park, Christopher Lim. (1998) "Turbulent Relations: Redirecting U.S. Foreign Policy Toward North Korea." *Harvard International Review* 20 (3): 32–35.

Sullivan, Kevin, and Mary Jordan. (1999) "The Last Fortress: Our Futile Search for North Korea." *The Washington Post*, 1 August.

Yonhap News Agency/British Broadcasting Corporation. (2000) "North Korea to Submit Implementation Report on Human Rights Convention." Seoul: Yonhap News Agency/British Broadcasting Corporation.

NORTH KOREA—POLITICAL SYSTEM

Following most of the political systems in Communist countries, North Korea (Democratic People's Republic of Korea, or DPRK) adopted the party-dominated structure. At a glance, the North Korean political system resembles the separation of powers in Western democratic countries: a Cabinet, Supreme People's Assembly (SPA), and a Court are the institutions of the state. But all of the political institutions, including the military and auxiliary organizations, were at first under the tight control of the single mass party, the Korean Workers Party (KWP). Full-time party cadres and organizations take positions in various levels of the institutions of state and exercise power in the name of the party's guidance. The constitution of North Korea reads "The Democratic People's Republic of Korea functions in all aspects of affairs under the leadership of the Korean Workers Party" (Article 11).

Kim Il Sung (1912–1994) and his son Kim Jong Il (b. 1941) have ruled the party. The party has dominated society, but father and son have exercised absolute power in the party. Since the death of Kim Il Sung, the party's role has been subordinated to that of the military. Now the junior Kim rules the society through the military as well as through the party.

Consolidation of Kim Il Sung's Power

Even though the Communist movement in Korea may date back to the 1920s, the history of the KWP began with the power competition between Kim Il Sung's faction and other Communist factions right after the end of Japanese colonial rule in August 1945. Kim's major competitors were a Soviet faction and a Yan'an faction with Chinese training. A Seoul-based Communist faction joined the competition after it escaped the control of the U.S. Army military government (1945–1948) in the southern part of Korea. Kim's faction won out before the start of the Korean War in June 1950 and completely dominated the KWP by the mid-1950s.

Kim's win may be attributed to the assistance of the Soviet army at the initial stage of the power competi-

U.S. Secretary of State Madeleine Albright with Kim Young Nam, president of North Korea's Supreme People's Assembly, during her trip to North Korea in October 2000. (AFP/CORBIS)

PREFACE TO THE DEMOCRATIC PEOPLE'S REPUBLIC OF KOREA (NORTH KOREA)

Adopted: 1 September 1998

The Democratic People's Republic of Korea is a socialist fatherland of Juche which embodies the idea of and guidance by the great leader Comrade Kim Il Sung.

The great leader Comrade Kim Il Sung is the founder of the DPRK and the socialist Korea.

Comrade Kim Il Sung founded the immortal Juche idea, organized and guided an anti-Japanese revolutionary struggle under its banner, created revolutionary tradition, attained the historical cause of the national liberation, and founded the DPRK, built up a solid basis of construction of a sovereign and independent state in the fields of politics, economy, culture and military, and founded the DPRK.

Comrade Kim Il Sung put forward an independent revolutionary line, wisely guided the social revolution and construction at various levels, strengthened and developed the Republic into a people-centered socialist country and a socialist state of independence, self-sustenance, and self-defense.

Comrade Kim Il Sung clarified the fundamental principle of State building and activities, established the most superior state social system and political method, and social management system and method, and provided a firm basis for the prosperous and powerful socialist fatherland and the continuation of the task of completing the Juche revolutionary cause.

Comrade Kim Il Sung regarded believing in the people as in heaven as his motto, was always with the people, devoted his whole life to them, took care of and guided them with a noble politics of benevolence, and turned the whole society into one big and united family.

The great leader Comrade Kim Il Sung is the sun of the nation and the lodestar of the reunification of the fatherland. Comrade Kim Il Sung set the reunification of the country as the nation's supreme task, and devoted all his work and endeavors entirely to its realization.

Comrade Kim Il Sung, while turning the Republic into a mighty fortress for national reunification, indicated fundamental principles and methods for national reunification, developed the national reunification movement into a pan-national movement, and opened up a way for that cause, to be attained by the united strength of the entire nation.

The great leader Comrade Kim Il Sung made clear the fundamental idea of the Republic's external policy, expanded and developed diplomatic relations on this basis, and heightened the international prestige of the Republic. Comrade Kim Il Sung as a veteran world political leader, hewed out a new era of independence, vigorously worked for the reinforcement and development of the socialist movement and the nonaligned movement, and for world peace and friendship between peoples, and made an immortal contribution to the mankind's independent cause.

Comrade Kim Il Sung was a genius ideological theoretician and a genius art leader, an ever-victorious, iron-willed brilliant commander, a great revolutionary and politician, and a great human being. Comrade Kim Il Sung's great idea and achievements in leadership are the eternal treasures of the nation and a fundamental guarantee for the prosperity and efflorescence of the DPRK.

The DPRK and the entire Korean people will uphold the great leader Comrade Kim Il Sung as the eternal President of the Republic, defend and carry forward his ideas and exploits and complete the Juche revolution under the leadership of the Workers' Party of Korea.

The DPRK Socialist Constitution is a Kim Il Sung constitution which legally embodies Comrade Kim Il Sung's Juche state construction ideology and achievements.

Source: The People's Korea: DPRK Socialist Constitution. Retrieved 8 March 2002, from: http://www.korea-np.co.jp/pk/dprk_constitution/category33.htm.

tion, rather than the aid of the Soviet faction, which consisted of ideologues of the second generation of Korean immigrants, who had no connection to the Soviet military. The Soviet army, originally deployed to disarm the defeated Japanese troops, disarmed the Yan'an faction's anti-Japanese forces when the latter entered Korea. It is noteworthy, however, that Kim's advantage did not necessarily guarantee his hegemonic role in the party. In order to pave the way for socialist transformation politics—such as land reform and nationalization of major industries—before the launch of the DPRK in 1948, Kim's faction had to rely upon a coalition with the Soviet and Yan'an factions. Moreover, in order to extend the organizational base at the local level, the faction asked for the assistance of the Soviet army's advisory group as well as the indigenous Communists.

Kim was able to achieve supreme power during the Korean War (1950–1953). Before the war broke out, the Communist faction from the South asserted that South Koreans would massively support the North Korean army's marching into Seoul to subvert the South Korean government. That turned out not to be the case, however, and thus members of the Seoul-based Communist faction were purged from the KWP. Kim's attack on his rivals was highlighted at the August Factional Incident in 1956, in which he expelled several high officials of the Soviet and Yan'an factions from the party. The Soviet and Yan'an factions maintained that the party had to give priority to agriculture and light industry because of the sharp shortage of food and daily consumer goods, whereas Kim stressed heavy industry, saying that its development would boost the economy in general. Kim not only took advantage of this conflict to eliminate his opponents and to consolidate his power in the party, he also succeeded in implementing the development strategy of "heavy industry first, followed by light industry and agriculture." The supremacy of Kim's power in the party gradually developed into a personality cult and dictatorship during the 1960s.

Emergence of Kim Jong Il

According to the KWP Act, the party is organized under the principle of democratic centralism, through which cadres of lower party units select members of higher offices, who then make the decisions that determine the roles and procedures of the lower level. Formally, the highest authority in the party should be the party congress, whose functions are taken over by the party central committee when it is in recess. Informally, however, the Organization Department in the secretariat has maintained power to supervise systematically and inspect the operation of the KWP as a whole.

The tradition of the Organization Department's predominant role began when the current leader, Kim Jong Il, emerged as de facto successor to his father in 1973. At that time, the junior Kim became a secretary in charge of the Organization Department as well as of the Department of Propaganda and Agitation. On the one hand, by utilizing the Department of Propaganda and Agitation, he became the only authoritative interpreter of Juche, the official ideology of self-reliance, and proclaimed "Kimilsung-ism" to promote his father's personality cult. On the other hand, with the Organization Department he came to be deeply involved in the personnel affairs of the Cabinet and military as well as of party cadres. He also transformed the department into his personal power base by requiring all the documents and reports made by other departments to pass through the Organization Department before being implemented as policies.

Strengthening of the KWP in general and the predominant role of the Organization Department in particular resulted in the concentration of power within the party, but also in the pervasiveness of Kim Jong Il's influence on every aspect of society. As a move to ensure power succession to himself, the junior Kim proclaimed Ten Principles for the Establishment of the Monolithic Idea to induce subordination to Kim Il Sung's absolute authority. As the principles became the standard by which the loyalty of the party cadres and members was tested, the North Korean political system became even more strictly controlled. The ten principles are as follows: (1) fight at the risk of one's life for the dissemination of Kim Il Sung's revolutionary idea, (2) serve Kim with highest loyalty, (3) respect Kim's authority without question, (4) believe in Kim's revolutionary idea and his instructions, (5) maintain the principle of unconditionality in implementing Kim's instructions, (6) strengthen the ideological unity and revolutionary integrity centered around Kim, (7) follow and learn from Kim's Communist dignity, revolutionary work style, and mass line, (8) keep Kim's political life in one's heart and recompense him with strong trust for his high political integrity and concern, (9) establish strong organizational discipline following Kim's monolithic guidance, and (10) succeed and complete Kim's revolutionary works from generation to generation. It is notable that of these principles, the tenth suggested the political succession from Kim Il Sung to Kim Jong Il. That is, the junior Kim presented the disciplinary principles so as to enhance his own authority as well as the personality cult around his father.

The New Constitution

With the death of Kim Il Sung in July 1994, Kim Jong Il succeeded at once. The junior Kim has taken tight control of the military, a potential arbiter in the process of power transition, since the early 1990s, when he monopolized core offices dealing with the armed forces. He was appointed Supreme Commander of the People's Army in 1991, Marshal of the Republic in 1992, and Chairman of the National Defense Committee (NDC) in 1993. He did not have to exercise power over the military through the institutional mechanisms of the KWP. He gave orders and instructions to the armed forces directly and could divide and rule the two power-base institutions, the military and the party. The military swore a loyalty oath to the junior Kim as soon as Kim Il Sung died.

It should be noted that the junior Kim's formal succession was not completed until September 1998, when the Supreme People's Assembly amended the constitution. Most observers of North Korea expected that he would take the office of state president, but this did not happen. Instead, under the new constitution, in which there is no presidency, he appointed himself chairman of the NDC again, which was strengthened in its status and function.

According to the new constitution, power is formally divided into three institutions: the NDC, Presidium of the SPA, and Cabinet. When Kim Il Sung was named eternal president of the DPRK, the office of state president was abolished in the new constitution of 1998. Since 1998, the chairman of the SPA represents the state and performs ceremonial functions in foreign affairs, whereas the SPA in general operates as a legislative body. In the absence of a state president, the chairman of the NDC is the highest post. The Cabinet is expected to play a more active role in internal affairs such as economy and administration.

Under the new constitution, the NDC's role and status were strengthened. The NDC is defined as the highest guiding organ of the military and the managing organ of military matters. As chairman of the NDC, Kim Jong Il is in firm control of all the armed forces, including not only the regular army, navy, and air force but also the border control force and the worker-farmer's corps. Furthermore, the chairman of the NDC is in charge of all political and economic matters as well. In this regard, Kim is the true head of state, while the head of the SPA has a more ceremonial role.

Given this authority structure, the constitutional change implies several points. First, by naming his father the eternal president, Kim Jong Il intended to extend Kim Il Sung's charisma and legitimacy as the founding father of the DPRK. Second, Kim Jong Il was able deliberately to avoid the burdens of being the formal head of state: meeting with foreign diplomats and public appearances, which he has seldom liked. Third, he has also avoided responsibility for North Korea's economic devastation by providing the Cabinet and local government with more formal authority in economic affairs than before, while keeping actual power over domestic and foreign affairs.

Kim Jong Il's era under the new constitution is one in which the relationship between party and military have been restructured. Since Kim Il Sung's death, the junior Kim has ruled North Korea with the title of Supreme Commander of the People's Army. The status of the military has been enhanced to the point that it appears to dominate the North Korean political system. All the social sectors have been forced to demonstrate military spirit and adopt military methods. To resort to military leadership necessarily brings a change in the relationship between party and military. The change is best reflected in an editorial of the party organ, *Rodong Shinmun*, on 16 February 1997: "If it were not for the People's Army, our people, our state, and our party could not exist."

Whereas the Leninist tradition is that the Communist Party guides the military, in North Korea the KWP no longer exercises absolute control over the People's Army, nor is the military under the party's bureaucratic guidance. The political officers in charge of party work still remain in the military to promote loyalty to Kim Jong Il among the men, but their function does not depend upon the party's guidance. In a closed-session speech delivered to high-ranking party officials in December 1996, Kim Jong Il was quoted as saying that the party's morale was so degraded that party cadres would benefit from getting an ideological education from the political officers of the military.

Meanwhile, the new constitution has given the Cabinet more responsibility and power to run the crippled economy. Now the Cabinet has the right to supervise and control local governments and local economies. With the adoption of the new constitution, the old tradition that a local party secretary simultaneously held the office of head of local government is no longer the case. Accordingly, the local government comes to be relatively independent of the local party, particularly in economic affairs, and it is under the control of the Cabinet in the hierarchical sense.

It is also notable that the local government's relative independence from the local party has not brought any significant change in the overall relationship between party and government. The relationship is still often compared to the relationship between the man steering a boat and the man rowing it. The party steers the government, which does the rowing. Even though the party's influence has lessened in recent years, especially in military affairs, it still guides the government. There are two reasons for that. On the one hand, the ruling elite in North Korea attributes the demise of the socialist bloc in Eastern Europe to the failure of the party's dominance of society. They also emphasize the significance of the party's tight control over other segments of society. On the other hand, most of Kim Jong Il's supporters are in the party, and the party at large is his most loyal supporter. Furthermore, Kim Jong Il himself started his career as a party cadre, and his power succession began within the structure of the party. Therefore, the fact that the government gained in status in the new constitution does not affect the guiding role of the party over the government.

Sung Chull Kim

See also: **Juche; Kim Il Sung; Kim Jong Il**

Further Reading

Ok, Tae Hwan, and Hong Yung Lee, eds. (1994) *Prospects for Change in North Korea*. Berkeley, CA: Institute of East Asian Studies, University of California.

Scalapino, Robert A., and Chong-Sik Lee. (1972) *Communism in Korea*. 2 vols. Berkeley and Los Angeles: University of California Press.

Scalapino, Robert A., and Jun-Yop Kim, eds. (1983) *North Korea Today: Strategic and Domestic Issues*. Berkeley, CA: Institute of East Asian Studies, University of California.

NORTH KOREA–SOUTH KOREA RELATIONS

The division of the Korean Peninsula into North and South is a legacy of the Japanese occupation that began before annexation in 1910 and ended in 1945 with the reoccupation of the peninsula by Soviet troops in the north and U.S. troops in the south. Officially, the solidification of the division of the Korean Peninsula occurred in 1948 after elections were held in the Republic of Korea (ROK) and the Democratic People's Republic of Korea (DPRK) and the majority of the foreign troops returned home. Since that time the two Koreas have fought one major bloody war (1950–1953) and have engaged in numerous confrontations along the thirty-eighth parallel. On occasion they have also approached the negotiating table with hopes of putting an end to the conflict while setting the groundwork for the establishment of amicable relations leading to eventual reunification. Since 1988, there has been trade between the two Koreas.

A Korean man, who had fled to the south from the north during the Korean War, hands South Korean president Kim Dae Jung a family picture prior to Kim's departure for North Korea to engage in cooperation talks in June 2000. (AFP/CORBIS)

The Division of Korea

The Korean Provisional Government in Shanghai was a weak coalition of Korean refugees who had fled Japan-controlled Korea over the initial decade of Japanese rule. It was formed in 1919 and lasted until the end of World War II. While some members of this group believed Korea's independence would best be secured through diplomacy with the West, others felt the necessity of military force to drive the Japanese from the peninsula. The group split, with the former faction making its way to the United States and the latter primarily to the Soviet Far East and Manchuria. At the end of World War II, the respective groups rode in on the coattails of the occupation forces, the Soviets supporting Kim Il Sung (1912–1994) and the military faction, and the United States supporting Syngman Rhee (1875–1965) and the diplomacy faction.

The decision to divide the peninsula into two regions was hastily made on the evening of 10 August, less than a week before the Japanese surrender. Dean Rusk, a major in the U.S. military who later served in several cabinets in the United States, and Colonel Charles H. Bonesteel, another American who was later commander of American forces in the ROK, who were entrusted with determining the line of division, chose the thirty-eighth parallel, giving the United States control of Seoul, the capital. This division was accepted and respected by Moscow. Both sides believed the division would last until peninsular elections could be held and the country returned to independence. But North–South politics, supported by Cold War ideological differences, cemented the division between the two states, preventing the realization of elections at a national level.

The Korean War Era

Relations between the two sides were never good, with both the United States and the Soviet Union installing leaders generally friendly toward their respective ideologies, leaders who grew increasingly negative toward the other. Even though history tells us that war officially broke out on 25 June 1950, border clashes had been occurring since 1949. Other confrontations in the southern half of the peninsula, which included peasant rebellions and guerrilla warfare, demonstrated opposition first to U.S. occupation of the country and later to the conservative rule of Syngman Rhee. To the north, the Communist regime apparently enjoyed better success in repressing opposition forces. The Korean War lasted until 1953, with the ROK being rescued by a U.S.-directed United Nations force and the DPRK by the Communist regime in mainland China. The latter's participation came primarily as a result of threats by U.S. commander Douglas MacArthur to carry the war into Chinese territory. The war left heavy material damage to both sides and caused millions of deaths and family displacements. In 1953 the Armistice Agreement ended the hot war but wrapped the relations of the two countries in a Cold War atmosphere.

Other Confrontations

Since 1953 there have been numerous hostile and confrontational incidents instigated from both sides of the thirty-eighth parallel. The North Koreans were accused of initiating an attack on the South Korean presidential mansion in 1968, of attempting to sneak spies into the south using a submarine in 1996, and of instigating battle along a disputed water boundary in the West Sea in 1999. Team Spirit and other military games conducted by the South Korean and U.S. forces are viewed by the DPRK as intimidation ploys. Since the mid-1950s the North Koreans have also felt threatened by the cache of nuclear weapons stored in South Korea, as well as by U.S. threats to use the weapons, primarily during the Korean War.

Movement toward Reunification

But there have been signs of reconciliation. In 1972, for example, the inter-Korean Red Cross met at the demilitarized zone (DMZ) town of Panmunjom. These talks resulted in the composition of the Joint North–South Communique of 4 July, which stated the aspiration of the two Koreas to seek unification without the help of a third party. In 1994, Korean president Kim Young Sam agreed to meet with North Korean leader Kim Il Sung. However, the latter Kim's untimely death put an end to those plans. With the North's nuclear program apparently frozen since 1994, the two sides have engaged in productive discussion to resolve their differences. This discussion paved the way for the North–South summit that took place in P'yongyang in June 2000. Since then, however, Kim Jong Il's refusal to visit Seoul and less amicable relations between the U.S. and the DPRK have frozen the progress made during the 1990s.

Over this time several scenarios for Korean unification have been proposed. No one predicts the course of unification to be free of confusion or even violence. Pessimists envision either the total economic and political collapse of the DPRK, or a desperate military attempt at unification by the North, bringing about its eventual absorption by the South. Either scenario predicts economic chaos throughout the Northeast Asian region as well as a massive refugee movement from the North to either the ROK or to a third country, possibly Japan or the United States. The problems associated with these scenarios, and the recent economic difficulties experienced by the ROK, have caused some to consider "soft landing" scenarios in which the economic health of the DPRK is strengthened to prepare it for its inevitable absorption by the South. A third option has been put forth by both the North and the South from the early 1970s: that of a one-country, two-system confederation arrangement in which the two states would gradually begin to work together toward a unification conducted upon more equal terms. Few, if any, see Korean unification as occurring suddenly, as it did in Germany, but rather as a gradual process.

Mark E. Caprio

See also: **Korean War; North and South Korean Economic Ventures**

Further Reading

Cumings, Bruce. ([1981] 1990) *The Origins of the Korean War*. Vol. 1. Princeton, NJ: Princeton University Press.

Kihl, Young Hwan, ed. (1994) *Korea and the World: Beyond the Cold War*. Boulder, CO: Westview Press.

NORTH KOREA–UNITED STATES RELATIONS Interaction between the Democratic Republic of North Korea (DPRK) and the United States has long been filled with animosity, tension, and confrontation. In 2002 there are no official diplomatic relations between these two countries.

The DPRK's version of Korean history depicts Americans as the root cause for the division of the Korean Peninsula along the thirty-eighth parallel in 1948. Communist North Korea maintains that the United States, with United Nations backing, illegally helped in establishing an opposing Republic of Korea (ROK) government in the south of the peninsula. During the height of the Cold War, North Korea accused the United States of turning South Korea into an American colony in order to strengthen its influence and colonize the whole of the Korean Peninsula.

When the United States provided weapons and training for the South Korean Army in the late 1940s and early 1950s, the DPRK condemned the Americans for initiating the Korean War (1950–1953) between North and South Korea. In the aftermath of the war, the U.S.–ROK Mutual Defense Treaty of 1965, which protects the ROK from any aggressive moves from the North, as well as positioning 37,000 U.S. troops in various military bases in South Korea, led North Korea to perceive the United States as the foremost threat to its survival and security. Repeatedly North Korea has demanded that the United States withdraw its troops from South Korean soil because it sees American security commitments to the ROK as the main stumbling block in achieving the reunification of the Korean Peninsula.

Relations between P'yongyang and Washington further deteriorated when, in 1968, North Korea captured the USS *Pueblo*, a U.S. intelligence ship, claiming the Americans were spying around its coast. In another incident, DPRK soldiers killed several American soldiers with axes at the border village of Panmunjom in 1976. In the 1990s, a new pattern emerged in P'yongyang's relations with Washington whereby North Korea now used its nuclear capabilities as a bargaining chip in gaining economic assistance from the United States. In return for freezing its reactors that are capable of manufacturing weapons-grade plutonium, the United States agreed to furnish the DPRK with two light-water nuclear reactors and heavy oil.

But the American policy of simultaneously imposing economic and trade sanctions and labeling the DPRK as a "rogue state" hampered efforts at reconciliation. There was marked progress when Jo Myong-rok, second in command after Kim Jong Il, made a landmark visit to Washington in October 2000 to attempt a rapprochement with the United States. Shortly thereafter, Secretary of State Madeline Albright from the Clinton administration visited P'yongyang. However, North Korea believes that the George W. Bush Republican leadership in Washington that took office in 2001, which has blacklisted it as a terrorist-supporting country (part of the "axis of evil"), and uses the label to justify its plans for a missile defense system, will isolate the DPRK from the rest of the world. In the 2002 climate, chances for normalizing relations between the two countries were practically nonexistent.

Geetha Govindasamy

See also: **North Korea—Political System; North Korea–South Korea Relations**

Further Reading

O'Neill, Aloysius. (1992) "U.S. Policy toward Northeast Asia and Prospects for U.S.–North Korean Rapprochement." *The Journal of Unification Studies* 15.

Kim, Gye Dong. (1993) "North Korea's Improvement of Relations with U.S.A. and Japan: The Possibilities and Limits." *East Asian Review* 15, 1.

Kim, Hong Nack. (1992) "North Korea's Policy toward Japan and the United States." *The Journal of East Asian Affairs* 6, 2.

Lee, Chae Jin. (1993) "U.S. Policy toward North Korea in the 1990s." *Korean Studies* 16.

Mazarr, Michael J. (1995) *North Korea and the Bomb: A Case Study in Nonproliferation.* New York: St. Martin's Press.

Sigal, Leon V. (1998) *Disarming Strangers: Nuclear Diplomacy with North Korea.* Princeton, NJ: Princeton University Press.

NORTH KYONGSANG PROVINCE (2000 pop. 2.8 million). North Kyongsang Province (Kyongsang pukto) is located in South Korea in the southeastern region of the Korean Peninsula. It contains the major urban center of Taegu, with a population of 2.5 million, and the important cultural area of Kyongju, the capital of the Shilla kingdom (57 BCE–935 CE). It is bordered by the Sobaek Mountains to the north and west, South Kyongsang Province to the south, and the Sea of Japan (East Sea) to the east. Due to the rugged topography of the surrounding mountains, subareas within the region share cultural traits, such as a dialect and customs, which are quite different from those of outlying regions. Both Kyongsang provinces are also known as *Yongnam* ("south of the mountain passes"), attesting to the historical importance that mountains have played in fostering regional characteristics.

North Kyongsang Province has a large industrial agglomeration, due mainly to heavy investments in the region by the South Korean government since the 1960s. Steel, shipbuilding, automobile, and petrochemical factories are concentrated along the southeast coast beginning in P'ohang and extending into South Kyongsang Province. The northwestern part of the province also has two major clusters of industries around Taegu and Kumi, which specialize in textiles and electronics.

North Kyongsang Province boasts two Buddhist sites, Pulguk Monastery and the Sokkuram Grotto, both constructed between 751 and 775 CE, which have been named as cultural sites on the UNESCO World Heritage List. It also preserves a regional version of the mask dance at Hahoe Village, near Andong, called the *Hahoe Pyolsin kut*, which was performed during village festivals on the second day of the first moon according to the lunar calendar.

Richard D. McBride II

Further Reading

Eckert, Carter J., et al. (1990) *Korea Old and New: A History*. Seoul: Ilchokak.

Korean Overseas Culture and Information Service. (1999) *A Handbook of Korea*. 10th ed. Seoul: Korean Overseas Culture and Information Service.

Lee, Ki-baik. (1984) *A New History of Korea*. Trans. by Edward W. Wagner. Cambridge, MA: Harvard University Press.

NORTH P'YONGAN PROVINCE

NORTH P'YONGAN PROVINCE (2002 est. pop. 3.1 million). North P'yongan Province (P'yongan pukto), located in northwestern North Korea (Democratic People's Republic of Korea), has an area of 12,383 square kilometers. The province borders the Yalu (Amnok) River separating North Korea and China (People's Republic of China). It also faces the Yellow Sea to the west.

The provincial capital is at Sinuiju, which is close to the mouth of the Yalu River and the border with China. In the first half of the twentieth century, Sinuiju was an important connection point for trains connecting Korea and Manchuria. Sinuiju and Kusong are the two designated cities, and there are twenty-three counties (*kun*).

The region is highly industrialized because of its location and abundance of hydroelectric power. Arms, machinery, textiles, clothing, footwear, foodstuffs, and daily necessities are some of the key manufactured goods. Rice, corn, beans, livestock, fruits, and sericulture make up the predominant agricultural sectors. The province's location on the Yellow Sea also enables deep-sea and coastal fishing.

North P'yongan Province is noted as well for its beautiful landscape of mountains, waterfalls, and caves. The area also has many historical points of interest, such as Buddhist temples.

Jennifer Jung-Kim

Further Reading

Cho, Chung-Kyung, Phyllis Haffner, and Fredric M. Kaplan. (1991) *The Korea Guidebook*. 5th ed. Boston: Houghton Mifflin.

Storey, Robert, and Alex English. (2001) *Korea*. 5th ed. Berkeley, CA: Lonely Planet Publications.

NORTHERN EXPEDITION The Northern Expedition (1926–1928) was the major military effort by the Chinese Nationalist regime under Chiang Kai-shek (Jiang Jieshi; 1887–1975) to move north from Guangdong in southeast China in July 1926 to unify the country under the Guomindang (Chinese Nationalist Party) and to end the power of the warlords that so weakened and divided China.

The campaign reflected at least initially the Nationalist-Communist alliance; Communist cadres preceded the advance of Nationalist armed forces and thereby helped in building popular support among peasants and workers. However, bribery was also used to convince local warlords to accept nominal Nationalist control of much of China.

There were some successes. Within several weeks after its start in June 1926, the National Revolutionary Army seized Changsha, the capital of Hunan Province in central China, and the great port area of Wuhan on the Chang (Yangtze) River in September, Fuzhou in southeastern China in December, and Shanghai and Nanjing the following March, by which time Chiang's forces controlled much of central China.

The Nationalist movement was divided into right and left wings, and the left wing—both the Nationalist and Communist followers—settled into Wuhan, one of the great industrial areas in largely agrarian China, while the right wing of the Guomindang moved to the more strategic lower Chang area and the Nanjing-Shanghai axis.

Soon after capturing Shanghai, in April 1927, Chiang turned on the Communist movement and with the assistance of foreign forces and the Shanghai underworld destroyed the so-called urban Communists in a reign of terror, ending the alliance and forcing the surviving Communist cadres to flee with Mao Zedong to Jiangxi Province in the southeastern countryside; here they regrouped and later began their Long March in 1934.

One outcome of the Northern Expedition was the decimation of the power of the urban and Soviet-allied Chinese Communist movement and its transformation to a more agrarian-based Marxist movement under the leadership of Mao Zedong and his colleagues. Other significant results were the strengthening of Chiang's leadership, the continuing power of warlords to influence government actions, a decision by Japan to invade the divided China, and later ties between the Nationalists and Western nations.

Charles Dobbs

Further Reading

Botier, George F. (1979) *A Short History of Nationalist China, 1919–1949.* New York: Putnam.

Jordan, Donald A. (1976) *The Northern Expedition: China's National Revolution of 1926–1928.* Honolulu: University of Hawaii Press.

NORTHERN TERRITORIES

NORTHERN TERRITORIES (2001 est. pop. 29,000). The Northern Territories are a group of islands in the Kurile chain north of the Japanese island of Hokkaido. Historically the islands and the island of Sakhalin have been claimed by both Russia and Japan. In 1855, the two nations agreed that the two largest islands in the Kuriles, Kunashiri and Etorofu, belonged to Japan and that Sakhalin would be shared. In 1875, it was agreed that all the Kuriles belonged to Japan and that Sakhalin belonged to Russia. Japan's victory in the Russo-Japanese War (1904–1905) resulted in Japan acquiring the southern portion of Sakhalin Island (south of 50 degrees north latitude) through the Treaty of Portsmouth.

Russia, and then the Soviet Union, long sought to reacquire the islands, and the Kuriles were promised to Joseph Stalin at the 1945 Yalta Conference. In the 1951 peace treaty signed by Japan and the Allies (with the exception of the Soviet Union), Japan renounced any claim to Sakhalin or the Kuriles. However, because Japan and the Soviet Union never concluded a peace treaty, the issue of rightful control of the islands continues to be a sticking point. The islands are currently inhabited by Russians and ethnic Koreans brought there during the Japanese occupation of Korea.

Thomas P. Dolan

Further Reading

Hasegawa, Tsuyoshi. (1998) *The Northern Territories Dispute and Russo-Japanese Relations.* Berkeley: University of California Institute of International Studies.

NORTH-WEST FRONTIER PROVINCE—SARHAD

NORTH-WEST FRONTIER PROVINCE—SARHAD (2002 est. pop. 19.5 million). The smallest province (74,522 square kilometers) of the federal state of Pakistan, North-West Frontier Province (NWFP) by its very name reveals its geographical position. The region is surrounded by Afghanistan to the west and north, the Pakistani provinces of Baluchistan to the south and Punjab to the east, and the territory of Jammu and Kashmir, contested with India, to the northeast.

The NWFP's terrain is characterized by harsh mountain ranges, high plains bounded by stony hills, and narrow mountain passes, such as the famous Khyber Pass, a gateway between India and Afghanistan. The great Hindu Kush range crosses the region; its highest peak is the Tirich Mir (7,690 meters). The main rivers are the Kabul, which flows from east to west, the Kunar, Kandia, Kurram, Gumal, and Swat. The vale of Swat is considered one of the most beautiful valleys in the country, with historical-period architecture and earlier archaeological remains dating back to 3000 BCE.

The heart of the province is the large and fertile vale of Peshawar, which was once the center of the Ghandara kingdom (sixth century BCE–tenth century CE), a civilization of the Indian subcontinent. The city of Peshawar, founded 2,000 years ago, is the present capital of the province and the main urban center of the region. During the Soviet occupation of Afghanistan (1979–1988), the city hosted crowds of Afghan refugees and became the headquarters of the mujahideen (Islamic warriors), a group fighting against the Red Army, and the Communist government of Kabul.

Islam was effectively brought to the region by the Turkic dynasty of the Ghaznavids at the end of the tenth century. From then on, the region passed successively to Ghurid, Afghan, Mughal, Pashtun, and Sikh rule. The British occupied the NWFP in 1849 following the Second Sikh War and strongly fortified it, since they considered this region a strategic pillar for the defense of their empire in India. Nevertheless, they always faced problems in keeping the NWFP under control, especially in the so-called tribal areas. There, fierce Pashtun tribes (called Pathan by the British) strenuously fought against the British Army to maintain their autonomy and their traditional laws. After the Partition of India in 1947, the NWFP joined the new state of Pakistan, the special status of the Pashtun tribal areas remaining unchanged.

The ethnic group of the Pashtun, divided into many tribes, clans, and subsections, represents the overwhelming majority of the population, which is mostly rural (79 percent of the total population, according to 1999 estimates), except for the area of Peshawar.

Riccardo Redaelli

Further Reading

Collin, Davies C. (1932) *The Problem of the North West Frontier, 1890–1908*. Cambridge, U.K.: Cambridge University Press.

Rashid, Ahmed. (2000) *Taliban: Islam, Oil and the New Great Game in Central Asia*. London: I. B. Tauris.

Spain, James. (1963) *People of the Khyber: The Pathans of Pakistan*. New York: Praeger.

———. (1995) *Pathans of the Latter Day*. Karachi, Pakistan: Oxford University Press.

Swinson, Arthur. (1967) *North-West Frontier: People and Events, 1839–1947*. London: Hutchinson.

NO-RUZ No-ruz (also, Nau rooz, Noruz, Now ruz; new day) is a Persian expression referring to the Persian New Year. It takes place on the first day of spring (21 March) and heralds the beginning of thirteen days of celebration. A few weeks before No-ruz, Iranians commonly do spring cleaning in their homes in preparation for the arrival of the New Year. Picnics are a common tradition on the thirteenth day. In addition, people take to the streets to participate in celebrations by playing drums and singing songs. Some also dress up in brightly colored satin outfits and wear makeup, to portray Haji Firuz (bards). The frequent themes during No-ruz celebrations are good and evil or death and rebirth.

An elaborate dinner takes place on No-ruz. Usually, a traditional centerpiece, called the *haft-sin* (seven esses), is placed on the dinner table. The seven esses refer to the seven items in the arrangement that all begin with the letter *s* in the Persian language and which can include sumac (a spice), *serkeh* (vinegar), *samanu* (wheat pudding), *sabzi* (greens), *sonbol* (hyacinth), *senjed* (a type of Iranian fruit), *sekeh* (coin), *sib* (apple), and *sir* (garlic). These items are offered as symbols to bring good luck and prosperity in the coming year.

Houman A. Sadri

Further Reading

Fardjan, Faridah, and Meyer Azaad. (1972) *Uncle New Year: An Original Persian Folk Story*. Minneapolis, MN: Carolrhoda Books.

Ghanoonparvar, Mohammad R. (1982) *Persian Cuisine*. Lexington, KY: Mazda.

Ghirshman, Roman. (1978) *Iran*. Harmondsworth, Middlesex, U.K.: Penguin Books.

Miskub, Shahrokh. (1992) *Iranian Nationality and the Persian Language*. Washington, DC: Mage.

NOW RUZ. See **No-ruz.**

NU SHOOTING Nu shooting is a form of archery indigenous to southwestern China and associated with the non-Han Nu ethnic minorities of the region. It is distinguished from other forms of archery by the use of a wooden bow and arrow and bamboo arrowheads. The Chinese government promotes Nu shooting as an authentic "minority sport" and organizes tournaments where challengers shoot at targets from various distances, horseback, and standing and kneeling positions.

David Levinson

Further Reading

Ma Yin, ed. (1989) *China's Minority Nationalities*. Beijing: Foreign Language Press.

NU, U (1907–1995), Myanmar political figure and writer. Myanmar (Burmese) leader U Nu, born in Wakema, Myaungma District, in 1907, received a B.A. from Rangoon University in 1929. He became headmaster and later superintendent at Pantanaw High School and worked briefly under U Thant (1909–1974), who later became UN secretary-general. He completed a law degree at Rangoon University in 1935. In the same year he was elected president of the newly established Rangoon University Student Union. His expulsion from the university jointly with nationalist leader Aung San (1915–1947) gave the impetus for the 1936 university strikes and marked the beginning of his political career. Aung San convinced him to join the Burmese nationalist movement the Dobama in 1938, where they were both elevated to the executive committee, causing a rift among the membership. He became known as Thakin Nu at that time. Outbreak of war in Europe in September 1939 spurred renewed demands for national independence, and U Nu's involvement caused him to be sentenced to two years in prison on 15 July 1940. During his imprisonment, he wrote a number of plays. Freed in the wake of the Japanese invasion of Burma on 9 December 1941, he subsequently became general secretary of the united Dobama-Sinyetha Party and served in Ba Maw's (1893–1977) government under the Japanese as minister of foreign affairs (1943) and as minister of information (1944).

After Aung San's assassination in 1947, U Nu was invited to be chair of the Anti-Fascist Peoples' Freedom League (AFPFL), the dominant party in the country. On 17 October 1947, he concluded the Nu-Attlee agreement on Burma's national independence and became Burma's first prime minister on 4 January 1948 at national independence, serving until 1962 with brief interludes in the 1956–1957 period to reorganize the AFPFL. He became leader of the "Clean" AFPFL faction in 1958. Between 1958 and 1960, he invited a "caretaker" government headed by General Ne Win to deal with the nation's security issues. U Nu won the office again in the 1960 election and declared Buddhism the national religion in the same year, which caused considerable opposition among non-Buddhists. As prime minister, U Nu failed to address politically ethnic and Communist insurgency, and he overemphasized Buddhism (the grounds for his electoral appeal) as a solution to national unity at the expense of a more inclusive approach to religions in general.

Ne Win's 1962 military coup put an end to electoral government and U Nu's role within it. He placed U Nu in prison. After his release on 27 October 1966, U Nu left the country in February 1969, and at a news conference that was held in London on 27 August 1969 he declared himself to be the "legal prime minister" of Burma. Subsequently, he was based in Bangkok, where he tried to organize Burmese resistance in the Thai-Burma border region. However, he left Thailand for India in June 1973. Under an amnesty declared by the Council of State (by Ne Win), U Nu returned to Burma on 29 July 1980, where he became a monk for a while and where he got involved in Buddhist missionary work, including the Burma Pitaka Association, which he founded. He again proclaimed himself to be the legal prime minister and declared an interim government on 9 September 1988, but this met with little or no support. His time as a politician had by then ended. For refusing to disband his "government," U Nu was put under house arrest on 29 December 1989 but was released on 23 April 1992. He died in Rangoon on 14 February 1995.

U Nu is remembered for his interest in Buddhism and in literature and translation. He set up the Nagani book club in 1939, which translated major political tracts for the Burmese readership. Also, between 1954 and 1955 he initiated the Sixth Buddhist Sangayana (Sixth Buddhist Synod), only the second to be held in Burmese history, to ensure the purity of the Buddhist canon.

Gustaaf Houtman

See also: **Anti-Fascist People's Freedom League Myanmar; Aung San; Myanmar—History; Myanmar—Political System; Ne Win, U**

Further Reading

Ba Maw, U. (1959) "U Nu Psychoanalyzed." *The Nation.* (October).

Butwell, Richard A. (1962) "The Four Failures of U Nu's Second Premiership." *Asian Survey* 2 (March).

———. (1969) *U Nu of Burma.* Stanford, CA: Stanford University Press.

———. (1975) *U Nu, Saturday's Son.* New Haven, CT: Yale University Press. (Includes an autobiography written originally in Burmese by U Nu himself, translated by U Law Yone, and edited by Dr. Kyaw Win.)

Nu, U. (1954) *Burma under the Japanese: Pictures and Portraits.* Ed. and trans. by John Sydenham Furnivall. New York: St. Martin's.

———. (1957) *The People Win Through: A Play.* New York: Taplinger.

Sarkisyanz, Manuel. (1961) "On the Place of U Nu's Buddhist Socialism in Burma's History of Ideas." In *Studies on Asia*, edited by Robert K. Sakai. Lincoln, NE: University of Nebraska Press.

Trager, Frank N. (1963) "The Failure of U Nu and the Return of the Armed Forces in Burma." *The Review of Politics* 25.

NUCLEAR ALLERGY

NUCLEAR ALLERGY Japan is often described as having an "allergy" to anything even remotely related to nuclear weapons. This allergy sometimes extends to nonmilitary uses of nuclear technology. Even so, the Japanese government has actively pursued nuclear power as a source of energy, despite public reservations stemming from Japan's history as the only country to experience the hostile use of nuclear weapons. The collective social and psychological scare left by the U.S. decision to use atomic bombs at the end of World War II has had lasting political implications.

The nuclear allergy toward weapons became institutionalized in 1967 when the then–prime minister Sato Eisaku delineated Japan's three nonnuclear principles. First, Sato pledged that Japan would not produce nuclear weapons. Second, Japan would not possess nuclear weapons in its self-defense arsenal. Finally, Japan would not permit other countries, notably the United States, to have nuclear weapons on Japanese soil. These principles were partially responsible for

Sato's sharing the 1974 Nobel Peace Prize. The third principle, it turns out, was not met, as the United States did at times transport and store nuclear weapons on Japanese soil, apparently without the Japanese government's knowledge. Furthermore, the nonnuclear stance was an easy foreign policy position to adopt, since Japan was under the American nuclear umbrella. Nevertheless, the anti–nuclear weapons stance has been a mainstay of Japanese foreign policy.

It is worth noting that while the Japanese public and government may be allergic to nuclear weapons there is an uneasy yet substantial role for nuclear *power* in Japan. Japan's penchant for nuclear power results in part from the long-held view of the country as a small island devoid of natural resources and in need of energy self-sufficiency. Moreover, the 1973 oil shock taught the Japanese government that the country was too sensitive to disruptions in fossil fuel supplies and hence that it should increase domestic electricity-generating capacity. The net result is Japan's uncomfortable embrace of nuclear power while it rejects nuclear weapons.

Jonathan R. Strand

Further Reading

Pempel, T. J. (1975) "Japan's Nuclear Allergy." *Current History* (April): 169–173.

Samuels, Richard J. (1994) *Rich Nation, Strong Army: National Security and the Technological Transformation of Japan.* Ithaca, NY: Cornell University Press.

Suzuki, Tatsujiro. (1991) "Japan's Nuclear Dilemma." *Technology Review* 94 (October): 41–49.

NUCLEAR ARMS Emerging strategic trends indicate that the security environment in the Asia-Pacific region is becoming more complex and uncertain, with the gradual diffusion of power and proliferation of nuclear and ballistic-missile capabilities. The Asia-Pacific region is now home to the largest number of states possessing nuclear weapons (NWS) in the world. In addition to the two nuclear superpowers—Russia and the United States—China, India, and Pakistan possess sizable nuclear arsenals. Australia, Japan, and South Korea enjoy the protection of the U.S. extended nuclear deterrence umbrella and either have some American nuclear weapons deployed on their territory or provide special facilities to the nuclear-armed U.S. forces. Several East Asian countries can assemble nuclear devices on short notice—Japan, North Korea, South Korea, and Taiwan. In Southwest Asia, Iran is believed to be working on nuclear weapons and missile programs. While the threat of a global nuclear Armageddon has receded, there is now a real danger that nuclear weapons will be used in regional conflicts, by terrorist groups, by separatist forces seeking independence, or by rival factions in a coup d'état, perhaps accidentally, due to weak command and control systems.

The nuclear proliferation that occurred after the Cold War shows that international nonproliferation measures cannot prevent the spread of nuclear weapons in regions where heavily armed and often antagonistic neighbors confront each other, as in the case of the two Koreas, China and Taiwan, China and India, or India and Pakistan. Proliferation is closely related to the security dilemma rooted in the belief held by many in the three divided Asian countries of Korea, China, and India that the possession of such weapons is essential to their very survival and long-term security. Such an attitude does not portend well for the future of the global nuclear nonproliferation (NNP) regime.

The Global Nuclear Nonproliferation Regime

The global NNP regime is an outgrowth of steps taken during the second half of the twentieth century to halt the horizontal spread of nuclear weapons. Several key components of the NNP regime include the Vienna-based International Atomic Energy Agency (IAEA), founded in 1957; the 1963 Partial Test Ban Treaty banning the testing of nuclear weapons in the atmosphere, in outer space, or underwater; the 1968 Nuclear Non-Proliferation Treaty (NPT), which was extended indefinitely in 1995; the London-based Nuclear Suppliers' Group, formed in 1974, which requires IAEA safeguards on all of its participants' nuclear exports; the 1987 Missile Technology Control Regime aimed at halting the proliferation of nuclear-capable ballistic missiles and other unmanned delivery systems; the 1995 Wassenaar Arrangement (a successor to the Cold War era's COCOM, or Coordinating Committee on Multilateral Export Controls) covering conventional weapons and duel-use exports; the Zangger Committee, which regulates nuclear-related exports; and the 1996 Comprehensive Test Ban Treaty (CTBT—yet to come into force), which constrains all states from conducting nuclear tests (but allows computer-simulated, zero-yield, and subcritical tests). In addition the nuclear weapons-free zones (NWFZs) in Latin America (including the Argentine-Brazilian bilateral arrangement), the South Pacific, Southeast Asia, and Africa have further strengthened the NNP regime. In 1997 the five Central Asian states issued the Tashkent statement, which proposed an NWFZ in that area.

POLICY AND REALITY IN NUCLEAR SOUTH ASIA

The following text is from a resolution passed by the All India Congress Committee in November 1963. Despite the support for a ban on nuclear weapons, India and Pakistan each had substantial arsenals as of 2002, and the region remained, in the view of many experts, a likely scene for regional nuclear war.

> The Committee welcomes the recent Nuclear Test Ban Agreement. This has provided a beginning, however small, in lowering world tensions and given some hope of wider and more significant relaxations which can lead to the ultimate ending of the cold war. This Agreement is a limited one and by itself does not ensure peace. Nevertheless, the Agreement repudiates the cold war attitude and approach and has been recognised as a beginning and reversal of the cold war approach. It is, therefore, to be welcomed. The Committee hopes that this approach will be continued and the Agreement will be followed by a halt in the armament race, particularly in nuclear arms, and that the manufacture, stockpiling and use of nuclear weapons or traffic in them will be prohibited by international agreement.
>
> *Source:* Jagdish Saran Sharma. (1965) *India's Struggle for Freedom: Select Documents and Sources*. Vol. II. Delhi: S. Chand & Co., 211.

The overall record of the global NNP regime has been a mixture of success and failure. On the positive side, five decades of international efforts at curbing the spread of nuclear weapons created a political and normative climate in which no state can easily declare its nuclear intentions. The unsuitability of nuclear weapons in most military situations may also render them inappropriate for use in many conflicts. In recent years a number of nuclear-capable states—notably Argentina, Brazil, South Africa, and the former Soviet republics of Ukraine, Belarus, and Kazakhstan—have agreed to abandon or dismantle their nuclear weapons capabilities. With the exception of only four countries in the world—Israel, India, Pakistan, and Cuba—all countries have acceded to the NPT, making it the most extensive multilateral control measure regulating nuclear arms. In this sense the regime has been fairly successful.

On the negative side, the campaign for nuclear disarmament appears to be faltering just when success seemed at hand. Since the mid-1980s attempts at nuclear disarmament have been seriously undermined by developments such as the emergence of new suppliers of nuclear technology (notably China), growing trade in delivery systems, and an increase in the number of threshold or new NWSs. When they exploded ten nuclear bombs during two weeks in May 1998, India and Pakistan not only fundamentally altered the Asian nuclear balance of power but also demonstrated that nuclear might represents, as Samuel P. Huntington foresaw in *The Clash of Civilizations* (1996: 192), "the central phenomenon of the slow but ineluctable diffusion of power in a multicivilizational world." Apart from the five declared NWSs (the United States, Russia, Britain, France, and China) and two new self-declared NWSs (India and Pakistan), several other nations (Israel, Japan, North Korea, Taiwan, and Iran) are widely believed to have made significant progress toward acquiring nuclear weapons capability. Many signatories to nonproliferation treaties retain an interest in joining the exclusive nuclear club: for example Iraq and North Korea maintained clandestine nuclear weapons programs that were exposed following the 1991 Persian Gulf War and in 1994, respectively. The degree to which a small country like North Korea manipulated major powers with its "nuclear/missile card" was not lost on the Taiwanese, who argue that Taiwan should have its own nuclear weapons program to counter forcible reunification with mainland China. Vietnam also seems keen to acquire nuclear and missile technology.

China bears a great deal of responsibility for recent nuclear proliferation in Asia, in view of the assistance it provided to the nuclear and missile programs of Pakistan and North Korea to countervail its Asian strategic rivals, India and Japan. Beijing's proliferation activities helped create the contexts in which India decided to unveil its nuclear weapons and Japan decided to opt for the U.S.-backed Theater Missile Defenses in East Asia. (Theater Missile Defenses are aimed at erecting a defense shield to protect the U.S. forces and bases in the Asia-Pacific region from long-range ballistic missile attacks from enemy forces—rogue states and nonstate actors, such as al-Qaeda.) Though some countries helped by China—Argentina, Brazil, and South Africa—eventually renounced their nuclear weapons programs, others (for example, Iran) continue to pose formidable challenges to the nonproliferation regime. For their part the five acknowledged NWSs continue technological and research efforts to update their weapons capacities, reaffirming the stance that their possession of such weapons is necessary for strategic deterrence, balance, and national security. Nunclear weapons have obviously not lost their value as instruments of power.

Nuclear Arsenals

Much like the United States and Russia, China possesses a complete triad of ground-, sea-, and air-based nuclear deterrents. Unlike Moscow's and Washington's arsenals of about 3,000 warheads each, however, Beijing possesses roughly 450 to 500 nuclear warheads, making it the third-largest NWS. The nuclear arsenals of the United States, Russia, and China include strategic bombers, submarine-launched ballistic missiles, modern short-range and long-range (intermediate and intercontinental) ballistic missiles armed with miniaturized multiple independent reentry vehicles, tactical nuclear weapons, neutron bombs, and advanced command, control, communications, computer processing, and intelligence. The nuclear arsenals of new entrants to the nuclear club are much smaller. India is estimated to have 70 to 100 nuclear warheads and Pakistan 30 to 50 warheads, and their delivery systems consist of short- and intermediate-range ballistic missiles and fighter aircraft such as the Mirage 2000, Jaguars, and F-16s.

North Korea's nuclear arsenal is the subject of much debate and speculation; it probably does not exceed five to seven nuclear bombs. South Korea operates many nuclear power reactors and possesses the technical capacity to manufacture nuclear weapons if it decides to do so. Should the United States reduce its military commitment to South Korea's defense, or if relations with North Korea deteriorate badly, South Korea might reconsider its nuclear options. On the other hand Seoul could inherit North Korea's nuclear weapons capabilities following the reunification of the two Koreas—a prospect that would cause anxiety in Japan. Japan has a sizable plutonium stockpile, missile capability, and a modern and highly capable self-defense force, as well as an extensive nuclear power industry; furthermore the country is building large-scale reprocessing facilities to extract weapons-grade plutonium from spent reactor fuel.

Nuclear Strategies

The United States and the North Atlantic Treaty Organization (NATO) have reaffirmed the centrality of nuclear weapons in their military doctrine and collective security strategy. The nuclear strategies of both Washington and Moscow do not rule out the use of nuclear weapons to counter nonnuclear threats to their security. At the beginning of the twenty-first century Chinese nuclear strategy shifted from one of "minimum deterrence" to one of "limited deterrence." In effect Beijing now seeks to deter the use of conventional, tactical, and long-range strategic nuclear weapons by the enemy and to control escalation in the event of a nuclear confrontation. Under a "limited deterrence" doctrine, China would have to acquire capability to target the enemy's forces as well as cities, which would require increased accuracy and expanded deployments. For their part India and Pakistan claim to adhere to a "credible minimum deterrence" posture. China and India are the only nuclear powers to adopt a policy of "no first use" (NFU); that is, they will not be the first to use nuclear weapons but will launch a second-strike counterattack if nuclear weapons are used against them. The value of an NFU pledge in crisis situations, however, remains to be tested. During the 1996 Taiwan missile crisis China's NFU commitment did not stop it from issuing to the United States a nuclear threat to the effect that Washington valued Los Angeles and San Francisco more than Taipei. The Bush administration is contemplating the resumption of nuclear testing even as it has announced plans to cut down the size of the U.S. nuclear arsenal.

Future Uncertain

The momentous political changes and the global nuclear balance of power since the end of the Cold War have thrown up both challenges and opportunities for the global nonproliferation regime. The Cold War may have terminated, but the same is not true for regional conflicts. As the twenty-first century dawned, many circumstances increased the relevance of nuclear weapons as a strategic equalizer for second-tier NWSs like China and possibly as a hedge against great-power intervention for nonnuclear countries: the lessons learned in the 1991 Persian Gulf War and the 1999 Kosovo military operations; the overarching military dominance of the United States, driven by the ongoing information technology–based revolution in military affairs; the relative cheapness of nuclear deterrents compared with modern conventional weaponry; the relatively easy access to nuclear technology and fissile material; and the new U.S. focus on building national and theater missile defenses. For example, the coalition of international forces led by the United States might not have launched the Persian Gulf War if Iraq had been bristling with nukes. North Korea might not have been rewarded with diplomatic and financial inducements, including billions of dollars in fuel and food aid, had it possessed nuclear capability.

The nuclear dimension in twenty-first-century Asia will not only grow more complex and potentially troublesome but also may become difficult to manage. In asymmetric conflicts, biological and chemical weapons of mass destruction will indeed become the "poor man's nukes." Reversal of the nuclear arms reductions mandated by the Strategic Arms Reduction Talks (START), amendment or reinterpretation of the 1972 Anti-Ballistic Missile Treaty to permit the deployment of national and theater missile defenses by the United States, or both actions, would increase Russia's and China's strategic vulnerability. Such actions could ignite another nuclear arms race among the United States, Russia, and China; could force India and perhaps Japan to expand their nuclear arsenals; and could motivate threshold states and nuclear aspirants to pursue nuclear weapons programs. In the worst-case scenario many nations might reverse previous commitments to forgo the acquisition of nuclear weapons. Signing the NPT or CTBT is by no means a guarantee that a country has no nuclear ambitions. As the number of new and potential nuclear states grows around China's borders, Beijing is likely to increase its arsenal. Indeed China's modernization of its nuclear force may become a determining factor in shaping the second nuclear age in the twenty-first century. A nuclear weapons convention based on the Chemical Weapons Convention and the Biological Weapons Convention may offer one solution, but none of the permanent members of the United Nations Security Council is contemplating the idea of dismantling its nuclear weapons.

The Asia-Pacific area is gradually moving toward multiple nuclear-deterrence games, multiple nuclear balances of power. Conceivably the future will present many heretofore unknown situations: for example (1) a new global nuclear balance of power (China-United States-Russia); (2) new regional nuclear balances (China and India, India and Pakistan, Israel and Iran); (3) the dangers of nuclear gang-up (China and Pakistan versus India, Pakistan and Iran versus India); (4) nuclear ambiguity (the Korean Peninsula); and (5) nuclear anonymity (Japan, Taiwan). Sudden, unexpected nuclear crises could emerge between China and the United States, North Korea and Japan, China and India, and India and Pakistan.

J. Mohan Malik

Further Reading

Bracken, Paul. (1999) *Fire in the East: The Rise of Asian Military Power and the Second Nuclear Age.* New York: HarperCollins.

Cordesman, Anthony H. (2002) *Proliferation in the "Axis of Evil": North Korea, Iran, and Iraq.* Washington, DC: Center for Strategic and International Studies.

Huntington, Samuel P. (1996) *The Clash of Civilizations and the Remaking of World Order.* New York: Simon and Schuster.

Malik, J. Mohan. (2000) "China and the Nuclear Non-Proliferation Regime." *Contemporary Southeast Asia* 22, 3 (December): 445–478.

Ungerer, Carl, and Marianne Hanson, eds. (2001) *The Politics of Nuclear Non-Proliferation.* St. Leonards, U.K.: Allen and Unwin.

NUKUS (2002 pop. 254,000). Nukus became the capital of the Karakalpak Autonomous Republic in Uzbekistan in 1939. Located in southwestern Uzbekistan, Nukus lies at the head of the Amu Dar'ya River delta. The population consists mostly of Turkic-speaking Karakalpaks ("black hat people"), Uzbeks, and Turkmen. Culturally Karakalpaks are more closely related to Kazakhs than to Uzbeks. Historically they have been successively dominated by aggressive Kazakhs, area chieftains, and Russia. Under Soviet rule the Karakalpaks progressed through various stages of nationhood, and the region became the autonomous republic of Karakalpakstan in Uzbekistan in 1936, at which time Nukus became a city.

Today Nukus's autonomy as the capital is shaky. The city is isolated, poor, desolate, unhealthy, windy, and subject to frequent sandstorms (in which environmental pollutants become airborne). Its unhealthy condition reflects a regional catastrophe: to irrigate crops, water has long been diverted from the Amu Dar'ya, causing severe shrinkage of the Aral Sea for a distance of some 100 kilometers to the north, as well as harsh environmental pollution. In the late 1980s people left the surrounding countryside and moved to Nukus, which became the fastest-growing city in Uzbekistan.

Nukus is home to Nukus State University, the Uzbek Academy of Sciences, and the Igor Savitsky Art Gallery, containing works by artists whom Soviet dictator Joseph Stalin banished to Nukus in the 1930s. Before the Soviet Union's collapse illegal chemical weapons were developed in the city, and its economy was then much healthier. Today Nukus is a center for such products as cotton, rice, alfalfa, footwear, and furniture.

Gary Mason Church

Further Reading

MacLeod, Calum, and Bradley Mayhew. (1997) *Uzbekistan: The Golden Road to Samarkand.* 2d ed. Lincoln, IL: Odyssey/Passport.

NUR JEHAN (1925–2000), South Asian singer. A singer of the Indo-Pakistan subcontinent, Nur Jehan was a symbol of beauty and sensuousness for five decades. Born in the village of Damsel in Pakistan, she began her singing career at the age of five on a stage in Calcutta (Kolkata) and acted in a Punjabi movie at the age of nine. Her first film, *Umeed* (Hope), was made in 1941 and she migrated to Pakistan six years afterward. She achieved fame with the films *Chaudhri* (Village Chief), in Punjabi, and *Khandaan* (Family), in Urdu. Her dramatic talent, charming face, and resonant voice made her the heartthrob of South Asia.

Nur Jehan had remarkable stamina and could sing for hours. Her personal life was equally colorful. She was involved with such figures as Hassan Rizvi, Ejaz Durrani, and Yusuf Khan. Her death on 23 December 2000, after a protracted illness, created a void that will be difficult to fill. Future generations will continue to enjoy her films, such as *Bari Maa* (Elder Mother), *Dost* (Friend), *Anomal Gharri* (Priceless Time), *Koel* (Cuckoo), *Lal Haveli* (Red Palace), *Mirza-Sahiban* (Sir), *Gaon Ki Ghori* (Village Damsel), and *Jugnu* (Glow Warm), and will be captivated by her mellifluous voice.

Patit Paban Mishra

Further Reading

Gazdar, Mushtaq. (1998) *Pakistan Cinema: 1947–1997.* Oxford, U.K.: Oxford University Press.

NUR MISUARI (b. 1940), Philippine Muslim political leader. Nuruladji Misuari is the founding chairman of the Moro National Liberation Front (MNLF), and was, from 1996 to 2001, governor of the Autonomous Region of Muslim Mindanao (ARMM). He is a Tausug Muslim from Mindanao-Sulu. While at the University of the Philippines in the 1960s, Misuari became a founding member of the Leftist Kabataan Makabayan and, in 1967, established the Muslim National League and edited its paper, *Philippine Muslim News*. He was subsequently one of a group of young Philippine Muslims who undertook guerrilla training in Malaysia and returned to Mindanao-Sulu to form the MNLF, which from the early 1970s led the Muslim insurgency against the Marcos government. From the mid-1970s, he was based overseas.

Following a split in the MNLF in 1977, Misuari was recognized as leader of the dominant Moro faction by both the Organization of Islamic Conference and the Philippine government, who continued to negotiate with him for a settlement of the armed conflict in the southern Philippines. In 1986, he returned to the Philippines at the invitation of President Aquino but did not accept proposed autonomy arrangements and again left for overseas. In 1996, Misuari signed a Peace Agreement with the Ramos administration and returned to the Philippines, where he became head of the Southern Philippines Council for Peace and Development (SPCPD), established under the 1996 agreement, and was elected governor of the ARMM, created under the 1987 constitution.

In 1999, Misuari survived a challenge to his leadership of the ARMM from within the MNLF and his term as governor was extended. But in August 2001, his position was again challenged by a faction identifying itself as the Executive Council of the Fifteen, and in the ARMM elections of November that year, following a disappointing, though predictable, vote against expansion of the ARMM, the ruling national coalition did not back Misuari's candidacy. Misuari boycotted the elections and attacked government troops in northwest Mindanao. He was subsequently arrested in Malaysia.

Ronald J. May

Further Reading

Che Man, Wan Kadir bin. (1990) *Muslim Separatism: The Muslims of Southern Philippines and the Malays of Southern Thailand.* Singapore: Oxford University Press.

NURBAKHSHIYA Nurbakhshiya refers to a distinctive Muslim religious group that originated in late medieval Central Asia and Iran and currently survives in the form of small communities in Baltistan, Pakistan, and Ladakh, India. Both these regions are part of the territory of the state of Jammu and Kashmir, contested between Pakistan and India since 1947. The group owes its name to Sayyid Muhammad Nurbakhsh (d. 1464), who proclaimed himself the Mahdi (Muslim messiah) in Khuttalan (present-day Tajikistan) in 1423 and spent his life trying to propagate his mission.

A significant community of Nurbakhshis survived him in Iran, from where the movement was transferred first to the Timurid court of Husayn Bayqara in Herat, Afghanistan, and then to Kashmir, India, in the fifteenth and sixteenth centuries. Under the leadership of Shams al-Din ʿIraqi (d. 1526), the Nurbakhshis were a major religious faction vying for political as well as cultural dominance at the time of Mughal expansion into Kashmir in the sixteenth century. They lost their struggle, however, and were heavily persecuted by the Turko-Mongol general Mirza Haydar Dughlat (d. 1551), who forced members of the community to seek refuge in the remote mountainous region of Baltistan. The modern Nurbakhshi community derives from the transplantation of the tradition to Baltistan.

Contemporary Nurbakhshis constitute a minority in both Baltistan and Ladakh, where the majority of the population is Twelver Shiʿi Muslim (adherents of a sect that believes in the succession of twelve distinct imams or leaders after the prophet Muhammad's death) in the former and Buddhist in the latter region. The Nurbakhshis were subjected to a campaign of "normalization" through conversion by Twelver Shiʿi and Sunni Muslims throughout the twentieth century, and the community is now divided into numerous factions. One subgroup, which calls itself Sufiyya Nurbakhshiya, favors retaining a distinct sectarian identity, while a significant proportion of the remaining population has shifted to a closer identification with Twelver Shiʿism. The latter group calls itself Imamiyya Nurbakhshiya and now includes Pir Shams al-Din Sayyid Muhammad Shah Nurani, the hereditary religious leader of the community, who resides in Kiris, Baltistan. The Sufiyya Nurbakhshiya has pursued an active publishing program in the past few decades, including, most notably, the serial *Nava-yi sufiyyu* ("The Sufi Voice," issued from Islamabad) and various books in Urdu by Ghulam Hasan Nurbakhshi.

The Nurbakhshiya's religious perspective attempts to subvert Islamic sectarian differences by proposing an overarching religious system based on the theories and practices of Sufism. Nurbakhsh's own works were directed toward dissolving sectarian boundaries, though the Iranian Sufi tradition linked to him after the sixteenth century identified itself as Twelver Shiʿi due to the effects of the religious policy of the Safavid dynasty (1501–1722). Some Nurbakhshis of Pakistan continue the antisectarian stance today by presenting their version of Islam as an antidote to the violent Sunni-Shiʿi confrontation that has plagued the country since the 1980s.

Shahzad Bashir

Further Reading

Bashir, Shahzad. (2002) *Messianic Hopes and Mystical Visions: The Nurbakhshiya between Medieval Mahdism and Modern Survival.* Columbia, SC: University of South Carolina Press.

Elias, Jamal. (2000) "A Second ʿAli: The Making of Sayyid ʿAli Hamadani in Popular Imagination." *Muslim World* 90, 3 and 4 (Fall): 395–419.

Holzwarth, Wolfgang. (1997) "Islam in Baltistan: Problems of Research on the Formative Period." In *The Past in the Present: Horizons of Remembering in the Pakistan Himalaya.* Edited by Irmtraud Stellrecht. Cologne, Germany: Rüdiger Köppe Verlag, 1–30.

Rieck, Andreas. (1995) "The Nurbachshis of Baltistan—Crisis and Revival of a Five Centuries Old Community." *Die Welt des Islams* 35, 2: 160–165.

NUSA TENGGARA Nusa Tenggara is a chain of medium-sized and small islands in the southeastern part of Indonesia, also known in English as the Lesser Sunda Islands. Bordered by Bali to the west, East Timor to the east, and Australia to the south, the region is divided into two administrative and cultural units: the provinces of West Nusa Tenggara and East Nusa Tenggara. The topographical conditions vary from mostly lush land in the western islands to arid savanna in the eastern ones. These islands are also marked by a chain of active and nonactive volcanoes, which extends from the northern part of Sumatra to the south and east across Java. Among the important volcanoes in this part of Indonesia are Mount Rinjani on the island of Lombok, Mount Tambora on the island of Sumbawa, both in West Nusa Tenggara, and Mount Kelimutu with its fabled three-colored lake on the island of Flores in East Nusa Tenggara.

West Nusa Tenggara Province consists of two main islands, Lombok and Sumbawa, and hundreds of small islands around them. Its population in 2000 was 3.8 million people. The capital of the province is Mataram on Lombok Island. There are four main ethnic groups in this province. The Balinese from the neighboring island of Bali are Hindu. The largest ethnic group is the Sasak, living mostly on Lombok, while the other two, the Samawa and the Bima, are on Sumbawa Island. These last three ethnic groups make up more than 90 percent of the population of the province and are predominantly Muslims.

The neighboring East Nusa Tenggara Province consists of three main islands, Flores, Timor (the western side), and Sumba, as well as more than five hundred small islands, roughly half of which are yet to be named. One of these islands, Komodo, is the only site in the world where the giant monitor lizard, known as the Komodo dragon, can be found. The province's capital city is Kupang in the western part of Timor Island. East Nusa Tenggara is the driest province in Indonesia, with average rainfall of only 500–2,000 millimeters per year. While Muslims predominate in West Nusa Tenggara and most of the rest of Indonesia, East Nusa Tenggara's 4 million people (2000 census) are predominantly Catholics (56 percent) and Protestants (35 percent). Muslims are a relatively small minority in the province, with 8 percent of the population. The relatively high proportion of Catholics in this province is mostly due to the influence of the Portuguese, who had in the past established a strong presence in this area and in neighboring East Timor.

Irman G. Lanti

Further Reading

Hicks, David. (1990) *Kinship and Religion in Eastern Indonesia.* Göteborg, Sweden: Acta Universitatis Gothobur gensis.

Magenda, Burhan Djabier. (1989) "The Surviving Aristocracy in Indonesia: Politics in Three Provinces of the Outer Islands." Ph.D. diss., Cornell University.

NUSRAT FATEH ALI KHAN (1948–1997),

Qawwali singer. Nusrat Fateh Ali Khan, the internationally acclaimed *qawwali* (a South Asian devotional musical tradition that is over six hundred years old), singer, was born in Faisalabad, Pakistan, into a prominent lineage of Sufi singers. *Qawwali* is traditionally performed at a *dargah* (Sufi shrine) and incorporates in its structure the classical forms of *raag* ("melody") and *taal* ("rhythm"). Lyrically *qawwali* draws from the compositions of medieval South Asian mystical poets and employs metaphorical language and symbolic imagery to illustrate the pain of separation from God and the ecstasy of reunion. Nusrat's *qawwali* music appealed to diverse cultural and linguistic groups throughout the Indian subcontinent and featured Sufi compositions from a wide array of languages, including Persian, Arabic, Punjabi, Urdu, Hindi, Braj, and Rajasthani. His mesmerizing voice often sent his audience into a musical trance and earned him the esteemed title *Shahen-Shah* ("the king of kings"). Nusrat's worldwide fame eventually increased due to his eclectic collaborations with popular musicians (Peter Gabriel, Eddie Vedder, Bally Sagoo) and his unique contributions to film scores (*Last Temptation of Christ, Dead Man Walking, Bandit Queen*). He died on 16 August 1997 in London, England, from kidney failure complications.

Varun Soni

Further Reading

Ehrlich, Dimitri. (1997) *Inside the Music: Conversations with Contemporary Musicians about Spirituality, Creativity, and Consciousness.* Boston: Shambhala Publications.

Qureshi, Regula Burckhardt. (1995) *Sufi Music of India and Pakistan: Sound, Context and Meaning in Qawwali.* Chicago: University of Chicago Press.

Ruby, Ahmed Aqeel. *Nusrat Fateh Ali Khan: A Living Legend.* Trans. by Sajjad Haider Malik. Lahore, Pakistan: Words of Wisdom, 1992.

OCHIRBAT, PUNSALMAAGIYN (b. 1942), President of Mongolia. Punsalmaagiyn Ochirbat was the first democratically elected president of Mongolia. Born in Zavhan Province, Mongolia, he was educated first in Ulaanbaatar and later earned advanced degrees in mining engineering in the Soviet Union. In 1966, Ochirbat began his career as an adviser in Mongolia's Ministry of Industry. Ten years later, he was appointed minister of fuel, power industry, and geology.

In 1976, Ochirbat also served as a deputy in the People's Great Assembly, Mongolia's parliament. Upon the resignation of former Mongolian People's Revolutionary Party (MPRP) leader Jambyn Batmonkh (b. 1926), Ochirbat was designated head of state in March 1990.

After the collapse of communism, the 1992 constitution changed the name of the country from the Mongolian People's Republic to Mongolia and called for new presidential elections to take place in 1993. Ochirbat ran for election against the MPRP candidate, Lodongiyn Tudev, under the banner of two democratic parties, the Mongolian National Democratic Party and the Mongolian Social Democratic Party. Ochirbat won this first democratic election in Mongolia with 57.8 percent of the vote, thus becoming the country's first president. However, he failed to win the election in 1997, losing to Natsagiin Bagabandi.

Timothy May

Further Reading

Dashpurev, D., and S. K. Soni. (1992) *Reign of Terror in Mongolia, 1920–1990*. New Delhi: South Asian Publishers.

Sanders, Alan. (1996) *Historical Dictionary of Mongolia*. Lanham, MD: Scarecrow Press.

OCTOBER 6 CRISIS—THAILAND The catalyst for the dramatic October 1976 political confrontation was the return to Thailand in mid-September of former Field Marshall Thanom Kittikachorn as a Buddhist monk, ostensibly to earn merit for his ailing ninety-one-year-old father. Thanom had been ousted in an October 1973 student uprising. Thanom's return led to student-led demonstrations calling for his expulsion from Thailand. Two political activists distributing anti-Thanom leaflets were found hung, which precipitated the political drama that followed. Students were convinced that police were involved in the hangings. As part of their demonstration, students organized a mock hanging of those lynched. Photos of the mock hanging were published on the front pages of several major newspapers. One of the student actors showed a remarkable resemblance to the crown prince of Thailand. The political right interpreted this as the student left insulting the revered institution of the monarchy. Whether the photos might have been intentionally doctored as a political "dirty trick" remains an unresolved issue.

In response to the alleged mock hanging of the crown prince, police and right-wing activists surrounded Thammasat University, where approximately two thousand demonstrators had spent the night. At 7:30 A.M. on 6 October, hundreds of police, including special riot squads and border patrol units, followed by right-wing groups such as the Red Guard, stormed the campus in response to an alleged firing of heavy weapons from within the campus. By noon, nearly all the students had been flushed from the buildings. Approximately 1,700 students were arrested for lèse majesté. It is estimated that approximately thirty students were killed and one hundred injured in the assault.

After the assault on Thammasat, later in the day, the military seized control of the government and called itself the Administrative Reform Council. Thus, Thailand's three-year experiment with democracy came to a crashing halt, and the 6 October coup ushered in Thailand's most repressive regime of the modern era.

To understand the trauma and tragedy of 6 October, it is critically important to understand the local regional context. Only the year before, Laos, Vietnam, and Cambodia all had become Communist, with Pol Pot leading the latter nation into the horror of the killing fields. The monarchy was abolished in both Laos and Cambodia. Thus, the Thai right was paranoid about the growing influence of the left in Thailand. In a real irony of history, this dramatic shift to the right in Thai politics occurred on the very same day that the Gang of Four was arrested in China.

Gerald W. Fry

Further Reading

Coordination Committee for the 20th Anniversary of October 6. (1996) *Tula: Raw Kugh Phuu Borisut* (October: We are Innocent). Bangkok, Thailand: Phim Dii Ltd.

Keyes, Charles F. (1987) *Thailand: Buddhist Kingdom as Modern Nation-State*. Boulder, CO: Westview Press.

Nations, Richard. (1976) "October Revolution—Part II." *Far Eastern Economic Review* 94, 42 (October 15): 10–11.

Wright, Joseph J., Jr. (1991) *The Balancing Act: A History of Modern Thailand*. Bangkok, Thailand: Asia Books.

OE KENZABURO (b. 1935), Japanese novelist, nonfiction essayist, and winner of the 1994 Nobel Prize for literature. Oe Kenzaburo is known throughout the world by translations of his work as a weaver of historical, mythical, and sexually grotesque novels and in Japan for his notoriously impenetrable wordplay and solipsistic tales. Oe was born on the southwestern island of Shikoku and took the position of posing moral and stylistic challenges to the status quo of the metropolis, a position that became more and more tenuous as his stature in the literary world continued to rise.

Among the last generation of children to be educated under the wartime imperial regime, in the postwar period Oe studied French existentialist literature at Tokyo University. His morbid stories of students

Oe Kenzaburo in Cambridge, Massachusetts, in June 2000 to receive an honorary doctorate from Harvard University. (REUTERS NEWMEDIA INC./CORBIS)

working grotesque jobs dealing with human and canine corpses in order to earn enough money to study won him early recognition for bringing European-style angst to the circumstances of postwar Japan.

In 1958, he was awarded the Akutagawa Literary Prize for his novella *Shiiku* (The Catch), the tale of a young boy's realization that both godlike figures in his life, the black American paratrooper stranded in his village and the emperor, are mortals. After the experiences of both the death threats he received in response to his "Sebunchin" (*Seventeen*, 1960), a story based on two actual assassinations by seventeen-year-old students, and the birth of his son, who was diagnosed with a brain hernia, as fictionalized in *Kojintekina taiken* (A Personal Matter, 1964), Oe's work assumed a more humanistic tone. His reflections on the survivors of the atomic bomb, *Hiroshima nooto* (Hiroshima Notes, 1965), and his epic novel of an antihero encountering his mythical and historical family roots, *Man'en gannen no futtoboru* (Football in the First Years of Man'en, 1967, translated as *The Silent Cry*), incorporated homages to William Butler Yeats, William Blake, and Dante Alighieri.

Arguing that he was a pacifist and a democrat, Oe refused the Emperor's Order of Culture within months of receiving the Nobel Prize. His more recent trilogy, *Moegaru midori no ki* (Burning Green Tree), is an amalgam of *Until the 'Savior' Gets Socked* (1993), *Vacillating* (1994), and *On the Day of Grandeur* (1995) that combines themes of a vanishing mythic order on the periphery of modernized Japan with an existential interrogation of ethics through the depiction of everyday life.

J. Abel

Further Reading

Lewell, John. (1993) *Modern Japanese Novelists: A Biographical Dictionary*. New York: Kodansha.

Treat, John Whittier. (1987) "*Hiroshima nooto* and Oe Kenzaburo's Existentialist Other." *Harvard Journal of Asiatic Studies* 47, 1 (June): 97–136.

OGASAWARA Thc Ogasawara (or Bonin) Islands lie between the Japanese mainland and the Marianas in the North Pacific. The first known inhabitants were a tiny group of American, European, and Pacific Islander settlers who arrived on the main island of Chichijima in 1830. Others soon followed, creating an ethnically and linguistically diverse community in which English (probably a pidgin variety) became the language of communication. In the 1870s, Japan proclaimed ownership of the islands, naturalizing the inhabitants and promoting Japanese settlement. The original settlers became increasingly incorporated into Japanese society but sustained a separate identity through their maintenance of English and Christianity.

Toward the end of World War II, the entire civilian population was evacuated to mainland Japan. Following the war, the U.S. Navy established a base on the islands, allowing only those islanders of non-Japanese heritage (commonly called "Westerners") to return. For a quarter century, these Bonin Islanders worked and studied in an English-speaking environment. During this period, the navy severely restricted movement to and from the islands and secretly stored nuclear missiles there. In 1968, the United States abruptly returned the islands to Japan. Many displaced prewar families returned to their birthplace, along with new migrants from the Japanese mainland. At the end of the twentieth century, the islands have been largely culturally and linguistically incorporated into Japan, although many descendants of the original settlers remain.

Daniel Long

Further Reading

Cholmondeley, Lionel B. (1915) *The History of the Bonin Islands*. London: Archibald Constable and Co.

Head, Timothy E., and Gavan Daws. (1968) "The Bonins—Isles of Contention." *American Heritage* 19, 2: 58–64, 69–74.

Long, Daniel. (1999) "Evidence of an English Contact Language in the 19th Century Bonin (Ogasawara) Islands." *English World-Wide* 20, 2: 251–286.

OH SADAHARU (b. 1940), Japanese baseball player. Oh hit 868 home runs during a 22-year career with the Yomiuri Giants from 1959 to 1980. Born in Tokyo, Oh joined the Giants in 1959 out of Waseda Jitsugyo High School. Originally a pitcher, he was switched to first base because of his hitting prowess and was noted for his famous "flamingo" hitting style. He won fifteen home run crowns, two triple crowns, and was a nine-time MVP and gold-glove winner as well as an eighteen-time all-star. He led the Giants to nine straight Japan Series championships in the 1960s and 1970s, and passed Henry (Hank) Aaron as world record holder for home runs on 3 September 1977. By the time he retired in 1980, he had passed Aaron's mark by a remarkable 113 home runs. Nevertheless, as the son of a Chinese father and Japanese mother, Oh suffered discrimination throughout his life and career because of his mixed ancestry. Since his retirement, Oh has stayed in the game as a manager, first with the Giants and later with the Fukuoka Daiei Hawks. He was elected into the Japanese baseball hall of fame in 1994, his first year of eligibility.

Todd S. Munson

Further Reading

Oh Sadaharu and David Faulkner. (1984) *Sadaharu Oh: A Zen Way of Baseball*. Tokyo: Kodansha International.

OIL AND MINERAL INDUSTRIES—CENTRAL ASIA The five Central Asian republics (Kazakhstan, Turkmenistan, Uzbekistan, Kyrgyzstan, and Tajikistan) are considered emerging oil- and mineral exporting markets by much of the international business and policy communities. Oil in Kazakhstan, gas in Turkmenistan, and mineral wealth in Uzbekistan, Kyrgyzstan, and even Tajikistan have prompted significant investment in the region in the hope of realizing great profits. However, transportation and geopolitical obstacles stand in the way of the successful exploitation of these resources.

Kazakhstan

As the leading oil-producing state in Central Asia, Kazakhstan has been a much-courted country for oil field rights and pipeline routes. Proven oil reserves are between 10.0 and 17.6 billion barrels, with "potential" reserves more than three to four times as much. Gas reserves are a modest 1.8 trillion cubic meters. These reserves are located largely in the western portion of the country and offshore in the Kazakh sector of the Caspian Sea. Specifically the Tengiz (onshore) and Kashagan (offshore) oil fields are of great importance to Kazakhstan, as is the Karachaganak field for both oil and gas. Currently there are three refineries in the country—Pavlodar, Atyrau, and Shymkent—and there is a pressing need to export unrefined oil to other countries to gain foreign currency.

Mineral deposits, on the other hand, are located in the central and eastern parts of the country and include major deposits of coal, iron ore, manganese, chrome ore, nickel, cobalt, copper, molybdenum, lead, zinc, bauxite, gold, and uranium. The coal deposits in the northern regions are critical for local energy needs and for southern Russia.

Turkmenistan

In contrast to Kazakhstan, Turkmenistan has a wealth of gas deposits and not much oil. At present proven reserves are 2.7 to 4.3 trillion cubic meters of gas and only 1.7 billion barrels of oil both onshore and offshore. The gas fields are located in a stretch of territory running due west of Ashgabat to the region around the port city of Turkmenbashi. Off the Turkmenistan coast of the Caspian Sea lie considerable deposits, the ownership of which is currently disputed by Turkmenistan and Azerbaijan. Turkmenbashi is developing into a major transit hub for natural gas, and it is hoped that the country will export gas via multiple routes through Russia, Iran, and across the Caspian. In the oil sector there are refineries in Chardzhou and Turkmenbashi, which currently process much of the oil extracted. Mineral deposits are minimal, with some coal located in the western portion of the country.

Uzbekistan

Uzbekistan's oil and gas deposits are enough to make the country self-sufficient and allow it to export modest amounts to regional markets. There are 0.6 billion barrels of oil and between 2.1 and 2.5 trillion cubic meters of gas of proven reserves. Uzbekistan's three oil refineries are located in the cities of Fergana and Bukhara and the area of Alty-Arik. Well-established pipelines for natural gas cover much of the Central Asian region.

Uzbekistan is a country with significant mineral wealth. Among the most important mineral deposits found in the country are coal, gold, uranium, silver, copper, lead, zinc, tungsten, and molybdenum, located in the central (Navoi) and eastern (Fergana) regions of the country. While most of the mining sector is state run, some foreign companies are involved in joint ventures, including Newmont Mining, which is currently operating in Navoi.

Tajikistan

Tajikistan has minimal oil and gas deposits, with less than 10 million barrels of oil and 5.6 billion cubic meters of gas. While there are claims of more significant finds, these have not as yet been verified. Tajikistan must rely on Kazakhstan, Uzbekistan, and Turkmenistan for oil and gas, as well as for refining the modest amount of oil and gas extracted in the country.

Mineral deposits are more significant, with large areas of the eastern part of the country—the Pamir range—still unexplored. Tajikistan is endowed with significant strategic minerals, such as uranium, mercury, brown coal, lead, zinc, antimony, and tungsten. During the Soviet period these resources were critical to Tajikistan's nuclear program. The Tajik government sees the economic benefit of using these resources as export commodities in the future.

Kyrgyzstan

Kyrgyzstan has less than 10 million barrels of oil and less than 5.6 billion cubic meters of gas of proven reserves, much like Tajikistan. While Kyrgyzstan must rely on oil and gas imports from Uzbekistan and Kazakhstan, it does have a small oil refinery in Jalal-Abad, which addresses local needs in that district. However, unlike Tajikistan, there is no claim to greater fossil-fuel wealth, and the country is trying to use hydropower in lieu of importing oil and gas from Kazakhstan and Uzbekistan.

Mineral deposits are almost the country's only resource. There are significant deposits of gold and rare-earth metals, coal, nepheline, mercury, bismuth, lead, and zinc. Gold is abundant in the high mountain ranges that make up nearly 45 percent of the country's terrain. The Canadian mining company Camoco is involved in a major joint-venture operation in the Kumtor mining region, which has gold and strategic minerals.

Obstacles Facing the Oil and Mineral Industries

The obstacles to realizing this Central Asian oil and mineral wealth are daunting. The first is the international market and oil prices. As long as oil prices remain relatively high, companies find it profitable to exploit the reserves in the region. Given that it costs an additional $2 to $4 per barrel to transport oil from Central Asia above what it costs to transport oil from almost any other place in the world, companies may balk at relying on the region for primary supplies. Mineral prices have been unusually low in the 1990s and the early 2000s, especially in the gold and silver markets, which translates into weak profits for companies operating in Kyrgyzstan and Uzbekistan.

A second obstacle is the transportation routing. Oil pipelines through Russia, China, Iran, the South Caucasus, and into Turkey and even Afghanistan have been proposed but not built. The politicking alone takes considerable time and has, in the case of the Afghan gas pipeline route, ultimately thwarted efforts to construct anything. At present the major pipeline options include the Caspian Pipeline Consortium (CPC), which runs through southern Russia and onward to the port of Novorossiysk, where it is shipped through the Black Sea and the Bosporus. A rival route is the Baku-Tbilisi-Ceyhan pipeline, which when completed will carry oil and gas across the southern Caucasus and eastern Turkey to the Mediterranean port of Ceyhan, Turkey. This project is supported by the U.S. government, among others. Lesser projects include a pipeline into Iran that would join the existing Iranian network that runs to the Persian Gulf and a pipeline from western Kazakhstan to western China (Xinjiang Province) and onward to the eastern portion of China and possibly Japan. Functioning at present are the CPC and a modest pipeline from Baku, Azerbaijan, to Supsa, Georgia, which transports Kazakh oil that is barged across the Caspian Sea to Baku.

A third obstacle to the oil and mineral industries is the lack of reliable rule of law in the region. While international companies may be willing to operate in countries in which their assets are not always protected by local law, the situation in the Central Asian states is ultimately detrimental to foreign investment. Of major concern for foreign investors is the high level of corruption. Often finders' fees must be paid to government officials to gain the rights to certain properties—and even these deals can be renegotiated at later dates. Given that generational leadership changes are anticipated in each Central Asian country over the next decade or two, there is a serious question about the abilities of succeeding governments to carry on positive relations with foreign oil and mineral companies. Corruption at lower levels is also endemic, especially when dealing with contractors and suppliers for building materials and support structures for oil and gas fields and mines.

Central Asia is endowed with significant oil and mineral wealth, but the concomitant problems most likely mean that the profit potential will remain unrealized or at best have a modest impact on the economies.

Roger D. Kangas

Further Reading

Ebel, Robert E. (1997) *Energy Choices in the Near Abroad: The Haves and Have-Nots Face the Future.* Washington, DC: CSIS.

Kangas, Roger. (2001) *The Caspian and Central Asian Oil and Gas Report: Developing the Energy Sector's New Frontier.* London: SMI.

Olcott, Martha Brill. (1999) "Pipelines and Pipe Dreams: Energy Development and Caspian Society." *Journal of International Affairs* 53, 1 (Fall): 305–323.

Rumer, Boris, ed. (1996) *Central Asia in Transition: Dilemmas of Political and Economic Development.* Armonk, NY: M. E. Sharpe.

Soglio, Ronald, and Amy Jaffe. (1998) *The Economics of Pipeline Routes: The Conundrum of Oil Exports from the Caspian Basin.* Energy study prepared by the James A. Baker III Institute for Public Policy. Houston, TX: Rice University Press.

OIL INDUSTRY—WEST ASIA

The countries of the Persian Gulf region sit atop 65 percent of the world's total oil reserves, and Western Asia's critical importance to the world oil market is obvious. Iraq has 11 percent of world oil reserves, and Iran has 9 percent. In 2000, all Persian Gulf producers accounted for nearly 28 percent of the world's total oil production, and most observers expect this share to rise in the future. Turkey does not have major oil reserves or production but serves as an important transit route for Iraqi oil exports and potentially for exports from Azerbaijan and Central Asia. Besides being important to the world oil market, the oil industries of most Persian Gulf countries make up a disproportionate share of their economies and are the main sources of hard-currency inflows and government revenues.

Iran

The British initially developed Iran's oil industry in the early 1900s. The first drilling concession was awarded to a British subject, William Knox D'Arcy, in 1901, and the first major discovery of oil in commercial quantities occurred in May 1908. From this discovery was born the Anglo-Persian (later Anglo-Iranian) Oil Company, which built the initial pipeline and refining infrastructure needed to make use of the oil and acquired a tanker fleet for overseas distribution.

Foreign control of Iran's oil industry generated much resentment, and for several decades Iranian leaders struggled to gain greater control and more equitable distribution of revenues. In November 1932, Shah Reza Pahlavi announced his intention to terminate the Anglo-Persian oil concession. After five months of negotiations, a new agreement was signed in April 1933, providing a guaranteed minimum royalty level independent of world oil prices and a partial "Persianization" of the company's workforce.

Tensions over royalties mounted again in the years following the Second World War, and in 1951 the newly appointed prime minister, Mohammed Mosaddeq, announced that Anglo-Iranian Oil would be nationalized. Britain imposed an embargo on Iranian oil, and Mosaddeq was deposed in August 1953, in a coup backed by Britain and the United States. Afterward a consortium dominated by Anglo-Iranian, but also including Royal Dutch Shell and a number of U.S. companies, was formed to manage oil production in Iran. Iran's National Iranian Oil Company (NIOC) nominally owned the oil reserves, but real control rested with the foreign firms. Power gradually shifted toward NIOC, however, and by 1973 Shah Mohammed Reza Pahlavi had instituted a system in which NIOC was recognized as the operator of Iran's oil industry, with the foreign firms functioning as service contractors. Iran was a founding member of the Organization of Petroleum Exporting Countries (OPEC), and while it did not side with Arab members during their oil embargo of 1973–1974, it did make production cuts in the mid-1970s to help the cartel sustain high prices.

In the aftermath of the Iranian Revolution of 1978–1979, which overthrew the shah and brought to power a government dominated by Ayatollah Ruhollah Khomeini, most foreign firms withdrew from Iran, and the country's oil exports experienced a dramatic decline. This second "oil shock" contributed to a rapid rise in world oil prices, which in turn had negative effects on the world's developed economies. Iran's oil production gradually recovered during the 1980s, when some foreign firms returned and local expertise became more available, but the Iran-Iraq War of 1980–1988 led to attacks on tankers and on Iran's main oil-export terminal at Khark Island.

By 2000, Iran's oil production had reached 3.7 million barrels per day (bbl/d), still far below the 6 million bbl/d peak it had reached in 1974 but well above the 1.4 million bbl/d low point it reached in 1981, after the revolution. Iran is expected to continue expanding its production and is again courting investment by foreign oil companies. The country's constitution forbids foreign ownership of oil reserves, so that these investments take the form of "buyback" contacts, which guarantee the foreign partner a set rate of financial returns.

Iraq

The first discovery of commercial quantities of oil in Iraq took place in October 1927, but the country had long been thought to hold major oil reserves due to oil seepages at ground level and other geological clues. The Iraq Petroleum Company (IPC), which was British led but included American and French firms among its owners, carried out the early development of the oil industry in Iraq.

As with other Persian Gulf oil producers, foreign control of the industry eventually led to local resentment and calls for nationalization. In the wake of a rising tide of Arab nationalism in the late 1950s, the Iraqi monarchy and the government of the prime minister Nuri as-Said were overthrown by a military coup in July 1958. The new government of Abdul Karim Kassem modified the terms of the IPC concession, eliminating over 99 percent of the land area it covered and allowing IPC to retain only the immediate locations of currently operating production facilities. The IPC consortium continued to produce oil, but it drastically curtailed investment in production capacity. As a result, Iraq's oil production increased only slightly during the 1960s, a period when world demand was surging and Iran and Saudi Arabia saw rapid increases in production. Iraq completely nationalized IPC in 1972, during a period when major oil producers worldwide were ending foreign control of their oil industries.

Since then, developments in Iraq's oil industry have been dominated by politics, and Iraq has failed to attain its full potential as an oil producer. After strong production increases in the late 1970s, Iraqi crude oil production peaked at slightly less than 3.5 million bbl/d in 1979. Saddam Hussein's decision to launch a war against Iran in September 1980, however, resulted in chaos in the Iraqi oil industry, and production fell to 1 million bbl/d in 1981. Combined with developments in Iran, this drop in production led to the highest oil prices ever, adjusted for inflation. From 1984 onward, production began to recover and reached 2.9 million bbl/d by 1989.

After Iraq's August 1990 invasion of Kuwait, however, the United Nations Security Council imposed sanctions on Iraq, which prohibited oil exports. Production plummeted to only 305,000 bbl/d in 1991. In

May 1996, under pressure from humanitarian organizations, the United Nations Security Council passed a resolution allowing Iraq to begin limited oil sales. The Oil for Food program has since been expanded, and restrictions on export volumes have been removed, but revenues are still routed through an escrow account controlled by the United Nations. In 2000, Iraq's oil production had rebounded to nearly 2.6 million bbl/d. In addition to the Oil for Food program sales, Iraq is known to smuggle out substantial quantities of crude oil and petroleum products in violation of sanctions.

Turkey

Turkey does not have substantial oil reserves, but it is important as a transit route between oil producers in the Middle East and Central Asia and consumers in Europe. Turkish crude oil production in 2000 was slightly under 59,000 bbl/d. Much of Iraq's crude oil exports crosses Turkey via a pipeline from northern Iraq to the Turkish Mediterranean port of Ceyhan. A proposed pipeline would also link oil fields near Baku in Azerbaijan with the Ceyhan export terminal and might carry crude oil from Kazakhstan to the Mediterranean as well. In addition to pipelines, some oil is exported from the Black Sea region by tanker via the Bosporus Straits.

Greg Priddy

Further Reading

United States Energy Information Administration. (2001) *International Energy Annual.* Washington, DC: U.S. Government Printing Office.

———. (2001) "Iran Country Analysis Brief." Retrieved 17 January 2002, from: http://www.eia.doe.gov/cabs/iran.html.

———. (2000) "Iraq Country Analysis Brief." Retrieved 17 January 2002, from: http://www.eia.doe.gov/cabs/iraq.html.

———. (2000) "Turkey Country Analysis Brief." Retrieved 17 January 2002, from: http://www.eia.doe.gov/cabs/turkey.html.

Yergin, Daniel. (1991) *The Prize: The Epic Quest for Oil, Money, and Power.* New York: Simon and Schuster.

OITA (2002 est. pop. 1.2 million). Oita Prefecture is situated in the northeast of Japan's island of Kyushu, where it occupies an area of 6,338 square kilometers. Oita's primary geographical features are the Kyushu Mountains, a volcanic chain, and coastal plains. Oita is bordered by the Inland Sea and by Miyazaki, Kumamoto, and Fukuoka prefectures. Once known as Toyo Province and later divided into Buzen and Bungo, it assumed its present name in 1871 and its present borders in 1876.

The prefecture's capital is Oita city, situated on Beppu Bay. A provincial government seat in ancient times, Oita in the early 2000s is an important transport center and industrial zone with plants for processing oil, metals, and chemicals, as well as wood pulp and foodstuffs. The prefecture's other important cities are Beppu, Nakatsu, Hita, and Saiki.

Archeological artifacts of the Jomon (10,000 BCE–300 BCE) and Yayoi (300 BCE–300 CE) cultures indicate early cultivation of the region. The primary economic activity remains agriculture, mainly rice, vegetables, mandarin oranges, and loquats, along with the breeding of cattle. Fishery and forestry flourish as well. Visitors are drawn to hot spring resorts and to the ancient rock-carved Buddhist sculptures in the Kunisaki and Usuki areas. Mountainous and coastal scenic destinations range from Aso Kuju National Park to the Inland Sea National Park.

E. L. S. Weber

Further Reading

"Oita Prefecture." (1993) *Japan: An Illustrated Encyclopedia.* Tokyo: Kodansha.

OKAYAMA (2002 est. pop. 2 million). Okayama Prefecture is situated in the western region of Japan's island of Honshu, where it occupies an area of 7,092 square kilometers. Okayama's primary geographical features are a mountainous north, the central highland Kibi Kogen, and the coastal plains, along with reclaimed land in Kojima Bay. The main rivers are the Yoshigawa, Asahigawa, and Takahashigawa. Okayama is bordered by the Inland Sea and by Tottori, Hyogo, and Hiroshima prefectures. Once divided into Bizen, Bitchu, and Mimasaka provinces, Okayama Prefecture assumed its present name in 1871 and its present borders in 1876.

The prefecture's capital is Okayama city, which evolved from a settlement around Okayama Castle, completed in 1573. It is home to Okayama University, noted for an active foreign exchange program that enrolls students from twenty-five countries. Among the city's historic sites are the 1686 garden Korakuen and the Orient Bijutsukan, one of the nation's first museums to focus on Asian and Middle Eastern art. The city's industrial base includes chemicals, rubber, textiles, and agricultural machinery fabrication. The prefecture's other important cities are Kurashiki, Tsuyama, and Tamano.

Okayama's history dates back to the Yayoi culture (300 BCE–300 CE), as indicated by archaeological excavations. The region was ruled by a series of Ikeda family warlords until the end of the Edo period (1600/1603–1868).

In the early 2000s, the prefecture continues to produce rice, tobacco, *igusa* fiber for tatami mats, and fruit, including hothouse grapes and peaches. Recent decades have seen the rise of the steel and petrochemical industries. A leading attraction is Kurashiki with its distinctive architecture, traditional merchant quarter, and folk art museums.

E. L. S. Weber

Further Reading

"Okayama Prefecture." (1993) *Japan: An Illustrated Encyclopedia*. Tokyo: Kodansha.

OKINAWA (2001 est. pop. 1.15 million). Okinawa is the largest island of Japan's Ryukyu Islands, which make up the southern half of the Nansei Islands, lying between Kyushu, Japan, and Taiwan. Approximately 50 inhabited islands and 110 uninhabited ones make up the Ryukyu Islands, which are further divided into three groups: the Okinawa Islands, the Miyako Islands to the south, and the Yaeyama Islands in the far south. The main island of Okinawa is 1,286 square kilometers in area and 105 kilometers in length, running north to south, and is subtropical in climate. Okinawa's largest city, Naha, is the capital of Okinawa Prefecture, which has a population of 1.31 million (1.15 million of whom live on the main island).

Historically, the Ryukyu Islands were the domain of the Ryukyu kingdom, created in 1429 when the Sho dynasty was formed after unifying the islands. The second Sho dynasty was founded in 1470 and lasted for four centuries, although it continued the custom (begun in 1372) of sending tributary missions to China to legitimize its rule and to gain trade benefits. In 1609, the Satsuma clan of Kyushu invaded the Ryukyu Islands and took the king hostage. He eventually agreed to sign a treaty that preserved the Ryukyu kingdom's nominal independence but in fact placed the islands under Satsuma's control. This relationship was concealed from China in order for Satsuma to continue to benefit from the kingdom's trade relations with China. This period of "dual subordination" ended officially in 1879, when the islands became an administrative part of modern Japan as Okinawa Prefecture. Toward the end of World War II, on 1 April 1945, the main island of Okinawa was invaded by U.S. forces preparing to attack mainland Japan. Okinawa continued under U.S. military control until 1972, when administrative rights over the Ryukyu Islands were returned to Japan. Representative of the strategic importance of the islands, the agreement allowed for U.S. forces to continue to be stationed on bases in Okinawa after reversion.

The bases have been both a source of friction, due to the disruption in the daily lives of the local residents, and a source of income for the prefecture due to the base-related income, rental fees, and compensation paid by the national government. Currently, U.S. facilities occupy close to 19 percent of the main

GUSUKU SITES OF THE RYUKYU KINGDOM—WORLD HERITAGE SITE

The Ryukyu Islands just off of Okinawa, Japan, were designated a World Heritage Site by UNESCO in 2000. The ruined castles and cities of the Ryukyu kingdom graphically illustrate the extensive contacts that the society had with nearby cultures and its unusual religion.

OKINAWA AND JAPAN

This description of Okinawa from the late nineteenth century suggests that it was seen as a cultural backwater to Japan.

> The streets in the towns present a most desolate appearance. On each side of these is a blank stone wall of about ten or twelve feet high, with openings in them here and there sufficiently wide to admit of access to the houses which are behind. Every house is surrounded by a wall, and from the street they convey the impression of being prisons rather than ordinary dwellings.

Source: Edward S. Morse ([1896] 1961) *Japanese Homes and Their Surroundings*, New York: Dover Publications, 341.

island, although the U.S. and Japanese governments have been attempting to consolidate and reduce the presence.

The subtropical climate of Okinawa allows it to grow pineapples, sugarcane, sweet potatoes, orchids, and other plants for sale in mainland Japan. Likewise, its rich culture, rhythmic music and dance, and beautiful seas and shorelines make it attractive to tourists, although high domestic airfares have made other destinations, including those abroad, comparatively cheaper.

Robert D. Eldridge

Further Reading

Eldridge, Robert D. (2001) *The Origins of the Bilateral Okinawa Problem: Okinawa in Postwar U.S.-Japan Relations, 1945–1952.* New York: Routledge-Garland.

Kerr, George H. (2000) *Okinawa: The History of an Island People.* Rev. ed. Boston: Tuttle Publishing.

Sarantakes, Nicholas E. (2000) *Keystone: The American Occupation of Okinawa and U.S.-Japanese Relations.* College Station, TX: Texas A&M University Press.

OLD ORDER The designation "Old Order" refers to the rule of Indonesia's first president, Sukarno (1901–1970), consisting of two phases: (1) parliamentary democracy (1950–1959) and (2) "Guided Democracy" (1959–1965). Sukarno's priorities were to maintain national unity and to boost the development of a national identity in the face of continuous Islamist and secular separatist rebellion. In 1957, Sukarno began to propose an alternative form of government, stating that parliamentary democracy was not conducive to achieving national unity. The final implementation of what Sukarno termed Guided Democracy, blending the three ideologies dominant in Indonesia (nationalism, Islam, and communism), in 1959 invested him with strong executive powers.

After the success of the Bandung Conference in 1955, Sukarno increasingly aspired to Third World leadership. In 1962, he succeeded in wrenching Irian Barat from the Dutch. In January 1965 he initiated Indonesia's withdrawal from the United Nations after his opposition to the international recognition of Malaysia had failed. His autocratic manner, his failure to solve the nation's economic problems, and his continuous support for the Indonesian Communist Party in spite of growing criticism on the part of the armed forces and Muslim factions led to his final downfall shortly after the abortive coup d'état of 30 September 1965.

Martin Ramstedt

Further Reading

Agung, Ide Anak Agung Gde. (1990) *Twenty Years of Indonesian Foreign Policy 1945–1965.* Yogyakarta, Indonesia: Duta Wacana University Press.

Cribb, Robert, and Colin Brown. (1995) *Modern Indonesia: A History since 1945.* New York: Longman Publishing.

Dahm, Bernhard. (1971) *History of Indonesia in the Twentieth Century.* London: Pall Mall Press.

Legge, John D. (1972) *Sukarno: A Political Biography.* New York: Penguin Press.

OLYMPICS No Asian athletes competed in Athens when the Olympic Games were revived in 1896, but an Indian athlete and an Iranian athlete may have competed at the second modern Olympic Games in Paris in 1900. In 1908, Turkey's Selim Sirry Bey became the first Asian member of the International Olympic Committee (IOC). Japan's Kano Jigoro, the inventor of judo, followed in 1909. Three years later, Japan's National Olympic Committee (NOC), headed by Kano, was the first Asian NOC to be recognized by the IOC. Two Japanese runners competed in the 1912 games (in Stockholm), the first Asian athletes whose Olympic participation can be documented.

India's D. J. Tata joined the IOC in 1920, but, with the exception of numerous victories in field hockey, few South Asian athletes have been Olympic victors. Although C. T. Wang became an IOC member in 1922, no Chinese athlete competed until 1932. That year, Liu Changchun was joined in Los Angeles by an 8-man Philippine team, a 16-man Indian team, and a Japanese team that numbered 101 men and 16 women. In the many early Olympics in which Turkish and Iranian athletes competed, their best performances were usually in weightlifting and wrestling, two sports practiced in traditional Turkish and Iranian "houses of strength."

At Los Angeles in 1932, Japanese swimmers stunned the athletic world by winning four gold, two silver, and five bronze medals. Japan's track-and-field athletes, who had also begun to win medals at the 1932 games, competed strongly in the 1936 games in Berlin, where Korea's Sohn Kee-Chung, competing as a member of the Japanese team, won the marathon.

At the 1936 games, the IOC voted to hold the next Olympics in Tokyo, but these games were doomed by Japan's 1937 invasion of China. Japan's military government concluded that scarce resources were better spent on weaponry than on sports facilities. When the games were revived in 1948, Japan, having lost the Pacific part of World War II, was not among the thirteen Asian nations that sent three hundred men and one woman to London.

Asians on USSR Team

By 1952, a number of Asian men and women competed as members of the USSR's first Olympic team, but the world's most populous nation was represented by the Republic of China (ROC), established on Taiwan, rather than by the People's Republic of China (PRC), which had controlled the mainland since the Chinese civil war ended in 1949. Although the IOC had invited a team from the PRC to participate in Helsinki, the team arrived after the games had begun. The PRC refused to compete in Melbourne in 1956 after the IOC rejected the PRC's demand that the ROC's athletes be barred from the games. The PRC boycotted the Olympics from 1960 (Rome) through 1980 (Moscow).

In the course of its protracted conflict with the IOC, the PRC had an ally in Indonesia, which had joined the Olympics in 1952 (after achieving independence from the Netherlands). In 1963, Indonesia's dictator, Sukarno, refused to invite the ROC to the IOC-patronized Asian Games in Jakarta. When the IOC responded by suspending the Indonesian NOC, Sukarno, with strong support from the PRC and North Korea, launched a rival to the Olympic Games, the Games of the New Emerging Forces (GANEFO), which attracted forty-eight mostly Asian and African teams to Jakarta. GANEFO sank into oblivion after the IOC decided, in 1964, to forgive a more or less repentant Indonesian NOC. The IOC, however, banned individual athletes from the 1964 Olympics if they had competed in GANEFO. Angered by this ban, North Korea boycotted the 1964 games in Tokyo.

The IOC was more tolerant of Israel's exclusion from the Asian Games and from the IOC-patronized Mediterranean Games (which began in 1951). The IOC reclassified Israel as a European nation. Since 1996, the IOC has allowed Palestine to compete as an Asian nation, but Israel continues to be classified as European.

The 1964 games were the first to be held in Asia. As a favor to the Japanese hosts, the IOC voted to include judo among its "sports obligatoires." Ironically, in the open class, Japan's Kaminago Akio was upset by Anton Geesink of the Netherlands. There was compensation. The Japanese women's volleyball team, "the Witches of the East," overcame an 8 14 last set deficit and upset the favored USSR team. These games, beautifully documented in filmmaker Ichikawa Kon's *Olympics*, were the zenith in Japan's Olympic trajectory. With sixteen gold, five silver, and eight bronze medals, the hosts were third in the unofficial standings.

Japanese sports administrators had another moment of glory in 1972 when the Winter Olympics were held in Hokkaido. Eight years later, Japan's NOC was coerced by its own government to comply with demands issued from Washington. In order to protest the USSR's invasion of Afghanistan, the United States insisted that Japan boycott the 1980 Olympics, which were held in Moscow. The Japanese were joined in this boycott by Iran, Pakistan, and a number of other Islamic nations motivated more by religious solidarity than by Cold War politics. North Korea participated in the USSR-led tit-for-tat boycott of the 1984 Olympics in Los Angeles.

North Korean Boycott

North Korea also boycotted the 1988 Olympics in Seoul, the second summer games to be held in Asia. The motive for this boycott was the IOC's refusal to allow North Korea to host more than four sports at the 1988 games. North Korea rejected the IOC's offer of archery and table tennis, along with some of the cycling and soccer competitions. At Seoul, the host team shocked the Japanese by winning six of judo's eight weight classes.

In the course of the next twelve years, at Barcelona (1992), Atlanta (1996), and Sydney (2000), the PRC finally surpassed Japan as Asia's dominant Olympic power. At Barcelona, Chinese athletes earned sixteen gold medals, more than the combined total of all the other Asian teams. At Atlanta, the number of Asian NOCs rose as a result of the IOC's acceptance of teams from Kazakhstan and other nations that had been part of the USSR. Despite the increased number of Asian opponents, the Chinese won twenty-eight gold medals, whereas the combined total won by other Asian athletes was a meager twelve. Another sign of the PRC's dominance was the decision of the IOC, in 2001, to accept Beijing's bid to host the 2008 Olympics.

Speed skaters from the PRC won that nation's first Winter Olympics medals in 1992, but, at the close of the twentieth century, Japan remained the only Asian nation with a significant presence at the winter games. Japanese speed skaters, figure skaters, and skiers did well at Albertville (1992) and Lillehammer (1994). On their home snow and ice at Nagano (1998), Japanese winter athletes were even more successful. Among the most memorable images of the Nagano games was that of ski jumper Harada Masahiko leaning forward and soaring 137 meters to secure the gold medal that his mistimed jump had cost him four years earlier at Lillehammer.

Further Reading

Guttmann, Allen. (2001) *The Olympics*. Rev. ed. Urbana, IL: University of Illinois Press.

OMAR, MULLAH MUHAMMAD (b. 1959), Taliban leader and ruler of Afghanistan. Mullah Muhammad Omar, member of the Pashtun ethnic group, is the leader of the Taliban, formerly the ruling group in Afghanistan. His experiences are both military and religious. Before the Soviet intervention in Afghanistan, he was head of a *madrasah* (Islamic religious school). During the jihad (holy war) against Soviet power, he was a mujahideen (guerrilla fighter) and commander in Kandahar Province, the Taliban stronghold in the southern part of the country. Following the Soviet defeat, Omar eventually returned to his religious role and currently holds the supreme religious title of Amir Al-Mu'minin (Leader of the Faithful). Until 2001, he was also the ultimate political authority in Afghanistan.

Under Omar's leadership since the mid-1990s, Afghanistan suffered from Taliban oppression. Focusing on internal affairs, Omar led the Taliban to reject unstable civil law in favor of an idiosyncratic interpretation of Islamic *shari'a* law. Taliban rule was perceived by the international community, and by many Afghans, as harsh, severe, and indifferent to human rights, particularly in the case of women. Through the Taliban Office of the Promotion of Virtue and the Prevention of Vice, women were denied the right to freedom of expression, movement, education, employment, health care, and religious expression. The most visible sign of their oppression was the mandatory enforcement of the *chaadaree* or *burqa*, a full-body covering.

Omar's alignment with the renegade Osama bin Laden and his terrorist group made him an adversary of the coalition of Western forces supporting the Afghan groups that defeated the Taliban in 2001.

M. Catherine Daly

Further Reading

Burhan, E., and T. Gouttierre. (1983) *Dari for Foreigners*. Omaha, NE: Center for Afghanistan Studies.

Magnus, R., and E. Naby. (1998) *Afghanistan: Mullah, Marx, and Mujahid*. Boulder, CO: Westview Press.

Marsden, P. (1998) *The Taliban: War, Religion, and the New Order in Afghanistan*. Karachi, Pakistan: Oxford University Press.

Rashid, A. (2000) *Taliban. Militant Islam, Oil, and Fundamentalism in Central Asia*. New Haven, CT: Yale University Press.

ONN BIN JAAFAR' (IC BIN) (1895–1962), Malaysian politician. As a young man, Jaafar supported a single Malay nation, composed of the territories of present-day Malaysia and Indonesia, though he later distanced himself from that position. Jaafar joined the British colonial civil service and rose to the post of chief minister, the highest office in the local government of a constituent state of Malaysia.

Following World War II, a unified Malay opposition led by Jaafar confronted the British, who expected to reassert their colonial authority. In March 1946, Jaafar convened the All Malaya Congress in Kuala Lumpur. Two hundred delegates, representing forty-one Malay organizations, attended. The congress supported the formation of a single Malay political association, and Jaafar founded the United Malays National Organization (UMNO) in May 1946, becoming its president. Jaafar, however, split with UMNO's leadership over the issue of race. Jaafar envisioned UMNO being a multiethnic party that included representatives from the country's Indian and Chinese communities, who made up more than one-third of the population. In 1950, the UMNO membership rejected Jaafar's proposal, opting for the continuation of communal parties based along racial/ethnic lines. In 1951, Jaafar left UMNO and founded the multiethnic Independence of Malaya Party (IMP). The IMP never won a large base of popular support or was able to challenge the UMNO-led coalition's monopoly on power.

Jaafar was succeeded by Tunku Abdul Rahman (1903–1990), who negotiated independence and the establishment of the Federation of Malaya on 31 August 1957, becoming the nation's first prime minister. Jaafar was the father of Tun Hussein bin Dato Onn (1922–1990), who served as Malaysia's third prime minister from 1976 to 1981.

Zachary Abuza

OOTACAMUND (2001 est. pop. 94,000). Udhagamandalam (Ootacamund, Ooty) is a town and district headquarters in the Nilgiri Hills of Tamil Nadu State, India. It was founded by John Sullivan (1788–1855) in 1821. The average elevation is about 2,200 meters, but the town is surrounded by hills reaching as high as 2,636 meters.

Ootacamund was the first Indian "hill station," a health haven for European residents. It was for many years the summer headquarters of the Madras government, and, after Independence in 1947, it developed a strong tourist economy, catering especially to middle-class Indians. It is noted for the 155-year-old Botanical Gardens, Government House, and the artificial Ooty Lake, which John Sullivan created by damming a small valley. Aside from tourism, the main

THE VICEROY OF INDIA ON OOTACAMUND IN 1877

"For the first time I have seen Ootacamund. *Having* seen it, I affirm it to be a paradise, and declare without hesitation that in every particular it far surpasses all that its most enthusiastic admirers and devoted lovers have said to us about it. The afternoon was rainy and the road muddy, but such beautiful *English* rain, such delicious *English* mud. Imagine Hertfordshire lanes, Devonshire downs, Westmoreland lakes, Scotch trout streams and Lusitanian views!"

Source: Lord Lytton, Viceroy of India, [Letter] (1877), as quoted in *The Sahibs* (1948), edited by Hilton Brown. London: William Hodge & Co., 27.

industry is the production of raw film stock at a modern factory that the government created to employ local college graduates.

The town has bus and rail connections with all parts of southern India, but there is no local airport because there is no flat land. Coimbatore, 80 kilometers away, has the nearest airport.

The original inhabitants of Ootacamund were Todas, a few dozen of whom still live there in three small hamlets. The town's name comes from their language: it means "one-stone hamlet." Today the town's population consists mainly of Tamilian and Kanarese immigrants as well as urban members of the local Badaga agricultural community.

Paul Hockings

Further Reading

Panter-Downes, Mollie. (1967) *Ooty Preserved: A Victorian Hill Station in India*. New York: Farrar, Straus, and Giroux.

Price, John Frederick. (1908) *Ootacamund: A History*. Madras: Superintendent, Government Press.

OPEN DOOR POLICY The United States initially formed its Open Door policy to trade and relations with China in 1899, when Japan and the European nations were debating the division of China. Secretary of State John Hay issued the first Open Door notes in September to Great Britain, Germany, and Russia, and in November to Japan, Italy, and France. The ultimate historical significance of U.S. Open Door policy was that it was the first step toward the transformation of international relations in China from European to American principles. According to the European principle, each power tries to acquire an exclusive sphere of interest, inheriting the accompanying administrative responsibilities. The American principle sought cooperation among the major nations to "develop" China through informal means, leaving the heavy burden of administrative responsibilities to China.

Core Demands

Hay made one short-term and four long-term core demands. First, in reaction to the rapidly changing situation in China, he sought to secure immediate equal treatment in trade and navigation in China, especially in the so-called sphere of interest. Second, maintaining China's administrative integrity was a long-term objective. Washington intended to enjoy the maximum benefits from free trade without shouldering costly administrative responsibility. Third, Hay addressed China's administrative reform as another long-term objective because the weak central government could not control local antiforeign upheavals, which precipitated direct intervention from European powers. Fourth, the United States pursued cooperation among the powers in China. Concerted action was necessary to prevent the traditional Chinese diplomacy of playing one power off against another. Finally, Hay sought to give international legitimacy to the Open Door policy by requesting that all the international powers state in writing that they would observe the basic ideas of the Open Door policy.

Each power reluctantly agreed to accept the notes on the condition that the other powers did the same. All the powers eventually recognized the principle of the Open Door policy in China, and in March 1900, Hay regarded each power's response to the Open Door notes as "final and definitive." Facing the Boxer Rebellion, the United States issued the second Open Door notes in July 1900, but the basic objectives remained the same. The United States had taken the first step toward establishing the American principle as a mode of international relations in China.

Yone Sugita

Further Reading

Anderson, David L. (1985) *Imperialism and Idealism: American Diplomats in China, 1861–1898*. Bloomington, IN: Indiana University Press.

LaFeber, Walter. (1963) *The New Empire: An Interpretation of American Expansion, 1860–1898*. Ithaca, NY: Cornell University Press.

McCormick, Thomas J. (1967) *China Market: America's Quest for Informal Empire, 1893–1901*. Chicago: Quadrangle Books.

Young, Marilyn B. (1968) *The Rhetoric of Empire: American China Policy, 1895–1901*. Cambridge, MA: Harvard University Press.

OPERA—VIETNAM

Called *hat tuong* in northern Vietnam and *hat boi* in southern Vietnam, Vietnamese opera is considered the classical operatic theater of Vietnam. *Hat boi* translates as "song and gesture," emphasizing the prominence of singing and acting in this highly stylized and refined performance art.

Various similarities to Chinese opera are obvious, although the degree of Chinese influence on the artistic development of Vietnamese opera is disputed. However, due to the proximity of the two nations and centuries of political and cultural influences from China, significant parallels in performance conventions and play content can be observed today. The first documented contact dates from the thirteenth century. In 1285, a Chinese opera troupe was captured by the Vietnamese army and subsequently engaged to teach its art to Vietnamese court performers under Emperor Tran Nhan Tong (1258–1308). In subsequent centuries, Vietnamese opera solidified as classical court entertainment, reaching its artistic zenith during the nineteenth century under the Nguyen dynasty (1802–1955). Two emperors especially supported the development of court opera: Gia Long (1762–1820), who had a permanent opera stage built in his palace; and his son, Emperor Minh Mang (1792–1841), who repeatedly invited Chinese performers to train his court troupe.

Clear similarities to Chinese opera can be seen in the division of plays into martial and civil categories, in the division of the characters into specific role types, in costuming, and in the use of highly stylized makeup for painted face characters. Staging conventions are also similar to Chinese opera: plays are performed on a basically bare stage with a painted backdrop and with a table and two chairs placed center stage. The most obvious differences can be found in the distinctly Vietnamese interpretation of the Chinese story material, the addition of indigenous historical and fictional tales, the use of the Vietnamese language, and the integration of a unique musical style originating from Champa, an early Hinduized kingdom in southern Vietnam. The orchestra, led by the lead drummer, consists of percussion instruments such as several drums, clappers, gongs, and cymbals and melodic instruments consisting of a two-stringed fiddle, flute, lute, and a reed oboe. Another clear distinction is the absence of the use of "water-sleeves," a prominent feature in Chinese opera. Also, contrary to the practice of male actors portraying female characters in traditional Chinese opera, Vietnamese opera has always had female actors portray female characters.

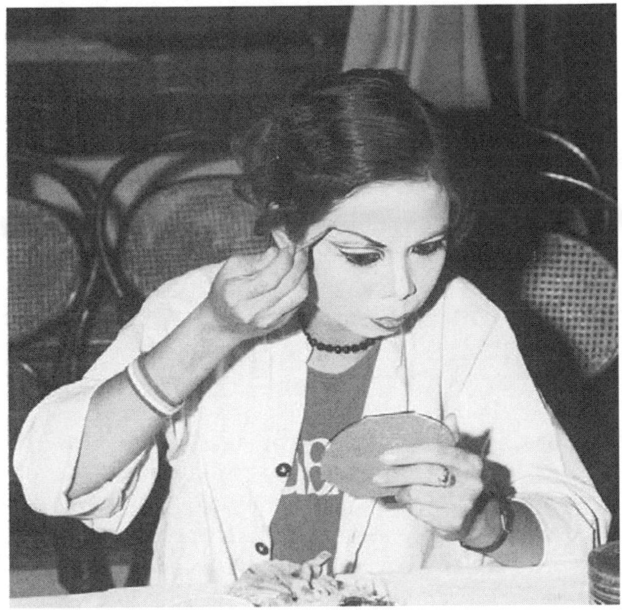

A performer in a classic opera applies her makeup at the Dao Tan Theater in Qui Nhon. (PAPILLO/CORBIS)

After 1945, court support for Vietnamese opera collapsed. However, a few commercial troupes are still performing today. The Vietnamese government is promoting this classical art form, which, despite strong Chinese influences, has developed into a uniquely Vietnamese cultural treasure.

Kirstin A. Pauka

Further Reading

Brandon, James R., ed. (1993) *Cambridge Guide to Asian Theatre*. Cambridge, U.K.: Cambridge University Press.

Huynh, Khac Dung. (1970) *Hat Bùi: Théâtre Traditionnel du Viet-nam*. Saigon, Vietnam: Kim Lai An Quan.

Mackerras, Colin. (1987) "Theatre in Vietnam." *Asian Theatre Journal* 4, 1 (Spring 1987): 1–28.

Miettinen, Jukka. (1992) *Classical Dance and Theatre in South-east Asia*. Singapore: Oxford University Press.

OPIUM

The sap of the poppy plant *Papaver somniferum* was used as a medicinal in China as early as the Tang dynasty (618–907 CE). By 1700 it was being smoked or eaten recreationally in Java, and the habit

A farmer cutting an opium poppy head in north Thailand. (MICHAEL FREEMAN/CORBIS)

spread throughout Asia. Opium became a very important part of Asia's political economy by 1800. After World War II, nonmedical opiate use became completely illegal throughout Asia, although illicit use and production remained important in some areas. India is currently the world's leading producer of licit opium derivatives.

The British and Dutch East India companies were important early producers and distributors of opium, and opium profits were crucial to the British and Dutch empires. Opium use was usually associated with the Chinese, and it spread rapidly in Chinese overseas communities and China proper after 1800. The India-China opium trade was one of the most lucrative trades of the nineteenth century. The Chinese government attempted to stop imports of Indian opium (and outflows of Chinese silver) in the First Opium War. After its defeat in this war, China became the center of the international trade. By 1906, China was consuming 22,000 tons of opium a year, much of it domestic, but also importing opium from India, Persia, and Turkey. The colonial states of Southeast Asia also consumed a lot of Indian and Persian opium, usually distributed by state monopolies. British India, the main supplier, exported more than 6,000 tons of opium a year in the late 1800s.

As the medical profession began to claim that opium was an individual and societal danger in the late nineteenth century, the European empires were increasingly pressured to end their involvement in the trade. The evolution of modern nationalism in China and elsewhere also led to campaigns to end the trade. By 1900, most Asian states had begun exercising closer control to increase revenue, and most announced plans to gradually eliminate opium sales. The 1912 Hague and 1925 Geneva conventions formally limited the international flow of opium. Japan expanded its opium sales to finance its takeover of Manchuria and later the invasion of China, but major states limited or even reduced their involvement in opium sales. None of the colonial opium monopolies continued after World War II. Despite this, much opium is still produced, especially in the "Golden Triangle" of northern Thailand and Myanmar (Burma), and its sale and export have remained important both to criminals and to minor state formations such as the regime of Khun Sha in Myanmar.

Alan Baumler

Further Reading

Brook, Timothy, and Bob Wakabayashi, eds. (2000) *Opium Regimes: China, Britain, and Japan*. Berkeley and Los Angeles: University of California Press.

Trocki, Carl. (1999) *Opium, Empire and the Global Political Economy: A Study of the Asian Opium Trade 1750–1950*. London: Routledge.

Westermeyer, Joseph. (1982) *Poppies, Pipes, and People: Opium and Its Use in Laos*. Berkeley and Los Angeles: University of California Press.

OPIUM WAR The First Opium War (1839–1842) was the beginning of active foreign aggression against China. The war began over Chinese attempts to prohibit British importation of opium. After China's defeat, the opium trade continued, but China also lost Hong Kong and was forced to open treaty ports to foreign trade and to accept the unequal treaties, which limited China's control over its foreign affairs.

Opium imports became a serious concern for the Qing dynasty court in the 1820s, as the court was worried about the effects of opium smoking on officials and soldiers and the supposed drain of silver out of the country. In the 1830s, a debate took place over whether these problems were best dealt with by legalizing and regulating opium or by prohibiting it. Prohibition won, and Lin Zexu was sent to Guangzhou (known popularly by its English name, Canton) to bring about the end of the trade.

The British in Canton were already unhappy that the Chinese government forbade them to trade in other ports, forced them to trade with a group of monopoly merchants (the Cohong) in Canton, and forbade the trade in opium, forcing the British to smuggle it or forgo the enormous profits it brought. British merchants were also unhappy at being subjected to Chinese law, which they regarded as barbaric. The McCartney mission of 1793 and the Amhurst mission of 1816 were intended to win the British full access to Chinese markets and European-style diplomatic relations with China, but both were failures.

Lin Zexu seized and destroyed the British opium at Canton and demanded that foreign merchants pledge not to import opium again. The British took these actions to be justification for war and sent a naval and military force from India. Fighting began in June of 1840. British strategy was to seize the island of Zhoushan, near the mouth of the Chang (Yangtze), and then sail north to Tianjin and demand payment for the seized opium and a complete revision of the relationship between the two countries. The British easily defeated all the Chinese naval and land forces they faced. The Qing court was eventually forced to agree to the Treaty of Nanjing. The Second Opium War 1856–1858 (also called the Arrow War) resulted in the 1858 Treaty of Tianjin, which further opened China to foreign penetration. These treaties were the foundation of the system of unequal treaties that would govern China's relations with the imperialist powers until World War II. The opium trade continued and grew, and the political and economic dislocations caused by the war and the treaty were key causes of the Taiping Rebellion, which lasted from 1851 to 1864.

Alan Baumler

Further Reading

Chang, Hsin-pao. (1964) *Commissioner Lin and the Opium War*. Cambridge, MA: Harvard University Press.

Polachek, James M. (1992) *The Inner Opium War*. Cambridge, MA: Harvard University Press.

Waley, Arthur. (1958) *The Opium War through Chinese Eyes*. London: Allen & Unwin.

ORAL (2002 est. pop. 185,000). A city located in north central Kazakhstan on the Ural River, Oral currently serves as the administrative center of the Batys Qazagstan Oblasy (West Kazakhstan Province). Founded in the first half of the seventeenth century, the city was called Yaitski Gorodok (Ural City), and the Ural River was known as the Yaits. It served as the headquarters for the Yaits Cossacks. Yaitski Gorodok was a center of the rebellion led by Stenka Razin (d. 1671), a Cossack who fomented revolt (1667–1671) until captured by the Russian czarist army and executed.

Less than a century later, the town and the Yaits Cossacks were heavily involved in the rebellion led by the Cossack Emelyan Pugachov (1726–1775) in 1773–1774 against Catherine II (1729–1796); he too was captured in 1774 and executed. In 1775, the Yaits Cossacks lost all autonomy, and the city, the Cossacks, and the river all had their names changed (the city to Uralsk, the river and Cossacks to Ural) to discourage people from thinking about the uprising.

From 1775 until 1917, Uralsk was assigned to different provinces and regions but remained part of the Russian empire and an important regional center. During the Russian Revolution, it was captured by Red Army troops in July 1919. After the dissolution of the Soviet Union in 1991, the government of Kazakhstan renamed Uralsk and its surrounding oblast. Oral today remains an important city in sparsely inhabited western Kazakhstan.

Andrew Sharp

ORANG ASLI The Orang Asli ("indigenous or native people") are the indigenous population of the Malay peninsula. There were three waves of Orang Asli immigration onto the Malay Peninsula. The Orang Asli Negritos were the first and now inhabit the most geographically isolated area: the dense forests of the northern half of the peninsula. Although their origins are unclear, it is thought they came from the Andaman Islands about 10,000 years ago. Numbering around 2,000, they are the most physically distinctive of the Orang Asli, being short and dark with frizzy hair. Traditionally, they lead a nomadic lifestyle, gathering roots and fruits and killing birds and small animals with darts from blowpipes. Larger animals, such as deer and wild pigs, are caught in traps or snares. All game, irrespective of who catches it, is shared among the members of the group.

The Senoi, considered to be the second major influx of Orang Asli, arrived on the peninsula around 6,000–8,000 years ago. Now numbering about 35,000, they are found in the central mountains of Malaysia, in the states of Perak, Pahang, and Selangor. On the whole they are smaller than Malays and have broad faces, prominent cheekbones, and wavy hair. They speak a language related to that of the Mon-Khmer people. The Senoi never put their dwellings near trees because of the danger of collapse during thunderstorms, of which they have an extraordinary fear, and which they believe are a punishment sent by the spirits of ancestral deities for sinning on earth. The Senoi are traditionally shifting cultivators, slashing and burning the forest to clear fields, and moving on to new areas only when the soil is exhausted. The Senoi commonly burn a house after a death occurs in it; today this is probably the only reason for leaving an area and setting up a home elsewhere. Destroying the house frightens the spirit, and by moving elsewhere they leave it behind. Spirits of the dead are greatly feared by the Senoi, and burial grounds are always situated across a river from the village, since the spirits, they believe, find it difficult to cross water.

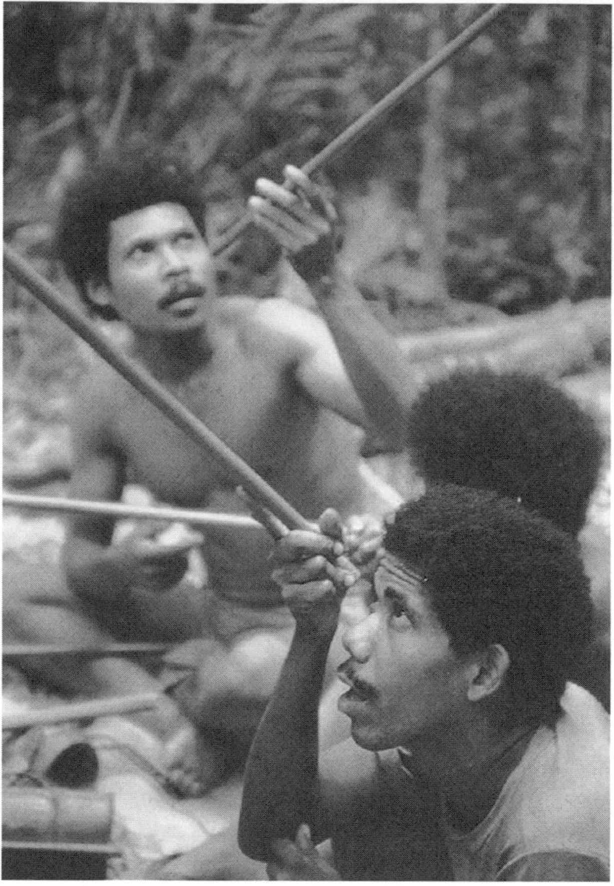

Orang Asli men in Malaysia inspecting their blowguns. (FARRELL GREHAN/CORBIS)

The Semelai subgroup of Orang Asli, who came to the peninsula about 4,000 years ago, are considered the earliest precursors of the Malays. Numbering about 25,000, and living mainly in the southern states, these are the Orang Asli who have integrated most with the Malays; the majority speak standard Malay, have Malay names, and follow a Malay lifestyle, without, however, being Muslim or considering themselves Malays. One exception is the 2,000 or so Orang Laut (sea people) from the state of Johor, who have been Muslim for centuries.

Because of contact with modern society, some Orang Asli have become unwilling to continue their traditional lifestyles. Many, however, are apparently not benefiting from this contact and instead are losing the traditional skills and knowledge that have for so long maintained them. Education, although available, shows no sign of helping the younger generation bridge the gap. Many Orang Asli children are reluctant to leave their villages in order to attend secondary schools, where they believe other races look down on them.

Kog Yue Choong

Further Reading

Shuttleworth, Charles. (1981) *Malaysia's Green and Timeless World: An Account of the Flora, Fauna, and Indigenous Peoples of the Forests of Malaysia*. Kuala Lumpur, Malaysia: Heinemann Educational Books (Asia) Limited.

ORANGUTAN The orangutan *(Pongo pygmaeus)*, whose name means "Man of the Woods" in Malay, is divided into two subspecies, one inhabiting the island of Sumatra and the other Borneo. This highly endangered primate is one of four still-existing species of great apes. The species is sexually dimorphic (occurring in two forms, one male and one female), with adult females averaging 45 kilograms and males 90 kilograms in weight. Height ranges between 1.2 and 1.6 meters when standing on both feet. The orangutan has dark skin but is covered with long orange hair, except on the face.

These diurnal (active in the daytime) apes are widely dispersed in the primary rainforest, where they eat fruits, leaves, bark, rotten wood, insects, and occasionally bird eggs. Females and young live mainly in the trees, traveling primarily by arm swinging, while the larger males more frequently forage and move, using all four limbs, on the forest floor. They build individual sleeping nests high in the trees at night, although juveniles and infants sleep with their mothers.

Females become sexually mature at about twelve years and have infants that weigh about 1.5 kilograms after nine months' gestation. The infants are carried and nursed for four to five years, and the interval between births is from five to eight years. Juveniles are dependent for protection and guidance in foraging on their mothers until they are eight or nine years old, when as subadults they leave their mothers for longer periods and interact with other subadults. Males do not mature until they are sixteen to twenty years old, when they must find or fight for a territory overlapping the ranges of several females. They defend this territory by calling loudly every day (long calls), which notifies other males to avoid them and attracts sexually receptive females. Lifespan is up to forty years.

Anne Zeller

Further Reading

Galdikas, Biruté M. F. (1995) *Reflections of Eden*. New York: Little, Brown.

———, and Nancy Briggs. (1999) *Orangutan Odyssey*. Intro. by Jane Goodall. New York: Harry N. Abrams.

ORGANIZATION OF PETROLEUM EXPORTING COUNTRIES Before the Organization of Petroleum Exporting Countries (OPEC) was established in 1960, international oil companies with concessions in the Middle Eastern oil countries controlled crude-oil prices and thus the amounts paid to the oil-producing countries; when the price of oil fell because supply exceeded demand, payments to the oil countries dropped as well. OPEC was organized as a voluntary intergovernmental organization whose basic aims are to coordinate and unify the petroleum policies of its member countries and to safeguard their interests. OPEC links countries whose main source of export earnings is petroleum.

To achieve their aims OPEC countries use various means, such as setting crude-oil prices according to world demand, imposing an overall production ceiling, and allocating production quotas. OPEC has also sometimes used oil as a political tool.

Formation and Membership

OPEC was established in Baghdad, Iraq, in September 1960. The organization was formed by five founding members: Iran, Iraq, Kuwait, Saudi Arabia, and Venezuela. In the 1960s five more countries became members: Qatar (1961), Indonesia (1962), Libya (1962), Abu Dhabi (1967), and Algeria (1969). In 1974 the United Arab Emirates, of which Abu Dhabi is the dominant member, took Abu Dhabi's place. The membership was raised to thirteen with the admission of Nigeria (1971), Ecuador (1973), and Gabon (1975). Two countries withdrew in the 1990s: Ecuador (1992) and Gabon (1996).

Organizational Structure

OPEC's headquarters are in Vienna, Austria. The organizational structure includes several bodies. The Conference, which consists of high-ranking representatives of the member countries, is OPEC's "supreme authority." Meeting at least twice a year, the Conference formulates general policies for OPEC, decides on new members, considers and approves the budget, and appoints the secretary-general.

The OPEC secretariat is directed by the board of governors and run by the secretary-general and by various bodies, including the Ministerial Monitoring Committee and the Economic Commission. The main functions of the secretariat include (1) collecting information and studying and reviewing all matters of common interest relating to the petroleum industry; (2) making studies and preparing proposals whenever requested by the board of governors; and (3) implementing the decisions taken by the Conference.

The board of governors directs the management of OPEC's affairs. It is charged with implementing the decisions of the Conference and drawing up the annual budget. The Ministerial Monitoring Committee ensures the stability of the world petroleum market by monitoring price evolution and preparing long-term strategies. The Committee is normally convened four times a year.

Oil and Gas Resources and Current Oil Production

Estimates of OPEC's oil and gas resources are made at regular intervals. At the end of the 1990s OPEC-member countries controlled unique oil and gas reserves. OPEC countries possess more than 75 percent of the world's known reserves of crude petroleum and about 44 percent of the world's known resources of natural gas. OPEC produces about 40 percent of the world's crude oil and about 14 percent of the world's natural gas. OPEC's oil exports represent about 60 percent of all oil traded internationally. Eighty-five percent of OPEC's total oil and 79 percent of its total gas reserves are concentrated in Asian OPEC countries (that is, OPEC member countries other than Venezuela, Libya, Nigeria, and Algeria).

The main producers are the Asian countries in the Persian Gulf region, which are especially rich in oil: Iran, Saudi Arabia, and Kuwait together contain more than 40 percent of the world's oil reserves. Saudi Arabia and Iran could probably sustain current production levels into the second half of the twenty-first century; current production levels in Iraq, the United Arab Emirates, and Kuwait may be sustainable into the twenty-second century.

Major Events in OPEC History

The first OPEC Conference was held in Baghdad in September 1960. The conference agreed to limit annual growth in output to secure adequate prices in 1965. The tax levied by OPEC members on the income of the petroleum companies was raised to 55 percent in 1970. In 1973 the Arab oil-exporting nations imposed an embargo on the United States and the Netherlands and increased prices to America's Western European allies because of their support of Israel in the Yom Kippur War. As a result, the price of crude oil quadrupled from $3 in October 1973 to $12 per barrel in January 1974. The Arab nations lifted the embargo in March 1974, after a proposal for an Israeli withdrawal from captured Syrian territory.

The OPEC Fund for International Development was created in 1976. The main goal of this financial institution is to help low-income countries in pursuit of their social and economic advancement. All developing countries, with the exception of OPEC member states, are in principle eligible for assistance.

The Iranian Revolution and the Iran-Iraq War led to another increase in crude oil prices, which more than doubled from $14 in 1978 to $35 per barrel in 1981. In 1982, for the first time in OPEC's history, the member countries agreed to defend the Organization's price structure by imposing an overall production ceiling of 18 million barrels per day. During the first half of 1986 petroleum prices dropped to below $10 per barrel, probably because some OPEC members ignored the production ceiling.

In August 1990 Iraq invaded Kuwait. After the United Nations imposed an international embargo on petroleum exports from both countries, the price of crude oil instantly increased to $25 per barrel. During the 1990s the price continued to fluctuate and reached its lowest level of $9.90 per barrel in February 1999. Following an OPEC agreement from 23 March 1999 to cut oil production by 1.7 million barrels per day, the price of crude oil rebounded sharply. During 1999, 2000, and the first eight months of 2001 they were high, especially in late 2000 when the price of crude oil was above $30 per barrel. Prices fell sharply in late September and October 2001, due to economic recession in the United States and some other countries.

Different political and economic forces are shaping the future of OPEC. In the global context the demand for oil will continue to rise, unless a cheap alternative source of energy is discovered. Thus OPEC could maintain or even increase its role on the world oil market, especially taking into consideration the lack of major oil finds in the last twenty years. From the other side, OPEC member nations often pursue their own interests, and compliance with OPEC decisions is limited to circumstances when the interests of all member nations converge.

Dimitar L. Dimitrov

Further Reading

Ahrari, Mohammed E. (1986) *OPEC: The Failing Giant.* Lexington, KY: University Press of Kentucky.

Al-Chalabi, Fadhil J. (1980) *OPEC and the International Oil Industry: A Changing Structure.* Oxford: Oxford University Press.

Allen, Loring. (1979) *OPEC Oil.* Cambridge, MA: Oelgeschlager, Gunn, and Hain.

Lukman, Rilwanu. (1995) "Political and Economic Issues Affecting Capacity Expansion: The OPEC Point of View." *OPEC Bulletin* (June): 14–16.

ORIENTAL ORTHODOX CHURCH The Oriental Orthodox Church is a group of distinct churches that have their origins in the Middle East. The term is used to avoid confusion with the Eastern Orthodox Church. Oriental Orthodox Churches include the Syrian Orthodox Church (also known as the Jacobite Church), the Armenian Gregorian Apostolic Orthodox Church, and, outside Asia, the Coptic (Egyptian) Orthodox Church, of which the Ethiopian Orthodox Church is a branch. These churches resemble the Eastern Orthodox Church in liturgy and structure, but they reject the findings of the Council of Chalcedon (451 CE), which defined Christian orthodoxy. For this reason they are also known as the non-Chalcedonian churches. Specifically, these churches reject the teaching that Christ is "of like nature" (Greek *homoiousion)* with God the Father, asserting instead that he is "of the same nature" *(homoousion).* From this precept they take the name Monophysite (one body).

The Syrian Orthodox Church was persecuted as heretical under the Byzantine empire, but under Islamic rule it attained the status of "protected community" *(dhimmi).* Today its members account for approximately 10–12 percent of the population of Syria. A tiny community survives in southeast Turkey, where it is subject to pressures of assimilation and emigration. The patriarch of the church, formerly resident at the monastery of Deir az-Zafferan near Mardin in Turkey, now lives in Damascus, Syria. An ancient Syrian Orthodox community, tracing its origin to the mission of the Apostle Thomas, exists in Karnataka State, India. The church also exists in émigré communities in Africa, the Americas, Australia, and Europe. The church uses Syriac, an ancient Semitic language closely related to biblical Aramaic, as its liturgical language, although 99 percent of its followers are Arabic speakers.

The Armenians claim to have been the first people to have adopted Christianity as a state religion, the ancient Armenian state having been outside the Byzantine empire. Ninety percent of Armenians worldwide belong to the Armenian Orthodox Church, and there is a strong identification between the membership of the Armenian church and the Armenian nation. The church is held to have been the preserver of Armenian identity against Muslim Turks and Iranians. As such, the Soviet authorities permitted the church's leader, the catholicos, to remain in his traditional seat of Echmiadzin after the Soviet takeover of Armenia. This legitimized the USSR as the protector of the Armenian nation after the genocide of 1915 (which Turkey denies) in which the large Armenian population of eastern Anatolia was either massacred or forced across the desert to Syria, where large Armenian communities of Anatolian origin remain. Outside Armenia itself, diaspora communities are to be found across the Middle East, especially in Iran, Syria, and Israel/Palestine.

Both the Syrian and Armenian Churches have so-called Uniate branches in communion with the Roman Catholic Church. Two other Uniate churches originated as non-Chalcedonian churches. These are the Maronite Church, the dominant Christian confession in Lebanon, and the Nestorian, or Assyrian, Church, with its leadership in Baghdad, Iraq, and followers in Iran, Turkey, and Syria, where many adherents fled after persecution in Iraq in the early twentieth century.

Will Myer

Further Reading

Challiot, C. (1998) *The Syrian Orthodox Church of Antioch.* Geneva, Switzerland: Inter-Orthodox Dialogue.

Mar, Gregorios. (1982) *The Orthodox Church in India.* New Delhi: Sophia Publications.

Nersoyan, T. (1996) *Armenian Christian Historical Studies.* New York: St. Vartan Press.

Ramet, P. (1988) *Eastern Christianity and Politics in the Twentieth Century.* Durham, NC: Duke University Press.

Vogt, K., and N. van Doorn-Harner, eds. (1997) *Between Desert and City: The Coptic Orthodox Church Today.* Oslo, Norway: Novis-farlag.

ORIENTALISM

ORIENTALISM Orientalism refers to two intellectual trends in the West: the appearance or deliberate cultivation in literature and art of stylistic and aesthetic traits reminiscent of Asian cultures, which began in eighteenth-century Europe; and, in the eighteenth and nineteenth centuries, the scholarly study of premodern Asia, especially philology (the study of language and linguistics) and other text-based pursuits, by Europeans and Americans. The fields of anthropology, sociology, and cultural, political, and economic history, insofar as they address Asia, have since been called Orientalist as well.

The First Orientalists

The earliest Orientalists, mostly trained in the Greco-Roman classics, were interested in recovering ancient texts, often seeing this as a way to open a window onto the origins of culture, which was itself a major preoccupation in the nineteenth century. Scholars studied the relationships between ancient languages and cultures and focused attention on religious and legal texts. John Selden (1584–1654), an English legal antiquarian and politician, became a recognized authority on Near Eastern polytheism and Jewish law. The German biblical scholar Johann Gottfried Eichhorn (1752–1827) challenged pious traditions by showing the common origins of the Bible and other Semitic texts. A. H. Anquetil-Duperron (1731–1805), a French scholar, brought Zoroastrian manuscripts to France in the early 1760s. Eugène Burnouf (1801–1852), the son of a French classicist, published works on the Pali language of the Theravada Buddhists, on Zoroastrian liturgy in the Avesta, and on Sanskrit mythological texts, for which he was appointed professor of the Sanskrit language at the Collège de France (1832–1852).

Orientalists as Diplomats and Administrators in Asia

Some of the first Orientalists got their start accompanying diplomatic missions to Asia. Antoine Galland (1646–1715), a French scholar who accompanied the French ambassador to Constantinople in 1670–1675, studied Arabic, Persian, and Turkish there. He later published *Mille et une nuits*, the first translation of *Arabian Nights' Entertainments* into a European language, as well as French translations of collections of Indian fables and the Qur'an. Likewise, Heinrich Julius Klaproth (1783–1835), a German who had taken part in a Russian visit to China in 1805, published a two-volume ethnographic and linguistic study of the Caucasus.

In other cases, Orientalists went to Asia as army officers or colonial administrators. Sir William Jones (1746–1794), an English scholar and translator of Greek, Latin, Arabic, and Persian who became a British supreme-court judge in Calcutta, undertook the study of Sanskrit to compile an authoritative digest of Hindu law that might be used in the courts. He founded the Asiatic Society of Bengal in 1784, and in his presidential discourse of 1786 he was the first to propose that Sanskrit and Greek shared a common ancestry, to which most other languages of Europe also belonged. Another example is Sir Henry Rawlinson (1810–1895), a British army officer assigned in 1833 to reorganize the army of the shah of Iran. He deciphered and wrote a linguistic analysis of the Old Persian section of the cuneiform inscription of Darius the Great at Bisitun, Iran (1837, 1846–1851), which paved the way for the decipherment of the Mesopotamian cuneiform script.

Orientalists as Public Intellectuals

By the late nineteenth century, some Orientalists had become celebrities and public intellectuals. The controversial British explorer and polymath Sir Richard Burton (1821–1890) captivated the reading public with prolific accounts of his adventures in Asia and Africa; he also produced thirty volumes of translations from numerous languages, including *The Arabian Nights* (sixteen volumes, 1885–1888) and the *Kama Sutra*, a Sanskrit treatise on the erotic arts (1883). Burton also wrote one of the first ethnological treatises, *Sind, and the Races That Inhabit the Valley of the Indus* (1851).

Equally famous, at least in learned circles, was Friedrich Max Müller (1823–1900), often called the founder of the field of comparative religion. German-born, he became a professor at Oxford University; he established his reputation with his edition of the Rig Veda, the oldest extant Sanskrit work, and with his influential essays on comparative mythology, religion, and linguistics. The fifty-one-volume series of translations that he edited, *Sacred Books of the East* (1879–1910), helped win acceptance for the idea that non-Western traditions could be viewed as religions comparable to Christianity or Judaism, each with a body of scriptures.

Since the end of the colonial era, philological studies have continued, although they have lost much of the prestige they had in the nineteenth and early twentieth centuries. For the most part, interest (and funding) has shifted to political science, social anthropology, and the history of the last few centuries.

Said's Critique

In 1978, Edward Said (b. 1935), a professor of English and comparative literature at Columbia University and a Palestinian by birth, wrote a book called *Orientalism* in which he criticized the conceptual foundations and principal methods of such scholarship. Said's approach was shaped by the writings of the French poststructuralist philosopher Michel Foucault (1926–1984) and the Italian Marxist Antonio Gramsci (1891–1937). From Foucault he took the notion of discourse theory and the insight that the production and possession of knowledge are sources of power. But he objected to the diffuseness of Foucault's conception of power and appealed to Gramsci's hegemony theory (which argues that elite social groups use cultural institutions, such as schools, parties, and the media, rather than naked force, to secure and extend their dominance, so that this dominance seems natural and appropriate).

Analyzing British, French, and American writing on the Arab societies of North Africa and the Middle East, Said argued that Western scholars systematically misunderstood and misrepresented these societies, due largely to the nature of their relationship to them (one of cultural superiority and imperial dominance). His conclusions have subsequently been extended to apply to Western scholarship on Asia in general. At the same time, his study extended its purview beyond scholarly works to include journalism, travel writing, and other types of literature, so that "Orientalism" as he defined it is in fact the sum of all Western literary and artistic expressions relating to Asia.

Said traced the roots of modern Orientalism back to ancient Greek depictions of the East and outlined its later development by littérateurs (Dante Alighieri, 1265–1321; Geoffrey Chaucer, 1342–1400; William Shakespeare, 1564–1616). According to him, the Orientalist vision of the East was well established as a literary trope long before the colonialist period; he claimed in fact that "colonial rule was justified in advance by Orientalism, rather than after the fact" (Said 1978: 39).

Beginning with the Egyptian expedition of Napoleon Bonaparte (1769–1821), "the Orientalist's special expertise was put directly to functional colonial use" (Said 1978: 80). For Said, the work of Sir William Jones exemplifies the double task of Orientalism: to describe, tabulate, analyze, and codify the Orient "scientifically," always in comparison with the Occident; and to use the knowledge thus generated to master and rule the Orientals. Thus Jones attempted to codify and apply in the courts a traditional Hindu law based on Sanskrit texts, as part of the East India Company's policy of governing Indians by their own codes.

Said argued that, although Orientalism adopts the posture of an objective scientific pursuit, it has from the first been motivated and sustained by a political purpose: the governance of colonial territories. Imperial administrators like Lord Curzon (1859–1925), viceroy of India, acknowledged that knowledge of the culture and sensibilities of the people of the East were indispensable for securing colonial dominance. With the end of the European empires and a decline in the popularity of philology, Said argued, the Orientalist enterprise increasingly took a new form: area-studies fields, which created expertise to be made available to governments and policy-making institutions.

Said argued that Orientalism helped the West to construct an image of itself by projecting every trait opposite to that of the West's onto the screen of a backward and decadent Orient. He made this argument by psychologizing the West's relationship to the East as self to "other." The Oriental was reduced to a stereotype, springing from the notion that it is possible to define the essential nature of Arabs or Muslims. Orientals, he claimed, are routinely characterized as sensuous, childlike, irrational, mendacious, and culturally passive and static. Such traits are supposedly exemplified in the person of the "Oriental despot," whose state is said to be the characteristic political institution of the East. Defining the Orient in this way provided a rationale for Western imperialism and colonialism: the destiny of Western power is to introduce reason and order into the Orient.

Said's critique of Orientalism became one of the most important foundations for what has been called colonial-discourse theory or, more broadly, postcolonial studies (the study of the relationships between European nations and the societies they formerly colonized). Another notable ramification of this field is subaltern studies, an approach to Indian history led by the Indian historian Ranajit Guha (b. 1923) and inspired by the work of Gramsci, which aims to write the history of subaltern peoples by recovering their own voices and agency. These approaches share a recognition that knowledge is intertwined with the exercise of power, as well as a postmodernist skepticism of all claims to objectivity.

Criticisms

Although widely praised in literary critical circles from the start, Said's book has been criticized from a variety of angles. First, representatives of Asian studies in a wide range of disciplines sharply objected to the suggestion that they were willfully or unwittingly complicit in their governments' programs for colonization and for political and economic domination, even in the postcolonial era. Philologists, for example, insisted that their painstaking analyses of ancient texts were only distantly related to any political agenda. Many objected to the suggestion that the field as a whole displays cynicism and bad faith. It has been observed that Said essentialized the Orientalist and elided all differences of approach or discipline. He made little distinction between eighteenth- and nineteenth-century views of the East and those of his scholarly contemporaries.

Furthermore, it can be pointed out that the charges laid at the door of Orientalists and of Westerners in general apply also to Asians and to people everywhere. Jones, for instance, is faulted for "an irresistible impulse always to codify, to subdue the infinite variety of the Orient to 'a complete digest'" (Said 1978: 78), but the Sanskrit legal works he consulted were deliberate codifications already, designed by Brahman scholars to consolidate and extend their own authority. Said's fallacy, by this reasoning, is to demonize Europeans in particular for behaving as the privileged and powerful do everywhere; indeed, the colonized of modern times were often the colonizers of earlier eras and produced "Orientalisms" of their own. Moreover, many critics note that scholarship on Asia is no longer in the hands of Westerners alone, and that the academic climate has changed considerably, partly in response to the arguments of Said.

On the other hand, criticisms also emerged from the vanguard of literary, social, and political theorists. Notable among these are Dennis Porter (b. 1933) and Aijaz Ahmad (b. 1945). Porter, a literary critic interested in travel writing, found Said's literary analysis too blunt: his sources (said Porter) are inadequately historicized, and literary texts are not treated any differently than are obviously ideological texts. Porter pointed to the fact that aesthetic products follow more than simply ideological imperatives. At the heart of this problem, Porter saw an incompatibility between Foucault's discourse theory and Gramsci's understanding of hegemony.

Aijaz Ahmad, an Indian Marxist critic, objected to Said's acceptance of the Nietzschean tenet that all communication is distorting and all truths illusory, an article of faith in late-twentieth-century French cultural criticism. This claim, which Ahmad called irrational and antihuman, allowed Said to dispense with considerations of class, gender, and even historical process. Ahmad also noted the totalizing character of Said's Orientalism. All other forms of oppression are subordinated to Orientalism, and all Westerners and everything they have said and done are by definition Orientalist. Ahmad alleged that this formulation of oppression was particularly well received in the United States by mostly male Third World immigrant scholars of upper-class background who were not moved by theories of class-based and gender-based oppression, and who could represent themselves as oppressed despite the fact that people of their social class often benefited from the colonial order.

Timothy Lubin

Further Reading

Ashcroft, Bill, Gareth Griffiths, and Helen Tiffin. (1989) *The Empire Writes Back: Theory and Practice in Post-Colonial Literatures*. London: Routledge.

Said, Edward. (1978) *Orientalism*. London: Routledge & Kegan Paul.

Williams, Patrick, and Laura Chrisman, eds. (1994) *Colonial Discourse and Post-Colonial Theory: A Reader*. New York: Columbia University Press.

ORIGAMI Origami means literally "folded paper," from the Japanese words *ori* (to fold) and *kami* (paper). In the sixth century, the Chinese introduced this art to Japan, where it developed its characteristic subtlety, refinement, and restraint. Origami is ingenious in its use of simple creases to capture the essence of a subject. Purists feel that a single sheet of paper should only be folded with no cutting while others find this rule too limiting.

In the Heian period (794–1185), owing to the high cost of paper, origami was a pastime of the nobility; by the Muromachi period (1333–1573), paper became more available and origami's popularity grew. The Tokugawa period (1600/1603–1868) saw the publication of the earliest texts on origami: the *Sembazuru orikata* (Folding a Thousand Cranes, 1797), which showed how to fold a series of connected cranes from a single sheet of paper; and the *Kan no mado* (Window on Mid-Winter, 1845), the first comprehensive collection of directions.

The well-known paper crane *(tsuru)* has its origins in the Tokugawa period and is still a popular symbol. The crane carries with it auspicious messages for long life and good fortune. A chain of one thousand cranes strung together represents both good health and peace, as found draped over the memorial statue in the Hiroshima Peace Park of Sadako Sasaki (1943–1955), the young girl who died of leukemia as a result of her exposure to radiation from the atom bomb dropped on Hiroshima in 1945. Following the practice of folding one thousand cranes to have a wish granted, Sadako began to fold her cranes in the hope of getting well. When she realized that this particular wish was not to be, she instead wished for a peaceful world. She continued until she died, eventually folding 1,500 cranes.

Catherine Pagani

Further Reading

Brossman, Julia McLean, and Martin W. Brossman, eds. (1961) *A Japanese Paperfolding Classic: Excerpt from the "Lost"* Kan no mado. Washington, DC: Pinecone Press.

Engel, Peter. (1989) *Folding the Universe: Origami from Angelfish to Zen.* New York: Random House.

Kasahara Kunihiko. (1988) *Origami Omnibus.* New York: Japan Publications.

ORISSA (2001 est. pop. 36.7 million). The state of Orissa, with an area of 155,707 square kilometers, is situated on the southeastern part of India. It is surrounded by the states of Bihar, Andhra Pradesh, and Chattisgarh and the Bay of Bengal. Bhubaneshwar is the capital city. Located in the tropical zone, the state has an average rainfall of 150 centimeters. The longest earthen dam in the world, the Hirakud Dam, is located in Orissa on the Mahanadi River.

A place of cultural synthesis and racial amalgamation, Orissa has a long tradition of maritime, commercial, and cultural contact with Southeast Asia. Its territory once extended from the Ganges River in the north to the Godavari River in the south. Its decline began in the middle of the sixteenth century, when parts of it were annexed by neighboring powers. It became a separate province on 1 April 1936.

The majority of the people are Hindus and speak the Oriya language. Tribal peoples constitute 22 percent of the population, one of the largest concentrations in India. Some 87 percent of the population is settled in rural areas. There are only 124 urban units, and only eight cities have a population of more than 100,000.

About 73 percent of the people are dependent on farming. Rice, pulses, oilseed, jute, coconuts, turmeric, and sugarcane are some of the important crops. The manufactured products of the state are textiles, paper, leather goods, cement, and steel. In spite of abundance of natural resources such as iron, coal, zinc, and forest goods, poverty is widespread. Orissa has the highest percentage of people in India (48.6 percent) living below the poverty line. The average annual income is only about $100. The literacy rate is 49.1 percent. Natural calamities such as drought, cyclones, heat waves, and floods are recurring features.

The poverty of the state contrasts with its rich cultural traditions. The magnificent temples of Konark, Lingaraj, and Jagannatha show that Orissan artists have remarkable dexterity in creating objects of art. The appliqué handicrafts, elegant *sambalpuri* clothes, silver filigree works, *patachitra* (cloth painting), and stone sculptures produced in the state are widely acclaimed.

Patit Paban Mishra

Further Reading

Jena, B. B. (1981) *Orissa: People, Culture, and Polity.* New Delhi: Kalyani.

Mishra, P. K., and J. K. Samal, eds. (1997) *Comprehensive History and Culture of Orissa.* New Delhi: Kaveri.

ORIYAS The Oriyas live mainly in the province of Orissa in eastern India, which became a state on 1 April 1936. The bordering states of Andhra Pradesh, Bihar, Chaatisgarh, and West Bengal have been influenced by different cultural traditions and have produced a unique Oriya culture. Forging a link between north and south India, the Oriyas have had a long experience of commercial, cultural, and military expansion. The Oriyas belong mainly to proto-Australoid and western brachycephalic stock and speak the Oriya language. With some twenty-two million speakers, Oriya is a direct descendent of Magadhi and its script a derivative of Bengali.

The Orissan empire once stretched from the Ganga River in the north to the Godavari River in the south. Maritime activities of the Oriyas made them a prosperous people, who contributed to the cultural rapprochement between India and Southeast Asia. The Oriyas are mostly Hindus, though a strong tribal influence can be found in their religion; they have built the magnificent temples of Konark, Lingaraj, and Jagannatha. Beautifully woven *samblapuri* clothes, silver filigree works, and *Odissi* dance are examples of Oriya artistry. The settlement pattern of the people is mainly rural, and agriculture is the main occupation.

Patit Paban Mishra

Further Reading

Jena, B. B. (1981) *Orissa: People, Culture, and Polity.* New Delhi: Kalyani.

Mishra, P. K., and J. K. Samal. (1997) *Comprehensive History and Culture of Orissa.* New Delhi: Kaveri.

OSAKA (2002 est. prefectural pop. 8.9 million). Osaka is Japan's second city of commerce, industry, and trade. Situated in central Honshu Island on Osaka Bay along the Inland Sea, the city is at the heart of the Hanshin Industrial Zone. The city proper (2002 estimated population 2.6 million) consists of twenty-six wards. It is the capital of Osaka Prefecture.

From the fourth to sixth centuries CE, Osaka, then known as Naniwa, lay close to the developing Yamato state, which eventually became Japan. Its port a conduit for culture from China, Naniwa itself was an imperial capital several times before the 710 founding of Nara as Japan's first permanent capital. In 1586, the city returned to prominence when national unifier Toyotomi Hideyoshi (1537–1598) erected Osaka Castle. With the defeat of his son in 1615, power shifted to Edo (present-day Tokyo). In the following centuries, Osaka flourished as a trade center. Its wealthy merchant class patronized the arts, fostering the development of Kabuki and of Bunruku puppet theater.

World War II bombing destroyed most of Osaka's traditional wooden buildings and many transport canals. The rebuilt city became a base for modern heavy industry. Today visitors are drawn to the replica of Osaka Castle, the Sumiyoshi Matsuri (a festival), and the various historic museums, Buddhist temples, and Shinto shrines.

Osaka Prefecture occupies an area of 1,869 square kilometers. It is bordered by Osaka Bay, and by Kyoto, Nara, Wakayama, and Hyogo prefectures. Once divided into Settsu, Kawachi, and Izumi provinces, it assumed its present name and borders in 1887. Today over two-thirds of the prefecture's industry is devoted to heavy manufacturing and chemicals; the newer factory complexes occupy land reclaimed from Osaka Bay. Visitors are drawn to the area's national parks and to Expo Memorial Park, built for Osaka's Expo '70 international exposition.

E. L. S. Weber

Further Reading

McClain, James L., and Osamu Wakita, eds. (1999) *Osaka: Merchants' Capital of Early Modern Japan.* Ithaca, NY: Cornell University Press.

Ropke, Ian M., and Jon Woronoff, eds. (1999) *Historical Dictionary of Osaka and Kyoto.* Metuchen, NJ: Scarecrow Press.

OSAKA ACTION PLAN On 18–19 November 1995, the eighteen-member Asia-Pacific Economic Conference (APEC) held its annual meeting in Osaka, Japan, and produced the largely ineffective Osaka Action Plan. While some substantive measures were adopted, this economic summit conference accomplished little beyond reiterating the more comprehensive agreement reached the year before in Bogor, Indonesia.

The relatively scanty result of the Osaka Conference was due, in part, to a split in the APEC membership. The United States was the most prominent of several countries that pressed for a strict commitment to liberalized Asian trade, enforceable by reference to unequivocal trade rules. Japan, in concert with like-minded nations, was reluctant to hurry the liberalization process and preferred more ambiguous enforcement with greater national flexibility. On the whole, the Japanese position prevailed.

The Bogor Declaration, which had set 2010 as the year for free commercial intercourse among developed economies and 2020 for less-developed nations, was repromulgated at Osaka. This second declaration at Osaka was less substantive and was restricted largely to lofty-sounding sentiments. For instance, the members pledged "to ensure the transparency of their laws, regulations, and administrative procedures affecting the flow of goods, services, and capital among APEC economies" ("Regional Affairs" 1995: 40829). Liberalization of trade was, in a few areas, moved slightly ahead of schedule. Otherwise, the Osaka Declaration was largely humdrum. While U.S. president Bill Clinton had attended the Bogor Conference, the American government merely sent its secretary of state, Warren Christopher, to Osaka.

Robert K. Whalen

Further Reading

"Regional Affairs." (1995) *News Digest* (November): 40829.

"Shrinking the Pacific." (1997) *McClean's Magazine* 110 (November): 69.

U.S. Department of State. (1995) *U.S. Department of State Dispatch.* Vol. 6. Washington, DC: U.S. Department of State.

OSH (2000 est. pop. 300,000). Between 2,500 and 3,000 years old, Osh is one of Central Asia's oldest settlements. Largely rebuilt during the twentieth century, it is located in southwestern Kyrgyzstan near the Uzbekistan border in the eastern section of the Fergana Valley. Its name has been known since at least the ninth century and is thought to have originated with an Iranian people known as the Ush, who used to live in the area. As early as the eighth century, Osh was a silk-production center along the Silk Road, and it remained a major trade post until the fifteenth century.

In the city's center is one of Central Asia's most sacred sites: a hill called Takht-i-Suleyman (Solomon's Throne), where the Prophet Muhammad is thought to have prayed and where Muslim pilgrims began visiting in the tenth century. Although Osh is an important Kyrgyzstan center, its population is mostly Uzbek. Consequently, ethnic discord has existed since Soviet dictator Stalin's rule and erupted into violence in 1990 when Uzbeks and Kyrgyz fought over land and water supplies and three hundred to one thousand were killed. Kyrgyz city government also oversees Uzbek-dominated local business. Osh has two universities, a sanatorium, and an airport. Economic activity has been aided by beneficial reforms and consists of the Jayma bazaar; opium and silk trade; sheep grazing; mining of zinc, lead, and coal; food processing; and the production of silk, cotton, and wool.

Gary Mason Church

Further Reading

MacLeod, Calum, and Bradley Mayhew. (1997) *Uzbekistan: The Golden Road to Samarkand.* 2d ed. Lincoln, IL: Odyssey/Passport.

Mayhew, Bradley, Richard Plunkett, and Simon Richmond. (2000) *Central Asia.* Oakland, CA: Lonely Planet.

OTTOMAN EMPIRE The Ottoman empire expanded from a small territory near Constantinople to capture the remnant of the Byzantine empire in the late thirteenth century, reviving many of its institutions and synthesizing an elaborate, centralized Sunni Islamic state. Suleyman the Magnificent (1494–1566) ruled the empire at its greatest extent; at that time it reached from the Near East west to the Balkans and south to North Africa. Although the empire began to slowly shrink after Suleyman, it persisted until overthrown in the early twentieth century.

Rise of Ottomans

Before the fourteenth century the Turkish tribe of Osman (from which "Ottoman" is derived) migrated westward to the Byzantine border and intermarried into the Byzantine royal family. Expansion began with Murad I (1326–1389), who made the Byzantine emperor a vassal, conquered parts of the Balkans, and routed the Serbs (1389). Bayezid (1360–1424), the first Ottoman ruler to assume the title of sultan, continued the advance but ended his life as a captive of Timur (Tamerlane), the Turkic conqueror who campaigned through much of Central and Western Asia.

Imperial Expansion

After dynastic civil war, the austere and determined Mehmed II the Conqueror (1432–1481), often considered the real founder of the empire, introduced European artillery expertise and dragged his newly built fleet across the headland of Pera (modern Beyoglu, European Turkey north of the Golden Horn) into the enclosed waters of the Golden Horn, an inlet of the Bosporus, to assault simultaneously the seaward and landward walls of Constantinople and to capture the city. He renamed it Istanbul and turned Hagia Sophia into a mosque.

Selim the Grim (1470–1520) created an Ottoman navy, which successfully countered the Venetians and captured Mesopotamia, Syria, and Egypt from the Mamluk sultans, thereby acquiring the holy cities of Mecca and Medina. Suleyman the Magnificent, whose reign represented the flowering of Ottoman culture, presided over the apogee of Ottoman importance and expansionism. He advanced into Europe and conquered the Hungarians (1526) but unsuccessfully besieged Vienna (1529) and Malta (1565). During Suleyman's reign the empire rimmed the whole eastern Mediterranean from the Persian Gulf to Hungary; it encompassed self-governing minorities of various

SVLTAN MVSTAPHA, FILS DE SVL-
tan Solyman. Chapitre. 146.

An illustration of an Ottoman sultan in ceremonial garb. (BETTMANN/CORBIS)

Muslim sects, as well as Armenian, Syrian, Coptic, and Greek Christians, Jews, and Yezidis (fire worshipers).

Ottoman naval expansion confronted Venice; defeated at Lepanto (1571), the fleet was rebuilt in a few months, but land wars with Persia (1575–1624) went badly due to mass desertions caused by the devaluation of the currency and hence underpayment of troops as Mexican silver flooded Europe. Viziers of the Koprulu family restored internal and naval peace, but after the defeat at Vienna (1683), Mustafa II (1664–1703) was forced to deal with foreign powers as equals in the Treaty of Carlowitz (1699), and some Balkan lands were lost.

Later History

Until the reforms of Mahmud II (1785–1839), weak sultans could not control the military or update its weaponry; from 1774 onward, the empire lost territory to expansionist Russia, nationalist movements, and rebellious governors. Protection and loans from Britain and France kept the empire alive long enough to become an ally of Germany in World War I.

Nationalist movements began in imitation of the French Revolution; Greece rebelled in 1821, and France, England, and Russia forced Mahmud II to accept Greek independence through the terms of the Treaty of Adrianople (1829). The Janissaries, an Ottoman military elite, had become rebellious Praetorian guards, responsible for deposing five sultans, until Mahmud II eliminated them and introduced far-ranging religious, legal, and military reforms.

Abdulhamid II (1842–1918) introduced the first constitution (1876) but later suspended it (1878) and ruled through autocratic despotism enforced by secret police. His reign saw the Armenian massacres (1895–1896). The rise of the Young Turk nationalist society, in response to the sultan's autocracy, caused him to reinstate the constitution in 1908.

Taking advantage of Ottoman military and administrative reorganization, a Russian aggressive move in 1826 enabled the Egyptian Pasa Mehmet, in a bid for independence, to strike northward through Palestine and Syria to central Anatolia. The British fleet ensured a reversion almost to the status quo, but the Ottoman empire's weakness was evident. Russia used religion to foment discontent among Orthodox Christian Ottoman subjects; Russia's massive defeat in the Crimean War (1854–1856) did not deter the Russian invasion of Ottoman Bulgaria in 1877. By the terms of the Conference of Berlin (1878), the Ottomans lost more territory: Romania and Bulgaria became independent, and Bosnia and Herzegovina went to Austria.

Britain moved in to guarantee the empire's borders in exchange for Cyprus and occupied Egypt to suppress nationalist unrest and maintain the route to India (1882). Uneasy peace ensued until eventually the Young Turk movement deposed the sultan and imposed constitutional government under the military triumvirate of Talat Pasa, Cemal Pasa, and Enver Pasa (1908). The Young Turks, crushing all opposition, disastrously led the empire on the losing side in the Balkan wars and World War I. Following the War of Independence (1919–1922), the new republican government, under Mustafa Kemal Ataturk (1881–1938), abolished the sultanate on 1 November 1922.

Character of the Ottoman State

The Ottoman state was organized around the idea of Islamic conquest of Christian states, and its military was based on a unique slave army called the *devshirme*. Christian boys were converted to Islam and educated for the select Janissary forces and for the civil service. Military fief holders *(sipahi)* served as cavalry in exchange for the revenue of their estates. After Suleyman, overpopulation, currency devaluation, and tribalism began to fragment the state.

During the early reigns, monopolies of silks, cottons, and metals brought prosperity, but the empire failed to enter an industrial age, relying on favorable tariffs to encourage imports and exports and, in the nineteenth century, on foreign contractors for the construction of railways and telegraph systems. Massive overspending, largely on trappings of royalty, led to debt restructuring and put large parts of the taxation system in foreign hands (1881).

Despite their belief in the mission of Islamic conquest of Christian states, the Ottomans adopted an enlightened policy of encouraging the coexistence of *millets* (self-governing communities of coreligionists) in the state. Each *millet*'s religious leader administered his community's legal and educational systems and collected a capitation tax for the Ottoman government in lieu of military service. Many Christian churches continued in use, although construction of new ones was forbidden until the nineteenth century. Forced population movements created enclaves of skilled Christian craftspeople, especially until the sixteenth century; it was Ottoman policy to move captured people in accordance with the political and economic needs of the empire.

Islam in the Ottoman Empire

From 1517, when the Ottomans conquered Mecca and Medina, the sultan was also nominally caliph, or leader of the faithful, and the Ottoman empire acquired theoretical leadership privileges over all Sunni Muslim states. The ulama, or religious hierarchy of mullahs, supported the sultan by validating his actions under Islamic law. Religious charitable foundations *(vakif)* provided mosques, schools, and hospital complexes supported by an income from trade. Pan Islamism as an ideology was not actively promoted until the time of Abdulhamid II; this movement, along with the Greek War of Independence, missionary activity, discriminatory taxes favoring Christians, and concessions made by the Tanzimat (reform) movement, led to Muslim resentment against Christian minorities.

Ottoman Culture

Ottoman art ignored the Muslim prohibition against depicting the human form and continued the Persian tradition of miniature painting and the Seljuk tradition of pottery and tile decoration. The imperial mosques, built by the famous architect Sinan (1489–1588), set the standard for later Turkish religious architecture. Sinan's mosques, finished with marble, Iznik tiles, and carving, and filled with rare carpets, are as impressive as Hagia Sophia; later Ottoman palaces were Victorian Gothic fantasies in white marble and glass set in tulip-filled gardens. Poetry was based on Persian models; the court spoke and wrote Arabic, Persian, Greek, and Turkish. The language of officialdom was Ottoman Turkish.

Impact of Ottoman Rule

The Ottoman empire united under one banner and under a fair system of government the rival monotheistic religions and many Indo-European and Turkish ethnic groups in an impressive and unequaled example of tolerance. Although it had been eroded by Russian and European aggression, at its end the empire included Syria and Arabia, present-day Libya and Rhodes, and parts of the Balkans. The last parliament of the Ottoman administration (1909) included 147 Turks, 60 Arabs, 27 Albanians, 26 Greeks, 14 Armenians, 10 Slavs, and 2 Jews. Foreign pressures and promotion of nationalist prejudices eroded the basis of this society; loss of this cultural diversity has proved to be a tragic legacy for modern Turkey's culture and economy.

Kate Clow

Further Reading

Kinross, Patrick. (1977) *The Ottoman Centuries.* New York: Morrow Quill.

Lewis, Bernard. (1982) *The Muslim Discovery of Europe.* London: George Weidenfeld and Nicolson.

Wheatcroft, Andrew. (1994) *The Ottomans.* London: Penguin Books.

OVERSEAS ECONOMIC COOPERATION FUND

OVERSEAS ECONOMIC COOPERATION FUND The Overseas Economic Cooperation Fund (OECF; in Japanese, Kaigai Keizai Kyoryoku Kikin) was Japan's primary bilateral official development assistance (ODA) loan facility. It was established in 1961 as a public agency *(tokushu hojin)* under the formal supervision of the Economic Planning Agency. In 1999, it was consolidated with the Japan Export-Import Bank to form the Japan Bank for International Cooperation (JBIC). At its inception, the OECF was intended to promote the development of new sources of raw materials for Japan by extending project loans to Japanese firms and taking equity positions in their resource development projects. In 1965, the task of giving ODA loans to developing country governments was added to the original OECF mandate.

Financed mainly by Japan's so-called second budget, the OECF grew to be the single largest source of bilateral ODA in the world, providing some 40 percent of Japan's $15 billion in ODA spending in 1999. Its consolidation with the Japan Export-Import Bank was the result of administrative reform efforts to streamline government by reducing the number of government agencies and corporations. Folding OECF into JBIC is expected to weaken Japan's ability to manage its ODA as a distinctive policy area with special needs, but it should improve its ability to coordinate its ODA lending with other forms of development finance.

David Arase

Further Reading

Arase, David. (1995) *Buying Power: The Political Economy of Japan's Foreign Aid.* Boulder, CO: Lynne Rienner.

Overseas Economic Cooperation Fund. (1982) *OECF 20-nen shi* (A History of OECF's Twenty Years). Tokyo: Overseas Economic Cooperation Fund.

OZAL, TURGUT

OZAL, TURGUT (1927–1993), Turkish politician. Turgut Ozal was one of the most controversial political leaders in Turkey. He was born in Malatya, a southeastern province of Turkey; his father was a minor bureaucrat and his mother an elementary school teacher. Ozal studied at the Istanbul Technical University on a government scholarship. After graduation, he worked at the Electrical Power Resources Survey and Development Administration and was then sent to the United States for further training.

On his return he worked at the State Planning Organization (SPO) in lieu of mandatory military service and in 1996 became the head of the SPO. Following the Turkish army's 1971 military intervention into the government, Ozal left Turkey for a position with the World Bank. He returned to Turkey in 1973 to work in the private sector.

His first political encounter was with the National Salvation Party. He was defeated as a parliamentary candidate from the Izmir district in the 1977 general election. In the Justice Party minority government of 1980, Ozal was appointed acting head of the State Planning Organization and minister of state in charge of economic affairs. He implemented the 24 January measures, which promoted less governmental control over the economy, devaluation of the Turkish currency, reform of the taxation system, liberalization of interest rates, and price increases.

Following the 1980 military intervention, the junta leaders appointed Ozal deputy prime minister responsible for the economy. He resigned from this post in 1982 due to the failure of his free-market policies, especially the liberation of interest rates, which led to the so-called banker scandal. The collapse of the system of independent money brokers, whereby individuals collected money at enormously high interest rates, caused thousands of people to lose their savings.

Ozal returned to politics in the 1983 general election. The military junta allowed only three parties to participate, one of them being Ozal's Motherland Party, which won 45 percent of the vote. Ozal's tenure as prime minister lasted ninety-six months. In 1989, after Kenan Evren's term of presidency ended, Ozal was elected the eighth president of the Turkish Republic. During his presidency he expanded the powers of his office to give the president greater authority in domestic and foreign policy. He held this post until his death in April 1993.

Ozal was a conservative and a defender of the free-market economic model that favored minimal state intervention in the economy. Privatization was a main element of his platform. While some praised him as a champion of freedom, his critics argued that he allowed the police and security forces to disregard human rights and turned a blind eye to bribes and corruption.

H. Ayla Kilic

Further Reading

Emin, Fatih. (1993) *Turgut Ozal, 1983–1993.* Istanbul, Turkey: Risale

Gokmen, Yavuz. (1992) *Ozal Sendromu* (The Ozal Syndrome). Ankara, Turkey: V. Yayinlari.

PACHINKO Along remote paddies and in the heart of Tokyo, neon lights pulse. Inside, day and night, thousands test their luck and skill at what could be called Japan's national pastime: pachinko.

Pachinko is an electric pinball game modeled after American mechanical versions from the early 1900s. In those mechanical models, players physically flipped a switch to propel small steel balls upward. The balls bounced off pins before falling into slots. A winning slot would produce more balls for play. A losing slot would swallow up the balls until the player had none left. Today's electric-powered models add more lights and flash and allow players to simply hold a knob steady in order to shoot the steel balls. Otherwise, however, pachinko rules remain the same.

Pachinko machines first found their way to Japan in the cosmopolitan years of the 1920s. However, because Western-inspired activities were increasingly discouraged during the war years of the next two decades, the game fell out of favor. In the postwar years, however, the populace craved new leisure activities. The first commercial pachinko parlor was opened in Nagoya in 1948. From there, parlors spread rapidly around the nation. Today, pachinko parlors can be found even in remote rural villages, and it is estimated that as many as one-quarter of the population ventures into the ear-shattering din of pachinko parlors at least occasionally. Particularly avid players dedicate their time to pachinko parlors as they would to a job. However, although the payoffs can be great, so can the losses.

Technically, gambling for cash payoffs is illegal. Players awarded bucket loads of winning pachinko balls take their winnings to a counter inside the parlor and receive small gifts such as chocolate bars or imitation gold bullion. It is commonly understood, however, that at a nearby offsite location, players can exchange their winning trinkets for real cash. As such, the pachinko industry is, in reality, a flourishing illegality mostly overlooked by law enforcement. Underworld connections to certain pachinko chains and illegal tax dodges have also brought disrepute to the business end of pachinko. Further, as in other gambling industries, pachinko has its fair share of addiction. It is clear from its ubiquitous presence, however, that pachinko remains a popular leisure activity in Japan, enjoyed by young and old, men and women, and persons from all walks of life.

Ann D. Brucklacher

Further Reading

Kiritani, Elizabeth. (1993) "Pachinko." In *Japan: An Illustrated Encyclopedia.* Tokyo: Kodansha.

———. (1994) "Pachinko: Japan's National Pastime." *Mangajin* 34 (April): 10–62.

Schilling, Mark. (1997) *Encyclopedia of Japanese Pop Culture.* New York: Weatherhill.

Tanioka Ichiro. (2000) *Pachinko and the Japanese Society: Legal and Socio-Economic Considerations.* Trans. by Osawa Minae, Madeleine Vedal, and Okamoto Miki. Osaka, Japan: Institute of Amusement Industries.

PACIFIC OCEAN The Pacific Ocean is the world's largest body of water, occupying almost one-third of the Earth's surface. It is about 155.5 million square kilometers (60 million square miles) in area, with a coastline of 135,663 kilometers (84,300 miles). It contains about 25,000 islands, most of them south of the equator. The ocean's average depth is 4,270 meters (14,000 feet); water temperature varies from freezing to about 29°C (84°F). The Pacific Ocean influences the climate of the surrounding land; much of Pacific Asia lies in the monsoon region and has distinct rainy and dry seasons. Tropical cyclones, or typhoons, are common. The Pacific Ocean's greatest resource is its fish (more than 60 percent of the world's fish catch); other important resources include petroleum, natural gas, minerals, and pearls. The eighteen members of Asia Pacific Economic Cooperation, an association of Pacific Rim nations, represent over half the world's gross national product, and trade among them represents more than 40 percent of world trade. Major Asian Pacific ports include Bangkok, Hong Kong, Kaohsiung, Manila, Pusan, Shanghai, Singapore, Vladivostok, and Yokohama. Contemporary issues in the Pacific include concerns over pollution and endangered marine animals, and disputes over fishing and territorial claims.

Michael Pretes

Further Reading

Lal, Brij Vilash, and Kate Fortune, eds. (2000) *The Pacific Islands: An Encyclopedia*. Honolulu: University of Hawaii Press.

Spate, Oskar. (1988) *Paradise Found and Lost*. Canberra, Australia: Australian National University Press.

PACIFIC RIM The region of land that surrounds the Pacific Ocean is called the Pacific Rim and includes more than thirty nations in Asia, Oceania, and North and South America. About 2.5 billion people live in this region, which is four-tenths of the population of the world, and the total gross domestic product in this region, which includes the two economic superpowers (the United States and Japan), accounted for 56 percent of the world gross domestic product in 1996. Now, economic growth in developing Asian nations is making the rest of the world pay more attention to this region, and this attention has led to a large-scale economic forum, the Asia-Pacific Economic Cooperation (APEC), which includes most of the nations of the Pacific Rim.

Furthermore, with the strengthening trend of bilateral trade and investment in this region, the term "Pacific Rim" no longer represents solely the geography of a region. In the period 1981–1983, 60 percent of all exports from APEC member nations were to the other APEC member nations. This figure increased to 69 percent in 1991–1993 and 71 percent in 1997. As for imports, they also increased, from 61 percent in 1981–1983 to 71 percent in 1991–1993 to 72 percent in 1997.

However, the continuing change in the balance of power between the United States and China and the increasing independence of Southeast Asian nations from the United States have led to less regional integration among North and South America, Southeast Asia, and Northeast Asia. This situation was accelerated by U.S. policies implemented during the Asian economic crisis in the late 1990s.

The emergence of the Pacific Rim as a major economic region represents a major shift in the world's regional power distribution. In the twentieth century, economic and political power resided in the nations on or near the Atlantic Ocean—Great Britain, the United States, France, and Germany. Earlier, economic power had been concentrated in Europe. The unification of Europe as the European Union is, in part, an effort to compete with Asia and the Pacific Rim.

Hiroshi Ohnishi

Further Reading

Flynn, Dennis O., Lionel Frost, and A. J. H. Lathan, eds. (1999) *Pacific Centuries: Pacific and Pacific Rim History since the Sixteenth Century*. New York: Routledge.

Simon, Denis Fred, ed. (1995) *Cooperation Strategies in the Pacific Rim: Global versus Regional Trends*. New York: Routledge.

PADRI WAR The Padri (or Paderi) War lasted from 1821 to 1837 and arose from a movement among the Minangkabau people of the central western coast of Sumatra both to purify Islamic practice and resist colonial rule. The Minangkabau social structure was matrilineal and highly decentralized. Their official ruler, the raja of Pagaruyung, had only nominal authority, while village chiefs *(panghulu)* held real power. In the early nineteenth century, Minangkabau believers returning from the hajj pilgrimage to Mecca brought back ideas of purifying the Islamic faith of their people. This involved eschewing traditional syncretic folk beliefs, gambling, drinking, and drug taking, and seeking to end their matrilineal traditions. The name of the movement was derived from Pedir, from where the pilgrims set sail for Arabia. The movement declared a jihad (holy war), and its followers imitated the purification movement of the Wahhabi of Arabia by wearing white robes and turbans. Poorer people were attracted to the movement, and as it acquired strength, political power resulted through influence on local village leaders. In particular, fines were levied for breaking the prohibitions of Islam. The new movement began to clash with the *panghulu*; even the raja was endangered, and most of the royal family was murdered in 1815.

While the British interregnum in the Dutch East Indies, under Sir Stamford Raffles, tolerated the movement, the Dutch return to Sumatra in 1819 altered the situation. The traditional leaders aligned themselves with the Dutch after war broke out in February 1821; however, they lost legitimacy in the eyes of the Minangkabau for this alliance—disastrous for their long-term survival. While Dutch troops were able to control the Padri movement, they refused to reinstate the displaced Minangkabau raja, establishing a Dutch regency instead. Inevitably this created more sympathy for the Padri movement, as some traditional leaders reconciled with Islamic forces. This allowed the Padri leader, Tuanku Imam Bonjol, to resist the Dutch in the city of Bonjol for fifteen years. The Dutch reached an understanding with Bonjol in order to conclude another war (1825–1830) on nearby Java. The final siege of Bonjol lasted months, due to the ferocious resistance of the residents. With the city of Bonjol destroyed and Iman Bonjol exiled elsewhere in the Indies, sporadic warfare occurred in the mountains for years afterwards. The Padri War is a classic case of how the Dutch exploited intracommunity divisions gradually to assume control of the entire archipelago.

Anthony L. Smith

Further Reading

Ricklefs, M. C. (1993) *A History of Modern Indonesia since c. 1300*. 2d ed. London: Macmillan Press.

Tarling, Nicholas, ed. (1992) *The Cambridge History of Southeast Asia, The Nineteenth and Twentieth Centuries*. Vol. 2. Cambridge, U.K.: Cambridge University Press.

PAGAN

PAGAN The city of Pagan (also spelled Bagan), the first capital of the Burman kings, is situated in central Burma (now Myanmar) in a sharp bend of the Irrawaddy River. The city was also known as Arimaddanapura, "the city that is a crusher of enemies," in the Pali language. Containing more than five thousand stupas and temples, the city is evidence of the architectural skill and religious worship of the Burmese. Pagan was founded in 849 BCE and became the capital of the Pagan dynasty (1044–1300) under King Anawrahta (1044–1077), during whose reign most construction took place. Pagan achieved its power by combining Burman military might, Mon architectual and artisan skills, and Indian Brahman political influence and by consolidating Theravada Buddhism with indigenous *nat* (spirit) worship. The largest and most important structures include the Mingalazedi (Blessing Stupa), Ananda Paya, and the Shwesandaw Paya. The city went into decline around 1234 under a series of weak kings. Mongol invasions from the north around 1287 led to the further decline of the city and its virtual abandonment. An earthquake in 1975 caused major damage to many of Pagan's structures, but restoration work has been largely successful in maintaining the city. Pagan is now the most visited tourist site in Myanmar.

Michael Pretes

Further Reading

Aung-Thwin, Michael. (1985) *Pagan: The Origins of Modern Burma*. Honolulu: University of Hawaii Press.

Htin Aung, Maung. (1967) *A History of Burma*. New York: Columbia University Press.

Strachan, Paul. (1990) *Imperial Pagan: Art and Architecture of Old Burma*. Honolulu: University of Hawaii Press.

PAGODAS, BURMESE

PAGODAS, BURMESE Myanmar (Burma) has thousands of religious structures—pagodas, temples, monasteries, ordination halls, nunneries, and resthouses. Many are of great antiquity; in Pagan, the ancient capital, no less than 2,217 religious structures are to be found in a sixteen-square-mile area. The most sacred of these, and the most subject to pilgrimage, are undoubtedly pagodas. Pagodas are technically better known as stupas, cone-shaped monumental structures built in memory of Buddha and often enshrining relics alleged to be of the Buddha himself or sacred images of him. In Burmese, pagodas are closely identified with the Buddha; the term is the same for both—*hpaya*. Unlike the temple, which usually has interior space, the pagoda consists mostly of a solid monument with little or no usable interior space. It is commonly surrounded, however, by ample platform space for worship and many ancillary buildings. The Shwezigon Pagoda in Pagan is where Anawratha placed the thirty-seven spirits *(nat)* at the foot of the pagoda, turning them into a coherent cult that defers to the Buddha. The Shwedagon Pagoda, north of Yangon (formerly Rangoon), is one of the largest and tallest pagodas in the world, and it attracts large numbers of pilgrims. Pagodas, and control over them, are deeply political—freedom fighters, such as Aung San (1915–1947) and his daughter Aung San Suu Kyi (b. 1945), gave their speeches there, and most kings and politicians of renown in Myanmar have built pagodas or have aspired to do so. It is assumed that the building of a

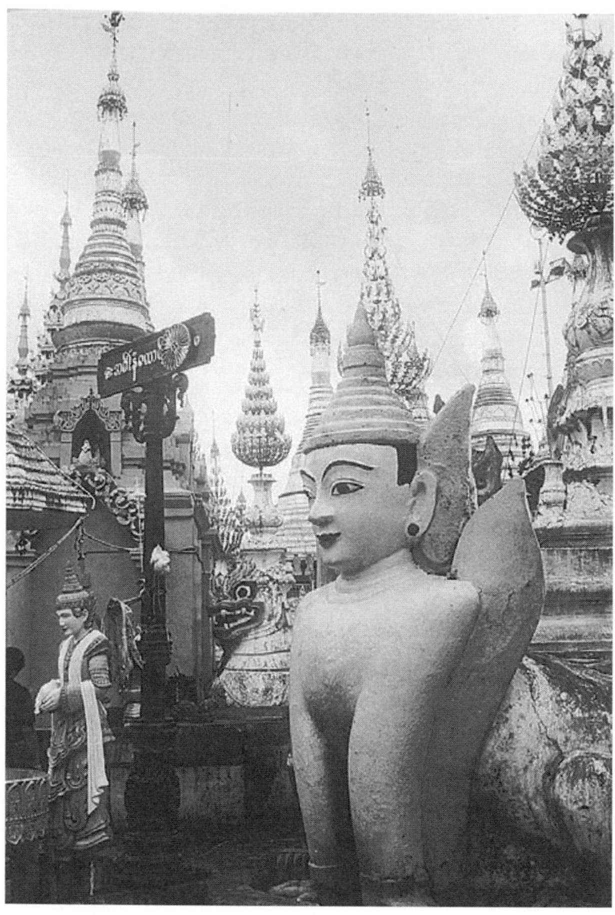

Personal deities and pagodas at the Shwedagon Pagoda in Yangon in 1996. (STEPHEN G. DONALDSON PHOTOGRAPHY)

pagoda would establish the builder on the path to *nibbana* (nirvana).

Gustaaf Houtman

Further Reading

Auboyer, Jeannine, et al. (1994) "Burma." In *Forms and Styles: Asia.* Cologne, Germany: Benedikt Taschen Verlag, 131–159.

Falconer, John, et al., and Kim Inglis, eds. (1998) *Myanmar Style: Art, Architecture, and Design of Burma.* Hong Kong: Periplus.

Shwedagon: Symbol of Strength and Serenity. (1997) Yangon, Myanmar: Yangon City Development Committee.

PAHANG (2002 est. pop. 1.3 million). Pahang, the largest state in Malaysia, is located in the east coast region. It covers an area of 35,965 square kilometers and has a population of approximately 1.3 million—74 percent Malay, 19 percent Chinese, 6 percent Indian, and 1 percent others. Kuantan, the state capital, is both a commercial center and a popular seaside resort. Gunung Tahan, the highest peak in the Malay Peninsula, forms a natural divider between east and west Pahang. Pahang is rich in natural resources, and two-thirds of the state are covered by rich tropical forest.

Pahang had always been a vassal until the end of the nineteenth century. As early as 1275, Java claimed Pahang as one of her dependencies. It paid tribute to Siam in the fourteenth century and Melaka in the 1450s. It came under the direct rule of the Johor sultanate in 1641 for two centuries. In 1858, the death of the *bendahara* (chief minister) Ali of Pahang resulted in a five-year civil war between his two sons that ended when the youngest, Wan Ahmad, declared himself *bendahara* in 1863. He assumed the title of sultan in 1881.

British intervention in the Malay States began around the 1870s. By 1887, Sultan Ahmad was persuaded to accept a British consul general, Sir Hugh Clifford. However, the atmosphere in Pahang grew tense between the British and the Malays. In 1888, the killing of a British Chinese subject compelled the sultan to accept a British resident. The role of the resident was to advise the sultan on how to improve the administration of his state. Although the resident was to have no executive powers, his advice had to be sought and implemented on all questions other than those touching on Malay religion and custom. It was a system used to exercise British influence over the Malay States. The three general aims were the establishment of law and order, the centralized collection of revenue, and the development of the resources of the states.

However, disputes and rebellions against the British, which became known as the Pahang War, dragged on until 1895, when Clifford forced the rebels to Kelantan, where they were eventually arrested. In 1896, Pahang became one of the Federated Malay States, along with Perak, Selangor, and Negeri Sembilan. In 1948, the Federated Malay States became part of the Federation of Malaya. The federation gained independence from British colonial rule in 1957. Together with Sabah and Sarawak, the federation formed Malaysia in 1963.

Yik Koon Teh

Further Reading

Andaya, Barbara Watson, and Leonard Y. Andaya. (1982) *A History of Malaysia.* London: Macmillan Press.

Eliot, Joshua, and Jane Bickersteth, eds. (1995) *Indonesia, Malaysia and Singapore Handbook.* Bath, U.K.: Trade and Travel Publications.

Linehan, W. (1973) *A History of Pahang.* Kuala Lumpur, Malaysia: The Malaysian Branch of the Royal Asiatic Society.

Ryan, N. J. (1969) *The Making of Modern Malaysia and Singapore: A History from Earliest Times to 1966.* Kuala Lumpur, Malaysia: Oxford University Press.

Winstedt, Richard O. (1982) *A History of Malaya.* Kuala Lumpur, Malaysia: Marican & Sons

———. (1966) *Malaya and Its History.* London: Hutchinson & Co.

PAHARI The Pahari, an ethnic group in northern South Asia numbering about 17 million, are culturally and linguistically distinct from their neighbors to the north and south. They live in a crescent-shaped area of the lower Himalayas extending from Kashmir to central Nepal and bordered on the south by the Indo-Gangetic Plain. They speak Pahari, an Indo-European language, which differs in dialect from east to west.

The Pahari live near water sources in small villages of around three hundred people. Men build and maintain the rows of rectangular, multistory houses of stone and adobe with traditional, ornately carved doors and appointments. They also maintain the livestock, which live on the ground floor of houses, near the kitchen and central living area. Hillsides are terraced and irrigated for agriculture, the Pahari's main economic activity. Wheat and barley are grown in the spring, and millet, maize, lentils, vegetables, and wet and dry rice are grown in the fall. Secondary income comes from the sale of buffalo- and cattle-milk products to neighboring populations as well as the sale of ginger, apricots, apples, and opium.

Pahari social organization is based on a hierarchical, male-centered, in-marrying caste system. Of the three caste categories (varnas) with descending orders of ritual purity in India—the Brahmans (priestly castes), the Kshatriya (royal, administrative, and warrior castes), and the Achut (performers of the most polluting tasks)—about 75 to 90 percent of the Pahari are Kshatriya. The Brahmans and Kshatriya own most of the land, and the low castes are their landless bonded labor. Only heads of high-caste households sit on village councils. These councils rule on matters of policy and social control. They also adjudicate cases of low-caste dispute and infraction. Commonly, punishment is violent physical sanction.

The governments of Kashmir, Himachal Pradesh, Uttar Pradesh, and Nepal allow elected Paharis to sit on governmental committees that deal with official matters. The Achut caste and women have seats reserved for them on these councils. Pahari women are active in economic and religious activities and in social relationships within villages. They work in agriculture, prepare all food, and handle household duties. Marriage takes place near the time of puberty, with a bride-price paid to the bride's family. Men are allowed to take more than one wife, although this option is practically open only to wealthy men. Women can divorce their husbands, although a woman must return the bride-price and forfeit her children to her husband. Children are raised together, despite sex, in a permissive, relaxed, and primarily female environment. At the age of eight, male children transfer to male care. High-caste boys are the only Pahari children who receive formal education.

Although overwhelmingly Hindu, Pahari religious traditions reflect their alpine existence. The Pahari virtually ignore Hindu dietary restrictions (except for the ban on beef), a number of great deities, most purity rituals, and caste-based restrictions on women. Animal sacrifice is still practiced, and Brahman priests, shamans, diviners, exorcists, and curers of either sex are all active in Pahari villages. Medicine incorporates herbal and ritual specialists, Ayurvedic medicine, and Western science to battle illness and disease. Nevertheless, the mortality rate (especially among infants) is extremely high.

Stephanie L. Ware

Further Reading

Berreman, Gerald D. (1972) *Hindus of the Himalayas: Ethnography and Change.* 2d ed. Berkeley and Los Angeles: University of California Press.

Raha, Manis Kumar, ed. (1987) *The Himalayan Heritage.* Delhi: Gian Publishing House.

PAHLAVI DYNASTY The reign of the Pahlavi dynasty (1925–1979) was a crucial and transitional period in Iranian history that began with Reza Shah Pahlavi (1878–1944) and ended with his son, Mohammad Reza Shah Pahlavi (1919–1980). For Iran, this was a time of rapid Westernization, secularization, and foreign influence, all of which ultimately contributed to the government's demise. Many of the sweeping changes introduced by the Pahlavis were unacceptable to the population, particularly to the religious community, and after the fall of the dynasty a conservative backlash erased most of the Pahlavi achievements.

Reza Shah Pahlavi

Known as Reza Khan, Reza Shah Pahlavi rose to power through the military, where he followed in the footsteps of his father, also a military officer. Reza Khan attained the position of colonel when he became

Mohammad Reza Shah Pahlavi and Queen Saroya in Tehran in July 1951. (BETTMANN/CORBIS)

commander of the elite Cossack Brigade. In February 1921, with the support of Britain, Reza Khan's forces marched into the capital and pressured the ruler of that time, Ahmad Shah Qajar, to appoint Sayyid Zia ad Din Tabatabai premier. Later Reza Khan was himself appointed premier after serving as defense minister. Due to his military victories Reza Khan was initially popular with the people, and as a result the *Majlis* (Parliament) eventually removed Qajar from power and named Reza Khan first regent (October 1925). Within two months he had been declared *shah-en-shah* (king of kings) of Iran. In spring 1925 Reza Shah chose Pahlavi (the name of the Middle Persian language used in the seventh century, particularly in Zoroastrian texts) as his family name. With this symbolic gesture he began the Pahlavi dynasty, representing Persian rule over the Persian people after many centuries of foreign dynasties.

During his reign Reza Shah worked to modernize Iran and to strengthen its economy and transportation system by using the funds generated by oil revenues. He increased revenues by raising tariffs on imports, revoking the economic concessions previously given to European countries, and in 1932 insisting that the Anglo-Persian Oil Company increase oil royalties to Iran and decrease the company's concessionaire area by 80 percent. He created a national civil service and a police force and built 22,400 kilometers of roads as well as the Trans-Iranian Railway. This improvement in the transportation infrastructure was intended to strengthen the economy by fostering industrialization.

In terms of the cultural and religious environment of Iran's society, Reza Shah swung the pendulum from Islamic traditions to secularism. He reduced the number of clerics in the *Majlis* from 40 percent to zero over the course of elections. He increased the powers of the secular state courts while diminishing those of the Islamic law courts. In an effort to homogenize the diverse population, he instituted a law requiring all men to wear Western-style clothes, and he required all public places and educational organizations to be opened to women. As might be expected, these rapidly introduced Westernizing policies were not welcomed by the religious community.

Events outside the country led Reza Shah to hand over control to his son in 1941. Reza Shah had began to disrupt Britain's and Russia's political and economic hold on Iran by building ties to Germany in the 1930s. He declared Iran a neutral country when World War

II broke out, because Germany had become a major Iranian trade partner by that time. This neutrality, however, was not respected by Britain and Russia, whose troops invaded Iran in August 1941 on five fronts. Reza Shah was forced to abdicate in favor of his oldest son, Mohammad Reza, who came to power on 16 September 1941. Reza Shah left Iran for Mauritius and ultimately for South Africa, where he died in 1944.

Mohammad Reza Shah Pahlavi

Although his father had relinquished the throne, his son held power mainly due to the presence of British and Russian troops in Iran. Mohammad Reza Shah Pahlavi, known as "the Shah," was forced to permit the foreign troops to use Iranian territory as needed during World War II while the Shah worked to gain support from his people, including the disaffected clerics who had disliked his father's secular policies. When the war ended, first the British and then the Soviet troops withdrew from Iran in 1946. The latter forces, however, left the monarch to deal with Russian-incited and -supported uprisings in Kurdistan and Azerbaijan. The goal of both uprisings was to establish political autonomy for the rebels, but successful containment of these rebellions at last established the Shah's control over all of Iran.

Mohammad Reza Pahlavi ruled as an absolute dictator, partly in response to an attempt on his life in February 1949. The rapid movement toward modernization that he fostered, along with his powerful security buildup, his authoritarian rule, the growing distance between rich and poor, and opposition by the religious community led to his eventual overthrow.

A showdown with Iran's premier, Mohammad Mosaddeq (1880–1967), compelled the Shah to nationalize the British-owned Anglo-Iranian Oil Company in 1951. In 1953, further disputes with Mosaddeq forced the Shah to flee to Rome, but the United States and Great Britain used the Central Intelligence Agency (CIA) and the British MI6 to bring about a pro-Shah coup. With Mosaddeq overthrown, the Shah returned to Iran.

Previously Russia and Britain had been the main outsiders involved in the power struggles in Iran, but the United States became the dominant actor in the region following the 1953 coup. The Shah encouraged this influence by brokering several economic and political deals with the United States. The National Iranian Oil Company gave U.S. companies a contract to run Iran's petroleum industry. Iran joined the pro-Western Baghdad Pact in 1955 and agreed to adhere to the Eisenhower Doctrine in 1957. To silence internal opposition, the Shah created the Savak (*Sazman-e Amniyat Va Ittilaat-e Keshvar*—Organization of National Security and Intelligence), a secret security and intelligence force with strong connections to the CIA and to Israel's Mossad. In 1962, the Shah instituted a major land reform by allotting peasants land formerly in private hands; in 1951, he had begun to turn royal lands over to small farmers. Nevertheless the lives of most people did not benefit from the Shah's innovations; such luxuries as electricity and access to adequate health care were not available to them.

The U.S. influence in Iranian affairs created resentment and opposition. The Shah decided to dissolve the *Majlis* so that he could rule by decree and avoid opposition to his policies, an act that further alienated the population. In early 1963, the Shah introduced an economic and social program called the White Revolution, which apparently received 91 percent approval, mainly because the regime had ruthlessly quashed the opposition. Ayatollah Ruhollah Khomeini (1900?–1989) was particularly vocal in his objection to this program and was arrested as a result. The Shah had to use excessive force to quell riots that broke out in protest to the ayatollah's imprisonment, but this action caused a worldwide reaction. Human-rights organizations and Western governments pressured the Shah to adhere to democratic principles. When the Shah loosened his iron fist, the ayatollah's supporters regained strength, and the monarch exiled Khomeini.

Mohammad Reza Shah Pahlavi and Iran grew increasingly important as the Middle East oil-producing countries made themselves felt internationally. As Iran's stature grew internationally, opposition to the Shah by the religious conservatives also grew. With Iran's oil revenues, the Shah launched ambitious economic five-year plans for rapid economic development in the agricultural and industrial sectors. Rapid growth, however, also resulted in housing shortages, inflation, pollution, and corruption; the distance between the wealthy few, including the Shah and his family, who enjoyed a luxurious lifestyle, and the rest of the population grew greater. In the 1970s, the religious opposition managed to infiltrate the military and to bring the oil industry to a standstill through massive strikes. The Shah finally tried to placate the opposition by appointing one of their own, Shahpur Bakhtiar, as prime minister, but this effort was seen as too little too late.

Under the guise of taking a vacation in Egypt, the Shah left Iran on 16 January 1979. Soon after, Ayatollah Khomeini returned to Iran and established the Islamic Republic regime. The Pahlavi dynasty came to an end, along with a 2,500-year-old tradition of monarchy in Iran. The ayatollah insisted on extraditing the Shah, who had secretly entered the United States for medical treatment, but the United States denied his demand. Escalating hostility between the two countries led to the taking of hostages in the U.S. embassy in Tehran. In early 1980, after months of traveling from country to country in search of a place to stay, the Shah went to Cairo at the invitation of the Egyptian president Anwar Sadat and died soon after.

Houman A. Sadri

See also: **Islamic Revolution**

Further Reading

Cleveland, William L. (1994) *A History of the Modern Middle East*. Boulder, CO: Westview Press.

Graham, Robert. (1978) *The Illusion of Power*. London: Croom Helm.

Pahlavi, Mohammad Reza. (1980) *Answer to History*. New York: Stein and Day.

Saikad, Amin. (1980) *The Rise and Fall of the Shah*. Princeton, NJ: Princeton University Press.

PAIK, NAM JUNE (b. 1932), Korean-born artist. Nam June Paik is recognized worldwide as the father of video art. He has produced a large number of video art works using television as a creative medium and diverting it from its conventional position and connotation.

Paik lived in Germany in the early 1960s and was an important member of the post–neo-Dada collective Fluxus. He was inspired by the Fluxus group's concert-based style, where different elements are referred to, including sounds, objects, and objects that produce sound. Through his own avant-garde works, Paik devoted himself to breaking down the barriers between high art and pop culture and to linking the world of art, media, technology, pop culture, and the avant-garde.

In 1963, Paik produced his first musical and video work, using a revolutionary way of electromagnetically deforming pictures. He was also the first artist to take advantage of Sony's portable video kit, the "portapak," with which he filmed Pope Paul VI's 1964 visit to New York. Paik showed the recording the same evening at the Café à Gogo. Paik's work calls into question the communication codes of a society accustomed to the institutional style of television and suggested an alternative type of television. In 1977, he conducted experiments with satellite transmission and sculpted constructions with stacked TV monitors that formed a monumental pyramid, a robot, and an aquarium. One of his impressive cybernetic installation works is *The More the Better*, produced in 1988, a media tower composed of 1,003 TV monitors, for the Seoul Olympic Games. The provocative and prophetic style of Paik's video installation has contributed to the creation and development of a new trend in postmodern art around the world.

Seong-Sook Yim

Further Reading

Hanhardt, John G. (1982) *Nam June Paik*. New York: Whitney Museum of American Art, in association with W. W. Norton.

Stooss, Toni, and Thomas Kellen. (1993) *Nam June Paik: Video Time, Video Space*. New York: H. N. Abrams.

PAINTING—CHINA In Chinese culture, painting joins poetry and calligraphy as one of the "three perfections" of the scholar-gentleman. These three art forms use essentially the same materials: ink, brush, and silk or paper and depend on line to give expression to ideas. Of these materials, the brush is of greatest importance, particularly in painting and calligraphy, where the quality of the line is essential. The brush's flexibility, thickness, and readiness to absorb the ink contribute to the great variety of strokes an artist can achieve.

Early Chinese Painting

Evidence of painting in China appears as early as the Neolithic age in the swirling abstract patterns found on Yangshao painted pottery. In the Shang (1766–1045 BCE) and Zhou (1045–256 BCE) dynasties, bronze decor offers information on the further development of pictorial art. These images and patterns were symbolic and were thought to carry special powers. It was at this time that wall paintings were also produced. Though the archaeological remains are few and fragmentary, early texts confirm that surfaces were covered in painted designs. Painting was found in other media as well: During the Warring States period (475–221 BCE), painted lacquers and silks, especially those found in tombs from the state of Chu, reflect the energy devoted to the development of regional artistic styles.

Han Dynasty

During the Han dynasty (206 BCE–220 CE), painting in China came into its own. The Han inherited the practice of painting murals from its predecessors in the Warring States (475–221 BCE) and Qin dynasty (221–206 BCE). Owing to the increasing influence of

Confucian thought, the subjects of Han painting included models of proper moral and social behavior. Unfortunately, much of what is known about painting is found only in written records: extant visual evidence of painting is provided by the stone reliefs, tomb murals, pictorial clay tiles, painted lacquer, and only a few paintings on silk. Among the most important finds are the paintings from the tombs at Mawangdui in Changsha, Hunan. The well-known T-shaped silk banner shows images from Chinese mythology as well as from the realm of humans.

Stone and clay tile reliefs, though different from paintings, give a more complete sense of the Han dynasty use of pictorial space. Confucian themes, interest in the afterlife, and human activity are found on the incised, stamped, or molded tomb decorations. These, in conjunction with the fragmentary paintings found on tomb walls, show the Han artisan's ability to depict receding space and the interest in observing from nature.

North and South Dynasties Period

The earliest known Chinese painting masters come from the period following the collapse of the Han. It is also a period of the first treatises on painting and calligraphy. The earliest and most influential is Xie He's (c. 500–c. 535) *Six Canons of Painting*, a work that outlines early painting theory. While little painting remains from this period (owing largely to political and social upheaval), the fragments and copies of works tell of a strong interest in Confucian subjects. One such work, attributed to Gu Kaizhi (c. 344–c. 406), is the handscroll *Admonitions of the Instructress to the Ladies of the Palace*. Rendered in ink and color on silk, this work combines image and text to offer rules for proper behavior. The figures are of central importance, showing great mastery of fluttering robes and drapery. But other important pictorial works are not paintings at all. The engraved stone sarcophagus illustrating tales of filial piety, now in the Nelson-Atkins Museum of Art in Kansas City, Missouri, and dating to the sixth century, not only details the Confucian theme of respect for elders but also shows the beginning of landscape elements in art and a growing confidence in depicting space.

Buddhism, introduced during the Han dynasty, began to flourish during the North and South dynasties (220–589 CE). The greatest wealth of wall paintings is found at the Buddhist cave-temple site of Dunhuang, on the eastern edge of the Gobi desert. Activity at Dunhuang began in the fourth century and continued over several hundred years; the paintings here combine Chinese and Central Asian elements and are characterized by a vitality unequaled in early Chinese art.

Sui and Tang Dynasties

China was reunited after centuries of disunion under the rulers of the short-lived Sui dynasty (581–618 CE). While the period lasted only thirty-seven years, its chief role was to set the stage for the succeeding Tang dynasty (618–907 CE), China's most glorious and cosmopolitan period, when painting achieved great heights.

During the Tang, the first imperial painting academy was established at the court. This academy attracted many notable artists, such as Yan Lide (d. 656) and his brother, Yan Liben (d. 673); Wu Daozi (flourished 720–760), the great master of the monochrome technique; Li Sixun (651–716) and his son Li Zhadao (c. 675–741), famous for their colorful landscapes in the "blue-and-gold" style; and the well-known horse painter Han Gan (flourished 742–756). Few paintings that can be firmly attributed to these artists have survived, but there are enough extant examples to give a sense of the overall character of their work. Yan Lide and Yan Liben, for example, epitomize early Tang figure painting. Here, the figures were first outlined in black, and the colors were then filled in, using some shading. Wu Daozi created a monochromatic technique known as *baimiao*, or "white line," which focused on calligraphic line. This simple style would influence later landscape artists and contrasted sharply with the strongly colored and more complex landscape paintings of Li Sixun and Li Zhaodao. The poet and painter Wang Wei (699–759) is associated with the creation of the true monochrome landscape painting, where the focus was not on a narrative but rather on nature.

Wall paintings were an important medium for Tang painters. Painting continued at Dunhuang, and these paintings offer insight into the richness of Tang culture and society through the themes, styles, and extent of foreign influence found in these works. Other important extant Tang wall paintings are found in tombs. Three well-known and fine examples come from the tombs of members of the Tang imperial family, constructed in 706. The walls are covered with paintings of hunting, polo, ceremonial processions, and a variety of auspicious symbols, showing the grace and elegance of Tang figure painting as a whole.

Five Dynasties Period and Song Dynasty

The Song Dynasty (960–1279) was a period of great intellectual and artistic attainments as well as one of political decline. The abundant leisure and patronage necessary for the arts, combined with the rise of Neo-Confucianism, created the intellectual and artistic environment in which landscape painting reached its zenith. Song paintings provided the models that would inspire artists into the Qing dynasty (1644–1912).

The most characteristic style of landscape painting of the Northern Song period (960–1126) is the monumental landscape, in which artists broke free from any Tang influence and created a style that was purely of the Song dynasty. The early masters of this style are Li Cheng (919?–967?) and Fan Kuan (flourished c. 990–1030). Their works, and those of their followers, embody the realism and rationalism characteristic of this period. Depth and distance are achieved with mists and towering mountains, detailed foregrounds of rocks, and aged, weathered trees. This style reached a climax under Li Cheng's student, Guo Xi (c. 1020–c. 1090). His masterwork, *Early Spring*, stands out as one of the most important works in the history of Chinese painting. Near the end of the Northern Song dynasty, the monumental landscapes were scaled down into small scenic views. Through the use of mists and bird's-eye perspectives, these paintings were softer and more poetic in feeling, as embodied in the work of Mi Fu (1051–1107) and his son, Mi Youren (1072–1151).

During the Northern Song, China's first important painting academy came into existence, formed under the Huizong emperor (1082–1135) in the twelfth century. Here, artists were encouraged to paint in a more literal style that went beyond mere technical performance to capture the subject, usually birds and flowers. Huizong himself was a gifted painter and calligrapher in his own right as well as an important collector and connoisseur, and several of his works are extant. Unfortunately, Huizong's skills did not extend to military matters; he was captured by the invading Jin armies in 1126 and died in prison. However, the newly established Southern Song dynasty (1126–1279) continued Huizong's so-called "academy style" in the new capital of Hangzhou.

The early years of the Southern Song academy featured artists who had worked previously in the north, including bird-and-flower painters and landscapists. However, painting also experienced its own developments, seen in the work of landscape painters Ma Yuan (flourished c. 1190–c. 1225) and Xia Gui (c. 1180–1230), who created the Ma-Xia style. In these works, the artist focused on a particular view of the natural world and made dramatic use of empty space by eliminating some detail and highlighting the extremes of foreground and distance.

Also working at this time were the Chan Buddhist painter-priests who enjoyed more spontaneity with their brush and ink in capturing the essence of their subjects, as embodied in the work of Muqi (c. early thirteenth century–after 1279).

Yuan Dynasty

The Mongol conquests of the Southern Song empire in the fourteenth century devastated the Chinese. Although the Mongols were able to employ some Chinese scholars at their court, most refused to serve these "barbarian" rulers and dedicated themselves instead to poetry, painting, and calligraphy. Because of this, the short-lived Yuan dynasty (1279–1368) saw an incredible development in the arts and produced some of China's greatest masters.

One artist who was criticized for serving the Mongols was Zhao Mengfu (1254–1322). A descendant of the Song imperial line, Zhao took a post in the Yuan bureaucracy and distinguished himself as a painter of great repute. His finely colored handscroll, *Autumn Colors on the Qiao and Hua Mountains*, with its competent and varied, interwoven and textured brush strokes, stands as one of the great paintings of this period.

Near the end of the Yuan dynasty, the artist's studio became a focal point for the gathering of amateur literati artists *(wenren)* for whom painting was not a means of livelihood, as it was for professional painters, but was done for enjoyment and personal expression. The most famous of these Yuan literati painters is a group known as the Four Great Masters: Huang Gongwang (1269–1354), Wu Zhen (1280–1354), Ni Zan (1301–1374), and Wang Meng (1308–1385). These men refused to serve the Mongol bureaucracy and emphasized an art-for-art's-sake attitude. They preferred landscapes to other subjects and worked with ink on paper; the purity and sharpness of these media highlighted their careful, almost calligraphic, brushwork. They worked in a variety of styles, making reference to earlier artists, and their theories of painting were extremely influential to later artists.

Ming Dynasty

By the mid-fourteenth century, the Mongols were driven out and China was once again ruled by the Chinese under the emperors of the Ming dynasty (1368–1644). With this new rule came the strong desire to return to Chinese traditions and eliminate any memory of "barbarian" rule.

Painting tended to be rather conservative, because artists looked to the past and emulated the styles of the old masters of the Tang and the Song dynasties. The distinctions between the amateur and professional painters continued in the two principal schools: the Zhe school, named for the southeastern Chinese province of Zhejiang and consisting of professional and court painters; and the Wu school, named after the Wu district near Suzhou, where many of the scholar-painters lived. The more conservative trend in the Ming is seen in the works of the artists associated with the Zhe school. These painters looked to Ma Yuan and Xia Gui of the Song dynasty as their source of inspiration and had a strong influence on later artists. One of the most famous practitioners of this school is Dai Jin (1388–1462), whose role in its development was so central that the school's name comes from Dai's home province. The Wu school artists, whose leading masters were Shen Zhou (1427–1509) and Wen Zhengming (1470–1559), looked to the paintings of the Four Great Masters of the Yuan dynasty for inspiration. However, it was not always easy to maintain the distinctions between the professional painters working in the styles of the Song dynasty and the amateurs who based their work on the artists of the Yuan dynasty, as seen in the works of three mid-Ming masters Zhou Chen (d. c. 1536), Tang Yin (1470–1523), and Qiu Ying (flourished c. 1522–1552), who worked in a variety of styles and were tremendously influential.

By the late sixteenth century, new impetus in the arts was provided by the theorist and painter Dong Qichang (1555–1636). In looking at the division between northern and southern schools of Chan Buddhism that began in the Tang dynasty, Dong felt that painting could similarly be divided into two schools that could also be traced back to the Tang. The Northern school was based on the colored landscape style of Li Zhaodao and included Song artists Ma Yuan and Xia Gui. The Southern school began with Wang Wei and included among its practitioners the Four Great Masters of the Yuan. Dong's theory was particularly influential with the orthodox artists of the early Qing dynasty and has provided food for thought for centuries of art historians.

Qing Dynasty

The Qing dynasty, under the rule of the Manchus, saw the high point of the classical traditional in painting. During this period, there were two basic trends: a conservative continuation of late Ming style, based on the writings of Dong Qichang; and an original, innovative trend that was not based on any one particular school.

The conservative style is best seen in the works of the Four Wangs: Wang Shimin (1592–1680), Wang Jian (1598–1677), Wang Hui (1632–1717), and Wang Yuanqi (1642–1715). The most traditional of the group was the earliest, Wang Shimin, who assimilated Song and Yuan styles; the most original was Wang Yuanqi, who is closer to the individualists than the others in his group.

In contrast were the individualist painters. Some, like their predecessors in the Yuan dynasty, did not want to serve under a foreign rule and retired from official life to paint and write poetry. Zhu Da (also called Bada Shanren, 1626–1705) is known primarily for his abbreviated style, capturing his subjects with a minimum of well-placed and spontaneous brush strokes. The monk-painter Kuncan (also called Shiqi, 1612–1673) produced more complex paintings of varied and textured strokes than Zhu Da and made effective use of color. Yuanji (also called Shitao and Daoji, 1642–1707) made use of much deeper color, bold washes, and elegant detail in his paintings. One of the most forceful of the individualists was Gong Xian (c. 1619–1689), whose style is characterized by rich velvety ink and gloomy, somber landscapes. The work of the monk-painter from south China, Hongren (1610–1664), in contrast, features spare landscapes composed of refined and simple brushstrokes first seen in the work of Ni Zan of the Yuan dynasty.

The presence of European artists in the eighteenth century influenced painting at the Qing court. The Italian Jesuit Giuseppe Castiglione (Lang Shining, 1688–1766) spent many years in Beijing and combined Western realism with Chinese conventions. His work, while greatly admired by the Qing rulers, was little appreciated by the Chinese literati.

However, the political turmoil of the twentieth century—led by the collapse of the Qing dynasty in 1911 and followed by the May Fourth Movement of 1919, the War of Resistance against Japan of 1937–1945, the founding of the People's Republic of China (PRC) in 1949, and the Cultural Revolution of 1966–1976—redefined Chinese art. Traditional literati painting faced opposition as artists began to look outside China for inspiration. Artists who advocated the reform of traditional painting in the early part of the twentieth century included Chen Shuren (1883–1949) and the brothers Gao Jianfu (1879–1951) and Gao Qifeng (1889–1933), all members of the Lingnan School in Guangzhou. Gao Jianfu had considerable influence on a young Xu Beihong (1895–1953), the best-known artist to blend French academic and Chinese styles. In contrast, Lin Fengmian (1900–1991), another modern master, was heavily influenced by the postimpressionists and fauvists.

With the establishment of the PRC in 1949, art became a tool for the ideologies of the Communist Party and reflected Marxist views on class, as outlined in Mao Zedong's "Talks at the Yan'an Forum on Art and Literature" of 1942. According to Mao, art should serve the masses and further the revolutionary cause. Mao's Cultural Revolution created further upheaval.

Artists faced persecution, and many were sent to the countryside to be "reeducated" and to learn from the peasants. Art at this time was symbolic of party policy and was produced on a huge scale for wide distribution, as evidenced in the two- and three-dimensional portraits of Mao that appeared throughout China at this time. Following Mao's death in 1976, which marked the end of the Cultural Revolution, came a general relaxation of government control in the arts and an openness to Western modernism that was embraced by China's young artists. Although Western styles continue to be influential, Chinese painters are also looking to their own long artistic tradition to create works that are a synthesis of China's deeply rooted culture with current international styles and techniques.

Catherine Pagani

See also: **Calligraphy—China**

Further Reading

Cahill, James. (1960) *Chinese Painting.* Lausanne, Switzerland: Skira.

Fong, Wen C. (1992) *Beyond Representation: Chinese Painting and Calligraphy, 8th–14th Century.* New Haven, CT: Yale University Press.

Loehr, Max. (1980) *The Great Painters of China.* Oxford: Phaidon.

Murck, Alfreda, and Wen C. Fong, eds. (1991) *Words and Images: Chinese Poetry, Calligraphy, and Painting.* New York: Metropolitan Museum of Art.

Sirén, Osvald. (1956–1958) *Chinese Painting: Leading Masters and Principles.* 7 vols. New York: Ronald Press.

Yang Xin, Richard M. Barnhart, et al. (1997) *Three Thousand Years of Chinese Painting.* New Haven, CT: Yale University Press.

PAINTING—JAPAN

The earliest surviving paintings in Japan date from the Kofun period (300–710 CE), when large tomb mounds *(kofun)* were constructed for all classes of society and ornamented with various painted designs. Distinctive among them is the black-and-red wall painting found in the mid-Kofun Takehara Tomb in Fukuoka, which contains among its elements a red-spotted animal, a horse and groom, and a boat with waves, all flanked by two standing fans. The recently excavated Takamatsu Tomb of the late seventh century, near Asuka, contains a set of wall paintings that are evidence of contact between China and Japan. The complex imagery in yellow, blue, red, orange, and green covers three walls (the south wall was damaged in the past by pillagers) and the ceiling, and includes mythological beasts, the constellations, and groups of men and women arranged according to Chinese principles of yin and yang.

Late Kofun (552–710 CE) and Nara (710–794 CE) Periods

In the sixth century, Japan established close cultural ties with China and Korea. Buddhism appeared at this time, imported from China via Korea, bringing with it elements of Chinese culture including artistic styles and subject matter. The Tamamushi Shrine, named for the wings of the jade beetle *(tamamushi)* that were once used to adorn the piece, dates from the Asuka period (552–645 CE). Its three-dimensional model of a Buddhist temple is evidence not only of Buddhist architecture in Japan but also contains the only extant paintings from the period, found on the four sides of its lacquered wood base. Worshipers would have circumambulated it in the same manner they did a Buddhist stupa: walking clockwise around the shrine and viewing the images as an aid to meditation and as a method of learning about Buddhist beliefs. It is found today at the temple complex of Horyuji. Horyuji holds some of the best examples of painting from the Hakuho period (645–710 CE); these are strongly related to Chinese paintings of the Tang dynasty (618–907 CE). Originally adorning the walls of the *kondo* (main worship hall), these early eighth-century paintings of enthroned Buddhas in their paradises were heavily damaged by fire in 1949.

The Tang influence carried into the Nara period. A set of folding screen panels of the mid-eighth century in the Todaiji temple complex show beautiful, full-figured, elegant women, each underneath a tree, in the Tang style. A new painting format, the narrative handscroll *(emakimono)* also emerged at this time. The *E inga kyo* (Sutra of Cause and Effect) is the first extant example of the *emakimono,* which would become a major Japanese painting format in centuries to come.

Heian Period (794–1185)

During the Heian period, the wealthy nobility refined court culture, with a resulting rise in the secular arts, and an emphasis on native Japanese styles. Chinese models continued to be adapted in the early Heian period. During this period, the esoteric schools of Shingon and Tendai Buddhism were introduced from China. The complex ideas and rituals associated with the Shingon sect took form in mandala paintings, which are abstractions of the spiritual universe. The believer focused on these images and through meditation learned to re-create the elements of the paintings in his or her own mind. Now in the Kyoogokokuji, the oldest mandala paintings in Japan are the *Taizokai* (Womb World) and the *Kongokai* (Diamond World), done in color on silk; they are thought to be ninth-century copies of Chinese originals.

There was also a rise in the worship of Amida Buddha and the belief in rebirth in Amida's Western Paradise. Paintings depicted *raigo*, the glorious ceremony when Amida, accompanied by attendant bodhisattvas, welcomed the deceased into his paradise.

In the later Heian period, the nobility's interest in Japanese literature and art resulted in the conscious decision to move away from Chinese models. This was especially true in secular painting, in which there was more freedom of expression. The terms *kara-e*, Chinese pictures, and *yamato-e*, referring to Japanese scenes and subjects, came into use at this time and reached a pinnacle in the eleventh century. One of the most striking examples of Japanese aesthetics and themes is found in the extant illustrations from the twelfth-century scrolls depicting the *Genji monogatari (The Tale of Genji)*. One of only four sets of *emakimono* to survive from the late Heian period, the *Genji* images show two painting conventions that are purely Japanese: roofless architecture (blown-off roof) that allows the viewer to peer down on the activity taking place inside structures, and the minimal facial details, called "line for eye and hook for nose."

Early Feudal Period (1185–1573)

The surface tranquillity of the Heian period was shattered by the Gempei wars (1180–1185), which ushered in an era of conflict and military dominance. Buddhism underwent changes as well, including the popular acceptance of Pure Land Buddhism, and the introduction from China of Zen Buddhism.

The thirteenth century witnessed a strong interest in *emakimono*. The diary of Murasaki Shikibu *(Murasaki Shikibu nikki)*, the author of *Genji Monogatari*, chronicled life at court; it inspired an *emakimono* whose surviving images tell of the nobility's interest in the past.

The interest in history is also revealed in another *emakimono*, *Heike monogatari emaki* (Scroll of the Tale of the Heike, second half of the thirteenth century), which tells of a conflict in 1160 between the rival Minamoto and Taira clans. One of the most dramatic scenes in Japanese painting is the burning of the retired emperor's Sanjo Palace. This long section features flames and warriors, as well as servants fleeing and ladies of the palace flinging themselves down a well to avoid the rampaging warriors.

Pure Land Buddhism addressed the pessimistic mood brought about by the horrors of war by encouraging the notion that through devotion to Amida Buddha, one could achieve enlightenment. As Amida became the central focus of worship, the mandala and *raigo* paintings acquired new imagery focusing primarily on the Western Paradise. One such work is the thirteenth-century *Taima Mandara*. Based on an eighth-century tapestry version, the mandala depicts Amida's paradise in great detail and its borders provide visual references to key religious concepts.

The years of the Gempei wars had an effect on the development of gruesome paintings known as *rokudoe* that depicted the different levels of rebirth: the realms of unenlightened beings, humans, animals, fighting demons, starving ghosts, and beings in hell. While these realms had been described in Heian-period texts, the nobility had chosen to believe that they would be reborn into a paradise. The pessimism caused by the horrors of war gave the impression in the late twelfth and thirteenth centuries that one could just as easily be reborn into one of the six realms instead. Three sets of *emakimono* graphically illustrate possible fates: the *Yamai no soshi* (Notebook of Illnesses), the *Jigoku zoshi* (Hell Scrolls), and the *Gaki zoshi* (Scroll of Hungry Ghosts).

The introduction at the end of the twelfth century of Zen Buddhism (Chan in Chinese, from the Sanskrit *dhyana*, meaning meditation) had a profound effect on Japanese culture. Different types of Zen painting developed and subjects included famous Zen practitioners, Buddhist deities, and landscapes. Some artists were priest-painters, such as the versatile artist Kichizan Mincho (1352–1431), who worked in color on silk, as well as ink on paper, and painted a variety of themes. The Zen style of monochrome ink painting is best exemplified by Kao Ninga (mid-fourteenth century), who depicted his subjects with quick, spontaneous brushstrokes of varying thickness and tone. The greatest of the Zen painters, however, is Sesshu Toyo (1420–1506), whose characteristic landscapes utilize the *haboku* (broken-ink technique), in which the artist appears to have splashed the ink on the paper. Another Zen subject is the *koan* (mental puzzle), used to aid in achieving enlightenment. A painting by Josetsu (a fourteenth- or early-fifteenth-century priest), *Catching a Catfish with a Gourd*, illustrates the problem of catching a wriggling fish with an unlikely object. Zen monochrome ink paintings, such as those mentioned here, have their roots in Chinese painting of the Song dynasty (960–1279), as exemplified in the works of the Chan Buddhist artist Mu Qi (late thirteenth century).

Momoyama Period (1573–1600)

The ten-year Onin War that began in 1467 devastated the capital and brought a period of political and social instability that was felt for nearly one hundred years. In the end, a new elite emerged consisting of feudal lords who controlled domains and acted as

Bamboo and Poppies, a screen painting by Kano Shigenobu, c. 1625. (SEATTLE ART MUSEUM/ CORBIS)

advisers to the shogun. The painting of this period reflects this change: during the first phase, the art is exuberant; in the second half of the Momoyama period, there is a return to earlier styles.

Painting in the first phase of the early sixteenth century is characterized by the lavish use of gold leaf and strong colors in striking patterns on *fusuma* (sliding-door panels) and *byobu* (folding screens). The second phase began in the late sixteenth century, when art showed an interest in traditions of the past, particularly *yamato-e* themes. This trend was led by the wealthy merchant class, which became interested in cultural pursuits such as literature and the tea ceremony.

Practitioners of the first style often were members of the Kano school, especially the father-and-son artists Kano Eitoku (1543–1590), who used gold leaf and brilliant colors on grounds, and Kano Mitsunobu (1565?–1608), who at the death of his father became the head of the Kano school in Kyoto. Other artists developed their own individual style from Eitoku's aesthetic, including the painter Hasegawa Tohaku (1539–1610). Tohaku used color and detail to great effect and was influenced by the brightly colored, decorative screens of the Kano school; however, he also looked to earlier monochrome ink styles of the Zen tradition. Sotatsu (1600–1640) is best known for reviving *yamato-e* painting by incorporating classical themes in his work.

Genre painting was another major development in Momoyama art and continued into the seventeenth century, when it inspired the subjects of mass-produced woodblock prints. An interest in the activities of commoners first found expression in paintings showing bird's-eye views of the area in and around Kyoto. As this interest developed, the subjects became more intimate and featured groups of figures engaged in leisure activities such as reading and playing music.

Edo Period (1600/1603–1868)

The Edo period began when Tokugawa Ieyasu became the ruler of Japan; it was a time of peace brought about by strict government controls. The arts commissioned by the ruling military class of this period show conservatism through the patronage of Kano school artists, who worked in traditional themes. Kano Tanyu (1602–1674), grandson of Kano Eitoku, carried the work of his family into the seventeenth century. Toward the end of the seventeenth century, however, the wealth of the rising merchant class *(chonin)* had a pronounced influence on the arts. Merchants wanted art to reflect their own surroundings—teahouses, the theater, and female entertainers.

One departure from the conservatism that marks this period is the development of Rinpa painting, which had its origins in the work of Sotatsu in the Momoyama period. The school was named for Ogata Korin (1658–1716), the school's most famous practitioner (the last syllable of the artist's name was combined with the term for "school," *pa*), and favorite subjects included themes from literature, such as *The Tale of Genji*, as well as flowers of the four seasons. Korin continued the decorative style of Sotatsu and created simplified, rhythmic, and bold designs using flat blocks of color against gold backgrounds.

Edo-period art was also inspired by works of Western artists. Called first *yofuga*, and later *yoga*, this style of painting used Western and Japanese materials and was characterized by its emphasis on perspective, shading, and realism. *Yofuga* was popularized by Hiraga Gennai

(1728–1779), who learned Dutch in Nagasaki, where the European traders resided. Gennai passed his ideas to his best student, Shiba Kokan (1738–1818), who worked at perfecting his command of Western artistic techniques.

Zen painting and calligraphy continued, but as Buddhism in general played less of a role in the everyday life of the Japanese people, these works of art, known as *zenga*, were produced by and for Zen masters to be used as visual aids for meditation. Landscapes were no longer the primary subject; instead, artists focused on the *koan* as a teaching tool. The most influential of these painters was Hakuin Ekaku (1685–1768), whose distinctive work includes the single character *mu* (nothingness) and an illustration of his own *koan*, the sound of one hand clapping.

Bunjinga (literati painting), also called *nanga* (southern painting, from its roots in China's Southern Song dynasty), the art of the literati, also found expression in the Edo period. The idea of freedom of expression was introduced from China in the seventeenth century and stressed that the arts of painting and calligraphy were the pursuits of the true scholar-gentleman. *Bunjinga* artists included Ike Taiga (1723–1776), Yosa Buson (1716–1783), Okada Beisanjin (1744–1820), Uragami Gyokudo (1745–1820), and Tani Buncho (1763–1840). These works varied widely in both style and content, from landscapes in ink and color on paper to strongly colored and intricately detailed bird-and-flower paintings on silk.

The Early Modern Period

The Tokugawa shogunate fell in 1868, ushering in the Meiji Restoration (1868–1912) and the beginning of Japan's modern period. The early years of the Meiji were devoted to rapid Westernization, and Western experts, including artists and architects, were brought to Japan to teach at the Technical Fine Arts School, where *yoga* was studied under the direction of Antonio Fontanesi (1818–1881), a follower of the Barbizon school. The brown and gold palette of the Barbizon school, however, clashed with the soft purples and blues of the Impressionists, which were brought to Japan by students who had spent time in Paris, including Kuroda Seiki (1866–1924).

In the 1880s, a backlash against things Western resulted in the promotion of Japan's own artistic traditions. Ernest Fenollosa (1853–1908), an American and a strong advocate for Japanese art, encouraged the study of traditional arts by establishing the Kangakai (Painting Appreciation Society), whose artists sought a balance between traditional art and new painting styles. Painters Kano Hogai (1828–1888) and Hashimoto Gaho (1835–1908) were the first practitioners, and their ideals were transmitted to the next generation and into the twentieth century.

Catherine Pagani

Further Reading

Akiyama Terukazu. (1961) *Japanese Painting*. Geneva, Switzerland: Skira.

Elisseeff, Danielle, and Vadime Elisseeff. (1985) *Art of Japan*. Trans. by I. Mark Paris. New York: Harry N. Abrams.

Ishizawa Masao et al. (1982) *The Heritage of Japanese Art*. New York: Kodansha.

Mason, Penelope. (1993) *History of Japanese Art*. New York: Harry N. Abrams; Englewood Cliffs, NJ: Prentice Hall.

Rosenfield, John M. (1979) *Song of the Brush*. Seattle, WA: Seattle Art Museum.

PAINTING—KOREA

Korean painting has developed continuously from ancient times to today. Accepting foreign art trends selectively, Korean artists greatly influenced the development of ancient Japanese painting and have cultivated their own independent painting style and aesthetic sense.

Korean painting was first produced in the period of the three kingdoms: Koguryo (37 BCE–668 CE), Paekche (18 BCE–663 CE), and Shilla (57 BCE–935 CE). Despite their close interrelationship, the painting styles of each kingdom were distinct: Koguryo painting was noted for its energetic style, Paekche for its elegance, and Shilla for its speculative and meticulous subjects, as shown in *Heavenly Horse*, a painting of a white horse excavated from a tumulus built in the fifth to sixth century ce. After Shilla's unification of the Korean Peninsula in 668, popular subjects included portraits of royal courtiers, blue-green landscapes, and religious themes. Buddhism, the state religion, provided abundantly elaborate subjects for paintings. During the Koryo kingdom (918–1392), Buddhist art flourished with a greater variety of subject matter and painting styles. Two typical works from this period are *Avalokitesvara Holding a Willow Branch* and *Frontispiece for Avatamsaka Sutra*. The former is a graceful and colorful image on silk of the bodhisattva of compassion, featuring delicately rendered transparent drapery and a subtle suggestion of movement; the latter's elegant style reveals the influence of Mahayana Buddhism among the aristocracy. Artists of that time painted not only for practical purposes but also for aesthetic appreciation and spiritual cultivation.

Choson-Dynasty Painters

During the Choson dynasty (1392–1910), distinguished scholar-painters and talented painters from

Landscape with Two Men on a Boat by Cho Suk Jin in the late nineteenth century. (SEATTLE ART MUSEUM/CORBIS)

the Royal Academy of Painting, or Tohwaso, developed a firm Korean tradition of painting based on actual Korean scenes as opposed to the stylized landscapes of Chinese Song dynasty (960–1279) painting traditions, using more advanced techniques for composition, brushwork, and treatment of space. Despite the pervasive influence of the Chinese Southern Song (1126–1279) school style, Korean painters invented their own techniques and expressed their own style. The paintings of An Kyon (b. 1499) and Prince Anp'yong (1418–1453), which depicted trees, flowers, and animals, played a vital role in the development of ink painting in Japan. Chong Son (1676–1759) and his followers, meanwhile, developed their own style of true-view landscape painting by sketching actual local scenes and portraying actual landscapes. *Diamond Mountains* and *Clearing after Rain on Mount Inwang* exemplify this new style, which reflected indigenous self-awareness and interest in Korean culture, appealing specifically to Koreans. The creative and realistic interpretation of nature, as well as the refined brushwork and coloring techniques, heavily influenced the folk paintings of future generations.

Kim Hong-do (b. 1745) and Sin Yoon-bok (b. 1758) were outstanding painters who expressed their national awareness by depicting scenes of Korean daily life with humor and affection. Their works are true examples of genre painting. Kim Hong-do and his followers painted in a realistic style humorous scenes from everyday life of the common folk in typical Korean costume, as exemplified in *Village School*, *Blacksmiths*, and *Threshing*. Sin Yoon-bok chose as subjects members of the aristocracy rather commoners, even though he shared an interest in painting Korean daily life in the manner of Kim Hong-do and his followers. Sin's genre paintings, such as *Amusement by the Lotus Pond*, depicted for the first time intimate romantic scenes of noblemen and courtesans, subject matter considered unvirtuous by the conservative Confucian society.

From 1850 to 1910, the final decades of the Choson dynasty, realistic landscape and genre paintings revealing unique Korean characteristics declined, giving way to the Ch'usa school style, which advocated an intellectual and spiritual approach to painting using simple and condensed brushwork but also incorporating a new ornamental and semicursive calligraphic style. Kim Chong-hi (1786–1865) and his followers developed the Ch'usa school, producing prolific ink brush works and calligraphy. *Orchid* and *Landscape in Winter* demonstrate the economy with which scholar-painters of the literati conveyed a heightened sense of spirituality.

During these years, several social and political upheavals caused a decline in Korean painting. Chang Sung-op (1843–1897) stood out in this period of relative artistic stagnation. He depicted a wide range of subjects, using powerful brushwork and vivid coloring; his works exercised an influence over modern Korean painting. During this period, Jesuit missionaries also brought the Western painting techniques of shading and perspective to Korea, although they remained far from prevalent.

Painting in the Twentieth Century

The traditional styles of Korean painting deteriorated drastically during the Japanese colonial regime (1910–1945) because the Japanese government enforced brutal policies aimed at obliterating Korean cultural identity. Traditional Korean painting was deliberately excluded from all academic studies. However, in 1918, Korean artists founded the Calligraphy and Painting Society, whose members organized nationalistic art survival movements through fifteen annual exhibitions. After Korea's liberation from Japan in 1945, the Korean painting tradition was revived. Artists developed new painting styles, mainly owing to the National Art Exhibition, which was established with the sponsorship of the Korean government. The annual exhibition gave promising young artists the opportunity to show their works. Also, several universities founded colleges of fine arts so that a new generation of artists could receive an appropriate education. But these efforts were suspended during the Korean War (1950–1953). In spite of hardships, many artists continued their work or study abroad. Some imitated modern abstract art; others simply depicted

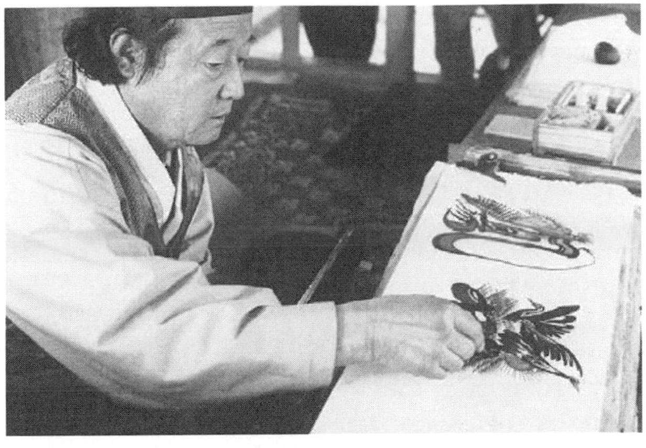

A traditional Korean painter demonstrating his skills at a folk festival at the Korean Folk Village near Suween, South Korea. (ROBERT HOLMES/CORBIS)

their tragic experiences and the horrors of war in a realistic style. Yi Chung-sop (1916–1956) is one of the academic realist artists who painted the suffering, poverty, and anguish of this period. He expressed his despair and depression by using distorted figures and violent brush strokes in paintings such as *A White Ox*. According to many critics, the cows frequently portrayed in Yi's sketches and paintings symbolize an imaginary utopia for the Korean people. Until the mid-1960s, many painters belonging to the Contemporary Artist Society also expressed their nihilist frustration and deep emotional scars caused by war by pursuing the so-called informal art movement, whose paintings were characterized by intense brushwork and irrational geometric abstraction, as in *Painting No. 1* by Pak So-bo.

Synthesizing Old and New

Since the 1970s, Korean artists have maintained active contact with Western modern art. Korean artists have participated in international exhibitions abroad and in internationally publicized art exhibitions in Korea. They have introduced such diverse art movements as pop art, neo Dada, performance art, hyperrealism, environment art, and conceptual art. However, other artists have kept alive their distinctive Korean cultural identity, expressing inner spirituality and longing for the past in an era of information technology in contemporary paintings that use neutral monochromatic coloring and techniques of tonal variation in light or dense ink quality, as exemplified, respectively, in *Joint 83-07* by Ha Jong-hyon and *Trees* by Song Su-nam.

Seong-Sook Yim

See also: **Calligraphy—Korea**

Further Reading

Ahn, Hwi-Joon, Won-yong Kim, and Young-na Kim. (1993) *Korean Art Tradition: A Historical Survey*. Seoul: Korea Foundation.

Covell, Jon Carter. (1985) *Korea's Colorful Heritage*. Seoul: Si-sa-youn-o-sa.

PAINTING—SOUTH ASIA The earliest remaining examples of painting in South Asia are Buddhist cave murals such as those in the monasteries at Ajanta in India. Here, two phases of painting, corresponding to the two phases of active patronage, may be distinguished, the earlier from the first century BCE and the later from the fifth century CE. The themes depicted are mainly stories from the *Jatakas* and scenes from the life of the Buddha. The murals are made with mineral colors on a specially plastered surface and, particularly in the later phase, are characterized by hieratic scaling (the size of figures often increasing with their spiritual importance), Buddha and Bodhisattvas shown in formal poses and with icongraphically determined physiognomy, and others depicted more realistically. Elements of three-dimensional modeling and perspective are mixed in with two-dimensional "flat" figuring introducing elements of realism in representations in which narrative interest clearly takes precedence over natural illusion.

Following Ajanta, few other fragmentary murals in cave or temple settings remain from medieval times; nor are there any extant examples of manuscript painting from before the eleventh century. Buddhist and Jain palm-leaf manuscripts exist from the eleventh century, showing illustrations of religious texts. These texts were venerated as sacred objects and offered as religious donations by patrons.

Extant eleventh- and twelfth-century Buddhist palm-leaf manuscripts come largely from regions in eastern India that were under the Pala kings, and they often have iconic scenes from the life of the Buddha on the inner surfaces of the wooden boards that bind the palm leaves and act as dividing elements between spaces in the text. Hieratic scaling and static figural postures executed using a rhythmic outline and filled in with flat, opaque mineral colors characterize the painting style.

The Jain manuscripts were mostly produced in the Gujarat region of western India. By the last quarter of the fourteenth century, the preferred medium for Jain manuscripts changed from palm leaf to paper, and the elongated palm-leaf format was gradually replaced by a rectangular form more suited to larger illustrations. The most popular of the illustrated Jain texts is a

Ajanta Cave 26: Stupa within nave shows several elements of early (fifth-century) Buddhist art in India. (GIAN BERTO VANNI/CORBIS)

history of the Tirthamkaras (a succession of twenty-four exemplary enlightened saviors of Jainism) known as the *Kalpa sutra*. A limited but bold color scheme is used, and flattened figures with rhythmic outlines as in the Buddhist tradition are shown. There is no attempt to depict spatial depth. A characteristic of the figures is their invariable presentation in profile with a protruding invisible eye.

The oldest extant illustrated Hindu manuscripts date to the second half of the fifteenth century and resemble Jain illustrations in their conventions. Hindu myths and epics from the Puranas and *Itihasa*s had by this time become standardized and pervasive in popular South Asian culture, and illustrations of episodes from some of these sources are common. From the early sixteenth century, a bold shift appears in this tradition, with the image gaining priority over the text. The by now standard rectangular form of the page is mostly occupied by the pictorial representation, with an abbreviated textual description in the upper margin and the extended text on the obverse of the page. This tradition made its appearance in Rajasthan and the western Gangetic kingdoms of northern India and is presumed to have had royal and other wealthy patronage. The contemporaneous rising popularity of medieval Vaishnavism, with its use of an erotic symbolism to describe the mystical pastimes of Krishna, must have played its part in fueling this production. The incorporation of a Vaishnavite mystical context into literary and courtly amorous narratives characterizes this painting tradition and initiates a thematic stream that continues through the history of South Asian painting. This tradition is named after one of its earliest manuscripts, the *Chaurapanchasika*, which is fifty stanzas about the poet's secret tryst with a princess on the eve of his execution. Other popular manuscripts from this tradition include the tenth chapter of the *Bhagavat purana*, dealing with the pastimes of Krishna, particularly his dalliances; the *Gita govinda*, a twelfth-century Sanskrit text from Bengal, also dealing with the loves of Krishna; the *Rasamanjari* (Inflorescence of Romantic Moods); the *Rasikapriya* (Connoisseur of Romance); and the *Ragamala* (Garland of Musical Modes). Although these paintings attempt a depiction of spatial depth, they are essentially flat, with stylized figures shown in static profile, making hieratic gestures in starkly simplified color planes. This painterly aesthetic, commonly known as the Rajput style, remained a viable South Asian idiom of painting, reasserting itself in various times and places throughout history.

The sixteenth century also witnessed the hegemonic rule of the Mughals in northern South Asia, resulting in a new school of painting, known commonly as Mughal painting. This school traces its roots to the mid-sixteenth-century rule of the second Mughal emperor, Humayun (1505–1556), who brought two master painters from the court of Tabriz, Abdus Samad and Mir Sayyid Ali, to found his atelier at Delhi in 1555. Within a year, Humayun died from an accidental fall and was succeeded by his son, Akbar (1542–1605), who had an abiding passion in the arts of painting and storytelling. Akbar quickly built up his father's atelier. Akbar's earliest commission was the illustration of the *Tutinama* (Tales of the Parrot), which utilized a large number of artists recruited from existing South Asian painting traditions working under the direction of the Persian masters, resulting in a distinctive hybrid style and aesthetic. Mixed perspective, structured visibility of interiors, and natural elements such as mountains and trees are taken from Persian prototypes; hieratic patterning, bold coloring, and narrative arrangements are reminiscent of indigenous traditions. A crowded swirl of highly individualized figure types laid out in a space divided using natural devices to give a sense of depth, a varied subtlety of coloring, and a judicious introduction of three-dimensional modeling to heighten the illusion of reality are innovations of the early Mughal style.

In the mid-sixteenth century, the Jesuits introduced Renaissance naturalism to Akbar's court. Space and volume began to be defined by light and shade. Aerial perspective was introduced, as well as atmospheric effects to depict spatial recession.

These techniques continued to gain prominence in paintings from the courts of Akbar's successors. The Mughal atelier remained as prolific under Akbar's son, Jahangir (1569–1627), although the thematic interest shifted from dynamic narrative episodes to carefully attentive portraiture, scenes of psychological interest, and detailed—albeit stylized—studies of flowers and animals. Although the Mughal atelier continued during the reign of Jahangir's son and successor, Shah Jahan (1592–1666), it seemed to lose its vitality and inventiveness; the paintings of this period are marked by a courtly stiffness and formalism and lack the boldness of color or composition of either Rajput paintings or earlier Mughal work. The Mughal atelier largely dispersed during the reign of the Islamic puritan Aurangzeb (1618–1707), the son and successor of Shah Jahan.

A Mughal period eighteenth-century painting, *Prince on a Brown Horse*. (BURSTEIN COLLECTION/CORBIS)

In the Deccan kingdoms of central India, small Islamic states had established themselves since the fourteenth century and developed independent cultural traditions. Among these, the most important were the kingdoms of Golconda and Bijapur, which remained independent until late in Aurangzeb's reign. With cultural roots in Persia and Turkey, these kingdoms developed their own painting traditions, known as the Deccani style, marked by rich coloration dominated by lavender, gold, and green, a jeweler's eye for decorative pattern, and mystical or fantastic stylizations.

In the late seventeenth century, after the dispersal of artists from Aurangzeb's court, further assimilation of Mughal thematic and stylistic idioms continued in the Hindu Rajput states. The earlier predominance of Hindu religious themes was complemented by formalized portraiture of the maharaja (prince), seen in court or in gardens or terraces with attendants, or in equestrian and hunting scenes. These scenes and some Mughal stylistic elements were mostly incorporated into flat decorative "Rajput" compositions in courts such as those of Kota and Mewar. The Bikaner paintings of this period, by contrast, show a much closer affinity to the naturalism of the Mughal style while making use of the decorative patterning and mystical palette of the Deccan courts. A highly accomplished and original Bikaner artist of this period, comparable to any contemporary Mughal artist, was Ruknuddin.

In Basholi in the Punjab Hills, however, reaction against the Mughal style spawned a powerful and vibrant style of painting. Religious texts were the main sources of inspiration; portraiture was restricted to iconic profiles of the seated maharaja. This style influenced painting in other hill states, such as Bahu, Chamba, Mankot, and Guler, and remained popular through the first quarter of the eighteenth century.

The Mughal court saw a brief and brilliant revival during the reign of Aurangzeb's grandson, Muhammad Shah (reigned 1719–1748). The idealized moody romanticism of the paintings produced under him, depicting courtly love and characterized by naturalistic atmospheric effects, carried over once more to inspire two of the finest and most charismatic schools of late Rajput and Pahari painting, those of Kishangarh and Kangra, respectively.

In the mid-eighteenth century, a fruitful collaboration between Raja Savant Singh (reigned 1748–1757) of the Rajput state of Kishangarh and the two master artists of his court, Bhavani Das and Nihal Chand,

The Kishangarh painting *A Love Scene* from the nineteenth century. (BURSTEIN COLLECTION/CORBIS)

both originally from Delhi, led to the formation of a distinctive style of painting. Extending the moody romanticism of the late Mughal court, Kishangarh painting of this period produced a large corpus of highly stylized depictions of the romantic fantasies of its patron with his court singer, Bani Thani, translated into images of Krishna and Radha, respectively. A surreal mysticism pushes amorous fantasy to the borders of the supernatural in these paintings.

A similar effect, using different means and developing a different and more refined aesthetic, appears in the mid-eighteenth century in the northern hill states of Guler, Jasrota, and Kangra, and is attributed to the efforts of two artist brothers, Manaku and Nainsukh, and their students. Nainsukh's work in the court of Raja Balwant Singh of Jasrota, can be said to originate the highly prized late Kangra school. The thematic mainstay of this school is the love of Radha and Krishna, stylistically raised to a high pitch of mystical evocation.

From the mid-eighteenth century, the British presence in South Asia exerted a powerful influence on courtly taste, pushing it toward photorealism. The advent of photography itself in the mid-nineteenth century contributed in no small measure to this change. Indigenous artists trained in earlier courtly styles now adapted their work to imitate the camera. Whereas some of these artists continued serving native patrons, particularly through portraiture, several were employed by the British to record scenes of South Asian life: its landscapes, flora, and fauna. The work of these artists forms a body known as the Company School. Added to this transformation in traditional painting is the work of European painters in South Asia as well as that of an educated urban class of native painters, tutored in European styles of painting.

Around the beginning of the twentieth century, a challenge and reaction to this trend was initiated by the Calcutta artist Abanindranath Tagore and his students as part of a nationalistic rethinking of identity. Artists of this Bengal School fashioned a distinctive style affiliated with pan-Asianism and an international antimaterialism, integrating elements of Rajput, Mughal, Japanese, and Pre-Raphaelite styles. From the second quarter of the twentieth century, international modernism increasingly influenced South Asian art, opening up a variety of creative adaptations. Today, the contemporary art scene in South Asia is among the most vibrant and prolific in the world, with increasing numbers of artists making bold forays into individualized modes of expression suited to the social, cultural, and local contexts of the subcontinent.

Debashish Banerji

Further Reading

Archer, W. G. (1973) *Indian Paintings from the Punjab Hills: A Survey and History of Pahari Miniature Painting*. 2 vols. London: H. M. Stationary Office.

Beach, Milo Cleveland. (1992) *Mughal and Rajput Painting*. Vol. 1, pt. 3 of *The New Cambridge History of India*. Cambridge: Cambridge University Press.

Brown, Percy. (1975) *Indian Painting under the Mughals, A.D. 1550 to A.D. 1750*. New York: Hacker Art Books.

Coomaraswamy, Ananda K. (1975 [1916]) *Rajput Painting: Being an Account of the Hindu Paintings of Rajasthan and the Punjab Himalayas from the Sixteenth to the Nineteenth Century, Described in Their Relation to Contemporary Thought*. 2 vols. New York: Hacker Art Books.

Randhawa, Mohindra Sinh, and John Kenneth Galbraith. (1968) *Indian Painting: The Scene, Themes, and Legends*. Boston.

Randhwa, Mohindra Sinh, and Doris Schreier Randhawa. (1980) *Kishangarh Painting*. Bombay.

Welch, Stuart Cary. (1978) *Imperial Mughal Painting*. London: Chatto and Windus.

Zebrowski, Mark. (1983) *Deccani Painting*. Berkeley: University of California Press.

PAK KYUNG-RI (b. 1926), Korean novelist. Pak Kyung-ri was born in the coastal city of Ch'ungmu in South Kyungsang Province. She started her career as a writer in the mid-1950s, with the publication of such short stories as "Kyesan" (Calculation) and "Hukhuk paekpaek" (Black and White) in *Hyondae munhak* (Contemporary Literature), one of the most prestigious South Korean literary journals. The two novels that followed in the early 1960s made her famous and established her as a prominent Korean novelist: *Kim yakkuk ui ttal tul* (Pharmacist Kim's Daughters) is a saga of sisters born to middle-class parents in a small southern coastal city; *Shijang kwa chonjang* (Marketplace and Battlefield) is a novel depicting the Korean War and how it completely destroys one happy middle-class family.

Pak wrote *T'oji* (Land) from 1969 to 1994 as a series in *Hyondae munhak*, and it was later published as a novel in sixteen volumes. It describes a family starting from the last period of the Choson dynasty in the nineteenth century through Japanese colonial rule, the liberation in 1945, the division of the nation by the United States and the Soviet Union, and the Korean War. It is a story of one family encompassing three generations, as well as a political, social, cultural, and economic history of modern Korea. Pak's novels have been translated into English, French, and German.

Choi Yearn Hong

Further Reading

Pak Kyung-ri. (1996) *Land*. London: Kegan Paul International.

PAKISTAN—PROFILE (2001 est. pop. 144.6 million). The country of Pakistan, located in the northwest corner of the Indian subcontinent, is officially named the Islamic Republic of Pakistan. It was

The multistory buildings in Karachi reflect the rapid urbanization Pakistan has experienced in recent years. (STAFFAN WIDSTRAND/CORBIS)

created on 14 August 1947 out of Muslim-majority territories in the northeast and northwest parts of British India. Initially consisting of two parts separated by approximately 1,600 kilometers of Indian territory, Pakistan split in 1971 when the eastern half seceded and became the Republic of Bangladesh.

Pakistan today consists of four provinces: Baluchistan, the North West Frontier Province (NWFP), the Punjab, and Sind. The federal capital, Islamabad, is a separate administrative unit and lies in the north-central part of the country. There are also two federally administered agencies, Gilgit and Baltistan, and a protected quasi-autonomous state, Azad (Free) Kashmir. The latter, annexed by Pakistan in the 1948 war with India, has its own government, although it remains under the protection and direct control of Pakistan.

While Pakistan's area is only the thirty-second largest in the world (making up around 0.7 percent of the earth's landmass), its population is widely assumed to be the world's seventh largest, though controversy surrounds the exact figures. The United Nations Development Programme estimated Pakistan's population at about 148 million in 1998; Pakistan's census conducted that same year, held after a contentious seventeen-year hiatus due to fears that a census could accentuate disputes between ethnic and sectarian groups, reported the country's population to be 130 million.

Geography

Nestled between India to the east, China to the northeast, Afghanistan to the northwest, Iran to the west, and the Arabian Sea to the south, Pakistan lies amid

PAKISTAN

Country name: Islamic Republic of Pakistan
Area: 803,940 sq km
Population: 144,616,639 (July 2001 est.)
Population growth rate: 2.11% (2001 est.)
Birth rate: 31.21 births/1,000 population (2001 est.)
Death rate: 9.26 deaths/1,000 population (2001 est.)
Net migration rate: -0.84 migrant(s)/1,000 population (2001 est.)
Sex ratio—total population: 1.05 male(s)/female (2001 est.)
Infant mortality rate: 80.5 deaths/1,000 live births (2001 est.)
Life expectancy at birth—total population: 61.45 years, male: 60.61 years, female: 62.32 years (2001 est.)
Major religions: Sunni Islam, Shiʿa Islam, Christianity, Hinduism
Major languages: Punjabi, Sindhi, Siraiki, Pashtu, Urdu (official), Balochi, Hindko, Brahui, English (official), Burushaski
Literacy—total population: 42.7%, male; 55.3%, female: 29% (1998)
Government type: federal republic
Capital: Islamabad
Administrative divisions: 4 provinces, 1 territory, 1 capital territory
Independence: 14 August 1947 (from UK)
National holiday: Republic Day, 23 March (1956) (proclamation of the republic)
Suffrage: 21 years of age, universal
GDP—real growth rate: 4.8% (2000 est.)
GDP—per capita (purchasing power parity): $2,000 (2000 est.)
Population below poverty line: 40% (2000 est.)
Exports: $8.6 billion (f.o.b., FY99/00)
Imports: $9.6 billion (f.o.b., FY99/00)
Currency: Pakistani rupee (PKR)

Source: Central Intelligence Agency. (2001) *The World Factbook 2001.* Retrieved 18 October 2001, from: http://www.cia.gov/cia/publications/factbook.

formidable neighbors. Its climate is generally arid, characterized by little rainfall, hot summers, cool or cold winters, and wide climactic variations between extremes of temperature at given locations: at one end, the warm, humid coastal area along the Arabian Sea, and at the other, the frozen, snow-covered, relatively inaccessible ridges of the Karakoram Range and other mountains in the far north. Less than a fifth of Pakistan's land area has the potential for intensive agricultural use. Nearly all of the cultivable land is actively under cultivation, though outputs are low by world standards.

The northern highlands region features some of the most rugged and famous mountains in the world, including the world's second-highest peak, K-2. Some of this region had once been part of the old Silk Road trading system that traversed Central Asia more than a thousand years ago, while other parts had been essentially cut off from the outside world because of the craggy and difficult terrain.

The Indus River plain consists of two major subdivisions corresponding roughly to the provinces of Punjab and Sind, which combine to be Pakistan's breadbasket. "Punjab" means the confluence of five rivers: the Indus, Jhelum, Chenab, Ravi, and Sutlej. The British attempted to harness the power of Punjab's rivers in the late nineteenth century by establishing an irrigation system in the southern part of the province, facilitating the emergence of intensive cultivation despite arid conditions.

The Baluchistan plateau, spotted with seismic fault lines, hosts an austere, dry terrain that has been compared to the surface of the moon. It has the lowest population density rates in the country.

Politics and Economics

Pakistan is constitutionally a parliamentary republic, though it has been ruled by military governments for much of its history. While the head of state is the president, the prime minister usually wields greater political influence. Three parallel legal systems exist: civil, religious, and military. The Council of Islamic Ideology, a constitutionally mandated organ, ensures that the country has no laws that are contradictory to the tenets of Islam.

Muhammad Ali Jinnah (1876–1948), credited as the country's founder, or Quaid-e-azam, died shortly after Pakistan's creation in September 1948. His Muslim League, which led Pakistan's independence movement, was unable to transform itself into a national, consensual political party. In October 1951, the assassination of Jinnah's political successor, Liaquat Ali Khan (1895–1951), further plunged the country into a crisis of civilian leadership at the national level, from which it has yet to recover completely.

Pakistan has had five periods of military rule: 1958–1969, led by Field Marshal Ayub Khan (1907–1974); 1969–1972, led by General A. M. Yahya Khan (1917–1980); 1977–1988, led by General Mohammad Zia ul-Haq (1924–1988); and 1999–present, led by General Pervez Musharraf (b. 1943). A civilian, Zulfikar Ali Bhutto (1928–1979), oversaw a democratic interregnum from the last four months of Yahya Khan's martial rule until 1977. Between 1988 and 1999, eight different civilian governments headed the country as the Pakistan People's Party of Benazir Bhutto (b. 1953) jockeyed for national political power with the Pakistan Muslim League of Nawaz Sharif (b. 1949). Following his assumption of the office of chief executive in October 1999, Pervez Musharraf brought charges of massive corruption against both Benazir Bhutto and Nawaz Sharif and has barred them from contesting national elections ever again.

Feudal, paternalistic relations continue to dominate political processes, especially in rural areas. Access to resources, services, jobs, state functionaries, and other benefits is mediated through powerful, influential patrons who, in most instances, are men.

Throughout the 1980s and 1990s, Pakistan's economy was constantly undergoing economic restructuring, albeit unsuccessfully, as far as bringing about viable reforms. The hyperinflation and economic stagnation that hit Pakistan's economy in late 1996 contributed to lowering people's already weak purchasing power; morale was further lowered as the government was forced to introduce austerity measures to prevent the economy from going into default. By the mid-1990s, debt servicing was twice as much as combined public spending in health and education.

Pakistan's low human-development position underscores what the political and economic turmoil of the past two decades has wrought. Adult literacy in 1998 was a dismal 44 percent (female adult literacy was even worse, 29 percent); Pakistan has one of the highest percentages of underweight children under the age of five years in the world (38 percent); and 44 percent of the population does not have access to proper sanitation. Runaway population growth rates in Pakistan threaten to reverse whatever gains have been made in the economic arena. The average gross national product growth rate was only marginally higher than the average population growth rate in the 1990s.

Separatist movements and ethnic crises have plagued Pakistan since its inception. At independence, many people feared that Pakistan might cease to exist; East Pakistan's secession in 1971—aided by India—further aggravated that anxiety. In the 1990s, separatist movements had been largely replaced by growing sectarian terrorism.

Society

Language remains an important marker of ethnic identity in Pakistan. Urdu (Pakistan's national language), Punjabi, and Sindhi, the most commonly spoken languages, as well as most of the more than twenty other languages in the country, belong to the Indo-Aryan branch of the Indo-European language family. Most of the remaining languages are related to early Dravidian.

Muslims make up 98 percent of Pakistan's population, with Shi'ites constituting roughly 12 to 15 percent of all Muslims. Minorities include Christians, Hindus, and Zoroastrians.

Pakistani social life revolves around family and the honor of women. A family's traditions have considerable bearing on its members, influencing perceptions of proper gender roles, occupational choices, whether to pursue an education, and alliances with others. Large extended families of the past provided ample opportunity for socialization, sustenance, protection, and regulation. Isolated individuals living apart from relatives remain uncommon; even male workers who have migrated to cities generally live with a relative or a friend of a relative. Children live with their parents until marriage; sons and their families—except in the most congested urban areas in the country—tend to live with their parents for their entire lives.

While distinctions based on *qaum* (tribe) remain significant social markers in the Punjab, particularly in rural areas, they have nowhere near the authority that tribal affiliation holds in the NWFP and Baluchistan. In the latter areas, patrilineally related lineages are the most significant bonds, with vendettas and feuds an intrinsic feature of social relations. Being irredentists (tribal members who recognize no legitimate authority other than that of their immediate tribal leader), Pakhtuns (the dominant ethnic group in the NWFP) and Baluchis (the dominant ethnic group in Baluchistan Province) have traditionally acknowledged only the legitimacy of their own groups' leaders.

In Sind, socioeconomic ties traditionally revolved around a few large dominant *waderas*, or landholding families. The remainder of people lived in persistent poverty. After independence, the millions of Hindus and Sikhs who left for India were replaced by roughly 7 million *muhajirs* (Muslims who fled from India to Pakistan at the time of partition in 1947), many of whom settled in the city of Karachi. Generally better educated than most native Sindhis, the refugees filled a vacuum in the province's commercial life and later provided the sociopolitical basis of the Muhajir Qaumi Movement, a political movement.

Urbanization has been occurring at an unprecedented rate in Pakistan, and 35 percent of Pakistanis now live in cities. Over half of all urban residents live in cities of more than a million people. Karachi and Lahore, the two largest cities, have estimated populations of 10 to 12 million and 7 to 8 million, respectively. The traditional hold—both economic and political—that local landlords enjoy in rural areas, especially in Punjab and Sind, virtually ensures the continuation of limited socioeconomic opportunities and mobility, which in turn are the greatest reasons for migration to urban areas.

Karachi has come to house the poorest slums in the country, particularly in the working-class neighborhoods of Orangi and Korangi. It has been ravaged by violence in the 1990s as contending ethnic groups vied to solidify their local power and control. Since the eruption of the civil war in Afghanistan, the city of Karachi had also become a destination point for a new kind of immigrant, refugees from Afghanistan escaping the turmoil in that country and the poverty and dependency of the refugee camps in NWFP and Baluchistan.

Pakistan was suddenly thrust to the center of the global political arena in the days following the terrorist attacks of 11 September 2001. As it had been a frontline state in the U.S. proxy war against the former Soviet Union in Afghanistan, it now became a frontline state in the war against global terrorism, particularly against the Taliban-led government of Afghanistan and Osama bin Laden's al-Qaeda organization. With Pakistan's unwavering support, military action succeeded in overthrowing the regime in Afghanistan in December 2001, and a new government has begun to take shape.

Anita M. Weiss

Further Reading

Ali, Imran. (1988) *The Punjab under Imperialism, 1885–1947.* New York: Columbia University Press.

Blood, Peter R., ed. (1995) *Pakistan: A Country Study*. Washington, DC: Area Handbook Series, Federal Research Division, Library of Congress.

Harrison, Selig S., Paul H. Kreisberg, and Dennis Kux, eds. (1999) *India & Pakistan: The First Fifty Years.* Cambridge, U.K., New York, and Melbourne, Australia: Cambridge University Press.

Hoodbhoy, Pervez, ed. (1998) *Education and the State: Fifty Years of Pakistan.* Karachi, Pakistan: Oxford University Press.

Khan, Shahrukh Rafi, ed. (2000) *Fifty Years of Pakistan's Economy: Traditional Topics and Contemporary Concerns.* Karachi, Pakistan: Oxford University Press.

Talbot, Ian. (1998) *Pakistan: A Modern History.* London and New York: St. Martin's Press.

Weiss, Anita M., and S. Zulfiqar Gilani, eds. (2001) *Power and Civil Society in Pakistan.* Karachi, Pakistan: Oxford University Press.

PAKISTAN—ECONOMIC SYSTEM

In August 1947, the partition of British India into the nations of India and Pakistan produced economic as well as political divisions. Britain had administered its Indian empire as a single economic unit. The partition not only caused population dislocations but also dissolved the integrated economy, and the greatest costs of this economic dislocation fell on Pakistan.

Early Stages of Pakistan's Economy

At independence Pakistan's basic physical infrastructure was extremely limited. It had only one seaport, Karachi. In Pakistan's eastern province, East Bengal, there were no port facilities. During the British period East Bengal's exports and imports had moved

In reaction to economic instability in 2001, customers of Pakistan's industrial bank seek to withdraw their funds. (AFP/CORBIS)

through the Indian port of Calcutta. Rail transport was almost nonexistent in East Pakistan and in the western provinces, and the railways ran from the interior to Karachi but not between the provinces. The world's largest irrigation system, developed by the British, was bifurcated due to the division of Punjab Province between India (which received the eastern portion) and Pakistan (which received the western portion).

Pakistan's private sector consisted of a small-scale trading class. Government services were also limited because few senior civil servants had opted for Pakistan. In short, Pakistan "was not only politically, socially, and administratively backward compared to the rest of India but was, economically, also the poorest part of the British Indian Empire" (Burki 1999: 95). The economy of the new nation was rural, with three-fourths of its gross domestic product (GDP) contributed by the agricultural sector. By 1949–1950 agriculture accounted for 53 percent of the GDP, while the services sector accounted for 39 percent. Industry was a low 8 percent of GDP.

Development of the Economic System

Pakistan's economic development began with government efforts to deal with refugee resettlement. The partition of British India had caused massive population movements, with Hindus and Sikhs leaving the western provinces of Pakistan to move to India and Muslims leaving India to settle in the provinces of Punjab and Sindh (in particular, Karachi) in Pakistan. The transfer of people numbered in the millions. Refugee relief became the first economic development problem confronting the government. Large-scale famine was avoided, and people were resettled.

Without a sizable business community, Pakistan filled the economic void through five-year planning and development of a public-enterprise sector. The first five-year plan, 1955–1960, did not meet its ambitious targets. The GNP growth rate for the decade of the 1950s was about 2.7 percent, while the population growth rate for the same period was approximately 1.8 percent.

The decade of the 1960s saw an improved GNP growth rate of about 6.8 percent, with a population growth rate of 2.8 percent. The government of Pakistan, headed by President Muhammed Ayub Khan, proclaimed the 1960s as the decade of development, and Pakistan was viewed by many as an economic model for other economically less developed countries to follow. The 1960s saw public enterprises playing an even larger role in the economy than in the 1950s.

Ayub's government also encouraged the growth of the private sector through incentives to family-controlled Pakistani businesses. In 1968, however, this strategy was criticized as promoting income inequalities, and Ayub's patronage of the so-called Twenty-Two Families (families engaged in business or industry, who had prospered from government concessions) was charged with creating and not alleviating poverty in the country.

With the transfer of power from military leadership to Zulfikar Ali Bhutto in December 1971, Pakistan's economic development switched gears. One target of Bhutto's wrath was the industrial families who had benefited from the Ayub regime and who were thus, by Bhutto's reasoning, enemies of his government. Beginning on 2 January 1972, just thirteen days after he became president, Bhutto nationalized thirty-one banks and large-scale industrial enterprises, and on 19 March 1972, he nationalized life insurance companies.

In engaging in this nationalization program, Bhutto discouraged domestic investment and increased the government's role in the economy. Each private unit nationalized became a public enterprise. By 1977 the government controlled all domestic banking (90 percent of the finance sector), 90 percent of the energy sector (electricity, gas, and oil), 11 percent of the industrial and manufacturing sector, 50 percent of the transportation and communications sector (with monopolies in air, rail, and shipping as well as telecommunications), and 70 percent of the mining sector.

An economic event that began in the 1970s had a positive impact on Pakistan's economy: the migration of Pakistani workers from the Middle East and South Asia to the oil-rich countries of the Gulf region. Over the next several decades, millions of Pakistanis worked in the Gulf states and sent home remittances. Worker remittances formed the single largest source of foreign exchange in Pakistan for several years. However, the decade of the 1970s witnessed a slowdown in economic growth (4.6 percent) and an increase in population growth rate (3.5 percent).

By the early 1980s individual countries and the international assistance community (the World Bank and the International Monetary Fund, in particular) had become disenchanted with government involvement in the economy and with public enterprises. The assistance agencies began to pressure nations such as Pakistan to disinvest and privatize their public-enterprise sectors. Pakistan initially resisted pressures to privatize. Because Pakistan was playing a central role as a conduit of arms and supplies to resistance groups fighting Russian troops in Afghanistan, Pakistan government officials thought Pakistan might be immune to such pressure.

Because Pakistan was a frontline state in the Afghanistan conflict, countries providing foreign assistance did not pressure Pakistan to make economic reforms to liberalize the economy, for fear that Pakistan would no longer support the resistance movements. Foreign aid continued to flow into Pakistan during the 1980s, helping to substitute for Pakistan's inability to tax its own citizens to further its economic development. The government of Pakistan could not tax its own citizens because of political pressure from elite groups, such as large landowners, whose income from agriculture was exempt from taxation.

As a result of massive amounts of foreign assistance and remittances from its overseas workers, the GNP in the 1980s grew at more than 6.0 percent, while population growth continued around 3.0 percent per annum. This rate of economic growth did not continue in the 1990s. On 1 October 1990, President George Bush suspended economic and military aid to Pakistan, based on new information concerning Pakistan's nuclear program, thus making Pakistan the first victim of the so-called Pressler Amendment to the U.S. Foreign Assistance Act. The Pressler Amendment prohibited the United States from providing economic and technical assistance to nations that were developing nuclear weapons capabilities. By this time, Pakistan was no longer a frontline state because the Soviet Union had withdrawn its troops from Afghanistan. Pakistan lost more than $500 million in capital flow from the United States in 1990–1991.

During the 1990s, Pakistan's economy grew on average around 3 percent per annum. Domestic savings and investment declined. The most recent data show that exports dropped by 10 percent, the national debt rose to $70 billion, which is equivalent to Pakistan's annual GDP, and its foreign exchange reserves could cover only about six weeks of imports.

Past Accomplishments and Future Prospects

Over the past five decades Pakistan's economy has moved away from agriculture to services and industry. Today the service sector accounts for 50 percent of GDP, while agriculture (at 26 percent) and industry (at 24 percent) follow. Although some attempts were made in the 1990s to liberalize the economy through limited government disinvestment and privatization, the government is still the main economic policymaker and manager of the economy.

Agenda items for economic reform in Pakistan might include maximizing domestic savings and aligning foreign inflows (foreign assistance and remittances, for example) with productive investment requirements to promote economic growth and poverty reduction. As a result of Pakistan's help in U.S. efforts to dismantle the terrorist network of Osama bin Laden by destroying the Taliban's control of Afghanistan, the economic sanctions imposed by the United States on Pakistan after Pakistan detonated its nuclear device were lifted in 2001. In addition, Pakistan will again receive U.S. economic and technical assistance. Such external assistance will have a positive impact on the economy.

Robert Laporte, Jr.

Further Reading

Birkhead, Guthrie S., ed. (1966) *Administrative Problems in Pakistan.* Syracuse, NY: Syracuse University Press.

Burki, Shahid Javed. (1999) *Pakistan: Fifty Years of Nationhood.* 3d ed. Boulder, CO: Westview Press.

Burki, Shahid Javed, and Robert LaPorte, Jr., eds. (1984) *Pakistan's Development Priorities: Choices for the Future.* Karachi, Pakistan: Oxford University Press.

Husain, Ishrat. (1999) *Pakistan: The Economy of an Elitist State.* Karachi, Pakistan: Oxford University Press.

"Pakistan: Cooking the Books." (2000) *The Economist* (8 April): 40–41.

Papanek, Gustav F. (1967) *Pakistan's Development: Social Goals and Private Incentives.* Cambridge, MA: Harvard University Press.

A teacher takes advantage of the warm weather and teaches the class outdoors in Hunza. (CHRISTINE OSBORNE/CORBIS)

PAKISTAN—EDUCATION SYSTEM

The educational system of Pakistan is among the least-developed in the world. The system was based on the British colonial educational system, which lasted until 1947. In that year, Pakistan gained independence as a result of the partition of the Indian subcontinent into the states of India and Pakistan. The colonial system was elitist; it was meant to educate a small portion of the population to run the government. Despite changes since independence, the Pakistani educational system has retained its colonial elitist character, a factor preventing the eradication of illiteracy.

Structure

The educational system in Pakistan is divided into five major levels. The pre-university education consists of four levels: the primary level (grades one to five), the middle level (grades six to eight), the high level (grades nine and ten, culminating in matriculation), and the intermediate level (grades eleven and twelve, leading to a diploma in arts or science). There is also a university level, which leads to undergraduate and graduate degrees.

The Pakistani educational system is highly centralized. The Ministry of Education is in charge of coordinating all institutions involved in academic and technical education, up to the intermediate level. For education programs above that level, there is a government-designated university in each of four Pakistani provinces of Sind, Punjab, Baluchistan, and the North West Frontier. These universities are responsible for coordinating instruction and examinations of all post-secondary institutions in their respective province. Apart from the Ministry of Education, other ministries may oversee certain degree programs of relevance to their activities.

Private and nonprofit schools and universities have begun to appear in Pakistan. These include the Lahore University of Management Sciences and the Aga Khan Medical University in Karachi. As privately funded universities, they provide an opportunity for higher education for a small percentage of people who do not have a chance to pursue their studies at publicly funded universities, which have limited annual admissions.

Performance

Despite the intentions of the Pakistani government, the educational system has failed to eradicate illiteracy in the post-independence era. It has also failed to train an adequate number of professionals to meet the needs of the country in different fields, which has been a major hindrance to the nation's economic development. The government-implemented reforms of the 1950s, 1960s, and 1970s did not address these deficiencies. By and large, they focused on replacing English, the colonial language of education, with Urdu, the language of most Pakistanis. The reforms of the 1970s also led to the nationalization of schools.

Facing the continued shortcomings of the educational system, the Pakistani government implemented new reforms in the late 1980s and early 1990s. These took the form of three major initiatives. The government privatized the schools nationalized in the 1970s. It also reversed the process of promoting Urdu as the language of education and encouraged a return to English language in the elite private schools. Finally, the government emphasized Pakistani studies and Islamic studies as two major fields in the curriculum. This was a shift from colonial education's emphasis on British history and English culture and literature.

The reforms of the post-independence era have improved the educational system and have increased the number of literate Pakistanis, but there are still basic shortcomings. Educational funding is low, and there is little political will to make improvements. In the 1999–2000 school year, government spending on education was about $1.8 billion, equal to 2.1 percent of Pakistan's gross national product (GNP). This amount represents a decrease from the period 1995–1997, when government expenditure on education equaled 2.7 percent of GNP, which itself was an insignificant figure for a country of approximately 144 million (2001 estimate), whose population is increasing at the annual rate of 2.4 percent.

Pakistan's expenditure on education is even significantly lower than that of India, a nation more or less at the same developmental level, with a much larger population and a heavier financial burden. During the period 1995–1997, India's expenditure on education was 3.2 percent of its GNP. In short, Pakistan's expenditure on education is not enough to meet the growing demand for educational services for the nation's increasing young population.

According to official statistics, the Pakistani literacy rate was 47 percent in 2000. This rate may be exaggerated, as the United Nations Development Programme (UNDP) statistics for 1998 suggest a literacy rate of 44 percent. According to the UNDP statistics for 1998, India's literacy rate was 55.7 percent, far above that of Pakistan.

The Pakistani educational system has demonstrated a discriminatory trend against women. This bias is evident in the pattern of literacy, which shows a strong correlation between gender and literacy rates. The illiteracy rate is very high among Pakistani women of all age groups. In 1998, the adult illiteracy rates were 42 percent for males and 71.1 percent for females. In the same year, the illiteracy rate for male youth and female youth was 25 and 53 percent, respectively. This gender-based discriminatory trend in education has contributed to the persistence of illiteracy and to a chronic shortage of educated people and has had a major impact on the continued underdevelopment of Pakistan.

Future Trends

The education system of Pakistan has been unable to meet the educational requirements of the Pakistanis. The system needs massive investment to increase the number of educational institutions and to train and recruit adequate numbers of educators at all levels. The Pakistani government has limited financial resources, which are inadequate to meet all of its needs. Added to large defense expenditures justified by the unstable relations between India and Pakistan, rampant corruption and a huge foreign debt (about $33 billion in 1998) further reduce the available resources for educational purposes. Unless the deteriorating Pakistani economy improves, there is little, if any, hope for a significant qualitative and quantitative change in Pakistan's educational system in the foreseeable future.

Hooman Peimani

Further Reading

Economist Intelligence Unit. (2000) *Country Profile, 2000: Pakistan-Afghanistan*. London: Economist Intelligence Unit.

Islam Seek. (2001) *Muslim Countries—Pakistan: Country Study*. Retrieved 15 June 2001, from: http://www.islamseek.com.

Library of Congress, Federal Research Division. (2001) *Pakistan—A Country Study*. Washington DC: Library of Congress. Retrieved 15 June 2001, from: http://lcweb2.loc.gov/frd/cs/pktoc.html.

United Nations Development Programme. (2000) *Human Development Report, 2000.* New York: UNDP.

World Bank. (2000) *World Development Indicators, 2000.* Washington, DC: World Bank.

PAKISTAN—HISTORY

Pakistan's history is often said to begin with the Arab invasion of the region of today's Sind in 611 BCE, but the territory of Sind had been mentioned earlier in Vedic literature. The nation of Pakistan was established on 14 August 1947 at the termination of the British Indian empire. The term *Pakistan* (pure land) alphabetically represents the Muslim majority areas of prepartition India: *P* for Punjab, *A* for Afghani regions (North West Frontier Province), *K* for Kashmir, *IS* for Indus-Sind, and *TAN* for Baluchistan. Bengal—a portion of which is present-day Bangladesh—was not originally included but was added by the British before partition.

Background

Joint expressions of Indian nationalism by Hindus and Muslims under the All India National Congress became ineffective after 1906, when the Indian nationalist movement was bifurcated on the basis of the Two-Nation theory, which said that British India should be partitioned into two nations on the basis of religion: one nation for Hindus and one for Muslims. From that point forward, both communities began to represent their constituencies with different platforms. Contrary to the popular notion that Pakistan originated for religious reasons, Pakistani nationalism derived from the nineteenth-century Muslim linguistic nationalism ignited by the replacement of Persian by English as the official language of the region. The linguistic factor inherent in the Hindu-Muslim conflict over the status of Hindi (spoken by more Hindus) and Urdu (spoken by more Muslims) as national languages is also salient to the Two-Nation Theory. Such differences led to separate political representation when the All India Muslim League was established under the leadership of Muhammad Ali Jinnah (1876–1948).

The idea of creating several independent Muslim states in Muslim-majority areas under British rule had already emerged, and the Muslim League formally adopted this position at the Lahore Convention (1940). Later, in the Pakistan Resolution, the Muslim League demanded a single Muslim state. To legitimize the Muslim League's demand, the legislative assembly of the Muslim-majority province of Sind was the first to pass a resolution in 1945 to support the idea of new Muslim states. After some regional adjustments, such as the division of Bengal and Punjab provinces, and despite reservations on the part of some conservative Hindu and Muslim groups, the British government acceded to the Muslim demand for a separate Muslim polity.

The new Islamic Republic of Pakistan was divided in two parts: East Pakistan (now Bangladesh) and West Pakistan (now Pakistan), separated by 1600 kilometers of Indian territory. East Pakistan included the East

Pakistani president Pervez Musharraf and Egyptian foreign minister Ahmed Maher, in Islamabad, November 2001, discuss the U.S. attack on the Taliban in Afghanistan. (AFP/CORBIS)

As part of the political instability that has marked Pakistan's leadership in recent years, protestors march in October 1999 following a bloodlesss coup by General Pervez Musharraf. (REUTERS NEWMEDIA INC./CORBIS)

TAKHT-I BAHI—WORLD HERITAGE SITE

One of the first World Heritage Sites to be so designated by UNESCO (1980), Takht-I-Bahi is an ancient hilltop Buddhist monastery near the citadel of Sahir-I-Bahol in Pakistan. The monastery has survived relatively intact since the first century CE.

Bengal province, and West Pakistan included Sind, West Punjab (including the Sindhu-Sagar Siraiki belt), Baluchistan, and the North West Frontier Province regions. Jinnah, as the first governor-general, deemphasized the religious nature of the new state in favor of secularism in the first session of the Pakistan Legislative Assembly. However, the postindependence emphasis on Islamic ideology as an integrative force binding together a multiethnic and multicultural country into a single nation-state did help to keep the country united.

The political and constitutional history of Pakistan has been somewhat unsteady. Pakistan has been ruled for more years by military than civilian governments and since independence has seen at least three major constitutions: 1956, 1962, and 1973. The 1973 constitution has been subjected to several suspensions and amendments under military rule. The goal of permanent democratization is reflected in the political party processes, although a decade (1989–1999) of civilian rule led to speculation that the Pakistani political culture requires a form of controlled democracy paving the road toward full-fledged future democracy. In addition, some problems originating in the partition, such as the dispute with India over Kashmir, have dominated the political and regional agendas.

Postindependence

Amid the postpartition migration of Muslims to Pakistan and Hindus to India, and with the Kashmir conflict simmering, a power struggle between Pakistan's landed aristocracy, immigrant leadership, and business groups, which began with the death of Jinnah, led to chaos and the assassination of the first prime minister, Liaqat Ali Khan (1895–1951). Although the government attempted to build new infrastructure, organize the bureaucracy and armed forces, and settle the issues of refugees versus natives, all these problems, along with limited state resources, limited Pakistan's reasonably fast progress toward economic and social development. Political differences among the provinces, particularly between East Pakistan and West Punjab province, the latter of which had a disproportionately large representation in the armed forces, created a political imbalance and led to the dismissal of Bengali leaders from the government and similar problems in other provinces. Threatened by the high demographic representation of East Pakistan in the government, the powerful West Punjabi governor, Ghulam Muhammad, on his own initiative amalgamated all four Pakistani provinces into a "One Unit" scheme (1955). On the surface, the West Punjabi establishment temporarily managed an artificial balance between East and West Pakistan, but the unpopular action ignited feelings of deprivation and generated subnationalist movements. The instability in East and West Pakistan ultimately led to civil war and the founding of Bangladesh in 1973.

Ayub Khan and the Post-Ayub Era

In October 1958, General Mohammad Ayub Khan (1907–1974), the commander in chief of the armed forces, suspended the 1956 constitution and took over the government. The coup d'état was carried out in time to prevent a probable vote in the Pakistan Legislative Assembly against the unpopular One Unit scheme in West Pakistan. Ayub Khan prolonged his rule for ten years. He introduced a new constitution in 1962, focusing on basic democracy, an indirect form of representation through officials elected at the village level, who voted for assembly members and also served as an electoral college for presidential elections.

KEY EVENTS IN MODERN PAKISTAN HISTORY

1906 The Two-Nation Theory becomes the dominant nationalistic agenda of Muslims in South Asia.

1940 At the Lahore Convention, support is given to the idea of Muslim states in Muslim areas of British rule.

1945 The legislature in Sind Province passes legislation supporting the creation of Muslim states.

1947 Pakistan becomes an independent nation.

1951 Liaqat Ali Khan, the first prime minister, is assassinated.

1955 The four West Pakistan provinces are united under the One Unit Scheme.

1958–1965 Period of rule of General Mohammad Ayub Khan, who comes to power in a military coup.

1965 Pakistan loses the first Indo-Pakistan War.

1969 National elections are held, followed by political instability.

1970 Pakistan loses the second Indo-Pakistan War.

1971–1977 During the rule of Zulfiqar Ali Bhutto stability is restored.

1973 Civil war results in East Pakistan becoming the independent nation of Bangladesh.

1977–1987 Bhutto is overthrown by Mohammad Zia-ul-Haq, whose regime is marked by political repression.

1988 The Pakistan People's Party comes to power through elections.

1990–1999 Period of political instability with several changes in leadership.

1999 General Parvaiz Musharraf comes to power in a military coup.

2001 Pakistan supports the United States in its attack on Afghanistan.

Despite some important achievements in agriculture and industry, Ayub Khan was compelled to resign over the outcome of the India-Pakistan war (1965) while celebrating a decade of development achievements. Ayub's successor, General Yahya Khan, consented to political reform. He abolished the One Unit plan and held national elections in 1969. Two major political parties, the Awami League in East Pakistan and the Pakistan People's Party in West Pakistan, emerged with an overwhelming majority vote in their respective constituencies. The neonationalist positions taken in the aftermath of elections in East and West Pakistan and disagreements over the formula for the transfer of power apparently led Yahya Khan to delay and postpone the transfer of political power to the newly elected leaders. The ensuing political riots, military response, and a civil war in East Pakistan graduated into another Indo-Pakistan war (1970), contributing to the fall of Dhaka (December 1970) and the creation of the Republic of Bangladesh.

Yahya Khan handed over the presidency of the rest of Pakistan to the West Pakistani populist leader Zulfiqar Ali Bhutto (1928–1979), chairman of the Pakistan People's Party. The Bhutto period (December 1971–July 1977) has been credited with achieving much desired stability and political reforms. However in July 1977, amid political crises created by the religious right, Bhutto was overthrown by General Mohammad Zia-ul-Haq (1924–1988), who later brought Bhutto to trial on questionable charges and sentenced him to death. Zia justified the military takeover and the abrogation of the constitution on the grounds that it was necessary for the Islamization of Pakistan. The Zia regime has been characterized as the most repressive in Pakistan's history. His mysterious death in an airplane crash (1987) led to increasing democratization as political repression was eased.

The Post-Zia Period

The elections of 1988 produced a victory for the Pakistan People's Party, with Benazir Bhutto (b. 1953) as the new prime minister. The Benazir government, however, was dismissed on corruption and mismanagement charges within eighteen months. Despite her political comeback in 1993, the prevailing mismanagement and corruption, as well as the intolerant attitude of the political opposition, led to her second dismissal. Her political rival and successor after each dismissal, Nawaz Sharif, also faced similar charges and a similar fate. By 1996, Benazir's Pakistan People's Party was defeated by the Muslim League and could not form a government even at the provincial level.

In October 1999, the chief of the Pakistan armed forces, General Parvaiz Musharraf, overthrew the Nawaz Sharif government. The Pakistani courts found both Benazir and Nawaz guilty of mismanagement and corruption, although both leaders have disputed the verdicts. Benazir remains in exile to avoid jail, while Nawaz faces additional charges. The new president, General Musharraf, has been advised by the Supreme Court of Pakistan to introduce economic and political reforms and elections to transfer political power to the democratically elected representatives by 2003. In 2001, he sided with the United States and supported its war on terrorism and invasion of Afghanistan while also cracking down on alleged extremists in Pakistan.

Aftab A. Kazi

Further Reading

Cloughly, Brian. (1999) *History of the Pakistan Army: Wars and Insurrections*. Karachi, Pakistan, and New York: Oxford University Press.

Dani, Ahmed Hassan. (1969) *Perspectives of Pakistan*. Islamabad, Pakistan: National Institute of Pakistan Studies, Quid-e-Azam University.

Kazi, Aftab A. (1987) *Ethnicity and Education in Nation-Building: The Case of Pakistan*. Lanham, MD: University Press of America.

Khan, Roedad. (1997) *Pakistan: A Dream Gone Sour*. Karachi, Pakistan: Oxford University Press.

Pasha, Ahmed Shuja. (1995) *Pakistan: A Political Study*. Lahore, Pakistan: Sang-e-Meel Publications.

Raza, Rafi, ed. (1997) *Pakistan in Perspective, 1947–1997*. Karachi, Pakistan: Oxford University Press.

PAKISTAN—HUMAN RIGHTS

PAKISTAN—HUMAN RIGHTS The state of Pakistan was created in 1947 as a homeland for Muslims. The result was mass rioting as people were displaced and forced to flee from their ancestral homes: Hindus and Sikhs fled to India from Pakistan, and many Muslims came to Pakistan from India. From its very inception, Pakistan was a Muslim state, in which non-Muslims had either been killed or forcibly expelled and their property seized. Given this background, civil- and human-rights abuses are not unexpected in Pakistan.

In the Universal Declaration of Human Rights (UDHR) adopted by the United Nations in 1948, great importance is placed on a person's right to life, liberty, and personal security. Although Pakistan has agreed with the UDHR, within an Islamic context there is abuse of human rights, especially of women, religious minorities, and children living in poverty.

Women and Human Rights in Pakistan

To Western eyes, women in Pakistan are treated as second-class citizens. Thus, a man can freely kill his wife if he considers that her words or actions have dishonored him or his family. According to the Human Rights Commission of Pakistan (HRCP), roughly 80 to 90 percent of women encounter domestic violence, which is socially tolerated because of the Islamic culture of male dominance over women. If a woman files a charge of rape, she herself faces being charged with adultery, according to the Hudood ordinances (laws that seek to harmonize the penal code with Islamic teaching). If a woman fails to prove that she did not consent to the sexual attack, she can be flogged or even publicly stoned, according to the law. Disproving consent, and therefore proving rape, can be difficult for women, since females or non-Muslims cannot be brought forward to testify; neither have any rights in an Islamic court. Added to this is the fact that police often rape women in custody.

Honor killings are also common in Pakistan. For example, in 1997 two hundred fifty women were burned alive because they dishonored their husbands, but only six husbands were arrested. Men are rarely if ever brought to justice, since numerous loopholes in the law make prosecution next to impossible. In 2000, there were eight hundred reported honor killings of women.

According to the U.S. State Department, Pakistan is a major player in the trafficking of women, most of whom end up in Saudi Arabia or the United Arab Emirates, where they are kept as sex slaves or house slaves.

Children and Human Rights in Pakistan

Children from poor families are also harshly treated, and their plight is completely ignored in Pakistan, according to the Commission of Inquiry for Women created by the U.S. State Department. They are frequently kidnapped or sold into slavery (bonded labor) or prostitution by their parents. Since there are no statutory-rape charges in Pakistan, girls sold into prostitution can be charged for adultery under the Hadood ordinances. Children, like women, suffer because the few laws that exist for their protection are rarely enforced.

It is also common to find children in the correctional system. Since there is no separate system for juvenile offenders, children are placed in the general prison population, where they are brutalized and abused by prisoners and guards. Such treatment violates the U.N. Conventions on the Rights of the Child. However, there is no legal will to ensure the protection of children.

According to the U.S. State Department, young boys are sold to the United Arab Emirates, where they are used as camel jockeys and are poorly fed, so that they do not gain weight.

Religious Minorities and Human Rights in Pakistan

Although Pakistan is largely Muslim, there are small pockets of Hindus, Sikhs, and Christians. It is often the practice that non-Muslims cannot own food stores, food-vending facilities, or restaurants; at times, they cannot frequent such establishments, the belief being that the touch of a nonbeliever defiles a Muslim.

This intolerant attitude in society has also found its way into the legal system in the shape of blasphemy laws, which have been created to punish blasphemers: those who defile the name of the prophet Muhammad are to be put to death; those who desecrate the Qur'an are to be imprisoned for life; and those who insult another person's religious beliefs may be imprisoned for up to ten years. According to the Human Rights Watch World Report of 1999, these laws are used to persecute non-Muslims and those deemed as non-Muslims (such as members of the Ahmadiya sect of Islam). As well, Muslims use these laws to settle scores or as a tool for intimidation. Those charged with blasphemy are in danger of being killed by lynch mobs, with the police merely standing by.

In 1999, a Christian man named Ayub Masih was sentenced to death for speaking favorably of Salman Rushdie's novel *The Satanic Verses*. Ayub Masih was shot in court by one of the men who brought the charge against him. Although Ayub Masih survived the attack, his assailant was not charged. In protest, the bishop of Faisalabad, a city in the Punjab, publicly committed suicide. The bishop's sacrifice accomplished nothing, since non-Muslims are still persecuted by way of these laws.

The Ahmadiyas, a Sufi-Muslim sect, have been completely disenfranchised in Pakistan. They have legally been declared non-Muslims and are forbidden to use Muslim forms and places of worship. In 1994 and again in 1992, the government of Pakistan issued a special ordinance in which Ahmadiyas were declared non-Muslims. They were charged with posing as Muslims in order to undermine the orthodox version of the faith. Ahmadiya mosques are routinely attacked, and people of the congregation murdered with impunity, since the police do little to interfere. Ahmadiyas are denied burial in Muslim cemeteries, and those already buried there are exhumed. The concept behind this action is again that of ritual pollution.

The police are often corrupt; they can arbitrarily arrest and detain citizens, and people in custody have reported abuses and attacks by the police. Aside from abusing prisoners, police routinely carry out extrajudicial killings of alleged criminals. These killings are reported to the press as "encounters" and always take place at night, in deserted areas, where there can be no eyewitnesses. The scenario is generally the same: the alleged criminals were being transported when friends of the criminals attacked the convoy in an attempt to free them; in the crossfire, all the prisoners were killed. Human-rights activists judge these encounters to be faked, nothing more than murder by the police. In 2000, there were 271 reported extrajudicial killings by the police. Various human-rights groups are actively seeking to change the status quo in Pakistan.

Nirmal Dass

Further Reading

Amnesty International. (1997) *Pakistan: Time to Take Human Rights Seriously*. New York: Amnesty International.

Jilani, Hina. (1998). *Human Rights and Democratic Development in Pakistan*. Lahore, Pakistan: Human Rights Commission of Pakistan.

Karim, Farhad. (1995) *Contemporary Forms of Slavery in Pakistan*. New York: Human Rights Watch.

Parekh, Vikram. (1999) *Prison Bound: The Denial of Juvenile Justice in Pakistan*. New York: Human Rights Watch.

Rehman, Javaid. (2000) *The Weaknesses in the International Protection of Minority Rights*. The Hague, Netherlands, and Boston: Kluwer Law International.

PAKISTAN—POLITICAL SYSTEM

The Islamic Republic of Pakistan was declared an independent and sovereign nation on 14 August 1947, when the British transferred political power to Muhammad Ali Jinnah (1876–1948) and his supporters in the Muslim League. The new nation was carved from areas of the former British Indian empire and included the provinces of Punjab, Sind, North West Frontier, and Baluchistan in the west and East Bengal in the east. Separating the western and eastern provinces were more than sixteen hundred kilometers of Indian territory.

As the first Islamic republic to be created, Pakistan, it was hoped, would become a homeland for Muslims on the Indian subcontinent. The intention of Pakistan's new leadership was to establish a parliamentary political system using the Westminster model of British parliamentary democracy as the template, with government authority vested in a legislature, an executive composed of a cabinet headed by a prime minister, and cabinet members drawn from the legislature. Recognizing the ethnic and linguistic diversity of its population, Pakistan's leaders envisioned a federal system of government whereby the central and provincial governments had both independent and shared powers.

In Karachi, members of the Jama'at-e Islami party protest the Indian occupation of Kashmir on 2 June 1999. (AFP/CORBIS)

Development of the Political System

On taking the oath of office as governor-general of the new republic, Muhammad Ali Jinnah (known to his followers as the *Quaid-e-Azam* or "Great Leader") appointed his lieutenant in the Muslim League, Nawabzada Liaqat Khan, as prime minister.

The First Decade, 1947–1958 Jinnah continued the viceregal system that the British had used to govern Pakistan as a colonial possession. Under this system, the governor-general dealt directly with senior civil servants, bypassing the civilian politicians who held ministerial positions. After Jinnah's death on 11 September 1948, Liaqat remained in the post of prime minister until his assassination on 16 October 1951. The power struggle between the offices of governor-general and prime minister then came to the fore, and this conflict has continued to reemerge throughout Pakistan's existence.

At independence, Pakistan had no constitution. The laws that substituted for a constitution were the Government of India Act of 1935 and the Independence of India Act of 1947, both enacted during the British colonial period. It was not until 23 March 1956 that Pakistan's first constitution was promulgated. The 1956 constitution maintained Pakistan's federal system, created a National Assembly, and changed the title of governor-general to president. Under the new constitution, the four western provinces were formed into one unit as West Pakistan, and East Bengal became the province of East Pakistan (the future Bangladesh).

The Ayub Khan Era, 1958–1969 Before elections could be held for a National Assembly and the two provincial assemblies, President Iskander Mirza abrogated the 1956 constitution on 7 October 1958, and General Muhammad Ayub Khan (1907–1970), commander in chief of the Pakistani army, was appointed chief martial-law administrator. In less than a month, Ayub removed Iskander Mirza as president and assumed total power on 28 October 1958. Thus Pakistan experienced its first military coup. Ayub appointed a commission to draft a second constitution that created a strong presidential political system. In the new constitution, the president has supreme power; the National Assembly rubber-stamps presidential decisions; the elections of the president and the members of national and provincial assemblies are indirect.

From independence and throughout the decades of the 1950s and 1960s, the people of Pakistan played almost no role in the governance of their country. Until 1971, the political elite, which included the Muslim League and the civil and the military services, governed with a heavy hand. No national elections based on universal suffrage (one person, one vote) were held. The military and civil services, created by the British, had changed little since independence. Although Ayub held indirect elections for the office of president and the national and provincial assemblies, the electorate was a group of eighty thousand so-called basic democrats, who were indirectly elected.

The Yahya Khan Interlude, 1969–1971 Ayub ruled Pakistan from 28 October 1958 until 25 March 1969, when General Agha Muhammad Yahya Khan (1917–1982), the commander in chief of the Pakistani army, forced him from office in Pakistan's second military coup. Yahya Khan then assumed the title of president and almost immediately abolished the 1962 constitution; eliminated the one-unit plan; reestablished the four provinces as separate political entities; and called for the National Assembly to be directly elected by the people. After its election, the National Assembly was charged to draft a third constitution. On 7 December 1970, Pakistan's first elections based on

PREAMBLE TO THE CONSTITUTION OF THE REPUBLIC OF PAKISTAN

Adopted 12th April 1973

Whereas sovereignty over the entire Universe belongs to Almighty Allah alone, and the authority to be exercised by the people of Pakistan within the limits prescribed by Him is a sacred trust;

And whereas it is the will of the people of Pakistan to establish an order:

Wherein the State shall exercise its powers and authority through the chosen representatives of the people;

Wherein the principles of democracy, freedom, equality, tolerance and social justice, as enunciated by Islam, shall be fully observed;

Wherein the Muslims shall be enabled to order their lives in the individual and collective spheres in accordance with the teachings and requirements of Islam as set out in the Holy Quran and Sunnah;

Wherein adequate provision shall be made for the minorities freely to profess and practise their religions and develop their cultures;

Wherein the territories now included in or in accession with Pakistan and such other territories as may hereafter be included in or accede to Pakistan shall form a Federation wherein the units will be autonomous with such boundaries and limitations on their powers and authority as may be prescribed;

Therein shall be guaranteed fundamental rights, including equality of status, of opportunity and before law, social, economic and political justice, and freedom of thought, expression, belief, faith, worship and association, subject to law and public morality;

Wherein adequate provision shall be made to safeguard the legitimate interests of minorities and backward and depressed classes;

Wherein the independence of the judiciary shall be fully secured;

Wherein the integrity of the territories of the Federation, its independence and all its rights, including its sovereign rights on land, sea and air, shall be safeguarded;

So that the people of Pakistan may prosper and attain their rightful and honoured place amongst the nations of the World and make their full contribution towards international peace and progress and happiness of humanity:

Now, therefore, we, the people of Pakistan,

Cognisant of our responsibility before Almighty Allah and men;

Congnisant of the sacrifices made by the people in the cause of Pakistan;

Faithful to the declaration made by the Founder of Pakistan, Quaid-i-Azam Mohammad Ali Jinnah, that Pakistan would be a democratic State based on Islamic principles of social justice;

Dedicated to the preservation of democracy achieved by the unremitting struggle of the people against oppression and tyranny;

Inspired by the resolve to protect our national and political unity and solidarity by creating an egalitarian society through a new order;

Do hereby, through our representatives in the National Assembly, adopt, enact and give to ourselves, this Constitution.

Source: Pakistani.org: "The Web for Pakistanis." Retrieved 8 March 2002, from: http://www.pakistani.org/pakistan/constitution/preamble.html.

universal suffrage were held. However, the results of the 1970 election were annulled due to the civil war that broke out on 25 March 1971. That conflict ended with the bifurcation of the nation and the creation of Bangladesh on 17 December 1971.

The Zulfikar Ali Bhutto Period, 1971–1977 Following the surrender of ninety thousand Pakistani troops in East Pakistan to the Indian army, President Muhammad Yahya Khan removed himself from office and appointed Zulfikar Ali Bhutto (1928–1979) as president. Bhutto's claim to national leadership was based on the results of the 1970 election, in which his party, the People's Party of Pakistan, won a majority of the seats in the four western provinces. One of his first acts as president was to remove or retire a number of Pakistani army generals to prevent another coup from taking place. Another of his immediate tasks was to convene the National Assembly (based also on the results of the 1970 election) to draft a third constitution for Pakistan. On 14 August 1973, the 1973 constitution went into effect. This constitution established a parliamentary system with the prime minister as the most important and powerful political official. The presidency was relegated to a largely symbolic office. Bhutto stepped down as president and assumed the office of prime minister. The third constitution also changed the title of the heads of the military branches from "commander" to "chief of staff," and the prime minister became the commander in chief of Pakistan's armed forces. This step was seen as an attempt to negate the power of the military. Bhutto also sought to reduce the power of the civil service by enacting a civil-service reform law coupled with a purge of approximately four thousand senior civil servants.

The Zia-ul-Haq Period, 1977–1988 By 1977, Bhutto was seeking continued legitimacy for his rule through national and provincial elections. When the results were announced, the opposition parties charged fraud and held street demonstrations that led to confrontations with the military. On 7 July 1977, Bhutto's appointee as chief of the army staff, General Mohammed Zia-ul-Haq (1924–1988), led the third military coup, suspended the 1973 constitution, dismissed the national and provincial assemblies, incarcerated Bhutto and members of the opposition, banned political parties, placed the country under martial law, and assumed the title of chief martial-law administrator.

During his eleven years of power, Zia ruled the country through the civil service and later through his handpicked politicians. Zulfikar Ali Bhutto was tried, convicted, and sentenced to death for conspiracy in the murder of a political opponent, and on 4 April 1979, Bhutto was executed. Zia initiated a program called Islamization, intended to neutralize the Muslim fundamentalist activists. He added amendments to the 1973 constitution that strengthened the role of the president (Zia assumed that title on 16 September 1978) and created a second legislative branch, the Senate, as a counterweight to the National Assembly. In 1985, Zia held nonpartisan elections for the national and provincial assemblies and shortly afterward revived the 1973 constitution as amended by him. He lifted the countrywide martial law on 30 December 1985.

The Post-Zia Period, 1988–Present

Zia died in the crash of a Pakistani air force C-130 military transport aircraft on 17 August 1988. The chairman of the senate, Ghulam Ishaq Khan, as acting president, called for elections, and elections for the national and provincial assemblies (on a partisan basis) were held in mid-November 1988. The People's Party of Pakistan (led by Zulfikar Ali Bhutto's daughter, Benazir) won a plurality of seats in the National Assembly and was asked by Ghulam Ishaq Khan to form a government. Thus after eleven years of military rule, civilians, selected through an electoral process based on universal suffrage, would again attempt to govern.

The political leadership structure created by Zia revolved around three power centers: the president, the prime minister, and the chief of the army staff. This troika, as it is referred to in Pakistan, was required to work together to be effective. Unfortunately conflict rather than cooperation marked the years of civilian governance following Zia's death. From 2 December 1988 to 12 October 1999, prime ministers were dismissed by presidents three times (August 1990, April 1993, and November 1996) and once by the chief of the army staff (October 1999). Neither Benazir Bhutto (prime minister from December 1988 to August 1990 and again from October 1993 to November 1996) nor Muhammad Nawaz Sharif (leader of the Muslim League and prime minister from November 1990 to April 1993 and again from February 1997 to October 1999) completed the terms for which they were elected. During his last term as prime minister, Nawaz pushed through legislation that eliminated the power of the president to dismiss elected governments and to appoint chiefs of staff of the armed forces, legally removing one leg (the president's) from the three-legged "power stool." He also attempted to place the chief of the army staff under the control of the prime minister, thus concentrating power into one position. In the manner of his military predecessor, Zia-ul-Haq, General Pervez Musharraf (b. 1943) assumed the title of chief executive after the 11 October 1999 coup and initiated an accountability process whereby Nawaz Sharif was convicted of hijacking and terrorism by an antiterrorism court and sentenced to life imprisonment. Furthermore, General Musharraf publicly vowed (on 7 February 2000) that power would never again be transferred to either Nawaz Sharif or Benazir Bhutto and stated that it would take five to ten years to "set things right in the country."

Pakistan has experienced over twenty-five years of governance by military leadership and only fifteen years of governance by democratically elected civilian leadership. Political power is concentrated in the central government, and the civil service plays a major role in the governance of the country. The outlook for a restoration of civilian-led government based on periodic democratic elections appears dim. General Musharraf has incarcerated some Islamists and prohibited others from staging protests against Pakistan's involvement in the elimination of the Taliban as the controlling power in Afghanistan and against the coalition and U.S. efforts to eliminate the terrorist group headed by Osama bin Laden.

Robert Laporte, Jr.

Further Reading

Burki, Shahid Javed. (1999) *Pakistan: Fifty Years of Nationhood.* 3d ed. Boulder, CO: Westview Press.

———. (1989) *Pakistan, A Historical Dictionary.* Metuchen, NJ: Scarecrow Press.

———. (1980) *Pakistan under Bhutto: 1971–1977.* London: Macmillan.

Burki, Shahid Javed, and Craig Baxter. (1991) *Pakistan under the Military: Eleven Years of Zia ul-Haq.* Boulder, CO: Westview Press.

Callard, Keith. (1957) *Pakistan: A Political Study.* London: Allen & Unwin.

LaPorte, Robert Jr. (1975) *Power and Privilege: Influence and Decision-Making in Pakistan.* Berkeley and Los Angeles: University of California Press.

Ziring, Lawrence. (1971) *The Ayub Khan Era: Politics in Pakistan, 1958–69.* Syracuse, NY: Syracuse University Press.

PAKISTAN PEOPLE'S PARTY

PAKISTAN PEOPLE'S PARTY The Pakistan People's Party (PPP) was founded by Zulfiqar Ali Bhutto (1928–1979), former foreign and prime minister and first PPP chairman, in December 1967 to launch a political movement that successfully led to the resignation of President Ayub Khan in 1969 and to national elections in 1970. Although the PPP is not a leftist party, its manifesto emphasized nationalizing banks, industries, insurance companies, schools, and colleges and promised land reform combining Islamic and mild socialist values to represent the PPP's diverse constituencies. The populist PPP won several elections, in 1970, 1977, 1988, and 1997. After the East Pakistan debacle (1971), Bhutto ruled residuary Pakistan as president and later as prime minister. PPP rule during the 1971–1977 period has been credited with the maintenance of relative stability in Pakistan. After the military takeover of 1977 that enforced Islamization, particularly after the controversial hanging of Bhutto in 1979, the PPP was severely repressed.

Since 1979, the PPP has been headed by Bhutto's wife, Nusrat Bhutto, and daughter, Benazir Bhutto (b. 1953). The Movement for the Restoration of Democracy brought the PPP back in power twice, in 1988 and 1993, with Benazir Bhutto as prime minister, only to be dismissed in 1990 and 1996, respectively. Since 1997, the PPP has been an opposition movement. Following her 1999 conviction for corruption, Benazir Bhutto has lived in exile, and the PPP, despite relative popularity, has experienced organizational problems.

Aftab A. Kazi

Further Reading

Akhund, Iqbal. (2000) *Trial and Error.* Karachi, Pakistan: Oxford University Press.

Bhutto, Benazir. (1988) *Daughter of the East: An Autobiography.* London: Mandarin.

Kazi, Aftab Ahmed. (1981) *The Politics of Civil-Military Relations in Pakistan.* Pittsburgh, PA: Center for International Security Studies, University of Pittsburgh Press.

Mahmood, Safdar. (2000) *Pakistan: Political Roots and Development.* Karachi, Pakistan: Oxford University Press.

Raza, Rafi. (1997) *Zulfiqar Ali Bhutto and Pakistan 1967–1977.* Karachi, Pakistan: Oxford University Press.

PAKUALAMAN

PAKUALAMAN In eastern Yogyakarta city lies the well-preserved Pakualaman Palace, home of the Pakualaman principality. The four palaces—namely Yogyakarta, Pakualaman, Surakarta, and Mangkunegaran—in the Yogyakarta and Surakarta regions each represent a different past political entity, but all are descendants of the Javanese Mataram kingdom.

Pakualaman itself is a relatively new principality, created by British Lieutenant-Governor Sir Thomas Raffles on becoming aware of correspondence between the royal households of Yogyakarta and Surakarta proposing they jointly oust the British from Java. In 1812 Raffles marched on the Yogyakarta *kraton* (palace) and its sultan, Hamengkubuwono II. British troops looted the *kraton*, destroying its archives and cultural treasures. The sultan's brother and former confidante, Natakusuma, who assisted the British, was rewarded with a territory of 4,000 households carved from Yogyakarta. Natakusuma took the title Paku Alam and is described in historical accounts as very savvy. He and his supporters adopted European manners and dressed in British cavalry uniforms for formal occasions (Carey 1992: 20), thus gaining greater access to Raffles' court. Paku Alam offered priceless Javanese artifacts to Raffles, well known for his interest in maritime Southeast Asia. Paku Alam is also thought to have informed the British of an alliance between Yogyakarta and Surakarta. While Paku Alam's independent territory was established in June

1812, the agreement was not formally sealed until 17 March 1813 when the Contract and Engagement between Britain and Paku Alam was signed (Carey 1992: 14). Contention with the British arose in October 1812, when Paku Alam attempted to claim more lands; Sepoy troops of the British garrison blocked further enlargement.

During World War II Paku Alam IIX forged an agreement with the Sultanate of Yogyakarta to accept a subordinate role to the main *kraton*. Both the sultan and Paku Alam supported the independence struggle led by Sukarno against the Dutch (1945–1949). In recognition of this, Yogyakarta retains a special status whereby the sultan of Yogyakarta is the provincial governor. In the interregnum after the death of Hamengkubuwono IX, Paku Alam IIX was appointed interim governor.

While most people living in the Yogyakarta area give their allegiance to the city's sultan, the princedom of Pakualaman has found a niche in promoting Javanese culture. Paku Alam and his immediate descendents (Paku Alam II and Paku Alam III) were all gifted in architecture, culture, and literature and did much to restore Javanese high culture in the Yogyakarta region after British destruction of the Yogyakarta *kraton*. The palace itself remains a repository of Javanese culture with displays of architecture, antiques, regular performances of Javanese gamelan orchestra, and other cultural arts.

Anthony L. Smith

Further Reading

Allan, Jeremy. (1989) *Yogyakarta*. Singapore: Times Editions.

Carey, Peter, ed. (1992) *The British in Java 1811–1816: A Javanese Account*. Oxford: Oxford University Press.

Koentjaraningrat. (1985) *Javanese Culture*. Singapore: Institute of Southeast Asian Studies and Oxford University Press.

PALAUNG STATE LIBERATION PARTY

The Palaung State Liberation Party is an armed opposition movement among the Palaung (Ta-ang) people of the Shan State of Myanmar (Burma). Related to the Wa, the Palaung and their villages are found in a number of districts in the state. The main military activities, however, have been centered in the northern mountains between Namhsan, Namkham, and the tea-growing valleys of the former Tawngpeng substate. In these areas a Palaung *sawbwa* (prince) traditionally ruled.

Palaung culture and politics have always been linked with wider developments in the Shan state. Like the Shans, most Palaungs are Buddhists. In 1963 the first Palaung insurgent group, the Palaung National Force (PNF), was established under the Shan State Army before setting out on its own three years later. In 1968 a damaging split occurred between PNF troops led by Kham Thaung and those headed by three sons of the last Tawngpeng *sawbwa*. Kham Thaung's troops came out on top, after which the surviving son, Chao Nor Far, merged his remaining soldiers with the Shan United Revolutionary Army based in the south of the state.

In 1976 the PNF was reconstituted as the Palaung State Liberation Party (PSLP) and joined the National Democratic Front. Kham Thaung died in 1979 from battle wounds, but the PSLP worked closely with the Kachin Independence Organization and the SSA and grew into an effective military force during the 1980s, with an estimated one thousand soldiers under arms.

In 1991 the PSLP was one of the first NDF groups to agree to a cease-fire with the State Law and Order Restoration Council (SLORC) government. Under the leadership of Aik Mone, the PSLP embarked on a number of peace and development schemes in its territory, designated as Shan State Special Region 7, with the expectation that this would eventually become a Palaung autonomous region in the country's future constitution.

Martin Smith

See also: **Ethnic Nationalism and Armed Conflict—Myanmar; Kachin Independence Organization; Myanmar—History; Myanmar—Political System; Shan State; State Law and Order Restoration Council—Myanmar; United Wa State Party**

Further Reading

Milne, Leslie. (1924) *The Home of an Eastern Clan: A Study of the Palaung of the Shan States*. Oxford: Clarendon.

Smith, Martin. (1999) *Burma: Insurgency and the Politics of Ethnicity*. 2d ed. London: Zed Books.

Tzang Yawnghwe, Chao. (1987) *The Shan of Burma: Memoirs of a Shan Exile*. Singapore: Institute of Southeast Asian Studies.

PALEOANTHROPOLOGY—CENTRAL ASIA

Central Asia, covering the territories of present-day Turkmenistan, Uzbekistan, Tajikistan, Kyrgyzstan, and Kazakhstan, was home to numerous prehistoric cultures. Their development was characterized by three main stages: a food collection economy of the Stone

Age (c. 800,000–6000 BCE), a food production economy of early agricultural communities (c. 6000 BCE), and more highly developed proto-urban civilizations in southern Central Asia (5000–2000 BCE) and more archaic stockbreeding cultures in the northern part of the region (4000–1000 BCE). (A proto-urban civilization is at an early developmental stage of urban civilization characterized mainly by the presence of large, dense settlements and the differentiation of the population into specialized occupational groups.) The rate of progress was mainly influenced by environmental conditions. Archaeological excavations in Central Asia reveal a wide range of localities, dated back to all the Stone Age subdivisions—the Paleolithic (Old Stone Age), Mesolithic (Middle Stone Age), and Neolithic (New Stone Age)—as well as to the Bronze Age.

Paleolithic (c. 800,000–10,000 BCE)

Occasional dissociated (unrelated) Lower Paleolithic (c. 800,000–100,000 BCE) implements have been found in the mountainous eastern part of Central Asia. These were a crudely made core (a piece of obsidian or stone from which flakes have been struck to make implements) and a primitive axe from the lower terrace of the Vakhsh River in northern Tajikistan, as well as stone flint workings from the Kuldara site in southern Tajikistan and the On-Archa site in the Tian Shan range in Kyrgyzstan. Similar finds were made near the port of Turkmenbashy in Turkmenistan, and in southern Kazakhstan at the Borikazgan, Tanirkazgan, Shabakty, Akkol-1, and Kazangap sites.

The most ancient Central Asian human remains (c. 650,000–600,000 BCE), along with a great variety of pebble tools, were excavated at the Sel-Ungur site in the Fergana Valley. The recovered artifacts were crudely made chopping tools, nondescript cleavers, amorphous cores, and triangular and oval hand axes. Lower Paleolithic multilayer sites (c. 200,000 BCE) were discovered in Uzbekistan, near its capital Tashkent (the Kulbulak site), and in southern Tajikistan (Karatau-1 and Lakhuti-1). Both culturally and historically, the Central Asian pebble cultures are connected with the pebble-tool zone in Southeast Asia and the northern part of the Indian subcontinent.

During the Middle Paleolithic (c.100,000 40,000 BCE) a cold and humid climate, together with an abundance of water, vegetation, and fauna species, made Central Asia a favorable human environment. Hundreds of Middle Paleolithic sites have been discovered throughout Central Asia. The most remarkable discovery was made in the Teshik-Tash cave of the Baisuntau Mountains in southern Uzbekistan. Aside from a considerable quantity of stone workings and burnt animal bones, the well-preserved skull and skeleton of a Neanderthal boy were recovered. The burial site, surrounded by wild goat horns, suggests the existence of primitive beliefs (because a funeral ritual had been observed) in Central Asia during the Middle Paleolithic.

Central Asian localities dating from the Upper Paleolithic (c. 40,000–10,000 BCE) are less numerous. In Upper Paleolithic cultures, a flint industry (frequently repeated microliths of a particular material or function) was predominant. Microliths are small (1–5 centimeters) stone tools, mainly thin blades with sharp cutting edges, usually geometric in shape. One of the earliest sites of the period was excavated near Turkmenbashy, where a great number of prismoid (in the form of a prism) cores were found. One of the best-studied Upper Paleolithic sites in Central Asia is the Samarqand campsite, which has three cultural layers. Other major Upper Paleolithic sites are Kapchigai and Hoji Gor in the Fergana Valley, Uchtut and Ijont in the Zeravshan Valley, Kulbulak, near Tashkent, Uzbekistan, and Shugnou and Yakshi in the Pamir Mountains in Tajikistan. The Yakshi site, at 2,000 meters above sea level, is one the highest known Paleolithic sites.

Mesolithic (c. 10,000–6,000 BCE)

The majority of the Mesolithic cultures in Central Asia developed a distinct blade-type industry, microlithic techniques, and tools of geometric shapes. Mesolithic cultures were found in the Caspian region, western Tajikistan, the Fergana Valley, and the eastern Pamir Mountains.

The Caspian group is the best studied and comprises the lower layers of the caves of Jebel and Dam-Dam-Chashma in the Balkhan Mountains, as well as the Kailiu Grotto in western Turkmenistan. Among the artifacts excavated were flint piercers, pointed scrapers, backed blades, and lunates (crescent-shaped flints with their inner edges untrimmed and the thick, rounded edges having small chips removed; used as arrowheads). The main activities of the eastern Caspian Mesolithic tribes were hunting and fishing. Cattle breeding had already begun, but due to the desert conditions, domesticated animals were not a major food source during the Mesolithic.

The sites in western Tajikistan are located along freshwater sources, mainly tributaries of the Amu Dar'ya River. One of the earliest of these is Kui Bulein, where blades with blunted edges, points (flint implements in the form of blunt darts, pointed at one end and oval or flat at the other), and geometric implements were found. Symmetrical trapezoids and a small lunate were recovered at the Chi-Chor-Chashma site. A cultural layer has not been preserved at either site; both are most likely the remains of temporary camps used by hunters.

The Fergana Valley group includes both open sites and caves. The Obi-Shir and Tash-Kumir caves yielded flint implements, distinguished by their large size, while the majority of the Fergana artifacts are markedly microlithic. A similar culture, with a wide use of microblades, was discovered in northern Afghanistan.

The culture of the eastern Pamirs comprises approximately twenty localities, including two large open sites—Karatumshuk and Oshkhona—which were summer campsites for roving hunters. The flint industry of this culture is distinctive. Crudely made discoid cores, scrapers, backed blades, arrowheads, and pebble choppers, retaining superficially archaic forms, are distinctly related to the Late Paleolithic of the Siberian-Mongolian tradition. Rock paintings of typical hunting scenes, executed in red ochre mixed with animal fat, were discovered in the Shakhty cave.

Neolithic And Aeneolithic Cultures (6000–2500 BCE)

The shift to a production economy during the Neolithic period (a global phenomenon known as the Neolithic revolution) led to profound changes in human society. The transition, which began with the domestication of animals and cultivation of plants, gradually diminished the importance of hunting, fishing, and plant gathering. With the introduction of copper and bronze, a higher level of productivity was reached. Wide use of firing furnaces and the potter's wheel, a greater variety of sophisticated tools, and stone and ceramic seals (devices for impressing characteristic marks into a soft surface to indicate ownership or authenticity) point to the establishment of a proto-urban civilization with crafts and incipient trade, which had been already separated from plant cultivation and stockbreeding.

The Djeitun culture (6000 BCE), located in the Kara Kum Desert of southern Turkmenistan and adjacent districts of Iran, is the earliest known agricultural civilization in Central Asia. Djeitun artifacts include microlithic flint geometric tools, polished flat discs of irregular shape, sandstone querns (handmills for grinding grain), pestles, mortars, and flat-bottomed clay pots made without the use of a wheel and decorated with simple painted patterns. All the sites (approximately twenty) were small villages, the largest of which—Chopan-depe—occupied an area of two hectares. The settlements consisted of one-room houses built of cylindrical clay bricks. Owing to the dry climate, primitive forms of irrigation, such as spring and summer flooding, were used. The Djeitun had domesticated sheep and goats, although hunting was still an important element of their everyday life.

Unlike Djeitun agrarians, Neolithic inhabitants of the Caspian area in Turkmenistan were fishermen and hunters. The main sites are the upper layers of the caves of Dam-Dam-Chashma and Jebel (5000—4000 BCE), where hand made round-based pottery with incised decoration, as well as notched blades, scrapers, trapezoids, and arrowheads, were excavated. Other sites in northern Turkmenistan are located east of the Caspian Sea (Hoja Su, Chagmak, and Janak) and in the Greater Balkhan Desert (Bash Kariz and Tash Arvat).

The largest Neolithic culture in the Khorezm area, along the lower Amu Dar'ya, is the Kelteminar (c. 5000–3000 BCE); the earliest occupation site is Janbaskala-4, in the Kyzyl Kum Desert. The Kelteminar artifacts include richly decorated round-based pots (early Kelteminar) and less decorated globular vessels with flat bases (late Kelteminar). The Kelteminar's main activities were fishing, hunting, food gathering, and incipient stock breeding.

The Neolithic culture of Djeitun in southern Turkmenistan was followed by a number of more developed Aeneolithic (transitional between Neolithic and Bronze Age) cultures, characterized by the use of copper. Excavations at the Anau mounds brought to light pottery, distinguished by its ample sand admixture, polished clay, and skilled firing. These are thin-walled, elegantly shaped vessels, mainly drinking bowls with concave bases. Other major Aeneolithic complexes in southern Turkmenistan, including the Chakmakli, Govich-depe, Koushut, and Monjukli sites, yielded pottery painted with rhomboids flanked by two triangles.

The lowest three cultural layers (5000–3000 BCE) of the major Aeneolithic-Bronze Namazga culture, located along the foothills of the Kopet Dag Mountains in Turkmenistan, marked the further growth of a food production economy, which resulted in a number of large agricultural settlements, where stock breeding almost totally replaced hunting. Weaving, as indicated by a large number of excavated baked-clay spindle whorls, was well developed. The largest settlements are Beurme, Karantki, and Tokai of the western zone, Kara-depe and Namazga-depe of the central zone, Chaachi-Sai and Meana-Sai of the eastern zone, and the Geoksyur Oasis north of the Kopet Dag. By the middle of the third millennium BCE, the Namazga-depe irrigation system was improved by the introduction of dykes, dams, and canals. Decorated pottery and figurines were far more sophisticated.

Sarazm, along the Zeravshan River in Tajikistan, near the Uzbek border, revealed totally unexpected urban settlements with painted pottery, giving evidence of direct contact with Baluchistan, Pakistan, in the early Aeneolithic period (c. 3000 BCE). These settlements were unexpected because the area had not been known for its developed urban settlements dated back as early as 3000 BCE.

The Neolithic Hissar culture in the mountainous eastern area of Central Asia is characterized by crude pebble tools. The main sites—Kun Bulien, Tutkaul, and Seyed, in southern Tajikistan—are located near sources of fresh water. The Hissar artifacts include arrowheads, polished axes, mortars and granite querns, bone piercers, and handmade point-based vessels (meant not to be stood on the flat end but rather to be dug into the earth) with textile impressions. The main occupations of the Hissar people were hunting, food gathering, agriculture, and stock breeding.

Bronze Age (2500–1000 BCE)

In Central Asia bronze replaced copper at the beginning of the third millennium BCE. Productive forms of economy further evolved that led to the appearance of larger proto-urban settlements with multiroom houses, defensive walls, and craftsmen's quarters.

The majority of Central Asian Early Bronze settlements (2500–2000 BCE) have been discovered in southern Turkmenistan. The largest sites are Ak-depe, Namazga-4, Altyn-depe, and Ulug-depe. Excavations at the best-studied site (Altyn-depe) yielded the remains of a 2-meter-thick fortification wall with towers, four collective funeral chambers, and ten building complexes. The typical pottery is a wheel-made red burnished ware with black spots. The few metal articles discovered include a vessel, makeup sticks with thickened ends, a spiral-headed pin, chisels, earrings, and punches (tools, usually short metal rods, variously shaped at one end for different uses). Cattle breeding continued to play a significant role. Two- and four-wheeled vehicles, most likely drawn by Bactrian camels, were used.

The most important Middle Bronze Age centers (2000–1600 BCE) in southern Turkmenistan were the urban settlements of Namazga-depe and Altyn-depe, where differences in social status of the inhabitants is evident in domestic architecture and funeral remains. A cult complex at Altyn-depe, built with one-meter thick blocks, suggests separation of a priestly class. Craft specialization is evident from the remains of mass-produced standardized, but elegant, pottery. Fields were artificially irrigated, although by less advanced techniques than those in use at the time in Mesopotamia.

The Late Bronze period (1500–1000 BCE) in southern Turkmenistan is characterized by the collapse of the major urban settlements in the piedmont zone (at the foot of mountains) and an overall decline in known settled areas. There are several possible explanations for this phenomenon, the most probable of which are environmental degradation and mass tribal migrations. Excavation sites at the Sumbar cemetery, the Namazga "tower," Tekkem-depe, Ulug-depe, and elsewhere have yielded bronze weapons, such as ribbed arrow and lance heads with new types of ornamentation. In Turkmenistan, Bronze Age sites also have been found in the Kelleli, Gonur, Auchin, Togolok, and Takhirbai Oases in Merv, along the Murgab River.

The Bronze Age in Khorezm, along the lowermost course of the Amu Dar'ya, is represented by the Tazabagyab culture (second millennium BCE), considered a southwestern extension of the Andronovo culture, spread into the neighboring steppe zone. The largest and best-studied Tazabagyab site is Kokcha-3, where a collective burial tomb has been excavated. The pottery items were cooking pots decorated with triangles. Bronze articles included awls, pendants, and bracelets.

Bronze Age sites in southern Uzbekistan have been recovered at four oases along the Surkhandarya River, and near minor streams emerging from the Baisuntau Mountains. Larger sites are Sapalli-tepe, Djarkutan, Buston, Bandikhan-1, Molali, and Buirachi-tepe. The most completely studied site, Sapalli-tepe, is remarkable for its planned architecture and rich and fairly well-preserved graves. The Bronze Age sites in this part of Central Asia do not appear to be as developed or densely occupied as the agricultural oases in Turkmenistan.

In northwestern Afghanistan, the Harappan civilization flourished in the small urban site of Shortughai, an advanced post on the Indus River, from 2600 to 1600 BCE. The post was started partly for the exploitation of lapis lazuli.

The Bronze Age along the lower Zeravshan River is represented by the Zamanbaba cemetery and settlement, comprising several oval earthen huts. The ceramics excavated were mostly hand made egg-shaped vessels with rounded or pointed bases and holes along the rim. Other artifacts include feeding troughs, cross-shaped beads, cylindrical clay pinheads, and metal mirrors. The Zamanbaba people were agriculturists and stockbreeders.

Along the middle section of the Zeravshan, the urban site of Sarazm declined, with evidence of intrusion from the neighboring Andronovo steppe culture.

The Fergana Valley had an established agricultural and stockbreeding economy, visibly influenced by the pastoral farming tribes of the neighboring steppe. The Kayrakkum culture spread over the western Fergana Valley, on the left bank of the Syr Dar'ya River. The Kayrakkum were farmers, stockbreeders, fishermen, and hunters. The proximity of copper ore deposits facilitated the development of a distinguished bronze industry and made mining an important part of the Kayrakkum economy as well.

The other Bronze Age culture discovered in the Fergana Valley is the Chust. The larger settlements are Dalverzin and Ashkal-tepe, although there were also smaller ones—Chust and Dekhkan. The inhabitants engaged in farming and stockbreeding; weaving was also of great importance. Among the implements discovered were bronze sickles, chisels, knifes, awls, and needles; weapons included arrowheads and spearheads; some horse harness equipment was also found. Chust pottery was made without the use of the potter's wheel. Thin-walled tableware, covered with red and black patterns, is very similar to that of southern Turkmenistan.

Assessment

The prehistoric development of human society in Central Asia proved the successive passage from a food collection to food production economy. The shift to agriculture and stockbreeding in Central Asia (the Neolithic revolution) made the rate of development and cultural differentiation between the southwestern and northeastern extremities of the region increasingly tense. Agrarian oases of Djeitun, Altyn-depe, and Namazga in southern Turkmenistan were almost a millennium ahead of the more archaic cultures of Khorezm, Fergana, and Hissar. Nevertheless, by the beginning of the first millennium BCE, when major urban settlements in southern Turkmenistan declined, their cultural achievements had been diffused farther northeastward into regions where farming had been at a very primitive level, or almost totally unknown. The intensified contacts between the Central Asian cultures, which led to their distinct drawing together, were further enhanced during the Iron Age, when recorded history began.

Natalya Yu. Khan

Further Reading

Belenitsky, Aleksandr. (1968) *Central Asia.* Geneva: Nagel Publishers.

Dani, Ahmad Hasan, and Vadim Mikhailovich Masson, eds. (1992) *History of Civilizations in Central Asia.* Paris: UNESCO Publishing.

Frankfort, Henri-Paul. (1989) *Foilles de Shortugai. Recherches sur l'Asie Centrale Protohistorique.* Paris: Editions Recherches sur les Civilisations.

Graves, Charles. (1994) *Proto-Religions in Central Asia.* Bochum, Germany: Brockmeyer.

Harris, David R., ed. (1996) *The Origins and Spread of Agriculture and Pastoralism in Eurasia.* Washington, DC: Smithsonian Institution Press.

Hiebert, Fredrik Talmage. (1994) *Origins of the Bronze Age Oasis Civilization in Central Asia.* Cambridge, MA: Harvard University Press.

Kohl, Philip L. (1984) *Central Asia. Paleolithic Beginnings to the Iron Age.* Paris: Editions Recherches sur les Civilisations.

———, ed. (1981) *The Bronze Age Civilization of Central Asia.* New York: M. E. Sharpe.

Masson, Vadim Mikhailovich, and Viktor Ivanovich Sarianidi. (1972) *Central Asia; Turkmenia before the Achaemenids.* Southampton, U.K.: Thames and Hudson.

Sinor, Danis. (1990) *The Cambridge History of Early Inner Asia.* Cambridge, U.K.: Cambridge University Press.

PALEOANTHROPOLOGY—EAST ASIA

In East Asia, the study of human origins and evolution, now known as paleoanthropology, began in 1923, with the discovery of Peking Man in a cave in China. The discoveries there followed on discoveries of early fossilized hominid remains in Java in the 1890s; similar discoveries were also being made during the 1920s and 1930s in Africa.

The First Discoveries

When Otto Zdansky, an Austrian geologist, discovered a worn and fossilized molar tooth at Zhoukoudian, forty-eight kilometers southwest of Beijing

DISCOVERY OF PEKING MAN—WORLD HERITAGE SITE

The site of the discovery of the Peking Man, located 42 kilometers southwest of Beijing, was designated a UNESCO World Heritage Site in 1987. The remains, dating from 18,000 to 11,000 BCE, are essential to understanding the prehistory of Asian societies.

PALEOANTHROPOLOGY—EAST ASIA

This is a description of the Cherchen Man, the most famous of the 3,000 year-old Caucasoid mummies found at Ürümchi, a stop along the ancient Silk Road. The desiccated corpses and their burial clothing and tapestries survived surprisingly well, giving archeologists clues to the genetic makeup and cultural origins of the mysterious mummies.

> His face is at rest, eyes closed and sunken, lips slightly parted; his hands lie in his lap, while his knees and head are tilted up—like a man who has just drifted off to sleep in a hammock. Visitors tend to tiptoe and lower their voices. A two inch beard covers his face, and his light brown hair has been twisted—plied from two strands, not braided from three—into two queues that hang halfway down to his chest. Here and there white hairs glint among the yellow-brown betraying his age—somewhere past fifty. He would have been an imposing figure in life, for he once stood six feet six inches tall.
>
> Bright ocher-yellow face paint curls across his temple, sprouting short rats on its outer cheek and reversing its curl as it meanders down to the flatland of his cheek before climbing across the great ridge of his nose—not a low bridged Asian nose but a veritable Sierra Nevada of a nose—to the far side. . . .
>
> Passing from the face, one's eye jumps between the violently colored leggings and the purply-red brown two-piece suit that covers most of the man's body. Originally the man wore soft white deerskin boots to above his knees—the left one is still there. But the right one has torn away, revealing horizontal stripes of gaudy red, yellow, and blue that put Ronald McDonald in the shade. . . .
>
> And his suit? By way of decoration on the plain-weave fabric, the tailor of the Cherchen Man's suit whipped bright red yarn as a sort of piping over the seams of both the shirt body and around the neck and front opening of the shirt. It produces a very subtle but very effective ornamentation—subtle because the piping is so fine and because its bright red color rests against the purply-red background. . . . Holding the man's shirtfront together is a waist cord plaited from yarns of five different colours: bright red, dark purply brown, blue, green, and yellow.

Source: Elizabeth Wayland Barber (1999) *The Mummies of Ürümchi.* New York: W. W. Norton & Company, 26–27.

(Peking), he recognized the similarities between it and the molar teeth of living people. The limestone deposits at Zhoukoudian also contained the remains of extinct mammal species, however, so that Zdansky realized that the humanlike tooth was extremely old. Subsequent work at Zhoukoudian between 1927 and 1937 by European, North American, and Chinese scholars, including Johan Anderson, Davidson Black, Pei Wenzhong, and Franz Weidenreich, confirmed the age and importance of the cave deposits at Zhoukoudian. By 1937 the fragmentary remains of at least thirteen skeletons of *Homo erectus* (an extinct relative of modern humans, who lived between 1.6 million and 200,000 years ago) had been recovered, along with broken mammal bones and associated cultural remains, such as stone tools. It is now known that the layers containing these fossil bones date to between 400,000 and 250,000 years before the present. (These layers at Zhoukoudian have been dated by using uranium series dating of bone, electron spin resonance of dental enamel, paleomagnetic sequences of sediments, and other methods. The results are reasonably consistent with the hominid fossils between 400,000 [bottom] and 250,000 [top] years ago.)

Later Excavations at the Peking Man Site

The archaeological deposits at Zhoukoudian became known as the "Peking Man" site. In one of the greatest scientific tragedies of the twentieth century, all the Zhoukoudian fossils discovered before World War II were lost during an attempt to send them to the United States after the Japanese army invaded China. Fortunately the German anatomist Franz Weidenreich had made detailed casts of the bones, and in association with his monographs, these enabled continued study of the fossils after they were lost.

After World War II, the Institute of Paleontology and Paleoanthropology in Beijing continued excavations at the Peking Man site and at other sections of the former cave complex. Between 1949 and 1966, five teeth, pieces of a tibia and humerus, and fragments of a skull and mandible were recovered.

Chinese archaeologists have identified thirteen layers in the excavated deposits at Zhoukoudian. *Homo erectus* remains and stone artifacts have been reported from Layers 3 to 9, with evidence of fire claimed for Layers 3, 4, 6, and 10. As well as *Homo erectus* fossil bones, the remains of more than ninety other mammal species have been recovered from the Peking Man site. These mammals included giant deer, hyena, saber-toothed cat, and horse. While some of these bones may be remains of *Homo erectus* meals, the majority are probably the result of carnivore activity in the caves.

Long-established interpretations of the excavated materials from the Peking Man site, including the evidence for fire, hearths, and stone- and bone-artifact manufacture, were challenged by Louis Binford (an American archaeologist) and his coworkers in the mid-1980s. They argued that natural processes rather than *Homo erectus* activity produced the ashlike deposits in the cave, and they claimed that many of the broken bones and stones were not artifacts. This opinion is generally accepted by North American and Western European scholars, although there is some resistance among Chinese scholars.

Homo erectus: Who, When, and Where?

At present the oldest reliably dated examples of *Homo erectus* remains come from the East African Rift Valley and are approximately 1.6 million years old. *Homo erectus* people appear to have evolved in Africa and then gradually spread through the tropical Old World (that is, the Eurasian landmass), reaching Java in Indonesia 800,000 years ago. The earliest *Homo erectus* examples from East Asia are those at the Chinese sites of Gongwangling and Chenjiawo in Shaanxi province in east-central China, dated to between 700,000 and 500,000 years ago. These dates are older than the Peking Man site (400,000 to 250,000 years ago). Pat Shipmann (an American archaeologist and science journalist specializing in interpreting faunal remains from archaeological sites) and others have argued that *Homo erectus* people were able to move out of Africa because hunting furnished more of their food than was the case with earlier human ancestors such as *Australopithecus*, who lived from around 5.3 million to around 1.6 million years ago. Those who depended on plant foods were limited in their movements by the often-restricted distributions of some preferred food-plant species.

Although *Homo erectus* people are known primarily from fragments of skull and jaw and isolated teeth, the discovery of more complete skeletal remains in East Africa has enabled a more thorough understanding of their appearance. At least in East Africa, they appear to have been as tall as modern people living in the same region. They had very long limbs and linearly shaped bodies, common among human populations living in hot climates today.

Much less is known about their East Asian descendants, but those who lived in the colder parts of their range probably were shorter and more robust than their African ancestors. While their body size was similar to modern humans, on average *Homo erectus* people had smaller braincases, larger teeth, and facial skeletons with heavier bones than *Homo sapiens* (the present human species). Above their eyes, a shelf of bone called a brow ridge projected; their foreheads receded; and their skulls were longer and generally flatter in shape. Areas of muscle attachment on the skull and other parts of the skeleton were more developed than in modern humans.

The Origins of Modern People in East Asia

At the time the initial discoveries were being made at the Peking Man site, the remains of other potential human ancestors had already been found in Java, Europe, and Africa. Franz Weidenreich noticed that there were anatomical differences between the fossil remains from different regions. His explanation of these physical differences linked variations among living people with geographic variations in the past. *Homo erectus* had spread over a large geographic area and had adapted to different regional environmental conditions. Variations in geographic adaptations, low population densities, limited interbreeding, and potential cultural differences between populations might have given rise to regional differences in physical appearance and physiology among ancient people. Weidenreich thought that these same factors were the origin of the geographic variations evident in human populations today. Furthermore he argued that anatomical features in modern East Asians were also present in Zhoukoudian *Homo erectus*. For Weidenreich this indicated that Peking Man was the direct ancestor of living Chinese people.

During the last twenty years, a protracted debate has been waged about the relationship of *Homo erectus* to modern humans, based on the analysis of genetic information in living populations, the recovery of deoxyribonucleic acid (DNA) from Neanderthal remains (Neanderthals, another extinct human species, date from approximately 100,000 to 35,000 years ago) and more recent fossils, and the comparison of the anatomical features in skeletal remains from different geographic areas. Most recently the comparison of Y chromosome and mitochondrial DNA information from living people with mitochondrial DNA from three northern European Neanderthal skeletons, and the appearance of early modern *Homo sapiens* skeletons in Africa, has indicated that *Homo erectus* is probably not a direct ancestor of our species. Our species appears to have evolved in Africa approximately 100,000 years ago and then moved out of Africa and displaced other species, including the Neanderthals. These anatomically modern humans reached Europe approximately 35,000 years ago and Australia at least 40,000 years ago.

There are now many *Homo erectus* and early *Homo sapiens* archaeological sites in East Asia, with the majority in eastern China. Unfortunately there is a gap in both the skeletal and archeological records between the first definitely modern people from sites like the Upper Cave at Zhoukoudian (not to be confused with the Peking Man site at Zhoukoudian), dated to between 20,000 and 15,000 years ago, and "archaic" *Homo sapiens* remains at sites like Dali and Mapa in China, which are between 300,000 and 100,000 years in age.

Clearly, however, people with East Asian facial features were not present in China before the Neolithic period, 10,000 to 7,000 years ago. (Modern Asian people have distinctive facial skeletons: for example, broad, flat cheekbones. Similar facial skeletons are common in the late Neolithic period from 8,000 years ago, but are not present in China before this time.) This finding supports the Y chromosome and mitochondrial DNA data obtained from modern populations, which indicate a recent African origin for all modern humans, and which exclude East Asian *Homo erectus* as an ancestor of living East Asians. East Asian people probably originated during a rapid expansion of Neolithic agriculturalists in the Chinese river valleys around 8,000 years ago.

Peter Brown

Further Reading

Binford, Louis, and C. Ho. (1985) "Taphonomy at a Distance: Zhoukoudian, 'The Cave Home of Beijing Man'?" *Current Anthropology* 26: 413–442.

Brown, Peter. (2001) "Chinese Middle Pleistocene Hominids and Modern Human Origins in East Asia." In *Human Roots—Africa and Asia in the Middle Pleistocene*, edited by Larry Barham and Kate Robson Brown. Bristol, U.K.: Western Academic & Specialist Press, 135–145.

Underhill, P. A., G. Rassarino, A. A. Lin, P. Shen, M. M. Lahr, R. A. Foley, P. J. Oefner, and L. L. Cavalli-Sforza. (2001) "The Phylogeography of Y Chromosome Binary Haplotypes and the Origins of Modern Human Populations." *Annals of Human Genetics* 65: 43–62.

Wu, Xinzhi, and Frank Poirier. (1995) *Human Evolution in China*. Oxford, U.K.: Oxford University Press.

PALEOANTHROPOLOGY—SOUTH ASIA

The scientific study of prehistoric human populations is called paleoanthropology. Paleoanthropologists examine human remains (including skeletons, of which some are fossilized) and archeological evidence of artifacts (including stone tools and other manufactured products of an extinct culture) in order to reconstruct lifeways of extinct populations for whom no written records may exist. Collaborating with paleoanthropologists are geologists and ecologists, who observe climatic and terrestrial changes; molecular biologists, who seek to reconstruct genetic relationships between ancient populations by DNA analysis; and geochronologists, who are able to determine the antiquity of skeletal and cultural remains through a variety of physical and biochemical techniques.

Human Settlement of the Indian Subcontinent

The scientific study of the archeology, skeletal biology, and ancient ecological settings of the prehistoric peoples of southern Asia (India, Pakistan, Sri

Lanka, Nepal, and the borderlands of these modern nations) reveals that humans inhabited this part of the world as early as 2 million years ago. This date falls within the Pliocene geological epoch that began about 5.2 million years ago. The fossil remains of the manufacturers of the crude chipped pebble tools discovered in geological deposits of this antiquity in the northwestern region of the Indian subcontinent have not been found. Until their skeletal remains are recovered, their genus and species identification within the human evolutionary tree remains uncertain. But the evidence of human occupation in South Asia from the archeological record left by later peoples, who achieved the making of technologically more advanced stone tools, is well established. At several archeological sites human skeletal remains have been unearthed and studied, including specimens from the Pleistocene epoch (popularly known as the Ice Age) that succeeded the Pliocene about 1.7 million years ago.

The stone implements are classified into prehistoric traditions according to their styles, raw materials, datable antiquity, and associated artifacts and traces of culturally distinctive lifeways. Succeeding the earliest chipped pebble tools, or "chopper-chopping tools," are the stone hand axes and cleavers of the Acheulian tradition of the Early and Middle Pleistocene geological subepochs (beginning about 1.4 million years ago and 780,000 years ago, respectively). From the Late Pleistocene subepoch (beginning about 130,000 years ago), one finds stone tools of the Mousterian (retouched flake tools) and Levalloisian (prepared-core flake tools) technological traditions. Blade and burin (bevel-pointed) tools appear in archeological sites dated to around 40,000 ago. All of these stone tool industries are included in a technological category called Paleolithic, or Old Stone Age. They are succeeded by the manufacture of small flake tools called microliths, which appear as early as 35,000 years ago in Sri Lanka and some 11,000 years ago in India and Pakistan, hence falling within the Late Pleistocene subepoch and the succeeding Holocene (also called the Recent, or Present Interglacial) epoch. Microlithic tools abound in post-Paleolithic, or Mesolithic, archeological sites throughout the Indian subcontinent.

The Socioeconomic Transition to Food Production

Paleolithic technological developments were followed by the domestication of plants and animals, which initiated both pastoralism and the establishment of sedentary life in villages, as well as development of new technologies, a cultural transition that has been called Neolithic (New Stone Age). By 7000 BCE, farming and herding practices were established in the northwestern sector of the Indian subcontinent; these gave rise to urban life by the end of the fourth millennium. Copper and bronze tools and weapons supplemented stone implements, hence these cultures have been assigned to a Bronze Age.

Among the advanced urban societies of this period were the Harappan (or Indus) civilization, located along the banks of the Indus river and its tributaries. From 3000 to 1700 BCE, this complex culture expanded over an immense domain from western Iran to the Himalaya mountains, the Punjab, southward to Gujarat in western India and the Ganges valley of north central India. Elements of the Harappan legacy survived among simpler food-producing village populations who used copper and bronze and who manufactured exquisite ceramics, but who did not continue the practices of a written script, grid-pattern streets indicative of carefully controlled city planning, standardized weights and measures, extensive trade contacts with the civilizations of Mesopotamia and the Persian Gulf, and other features of their Harappan predecessors. The post-Harappan tradition has been called the Chalcolithic (Copper) Age.

Agriculture and herding did not diffuse to central and southern India until after 2500 BCE, and there is no evidence of a Neolithic phase in Sri Lanka. Iron technology spread into these Indian regions after 1100 BCE. Many of the Iron Age villages erected large, upright standing stones, set up large boulders in circles or alignments, and built dolmens and stone-lined burial chambers covered with capstones. The Indian Iron Age is sometimes referred to as the Megalithic Age because of these giant stone monuments. This final era of South Asian prehistory survived in some localities until 50 CE. Even today, megalith building continues among some tribal populations. The Indian Iron Age ended with the dawn of the Indian early historic period, which emerged in the Ganges valley by the sixth century BCE, when the classical Buddhist, Hindu, and Jain religious and cultural traditions were established.

Research Methods

South Asian paleoanthropology includes the research of anthropologists concerned with the biological features of ancient peoples whose skeletal remains are preserved at the sites of these prehistoric cultural traditions. This record contains information that cannot be derived from other kinds of scientific investigations. Paleoanthropologists examine skeletal remains in order to determine the sex and age of the person at time of death. They observe evidence of trauma and disease from markers on bones and teeth, reconstruct living statures, analyze specific markers of occupational stress, note rates of growth and development, and establish the ancestral affinities of skeletal subjects. An individual skeleton or a cemetery series may reveal genetic affinities to other prehistoric groups or to living populations. The paleoanthropologist acquires these data from interpretations of measurements taken on bones and teeth with precision instruments and analysis of X-rays. Recorded are size, shape, and specific skeletal and dental traits, some of which are genetically inherited; others are due to cultural variables of habitual activities such as spear throwing, squatting as a resting posture, or bending over a metate (stone mortar) to mill coarse foods with a hand-held grinding stone. Paleoanthropologists collaborate with archeologists, paleoecologists, and geologists to reconstruct profiles of how the ancient peoples of South Asia evolved, adapted to different and changing ecological settings, and acquired their biological diversity.

South Asian Paleolithic Lifeways

South Asian peoples of the Paleolithic and Mesolithic tradition were hunter-gatherers who occupied natural caves and rock shelters but also settled along the banks of watercourses. The Narmada River is one of India's major waterways; its source is in the Himalaya Mountains and it flows across the north and central regions of India to empty into the Arabian Sea. Along the middle course of the Narmada Valley, near Hathnora village, the incomplete cranium of a late Middle Pleistocene human was found in 1982 by the geologist Arun Sonakia. In the vicinity of this fossil were stone tools of the Acheulian tradition and animal remains dated to 400,000–200,000 years ago. Examination of this fossil, called Narmada Man (though more likely a female than a male), indicates that it was an early member of our own species, *Homo sapiens*, but a number of its anatomical traits do not allow its classification with anatomically modern *Homo sapiens.* It therefore is identified as an anatomically archaic *Homo sapiens* (a taxonomic group to which some paleoanthropologists give the name *Homo heidelbergensis*).

In other parts of Asia the Acheulian tradition is associated with earlier members of the human family called *Homo erectus* (formerly called by the genus name *Pithecanthropus* and known popularly as the ape man). Evolving in Africa some 1.8 million years ago, *Homo erectus* migrated into Asia some 400,000 years later. Places of settlement and manufacturing sites are marked by tools of the Acheulian tradition that supplemented the older chopper-chopping tools as far eastward as northeastern India and Burma. The chopper-chopping tool tradition continued into East and Southeast Asia. The absence of Acheulian tools in these regions, even at localities where *Homo erectus* fossils have been found in China and Java, may be related to the timing of the diffusion of the Acheulian tradition out of Africa. That is, *Homo erectus* was already settled in Asia before Acheulian tools had been invented in Africa. In South Asia, tools of the Acheulian tradition were found at Hathnora in association with the human remains. The latter is identified as an anatomically archaic *Homo sapiens* rather than as *Homo erectus* because of its large cranial capacity, values obtained from cranial measurements, the formation and size of its brow ridges, and the thickness of the bones of the cranial vault. Some anatomical features of earlier humans are present, however. This picture may change if future discoveries turn up a *Homo erectus* fossil, but the present evidence demonstrates that the Acheulian tradition was practiced by more than one ancient species of humankind. Claims of finding ancestral human fossils from other localities within the Indian subcontinent, some of which were said to be of greater antiquity than the Narmada specimen, have not withstood scientific verification, but the prospect of discovery of additional Pleistocene fossils that are genuine and properly dated are excellent.

Biological Diversity and Change

Among Late Pleistocene fossils of the human family are those from northeastern Afghanistan's Mousterian (Middle Paleolithic) cave site of Darra-i-Kur, found in 1966, and a relatively large number of skeletons from the Sri Lankan cave sites of Fa Hien, Batadomba Lena, and Beli Lena Kitulgala, recovered in the 1970s. Microlithic tools are found with human skeletal remains in all of these Late Pleistocene to Middle Holocene sites as well as at several open-air burial and habitation sites. These and other archeological sites on the island have been assigned by some paleoanthropologists to a Mesolithic cultural tradition. Taken collectively, the Sri Lankan skeletons are all anatomically *Homo sapiens*, but they exhibit a high degree of muscular-skeletal robusticity (stoutly structured bones of the upper and lower extremities upon which muscular attachments are prominent, and pronounced development of cranial features such as brow ridges and bony attachments of the muscles of the neck). Molar and premolar teeth are large and the occlusal surfaces are heavily abraded.

There are other sites of microlith users who survived by hunting and gathering on the Indian mainland, some with human skeletons, as at Langhnaj in

Gujarat, Bagor in Rajasthan, and on the Gangetic plain at Sarai Nahar Rai, Mahadaha, and Damdama. Burials from the last three localities have yielded some forty or more skeletons. Although taller in stature than the Sri Lankan prehistoric people, these hunter-gatherers exhibit many of the same features of pronounced muscular-skeletal robusticity and large premolar and molar teeth. Although originally dated to the end of the Pleistocene, the Gangetic sites are now believed to have been inhabited as late as the third millennium BCE. Trade with sedentary village farmers and pastoralists occupying fertile valleys and plains may have taken place in this era, as at Langhnaj, where a copper knife of Harappan craftsmanship was recovered in the grave of one of the skeletons. As food-producing farmers and herders of the Neolithic tradition displaced the hunter-gatherers across much of the Indian subcontinent, the latter populations retreated to regions of relative isolation, some surviving as tribal groups to the present day.

Evolutionary Adaptations

In biology, evolution involves genetic changes in populations of living organisms from generation to generation. The fossil record of plants and animals, including humans, testifies to the fact that ancestral species differ anatomically from descendant species over the passage of time. The paleoanthropologist wants to know the origin, antiquity, and adaptive responses that account for anatomical diversity in different prehistoric human populations, including the role cultural behavior has played. Scientific studies of the ancient South Asian archeological and skeletal records and the reconstruction of different and changing environments leads to some of the following conclusions.

There is a trend toward reduction of muscular-skeletal robusticity and tooth size initiated by the socioeconomic transition from full-time hunting and gathering to domestication of plants and animals. Populations with the longest histories of farming and pastoral practices exhibit more gracile (slender) skeletal features than those encountered in populations where nature selected for more robust skeletal structures adaptive to a life of hunting large game and nomadic movement over extensive geographic territories. That is, the adaptive advantages of more powerful body structures among hunter-gatherer bands were not relevant to the sedentary food-producing lifeway, hence natural selection was "relaxed" and individuals with more gracile body builds were not at a disadvantage in their survival and opportunity to leave offspring with those adaptive traits. Also, certain cultural practices involving more complex technologies, trade contacts, and exploitation of a greater range of food resources contributed to those anatomical changes. Similar trends are found in other prehistoric populations outside of the Indian subcontinent.

As South Asia's prehistoric village communities increased in size and expanded into urban centers, as seen in the Bronze Age cities of the Harappan civilization and many centuries later in the Ganges Valley, health and rates of growth and development changed. Vectors of infectious diseases found a higher density of hosts in towns and cities than among nomadic hunting and gathering bands. Diseases such as tuberculosis, anemia, and dental caries (cavities), which leave characteristic markers on bones and teeth, may be diagnosed by paleoanthropologists. Other pathological conditions identifiable in a skeletal record are osteoarthritis and congenital conditions of abnormal growth and development. For example, it has been demonstrated that male infants were preferred over female infants among the Harappans since the female teeth bear markers of inadequate nutrition and higher incidences of episodes of interrupted growth. Among other physical changes related to cultural factors are the higher incidence of fractures of the skull in ancient village and urban site specimens than in those from hunting and foraging populations, the latter exhibiting higher frequencies of healed breaks of the bones of the lower limbs and torso. These differences may be related to trauma from interpersonal violence in the heavily populated towns and cities and to accidental incidences in the more dangerous and challenging life of nomadic hunter-gatherers. Changes in occlusal dental wear are often dramatic: the hunter-gatherers' severely worn teeth with their low frequencies of caries contrast remarkably with those of sedentary long-time food producers, whose teeth show less attrition but an increase in the number of pathological conditions, some of which are related to methods of food preparation and a high-carbohydrate diet.

All native South Asian populations existing today are genetically related to the ancient aboriginal peoples of this part of the world, although there has been some admixture with foreign populations coming from other parts of Asia, Europe, Arabia, and Africa. Certain prehistoric skeletal series are indicative of biological relationships to living populations of the subcontinent, while others appear to have no known descendants. Genetic affinities are of interest to paleoanthropologists, and from available evidence they do not perceive any mass migrations of peoples pouring into South Asia from some undefined place of origin in Central Asia, Africa, or elsewhere. This is a significant fact since there is a vast literature written by South Asian and Western historians about sudden demographic changes, in particular about the so-called Aryan invasion of India.

While it is true that the languages of Indo-Aryan or Indo-European stock are prevalent in Pakistan, northern India, and southern Sri Lanka, and that southern India is populated by speakers of two completely different linguistic stocks called Dravidian and Munda (also known as Australasian), the linguistic record is not concordant in any obvious way with the biological traits of prehistoric peoples in this part of the world. Attempts have been made to relate South Asian languages of these linguistic families to genetic affinities and theories of mass migrations, but these must be recognized as elements of cultural mythologies that bear political and religious considerations far removed from the data of paleoanthropological research.

Approaches to Paleoanthropological Research in South Asia

Paleoanthropology was conceived in South Asia as a synthesis of Western concepts of social progress, linear time, the Biblical creation story in Genesis, and the "noble savage" with Indian ideas about science and philosophy originating in the oral traditions that became the written Sanskrit and Pali literature of the Vedic texts. This synthesis continued during the several centuries of British colonial influence in India, and there was a reciprocal exchange of theories about human origins, antiquity, and humanity's place in nature with respect to the prehistory of the subcontinent. The myth of the Aryan conquest of this part of the world is one result of this synthesis. It is a unique intellectual development in paleoanthropology that has no counterpart in the paleoanthropological studies of other regions.

Another remarkable feature of South Asian paleoanthropology is that only a small number of native and foreign investigators are responsible for the considerable amount of research achieved by the close of the twentieth century. The contrast with the progress of paleoanthropology in Africa, North and South America, and Europe is striking. This difference in historical development may be due to several factors: the recognition that our earliest ancestors did not evolve in the Siwalik Hills of the Himalaya region, as had once been considered possible because of discoveries of fossil apes in this region; the fact that this part of the world did not yield any fossil remains of Pleistocene human ancestors until recently; and the policies of the governments of South Asian nations to provide minimal support for paleoanthropological research, preferring an investment in the biological anthropology of living populations. Nevertheless, the advancement of paleoanthropology in southern Asia has been remarkable in establishing a model for future research projects here and in other parts of the world. The employment of new analytical methods now available through achievements in computer science and the use of complex statistical methods hitherto impossible are solving questions of genetic affinities, biology, and lifeways of the earlier people of the subcontinent.

Kenneth A. R. Kennedy

Further Reading

Cohen, Michael, and George J. Armelagos, eds. (1984) *Paleopathology at the Origins of Agriculture.* Orlando, FL: Academic Press.

Deraniyagala, Siran U. (1992) *The Prehistory of Sri Lanka: An Ecological Perspective.* 2 vols. Colombo, Sri Lanka: Lakehouse Investments.

Kennedy, Kenneth A. R. (2000) *God-Apes and Fossil Men: Paleoanthropology of South Asia.* Ann Arbor: University of Michigan Press.

Kennedy, Kenneth A. R., Arun Sonakia, John Chiment, and K. K. Verma. (1991) "Is the Narmada Hominid an Indian *Homo Erectus?" American Journal of Physical Anthropology* 86, 4: 475–496.

Lukacs, John R., and J. N. Pal. (1993) "Mesolithic Subsistence in North India." *Current Anthropology* 34: 745–765.

PALEOANTHROPOLOGY—SOUTHEAST ASIA

In 1887, the Dutch anatomist Eugene Dubois (1858–1940) left the Netherlands for Sumatra in search of the missing link in the chain of human evolution. Dubois had been stimulated by the pioneering research on human evolution by Charles Darwin and Ernst Haeckel. A disciple of Haeckel, Dubois believed that the remote common ancestor of apes and humans had lived in Southeast Asia, rather than Africa, which was Darwin's choice. After failing to find fossil evidence in Sumatra, Dubois commenced fieldwork on the banks of the Solo River, near Trinil in central eastern Java in 1890. The following year his field team unearthed the fossilized skullcap of a primate that eventually became known as *Homo erectus.* In 1892, a short distance from the site of the original discovery, a complete human femur was also excavated. Although there has been considerable debate about the association between the skullcap and femur, Dubois believed the two bones to be from the same species. Dubois thought the small-brained biped more like an ape than a human and initially gave it the name *Anthropithecus erectus* ("erect manlike ape"), which he later changed to *Pithecanthropus erectus* ("erect ape-man").

Dubois was never comfortable with the notion that the Trinil fossils were closely related to *Homo sapiens*, and while his discoveries were widely applauded, his interpretation of their significance was not. The importance of *Pithecanthropus*, now *Homo erectus*, was reinforced by the more substantial discoveries at the "Peking Man" site, near Beijing, China, in the 1920s. Not only were a larger number of human-like fossils recovered, but stone tools and what was thought to be evidence of the use of fire were present as well. Particularly as a result of this cultural evidence, the scientific community became increasingly committed to thinking of *Homo erectus* as a direct ancestor of *Homo sapiens*. Unfortunately, until his death Dubois remained dismissive of the importance of the Chinese discoveries and the generally accepted view of the evolutionary position of his Trinil *Pithecanthropus*.

The next major discovery in Southeast Asia was also in Java. The Dutch Geological Survey conducted an excavation on the bank of the Solo River, near Ngandong, between 1931 and 1937. A large quantity of Pleistocene Age (1.8 million to 10,000 years ago) faunal remains were recovered, as well as parts of twelve *Homo erectus* skulls. While many paleoanthropologists have worked with the Ngandong fossils, the most notable are probably Ralph von Koenigswald and Franz Weidenreich. The major difficulty with Ngandong, and also with the majority of other Javan *Homo erectus* sites, is that it has proved extremely difficult to determine their exact age. Most of the bones at these sites have been transported by water; that is, the bones were not found where the animals died and may have been deposited and redeposited more than once. Stratigraphic relationships within the sites are also often complex, and while there may be volcanic sediments that can be dated using the potassium-argon method (K/Ar dating), the relationship of the fossils to the dated sediment is often questionable. While there is a broad consensus that *Homo erectus* was in Java between 800,000 and 300,000 years ago, there are also claims for dates as early as 1.8 million years, from Modjokerto in Java, and 100,000 years, from Ngandong.

SANGIRAN—WORLD HERITAGE SITE

A UNESCO World Heritage Site since 1996, the Sagiran Early Man site in Indonesia is one of the most important paleoanthropological sites in the world. Since the first hominid fossils were discovered at Sagiran in 1936, half of all hominid skeletons in the entire world have been found here.

Homo erectus: Who, When, and Where?

During the Pleistocene, global climates fluctuated and sometimes dropped an average of 5°C for periods of several thousand years, so that for some thousand-year periods, the temperature was on average 5° cooler than the average for the same areas today; the temperature then rose to modern averages before falling again, in roughly ten-thousand-year intervals. (This pattern was apparently more noticeable in the Northern Hemisphere, but the effect on sea levels was global.) These fluctuations resulted in the formation of very large glaciers in the Northern Hemisphere, spread of the Arctic and Antarctic ice sheets, and sea levels falling by as much as 100 meters. With major falls in sea level, many of the Southeast Asian islands were joined together, and Java was connected to the Asian mainland. This enabled the migration of terrestrial mammals, including *Homo erectus*, to Java, but it was probably difficult for mammals that could neither swim nor survive on rafts to progress further to the east.

Changes in climate would also have had a dramatic impact on vegetation, particularly on the distribution of rain forests and open woodland. This is important as it is usually argued that the food resources utilized by our prehistoric relatives would have been much more plentiful in open woodland habitats. Evidence of Pleistocene vegetation changes in Java is present in the mammal species preserved in fossil sites. For example, there were periods when orangutans, a rain-forest–dependent species, were common and others when they were not. If open woodlands and grasslands were the dominant vegetation types in Java during periods of low sea level, this would have enabled a more rapid colonization by *Homo erectus*. The proliferation of rain forests would have presented a serious challenge, and in combination with the tectonically active nature of Java, may have resulted in the extinction of *Homo erectus* in this part of the world.

The only reasonably complete skeleton of *Homo erectus* was recovered from the western shore of Lake Turkana, in the East African Rift Valley. This skeleton and other examples of *Homo erectus* from East Africa, China, and Java highlight the similarities to and differences from modern humans. They also demonstrate that there were geographic differences in the appearance of *Homo erectus*, and perhaps major cultural differences as well. In Africa and the Old World as far east as India, Early and Middle Pleistocene (1.8 million to 300,000 years ago) archaeological sites are characterized by a high proportion of bifacially flaked stone tools (tools flaked on both sides, as opposed to unifacial flaking). These tools, which are part of the Acheulian tradition (culture of populations in areas where this tool-making tradition flourished—Africa, Europe, India—first appearing around 1.5 million years ago in Africa), are uncommon in East Asia, and very few convincing stone tools of any type have been found at the Javan *Homo erectus* sites.

The Origins of Modern People in Southeast Asia

Fossil remains of *Homo erectus* have now been recovered from six separate sites in Java, with recent discoveries reported in Sambungmachan and Sangiran. In comparison with *Homo erectus* from Africa and China, the Javan skulls are longer and broader, with larger teeth, more projecting facial skeletons, more pronounced areas of muscle attachment, and a brow ridge that forms a straight bar rather than an arch over each eye. On average the examples of *Homo erectus* from Ngandong have a larger braincase volume than those from Trinil and Sangiran. This may be indicative of an evolutionary trend toward gradually increasing brain size in *Homo erectus*, as there is some evidence that the Ngandong fossils are newer than those discovered in Sangiran. Some researchers have seen this as evidence of a transition toward the modern human condition. Importantly, however, in Southeast Asia as well as on the Asian mainland, there is a substantial chronological gap between the known *Homo erectus* sites and the first evidence of *Homo sapiens*.

In Southeast Asia the earliest examples of *Homo sapiens* come from Niah Cave in Sarawak and Wadjak in Java. Unfortunately, there is some uncertainty over the age of the skeletons from these sites. Wadjak was excavated by Eugene Dubois in the 1890s, well before the development of modern archaeological dating methods. While Dubois thought Wadjak dated to the Pleistocene (older than 10,000 years), accelerator mass spectrometry (AMS) radiocarbon dating suggests an age of only 6,000 years. There is charcoal from Niah Cave radiocarbon-dated to approximately 40,000 years, but the association of the charcoal with the human skeleton is uncertain. Irrespective of the age of these sites, the appearance of modern humans in Australia by at least 40,000 years suggests that humans were present in Southeast Asia at the same time: there is no other way to reach Australia, even with a maximum fall in sea level during the Pleistocene.

The relationship between these modern people and earlier *Homo erectus* has been the subject of some debate. At least one researcher has argued for an evolutionary sequence linking Trinil, Ngandong, Wadjak, and Niah. This places *Homo erectus* as the direct biological ancestor of the first modern humans in the region. However, evidence from early human fossils from Africa and genetic evidence from living people makes this scenario unlikely. It is most probable that several waves of culturally and biologically different people passed through Southeast Asia over the last 40,000 years, and that these people subsequently colonized Australia, Melanesia, and the Pacific.

Peter Brown

Further Reading

Brothwell, Donald. (1960) "Upper Pleistocene Human Skull from Niah Caves." *Sarawak Museum Journal* 9: 323—349.

Reader, John. (1996) *Missing Links: The Hunt for Earliest Man*. London: Penguin.

Rightmire, Philip. (1990) *The Evolution of* Homo erectus*: Comparative Anatomical Studies on an Extinct Human Species*. Cambridge, U.K.: Cambridge University Press.

Santa Luca, A. P. (1980) *The Ngandong Fossil Hominids*. New Haven, CT: Yale University Press.

Underhill, P. A., et al. (2001) "The Phylogeography of Y Chromosome Binary Haplotypes and the Origins of Modern Human Populations." *Annals of Human Genetics* 65: 43–62.

Walker, Alan, and Shipman, Pat. (1996) *The Wisdom of the Bones: In Search of Human Origins*. New York: Knopf.

PALI CANON Pali is the archaic Prakrit language in which the Theravada canonical texts were orally transmitted from the time of the Buddha's death (486 BCE) until they were first written down in Sri Lanka by Sinhala monastic scribes around 100 BCE in the form of the Pali Canon. Related to Magadhi, Pali was probably spoken in central India during the Buddha's time. This would mean that Buddhist teachings were transmitted orally in Pali for more than three centuries before they were written down in the form we now know.

Together with the ancient commentaries, the Pali Canon constitutes the complete body of classical Theravada texts. It exists in various scripts as a large body of literature, amounting to many thousands of printed pages when translated into English. The Pali Canon, or *Tipitaka* (Three Baskets), is made up of three separate sections: the regulations of monastic life (Vinaya), the sermons of the Buddha (Sutta), and Buddhist philosophy (Abhidhamma). The Vinaya Pitaka is composed of injunctions by the Buddha against certain kinds of conduct. It imposes restraints on physical and verbal action of the ordained monks *(bhikkhu)* and female monks *(bhikkhuni)* and deals with transgressions of discipline. The Sutta Pitaka includes all discourses delivered by the Buddha in their entirety. These do not just concern the monastic community and are widely cited for their relevance also to the laity and are studied by them. Every *sutta* begins with "Evam me sutam" ("Thus have I heard"). The Abhidhamma Pitaka is the collection of classified and tabulated doctrines of the Buddha in terms of their ultimate and most abstract meanings.

If it were not for the concern with purity, the Pali Canon would not have been transmitted as accurately as it was from one generation to the next. This has been an extremely important factor within the monastic community through intergenerational transmission between monks. Royalty also expressed concern for the purity of the Tipitaka. For example, Burmese kings reinscribed the Tipitaka at the beginning of their reign. Also, external threats in particular motivated kings and politicians to take action to preserve the purity of the scriptures. Thus, in Burmese history, the only two Sangayanas were held at the beginning of the colonial period (King Mindon's Fourth Synod) and at the end (the Fifth Synod, held by Prime Minister U Nu), suggesting an urgent need to purify scriptures while under threat of external invasion.

Gustaaf Houtman

Further Reading

U Ko Lay, ed. (1990) *Guide to Tipitaka*. Delhi: Sri Satguru Publications.

Webb, Russell, ed. (1975) *An Analysis of the Pali Canon*. Kandy, Sri Lanka: Buddhist Publication Society.

PALM-LEAF MANUSCRIPTS

Societies in much of Southeast Asia, particularly Laos, and India used leaves of a type of palm tree, *bai lan*, as writing material. The leaves are cut into rectangular strips, and then a metal stylus is used to etch the text onto the leaves. In Lao manuscripts, rubber oil is rubbed into the engraving to darken the text on both sides of the leaf, and each side contains four lines of text. One book contains twenty sheets bound together. A typical story needs approximately five bundles, while an important epic such as the Lao *Ramayana*, *Phra Lak Phra Lam*, may require forty to fifty bundles. Each bundle is protected by a textile woven for this specific purpose. The manuscripts primarily documented religious stories, history annals, and, later, classical literature. Religious manuscripts included the Buddha's teachings, *Traipitika (Tipitaka)*, and *jataka* tales, the lives of the Buddha. Classical literature reached its height in the sixteenth century and included legends, historical events, and *jataka* tales adapted to include Lao settings and characters. Buddhist monks created the manuscripts, and temple libraries housed the manuscripts. Palm-leaf manuscripts are still kept in temple libraries as well as in museums in Laos, Thailand, France, and the United States.

Linda S. McIntosh

Further Reading

Khoret, Peter. (1994) "Lao." In *Traveler's Literary Companion to Southeast Asia*, edited by Alaister Dingwall. Brighton, U.K.: Passport, 120–153.

———. (1995) "Whispered So Softly It Resounds through the Forest, Spoken So Loudly It Can Hardly Be Heard: The Art of Parallelism in Traditional Lao Literature." In *Thai Literary Traditions*, edited by Manas Chitakasem. Bangkok, Thailand: Chulalongkorn University Press, 265–298.

PAMIR PEOPLES

The Pamirs (Mountain Tajiks) dwell in a high-altitude, mountainous knot located mostly in Tajikistan, on the disputed frontiers of Afghanistan, Pakistan, China, and the former Soviet Union. Within Tajikistan and these neighboring political states, the mountains are home to six million Tajiks, Kyrgyz, Uzbeks, and numerous other ethnic groups (Uygurs, Kazakhs, Russians, Jews, and Wahkis). The name Pamir Peoples, however, normally applies only to those Tajiks who live east of the Pamir crest in the Gorno-Badakshan Autonomous Oblast (GBAO), a poor, sparsely populated, and semiautonomous administrative unit with little political influence (not to be confused with the even poorer Badakshan Province in adjacent northeast Afghanistan).

Tajiks descend from the old pre-Turkic Iranian population and are one of the most ancient ethnic groups in Central Asia. Their language belongs to the Iranian branch of the Indo-European family and is a dialect of Persian. Persians first settled this region in 500 CE and were eventually absorbed into the Sasanid dynasty (224/228–651 CE). A succession of Arabs, neighboring Uzbeks, and Afghans overwhelmed them between 500 to 1400 CE. During this time, they developed a sedentary agricultural lifeway, the only Central Asians that were not primarily animal herders. Initially, Tajik indicated all "settled people" but evolved to distinguish the Iranian (Tajik) from Turkic (other Central Asian) subjects of the Arab empire that stretched from North Africa to Central Asia. Western penetration began in the late 1700s and for

A man on a horse below Mustagh Ata mountain in the Pamirs in western China. (GALEN ROWELL/CORBIS)

the next two hundred years, imperial Britain, czarist Russia, and China played the great game of political and military maneuvering for control of Central Asia. The struggle ended in the 1890s with Russian ascendancy of the Pamir. Through eons of political change in Badakshan, the Pamir became a cultural refuge where ancient habits and beliefs persevered.

In the early 2000s, five million ethnic Tajiks live mostly in Tajikistan as two distinct cultural groups: the majority lowland Tajiks of western Tajikistan, and the minority Mountain Tajiks who settle the deep canyons of the eastern Pamir and the north bank of the Pianj River (which later becomes the Amu Darya/Oxus). Interspersed with and included among Mountain Tajiks are six Pamiri clans (Iagnob, Iazgulem, Rushan, Shuganan, Vakhan, and Vanch) of almost pure ancient Iranian heritage. Collectively, they number 170,000 people and use Mountain Tajik, Pamirian (*pomir*), or Badakshani to describe their ethnicity. Relative to lowland Tajiks they are of fairer skin and taller. They follow Ismaili and Zoroastrian religious beliefs, while the western Tajiks are predominantly Sunni Muslims.

GBAO is an enclosed geographical dead end. Political restraints forbid travel into adjacent China and Afghanistan all year, and from October to March winter snows block the road to western Tajikistan. There is intermittent winter road access to Kyrgyzstan (Osh), but for the most part, GBAO is totally isolated for the six to seven winter months each year. Farming (wheat, barley, maize, apples, pears, walnuts, and apricots), animal husbandry (sheep and goats), mining of piezo-optic quartz for jewelry, and the production of woolen products (socks and scarves) are the main economic pursuits.

Following Tajik independence in 1991, sharply reduced subsidies from Moscow triggered acute shortages of food, medical supplies, and fuel. The education and agricultural sectors also declined precipitously so that this region is among the poorest in the former Soviet Union. The recent Tajik peace accords, a new road project between China and Eastern Tajikistan, and direct aid from the nongovernmental Aga Khan Foundation should provide some immediate relief and promote long-term economic development.

Stephen F. Cunha

Further Reading

Cunha, Stephen. (1997) "Reconciling Development, Conflict, and Conservation in Tajikistan." *American Geographical Society Focus* 44:1.

Wixman, Ronald. (1988) *The Peoples of the USSR: An Ethnographic Handbook*. Armonk, NY: M. E. Sharpe.

PAMIR RANGE The Pamirs form a complex mountain knot where the Hindu Kush, Karakoram, Alayskiy, Tian Shan, and Kunlun Shan converge. This "Roof of the World" results from the colliding Eurasian and Indian Ocean tectonic plates. The echelon grouping of ranges extends 135,000 square kilometers and reaches above 7,000 meters on three summits. Peak Communism (7,495 meters) was the highest mountain in the former Soviet Union. The 75-kilometer-long Fedchenko Glacier is one of the largest between Alaska and Antarctica.

Intercepted moisture from the Gulf of Arabia and the Mediterranean Sea sustains the Amu Dar'ya and Syr Dar'ya Rivers, Central Asia's lifelines and principal tributaries to the Aral Sea. The snow leopard *(Panthera uncia)*, Asiatic brown bear (*Ursus arctos isabellinus)*, and Marco Polo sheep *(Ovis poli)* thrive in the upper elevations, while riparian birch forests and juniper stands provide vital habitat for numerous other species.

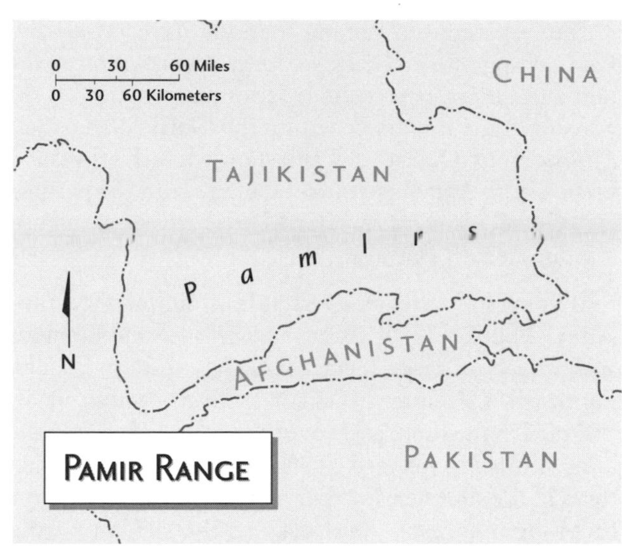

IT'S COLD AT THE TOP OF THE WORLD

This nineteenth century traveler's account makes it very clear just how cold it can get in the Pamir mountains at night and how hot during the day.

> The cold is still intense and on the increase, the thermometer *inside* our akois going down to zero every night, while the one hanging on the outside of the akoi averages about six or seven below. We find it very difficult to keep warm, and begin to fear that we shall lose some of our horses, as they are all loose on the hill and, having no horse-clothing, they must suffer badly at nights.
>
> The extraordinary part of this climate lies in the fact that the colder it gets at nights the warmer it is in the daytime. Since the thermometer has taken to going down below zero at night, it has also registered maximum temperatures of 100 to 106 in the sun's rays during the daytime, consequently the snows have been melting fast on the hills, and we have had no fresh snow-storms for some time. Had it not been for this, my last wounded *Ovis Poli* would never have been found. Yesterday a poor little half-frozen martin flew into Robert's akoi, and it perched there on a rope that is stretched across the inside, but whether it will live or not is a question, as there are no flies at this altitude or at this season for it to eat.
>
> *Source:* The Earl of Dunmore. (1894) *The Panmirs; Being a Narrative of a Year's Expedition on Horseback through Kashmir, Western Tibet, Chinese Tartary, and Russian Central Asia.* London: John Murray, 124–125.

Since antiquity, warring factions have prized the Pamir Range for its strategic location between mountain and desert, ocean and interior. Approximately 90 percent of the Pamirs lie within the Gorno-Badakshan Autonomous Oblast of Tajikistan, while Kyrgyzstan, Uzbekistan, Afghanistan, and China claim the periphery. Camel caravans traversed here between the tenth and nineteenth centuries.

The region remains a veritable ethnolinguistic museum. The Tajiks of Iranian heritage grow potatoes and wheat on river terraces in the western Pamirs. Pamirians (Mountain Tajiks) cultivate wheat, fruit, and nuts in the more arid canyons of the eastern mountains. Both groups lead goats and sheep to high pastures in the summer. Further east, the nomadic Kyrgyz of Mongol ancestry herd yaks in the shadow of the eastern Pamir Mountains and adjacent Pamir Plateau.

During the nineteenth century "Great Game," imperial Great Britain, czarist Russia, and China coveted the Pamirs to protect their adjacent colonial interests. The Soviets gained control until their empire dissolved in 1991, although their rule still infiltrates every facet of Central Asian economy, society, and political life. Long-suppressed ethnoreligious fervor erupted into civil war just six months after independence. The conflict still simmers between periods of fragile peace accords brokered by the United Nations and Russia.

Stephen F. Cunha

Further Reading

Cunha, Stephen F. (1997) "Summits, Snow Leopards, Farmers, and Fighters: Will Politics Prevent a National Park in the High Pamirs of Tajikistan?" *Focus* 66: 1.

Olufsen, Ole. (1904) *Through the Unknown Pamirs: The Second Danish Pamir Expedition, 1898–99*. London: William Heinemann.

PAMUK, ORHAN (b. 1952), Turkish novelist. Orhan Pamuk is a popular literary figure in Turkey. Born in Istanbul, he studied architecture and journalism and began writing in 1974. His first novel, *Cevdet Bey ve Oğulları* (Cevdet Bey and Sons) was published in 1982, after an eight-year search for a publisher, and gained him national recognition. Following *Sessiz Ev* (The House of Silence, 1982) and *Beyaz Kale* (1985; English translation The White Castle, 1991), his 1990 landmark novel *Kara Kitap* (The Black Book, 1994) has become one of the most controversial works in Turkish literature and extended his recognition to international circles. His following novels, *Yeni Hayat* (1994; The New Life, 1997), *Benim Adım Kırmızı* (1998; My Name Is Red, 2001), and *Kar* (Snow, 2001) are bestsellers in Turkey. His works have been translated into many languages and have received many awards.

Orhan Pamuk's writing fueled the discussion on postmodernism in Turkish literature. His style of using religious and historical themes in postmodernist forms drew criticism from both traditional intellectuals for exploiting the past and postmodernist intellectuals for being too populist. His unconventional use of the language has drawn much criticism from traditional literary circles. With all his work, the controversy around it, and its commercial success, Orhan Pamuk is a reflection of post-1980 Turkey's social transformation.

Mujdat Pakkan and Nazan Haydari

Further Reading

Esen, Nuket, ed. (1992). *Kara Kitap Üzerine Yazılar* (Notes on Black Book). Istanbul, Turkey: Iletisim.

Pamuk, Orhan. (1994) *The Black Book (Kara Kitap).* Trans. by Guneli Gun. New York: Farrar, Straus & Giroux.

———. (1997). *The New Life (Yeni Hayat).* Trans. by Guneli Gun. New York: Farrar, Straus & Giroux.

PANCASILA The Pancasila, or Five Pillars, contained in the preamble of the Indonesian constitution, have formed the foundation on which the Indonesian state ideology has been based since its independence. They comprise (1) belief in one God, (2) just and civilized humanitarianism, (3) national unity, (4) democracy based on the wise guidance of representative consultation, and (5) social justice. They were originally formulated by the eminent leader of the Indonesian independence movement, Sukarno, who for the first time publicly proclaimed them in his speech to the Preparatory Committee for the Independence of Indonesia on 1 June 1945 (celebrated in Indonesia as the "Birth of the Pancasila"). Designed to integrate Western democratic, nationalist, modernist Islamic, communist, and indigenous ideas on political organization, the Pancasila made Indonesia a religious state, albeit not an Islamic theocracy. Religion had been put forward as the first and foremost principle in order to appease the radical Muslims among the delegates of the Preparatory Committee, who had drafted a provision ("Jakarta Charter"), demanding the implementation of the *shari'a* (Islamic law) as the sole juridical guideline for all Indonesian Muslims. This had, however, been rejected by the majority of delegates. When Indonesia finally acquired full independence as a unitary nation-state in 1950, a provisional constitution was drafted that ratified the Pancasila as state ideology.

In 1955, the Constituent Assembly was formed in order to pass the final constitution of the Indonesian state. The issue of an Islamic state was again brought up, underpinned by the Darul Islam rebellion in various parts of the country. In 1959, Sukarno dissolved the Constituent Assembly, which had still not arrived at a conclusion, and reinstalled the constitution of 1945 as the only valid constitution of Indonesia. At the same time, on the basis of the Pancasila, he proclaimed his concept of "guided democracy," which had by now acquired a more authoritarian notion boosting the autocratic position of the president (i.e., Sukarno). This notion was taken over and reinforced under Suharto's "New Order" regime. In 1975, he decreed that the Pancasila were to be introduced into the curriculum of all educational institutions in order to forestall the intrusion of socially destabilizing ideologies. His P4 decree of 1978 and his decree of 1985, which established the Pancasila as the sole ideological foundation of all social, religious, and political organizations, were geared to boost the realization of the Pancasila society. Thus entwined with Suharto's New Order ideology, the Pancasila experienced a crisis of legitimacy after Suharto had to step down in May 1998.

Martin Ramstedt

Further Reading

Cribb, Robert, ed. (1991) *Islam and the Pancasila.* South East Asian Monograph, no. 28. Townsville, North Queensland, Australia: James Cook University of North Queensland, Centre for Southeast Asian Studies.

Dahm, Bernhard. (1969) *Sukarno and the Struggle for Indonesian Independence.* Ithaca, NY, and London: Cornell University Press.

Ramage, Douglas E. (1997) *Politics in Indonesia. Democracy, Islam, and the Ideology of Tolerance.* London and New York: Routledge.

Vatikiotis, Michael R. J. (1993) *Indonesian Politics under Suharto.* London and New York: Routledge.

Wandelt, Ingo. (1989) *Der Weg zum Pancasila-Menschen. Die Pancasila-Lehre unter dem P4-Beschluss; des Jahres 1978. Entwicklung und Struktur der indonesischen Staatslehre.* Frankfurt, Bern, New York, and Paris: Peter Lang.

PANDA The panda, or giant panda (*Ailuropoda melanoleuca*), is a bearlike animal native to China. The Chinese name is *da xiong mao* (great bear cat). Pandas are black and white in color, and adults are normally 160–180 centimeters in length and 85–110 kilograms in weight. Their scientific classification, as either members of the bear or raccoon family, is still disputed. Pandas live in cool, wet bamboo forests between 1,200 and 3,400 meters above sea level. Their diet consists almost entirely of bamboo leaves, stems, and shoots; they occasionally eat other plants and even meat. Pandas are found in six isolated mountain ranges in central China, in the provinces of Shaanxi, Gansu, and Sichuan. Pandas were mentioned in Chinese texts more than two thousand years ago, but they first became known to Western science only in 1869. Today there are an estimated six hundred to one thousand pandas in the wild, but they are greatly endangered because of dwindling habitat, largely due to logging and forest clearance. Pandas, because of their rarity and distinctive appearance, have long been considered a Chinese cultural treasure and symbol.

A young panda sitting in a patch of wildflowers in Sichuan, China. (KEREN SU/CORBIS)

Michael Pretes

Further Reading

Schaller, George B., Hu Jinchu, Pan Wenshi, and Zhu Jing. (1985) *The Giant Pandas of Wolong.* Chicago: University of Chicago Press.

Zhu Jing, and Li Yangwen, eds. (1980) *The Giant Panda.* Beijing: Science Press.

PANDIT Pandit is a category of Brahmans in India who are religious teachers (from the Sanskrit *pandita*, a learned man). In particular, they are people skilled in the literature of Sanskrit and in Hindu law, religion, and philosophy. Until 1862 the East India Company maintained a person known as the pundit (pandit) of the Supreme Court, whose job was to inform the English judges on points of Hindu law.

The pandits of Kashmir are one well-studied example of this widespread category, also known throughout northwestern India as Saraswat Brahmans.

They take their name from the former Saraswati River, now lost in the Thar Desert, or else from the goddess Saraswati, to whom they are devoted. The pandits of Kashmir, however, are primarily farmers, growing wheat, maize, paddy, fruits, and vegetables. Other occupations include shop keeping and the civil service. Pandits form scarcely 4 percent of the mainly Muslim population of the state of Kashmir and Jammu. They are the descendants of a handful of Brahman families who survived the arrival of Islam and Sufism in the mid-fourteenth century. It was only in the eighteenth century that they took on the semiofficial designation of pandit under the relatively tolerant Mughal emperors, under whose rule Kashmir fell.

Pandits follow a nondualistic school of philosophy known as Kashmiri Saivism. In the twentieth century, the best-known family of Kashmiri pandits was that of Jawaharlal Nehru and Indira Gandhi, his only daughter, who both became prime ministers of India.

Paul Hockings

Further Reading

Madan, Triloki Nath. (1989) *Family and Kinship: A Study of the Pandits of Rural Kashmir.* 2d ed. New Delhi, India: Oxford University Press.

PANDYA Pandya was an Indian dynasty ruling much of the southern Tamil-speaking area in ancient times. The dynasty was first mentioned in the fourth century BCE by the Sanskrit grammarian Katyayana and rose to influence in the sixth century CE. The earliest Pandyan king to whom a definite name and date can be ascribed is Nedum-Cheliyan, in the second century CE. Ancient writers repeatedly refer to the wealth of the kingdom, which had an extensive trade network reaching overseas. As the kingdom expanded, however, this led to clashes with several neighboring powers, including the Cholas, Kongu, the Pallavas, and the Chalukyas. The Pandyas were defeated and eclipsed by the Chola empire, but as this power began to decline in the thirteenth century, the Pandyas again emerged. Their territory was roughly that of the modern districts of Madurai, Tirunevelli, and Kanyakumari, and their capital was at Madurai. The dynasty was probably matrilineal, like that more recently in the royal house of Travancore. Marco Polo twice visited the Pandya kingdom, in 1288 and 1293, and was much impressed. In 1310 the eunuch general of the Delhi sultan, Malik Kafur, raided and brought an abrupt end to the Pandya dynasty. Thereafter, they were no more than local chieftains, retaining some land near Madurai.

Paul Hockings

Further Reading

Nilakanta Sastri, K. A. (1955) *A History of South India from Prehistoric Times to the Fall of Vijayanagar.* Madras, India: Oxford University Press.

PANGKOR TREATY The Pangkor Treaty (1874) set the stage for the establishment of British colonial rule in the Malay States (present-day peninsular Malaysia). Under terms of the treaty, the chieftains acknowledged the ascension of Abdullah (reigned 1874–1875), one of several claimants to the Perak sultanate. Abdullah, in turn, accepted the appointment of a British officer to be known as the resident, whose advice had to be sought and acted upon in all matters except those relating to Malay customs and practices and the Islamic religion. Sir Andrew Clarke, governor of the Straits Settlements (1873–1875), initiated the meeting that resulted in this treaty.

A combination of economic, geopolitical, and humanitarian considerations prompted the British to seek the Pangkor Treaty. Tin production and trade had been disrupted by a chaotic state of affairs in the western Malay States—caused by disputes among warring chiefs over control of tin fields—and by rivalries between Chinese organizations in the tin industry and piracy in the Strait of Malacca. Tin, by the last quarter of the nineteenth century, had become increasingly important owing to the expanding tinplate industry. The British also feared that rival European powers Germany and France might take advantage of the anarchy in the peninsular Malay States to establish hegemony. Undoubtedly there was widespread suffering due to the troubles, but humanitarian considerations were at best secondary to the economic and geopolitical considerations.

Although under instructions to study the situation and report on the steps to be taken, Clarke decided instead that action was warranted. Armed with a letter dated 30 December 1873 by Abdullah, who appealed to Clarke to mediate and expressed willingness to receive a British resident, Clarke convened a meeting at Pangkor in mid-January 1874. Rival Chinese mining factions were also invited to negotiate an amicable settlement.

Clarke's treaty was endorsed by British Prime Minister Benjamin Disraeli's Conservative government (1874–1880). Similar treaties were contracted with other peninsular Malay States: Selangor (February 1874), Sungai Ujong (December 1874), and Pahang (August 1888).

The Pangkor Treaty was a watershed in the history of Malaysia. It initiated a British forward movement into the Malay Peninsula, and by introducing the British resident system, it implemented British indirect rule, thereby setting the stage for the economic exploitation of the Malay States that subsequently brought about a plural society.

Ooi Keat Gin

Further Reading

Cowan, Charles Donald. (1961) *Nineteenth-Century Malaya: The Origins of British Political Control.* London: Oxford University Press.

Khoo, Kay Kim. (1972) *The Western Malay States, 1850–1873: The Effects of Commercial Development on Malay Politics.* Kuala Lumpur, Malaysia: Oxford University Press.

Mohamed, Amin, and Malcolm Caldwell, eds. (1977) *Malaya: The Making of a Neo-Colony.* London: Spokesman.

Sadka, Emily. (1968) *The Protected Malay States, 1874–1895.* Kuala Lumpur, Malaysia: University of Malaya Press.

PANINI (c. 520–460 BCE), Sanskrit grammarian. There is controversy regarding the dates of Panini, but most scholars believe that he lived in the fifth century BCE. He was born in Shalatura, near Attock in present-day Pakistan.

Panini's magnum opus, *Astadhyayi*, consists of four thousand sutras or Vedic precepts divided into eight chapters. It deals with the rules of Sanskrit grammar and systemizes such basic elements as nouns, verbs, and sentence structure. *Astadhyayi* covers phonetics, phonology, and morphology, making it a source text for Indian linguistics.

The *Astadhyayi* also gives insight into the religious and social development of the period. For instance, reference to bhakti (religious devotion) can be found in the discussion of the word Vasudevaka. (The word is a name for a person whose religious devotion is focused on Vasudeva.) There are also references to different categories of lowly born people, such as *aniravasita* (those living within society) and *niravasita* (those living outside society), and Panini also mentions women students pursuing Vedic knowledge.

His scientific study of grammar made Panini one of the luminaries in Sanskrit language. Some have seen *Astadhyayi* as a precursor of modern formal language theory. Panini's work systematizing the grammar of Sanskrit in *Astadhyayi* kept the Sanskrit language largely unchanged for about two millennia. He himself died after being attacked by a lion.

Patit Paban Mishra

Further Reading

Sharma, Ramanath, trans. (1998) *The Astadhyayi of Panini.* New Delhi, India: Munshiram.

Vasu, Srisa C., trans. (1980) *The Astadhyayi of Panini.* Columbia, MO: South Asia Books.

PANJABI Panjabi (or Punjabi) is an Indo-Aryan language spoken in a contiguous region in northwestern India and northeastern Pakistan. In India, it is one of the recognized national languages and the official state language of Punjab. Approximately 2.79 percent of the population of India, estimated in March 2001 at over one billion, are Panjabi speakers, yielding approximately 28 million speakers. In Pakistan, 48 percent of the population (estimated at 142,392,000) speak Panjabi, giving around 72 million speakers. Panjabi speakers also live in North America, Europe, East Asia, and East Africa.

The main dialect clusters are those of eastern Punjab, the central dialect (Majhi), and western varieties in Pakistan that constitute a complex dialect continuum. Older literature refers to western varieties of Panjabi as Lahnda or Lahndi.

In India, Panjabi is written in the Gurmukhi script, traditionally attributed to Guru Angad (1504–1552 CE), but with earlier roots; in Pakistan it is written in the Urdu script. Important figures in Panjabi literature include Sheikh (Baba) Farid (1173–1265), the Sikh Gurus, and the Sufi poets Shah Husain (1538–1601) and Bulleh Shah (1680–1758). The folk romance *(qissa) Hir-Ranjha* of Waris Shah (1735–1790?) is the best known Panjabi work of the eighteenth century. Eminent contemporary literary figures in India are Mohan Singh 'Mahir' (1905–1978) and Amrita Pritam (b. 1917). In Pakistan, Shafqat Tanveer Mirza (b. 1932), and Nasreen Anjum Bhatti (b. 1948) are important.

Linguistic Summary

In the Panjabi consonant system, voiced-voiceless, aspirated-unaspirated, and dental-retroflex oppositions are phonological. In the vowel system, nasalization and three phonemic tones are distinctive.

Nouns distinguish number (singular and plural) and gender (masculine and feminine). Some nouns bear a characteristic mark of gender.

Basic verb forms are constructed on the stem, the imperfective participle, or the perfective participle. Panjabi is a split-ergative language, in which perfective tenses of transitive verbs agree with an unmarked direct object (not with the subject). The normal word order in a sentence is subject, object, verb.

Elena Bashir

See also: **Indo-Aryan Languages**

Further Reading

Masica, Colin P. (1991) *The Indo-Aryan Languages.* Cambridge, U.K.: Cambridge University Press.

Sekhon, Sant Singh. (1993) *A History of Panjabi Literature.* 2 vols. Patiala, India: Publication Bureau, Punjabi University.

PAN-PHILIPPINE HIGHWAY The Pan-Philippine Highway, sometimes known as the Maharlika Highway, is a 2,500-kilometer (1,550-mile) network of sealed roads, expressways, interchanges, bridges, and ferry services that links the main islands of the Philippine archipelago: Luzon, the Visayas, and Mindanao. The transport development program was proposed in 1965 and was supported by loans and grants from foreign-aid institutions, including the World Bank. It was a major achievement in road construction, and government planners believed that the Pan-Philippine Highway, in conjunction with other road construction, would stimulate agricultural production by reducing transportation costs, encourage social and economic development outside the major urban centers, and expand industrial production for domestic and foreign markets. Rebuilt and improved in 1997 with assistance from the Japanese government, the highway was dubbed the Philippine-Japan Friendship Highway. A campaign to encourage domestic tourism launched in 1998 by the Department of Tourism saw twenty-six sections of the highway in Luzon and seven areas in the Visayas, Mindanao, and the Bicol region designated as Scenic Highways with developed amenities for travelers and tourists.

Daniel Oakman

Further Reading

Francisco, Stella Amor J., and Jayant K. Routray. (1992) *Road Transport and Rural Development: A Case Study in the Philippines.* Bangkok, Thailand: Asian Institute of Technology.

"The Proposed Pan-Philippine Highway." (1965) *The Journal of the American Chamber of Commerce of the Philippines* 41, 11 (November): 564–565.

P'ANSORI The Korean performance technique *p'ansori* (from *p'an,* meaning "performance," "performance space," or "event," and *sori,* meaning "sound," "voice," or "singing") features solo story-singing *(sori)* alternated with spoken passages *(aniri).* The earliest known records of its performance date to about three centuries ago in the southwestern provinces of the Korean Peninsula. *P'ansori* was designated in 1963 as Korea's Intangible Cultural Asset (Muhyong munhwajae) No. 5, and select singers as its "Preservers" (Poyuja). In *p'ansori,* a singer stands on a straw mat, and the drummer is seated to the left of the singer with a drum *(puk);* during the performance, the drummer and members of the audience freely utter stylized cries of encouragement *(ch'uimsae),* which blend rhythmically with the singing. The early singers emerged among the male performing artists *(kwangdae),* whose performance function included musical accompaniment for the regional shamanic ritual *(kut).* In the latter part of the nineteenth century, however, women began to participate in *p'ansori.* Additionally, in the nineteenth century, as a consequence of royal and aristocratic patronage, *p'ansori* narratives became selected and the lyrics refined. *P'ansori* appealed to both upper and lower classes.

Today, five narratives *(obat'ang)* are practiced, and they are believed to uphold the five Neo-Confucian cardinal virtues: *Ch'unhyang ka* (The Song of Ch'unhyang), for wifely chastity; *Shim Ch'ongga* (The Song of Shim Ch'ong), for filial piety; *Hungboga* (The Song of Hungbo), for sibling order; *Sugungga* (The Song of the Underwater Palace), for royalty; and *Chokpyokka* (The Song of the Red Cliff), for gentlemanly faith. *P'ansori* singing utilizes several rhythmic cycles *(changdan): chinyang* (slow six beats), *semach'i* (faster *chinyang*), *chungmori* (medium twelve beats), *chungjungmori* (faster twelve beats), *chajinmori* (syncopated four beats), *hwimori* (fast four beats), *onmori* (ten beats asymmetrically split), and *tanmori* (medium six beats, the first half of *chungmori*).

Chan Park

PAO NATIONAL ORGANIZATION The Pao National Organization (PNO) is the main armed opposition force among the Pao (Pa-oh, Taungthu) people in rural districts around Taunggyi in southwestern Shan State in Myanmar (Burma). Pao nationalists took up arms with the Karens, to whom they are related, in 1949 shortly after Burma's independence. More than 100,000 Paos inhabit rural districts of the Karen and Mon States. Militant Pao nationalism, however, has mostly been expressed within the context of Shan State, where more than 500,000 Paos live. Most Paos are Buddhists.

During the 1950s, the main drive of the Pao movement was against the traditional rule of the Shan *sawbwas* (princes). In 1958, some 1,300 Pao guerrillas laid down their weapons under the "arms for democracy" program of Prime Minister U Nu. One year later, the *sawbwa* system was abolished.

Following the 1962 coup of General Ne Win, however, the Pao armed movement quickly revived under a new name, the Shan State Nationalities Liberation Organization (SSNLO). In 1973, an ideological split occurred between the SSNLO supporters of Tha Kalei, who allied himself with the Communist Party of Burma, and a pro-federalist movement led by the veteran politician "Thaton" Hla Pe (1910–1975). Following Hla Pe's death, leadership was taken over by a former Buddhist monk, Aung Kham Hti, who reestablished the PNO in 1976 and joined the National Democratic Front.

Sporadic fighting continued between the two factions until 1989 when Buddhist monks brokered peace talks. The following year, above-ground Pao candidates won three seats in the 1990 general election, precipitating another reorientation in Pao politics. In 1991, the PNO arranged a cease-fire with the State Law and Order Restoration Council government, followed in 1994 by the SSNLO. A Pao self-administered region was promised in the cease-fire areas designated as Southern Shan State Special Region 6, and both Pao forces opened offices in the towns to embark on a variety of social and development programs.

Martin Smith

Further Reading

Hackett, W. (1953) "The Pao People of Shan State." Ph.D. diss., Cornell University.

Smith, Martin. (1999) *Burma: Insurgency and the Politics of Ethnicity*. 2d ed. London: Zed Books.

Tzang Yawnghwe, Chao. (1987) *The Shan of Burma: Memoirs of a Shan Exile*. Singapore: Institute of Southeast Asian Studies.

PAPER CRAFTS AND ARTS—KOREA The first form of paper in Korea appeared in the Three Kingdoms period (57 BCE–668 CE) and was made from pulp of hemp or ramie. Papermaking became an important industry with the invention of mulberry paper in the Koryo period (918–1392).

Koreans have had a long tradition of paper crafts, making products ranging from kites, flowers, fans, pouches, and boxes to larger items like chests and desks. Sliding doors were covered with paper, and floors were covered in layers of paper and varnish. In the early Choson period (1392–1910), a specially treated paper was used to make armor that was waterproof, warm, and resilient to attack.

Paper crafts are functional and also utilitarian in their use of scrap or used paper. They are also beautiful with their bright dyes and geometric patterns or flora and fauna motifs. One traditional paper craft technique uses layers of paper pasted together and shaped to form pouches, small baskets, and masks. Bamboo or wooden frames provide additional support for larger items. Kitchen items like bowls are made by using bits of paper soaked in water, then crushed and mixed with glue. A third technique weaves paper cords to make shoes, jars, and baskets. Varnish is used as a waterproof sealant.

Jennifer Jung-Kim

Further Reading

Korean Overseas Information Service. (1995) *Paper Crafts*. Korean Heritage Series no. 8. Seoul: Korean Overseas Information Service.

PARACEL ISLANDS are a small group of about fifteen to thirty low coral islands and reefs located in the potentially oil-rich South China Sea about 280 kilometers southeast of Hainan Island, or about one-third of the way from central Vietnam to the northern Philippines. Stimulated by the strategic location and the possibility of nearby off shore oil deposits, the People's Republic of China (PRC), Taiwan, and Vietnam all lay claim to all or part of the Paracels Islands. The United Nations Law of the Sea provides for peaceful resolution of disputed seabed territory. The Paracels fall under U.N. jurisdiction in regard to such disputes between China, Taiwan, and Vietnam. The islands were originally part of Vietnam and then part of French Indochina until World War II, when they were occupied by the Japanese. After the war, they passed briefly to China in 1945 (when an airfield was constructed), and then to the Republic of Vietnam. The Republic of Vietnam occupied the islands until 1974, when China seized them by force. The Paracel Islands have a total coastline distance of about 518 kilometers, have a high point of fourteen meters, have a tropical climate, have no natural resources (though their economic zone includes oil and natural gas deposits) or arable land, and are most susceptible to typhoons as their biggest natural hazard.

Richard B. Verrone

Further Reading

Admiralty, Naval Intelligence Divison, Great Britain. (1943) *Indo-China*. London: Her Majesty's Stationery Office, Geographical Handbook Series.

Tucker, Spencer C., ed. (1998) *Encyclopedia of the Vietnam War*. Oxford, U.K: Oxford University Press.

Lee, Ki-baik. (1984) *A New History of Korea*. Trans. by Edward W. Wagner. Seoul: Ilchokak.

PARHAE KINGDOM The kingdom of Parhae (698–926) rose from the ashes of the Korean Koguryo kingdom and as a revival of it. Following the collapse of Koguryo at the hands of Tang China, which had allied itself with Shilla, enabling that kingdom to unify most of the Korean Peninsula, many of the Tang's Koguryo prisoners of war were relocated in southwestern Manchuria. Rebellion broke out in the area, and former Koguryo general Tae Cho-yong and his followers seized control, migrated northwest to the Jilin area, and consolidated their power. These followers consisted of much of the former Koguryo aristocracy, who clearly believed that they had revived the former state. Tae proclaimed himself king and was recognized as ruler of the state of Chin by the Tang in 698. In 713, Chin was renamed Parhae. At its height in the ninth century under King Son (known as Tae Insu; reigned 818–830), Parhae stretched from the northern provinces of present-day Korea to encompass the whole of northeastern Manchuria and the Liaodong Peninsula. It had a largely agriculture-based economy that traded cereal grains and handcrafted products, mainly with Tang China.

Parhae's prosperity reached its height in the first half of the ninth century during the reign of King Son. By this time, the kingdom regained much of the former Koguryo territory, except that in eastern Manchuria and south of Pyongyang. Both Parhae and Shilla established peaceful diplomatic relations with Tang China and began to assimilate Tang culture and institutions, which allowed their cultures to flourish.

By the late ninth century, the political confusion and violence that was to lead to the downfall of the Tang dynasty was also adversely affecting Parhae. The strengthening Khitan tribe conquered Parhae in 926 and would go on to dominate much of northern China and Manchuria. On the Korean Peninsula, the Koryo kingdom (918–1392) replaced Shilla, and many of the Parhae ruling class, who were descendants of the Koguryo people, moved south to join the newly formed dynasty of Koryo.

David E. Shaffer

Further Reading

Eckert, Carter J., Ki-baik Lee, Young Ick Lew, Michael Robinson, and Edward W. Wagner. (1990) *Korea: Old and New*. Seoul: Ilchokak.

Henthorn, William E. (1971) *A History of Korea*. New York: Free Press.

PARK CHUNG HEE (1917–1979), Third president of the Republic of Korea. Park Chung Hee (Pak Chong-hui) gained political control of South Korea through a military coup on 16 May 1961. He first ruled through a military junta called the Supreme Council for National Reconstruction, before winning the 1963 presidential elections (thereby establishing the Third Republic). He was reelected in 1967, 1971, 1972 (when the Fourth Republic was founded through the *Yushin* constitutional reforms, formulated to allow Park to remain in power), and 1978.

Park's political longevity was derived from institutional, social, and international support as well as from South Korea's economic development in the 1970s, hostilities between North and South Korea, and Cold War politics. Park was assassinated on 26 October 1979 by Kim Jae Kyu (1926–1980), an old friend of Park and at that time the head of the Korean Central Intelligence Agency.

Park was born near Taegu in North Kyongsang province in present-day South Korea. He was educated in the Manchukuo Military Academy and the Japanese Imperial Military Academy and served in the Japanese army. After World War II, Park received advanced training at the Korean Military Academy and in the U.S. Army. Rising through the ranks, Park was a major general at the time of the 1961 military coup. Park's rule was noted for his acceptance of a police state and his use of military strength, as well as economic growth.

Jennifer Jung-Kim

President Park Chung Hee relaxing in May 1967 in Seoul. (BETTMANN/CORBIS)

Further Reading

Eckert, Carter J., and Ki-baek Yi. (1990) *Korea Old and New: A History*. Seoul: Ilchogak.

Saccone, Richard. (1993) *Koreans to Remember: 50 Famous People Who Helped Shape Korea*. Elizabeth, NJ: Hollym.

PARSI The Parsis, numbering no more than eighty thousand, are a cultural and religious community centered in Mumbai (Bombay) but also living in some towns and villages of Gujarat State. Originally from Persia, they sought refuge from Islam at Sanjan on the west coast of India in (traditionally) 716 CE. Their identity hinges on their practice of Zoroastrianism, one of the world's monotheistic religions. The prophet Zoroaster's (Zarathushtra, c. 628–c. 551 BCE) teachings were preserved in the Avesta, a fragmentary compilation of praise and prayers to Ahuramazda and various guardians of the universe. Zoroastrianism includes the belief in two contending principles of Ahuramazda the good and Ahriman the evil, with men being soldiers in the army of Ahuramazda, and the worship of fire, in the home as well as in fire temples, as a symbol of life. There is a hereditary priesthood. The major life cycle ritual is the *Navjot*, an initiation ceremony for both sexes around the age of seven. The Parsis of India still expose corpses to birds of prey in stone structures known as towers of silence. Parsis have a 365-day calendar and celebrate communal feasts known as *Ghambars*, originally tied to the agricultural cycle. There is a strict rule of endogamy, and children of non-Parsi fathers were once denied Parsi status.

Although they began as an agrarian people, the Parsis moved into many other professions, especially under British rule when they accepted modern education. They contributed outstanding members to education, arts, sciences, jurisprudence, finance, politics, and the Indian civil service, out of all proportion to their numbers. Their most enduring efforts, however, have been in entrepreneurship. In the early twentieth century, individual Parsis built empires in shipbuilding, textiles, iron and steel works, banking, and overseas trade. The community has a well-deserved reputation for philanthropy, including endowing fire temples and schools and funds for the welfare of their community.

Since the 1950s many younger, well-educated, professional Parsis have emigrated, and sizable groups live in Canada, the United States, Australia, and Britain. Parsis tend to form social and religious organizations to keep alive as many cultural traditions as possible. Because exogamy is more common among the offspring of the emigrants, children of mixed marriages are now accepted into the community. The greatest challenge facing the Parsis is a precipitous decline in numbers. Due to late marriages, low birthrates, and high economic expectations of the young, demographers have predicted that the Parsis will die out well before the end of the twenty-first century if current trends persist.

W. D. Merchant

Further Reading

Kulke, Eckehard. (1974) *The Parsis in India: A Minority as Agent of Social Change*. Munich, Germany: Weltforum Verlag.

Modi, Jivanji Jamshedji. (1986) *The Religious Ceremonies and Customs of the Parsees*. Mumbai (Bombay), India: Society for the Promotion of Zoroastrian Religious Knowledge and Education.

PARTAI KEBANGKITAN BANGSA The Partai Kebangkitan Bangsa (National Awakening Party, PKB) emerged as one of the more serious contenders among the many political parties that sprang up in Indonesia after the fall of President Suharto in May 1998. Established on 23 July 1998, PKB was inspired by the secular and liberal outlook of Abdurrahman Wahid (b. 1940), the leader of the traditionalist Muslim organization Nahdlatul Ulama (NU) and one of the cofounders of PKB. Because Wahid was suffering from the effects of a stroke, PKB was chaired by Matori Abdul Djalil. Due to its loyalty to the Pancasila, the five principles of the state philosophy as contained in the preamble of the Indonesian constitution of 1945, PKB could not mobilize the Islamist base of the 35-million-member NU. Thus it faced strong competition from other Muslim parties, such as the Partai Persatuan Pembangunan (Unification and Development Party, PPP), Partai Amanat Nasional (National Mandate Party, PAN), and others. PKB, however, formed a coalition with Megawati Sukarnoputri's secular Partai Demokrasi Indonesia-Perjuangan (Fighting Party for Indonesian Democracy, PDI-P). In the general elections of June 1999, PKB ranked as the fourth-strongest party, behind PDI-P, Golongan Karya (Functional Groups [the former government party under Suharto], Golkar), and PPP. Shortly before the presidential elections of October 1999, PKB unexpectedly joined the Islamic Central Axis alliance under the leadership of the PPP, which proposed Wahid as its presidential candidate. Competing against Megawati, Wahid won the election, while Megawati became his vice president.

Martin Ramstedt

Further Reading

Emmerson, Donald K., ed. (1999) *Indonesia beyond Suharto: Polity, Economy, Society, Transition*. London: East Gate.

Forrester, Geoff. (1999) *Post-Suharto Indonesia: Renewal or Chaos?* Singapore: Institute of Southeast Asian Studies; Leiden, Netherlands: KITLV (Royal Institute of Linguistics and Anthropology).

Pompe, Sebastiaan. (1999) *De Indonesische Algemene Verkiezingen 1999*. Leiden, Netherlands: KITLV (Royal Institute of Linguistics and Anthropology) Uitgeverij.

PARTAI PERSATUAN PEMBANGUNAN

In 1973, the Indonesian New Order government of Suharto merged all existing political parties into two parties—the Partai Demokrasi Indonesia (PDI; Indonesian Democratic Party) and the Partai Persatuan Pembangunan (PPP; United Development Party)—in order to minimize real opposition from popular political agencies such as the Partai Nasional Indonesia (PNI; Indonesian National Party) or the Nahdlatul Ulama (NU). The resultant "opposition parties" PDI and PPP served more as an alibi for the supposedly democratic New Order government, which appeared to tolerate a multiparty system, than as forums for true opposition. Through intimidation, violence, and election fraud, Suharto ensured that open support for these parties on the part of the masses remained small. Hence, the hegemony of the government party Golongan Karya (Golkar) was never threatened, and in effect Suharto did sponsor a one-party system.

Whereas the Christian-backed PDI had a nationalist and secular agenda, the PPP had a strong Islamic profile, having incorporated the four Muslim parties Nahdlatul Ulama, Parmusi, Persatuan Tarbiyah Islamiyah (PERTI), and Partai Sarekat Islam. It was, however, weakened by deep internal divides due to the divergent political orientations of its members. Under heavy state pressure, the PPP replaced Islam with the Pancasila (the five principles of the Indonesian state philosophy, consisting of belief in one God, humanity, national unity, democracy, and social justice) as its sole ideological fundament in 1984. In protest, the Nahdlatul Ulama withdrew from the party, while many other members shifted their loyalty to Golkar. Nevertheless, the PPP remained the sole political forum for Muslim interests until the fall of Suharto in May 1998. In the ensuing reformation era, it enhanced its Islamic profile, thereby gaining in influence, and formed the Central Axis (Poros Tengah) alliance with other emerging Muslim parties. As the leader of this Islamic alliance, which unexpectedly proposed Abdurrahman Wahid (b. 1940) as candidate for the presidential election of October 1999, the PPP helped to prevent Megawati Sukarnoputri, the candidate of the Partai Demokrasi Indonesia-Perjuangan, winner of the June general elections, from winning the election.

Martin Ramstedt

Further Reading

Cribb, Robert, and Colin Brown. (1995) *Modern Indonesia: A History since 1945*. New York: Longman Publishing.

Emmerson, Donald K., ed. (1999) *Indonesia Beyond Suharto: Polity, Economy, Society, Transition*. London: East Gate

Forrester, Geoff. (1999) *Post-Suharto Indonesia: Renewal or Chaos?* Singapore: Institute of Southeast Asian Studies; Leiden, Netherlands: KITLV (Royal Institute of Linguistics and Anthropology).

Pompe, Sebastiaan. (1999) *De Indonesische Algemene Verkiezingen 1999*. Leiden, Netherlands: KITLV (Royal Institute of Linguistics and Anthropology) Uitgeverij.

Ramage, Douglas E. (1997) *Politics in Indonesia. Democracy, Islam, and the Ideology of Tolerance*. London and New York: Routledge.

Vatikiotis, Michael R. J. (1993) *Indonesian Politics under Suharto*. London and New York: Routledge.

PARTI RAKYAT BRUNEI Parti Rakyat Brunei is a political party established in Brunei in 1956 and modeled on Malaya's left-leaning Parti Rakyat Malaya. Independence for Brunei, a British protectorate since 1888, was its main agenda. Although it did not favor dissolution of the sultanate, the PRB wanted national leadership to shift from the palace to the *rakyat* (people) through democratization in the government.

The PRB rejected the notion of membership in federation with Malaysia, proposed by Malaya's Tunku Abdul Rahman Putra al-Haj in 1961, believing that entry into Malaysia would dash all hopes of a revival of Brunei hegemony and would result in the loss of Brunei's unique identity. At the time, the PRB's membership of 26,000 people represented more than a quarter of Brunei's population; nevertheless, the government of Brunei favored federation with Malaysia. On 5 December 1962, the PRB submitted a motion demanding Sarawak and British North Borneo be returned to Brunei, that a federation of the three British Borneo territories be created, that Brunei reject entry into Malaysia, and that Brunei become independent in 1963. The motion was rejected, and the PRB launched a coup that it had originally planned for April or May of 1963. British forces quashed the rebellion, and Sultan Omar Ali Saiffuddin III of Brunei declared a state of emergency and outlawed the PRB. Some 3,000 PRB participants in the revolt were captured; others fled abroad. A. M. Azahari (Sheikh Ahmad Azahari bin

Sheikh Mahmud, b. 1929), leader of the PRB, was in Manila when the revolt occurred; he sought refuge in Jakarta.

On 13 July 1973 PRB detainees who had refused to renounce the party staged a dramatic escape and reconstituted the party in exile. In December, an Ad Hoc Committee for the Independence of Brunei was established in Kuala Lumpur. Subsequently on 7 May 1974, the PRB was formally reactivated with the naming of an executive committee with Azahari as president.

Throughout the 1970s the PRB actively garnered moral and material support from various quarters, including the United Nations, Malaysia, Indonesia, and the Philippines. The PRB's perseverance resulted in a U.N. resolution on Brunei (13 November 1975) that established principles of succession and legitimacy that any government established in Brunei should meet. However, despite Brunei's independence from Britain on 31 December 1983, the PRB continued to be outlawed, and several detainees remained in custody. PRB leaders remained in exile. The PRB is now dormant, and its political future is uncertain.

Ooi Keat Gin

Further Reading

Hussainmiya, Bachamiya Abdul. (1995) *Sultan Omar Ali Saifuddin III and Britain.* Kuala Lumpur: Oxford University Press.

Ranjit Singh, D. S. (1991) *Brunei 1839–1983: The Problems of Political Survival.* Kuala Lumpur, Malaysia: Oxford University Press.

Saunders, Graham. (1994) *A History of Brunei.* Kuala Lumpur, Malaysia: Oxford University Press.

Zaini Haji Ahmad, ed. (1987) *Partai Rakyat Brunei: The People's Party of Brunei. Selected Documents/Dokumen Terpilih.* Kuala Lumpur, Malaysia: INSAN.

PASHTO Pashto, or Pakhto, is a language that has its origins in the northeastern group of the Iranian languages; it is considered the language of the Pashtun people. It is believed that at least 10 million people speak Pashto. Not only is it one of the official languages spoken in Afghanistan (Dari is the other official language), but other communities, such as the people in the North West Frontier and Baluchistan provinces of Pakistan, speak it as well.

Several Pashto dialects exist, the main ones being the western or southwestern and the eastern or northeastern. The former is often referenced as Pashto, while the latter is called Pakhto. One of the differences between the two dialects is that the speakers use different symbols or letters to represent the same sound. To compensate for these differences and thus create a sense of unity among the speakers of Pashto, completely separate letters were devised to replace those that caused the confusion. Current deviations of written Pashto occur between the Pashto written in Afghanistan and that in Pakistan. Pakistani people are rarely taught Pashto in school, so that the Pakistani Pashto-speaking population tends to spell phonetically.

Some historical accounts state that Pashto first appeared in written form in a work by Bayazid Ansari (c. 1525–c. 1581), an Afghan religious leader who declared that he had received divine instruction to write his work in Pashto. Ansari's work is believed to be the earliest existing written piece in Pashto.

Houman A. Sadri

Further Reading

Adamec, Ludwig W. (1997) *Historical Dictionary of Afghanistan.* 2d ed. Lanham, MD: Scarecrow Press.

Cleveland, William L. (1994) *A History of the Modern Middle East.* Boulder, CO: Westview Press.

Norton, Augustus Richard, ed. (1996) *Civil Society in the Middle East.* Leiden, Netherlands, and New York: Brill.

Rubin, Barnett R. (1995) *The Fragmentation of Afghanistan: State Formation and Collapse in the International System.* New Haven, CT: Yale University Press.

PASHTUN Pashtun (Pakhtun, Pushtoon) refers to the predominant ethnic group of Afghanistan, which has for centuries represented the political and military elite. Before the eighteenth century, the Pashtan were also known as Afghans, but with the creation of modern Afghanistan in 1747, that name came to identify any person born in the country and lost its distinctive ethnic connotation. The difference between the words "Pashtun" and "Pakhtun" is purely phonetic. The term "Pathan" is less accurate; adopted by the English during the colonial period, it is still in use in the present state of Pakistan to identify the Pashtun people who have settled within Pakistan's borders.

Pashtun origins are still disputed. Though Pashtun traditions claim a Jewish origin—the common tribal ancestor being Afghana, a grandson of King Saul of Israel—the language belongs to the Indo-European stock. Between the thirteenth and sixteenth centuries, the Pashtun extended their influence over the Afghan region, migrating also toward the western borders of the Indian subcontinent. In 1747, the Ghilzays, a powerful Pashtun tribe with many subdivisions, invaded the Persian empire, putting an end to the Safavid dy-

Pashtun soldiers in Kandahar, Afghanistan, in December 2001. (REUTERS NEWMEDIA INC./ CORBIS)

nasty (1501–1722/1736). Also in 1747, the Pashtun Abd'ali commander, Ahmad Shah (1722—1773), established himself as first amir (king) of Afghanistan, and the Abd'alis became the predominant tribe of the country. Thereafter, the Abd'alis were known as Durranis, from Ahmad Shah's appellative *Durr-i Durran* (Pearl of Pearls).

The Pashtun traditionally have a strong and distinctive tribal structure, organized into tribal subsections (tribes, clans, subclans) according to the male bloodline descent from an eponymous ancestor. The two main groups of tribes are the Durranis, who held the principal political positions, and the Ghilzays, but there are at least sixty tribes of different importance and size. The powerful nomadic traditions and close links with the practice of transhumance and animal husbandry gave them great mobility over, and knowledge of, the harsh Afghan territory, enhancing their warfaring attitudes against any external aggression. Indeed, Pashtun have always been attracted to the military life, while blood feuds and disputes are even today a characteristic of inter- and intratribal relations.

These warrior traditions have been "codified" in the Pakhtunwali, the unwritten code observed by Pashtun warriors to preserve their honor. Basic elements of this code are hospitality, the blood feud, the right/duty of asylum, and the defense of the honor of the women of one's own tribal subsection. From a religious point of view, Pashtun are Sunni Muslims.

In 1999, Pashtun in Afghanistan were estimated to be almost 10 million (38 percent of the total population), settled mainly in the Kabul area, in Kandahar, and along the eastern borders. In Pakistan, there were around 15 to 16 million Pashtun, concentrated in North West Province and Baluchistan.

Riccardo Redaelli

Further Reading

Caroe, Olaf. (1983) *The Pathans: With an Epilogue on Russia*. New enlarged ed. Karachi, Pakistan: Oxford University Press.

Dupree, Louis. (1980) *Afghanistan*. New enlarged ed. Princeton, NJ: Princeton University Press.

PASHTUNWALI Pashtunwali is the Pashtun code of life. The Pashtun, speaking an east Iranian dialect called Pashto, live on both sides of the border between Pakistan and Afghanistan. Although predominantly Muslim, the Pashtun live according to a cultural code, Pashtunwali, which demands courage, hospitality (e.g., giving shelter to anyone who seeks protection), and revenge—unless the aggressor seeks public pardon. Pashtunwali, however, never forgives shame-causing crimes, especially those involving a woman's honor. Pashtun society is well known for its generations-long cycles of revenge murder. Conflict resolution in the case of murder involves public pardon, forgiveness, the ceding of land, or the giving in marriage of a woman from the aggressor's family to a member of the aggrieved family. Pashtunwali is driven by *nang* (honor) and *tor* (shame). As a compendium of cultural customs, Pashtunwali guides a Pashtun's every public behavior and action. Sometimes its many expectations make it difficult for even the staunchest Pashtun to live by the letter and spirit of the Pashtunwali code. "To be a Pashtun is a curse," says a Pashto proverb, "but not to be a Pashtun is a shame."

Abdul Karim Khan

Further Reading

Ahmed, Akbar S. (1980) *Pashtun Economy and Society: Traditional Structure and Economic Development in a Tribal Society*. London: Routledge and Kegan Paul.

Caroe, Olaf. (1958) *The Pathans, 550 bc–ad 1957*. London: Macmillan.

PATHET LAO The Pathet Lao has been the predominant twentieth-century revolutionary movement in Laos. The literal meaning of Pathet Lao is Lao nation, Lao country, or land of the Lao, reflective of its strong nationalistic orientation.

The Pathet Lao originated from the Vietnamese communists' resistance in 1945 to the return of French colonial rule. The actual first use of the term occurred in 1950 in a special manifesto issued by the Congress of the Free Laos Front organized by Lao radical leaders opposed to the French and their colonial rule. The emergence of the Pathet Lao as a separate political force resulted from the split within the Lao Issara (Lao independence movement) in March of 1949. In 1949 an accommodation was reached between the center-right of the former Lao Issara movement and the French, resulting in the neocolonial rule opposed by the Pathet Lao and its leaders.

The major leaders of the Pathet Lao were Kaysone Phomvihan, Prince Souphanouvong (the "Red Prince"), and Nouhak Phoumsavan. All three of these leaders had close ties to Vietnam. Among them, Kaysone is clearly considered the revolutionary nationalist hero of Laos.

After the Geneva Conference in 1954, Laos was split into two zones, with the Pathet Lao dominant in the northeastern areas of Sam Neua and Phong Saly. They referred to their areas as liberated zones. They continued their revolutionary struggle against the French and later American-influenced neocolonial regimes. Eventually, through armed revolutionary struggle, the Pathet Lao achieved power in the latter part of 1975, and the Lao People's Democratic Republic was declared on 2 December 1975.

The formal party structure of the Pathet Lao was the Lao People's Revolutionary Party (LPRP), established in 1955 as the clandestine core organization within the Neo Lao Hak Sat (Lao Patriotic Front), which continues to rule Laos at the present time, and is normally simply referred to simply as the Party. The future of the LPRP fundamentally depends on the extent to which it remains faithful to the revolutionary ideals of the Pathet Lao and demonstrates genuine commitment to and success in improving the welfare of the Lao people.

Gerald W. Fry

Further Reading

Chomsky, Noam. (1970) *At War with Asia*. London: Fontana/Collins.

Decorney, Jacques. (1970). "Life in the Pathet Lao Liberated Zone." In *Laos: War and Revolution*, edited by Nina S. Adams and Alfred W. McCoy. New York: Harper & Row, 411–423.

Kaysone Phomvihane. (1981) *Revolution in Laos: Practice and Prospects*. Moscow: Progress.

Langer, Paul F., and Joseph J. Zasloff (1970). *North Vietnam and the Pathet Lao: Partners in the Struggle for Laos*. Cambridge, MA: Harvard University Press.

Zasloff, Joseph. (1973) *The Pathet Lao: Leadership and Organization*. Santa Monica, CA: Rand Corporation.

PATNA (2001 est. pop. 1.4 million). Patna (ancient Pataliputra) is the capital of Bihar State in northern India, 300 miles northwest of Calcutta on the south bank of the Ganges. The river is triple its usual width here and is crossed by the Mahatma Gandhi Seti, one of the largest bridges in the world.

Kunika Ajatasatru, second in the line of Magadh kings and heir of King Bimbisara, the philosopher-king of Kashi, ascended the throne of Magadh in 493 BCE. He fortified the small village of Pataligrama, which later came to be known as Pataliputra. The city was established by Ajatasatru's son Udayi to fulfill the Buddha's prophecy of a great city on that site. It was the capital of the Mauryan and Gupta empires and one of the subcontinent's most important cities for nearly a thousand years. The first Mauryan emperor, Candragupta (d. c. 297 BCE), expanded his domain to the Indus; his grandson Asoka (d. c. 238 BCE) extended it further. The city declined under medieval feudalism, until the sultanate revival in the sixteenth century under the rule of Mughal emperor Sher Shah. The English and Dutch East India Companies established factories in 1640 and 1666. The English began governing in 1766 and made Patna a provincial capital in 1912.

The symbol of the city is the beehive-shaped Golghar, a granary built in 1786. The Har Mandir Sahib shrine commemorates the Sikh guru Gobind Singh (1666–1708). In his honor the old quarter of the city is called Patna Sahib.

Roger Davis

Further Reading

Ahmad, Qeyamuddin. (1988) *Patna through the Ages: Glimpses of History, Society, and Economy.* New Delhi: Commonwealth.

Singh, Kanak. (1991) *History of Freedom Movement in Bihar: A Case Study of Patna City.* Patna, India: Janaki Prakashan.

PDP. See **Phalang Dharma Party.**

PEGU

(2002 est. pop. 228,100). Pegu (Bago), located on the banks of the Pegu (Bago) River, eighty kilometers northeast of Yangon (Rangoon), is the third-largest city in Myanmar (Burma). It is the capital of Pegu (Bago) Division, which has a population of 4.85 million (1997 est.) and is a major agricultural and rice-producing region. Its road and rail links are to be augmented by the new Hanthawaddy International Airport (scheduled for completion in 2004).

Pegu has an ancient history and was once known as Hamsavati (Hanthawadi), after the mythical bird associated with the city's founding. From 1365 to 1539 Pegu was the capital of the independent Mon kingdom of Lower Burma, whose rulers included King Razadarit (1385–1423), Queen Shin Sawbu (1453–1472), and King Dhammazedi (1472–1492). Fifteenth- and sixteenth-century European travelers left accounts of Pegu's splendor and prosperity. From 1539 to 1599 it was the capital of a united Burmese kingdom (the first Toungoo dynasty) until besieged and sacked by Arakanese invaders. Thereafter, years of warfare and the silting of its river port contributed to Pegu's decline and depopulation. In 1635, King Thalun abandoned Pegu altogether, transferring the capital to Ava in Upper Burma. Although resurgent Mon forces conquered Ava in 1752, their victory was short-lived. Any hopes for the restoration of the old Mon kingdom of Pegu were quashed by the rise of King Alaungpaya, founder of the Konbaung dynasty, who conquered and sacked Pegu in 1757. Pegu was annexed by the British in 1852 and developed into a major administrative and trading center for agricultural and forest products.

Pegu's most notable Buddhist monuments are Shwe-maw-daw Temple, Kalyani Thein (Ordination Hall, rebuilt in 1954 on the site of the 1476 original), the Shwe-thalyaung reclining Buddha image, and the four-faced Kyaik-pun image. In the 1990s, an ancient palace site was excavated and the palace of King Bayinnaung (1551–1581) lavishly reconstructed.

Patricia M. Herbert

Further Reading

Guillon, Emmanuel. (1999) *The Mons, A Civilization of Southeast Asia.* Translated and edited by James V. Di Crocco. Bangkok, Thailand: Siam Society.

PEKING UNIVERSITY

Peking University is the oldest and best comprehensive university in China. It was founded in December 1898 under the Qing dynasty (1644–1912) and was originally named the Metropolitan University. After the Republic of China was established, the university changed its name to Peking University in May 1912, and it retained this name after the People's Republic of China was established on 1 October 1949.

Peking University has a liberal tradition of academic freedom. In 1919 it played a leading role in the May Fourth intellectual and social movement and became a center for the Chinese new culture movement to adopt a popular speaking language instead of that of the traditional classic literature. Marxism in China was first developed at Peking University by Professors Chen Duxiu (1889–1942), Li Dazhao (1889–1927), and Mao Zedong (1893–1976), who then worked in the university's library.

When the Japanese invaded China in World War II, the university was moved to Kunming, Yunnan Province. When the university moved back to Beijing in 1946, it consisted of six colleges with a total of 3,000 students. Enrollment increased to 10,671 students in 1952 but declined during the Cultural Revolution (1966–1976).

In 2001 Peking University is a comprehensive university, offering five fields of study: humanities, social sciences, science, medicine and information, and engineering. With a total enrollment of 36,982 students, it has 16 colleges, 19 departments, 80 undergraduate programs, 177 masters programs, and 155 doctoral programs. At present, it also has 98 research institutes and 126 research centers.

The presidents of Peking University have been well-known scholars, including Yan Fu, the most famous Chinese translator of Western classics to Chinese; Cai Yuanpei, the famous educator; Hu Shi, the philosopher and author; and Ma Yinchu, the economist.

Chang Teh-Kuang

Further Reading

Nee, Victor. (1969) *The Cultural Revolution at Peking University*. New York: Monthly Review Press.

Peking University. (2001) "Faculty & Enrollment & Teaching." Retrieved 14 December 2001, from: http://www.pku.edu.cn/eabout/faculty.htm.

———. (2001) "History of Peking University." Retrieved 14 December 2001, from: http://www.pku.edu.cn/eabout/pku-history.htm.

PENANG (1995 est. pop. 1.2 million). Penang or Pulau Pinang ("Betel Nut Island" in Malay) is located in northwestern peninsular Malaysia. Today the "Pearl of the Orient" comprises the island of Penang and Seberang Perai (formerly Province Wellesley), a narrow strip on the peninsular Malaysian mainland. These are separated by a channel and linked by the Penang Bridge and a twenty-four-hour ferry service. The population is approximately 38 percent Malay, 50 percent Chinese, and 11 percent Indian. The capital of Penang is Georgetown, the seat of administration and the state's commercial hub. Penang is well known for its golden beaches.

Before 1786, Penang was part of the Kedah state. Kedah paid tribute in the form of "golden flowers" to its powerful neighbor, Siam, and was also in constant danger of a Bugis invasion from the south. The history of modern Penang began in 1786, when Englishman Francis Light persuaded the sultan of Kedah to lease Penang to the British East India Company in return for protection against the Bugis and Siamese.

After it became obvious that the British had no intention of fulfilling the agreement, the sultan of Kedah assembled a fleet to recapture Penang but was defeated. A treaty was signed to confirm the British occupation of Penang. The island was originally named Prince of Wales Island and later renamed Georgetown after King George III. In 1800, the Sultan of Kedah ceded a strip of land on the mainland, which Francis Light named Province Wellesley after Colonel Arthur Wellesley, then governor of India. In 1826, Penang formed part of the Straits Settlement with Melaka and Singapore. It became a major trading center. In 1948, it became one of the states of the Federation of Malaya. The federation gained independence from the Britain in 1957. Together with Sabah and Sarawak, the federation formed Malaysia in 1963.

Yik Koon The

Further Reading

Andaya, Barbara Watson, and Leonard Y. Andaya. (1982) *A History Of Malaysia*. London: Macmillan Press.

Eliot, Joshua, and Jane Bickersteth, eds. (1995) *Indonesia, Malaysia, and Singapore Handbook*. Bath, U.K.: Trade and Travel Publications.

Winstedt, Richard. (1966) *Malaya and Its History*. London: Hutchinson & Co.

PENINSULAR THAILAND Like an elephant's trunk, peninsular Thailand stretches roughly 800 kilometers south of the capital, Bangkok, to the Malaysian border. Wedged between the Gulf of Thailand in the east and Myanmar (Burma) and the Andaman Sea in the west, the peninsula is only about 234 kilometers wide at its widest, narrowing in parts to only about 30 kilometers. However, peninsular or southern Thailand also encompasses a number of islands off both coasts.

One of the country's most interesting regions, the peninsula plays a vital role in the economic and cultural makeup of Thailand. Distinct from the rest of the country, the four southernmost provinces of peninsular Thailand are closely linked to the Malay culture of Malaysia and Indonesia. While representing only about 5 percent of the total Thai population, Muslims are predominant in the peninsula. So too is an ethnic Chinese population that adds to the region's cultural and linguistic diversity. Even the Thai spoken in the south is distinct; it is often referred to as *paasaa paak tai*, or "language of the south."

Although peninsular Thailand is largely rural, several metropolitan centers exist. The biggest, Hat Yai, has a population of around 200,000, making it one of the larger cities in the country and a vibrant commercial center. Other cities include the fishing port of Songkhia and the major tourist center of Phuket. The split between rural and urban in the region reflects the cultural diversity as well, with the Chinese dominating the large towns and cities and the Muslim Thais inhabiting the countryside.

This diversity has, however, been problematic for Thailand. Historically, rebellions and strong separatist feelings have distanced the region from the rest of the country. A Communist insurgency during the 1950s, 1960s, and 1970s was based in peninsular Thailand (as well as in the northeast) and was closely associated with the Chinese population. Armed revolts in the area have long since ended, and in fact the region has become a stronghold for a major national political organization, the Democratic Party. Peninsular Thailand has however retained much of its uniqueness, and differences with the government in Bangkok are not uncommon.

With access to the seas, fishing is a major industry in peninsular Thailand. In fact, the region is one of the most important fishing centers in Southeast Asia. Large rubber plantations and a variety of agricultural and mining interests also contribute to the local economy. Unlike other regions of the country, which frequently endure droughts, peninsular Thailand has a high and consistent amount of rainfall, enriching its agricultural prosperity. Tourism is one of the largest industries in the area as well, particularly on resort islands such as Phuket and Koh Samui. Thailand's largest island, Phuket, is also its richest province. Noted for its diverse peoples, spectacular scenery, and resource wealth, the peninsula offers much to the cultural and economic fabric of Thailand.

Arne Kislenko

Further Reading

Chutima, Gawin. (1990) *The Rise and Fall of the Communist Party of Thailand (1973–1987).* Canterbury, U.K.: University of Kent at Canterbury, Centre of South-East Asian Studies.

Dixon, Chris. (1998) *The Thai Economy: Uneven Development and Internationalization.* London: Routledge.

Forbes, Andrew D. W., ed. (1988) *The Muslims of Thailand.* Gaya Bihar, India: Centre for South East Asian Studies.

Keyes, Charles F. (1987) *Thailand, Buddhist Kingdom as Modern Nation-State.* Boulder, CO: Westview Press.

McVey, Ruth. (2000) *Money and Power in Provincial Thailand.* Honolulu, HI: University of Hawaii Press.

Reynolds, Craig J. (1987) *Thai Radical Discourse: The Real Face of Thai Feudalism Today.* Ithaca, NY: Southeast Asia Program, Cornell University.

PEOPLE POWER MOVEMENT People Power Movement refers to the popular uprising that ousted Philippine president Ferdinand E. Marcos in February 1986. Also known as the EDSA Revolution, the uprising was in reaction to the massive fraud and violence unleashed by the government to ensure that Marcos and vice presidential candidate Arturo Tolentino would win the so-called snap elections that Marcos had called earlier that month. The opposition ticket was headed by Corazon Aquino, wife of former Senator Benigno "Ninoy" Aquino, who was assassinated in 1983 by elements of the Philippine military as he debarked his plane at the Manila International Airport (since renamed Ninoy Aquino International Airport). Many believed that Aquino and her running mate, Salvador Laurel, would have won had the elections been fair and honest. Massive demonstrations were held in front of Malacanang (the presidential palace) and two military camps located at Epifanio de los Santos Avenue (EDSA). The peaceful uprising became a model for other countries wishing to change their government without resort to a military coup or a bloody revolution.

Josie Hernandez de Leon

Further Reading

de Leon, Josie H. (1986) "Electoral Manipulation: The Case of the February 1986 Presidential Elections." *Philippine Journal of Public Administration* 30, 2: 154–183.

PEOPLE'S ARMY OF VIETNAM The People's Army of Vietnam (PAVN) is the Vietnamese armed forces. It includes the army, the navy, the air force, and several paramilitary units. It was created in May 1945 during a conference of the Indochinese Communist Party, and it consisted of the union of a number of revolutionary forces, such as the Armed Propaganda Brigades and the Viet Minh. Originally called the Vietnamese Liberation Army, it became known as the PAVN following the 1954 Geneva Agreements at the end of the war with France (French, or First, Indochina War; 1946–1954). The PAVN received world recognition at the time because the Geneva Agreements stipulated that the Democratic Republic of Vietnam (DRV) could keep its existing armed forces. PAVN troops were divided into three broad categories: the PAVN Regular Force (the army, navy, and air force), the Regional Force (infantry units located in distinct areas), and the Militia Self-Defense Force (local troops organized at the village or city level).

The PAVN fought against Japanese occupation forces in 1945, against French forces during the war with France, and against American and Army of the Republic of Vietnam (ARVN) forces during the Vietnam War (Second Indochina War; 1954–1975). Following the reunification of Vietnam in 1975, the PAVN was called upon to participate in the nation's postwar reconstruction. A number of troops were demobilized and transformed into economic development units. This proved to be short-lived because in 1978, PAVN troops participated in a military intervention of Cambodia and remained in that nation for ten years. In 1979, the PAVN defended Vietnam's northern border against the threat of Chinese attack and invasion.

Over the years, with military and material assistance from the Soviet Union and the People's Republic of China, the PAVN evolved from a poorly equipped guerrilla army to a modern, more conventional military force. Presently, the PAVN boasts an estimated 1.5 million troops, and an estimated 13 million Vietnamese men and women can be mobilized if necessary. The PAVN operates under the direction of a number of Vietnamese governmental and Communist Party institutions: the National Assembly, the Ministry of Defense, the National Defense Council, the Politburo, and the Central Military Party Committee. In addition, a few members of the PAVN's high command often serve on governmental and party committees.

Micheline R. Lessard

Further Reading

Duiker, William. (1981) *The Communist Road to Power in Vietnam.* Boulder, CO: Westview Press.

Kahin, George McT. (1987) *Intervention: How America Became Involved in Vietnam.* New York: Anchor.

Karnow, Stanley. (1983) *Vietnam: A History.* New York: Viking.

CHAIRMAN MAO ON THE PEOPLE'S LIBERATION ARMY

The Three Main Rules of Discipline are as follows:

Obey orders in all your actions
Do not take a single needle or piece of thread from the masses.
Turn in everything captured.

The Eight Points for Attention are as follows:

Speak politely.
Pay fairly for what you buy.
Return everything you borrow.
Pay for anything you damage.
Do not hit or swear at people.
Do not damage crops.
Do not take liberties with women.
Do not ill-treat captives.

Source: Mao Zedong (1976) *Quotations from Chairman Mao Tsetung.* Beijing: Foreign Language Press, 256–257.

PEOPLE'S LIBERATION ARMY The People's Liberation Army (PLA) is the collective name for the ground, air, naval, and strategic forces of the Communist Chinese military. The current PLA is one of the largest military forces in the world. Its army, which numbers more than three million, is the largest in the world. It also has a fairly sizeable navy and air force, and its nuclear forces, while small compared to those of the United States and Russia, rank as the fourth largest. However, many of its weapons and equipment are antiquated and limited in their ability to project military force beyond China's borders.

The origins of the PLA date back to 1 August 1927, when the Chinese Workers' and Peasants' Red Army was established by the Chinese Communists to fight a guerrilla war against the Nationalist (Guomindang) forces led by Chiang Kai-shek (1887–1975). During the Maoist period (1949–1976), the PLA was transformed from a loosely organized guerrilla army into a professional fighting force closely resembling the Soviet model, although there was always some tension between those who favored further professionalization and those who wanted the PLA to remain a revolutionary organization.

The PLA has historically been deeply involved with the governance of the country, although it has always remained subordinate to Chinese Communist Party (CCP) rule. Top party leaders, including Mao Zedong (1893–1976) and Deng Xiaoping (1904–1997), have historically had extensive experience in, and connections with, the Red Army. The PLA forms one of the three pillars of power in the Chinese Communist political system, alongside the CCP and the Chinese state or government. It enjoys equal rank with the State Council, the highest governmental body, and answers only to the Military Affairs Commission of the CCP. It is the Communist Party, in other words, and not the government that commands the PLA. In fact, party control over the PLA has been so important that the only official position held by Deng Xiaoping, China's preeminent leader during the 1980s, was chairman of the Military Affairs Commission. Another indication of the PLA's involvement in domestic affairs is that it runs a vast network of military industries and transportation links that accounts for a significant part of the nation's economic output. During the 1980s and 1990s, China's leaders have sought to further professionalize and modernize the PLA in an effort to disentangle it from domestic affairs and redirect its mission toward external security.

Shawn Shieh

Further Reading

Jencks, Harlan W. (1982) *From Muskets to Missiles: Politics and Professionalism in the Chinese Army, 1945–1984.* Boulder, CO: Westview Press.

Joffe, Ellis. (1987) *The Chinese Army After Mao.* Cambridge, MA: Harvard University Press.

Shambaugh, David, and Richard H. Yang, eds. (1997) *China's Military in Transition.* Oxford, U.K.: Clarendon Press.

PERAK (2002 est. pop. 2.1 million). Perak, which in the Malay language means "silver," covers an area of 21,005 square kilometers on the west coast of the Malay Peninsula and has a population of more than 2 million—48 percent Malay, 36 percent Chinese, 14 percent Indian, and 2 percent others. Ipoh, its capital, has become one of the largest cities in Malaysia. Its rich deposit of tin was its major trade until the tin slump of 1983. Perak managed to restructure its economy to focus on industry, business, and investment.

The origin of the present sultanate can be traced to the Melaka sultanate. The last sultan of Melaka was Sultan Mahmud (d. 1528), who reigned from 1488 to 1511. In 1511, Melaka was captured by the Portuguese. Sultan Mahmud fled to Johor. He was succeeded by his younger son, Alauddin, who became the sultan of Johor. Mahmud's eldest son, Muzaffar Shah, set out for Perak and established his court there. He became the first sultan of Perak in about 1529.

Perak, with its rich tin deposits, had attracted constant threats to its sovereignty, starting with the Acehnese in the sixteenth century. After 1641, the Dutch attempted to establish a monopoly over the tin trade but without great success. In the eighteenth century, threats came from the Bugis in the south and the Siamese in the north.

The growing importance of tin ore on the world market led to an influx of Chinese miners into the tin fields of Larut. In the 1860s and 1870s, factional feuds among the Chinese miners and disputes over succession to the throne led to British intervention under the Pangkor Treaty in 1874. Before the 1870s, the British had a policy of noninvolvement in the affairs of the Malay States, although Britain had extensive trading business there. British intervention settled the dispute among the Chinese miners, and the Pangkor Treaty recognized Abdullah as the sultan of Perak (reigned 1874–1875). A British resident, James Wheeler Woodford Birch, was also appointed to Perak. The role of the resident was to advise the sultan on how to improve the administration of his state. Although the resident was to have no executive powers, his advice was to be sought and followed on all questions other than those touching on Malay religion and custom. It was a system used to exercise British influence over the Malay States. The three general aims were the establishment of law and order, the centralized collection of revenue, and the development of the resources of the states.

However, opposition from the Perak chiefs resulted in the assassination of Birch in 1875. Under Sir Hugh Low from 1877 to 1889, Perak became a model for the development of the British resident system. In 1896, Perak, together with Selangor, Negeri Sembilan, and Pahang, formed the Federated Malay States. In 1948, the Federated Malay States became part of the Federation of Malaya. The federation gained independence from British colonial rule in 1957. Together with Sabah and Sarawak, the federation formed Malaysia in 1963.

Yik Koon Teh

Further Reading

Andaya, Barbara Watson, and Leonard Y. Andaya. (1982) *A History of Malaysia.* London: Macmillan Press.

Eliot, Joshua, and Jane Bickersteth, eds. (1995) *Indonesia, Malaysia, and Singapore Handbook.* Bath, U.K.: Trade and Travel Publications.

Ryan, N. J. (1969) *The Making of Modern Malaysia and Singapore: A History from Earliest Times to 1966.* Kuala Lumpur, Malaysia: Oxford University Press.

Winstedt, Richard O. (1982) *A History of Malaya.* Kuala Lumpur, Malaysia: Marican & Sons.

———. (1966) *Malaya and Its History.* London: Hutchinson & Co.

Winstedt, Richard O., and R. J. Wilkinson. (1974) *A History of Perak.* Kuala Lumpur, Malaysia: Malaysian Branch of the Royal Asiatic Society.

PERANAKAN The word "Peranakan" is Malay for someone who is "local born" of mixed ancestry, but it is now almost exclusively used to refer to the Chinese community. Chinese Peranakan communities emerged in Java (and to a lesser extent in southern Sumatra and coastal Kalimantan) during the eighteenth century and functioned as a merchant class under the Dutch authorities. The Chinese settlers, invariably male, married local women, forming a mixed community that then remained apart from indigenous society. While earlier Chinese migrants, starting with the Mongol incursions of the late 1200s, had been absorbed into the local population, the Peranakan communities remained distinct but adopted aspects of Javanese society.

The Peranakan communities adopted the Malay language, mixing in elements of Javanese, Sundanese, and their native Hokkien. Their cuisine was a mixture of Chinese and Javanese cooking, although with elements unknown in either culture, while their traditional clothing was also unique. Traditionally, they preferred the Chinese style of housing. Peranakan culture formed a "third," or "intermediary," culture in the sense that it combined Chinese and Indonesian elements but also included unique customs. What continued to separate the Peranakan—and mark them as Chinese to the indigenous peoples of Java—was their nonconversion to Islam (unlike earlier Chinese settlers); thus they remained Buddhist and/or Confucian or became Christian in some cases. By the early nineteenth century, the arrival of women with a more diverse group of Chinese migrants from Hokkien-, Hakka-, and Cantonese-speaking areas created a new type of settler community, which the Indonesians called Totok (pure blood). The Peranakan communities have tended, over time, to merge with the Totok communities through intermarriage, thus blurring the boundaries.

Anthony L. Smith

Further Reading

Cushman, Jennifer, and Wang Gungwu, eds. (1988) *Changing Identities of the Southeast Asian Chinese since World War II.* Hong Kong: Hong Kong University Press.

Skinner, G. William. (1996) "Creolized Chinese Societies in Southeast Asia." In *Sojouners and Settlers: Histories of Southeast Asia and the Chinese*, edited by Anthony Reid. Sydney: Allen & Unwin, 51–93.

PERGAMON The ancient city of Pergamon, located on the site of the present-day city of Bergama in Izmir, Turkey, flourished in the third and second centuries BCE. It allied itself with Rome and after becoming Roman in 133 BCE was known as Pergamum.

The kingdom of Pergamon surrendered to Alexander of Macedon in 334 BCE and after Alexander's death in 323 BCE was claimed by Lysimachus, one of Alexander's generals, in 301 BCE. Lysimachus used the acropolis of Pergamon to guard his riches. Philetaerus, at first an ally of Lysimachus, changed sides and supported Seleucus I, another of Alexander's generals, a tactic that won him the rulership of Pergamon. Phile-

The ruins of the Temple of Trajan at the site of an ancient Greek city in Pergamon, c. 1997. (RICHARD T. NOWITZ/CORBIS)

taerus ruled over the kingdom from 282 to 263 BCE; his successor, his nephew Eumenes I, governed until 241 BCE and left a wealthy kingdom to his cousin Attalus I, founder of the Attalid dynasty that controlled the city-state until 133 BCE.

Attalus (reigned 241–197 BCE) enlarged the kingdom to include Bythnia, Lydia, Cappadocia, and land as far away as Antalya; conquered the invading Gauls and the Seleucid king Antiochus III; and allied the kingdom with Rome. Attalus founded a library in the well-fortified, magnificently constructed city, which became a major literary center in Asia Minor as well as a center of Hellenistic sculpture.

Eumenes II, Attalus's son, expanded the kingdom still further and developed the library to challenge the library of Alexandria. The immense altar of Zeus, a masterpiece of Hellenistic architecture and sculpture constructed in Eumenes II's reign, is decorated around the base with a heroic frieze almost 120 meters long, depicting the battle of Gods and Giants; a smaller frieze celebrating the founding of Pergamon adorns the main colonnaded court. The dramatic conflicts of the figures on the large frieze suggest the power and divinity inherent in nature, which Greeks saw as their gods.

Pergamon continued to prosper, but Attalos III, the last ruler of the dynasty, had no heirs and at his death bequeathed his kingdom to Rome. Pergamon became Pergamum, the first Roman-ruled possession in Asia Minor and capital of the Roman province of Asia.

Ancient Monuments of Pergamon

The city was founded on a steep acropolis and expanded under later kings and the Romans to the plain below; it varies in altitude from 60 to 335 meters. On the oldest part of the site, the acropolis, stand temples to Athena, the altar dedicated to Zeus and probably to all the gods, royal palaces designed to glorify the Hellenistic rulers, and a *heroon*, or shrine to a hero, where the Attalid dynasty was worshiped. The library, which attracted distinguished scholars, included books written on parchment—specially treated skins of young animals, particularly sheep, calf, or goat (from the Greek *pergamene*, "of Pergamum"; Pergamon was famed for its fine parchment). In 40 BCE Mark Antony sent some of the 200,000 books to Cleopatra to restock the library of Alexandria after a disastrous fire.

Below the original walls and rising above the temple of Dionysus, the huge Greek theater was partly cut into natural rock; there were eighty rows in the *cavea*, or circle of seats, and two *diazomas*, horizontal passages that allowed people to cross the seating area. A huge gymnasium, with divisions for teaching infant, junior, and senior boys, included baths supplied through clay pipes. From the second century BCE, aqueducts made of earthenware pipes were constructed to supply drinking water; that from the spring at Madradag Hill was made up of 240,000 separate clay pipes. Later a pressurized lead-piped system and an eighty-kilometer-long Roman aqueduct led to cisterns and holding tanks.

The Romans added a temple dedicated to the imperial cult and a Serapeion, the temple of an Egyptian deity worshiped in the Greco-Roman world. The Serapeion, 260 by 100 meters, was built of red brick and had ducted sacred pools. A sacred way led to a temple of Asklepios, the Greek god of medicine; his temple functioned as a sort of hospital, where the god appeared to patients in dreams, offering diagnosis and cures.

Later Pergamum

The Greek physician Galen (129–c. 199 CE) was born in Pergamum and ministered to the gladiators there. From 161 Galen was in Rome, at the court of Marcus Aurelius, and then was physician to the Roman emperor Commodus. Galen's writings formed the basis of Greco-Roman and Arabic medicine. Pergamum was also an early center of Christianity and the seat of one of the seven churches of Asia, founded by Saint Paul. The city continued as a commercial center during the Byzantine and Ottoman empires.

Discovery

The ancient ruins of Pergamon, which surround the modern city of Bergama, were rediscovered in 1868 by a railway engineer, Carl Humann, who found fragments of the sculptures of the Zeus altar. From 1878 on, the immense altar was excavated under the sponsorship of the Prussian government, and the remains were taken to Berlin and installed in the Pergamon Museum, where they may be seen today. Despite this loss, ancient Pergamon is still a magnificent Hellenistic city whose sights attract numerous visitors.

Kate Clow

Further Reading

Akurgal, Ekrem. (1969) *Ancient Civilizations and Ruins of Turkey*. Istanbul, Turkey: Haslet Kitabevi.

Darke, Diana. (1989) *Discovery Guide to Aegean and Mediterranean Turkey*. 2d ed. London: Michael Haag, Ltd.

PERIPATETICS The people whom anthropologists commonly call peripatetics (from the Greek *peripatetikos*, meaning to walk up and down, discoursing while walking) are known in South and West Asia by a variety of terms, among them Gypsies, Lambadis, and Banjaras. They consist of innumerable small, nomadic groups, often no more than one extended family in size, who move through the countryside performing a wide range of tasks. Many of these occupations have given rise to the particular name of a group, like the Banjaras, carriers of rice and salt. The peripatetics fill an economic niche wherever they go. Some perform a variety of services through the distribution of minor products, such as trinkets, forest produce, or magical amulets. Others are religious mendicants who give the faithful the opportunity of acquiring merit by feeding these beggars. Yet others are street beggars or fortune-tellers of a more secular nature. Many groups are involved in performances, from displaying wild animals or performing acrobatic feats to clairvoyance and prostitution.

In South Asia the great majority of peripatetics are Hindu, but some are Muslim or Sikh, and others may claim to be Christian. In every case the nomadism of these people is distinct from the purposive nomadism of transhumant pastoralists like the Gujjars, who move their herds over a fixed route every year to find better pasture. Nonetheless some peripatetics have herds, usually of camels, goats, or pigs, which have their own niche in the landscape.

There are no reliable census figures for such people, and they tend to keep their distance from all kinds of officials, especially the police. There may be some 10 million in South Asia, but there is no source against which to check this figure.

The subculture of peripatetics has its economic specializations, but in other respects it is consonant with that of other castes in the area where the group resides. In the Indian state of Andhra Pradesh, for example, the peripatetics normally speak Telugu like everyone else, but they may use additional languages if they move much outside that state. Some groups have their own "secret" languages or dialects. Their worship is commonly like that of neighboring Hindu castes. Their marriage preferences are usually similar to those of other castes in the area as well.

Paul Hockings

PERLIS (2002 est. pop. 209,000). At 759 square kilometers, Perlis is the smallest state in Malaysia. It lies in the northwestern corner of the Malay Peninsula and borders Thailand to the north and the Strait of Malacca to the west. Perlis was originally part of the state of Kedah, which lies to its south. However, the Thais decided to create another vassal principality when they conquered Kedah in 1821, and thus Perlis was formed. Perlis was later transferred to the British under the Treaty of Bangkok (1909). During the Japanese occupation of British Malaya from 1941 to 1945, Perlis, together with the states of Kedah, Kelantan, and Trengganu, was ceded to Thailand. After the war, Perlis became a member of the Federation of Malaya (1948) and, subsequently, a constituent state of independent Malaysia (1957).

The state's major land use is in agriculture (predominantly rice, sugarcane, and rubber). Mining, quarrying, and harvesting forestry products continue to be important economic activities as well. Since the 1970s, however, medium-scale manufacturing has assumed an increasing share of the state's gross domestic product.

Seng-Guan Yeoh

Further Reading

Haji Buyong Adil. (1981) *Sejarah Perlis*. Kuala Lumpur, Malaysia: Dewan Bahasa dan Pustaka.

Wan Hashim, Wan Teh, and Ismail Hamid. (1988) *Nilai budaya masyarakat desa*. Kuala Lumpur, Malaysia: Dewan Bahasa dan Pustaka.

PERSEPOLIS (literally "City of the Persians" in Greek) was one of the most important capitals of ancient Persia. While the exact date of its foundation is not known, it appears to have become prominent at the death in 522 BCE of Cambyses II, the son and successor of Cyrus the Great (c. 585–c. 529), when it replaced Pasargadae as the capital of the empire. It was called Parsa by the Persians and functioned as the principal royal residence of the Achaemenid kings. It is assumed that Darius I (550–486 BCE), who succeeded Cambyses II, began work on the main platform of the complex and its structures between 518 and 516 BCE, visualizing Persepolis as the grand focus of his vast empire. Additional monuments were then added to the city's infrastructure in the reigns of Xerxes I (c. 519–465 BCE) and Artaxerxes I (d. 425 BCE). This great prosperity lasted only two hundred years, and the city was plundered and burned by Alexander of Macedon in 330 BCE following his historic victory over the Persian armies. After its massive destruction, Persepolis was eventually abandoned and lay in ruins through the successive dynasties that controlled Persia until 1620, when its site was first identified.

PERSEPOLIS—WORLD HERITAGE SITE

The ruins of the ancient capital of the Achaemenid empire were designated a UNESCO World Heritage Site in 1979. Persepolis' monumental historical importance and its surprisingly well-preserved remains make it a highly significant archeological site.

Investigating the Ruins of Persepolis

In the following centuries, Persepolis and its impressive ruins were the focus of numerous historical and travel accounts. While these observations were condensed and published by George N. Curzon in *Persia and the Persian Question* in 1892, scientific research and examination of the site was not undertaken until the 1930s. Ernst Herzfeld became the first field director of the Oriental Institute's Persepolis Expeditions in 1931. Between 1931 and 1934, he excavated the grand eastern stairway of the Apadana (the royal reception hall), the smaller stairs of the Council Chamber, and the Harem of Xerxes on the Persepolis terrace. Erich F. Schmidt took charge in 1934 and continued the excavations of the complex until the end of 1939, when the onset of the war in Europe put an end to archaeological work in Iran.

Since the early excavations under Herzfeld had mainly uncovered palaces, until the first quarter of the twentieth century Persepolis was believed to consist largely of palaces of the Achaemenid sovereigns and their annexes and gardens. However, the later excavations, between 1934 and 1939, revealed several additional structures on the high terrace. These included an entrance hall, the few remaining columns of the Apadana, the ruins of Darius' small residence (the Tachara), those of the palace of Xerxes (the Hadish), and the ruins of a structure identified as the Harem. There was, in addition, a second reception hall, known as the Hall of a Hundred Columns, and the "Unfinished Gate." It was believed by scholars that the citadel and the royal treasury were on the mountain called Kuh-i Rahmat, and that the town itself was situated at Istakhr, about six kilometers away.

By the 1960s, several scholars had reexamined the excavations and concluded that palace structures were only part of the large ensemble of buildings. Furthermore, even the functions assigned to some of the structures were inaccurate. The royal Harem, for example, was a double line of enormous halls with no external openings or open spaces, and organized around a long central corridor. It was evidently closer in its form and organization to a large group of vaulted halls, marked on the ground by multiple bases of stone columns, indicating storage structures or elaborate warehouses. It was therefore highly likely that these buildings housed the extensive royal treasuries of the Achaemenid kings, truly a fitting function for this grand showcase of the empire. The vast storerooms were in turn enclosed by elaborate military quarters and a few palaces. The "royal towns" of which the historians spoke lay at the foot of the terrace on the level of the plain, protected by a double wall and a moat.

The Structure of Ancient Cities

The remains of Persepolis provide scholars with important evidence on the form and layout of cities in ancient Persia. Its layout and monuments coincide with the depictions of cities and military camps on surviving wall panels, such as those at Sennacherib's palace city at Nineveh—the cult center of Ishtar between 704 and 681 BCE. Those wall panels mainly described scenes of war, defeat, and the conquest of enemies; cities and urban foundations were here always represented as circular, oval structures with strong walls and defensive bastions. In addition, a moat usually surrounded the entire city, so that the attacking armies were either inside or outside this defensive barrier. Significantly, within the urban walls there also appeared the horizontal road connecting the longer axis of the oval enclosure created by the city walls. Prominent buildings, in addition to numerous tentlike structures, filled up the rest of the space.

Based on these reconstructions of Parthian and Sassanian cities, it is therefore likely that the terrace at Persepolis—the raised, protected eminence within its citadel—was the center of an immense urban region, stretching for several miles across the plain. This urban district of dense population was criss-crossed by a large network of irrigation canals. Furthermore, main streets radiated from the central citadel, dividing the city into sectors and delineating the various areas of this region. It is evident that cities such as Persepolis, including its extant remains and legendary accounts, were important sources of emulation for the creation of urban centers by civilizations of the Near and Middle East, Central Asia, and the Indian subcontinent.

Manu P. Sobti

Further Reading

Godard, Andre. (1965) *The Art of Iran.* Trans. by Michael Heron. New York and Washington: Frederick A. Praeger.

Schmidt, Erich Friedrich. (1940) *Flights over Ancient Cities of Iran.* Chicago: University of Chicago Press.

———. (1953–1970) *Persepolis I, II, and III.* Chicago: University of Chicago Press.

———. (1939) *The Treasury of Persepolis and Other Discoveries in the Homeland of the Achaemenians.* Chicago: University of Chicago Press.

Wilber, Donald N. (1989) *The Archaeology of Parsa, Seat of the Persian Kings.* New York: Darwin Press.

PERSIAN is the official language of Iran, a country historically known as Persia in Western literature. Persian, called Farsi in Iran, is the native language of over half of the present-day population of 70 million, as well as the medium for instruction, education, mass media, business, and administration among the different ethnic and linguistic communities throughout the country.

Persian is also spoken as a first language by some people in Afghanistan, Tajikistan, Uzbekistan, Pakistan, and India. In Afghanistan it is called Dari and with another Iranian language, Pashto, has official status. In Tajikistan, where Persian is the national language, it is called Tajiki.

Persian, Dari, and Tajiki differ from one another in vocabulary, pronunciation of some phonemes, and certain grammatical features, but the speakers of these languages can understand one another and can share the rich Persian literary and cultural heritage.

Iran is a country of considerable language diversity. Apart from Persian, there are other Iranian languages such as Kurdish, Baluchi, and Lori, not to mention non-Iranian (Azeri, Armenian, Arabic) languages spoken by members of various ethnic and religious minorities. Persian shows considerable dialectical variation; people in various parts of Iran speak their own dialects, such as Shirazi, Isfahani, Mashhadi, and Tehrani. The dialect of Tehran, the capital city, is considered the standard contemporary dialect of Persian.

Historical Development

Persian belongs to the Iranian branch of the Indo-Iranian language family, a major subgroup of the Indo European languages. On the basis of structural as well as historical characteristics, the ancient Iranian languages are classified into two genetically related groups: Western and Eastern.

The Western group consists of Old Persian and Median, whereas the Eastern group includes Scythian and Avestan. Old Persian is assumed to be the ancestor of Middle Persian, which in turn is the ancestor of Modern Persian. The historical development of Persian began as early as the sixth to third centuries BCE, when Old Persian was the official language of the Achaemenid empire (c. 559–c. 530 BCE). The Achaemenid dynasty developed a sophisticated culture, reflected in the cuneiform inscriptions of the kings, such as those discovered in the remains of the royal palaces at Persepolis in southern Iran and on the vast carved monument of Darius the Great at Bisitun in western Iran. (The Bisitun trilingual cuneiform inscriptions provided the key to translating Babylonian and Assyrian cuneiform, undertaken by the British officer Sir Henry Rawlinson in the 1840s.) The Persian cuneiform inscriptions, despite representing a limited corpus of roughly six hundred words, indicate that Old Persian, unlike Middle and Modern Persian, was a highly inflected language with seven cases, three genders, and singular, plural, and dual forms.

Middle Persian, called also Pahlavi, is the language spoken in southwestern Iran from the collapse of the Achaemenid empire to the ninth century CE, during the Islamic period. This language served as the official administrative and literary language of Iran under the rule of the Sasanid dynasty (224–651). A great body of literature and an abundance of material have been preserved in Middle Persian. This language was written in the Pahlavi script, an adaptation of the Aramaic script.

Middle Persian and Modern Persian overlapped, the emergence of Modern Persian coinciding with the Arab conquest of Iran and the conversion of the Iranians to Islam in the seventh century. The oldest records of this language date from the tenth century. Modern Persian is a modified evolutionary form of Middle Persian. Both languages are analytic and are similar in terms of syntactic and morphological characteristics. ("Analytic" means that syntactic relationships are represented by the use of uninflected function words instead of inflections. Inflectionally, both Middle and Modern Persian are much simpler than Old Persian, which was a synthetic or highly inflected language.) Modern Persian first flourished in the eastern and northern regions of Iran and has remained the official language of Iran from the tenth century to the present time.

Linguistic and Literary Characteristics

The modern post-Islamic period in the history of Persian is characterized by the language's strong tendency toward a simplified morphological and syntactic system as compared with Old Persian. During the modern period the Persian vocabulary has been affected by other Iranian and non-Iranian languages. Arabic had the greatest influence on the Persian language, since it was the cultural language of the Islamic world. The slow but constant penetration of thousands of Arabic words into Persian enriched the vocabulary and changed the phonemic and syntactic character of the language to some extent. It also led to the gradual introduction of Arabic script for writing Persian. Arabic was a simpler script than the complicated Middle Persian Pahlavi script. The Arabic alphabet was gradually modified to suit the Persian phonetic system. Four consonants (*p*, *č*, *ž*, and *g*) were added to the alphabet to represent Persian sounds absent in Arabic. Although the Arabic words that entered the Persian lexicon retain their original orthography (spelling), the pronunciation of some was adapted in accordance with the Persian phonetic structure.

Modern Persian literature has existed for at least one thousand years and has been considered by thinkers such as Goethe one of four main bodies of world literature. Among the treasury of works written in Persian by historians, philosophers, and poets, two noteworthy examples are the national epic poem the *Shahnameh* (Book of Kings), written by Firdawsi (c. 935–c. 1020) of Tus approximately one thousand years ago, and the mystical poems of Rumi (Jalal ad-Din ar-Rumi, c. 1207–1273) of Balkh, written about seven hundred years ago.

Shahla Raghibdoust

Further Reading

Aryanpur, Manoochehr, and Abbas Aryanpur Kashani. (1973) *A History of Persian Literature*. Tehran, Iran: Kayhan Press.

Natel Khanlari, Parviz. (1979) *History of the Persian Language*. Delhi: Idarah-i Adabiyat-i Delhi.

Rypka, Jam. (1968) *History of Iranian Literature*. Dordrecht, Netherlands: D. Reidel.

PERSIAN GULF The Persian Gulf links the Middle Eastern countries with the rest of the world, which accounts for its strategic importance in modern times. It is an arm of the Arabian Sea 885 kilometers long and 322 kilometers in maximum width; its area is 229,992 square kilometers and the average depth is 100 meters. The Persian Gulf lies between the Arabian Peninsula in the south and west and Iran in the north and northeast and is connected with the Arabian Sea and Gulf of Oman through the Straits of Hormuz. In addition to Iran along its entire northern shore, the countries bordering the Persian Gulf include Iraq at its northwestern tip and Kuwait, Saudi Arabia, Bahrain, Qatar, the United Arab Emirates, and Oman along its southeastern terminus at the Strait of Hormuz.

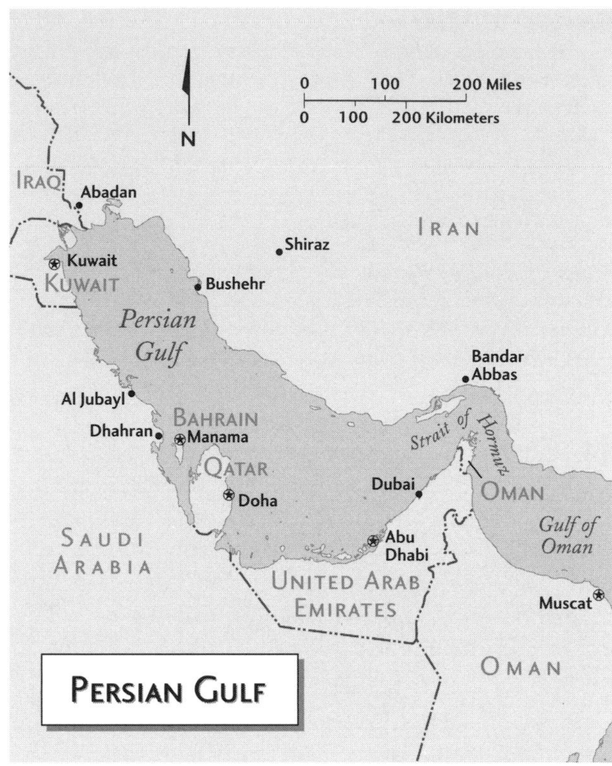

Since ancient times, the Persian Gulf linked the peoples of the Middle East with India in particular and the Indian Ocean region in general. During the Abbasid caliphate (750–1258), vessels from India, Africa, and the Far East regularly called at the port of Basra at the northwestern point of the gulf. Westerners began frequenting its waters in the sixteenth century: first the Portuguese, then the Dutch, English, French, and Americans.

Before the discovery of oil the most important commodities of the region were pearls and dates. The majority of the inhabitants, who in early modern times were predominantly Arabs even along the Persian shore, lived mainly through nomadic herding, fishing, and occasionally piracy.

Traditional pearl fishing began to decline after the introduction of cultivated pearls in the 1930s, and oil soon came to dominate the region's economic activities. Both land and offshore oil fields have been discovered, and today the Persian Gulf region accounts for approximately two-thirds of the world's oil reserves and one-third of the world's natural gas reserves. The region also currently accounts for nearly one-fourth of the world's oil production, and the traditional lateen-rigged sailing vessels have now been largely replaced by the constant traffic of large tankers.

The strategic importance of Persian Gulf resources has figured prominently in a number of recent border conflicts and policy disputes with major international involvement. While none of the states in the area remained immune from these conflicts, the most important ones have been the Iran-Iraq War (1980–1988) and the Gulf War between Iraq and the United Nations over Kuwait in 1991.

Oil wealth transformed the lives of the inhabitants, offering many of them employment in modern industries, improved health care, universal education, and modern means of communication. Traditional Islamic and tribal values continue to play an important role, though there are wide differences between the countries of the region in this regard. In some countries women have recently enjoyed greater employment opportunities and some social freedoms.

Thabit Abdullah

PERSIAN GULF WAR In March 1975, after years of more or less overt hostility, Iran and Iraq signed what appeared to be a comprehensive settlement of their differences, the Algiers Agreement. Under terms of the agreement, Iran undertook to cease supporting the Iraqi Kurds in their struggle against the Iraqi government. The agreement also promised a permanent resolution of the disputed border between the two nations, notably in the Shatt al Arab waterway, where it was agreed that it should follow the lowest or median point, the *thalweg*. For a few years, Baghdad and Tehran enjoyed a friendly relationship that was unprecedented, shattered only by the overthrow of the Iranian monarchy and the installation of the Islamic republic in 1979. Tensions mounted throughout 1979 and the first half of 1980, eventually leading to Iraqi president Saddam Hussein (b. 1937) ceremonially tearing up a copy of the Algiers Agreement on Iraqi television and setting in motion a war against Iran in September 1980.

The ten-year war that followed was both extremely costly and almost completely pointless. The bulk of the Iraqi Shiʿite population stood on the side of their nation rather than on the side of Shiʿa Islam (the form of Islam that predominates in Iran). The human and economic costs of the war were staggering. Western

A U. S. tank in the desert in Kuwait with oil wells burning in the background in March 1991. (DAVID & PETER TURNLEY/CORBIS)

sources estimate nearly 400,000 dead, roughly one-quarter Iraqi and three-quarters Iranian, and perhaps 750,000 wounded, with costs of $452.6 billion for Iraq and $644.3 billion for Iran.

In the course of the war, Iraq contracted substantial debts, both to its rich neighbors and to various G7 (Group of Seven economic summit) nations. Although no serious pressure was exerted upon Iraq to repay these debts, their extent in August 1988, when Iran and Iraq agreed to a cease-fire, certainly complicated the transition from a war to a peace economy. Another far-reaching consequence of the war was that Iraq emerged as a substantial military power. In 1979–1980, the Iraqi armed forces numbered 190,000 men; by 1987–1988, this number had more than quintupled, to around 1 million. In addition, Iraq had built up an important armaments industry whose products included a surface-to-surface missile based on the Soviet Scud. By 1989–1990, the scale of military production was beginning to give rise to serious international concern; it was widely known that Iraq was manufacturing chemical weapons and sophisticated missiles and was not far from acquiring the means to produce nuclear weapons. The essential components of all these were provided by firms in western Europe and the United States.

Iraq from 1988 to 1990

Although Iraq's economic situation after the war was certainly bad, it could not be described as desperate, given the nation's substantial oil reserves. But, although the reconstruction of the cities, the infrastructure, and industry was certainly an important goal, only $2.5 billion per year was allocated to reconstruction during the period 1988–1989, whereas $5 billion a year was allocated to rearmament. Hence the desperateness of Iraq's financial position was more an expression of Saddam Hussein's priorities than an objective fact.

At the same time, the efforts that were made to restructure the economy led to steep price rises and a rise in the cost of living generally; inflation was estimated at 45 percent for 1990, hitting those on fixed incomes hardest. This produced a deep sense of dislocation and discontent among wide sections of the population who had grown used to the state providing them with secure employment and subsidizing most essential items of consumption throughout the 1970s and 1980s.

Early in 1990, a combination of factors enabled Saddam Hussein to project himself as "embattled" once more. In February the Middle East division of Human Rights Watch (a nongovernmental organization dedicated to combating abuses of human rights) published a scathing denunciation of Iraq's human-rights record; in March, the Western media widely condemned Iraq's execution of a British journalist on charges of espionage; in April, a scandal erupted over the so-called Iraq supergun (a device that was to be capable of firing artillery over thousands of miles) and later over the discovery of essential parts for nuclear weapons in the baggage of Iraqi travelers passing through London's Heathrow Airport. In the spring of 1990, Iraqi officials lobbied Persian Gulf rulers to lower their oil production and also to push up oil prices to around $20 a barrel.

Iraq's Invasion of Kuwait

At the same time, Saddam Hussein was determined to provide Iraq with access to a deep-water anchorage on the gulf as an alternative to the port of Umm Qasr. He was casting his eyes on the Kuwaiti islands of Bubyan and Warba, which would provide an alternative harbor. In the spring of 1990, he demanded access to the islands and resuscitated Iraq's claim to that part of the Rumaila oilfield that ran across northern Kuwait and southern Iraq. He also castigated Kuwait for allegedly having the temerity to demand repayment of some of Iraq's debts and for having been instrumental in the campaign to keep oil prices low. At the end of July 1990, part of the Iraqi army was sent to the border, and on 2 August, when Kuwait refused to give in to these demands, Iraq invaded, and subsequently annexed, Kuwait.

Reaction to the invasion was swift. The United Nations Security Council passed a number of resolutions condemning Iraq; on 7 August, President George H. W. Bush ordered an immediate airlift of American troops to Saudi Arabia to defend it from possible Iraqi attack. Arab and Asian workers began to pour out of Kuwait across Iraq toward the Jordanian border, where they were crossing at the rate of ten thousand to fifteen thousand a day during August and September.

During the next few weeks, Iraqi troops killed large numbers of Kuwaitis; they also rounded up all Iraqis in Kuwait (many of whom were political refugees) and took them into custody. Several thousand Kuwaitis were arrested; many have not been seen since. Hospitals and other public buildings were stripped of their equipment, and looting of property and attacks on civilians became commonplace. The price of oil rose steadily, from about $20 per barrel before the invasion began to above $40 by mid-September 1990; neither Iraq nor Kuwait was exporting oil.

A number of individuals and groups made attempts at mediation; meanwhile, Saddam Hussein began to talk in terms of "linkage" with the Palestinian issue, to assert that Iraq would withdraw from Kuwait if Israel withdrew from the Occupied Territories. On 15 August, Iraq accepted Iran's peace terms for the Iran-Iraq War unconditionally, restoring the status quo in the Shatt al Arab waterway to what it had been under the Algiers Agreement of March 1975. At the end of November, the United Nations issued Resolution 678, which authorized member nations to use all necessary means to force Iraq to withdraw from Kuwait if it had not done so by 15 January 1991.

Counterattacks by the Anti-Iraq Coalition

During the autumn of 1990, the United States put together an anti-Iraq coalition of some thirty nations, including Egypt and Syria, almost of all of which sent token detachments to Saudi Arabia. In the end the coalition partners mustered half a million troops. When Saddam Hussein failed to respond to the ultimatum in Resolution 678, the United States and its allies began to bomb various targets in Iraq on 17 January 1991, causing large numbers of civilian deaths and considerable damage to the nation's infrastructure. Iraq retaliated by launching Scud missiles at targets in Israel and Saudi Arabia. After five weeks of bombing, a ground offensive, called Desert Storm, was launched on 24 February, ending with the rout and destruction of much of the regular Iraqi army on 27 February, when a cease-fire was declared. Iraqi troops had been driven out of Kuwait the previous day.

Analysis and Consequences of the Persian Gulf War

The decision to invade Kuwait probably had three principal roots: first, Saddam Hussein's almost pathological ambition and his desire to carve out a major leadership role for himself within the Arab world; second, the fact that he had created an enormous military machine that could not easily be run down; and third, the sense that the great changes taking place in eastern Europe would mean that the world balance of power had shifted decisively in favor of the United States and that neither he nor "the Arab masses" could continue to rely upon the Soviet Union and its allies.

For Iraq and Kuwait, the invasion and the war (the period between 2 August 1990 and 27 February 1991) resulted in at least 100,000 deaths among both military and civilian populations and 300,000 wounded. As many as 2.5 million people were displaced (in the sense of being forced to leave, or leaving, their homes and places of work). Over $170 billion in property and infrastructure damage was caused in Iraq and perhaps $60 billion worth in Kuwait, excluding the environmental harm caused by Iraq's sabotaging over seven hundred Kuwaiti oil wells. Of course, given that the cease-fire after the war with Iran was only a little over two years old in August 1990, the effect of this additional self-inflicted wound on an already ailing Iraqi economy was even more damaging than these figures suggest.

Peter Sluglett

Further Reading

Baram, Amatzia, and Barry Rubin, eds. (1993) *Iraq's Road to War*. Basingstoke, U.K.: Macmillan.

Farouk-Sluglett, Marion, and Peter Sluglett. (2001) *Iraq since 1958: From Revolution to Dictatorship*. 3d ed. London: I. B. Tauris.

O'Loughlin, John, Tom Mayer, and Edward S. Greenberg, eds. (1994) *War and Its Consequences: Lessons from the Persian Gulf Conflict*. New York: HarperCollins.

Schofield, Richard. (1991) *Kuwait and Iraq: Historical Claims and Territorial Disputes*. London: Royal Institute of International Affairs.

Tripp, Charles. (2000) *A Political History of Iraq*. Cambridge, U.K.: Cambridge University Press.

PERSIAN MINIATURE PAINTING The art of Persian miniature emerged as a means of illustrating books, usually accompanying works of poetry. Persian miniatures evolved in Iran during the rule of the Turkic Seljuk dynasty (1038–1157 CE). Miniatures in this period were characterized by ornamentally posed figures with almond eyes and round faces against a background of deep tones. The miniatures in this period were relatively crude but served as a model for later forms.

With the Mongol invasions and the rule of their successors, the Il-Khans (1256–1336 CE), the art of miniature developed rapidly in Iran. The Il-Khans adapted to Iranian culture and, wanting to imitate the previous rulers, maintained the services of notable artists. This period of miniatures witnessed the use of landscapes and the introduction of Mongol warriors.

The Il-Khans were succeeded by the rule of Timur and his Tartar hordes (1370–1405 CE). Under the rule of the Timurid dynasty, miniatures and bookmaking arts entered a new level of sophistication. During this era, a bookmaking academy was established in Herat. Here, Bihzad, considered the greatest miniaturist in Persian art, began his career. The *nasta'liq* script, a highly decorative writing that emerged in Herat, accompanied miniatures in this period.

The fourth period of miniature art began with the Safavid dynasty (1501–1722/1736 CE) that emerged in Tabriz, in northern Iran. In this period, miniature paintings evolved as a court art, portraying the shahs and his princes. Outdoor life was another theme during this period, characterized mostly by hunting themes. Miniatures were painted on palm leaves or canvas until the introduction of paper in Iran in the beginning of the sixteenth century. The traditional technique of painting miniatures begins with outlining the drawing in black and painting the colors into the outlined areas.

During the reign of Shah Abbas the Great (1587–1629 CE), the Safavid capital moved from Tabriz to Isfahan, inaugurating a new era in miniature painting. The most prominent artist during this period was Riza Abbasi, who initiated a new school in miniature painting, where the figures displayed a closer likeness to ordinary people. The Persian miniatures spread to the neighboring Ottoman and Mughal empires, as Iranian artists founded schools.

The art of Persian miniature declined with the rise of the Turkic Qajar dynasty (1794–1925 CE) in Iran. During this period, European cultural influences were already making themselves felt in the region. The schools of Persian miniature painting closed during this era and the masters of this art eventually died, taking their skills with them. Persian miniature in the modern era usually consists of skillful copies of the works of the Timurid and Safavid eras.

Ibrahim Marashi

Further Reading

Kubickova, Vera. (n.d.) *Persian Miniatures*. London: Spring Books.

Pope, Arthur Upham. (1970) *Masterpieces of Persian Art*. Westport, CT: Greenwood Press.

PERSIANS Persians are people of Indo European or Aryan origin that moved to the Iranian plateau from the east. The word "Persian" comes from the Persian word Parsa (its Arabic form is Fars), which referred to people from the region in the south of Iran. The majority of the Iranian people are of Persian ethnic background (over half of the population). Persians have experienced a history replete with foreign invasions, battles, and conquests, and have also contributed to the development of world science, art, and literature.

MEIDAN EMAN—WORLD HERITAGE SITE

Designated by UNESCO as a World Heritage Site in 1979, Meidan Eman is a labyrinthine network of mosques and arcades in Iran and a superb example of life in seventeenth-century Persia.

During the first millennium BCE, the Persians arrived in the southern and central area of Iran from the Caucasus region; they established themselves there by the seventh century BCE. Most likely, they had left their original lands because of overgrazing, overpopulation, and conflicts. A seventh-century BCE ruler was Hakamanish, known in Greek as Achaemenes. Hakamanish was the ancestor of Cyrus the Great (c. 585–c. 529 BCE), the founder of the Achaemenid empire. Through conquest, Cyrus the Great extended the Persian empire until it included Asia Minor and Babylonia; later he extended it east into Afghanistan and west as far as the Danube River.

Early Persian Dynasties and the Coming of Islam

Alexander of Macedon (356–323 BCE) defeated the Achaemenid empire in 330 BCE. Alexander the Great aimed to integrate the Greek and Persian cultures; to that end, in 324 BCE he ordered his officers and ten thousand soldiers to take Persian women as their brides. After the death of Alexander, the Seleucids and Parthians ruled the territory of the Persians. In 224 Ardeshir (reigned 224–241 CE) ousted the last of the Parthian kings and founded the Persian Sasanid dynasty (224–651 CE).

The Sasanid dynasty consolidated power and was able to achieve control over an area about the same size as that achieved under the Achaemenids. Culturally, they worked to remove Greek influences and to reinforce Persian ones. They established Zoroastrianism as the state religion.

Constant warfare with the Byzantines coupled with economic hardship opened the door for invasion. Eventually, fatal invasion came from the least likely place: Arabia. The Arab tribes had become united under the banner of Islam and mastered the use of light armored cavalry, a new style of warfare. In battles, they surprised the Persian heavy armed forces with their lightning-speed, hit-and-run attacks. The Arabs defeated the Persians, captured almost the entire territory of the empire, and incorporated Persia into the Islamic empire. The vast majority of Persians were gradually converted to Islam. Having no experience in running a large state, the Arabs adopted many Persian administrative and ceremonial practices. Moreover, although Arabic was the official language, Persian continued to be spoken throughout the region.

Persian History from the Mongols to the Pahlavis

In time, several dynasties of Persian descent emerged to revitalize Persian traditions. No one dynasty was able to achieve control over the entire territory of the former Persian empires, and the rivalry among them made it easy for the Mongols to conquer them early in the thirteenth century. The Mongol invasion had a devastating effect on the Persian population and infrastructure. Eventually, an Iranian dynasty, the Safavid dynasty (1501–1722) was established; it was followed by a number of smaller dynasties until the Qajar dynasty (1794–1925) came to power. The Qajars were of Turkic origin but were culturally Persianized. Persia's last dynasty was that of the Pahlavis, Reza Shah (1878–1944) and his son, Muhammad Reza Shah (1919–1980).

The Persian Cultural Legacy

The Persian empire was at its heyday during the Achaemenids. Politically, the Achaemenids organized their empire into provinces that were governed by satraps, who were appointed by the king. The satraps were given plenty of leeway in terms of governing their areas. Generally, the Persians were tolerant of the laws and customs of the people they conquered, and were in fact influenced by them. This live-and-let-live policy also fit with how the Persians perceived society, which they believed began with the family and worked upward to the nation-state. As long as the masses remained loyal, the rulers were not concerned with how the people behaved individually.

The Persian economy was sustained by agriculture, although craftsmanship and commerce were also important to its development. Under Darius the Great (550–486 BCE), the Persians gained a universal legal system upon which much of Iranian law is based. Darius the Great also incorporated gold and silver as the monetary systems of exchange.

There were generally four classes of people in ancient Persian society: priests, warriors, scribes, and an artisan-peasant class. The style recognized today as Persian, an eclectic synthesis of the styles of the peoples the Persians conquered, combined with native styles, is visible in Persepolis, which Darius the Great had made his capital. The pavilions and columned halls of Persepolis are Persian trademarks. The reliefs at Persepolis also demonstrate the Persian style with flair. Instead of telling a story, as Egyptian and Assyrian reliefs do, the Persian reliefs paint a picture of happy subjects paying tribute to their king and perhaps demonstrate the Persian policy of tolerance as revered by the masses and the artistic community.

Houman A. Sadri

Further Reading

Frye, Richard Nelson. (1975) *The Golden Age of Persia*. London: Weidenfeld and Nicolson.

Ghirshman, Roman. (1978) *Iran*. Middlesex, U.K.: Penguin Books.

Melville, Charles, ed. (1996) *Safavid Persia: The History and Politics of an Islamic Society*. New York: St. Martin's Press.

PESHAWAR (1998 est. pop. 998,000). Peshawar is an ancient city in Pakistan. It was established more than two thousand years ago by the Kushan kings of Gandhara. Since that time, it has changed names as often as it has rulers. Once known as the Lotus Land, City of Flowers, and the City of Grains, it was finally named Peshawar (the Place at the Frontier) by the Mughal emperor Akbar (reigned 1556–1605).

During the Kushan kings' rule in Peshawar, the city was an important Buddhist center and served as a pilgrimage site. After the worldwide decline of Buddhism, however, Peshawar lost its prestige and had little significance until the Mughal emperor Zahir-ud-din Muhammad (Babur) conquered South Asia in 1526 and built a fort there in 1530. His grandson not only renamed the city but also enhanced the existing bazaars and urban structures. The city received a further boost during the succeeding reign of Sher Shah (reigned 1540–1545), who decided to construct the Delhi-to-Kabul Shahi Road through the Khyber Pass. The latter serves as the western border of Pakistan. This road facilitated trade to Peshawar and its vicinity.

Today the city is well known for its extensive bazaars, which offer all types of handicrafts. One of the most famous bazaars is the Qissa Khwani (Storytelling) Bazaar, which still has many teahouses that honor the traditional profession of storytelling. In these teahouses, both tourists and the local people enjoy the artistic performance of storytellers recounting a variety of stories from epic sagas to romantic tales.

In the international scene, Peshawar's artistic merits have often been overshadowed by its military significance and affairs. As the city is a bridge between Afghanistan and Pakistan, it consequently provides Islamabad with economic, political, and security challenges as well as opportunities in relation to Afghan affairs. During the 1980s, it was the home base for the mujahideen, the Afghan guerrilla group that challenged the Russian-backed Afghan government and Soviet troops.

Further Reading

Albrecht, Herbert. (1974) *Living Conditions of Rural Families in Pakistan: A Classification of Rural Households as a Basis for Development Policies Using as Models Six Villages in the Peshawar District*, edited by Frithjof Kuhnen and translated by V. June Hager. Islamabad, Pakistan: Embassy of the Federal Republic of Germany in cooperation with USAID, Pakistan.

Dani, Ahmad Hasan. (1969) *Peshawar: Historic City of the Frontier*. Peshawar, Pakistan: Khyber Mail Press.

Nichols, Robert. (2001) *Settling the Frontier: Land, Law, and Society in the Peshawar Valley, 1500–1900*. Karachi, Pakistan: Oxford University Press.

Sehrai, Fidaullah. (1980) *A Brief Guide to Peshawar Museum*. Peshawar, Pakistan: Peshawar Museum.

PESTA MENUAI Sabah, an East Malaysian state that occupies the northwest tip of the island of Borneo, celebrates Pesta Menuai (Harvesting Festival) each May to mark the end of the rice-harvesting season. In the local Sabahan language of Kadazandusun this festival is called Tadau Kaamatan.

Pesta Menuai is celebrated to offer thanks to the gods for a bountiful harvest and to ask for their blessings for the coming season. The Kadazandusun people include the Unduk Ngadau Beauty Pageant as part of their Tadau Kaamatan. The celebration is in praise of the legendary Huminodun, who was a willing sacrifice for the sake of her father, and Unduk Ngadau is in praise of Huminodun's eternal youth and total beauty of heart, mind, and body. For those who are no longer involved in agriculture or have embraced nonanimistic religions, the festival is an occasion to renew friendships, have family reunions, and perform filial duties. It is celebrated with a feast of food and merrymaking not only in the villages but also in the towns. Open houses are held wherein friends and relatives are served traditional food.

Shanthi Thambiah

Further Reading

Charuruks, Irene Benggon, and Janette Padasian, eds. (1992) *Cultures, Customs, and Traditions of Sabah, Malaysia: An Introduction.* Kota Kinabalu, Malaysia: Sabah Tourism Promotion Corporation.

Evans, Ivor H. N. (1970) *Studies in Religion, Folk-Lore, and Customs in British North Borneo and the Malay Peninsula.* London: Frank Cass.

Yahaya Ismail. (1998) *The Cultural Heritage of Sabah.* Petaling Jaya, Malaysia: Dinamika Edition.

PETRONAS TOWERS The eighty-eight-story, 451.9-meter-tall Petronas twin towers in Kuala Lumpur, Malaysia, became the tallest buildings in the world when completed in 1996, replacing Chicago's Sears Tower, which had held the record since 1974. Designed by the American architect Cesar Pelli (b. 1926), each of the steel-clad towers is topped by a functionless spire, suggesting that their record-breaking height was not accidental. The two towers are joined by a 58.4-meter skybridge at the forty-first and forty-second stories, 170 meters above street level. Together, they form part of a larger development, the Kuala Lumpur City Centre (KLCC).

The towers are located at the northwest corner of KLCC, which is a northeastward expansion of Kuala Lumpur's main commercial district, the so-called Golden Triangle area, occupying the site of the former colonial racecourse. Piling and foundation work for the towers commenced in 1993 and experienced some difficulties owing to the limestone geology of the area. Rival Japanese- and South Korean–led consortia were responsible for construction of one tower each, the Japanese eventually winning the "race to the top" in April 1996. One tower is occupied by the national oil company, Petronas, whose name the towers bear. Multinational companies occupy the remaining space.

Timothy G. Bunnell

Further Reading

Crosbie, Michael J. (1998) *Cesar Pelli: Recent Themes.* Berlin: Berkhauser.

PETROPAVLOVSK (2000 pop. 200,000). Formerly called Kyzldzhar (Kyzyl-Dzhar), Petropavlovsk was founded in 1752 as a fort on a caravan route between Turkistan and western China and renamed for Saints Peter (Russian Pëtr) and Paul (Russian Pavl) in association with a church dedication. The city is located in northern Kazakhstan in the Virgin Lands Region (an uncultivated area extending from the Volga River to northern Kazakhstan and western Siberia that the Khrushchev regime attempted to cultivate from 1953, the project abandoned by 1970), west of Omsk and on the Ishim River.

As a fort Petropavlovsk expanded Russian settlement southward into the lands of the Kazakh nomads. It was a major trading post between Turkistan and western China for silk, carpets, and skins. By the time of the Russian Revolution in 1917, the city was a primary trading center between Russia and Central Asia. Petropavlovsk lies at the intersection of the Trans-Siberian and Trans-Kazakhstan railroads that transport coal, lumber, grain, and meats.

The city's industry began to develop in the late 1800s and strengthened during and after World War II. Before the Soviet Union's collapse Petropavlovsk's economic base was founded on four important defense factories. In the late 1990s that foundation became a Turkish-funded pasta plant. The city also produces grain, clothing, diesel engines, electrical insulation, timber, small motors, agricultural machinery, wood pulp, leather, and felt. Petropavlovsk has a teacher-training school, theater, and television station. It is a relaxed city with many Russians in the population, giving the city a strong Siberian character.

Gary Mason Church

Further Reading

Mayhew, Bradley, Richard Plunkett, and Simon Richmond. (2000) *Central Asia.* Oakland, CA: Lonely Planet.

PHALANG DHARMA PARTY Thailand's Phalang Dharma Party (PDP; pronounced "palang tam") was established on 9 June 1988 through the leadership of Chamlong Srimuang. Also, as its name (Moral Force Party) connotes, the party was established as a new kind of clean party that would not succumb to the money politics that has plagued Thailand for decades. Its members and candidates for parliament were to be individuals of high moral character. The party grew out of the informal Ruam Phalang (Collective Force) group and the Santi Asoke Buddhist

TABLE 1

Performance of the Phalang Dharma Party in Thai National Elections.

Election	Number of seats won	Percentage of total seats won
July 1988	14	3.9
March 1992	41	11.4
September 1992	47	13.1
July 1995	23	5.9
November 1996	1	0.3
January 2001	1	0.2

movement, which calls for a more authentic commitment to the original ideals of Buddhism.

The dramatic ebb and flow of Phalang Dharma's strength is directly linked to that of its founder, Chamlong Srimuang (b. 1935), the former governor of Bangkok and major general and Young Turk in the Thai military. Given his strong commitment to Buddhism, he is sometimes referred to as "half monk, half man" and is extremely modest in his personal lifestyle. The original problem of the party was that its strength was primarily in Bangkok. Though it expanded its support in the countryside, a major political confrontation that turned violent in Bangkok in May 1992 led to controversy and began to erode support for Chamlong and his party. Chamlong was the primary leader of a people-power movement opposing General Suchinda's (b. 1933) assumption of the prime ministership without being an elected member of parliament. There was considerable criticism of Chamlong from Thais, who accused him of sacrificing lives in the military suppression of the Bangkok demonstrations to pursue his own personal political agenda.

In the September 1992 national election, support for the party in Bangkok began to erode. In January 1993, Chamlong stepped down as leader of the party; he was replaced by a business tycoon, Boonchu Rojanastien. As more and more businesspeople became involved with the party, its initial idealism was severely eroded. The party also unwisely joined an unpopular coalition government in 1995. In the November 1996 election, the party won only one seat. In the January 2001 national election, there were 128 Phalang Dharma candidates but only one was elected. Phalang Dharma had lost its influence in Thai politics.

Gerald W. Fry

Further Reading

McCargo, Duncan. (1997) *Chamlong Srimuang and the New Thai Politics*. London: Hurst and Company.

Murray, David. (1996) *Angels and Devils: Thai Politics from February 1991 to September 1992—A Struggle for Democracy?* Bangkok, Thailand: White Orchid Press.

PHAN BOI CHAU (1867–1940), Vietnamese scholar. Phan Boi Chau was an anticolonial leader, and is often referred to as Vietnam's first modern nationalist. Phan began working against French colonialism in 1903. He initially advocated the reformation of the Vietnamese monarchy based on the Japanese Meiji model. Phan later discarded the idea of a reformed monarchy after observing in Canton the results of the successful 1911 nationalist revolution in China under Sun Yat-sen (1866–1925) and the Guomindang (Kuomintang). He then began a political crusade to create a Vietnamese democratic republic. To this end, he founded an exile regime in China, the Vietnam Restoration Society (Viet Nam Quang Phuc Hoi), and appointed Cuong De (1882–1951) as president and himself as vice president. This organization inspired increased underground resistance against the French in Vietnam, especially between 1912 and 1918. In 1925 French officials captured Phan in Shanghai and, after a brief trial, sentenced him to life in prison in Hanoi for his anticolonial activities. He eventually died under house arrest in Hue in 1940.

Vietnamese nationalists later reported that Ho Chi Minh (1890–1969) and his associate Lam Duc Tho sold information on Phan's locale to French officials that led to his arrest. After Lam publicly disclosed this in late 1945 and thus betrayed Phan, considered by the Vietnamese an anti-French hero, he was executed in front of his home by the Viet Minh.

Richard B. Verrone

Further Reading

Buttinger, Joseph. (1968) *Vietnam: A Political History*. New York: Praeger.

Duiker, William J. (1976) *The Rise of Nationalism in Vietnam, 1900–1941*. Ithaca, NY: Cornell University Press.

Marr, David. (1971) *Vietnamese Anti-Colonialism, 1885–1925*. Berkeley and Los Angeles: University of California Press.

PHIEU LE KHA (b. 1932), General secretary of the Vietnam Communist Party. Born in Thanh Hoa Province in 1932, Phieu Le Kha joined the Communist Party in 1949 and became a political officer in the Vietnam People's Army (VPA). He served during both the anti-French and anti-U.S. wars and later as the deputy political commissar of several military regions before becoming the chief political commissar and deputy commander of Vietnam's forces in Cambodia in the mid-1980s. His military career culminated in 1991 when he became head of the VPA's General Political Department, the top Communist Party official in the military. Lieutenant General Phieu joined the Vietnam Communist Party (VCP) Central Committee at the third plenum in June 1992, and his promotion through the party hierarchy was swift. He became a member of the Central Committee's secretariat in 1992 and of the Politburo in January 1994. At the Eighth VCP Congress in June 1996 he was elected to the Politburo's standing committee, a five-person board that deals with the day-to-day running of the country. At the Central Committee's fourth plenum, on 26 December 1997, he was elected VCP general secretary. Additionally, since 1992 he has served as a deputy to the National Assembly, the country's parliament. Phieu is an ideological conservative who has sought to limit the pace and scope of the economic reform program, known as *doi moi*, and has called for vigilance against corruption, Western democratic influences, and threats to undermine the VCP's monopoly of power through "peaceful evolution."

Zachary Abuza

Further Reading

Abuza, Zachary. (2001) *Renovating Politics in Contemporary Vietnam.* Boulder, CO: Lynne Rienner.

PHILIPPINE INDEPENDENT CHURCH

The Philippine Independent Church (PIC) was founded in August 1902 by the Filipino journalist and modern reformer Isabelo de los Reyes. It is also known as Iglesia Filipina Independiente or the Aglipayan Church, after its first bishop, Gregorio Aglipay y Labayan (1860–1940), an excommunicated Catholic priest and supporter of Philippine independence. Aglipay led the church from 1902 until his death and, having failed to win acceptance from the Vatican, aligned it with Unitarian Church. The new church was in part a reaction to the restricted role for native Filipino clergy in the Roman Catholic Church in the Philippines and was also, in part, an expression of Filipino nationalism and resistance to American control. The church is led by a supreme bishop *(obispo maximo)* who is elected by a general assembly of lay and clerical delegates. Since 1999 the supreme bishop has been the Rev. Thomas A. Millamena. PIC is a member of the World Council of Churches and has ties with Old Catholic chuches in Europe and the Anglican and Episcopal churches. Its clergy is trained at Saint Andrew's Theological Seminary, which serves the PIC and the Episcopal Church in the Philippines.

After attracting about 25 percent of the Philippine population soon after it was formed, the membership declined and the church was damaged by conflict among different factions and disputes over how far church doctrine should deviate from Roman Catholicism. After Aglipay's death in 1940 the church moved away from Unitarianism, and in 2002 PIC doctrine and practice is in general accord with the Episcopal Church. The church membership in the 1990s is estimated at between 2.5 and 4.5 million.

David Levinson

See also: **Catholicism, Roman—Philippines**

Further Reading

Achutegui, Pedro S. de (1961) *Religious Revolution in the Philippines: The Life and Church of Gregorio Aglipay, 1860-1940.* Manila: Ateneo de Manila.

PHILIPPINE LANGUAGES

About 110 distinct Philippine languages are spoken in the Philippines, an archipelago off the southeastern coast of mainland China, by 73 million Filipinos. The Philippine languages belong to the Western Malayo-Polynesian branch of the Austronesian language family, whose members include languages spoken in areas as far north as Hawaii and as far south as New Zealand, covering the area from Easter Island in South America to Madagascar off the coast of Africa. Within the language family, the Philippine languages are most closely related to the languages of Kalimantan, Sumatra, and Sulawesi in Indonesia; Sarawak and Sabah in Malaysia; and the Malagasy language in Madagascar.

Subgroupings

The Philippine languages are generally classified into three large subgroups, namely: (1) the Northern Philippine languages, spoken by a number of ethnolinguistic groups in the northern and central Luzon regions; (2) the Meso-Philippine languages, spoken by a large number of ethnolinguistic groups, more widely dispersed in the vast area from central to southern Luzon, parts of Mindoro and Palawan, the Visayan Islands, and parts of Mindanao; and (3) the Southern Philippine languages, spoken in parts of Zamboanga, Lanao, and Maguindanao. A number of languages belong to smaller subgroups: (4) the Ivatan languages, spoken on the northernmost islands of Batanes and Babuyan; (5) the Sama languages, spoken in the southern parts of Zamboanga and the islands of Sulu, Tawi-

tawi, and Basilan; (6) the South Mindanao languages, spoken in parts of Davao, South Cotabato, and Maguindanao; and (7) Sangil, spoken in Balut and the Sarangani Islands of Davao del Sur.

Sound System

The majority of the Philippine languages have the following consonants:

Place/ manner of articulation	Bilabial	Dental	Velar	Palatal	Glottal
Stops	p, b	t, d	k, g		q
Fricatives		s			h
Nasals	m	n	ng		
Tap		r			
Lateral		l			
Glide	w			y	

The *q* sound is the glottal stop. It is the sound that occurs between the two syllables of the English expression "Uh-oh!" Initial *p, t,* and *k* are not aspirated; that is, they are produced with no puff of air coming out of the mouth. The *ng* sound is like that of the final sound in the word "sing." In Philippine languages, it can be found in the word-initial, medial, and final positions. The *l* sound is articulated with the tongue flat from the tip to the back, with the tongue tip touching the back of the upper teeth. The *r* sound is produced with the tongue tip quickly tapping the upper gum ridge. All the other consonants are produced like the corresponding English sounds. A minority of languages have the sounds *f, v, ch, j,* and *z* in addition to the consonants listed above.

Many Philippine languages have a three-vowel system, others have a four-vowel system, a number have five vowels, and a small number have more than five. The most common vowel systems are as follows:

Three-Vowel System

Tongue position during articulation	Front	Central	Back
High	i		u
Mid			
Low		a	

Four-Vowel System

	Front	Central	Back
High	i		u
Mid		ə	
Low		a	

Five-Vowel System

	Front	Central	Back
High	i		u
Mid	e		o
Low		a	

The *i* sound is like the *i* in the word "marine." The *u* sound is like *oo* in "moon." The *a* sound is like *a* in "father." The *e* sound is like *e* in the word "bed." The *o* sound is like the *o* in "fork." The *ə* sound, or schwa, as it is commonly called by language scholars, is like the *e* in the word "father."

Word Formation

The most productive way of forming new words is through affixation. Most words are made up of affixes and roots. The roots are substantive, verbal, and adjectival in meaning, and the affixes indicate such things as aspect, focus, and mode. The specific meaning of a word is determined by the particular combination of the root and its affix.

For example, the Cebuano root *tuon* (study) may denote the variations in meaning depending on the affix added.

magtuon (v.)	to study
makatuon (v.)	be able to study
makigtuon (v.)	to study with someone
hinuon (adj.)	studious
tun-anan (n.)	place for studying

Reduplication or repetition of a word or part of a word is another productive way of forming new words in Philippine languages. It is used extensively to indicate information such as noncompleted action, intensity, plurality, and restriction.

The following are Ilokano examples:

kaan (v.)	eat
mangantu (v.)	will eat
mangan (v.)	to eat
mangmangan (v.)	is eating
napintas (adj.)	beautiful
napipintas (adj.)	beautiful (plural)
nakapinpintas (adj.)	very beautiful

Most roots may be verbalized, that is, used as verbs, by attaching a verbal affix to them. The examples here are from Kapampangan:

asan (n.)	fish
Mangasan	to go fishing
malan (n.)	dress

Magmalan	to dress up
pagal (adj.)	tired
mepagal (v.)	to become tired
maragul (adj.)	big
magmaragul (v.)	to be proud
bigla (adv.)	suddenly
Mebigla	to be surprised

Word Order

The basic word order in Philippine languages is predicate or comment followed by the subject or topic. The predicate can be a verb phrase, a noun phrase, an adjective phrase, or a prepositional phrase. The subject is a noun phrase that is in focus.

An important feature of Philippine languages is commonly called focus. Focus is the grammatical relation between the verb and a particular verbal complement marked by the topic marker. This complement is referred to as the topic. The meaning relationship of the topic to the verb (actor, goal, beneficiary, etc.) is indicated by the verbal affix.

The following are examples from Tagalog. The noun in focus is underlined.

Bumili ang bata ng mangga sa tindahan para sa nanay niya.

"The child bought some mangoes at the store for his mother."

Binili ng bata ang mangga sa tindahan para sa nanay niya.

"The child bought some mangoes at the store for his mother."

Binilhan ng bata ng mangga para sa nanay niya ang tindahan.

"The child bought some mangoes at the store for his mother."

Ibinili ng bata ng mangga sa tindahan ang nanay niya.

"The child bought some mangoes at the store for his mother."

Orthography

The major languages and a number of minority languages are written with the Roman alphabet, which was first introduced by the Spanish Catholic missionaries who came to the islands in the late sixteenth century. The major languages and some minority languages have extensive written literature. Before the colonization of the Philippines by the Spaniards, these languages had a writing system based on a syllabary that was probably of Indian origin. The syllabary consisted of seventeen symbols, three for vowels and the rest for consonants.

Major Languages and Common Regional Languages

Of the 110 languages spoken on the islands, 8 are considered major languages, each with at least two million native speakers. These are Cebuano (15.2 million), Tagalog (14.9 million), Ilocano (8 million), Hiligaynon (7 million), Bicol (3.6 milion), Waray (3 million), Kapampangan (2 millon), and Pangasinan (2 million) (1993–1995 data). Ilokano, Kapampangan, and Pangasinan belong to the Northern Philippine subgroup. The rest of the major languages belong to the Meso-Philippine subgroup. The other languages, with less than 2 million speakers each, are considered minor languages.

There are three common regional languages or lingua francas, languages used for everyday communication by speakers of different languages. These are Ilokano in northern and most of central Luzon, Tagalog in southern and parts of central Luzon, and Cebuano in the Visayas and Mindanao.

Filipino

Filipino is the Tagalog-based national language and one of two official languages of the country—the other being English. Following the mandate of the 1935 constitution, President Manuel Quezon proclaimed Tagalog as the basis of the national language in 1937. To free the national language from its ethnic ties and therefore to facilitate its acceptance, Tagalog was renamed Pilipino in 1959. However, the 1973 constitution rescinded the choice of Tagalog (Pilipino) as the basis of the national language. It stipulated that the National Assembly was to take steps toward the formation of a genuine national language to be called Filipino, which would incorporate elements from various Philippine languages. As predicted by Philippine language experts, after the 1987 constitutional deliberations, Pilipino was renamed Filipino and is characterized by an openness to borrowings from the other Philippine languages as well as from English, Spanish, and other foreign languages.

The 1980 Philippine census indicated that close to 75 percent of the population speaks a variety of Filipino. According to 1999 research data, there are approximately 57 million speakers of Filipino, including non-native speakers.

Filipino, like a number of other Philippine languages, has been influenced, principally in vocabulary, by the languages with which it has come into contact: Sanskrit (through Malay), Arabic, Chinese, English, and Spanish. It is still borrowing many terms from English. It is spoken as the mother tongue in the following Philippine provinces: Bataan, Batangas, Bulacan, Cavite, Laguna, Marinduque, Nueva Ecija, Occidental Mindoro, Oriental Mindoro, Quezon, and Rizal.

Teresita V. Ramos and Maria Sheila Zamar

Further Reading

Gonzales, Andrew B. (1977) "Pilipino in the Year 2000." In *Language Planning and the Building of a National Language*, edited by B. Sibayan and A. Gonzales. Manila, Philippines: Linguistic Society of the Philippines and PNC Language Study Center, 263–290.

———. (1987) "Language Agenda for the 21st Century: The Development of Filipino and the Maintenance of English." In *A Filipino Agenda for the 21st Century*, edited by F. Sionil Jose. Manila, Philippines: Solidarity Publishing House, 107–215.

———. (1991) "Cebuano and Tagalog: Ethnic Rivalry Redivivus." In *Language and Ethnicity*, edited by James R. Dow. Philadelphia: John Benjamins Publishing, 11–129.

———. (1996) "Language and Nationalism in the Philippines: An Update." In *Readings in Philippine Sociolinguistics*, edited by Ma. Lourdes S. Bautista. Manila, Philippines: De La Salle University Press, 228–239.

McFarland, Curtis B. (1996) "Subgrouping and Number of Philippine Languages, or How Many Philippine Languages Are There?" In *Readings in Philippine Sociolinguistics*, edited by Ma. Lourdes S. Bautista. Manila, Philippines: De La Salle University Press, 12–22.

Ramos, Teresita V., and R. Cena. (1990) *Modern Tagalog: Grammatical Explanations and Exercises for Non-Native Speakers*. Honolulu: University of Hawaii Press.

Ramos, Teresita V., and V. de Guzman. (1971) "Introduction." In *Tagalog for Beginners*. Honolulu: University of Hawaii Press, 1–7.

Summer Institute of Linguistics. (2001) "Ethnologue: Languages of the World." Retrieved 28 December 2001, from: http://www.ethnologue.com/web.asp.

Weber, George. (1989) "A Colorful Tropical Cocktail: Languages in the Philippines and the Austronesian Language Family." *Language International* 1, 1 (January/February): 13–17.

PHILIPPINE SEA The Philippine Sea is a section of the western Pacific Ocean, located to the east and north of the Philippines. It occupies a total area of around 5,726,000 square kilometers (2,700,000 square miles), or around 2.7 percent of the Pacific Ocean, stretching approximately 2,900 kilometers (1,800 miles) north-south and 2,300 kilometers (1,500 miles) east-west. The Philippine islands of Luzon, Samar, and Mindanao form the sea's southwest boundaries; Palau, Yap, and Ulithi form its southeast perimeter; the Mariana Islands, including Guam (U.S.), Saipan, and Tinian, mark its eastern limits; the Bonin and Volcano Islands lie to the northeast; Honshu, Shikoku, and Kyushu (Japan) bound it to the north; Okinawa's Ryukyu Islands (Japan) lie to the northwest; and Taiwan is to the west.

The deepest area of the sea is the Philippine Trench, at around 10,497 meters (34,438 feet), making it one of the world's deepest trenches. There are numerous seamounts, many of them volcanic mounts, rising from the sea floor and capped with corals. The warm Pacific North Equatorial Current flows across the southern part of the sea, making the Philippine Sea a great fishing ground. However, many typhoons originate in the sea and are particularly devastating in September and October.

Rafis Abazov

Further Reading

Peive, A. V., ed. (1980) *Geology of the Philippine Sea Floor.* Moscow: Nauka.

Shiki, T., ed. (1985). *Geology of the Northern Philippine Sea.* Tokyo: Tokyo University Press.

PHILIPPINES—PROFILE (2001 est. population 82.8 million). The Philippines is an archipelago, a group of 7,100 islands spread out over 800,000 square kilometers of ocean. The population is concentrated on eleven major islands, conveniently grouped into three: Luzon in the north is the largest, the smaller masses in the central region constitute the Visayan Islands, and in the south lies the second-largest island, Mindanao. Approximately 80 kilometers north of Luzon is Taiwan, 1,200 kilometers to the west is Vietnam, and some 7,700 kilometers across the wide expanse of the Pacific Ocean to the east lies Hawaii.

Volcanic eruptions formed the Philippine archipelago eons ago. This origin accounts for its irregular coastline, terrain, and climate. Periodic eruptions of its twenty active volcanoes, notably Pinatubo and Mayon, affect the varied tropical climate and environment. The temperature averages 27°C in the plains and 18°C in the mountains. The highest point is volcanic Mount Apo in Mindanao (2,954 meters). Parts of Manila, its capital and largest city, are below sea level and flood in heavy rainfall.

People

During Spain's 300-plus-year colonization of the country (1521–1898), the term "Filipino" originally identified a person of Spanish descent born in the Philippines. In the eighteenth century the term applied to Christianized Malays, the dominant ethnic group, distinguishing them from the aboriginal Aetas, a pygmy people living in the Mount Pinatubo area, and other minorities, such as the Ifugaos in the north, that did not convert to Christianity. Today the term qualifies groups, made distinct either by religion, ethnicity, or language; Muslim and Christian Filipino, for example, are religious categories, while American, Chinese and Indian Filipino are ethnic labels. The ethnic label also applies to mestizo (children of mixed ancestry) offspring. As mandated by the 1987 constitution, which restored democracy in the Philippines after a period of dictatorship, Filipino is now also the name of the official language. Based on Tagalog, it draws its vocabulary from seventy or more indigenous languages and may in time evolve as an authentic national language. In the meantime English is still widely used in education, government, and commerce.

The Spanish colonizers who came to the Philippines in the sixteenth century did not find a unified country. Three factors figured in the fragmentation: geography, ethnicity, and language. The sea was a natural divider for the islands of the archipelago. The mostly Malay settlers split between those that stayed in the plains and valleys and those who lived in the mountains, away from contact with the colonizers; these people did not become Christians. The Malays living in the lowlands lived in separate communities, each ruled by a *datu* (headman), while those in the highlands banded as tribes.

From the second to the ninth centuries CE, trade between the Philippines and other Asian countries flourished. Sailors and merchants from China and India stayed and to this day own the stores that sell canned goods, textiles, and appliances in towns and cities. Arab traders came in the middle of the thirteenth century and brought goods from Europe, but in the early fifteenth century they also brought Islam. The religion took hold in Mindanao and Sulu, islands close to Indonesia, which had already become Islamic. Given the predominant Malay stock of the people of both countries, the Filipinos and Indonesians are blood relations. The Muslims in Sulu and Mindanao, who evolved a more complex culture than the inhabitants of the other islands, were split into many ethnic groups but were united by Islam. They were ruled by numerous sultanates, also separated by sea and terrain. The Spanish, who attempted to subdue this region in the sixteenth century, referred to the Muslim

VIGAN—WORLD HERITAGE SITE

A UNESCO World Heritage Site since 1999, Vigan is a small sixteenth-century Spanish colonial town in the Philippines. Bearing witness to the considerable impact that European colonialism had on Philippine life, Vigan is unique in that it has retained its original planning and survived relatively intact.

PHILIPPINES

Country name: Republic of the Philippines
Area: 300,000 sq km
Population: 82,841,518 (July 2001 est.)
Population growth rate: 2.03% (2001 est.)
Birth rate: 27.37 births/1,000 population (2001 est.)
Death rate: 6.04 deaths/1,000 population (2001 est.)
Net migration rate: -1.01 migrant(s)/1,000 population (2001 est.)
Sex ratio: 0.99 male(s)/female (2001 est.)
Infant mortality rate: 28.7 deaths/1,000 live births (2001 est.)
Life expectancy at birth—total population: 67.8 years, male: 64.96 years, female: 70.79 years (2001 est.)
Major religions: Roman Catholic, Protestant, Muslim
Major languages: two official languages—Filipino (based on Tagalog) and English; eight major dialects—Tagalog, Cebuano, Ilocano, Hiligaynon or Ilonggo, Bicol, Waray, Kapampangan, and Pangasinan
Literacy—total population: 94.6%, male: 95%, female: 94.3% (1995 est.)
Government type: republic
Capital: Manila
Administrative divisions: 73 provinces and 61 chartered cities
Independence: 4 July 1946 (from United States)
National holiday: Independence Day (from Spain), 12 June (1898); note: 12 June 1898 is the date of independence from Spain, 4 July 1946 is the date of independence from the United States
Suffrage: 18 years of age; universal
GDP—real growth rate: 3.6% (2000 est.)
GDP—per capita: (purchasing power parity): $3,800 (2000 est.)
Population below poverty line: 41% (1997 est.)
Exports: $38 billion (f.o.b., 2000 est.)
Imports: $35 billion (f.o.b., 2000 est.)
Currency: Philippine peso (PHP)

Source: Central Intelligence Agency. (2001) *The World Book Factbook 2001.* Retrieved 5 March 2002, from http://www.cia.gov/cia/publications/factbook.

population as "Moros," or Moors. Their fight with these Muslims was an extension of the war against the Moors that they waged in Spain. Neither the Spanish nor the Americans who followed them were able to control the Moros successfully. This historical fact is celebrated in Moro ballads that also extol ritual suicide and jihad, or attack against infidels or Christians.

Christianity in the Philippines

The Philippines is the only Christian nation in Southeast Asia. Spanish friars brought Roman Catholicism with them in 1521, and American missionaries introduced Protestant Christianity in 1899. The Genesis story in the Bible parallels native myths of creation and belief in a supreme being, and facilitated the work of converting the people to Christianity.

For the majority of the Philippines' population, the Christian outlook eases the pain of their poverty. Christianity gives them hope and reinforces the coping mechanisms they have developed, such as *bahala na* (come what may), *pakikisama* (a sense of deep camaraderie), and *utang na loob* (a feeling of gratitude for acts of kindness). *Bahala na* complements the Christian virtue of hope and engenders either fatalism or a certainty of arriving at the Promised Land. *Pakikisama* works with Christian charity to heighten a sense of community and belonging. *Utang na loob*, alongside religious faith, takes on a peculiar notion of sin: not only does it violate a commandment; it is also an act of ingratitude against God.

Economy

The Philippine economy depends primarily on its agricultural and natural resources. It involves cultivating the crops, such as rice and sweet potatoes, needed to feed its rapidly increasing population, and exporting products such as lumber and fish to help pay for its imports. The manufacturing of such products as textiles and chemicals also helps maintain the balance of trade. The Philippines spends more on imports than it earns from exports of crops, minerals, and forest resources, however, an imbalance that has necessitated borrowing from the World Bank International Monetary Fund and reliance on foreign aid from countries such as Japan and the United States. Paying off the interest on these debts reduces revenues available for health, education, and welfare, the effect of which is revealed in the huge gap between the rich and poor, dramatized by the urban landscape of Manila, where squatters' shanties thrive alongside condominiums and high-rises. Estimates suggest that 70 percent of the Philippine population of nearly 80 million is poor.

A 1992 report by the U.S. embassy in Manila describes the Philippine economy as "stagnant" and "import-dependent and import-subsisting." It is a sad assessment that a country so rich in natural resources imports chickens and beef for fast-food franchises such as Kentucky Fried Chicken and McDonald's, and lumber for its custom-built houses. Several factors account for this stagnant economy, foremost among them the national government, which is perceived as weak, ineffectual, and slow to institute social and economic reform.

Colonial and Postcolonial History

The explorer Ferdinand Magellan arrived in the Philippines in 1521; he claimed the islands for Spain, following an "I was here first" policy that ran contrary to the treaty agreed upon by two superpowers of the sixteenth century, Spain and Portugal. To keep peace between the two neighboring countries, the Spanish pope had drawn an imaginary line through the globe and given to Spain all colonizable lands to the west and to Portugal the lands to the east. According to the pope's demarcation, Portugal should have colonized the Philippines, as it did Formosa (now Taiwan), which lies directly north.

In 1565 Miguel Lopez de Legazpi arrived from the Spanish colony of Acapulco and conquered the islands in earnest. The Spanish religious aim—converting the natives to Christianity—made them different from other European colonizers. Augustinian, Dominican, and Franciscan friars pursued this goal with zeal, learning the native languages, the better to spread the Word of God. In the process they enriched the vocabulary of each language; this achievement is recorded in the pamphlets and books the friars wrote, the first printed as early as 1593. Although praised for their work in lexicography, the Spanish are faulted for destroying the written culture of prehistoric Filipinos, which used an alphabet of three vowels and fourteen consonants. However, the oral literature has survived, preserved by tribes that were either not conquered or lived in mountainous regions inaccessible to the colonizers.

Spanish colonization was not total, but Spain installed a government that organized villages for tax purposes and control by appointed leaders, and created a class of property owners that evolved into the landed elite of today.

U.S. colonization began when its forces destroyed the Spanish fleet on Manila Bay on 1 May 1898 and later staged a mock land battle against Spanish soldiers. War against Spain had indeed been declared, but this prearranged victory in Manila and the subsequent payment of $20 million to Spain robbed Philippine revolutionaries of the opportunity to savor the independence that the leader Emilio Aguinaldo had declared on 12 June 1898. Filipinos staunchly resisted the U.S. takeover, and although U.S. officials declared their "insurrection" defeated in 1902, in fact it lasted for three more years. In the end, however, the Philippines became a U.S. colony.

U.S. colonizers attempted to restructure Philippine society. They introduced town government programs and educational theories based on U.S. models, but many of the policies failed. They did, however, succeed in making English the medium of instruction in public schools, and the Philippines became the third-largest English-speaking country in the world, after the United States and England.

The United States swelled the ranks of the landed elite by selling large tracts of real estate to wealthy Chinese and mestizos. Promising independence, in 1934 the United States allowed elections that enabled educated members of this class to participate in running the colonial government. Although the United States believed it was establishing a Philippine democracy, in retrospect, the system allowed the wealthy to dominate the country.

The Philippines finally was granted independence on 4 July 1946, almost a year after the end of World War II. Manuel A. Roxas became the first president. He and subsequent presidents were drawn from the ranks of the Philippines elite, and the majority of the population saw little social change during the decades that followed.

The Future In the twenty-first century, two forces are competing to shape the country's future: nongovernmental organizations (NGOs) and the New People's Army (NPA). NGOs (some 58,000 were registered in 1993) are working peacefully to promote the interests of farmers, the poor, women, and indigenous peoples. The NPA hopes to achieve the same goal with arms. It does not, however, have a broad national front or coalition (unlike, for instance, the Sandinistas, who successfully took control of Nicaragua in 1979), but it is active in all of the nation's seventy-three provinces. It gets political support and medical supplies from sympathizers in Europe, the United States, Canada, Japan, Australia, New Zealand, and Latin America. In the late 1980s North Korea was a likely source of arms. While NGOs attempt to work with the system, the NPA hopes to destroy it, seeking a victory similar to Mao Zedong's in China or Ho Chi Minh's in Vietnam. The NGOs are regarded as either optimistic or opportunistic and the NPA as one of the few remaining viable Communist insurgencies in the world today.

Recent events have conspired against the NPA. After the 11 September 2001 terrorist attacks that destroyed the twin towers of the World Trade Center in New York City, the United States launched a war against terrorism. Upon invitation from the Philippine government, the U.S. military promised $100 million in aid and 30,000 machine guns to help quell terrorism there. This action is in the tradition of U.S. intervention, which put down the Huk Communist insurgency in the 1950s, propped up the Marcos dictatorship in the 1970s and 1980s, and aided the beleagured Corazon Aquino regime when rebels in the military staged coups. What this new U.S. military presence portends is still uncertain.

Paulino Lim, Jr.

Further Reading

Agoncillo, Teodoro A. (1969) *A Short History of the Philippines.* New York: New American Library.

Brainard, Cecilia Manguerra, and Edmundo F. Litton. (1999) *Journey of 100 Years: Reflections on the Centennial of Philippine Independence.* San Francisco: Tiboli Press.

Broad, Robin, and John Cavanagh. (1993) *Plundering Paradise.* Berkeley and Los Angeles: University of California Press.

Fallows, James. (1987) "A Damaged Culture." *Atlantic Monthly* (November): 49–58.

Jones, Gregg R. (1989) *Red Revolution: Inside the Philippine Guerilla Movement.* Boulder, San Francisco, and London: Westview Press.

Lumbera, Bienvenido, and Cynthia N. Lumbera. (1982) *Philippine Literature: A History and Anthology.* Manila, Philippines: National Bookstore.

Mann, Jim. (2001) "A Risky Move by Filipinos." *Los Angeles Times* (24 January).

May, Glenn. (1980) *Social Engineering in the Philippines.* London: Greenwood Press.

Mendes, Helvecio. (1988) *Flowers on Fire in the Philippines.* Quezon City, Philippines: Claretian Publications.

Rafael, Vicente L. (1995) *Discrepant Histories: Translocal Essays on Philippine Cultures.* Philadelphia: Temple University Press.

San Juan, Epifanio, Jr. (2000) *After Colonialism: Remapping Philippines-United States Confrontations.* Lanham, MD: Rowman & Littlefield.

Shackford, Julie. (1990) *The Philippines: Historical Overview.* Honolulu: University of Hawaii.

Schirmer, Daniel B., and Stephen Rosskamm Shalom. (1987) *The Philippines Reader: A History of Colonialism, Neocolonialism, Dictatorship, and Resistance.* Boston: South End Press.

Silliman, G. Sidney, and Lela Garner Noble, eds. (1998) *Organizing for Democracy: NGOs, Civil Society, and the Philippine State.* Honolulu: University of Hawaii Press.

United States Embassy (Philippines). (1993) *Foreign Economic Trends and Their Implications for the U.S.* Manila, Philippines: United States Embassy.

PHILIPPINES—ECONOMIC SYSTEM Before the Spanish colonization of the Philippines, which began in the sixteenth century, the Philippines had never been ruled by a single state, though a sultan state was established in the Sulu archipelago of the southern Philippines around the mid-fifteenth century under Islamic influence. Some historians say that if the Spanish conquest had been delayed for half a century, Luzon and Visayan islands (in the northern and central Philippines) might also have been placed under the influence of Islamic culture.

At the time of the Spanish conquest, a hamlet or village *(barangay)* served as the basic community unit for the inhabitants in most of the Philippine islands. *Barangays* were usually located near seashores, riversides, or lakefronts. *Barangay* inhabitants supported themselves through various economic activities, such as slash-and-burn farming, lowland cultivation, fishing, and trading. Each *barangay* consisted of thirty to one hundred households, headed by a chieftain *(datu)*.

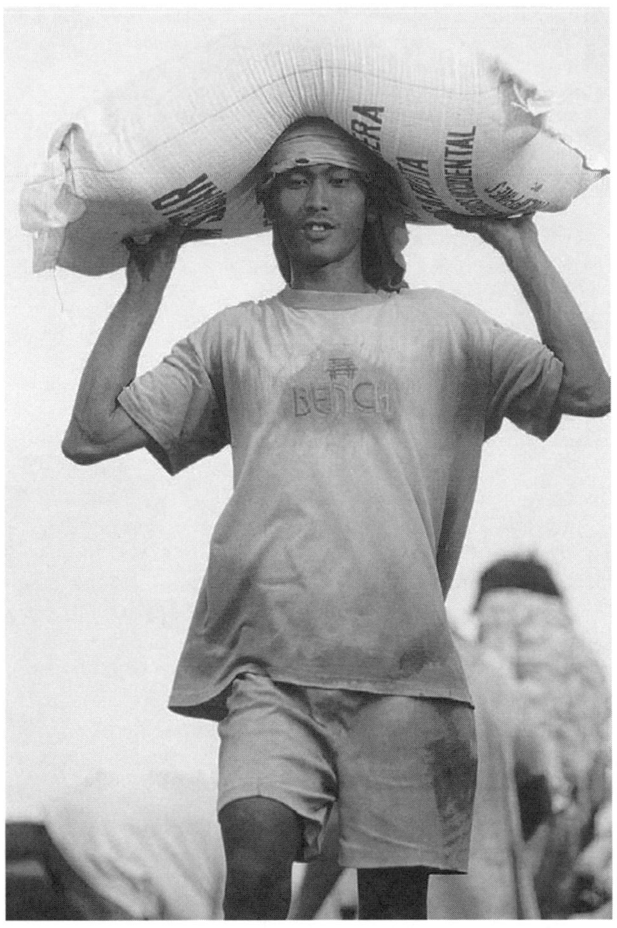

Despite the growth of industry, agriculture remains a major component of the Philippine economy. Here, a worker hauls 50-kilogram bags of raw sugar on the docks in Bacolod, Negrosuin, in Jauary 1996. (PAUL A. SOUDERS/CORBIS)

The community was composed of four different social groups: (1) the *datu* and his family; (2) the *timagua*, relatives of the *datu* or descendants of a previous *datu;* (3) the *aliping namamahay*, people who had their own house and a piece of land and had an obligation to give part of their products and their service to the *datu;* and (4) the *aliping saguiguilir*, the people who lived in the *datu*'s household, rendering various services for him. Most of the *aliping saguiguilir* were captives, criminals, or debtors.

In some cases, several *barangays* composed a unified larger village with several hundred households or more. In other areas, several independent *barangays* organized a kind of federation as an early stage of regional political unity. Domestic commerce among *barangays* and inter-island trading were observed. With goods for barter, boats sailed from Luzon to Visayan and Mindanao islands. Trade was also conducted with other Asian countries such as China, Japan, Siam, Cambodia, Borneo, Sumatra, and Java.

The *Encomienda*, Galleon Trade, and Economic Reform under Spain

At the onset of colonization, Spain introduced the *encomienda* system to govern the inhabitants of the islands. Under the *encomienda* system, the Spanish crown vested in its military officers as a reward for conquest the right to govern the inhabitants, to collect taxes, and to require them to provide unpaid labor. The Spaniards given *encomiendas* were called *encomenderos*. They accepted their obligations to protect the inhabitants, to support evangelization by Catholic priests, and to defend their jurisdictions from outside aggression. However, most of the *encomenderos* abused their rights, tyrannized the people, and did not help the priests convert the population to the Catholic faith. Catholic priests repeatedly petitioned the Spanish crown to stop the abuses of the *encomenderos*, but in vain.

However, the *encomiendas* were hereditary only for two or three generations and had to be returned to the Crown afterward. With the difficulty of collecting taxes, the *encomienda* system gradually became unpopular, even among *encomenderos;* it began to decline in the mid-seventeenth century and disappeared by the end of the eighteenth century.

Agriculture and commerce in the Philippine islands did not undergo radical changes for the local population during the Spanish colonization that lasted from the mid-sixteenth century to the mid-eighteenth century. This was because Spain maintained the Philippine colony financially, relying heavily on the galleon trade. Large galleons transported goods between Manila and Acapulco, Mexico. In this trading system, Manila served as an entrepôt between China and Mexico, sending Chinese goods such as silk or porcelain to Acapulco in exchange for Mexican silver. This trade was administered by the Philippine colonial government and handled exclusively by the Spaniards in Manila. It brought an enormous amount of tariff income to the colonial government as well as wealth to the Spaniards.

While the Philippines was tied to Mexico through the galleon trade, the colonial government received a subsidy called the *situado* from Mexico. This system was created at the end of the sixteenth century to address the serious financial deficit run up by Philippine colonial government because of heavy military expenditures. With Mexico's independence from Spain in 1812, both the galleon trade and the *situado* were abolished.

FIVE LARGEST COMPANIES IN THE PHILIPPINES

According to *Asia Week*, the five largest companies in the Philippines are as follows.

Company	Sector	Sales ($ in millions)	Rank in Asia
Manila Electric	Energy	2,422.1	551
National Power	Energy	2,265.6	598
San Miguel	Beer, Food Packaging	2,007.3	673
Petron	Oil Refining	1,990.6	679
Pilipinas Shell Petroleum	Oil Refining	1,891.5	709

Source: "The Asia Week 1000." (2001) *Asia Week* (9 November): 114.

The British occupation of Manila in 1762–1764 marked a watershed in Spanish colonial policy toward the Philippines. With the rise of British influence in Asia, the Philippine colonial government emphasized the need to exploit natural resources and to develop agriculture as well as trade and commerce. In 1779 Governor-General José Basco y Vargas formulated a general economic plan aimed at financial self-sufficiency and diversification of foreign trade in the Philippines. In 1781 he founded the Sociedad Económica de Amigos del País (Economic Society of Friends of the Country) to promote the cultivation of new agricultural products such as coffee, sugar, Manila hemp *(abaca)*, pepper, and others. Then in 1782 the tobacco monopoly was introduced, and in 1785 the Real Compañía de Filipinas (Royal Company of the Philippines) was established, following the examples of the British and Dutch East India Companies.

The aim of the tobacco monopoly was to develop tobacco cultivation and export to provide new income to the government. The government first designated Manila and several provinces in the Central Luzon Plain as tobacco-planting areas. The plantations in these areas failed, and in the early nineteenth century tobacco planting was transferred to the Cagayan valley in northern Luzon. The tobacco monopoly was abolished in the early 1880s, in response to rampant graft and corruption among local officials and government agents and destitution among the general public in tobacco-planting areas. For its part, the Real Compañía de Filipinas had already suffered heavy losses by the end of the eighteenth century and was abolished in 1834. Although its aim had been to encourage direct trade between Spain and the Philippines or other Asian countries, it had passively waited for other European ships to bring commodities to Manila. In addition, it faced the objections of Manila's galleon traders, whose interests were threatened by its existence.

The Rise and Expansion of the Export Economy

The abolition of the Real Compañía de Filipinas marked the end of the Spanish monopoly on foreign trade with the Philippines. In 1834, Spain officially opened Manila to the world market; in 1855, Iloilo, Sual, and Zamboanga; Cebu in 1860; and Legaspi and Tacloban in 1873. The opening of ports to foreign trade stimulated the Philippine economy in the late nineteenth century. The production of Manila hemp, sugar, and tobacco as export crops grew rapidly, while cotton textiles were massively imported. Britain was the major trade partner in both exports and imports throughout the late nineteenth century; the United States played an important role only for exports (particularly Manila hemp); Hong Kong and Singapore also played important roles as entrepôts for the Philippine-British trade.

The rise of the export crop economy changed the socioeconomic structure of the Philippines. With the importation of foreign textiles, the indigenous textile industry declined. Rice was imported mainly from Saigon from the 1870s. Foreign firms, particularly British and American agency houses, served as merchant banks extending credit facilities for the production of export crops. Chinese merchants appeared in various regions of the country, engaging in commercial activities and extending loans to small cultivators. Large estates called haciendas emerged; the Catholic Church, Spaniards, and Spanish and Chinese mestizos (children of intermarriage between foreigners and indigenous people) accumulated wealth as large landlords, while massive numbers of inhabitants were reduced to the status of sharecroppers *(kasamas)*. Particularly in several provinces near Manila, religious orders owned vast tracts of land. For example, in Cavite Province in southern Luzon, religious orders controlled one-third of the agricultural lands at the end of the nineteenth century. These so-called friar lands became a hotbed for Filipino uprisings for independence from Spain at the century's end.

Through the Philippine independence struggle against Spain (1896–1898) and the Philippine-American War (1899–1902), the Philippines changed its colonial master from Spain to the United States. By the mid-1920s the United States had become a major trading partner of the Philippines, which exported agricultural products such as sugar, coconut products (copra and coconut oil), Manila hemp, and tobacco, while importing cotton textiles, iron, steel, and other manufactured products. Japan became another important trade partner from the 1920s. The Philippines exported Manila hemp to Japan and imported cotton goods from it. Most of the Manila hemp exported to Japan was produced on Japanese plantations in Davao, Mindanao Island. It was said that by the outbreak of the Pacific War approximately 20,000 Japanese lived in Davao, composing the largest Japanese population in Southeast Asia.

With the expansion of the export economy of the Philippines, the United States invested in sugar and coconut processing and in public utilities (railroads and electricity production and distribution). However, by the late 1930s the level of Filipino investment exceeded that of the United States in sugar manufacturing, mining, and forestry. In general, the Philippines was not considered a profitable market for U.S. investors for two reasons. First, under the Public Land Act of 1903, purchase of public lands was limited to 16 hectares for American individuals and 1,024 hectares for American private corporations. Second, the Jones Law was enacted in 1916, providing for the future independence of the Philippines. This discouraged further U.S. investments in the Philippines. The relatively small share of investments was also visible in banking and financing. It was not the U.S. banking sector but the Philippine National Bank, a semigovernmental bank, that provided massive loans for the export sector, thereby being instrumental in developing the processing sector of agricultural export products.

Indeed, in spite of those limitations and detrimental factors, Americans actively maintained their interests in various sectors of the Philippine economy. Chinese merchants continued to keep their influential positions in commercial sectors in various local areas, as in other Southeast Asian countries. Nevertheless, it is important to note here that the Filipino landed elite also strengthened their economic base during the American colonial period. These were landlords in rice lands, sugar lands, or coconut plantations, who owned from one hundred hectares to several thousand hectares or even more in rare cases. Most of them were descendants of Spanish or Chinese mestizos who emerged as landlords in the late nineteenth century. They increased their landholdings, and some of them initiated investments in sugar manufacturing. As the Philippine economy was restructured in the U.S. trade sphere, privileged Filipino landlords and entrepreneurs stabilized their prominent economic status and functioned as an oligarchy as the gap widened between the rich and the poor.

Industrialization and Its Aftermath

The outbreak of the World War II in the Pacific in 1941 changed the fate of the Philippines. Under the Japanese occupation the Philippine economy was totally destroyed. Throughout the American period, the Philippines had imported rice mainly from French Indochina, and under the Japanese occupation food shortages became a serious problem. The Japanese military administration planned to exploit various mineral resources and to convert sugar fields into cotton lands, but these initiatives failed due to anti-Japanese guerrilla activities. When the war was over in 1945, the Philippine economy remained at a standstill and had to be restored from the devastation caused by the war and occupation. The restructuring of the Philippine economy after independence in 1946 encompassed three main tasks: (1) building multilateral trade relations, (2) solving agrarian unrest, and (3) initiating industrialization for economic growth.

The path of multilateral trade relations did not immediately open after independence. This was because of the prolonged preferential trade relations with the United States under the Bell Trade Act of 1946, and later the Laurel-Langley Agreement of 1955, which finally expired in 1974. For over two decades the Philippines maintained bilateral trade relations with the United States, with sugar and coconut oil as major export commodities. In the late 1970s Philippine trade with Japan expanded, ranking second after trade with the United States in total trade in the 1980s and 1990s. And since the 1980s Korea, Singapore, Hong Kong, Taiwan, and Malaysia have emerged as important trade partners of the Philippines.

Large landholdings and tenancy caused agrarian unrest after independence. It was particularly so in the Central Luzon Plain in the early 1950s with the peasant uprising called the Huk Movement. However, the agrarian reform programs in the 1950s and 1960s were very limited in their aims and scope. In 1972 President Ferdinand Marcos declared martial law and implemented agrarian reforms in rice- and corn-growing areas in the name of building the "New Society."

Indeed, it was under the Marcos regime that the colonial structure of the Philippine economy was gradually transformed. In the 1950s and 1960s, the Philippines, like other Southeast Asian countries, took import substitution (encouraging industries to produce manufactured goods for the domestic market, thereby reducing imports) as the basic principle of industrialization, aiming to strengthen the manufacturing sector for the domestic market. In the 1970s, on the other hand, emphasis was given to export-oriented industrialization, under the liberalization of foreign investments. From the late 1970s, exports of electronics and garments rapidly increased, exceeding those of coconut oil and sugar by the early 1980s. In the political turmoil of the 1980s, however, the economy of the Philippines stagnated under the load of swelling foreign debts, mismanagement of giant corporations, and increasing unemployment. In 1987 a new agrarian reform law was enacted under the government of Corazon Aquino; it broadened the Marcos reforms to include all agricultural lands. Under the agrarian reform programs, the traditional sharecropping system almost disappeared in rice lands; however, the discrepancy among peasants and landless rural workers widened because lands were given to former tenants but not to rural workers. On the other hand, in the newly covered areas of agrarian reform such as sugar and coconut lands, rural workers are among the beneficiaries for land transfers, but due to resistance from landlords, the agrarian reform has not been effectively implemented. In the 1990s, the Philippines' economic growth lagged behind that of other nations in the region, and the government has made efforts to catch up economically with them. Diversification of export industries, while tackling the serious poverty problems, will be an important economic strategy for the Philippines in the years to come.

Yoshiko Nagano

Further Reading

Corpuz, Onofre D. (1989) *The Roots of the Filipino Nation*. 2 vols. Quezon City, Philippines: Aklahi Foundation.

Doeppers, Daniel F. (1984) *Manila, 1900–1941: Social Change in a Local Colonial Metropolis*. New Haven, CT.: Yale University Southeast Asia Studies.

Golay, Frank. (1961) *The Philippines: Public Policy and National Economic Development*. Ithaca, NY: Cornell University Press.

Ikehata, Setsuho, and Ricardo Trota Jose, eds. (1999) *The Philippines under Japan: Occupation Policy and Reaction*. Quezon City, Philippines: Ateneo de Manila University Press.

Legarda, Benito J., Jr. (1999) *After the Galleons: Foreign Trade, Economic Change, and Entrepreneurship in the Nineteenth-Century Philippines*. Madison: University of Wisconsin–Madison Center for Southeast Asian Studies.

McCoy, Alfred W., and Ed C. de Jesus, eds. (1982) *Philippine Social History: Global Trade and Local Transformations*. Quezon City, Philippines: Ateneo de Manila University.

Schurz, William Lytle. (1939) *The Manila Galleon*. New York: E. P. Dutton and Co.

Wickberg, Edgar. (1965) *Chinese in Philippine Life, 1850–1898*. New Haven, CT: Yale University Press.

Yoshihara, Kunio. (1985) *Philippine Industrialization: Foreign and Domestic Capital*. Singapore: Oxford University Press.

PHILIPPINES—EDUCATION SYSTEM

The modern education system in the Philippines has been strongly influenced by the colonial past and by a strong government lead in raising standards of education during the 1980s and 1990s. In terms of primary and secondary school enrollment, the Philippines traditionally was considered among the top countries in Southeast Asia. The country established a relatively strong education system to meet the demands of its young and rapidly growing population and of the rapidly growing national economy.

Education in the Sixteenth through Nineteenth Centuries

During the precolonial era, many Philippine traders used Arabic script in daily life, and some historical evidence suggests that many urban settlers could read and write. With Spanish colonization and the arrival of Spanish missionaries in the early sixteenth century, the education system in the Philippines developed under a strongly Spanish influence. Missionaries established and ran a number of religious schools, and in the early seventeenth century the first Western-style higher education institutions were established to meet the commercial and administrative needs of the colony. In 1611 the Spanish opened Santo Tomas College, which attained university status in 1644, becoming the oldest university in the Philippines and one of

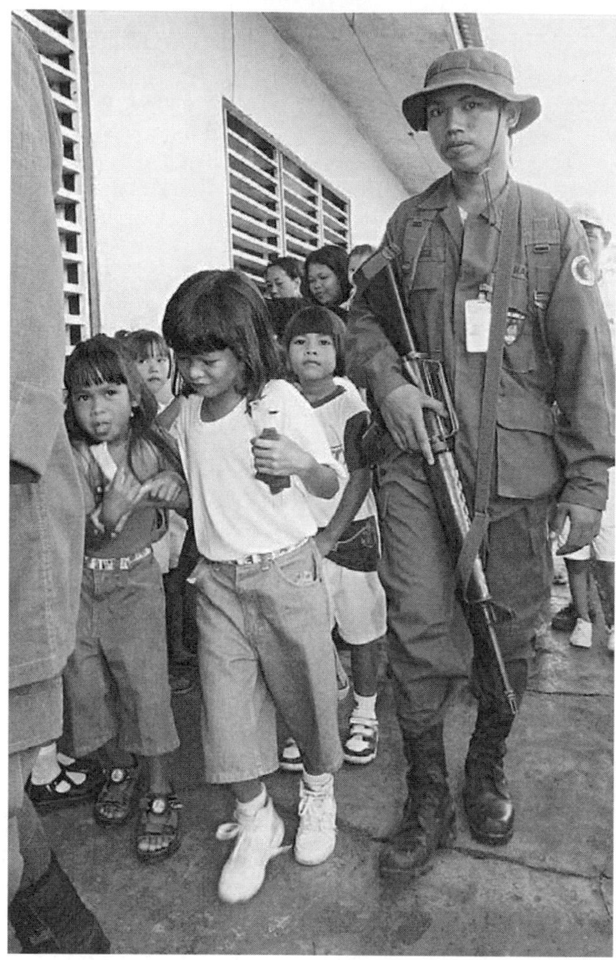

A police officer guards children at an elementary school in the southern Philippines in June 2000. Fighting between Muslim separatists and government forces have raised fears about the children's safety. (AFP/CORBIS)

the oldest in the region. During the Spanish era, however, education was a privilege of the upper class, rich individuals, and the nobility.

Education from 1899 to 1946

With U.S. occupation of the Philippines in 1899, the situation changed dramatically. In 1900 the new colonial administration introduced universal primary education, making the Philippines one of the first countries in Asia to adopt such an educational regime. This contributed to a rapid rise in the number of public and private primary schools as well as higher-education institutions. Importantly, the Philippines had more private higher institutions than public universities in the 1930s. According to various estimates, the literacy rate doubled, from around 25 to 30 percent at the beginning of the twentieth century to around 50 percent in the 1930s, but there was a huge regional disparity in school admissions, and the government was too slow to move toward eliminating mass illiteracy. World War II halted social and economic development in the Philippines archipelago, as it brought large-scale destruction during the Japanese occupation and the United States–led liberation of the country in 1945.

Education after Independence

The Philippines became an independent republic in 1946, and the new government launched a series of national development plans in the field of education, with the target of total elimination of illiteracy in the country. Between 1946 and 2001, primary school enrollments rose from 4 million to 12.8 million, while secondary school enrollments rose from 0.5 to 5.4 million. By the late 1990s, more than 95 percent of primary school–age children were enrolled in public or private schools, and the Philippines became one of the highest-ranked nations in Asia in terms of school enrollments. The adult literacy rate reached 94.8 percent; it was even higher in the major urban areas of Luzon Island, but lower in many areas of Mindanao Island and the Eastern Visayan.

General primary education is mandatory and free, and citizens have the right to receive free tertiary education on a competitive basis. The Ministry of Education, Culture, and Sports regulates the national system of education and sets the national standards. Filipino and English are the two major languages of instruction, but the state provides support for education in the languages of other ethnic groups, including ethnic minority groups. The major problems in relation to providing quality education are the scattered nature of the Philippine archipelago; the presence of cultural minority (including Muslim) groups and small indigenous groups, speaking eight major Philippine languages and several minor languages; and the escalation of conflict in the southern Philippines in the late 1990s.

Primary and Secondary Education Presently, children at the age of six begin a four-year compulsory primary education program; for the first two years, the vernacular language used in the school's locality is the auxiliary medium of instruction, but only as a means of facilitating the students' understanding of concepts in either English or Filipino. At the age of ten, children enroll in a two-year intermediate education program, and at the age of twelve, they enter a four-year secondary education program. On completion of secondary school, pupils receive a high school diploma.

EDUCATION IN THE PHILIPPINES—PAST AND PRESENT

The modern Philippines education system is based on the United States model with a clear separation of church and state. But it was not always that way. During the period of Spanish rule, Roman Catholic teachings were an important part of the curriculum.

Regulations Prescribed by the Decree of 1863 for Primary Schools.

The teaching in the schools for natives shall comprise:

(1) The Christian doctrine and principles of morality and sacred history.

(2) Reading.

(3) Writing.

(4) Practical teaching of the Castilian language.

(5) Principles of arithmetic including the four rules for integers, common fractions, decimals, and denominate numbers, with principles of the decimal metric system, and its equivalents in the usual weights and measures.

(6) Principles of general geography and Spanish history.

(7) Principles of practical agriculture, with application to the products of the country.

(8) Rules of courtesy.

(9) Vocal music.

The primary teaching of girls will include all the above except Nos. 6 and 7, and the needlework suitable to their sex. (Art. 1)

Primary instruction is obligatory for all the natives between the ages of 7 and 12. The teacher shall have especial care that the scholars have practical exercise in speaking the Castilian language. Primary instruction shall be free for children whose parents are not known to be wealthy. Paper, copybooks, ink, and pens, will be free to all the children. (Art. 2, 3, and 4)

The parish priest shall direct the teaching of Christian doctrine and morality. (Art. 6)

The Christian doctrine shall be taught by the catechism which is in use, and approved by ecclesiastical authorities. For reading, the syllabary prescribed by the superior civil governor, the Cathecism of Astete, and the Cathecism of Fleuri, shall be used. For writing, the *Muestras de caracter Espanol* by Iturzaeta shall be used. (Art. 7)

Teachers of *entrada* shall receive from 8 to 12 pesos per month; those of *ascenso*, from 12 to 15; those of *termino* of the second grade from 15 to 20. In addition teachers shall enjoy the following advantages:

(1) A dwelling apartment for themselves and family in the schoolhouse, or reimbursement if they rent one.

(2) The fees paid by well-to-do chuldren.

(3) The privileges and exemptions and pension mentioned in Arts. 12, 13, and 14 of the Royal decree. (Arts. 23 and 24)

Women teachers for girls must be at least 25 years old, and shall possess the other qualifications that are demanded from the male teachers. They shall receive monthly pay of 8 pesos if they have a certificate, and 6 if the contrary be true, and all the fees of wealthy girls. They shall also have the right to live in the school, and in case they do not live there, to a reimbursement to pay their rent. (Arts. 26, 28)

Source: Emma H. Blair and James Robertson, eds. (1903–1909) *The Philippine Islands*, Cleveland, OH: Arthur H. Clark, Co., 46: 81.

There are several compulsory subjects, including English, Filipino, mathematics, practical arts, science, social studies, youth development training, and citizens' army training.

According to official figures, in 1997 there were 6,362 pre-primary educational establishments, attended by 452,000 children, with 9,644 teachers. Approximately 37,640 primary schools, with 342,000 teachers, provided education for 12 million pupils, and 5,880 secondary schools with 154,700 teachers provided education for approximately 5 million students. The official statistics state that the Philippines achieved 100 percent enrollment of relevant age-group children at primary schools.

Tertiary Education After completing secondary school, students may continue their education at a non-university-level institution (i.e., technical or vocational) or at a university. As a prerequisite for university entry, secondary school graduates must take the National Secondary Aptitude Test. Most education programs at tertiary level are conducted in Filipino and English; students are required to take three courses in Filipino and three in English as part of the general education curriculum during their first two years. Students must study for four years and acquire between 120 and 190 credits to obtain a bachelor's degree.

Students may continue their education at a post-graduate level, but to do so they must achieve at least the score of 85 or a B grade at the bachelor's level. A master's degree takes between two and four years of study. Alternatively, students may undertake diploma or certificate courses of various durations. Upon completion of their master's degree, students may enter a three- to four-year doctorate program, which combines course work and a dissertation.

Official figures for 1997 listed approximately sixty universities throughout the Philippines, both private and publicly owned, which were attended by approximately 260,000 students, and seventy-three private institutions, attended by approximately two million students. Private universities charge between $1,500 and $5,000 per academic year (1999–2000 academic-year estimates). Traditionally, a large number of middle-class and upper-middle-class families send their children to study at various universities abroad, with the United States and Canada the most popular destinations. However, many students (estimated at 12–18 percent) choose to remain in their host countries upon completing their education.

During the 1990s, there was serious concern about the quality of the education system in the Philippines and about regional disparities in educational services. There is a high percentage of dropouts from intermediate and secondary schools. Some problems were related to limited government expenditure on education. According to the United Nations Development Report (2000), between 1985 and 1997 the government significantly increased its expenditure on education—from 10,500 million to 100,000 million pesos (or from 1.94 percent to 4.0 percent of gross national product). However, this increase was offset by the rapidly growing population (36.87 percent of the population is below the age of fourteen, according to 2002 estimates) and by inflation.

Rafis Abazov

Further Reading

Asian Development Bank. (1999) *Philippine Education for the 21st Century (1998 Philippines Education Sector Study).* Manila, Philippines: Asian Development Bank.

Heaver, Richard A., and Joseph M. Hunt. (1995) *Improving Early Childhood Development: An Integrated Program for the Philippines (Directions in Development, (World Bank).* Washington, DC: World Bank.

Swinerton, Nelson E. (1991) *Philippine Higher Education.* Westport, CT: Praeger.

Synott, John P. (2001) *Teacher Unions, Social Movements, and the Politics of Education in Asia: South Korea, Taiwan, and the Philippines.* Burlington, VT: Ashgate.

United Nations Development Program. (1999) *Philippines: Human Development Report, 2000.* Manila, Philippines: UNDP.

PHILIPPINES—HISTORY

The Philippines is a multiethnic and multireligious nation. The major groups are the majority Christian Filipinos, Muslim Filipinos who live mainly on Mindanao and the Sulu archipelago in the south, and indigenous peoples in mountainous regions. The islands have been occupied for about 30,000 years and have been part of the world economy since the beginning of Spanish colonial rule in 1571. Philippine history can be divided into six periods: ancient and precolonial, Spanish colonial period (1571–1898), Philippine revolution (1896–1902), American colonial period (1898–1946), Japanese occupation (1941–1945), independence (1946–present).

Ancient and Precolonial Periods

The Philippine islands were first occupied by humans from about 30,000 to 25,000 years ago by people from mainland Southeast Asia. These people were hunter-gatherers and are the ancestors of the modern Philippine population group known as Negritos for their physical appearance, thought to resemble that of

KEY EVENTS IN PHILIPPINE HISTORY

c. 30,000 BCE First human occupation of the islands
c. 3,000 BCE Malays from Southeast Asia settle on the islands.
14th century CE Islam arrives in the southern islands from Borneo.
1521 Ferdinand Magellan arrives and dies in the Philippines.
1571 Miguel Lopez de Legazpi establishes Manila as the Spanish capital.
1600 Much of the Philippines is under Spanish colonial rule.
1650s The *encomienda* system begins to decline.
1762–1764 The British occupy Manila.
1780s The economy is reformed to stress agriculture and export.
1834 Manila is opened to the world market.
1880–1895 The propaganda movement agitates for political reform.
1896–1898 The Philippine revolution ends Spanish rule.
1898 Through the Treaty of Paris the United States gains control of the Philippines from Spain.
1899–1902 The Philippine-American War begins the era of American rule.
1916 The United States grants the Philippines more political autonomy.
1934–1935 A commonwealth government is instituted.
1942–1945 The Philippines is occupied by Japan.
1944 The American re-occupation of the islands begins.
1946 The Philippines becomes an independent nation.
1942 The Huk rebellion begins on Luzon and lasts into the 1950s.
1960s Anti-American movements develop.
1969 The Moro National Liberation Front is founded on Mindanao.
1972 President Ferdinand Marcos declares martial law which lasts until 1981.
1983 Opposition leader Benigno Aquino is assassinated.
1986 Corazon Aquino is elected president. Marcos flees the country.
2001 Gloria Macapagal-Arroyo becomes president.

Africans. There is no evidence that they migrated from Africa, as suggested in some popular accounts. The Negritos today are a threatened population of about 15,000 who are being rapidly assimilated into the general population.

Beginning in about 3,000 BCE heavier migration began as a succession of Malays from Borneo, Sumatra, and mainland Southeast Asia arrived and established communities on the coasts and along rivers. The typical community *(barangay)* had from thirty to a hundred families and was headed by a chieftain. They subsisted through hunting, gathering, fishing, slash-and-burn agriculture, and trading. There were also several larger settlements, such as the one at the site of Manila, which served as trading centers with China, Japan, India, and Southeast Asian states. Some communities at times came under the control or influence of Southeast Asian states, the most important being the Majapahit empire of Java in the thirteenth century.

Islam arrived in the southernmost islands in the fourteenth century via Arab traders from Borneo. It then spread northward and at the time of Spanish arrival in the sixteenth century was taking hold in the central islands and the northern island of Luzon. At that time the peoples of the southern island of Mindanao and the Sulu Archipelago were mainly Muslim.

Spanish Colonial Period

In 1521 Ferdinand Magellan (1480–1521) a Portuguese navigator sailing for Spain, reached the islands. Magellan died there in battle in April of the same year, but survivors brought word of the islands back to Spain. In 1565 Miguel López de Legazpi (c. 1510–1572) established the first Spanish settlement (San Miguel, on Cebu), and in 1571 he founded Manila on Luzon. The islands were named for King Philip II of Spain. The colony was considered a province of New Spain and was administered from Mexico City.

MAGELLAN'S ARRIVAL IN THE PHILIPPINES

The Philippines were colonized by Spain following Magellan's arrival in the islands in 1521. The following extract from the account of the voyage kept by Magellan's companion Antonio Pigafetta tells of their arrival and first impressions.

Arrival at the Philippines

At dawn on Saturday, March 16, 1521, we came upon a high land at a distance of three hundred *leguas* from the islands of Latrroni, and island named Zamal (Samar). The following day the captain-general desired to land on another island which was uninhabited and lay to the right of the above mentioned island in order to be more secure and get water and have some rest. He had two tents set up on the shore for the sick and had a sow killed for them. On Monday afternoon, March 18, we saw a boat coming toward us with nine men in it. Therefore, the captain-general ordered that no one should move or say a word without his permission. When those men reached the shore, their chief went immediately to the captain-general giving signs of joy because of our arrival. Five of the most ornately adorned of them remained with us, while the rest went to get some others who were fishing, and so that all came. The captain-general seeing that they were reasonable men, ordered food to be set before them, and gave them red caps, mirrors, combs, bells, ivory, bocasine, and other things. When they saw the captain's courtesy, they presented fish, a jar of palm wine, which they call *uraca* (i.e. arrack), figs more than one *palmo* long (i.e. bananas), and others which were smaller and more delicate, and two cocoanuts. They had nothing else then, but made us signs with their hands that they would bring *umay* or rice, and cocoanuts and many other articles of food within four days. . . .

Those people became very familiar with us. They told us many things, their names and those of some of the islands that could be seen from that place. Their own island was called Zuluan and it is not very large. We took great pleasure with them, for they were very pleasant and conversable. In order to show them greater honor, the captain-general took them to his ship and showed them all his merchandise—cloves, cinnamon, pepper, ginger, nutmeg, mace, gold, and all things in the ship. He had some mortars fired for them, whereas they exhibited great fear, and tried to jump out of the ship. They made signs to us that the above said articles grew in that place where we were going. When they were about to retire they took their leave very gracefully and neatly, saying that they would return according to their promise. The island where we were is called Humunu; but inasmuch as we found two springs there of the clearest water, we called it Acquada da li buoni Segnialli (i.e. the Watering place of good Signs) for there were the first signs of gold which we found in those districts. We found a great quantity of white coral there, and large trees with fruits a trifle smaller than the almond and resembling pine seeds. There are also many palms, some of them good and others bad. There are many islands in that district, and therefore we called them the archipelago of San Lazaros, as they were discovered on the Sabbath of St. Lazarus. They lie in X degrees of latitude toward the Arctic pole, and in a longitude of one hundred and sixty one degrees from the line of demarcation.

At noon on Friday, March 22, those men came as they had promised us in two boats with cocoanuts, sweet oranges, a jar of palm-wine, and a cock, in order to show us that there were fowls in that district. They exhibited great signs of pleasure at seeing us. We purchased all those articles from them. Their seignior was an old man who was painted (i.e. tattooed). He wore two gold earrings (*schione*) in his ears, and the others many gold armlets on their arms and kerchiefs about their heads. We stayed there one week, and during that time our captain went ashore daily to visit the sick, and every morning gave them cocoanut water from his own hand, which comforted them greatly. These are people living near that island who have holes in their ears so large that they cam pass their arms through them. Those people

CONTINUED ON NEXT PAGE

CONTINUED FROM PREVIOUS PAGE

are *caphri*, that is to say heathen. They go naked with a cloth woven from the bark of a tree about their privies except for some of the chiefs who wear cotton cloth embroidered with silk at the ends by means of a needle. They anoint themselves with cocoanut and with bean-seed oil, as a protection against sun and wind. They have very black hair that falls to the waist, and use daggers, knives, and spears ornamented with gold, large shields, fascines, javelins, and fishing nets that resemble *rizali*, and their boats are like ours.

Source: Emma H. Blair and James Robertson, eds. (1903–1909) *The Philippine Islands*. Cleveland, OH: Arthur H. Clark, Co., I: 97.

The Spanish called the Muslims Moros (after the Moors, or North African Muslims, who had ruled Spain), considered them enemies, and initiated a campaign to eradicate Islam from the islands that has continued in various forms into the twenty-first century. By the end of the sixteenth century, most regions except for parts of Muslim Mindanao and the Sulu Archipelago were under Spanish control.

Spain governed the colony under the *encomienda* system, under which Spanish settlers colonized the land for the crown and were given the right to collect taxes and exploit the labor of the indigenous Filipinos. The crown also supported Catholic missionaries, who converted many Filipinos but did not allow the establishment of a native clergy.

By the middle of the seventeenth century, complaints about abuses of the *encomienda* system as well as difficulties encountered in collecting taxes caused it to be abandoned and replaced with a new system based on local rule. Indigenous leaders were placed in charge and allowed to collect taxes and own land, with the Spanish governor-generals having considerable power over local and regional affairs. Also enjoying considerable power were the village priests, who, as the only people in the villages who spoke both Spanish and the indigenous languages, served as intermediaries between the colonists and the colonized. The new system created local elites of native Filipinos and also created an ethos of local rule that continues to the present. Economically, the colony served as a trading post, with Manila the main port, for silk and porcelain from China and silver from Mexico. Many of the traders were Chinese, who retain that role in the modern Philippines, although the products are now different.

Spanish control was at times under threat from the Portuguese, Dutch, English (who occupied Manila from 1762–1764), Chinese, and the Filipinos themselves. These threats led the Spanish colonial government to reform the economy, switching from a focus on trade to a strong agricultural base. Reforms began late in the century and included the growing of agricultural products such as coffee, sugar, and Manila hemp (abaca); the tobacco monopoly, which began in 1782; and the founding of the Real Compañía de Filipinas (Royal Company of the Philippines) in 1785. In 1834, Manila was opened to the world market, followed by several other ports over the next fifty years. The new trade opportunities stimulated the agricultural sector, and hemp, sugar, and tobacco became major exports while cotton textiles were imported. Britain was the major trade partner.

The new economy produced a new socioeconomic order with British banks, Chinese merchants, and much of the land owned by wealthy Spaniards, Spanish and Chinese mestizos, and the Catholic Church. Most Filipinos were poor peasants working land owned by others. This new order set the stage for the Philippine Revolution of 1896–1902, which was marked by peasant revolts, resentment of Church wealth, and the support of a small but active group of Filipino intellectuals.

Philippine Revolution

The Philippine Revolution entailed the struggle for independence from Spain from 1896 to 1898 and the Philippine-American War from 1899 to 1902.

Philippine nationalism emerged in the mid-nineteenth century. An early issue was Church discrimination against indigenous secular priests, who were forced to leave their parishes. Spanish colonial officials oppressed the movement, and arrested and executed the leaders (Mariano Gomez, José Burgos, and Jacinto Zamora) in 1872. This movement was followed by the propaganda movement (1880–1895), led by Filipino intellectuals who had been educated in Europe, such as José Rizal (1861–1896) and Marcelo H. Del Pilar (1850–1896). They protested the mistreatment of the Filipinos and called for basic humanitarian reforms, and while the movement was repressed and

A PRIMER FOR PHILIPPINE INDEPENDENCE

The following text written by Philippine patriot Andres Bonifacio is one of several written to prepare the Philippine people for revolution against Spain.

Of old, previous to the arrival of the Spaniards, these Islands were governed by our own compatriots who were then living in the greatest abundance and prosperity. These maintained good relations with their neighbors, especially with the Japanese, and traded with them in commodities of all sorts. The result was that wealth and good customs were a common patrimony; young and old, the women included, knew how to read and write, using their own alphabet. But the Spaniards came, with the pretense of peace. The persons then governed us flattered by their honeyed tempting words, allowed themselves to be deceived by their offers to guide us on the paths of wisdom and increased prosperity. They were, however, obliged to comply with the ritualistic customs of the islanders, to give binding force to their compacts by means of an oath of peace, which consisted in taking a small quantity of blood from the veins of the contracting parties and then drinking the blood so mixed, as evidence that they were to be absolutely true and loyal to their allies. This was called the Pact of Blood (which was included) between King Sikatuna and the representative of the King of Spain, Legazpi.

Since then, for over 300 years, we have been supplying (the wants) of the race of Legazpi with largesse and have enriched them with abundance, despite the hunger that we ourselves have suffered. We have wasted our wealth and blood and even given our lives in their defence; we have even fought our compatriots who could not willingly submit to their yoke; we have combated the Chinese and the Dutch who attempted to wrest these Islands from them.

Now after all this, what comfort or liberal concession have they bestowed upon us in exchange for all our sacrifices? How have they kept the contract, the cause, precisely of our sacrifices? Our munificence they have rewarded with treachery, and far from guiding us on the path of knowledge, they have blinded us and contaminated us with their infamous procedure. They have endeavored to make us abandon our good customs; they have initiated us in a false belief and have dragged the honor of the people into the mire. And if we dare beg for a scrap of love, they give us banishment instead and tear us away from our beloved children, our wives, and our old parents. Every sigh that we utter they brand as a sin and immediately punish it with implacable ferocity.

Now nothing is to be seen of popular tranquility, now our peace is constantly being disturbed by incessant rumors of complaints and prayers, of the wailing and grief of orphans, widows, and parents of countrymen, ours whom the dominator has wronged; of the tears of mothers whose sons have been put to death; of the wail of tender children whom cruelty has made orphans, and each tear is like a drop of molten lead that lacerated our suffering wounded heart; now they tighten more and more the links of the chains of vassalage that dishonor every man of integrity. What, then, must we do? The sun of reason that shines in the East clearly shows into our eyes which, alas! have been blinded so long, the way we must follow; by its light we can see the death-dealing claws in the outstretched hands of the malevolent. Reason tells us that we can not expect anything but suffering upon suffering, treachery upon treachery, contempt upon contempt, and tyranny upon tyranny. Reason tells us that we must not waste our time waiting in vain for promises of felicity that will never come, that will never materialize. Reasons tells us that we must rely upon ourselves alone and never entrust our rights to life to anybody. Reason teaches us to be united in sentiment, thought, and purpose, so that we may acquire the strength necessary to crush the evil that is affecting our people.

It is time that the light of truth should shine; time that we should show determination, honor, shame and mutual cooperation. The

CONTINUED ON NEXT PAGE

CONTINUED FROM PREVIOUS PAGE

> time is come now to diffuse the gospel that shall tear the tough web obscuring our intellect, and that the islanders should see whence come their misfortunes. Now it will be made evident that every step we are taking is on the unstable ground, on the brink of a horrible abyss of death, dug by our wily enemy.
>
> Therefore, oh my compatriots! let us scatter the mist that befogs our intellect and let us consecrate all our force to the good cause, in the ultimate prosperity, so anxiously desired by us, of the land of our birth.
>
> *Source:* Nicolas Zafra. (1967) *Philippine History through Selected Sources*. Quezon City, Philippines. Alemar-Phoenix Publishing House, 212–213.

failed to produce reforms, it did succeed in developing a national consciousness among Filipinos.

Rizal published two political novels, *Noli Me Tangere* (Touch Me Not) in 1887 and *El Filibusterismo* (The Rebel) in 1891, in which he described vividly the oppression of Spanish colonial rule and the role of the priests. He returned to Manila and organized La Liga Filipina (The Philippine League), a secret society, on 3 July 1892. He was arrested on 6 July and exiled to Mindanao. Some members of La Liga Filipina, including Andres Bonifacio (1863–1897) founded another secret society, Kataastaasang Kagalanggalangang Katipunan ng mga Anak ng Bayan (The Highest and Most Honorable Society of the Sons of the Country), or Katipunan for short, on 7 July and called for an armed revolution. On 30 August 1896 the Philippine revolution broke out in Manila and gathered strength following the execution of Rizal on 30 December. However, the revolution went awry when the leadership shifted to Emilio Aguinaldo (1869–1964), municipal mayor of Kawit, Cavite (1894–1897), in May 1897. On 12 June 1898 Aguinaldo declared independence.

At this point the United States intervened, and the Philippines was bought by the United States from Spain in the Treaty of Paris on 10 December 1898. The revolutionary government established the República Filipina (Philippine Republic) on 23 January 1899 and promulgated a constitution, but the Philippine-American War broke out on 4 February 1899, less than two weeks later, and Aguinaldo was captured on 23 March 1901. Although on 4 July 1902 the United States declared control of the Philippines, resistance continued until 1910. About 500,000 Filipinos were killed during the revolution. The United States also occupied Muslim areas in the south, and Sultan Jamal ul Kiram II (d. 1936) of Sulu surrendered under the Carpenter Agreement in 1915.

American Period

The Philippine Organic Act of 1 July 1902 provided the framework for the new colonial government. American rule introduced a modern secular educational system (1901), separation of church and state, a legislative assembly (1907) and a party system. The municipal governments were still administered by Filipino local leaders, and wholesale and retail trade was controlled by ethnic Chinese. American colonial policy toward the Philippines varied depending on whether the Republican or Democratic Party was in power, with the Democrats generally favoring more autonomy for the Philippines. For example, from 1913–1921, when the U.S. president was a Democrat, the Filipinization program was initiated, and Filipinos held a majority of the civil-service positions. In 1916 the Philippine Autonomy Act (Jones Act) granted more autonomy to the Filipinos. The Philippine Independence Act (Tydings-McDuffie Law) was enacted by the U.S. Congress in 1934, and in 1935 a commonwealth government was instituted. Full independence was planned for 1946.

The United States could not take full economic control of the Philippines until 1909, as the Treaty of Paris provided for a ten-year period during which Spanish ships and goods could enter the Philippines on the same terms as American ships and goods. In 1909 the U.S. Congress passed the Payne-Aldrich Tariff Act, which permitted free entry of all Philippine products except rice, sugar, and tobacco. These exceptions were abolished by the Underwood-Simmons Act in 1913. Under free-trade relations, the Philippine economy grew rapidly, as products such as sugar and Manila hemp were exported to the United States and American manufactured products imported. In the 1930s, the United States took about 80 percent of the Philippines' total exports and accounted for about 65 percent of its total imports.

Japanese Occupation

The Japanese invaded the Philippines on 8 December 1941, occupied Manila on 2 January 1942, and established a military administration the following day. Retreating American and Filipino forces surrendered on Corregidor and Bataan. Japanese occupation was harsh, and many Filipinos lacked the basic necessities of life (many starved), were forced to perform labor, were tortured, and suffered the plundering of their homes and communities. This deprivation of human rights continues to inform Filipino views of Japan and the Japanese. Filipino resistance was centered in central Luzon and communists played a leading role. In 1944 U.S. forces aided by Filipino guerrillas reoccupied the islands. The Battle of Leyte Gulf, the largest naval battle in history, was a major defeat for the Japanese and eased the way for the American re-occupying forces. Nonetheless, fighting was fierce, and the Japanese forces did not surrender until 3 September 1945. The Philippine government estimated that more than one million Filipinos were wounded or killed during the occupation.

The Independent Philippines

When the Philippines became an independent nation on 4 July 1946, it was in much worse condition than it had been before World War II. Rehabilitation was accomplished largely through a series of treaties with and support provided by the United States: The Treaty of General Relations, the Philippine Trade Act Agreement (Bell Trade Agreement), and the Military Bases Agreement. The trade agreement provided for reciprocal free trade until 1954, after which there would be gradual imposition of duties on specific products until 1973. The Military Bases Agreement provided for the use of twenty-three military and naval bases by the United States, originally for ninety-nine years. The Mutual Defense Treaty (Mutual Defense Pact) signed on 30 August 1951 provided for mutual aid in an external attack.

The Philippines' dependence on the United States led to the rise of antigovernment and anti-imperialism movements, the most important of which was the Hukbalahap (Huk) movement. The Huk movement began in 1942 in central Luzon; its full name was Hukbo ng Bayan Lapan sa Hapon (People's Army against the Japanese). The movement was led by the Partido Komunista ng Pilipinas (the old Communist Party of the Philippines, formed in the 1930s). After the war, the Huks were disappointed with the Philippines' dependence on the United States and the oligarchy of Filipino landlords. They changed the full name to Hukbong Mapagpalaya nang Bayan (People's Liberation Army) and started a peasant revolt, demanding equitable distribution of the land and harvest. They nearly captured Manila in 1950. Their leader surrendered in 1954, but the movement continued its activities into the 1970s. Successive presidents launched land-reform programs to maintain social stability, but tenant farmers were dissatisfied with those watered-down bills.

Anti-American nationalism movements led by urban laborers, students, and intellectuals gained power in the 1960s. The Communist Party of the Philippines (CPP) refounded in 1968, adopted the tenets of Maoism. The New People's Army (NPA) was organized as the military arm of the CPP in 1969. In the south, the Moro National Liberation Front (MNLF) was formed in 1969; it demanded independence for Muslim-dominated areas. Meanwhile economic conditions worsened due to inflation and unemployment.

President Ferdinand Marcos (1916–1989) declared martial law in 1972. The military arrested several thousand people including opposition politicians, journalists, student leaders, intellectuals, and labor union leaders. Martial law was lifted in 1981, but after opposition leader Benigno Aquino, Jr. (1932–1983) was assassinated at Manila International Airport in 1983, many more Filipinos joined the protest movement against Marcos's dictatorship. In the election of 1986 Corazon Cojuangco Aquino (b. 1933), widow of Benigno, was elected president, and Marcos and his family went into exile in Hawaii.

In 2001 Vice President Gloria Macapagal-Arroyo (b. 1947) was sworn in as the new president of the Philippines. She came to power through a peaceful "People Power" movement that led to the resignation of President Joseph Estrada (b. 1937) over charges of corruption and cronyism. The Philippines restored democracy for a second time, but economic reform and continuing resistance from Muslims in the south remain serious issues.

Shinzo Hayase and David Levinson

Further Reading

Agoncillo, Teodoro A. (1956) *The Revolt of the Masses: The Story of Bonifacio and the Katipunan*. Quezon City, Philippines: University of the Philippines.

Blair, Emma Helen, and James Alexander Robertson, eds. ([1903–1909] 1973) *The Philippine Islands 1493–1898*. Reprint ed. Rizal, Philippines: Cachos Hermanos.

Constantino, Renato. (1975) *The Philippines: A Past Revisited*. Quezon City, Philippines: Tala Publishing Services.

Constantino, Renato, and Letizia R. Constantino. (1978) *The Philippines: The Continuing Past*. Quezon City, Philippines: The Foundation for Nationalist Studies.

Ileto, Reynaldo C. (1979) *Pasyon and Revolution: Popular Movements in the Philippines, 1840–1910.* Quezon City, Philippines: Ateneo de Manila University Press.

———. (1998) *Filipinos and Their Revolution: Events, Discourse, and Historiography*, Quezon City, Philippines: Ateneo de Manila University Press.

McCoy, Alfred W., and Ed. C. de Jesus, eds. (1982) *Philippine Social History: Global Trade and Local Transformations.* Quezon City, Philippines: Ateneo de Manila University Press.

Steinberg, David J. (2000) *The Philippines: A Singular and a Plural Place.* 4th ed. Boulder, CO: Westview Press.

PHILIPPINES—HUMAN RIGHTS

The present Philippine constitution (1987) adopts a broad definition of human rights that includes not only civil and political rights but also economic, social, and cultural rights, as well as the rights of special groups such as women, the disabled, and indigenous cultural communities. It guarantees its citizens certain basic rights, such as the right to free speech, association, and religion. In addition, the Philippine constitution prohibits the use of torture, force, and secret detention for those accused. The constitution also directs the state to enact laws that protect and enhance the rights of all people to human dignity, that reduce inequalities, and that support diffusing wealth and political power for the common good.

The Philippines' National Commission on Human Rights (NCHR) was one of the first such agencies in Asia. Its primary task is to investigate complaints of human-rights violations. On the international level, the Philippines is a signatory to the U.N. Universal Declaration of Human Rights and has acceded to several important U.N. covenants and protocols on human rights, most notably the International Covenant and Optional Protocol on Civil and Political Rights and the International Covenant on Social, Economic, and Cultural Rights. In 1996, activists from academia, nongovernmental organizations (NGOs), and the NCHR formed the Working Group which has been pursuing the creation of a regional human-rights organization within the Association of Southeast Asian Nations (ASEAN). Despite these initiatives, however, violations of human rights continue across the country. These violations are monitored by organizations such as Task Force Detainees of the Philippines (TFDP), the Philippine Association of Human Rights Advocates, and Amnesty International Philippines.

Civil and Political Rights

The constitution of 1987, written under the administration (1986–1992) of President Corazon Aquino

In October 2000, Filipinos in Hong Kong, where they number about 160,000, protest the rule of Philippine president Joseph Estrada, which they claim is corrupt and violates Filipino human rights. (AFP/CORBIS)

(b. 1933), provided legal and institutional guarantees for the protection of human rights. It was a response to the political and economic excesses of the regime of Ferdinand Marcos (1917–1989), who controlled the Philippines from 1966 to 1986; those excesses included arbitrary arrests and detentions of citizens, extrajudicial killings, disappearances, and kidnappings, as well as widespread poverty, hunger, and malnutrition. Nevertheless, human-rights abuses have continued to be a serious problem in the post-Marcos years, especially among Philippine military and paramilitary groups and the Philippine police. Reports of human-rights violations have consistently followed Philippine military operations conducted against Muslim secessionist groups and criminal gangs in Mindanao. These have included indiscriminate bombardment of numerous Muslim villages and towns, mass displacements of as many as 200,000 people from their homes, killings, and disappearances. Arbitrary arrests and torture have been regularly resorted to as a means of extracting information regarding these secessionist groups and criminal gangs.

Aside from government forces, insurgent groups such as the New People's Army (NPA) and extremist Islamic groups such as the Abu Sayyaf have also been implicated in human-rights violations. The NPA does not refrain from using children as armed combatants and noncombatants, committing extrajudicial killings, kidnappings, torture, and detentions. The Abu Sayyaf has committed acts of murder, beheadings, torture, kidnapping, and rape.

The Rights of Prisoners Although every accused is guaranteed a fair and speedy trial, the court system, with its poorly paid and overburdened judges and prosecutors, has remained susceptible to corruption and to the influence of the wealthy and powerful. With regard to the rights of prisoners against physical and psy chological maltreatment and degrading punishment, recent reports from human-rights organizations draw an alarming picture. Philippine prisons often hold three times as many prisoners as they were designed for. Sometimes women and children are put together with male prisoners, which leads to rape and physical abuse. Prisoners are forced to live in inhumane conditions not only because of the density of the prison population, but also because of the lack of sanitary facilities and maintenance. In 2000, human-rights groups reported that sanitary facilities were insufficient, that there were not enough dispensers of clean water, and that in some cases prisoners had to endure knee-high waters after strong rains. Many prisoners suffer from health problems such as tuberculosis and other diseases.

The Death Penalty In 1998, then-President Joseph Estrada (b. 1937) reintroduced the death penalty, despite strong opposition from human-rights organizations. In 2000, the death penalty was suspended in observance of the Catholic Church's Jubilee Year. Of the roughly 1,500 people due to be executed, most came from the poorest sectors of society and could not afford the services of legal counsel. There is a move in the Philippine Senate to abolish the death penalty. The House appears to be divided on the issue, but President Gloria Macapagal-Arroyo (b. 1947) and the powerful Roman Catholic Church support the Senate move to review the controversial legislation.

The Right to Vote Philippine citizens living abroad, numbering around 5–6 million in 2000, pay taxes that constitute a sizable portion of the national income but are effectively disenfranchised because the government has not yet passed a law allowing absentee voting as required by the constitution.

Looking to the Future

Since 1987 important steps have been taken to improve the human-rights situation in the Philippines. At midyear 2000, there were more than 14,000 local human-rights officers nationwide. However, the examples above illustrate that there is still a long way to go to reach the goals proudly set in the constitution. President Gloria Macapagal-Arroyo faces enormous tasks. The further improvement of the human-rights situation in the Philippines depends on the strengthening of the judicial system, the establishment of an absentee voting system, the successful fight against corruption, and the reconsideration of the death penalty. Moreover, as a signatory to the Covenant on Economic, Social, and Cultural Rights, the country needs to strengthen the economy, fight poverty, bridge the gap between the rich and the poor, and provide a peaceful solution to the problems of Muslims in Mindanao and other minority groups in the archipelago. At the very least, the Philippines needs to curb the strong political influence of the Philippine military in Philippine society.

Martina H. Timmermann

Further Reading

De Boer, Evert, Huub Jaspers, and Gerard Prickaerts. (1996) *We Did Not Learn Human Rights from the Books: The Philippines and Human Rights in the Period 1986 to 1996.* In collaboration with the Justice, Peace, and Integrity of Creation Commission (JPIC) of the Association of Major Religious Superiors in the Philippines (AMRSP). Quezon City, Philippines: Claretian Publications.

Gowing, Peter. (1988) *Understanding Islam and the Muslims in the Philippines.* Quezon City, Philippines: New Day Publishers.

Institute of Human Rights, University of the Philippines Law Center. (1999) *1999 Philippine Peace and Human Rights Review.* Quezon City, Philippines: U.P. Law Center Printery.

Philippine Alliance of Human-Rights Advocates. (2000) *Human Rights at the Close of the 20th Century.* Quezon City, Philippines: Philippine Human Rights Information Center.

Task Force Detainees of the Philippines (TFDP). (1999) *Task Force Detainees of the Philippines: A Pioneer in Human Rights. 25 Years of Struggle for People's Dignity 1974–1999.* Quezon City, Philippines: TFDP.

U.S. Department of State. (2001) *Philippines. Country Reports on Human Rights Practices, 2000.* Washington, DC: Bureau of Democracy, Human Rights, and Labor.

PHILIPPINES—POLITICAL SYSTEM

Vice President Gloria Macapagal-Arroyo was sworn in as the new president of the Philippines on 20 January 2001. Her assumption of power resulted from a peaceful demonstration of "People Power," which forced the resignation of President Joseph Estrada over charges of corruption and cronyism. This is the second time in postwar Philippine politics that a president has been replaced through populist action. The first time was in February 1986, when Corazon Aquino became president after a mass outpouring of popular support for her against then-President Ferdinand Marcos. Although formal institutions exist providing a mechanism for change of government, it appears that when these institutions impede what people perceive as good governance, they are willing to explore other avenues.

Formal Structure of Government

From the time when the Philippines declared itself a sovereign state in 1898, the nation has had four major constitutions: the 1899 constitution, which established the first republic in Asia; the 1935 constitution, which served as the basic law during the period of self-government while the Philippines was still under

American rule and after it became independent in 1946; the 1973 constitution, which allowed Ferdinand Marcos to continue to hold office as president; and the 1987 constitution, upon which the present government is based, which essentially restored institutions and processes dismantled by Marcos during his regime. The 1987 constitution describes the Philippine political system as republican and democratic. It is a unitary system in that power resides in a central authority, and whatever power lower levels of government possess has been delegated to them either by Congress or through executive orders. The formal political structure of the Philippines is patterned on that of the United States, in which the president wields executive power, Congress formulates laws, and an independent judiciary ensures that laws are uniformly upheld.

The Executive Branch As chief executive, the president has the power to execute laws. The president is assisted by a cabinet, which currently comprises twenty-three departments. Among the more important departments are Foreign Affairs, National Defense, Finance, Interior and Local Government, Justice, and Trade and Industry. Both president and vice president are elected at large for a six-year term with no possibility of reelection. This means that the president and vice president could belong to different political parties. The vice president succeeds the president in case of death, resignation, or incapacity. In some instances, the vice president is assigned a government portfolio; Vice President Teofisto Guingona is concurrently serving as secretary of foreign affairs. Controversies regarding the results of the election of president and vice president are decided by the Supreme Court.

The Legislative Branch The Philippine Congress is a bicameral body, the upper house being the Senate and the lower house being the House of Representatives. These two houses possess equal power, although budgetary bills must originate in the lower house, while treaty ratification rests exclusively with the upper house.

With only twenty-four seats, the Philippine Senate is one of the smallest upper chambers among countries with bicameral legislatures. Its members are nationally elected for six-year terms on a staggered basis, twelve senators being elected every three years. Senators may serve for a maximum of two terms or twelve consecutive years. In the May 2001 elections, thirteen Senate seats were contested. The extra seat became vacant when Senator Guingona assumed the vice presidency, which became vacant when Macapagal-Arroyo took over as president. Guingona, who was nominated by Macapagal-Arroyo to succeed her, had been Senate minority leader.

The constitution states that the House shall comprise not over 250 members, apportioned by area and population, and that party-list representatives shall not exceed 20 percent of the total members. Members are elected for three-year terms and can serve for a maximum of three consecutive terms. The House of Representatives is presided over by a speaker.

Both the Senate and the House of Representatives have working committees organized according to sectoral or functional interests. These committees conduct inquiries in aid of legislation and call upon government officials and the private sector, including concerned citizens, to appear before them. Senators and representatives can file bills on almost any subject for legislation, but the Senate is traditionally expected to file bills of national import; the House of Representatives, on the other hand, generally concentrates on constituent concerns.

Congress also functions as the sole judge regarding any election contest that pertains to its members. For the Senate, there is the Senate Electoral Tribunal, which is composed of three justices of the Supreme Court and six senators chosen on the basis of proportional representation from parties represented in the Senate; for the House, there is the House Electoral Tribunal, which is composed of three justices of the Supreme Court and six representatives chosen on the basis of proportional representation from parties of organizations registered under the party-list system.

Congress, through the Commission on Appointments, also confirms (or rejects, as the case may be) presidential appointments for heads of executive departments, ambassadors and other public ministers and consuls, officers of the armed forces from the rank of colonel or navy captain, and officials of constitutional bodies such as the Civil Service Commission, the Commission on Elections, and the Commission on Audit. The Commission on Appointments is chaired by the president of the senate, with twenty-four members, twelve of whom are senators and twelve of whom are representatives.

The Judiciary Judicial power is vested in the Supreme Court and in the lower courts. Members of the judiciary are chosen by the president from a list of nominees provided by the Judicial and Bar Council, a constitutional body composed of representatives from the executive, legislative, and judicial branches of government, the legal profession, and the private sector. Once appointed, judges have secure tenure and can serve until the age of seventy or until they become incapacitated.

Constitutional Commissions The constitution also provides for independent constitutional commissions, namely, the Civil Service Commission, the Commission on Elections, and the Commission on Audit. The Civil Service Commission administers the civil service, comprising all governmental agencies, including corporations that are owned or controlled by the government. The Commission on Elections administers all laws relating to conducting an election, plebiscite, initiative, referendum, or recall. It has jurisdiction over contested elections of officials other than members of Congress, the president, and the vice president. The Commission on Audit examines, audits, and settles all accounts pertaining to government revenues and expenditures. The members of these commissions are appointed by the president subject to confirmation by the Commission on Appointments of Congress. They have a term of seven years without reappointment.

Local Governments The lowest political unit in the Philippines is the *barangay* (village). The *barangay* is administered by a council headed by a *punong barangay* (chairperson). Several *barangays* make up a city or municipality. A *barangay* consists of at least two thousand residents for municipalities and five thousand for cities. A province consists of municipalities and sometimes what are called component cities. Other cities are run independently of the province and have their own charters. There are also subnational administrative units composed of several provinces linked by common characteristics such as ethnicity or language. At all these levels, officials are elected by their constituencies.

People Power

In addition to these formal structures, structures such as the media and nongovernmental organizations allow people active involvement in national affairs. Unique to Philippine democracy is the concept of "People Power," a mass movement that at critical times is crucial in the political process, specifically, in deciding who should be president. In the case of Corazon Aquino, the people determined that the 1986 election was neither fair nor free. They staged massive demonstrations until Ferdinand Marcos was deposed. In the case of Gloria Macapagal-Arroyo, the people determined that Joseph Estrada was inept and corrupt and unfit to be president. Again, massive demonstrations were staged until Estrada was forced from office. The jury is still out as to whether this method of changing governments will become a more frequent occurrence in Philippine politics.

Josie Hernandez de Leon

Further Reading

Chan Robles Virtual Law Library. Retrieved 22 January 2002, from: http://www.chanrobles.com/localgov.htm.

Constitution of the Republic of the Philippines. (1986) Manila, Philippines: Constitutional Commission.

PHILIPPINES–UNITED STATES RELATIONS

U.S. business connections to Spain's Asian colony *Las Islas Filipinas* ("the Philippine Islands") emerged before the Spanish-American War of 1898 swamped the Philippine Revolution. Since 1898, however, relations between the two nations have included warfare, colonial rule, and an evolving bilateral relationship between unequally matched partners.

Armed conflict (1898–1902) marked the first phase of this unequal relationship. An administratively diverse colonial period (1902–1946) ensued. This led to increasing autonomy for the Filipino elite, divided loyalties during World War II, and a brief return to U.S.-supervised self-rule after Japan's defeat. A diverse period of constitutional independence followed during the next six decades.

From the Revolutionary Malolos Republic Through World War II

The *Kataastaasan Kagalanggalang Katipunan ng mga Anak ng Bayan* ("Highest and Most Honorable Society of the Country's Offspring") movement launched the Philippine Revolution of 23 August 1896 and led the struggle for independence. That movement was overtaken by the Spanish-American War of 1898. During September 1898–January 1899, Filipino delegates in Malolos ratified President Emilio Aguinaldo's 12 June 1898 Declaration of Independence and ratified a *Constitución Política* ("Political Constitution"). The Malolos Republic is also called the First Philippine Republic.

On 4 February 1899, fighting broke out between U.S. infantry and Filipino soldiers. Against harsh domestic dissent by Americans such as Grover Cleveland and Samuel Clemens in the Anti-Imperialist League, Presidents William McKinley (served 1897–1901) and Theodore Roosevelt (served 1901–1909) dismissively characterized the war as an insurrection. And on 8 September 1902, the Civil Commission declared that peace existed in the Philippine Islands, although armed resistance continued. Asia's first constitutional republic became the United States' first Asian colony, rearranging the Asia-Pacific imperial checkerboard. U.S. tutelage pleased many in the wealthy, educated class of Filipinos. More than most of their European counterparts in Asia, U.S. colonialists integrated the social and economic elite into colonial administration. Except in

PHILIPPINE INDEPENDENCE

The following text highlights some steps agreed to by the United States and the Philippines designed to move the Philippines to United States Commonwealth status in 1936.

Section 1. The Philippines Legislature is hereby authorized to provide for the election of delegates to a constitutional convention, which shall meet in the hall of the house of representatives in the capital of the Philippine Islands, at such time as the Philippine Legislature may fix, but not later than October 1, 1934, to formulate and draft a constitution for the government of the Commonwealth of the Philippine Islands, subject to the conditions and qualifications prescribed in this Act. . . .

Section 2. (a) The constitution formulated and drafted shall be republican in form, shall contain a bill of rights, and shall, either as a part thereof or in an ordinance appended thereto, contain provisions to the effect that, pending the final and complete withdrawal of the sovereignty of the United States over the Philippine Islands:

(1) All citizens of the Philippine Islands shall owe allegiance to the United States.

(2) Every officer of the government of the Commonwealth of the Philippine Islands shall, before entering upon the discharge of his duties, take and subscribe an oath of office, declaring, among other things, that he recognizes and accepts the supreme authority of and will maintain true faith and allegiance to the United States.

(3) Absolute toleration of religious sentiment shall be secured and no inhabitant or religious organization shall be molested in person or property on account of religious belief or mode of worship.

(4) Property owned by the United States, cemeteries, churches, and parsonages or convents appurtenant thereto, and all lands, buildings, and improvements used exclusively for religious, charitable, or educational purposes shall be exempt from taxation.

(5) Trade relations between the Philippine Islands and the United States shall be upon the basis prescribed in section 6.

(6) The public debt of the Philippine Islands and its subordinate branches shall not exceed limits now or hereafter fixed by the Congress of the United States; and no loans shall be contracted in foreign countries without the approval of the President of the United States.

(7) The debts, liabilities, and obligations of the present Philippines government, its Provinces, municipalities, and instrumentalities, valid and subsisting at the time of the adoption of the constitution, shall be assumed and paid by the new government.

(8) Provision shall be made for the establishment and maintenance of an adequate system of public schools, primarily conducted in the English language.

(9) Acts affecting currency, coinage, imports, exports, and immigration shall not become law until approved by the President of the United States.

(10) Foreign affairs shall be under the direct supervision and control of the United States.

(11) All acts passed by the Legislature of the Commonwealth of the Philippine Islands shall be reported to the Congress of the United States.

(12) The Philippine Islands recognizes the right of the United States to expropriate property for public uses, to maintain military and other reservations and armed forces in the Philippines, and, under order of the President, to call into service of such armed forces all military forces organized by the Philippine government.

(13) The decisions of the courts of the Commonwealth of the Philippine Islands shall be subject to review by the Supreme Court of the United States. . . .

(14) The United States may, by Presidential proclamation, exercise the right to intervene for the preservation of the government of the Commonwealth of the Philippine Islands and for the maintenance of the government as provided in the constitution thereof, and for the protection of life, property, and individual liberty and for the discharge of government

CONTINUED ON NEXT PAGE

CONTINUED FROM PREVIOUS PAGE

obligations under and in accordance with the provisions of the constitution.

(15) The authority of the United States High Commissioner to the government of the Commonwealth of the Philippine Islands, as provided in this Act, shall be recognized.

(16) Citizens and corporations of the United States shall enjoy in the Commonwealth of the Philippine Islands all the civil rights of the citizens and corporations, respectively, thereof.

Source: Nicholas Zafra. (1967) *Philippine History through Selected Sources.* Alemar, AZ: Phoenix Publishing House, 309.

education and foreign policy, the United States yielded administrative control of the Philippines to the *ilustrados* ("enlightened ones"), as the elite were called. Key U.S. statutes were the Philippine Bill of 1 July 1902 (which provided for an elected assembly while the upper house members appointed by the U.S. President) and the Jones Law (which pledged to give the Philippines independence after a stable government was in place). The United States directly conducted all foreign relations affecting its Southeast Asian colony.

An unusual bloc of U.S. idealists, protectionists, and racists supported independence for the Philippines. Responding to the Tydings-McDuffie Act of 1934, Filipino delegates to the 1934–1935 Convention instituted a form of presidentialism for the preindependence Commonwealth and future Third Republic that was more centralized than that of the United States.

Japan was the third colonial power to rule the Philippines in less than fifty years, invading and quickly defeating the United States. The Filipino elite responded in disarray. In the face of Japan's advances, a refugee cohort fled to Washington, D.C. Remaining in the Philippines, Japan-educated José P. Laurel, Sr., led legislators elected in November 1941 and others to collaborate in the Japan-sponsored Second Republic (1943–1945). In the countryside, guerillas also were divided. Nonetheless, intense resistance from the mainly Filipino United States Armed Forces in the Far East and other guerrillas fighting under socialist and Communist leadership shocked the Japanese. Once U.S. forces had been defeated, the Japanese hoped to be greeted as leaders of a pan-Asian campaign against Caucasian colonial powers and underestimated the power of the promise of independence the United States had already made to Filipinos.

Although Japan only offered a fictive independence, the Second Republic provided useful training for future leaders of the successor Third Republic (1946–1972). For example, Laurel's minister of foreign affairs was Claro M. Recto, later a senator and seminal critic of U.S. neocolonialism. Laurel is credited with thwarting a Japanese plan to conscript all young Filipino men into the Japanese Imperial Army. At least 500,000 war deaths occurred during U.S. bombing campaigns from October 1944 to April 1945, along with considerable destruction of roads, buildings, and livestock.

The Post–World War II Era

Before constitutional independence devolved on the Philippines, it joined in cofounding the United Nations. However, the Philippines' early admission to the United Nations was partly a response to the Japan-sponsored Second Republic and part of a United States–United Kingdom trade-off with the Soviet Union's Josef Stalin (1879–1953). The Soviet leader insisted that certain satellite Soviet republics be admitted, and the Philippines was admitted in exchange. In its first decade, the Philippines' delegation to the United Nations acted in concert with the United States.

On 4 July 1946, the Philippines became an independent nation, with President Manuel Roxas (served 1946–1948) of the Commonwealth becoming the first president of the Third Republic. Roxas, ten senatorial candidates on his party's ticket, and six cabinet members had collaborated with Japan. As the United States and Soviet Union increasingly confronted one another through proxy military conflicts in Asia and elsewhere, Cold War politics dominated the first four and a half decades of Philippines-U.S. relations.

During 1946–1947, the Bell Trade Act and the Tydings Rehabilitation Act gave the United States unusual trade and investment advantages. Token World War II–related damages payments from the United States at the rate of twelve cents on the dollar were made in exchange for a plebiscite ratifying a humiliating "Parity Amendment," which treated U.S. investors the same as Filipinos.

The Bell Trade Act of 1947 and the 1955 Laurel-Langley amendments diverted the Philippines from industrialization based on import substitution. Exports to the

THE END OF THE PHILIPPINE REPUBLIC

The following oath of allegiance to the sovereignty of the United States by Philippine president Emilio Aguinaldo on 1 April 1901 marked the end of the Philippine Republic and the beginning of U.S. control, which ended in 1946.

> The effects of the war which only recently have come to my knowledge have fully convinced me that complete termination of hostilities and the establishment of lasting peace are not only desirable but absolutely essential to the welfare of the Philippines.
>
> The Filipinos were never depressed because of the weakness of their forces, nor did they feel discouraged. Courageously they launched themselves into every undertaking which called forth strength and fortitude. However, the time has come when they find themselves faced by an irresistible force which, while impeding their progress, nevertheless enlightens their minds, pointing out to them another path, the cause of peace which the majority of their countrymen have gladly embraced, confident that, under the protection of the American people, they would obtain all the liberties promised to them and which they are even now beginning to enjoy.
>
> The country clearly wants peace. Let it be so. Enough of blood, tears and desolation! These desires can not be ignored by those who are still in arms but whose firm resolve is none other than to serve the country whose will is now unmistakable.
>
> Now that I have come to know this will, I respect and obey it. And, after mature deliberation, I make it known to the world that I can not be deaf to the voice of a people longing for peace nor to the cries of thousands of families anxiously awaiting the freedom magnanimously promised to their beloved ones by the North American Nation.
>
> In recognizing and accepting the sovereignty of the United States, as I now do without any reservation, I believe I am serving you, my Country. May happiness be ever yours.

Source: Nicolas Zafra. (1967) *Philippine History through Selected Sources*. Quezon City, Philippines: Alemar-Phoenix Publishing House, 256.

United States, 59.9 percent of all exports from the Philippines in 1946, fell to a 28.5 percent share in 1975, the first year after the Laurel-Langley Agreement expired. In the same thirty-one-year period, the share of imports from the United States fell from 87.0 percent to 21.8 percent.

In early 1947, twenty-three U.S. military establishments were scattered throughout the archipelago. Under economic duress as a result of damages incurred during World War II, the Philippines endorsed a ninety-nine-year Military Bases Agreement (1947–2046). The administration of President Ferdinand Edralin Marcos (served 1965–1986) reduced this span. The 1966 Narciso Ramos-Dean Rusk executive agreement allowed an optional twelve-month phase-out period beginning as early as 1991. The bases continue to provide the United States with opportunities for ongoing and easy access to and influence with key officers in the Armed Forces of the Philippines. Earlier, the bases had facilitated U.S. participation in the multilateral colonial suppression of China's Boxer Rebellion (1900) and in the Allied intervention in the Russian Civil War of 1918–1922. Needless to say, the availability of military bases to the United States in postindependence Philippines generated resentment in other newly independent Asian countries. The Philippines supported the U.S.-led United Nations forces with four battalion combat teams in the Korean War (1950–1953) underwritten by U.S. mutual security funds. There was another downside: U.S. bases made the Philippines a target for Soviet missiles.

In seven major Asian capitals where the Philippines had no diplomats until 1955, the United States represented its former colony, and at least as late as 1964, Filipino diplomats in three Asian countries relied on U.S. embassies to transmit cables to Manila.

Claims that the Philippines was a U.S. puppet need to be case-specific. Such claims need to distinguish between views shared by ruling groups in the two countries and evidence of heavy-handed pressure that might have forced the Philippines to act in a way it might otherwise have avoided. For example, the Philippines under President Elpidio Quirino (served 1948–1953) refused to sign the San Francisco Peace Treaty, later negotiating a separate settlement with Japan. President Diosdado Macapagal (served 1961–1965) disturbed U.S. President John F. Kennedy (served 1961–1963) by reviving a longstanding claim to Sabah (North Borneo) when Malaya was about to become Malaysia. And just because the United States benefited from the military bases is not sufficient evidence to prove that presidents of the Philippines felt threatened by foreign invasion. Rather, presidents of the Philippines often exploited U.S. desires to extract concessions. This point need not be conflated with arguable assertions that Filipinos benefited from those concessions. Nonetheless, relations were close. However, Filipinos increasingly accepted the need for *isang malayang patakarang panlabas* ("independent foreign policy").

The Philippines-United States Military Assistance Agreement of 20 March 1947 established a joint U.S. military assistance group. Extended indefinitely in 1953, it directed a civil war against the *Hukbong Mapagpalaya ng Bayan* ("National Liberation Army"), a leftist agrarian social movement. The agreement made the armed forces of the Philippines dependent on the United States as a source for arms and munitions even if other foreign equipment was more reasonably priced.

The Mutual Defense Treaty (MDT) of 30 August 1951 remained in force fifty years later. Contrary to the hopes of disappointed Filipino politicians, this agreement did not elicit a U.S. commitment to defend the Philippines in conflicts over the Spratly Islands and other disputed islands in the South China Sea.

The Philippines signed the South East Asia Collective Defense Treaty ("Manila Pact"), its controversial protocol (on Laos, Cambodia, and South Vietnam), and the Pacific Charter with the United States and other allies on 8 September 1954. The Philippines participated in the follow-up 23–25 February 1955 Bangkok Conference to organize the South East Asia Treaty Organization (SEATO). A desire for greater respect from independent Asian countries left the Philippines increasingly disillusioned with SEATO (1955–1976).

Implementing memoranda from the U.S. National Security Council in 1949 and 1954, officials in the Departments of State and Defense joined with other members of the executive branch, congressional representatives, journalists, and academics in promoting regional cooperation among anticommunist Southeast Asian governments. That sustained encouragement reinforced the views of presidents and diplomats of the Philippines who cofounded the Association of South-East Asia (ASA), South East Asian Association for Regional Cooperation (SEAARC) and Association of Southeast Asian Nations (ASEAN) in the 1960s.

Having criticized President Macapagal for considering a U.S. request to send Filipino troops to the Vietnam War, newly elected President Ferdinand Edralin Marcos outmaneuvered his congressional opponents and sent an engineering battalion to Vietnam. That contingent included West Point graduate and future President Fidel V. Ramos (served 1992–1998). Later, U.S. Congressional investigations revealed that, in exchange, Marcos wangled secret concessions from U.S. President Lyndon B. Johnson (1963–1969) to help construct schoolhouses and roads throughout the Philippines. These facilitated Marcos's reelection in 1969. Naval and air bases provided key logistical support for U.S. bombing in Vietnam—a source of criticism during Marcos's two elected terms of office. Marcos's tolerance of U.S. military facilities made his martial law regime tolerable to four U.S. presidents from 1972 to 1986.

The Marcos regime collapsed in the face of a failed February 1986 "snap election," vote fraud, boycotts, a military revolt led by Ramos, and internationally televised reporting of a massive civilian protest. President Corazon Cojuangco Aquino (served 1986–1992) promised the United States Congress that the Philippines would pay foreign debts owed to U.S. banks, even though those questionable Marcos-era loans sapped the economy. Despite a long personal friendship with Marcos and open misgivings about Aquino, U.S. President Ronald W. Reagan (served 1981–1989) endorsed her role in redemocratizing the Philippines.

Aquino's arguable electoral legitimacy left her vulnerable in the face of substantive and procedural foreign affairs–related resolutions at the 1986 Constitutional Commission. Aquino needed an overwhelming "yes" vote in the February 1987 constitutional plebiscite and, therefore, resigned herself to amendments that would limit her ability to extend the Military Bases Agreement. During an attempted 1989 coup d'état against Aquino, her indebtedness to the United States was highlighted when fighter jets from U.S. bases buzzed rebel positions. Later, U.S. naval and air facilities provided key logistical support for U.S. operations in the Persian Gulf War. Further, the presence of nuclear weapons—neither admitted nor denied by the United States—posed concomitant dangers of accidental explosion and other types of radiation and toxic-waste clean-up hazards. To the chagrin of the GABRIELA federation of women's organizations, antinuclear groups, the National Democratic Front, and conservative Filipino nationalists, U.S. bases encouraged local prostitution under the euphemistic guise of rest and recreation. Supported by the Anti-Bases Movement in the twilight of the Cold War, the Senate rebuffed Aquino, rejecting an extension of the Military

Bases Agreement on 16 September 1991. This led to a phase-out of U.S. military presence in the Philippines by December 1992.

By the early 1990s, new annual foreign direct investment from South Korea, Japan, Singapore, and Taiwan exceeded that from the United States. Following the 1992 shutdown of the naval facility at Subic Bay and the advent of the North American Free Trade Agreement, new political, economic, and cultural pressures shaped relations between Washington and Manila.

In the late 1990s, unfinished business from that era included unpaid World War II veterans benefits, paternity suits initiated in U.S. federal district courts on behalf of Amerasian children, and toxic-waste cleanup issues at former military base sites.

During the twentieth century, Filipinos became intimately familiar with American popular culture. But continuing eastward across the Pacific, the culture of the Filipino diaspora (immigrants and their descendants) changed the United States. In the 1990s, voters twice elected Benjamin J. Cayetano, son of an immigrant Filipino waiter, as governor of Hawaii. By 1992, Philippine languages collectively had become the second-fastest-growing second-language group spoken in homes throughout the United States. And by June 2001, Filipinos in the United States numbered over 2 million.

Summary and Prospects

Colonialism and Cold War priorities dominated Philippines-U.S. relations from the late nineteenth century until the early 1990s. Despite its claims of enlightened rule, the United States took advantage of the unequal relationship. Weakened by World War II, the Philippines' constitutional independence was attenuated for over a decade by neocolonial political, military, and economic measures. Other Asian countries often felt that the Philippines toed the U.S. line too closely, particularly in its inability to pursue alternatives other than those promoted by the United States. The U.S. military occupied or traveled through the archipelago's land, waters, and airspace from 1898 to 1992, except for thirty months during World War II, but the relationship between the United States and Philippines also made possible the migration of large numbers of Filipinos into the United States.

It was expected that the period after 1992 would open a new chapter in bilateral relations. However, a 1998 Philippines-U.S. Visiting Forces Agreement (VFA) allowed U.S. forces to return to the Philippines, albeit not permanently. In the twenty-first century, the United States remains the most important bilateral partner of the Philippines but is no longer as overwhelmingly dominant as it once was. On the occasion of the fiftieth anniversary of the U.S.-Philippines Mutual Defense Treaty in 2001, Philippines president Gloria Macapagal-Arroyo and U.S. president George W. Bush renewed their commitment to the United States-Philippines alliance. Whether or not this new century will result in a more egalitarian relationship between the United States and the Philippines remains to be seen.

Both the VFA and the MDT served as the rationale for the presence in 2002 of U.S. troops in the southern Philippines, where they engaged in a military operation together with the Philippines' armed forces to flush out elements of the Abu Sayyaf, a terrorist organization in Muslim Mindinao. While the Cold War has ended, U.S. priorities still frame U.S.-Philippines relations. As of 2002, that priority has become the war on terrorism.

Vincent Kelly Pollard

Further Reading

Castro, Pacifico A.,ed. (1983) *Agreements on U.S. Military Facilities in Philippine Military Bases, 1947–1982*. Bilateral Reference Series, no. 7. Manila, Philippines: Foreign Service Institute.

Cullather, Nick. (1994) *Illusions of Influence: The Political Economy of United States-Philippines Relations, 1942–1960*. Stanford, CA: Stanford University Press.

Golay, Frank Hindman. (1998) *Face of Empire: United States-Philippine Relations*. University of Wisconsin-Madison Center for Southeast Asian Studies Monograph no. 14. Quezon City, Philippines: Ateneo de Manila University Press.

Hess, Gary R. (1987) *The United States' Emergence as a Southeast Asian Power, 1941–1950*. New York: Columbia University Press.

Pollard, Vincent Kelly. (1998) "Electioneering, Constitution Writing and Foreign Policy Making During Early Redemocratization." *Philippine Journal of Political Science*, combined issues 39–42: 73–125.

———. (1995) "Two Stages in American Promotion of Asian Regionalism: United States-Southeast Asia-Japan Relations, 1945–1970." *Bulletin of Asian Studies* 5: 89–97.

Salonga, Jovito R. (1994) *The Senate That Said No: A Four-Year Record of the First Post-EDSA Senate*. Quezon City, Philippines: University of the Philippines Press.

Schirmer, Daniel B., and Stephen Rosskamm Shalom, eds. (1987) *The Philippines Reader: A History of Colonialism, Neocolonialism, Dictatorship, and Resistance*. Boston: South End Press

Development along the Tonle Sap River in 1991. (MICHAEL S. YAMASHITA/CORBIS)

Wurfel, David. (1990) "Philippine Foreign Policy." In *The Political Economy of Foreign Policy in Southeast Asia*, edited by David Wurfel and Bruce Burton. Basingstoke, UK: Macmillan, 146–176.

PHNOM PENH (1998 est. pop. 862,000). Phnom Penh is the capital and largest city in Cambodia. It originally was called Chadomukh (Four Faces) and later was renamed Phnom Penh (Phnom means hill, on which an wealthy woman, named Penh, had a Buddhist sanctuary built). Though the founding dates back to 1434, the city's real development started only after King Norodom of Cambodia left his residence in Udon in 1866 to set up a new capital. King Norodom signed a protectorate treaty with France and during the next fifty years the population of the city increased to about seventy thousand inhabitants. The original, one-street settlement along the Tonle Sap River expanded on a square layout. Swampy areas were gradually filled in, and in 1914 a grid scheme of streets west of old Phnom Penh formed the new city. In the following years, this urban terrain was enlarged farther west and northwest. With the modernization came drinking water, a sewage system, electrical power plants, and facilities for a large river port. From 1935 onward, a central market and the railway station were opened and a technical college and museums were built and enlarged. In 1953, the year of the official independence of Cambodia, Phnom Penh had about 350,000 inhabitants.

Even if the traditional royal, Buddhist, and commercial foci were still concentrated in the heart of the city, the colonial influence was clearly reflected in the newly allocated functions associated with French power, and in the "quartiers" that originated from the astute use of Western town planning concepts. With its large tree-lined boulevards and public gardens, Phnom Penh had the flair of a French provincial city with a tropical climate and a multiethnic population.

During the Vietnam War, South Vietnamese troops and U.S. bombers invaded Cambodia, and more than 750,000 refugees settled in Phnom Penh. When the Communist Khmer Rouge took control of Cambodia in 1975, all city dwellers were forced to move into the countryside. Phnom Penh remained a ghost town for nearly four years. After the Vietnamese intervention in 1979, a rapid repopulation took place, as not only former inhabitants but also rural people flooded in, drawn by the possibility of better income than could be made in the provinces. Today Phnom Penh still suffers from its difficult past, but as the home of nearly a million inhabitants and all central state offices and functions, including the impressive royal palace, the parliament, and the national museum, as well as schools through university level, the international airport, and textile and agricultural industries, it once again is the undisputed capital and prime city of Cambodia.

G. R. Zimmermann

Further Reading

Igout, Michel. (1993) *Phnom Penh: Then and Now*. Bangkok, Thailand: White Lotus.

Someth Uk. (1975) *Phnom Penh et son évolution urbaine*. Paris: Planification, Habitat, Information.

Zimmermann, Gerd R. (1997) *Phnom Penh as the "Primate City" of Cambodia and Its Rival since 1979*. ASIEN 63: 56–70. Hamburg, Germany: Universitat Braunschweig.

PHNOM PENH EVACUATION On 17 April 1975 the five-year civil war between Cambodia's ruling regime and a Communist insurgency finally ended. To many commentators, the Communist victory had been inevitable. Disciplined and ruthless, the Communists (popularly known as the Khmer Rouge, or Red Khmer) had quickly gained the ascendancy against the army of the corruption-riddled Khmer Republic when the civil war began in 1970. While the Republican cause was prolonged by the military support of the United States, the victorious march of Communist troops into Phnom Penh in April 1975 surprised few observers. Over the week following their victory, before the new regime closed it doors and veiled Cambodia in a shroud of secrecy, the world was given a glimpse of the terror that Cambodia's new rulers would unleash on the unsuspecting Cambodian people.

The decision to evacuate Phnom Penh had been made by the Central Committee of the Communist Party in February 1975. When the Communist troops finally arrived in the city, many were still unaware of the decision. While troops from the Communists' southwest and northern zones appeared to be aware of the order to evacuate the city, many troops from the east had no idea of the plans of their superiors. Many of the regime's survivors who lived in Phnom Penh at the time have recalled that their first contact with the Communist soldiers involved no calls for evacuation. Others were immediately ordered, often at gunpoint, to leave the city. Over the next few days, the evacuation order became clear. The entire population of Phnom Penh, swelled to overflowing because of the influx of internally displaced persons during the fighting, was ordered to move to the countryside. There were to be no exceptions—the elderly, women with babies, even hospital patients, were forced to join the exodus.

Historians and analysts have long speculated about the reasons behind the evacuation. It has been argued that the evacuation of the cities was ordered as a solution to a looming food crisis, to prevent a possible epidemic of disease, or to forestall and negate any possible resistance. It seems clear, however, that the rationale for ordering the evacuation was, simply, that it suited the ideological agenda of Cambodia's new rulers. Cities were representations of capital, Western ideas and thinking, Western institutions, the exploitation of the poor, and corruption. In a society that was to be built upon the notion of absolute equality, there remained little room for highly populated urban centers.

David M. Ayres

See also: **Khmer Rouge; Killing Fields**

Further Reading

Becker, Elizabeth. (1998) *When the War Was Over: Cambodia and the Khmer Rouge Revolution*. New York: Public Affairs.

Chandler, David. (1991) *The Tragedy of Cambodian History: Politics, War, and Revolution since 1945*. Bangkok, Thailand: Silkworm Press.

Kiernan, Ben. (1996) *The Pol Pot Regime: Race, Power, and Genocide in Cambodia under the Khmer Rouge, 1975–1979*. New Haven, CT: Yale University Press.

Ponchaud, Francois. (1978) *Cambodia: Year Zero*. Trans. by N. Amphoux. London: Allen Lane.

PHRA PATHOM CHEDI The largest and probably earliest Buddhist monument of Thailand, situated about 56 kilometers southwest of Bangkok in the town of Nakhon Pathom, formerly Nakhon Chaisri. The name of the monument, translated as "The First Holy Stupa," originates from Sanskrit *(brah pathama cetiya)*. Nakhon Pathom is one of the oldest settlements of Thailand, dating back to around 150 BCE, as proved by the stone "wheels of law" *(dharma cakra)* and "Buddha's footprints" found at the *chedi*. The first original structure that is now inside the *chedi* was 39 meters high and built in the style of the great stupa at Sanchi under the leadership of Indian missionary monks. The indigenous Mon population was converted to Buddhism as is proved by inscriptions in archaic Mon language. The *chedi* is considered sacred since it is said to contain relics of the Gautama Buddha. The monument was built over and restored several times, and the present monument, 120 meters in height, is the 1853 realization of King Mongkut, Rama IV (1851–1868).

The monument is part of a Buddhist monastery, which is a center of Dhamma or dharma related activities in Thailand. Phra Pathom Chedi becomes a place of pilgrimage every year in November, when festive ceremonies are carried out to pay homage to the *chedi* and to the Buddha and his teachings.

Jana Raendchen

Further Reading

Coedès, George. (1996) *The Indianized States of Southeast Asia*, 3d ed., edited by Walter F. Vella. Honolulu, HI: University of Hawaii Press.

Namphawan, K. (1999) "Phra Pathom Chedi." In *Saranukrom Watthanatham Thai—Phak Klang*. Vol. 9. Bangkok, Thailand: Munithi Saranukrom Watthanatham Thai, 4062–4065.

Pierre, D. (1959) *L'archéologie Mône de Dvaravati*. Paris: École Francaise d'Extrême-Orient.

PHUKET (2002 pop 246,000). The granite island of Phuket is the largest island in the nation of Thailand. It is located in southwest Thailand off the western Malay Peninsula in the Andaman Sea. The island was known as Ujong Salang (Cape Salang) to the Malays and was called Junkceylon by Europeans, possibly a corruption of Ptolemy's name for a cape passed on the way to the Malay Peninusula, "Jang Si Lang." Along with Penang (Malaysia) and Medan (Indonesia), Phuket is part of the northern growth triangle.

The name also refers to the seaport town of Phuket, located at the southern end of this island, as well as to its provincial name. It is a principal port for the nation and the provincial capital. The port typically draws shipping traffic from the Indian Ocean.

Phuket's earliest inhabitants may have been the Chao Lam, or "sea gypsies," a short-statured people who traveled the coastal regions by boat. Indian immigrants settled all along its coast in the fourth century CE, flourishing there through the thirteenth century, when Tai rule was first extended to Phuket. European trade in the area began in the seventeenth century. The Burmese, who had destroyed the Tai kingdom of Ayutthaya in 1769, turned their attention to Phuket in 1785 but were successfully repulsed. From then on, Phuket was largely in Siam's sphere of influence, although Europeans retained trading concessions on the island. Phuket did not become a province of Thailand until 1933.

The Sarasin Bridge connects the island to the mainland. Most residents are Thai. Other ethnic groups represented on the island include Muslim Malays; Chao Lam (people of the sea); Chinese; expatriates from Australia, New Zealand, and Canada; and residents of Indian and Arabic descent.

The Chinese mined tin on Phuket for centuries. Demand for the mineral is in decline, and with concerns about the adverse impact of mining on aquatic life such as coral reefs, local officials are attempting to convert the mining sites. These sites are reportedly being transformed to provide more tourist facilities such as resort hotels and golf courses.

Other commerce on Phuket includes trade in rubber and charcoal; there is also fishing and agriculture. Major crops include coconuts, pineapples, bananas, cashews, and rice. Although farming is important to the local economy, land is being taken out of production and developed to accommodate continued growth.

In the 1980s, improvements were made throughout the city so that Phuket could be internationally marketed as a tourist destination. Commercial attractions including shops for arts and crafts, restaurants, and the like have been added. Phuket is known as the Pearl of the South for its natural attractions such as Phra Taew National Park and its waterscapes that entice vacationing scuba divers. The island is also considered one of the world's top beach resorts.

Linda Dailey Paulson

Further Reading

Smyth, H. Warington. ([1898] 2001) *Five Years in Siam (1891–1896)*. Vol. 1: *The Menam Valley, Lao States, Ratburi, Tenasserim, and Phuket*. Reprint. Bangkok, Thailand: White Lotus Press.

Thailand Information Center. (2001) "The Island of Phuket." Retrieved 13 March 2002, from: http://mitglied.lycos.de/phi/index-history.phukete.html.

PHUMISAK, CHIT (1930–1966), Thai historian and philologist. Chit Phumisak, a well-known scholarly writer and intellectual, analyzed Thai society and history from a Marxist perspective, and his ideas became a basis for Marxism-oriented ideological changes of the Communist Party of Thailand (CPT) after 1976, when state anticommunist propaganda reached a climax under the military regime of Thanin Kraivichian.

Chit Phumisak was born on 25 September 1930 in Prachinburi Province into the family of an excise official. He was forced to change his given name, Somchit, to Chit (to indicate male gender clearly) when Field Marshal Phibul Songkram became prime minister for a second time in 1948.

While still a student of philology at Chulalongkorn University in Bangkok (1950–1956), Phumisak worked as literary critic, essayist, and poet for newspapers and journals such as *Thai Mai*, *Phim Thai*, and *San Seri*. After graduating, he became a reader at Pethburi Teacher's College. The essentially antinationalist, progressive, Marxism–oriented works that he wrote until 1957, especially his *Chomnaa sakdinaa Thai* (The Face of Thai Feudalism), were interpreted by the Sarit Thanarat regime as direct threats against the Thai state.

For criticizing the military government, Phumisak was imprisoned from 1958 to 1964, together with many other intellectuals. During that time he translated Maxim Gorki's *Mother* and Premchand's *Godana* into Thai, and he wrote one of his most important works, *Khwaampenmaa khoong kham Sayaam, Thai, Lao lae Khoom* (The Origins of the Terms Siam, Thai, Lao and Khom), which could be published only after his death.

After his release from prison, Phumisak joined the CPT and went to northeast Thailand (Isan) to participate in the Communist insurgency. He died in an armed struggle in Sakhon Nakhon Province on 5 May 1966.

Chit Phumisak's works, including the poems and songs he had written under the pseudonyms Kawi Kanmuang and Kawi Srisayam, were reissued in high numbers after the 14 October 1973 peaceful student uprising. After 1976 Phumisak became an iconic figure for the Marxist wing of the CPT, which was formed mainly by Thai intellectuals.

Jana Raendchen

Further Reading

Muanmil, Prathip. (1999) *100 nakpraphan Thai* (100 Thai Writers). Bangkok, Thailand: Chomromdek.

Phumisak, Chit. (1957) *Chomnaa sakdinaa Thai* (The Face of Thai Feudalism). Bangkok, Thailand: Nitisart.

———. (1997) *Khwaampenmaa khoong kham Sayaam, Thai, Lao lae Khoom* (The Origins of the Terms Siam, Thai, Lao, and Khom). 4th ed. Bangkok, Thailand: Saysong Suksit.

———. (1957) *Silapa phuea chiiwit, silapa phuea prachachon* (Art for Life, Art for the People). Bangkok, Thailand: Nitisart.

Swastisri, Suchart, ed. (1974) *Chit Phumisak: Nak rop khoong khon run mai* (Chit Phumisak: Fighter of a New Generation). Bangkok, Thailand: Sangkhomsart Parithat.

PHYA THAKSIN (reigned c. 1767–1782), liberator of Siam. After the Burmese devastation of Ayutthaya in April 1767, it was the half-Chinese General Phya Taksin, the governor of Tak province and later king of Siam (present-day Thailand), who restored the pride of Siam. He, along with five hundred soldiers, left the doomed capital and reached the safe sanctuary of the eastern shore of the Gulf of Siam. With an expanded army of five thousand, he established himself as king of Siam in the town of Thonburi, which became the new capital. The Chinese from his paternal home, Chaozhu, supplied the labor force and building material he used to build his new capital.

Taksin endeavored to rally the Siamese people. He brought central and border provinces under Thonburi. His army repelled Burmese attacks in 1773 and 1776. Vietnamese influence over Cambodia diminished temporarily and was replaced by Siamese influence over the country after Taksin installed his puppet Ang Nhon as ruler of Cambodia in 1771. The kingdom of Luang Prabang became an ally to Siam in 1774, throwing off the Burmese domination established with the help of the kingdom of Vientiane in 1771. In turn Vientiane, whose ruler defied Taksin by maintaining an alliance with Siam's enemy Burma, was occupied by Siam in 1778. The famous Emerald Buddha, in Vientiane's possession since 1564, was brought to Bangkok at that time.

A patron of arts and literature, Taksin was also a devout Buddhist. Toward the end of his life he claimed mystical powers and sainthood and was accused of insanity. The hostility of Buddhist monks toward Taksin's demand of obeisance led to his downfall and imprisonment. His bravery as the liberator of Thailand earned him the epithet "the Great."

Patit Paban Mishra

Further Reading

Hall, D. G. E. (1968) *A History of South-East Asia.* London: Macmillan.

Tarling, Nicholas, ed. (1992) *The Cambridge History of Southeast Asia.* Vol. 1. Cambridge, U.K.: Cambridge University Press.

PIBUL SONGGRAM (1897–1964), prime minister of Thailand. Born Plaek Khittasangkha, Pibul Songgram received French military training and rose from humble origins to become a second-echelon leader of the military coup that established a constitutional monarchy in 1932. In 1933, he participated in the ouster of Prime Minister Phya Manopakam and was involved in suppressing Prince Boworadet's royalist, antigovernment rebellion. He became minister of defense in 1934 and prime minister in 1938. In 1939, as part of his modernity platform, he changed the name of the country from Siam to Thailand (later naming himself field marshal). Pibul held the post of prime minister longer than any other leader in Thailand.

In June 1940, after France fell to Nazi Germany, Pibul aligned Thailand with Japan to avoid a destructive takeover by Japan and to regain territory lost to French colonialism. In 1944 he resigned as prime minister to make way for a noncollaborationist government to deal with the victorious Allied powers. Although he was arrested for war crimes by his successor, Kowit Aphaiwong, charges were later dropped.

In 1947, Pibul led a coup against Kowit, and in 1948 he again became prime minister. With the military rent with factions, he survived attempted coups in 1949 and 1951. In 1952, after new elections under a revised constitution that assigned more than one hundred parliamentary seats to unelected military officers, he appointed a cabinet that favored one of the factions; in 1957 that faction won parliamentary elections amid charges of vote rigging. In 1958, Pibul's government was toppled in a military coup led by Field Marshal Sarit Thanarat, the leader of the other faction. Pibul then fled into exile and died in Japan.

Michael Haas

Further Reading

Ray, Jayanta Kumar. (1972) *Portraits of Thai Politics*. Tokyo: Orient Longman.

PIG In the wild, pigs (also called hogs or swine) are native to most regions of the earth except Australasia and Antarctica. The pig belongs to the family of Suidae, nonruminant ungulates, and are hoofed herbivorous mammals. They prefer boggy, wooded country. Families with up to twelve piglets scavenge together, using their sensitive snouts to root up food.

The commonest species of pig, *Sus scrofa*, was native to Europe, North Africa, and the western half of Asia. This species became one of the earliest domesticates and today is found wherever farmers live, except in Islamic countries.

Easily tamed, wild boars and sows were domesticated in western Asia during the Neolithic period, in the seventh millennium BCE. Pigs are the only farm animals that eat whatever humans do; they can also scavenge a wide variety of foods. Not only do they give valuable meat and fat and reproduce easily, but their bristles and manure are valuable. Their milk is not used.

The Chinese pig was also domesticated in the Neolithic period, either from *S. leucomystax*, a species of white-whiskered swine native to China, Taiwan, and Japan, or from the East Indian wild boar *(S. vittatus)*. Chinese domestic stock was introduced to Europe and interbred with the European pig.

Pork is widely esteemed in the cuisine of most countries, especially in East Asia, except among Jews, Sikhs, and Muslims, groups that consider its flesh defiling. Buddhists and upper-caste Hindus also do not eat pork or any kind of flesh.

Paul Hockings

PILGRIMAGE—SOUTH ASIA Pilgrimage is the practice of journeying to sites where religious powers, knowledge, or experiences are deemed especially accessible. Such journeys are increasingly popular throughout South Asia, facilitated by ever-improving transportation. Every major South Asian religious tradition has its sacred geography, chartered in myth, oral traditions, and history. Movement over actual kilometers, whether five or five hundred, is critical to pilgrimage, for what is important is not just visiting a sacred place but leaving home. At the level of folk religion or popular practice and belief, religious journeys for South Asian Hindus, Buddhists, Jains, Muslims, and Sikhs have much in common. Christians in the subcontinent also have important pilgrimage traditions, but they are not covered in this article. Sacred places offer travelers physically and aesthetically potent experiences, from climbing hills to partaking of blessed meals or hearing devotional readings and musical performances.

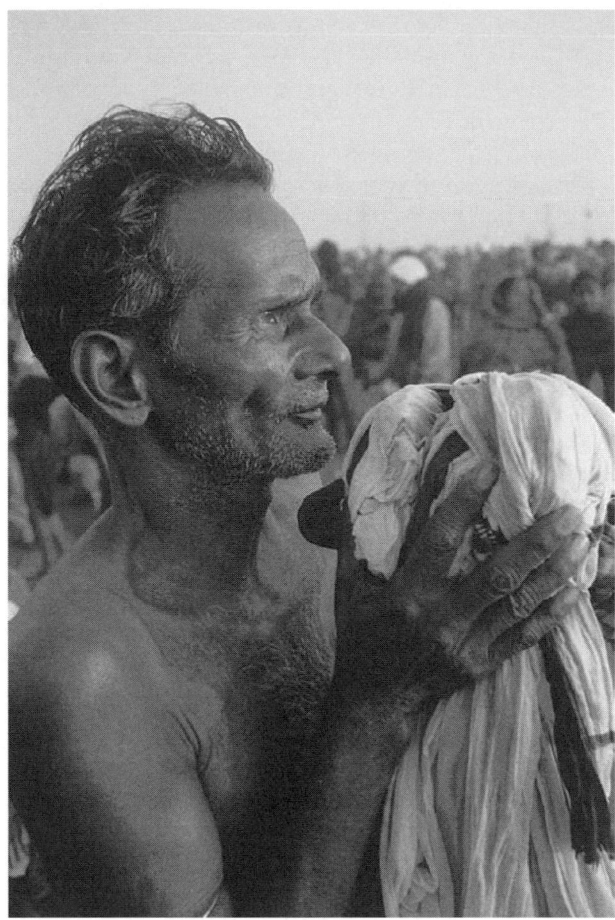

A pilgrim prepares to bathe in the sacred waters of the Hooghly River at Sagar, India. (EYE UBIQUITOUS/CORBIS)

Power originating in one sacred place may be transferred to another site. For example, the Buddha is said to have attained enlightenment under a particular tree in northeastern India. According to legend, over two thousand years ago a branch from this tree was miraculously established at the Buddhist temple complex of Anuradhapura, in Sri Lanka, and its worship has continued through the centuries. In Nepal, the land of the Buddha's birth, many replicas of major Indian temples offer Nepalese Buddhist pilgrims blessings equal to those available in the original sites. Similar collapses of space are common in Hindu ideas about sacred centers.

CAPE COMORIN

Cape Comorin (or Kanyakumari) is a headland marking the southernmost point of the Indian Peninsula, and a place highly sacred to Hindus as a pilgrimage site where "three seas" meet, or where the Arabian Sea and the Bay of Bengal merge with the Indian Ocean. It is also the only place in India where the sun rises in the sea and sets in the sea. The headland is a circular low sandy point, though the Western Ghats terminate only two kilometers away.

There is a town here (population 25,000 in 2001) and an important temple. The place is famed in Hindu mythology and is especially associated with Kumari or Kanniyammal, the "virgin goddess." In front of her temple is a rocky pool where pilgrims bathe. There are also popular memorials to Swami Vivekananda and Mohandas K. Gandhi.

Paul Hockings

Hindu Pilgrimage

The Hindu practice of pilgrimage is rooted in ancient scriptural charters. According to textual scholars, the earliest reference to Hindu pilgrimage is in the Rig Veda (c. 1000 BCE), in which the "wanderer" is praised. Numerous later texts, including the epic *Mahabharata* (c. 300 BCE) and several of the mythological Puranas (c. 300–750 CE) elaborate on the capacities of particular sacred sites to grant boons, including health, wealth, progeny, and deliverance after death. Texts enjoin Hindu pilgrims to perform rites on behalf of ancestors and recently deceased kin. Sanskrit sources as well as devotional literature in regional vernacular languages praise certain places and their miraculous capacities.

The Sanskrit and Hindi word for a pilgrimage center is *tirtha*, literally a river ford or crossing place. The concept of a ford is associated with pilgrimage centers not simply because many are on riverbanks but because they are metaphorically places for transition, either to the other side of particular worldly troubles or beyond the endless cycle of birth and death.

The institution of pilgrimage is an integrating force among the linguistically and culturally diverse Hindu peoples of the Indian subcontinent. The four places *(car dham)* are a widely recognized set of sacred centers in the four cardinal directions: Kedarnath in the north, Dvarka in the west, Puri in the east, and Rameswaram in the south. A pilgrim who visits all four circumambulates India. Other important Hindu pilgrimage centers include Haridwar, Gaya, Prayag, Varanasi, and Vrindavan in northern India and Cidambaram, Madurai, Sabari Malai, and Tirupati in southern India. Most pilgrimage centers hold periodic religious fairs called *melas* to mark auspicious astrological moments or important anniversaries.

Buddhist and Jain Pilgrimage

During the period 566–486 BCE, two new schools of religious teachings, Buddhism and Jainism, emerged in India. Each was founded by an individual teacher, and in each, pilgrimage centers commemorate the life of the founder, as well as later important leaders and holy persons. Buddhist and Jain pilgrimage centers exist throughout India, and major Buddhist shrines flourish in Nepal and Sri Lanka. Whereas many Buddhist shrines developed around putative relics of the Buddha's body, Jains have no reverence for physical remains.

The best-known Buddhist pilgrimage centers in India are associated with important events in the Buddha's life. Two of these are Bodh Gaya in Bihar, northeast India, where the Buddha is said to have achieved enlightenment under the *bodhi* (enlightenment) tree, and Sarnath in Uttar Pradesh, India, where he preached his first sermon. Notably both sites are on the outskirts of more ancient Hindu places of pilgrimage, Gaya and Varanasi. Distinctive to Jain shrines are the somewhat abstract stone images, often beautifully sculpted, of *tirthankaras* (Jain teachers).

Islamic Shrines

A strong Islamic presence on the Indian subcontinent dates back to the eighth century CE. In South Asia as elsewhere, Muslims have for centuries practiced shrine pilgrimage known as *ziyarat* or visiting. Muslim shrines usually develop around saints' tombs. However, the custom of visiting a saint begins during

THE MYSTICAL PULL OF THE GANGES

"I think I now behold the group we formed [on the banks of the Hugly]—the white dresses of the ladies, making them to look like spirits walking in a garden, and honest Augustus, with his *solah topee*, looking down on his shoes, and saying agreeable things: the shadows of evening closing around us; the huge fox bats sailing heavily overhead; the river spreading its broad surface before us; the boats moving across it afar, their oars dabbling as it were in quicksilver; the mists rising slowly from neighbouring groves, and then the stilly tranquil hour, broken only by the plash of passing oars, the sound of a distant gong, or the far-off music of a marriage ceremony, or the hum and drumming of the bazaar—those drowsy sounds of an Indian eve. It was a bit of still life to be ever remembered."

Source: Francis J. Bellew. (1843) *Memoirs of a Griffin* or a *Cadet's First Year in India*, as quoted in *The Sahibs* (1948), edited by Hilton Brown. London: William Hodge & Co., 125.

the saint's lifetime, when a particular holy person gains a reputation for teaching, healing, and miracles. The more celebrated Islamic shrines develop into large complexes called *dargahs* (palaces or royal courts).

Tombs of the Chishti Sufi saints, who flourished during the thirteenth and fourteenth centuries in India, stand out as places of pan-Islamic pilgrimage significance. The *dargah* of Muʿinuddin Chishti in Ajmer, Rajasthan, India, where the Mughal emperor Akbar (1542–1605) made annual pilgrimages, is generally accepted as the most important and is revered by Hindus as well as Muslims. Muslim shrines celebrate annual festivals known as *'urs*, which are similar to Hindu *melas*.

Sikh Shrines

The founder of the Sikh religion, Guru Nanak (1469–1539), spoke against pilgrimage, calling it a superficial practice. Nonetheless, a strong tradition of visiting places sacred to their own history exists among Sikhs. Sikh shrines are often associated with the ten Sikh gurus' lives and travels. They are called *gurdvaras* (the dwelling places of the gurus). Most celebrated is the Darbar Sahib (reverenced court), known in English as the Golden Temple, in Amritsar, Punjab, India. Among their unique features, the *gurdvaras* enshrine Sikhism's sacred book, the Guru Granth Sahib, and house the *langar* or pilgrims' kitchen, where the needy receive free food.

Ann Grodzins Gold

Further Reading

Aitken, Molly Emma, ed. (1995) *Meeting the Buddha: On Pilgrimage in Buddhist India*. New York: Riverhead Books.

Bhardwaj, Surinder Mohan. (1973) *Hindu Places of Pilgrimage in India: A Study in Cultural Geography*. Berkeley and Los Angeles: University of California Press.

Buitenen, J. A. B. van, trans. and ed. (1976) "The Tour of the Sacred Fords." In *The Mahabharata*. Vol. 2. Chicago: University of Chicago Press, 366–455.

Dundas, Paul. (1992) "Pilgrimage and Holy Places." In *The Jains*. New York: Routledge, 187–194.

McLeod, Hew. (1997) "The Principal Gurdwaras." In *Sikhism*. New York: Penguin Books, 153–162.

Troll, Christian W., ed. (1989) *Muslim Shrines in India*. Delhi: Oxford University Press.

PILIPINO. See **Philippine Languages.**

PINGYAO, ANCIENT CITY OF UNESCO listed China's ancient city of Pingyao, located in Shanxi Province, as a site on its World Heritage List in 1997. Pingyao dates to the Western Zhou dynasty (1045–771 BCE) and is one of China's premier examples of an ancient city. The impressive city wall, measuring 6,163 meters and renovated in 1370, still encloses streets, shops, temples, government offices, and residences from the Ming (1368–1644) and Qing (1644–1912) dynasties. Mingqing Street, the commercial center of old Pingyao, is lined with well-preserved stores from the two dynasties. Cultural relics in the area date as far back as the Tang (618–907 CE) and Song (960–1279) dynasties. The Shuanglin Temple, first built in 571, contains more than 2,000 colored clay figurines representing the craftsmanship of ancient China. In addition to its cultural importance, Pingyao also holds commercial distinction. Pingyao merchants often conducted their business in other provinces, while maintaining their Pingyao identity. The mobility and native ties of the merchants contributed to their developing China's first remittance firms, or banks, turning Pingyao into a financial center in the nineteenth century. Wealthy merchants, in turn, built magnificent residences, adding to the city's architectural and cultural wealth.

Jennifer Rudolph

Further Reading

Geng Yanbo, ed. (1999) *Wang Kia Da Yuan* (The Wang Family Compound). Taiyuan, Shanxi Province, China: Shanxi Jingji Publishing House.

Li Peiyi, ed. (2000) *Pingyao Gucheng* (The Old Town of Pingyao). Beijing: The Great Wall Publishing House.

Zhang Chengde, and Fan Duixiang, eds. (1997) *Pu Shang Zhai Yuan—Qiao Jia* (Residential Courtyards of Shanxi Merchants—The Qiao Family Compound). Taiyuan, China: Shanxi Renmin Publishing House.

PIRACY IN SOUTHEAST ASIA Piracy has been a feature of maritime Southeast Asia since it was first navigated. In 414 CE, a Chinese traveler, Fah Hsien, noted the perils of piracy in Southeast Asia (Miller 1970: 14). In ancient times, Southeast Asian kingdoms commonly used piratical violence to compete with one another. The trading empire of Srivijaya (established around 682 CE) was destroyed in this way by the Javanese kingdom Majapahit.

Piracy was a disruptive factor in the trading routes to India and China and came to be a major nuisance to the colonial powers on their arrival in the region. In earlier colonial times many acts of piracy enjoyed official sanction from sultans, princes, and aristocrats of the region. Some small kingdoms in Southeast Asia used pirates to plunder ships and coastal villages as a source of illegal revenue. Determining the identity of the pirates was difficult as established villages could resort to piracy to supplement income from other commercial activities such as fishing, farming, or trading.

From the point of view of the peoples of Southeast Asia, growing European incursions into their seas and lands represented subjugation, thus what constituted piracy could be said to be relative. The vessels of colonial nations were also known to engage in acts of piracy against each other and indigenous boats. Before the overall problem was brought under control in the latter half of the nineteenth century, local pirate fleets, sometimes consisting of thousands of men, could be used to devastating effect against colonial shipping. Using small ships *(perahu)* in hit-and-run raids, the pirates could easily hide in the myriad of bays, rivers, mangrove swamps, and forests. The problem areas were the Malay Peninsula, the Sekrang and Sarebus Rivers of Borneo, the Sulu Islands, and Mindanao. These pirates were feared for their ruthlessness (those from the South Philippines were infamous for their love of hand-to-hand combat) and accounts exist of their barbarity, which were taken from the few survivors. Many captives, whether from Europe or Southeast Asia, if not tortured and killed, were sold into slavery.

But considerable opposition was to come from the well-armed vessels of the colonial powers. The British, Dutch, and Spanish navies were only able to break the pirate threat by seeking out their inland bases. The British Royal Navy decided to destroy piracy on the high seas and put considerable effort into locating and eliminating pirates in many places around the world—even sailing up rivers or traveling deep inland. The advent of the steam warship made pursuit far easier regardless of wind direction, which was a considerable advantage over the small sailing craft of the Southeast Asian pirates. However, piracy has never disappeared from Southeast Asia. It enjoyed a revival in the chaotic aftermath of World War II but was under relative control again within the next few decades. Even so, the region remains the most dangerous area for piracy. Of 1,243 cases of reported piracy worldwide in 1998 (and there are many unreported cases), nearly half—579—occurred in Southeast Asia.

Anthony L. Smith

Further Reading

Miller, Harry. (1970) *Pirates of the Far East*. London: Robert Hale & Company.

Renwick, Neil, and Jason Abbott. (1999) "Piratical Violence and Maritime Security in Southeast Asia." *Security Dialogue* 30, 2: 183–196.

Rutter, Owen. (1930) *The Pirate Wind: Tales of the Sea-Robbers of Malaya*. Singapore: Oxford University Press.

Tarling, Nicholas. (1963) *Piracy and Politics in the Malay World: A Study of British Imperialism in Nineteenth Century South-East Asia*. Melbourne, Australia: Cheshire.

Tangliacozzo, Eric. (2000) "Kettle on a Slow Boil: Batavia's Threat Perceptions in the Indies' Outer Islands, 1870–1910." *Journal of Southeast Asian Studies* 31, 1: 70–100.

PKB. See **Partai Kebangkitan Bangsa.**

PLAIN OF JARS Like Easter Island with its strange, huge carved-stone figures, the Plain of Jars in northern Laos, amid the mountains of the Annamese Cordillera, is full of mystery. What people carved the huge stone jars and when? How did they transport the stone from the quarry to the plain? What purpose did the jars serve?

Tran Ninh is the Vietnamese name for the Plain of Jars; Thong Hai Hin is its name in the Lao language. The jars range from one to three meters in height and weigh six hundred kilograms on average. More than three hundred lie across the plain. According to local legends, the jars were the leftovers of an enormous banquet celebrating the victory of a sixth-century ruler, but archaeologists believe that the jars are as old as fifteen hundred to two thousand years and thus much earlier than the mythical banquet.

In the 1930s, a French archaeologist, Madeleine Colani, studied the jars and excavated the earth around them. She found the remains of stone, glass, and clay beads, shells, bronze bracelets, and bronze and iron tools possibly used to carve the jars, which she thought were about two thousand years old. Colani presumed that the jewelry had originally been burial gifts for the deceased whose cremated remains had rested inside the jars. When exploring a large cave near the Plain of Jars, Colani found traces of heavy burning on one wall and suggested that the cremations had occurred there.

Colani connected the Plain of Jars with two other sites: one in the North Cachar Hills of northeastern India some one thousand kilometers to the northwest, where roughly similar stone jars containing bones had been discovered in 1928, and the other at Sa Huynh south of Da Nang in Vietnam, where similar jars holding some human remains had been buried in the sand along the South China Sea. Colani then concluded that these three jar locations marked an ancient caravan route, perhaps traveled by traders of salt, from the coast of Vietnam through Tran Ninh all the way to India. Most scholars agree with Colani's dating of the jars somewhere between 500 BCE and 100 CE, although her reconstruction of the historical context must remain speculative until more complete evidence emerges.

History of the Plain of Jars Region

By 100 CE, along the coasts and river valleys of Southeast Asia, Indian-inspired cultures had begun to develop; the kingdoms of Angkor, Champa, and Pagan, in today's Cambodia, Vietnam, and Myanmar (Burma), flourished, but the first kingdom in present-day Laos arose only in 1353. By this late date, the inhabitants of Laos would have had no knowledge of the people who made the stone jars lying about the plain near the first capital city of Luang Prabang.

Today the official Lao name of the region is the province of Xieng Khuang, which is populated mainly by Lao Phuan, Khmu (belonging to the Mon-Khmer language family), and Hmong (belonging to the Sino Tibetan language family) ethnic groups. The Plain of Jars was the center of the Lao kingdom of Muang Phuan, which was incorporated as a tributary state into the Lao kingdom of Lan Xang ("land of a million elephants") in the fourteenth century. The Phuan (also Lao Phuan or Tai Phuan) are an ethnic group belonging to the Tai language family, linguistically and culturally closely related to the Lao of the Mekong Valley. From 1434, Muang Phuan paid tribute to Hanoi and was called Tran Ninh Prefecture by the Vietnamese.

The attempt to absorb the region into the Vietnamese state met with strong opposition, which resulted in the Vietnamese invasion of Lan Xang in 1478. After this, Muang Phuan had to pay tribute to both Hanoi and Lan Xang until the division of Lan Xang in the early eighteenth century, when Muang Phuan fell increasingly under Vietnamese influence.

In the 1830s, the region came under Siamese control, and many Phuan families were forced to resettle west of the Mekong Delta (today's Thailand). In 1893, according to the Franco-Siamese Treaty, Muang Phuan became part of French Laos.

The region around the Plain of Jars has thus seen centuries of warfare as armies of the Southeast Asian kingdoms fought for power in the area, but the most intense combat occurred from the mid-1960s until the early 1970s, after the region had fallen to combined Neutralist and Pathet Lao (Communist) forces in 1960. The plain was heavily bombed; American aircraft jettisoned their undropped bombs when they returned from raids on North Vietnam, and Pathet Lao and U.S.-backed troops fought here. Yet, amazingly, recent visitors to the Plain of Jars have confirmed that the jars survived largely intact, perhaps deliberately spared by the various armies who fought there.

Jana Raendchen

Further Reading

Colani, Madeleine. (1935) *Megalithes du Haut-Laos (Hua Pan, Tran Ninh)*. Paris: Les Éditions d'art et d'histoire.

Saemlamchiak, Photi. (1994) *Tamnaan thai phuan* (Thai Phuan Annals). Bangkok, Thailand: Samakkhisarn.

Saenmani, Khamhung, and Volker Grabowsky. (2001) *Kaap Muang Phuan*. Vientiane, Laos: National University of Laos.

Smuckarn, Snit, and Kennon Breazeale. (1988) *A Culture in Search of Survival: The Phuan of Thailand and Laos*. Monograph Series, no. 31. New Haven, CT: Yale University Press.

Stuart-Fox, Martin. (1998) *The Lao Kingdom of Lan Xang: Rise and Decline*. Bangkok, Thailand: White Lotus.

Stuart-Fox, Martin, and Mary Kooyman. (1992) *Historical Dictionary of Laos*. Metuchen, NJ, and London: Scarecrow Press.

PLAZA ACCORD In September 1985, the Group of Five, or G-5, countries—the United States, Japan, the United Kingdom, Germany, and France—meeting at the Plaza Hotel in New York announced the signing of the Plaza Accord. One main purpose of this agreement was to lower the value of the dollar vis-à-vis the yen. At the time, Japan had a large trade surplus with the United States. It was thought that by weakening the dollar and strengthening the yen American exports would be cheaper and hence sell more in Japan and elsewhere. More important, as a result of the strengthening of the yen, Japanese exports would be more expensive and hence sell less in the United States.

The Plaza Accord was the result of several rounds of secret negotiations among the G-5 earlier in 1985. The group set aside around $18 billion to intervene in global markets to weaken the dollar and, it was thought, improve the export position of American corporations. In an almost unprecedented example of policy coordination, the yen rose in value from around 240 to the dollar to about 200 by the end of 1985. By 1987, it had doubled in value vis-à-vis the dollar. It seemed that the G-5's intervention in the market had worked. But the effect on the U.S. trade deficit was minimal. Thus, while the Plaza Accord marked an important milestone in G-5 cooperation, it did not improve the U.S. trade balance.

There are two primary reasons that strengthening the yen did not lead to a reduction in the U.S. trade deficit. First, Japanese corporations cut prices to compensate partially for the increase in the yen's value. This, along with an interest-rate cut by the Bank of Japan, provided breathing room for Japanese firms. Second, many Japanese corporations began to export production to other areas of Asia and to the United States itself. Japanese firms already had ties with firms in other Asian countries, but the price pressures of a strong yen following the Plaza Accord led to deepening regional integration. Products that were previously exported from Japan were now being exported to the United States from other countries and therefore were counted not as Japanese exports but as Malaysian, Thai, or another country's exports.

Jonathan R. Strand

Further Reading

Encarnation, Dennis J. (1992) *Rivals Beyond Trade: America Versus Japan in Global Competition*. Ithaca, NY: Cornell University Press.

Lincoln, Edward J. (1993) *Japan's New Global Role*. Washington, DC: Brookings Institution.

Murphy, R. Taggart. (1997) *The Weight of the Yen*. New York: W. W. Norton.

PLOWING RITUAL—VIETNAM In feudal Vietnam, from the eleventh to the nineteenth centuries, the king had absolute control of the land, the people, and the spirits. While not divine, he stood between the people and heaven, and among the most important of his symbolic roles was to serve as the high priest of agriculture.

In 987 CE, King Le Dao Hanh carried out for the first time the annual rite of plowing a small plot of rice paddy land set aside for the purpose of ensuring that the Vietnamese people had enough to eat. The king first made an offering to the God of Agriculture, known to the Vietnamese as Than Nong (the spirit of agriculture), and to the legendary Chinese emperor Shen Nung, who was credited with introducing agriculture to both the Chinese and the Vietnamese. Then the king himself plowed a few furrows of land. The rice crop from this land was later used by the king for making ceremonial offerings.

In 1038, during the Ly dynasty (1010–1225), court officials asked the king if it was proper for him to perform such a menial task. The king responded by asking where he would get proper rice for his ritual needs and how he could set an example for his people if he did not plow the consecrated royal fields. He then plowed three furrows of land with his own hands.

In 1048, two altars were constructed, one to the God of Earth (Xa) and the other to the God of Cereals (Tac). At the start of each of the four seasons of the year, offerings were made to these two gods, who came to symbolize not only agricultural fertility but the nation itself. The king's role as a national high priest of agriculture in Vietnam would continue for a thousand years with only minor variations.

Toward the end of the dynastic period in Vietnam, the king ceased to perform the plowing ceremony himself as had his predecessors. Instead, he assigned a high-ranking official to perform the plowing on his behalf. The king's representative would plow exactly nine furrows in the consecrated fields in the middle of the night on the twelfth day of the fifth lunar month. Subsequent work in this field would be carried out by local farmers. When the last king of Vietnam renounced the throne in 1945, all such rituals, like the kingship itself, came to an end.

Neil Jamieson

Further Reading

Phoung Quynh. (1995) *Traditional Festivals in Vietnam*. Hanoi, Vietnam: Giao Publishers.

POETRY—CHINA During the high tide of their "literary revolution" of the 1920s, China's poets experimented widely with European images, rhythms, and literary trends. The strongest influence initially was that of romanticism, as seen in the work of Guo Moruo (1892–1978); during the 1930s younger poets were more attracted by imagism and symbolism. Although the extended war with Japan (1937–1945) and subsequent civil strife brought attention to China's rich body of traditional folksongs as the vehicle for new, patriotic content, postwar poets produced a remarkable body of modernist verse. This tradition was later continued on Taiwan in the 1960s and 1970s. In the People's Republic, leftist political movements enforced the production of verse simple enough to be appreciated by unlettered farmers and workers, but this provoked a strenuous reaction after the death of Mao Zedong in 1976. Within a few years *menglong* (misty) poets appeared; in marked contrast to their predecessors, who produced public poetry, these younger poets developed very personal styles and levels of significance. By the end of the century, China's poets were freely experimenting with a variety of styles, influenced both by twentieth-century trends abroad and their own literary heritage.

Throughout the twentieth century many readers felt that these engagements with other literatures were less than successful, in some cases reflecting the cadences of other languages more than of Chinese. Twentieth-century poets had generally written free verse in colloquial language; this was a dramatic shift from the indigenous poetic tradition in which verse was carefully structured in a few conventional forms. Similarly, the diction of classical verse was rich and seldom utilized true spoken language. Poetry had for three thousand years been the vehicle for the highest levels of literary art; to memorize large numbers of poems was necessary if one was to be considered learned. Even today students learn selected works of major historical poets for recitation. Consequently, the past still exerts its influence on writers of the twenty-first century, despite its associations with old China's political elite.

The Roots of Chinese Poetry

China's earliest poetry was compiled into the *Shijing* (most often called The Book of Songs in English), by Confucius (551–479 BCE) some would argue. Certainly it has regularly been considered a source for proper moral conduct as well as of inspiration for later writers. Its imagery is rich, and its range of subjects very broad, from the founding myths of the royal house through the banquets of the nobility to the daily cares and joys of the common people. Some of these short poems seem very much like folk songs; their immediacy has moved readers through the ages. A second major collection appeared about six hundred years later; named *Chuci* (Songs of the South), it preserved poetry generally associated with the lands south of the Chang (Yangtze) River. The older stratum of the text is associated with the court minister Qu Yuan (fourth–third centuries BCE). Exiled due to the slander of jealous rivals, he wrote of his loyalty and longing for recognition in the form of a very lengthy allegory. Other poems in the collection are about Qu Yuan, and some of the more interesting clearly refer to religious rituals of the period, using rhythms quite different from those of the northern tradition.

Traditional Forms: *Fu*, *Shi*, and *Ci*

Inspired, most likely, by the long compositions in the *Chuci*, poets of China's first great dynasty, the Han (206 BCE–220 CE), compiled lengthy *fu* (rhyme prose or rhapsodies) that incorporated lush descriptions of objects, buildings, landscapes, human activities such as hunting, and even emotional states in alternating prose and rhymed verse. The greatest of these writers was Sima Xiangru (179–118 BCE), who recounted the pleasures of his king; other Han writers such as Yang Xiong (53 BCE–18 CE) insisted that *fu* should serve to criticize excesses, not to encourage them.

Fu were meant to be read aloud; their varying cadences, alliteration, and complex rhyming schemes were designed to delight the ear. Virtually all other Chinese poetry was lyrical, often intended literally to be sung. By the end of the Han dynasty, writers drew on the subjects of folk songs, love, separation, and death to begin a new tradition of occasional verse that continues to this day. These poems, called generally *shi* (lyrical verse), have lines of all the same length; the most common form is the five-syllable line, which in monosyllabic Chinese originally meant five-word lines. *Shi* poems were often written in couplets, with the second lines of all the couplets rhyming with one another. Most are relatively short. During the Tang period (618–907), strictly regulated verse forms developed; these, called *jinti shi* (modern-style verse), prescribed even the tonal patterns of syllables in each line. These "modern" forms were generally either four or eight lines in length and were written alongside the freer, earlier *gushi* (ancient style) forms. Both forms continued to be written through the Ming (1368–1644) and Qing (1644–1912) periods.

A new form, the *ci*, or song lyric, developed among Tang-period entertainers in response to popular music imported from Central Asia. Instead of all lines having the same length, these new poems were written to fit the varying lines of Central Asian melodies. Later, when the music had been forgotten, poets (even those of the twentieth century, such as Mao Zedong) would "fill in" the patterns of line length, tonal sequence, and rhyme scheme found in early poems written to fit these named, but lost, melodies. From the late Tang onward, poets generally composed *ci* that fit those original patterns, although there were efforts to update the melodies used for writing new song lyrics during the Mongol Yuan dynasty (1279–1368) and subsequent dynasties as arias, for the theater became the primary venue for sung verse. Some poets viewed the *ci* as inadequate for serious composition, but for others, the full range of poetic topics was written into both *shi* and *ci*. Poetry in the *ci* form reached its first peak of development during the Song period (960–1279) and its second during the seventeenth century in the hands of Ming poets, such as Chen Zilong (1608–1647), and Qing poets, including the Manchu writer Nalan Xingde (1655–1685).

TAO QIAN, TROUBLED POET

Surely the best-loved early Chinese poet now is Tao Qian (365–427). After a fitful career in the bureaucracy, Tao retired to live as a farmer. Many of his poems, such as the one below, seem to celebrate the simple life, but others hint darkly at hunger, frustration, even despair at his situation in life.

Poems After Drinking Wine, No. 5

I built my hut beside a traveled road
Yet hear no noise of passing carts and horses.
You would like to know how it is done?
With the mind detached, one's place becomes remote.
Picking chrysanthemums by the eastern hedge
I catch sight of the distant southern hills:
The mountain air is lovely as the sun sets
And flocks of flying birds return together.
In these things is a fundamental truth
I would like to tell, but lack the words.

Robert E. Hegel

Source: James Hightower, trans. (1977) *The Poetry of T'ao Ch'ien*. Oxford: Oxford University Press, 130.

Major Poets

China's great poets are legion, but those of the Tang dynasty are generally considered the best. The great triad of Du Fu (712–770), Li Bai (or Li Bo, 701–762), and Wang Wei (d. 761) are considered to embody the teachings of Confucianism, Taoism, and Buddhism, respectively. Other poets brought a very personal voice to their poems, such as the reclusive Tao Qian (365–427) and the failed statesman Su Shi (Su Dongpo, 1037–1101). Many were exceptionally capable craftsmen, but China's literary history is crowded by people who dashed off poems to commemorate special occasions (banquets, birthdays, leave-taking). And although most of the best-known poets were men, China produced a striking number of distinguished women poets. Perhaps the most famous is Li Qingzhao (1084?–c. 1151)who, widowed early from her constant literary companion, left a legacy of haunting poems of love and loss. The Ming and Qing periods produced literary societies of women whose many members often never met but who maintained long correspondences in verse as the vehicle to convey their deepest feelings.

Themes

Certainly a large percentage of Chinese poetry has been devoted to love, given the system of arranged marriages that persisted for so many centuries. But poems in China have conveyed the most profound as well as the most lighthearted of emotions, have captured the daily lives and aspirations of so many, and have narrated significant (and insignificant) events over more than two millennia. There are no better examples of this range of experience than the poems of Song-period poets Su Shi and Mei Yaochen (1002-1060). Religious thoughts have motivated many poets, but because there is no fundamental dichotomy between religious and secular lives, the world is present even in religious poetry—see, for example, poems by painters Wang Wei ("Twenty Views of Wangquan") and Shen Zhou (1427–1509). So, too, is wine, the favored companion for versification. Li Bai is especially known for his wine poems ("Bring the Wine"), while his contemporary Du Fu wrote many that describe people's suffering in times of war and famine ("The Old Man With No Family to Take Leave Of").

Not only has poetry been the greatest of Chinese art forms, but it has also been one of the clearest mirrors for reflecting the experience of this major segment of humanity over an enormous span of time. Enormous numbers of poems survive: over fifty thousand from the Tang period alone, along with hundreds of thousands from later periods.

Robert E. Hegel

See also: **Chuci; Ci; Du Fu; Guo Moruo; Li Bai; Literature—China; *Quan Tasngshi*; Shi; *Shijing***

Further Reading

Chang, Kang-i Sun. (1986) *Six Dynasties Poetry*. Princeton, NJ: Princeton University Press.

Chang, Kang-i Sun, and Haun Saussy, eds. (1998) *Chinese Women Poets: An Anthology of Poetry and Criticism*. Stanford: Stanford University Press.

Chaves, Jonathan, trans. and ed. (1986) *The Columbia Book of Later Chinese Poetry (1279–1911)*. New York: Columbia University Press.

Graham, A. C., trans. (1965) *Poems of the Late T'ang*. Harmondsworth, U.K.: Penguin.

Hawkes, David, trans. (1989) *The Songs of the South*. Oxford: Clarendon Press.

Hightower, James, trans. (1977) *The Poetry of T'ao Ch'ien*. Oxford: Oxford University Press.

Liu, James J. Y. (1982) *The Interlingual Critic: Interpreting Chinese Poetry*. Bloomington, IN: Indiana University Press.

Owen, Stephen. (1981) *The Great Age of Chinese Poetry: The High T'ang*. New Haven, CT: Yale University Press.

———. (1985) *Remembrances: The Experience of the Past in Classical Chinese Literature*. Cambridge, MA, and London: Harvard University Press.

Waley, Arthur, trans. (1996) *The Book of Songs*, edited by Joseph R. Allen. New York: Grove Press.

Watson, Burton, trans. (1971) *Chinese Rhyme-Prose in the Fu Form from the Han and the Six Dynasties Period*. New York: Columbia University Press.

———, trans. and ed. (1984) *The Columbia Book of Chinese Poetry: From Early Times to the Thirteenth Century*. New York: Columbia University Press.

Yeh, Michelle. (1991) *Modern Chinese Poetry: Theory and Practice since 1917*. New Haven, CT: Yale University Press.

———, trans. and ed. (1992) *Anthology of Modern Chinese Poetry*. New Haven, CT: Yale University Press.

Yu, Pauline, ed. (1987) *The Reading of Imagery in the Chinese Poetic Tradition*. Princeton, NJ: Princeton University Press.

POETRY—INDIA

Indian poetry has come a long way from the earliest period of sacred writings, love lyrics, and court poetry. Beginning in the Rig Vedic period, around 1500 BCE, classical poetry continued until the middle of the ninth century CE. Sanskrit epics, like the *Mahabharata* and the *Ramayana*, and the works of Kalidas dominated the scene. Ilanko Adigal (ninth century CE) wrote epics in Tamil. The following period saw the birth of modern Indian languages, and poetry was characterized by a drift from classical languages, the introduction of bhakti (devotional) poetry, the grown of Perso-Arabic literature, and the development of Urdu.

Poetic Traditions

Western models greatly influenced Indian poetry at the beginning of the nineteenth century. Realism, social awareness, concern for the downtrodden, anticolonial sentiments, and Western philosophy inspired Indian poets. A sense of unity, which derives from geographical, historical, ritualistic, and behavioral patterns, is present throughout the history of the Indian people. The concept of *Bharatavarsa* is a part of the common psyche of Indians, and this is reflected in the literature. India, that is, Bharata, existed as an entity from time immemorial. The image of India was not so much a territorial unit as one referring to history, culture, mythology, tradition. Although they may be subdivided into different groups, Indians form one community, and their poetry reflects their common hopes and aspirations.

The Nineteenth Century

The year 1800 is regarded as a landmark in the history of Indian literary activities. Although the printing press appeared in the mid-sixteenth century in Goa, the establishment of the Serampore Mission Press in 1800 ushered in a new era of communication. The traditions of manuscript and scribal writings ended. Works in Hindi, Bengali, Gujarati, Oriya, and other modern Indian languages were published. The printed script and new literary forms like the ode and sonnet stimulated the growth of a new kind of poetry, but a longing for Indian classical literature and society continued.

The creation of modern Indian poetry was slow, and there was no uniformity of pattern. Poetry in Bengali and Marathi took the lead, while poetry in languages like Hindi, Oriya, Kannada, Telugu, and Assamese lagged behind. The influence of classical and medieval poetry continued in places where English education was not an influence.

Michael Madhusudan Dutt (1827–1873) brought about significant changes in Bengali poetry by adopting new poetic forms, yet his magnum opus *Meghnadvadha* (Killing of Meghanad) was based on a story from the *Ramayana*. Altaf Husain Hali (1837–1914) broke away from the convention of *ghazal* (songs), and his *Madd-wa-Jazr-e-Islam* (Ebb and Flow of Islam) reflected resurgent Islam. Bharatendu Harishchandra (1846–1884), Lakshminath Bazbarua (1868–1938),

Radhanath Ray (1848–1908), Lachman Raina Bulbul (1812–1884), Rajaraja Varma (1863–1918), and other writers broke new grounds in Hindi, Gujrati, Assamese, Oriya, Telegu, Tamil, Marathi, Kashmiri, and Malalyam.

The Twentieth Century

The poetry of the twentieth century dealt with disillusionment with British rule, the struggle for freedom, the trauma of partition, and the glorification of the past. Poets also concerned themselves with the rural-urban dichotomy, East-West relations, social problems, Marxism, existentialism, the shift from liberal humanism to feminism, a fresh approach to sexuality and morality, and a concern for the underprivileged of society. Poetry became the instrument of momentous social, political, and economic change. New poetic forms and styles were discovered to delineate changing ideologies.

The towering figure of Rabindranath Tagore (1861–1941) dominated the literary scene. His spirit of reason and freedom found expression in the *Gitanjali* (Offering of Songs), for which he received the Nobel Prize in 1913. He represented the new spirit of the country and made a strong impact on both Bengali and non-Bengali poetry. The imagery of Jibanananda Das (1899–1954) and psychological probing in the poetry of Buddhadeva Bose (1908–1974) also added new dimensions to Bengali poetry. Chaoba Singh (1896–1951), Lamabam Kamal Singh (1899–1935), and Anganghal Singh (1892–1944) set new trends in Manipuri poetry. Romanticism, nationalism, and mysticism marked Assamese poetry. Mysticism, nationalism, and concern for the downtrodden distinguished the writings of the woman poet Kuntala Kumari Sabat (1900–1938), who wrote in Oriya.

Patriotic fervor characterized the poetry of Subramania Bharati (1882–1921), the greatest poet in modern Tamil, whose *Kuyil Pattu* (Song of the Cuckoo, 1912) is a noted work. Bharatidasan (1891–1964) was the author of *Kudumba Vilakku* (The Light of the Home). The free verse of Balvantrai Kalyanrai Thakore (1869–1952) and the modernity of Umashankar Joshi (1911–1988) set trends in Gujrati poetry. The new poetry in Marathi began with the *Kahi Kavita* of B. S. Mardhekar (1909–1956). Namdev Dhasal (b. 1946) wrote about the Dalit (untouchables).

Samad Mir (1894–1959) continued the Sufi mystic tradition in Kashmiri poetry in the twentieth century. The psyche of a woman confined by orthodoxy and the trauma of partition is superbly depicted in the writings of the Punjabi poet Amtira Pritam (b. 1917). Muhammad Iqbal (1877–1938) was the greatest Urdu poet of the Indian subcontinent in modern times. Left-leaning ideology is marked in the poetry of other Urdu poets such as Faiz Ahmad Faiz (1911–1984), Jan Nishar Akhtar (1914–1979), and Ali Sardar Jafri (1913). Romanticism, or *Chayavad*, became the hallmark of Hindi poetry, evident in the writings of Suryakant Tripathi (1899–1961), Sumitranandan Pant (1900–1977), Jaishankar Prasad (1889–1937), Mahadevi Verma (1907–1987), and others. Sachchidananda Hirananda Vatsyayana (1911–1987) triggered the new trend in Hindi poetry known as *Nai Kavita* (new poetry movement), known earlier as *prayogvad*, which searched for new values. Raghuvir Sahay (1929–1990) dealt with the problems of women with a rare sensitivity. Sri Aurobindo (1872–1950), Sarojini Naidu (1879–1949), Nissim Ezekiel (b. 1924), A. K. Ramanujan (1929–1993), Kamala Das (1934), Dom Moraes (b. 1938), and Vikram Seth (b. 1952) are among India's poets writing in English.

Modern Indian poetry found its place in world literature by adopting new styles, keeping in tune with various contemporary trends, portraying the problems of society, and retaining its own uniqueness. An emphasis on realism and concern for individuals are hallmarks of Indian poetry. Although Indian poets write in many different languages, poetry, like other art, is a unifying force. Indian poetry expresses shared Indian feelings and ideas.

Patit Paban Mishra

See also: **Literature, Bengali; Literature—India; Literature, Sanskrit**

Further Reading

Das, Sisir Kumar. (1991) *A History Of Indian Literature, 1800–1910.* New Delhi: Sahitya Akademi.

———. (1995) *A History Of Indian Literature, 1911–1956.* New Delhi: Sahitya Akademi.

Desouza, Eunice. (1997) *Nine Indian Women Poets: An Anthology.* Oxford: Oxford University Press.

Dharwadker, Vinay, and A. K. Ramanujan, eds. (1998) *The Oxford Anthology of Modern Indian Poetry.* Oxford: Oxford University Press.

George, K. M., ed. (1984) *Comparative Indian Literature.* 2 vols. New Delhi: Macmillan.

Gokak, V. K. (1975) *Integral View of Poetry: An Indian Perspective.* Columbia: South Asia Books.

Jotwani, Motilal. (1979) *Contemporary Indian Literature and Society.* New Delhi: Heritage.

Narasingha, C. D., ed. (1970) *Indian Literature of the Past Fifty Years, 1917–1967.* Mysore, India: Mysore University Press.

POETRY—IRAQ One way of dealing with Iraqi poetry is to speak of it in terms of both history and cultural dynamics. Premodern poetry (1258–1920) begins with the invasion of Baghdad by the Mongols. The era of postindependence poetry starts with the end of British colonial rule in 1920. The modern era finds its origins in the free verse poets of the 1940s.

Premodern Poetry

After the fall of Baghdad to the Mongol Hulagu Khan, who ransacked the Muslim capital in 1258, Iraqi literature suffered greatly until the late nineteenth century. Aside from Safi al-Deen al-Hilli (d. 1349), there were no major figures before the late emergence of ʿAbd al-Ghaffar al-Akhras (1804–1874), Musa al-Talaqani (1814–1880), Haydar al-Hilli (Hillah, 1827–1887), ʿAbd al-Ghani Jamil (1780–1863), and, a little later, Muhammad Saʿid al-Habubi (d. 1915).

With the exception of the latter, the tendency among the premodern poets is toward classical themes and techniques of poetry. They wrote panegyrics, elegies, and satire along with poetry of wit and religious benedictions. Their contribution lies, however, in bringing back to the desolate cultural scene some exuberance and life, endowing it not only with rhetorical embellishments and poetic resonance but also with some politics of engagement. Haydar al-Hilli built on tradition, but he paved the way for further innovation. ʿAbd al-Ghani Jamil, on the other hand, voiced political opposition against foreign occupation and misuse of people, their lands, and resources. He targeted the Ottomans, and his poetry offers a political record of the struggle for national independence. Yet the real contribution to innovation came from the faqih (theologian) and sheikh Muhammad Saʿid al-Habubi. He practiced every mode of poetry and wrote elegant and secular *muwashshahat* (strophic songs in colloquial language) on wine and love, which surprised his students at the religious schools and made many speculate on the sheikh's career. Witty and eloquent, the sheikh made it clear that he wrote within a convention irrespective of moral constraints. He wrote no political verse despite the fact that he led, in 1914, an army of followers against the British forces near the Shu'ayiba, south of Iraq, where he was wounded and later died.

Postindependence Poetry

Muhammad Saʿid al-Habubi's poetic practice within a new understanding of the sacred and the profane can serve as a bridge to the second or postindependence stage in Iraqi poetry. This is marked by an upsurge of national poetics and free manipulation of themes and techniques that only fall short of the culminating innovative stance of the late 1940s, usually associated with the free-verse movement. The known figures of the national period were also poets of major caliber in the history of Iraqi cultural life.

Living through the disintegration of the Ottoman empire and the British occupation after the World War I, these poets were aware of their national agenda. Their registers vary, but all responded to the spirit of the times as well as the national needs and aspirations of the Iraqis. They were a postwar generation, but they were also strongly committed to national issues. Thus, Maʿruf al-Rusafi (1875–1945) was opposed to the British and to the so-called independence mandated by the British (1920–1958). He defied the installation of a king brought from outside the country and wrote openly in that direction. He called for freedom of expression, parliamentary elections, and genuine democracy. Gertrude Bell, the British press secretary in Baghdad, censored his poetry, but he continued writing in defiance of the British and their puppet regime. His themes and concerns touch also on emancipation of women, equal opportunities for all, and reform at large.

His counterpart was Jamil Sidqi al-Zahawi (1863–1936), whose concerns were mainly social and scientific. He thought of poetry as an appropriate medium for the discussion of scientific discovery, biological evolution, and other issues, which had never been thought of as poetic subjects. He practiced strophic poetry, and although he believed strongly in the need to go beyond classical tenets of composition, his poetry never went beyond classical meters and their variants.

Both Ali al-Sharqi (1890–1964) and Ahmed al-Safi al-Najafi (1897–1977) brought a new spirit to Iraqi poetry. The latter was no less committed to national issues than his immediate predecessor al-Rusafi, but his poetry speaks more of exile, nostalgia, and love. Al-Sharqi brought into Iraqi poetry refined elegance and smooth eloquence and is more tuned to modernism. He was distinguished, too, for his urban sensibility that goes beyond the limitations of oratory and classical composition. But the whole postindependence poetry movement is culminated in Muhammad Mahdi al-Jawahiri (1900/1903–1997). Writing and reciting poetry in the classical mode, and attuned to experimentation in images, al-Jawahiri fits well, nevertheless, in the early Iraqi style of Abu al-Tayyib al-Mutanabbi (d. 965). Al-Jawahiri's political concerns involved him in a struggle not only against the British and their puppet regime but also against national regimes since 1958. His political career and his poetics endear him to a large audience in Iraq and the Arab world. But his poetry is known for its variety, as he treads in love, wine, nostalgia, and exile. Indeed, al-Jawahiri posed a real challenge to the innovators of the free-verse movement, for his spontaneity and eloquence could not be challenged or surpassed.

Modern Poetry

The free-verse movement of the late 1940s, which spanned the Arab world, has its originators in Iraq. Nazik al-Mala'ikah (b. 1923) was the pioneer, as she explains in her book *Qadaya al-Shi'r al-Mu'asir* (Issues in Contemporary Poetry).

In pace with the Arab world's complex postwar situation, poets recognized the limits of conventional poetics. On the other hand, they were in touch with Anglo-American and Russian culture. The modernist trend worldwide drew attention to their ancient culture with its regeneration myths. Poets like Badr Shakir al-Sayyab (1926–1964), 'Abd al-Wahhab al-Bayati (1926–1999), and Nazik al-Mala'ikah practiced new forms and delved into new and surprising themes. Poets like Hussein Mardan (1927–1972) might flout tradition and morality in a Baudelairean fashion, celebrating vagrancy and vice, but others had agendas of great political and social commitment. The regeneration myth received attention in the 1950s, but disillusionment in the 1960s drove poets to identify with Christ, Islamic martyrs, and exiles and victims of repression and occupation. Poetry since the 1960s tends to manage its lineage through textual affiliation with forebears in a poetic tradition that goes back to the tenth century. There is a selective engagement with the works of the past, which are drawn on to help the poet find a sense of identity. The issue at hand is to come out with a stratagem that identifies the new poet's position obliquely, while examining tradition with a critical and discriminating sense. The outcome brings the past and the present in focus, with the new poet creating from the voices of the past a unified new voice and perspective.

Mushin Jassim al-Musawi

Further Reading

Badawi, Muhammad Mustafa. (1975) *A Critical Introduction to Modern Arabic Poetry*. Cambridge, U.K.: Cambridge University Press.

Al Musawi, Muhsin Jassim. (2000) "Dedications as Poetic Intersections." *Journal of Arabic Literature* 31, 1: 1–37.

POETRY—JAPAN

According to legend, the first poem in Japan was spoken by the god Susanoo no Mikoto when he built his palace in the land of Izumo. In his preface to the *Kokinwakashu* (c. 905), the first imperial anthology of poetry written in Japanese, the poet Ki no Tsurayuki (d. c. 945) also dates poetry to the age of the gods. This essay emphasizes written poetry and covers primitive song, court poetry, renga and haikai, and modern verse.

Primitive Song

In the early eighth century Japanese primitive songs were taken down from the words of reciters *(kataribe)* and also preserved as prayers in Shinto ceremonies. The earliest songs have no fixed prosody, that is, no set number of syllables and no regular alternation of long and short lines. These songs celebrate the daily lives of the early Japanese and reflect themes of love, work, awe and respect for nature, victory in battle, reverence, and praise.

One of the earliest written sources of Japanese song is the *Kojiki* (Record of Ancient Matters, c. 712). The *Kojiki* was compiled and presented to the Empress Gemmei (reigned 707–715) by O no Yasumaro (d. 723) in the Nara period (710–794). Although the *Kojiki* was commissioned to give the imperial house added legitimacy in an account of its divine origins, it also preserves a number of *uta* (poems or songs), mostly on the theme of love.

Japanese primitive song also was preserved in the form of ancient ritual prayers *(norito-goto)*, divinely imparted magic words spoken in a sacred place. Primitive *norito* were thought to have been the words of the Shinto gods and spirits *(kami)*. With the development of court ritual, however, they became prayers from men spoken in worship of the gods, that is, as prayers of petition, mystical and powerful incantations, and blessings to insure longevity.

By the mid-seventh century, Japanese poetry had come to be composed in a pattern of alternating five- and seven-syllable phrases. In the seventh and eighth centuries, the two major forms of verse were the *choka* or *nagauta* (long poem) and the *tanka* (short poem), both of which were considered to be *waka* ("Japanese" poetry as distinct from Chinese poetry). The *choka* was made up of an indefinite number of pairs of five- and seven-syllable lines, ending with an additional seven-syllable line, while the *tanka* had just thirty-one syllables in the pattern 5-7-5-7-7. In later ages the word *waka* was used to denote this form only, for the *choka*, although well represented in the oldest extant poetry anthology, the *Man'yoshu* (c. 759), waned during the Nara period, leaving *tanka* the normative form of Japanese verse.

Court Poetry

In the late ninth century Emperor Daigo (reigned 897–930 CE) ordered four poets, including Ki no Tsurayuki, to compile the *Kokinwakashu* (Collection of Ancient and Modern Poems), or *Kokinshu*. In his preface, Tsurayuki wrote what is regarded as the first statement on poetics in Japanese literature: A good poem should achieve a balance between *kotoba* (words) and *kokoro* (heart), a critical standard representing an ideal of balance between content and form that was borrowed from the Chinese *Shijing* (Classic of Poetry, eighth–sixth centuries BCE). In the Heian period (794–1185) all refined people wrote poetry; indeed, it was a major mode of discourse. Tsurayuki and the other compilers of the *Kokinshu* lauded a style of poetry characterized by elegance and refined diction—a style that remained popular into the late twelfth century. The aesthetic ideals of the period included *aware* (sensitivity to the sadness of things), *miyabi* (courtliness), and *en* (luxuriant beauty).

Poetry was composed for formal occasions, such as for court observances and poetry matches, but poems were also exchanged informally between acquaintances, and an exchange of poems was a requisite of courtship. As men and women seldom saw each other face to face, poems passed to one another by intermediaries served as a way to become acquainted. Once an affair was embarked upon, poems were used to seek and give reassurance, to berate the beloved for his or her fickleness, and to express sorrow and regret when the affair drew to a close. Female poets were as highly regarded as male poets during this era; among the most famous are Izumi Shikibu (975?–1035?), Akazome Emon (flourished 976–1041), Murasaki Shikibu (d. 1014?), and Sei Shonagon (965?–1017?).

Near the end of Heian period (794–1185) *shakkyoka*, or Buddhist poetry, came to be accepted as an official theme of court poetry. *Shakkyoka* are based on the sutras, texts, doctrines, ceremonies, and rituals of Buddhism. Buddhist thought and practice permeated the lives of Heian aristocrats and deeply influenced court ritual and observance as well as the writing of poems. Buddhist monks and nuns sought to define the relationship between *waka* composition and religious life. A reconciliation between the way of poetry *(kado)* and the way of Buddhism *(butsudo)* was found in the idea of *hosshin*, a force to which a person is connected and which will bring about his or her enlightenment. Thus the proximity of one's poetry to the teachings of the Buddha was thought to create a connection between poet, poetry, and Buddhism. *Shakkyoka* sequences are found primarily in the imperial anthologies of poetry dating from the *Goshuishu* (1086) through the *Shinkokinshu* (1216), and in private and personal anthologies of the Heian and Kamakura (1185–1333) periods.

Renga* and *Haikai

Renga, or linked verse, were known even in the days of the *Kojiki*, when two people would participate in the creation of one *tanka*, one person composing the first seventeen-syllable *kami no ku* (the 5-7-5 portion), and the other composing the remaining fourteen-syllable *shimo no ku* (the 7-7 portion). From the end of the twelfth century it became a popular pastime for groups of people to compose extended *renga* (5-7-5, 7-7, 5-7-5, 7-7, and on and on), and during the fourteenth century the form became highly refined, governed by increasingly complicated rules regarding subject matter and vocabulary. Among the most famous *renga* masters were the monks Shinkei (1406–1475) and Sogi (1421–1502).

In response to the high seriousness of *renga*, *haikai no renga*, or *haikai*, developed: its form was the same, but the subject matter was much broader, including not only such elegant topics as the moon and cherry blossoms but also everyday inconveniences such as fleas and lice.

In both *renga* and *haikai*, the opening verse, or *hokku* (first verse), was especially important. The undisputed master of the *hokku* is Matsuo Basho (1644–1694). In the modern era, the poet Masaoka Shiki (1867–1902) coined the term "haiku" to refer to verses composed in this form (5-7-5) but abandoned the linked verse concept as outdated; the word haiku was then applied retroactively to the *hokku* of Basho.

In his poetry, Basho is less concerned with what people are doing and feeling than with the world of nature as it reflects the nature of truth. He attempts to penetrate the essence of a thing, a practice central to Chan/Zen Buddhism. These elements are clear in the following *hokku* from Basho's travel diary *Oku no Hosomichi (The Narrow Road to the Deep North).*

Silence—
the cicada sound
penetrates the rocks.

(Translation by Lea Millay)

Other poets known for their composition of *hokku* are Yosa Buson (1716–1783) and Kobayashi Issa (1763–1827).

Modern Poetry

With the opening of Japan to the West in the 1850s, and increased contact after the Meiji Restoration of

1868, Japanese poets became exposed to the poetic traditions of Europe. In response to that exposure, literary critics began to call for similar poetry in Japanese. The first collection of modern poetry, *Shintaishi-sho* (Selection of Poems in the New Style), was published in 1882. As the *shintaishi* developed into *gendaishi* (modern-style verse) over the next several decades it was particularly influenced by the French symbolists and made use of vernacular Japanese (traditional poetry was still composed in classical Japanese, which the spoken language had long since grown away from).

Not all the poets of the Meiji period (1868–1912) embraced Western influence. Some poets, such as Masaoka Shiki and Yosano Akiko (1878–1942) sought successfully to revitalize traditional Japanese verse forms. *Waka* saw a further spectacular resurgence of popularity in the 1980s, when Tawara Machi (b. 1963), a schoolteacher in her twenties, published *Sarada Kinenbi* (Salad Anniversary), an anthology of *waka* that mixed classical locutions and modern situations to express the age-old themes of lost love and regret. Like generations of Japanese poets before her, Tawara Machi creates slender verses that have a powerful effect completely disproportional to their length.

S. Lea Millay

Further Reading

Bowring, Richard. (1982) *Murasaki Shikibu: Her Diary and Poetic Memoirs.* Princeton, NJ: Princeton University Press.

Brower, Robert, and Earl Miner. (1961) *Japanese Court Poetry*. Stanford, CA: Stanford University Press.

Cranston, Edwin A. (1993) *A Waka Anthology: The Gem-Glistening Cup*. Stanford, CA: Stanford University Press.

Hass, Robert. (1994) *The Essential Haiku: Versions of Basho, Buson, and Issa*. Essential Poets, no. 20. Hopewell, NJ: Ecco Press.

Hirshfield, Jane, and Mariko Aratani. (1990) *The Ink Dark Moon: Love Poems by Ono no Komachi and Izumi Shikibu, Women of the Ancient Court of Japan*. New York: Vintage Books.

Kamens, Edward. (1990) *The Buddhist Poetry of the Great Kamo Priestess: Daisaiin Senshi and Hosshin Wakashu*. Ann Arbor: Center for Japanese Studies, University of Michigan.

Konishi Jin'ichi. (1984–1991) *A History of Japanese Literature*. Vols. 1–3. Trans. by Aileen Gatten and Nicholas Teele (vols. 1–2) and Gatten and Mark Harbison (vol. 3). Princeton, NJ: Princeton University Press.

Matsuo Basho. (2000) *Narrow Road to the Interior and Other Writings*. Trans. by Sam Hamill. Boston: Shambhala.

McCullough, Helen Craig. (1985) *Brocade by Night:* Kokin Wakashu *and the Court Style in Japanese Classical Poetry*. Stanford, CA: Stanford University Press.

Millay, S. Lea. (2000) "The Voice of the Court Woman Poet." In *Crossing the Bridge: Comparative Essays on Medieval European and Heian Japanese Women Writers*, edited by Barbara Stevenson and Cynthia Ho. The New Middle Ages Series, no. 12. New York: St. Martin's Press.

Miner, Earl, Hiroko Odagiri, and Robert Morrell, eds. (1985) *The Princeton Companion to Classical Japanese Literature*. Princeton, NJ: Princeton University Press.

Sato, Hiroaki,and Burton Watson. (1981) *From The Country of Eight Islands: an Anthology of Japanese Poetry*. Seattle: University of Washington Press.

Yosano Akiko. (1987) *Tangled Hair (Midaregami)*. Trans. by Sanford Goldstein and Seishi Shinoda. Tokyo: Tuttle.

POETRY—KOREA

POETRY—KOREA The history of poetry in Korea is long and varied, with different genres prevailing in the different political and cultural periods. Throughout much of Korea's history, writers of poetry tended to be of the aristocratic class, government officials for whom the ability to write poetry was an indication of their upbringing and their ability to serve their nation well. Folk beliefs, Buddhism, Confucianism, and Western thought have all, in turn, exerted a strong influence on Korean poetry.

Korean traditional poetry on the whole can be characterized as being centered on the self, through which the reader can relate to his or her own experiences and proceed to discover their universality. Because of its Buddhist and Confucian underpinnings, Korean poetry tended to be transcendent, seeking the ultimate in freedom, liberation, and wisdom. The subject matter tended to be concrete objects or events—a gnarled pine, spring rain, night on the river—and written spontaneously. Traditional poetry also tended to be related to nature and to deal with it conceptually. With roots reaching back to ancient animism, something in nature was not viewed merely as a physical object but rather as a medium through which a universal essence could be captured. This romance with nature remains embodied in the poetry of today.

Poetry in Chinese

The oldest form of poetry written in Korea and that with the greatest longevity is *hanshi* (poems in Chinese). *Hanshi* dates back to at least the Three Kingdoms period (first century BCE–seventh century CE) when King Yuri (reigned 19 BCE–18 CE) of the Koguryo kingdom (37 BCE–668 CE) is recorded as having written such poems, and the genre survived into the early twentieth century. As the Korean language at the time had no script of its own, Chinese characters as well as Chinese syntax was employed in writing *hanshi*, as it was for Korean in general. Unlike its

Chinese cousin, which consisted of five or seven characters per foot, Korean *hanshi* generally consisted of four. As only the upper class was schooled in Chinese characters and the art of writing them with ink brushes, *hanshi* and all other types of early Korean poetry did not reach beyond the aristocracy. The rich content of *hanshi* was recited by chanting, and common subjects were scenic views, love, and loyalty as well as self-reflection and self-ridicule.

Shilla Poetry

The first uniquely Korean poetic form to appear was the *hyangga* songs of the Shilla period (57 BCE–935 CE). Two dozen remaining works from the mid-sixth to late ninth centuries are four-line, eight-line, and ten-line poems. The four-line poems tend to resemble folk ballads, whereas the ten-line poems have a more highly developed structure of three parts of four, four, and two lines. The extant eight- and ten-line *hyangga* were composed for memorial and other ceremonial use. They were written by Buddhist priests and by warriors of the elite *hwarang* youth troops and were sung instead of merely recited. Contributing to the distinctness of *hyangga* is that while they were written in Chinese characters, at times the characters were employed only for their meaning, being pronounced instead with the synonymous native Korean word. At other times, characters are used merely for their pronunciation, their original meaning discarded to substitute for Korean syntactic particles and connectives. Unlike *hanshi*, which was written in Chinese syntax, *hyangga* was sung purely in the Korean language of the period.

Koryo Songs

Koryo kayo (Koryo songs) gradually replaced *hyangga* as the Koryo dynasty (918–1392) took over rule from Shilla. Also referred to as *changga* (long songs), they differed from *hyangga* in that they were longer, with a freer, less disciplined form, and were daringly direct in nature. *Koryo kayo* were transmitted orally throughout the entirety of the Koryo period, not written down until well into the fifteenth century. A new poetic form was introduced into the later *Koryo kayo* of the thirteenth through sixteenth centuries that became known as *pyolgok* (special tunes). The extended form of *pyolgok* consisted of numerous stanzas, and they were referred to as *kyonggi* songs. They were based on the Chinese characters and Chinese classics of the aristocracy and reflected Confucian thought. The short-form *pyolgok*, on the other hand, structure the entire piece into a single stanza. Disparagingly referred to as *sogyo* (commoner's ditty) by the aristocratic class for not conforming to their Confucian norms, they nevertheless contained a subtlety and delicacy to their lyrics.

Choson Verse

The creation of a phonetic alphabet for Korean in 1446 signaled a boon for the writing of poetry in the Choson dynasty (1392–1910). Although *shijo* (tunes of the times) had their beginnings in the late Koryo period, it was in the fifteenth century that the genre began to flourish and did so for five hundred years. These short, witty epigrams expressing a single thought or observation became the first truly Korean vernacular verse and had a greater influence on modern poetic form than any other Korean verse form. The basic form of *shijo*, *pyong-shijo*, consists of three lines of fourteen to sixteen syllables with each line divided into four feet of three to four syllables each. The two variations of the basic form are *os-shiji*, which has a slightly extended first or second line, and *sasol-shijo*, in which the first two lines are highly extended and the third line less so.

Characteristic of classical *shijo* is a sensibility expressed through the simplicity of unadorned emotion. They deal with a wide range of subjects including love, sorrow, the virtue of a life of hardship, the delights of nature, and human existence. The first of the great *shijo* poets, the controversial bureaucrat Chong Chol (1536–1593), expresses great sensitivity and a desire for self-perfection in *Rain on a Lotus Leaf*:

> A sudden shower
>   spatters a lotus leaf,
> But I cannot find
>   the track of water.
> I wish my heart was like that leaf,
>   that nothing ever stained it.
>
> (O'Rourke 1982: 21)

Characteristic of modern *shijo* is that each work is titled, they are relatively free in form and quite commonly break the rules of versification, they are intended to be read as opposed to listened to, and they favor the use of sensitive expression and metaphor.

With the appearance of the Korean alphabet, a new vernacular verse genre, *kasa*, emerged. Like the *Koryo kayo* before it, a *kasa* was meant to be sung. It has the form of four feet per line with three or four syllables to each line and no limit on the number of lines. *Kasa* can be characterized as a hybrid of musical verse and prose, as an essay set to rhythm. During the early part of the Choson period, *kasa*, like concurrently popular *shijo*, was written by aristocrats, but in the later Choson period, commoners began to compose *kasa* and it was enjoyed by both classes. Recurring *kasa* themes include contemplation of nature for spiritual enlightenment, gentlemanly virtues, and the metaphor of male-female love to express the sovereign-subject loyalty relationship. The *kasa* of the late Choson period tended to be longer in length and more prosaic in nature.

Modern Poetry

The opening of Korea at the end of the Choson period saw an influx of Western ideas that had enormous ramifications for all aspects of society and culture, including the formation of a new and modern poetry. Both the adoption of free verse and the reconstruction of the traditional folk ballad, especially by Kim Sowol (1902–1934), set the foundations for modern Korean poetry in the 1930s. The poetry of the late 1920s and early 1930s, led by Chong Chi-yong (b. 1903), was steeped in imagery, representing Korea's first experimentation with modernism. The poetry of the late 1930s and early 1940s, the harshest years of the Japanese colonial period (1910–1945), captured the emotions of the people in their plight. Yun Tong-ju (1917–1945) succinctly captures this in *The Sorrowful Race:*

> White towels are wrapped around black heads,
> White rubber shoes are hung on rough feet.
>
> White blouses and skirts cloak sorrowful frames,
> And white belts tightly tie gaunt waists.
>
> (Shaffer 1999: 26)

After liberation in 1945 and the ravages of the Korean War (1950–1953), much of the most acclaimed poetry has dealt with the excesses of political power and the plight of the oppressed. Most noted for their works in this area are Shin Kyoung-rim (b. 1936), Ko Un (b. 1933), and Kim Chi-ha (b. 1941). Probably most highly regarded of Korean's modern poets is the prolific So Chong-ju (1915–2000), who took Korean myth, legend, and historical anecdote and crafted them into masterpieces. While the popularity of poetry seems on the wane in much of the world, it enjoys great popularity among the people of Korea.

David E. Shaffer

See also: **Literature—Korea; So Chong-ju; Yi Kyu-bo; Yun Son-do**

Further Reading

Anthony of Taize, Brother, and Young-Moo Kim. (1993) *The Sound of My Waves: Selected Poems by Ko Un*. Ithaca, NY: Cornell University.

Kim, Joyce Jaihiun. (1974) *The Immortal Voice: An Anthology of Modern Korean Poetry*. Seoul: Inmun Publishing.

Ko, Won. (1970) *Contemporary Korean Poetry*. Iowa City: University of Iowa Press.

Koh, Chang-soo. (1984) *Best Loved Poems of Korea*. Elizabeth, NJ: Hollym International Corp.

Lee, Sung-il. (1998) *The Moonlit Pond: Korean Classical Poems in Chinese*. Port Townsend, WA: Copper Canyon Press.

McCann, David. (1986) *Unforgettable Things: Poems by So Chongju*. Seoul: Si-sayong-o-sa.

———. (1980) *The Middle Hour: Selected Poems of Kim Chi Ha*. Stanfordville, NY: Human Rights Publishing Group.

O'Rourke, Kevin. (1982) *The Cutting Edge: A Selection of Korean Poetry, Ancient and Modern*. Seoul: Yonsei University Press.

———. (1995) *Poems of a Wanderer: Selected Poems of Midang So Chong-ju*. Dublin, Ireland: Dedalus Press.

———. (2000) "Kevin O'Rourke's Korean Poetry Page." Accessed 6 January 2002, from http://korea.insights.co.kr/english/poem.

Rutt, Richard. (1998) *The Bamboo Grove: An Introduction to Sijo*. Ann Arbor: University of Michigan Press.

Shaffer, David E. (1999) *The Heavens, the Winds, the Stars and Poetry: The Works of Yun Tong-ju*. Seoul: Hakmun Publishing.

POETRY—PHILIPPINES

The history of Philippine poetry can be described in four major literary periods: precolonial (before 1521), Spanish colonial (1521–1898), U.S. colonial (1898–1946), and contemporary (1946–present). A strong indigenous oral tradition is interwoven with the Spanish and U.S. colonial influences of culture and language. Poetry has been written in Tagalog (the national language) and in the eighty-seven regional dialects, as well as in the Castilian Spanish of Miguel de Cervantes and Lope de Vega and the American English of Walt Whitman and Mark Twain.

Precolonial Poetry

An indigenous oral tradition of *bugtong* (riddles) and *sawikain* (proverbs) played a central part of community life in villages of precolonial Philippines. Short four-line poems called *tanaga* evolved from this oral tradition. Each line contained seven or eight syllables, and at the heart of the poem was a cryptic metaphor called a *talinghaga*. Popular folk musical verse was divided into several categories: the *diona*, *talindao*, and *auit* (songs sung at home); *indolanin* and *dolayanin* (street songs); *hila*, *soliranin*, and *manigpasin* (rowing songs); *holohorlo* and *oyayi* (cradle songs); *ombayi* (songs of sadness); *omiguing* (songs of tenderness); *tagumpay* (triumphant songs); *dopayanin* (boat songs); *hiliriao* (drinking songs); and *diona* (wedding songs). Through these verses the local history, politics, and culture were passed from generation to generation. The most skilled poets would memorize epic cycles that took two to four days to recite during all-night dramatic performances. Two examples of precolonial epics that survive today are *Biag ni Lam-ang* (Legend of Lam-ang) in Ilocano (a northern Luzon dialect) and *Ibalon* in Bicol (a southern Luzon dialect).

Poetry in the Spanish Colonial Period

With the arrival of the Spanish colonizers Ferdinand Magellan (1521) and Miguel Lopez de Legazpi (1571) came priests and their tradition of European Catholicism. *Satanas* (Satan) first appeared in Tagalog poetry, and the Christian themes of sin, guilt, and retribution became central concerns of the native population. In 1610, Tomas Pinpin, a Filipino poet working for the Dominican printing press in Bataan (a town outside Manila), wrote a book entitled *Librong Pagaaralan nang manga Tagalog nang Uicang Castila* (A Book in Which Tagalogs May Study the Spanish Language). In this book Pinpin inserted six *auit* that had alternating Spanish and Tagalog lines. This type of bilingual poetry was written by a group called the Ladino Poets.

Metrical romances called *awit* or *korido* were also popular with the literary crowds. The most influential Tagalog romance of the period was the politically cryptic *Florante at Laura* (Florante and Laura; 1838), written by Francisco Baltazar, also known as Balagtas (1788–1862). The first book of poetry written in Spanish by a Filipino was *Sampaguitas y Poesias Varias* (Sampaguitas and Other Poems; 1880) by Pedro Paterno (1858–1911), which was printed in Spain. Paterno, Marcelo H. Del Pilar (1850–1896), Jose Rizal (1861–1896), and Isabelo De Los Reyes (1864–1918) were literary and political figures called *Ilustrados* (enlightened ones) who were living in Madrid and working to attain political freedom for the natives back in the Philippines. The first Filipino female poet to attain outside recognition was Leona Florentino (1849–1884), whose poems were exhibited in the Exposition Filipina in 1887 in Madrid and in the 1889 Exposition Internationale in Paris.

Poetry in the U.S. Colonial Period

In 1898, the U.S. president William McKinley (1843–1901) announced that it was the United States' moral duty to take possession of the Philippine Islands because the Filipinos had to be civilized, educated, and Christianized. After U.S. soldiers "pacified" the native population during the Philippine-American War (1899–1902), thousands of U.S. teachers were sent throughout the archipelago to teach the Filipinos the English language. In just a few years, English became the privileged form of expression for poets, prose writers, and dramatists.

The earliest Filipino poems written in English were published in 1905 in Berkeley, California, in *The Filipino Students' Magazine*, which was edited by *pensionados* (Philippine-American government scholars). The first book of poetry written in English, *Azucena* (1925) by Marcelo De Gracia Concepcion (1895–1954), was published in the United States by G. P. Putnam's Sons. The most influential Filipino poet, Jose Garcia Villa (1908–1997), lived most of his adult life in New York City. His books are *Have Come, Am Here* (Viking Press, 1942), *Volume Two* (New Directions, 1949), and *Selected Poems and New* (McDowell, Obolensky, 1958). Another early immigrant Filipino poet was Carlos Bulosan (1911–1956), who published political poems in American magazines like *The New Yorker*, *Poetry* (edited by Harriet Monroe) and *Saturday Evening Post*. In Manila in 1940, the Commonwealth Literary Prize in English poetry was given to Rafael Zulueta Da Costa (1915–1990) for *Like the Molave and Other Poems*. Native themes were well represented by such local poets as Fernando Ma Guerrero (1873–1929), Lope K. Santos (1879–1965), Jose Corazon De Jesus (1896–1932), Amado V. Hernandez (1903–1970), Alejandro G. Abadilla (1904–1969), Angela Manalang Gloria (1907–1999), and Trinidad Tarrosa Subido (1912–1993).

Contemporary Poetry

The declaration of formal independence from the United States on 4 July 1946 brought a sense of a new beginning to the people and poets of the Philippines. A generation of poets who studied at the famed Iowa Writer's Workshop at the University of Iowa in the 1950s—Bienvenido N. Santos (1911–1996), Ricaredo Demetillo (1920–1998), Dominador I. Ilio (b. 1913), and Edith Tiempo (b. 1919)—came back to the Philippines with the literary ideals of the American New Criticism. The 1970s and 1980s proved to be a politically aware era for Filipino poets, who were writing under the censorship of the dictatorial regime of Ferdinand Marcos (1965–1986). As a reaction to the 1983 assassination of Benigno Aquino, Jr., a leading anti-Marcos politician, several poets formed a literary organization called PLAC (Philippine Literary Arts Council) to protest the abuses of the government. One of its leading founders was Alfred A. Yuson (b. 1945), whose neorealist books of poems are *Dream of Knives* (1986) and *Trading in Mermaids* (1993). Current trends in Filipino poetry are best exemplified by the pyrotechnic imagination of Eileen R. Tabios (b. 1960), whose book of poetry *Beyond Life Sentences* (1998) won the National Book Award given by the Manila Book Critics Circle. Her poems incorporate the American precision of Marianne Moore, the experimental joie de vivre of Paul Valery, and the imagistic intensity of Pablo Neruda.

Nick Carbo

Further Reading

Abad, H. Gemino. (1999) *A Habit of Shores: Filipino Poetry and Verse from English, 60's to the 90's.* Quezon City, Philippines: University of the Philippines Press.

Abad, H. Gemino, and Edna Z. Manlapaz, eds. (1989) *Man of Earth: An Anthology of Filipino Poetry and Verse from English, 1905 to the Mid-50's.* Quezon City, Philippines: Ateneo de Manila University Press.

Carbo, Nick. (1996) *Returning a Borrowed Tongue: An Anthology of Filipino and Filipino American Poetry.* Minneapolis, MN: Coffee House Press.

Carbo, Nick, and Eileen Tabios, eds. (2000) *Babaylan: An Anthology of Filipina and Filipina American Writers.* San Francisco: Aunt Lute Books.

POETRY—VIETNAM

Chinese chronicles trace the mythic origin of the Vietnamese to a union between a dragon king from the watery south and an immortal fairy queen from the mountainous north some four thousand years ago. Vietnam's history of poetic activity may be as ancient, based on the rich musicality of the Vietnamese language with its six tones and an age-old love of folk song that endures in modern Vietnamese culture. By the end of the tenth century CE, literary intelligentsia influenced by Chinese poetics developed a written poetic tradition in *chu Han* (Chinese script). By the fifteenth century, a demotic form of Vietnamese writing known as *chu nom*, or *nom*, became popular, fostering poetic license to alter strict Chinese metrical patterns to suit Vietnamese language and folk song forms. *Chu Han* and *nom* poems persisted until French colonization (1859–1945), when *quoc ngu* (romanized Vietnamese) gradually superseded these two scripts. *Quoc ngu* eventually enabled many poets, who had also become enamored of French romanticism, to discard any restrictive residue of Chinese poetics and create new experimental forms of poetry. During the thirty years of struggle for independence (1945–1975), poets split over ideological differences as the country became divided into North and South. After reunification in 1975, poets and writers were strongly encouraged to compose verse in *quoc ngu* with themes complementary to socialist realism. In the early 2000s, poetic freedom of expression remains somewhat circumscribed in Vietnam.

Folk Songs *(ca-dao)*

Vietnam's rich oral tradition of folk poetry, *ca-dao* (unaccompanied songs), is the lyrical expression of peasants and village folk. While most *ca-dao* were orally transmitted over generations, it is possible that literati who remained close to rural life composed *ca-dao* anonymously. Sometimes bawdy in content, often playful and irreverent, these folk songs ironically reflect social inequities and the vicissitudes of life, village customs and mores, romantic love, and the splendor of Vietnam's landscape. Since folk songs are closely attuned to Vietnamese tastes and feelings, they are even used in schools for teaching children geography, history, and other subjects. Parts of well-known folk songs also can be included in more formal poems. The importance of *ca-dao* in Vietnamese culture was recognized by Nguyen Van-Ngoc, who compiled the first systematic collection, *Tuc-ngu phong-dao* (Proverbs and Folk songs) in 1928.

Folk songs are found in a wide range of forms, from two-syllable to six- and eight-syllable verse using both medial and final rhymes, and rules for tone harmony give the verse a musical quality. The most popular form is *luc-bat* (six-eight) meter in which the first line has six syllables and the second line eight syllables. These couplets can be expanded into long verse narratives *(truyen nom)*, as in *The Tale of Kieu. Luc-bat* couplets and narrative verse alike follow a rhyme scheme such that the final syllable of the first line rhymes with the sixth syllable of the second line, and the eighth syllable (the final syllable) of the second line rhymes with the sixth syllable of the third line, and so forth.

Traditional Poetry *(tho cu)*

Vietnam was essentially a province of China from 111 BCE to 939 CE. By the end of the tenth century, the art of composing classical Chinese verse became one of the most highly regarded activities of the Vietnamese literati. Ultimately, the Ly dynasty (1009–1225) officially mandated that classical Chinese be used for education and governmental business. By adopting China's Neo-Confucian traditions, the Ly monarchs may have hoped to forestall further Chinese domination. These adopted Chinese traditions included the Song dynasty (960–1267)–style civil-service examinations, requiring knowledge of Chinese poetry and the ability to compose it. Once integrated into the civil-service examination system, verse writing in classical Chinese became a major concern of Vietnamese scholars, a concern that persisted until the traditional examination system was abolished in 1918.

Chinese classical poetry was governed by strict rules prescribing the number of lines, tone harmony, rhyming patterns, and parallelism of words, phrases, and sentences. It was typically based upon Chinese Tang-dynasty (618–907 CE) metrical rules for seven-syllable octets. The popular *bat cu* form has eight lines, each consisting of seven monosyllabic words. The caesura is always after the fourth word. The tone of each word is fixed and the rhyme is the same pattern throughout the poem. The first two lines form an introduction, the last two a conclusion. The subject matter, imagery, and language of classical verse also were formalized, circumscribing the poet's ability to express much spontaneous emotion. Nevertheless, some Vietnamese scholar-poets developed this Chinese style of traditional poetry into their own distinctive genre by incorporating indigenous imagery and imparting a dynamic quality to their poems.

Some of the first recorded classical poems in Chinese were by Vietnamese Buddhist monks and reflect religious themes, such as the transitory nature of the world and the aesthetics of solitude. Poems by the literati, such as Truong Han-Sieu (d. 1354), and Chu (Van) An (1292–1370), explored a variety of subjects, including patriotism, the importance of moral virtues, filial piety and loyalty to the king, and the joys and sorrows of life, including romantic love. During the Late Le dynasty (1428–1788) this genre was promoted by the poet-monarch Le Thanh-Tong (1460–1497), who established the Tao Dan group, which was known for developing a new style of classical poetry *(vinh-su)* to praise historical events. Both monks and scholars continued to use classical Chinese for regulated verse and prose, but by the Early Le dynasty (980–1009) they may also have written in *nom* to compose eight-line stanzas or long narratives in the native *luc-bat* meter or its variants.

Chu Nom ("southern writing"), or *Nom* is the term for native or demotic characters created from the Chinese ideographs. *Nom* graphs were used for their phonetic and semantic value; sometimes they were used only as indicators of the semantic meaning of a Vietnamese word or its pronunciation. This novel script may have been created by the time Sino-Vietnamese pronunciation became established, around the eleventh century. It was already widely used under the Tran dynasty (1225–1400). Very little Vietnamese *nom* poetry has survived from prior to the time of Nguyen Trai (1380–1442), who edited some important *nom* texts, including *Quoc-am thi-tap* (Collected Poems in National Language). During the Tran and Late Le dynasties, writers in *nom* wrote reflective poems about the intrigues and artificiality of court life, or eulogies on nature in which a sense of peace and authenticity was sought.

Verse in *nom* achieved its height in the eighteenth century. The most popular of the *nom* narratives is *The Tale of Kieu (Truyen Kieu* or *Kim Van Kieu)*, by Nguyen Du (1765–1820). It is a romantic tale of tragic karmic consequences, admired for its pathos and lyrical beauty. Other well-known long lyrical poems from this period include *Cung oan ngam khuc* (A Royal Concubine's Complaint) by On Nhu Hau (1741–1798), lamenting the fate of a beautiful concubine trapped in a restrictive palace culture, and *Chinh-phu ngam* (Lament of a Warrior's Bride) by the female poet Doan Thi-Diem (1705–1746), depicting the tragedy of a forlorn wife waiting in vain for her husband to return from war.

Both *chu Han* and *nom* were utilized by some poets well into the twentieth century, but ultimately they were superseded by the popularity of poetry in *quoc ngu* (romanized script). Classical poets like Nguyen Khuyen (1835–1909) and Tran Te Xuong (1870–1907), who lived at the end of the nineteenth century, were sad to see their traditional world disintegrate as rapid changes wrought by French occupation transformed Vietnamese society. During this era the poets Nguyen Dinh-Chieu (1822–1888) and Bui Huu-Nghia (1807–1872) wrote patriotic verse in resistance to French colonization, and the scholar and poet Phan Chau-Trinh (1872–1926) was imprisoned for this patriotism. Chu Manh Trinh (1862–1905) and Duong Khue (1839–1902) wrote defeatist verse, while Tran Te-Xuong (1870–1907) created satirical poetry about corrupt bureaucrats. Other poets simply retired in disgust from colonial office to live a reclusive existence.

Modern Poetry

The establishment of the French presence in Vietnam by the end of the nineteenth century caused both economic and social upheavals. During the colonial period (1862–1945), books in Chinese were gradually superceded by those in *nom* and then in *quoc ngu*, codified by a Jesuit missionary, Alexandre de Rhodes (1591–1660), in 1651. This vernacular script was used predominantly in Catholic circles until colonial bureaucrats promoted it to the non-Catholic press and encouraged French colonials living in Vietnam to read Vietnamese in *quoc ngu*. After 1920, the explosion of *quoc ngu* newspapers provided a popular venue for the publication of a new type of Vietnamese poetry.

By 1932 a new type of verse launched by the poet Phan Khoi (1887–1958)—inspired by French romanticism, realism, and the alienation caused by a rapidly changing colonial society—became progressively more important. This New Poetry *(tho moi)*, popularized by

Nguyen Khac-Hieu (1888–1939), was written without restrictions on rhyming pattern, line length, or emotional expression. From 1932 to 1940, the New Poetry movement revolved around young poets following master poet The-Lu (1906–1989), assisted by the literary group Tu-Luc Van Doan ("Self-Reliance") and their periodical titled *Phong-hoa*, which published the poems. These young poets, from the urban middle class, reflected a sense of failed individualism, melancholy, and alienation as second-class colonial citizens in their own country. During the 1930s, they became preoccupied with an important debate about the use of poetry: the "art for art's sake" or "art for the sake of life" controversy. French influence was strongest in the south, where poets completely rejected rhyme for assonance and adopted new techniques, such as enjambment, alliteration, and caesura. Some poets continued to write in the classical forms as well.

From 1940, poets drifted in different ideological directions as nationalism developed in reaction to the colonial policies of the Vichy regime in France and the subsequent defeat of Japan in World War II. Some accomplished poets, such as Huy-Can (b. 1919), and To-Huu (b. 1920), became deeply involved in the quest for independence. Poets in the north, who had been part of the New Poetry movement in the 1930s, shifted from a 1930s style of romantic, alienated individualism or a 1940s style of rural realism to a more ideologically relevant socialist realism. Xuan Dieu (1917–1985) and like-minded northern poets became involved in the Literary Association for National Salvation and used poetry to reform the thoughts of local soldiers and cadres. Meanwhile, poets in the south retained more French influence and continued to write free verse dealing with a wider spectrum of subjects and experimental forms. Ideological differences were exacerbated by the partition of Vietnam at the seventeenth parallel in 1954.

Following the partition, there were two distinct directions for poetry: socialist realism in the north and the deepening development of New Poetry in the south. Northern poets who continued to protest against the ideological direction of socialist realism were soon silenced by the political dictum of "art for the sake of life," while poets in the south remained adamant about "art for the sake of art." Northern poet Che Lan-Vien (1920–1988) wrote unsympathetically of an unreformed northern poet shipped off to a work camp: "What good is all that futile verse that flows like water / And does not serve the people so much as a single bowl of rice?" (translated by Neil Jamieson).

Many poets in the south, such as Thanh Tm Tuyen (b. 1936) and Nguyen Sa (b. 1930), who had fled the north in their childhood, continued to develop the New Poetry style. Female poets such as Nguyen Thi Hoang (b. 1939) became more prominent during the 1960s. She wrote of the pain and conflict of Saigon's youth in a poem titled "Confession" (1963): "my misery knows no bounds. / Night after night I strain to listen to the vespers / While agonizing over a hundred lonely griefs" (translation by Nguyen Dinh Tuyen). During the 1960s and 1970s, as the entire country became progressively engulfed in a bitter civil war with American involvement, poets on both sides took the tragedy of war as the subject of their poetry.

When Vietnam was reunified under Communist control in 1975, southern poetry written between 1954 and 1975 was harshly suppressed. Poets in the former Republic of Vietnam fled the country, unwilling to be restricted to writing in a style of socialist realism. Those who could not escape were sent to reeducation camps. In reaction to his forced imprisonment, Ha Thuc Sinh penned the following lines: "Do not die, Poetry / When I need you so much! / Be like a sharp knife / That I may yet have a weapon to fight the enemy" (translated by James Banerian).

Vietnamese poetry in the early 2000s is a highly regarded genre. Bookstalls selling miniature pocket-size collections of both traditional and modern poetry can be found along the bustling roads of any major city. Poetry continues to be published in journals and newspapers by poets usually aligned with specific writers' associations situated in Hanoi, Hue, or Ho Chi Minh City. Poems continue to be recited at gatherings of friends, and folk songs continue to be sung by peasants for their pleasure. After so many years of writing in the style of socialist realism, poets may enjoy a wider but still limited freedom of expression with the new *doi moi* (renovation) policy implemented in 1986.

Teri Shaffer Yamada

See also: **Chu Nom; Ho Xuan Huong; Literature—Vietnam; Tu Luc Van Doan; Sino-Vietnamese Culture**

Further Reading

Balaban, John. (1980) *Ca Dao Viet Nam: A Bilingual Anthology of Vietnamese Folk Poetry.* Greensboro, NC: Unicorn Press.

———, trans. (2000) *Spring Essence: The Poetry of Ho Xuan Huong.* Port Townsend, WA: Copper Canyon Press.

Bowen, Kevin, Nguyen Ba Chung, and Bruce Weigl, eds. (1998) *Mountain River: Vietnamese Poetry from the Wars, 1948-1993.* Amherst: University of Massachusetts Press.

Bowen, Kevin, and Nguyen Ba Chung, trans. (1999) *Distant Road: Selected Poems of Nguyen Duy*. Willimantic, CT: Curbstone Press.

Durand, Maurice M., and Nguyen Tran Huan. (1985) *An Introduction to Vietnamese Literature*. Trans. by D. M. Hawke. New York: Columbia University Press.

Ha Thuc Sinh *If I Should Live to Return: Report to the Free World*. Trans. by James Banerian. Distributed for the translator by Dalley Book Service.

Huynh Sanh Thong. (1979) *The Heritage of Vietnamese Poetry*. New Haven, CT: Yale University Press.

Huynh Sanh Tong, ed. and trans. (1996) *An Anthology of Vietnamese Poems: From the Eleventh through the Twentieth Centuries*. New Haven, CT: Yale University Press.

Jamieson, Neil. (1992) "Shattered Identities and Contested Images: Reflections of Poetry and History in Twentieth-Century Vietnam." *Crossroads* 7, 2: 70–134.

Linh Dinh. (1996) "The Cat Sits on a Palm Tree: An Introduction to the Folk Poems, Proverbs, and Riddles of Viet Nam." In *North Viet Nam Now: Fiction and Essays from Ha Noi. Viet Nam Forum* 15. New Haven, CT: Yale University Council on Southeast Asia Studies, 135–159.

Ly Chanh Trung. (1960) *Introduction to Vietnamese Poetry*. Vietnam Culture Series, no. 3. Saigon, Vietnam: Ministry of Culture.

Nguyen Cong Tru. (1987) "Fourteen Poems." Trans. by Huynh Sanh Thong. *Viet Nam Forum* 9. New Haven, CT: Yale University Council on Southeast Asia Studies, 79–91.

Nguyen Du. (1983) *The Tale of Kieu*. Trans. by Huynh Sanh Thong. New Haven, CT: Yale University Press.

Nguyen Dinh Hoa. (1994) *Vietnamese Literature: A Brief Survey*. San Diego, CA: San Diego State University.

Nguyen Ngoc Bich. "The Poetic Tradition of Vietnam." In *Some Aspects of Vietnamese Culture*, edited by Nguyen Din Hoa. Monograph Series, no. 2. Carbondale, IL: Center for Vietnamese Studies, 19–38.

———, ed. and trans. (1975) *A Thousand Years of Vietnamese Poetry*. New York: Alfred A. Knopf.

———, ed. (1989) *War and Exile: A Vietnamese Anthology*. Springfield, VA: Vietnamese PEN Abroad.

POJAGI *Pojagi*, or *po*, are Korean cloths (most often silk or ramie) used to cover, store, or carry items. They range in size, color, and design depending on function. Most commonly, they are square or rectangular so the opposite corners can be tied together to hold their contents securely.

Pojagi have long been a part of Korean culture but flourished in the Choson dynasty (1392–1910). They are still prevalent today for formal gift-giving, storage, and as a practical alternative to shopping bags in an environmentally conscious society. Some of the most common forms of *pojagi* are the table *po* (*sangpo*) to cover food, blanket *po* (*ibulpo*) to store bedding, and everyday *pojagi* to carry items.

Most *pojagi* are of patchwork design, allowing for thrifty use of fabric remnants, and are also highly artistic in their use of color and design. They often incorporate bright colors and geometric patterns. There are embroidered *pojagi* (*supo*) bearing floral motifs for more formal uses.

The *pojagi* for wedding rituals are double-faced in blue and red, the two traditional wedding colors. Two varieties include the bridal chest *po* (*hampo*) and ceremonial present *po* (*yedanpo*) to wrap gifts between the bride and groom's families, respectively.

Jennifer Jung-Kim

Further Reading

Korean Overseas Information Service. (1995) *Pojagi Wrapping Cloths*. Korean Heritage Series no. 9. Seoul: Korean Overseas Information Service.

POL POT (1925–1998), leader of Khmer Rouge guerrillas of Cambodia. Saloth Sar, as Pol Pot was originally named, lived comfortably as a child with his father (a prosperous landowner), along with his brother, sister, and female cousin, under the protection of King Sisowath and King Monivong of Cambodia. For a time Saloth Sar lived in the royal palace, where he witnessed the feudalistic practices, including his sister and cousin's becoming royal consorts, experiences that might have affected his later political thinking.

Because of his family's status, Saloth Sar attended several French-language schools (a privilege afforded few Cambodians) but failed to earn a high school diploma. He subsequently lived in a Buddhist monastery as a novice monk for a few months.

In 1949 Saloth Sar's fluency in French and his family's political connections earned him a scholarship to study in France, but there he neglected academics to study left-wing politics. As a result, he was forced to return to Cambodia when he failed his exams, shortly after joining the French Communist Party in 1952. Before returning, however, he spent time in Yugoslavia working in a labor battalion.

After Cambodia's independence Saloth Sar led a double life, teaching in a private school in Phnom Penh (1954–1963) and commanding the country's Communist Party. In 1965 he visited China and was inspired by the Cultural Revolution, which he saw as a meaningful revolutionary model. Supported by Chinese officials, he returned to Cambodia and spent the

One of the few photos of Pol Pot hangs in the Tuoi Sieng Museum in Phnom Penh, which had been a Khmer Rouge prison and torture center. (PABLO SAN JUAN/CORBIS)

next four years refining the radically utopian ideology he was to practice as Pol Pot.

After Cambodia's ruler Prince Norodom Sihanouk was overthrown in a pro-American coup in 1970, the Khmer Rouge (Cambodian Reds, or Communists)—a term the prince derisively applied to Pol Pot's rebels—waged guerrilla warfare against the Cambodian army. Intensive U.S. bombing of the Cambodian countryside no doubt increased the popularity of the Khmer Rouge. Eventually occupying the capital of Phnom Penh in April 1975, the guerrillas forced the city's 2 million residents—and those of other towns—into the countryside within two days to work in agricultural communes. During the next four years, nearly 2 million people were murdered or died horribly from overwork, disease, or starvation, as Pol Pot brutally took Cambodia back to "Year Zero," in the process destroying the country's economy and society.

In 1979 the Vietnamese entered Cambodia and drove the Khmer Rouge from power, but for nearly two decades Pol Pot and his army hid in the jungles of Thailand and northern Cambodia and terrorized the Vietnamese-dominated Cambodian government and the local population. Soldiers led by Ta Mok, his former comrade, arrested Pol Pot in 1997 after he had ordered some subordinates killed. On 15 April 1998, while listening to the Voice of America, Pol Pot learned that Ta Mok intended to deliver him to an international tribunal for trial. Before midnight he was dead, allegedly from heart failure, though some suspect suicide or even murder.

Greg Ringer

Further Reading

Becker, Elizabeth. (1998) *When the War Was Over: Cambodia and the Khmer Rouge Revolution.* Washington, DC: Public Affairs.

Chandler, David. (1999) *Brother Number One: A Political Biography of Pol Pot.* 2d ed. Boulder, CO: Westview Press.

Chandler, David, Ben Kiernan, and Chanthou Boua, eds. (1988) *Pol Pot Plans the Future: Confidential Leadership Documents from Democratic Kampuchea, 1976–1977.* New Haven, CT: Yale Council on Southeast Asia Studies.

Heder, Stephen R. (1991) *Pol Pot and Khieu Samphan.* Clayton, Victoria, Australia: Monash University, Centre of Southeast Asia Studies.

Kiernan, Ben. (1985) *How Pol Pot Came to Power: A History of Communism in Kampuchea, 1930–1975.* London: Verso.

———. (1998) *The Pol Pot Regime: Race, Power, and Genocide in Cambodia under the Khmer Rouge, 1975–79.* New Haven, CT: Yale University Press.

POLITICAL PARTICIPATION, UNOFFICIAL—CHINA When individuals or groups become active in the family, at work, and in clubs, the economy, or politics in order to achieve or influence certain aims in public life, such actions can be called political participation. China's traditional political culture allowed the vast majority of the population only a small degree of formal participation. Confucianism defined duties (to the ruler, to the state, to the family), but no rights. Independent political institutions and parallel power structures were always suppressed. One exception was the concept of the Mandate of Heaven, which permitted people to rebel in order to depose an incompetent ruler, should the state be in political, economic, and social decline. Locally, self-governing villages and communities enjoyed a relatively large degree of autonomy. Clans, kinship groups, secret societies, temple organizations, guilds, and regional groupings organized their own social spheres. Also, the assertion of interests against those of state and bureaucracy happened informally through connections, corruption, negotiation, and strategy.

Political Participation before 1949

Toward the end of the empire (1912) and during the republic (1912–1927), the basis for a legal system with laws and law courts began to develop, and political parties, professional organizations, literary and artistic circles, and mass media emerged. At the beginning of the 1930s, there were attempts to introduce general elections for the offices of heads of villages or communities. The strengthening of authoritarian structures between 1912 and 1949 limited the development of a civil society largely autonomous of the state, which could have led to democratic forms of participation.

Communist Control of Political Participation

The Chinese Communist Party (CCP) initially allowed alternative forms of political participation in the regions it controlled. After the founding of the People's Republic (1949), however, the CCP monopolized political and public life. Calls for freedom of speech and participation in politics were soon put to an end (for example, Mao Zedong's Hundred Flowers Campaign, a brief period of open criticism of the government, which was ended in 1957). As obvious dissatisfaction with the CCP and its structures became apparent, critics were arrested as right-wingers and punished. From then on, such movements were subject to stronger political and ideological control.

Mao's "mass line" was supposed to be the central instrument for the articulation of people's interests and participation in society. In theory it involved consultations between the population (mainly farmers) and functionaries, with the aim of adapting the party's politics to the actual situation. However, the decisive partner in these consultation processes was always the CCP, which gathered and then interpreted the opinion of the masses according to its own aims and ideas. It sought the people's support, not their participation.

The CCP launched political campaigns in which the masses were to be mobilized to help reach economic or political aims. Divergent opinions or new forms of organizations were tolerated only as long as they echoed the aims of the dominant opinion in the political elite. Mass mobilization was carried out by the party leadership and was supervised by the political elite. The participation mechanisms promoted by the CCP (criticism and self-criticism, wall news sheets, ideological study groups) tended to become ritualized and were more a means of social control than of fostering political participation.

Political Participation in the Era of Reform

Social pluralization in the course of China's reform policies since 1979 has opened up possibilities for more social involvement. New and existing social groups that were not represented in the CCP (private entrepreneurs, professional groups, migrant workers, ethnic minorities, and religious groups) have sought economic, social, and political participation and the creation of channels for the expression and pursuit of their interests. This is true for both formal and informal structures. Formal participation can take place both in the CCP and outside it: in the mass organizations (unions, Communist Youth League, Women's Federation, People's Militia), in the so-called Political Consultative Conferences, in non-Communist parties, and in many new associations and clubs. Such associations articulate interests; that is, they produce social input that influences political decision-making processes. The increasing separation between the public and private spheres and the state's retreat from many areas of society give these associations more room to maneuver, widen their autonomy, and create and articulate a social counterweight to state actions, all of which provide more space for direct participation. This is also true for elections at county, township, or village level, which were institutionalized and subject to new laws in the first half of the 1980s. Particularly at village level, the village-leadership elections may lead to a type of grassroots democracy, although until now these elections have often taken place in only modified or limited form.

Informal Political Participation

At the informal level, the creation or use of *guanxi* ("personal connections") can be used to influence decisions or push interests. *Guanxi* function through networks, patronage, bribes and other forms of corruption, and nepotism. They are a permissible means of seeking compromises and negotiating interests as long as they do not disrupt the political framework set up by the CCP. The informal level also includes illegal forms of political participation, such as organizing illegal demonstrations or strikes, refusing to pay taxes, or forming illegal interest groups (trade unions, secret societies, underground churches, regional groups).

Additionally, a kind of regionalism is developing in the form of increased regional and local autonomy based on economic practices. In areas with strong local economies, local interests are prioritized over state interests. Communities report lower than actual profits in order to pay fewer taxes and use the money for local development, or they turn to protectionism (import or export bans for products to or from other provinces) to safeguard their own markets. This regional autonomy can also include negotiating how much income tax must be passed on to the central government, developing independent foreign trade in goods and currency, or deviating from central policies. These phenomena are a kind of regional participation, because they lead to more involvement in decisions in the interests of the region or the community, even if they are in the form of deviation from official policies.

Such informal patterns make it clear that participation and decision-making structures in China cannot be explained by the analysis of formal channels only. Where there are few opportunities for formal participation, informal means of advancing particular interests also exist.

In order to implement its policies and widen its popular support, the CCP has been trying to include more people and groups in discussion and consultation processes. Interest groups, which had not been integrated into existing structures or which were outside official discourse, have furthered this attempt to widen participation. The discourse is limited in the sense that those involved have to accept the political system and the leadership of the CCP. However, groups that in the past had no means of expressing their needs and desires now have the opportunity to articulate their interests.

Collective Action by Social Groups

China's peasant population has made use of specific forms of protest behavior that are highly effective. Protest activities include supplying falsified (reduced) harvest figures; claiming that the amount of cultivable land is less than it really is and that income is lower than it really is; giving the worst-quality products to the state; refusing to cooperate with state directives; engaging in tax evasion, negligence, and theft or destruction of state property; and organizing informal interest groups. This kind of everyday resistance, which can be seen as political participation and articulation of interests by the weakest in society, can in the long term lead to political changes because of its high social and economic costs. In societies where there is no other way to express dissatisfaction, such behavior is the peasants' only means of resistance.

One example of such collective action was taken at the end of the 1970s. Due to stagnation and poverty, farmers in poor areas spontaneously began to divide collectively held land among themselves and to return to family-run farming. The economic success of these measures led to the CCP's approving them as "agricultural reform," which was then implemented across the whole country. In this case, collective action initiated political change. It provided the solution for economic difficulties and was therefore approved by members of the Party leadership.

Finally, at the level of the individual, means of political participation include *guanxi* networks and bribery. Gift giving, hospitality, bonuses, and "donations" from entrepreneurs to functionaries are all means by which individuals attempt to gain a voice in political decision making.

Although direct participation in Chinese power structures is still dependent on membership in the CCP, political power and political influence do not stem only from membership in the party. Today China's people have more and more opportunity to voice their interests and to participate in the political life of the nation outside the CCP and formal structures.

Thomas Heberer

See also: **Guanxi; Social Associations—China**

Further Reading

Christiansen, Flemming. (1996) *Rai Shirin: Chinese Politics and Society*. London and New York: Prentice Hall/Harvester Wheatsheaf.

Gao, Bingzhong. (2001) "The Rise of Associations in China and the Question of Their Legitimacy." *Social Sciences in China* (spring): 73–87.

Heberer, Thomas, and Wolfgang Taubmann. (1998) *Chinas Ländliche Gesellschaft im Umbruch*. Opladen, Germany: Westdeutscher Verlag.

Heberer, Thomas, and Kerstin K. Vogel, eds. (1997) *Frauen-Los!?: Politische Partizipation von Frauen in Ostasien*. Münster, Germany: Lit-Verlag.

Lieberthal, Kenneth. (1995) *Governing China: From Revolution through Reform*. New York: W. W. Norton.

Pearson, Margaret M. (1994) "The Janus Face of Business Associations in China: Socialist Corporatism in Foreign Enterprises." *Australian Journal of Chinese Affairs* (January): 25–48.

Saich, Tony. (2000) "Negotiating the State: The Development of Social Organizations in China." *China Quarterly* (March): 124–141.

Shi, Tianjian. (1997) *Political Participation in Beijing*. Cambridge, MA: Harvard University Press.

Shue, Vivienne. (1994) "State Power and Social Organization in China." In *State Power and Social Forces: Domination and Transformation in the Third World*, edited by Joel S. Migdal, Atul Kohli, and Vivienne Shue. Cambridge, U.K., New York, and Melbourne, Australia: Cambridge University Press, 65–88.

Unger, Jonathan. (1996) "Bridges: Private Business, the Chinese Government, and the Rise of New Associations." *China Quarterly* (September): 63–88.

POLO, MARCO (1254–1324), Venetian trader and explorer. Marco Polo, born into a Venetian trading family with Eurasian connections, went along with family members overland to Mongol China, where he spent some seventeen years (1275–1292) and may have held some official position. He traveled extensively (mostly by sea), and finally returned to Italy in 1295. Shortly thereafter, while a prisoner of war of the Genoese, he dictated his memoirs to a fellow prisoner who also happened to be a writer of romances, and who may have embellished what he heard considerably. There also exist several alternative versions in a variety of languages (the original was in Old French), which vary considerably in detail and in overall coverage. In any case, the memoirs were an immediate sensation, and few books have been more translated or have had as great an impact upon the European imagination as have Marco Polo's travels.

Marco Polo's Impressions of Mongol China

During Marco Polo's time, most of Eurasia was divided up among various competing khanates, successors to a unified Mongol empire. The largest was Mongol China, which included a substantial part of Central Asia as well as what is now China. Marco Polo's account naturally contains extensive information about it since he spent most of his time there. What most impressed him, besides daily life at the exotic court of Khubilai Khan (1215–1294), was the sheer wealth of much of the society that he saw. He makes this clear in his description of the former Song dynasty capital of Hangzhou (called Kinsay, from a Song term designating its status as a "temporary" capital after the Song loss of northern China). According to Marco, the sheer well-being of the inhabitants and level of economic activity there—in its many markets, for example, frequented daily by more people than lived in any Italian city—was almost beyond belief. It was Marco Polo's descriptions of the wealth of the East, above all, that drew European attentions during the fourteenth- and fifteenth-century Age of Exploration, when Marco Polo's book was required reading for anyone interested in the East, including Columbus.

Marco Polo's Other Travels

In addition to China, Marco or his family visited the other khanates of the Mongolian world, including the Golden Horde, which ruled Russia, the Russian steppe, the Volga basin, and associated areas; the Il-Khanate of Iran, through which young Marco traveled on the way to China and by which he returned; and the domains of the Chagatai house in Turkistan, also crossed during Polo's outbound journey. He also heard of, or personally touched on, a great many other areas as well. For example, in some official capacity, he not only visited southwest China and Yunnan, an area which had only recently been made a part of China by Mongol conquest, but also Burma, invaded several times by the Mongols. He left behind as a result a valuable first-hand account that is the earliest detailed European notice of the area. He was also the first European writer to mention Japan, although he did not visit it. Before

A miniature painting from Maudeville's *Book of Marvels* shows Marco Polo before Kubilai Khan. (BETTMANN/CORBIS)

returning to Europe, Marco Polo not only visited Manzi, or south China, but also sailed through insular southeast Asia, including Java, the Indian Ocean, and Persian Gulf, then made a final return lap through Il-Khanate domains, the empire of Trebizond (on the southeastern shores of the Black Sea), and Byzantium.

Legend and Folklore in Marco Polo's Memoirs

In addition to providing often quite accurate factual information about the countries that he visited, Marco Polo's memoirs are a treasure trove of legend. They speak at length of Prester John, the supposed Christian king of the East whose realm was a primary target of early explorers in later centuries. He also repeats many interesting travelers' tales about various superstitions associated with the deserts of Central Asia. There is, for example, the Island of Women, one of a pair of mythical islands divided by sex, or the Dry Tree that had stood since ancient times in an immense plain. Some of the travelers' tales, like that of the Dry Tree, were of great antiquity and for that reason are of great interest to folklorists.

In all of this, perhaps the most valuable information of all is Marco Polo's independent testimony on how Mongol China actually worked. Like the Persian historian Rashid ad-Din (1247–1318), he describes a regime more Mongolian than Chinese, one in which Khubilai and his court moved with the seasons in the traditional Mongolian way and engaged in typical Mongolian occupations while doing so, including much-loved hunting.

Marco Polo and Revisionist History

Marco Polo's descriptions of China and other parts have always seemed a little larger than life to some, and of late there has been a major effort to discredit him. Marco Polo's book does have its problems, but this effort is largely based upon a misappraisal of the environment he describes. It was not very Chinese, but if Marco preserves a Turkic nickname for a Chinese city, this was because he lived in a heavily Turkicized environment. Similarly, if he was thinking in Persian much of the time, this is also only to be expected given the dominance of Persian culture at the Mongol court.

Paul D. Buell

Further Reading

Franke, Herbert. (1966) "Sino-Western Contacts under the Mongol Empire." *Journal of the Royal Asiatic Society: Hong Kong Branch*, 6: 49–72.

Pelliot, Paul. (1959–1973) *Notes on Marco Polo*. 3 vols. Paris: Impremerie Nationale, Librairie Adrien-Maisonneuve.

Rachewiltz, Igor de. (1999) "F. Wood's *Did Marco Polo Go To China?* A Critical Appraisal by I. de Rachewiltz." Retrieved 6 February 2002, from: http://rspas.anu.edu.au/eah/Marcopolo.html.

Yule, Henry, and Henri Cordier. ([1903–1920] 1975) *The Book of Ser Marco Polo, the Venetian*. 2 vols. Reprint ed. Amsterdam: Philo Press.

POLONNARUVA Polonnaruva was an ancient Sri Lankan capital that became a residence of Ceylon's kings in the fourth century CE and flourished owing to its proximity to the Mahaweli River and its location on the route to southern Sri Lanka, east of the central highlands. It became a second capital in the eighth century and succeeded Anuradhapura as the sole capital after the destruction of that city in 993. The invading Cholas made Polonnaruva their capital, as did the Sinhalese who overthrew them. The city reached its height under King Parakramabahu I (reigned 1153–1186), who built a walled city containing extensive gardens, monastic and temple complexes, and many monuments in brick and stone, all watered by a vast man-made lake. It was deserted in the thirteenth century after a series of invasions and the spread of malaria drove the political centers to the coasts. The ruins of monuments built by the Cholas and Parakramabahu I are well preserved. A modern town arose in the twentieth century after the restoration of the ancient irrigation reservoirs and the suppression of malaria. It has become a major tourist destination and in 1982 was named to the UNESCO World Heritage List.

Patrick Peebles

Further Reading

Saparamadu, S. D., ed. (1995) *The Polonnaruva Period. Special Number on the Polonnaruva Period issued in Commemoration of the 800th Anniversary of the Accession of King Parakrama Bahu the Great. Ceylon Historical Journal* 4.

Smith, Bardwell. (1986) "The Pursuit of Equilibrium: Polonnaruwa as a Ceremonial Center." *Journal of Developing Societies* 2: 193–207.

PONDICHERRY (2001 pop. 808,000). The union territory of Pondicherry consists of the former French settlements of Pondicherry, Karaikal, Mahe, and Yanam, which lie scattered in South India. These were transferred to the Indian Union in 1954. The capital, Pondicherry, lies on the southeastern coast of India. It is bounded on the east by the Bay of Bengal and on the other three sides by the state of Tamil Nadu. Karaikal is situated on the east coast, about 150 kilometers south of Pondicherry. Mahe lies on the western coast and is surrounded by the state of Kerala, while Yanam is situated on the East Godavari district of Andhra Pradesh.

Nearly 45 percent of the people in Pondicherry are engaged in agriculture. Food crops include rice, millet, and pulses, while sugarcane, peanuts, and cotton are the major cash crops. Modern industries have also come up in Pondicherry. The principal industries include textiles, computers, electronic goods, biopolymers, pharmaceuticals, leather goods, and a range of consumer products.

The capital Pondicherry had been the headquarters of the French colonies in India since the seventeenth century and has a rich French cultural heritage. The French Boulevard Town, Sri Aurobindo Ashram, and Auroville Museum are some places of interest to tourists.

Sanjukta Das Gupta

Further Reading

Miles, William F. S. (1995) *Imperial Burdens: Countercolonialism in Former French India.* Boulder, CO: Lynn Reinner Publications.

Mittal, Arun. (2000) *Visit Pondicherry.* Mumbai, India: Bharatiya Vidya Bhavan.

PORCELAIN—EAST ASIA

Porcelain (ceramic ware made with kaolin, a fine white clay) was first made in China around 850 CE during the Tang dynasty (618–907). An Islamic traveler who had visited China in 851 described clay vessels that looked to him like glass. There is available evidence that fine white stoneware (pottery made from high-firing clay other than kaolin) was being made in China as long ago as 1400 BCE, and Chinese potters appear to have been acquainted with kaolin in the Han dynasty (206 BCE–220 CE). The forerunner of the modern-day porcelain was not made until the Tang dynasty, several centuries later. This Tang-dynasty porcelain is known as hard-paste or true porcelain. It was produced by mixing kaolin, which is formed by the decay of feldspar, a chief constituent of granite, together with petuntse, a form of feldspar found only in China. Kaolin is the essential ingredient for the manufacture of porcelain. It is found throughout the world and known for its white firing characteristics (that is, the fact that the finished product appears white rather than gray or brown or rust-colored) and high fusion temperature (that is, the high heat required to turn the constituent ingredients into porcelain). Chemically, kaolin comprises kaolinite, muscovite, quartz, feldspar, and anastase. Kaolin and petuntse are fused together by firing in a kiln, first at 980°C, then dipped in glaze and refired at a higher temperature of about 1300°C. Petuntse is responsible for binding the clay particles together and giving porcelain its translucency. The high temperatures used in the firings in the kiln vitrify the ceramic body; that is, they give it its glassy characteristics.

Some of the most beautiful Chinese porcelain wares were made during the Song dynasty (960–1279), including eggshell porcelain, which was thinner and more translucent than previously manufactured porcelain. Ding ware, which was produced in northeastern China, has a molded design which is emphasized by its typical ivory-colored glaze. There were two other types of porcelain that were produced during the Song dynasty, although slightly later. These were the Longchuan and Jingbai wares. The Longchuan wares were near-white ceramic bodies under a bluish-green translucent glaze (celadon) reminiscent of green jade, a favorite stone among the Chinese. This ware showed to great advantage the incised or molded decoration of the period. Jingbai ware, made in Jiangxi (which eventually became the center of Chinese porcelain manufacture), was delicately formed. It was distinguished by a pale blue glaze with decorations of incised flowers and foliage.

Porcelain was not widely made in China until the Yuan dynasty (1297–1368). It was also only at this time that the Chinese started to use a kaolin-based compound to produce a material that when fired in the kiln at very high temperatures turned both white and translucent.

The Spread of Porcelain to Europe

Porcelain's origins in China led to it being called "china." China was first brought to Europe in the twelfth century; Portuguese traders began importing it in the sixteenth. Sometime between then and the beginnings of porcelain manufacture in Europe in the late eighteenth century, the Portuguese introduced the name "porcelain." Today, the terms *china* and *porcelain* are used interchangeably. The only clear effort to delineate between china and porcelain is to use *china* to refer to figurines and items for use with meals. Porcelain, on the other hand, is taken to be a broader term that has been applied to a wider range of products. So reference is made to a tea set that is made from either china or porcelain, but the material used to make a toilet is porcelain.

The Chinese technique for manufacturing porcelain remained a secret. During the medieval period, Europeans, whose appetite for the aesthetic beauty of kaolin clay seemed insatiable, tried experimenting with various materials in the hope of discovering the Chinese formula; it was not discovered until the early eighteenth century. In the meantime, China exported its porcelain wares, especially its blue and white ware (porcelain decorated with cobalt-blue designs under a clear glaze) in ever increasing quantities, beginning in the sixteenth century. Such exports were conducted largely through the British and Dutch East India Companies. By 1700, there was a vast trade in porcelain. The wares of the Ming dynasty (1368–1644) were particularly prized.

Ming-Dynasty and Qing-Dynasty Ware

Ming potters paid more attention to painted designs and less to the forms of the wares. There was great success with the production of the blue and white wares. During the reign (1505–1521) of the Zhengde emperor (1491–1521), wares with a yellow ground were made when the art of fusing enamels or colored glass onto the surface of the glaze was perfected.

The well-known center for porcelain manufacture, Jingdezhen (in Jiangxi), reached its peak during the reign of the great Qing emperor Kangxi (1654–1722, reigned 1661–1722). This center produced numerous wares for the use of the court as well as large quantities of porcelain to satisfy the demands of the European market. Wares of exceptional beauty would be produced to commemorate the birthdays of emperors. Especially popular during the reign of Kangxi was *famille verte*, wares in which various shades of green predominate. Then a black enamel background was used, giving rise to the name *famille noire* and later the *famille rose* that included a range of rose pink enamels. These wares were popular during the reign (1726–1795) of the Qianlong emperor (1711–1795), the grandson of the Kangxi emperor. Most of the enamel was then added in Guangzhou (Canton), which was the primary trading port.

Japanese Porcelain

True porcelain was made in Japan only after the early part of the seventeenth century. Only then were the necessary clay materials discovered in Hizen. The Japanese used a purple-toned underglaze blue (that is, a blue underglaze design) on a grayish-colored ceramic body. The later wares from Japan that were popular in Europe were painted in rich vermilion and other colors and decorated with a profusion of flowers together with gilding. This decorative style was known as Imari, which was the name of the seaport from which these porcelains from Arita were being shipped.

Some of the finest porcelain created in Japan is decorated in Kakiemon style. This style is named after a family of potters in Arita who were credited with having introduced, during the middle of the seventeenth century, the use of enamel painting in soft reds, greenish-blue, turquoise, yellow, and the occasional underglaze blue.

Korean Porcelain

Much early Korean porcelain, such as that of the twelfth century, has been found to be so like the Chinese Ding ware that it is difficult to distinguish. Collectors consider Korean wares far more delicate and elegant than the Chinese, at least in the forms. The techniques for making Korean celadon (manufactured during the Koryo dynasty, 918–1392) were later lost, but recent research has come close to discovering the lost techiques.

Ooi Giok Ling

Further Reading

Honey, W. B. (1945) *The Ceramic Art of China and Other Countries of the Far East*. London: Faber and Faber.

Payton, M., and G. Payton. (1973) *The Observer's Book of Pottery and Porcelain*. London: Frederick Warne & Co.

POROS

POROS (c. fourth century BCE), ruler in the Punjab. Poros is the classical Greek name of a ruler in the Punjab (northwestern India) who was also called Parvataka. His kingdom lay between the Jhelum and the Chenab Rivers. In 326 BCE, instead of submitting to Alexander of Macedon as his neighbors in Taxila had, Poros fought a remarkable battle, which Alexander found to be one of the toughest he had ever undertaken. The Punjabi's strategy was to form a square with his slow-moving infantry, longbow archers, and war elephants. However, his forces were no match for the faster and more mobile Greek cavalry, especially as Alexander had trained his troops to counter elephants. Though he was wounded and beaten, Poros did not flee from the battlefield. Alexander was so impressed with the king's personality that he befriended Poros and reinstated him in his kingdom, perhaps even increasing its territory. After Alexander departed from India, the Punjab was liberated from the Greek thrall by Chandragupta Maurya. Poros's role in the liberation is unknown.

Paul Hockings

Further Reading

Rapson, E. J., ed. (1922) *Ancient India*. Vol.1 of *The Cambridge History of India*. Cambridge, U.K.: Cambridge University Press.

PORTUGUESE IN SOUTHEAST ASIA

PORTUGUESE IN SOUTHEAST ASIA In the fifteenth century, Spain and Portugal, as both formal allies and trading rivals, began to circumnavigate the globe to seek out new lands to expand trading networks and to spread Catholicism. A papal edict of 1493 divided the "New World" (or non-European world) between Spain and Portugal. This edict had assumed that the world was flat, but the circumnavigation of the globe by Ferdinand Magellan (c. 1480–1521) in 1521 led to the 1529 Treaty of Saragossa to divide Asia. The treaty gave the Spanish a free hand in the Philippines, while the Portuguese had sole rights to the islands that now form Indonesia.

Growth of Portuguese Control

Arab traders dominated the lucrative trade from the spice-producing islands of what is now Indonesia. Portugal, a small and somewhat poor nation, excelled at seafaring. The skilled Portuguese navigator Vasco da Gama (c. 1460–1524) arrived on India's southwest coast, at Calicut (Calcutta), in 1498. Da Gama was followed by Afonso de Albuquerque (1453–1515), appointed viceroy of India in 1509, who established a number of imperial possessions for Portugal. The Portuguese established a series of strategic ports and small territories in western Africa, Arabia, and southern and eastern Asia to control the trading routes to the Spice Islands of what is now Indonesia. The aim of the Portuguese was to secure key ports rather than to conquer territory. By the sixteenth century the Portuguese sphere of influence included African, Arabian, and South Asian ports as well as North Sumatra, Melaka, Bantam (West Java), Manado (North Sulawesi, Indonesia), parts of Maluku, Ambon, and the island of Timor in maritime Southeast Asia, and Macao and Taiwan in East Asia. Trading posts were also set up, with permission from local potentates, in Ayutthaya (a kingdom in what is now Thailand), Cambodia, and Myanmar (Burma). A crucial event was the capture of Melaka, the strategic Malayan trading city that lies on the all-important Strait of Malacca, in 1511. Control of Melaka gave Lisbon a monopoly on the spice trade to Europe. When Albuquerque finally captured it, his troops slaughtered the local Muslim population, while the sultan fled to Johor, where he rallied his forces for a counterattack. Until the arrival of the Spanish in the Philippines in 1564, the Portuguese were without European rivals in the region.

Portugal used a series of "factories" (handling posts) to process the raw commodities and used naval power to dominate the trading routes, although they never gained complete hegemony. However, the spice was tremendously lucrative, with the value of the trade in the sixteenth century being worth several times the entire revenue collected in Portugal itself. The Portuguese discovered that there was little that Southeast Asians wished to buy from Europe, but there were commodities they wanted from elsewhere. Thus the trading network that linked the various parts of Africa, Arabia, and Asia enriched the Portuguese middlemen, who took the profits back to Portugal: ivory and gold from Africa, textiles from India, spice from Indonesia, and manufactured goods from China.

Limitations and Decline of Portuguese Control

The spread of Portuguese religion and culture was, on the whole, far less successful. The rough and often violent behavior of the Portuguese sojourners left a very poor impression on the peoples of Southeast Asia, vast numbers of whom had adopted the Islam of Arab and Indian traders. The peoples of the Malay Peninsula and the Spice Islands favored trading with their coreligionists in the Middle East. For the Portuguese forces, occupation of their Southeast Asian possessions was hazardous, with fifteen major assaults by sultans in Johor, Aceh, and Java between 1513 and 1616. The Portuguese had also adopted the regular tactic of piracy against Muslim vessels, in the name of Christianity, which helped to undermine any pretensions to legitimacy they might have had. Opposition to the Portuguese solidified the power of emerging sultanates of neighboring areas that, hitherto, had only nominal control over the people in whose name they governed. The Portuguese also began to suffer severe domestic problems, in part because of the tremendous loss of men in the colonies due to conflict, piracy, and disease. The Dutch, on their arrival in the region in the seventeenth century, were able to displace the Portuguese in their key strongholds, notably by conquering Melaka in 1641. The Portuguese withdrew gradually from almost all of their ports but were able to hold the eastern part of Timor, creating the separate territory of East Timor.

One Portuguese legacy was the adoption of new words into Bahasa (Malay), particularly for new technologies of the time, which are still in use to this day. There is a smattering of Portuguese surnames around Southeast Asia, particularly in Melaka, denoting the descendants of marriages between Portuguese sailors and local women, which were quite common in colonial times.

Anthony L. Smith

Further Reading

Dixon, Chris. (1991) *South-East Asia in the World-Economy*. Cambridge, U.K.: Cambridge University Press.

Osborne, Milton. (1995) *Southeast Asia: An Introductory History*. St. Leonard's, Australia: Allen & Unwin.

Tarling, Nicholas. (1966) *A Concise History of Southeast Asia*. Singapore: Donald Moore Press.

Belarus
Ukraine
Moldova
Romania
Bulgaria
Black Sea
Georgia
Caucasus Mts.
T'bilisi
Istanbul
Ankara
Turkey
Armenia
Yerevan
Azerbaijan
Baku
Caspian Sea
Greece
Adana
Nicosia
Cyprus
Lebanon
Israel
Syria
Jordan
Euphrates
Tigris
Baghdad
Iraq
Zagros Mountains
Iran
Tehran
Kuwait
Persian Gulf
Qatar
Saudi Arabia
United Arab Emirates
Oman
Yemen
Red Sea
Egypt
Sudan
Eritrea
Djibouti
Somalia
Ethiopia
Uganda
Kenya
Democratic Republic of the Congo
Rwanda
Burundi
Tanzania
Zambia
Zimbabwe
Mozambique
Madagascar
Mauritius
Port Louis
Réunion
60°E
Kazakhstan
Astana
Aral Sea
Syr Dar'ya
Amu Dar'ya
Kara-Kum
Lake Balkash
Almaty
Bishkek
Kyrgyzstan
Tian S
Tashkent
Fergana Valley
Uzbekistan
Turkmenistan
Ashgabat
Dushanbe
Tajikistan
Pamirs
Taklimak Desert
Kabul
Peshawar
Islamabad
Jammu and Kashmir
Afghanistan
Lahore
Himalay
Indus River
Pakistan
New Delhi
Nepa
Kath
Ganges River
Karachi
India
Mumbai
Arabian Sea
Madras
Lakshadweep
Sri Lan
Colombo
Maldives
Male
N
R
0 500 1000 Miles
0 500 1000 Kilometers
Indian